THE CIA
WORLD FACTBOOK
1992

Contents

THE CIA WORLD FACTBOOK 1992

Afghanistan Geography

Total area: 647,500 km2
Land area: 647,500 km2
Comparative area: slightly smaller than Texas
Land boundaries:
    5,529 km total; China 76 km, Iran 936 km, Pakistan 2,430 km, Tajikistan
    1,206 km, Turkmenistan 744 km, Uzbekistan 137 km
Coastline:
    none - landlocked
Maritime claims:
    none - landlocked
Disputes:
    Pashtunistan issue over the North-West Frontier Province with Pakistan;
    periodic disputes with Iran over Helmand water rights; Pakistan, Saudi
    Arabia, and Iran continue to support clients in country; power struggles
    among various groups for control of Kabul, regional rivalries among emerging
    warlords, and traditional tribal disputes continue
Climate:
    arid to semiarid; cold winters and hot summers
Terrain:
    mostly rugged mountains; plains in north and southwest
Natural resources:
    natural gas, crude oil, coal, copper, talc, barites, sulphur, lead, zinc,
    iron ore, salt, precious and semiprecious stones
Land use:
    arable land 12%; permanent crops NEGL%; meadows and pastures 46%; forest and
    woodland 3%; other 39%; includes irrigated NEGL%
Environment:
    damaging earthquakes occur in Hindu Kush mountains; soil degradation,
    desertification, overgrazing, deforestation, pollution
Note:
    landlocked

:Afghanistan People

Population: US Bureau of the Census - 16,095,664 (July 1992), growth rate 2.4%
(1992)
   and excludes 3,750,796 refugees in Pakistan and 1,607,281 refugees in Iran;
   note - another report indicates a July 1990 population of 16,904,904,
   including 3,271,580 refugees in Pakistan and 1,277,700 refugees in Iran
Birth rate: 44 births/1,000 population (1992)
Death rate: 20 deaths/1,000 population (1992)
Net migration rate: 0 migrants/1,000 population (1992); note - there are flows across
the border
   in both directions, but data are fragmentary and unreliable
Infant mortality rate: 162 deaths/1,000 live births (1992)
Life expectancy at birth: 45 years male, 43 years female (1992)
Total fertility rate: 6.4 children born/woman (1992)
Nationality:
   noun - Afghan(s); adjective - Afghan
Ethnic divisions:
   Pashtun 38%, Tajik 25%, Uzbek 6%, Hazara 19%; minor ethnic groups include
   Chahar Aimaks, Turkmen, Baloch, and others
Religions:
   Sunni Muslim 84%, Shi`a Muslim 15%, other 1%
Languages:
   Pashtu 35%, Afghan Persian (Dari) 50%, Turkic languages (primarily Uzbek and
   Turkmen) 11%, 30 minor languages (primarily Balochi and Pashai) 4%; much
   bilingualism
Literacy:
   29% (male 44%, female 14%) age 15 and over can read and write (1990 est.)
Labor force:
   4,980,000; agriculture and animal husbandry 67.8%, industry 10.2%,
   construction 6.3%, commerce 5.0%, services and other 10.7%, (1980 est.)
Organized labor:
   some small government-controlled unions existed under the former regime but
   probably now have disbanded

:Afghanistan Government

Long-form name:
   Islamic State of Afghanistan
Type:
   transitional
Capital: Kabul
Administrative divisions:
   30 provinces (velayat, singular - velayat); Badakhshan, Badghis, Baghlan,
   Balkh, Bamian, Farah, Faryab, Ghazni, Ghowr, Helmand, Herat, Jowzjan, Kabol,
   Kandahar, Kapisa, Konar, Kondoz, Laghman, Lowgar, Nangarhar, Nimruz,
   Oruzgan, Paktia, Paktika, Parvan, Samangan, Sar-e Pol, Takhar, Vardak,
   Zabol; note - there may be a new province of Nurestan (Nuristan)
Independence:
   19 August 1919 (from UK)
Constitution:
   the old Communist-era constitution probably will be replaced with an Islamic

2

constitution

Legal system:

a new legal system has not been adopted but the transitional government has declared it will follow Islamic law (Shari`a)

National holiday:

28 April, Victory of the Muslim Nation; 4 May, Remembrance Day for Martyrs and Disabled; 19 August, Independence Day

Executive branch:

a 51-member transitional council headed by Sibghatullah MOJADDEDI rules Kabul; this body is to turn over power to a leadership council, which will function as the government and organize elections; Burhanuddin RABBANI will serve as interim President

Legislative branch:

previous bicameral legislature has been abolished

Judicial branch:

an interim Chief Justice of the Supreme Court has been appointed, but a new court system has not yet been organized

Leaders:

Chief of State and Head of Government:

Interim President Burhanuddin RABBANI; First Vice President Abdul Wahed SORABI (since 7 January 1991); Prime Minister Fazil Haq KHALIQYAR (since 21 May 1990)

Political parties and leaders:

the former resistance parties represent the only current political organizations and include Jamiat-i-Islami (Islamic Society), Burhanuddin RABBANI; Hizbi Islami-Gulbuddin (Islamic Party), Gulbuddin Hikmatyar Faction; Hizbi Islami-Khalis (Islamic Party) Yunis Khalis Faction; Ittihad-i-Islami Barai Azadi Afghanistan (Islamic Union for the Liberation of Afghanistan), Abdul Rasul SAYYAF; Harakat-Inqilab-i-Islami (Islamic Revolutionary Movement), Mohammad Nabi MOHAMMADI; Jabha-i-Najat-i-Milli Afghanistan (Afghanistan National Liberation Front), Sibghatullah MOJADDEDI; Mahaz-i-Milli-Islami (National Islamic Front), Sayed Ahamad GAILANI; Jonbesh-i-Milli Islami (National Islamic Movement), Ahmad Shah MASOOD and Rashid DOSTAM; Hizbi Wahdat (Islamic Unity Party), and a number of minor resistance parties; the former ruling Watan Party has been disbanded

Suffrage:

undetermined; previously universal, male ages 15-50

Elections:

the transition government has promised elections in October 1992

Communists:

the former ruling Watan (Homeland) Party has been disbanded

:Afghanistan Government

Other political or pressure groups:

the former resistance commanders are the major power brokers in the countryside; shuras (councils) of commanders are now administering most cities outside Kabul; ulema (religious scholars); tribal elders

Member of:

Has previously been a member of AsDB, CP, ESCAP, FAO, G-77, IAEA, IBRD, ICAO, IDA, IDB, IFAD, IFC, ILO, IMF, INTELSAT, IOC, ITU, LORCS, NAM,

OIC,
UN, UNCTAD, UNESCO, UNIDO, UPU, WFTU, WHO, WMO, WTO; note - the new
government has not yet announced whether it will continue to be a member of
these bodies; the former resistance government in exile (Afghan Interim
Government) was given membership in the OIC in 1989

Diplomatic representation:
previous Minister-Counselor, Charge d'Affaires Abdul Ghafur JOUSHAN;
Chancery at 2341 Wyoming Avenue NW, Washington, DC 20008; telephone (202)
234-3770 or 3771; a new representative has not yet been named

US:
Charge d'Affaires (vacant); Embassy at Ansari Wat, Wazir Akbar Khan Mina,
Kabul; telephone 62230 through 62235 or 62436; note - US Embassy in Kabul
was closed in January 1989

Flag:
a new flag of unknown description reportedly has been adopted; previous flag
consisted of three equal horizontal bands of black (top), red, and green,
with the national coat of arms superimposed on the hoist side of the black
and red bands; similar to the flag of Malawi, which is shorter and bears a
radiant, rising red sun centered in the black band

:Afghanistan Economy

Overview:
Fundamentally, Afghanistan is an extremely poor, landlocked country, highly
dependent on farming (wheat especially) and livestock raising (sheep and
goats). Economic considerations, however, have played second fiddle to
political and military upheavals during more than 13 years of war, including
the nearly 10-year Soviet military occupation (which ended 15 February
1989). Over the past decade, one-third of the population fled the country,
with Pakistan sheltering more than 3 million refugees and Iran about 1.3
million. Another 1 million probably moved into and around urban areas within
Afghanistan. Although reliable data are unavailable, gross domestic product
is lower than 12 years ago because of the loss of labor and capital and the
disruption of trade and transport.

GDP:
exchange rate conversion - $3 billion, per capita $200; real growth rate 0%
(1989 est.)

Inflation rate (consumer prices):
over 90% (1991 est.)

Unemployment rate: NA%

Budget:
revenues NA; expenditures NA, including capital expenditures of NA

Exports:
$236 million (f.o.b., FY91 est.)
commodities:
natural gas 55%, fruits and nuts 24%, handwoven carpets, wool, cotton,
hides, and pelts
partners:
mostly former USSR

Imports:

$874 million (c.i.f., FY91 est.)
commodities:
food and petroleum products
partners:
mostly former USSR
External debt: $2.3 billion (March 1991 est.)
Industrial production:
growth rate 2.3% (FY91 est.); accounts for about 25% of GDP
Electricity:
480,000 kW capacity; 1,450 million kWh produced, 90 kWh per capita (1991)
Industries:
small-scale production of textiles, soap, furniture, shoes, fertilizer, and
cement; handwoven carpets; natural gas, oil, coal, copper
Agriculture:
largely subsistence farming and nomadic animal husbandry; cash products -
wheat, fruits, nuts, karakul pelts, wool, mutton
Illicit drugs:
an illicit producer of opium poppy and cannabis for the international drug
trade; world's second-largest opium producer (after Burma) and a major
source of hashish
Economic aid:
US commitments, including Ex-Im (FY70-89), $380 million; Western (non-US)
countries, ODA and OOF bilateral commitments (1970-89), $510 million; OPEC
bilateral aid (1979-89), $57 million; Communist countries (1970-89), $4.1
billion; net official Western disbursements (1985-89), $270 million
Currency:
afghani (plural - afghanis); 1 afghani (Af) = 100 puls

:Afghanistan Economy

Exchange rates:
afghanis (Af) per US$1 - 550 (May 1992, free market exchange rate), 900
(free market exchange rate as of November 1991), 850 (1991), 700 (1989-90),
220 (1988-89); note - these rates reflect the bazaar rates rather than the
official exchange rates
Fiscal year: 21 March - 20 March

:Afghanistan Communications

Railroads:
9.6 km (single track) 1.524-meter gauge from Kushka (Turkmenistan) to
Towraghondi and 15.0 km from Termez (Uzbekistan) to Kheyrabad transshipment
point on south bank of Amu Darya
Highways:
21,000 km total (1984); 2,800 km hard surface, 1,650 km bituminous-treated
gravel and improved earth, 16,550 km unimproved earth and tracks
Inland waterways:
total navigability 1,200 km; chiefly Amu Darya, which handles steamers up to
about 500 metric tons
Pipelines:
petroleum products - former USSR to Bagram and former USSR to Shindand;
natural gas 180 km
Ports:

Shir Khan and Kheyrabad (river ports)
Civil air:
  2 Tu-154, 2 Boeing 727, 4 Yak-40, assorted smaller transports
Airports:
  41 total, 37 usable; 9 with permanent-surface runways; none with runways
  over 3,659 m; 10 with runways 2,440-3,659 m; 18 with runways 1,220-2,439 m
Telecommunications:
  limited telephone, telegraph, and radiobroadcast services; television
  introduced in 1980; 31,200 telephones; broadcast stations - 5 AM, no FM, 1
  TV; 1 satellite earth station

:Afghanistan Defense Forces

Branches:
  the military currently is being reorganized by the new government and does
  not yet exist on a national scale; some elements of the former Army, Air and
  Air Defense Forces, National Guard, Border Guard Forces, National Police
  Force (Sarandoi), and Tribal Militias remain intact and are supporting the
  new government; the government has asked all military personnel to return to
  their stations; a large number of former resistance groups also field
  irregular military forces; the Ministry of State Security (WAD) has been
  disbanded
Manpower availability:
  males 15-49, 3,989,232; 2,139,771 fit for military service; 150,572 reach
  military age (22) annually
Defense expenditures:
  the new government has not yet adopted a defense budget

Albania Geography

Total area: 28,750 km2
Land area: 27,400 km2
Comparative area: slightly larger than Maryland
Land boundaries:
  720 km total; Greece 282 km, Macedonia 151 km, Serbia and Montenegro 287 km
  (114 km with Serbia, 173 km with Montenegro)
Coastline:
  362 km
Maritime claims:
 Continental shelf:
  not specified
 Territorial sea:
  12 nm
Disputes:
  Kosovo question with Serbia and Montenegro; Northern Epirus question with
  Greece
Climate:
  mild temperate; cool, cloudy, wet winters; hot, clear, dry summers; interior
  is cooler and wetter
Terrain:
  mostly mountains and hills; small plains along coast
Natural resources:
  crude oil, natural gas, coal, chromium, copper, timber, nickel

Land use:
   arable land 21%; permanent crops 4%; meadows and pastures 15%; forest and
   woodland 38%; other 22%; includes irrigated 1%
Environment:
   subject to destructive earthquakes; tsunami occur along southwestern coast
Note:
   strategic location along Strait of Otranto (links Adriatic Sea to Ionian Sea
   and Mediterranean Sea)

:Albania People

Population: 3,285,224 (July 1992), growth rate 1.1% (1992)
Birth rate: 23 births/1,000 population (1992)
Death rate: 5 deaths/1,000 population (1992)
Net migration rate: —6 migrants/1,000 population (1992)
Infant mortality rate: 27 deaths/1,000 live births (1992)
Life expectancy at birth: 71 years male, 78 years female (1992)
Total fertility rate: 2.8 children born/woman (1992)
Nationality:
   noun - Albanian(s); adjective - Albanian
Ethnic divisions:
   Albanian 90%, Greeks 8%, other 2% (Vlachs, Gypsies, Serbs, and Bulgarians)
   (1989 est.)
Religions:
   all mosques and churches were closed in 1967 and religious observances
   prohibited; in November 1990, Albania began allowing private religious
   practice; estimates of religious affiliation - Muslim 70%, Greek Orthodox
   20%, Roman Catholic 10%
Languages:
   Albanian (Tosk is official dialect), Greek
Literacy:
   72% (male 80%, female 63%) age 9 and over can read and write (1955)
Labor force:
   1,500,000 (1987); agriculture about 60%, industry and commerce 40% (1986)
Organized labor:
   Independent Trade Union Federation of Albania; Confederation of Trade Unions

:Albania Government

Long-form name:
   Republic of Albania
Type:
   nascent democracy
Capital: Tirane
Administrative divisions:
   26 districts (rrethe, singular - rreth); Berat, Dibre, Durres, Elbasan,
   Fier, Gjirokaster, Gramsh, Kolonje, Kore, Kruje, Kukes, Lezhe, Librazhd,
   Lushnje, Mat, Mirdite, Permet, Pogradec, Puke, Sarande, Shkoder, Skrapar,
   Tepelene, Tirane, Tropoje, Vlore
Independence:
   28 November 1912 (from Ottoman Empire); People's Socialist Republic of
   Albania declared 11 January 1946
Constitution:

an interim basic law was approved by the People's Assembly on 29 April 1991;
a new constitution is to be drafted for adoption in 1992

Legal system:

has not accepted compulsory ICJ jurisdiction

National holiday:

Liberation Day, 29 November (1944)

Executive branch:

president, prime minister of the Council of Ministers, two deputy prime
ministers of the Council of Ministers

Legislative branch:

unicameral People's Assembly (Kuvendi Popullor)

Judicial branch:

Supreme Court

Leaders:

Chief of State:

President of the Republic Sali BERISHA (since 9 April 1992)

Head of Government:

Prime Minister of the Council of Ministers Aleksander MEKSI (since 10 April
1992)

Political parties and leaders:

there are at least 18 political parties; most prominent are the Albanian
Socialist Party (ASP), Fatos NANO, first secretary; Democratic Party (DP),
Eduard SELAMI, chairman; Albanian Republican Party (RP), Sabri GODO; Omonia
(Greek minority party), leader NA (ran in 1992 election as Unity for Human
Rights Party (UHP)); Social Democratic Party (SDP), Skender GJINUSHI; note -
in December 1990 then President ALIA allowed new political parties to be
formed in addition to the then AWP for the first time since 1944

Suffrage:

universal and compulsory at age 18

Elections:

People's Assembly:

last held 22 March 1992; results - DP 62.29%, ASP 25.57%, SDP 4.33%, RP
3.15%, UHP 2.92%, other 1.74%; seats - (140 total) DP 92, ASP 38, SDP 7, RP
1, UHP 2

Member of:

CSCE, EBRD, ECE, FAO, IAEA, IBRD, IMF, INTERPOL, IOC, ISO, ITU,
LORCS, OIC,
UN, UNCTAD, UNESCO, UNIDO, UPU, WFTU, WHO, WMO

Diplomatic representation:

Minister-Counselor, Charge d'Affaires ad interim (30 April 1991) Sazan Hyda
BEJO; chancery (temporary) at 320 East 79th Street, New York, NY 10021;
telephone (212) 249-2059

US:

Ambassador (vacant); Embassy at Rruga Labinoti 103, room 2921, Tirane
(mailing address is APO AE 09624); telephone 355-42-32875; FAX 355-42-32222

:Albania Government

Flag: red with a black two-headed eagle in the center

:Albania Economy

Overview:
  The Albanian economy, already providing the lowest standard of living in
  Europe, contracted sharply in 1991, with most industries producing at only a
  fraction of past levels and an unemployment rate estimated at 40%. For over
  40 years, the Stalinist-type economy has operated on the principle of
  central planning and state ownership of the means of production. Albania
  began fitful economic reforms during 1991, including the liberalization of
  prices and trade, the privatization of shops and transport, and land reform.
  These reform measures were crippled, however, by the widespread civil
  disorder that accompanied the collapse of the Communist state. Following
  their overwhelming victory in the 22 March 1991 elections, the new
  Democratic government announced a program of shock therapy to stabilize the
  economy and establish a market economy. In an effort to expand international
  ties, Tirane has reestablished diplomatic relations with the former Soviet
  Union and the US and has joined the IMF and World Bank. The Albanians have
  also passed legislation allowing foreign investment. Albania possesses
  considerable mineral resources and, until 1990, was largely self-sufficient
  in food; however, the breakup of cooperative farms in 1991 and general
  economic decline forced Albania to rely on foreign aid to maintain adequate
  supplies. Available statistics on Albanian economic activity are rudimentary
  and subject to an especially wide margin of error.
GNP:
  purchasing power equivalent - $2.7 billion, per capita $820; real growth
  rate —35% (1991 est.)
Inflation rate (consumer prices):
  100% (1991 est.)
Unemployment rate: 40% (1992 est.)
Budget:
  revenues $1.1 billion; expenditures $1.4 billion, including capital
  expenditures of $70 million (1991 est.)
Exports:
  $80 million (f.o.b., 1991 est.)
 commodities:
  asphalt, petroleum products, metals and metallic ores, electricity, crude
  oil, vegetables, fruits, tobacco
 partners:
  Italy, Yugoslavia, Germany, Greece, Czechoslovakia, Poland, Romania,
  Bulgaria, Hungary
Imports:
  $147 million (f.o.b., 1991 est.)
 commodities:
  machinery, machine tools, iron and steel products, textiles, chemicals,
  pharmaceuticals
 partners:
  Italy, Yugoslavia, Germany, Czechoslovakia, Romania, Poland, Hungary,
  Bulgaria
External debt: $500 million (1991 est.)
Industrial production:
  growth rate —55% (1991 est.)
Electricity:

9

1,690,000 kW capacity; 5,000 million kWh produced, 1,530 kWh per capita (1990)

Industries:

food processing, textiles and clothing, lumber, oil, cement, chemicals, basic metals, hydropower

:Albania Economy

Agriculture:

arable land per capita among lowest in Europe; over 60% of arable land now in private hands; one-half of work force engaged in farming; wide range of temperate-zone crops and livestock; severe dislocations suffered in 1991

Economic aid:

$190 million humanitarian aid, $94 million in loans/guarantees/credits

Currency:

lek (plural - leke); 1 lek (L) = 100 qintars

Exchange rates:

leke (L) per US$1 - 50 (January 1992), 25 (September 1991)

Fiscal year: calendar year

:Albania Communications

Railroads:

543 km total; 509 1.435-meter standard gauge, single track and 34 km narrow gauge, single track (1990); line connecting Titograd (Serbia and Montenegro) and Shkoder (Albania) completed August 1986

Highways:

16,700 km total; 6,700 km highways, 10,000 km forest and agricultural cart roads (1990)

Inland waterways:

43 km plus Albanian sections of Lake Scutari, Lake Ohrid, and Lake Prespa (1990)

Pipelines:

crude oil 145 km; petroleum products 55 km; natural gas 64 km (1988)

Ports:

Durres, Sarande, Vlore

Merchant marine:

11 cargo ships (1,000 GRT or over) totaling 52,886 GRT/76,449 DWT

Airports:

12 total, 10 usable; more than 5 with permanent-surface runways; more than 5 with runways 2,440-3,659 m; 5 with runways 1,220-2,439 m

Telecommunications:

inadequate service; 15,000 telephones; broadcast stations - 13 AM, 1 TV; 514,000 radios, 255,000 TVs (1987 est.)

:Albania Defense Forces

Branches:

Army, Coastal Defense Command, Air and Air Defense Forces, Interior Ministry Troops, Border Troops

Manpower availability:

males 15-49, 886,032; 731,072 fit for military service; 33,028 reach military age (19) annually

Defense expenditures:

exchange rate conversion - 1.0 billion leks, NA% of GNP (FY90); note - conversion of defense expenditures into US dollars using the current exchange rate could produce misleading results

Algeria Geography

Total area: 2,381,740 km2
Land area: 2,381,740 km2
Comparative area: slightly less than 3.5 times the size of Texas
Land boundaries:
    6,343 km total; Libya 982 km, Mali 1,376 km, Mauritania 463 km, Morocco 1,559 km, Niger 956 km, Tunisia 965 km, Western Sahara 42 km
Coastline:
    998 km
Maritime claims:
  Territorial sea:
    12 nm
Disputes:
    Libya claims about 19,400 km2 in southeastern Algeria; land boundary disputes with Tunisia under discussion
Climate:
    arid to semiarid; mild, wet winters with hot, dry summers along coast; drier with cold winters and hot summers on high plateau; sirocco is a hot, dust/sand-laden wind especially common in summer
Terrain:
    mostly high plateau and desert; some mountains; narrow, discontinuous coastal plain
Natural resources:
    crude oil, natural gas, iron ore, phosphates, uranium, lead, zinc
Land use:
    arable land 3%; permanent crops NEGL%; meadows and pastures 13%; forest and woodland 2%; other 82%; includes irrigated NEGL%
Environment:
    mountainous areas subject to severe earthquakes; desertification
Note:
    second-largest country in Africa (after Sudan)

:Algeria People

Population: 26,666,921 (July 1992), growth rate 2.5% (1992)
Birth rate: 31 births/1,000 population (1992)
Death rate: 7 deaths/1,000 population (1992)
Net migration rate: 0 migrants/1,000 population (1992)
Infant mortality rate: 56 deaths/1,000 live births (1992)
Life expectancy at birth: 66 years male, 68 years female (1992)
Total fertility rate: 4.1 children born/woman (1992)
Nationality:
    noun - Algerian(s); adjective - Algerian
Ethnic divisions:
    Arab-Berber 99%, European less than 1%
Religions:
    Sunni Muslim (state religion) 99%, Christian and Jewish 1%
Languages:

Arabic (official), French, Berber dialects
Literacy:
  50% (male 63%, female 36%) age 15 and over can read and write (1987)
Labor force:
  3,700,000; industry and commerce 40%, agriculture 24%, government 17%, services 10% (1984)
Organized labor:
  16-19% of labor force claimed; General Union of Algerian Workers (UGTA) is the only labor organization and is subordinate to the National Liberation Front

:Algeria Government

Long-form name:
  Democratic and Popular Republic of Algeria
Type:
  republic
Capital: Algiers
Administrative divisions:
  48 provinces (wilayast, singular - wilaya); Adrar, Ain Defla, Ain Temouchent, Alger, Annaba, Batna, Bechar, Bejaia, Biskra, Blida, Bordj Bou Arreridj, Bouira, Boumerdes, Chlef, Constantine, Djelfa, El Bayadh, El Oued, El Tarf, Ghardaia, Guelma, Illizi, Jijel, Khenchela, Laghouat, Mascara, Medea, Mila, Mostaganem, M'Sila, Naama, Oran, Ouargla, Oum el Bouaghi, Relizane, Saida, Setif, Sidi Bel Abbes, Skikda, Souk Ahras, Tamanghasset, Tebessa, Tiaret, Tindouf, Tipaza, Tissemsilt, Tizi Ouzou, Tlemcen
Independence:
  5 July 1962 (from France)
Constitution:
  19 November 1976, effective 22 November 1976; revised February 1989
Legal system:
  socialist, based on French and Islamic law; judicial review of legislative acts in ad hoc Constitutional Council composed of various public officials, including several Supreme Court justices; has not accepted compulsory ICJ jurisdiction
National holiday:
  Anniversary of the Revolution, 1 November (1954)
Executive branch:
  president, prime minister, Council of Ministers (cabinet)
Legislative branch:
  unicameral National People's Assembly (Al-Majlis Ech-Chaabi Al-Watani)
Judicial branch:
  Supreme Court (Cour Supreme)
Leaders:
 Chief of State:
  President Mohamed BOUDIAF; assassinated 29 June 1992
 Head of Government:
  Interim Prime Minister Sid Ahmed GHOZALI (since 6 June 1991)
Political parties and leaders:
  National Liberation Front (FLN); Socialist Forces Front (FFS), Hocine Ait AHMED, Secretary General; the government established a multiparty system in

September 1989, and, as of 31 December 1990, over 30 legal parties existed
Suffrage:
universal at age 18
Elections:
National People's Assembly:
first round held on 26 December 1991 (second round canceled by the military after President BENJEDID resigned 11 January 1992); results - percent of vote by party NA; seats - (281 total); the fundamentalist FIS won 188 of the 231 seats contested in the first round; note - elections (municipal and wilaya) were held in June 1990, the first in Algerian history; results - FIS 55%, FLN 27.5%, other 17.5%, with 65% of the voters participating
President:
next election to be held December 1993
Communists:
400 (est.); Communist party banned 1962
Member of:
ABEDA, AfDB, AFESD, AL, AMF, AMU, CCC, ECA, FAO, G-15, G-24, G-77, IAEA,
IBRD, ICAO, IDA, IDB, IFAD, ILO, IMF, IMO, INMARSAT, INTELSAT, INTERPOL,
IOC, ISO, ITU, LORCS, NAM, OAPEC, OAS (observer), OAU, OIC, OPEC, UN, UNAVEM, UNCTAD, UNESCO, UNHCR, UNIDO, UPU, WCL, WHO, WIPO, WMO, WTO

:Algeria Government

Diplomatic representation:
Ambassador Abderrahmane BENSID; Chancery at 2118 Kalorama Road NW, Washington, DC 20008; telephone (202) 265-2800
US:
Ambassador Mary Ann CASEY; Embassy at 4 Chemin Cheich Bachir El-Ibrahimi, Algiers (mailing address is B. P. Box 549, Alger-Gare, 16000 Algiers); telephone [213] (2) 601-425 or 255, 186; FAX [213] (2) 603979; there is a US Consulate in Oran
Flag:
two equal vertical bands of green (hoist side) and white with a red five-pointed star within a red crescent; the crescent, star, and color green are traditional symbols of Islam (the state religion)

:Algeria Economy

Overview:
The oil and natural gas sector forms the backbone of the economy. Algeria depends on hydrocarbons for nearly all of its export receipts, about 30% of government revenues, and nearly 25% of GDP. In 1973-74 the sharp increase in oil prices led to a booming economy and helped to finance an ambitious program of industrialization. Plunging oil and gas prices, combined with the mismanagement of Algeria's highly centralized economy, has brought the nation to its most serious social and economic crisis since independence in 1988. The government has promised far-reaching reforms, including privatization of some public- sector companies, encouraging private-sector activity, boosting gas and nonhydrocarbon exports, and proposing a major overhaul of the banking and financial systems, but to date it has made only

13

limited progress.

GDP:
exchange rate conversion - $54 billion, per capita $2,130; real growth rate 2.5% (1990 est.)

Inflation rate (consumer prices):
30% (1991 est.)

Unemployment rate: 30% (1991 est.)

Budget:
revenues $16.7 billion; expenditures $17.3 billion, including capital expenditures of $6.6 billion (1990 est.)

Exports:
$11.7 billion (f.o.b., 1991 est.)
commodities:
petroleum and natural gas 97%
partners:
Netherlands, Czechoslovakia, Romania, Italy, France, US

Imports:
$9 billion (f.o.b., 1991 est.)
commodities:
capital goods 29%, consumer goods 30%
partners:
France 25%, Italy 8%, FRG 8%, US 6-7%

External debt: $26.4 billion

Industrial production:
growth rate —3% (1989 est.); accounts for 30% of GDP, including petroleum

Electricity:
6,380,000 kW capacity; 16,700 million kWh produced, 640 kWh per capita (1991)

Industries:
petroleum, light industries, natural gas, mining, electrical, petrochemical, food processing

Agriculture:
accounts for 11% of GDP and employs 24% of labor force; net importer of food - grain, vegetable oil, and sugar; farm production includes wheat, barley, oats, grapes, olives, citrus, fruits, sheep, and cattle

Economic aid:
US commitments, including Ex-Im (FY70-85), $1.4 billion; Western (non-US) countries, ODA and OOF bilateral commitments (1970-89), $925 million; OPEC bilateral aid (1979-89), $1.8 billion; Communist countries (1970-89), $2.7 billion; net official disbursements (1985-89), —$375 million

Currency:
Algerian dinar (plural - dinars); 1 Algerian dinar (DA) = 100 centimes

Exchange rates:
Algerian dinars (DA) per US$1 - 21.862 (January 1992), 18.473 (1991), 8.958 (1990), 7.6086 (1989), 5.9148 (1988), 4.8497 (1987)

:Algeria Economy

Fiscal year: calendar year

:Algeria Communications

Railroads:

4,060 km total; 2,616 km standard gauge (1.435 m), 1,188 km 1.055-meter gauge, 256 km 1.000-meter gauge; 300 km electrified; 215 km double track

Highways:

80,000 km total; 60,000 km concrete or bituminous, 20,000 km gravel, crushed stone, unimproved earth

Pipelines:

crude oil 6,612 km; petroleum products 298 km; natural gas 2,948 km

Ports:

Algiers, Annaba, Arzew, Bejaia, Djendjene, Ghazaouet, Jijel, Mers el Kebir, Mostaganem, Oran, Skikda

Merchant marine:

75 ships (1,000 GRT or over) totaling 903,179 GRT/1,064,246 DWT; includes 5 short-sea passenger, 27 cargo, 12 roll-on/roll-off cargo, 5 petroleum tanker, 9 liquefied gas, 7 chemical tanker, 9 bulk, 1 specialized tanker

Civil air:

42 major transport aircraft

Airports:

141 total, 124 usable; 53 with permanent-surface runways; 2 with runways over 3,659 m; 32 with runways 2,440-3,659 m; 65 with runways 1,220-2,439 m

Telecommunications:

excellent domestic and international service in the north, sparse in the south; 822,000 telephones; broadcast stations - 26 AM, no FM, 18 TV; 1,600,000 TV sets; 5,200,000 radios; 5 submarine cables; radio relay to Italy, France, Spain, Morocco, and Tunisia; coaxial cable to Morocco and Tunisia; satellite earth stations - 1 Atlantic Ocean INTELSAT, 1 Indian Ocean INTELSAT, 1 Intersputnik, 1 ARABSAT, and 15 domestic

:Algeria Defense Forces

Branches:

National Popular Army, Navy, Air Force, Territorial Air Defense, National Gendarmerie

Manpower availability:

males 15-49, 6,386,157; 3,928,029 fit for military service; 283,068 reach military age (19) annually

Defense expenditures:

exchange rate conversion - $867 million, approximately 1.8% of GDP (1992)

American Samoa Geography

Total area: 199 km2

Land area: 199 km2; includes Rose Island and Swains Island

Comparative area: slightly larger than Washington, DC

Land boundaries:

Coastline:

116 km

Maritime claims:

Contiguous zone:

12 nm

Continental shelf:

200 m (depth)

Exclusive economic zone:
  200 nm
 Territorial sea:
  12 nm
Disputes:
  none
Climate:
  tropical marine, moderated by southeast trade winds; annual rainfall
  averages 124 inches; rainy season from November to April, dry season from
  May to October; little seasonal temperature variation
Terrain:
  five volcanic islands with rugged peaks and limited coastal plains, two
  coral atolls
Natural resources:
  pumice and pumicite
Land use:
  arable land 10%; permanent crops 5%; meadows and pastures 0%; forest and
  woodland 75%; other 10%
Environment:
  typhoons common from December to March
Note:
  Pago Pago has one of the best natural deepwater harbors in the South Pacific
  Ocean, sheltered by shape from rough seas and protected by peripheral
  mountains from high winds; strategic location about 3,700 km south-southwest
  of Honolulu in the South Pacific Ocean about halfway between Hawaii and New
  Zealand

:American Samoa People

Population: 51,115 (July 1992), growth rate 3.9% (1992); about 65,000 American
Samoans
  live in the states of California and Washington and 20,000 in Hawaii
Birth rate: 37 births/1,000 population (1992)
Death rate: 4 deaths/1,000 population (1992)
Net migration rate: 6 immigrants/1,000 population (1992)
Infant mortality rate: 19 deaths/1,000 live births (1992)
Life expectancy at birth: 71 years male, 75 years female (1992)
Total fertility rate: 4.5 children born/woman (1992)
Nationality:
  noun - American Samoan(s); adjective - American Samoan; US, noncitizen
  nationals
Ethnic divisions:
  Samoan (Polynesian) 90%, Caucasian 2%, Tongan 2%, other 6%
Religions:
  Christian Congregationalist 50%, Roman Catholic 20%, Protestant
  denominations and other 30%
Languages:
  Samoan (closely related to Hawaiian and other Polynesian languages) and
  English; most people are bilingual
Literacy:
  97% (male 97%, female 97%) age 15 and over can read and write (1980)

Labor force:
  14,400 (1990); government 48%, tuna canneries 33%, other 19% (1986 est.)
Organized labor:
  NA

:American Samoa Government

Long-form name:
  Territory of American Samoa
Type:
  unincorporated and unorganized territory of the US;
  administered by the US Department of Interior, Office of Territorial and
  International Affairs; indigenous inhabitants are US nationals, not citizens
  of the US
Capital: Pago Pago
Administrative divisions:
  none (territory of the US)
Independence:
  none (territory of the US)
Constitution:
  ratified 1966, in effect 1967; note - a comprehensive revision is awaiting
  ratification by the US Congress (1992)
National holiday:
  Territorial Flag Day, 17 April (1900)
Executive branch:
  popularly elected governor and lieutenant governor
Legislative branch:
  bicameral Legislative Assembly (Fono) consists of an upper house or Senate
  and a lower house or House of Representatives
Judicial branch:
  High Court, district courts, and village courts
Leaders:
  Chief of State:
  President George BUSH (since 20 January 1989); Vice President Dan QUAYLE
  (since 20 January 1989)
  Head of Government:
  Governor Peter Tali COLEMAN (since 20 January 1989); Lieutenant Governor
  Galea'i POUMELE (since NA 1989)
Suffrage:
  universal at age 18; indigenous inhabitants are US nationals, not US
  citizens
Elections:
  Governor:
  last held 7 November 1988 (next to be held November 1992); results - Peter
  T. COLEMAN was elected (percent of vote NA)
  House of Representatives:
  last held November 1990 (next to be held November 1992); results -
  representatives popularly elected from 17 house districts; seats - (21
  total, 20 elected, and 1 nonvoting delegate from Swain's Island)
  Senate:
  last held 7 November 1988 (next to be held November 1992); results -

senators elected by county councils from 12 senate districts; seats - (18 total) number of seats by party NA

US House of Representatives:

last held 19 November 1990 (next to be held November 1992); results - Eni R. F. H. FALEOMAVAEGA reelected as a nonvoting delegate

Member of:

ESCAP, IOC, SPC

Diplomatic representation:

none (territory of the US)

Flag:

blue with a white triangle edged in red that is based on the fly side and extends to the hoist side; a brown and white American bald eagle flying toward the hoist side is carrying two traditional Samoan symbols of authority, a staff and a war club

:American Samoa Economy

Overview:

Economic development is strongly linked to the US, with which American Samoa does nearly 90% of its foreign trade. Tuna fishing and tuna processing plants are the backbone of the private-sector economy, with canned tuna the primary export. The tuna canneries and the government are by far the two largest employers. Other economic activities include a slowly developing tourist industry.

GNP:

purchasing power equivalent - $128 million, per capita $2,500; real growth rate NA% (1990)

Inflation rate (consumer prices):

4.3% (1989)

Unemployment rate: 12% (1991)

Budget:

revenues $126,394,000 (consisting of $46,441,000 local revenue and $79,953,000 grant revenue); including capital expenditures of $NA million (1990)

Exports:

$307 million (f.o.b., 1989)

commodities:

canned tuna 93%

partners:

US 99.6%

Imports:

$377.9 million (c.i.f., 1989)

commodities:

materials for canneries 56%, food 8%, petroleum 7%, machinery and parts 6%

partners:

US 72%, Japan 7%, NZ 7%, Australia 5%, other 9%

External debt: $NA

Industrial production:

growth rate NA%

Electricity:

42,000 kW capacity; 85 million kWh produced, 2,020 kWh per capita (1990)

Industries:
　tuna canneries (largely dependent on foreign supplies of raw tuna), meat
　canning, handicrafts
Agriculture:
　bananas, coconuts, vegetables, taro, breadfruit, yams, copra, pineapples,
　papayas, dairy farming
Economic aid:
　$21,042,650 in operational funds and $5,948,931 in construction funds for
　capital improvement projects from the US Department of Interior (1991)
Currency:
　US currency is used
Exchange rates:
　US currency is used
Fiscal year:　1 October - 30 September

:American Samoa Communications

Railroads:
　none
Highways:
　350 km total; 150 km paved, 200 km unpaved
Ports:
　Pago Pago, Ta'u
Airports:
　4 total, 4 usable; 2 with permanent-surface runways; none with runways over
　3,659 m; 1 with runways 2,440 to 3,659 m (international airport at Tafuna,
　near Pago Pago); small airstrips on Ta'u and Ofu
Telecommunications:
　6,500 telephones; broadcast stations - 1 AM, 2 FM, 1 TV; good telex,
　telegraph, and facsimile services; 1 Pacific Ocean INTELSAT earth station, 1
　COMSAT earth station

:American Samoa Defense Forces

Note: defense is the responsibility of the US

Andorra Geography

Total area:　450 km2
Land area:　450 km2
Comparative area:　slightly more than 2.5 times the size of Washington, DC
Land boundaries:
　125 km total; France 60 km, Spain 65 km
Coastline:
　none - landlocked
Maritime claims:
　none - landlocked
Disputes:
　none
Climate:
　temperate; snowy, cold winters and cool, dry summers
Terrain:
　rugged mountains dissected by narrow valleys
Natural resources:

hydropower, mineral water, timber, iron ore, lead
Land use:
  arable land 2%; permanent crops 0%; meadows and pastures 56%; forest and
  woodland 22%; other 20%
Environment:
  deforestation, overgrazing
Note:
  landlocked

:Andorra People

Population: 54,428 (July 1992), growth rate 2.2% (1992)
Birth rate: 11 births/1,000 population (1992)
Death rate: 4 deaths/1,000 population (1992)
Net migration rate: 15 migrants/1,000 population (1992)
Infant mortality rate: 7 deaths/1,000 live births (1992)
Life expectancy at birth: 74 years male, 81 years female (1992)
Total fertility rate: 1.3 children born/woman (1992)
Nationality:
  noun - Andorran(s); adjective - Andorran
Ethnic divisions:
  Catalan stock; Spanish 61%, Andorran 30%, French 6%, other 3%
Religions:
  virtually all Roman Catholic
Languages:
  Catalan (official); many also speak some French and Castilian
Literacy:
  NA% (male NA%, female NA%)
Labor force:
  NA
Organized labor:
  none

:Andorra Government

Long-form name:
  Principality of Andorra
Type:
  unique coprincipality under formal sovereignty of president of France and
  Spanish bishop of Seo de Urgel, who are represented locally by officials
  called veguers
Capital: Andorra la Vella
Administrative divisions:
  7 parishes (parroquies, singular - parroquia); Andorra, Canillo, Encamp, La
  Massana, Les Escaldes, Ordino, Sant Julia de Loria
Independence:
  1278
Constitution:
  none; some pareatges and decrees, mostly custom and usage
Legal system:
  based on French and Spanish civil codes; no judicial review of legislative
  acts; has not accepted compulsory ICJ jurisdiction
National holiday:

Mare de Deu de Meritxell, 8 September

Executive branch:
two co-princes (president of France, bishop of Seo de Urgel in Spain), two designated representatives (French veguer, Episcopal veguer), two permanent delegates (French prefect for the department of Pyrenees-Orientales, Spanish vicar general for the Seo de Urgel diocese), president of government, Executive Council

Legislative branch:
unicameral General Council of the Valleys (Consell General de las Valls)

Judicial branch:
civil cases - Supreme Court of Andorra at Perpignan (France) or the Ecclesiastical Court of the bishop of Seo de Urgel (Spain); criminal cases - Tribunal of the Courts (Tribunal des Cortes)

Leaders:

Chiefs of State:
French Co-Prince Francois MITTERRAND (since 21 May 1981), represented by Veguer de Franca Jean Pierre COURTOIS; Spanish Episcopal Co-Prince Mgr. Joan MARTI y Alanis (since 31 January 1971), represented by Veguer Episcopal Francesc BADIA Batalla

Head of Government:
Oscar RIBAS Reig (since January 1990)

Political parties and leaders:
political parties not yet legally recognized; traditionally no political parties but partisans for particular independent candidates for the General Council on the basis of competence, personality, and orientation toward Spain or France; various small pressure groups developed in 1972; first formal political party, Andorran Democratic Association, was formed in 1976 and reorganized in 1979 as Andorran Democratic Party

Suffrage:
universal at age 18

Elections:

General Council of the Valleys:
last held 11 December 1989 (next to be held December 1993); results - percent of vote by party NA; seats - (28 total) number of seats by party NA

Member of:
INTERPOL, IOC

Diplomatic representation:
Andorra has no mission in the US

:Andorra Government

US:
includes Andorra within the Barcelona (Spain) Consular District, and the US Consul General visits Andorra periodically; Consul General Carolee HEILEMAN; Consulate General at Via Layetana 33, 08003 Barcelona (mailing address APO AE 09646); telephone [34] (3) 319-9550

Flag:
three equal vertical bands of blue (hoist side), yellow, and red with the national coat of arms centered in the yellow band; the coat of arms features a quartered shield; similar to the flags of Chad and Romania that do not have a national coat of arms in the center

:Andorra Economy

Overview:

The mainstay of Andorra's economy is tourism. An estimated 13 million tourists visit annually, attracted by Andorra's duty-free status and by its summer and winter resorts. Agricultural production is limited by a scarcity of arable land, and most food has to be imported. The principal livestock activity is sheep raising. Manufacturing consists mainly of cigarettes, cigars, and furniture. The rapid pace of European economic integration is a potential threat to Andorra's advantages from its duty-free status.

GDP:

purchasing power equivalent - $727 million, per capita $14,000; real growth rate NA% (1990 est.)

Inflation rate (consumer prices):

NA%

Unemployment rate:　none

Budget:

revenues $NA; expenditures $NA, including capital expenditures of $NA

Exports:

$0.017 million (f.o.b., 1986)

commodities:

electricity

partners:

France, Spain

Imports:

$531 million (f.o.b., 1986)

commodities:

consumer goods, food

partners:

France, Spain

External debt:　$NA

Industrial production:

growth rate NA%

Electricity:

35,000 kW capacity; 140 million kWh produced, 2,800 kWh per capita (1991)

Industries:

tourism (particularly skiing), sheep, timber, tobacco, banking

Agriculture:

sheep raising; small quantities of tobacco, rye, wheat, barley, oats, and some vegetables

Economic aid:

Currency:

French franc (plural - francs) and Spanish peseta (plural - pesetas); 1 French franc (F) = 100 centimes and 1 Spanish peseta (Pta) = 100 centimos

Exchange rates:

French francs (F) per US$1 - 5.3801 January (1992), 5.6421 (1991), 5.4453 (1990), 6.3801 (1989), 5.9569 (1988), 6.0107 (1987); Spanish pesetas (Ptas) per US$1 - 100.02 (January 1992), 103.91 (1991), 101.93 (1990), 118.38 (1989), 116.49 (1988), 123.48 (1987)

Fiscal year:　calendar year

Highways:
  96 km

Telecommunications:
  international digital microwave network; international landline circuits to
  France and Spain; broadcast stations - 1 AM, no FM, no TV; 17,700 telephones

:Andorra Defense Forces

Note: defense is the responsibility of France and Spain

Angola Geography

Total area: 1,246,700 km2
Land area: 1,246,700 km2
Comparative area: slightly less than twice the size of Texas
Land boundaries:
  5,198 km total; Congo 201 km, Namibia 1,376 km, Zaire 2,511 km, Zambia 1,110
  km
Coastline:
  1,600 km
Maritime claims:
 Exclusive fishing zone:
  200 nm
 Territorial sea:
  20 nm
Disputes:
  civil war since independence on 11 November 1975; on 31 May 1991 Angolan
  President Jose Eduardo dos SANTOS and Jonas SAVIMBI, leader of the National
  Union for the Total Independence of Angola (UNITA), signed a peace treaty
  that calls for multiparty elections in late September 1992, an
  internationally monitored cease-fire, and termination of outside military
  assistance
Climate:
  semiarid in south and along coast to Luanda; north has cool, dry season (May
  to October) and hot, rainy season (November to April)
Terrain:
  narrow coastal plain rises abruptly to vast interior plateau
Natural resources:
  petroleum, diamonds, iron ore, phosphates, copper, feldspar, gold, bauxite,
  uranium
Land use:
  arable land 2%; permanent crops NEGL%; meadows and pastures 23%; forest and
  woodland 43%; other 32%
Environment:
  locally heavy rainfall causes periodic flooding on plateau; desertification
Note:
  Cabinda is separated from rest of country by Zaire

:Angola People

Population: 8,902,076 (July 1992), growth rate 2.7% (1992)
Birth rate: 46 births/1,000 population (1992)
Death rate: 19 deaths/1,000 population (1992)

Net migration rate: NEGL migrants/1,000 population (1992)
Infant mortality rate: 152 deaths/1,000 live births (1992)
Life expectancy at birth: 43 years male, 47 years female (1992)
Total fertility rate: 6.6 children born/woman (1992)
Nationality:
  noun - Angolan(s); adjective - Angolan
Ethnic divisions:
  Ovimbundu 37%, Kimbundu 25%, Bakongo 13%, Mestico 2%,European 1%, other
22%
Religions:
  indigenous beliefs 47%, Roman Catholic 38%, Protestant 15% (est.)
Languages:
  Portuguese (official); various Bantu dialects
Literacy:
  42% (male 56%, female 28%) age 15 and over can read and write (1990 est.)
Labor force:
  2,783,000 economically active; agriculture 85%, industry 15% (1985 est.)
Organized labor:
  about 450,695 (1980)

:Angola Government

Long-form name:
  People's Republic of Angola
Type:
  in transition from a one-party Marxist state to a multiparty democracy with
  a strong presidential system
Capital: Luanda
Administrative divisions:
  18 provinces (provincias, singular - provincia); Bengo, Benguela, Bie,
  Cabinda, Cuando Cubango, Cuanza Norte, Cuanza Sul, Cunene, Huambo, Huila,
  Luanda, Lunda Norte, Lunda Sul, Malanje, Moxico, Namibe, Uige, Zaire
Independence:
  11 November 1975 (from Portugal)
Constitution:
  11 November 1975; revised 7 January 1978, 11 August 1980, and 6 March 1991
Legal system:
  based on Portuguese civil law system and customary law; recently modified to
  accommodate multipartyism and increased use of free markets
National holiday:
  Independence Day, 11 November (1975)
Executive branch:
  president, prime minister, chairman of the Council of Ministers, Council of
  Ministers (cabinet)
Legislative branch:
  unicameral People's Assembly (Assembleia do Povo)
Judicial branch:
  Supreme Court (Tribunal da Relacaao)
Leaders:
 Chief of State:
  President Jose Eduardo dos SANTOS (since 21 September 1979)

Head of Government:
Prime Minister Fernando Jose Franca VAN DUNEM (since 21 July 1991)
Political parties and leaders:
the Popular Movement for the Liberation of Angola - Labor Party (MPLA), led
by Jose Eduardo dos SANTOS, is the ruling party that has been in power in
Angola's one-party system since 1975. The National Union for the Total
Independence of Angola (UNITA), led by Jonas SAVIMBI, has been in insurgency
since 1975, but as a result of the peace accords is now a legally recognized
political party. Some 30 other political parties now exist in Angola, but
few of them are viable and only a couple have met the requirements to become
legally recognized.
Suffrage:
universal at age 18
Elections:
first nationwide, multiparty elections to be held between September and
November 1992
Member of:
ACP, AfDB, CCC, CEEAC (observer), ECA, FAO, FLS, G-77, IBRD, ICAO,
IFAD,
ILO, IMF, IMO, INTELSAT, INTERPOL, IOC, ITU, LORCS, NAM, OAU,
SADCC, UN,
UNCTAD, UNESCO, UNIDO, UPU, WCL, WFTU, WHO, WIPO, WMO, WTO
Diplomatic representation:
none; note - US Liaison Office (USLO) established after Peace Accords in May
1991 as a precursor to establishing an embassy after election in 1992;
address - Luanda (USLO), BPA Building, llth floor, telephone [244] (2)
39-02-42; FAX [244] (2) 39-05-15
Flag:
two equal horizontal bands of red (top) and black with a centered yellow
emblem consisting of a five-pointed star within half a cogwheel crossed by a
machete (in the style of a hammer and sickle)

:Angola Economy

Overview:
Subsistence agriculture provides the main livelihood for 80-90% of the
population, but accounts for less than 15% of GDP. Oil production is vital
to the economy, contributing about 60% to GDP. In recent years, a bitter
internal war has severely affected the nonoil economy, and food has to be
imported. For the long run, Angola has the advantage of rich natural
resources in addition to oil, notably gold, diamonds, and arable land. To
realize its economic potential Angola not only must secure domestic peace
but also must reform government policies that have led to distortions and
imbalances throughout the economy.
GDP:
exchange rate conversion - $8.3 billion, per capita $950; real growth rate
1.7% (1991 est.)
Inflation rate (consumer prices):
6.1% (1990 est.)
Unemployment rate: NA%
Budget:

revenues $2.6 billion; expenditures $4.4 billion, including capital
expenditures of $963 million (1990 est.)
Exports:
  $3.9 billion (f.o.b., 1990 est.)
  commodities:
  oil, liquefied petroleum gas, diamonds, coffee, sisal, fish and fish
  products, timber, cotton
  partners:
  US, USSR, Cuba, Portugal, Brazil, France
Imports:
  $1.5 billion (f.o.b., 1990 est.)
  commodities:
  capital equipment (machinery and electrical equipment), food, vehicles and
  spare parts, textiles and clothing, medicines; substantial military
  deliveries
  partners:
  US, USSR, Cuba, Portugal, Brazil
External debt: $7.0 billion (1990)
Industrial production:
  growth rate NA%; accounts for about 60% of GDP, including petroleum output
Electricity:
  510,000 kW capacity; 770 million kWh produced, 90 kWh per capita (1991)
Industries:
  petroleum, diamonds, mining, fish processing, food processing, brewing,
  tobacco, sugar, textiles, cement, basic metal products
Agriculture:
  cash crops - coffee, sisal, corn, cotton, sugar, manioc, tobacco; food crops
  - cassava, corn, vegetables, plantains, bananas; livestock production
  accounts for 20%, fishing 4%, forestry 2% of total agricultural output;
  disruptions caused by civil war and marketing deficiencies require food
  imports
Economic aid:
  US commitments, including Ex-Im (FY70-89), $265 million; Western (non-US)
  countries, ODA and OOF bilateral commitments (1970-89), $1,105 million;
  Communist countries (1970-89), $1.3 billion; net official disbursements
  (1985-89), $750 million
Currency:
  kwanza (plural - kwanza); 1 kwanza (Kz) = 100 lwei
Exchange rates:
  kwanza (Kz) per US$1 - 180.0

:Angola Economy

Fiscal year: calendar year

:Angola Communications

Railroads:
  3,189 km total; 2,879 km 1.067-meter gauge, 310 km 0.600-meter gauge;
  limited trackage in use because of landmines still in place from the civil
  war; majority of the Benguela Railroad also closed because of civil war
Highways:
  73,828 km total; 8,577 km bituminous-surface treatment, 29,350 km crushed

stone, gravel, or improved earth, remainder unimproved earth

Inland waterways:

1,295 km navigable

Pipelines:

crude oil 179 km

Ports:

Luanda, Lobito, Namibe, Cabinda

Merchant marine:

12 ships (1,000 GRT or over) totaling 66,348 GRT/102,825 DWT; includes 11 cargo, 1 petroleum tanker

Civil air:

28 major transport aircraft

Airports:

309 total, 177 usable; 30 with permanent-surface runways; 2 with runways over 3,659 m; 15 with runways 2,440-3,659 m; 54 with runways 1,220-2,439 m

Telecommunications:

limited system of wire, radio relay, and troposcatter routes; high frequency radio used extensively for military links; 40,300 telephones; broadcast stations - 17 AM, 13 FM, 6 TV; 2 Atlantic Ocean INTELSAT earth stations

:Angola Defense Forces

Branches:

Army, Navy, Air Force/Air Defense, People's Defense Organization and Territorial Troops, Frontier Guard

Manpower availability:

males 15-49, 2,129,877; 1,072,323 fit for military service; 89,585 reach military age (18) annually

Defense expenditures:

exchange rate conversion - $NA, NA% of GDP

Anguilla Geography

Total area: 91 km2

Land area: 91 km2

Comparative area: about half the size of Washington, DC

Land boundaries:

Coastline:

61 km

Maritime claims:

 Exclusive fishing zone:

 200 nm

 Territorial sea:

 3 nm

Disputes:

Climate:

tropical; moderated by northeast trade winds

Terrain:

flat and low-lying island of coral and limestone

Natural resources:

negligible; salt, fish, lobster

Land use:
   arable land NA%; permanent crops NA%; meadows and pastures NA%; forest and woodland NA%; other NA%; mostly rock with sparse scrub oak, few trees, some commercial salt ponds

Environment:
   frequent hurricanes, other tropical storms (July to October)

Note:
   located 270 km east of Puerto Rico

:Anguilla People

Population: 6,963 (July 1992), growth rate 0.6% (1992)
Birth rate: 24 births/1,000 population (1992)
Death rate: 8 deaths/1,000 population (1992)
Net migration rate: —10 migrants/1,000 population (1992)
Infant mortality rate: 18 deaths/1,000 live births (1992)
Life expectancy at birth: 71 years male, 77 years female (1992)
Total fertility rate: 3.1 children born/woman (1992)

Nationality:
   noun - Anguillan(s); adjective - Anguillan

Ethnic divisions:
   mainly of black African descent

Religions:
   Anglican 40%, Methodist 33%, Seventh-Day Adventist 7%, Baptist 5%, Roman Catholic 3%, other 12%

Languages:
   English (official)

Literacy:
   95% (male 95%, female 95%) age 12 and over can read and write (1984)

Labor force:
   2,780 (1984)

Organized labor:
   NA

:Anguilla Government

Long-form name:
   none

Type:
   dependent territory of the UK

Capital: The Valley

Administrative divisions:
   none (dependent territory of the UK)

Independence:
   none (dependent territory of the UK)

Constitution:
   1 April 1982

Legal system:
   based on English common law

National holiday:
   Anguilla Day, 30 May

Executive branch:
   British monarch, governor, chief minister, Executive Council (cabinet)

28

Legislative branch:
unicameral House of Assembly
Judicial branch:
High Court
Leaders:
 Chief of State:
  Queen ELIZABETH II (since 6 February 1952), represented by Governor Brian G.
  J. CANTY (since NA 1989)
 Head of Government:
  Chief Minister Emile GUMBS (since March 1984, served previously from
  February 1977 to May 1980)
Political parties and leaders:
  Anguilla National Alliance (ANA), Emile GUMBS; Anguilla United Party (AUP),
  Hubert HUGHES; Anguilla Democratic Party (ADP), Victor BANKS
Suffrage:
 universal at age 18
Elections:
 House of Assembly:
  last held 27 February 1989 (next to be held February 1994); results -
  percent of vote by party NA; seats - (11 total, 7 elected) ANA 3, AUP 2, ADP
  1, independent 1
Member of:
 CARICOM (observer), CDB
Diplomatic representation:
 none (dependent territory of the UK)
Flag:
  two horizontal bands of white (top, almost triple width) and light blue with
  three orange dolphins in an interlocking circular design centered in the
  white band; a new flag may have been in use since 30 May 1990

:Anguilla Economy

Overview:
  Anguilla has few natural resources, and the economy depends heavily on
  lobster fishing, offshore banking, tourism, and remittances from emigrants.
  In recent years the economy has benefited from a boom in tourism.
  Development plans center around the improvement of the infrastructure,
  particularly transport and tourist facilities, and also light industry.
GDP:
  exchange rate conversion - $23 million, per capita $3,300; real growth rate
  8.2% (1988 est.)
Inflation rate (consumer prices):
  4.5% (1988 est.)
Unemployment rate: 5.0% (1988 est.)
Budget:
  revenues $13.8 million; expenditures $15.2 million, including capital
  expenditures of $2.4 million (1992 est.)
Exports:
 $NA
 commodities:
  lobster and salt

partners:
 NA
Imports:
 $NA
 commodities:
 NA
 partners:
 NA
External debt: $NA
Industrial production:
  growth rate NA%
Electricity:
  2,000 kW capacity; 6 million kWh produced, 867 kWh per capita (1991)
Industries:
  tourism, boat building, salt, fishing (including lobster)
Agriculture:
  pigeon peas, corn, sweet potatoes, sheep, goats, pigs, cattle, poultry
Economic aid:
  Western (non-US) countries, ODA and OOF bilateral commitments (1970-89), $38
  million
Currency:
  East Caribbean dollar (plural - dollars); 1 EC dollar (EC$) = 100 cents
Exchange rates:
  East Caribbean dollars (EC$) per US$1 - 2.70 (fixed rate since 1976)
Fiscal year: NA

:Anguilla Communications

Highways:
  60 km surfaced
Ports:
  Road Bay, Blowing Point
Civil air:
  no major transport aircraft
Airports:
  3 total, 3 usable; 1 with permanent-surface runways of 1,100 m (Wallblake
  Airport)
Telecommunications:
  modern internal telephone system; 890 telephones; broadcast stations - 3 AM,
  1 FM, no TV; radio relay link to island of Saint Martin

:Anguilla Defense Forces

Note: defense is the responsibility of the UK

Antarctica Geography

Total area: 14,000,000 km2 (est.)
Land area: about 14,000,000 km2
Comparative area: slightly less than 1.5 times the size of the US; second-smallest
continent
  (after Australia)
Land boundaries:
  none, but see entry on Disputes

Coastline:
17,968 km
Maritime claims:
none, but see entry on Disputes
Disputes:
Antarctic Treaty defers claims (see Antarctic Treaty Summary below); sections (some overlapping) claimed by Argentina, Australia, Chile, France (Adelie Land), New Zealand (Ross Dependency), Norway (Queen Maud Land), and UK; the US and Russia do not recognize the territorial claims of other nations and have made no claims themselves (but reserve the right to do so); no formal claims have been made in the sector between 90. west and 150. west, where, because of floating ice, Antarctica is unapproachable from the sea
Climate:
severe low temperatures vary with latitude, elevation, and distance from the ocean; East Antarctica is colder than West Antarctica because of its higher elevation; Antarctic Peninsula has the most moderate climate; higher temperatures occur in January along the coast and average slightly below freezing
Terrain:
about 98% thick continental ice sheet and 2% barren rock, with average elevations between 2,000 and 4,000 meters; mountain ranges up to 4,897 meters high; ice-free coastal areas include parts of southern Victoria Land, Wilkes Land, the Antarctic Peninsula area, and Ross Island on McMurdo Sound; glaciers form ice shelves along about half of the coastline, and floating ice shelves constitute 11% of the area of the continent
Natural resources:
none presently exploited; iron, chromium, copper, gold, nickel, platinum, and other minerals, and coal and hydrocarbons have been found in small, uncommercial quantities
Land use:
no arable land and no plant growth; ice 98%, barren rock 2%
Environment:
mostly uninhabitable; katabatic (gravity-driven) winds blow coastward from the high interior; frequent blizzards form near the foot of the plateau; a circumpolar ocean current flows clockwise along the coast as do cyclonic storms that form over the ocean; during summer more solar radiation reaches the surface at the South Pole than is received at the Equator in an equivalent period; in October 1991 it was reported that the ozone shield, which protects the Earth's surface from harmful ultraviolet radiation, had dwindled to its lowest level ever over Antarctica; active volcanism on Deception Island and isolated areas of West Antarctica; other seismic activity rare and weak
Note:
the coldest, windiest, highest, and driest continent

:Antarctica People

Population: no indigenous inhabitants; staffing of research stations varies seasonally
Population: Summer (January) population:
4,115; Argentina 207, Australia 268, Belgium 13, Brazil 80, Chile 256, China

NA, Ecuador NA, Finland 11, France 78, Germany 32, Greenpeace 12, India 60, Italy 210, Japan 59, South Korea 14, Netherlands 10, New Zealand 264, Norway 23, Peru 39, Poland NA, South Africa 79, Spain 43, Sweden 10, UK 116, Uruguay NA, US 1,666, Russia 565 (1989-90)

Summer only stations:

over 40; Argentina 7, Australia 3, Chile 5, Germany 3, India 1, Italy 1, Japan 4, New Zealand 2, Norway 1, Peru 1, South Africa 1, Spain 1, Sweden 2, UK 1, US numerous, Russia 5 (1989-90); note - the disintegration of the former Soviet Union has placed the status and future of its Antarctic facilities in doubt. Stations may be subject to closings at any time because of ongoing economic difficulties.

Winter (July) population:

1,066 total; Argentina 150, Australia 71, Brazil 12, Chile 73, China NA, France 33, Germany 19, Greenpeace 5, India 1, Japan 38, South Korea 14, NZ 11, Poland NA, South Africa 12, UK 69, Uruguay NA, US 225, Russia 313 (1989-90)

Year-round stations:

43 total; Argentina 6, Australia 3, Brazil 1, Chile 3, China 2, Finland 1, France 1, Germany 1, India 1, Japan 2, South Korea 1, NZ 1, Poland 1, South Africa 3, UK 5, Uruguay 1, US 3, Russia 6 (1990-91)

:Antarctica Government

Long-form name:

Type:

Antarctic Treaty Summary: Article 1:

area to be used for peaceful purposes only; military activity, such as weapons testing, is prohibited, but military personnel and equipment may be used for scientific research or any other peaceful purposes

Article 2:

freedom of scientific investigation and cooperation shall continue

Article 3:

free exchange of information and personnel in cooperation with the UN and other international agencies

Article 4:

does not recognize, dispute, or establish territorial claims and no new claims shall be asserted while the treaty is in force

Article 5:

prohibits nuclear explosions or disposal of radioactive wastes

Article 6:

includes under the treaty all land and ice shelves south of 60. 00' south

Article 7:

treaty-state observers have free access, including aerial observation, to any area and may inspect all stations, installations, and equipment; advance notice of all activities and of the introduction of military personnel must be given

Article 8:

allows for jurisdiction over observers and scientists by their own states

Article 9:

frequent consultative meetings take place among member nations

Article 10:
treaty states will discourage activities by any country in Antarctica that are contrary to the treaty

Article 11:
disputes to be settled peacefully by the parties concerned or, ultimately, by the ICJ

Article 12, 13, 14:
deal with upholding, interpreting, and amending the treaty among involved nations

Other agreements:
more than 170 recommendations adopted at treaty consultative meetings and ratified by governments include - Agreed Measures for the Conservation of Antarctic Fauna and Flora (1964); Convention for the Conservation of Antarctic Seals (1972); Convention on the Conservation of Antarctic Marine Living Resources (1980); a mineral resources agreement was signed in 1988 but was subsequently rejected; in 1991 the Protocol on Environmental Protection to the Antarctic Treaty was signed and awaits ratification; this agreement provides for the protection of the Antarctic environment through five specific annexes on marine pollution, fauna, and flora, environmental impact assessments, waste management, and protected areas; it also prohibits all activities relating to mineral resources except scientific research

:Antarctica Economy

Overview:
No economic activity at present except for fishing off the coast and small-scale tourism, both based abroad.

:Antarctica Communications

Ports:
none; offshore anchorage only at most coastal stations

Airports:
41 airport facilities at different locations operated by 14 national governments party to the Treaty; one additional air facility operated by commercial (nongovernmental) tourist organization; helicopter pads at 28 of these locations; runways at 9 locations are gravel, sea ice, glacier ice, or compacted snow surface suitable for wheeled fixed-wing aircraft; no paved runways; 16 locations have snow-surface skiways limited to use by ski-equipped planes - 9 runways/skiways 1,000 to 3,000 m, 4 runways/skiways less than 1,000 m, 5 runways/skiways greater than 3,000 m, and 7 of unspecified or variable length; airports generally subject to severe restrictions and limitations resulting from extreme seasonal and geographic conditions

:Antarctica Defense Forces

Note:
none; Article 7 of the Antarctic Treaty states that advance notice of all military activities and the introduction of military personnel must be given

Antigua and Barbuda Geography

Total area: 440 km2
Land area: 440 km2; includes Redonda
Comparative area: slightly less than 2.5 times the size of Washington, DC

Land boundaries:
  none
Coastline:
  153 km
Maritime claims:
  Contiguous zone:
  24 nm
  Exclusive economic zone:
  200 nm
  Territorial sea:
  12 nm
Disputes:
  none
Climate:
  tropical marine; little seasonal temperature variation
Terrain:
  mostly low-lying limestone and coral islands with some higher volcanic areas
Natural resources:
  negligible; pleasant climate fosters tourism
Land use:
  arable land 18%; permanent crops 0%; meadows and pastures 7%; forest and
  woodland 16%; other 59%
Environment:
  subject to hurricanes and tropical storms (July to October); insufficient
  freshwater resources; deeply indented coastline provides many natural
  harbors
Note:
  420 km east-southeast of Puerto Rico

:Antigua and Barbuda People

Population: 64,110 (July 1992), growth rate 0.4% (1992)
Birth rate: 18 births/1,000 population (1992)
Death rate: 6 deaths/1,000 population (1992)
Net migration rate: —8 migrants/1,000 population (1992)
Infant mortality rate: 20 deaths/1,000 live births (1992)
Life expectancy at birth: 71 years male, 75 years female (1992)
Total fertility rate: 1.7 children born/woman (1992)
Nationality:
  noun - Antiguan(s), Barbudan(s); adjective - Antiguan, Barbudan
Ethnic divisions:
  almost entirely of black African origin; some of British, Portuguese,
  Lebanese, and Syrian origin
Religions:
  Anglican (predominant), other Protestant sects, some Roman Catholic
Languages:
  English (official), local dialects
Literacy:
  89% (male 90%, female 88%) age 15 and over having completed 5 or more years
  of schooling (1960)
Labor force:

30,000; commerce and services 82%, agriculture 11%, industry 7% (1983)

Organized labor:

Antigua and Barbuda Public Service Association (ABPSA), membership 500;

Antigua Trades and Labor Union (ATLU), 10,000 members; Antigua Workers Union

(AWU), 10,000 members (1986 est.)

:Antigua and Barbuda Government

Long-form name:

Type:

parliamentary democracy

Capital: Saint John's

Administrative divisions:

6 parishes and 2 dependencies*; Barbuda*, Redonda*, Saint George, Saint
John, Saint Mary, Saint Paul, Saint Peter, Saint Philip

Independence:

1 November 1981 (from UK)

Constitution:

1 November 1981

Legal system:

based on English common law

National holiday:

Independence Day, 1 November (1981)

Executive branch:

British monarch, governor general, prime minister, Cabinet

Legislative branch:

bicameral Parliament consists of an upper house or Senate and a lower house
or House of Representatives

Judicial branch:

Eastern Caribbean Supreme Court

Leaders:

Chief of State:

Queen ELIZABETH II (since 6 February 1952), represented by Governor General
Sir Wilfred Ebenezer JACOBS (since 1 November 1981, previously Governor
since 1976)

Head of Government:

Prime Minister Vere Cornwall BIRD, Sr. (since NA 1976); Deputy Prime
Minister (vacant)

Political parties and leaders:

Antigua Labor Party (ALP), Vere C. BIRD, Sr., Lester BIRD; United
Progressive Party (UPP), Baldwin SPENCER

Suffrage:

universal at age 18

Elections:

House of Representatives:

last held 9 March 1989 (next to be held NA 1994); results - percent of vote
by party NA; seats - (17 total) ALP 15, UPP 1, independent 1

Other political or pressure groups:

United Progressive Party (UPP), a coalition of three opposition political

parties - the United National Democratic Party (UNDP), the Antigua Caribbean
Liberation Movement (ACLM), and the Progressive Labor Movement (PLM), the
UPP is led by Baldwin SPENCER; Antigua Trades and Labor Union (ATLU), head-
ed
  by Noel THOMAS
Member of:
  ACP, C, CARICOM, CDB, ECLAC, FAO, G-77, GATT, IBRD, ICAO, ICFTU,
IFAD, IFC,
  ILO, IMF, IMO, INTERPOL, IOC, ITU, NAM (observer), OAS, OECS, OPANAL,
UN,
  UNCTAD, UNESCO, WCL, WHO, WMO
Diplomatic representation:
  Ambassador Patrick Albert LEWIS; Chancery at Suite 2H, 3400 International
  Drive NW, Washington, DC 20008; telephone (202) 362-5211 or 5166, 5122,
  5225; there is an Antiguan Consulate in Miami

:Antigua and Barbuda Government

  US:
  the US Ambassador to Barbados is accredited to Antigua and Barbuda, and, in
  his absence, the Embassy is headed by Charge d'Affaires Bryant SALTER;
  Embassy at Queen Elizabeth Highway, Saint John's (mailing address is FPO AA
  34054); telephone (809) 462-3505 or 3506; FAX (809) 462-3516
Flag:
  red with an inverted isosceles triangle based on the top edge of the flag;
  the triangle contains three horizontal bands of black (top), light blue, and
  white with a yellow rising sun in the black band

:Antigua and Barbuda Economy

Overview:
  The economy is primarily service oriented, with tourism the most important
  determinant of economic performance. During the period 1987-90, real GDP
  expanded at an annual average rate of about 6%. Tourism makes a direct
  contribution to GDP of about 13% and also affects growth in other sectors -
  particularly in construction, communications, and public utilities. Although
  Antigua and Barbuda is one of the few areas in the Caribbean experiencing a
  labor shortage in some sectors of the economy, it was hurt in 1991 by a
  downturn in tourism caused by the Persian Gulf war and the US recession.
GDP:
  exchange rate conversion - $418 million, per capita $6,500 (1989); real
  growth rate 4.2% (1990 est.)
Inflation rate (consumer prices):
  7% (1990 est.)
Unemployment rate: 5.0% (1988 est.)
Budget:
  revenues $92.8 million; expenditures $101 million, including capital
  expenditures of $NA (1990 est.)
Exports:
  $33.2 million (f.o.b., 1990)
  commodities:
  petroleum products 48%, manufactures 23%, food and live animals 4%,
  machinery and transport equipment 17%

partners:
  OECS 26%, Barbados 15%, Guyana 4%, Trinidad and Tobago 2%, US 0.3%
Imports:
  $325.9 million (c.i.f., 1990)
  commodities:
  food and live animals, machinery and transport equipment, manufactures,
  chemicals, oil
  partners:
  US 27%, UK 16%, Canada 4%, OECS 3%, other 50%
External debt: $250 million (1990 est.)
Industrial production:
  growth rate 3% (1989 est.); accounts for 3% of GDP
Electricity:
  52,100 kW capacity; 95 million kWh produced, 1,482 kWh per capita (1991)
Industries:
  tourism, construction, light manufacturing (clothing, alcohol, household
  appliances)
Agriculture:
  accounts for 4% of GDP; expanding output of cotton, fruits, vegetables, and
  livestock; other crops - bananas, coconuts, cucumbers, mangoes, sugarcane;
  not self-sufficient in food
Economic aid:
  US commitments, $10 million (1985-88); Western (non-US) countries, ODA and
  OOF bilateral commitments (1970-89), $50 million
Currency:
  East Caribbean dollar (plural - dollars); 1 EC dollar (EC$) = 100 cents
Exchange rates:
  East Caribbean dollars (EC$) per US$1 - 2.70 (fixed rate since 1976)
Fiscal year: 1 April - 31 March

:Antigua and Barbuda Communications

Railroads:
  64 km 0.760-meter narrow gauge and 13 km 0.610-meter gauge used almost
  exclusively for handling sugarcane
Highways:
  240 km
Ports:
  Saint John's
Merchant marine:
  105 ships (1,000 GRT or over) totaling 364,891 GRT/552,475 DWT; includes 71
  cargo, 3 refrigerated cargo, 12 container, 3 roll-on/roll-off cargo, 1
  multifunction large load carrier, 1 oil tanker, 12 chemical tanker, 2 bulk;
  note - a flag of convenience registry
Civil air:
  11 major transport aircraft
Airports:
  3 total, 3 usable; 2 with permanent-surface runways; 1 with runways
  2,440-3,659 m; 2 with runways less than 1,220 m
Telecommunications:
  good automatic telephone system; 6,700 telephones; tropospheric scatter

links with Saba and Guadeloupe; broadcast stations - 4 AM, 2 FM, 2 TV, 2 shortwave; 1 coaxial submarine cable; 1 Atlantic Ocean INTELSAT earth station

:Antigua and Barbuda Defense Forces

Branches:
Royal Antigua and Barbuda Defense Force, Royal Antigua and Barbuda Police Force (including the Coast Guard)

Manpower availability:
NA

Defense expenditures:
exchange rate conversion - $1.4 million, 1% of GDP (FY91)

Arctic Ocean Geography

Total area: 14,056,000 km2
Land area: 14,056,000 km2; includes Baffin Bay, Barents Sea, Beaufort Sea, Chukchi Sea,
East Siberian Sea, Greenland Sea, Hudson Bay, Hudson Strait, Kara Sea,
Laptev Sea, and other tributary water bodies

Comparative area: slightly more than 1.5 times the size of the US; smallest of the world's
four oceans (after Pacific Ocean, Atlantic Ocean, and Indian Ocean)

Coastline:
45,389 km

Disputes:
some maritime disputes (see littoral states)

Climate:
persistent cold and relatively narrow annual temperature ranges; winters characterized by continuous darkness, cold and stable weather conditions, and clear skies; summers characterized by continuous daylight, damp and foggy weather, and weak cyclones with rain or snow

Terrain:
central surface covered by a perennial drifting polar icepack that averages about 3 meters in thickness, although pressure ridges may be three times that size; clockwise drift pattern in the Beaufort Gyral Stream, but nearly straight line movement from the New Siberian Islands (Russia) to Denmark Strait (between Greenland and Iceland); the ice pack is surrounded by open seas during the summer, but more than doubles in size during the winter and extends to the encircling land masses; the ocean floor is about 50% continental shelf (highest percentage of any ocean) with the remainder a central basin interrupted by three submarine ridges (Alpha Cordillera, Nansen Cordillera, and Lomonsov Ridge); maximum depth is 4,665 meters in the Fram Basin

Natural resources:
sand and gravel aggregates, placer deposits, polymetallic nodules, oil and gas fields, fish, marine mammals (seals, whales)

Environment:
endangered marine species include walruses and whales; ice islands occasionally break away from northern Ellesmere Island; icebergs calved from glaciers in western Greenland and extreme northeastern Canada; maximum snow cover in March or April about 20 to 50 centimeters over the frozen ocean and

lasts about 10 months; permafrost in islands; virtually icelocked from
October to June; fragile ecosystem slow to change and slow to recover from
disruptions or damage

Note:
 major chokepoint is the southern Chukchi Sea (northern access to the Pacific
 Ocean via the Bering Strait); ships subject to superstructure icing from
 October to May; strategic location between North America and Russia;
 shortest marine link between the extremes of eastern and western Russia,
 floating research stations operated by the US and Russia

:Arctic Ocean Economy

Overview:
 Economic activity is limited to the exploitation of natural resources,
 including crude oil, natural gas, fish, and seals.

:Arctic Ocean Communications

Ports:
 Churchill (Canada), Murmansk (Russia), Prudhoe Bay (US)
Telecommunications:
 no submarine cables
Note:
 sparse network of air, ocean, river, and land routes; the Northwest Passage
 (North America) and Northern Sea Route (Asia) are important seasonal
 waterways

Argentina Geography

Total area: 2,766,890 km2
Land area: 2,736,690 km2
Comparative area: slightly more than four times the size of Texas
Land boundaries:
 9,665 km total; Bolivia 832 km, Brazil 1,224 km, Chile 5,150 km, Paraguay
 1,880 km, Uruguay 579 km
Coastline:
 4,989 km
Maritime claims:
 Continental shelf:
 200 m (depth) or to depth of exploitation
 Exclusive economic zone:
 nm limits unknown
 Territorial sea:
 12 nm (overflight and navigation permitted beyond 12 nm)
Disputes:
 short section of the boundary with Uruguay is in dispute; short section of
 the boundary with Chile is indefinite; claims British-administered Falkland
 Islands (Islas Malvinas); claims British- administered South Georgia and the
 South Sandwich Islands; territorial claim in Antarctica
Climate:
 mostly temperate; arid in southeast; subantarctic in southwest
Terrain:
 rich plains of the Pampas in northern half, flat to rolling plateau of
 Patagonia in south, rugged Andes along western border

Natural resources:

fertile plains of the pampas, lead, zinc, tin, copper, iron ore, manganese, crude oil, uranium

Land use:

arable land 9%; permanent crops 4%; meadows and pastures 52%; forest and woodland 22%; other 13%; includes irrigated 1%

Environment:

Tucuman and Mendoza areas in Andes subject to earthquakes; pamperos are violent windstorms that can strike Pampas and northeast; irrigated soil degradation; desertification; air and water pollution in Buenos Aires

Note:

second-largest country in South America (after Brazil); strategic location relative to sea lanes between South Atlantic and South Pacific Oceans (Strait of Magellan, Beagle Channel, Drake Passage)

:Argentina People

Population: 32,901,234 (July 1992), growth rate 1.1% (1992)
Birth rate: 20 births/1,000 population (1992)
Death rate: 9 deaths/1,000 population (1992)
Net migration rate: NEGL migrants/1,000 population (1992)
Infant mortality rate: 34 deaths/1,000 live births (1992)
Life expectancy at birth: 67 years male, 74 years female (1992)
Total fertility rate: 2.8 children born/woman (1992)
Nationality:

noun - Argentine(s); adjective - Argentine

Ethnic divisions:

white 85%; mestizo, Indian, or other nonwhite groups 15%

Religions:

nominally Roman Catholic 90% (less than 20% practicing), Protestant 2%, Jewish 2%, other 6%

Languages:

Spanish (official), English, Italian, German, French

Literacy:

95% (male 96%, female 95%) age 15 and over can read and write (1990 est.)

Labor force:

10,900,000; agriculture 12%, industry 31%, services 57% (1985 est.)

Organized labor:

3,000,000; 28% of labor force

:Argentina Government

Long-form name:

Argentine Republic

Type:

republic

Capital: Buenos Aires

Administrative divisions:

23 provinces (provincias, singular - provincia), and 1 district**
(distrito); Buenos Aires, Catamarca, Chaco, Chubut, Cordoba, Corrientes, Distrito Federal**, Entre Rios, Formosa, Jujuy, La Pampa, La Rioja, Mendoza, Misiones, Neuquen, Rio Negro, Salta, San Juan, San Luis, Santa Cruz, Santa Fe, Santiago del Estero, Tierra del Fuego, Tucuman; note - the national

territory is in the process of becoming a province; the US does not recognize claims to Antarctica

Independence:
9 July 1816 (from Spain)

Constitution:
1 May 1853

Legal system:
mixture of US and West European legal systems; has not accepted compulsory ICJ jurisdiction

National holiday:
Revolution Day, 25 May (1810)

Executive branch:
president, vice president, Cabinet

Legislative branch:
bicameral National Congress (Congreso Nacional) consists of an upper chamber or Senate (Senado) and a lower chamber or Chamber of Deputies (Camara de Diputados)

Judicial branch:
Supreme Court (Corte Suprema)

Leaders:
 Chief of State and Head of Government:
President Carlos Saul MENEM (since 8 July 1989); Vice President (position vacant)

Political parties and leaders:
Justicialist Party (JP), Carlos Saul MENEM, Peronist umbrella political organization; Radical Civic Union (UCR), Mario LOSADA, moderately left of center; Union of the Democratic Center (UCD), Jorge AGUADO, conservative party; Intransigent Party (PI), Dr. Oscar ALENDE, leftist party; several provincial parties

Suffrage:
universal at age 18

Elections:
 Chamber of Deputies:
last held in three phases during late 1991 for half of 254 seats, total current breakdown of seats - JP 122, UCR 85, UCD 10, other 37
 President:
last held 14 May 1989 (next to be held NA May 1995); results - Carlos Saul MENEM was elected
 Senate:
last held May 1989, but provincial elections in late 1991 set the stage for indirect elections by provincial senators for one-third of 46 seats in the national senate in May 1992; total current breakdown of seats - JP 27, UCR 14, others 5

Communists:
some 70,000 members in various party organizations, including a small nucleus of activists

:Argentina Government

Other political or pressure groups:
Peronist-dominated labor movement, General Confederation of Labor

(Peronist-leaning umbrella labor organization), Argentine Industrial Union (manufacturers' association), Argentine Rural Society (large landowners' association), business organizations, students, the Roman Catholic Church, the Armed Forces

Member of:

AfDB, AG (observer), CCC, ECLAC, FAO, G-6, G-11, G-15, G-19, G-24, G-77, GATT, IADB, IAEA, IBRD, ICAO, ICC, ICFTU, IDA, IFAD, IFC, ILO, IMF, IMO, INMARSAT, INTELSAT, INTERPOL, IOC, IOM, ISO, ITU, LAES, LAIA, LORCS,

MERCOSUR, OAS, PCA, RG, UN, UNAVEM, UNCTAD, UNESCO, UNHCR, UNIDO, UNIIMOG,

UNTSO, UPU, WCL, WFTU, WHO, WIPO, WMO, WTO

Diplomatic representation:

Ambassador Carlos ORTIZ DE ROZAS; Chancery at 1600 New Hampshire Avenue NW,

Washington, DC 20009; telephone (202) 939-6400 through 6403; there are Argentine Consulates General in Houston, Miami, New Orleans, New York, San Francisco, and San Juan (Puerto Rico), and Consulates in Baltimore, Chicago, and Los Angeles

US:

Ambassador Terence A. TODMAN; Embassy at 4300 Colombia, 1425 Buenos Aires (mailing address is APO AA 34034); telephone [54] (1) 774- 7611 or 8811, 9911; Telex 18156 AMEMBAR

Flag:

three equal horizontal bands of light blue (top), white, and light blue; centered in the white band is a radiant yellow sun with a human face known as the Sun of May

:Argentina Economy

Overview:

Argentina is rich in natural resources and has a highly literate population, an export-oriented agricultural sector, and a diversified industrial base. Nevertheless, following decades of mismanagement and statist policies, the economy has encountered major problems in recent years, leading to escalating inflation and a recession during 1988-90. Since 1978, Argentina's external debt has nearly doubled to $58 billion, creating severe debt servicing difficulties and hurting the country's creditworthiness with international lenders. Elected in 1989, President Menem has implemented a comprehensive economic restructuring program that shows signs of reversing Argentina's economic decline and putting it on a path of stable, sustainable growth.

GDP:

exchange rate conversion - $101.2 billion, per capita $3,100; real growth rate 5.5% (1991 est.)

Inflation rate (consumer prices):

83.8% (1991)

Unemployment rate: 6.4% (October 1991)

Budget:

revenues $13.6 billion; expenditures $16.6 billion, including capital expenditures of $2.5 billion (1991)

Exports:
   $12 billion (f.o.b., 1991)
   commodities:
   meat, wheat, corn, oilseed, hides, wool
   partners:
   US 12%, USSR, Italy, Brazil, Japan, Netherlands
Imports:
   $8 billion (c.i.f., 1991)
   commodities:
   machinery and equipment, chemicals, metals, fuels and lubricants,
   agricultural products
   partners:
   US 22%, Brazil, FRG, Bolivia, Japan, Italy, Netherlands
External debt: $61 billion (January 1992)
Industrial production:
   growth rate 20% (1991 est.); accounts for 30% of GDP
Electricity:
   17,059,000 kW capacity; 47,357 million kWh produced, 1,450 kWh per capita
   (1991)
Industries:
   food processing, motor vehicles, consumer durables, textiles, chemicals and
   petrochemicals, printing, metallurgy, steel
Agriculture:
   accounts for 15% of GNP (including fishing); produces abundant food for both
   domestic consumption and exports; among world's top five exporters of grain
   and beef; principal crops - wheat, corn, sorghum, soybeans, sugar beets
Illicit drugs:
   increasing use as a transshipment country for cocaine headed for the US and
   Europe
Economic aid:
   US commitments, including Ex-Im (FY70-89), $1.0 billion; Western (non-US)
   countries, ODA and OOF bilateral commitments (1970-89), $4.4 billion;
   Communist countries (1970-89), $718 million
Currency:
   peso (plural - pesos); 1 pesos = 100 centavos

:Argentina Economy

Exchange rates:
   pesos per US$1 - 0.99076 (Feburary 1992), 0.95355 (1991), 0.48759 (1990),
   0.04233 (1989), 0.00088 (1988), 0.00021 (1987)
Fiscal year: calendar year

:Argentina Communications

Railroads:
   34,172 km total (includes 209 km electrified); includes a mixture of
   1.435-meter standard gauge, 1.676-meter broad gauge, 1.000-meter narrow
   gauge, and 0.750-meter narrow gauge
Highways:
   208,350 km total; 47,550 km paved, 39,500 km gravel, 101,000 km improved
   earth, 20,300 km unimproved earth
Inland waterways:

11,000 km navigable

Pipelines:

crude oil 4,090 km; petroleum products 2,900 km; natural gas 9,918 km

Ports:

Bahia Blanca, Buenos Aires, Necochea, Rio Gallegos, Rosario, Santa Fe

Merchant marine:

98 ships (1,000 GRT or over) totaling 1,235,385 GRT/1,952,307 DWT; includes
35 cargo, 6 refrigerated cargo, 6 container, 1 railcar carrier, 33 oil
tanker, 4 chemical tanker, 3 liquefied gas, 10 bulk; in addition, 2 naval
tankers and 1 military transport are sometimes used commercially

Civil air:

56 major transport aircraft

Airports:

1,702 total, 1,473 usable; 137 with permanent-surface runways; 1 with
runways over 3,659 m; 31 with runways 2,440-3,659 m; 326 with runways
1,220-2,439 m

Telecommunications:

extensive modern system; 2,650,000 telephones (12,000 public telephones);
microwave widely used; broadcast stations - 171 AM, no FM, 231 TV, 13
shortwave; 2 Atlantic Ocean INTELSAT earth stations; domestic satellite
network has 40 earth stations

:Argentina Defense Forces

Branches:

Argentine Army, Navy of the Argentine Republic, Argentine Air Force,
National Gendarmerie, Argentine Naval Prefecture (Coast Guard only),
National Aeronautical Police Force

Manpower availability:

males 15-49, 8,101,856; 6,568,885 fit for military service; 276,457 reach
military age (20) annually

Defense expenditures:

exchange rate conversion - $700 million, 1.5% of GDP (1991)

Armenia Geography

Total area: 29,800 km2

Land area: 28,400 km2

Comparative area: slightly larger than Maryland

Land boundaries:

1,254 km total; Azerbaijan (east) 566 km, Azerbaijan (south) 221 km, Georgia
164 km, Iran 35 km, Turkey 268 km

Coastline:

none - landlocked

Maritime claims:

none - landlocked

Disputes:

violent and longstanding dispute with Azerbaijan over ethnically Armenian
exclave of Nagorno-Karabakh; some irredentism by Armenians living in
southern Georgia; traditional demands on former Armenian lands in Turkey
have greatly subsided

Climate:

continental, hot, and subject to drought

Terrain:

high Armenian Plateau with mountain; little forest land; fast flowing
rivers; good soil in Aras River valley

Natural resources:

small deposits of gold, copper, molybdenum, zinc, alumina

Land use:

10% arable land; NA% permanent crops; NA% meadows and pastures; NA% forest
and woodland; NA% other; NA% irrigated

Environment:

pollution of Razdan and Aras Rivers; air pollution in Yerevan

:Armenia People

Population: 3,415,566 (July 1992), growth rate 0.8% (1992)

Birth rate: 22 births/1,000 population (1992)

Death rate: 7 deaths/1,000 population (1992)

Net migration rate: —7 migrants/1,000 population (1992)

Infant mortality rate: 35 deaths/1,000 live births (1992)

Life expectancy at birth: 68 years male, 74 years female (1992)

Total fertility rate: 2.7 children born/woman (1992)

Nationality:

noun - Armenian(s); adjective - Armenian

Ethnic divisions:

Armenian 93.3%, Russian 1.5%, Kurd 1.7%, other 3.5%

Religions:

Armenian Orthodox 94%

Languages:

Armenian 93%, Russian 2%, other 5%

Literacy:

NA% (male NA%, female NA%) age 15 and over can read and write (NA)

Labor force:

1,630,000; industry and construction 42%, agriculture and forestry 18%,
other 40%(1990)

Organized labor:

NA

:Armenia Government

Long-form name:

Republic of Armenia

Type:

republic

Capital: Yerevan

Administrative divisions:

none - all rayons are under direct republic jurisdiction

Independence:

Armenian Republic formed 29 November 1920 and became part of the Soviet
Union on 30 December 1922; on 23 September 1991, Armenia renamed itself the
Republic of Armenia

Constitution:

adopted NA April 1978, effective NA

Legal system:

based on civil law system

National holiday:
  NA
Executive branch:
  President, Council of Ministers, prime minister
Legislative branch:
  unicameral body - Supreme Soviet
Judicial branch:
  Supreme Court
Leaders:
 Chief of State:
  President Levon Akopovich TER-PETROSYAN (since 16 October 1991), Vice
  President Gagik ARUTYUNYAN (since 16 October 1991)
 Head of Government:
  Prime Minister Gagik ARUTYUNYAN (since November 1991), First Deputy Prime
  Minister Grant BAGRATYAN (since NA September 1990); Supreme Soviet Chair-
man
  - Babken ARARKTSYAN
Political parties and leaders:
  Armenian National Movement, Husik LAZARYAN, chairman; National
  Self-Determination Association, Pakvyr HAYRIKIAN, chairman; National
  Democratic Union, Vazgen MANUKYAN, chairman; Democratic Liberal Party,
  Ramkavar AZATAKAN, chairman; Dashnatktsutyan Party, Rouben
MIRZAKHANIN;
  Chairman of Parliamentary opposition - Mekhak GABRIYELYAN
Suffrage:
  universal at age 18
Elections:
 President:
  last held 16 October 1990 (next to be held NA); results - elected by the
  Supreme Soviet, Levon Akopovich TER-PETROSYAN 86%; radical nationalists
  about 7%
 Supreme Soviet:
  last held 20 May 1990 (next to be held NA); results - percent of vote by
  party NA; seats - (259 total); number of seats by party NA
Other political or pressure groups:
  NA
Member of:
  CSCE, NACC, UN, UNCTAD
Diplomatic representation:
  Charge d'Affaires ad interim, Aleksandr ARZOUMANIAN
  US:
  Ambassador (vacant); Steven R. MANN, Charge d'Affaires; Embassy at Hotel
  Hrazdan (telephone 8-011-7-8852-53-53-32); (mailing address is APO AE
  09862); telephone 8-011-7-885-215-1122 (voice and FAX); 8-011-7-885-215-1144
  (voice)

:Armenia Government

Flag:
  NA

:Armenia Economy

Overview:

Armenia under the old centrally planned Soviet system had built up textile, machine-building, and other industries and had become a key supplier to sister republics. In turn, Armenia had depended on supplies of raw materials and energy from the other republics. Most of these supplies enter the republic by rail through Azerbaijan (85%) and Georgia (15%). The economy has been severely hurt by ethnic strife with Azerbaijan over control of the Nagorno-Karabakh Autonomous Oblast, a mostly Armenian-populated enclave within the national boundaries of Azerbaijan. In addition to outright warfare, the strife has included interdiction of Armenian imports on the Azerbaijani railroads and expensive airlifts of supplies to beleagured Armenians in Nagorno-Karabakh. An earthquake in December 1988 destroyed about one-tenth of industrial capacity and housing, the repair of which has not been possible because the supply of funds and real resources has been disrupted by the reorganization and subsequent dismantling of the central USSR administrative apparatus. Among facilities made unserviceable by the earthquake are the Yerevan nuclear power plant, which had supplied 40% of Armenia's needs for electric power and a plant that produced one-quarter of the output of elevators in the former USSR. Armenia has some deposits of nonferrous metal ores (bauxite, copper, zinc, and molybdenum) that are largely unexploited. For the mid-term, Armenia's economic prospects seem particularly bleak because of ethnic strife and the unusually high dependence on outside areas, themselves in a chaotic state of transformation.

GDP:

$NA, per capita $NA; real growth rate —10% (1991)

Inflation rate (consumer prices):

91%

Unemployment rate: NA%

Budget:

revenues $NA; expenditures $NA, including capital expenditures of $NA

Exports:

$176 million (f.o.b., 1990)

commodities:

machinery and transport equipment, ferrous and nonferrous metals, and chemicals (1991)

partners:

NA

Imports:

$1.5 billion (c.i.f., 1990)

commodities:

machinery, energy, consumer goods (1991)

partners:

NA

External debt: $650 million (December 1991 est.)

Industrial production:

growth rate —9.6% (1991)

Electricity:

NA kW capacity; 10,433 million kWh produced, about 3,000 kWh per capita (1990)

Industries:
   diverse, including (in percent of output of former USSR) metalcutting
   machine tools (6.7%), forging-pressing machines (4.7%), electric motors
   (8.7%), tires (2.1%), knitted wear (5.6%), hosiery (2.3%), shoes (2.2%),
   silk fabric (5.3%), washing machines (2.0%); also chemicals, trucks,
   watches, instruments, and microelectronics

:Armenia Economy

Agriculture:
   only 10% of land area is arable; employs 18% of labor force; citrus, cotton,
   and dairy farming; vineyards near Yerevan are famous for brandy and other
   liqueurs

Illicit drugs:
   illicit producer of cannabis mostly for domestic consumption; used as a
   transshipment point for illicit drugs to Western Europe

Economic aid:
   NA

Currency:
   as of May 1992, retaining ruble as currency

Exchange rates:
   NA

Fiscal year: calendar year

:Armenia Communications

Railroads:
   840 km all 1.000-meter gauge (includes NA km electrified); does not include
   industrial lines (1990)

Highways:
   11,300 km total (1990); 10,500 km hard surfaced, 800 km earth

Inland waterways:
   NA km perennially navigable

Pipelines:
   NA

Ports:
   none - landlocked

Merchant marine:
   none:
   landlocked

Civil air:
   none

Airports:
   NA total, NA usable; NA with permanent-surface runways; NA with runways over
   3,659 m; NA with runways 2,440-3,659 m; NA with runways 1,220-2,439 m

Telecommunications:
   Armenia has about 260,000 telephones, of which about 110,000 are in Yerevan;
   average telephone density is 8 per 100 persons; international connections to
   other former republics of the USSR are by landline or microwave and to other
   countries by satellite and by leased connection through the Moscow
   international gateway switch; broadcast stations - 100% of population
   receives Armenian and Russian TV programs; satellite earth station -
   INTELSAT

:Armenia Defense Forces

Branches:
  Republic Security Forces (internal and border troops), National Guard; CIS
  Forces (Ground and Air Defense)
Manpower availability:
  males 15-49, NA; NA fit for military service; NA reach military age (18)
  annually
Defense expenditures:
  $NA, NA% of GDP

Aruba Geography

Total area: 193 km2
Land area: 193 km2
Comparative area: slightly larger than Washington, DC
Land boundaries:
  none
Coastline:
  68.5 km
Maritime claims:
 Exclusive fishing zone:
  12 nm
 Territorial sea:
  12 nm
Disputes:
  none
Climate:
  tropical marine; little seasonal temperature variation
Terrain:
  flat with a few hills; scant vegetation
Natural resources:
  negligible; white sandy beaches
Land use:
  arable land 0%; permanent crops 0%; meadows and pastures 0%; forest and
  woodland 0%; other 100%
Environment:
  lies outside the Caribbean hurricane belt
Note:
  28 km north of Venezuela

:Aruba People

Population: 64,692 (July 1992), growth rate 0.7% (1992)
Birth rate: 16 births/1,000 population (1992)
Death rate: 6 deaths/1,000 population (1992)
Net migration rate: —3 migrants/1,000 population (1992)
Infant mortality rate: 9 deaths/1,000 live births (1992)
Life expectancy at birth: 73 years male, 80 years female (1992)
Total fertility rate: 1.8 children born/woman (1992)
Nationality:
  noun - Aruban(s); adjective - Aruban
Ethnic divisions:

mixed European/Caribbean Indian 80%

Religions:

Roman Catholic 82%, Protestant 8%, also small Hindu, Muslim, Confucian, and Jewish minority

Languages:

Dutch (official), Papiamento (a Spanish, Portuguese, Dutch, English dialect), English (widely spoken), Spanish

Literacy:

NA% (male NA%, female NA%)

Labor force:

NA, but most employment is in the tourist industry (1986)

Organized labor:

Aruban Workers' Federation (FTA)

:Aruba Government

Long-form name:

Type:

part of the Dutch realm - full autonomy in internal affairs obtained in 1986 upon separation from the Netherlands Antilles

Capital: Oranjestad

Administrative divisions:

none (self-governing part of the Netherlands)

Independence:

none (part of the Dutch realm); note - in 1990, Aruba requested and received from the Netherlands cancellation of the agreement to automatically give independence to the island in 1996

Constitution:

1 January 1986

Legal system:

based on Dutch civil law system, with some English common law influence

National holiday:

Flag Day, 18 March

Executive branch:

Dutch monarch, governor, prime minister, Council of Ministers (cabinet)

Legislative branch:

unicameral legislature (Staten)

Judicial branch:

Joint High Court of Justice

Leaders:

 Chief of State:

 Queen BEATRIX Wilhelmina Armgard (since 30 April 1980), represented by Governor General Felipe B. TROMP (since 1 January 1986)

 Head of Government:

 Prime Minister Nelson ODUBER (since NA February 1989)

Political parties and leaders:

Electoral Movement Party (MEP), Nelson ODUBER; Aruban People's Party (AVP), Henny EMAN; National Democratic Action (ADN), Pedro Charro KELLY; New Patriotic Party (PPN), Eddy WERLEMEN; Aruban Patriotic Party (PPA), Benny NISBET; Aruban Democratic Party (PDA), Leo BERLINSKI; Democratic Action

(AD '86), Arturo ODUBER; Organization for Aruban Liberty (OHA), Glenbert CROES; governing coalition includes the MEP, PPA, and ADN

Suffrage:

universal at age 18

Elections:

Legislature:

last held 6 January 1989 (next to be held by NA January 1993); results - percent of vote by party NA; seats - (21 total) MEP 10, AVP 8, ADN 1, PPN 1, PPA 1

Member of:

ECLAC (associate), INTERPOL, IOC, UNESCO (associate), WCL, WTO (associate)

Diplomatic representation:

none (self-governing part of the Netherlands)

Flag:

blue with two narrow horizontal yellow stripes across the lower portion and a red, four-pointed star outlined in white in the upper hoist-side corner

:Aruba Economy

Overview:

Tourism is the mainstay of the economy, although offshore banking and oil refining and storage are also important. Hotel capacity expanded rapidly between 1985 and 1989 and nearly doubled in 1990 alone. Unemployment has steadily declined from about 20% in 1986 to about 3% in 1991. The reopening of the local oil refinery, once a major source of employment and foreign exchange earnings, promises to give the economy an additional boost.

GDP:

exchange rate conversion - $854 million, per capita $13,600; real growth rate 10% (1990 est.)

Inflation rate (consumer prices):

8% (1990 est.)

Unemployment rate: 3% (1991 est.)

Budget:

revenues $145 million; expenditures $185 million, including capital expenditures of $42 million (1988)

Exports:

$134.4 million (f.o.b., 1990)

commodities:

mostly petroleum products

partners:

US 64%, EC

Imports:

$488 million (f.o.b., 1990)

commodities:

food, consumer goods, manufactures

partners:

US 8%, EC

External debt: $81 million (1987)

Industrial production:

growth rate NA
Electricity:
   310,000 kW capacity; 945 million kWh produced, 15,000 kWh per capita (1990)
Industries:
   tourism, transshipment facilities, oil refining
Agriculture:
   poor quality soils and low rainfall limit agricultural activity to the
   cultivation of aloes, some livestock, and fishing
Economic aid:
   Western (non-US) countries ODA and OOF bilateral commitments (1980-89), $220
   million
Currency:
   Aruban florin (plural - florins); 1 Aruban florin (Af.) = 100 cents
Exchange rates:
   Aruban florins (Af.) per US$1 - 1.7900 (fixed rate since 1986)
Fiscal year: calendar year

:Aruba Communications

Highways:
   Aruba has a system of all-weather highways
Ports:
   Oranjestad, Sint Nicolaas
Civil air:
   Air Aruba has a fleet of 3 intermediate-range Boeing aircraft
Airports:
   government-owned airport east of Oranjestad accepts transatlantic flights
Telecommunications:
   generally adequate; extensive interisland radio relay links; 72,168
   telephones; broadcast stations - 4 AM, 4 FM, 1 TV; 1 sea cable to Sint
   Maarten

:Aruba Defense Forces

Note: defense is the responsibility of the Netherlands

Ashmore and Cartier Islands Geography

Total area: 5 km2
Land area: 5 km2; includes Ashmore Reef (West, Middle, and East Islets) and Cartier
   Island
Comparative area: about 8.5 times the size of The Mall in Washington, DC
Land boundaries:
   none
Coastline:
   74.1 km
Maritime claims:
 Contiguous zone:
   12 nm
 Continental shelf:
   200 m (depth) or to depth of exploration
 Exclusive fishing zone:
   200 nm
 Territorial sea:

3 nm
Disputes:
  none
Climate:
  tropical
Terrain:
  low with sand and coral
Natural resources:
  fish
Land use:
  arable land 0%; permanent crops 0%; meadows and pastures 0%; forest and
  woodland 0%; other - grass and sand 100%
Environment:
  surrounded by shoals and reefs; Ashmore Reef National Nature Reserve
  established in August 1983
Note:
  located in extreme eastern Indian Ocean between Australia and Indonesia, 320
  km off the northwest coast of Australia

:Ashmore and Cartier Islands People

Population: no permanent inhabitants; seasonal caretakers

:Ashmore and Cartier Islands Government

Long-form name:
  Territory of Ashmore and Cartier Islands
Type:
  territory of Australia administered by the Australian Minister for Arts,
  Sports, the Environment, Tourism, and Territories - Roslyn KELLY
Capital: none; administered from Canberra, Australia
Administrative divisions:
  none (territory of Australia)
Legal system:
  relevant laws of the Northern Territory of Australia
Diplomatic representation:
  none (territory of Australia)

:Ashmore and Cartier Islands Economy

Overview: no economic activity

:Ashmore and Cartier Islands Communications

Ports: none; offshore anchorage only

:Ashmore and Cartier Islands Defense Forces

Note:
  defense is the responsibility of Australia; periodic visits by the Royal
  Australian Navy and Royal Australian Air Force

Atlantic Ocean Geography

Total area: 82,217,000 km2
Land area: 82,217,000 km2; includes Baltic Sea, Black Sea, Caribbean Sea, Davis
Strait,
  Denmark Strait, Drake Passage, Gulf of Mexico, Mediterranean Sea, North Sea,

Norwegian Sea, Weddell Sea, and other tributary water bodies

Comparative area: slightly less than nine times the size of the US; second-largest of the
   world's four oceans (after the Pacific Ocean, but larger than Indian Ocean
   or Arctic Ocean)

Coastline:
   111,866 km

Disputes:
   some maritime disputes (see littoral states)

Climate:
   tropical cyclones (hurricanes) develop off the coast of Africa near Cape
   Verde and move westward into the Caribbean Sea; hurricanes can occur from
   May to December, but are most frequent from August to November

Terrain:
   surface usually covered with sea ice in Labrador Sea, Denmark Strait, and
   Baltic Sea from October to June; clockwise warm water gyre (broad, circular
   system of currents) in the north Atlantic, counterclockwise warm water gyre
   in the south Atlantic; the ocean floor is dominated by the Mid-Atlantic
   Ridge, a rugged north-south centerline for the entire Atlantic basin;
   maximum depth is 8,605 meters in the Puerto Rico Trench

Natural resources:
   oil and gas fields, fish, marine mammals (seals and whales), sand and gravel
   aggregates, placer deposits, polymetallic nodules, precious stones

Environment:
   endangered marine species include the manatee, seals, sea lions, turtles,
   and whales; municipal sludge pollution off eastern US, southern Brazil, and
   eastern Argentina; oil pollution in Caribbean Sea, Gulf of Mexico, Lake
   Maracaibo, Mediterranean Sea, and North Sea; industrial waste and municipal
   sewage pollution in Baltic Sea, North Sea, and Mediterranean Sea; icebergs
   common in Davis Strait, Denmark Strait, and the northwestern Atlantic from
   February to August and have been spotted as far south as Bermuda and the
   Madeira Islands; icebergs from Antarctica occur in the extreme southern
   Atlantic

Note:
   ships subject to superstructure icing in extreme north Atlantic from October
   to May and extreme south Atlantic from May to October; persistent fog can be
   a hazard to shipping from May to September; major choke points include the
   Dardanelles, Strait of Gibraltar, access to the Panama and Suez Canals;
   strategic straits include the Dover Strait, Straits of Florida, Mona
   Passage, The Sound (Oresund), and Windward Passage; north Atlantic shipping
   lanes subject to icebergs from February to August; the Equator divides the
   Atlantic Ocean into the North Atlantic Ocean and South Atlantic Ocean
   Kiel Canal and Saint Lawrence Seaway are two important waterways

:Atlantic Ocean Economy

Overview:
   Economic activity is limited to exploitation of natural resources,
   especially fish, dredging aragonite sands (The Bahamas), and crude oil and
   natural gas production (Caribbean Sea and North Sea).

:Atlantic Ocean Communications

Ports:

Alexandria (Egypt), Algiers (Algeria), Antwerp (Belgium), Barcelona (Spain), Buenos Aires (Argentina), Casablanca (Morocco), Colon (Panama), Copenhagen (Denmark), Dakar (Senegal), Gdansk (Poland), Hamburg (Germany), Helsinki (Finland), Las Palmas (Canary Islands, Spain), Le Havre (France), Lisbon (Portugal), London (UK), Marseille (France), Montevideo (Uruguay), Montreal (Canada), Naples (Italy), New Orleans (US), New York (US), Oran (Algeria), Oslo (Norway), Piraeus (Greece), Rio de Janeiro (Brazil), Rotterdam (Netherlands), Saint Petersburg (formerly Leningrad; Russia), Stockholm (Sweden)

Telecommunications:

numerous submarine cables with most between continental Europe and the UK, North America and the UK, and in the Mediterranean; numerous direct links across Atlantic via INTELSAT satellite network

Australia Geography

Total area: 7,686,850 km2
Land area: 7,617,930 km2; includes Macquarie Island
Comparative area: slightly smaller than the US
Land boundaries:

Coastline:

25,760 km

Maritime claims:

Contiguous zone:

12 nm

Continental shelf:

200 m (depth) or to depth of exploitation

Exclusive fishing zone:

200 nm

Territorial sea:

12 nm

Disputes:

territorial claim in Antarctica (Australian Antarctic Territory)

Climate:

generally arid to semiarid; temperate in south and east; tropical in north

Terrain:

mostly low plateau with deserts; fertile plain in southeast

Natural resources:

bauxite, coal, iron ore, copper, tin, silver, uranium, nickel, tungsten, mineral sands, lead, zinc, diamonds, natural gas, crude oil

Land use:

arable land 6%; permanent crops NEGL%; meadows and pastures 58%; forest and woodland 14%; other 22%; includes irrigated NEGL%

Environment:

subject to severe droughts and floods; cyclones along coast; limited freshwater availability; irrigated soil degradation; regular, tropical, invigorating, sea breeze known as the doctor occurs along west coast in summer; desertification

Note:

world's smallest continent but sixth-largest country

:Australia People

Population: 17,576,354 (July 1992), growth rate 1.4% (1992)
Birth rate: 15 births/1,000 population (1992)
Death rate: 7 deaths/1,000 population (1992)
Net migration rate: 7 migrants/1,000 population (1992)
Infant mortality rate: 8 deaths/1,000 live births (1992)
Life expectancy at birth: 74 years male, 80 years female (1992)
Total fertility rate: 1.8 children born/woman (1992)
Nationality:

noun - Australian(s); adjective - Australian
Ethnic divisions:

Caucasian 95%, Asian 4%, Aboriginal and other 1%
Religions:

Anglican 26.1%, Roman Catholic 26.0%, other Christian 24.3%
Languages:

English, native languages
Literacy:

100% (male 100%, female 100%) age 15 and over can read and write (1980 est.)
Labor force:

8,630,000 (September 1991); finance and services 33.8%, public and community
services 22.3%, wholesale and retail trade 20.1%, manufacturing and industry
16.2%, agriculture 6.1% (1987)
Organized labor:

40% of labor force (November 1991)

:Australia Government

Long-form name:

Commonwealth of Australia
Type:

federal parliamentary state
Capital: Canberra
Administrative divisions:

6 states and 2 territories*; Australian Capital Territory*, New South Wales,
Northern Territory*, Queensland, South Australia, Tasmania, Victoria,
Western Australia
Independence:

1 January 1901 (federation of UK colonies)
Constitution:

9 July 1900, effective 1 January 1901
Dependent areas:

Ashmore and Cartier Islands, Christmas Island, Cocos (Keeling) Islands,
Coral Sea Islands, Heard Island and McDonald Islands, Norfolk Island
Legal system:

based on English common law; accepts compulsory ICJ jurisdiction, with
reservations
National holiday:

Australia Day, 26 January
Executive branch:

British monarch, governor general, prime minister, deputy prime minister,
Cabinet
Legislative branch:
  bicameral Federal Parliament consists of an upper house or Senate and a
  lower house or House of Representatives
Judicial branch:
  High Court
Leaders:
  Chief of State:
    Queen ELIZABETH II (since February 1952), represented by Governor General
    William George HAYDEN (since 16 February 1989)
  Head of Government:
    Prime Minister Paul John KEATING (since 20 December 1991); Deputy Prime
    Minister Brian HOWE (since 4 June 1991)
Political parties and leaders:
  government:
    Australian Labor Party, Paul John KEATING
  opposition:
    Liberal Party, John HEWSON; National Party, Timothy FISCHER; Australian
    Democratic Party, John COULTER
Suffrage:
  universal and compulsory at age 18
Elections:
  House of Representatives:
    last held 24 March 1990 (next to be held by NA November 1993); results -
    Labor 39.7%, Liberal-National 43%, Australian Democrats and independents
    11.1%; seats - (148 total) Labor 78, Liberal-National 69, independent 1
  Senate:
    last held 11 July 1987 (next to be held by NA July 1993); results - Labor
    43%, Liberal-National 42%, Australian Democrats 8%, independents 2%; seats -
    (76 total) Labor 32, Liberal-National 34, Australian Democrats 7,
    independents 3
Communists:
  4,000 members (est.)

:Australia Government

Other political or pressure groups:
  Australian Democratic Labor Party (anti-Communist Labor Party splinter
  group); Peace and Nuclear Disarmament Action (Nuclear Disarmament Party
  splinter group)
Member of:
  AfDB, AG (observer), ANZUS, APEC, AsDB, Australia Group, BIS, C, CCC,
COCOM,
  CP, EBRD, ESCAP, FAO, GATT, G-8, IAEA, IBRD, ICAO, ICC, ICFTU, IDA,
IEA,
  IFAD, IFC, ILO, IMF, IMO, INMARSAT, INTELSAT, INTERPOL, IOC, IOM,
ISO, ITU,
  LORCS, MTCR, NAM (guest), NEA, NSG, OECD, PCA, SPC, SPF, UN,
UNCTAD, UNESCO,
  UNFICYP, UNHCR, UNIIMOG, UNTAG, UNTSO, UPU, WFTU, WHO, WIPO,

WMO, WTO, ZC

Diplomatic representation:

Ambassador Michael J. COOK; Chancery at 1601 Massachusetts Avenue NW, Washington, DC 20036; telephone (202) 797-3000; there are Australian Consulates General in Chicago, Honolulu, Houston, Los Angeles, New York, Pago Pago (American Samoa), and San Francisco

US:

Ambassador Melvin F. SEMBLER; Moonah Place, Yarralumla, Canberra, Australian

Capital Territory 2600 (mailing address is APO AP 96549); telephone [61] (6) 270-5000; FAX [61] (6) 270-5970; there are US Consulates General in Melbourne, Perth, and Sydney, and a Consulate in Brisbane

Flag:

blue with the flag of the UK in the upper hoist-side quadrant and a large seven-pointed star in the lower hoist-side quadrant; the remaining half is a representation of the Southern Cross constellation in white with one small five-pointed star and four, larger, seven-pointed stars

:Australia Economy

Overview:

Australia has a prosperous Western-style capitalist economy, with a per capita GDP comparable to levels in industrialized West European countries. Rich in natural resources, Australia is a major exporter of agricultural products, minerals, metals, and fossil fuels. Of the top 25 exports, 21 are primary products, so that, as happened during 1983-84, a downturn in world commodity prices can have a big impact on the economy. The government is pushing for increased exports of manufactured goods, but competition in international markets continues to be severe.

GDP:

purchasing power equivalent - $280.8 billion, per capita $16,200; real growth rate —0.6% (1991 est.)

Inflation rate (consumer prices):

3.3% (September 1991)

Unemployment rate: 10.5% (November 1991)

Budget:

revenues $76.9 billion; expenditures $75.4 billion, including capital expenditures of NA (FY91)

Exports:

$41.7 billion (f.o.b., FY91)

commodities:

metals, minerals, coal, wool, cereals, meat, manufacturers

partners:

Japan 26%, US 11%, NZ 6%, South Korea 4%, Singapore 4%, UK, Taiwan, Hong Kong

Imports:

$37.8 billion (f.o.b., FY91)

commodities:

manufactured raw materials, capital equipment, consumer goods

partners:

US 24%, Japan 19%, UK 6%, FRG 7%, NZ 4% (1990)

External debt: $130.4 billion (June 1991)

Industrial production:

growth rate —0.9% (1991); accounts for 32% of GDP

Electricity:

40,000,000 kW capacity; 155,000 million kWh produced, 8,960 kWh per capita (1991)

Industries:

mining, industrial and transportation equipment, food processing, chemicals, steel, motor vehicles

Agriculture:

accounts for 5% of GNP and 37% of export revenues; world's largest exporter of beef and wool, second-largest for mutton, and among top wheat exporters; major crops - wheat, barley, sugarcane, fruit; livestock - cattle, sheep, poultry

Illicit drugs:

Tasmania is one of the world's major suppliers of licit opiate products; government maintains strict controls over areas of opium poppy cultivation and output of poppy straw concentrate

Economic aid:

donor - ODA and OOF commitments (1970-89), $10.4 billion

Currency:

Australian dollar (plural - dollars); 1 Australian dollar ($A) = 100 cents

Exchange rates:

Australian dollars ($A) per US$1 - 1.3360 (January 1992), 1.2836 (1991), 1.2618 (1989), 1.2752 (1988), 1.4267 (1987)

:Australia Economy

Fiscal year: 1 July - 30 June

:Australia Communications

Railroads:

40,478 km total; 7,970 km 1.600-meter gauge, 16,201 km 1.435-meter standard gauge, 16,307 km 1.067-meter gauge; 183 km dual gauge; 1,130 km electrified; government owned (except for a few hundred kilometers of privately owned track) (1985)

Highways:

837,872 km total; 243,750 km paved, 228,396 km gravel, crushed stone, or stabilized soil surface, 365,726 km unimproved earth

Inland waterways:

8,368 km; mainly by small, shallow-draft craft

Pipelines:

crude oil 2,500 km; petroleum products 500 km; natural gas 5,600 km

Ports:

Adelaide, Brisbane, Cairns, Darwin, Devonport, Fremantle, Geelong, Hobart, Launceston, Mackay, Melbourne, Sydney, Townsville

Merchant marine:

85 ships (1,000 GRT or over) totaling 2,324,803 GRT/3,504,385 DWT; includes 2 short-sea passenger, 8 cargo, 8 container, 11 roll-on/roll-off, 1 vehicle carrier, 17 petroleum tanker, 2 chemical tanker, 4 liquefied gas, 1 combination ore/oil, 30 bulk, 1 combination bulk

Civil air:

about 150 major transport aircraft

Airports:
481 total, 440 usable; 237 with permanent-surface runways, 1 with runway
over 3,659 m; 20 with runways 2,440-3,659 m; 268 with runways 1,220-2,439 m

Telecommunications:
good international and domestic service; 8.7 million telephones; broadcast
stations - 258 AM, 67 FM, 134 TV; submarine cables to New Zealand, Papua New
Guinea, and Indonesia; domestic satellite service; satellite stations - 4
Indian Ocean INTELSAT, 6 Pacific Ocean INTELSAT earth stations

:Australia Defense Forces

Branches:
Australian Army, Royal Australian Navy, Royal Australian Air Force

Manpower availability:
males 15-49, 4,769,005; 4,153,060 fit for military service; 138,117 reach
military age (17) annually

Defense expenditures:
exchange rate conversion - $7.5 billion, 2.4% of GDP (FY92 budget)

Austria Geography

Total area: 83,850 km2
Land area: 82,730 km2
Comparative area: slightly smaller than Maine

Land boundaries:
2,591 km total; Czechoslovakia 548 km, Germany 784 km, Hungary 366 km, Italy
430 km, Liechtenstein 37 km, Slovenia 262 km, Switzerland 164 km

Coastline:
none - landlocked

Maritime claims:
none - landlocked

Disputes:
none

Climate:
temperate; continental, cloudy; cold winters with frequent rain in lowlands
and snow in mountains; cool summers with occasional showers

Terrain:
mostly mountains with Alps in west and south; mostly flat, with gentle
slopes along eastern and northern margins

Natural resources:
iron ore, crude oil, timber, magnesite, aluminum, lead, coal, lignite,
copper, hydropower

Land use:
arable land 17%; permanent crops 1%; meadows and pastures 24%; forest and
woodland 39%; other 19%; includes irrigated NEGL%

Environment:
because of steep slopes, poor soils, and cold temperatures, population is
concentrated on eastern lowlands

Note:
landlocked; strategic location at the crossroads of central Europe with many
easily traversable Alpine passes and valleys; major river is the Danube

:Austria People

Population: 7,867,541 (July 1992), growth rate 0.7% (1992)
Birth rate: 12 births/1,000 population (1992)
Death rate: 11 deaths/1,000 population (1992)
Net migration rate: 5 migrants/1,000 population (1992)
Infant mortality rate: 8 deaths/1,000 live births (1992)
Life expectancy at birth: 73 years male, 80 years female (1992)
Total fertility rate: 1.5 children born/woman (1992)
Nationality:
   noun - Austrian(s); adjective - Austrian
Ethnic divisions:
   German 99.4%, Croatian 0.3%, Slovene 0.2%, other 0.1%
Religions:
   Roman Catholic 85%, Protestant 6%, other 9%
Languages:
   German
Literacy:
   99% (male NA%, female NA%) age 15 and over can read and write (1974 est.)
Labor force:
   3,470,000 (1989); services 56.4%, industry and crafts 35.4%, agriculture and
   forestry 8.1%; an estimated 200,000 Austrians are employed in other European
   countries; foreign laborers in Austria number 177,840, about 6% of labor
   force (1988)
Organized labor:
   60.1% of work force; the Austrian Trade Union Federation has 1,644,408
   members (1989)

:Austria Government

Long-form name:
   Republic of Austria
Type:
   federal republic
Capital: Vienna
Administrative divisions:
   9 states (bundeslander, singular - bundesland); Burgenland, Karnten,
   Niederosterreich, Oberosterreich, Salzburg, Steiermark, Tirol, Vorarlberg,
   Wien
Independence:
   12 November 1918 (from Austro-Hungarian Empire)
Constitution:
   1920; revised 1929 (reinstated 1945)
Legal system:
   civil law system with Roman law origin; judicial review of legislative acts
   by a Constitutional Court; separate administrative and civil/penal supreme
   courts; has not accepted compulsory ICJ jurisdiction
National holiday:
   National Day, 26 October (1955)
Executive branch:
   president, chancellor, vice chancellor, Council of Ministers (cabinet)
Legislative branch:

bicameral Federal Assembly (Bundesversammlung) consists of an upper council or Federal Council (Bundesrat) and a lower council or National Council (Nationalrat)

Judicial branch:

Supreme Judicial Court (Oberster Gerichtshof) for civil and criminal cases, Administrative Court (Verwaltungsgerichtshof) for bureaucratic cases, Constitutional Court (Verfassungsgerichtshof) for constitutional cases

Leaders:

Chief of State:

President Thomas KLESTIL (since 8 July 1992)

Head of Government:

Chancellor Franz VRANITZKY (since 16 June 1986); Vice Chancellor Erhard BUSEK (since 2 July 1991)

Political parties and leaders:

Social Democratic Party of Austria (SPO), Franz VRANITZKY, chairman; Austrian People's Party (OVP), Erhard BUSEK, chairman; Freedom Party of Austria (FPO), Jorg HAIDER, chairman; Communist Party (KPO), Walter SILBERMAYER, chairman; Green Alternative List (GAL), Johannes VOGGENHUBER,

chairman

Suffrage:

universal at age 19; compulsory for presidential elections

Elections:

National Council:

last held 7 October 1990 (next to be held October 1994); results - SPO 43%, OVP 32.1%, FPO 16.6%, GAL 4.5%, KPO 0.7%, other 0.32%; seats - (183 total) SPO 80, OVP 60, FPO 33, GAL 10

President:

last held 24 May 1992 (next to be held 1996); results of Second Ballot - Thomas KLESTIL 57%, Rudolf STREICHER 43%

Communists:

membership 15,000 est.; activists 7,000-8,000

:Austria Government

Other political or pressure groups:

Federal Chamber of Commerce and Industry; Austrian Trade Union Federation (primarily Socialist); three composite leagues of the Austrian People's Party (OVP) representing business, labor, and farmers; OVP-oriented League of Austrian Industrialists; Roman Catholic Church, including its chief lay organization, Catholic Action

Member of:

AfDB, AG (observer), AsDB, Australia Group, BIS, CCC, CE, CERN, COCOM, CSCE,

EBRD, ECE, EFTA, ESA, FAO, G-9, GATT, HG, IADB, IAEA, IBRD, ICAO, ICC, ICFTU, IDA, IEA, IFAD, IFC, ILO, IMF, IMO, INTELSAT, INTERPOL, IOC, IOM,

ISO, ITU, LORCS, MTRC, NAM (guest), NEA, NSG, OAS (observer), OECD, PCA, UN,

UNCTAD, UNESCO, UNDOF, UNFICYP, UNHCR, UNIDO, UNIIMOG, UNTSO, UPU, WCL,

WFTU, WHO, WIPO, WMO, WTO, ZC

Diplomatic representation:

Ambassador Friedrich HOESS; Embassy at 3524 International Court NW, Washington, DC 20008; telephone (202) 895-6700; there are Austrian Consulates General in Chicago, Los Angeles, and New York

US:

Ambassador Roy Michael HUFFINGTON; Embassy at Boltzmanngasse 16, A-1091, Vienna (mailing address is APO AE 09108-0001); telephone [43] (1) 31-55-11; FAX [43] (1) 310-0682; there is a US Consulate General in Salzburg

Flag:

three equal horizontal bands of red (top), white, and red

:Austria Economy

Overview:

Austria boasts a prosperous and stable capitalist economy with a sizable proportion of nationalized industry and extensive welfare benefits. Thanks to an excellent raw material endowment, a technically skilled labor force, and strong links to German industrial firms, Austria occupies specialized niches in European industry and services (tourism, banking) and produces almost enough food to feed itself with only 8% of the labor force in agriculture. Improved export prospects resulting from German unification and the opening of Eastern Europe, boosted the economy during 1990 and to a lesser extent in 1991. GDP growth slowed from 4.9% in 1990 to 3% in 1991 - mainly due to the weaker world economy - and is expected to drop to around 2% in 1992. Inflation is forecasted at about 4%, while unemployment probably will increase moderately through 1992 before declining in 1993. Living standards are comparable with the large industrial countries of Western Europe. Problems for the 1990s include an aging population, the high level of subsidies, and the struggle to keep welfare benefits within budget capabilities. Austria, which has applied for EC membership, was involved in EC and European Free Trade Association negotiations for a European Economic Area and will have to adapt its economy to achieve freer interchange of goods, services, capital, and labor within the EC.

GDP:

purchasing power equivalent - $164.1 billion, per capita $20,985; real growth rate 3% (1991)

Inflation rate (consumer prices):

3.3% (1991, annual rate)

Unemployment rate: 5.8% (1991)

Budget:

revenues $47.7 billion; expenditures $53.0 billion, including capital expenditures of $NA (1990)

Exports:

$40 billion (1991)

commodities:

machinery and equipment, iron and steel, lumber, textiles, paper products, chemicals

partners:

EC 65.8%, (Germany 39%), EFTA 9.1%, Eastern Europe/former USSR 9.0%, Japan 1.7%, US 2.8%

Imports:
  $50.2 billion (1991)
  commodities:
  petroleum, foodstuffs, machinery and equipment, vehicles, chemicals,
  textiles and clothing, pharmaceuticals
  partners:
  EC 67.8% (Germany is 43.0%), EFTA 6.9%, Eastern Europe/former USSR 6.0%,
  Japan 4.8%, US 3.9%
External debt: $11.8 billion (1990 est.)
Industrial production:
  2.0% (1991)
Electricity:
  17,600,000 kW capacity; 49,500 million kWh produced, 6,500 kWh per capita
  (1991)
Industries:
  foods, iron and steel, machines, textiles, chemicals, electrical, paper and
  pulp, tourism, mining

:Austria Economy

Agriculture:
  accounts for 3.2% of GDP (including forestry); principal crops and animals -
  grains, fruit, potatoes, sugar beets, sawn wood, cattle, pigs, poultry;
  80-90% self-sufficient in food
Economic aid:
  donor - ODA and OOF commitments (1970-89), $2.4 billion
Currency:
  Austrian schilling (plural - schillings); 1 Austrian schilling (S) = 100
  groschen
Exchange rates:
  Austrian schillings (S) per US$1 - 11.068 (January 1992), 11.676 (1991),
  11.370 (1990), 13.231 (1989), 12.348 (1988), 12.643 (1987)
Fiscal year: calendar year

:Austria Communications

Railroads:
  6,028 km total; 5,388 km government owned and 640 km privately owned (1.435-
  and 1.000-meter gauge); 5,403 km 1.435-meter standard gauge of which 3,051
  km is electrified and 1,520 km is double tracked; 363 km 0.760-meter narrow
  gauge of which 91 km is electrified
Highways:
  95,412 km total; 34,612 km are the primary network (including 1,012 km of
  autobahn, 10,400 km of federal, and 23,200 km of provincial roads); of this
  number, 21,812 km are paved and 12,800 km are unpaved; in addition, there
  are 60,800 km of communal roads (mostly gravel, crushed stone, earth)
Inland waterways:
  446 km
Pipelines:
  crude oil 554 km; natural gas 2,611 km; petroleum products 171 km
Ports:
  Vienna, Linz (river ports)
Merchant marine:

31 ships (1,000 GRT or over) totaling 130,966 GRT/219,130 DWT; includes 26 cargo, 1 container, 4 bulk

Civil air:

25 major transport aircraft

Airports:

55 total, 55 usable; 20 with permanent-surface runways; none with runways over 3,659 m; 6 with runways 2,440-3,659 m; 4 with runways 1,220-2,439 m

Telecommunications:

highly developed and efficient; 4,014,000 telephones; broadcast stations - 6 AM, 21 (545 repeaters) FM, 47 (870 repeaters) TV; satellite ground stations for Atlantic Ocean INTELSAT, Indian Ocean INTELSAT, and EUTELSAT systems

:Austria Defense Forces

Branches:

Army, Flying Division, Gendarmerie

Manpower availability:

males 15-49, 2,011,895; 1,693,244 fit for military service; 51,788 reach military age (19) annually

Defense expenditures:

exchange rate conversion - $1.8 billion, 1% of GDP (1991)

Azerbaijan Geography

Total area: 86,600 km2

Land area: 86,100 km2; includes the Nakhichevan' Autonomous Republic and the Nagorno-Karabakh Autonomous Oblast; region's autonomy was abolished by Azerbaijan Supreme Soviet on 26 November 1991

Comparative area: slightly larger than Maine

Land boundaries:

2,013 km total; Armenia (west) 566 km, Armenia (southwest) 221 km, Georgia 322 km, Iran (south) 432 km, Iran (southwest) 179 km, Russia 284 km, Turkey 9 km

Coastline:

none - landlocked

Maritime claims:

NA

 Exclusive fishing zone:

NA nm; Azerbaijani claims in Caspian Sea unknown; 10 nm fishing zone provided for in 1940 treaty regarding trade and navigation between Soviet Union and Iran

Disputes:

violent and longstanding dispute with Armenia over status of Nagorno-Karabakh, lesser dispute concerns Nakhichevan'; some Azeris desire absorption of and/or unification with the ethnically Azeri portion of Iran; minor irredentist disputes along Georgia border

Climate:

dry, semiarid steppe; subject to drought

Terrain:

large, flat Kura Lowland (much of it below sea level) with Great Caucasus Mountains to the north, Karabakh Upland in west; Baku lies on Aspheson Peninsula that juts into Caspian Sea

Natural resources:

petroleum, natural gas, iron ore, nonferrous metals, alumina

Land use:

NA% arable land; NA% permanent crops; NA% meadows and pastures; NA% forest and woodland; NA% other; includes 70% of cultivated land irrigated (1.2 million hectares)

Environment:

local scientists consider Apsheron Peninsula, including Baku and Sumgait, and the Caspian Sea to be "most ecologically devastated area in the world" because of severe air and water pollution

Note:

landlocked; major polluters are oil, gas, and chemical industries

:Azerbaijan People

Population: 7,450,787 (July 1992), growth rate 1.6% (1992)
Birth rate: 26 births/1,000 population (1992)
Death rate: 7 deaths/1,000 population (1992)
Net migration rate: —3 migrants/1,000 population (1992)
Infant mortality rate: 45 deaths/1,000 live births (1992)
Life expectancy at birth: 65 years male, 73 years female (1992)
Total fertility rate: 2.9 children born/woman (1992)

Nationality:

noun - Azerbaijani(s); adjective - Azerbaijani

Ethnic divisions:

Azeri 82.7%, Russian 5.6%, Armenian 5.6%, Daghestanis 3.2%, other 2.9%; note - Armenian share may be less than 5.6% because many Armenians have fled the ethnic violence since 1989 census

Religions:

Moslem 87%, Russian Orthodox 5.6%, Armenian Orthodox 5.6%, other 1.8%

Languages:

Azeri 82%, Russian 7%, Armenian 5%, other 6%

Literacy:

NA% (male NA%, female NA%) age 15 and over can read and write (1992 est.)

Labor force:

2,789,000; agriculture and forestry 32%, industry and construction 26%, other 42% (1990)

Organized labor:

NA (1992)

:Azerbaijan Government

Long-form name:

Azerbaijani Republic; short-form name: Azerbaijan

Type:

republic

Capital: Baku (Baky)

Administrative divisions:

1 autonomous republic (avtomnaya respublika), Nakhichevan' (administrative center at Nakhichevan'); note - all rayons except for the exclave of Nakhichevan' are under direct republic jurisdiction;1 autonomous oblast, Nagorno-Karabakh (officially abolished by Azerbaijani Supreme Soviet on 26 November 1991) has declared itself Nagorno-Karabakh Republic

Independence:

28 May 1918; on 28 April 1920, Azerbaijan became the Soviet Socialist Republic of Azerbaijan; on 30 April 1992 it became the Azerbaijani Republic; independence declared 30 August 1991

Constitution:
adopted NA April 1978

Legal system:
based on civil law system

National holiday:
NA

Executive branch:
president, Council of Ministers

Legislative branch:
National Parliament (Milli Majlis) was formed on the basis of the National Council (Milli Shura)

Judicial branch:
Supreme Court

Leaders:
Chief of State:
President-elect Ebulfez ELCIBEY (since 7 June 1992)
Head of Government:
Prime Minister Rahim GUSEYNOV (since 14 May 1992)

Political parties and leaders:
NA

Suffrage:
universal at age 18

Elections:
National Parliament:
last held NA September 1990 (next expected to be held late 1992); results - seats - (360 total) Communists 280, Democratic Bloc 45 (grouping of opposition parties), other 15, vacant 20; note - these figures are approximate
President:
held 8 September 1991 (next to be held 7 June 1992); results - Ebulfez ELCIBEY (6,390 unofficial)

Other political or pressure groups:
Self-proclaimed Armenian Nagorno-Karabakh Republic

Member of:
CIS, CSCE, IMF, OIC, UN, UNCTAD

Diplomatic representation:
NA
US:
Ambassador (vacant); Robert MILES, Charge d'Affaires; Embassy at Hotel Intourist (telephone 8-011-7-8922-91-79-56) plus 8 hours; (mailing address is APO New York is 09862), telephone NA

:Azerbaijan Government

Flag:
three equal horizontal bands of blue (top), red, and green; a crescent and eight-pointed star in white are centered in red band

:Azerbaijan Economy

Overview:
   Azerbaijan is less developed industrially than either Armenia or Georgia,
   the other Transcaucasian states. It resembles the Central Asian states in
   its majority Muslim population, high structural unemployment, and low
   standard of living. The economy's most prominent products are cotton, oil,
   and gas. Production from the Caspian oil and gas field has been in decline
   for several years. With foreign assistance, the oil industry might generate
   the funds needed to spur industrial development. However, civil unrest,
   marked by armed conflict in the Nagorno-Karabakh region between Muslim
   Azeris and Christian Armenians, makes foreign investors wary. Azerbaijan
   accounts for 1.5% to 2% of the capital stock and output of the former Soviet
   Union. Although immediate economic prospects are not favorable because of
   civil strife, lack of economic reform, political disputes about new economic
   arrangements, and the skittishness of foreign investors, Azerbaijan's
   economic performance was the best of all former Soviet republics in 1991
   largely because of its reliance on domestic resources for industrial output.
GDP:
   $NA, per capita $NA; real growth rate —0.7% (1991)
Inflation rate (consumer prices):
   87% (1991)
Unemployment rate: NA%
Budget:
   revenues $NA; expenditures $NA, including capital expenditures of $NA (1992)
Exports:
   $780 million (f.o.b., 1991)
  commodities:
   oil and gas, chemicals, oilfield equipment, textiles, cotton (1991)
  partners:
   mostly CIS countries
Imports:
   $2.2 billion (c.i.f., 1990)
  commodities:
   machinery and parts, consumer durables, foodstuffs, textiles (1991)
External debt: $1.3 billion (1991 est.)
Industrial production:
   growth rate 3.8% (1991)
Electricity:
   6,025,000 kW capacity; 23,300 million kWh produced, 3,280 kWh per capita
   (1991)
Industries:
   petroleum and natural gas, petroleum products, oilfield equipment; steel,
   iron ore, cement; chemicals and petrochemicals; textiles
Agriculture:
   cotton, grain, rice, grapes, fruit, vegetables, tea, tobacco; cattle, pigs,
   sheep and goats
Illicit drugs:
   illicit producer of cannabis and opium; mostly for domestic consumption;
   status of government eradication programs unknown; used as transshipment
   points for illicit drugs to Western Europe
Economic aid:

NA
Currency:
as of May 1992, retaining ruble as currency
Exchange rates:
NA
Fiscal year: calendar year

:Azerbaijan Communications

Railroads:
2,090 km (includes NA km electrified); does not include industrial lines
(1990)
Highways:
36,700 km total (1990); 31,800 km hard surfaced; 4,900 km earth
Inland waterways:
NA km perennially navigable
Pipelines:
NA
Ports:
inland - Baku (Baky)
Merchant marine:
none - landlocked
Civil air:
none
Airports:
NA
Telecommunications:
quality of local telephone service is poor; connections to other former USSR
republics by landline or microwave and to countries beyond the former USSR
via the Moscow international gateway switch; Azeri and Russian TV broadcasts
are received; Turkish and Iranian TV broadcasts are received from INTELSAT
through a TV receive-only earth station

:Azerbaijan Defense Forces

Branches:
Republic Security Forces (internal and border troops), National Guard; CIS
Forces (Ground, Navy, Air, Air Defense)
Manpower availability:
males 15-49, NA; NA fit for military service; NA reach military age (18)
annually
Defense expenditures:
$NA million, NA% of GDP

The Bahamas Geography

Total area: 13,940 km2
Land area: 10,070 km2
Comparative area: slightly larger than Connecticut
Land boundaries:
none
Coastline:
3,542 km
Maritime claims:

Continental shelf:
  200 m (depth) or to depth of exploitation
  Exclusive fishing zone:
  200 nm
  Territorial sea:
  3 nm
Disputes:
  none
Climate:
  tropical marine; moderated by warm waters of Gulf Stream
Terrain:
  long, flat coral formations with some low rounded hills
Natural resources:
  salt, aragonite, timber
Land use:
  arable land 1%; permanent crops NEGL%; meadows and pastures NEGL%; forest
  and woodland 32%; other 67%
Environment:
  subject to hurricanes and other tropical storms that cause extensive flood
  damage
Note:
  strategic location adjacent to US and Cuba; extensive island chain

:The Bahamas People

Population: 255,811 (July 1992), growth rate 1.4% (1992)
Birth rate: 19 births/1,000 population (1992)
Death rate: 5 deaths/1,000 population (1992)
Net migration rate: 0 migrants/1,000 population (1992)
Infant mortality rate: 19 deaths/1,000 live births (1992)
Life expectancy at birth: 69 years male, 76 years female (1992)
Total fertility rate: 2.2 children born/woman (1992)
Nationality:
  noun—Bahamian(s); adjective—Bahamian
Ethnic divisions:
  black 85%, white 15%
Religions:
  Baptist 32%, Anglican 20%, Roman Catholic 19%, Methodist 6%, Church of God
  6%, other Protestant 12%, none or unknown 3%, other 2% (1980)
Languages:
  English; some Creole among Haitian immigrants
Literacy:
  90% (male 90%, female 89%) age 15 and over but definition of literacy not
  available (1963 est.)
Labor force:
  127,400; government 30%, hotels and restaurants 25%, business services
  10%, agriculture 5% (1989)
Organized labor:
  25% of labor force

:The Bahamas Government

Long-form name:
   The Commonwealth of The Bahamas
Type:
   commonwealth
Capital: Nassau
Administrative divisions:
   21 districts; Abaco, Acklins Island, Andros Island, Berry Islands,
   Biminis, Cat Island, Cay Lobos, Crooked Island, Eleuthera, Exuma, Grand
   Bahama, Harbour Island, Inagua, Long Cay, Long Island, Mayaguana,
   New Providence, Ragged Island, Rum Cay, San Salvador,
   Spanish Wells
Independence:
   10 July 1973 (from UK)
Constitution:
   10 July 1973
Legal system:
   based on English common law
National holiday:
   National Day, 10 July (1973)
Executive branch:
   British monarch, governor general, prime minister, deputy prime
   minister, Cabinet
Legislative branch:
   bicameral Parliament consists of an upper house or Senate and a lower
   house or House of Assembly
Judicial branch:
   Supreme Court
Leaders:
  Chief of State:
   Queen ELIZABETH II (since 6 February 1952), represented by
   Acting Governor General Sir Clifford DARLING (since 2 January 1992)
  Head of Government:
   Prime Minister Sir Lynden Oscar PINDLING (since 16 January 1967)
Political parties and leaders:
   Progressive Liberal Party (PLP), Sir Lynden O. PINDLING; Free National
   Movement (FNM), Hubert Alexander INGRAHAM
Suffrage:
   universal at age 18
Elections:
  House of Assembly:
   last held 19 June 1987 (next to be held by NA June 1992);
   results—percent of vote by party NA; seats—(49 total) PLP 32, FNM 17
   *** No entry for this item ***
Other political or pressure groups:
   Vanguard Nationalist and Socialist Party (VNSP), a small leftist party
   headed
   by Lionel CAREY; Trade Union Congress (TUC), headed by Arlington MILLER
Member of:
   ACP, C, CCC, CARICOM, CDB, ECLAC, FAO, G-77, IADB, IBRD, ICAO,
   ICFTU, IFC, ILO, IMF, IMO, INTELSAT, INTERPOL, IOC, ITU, LORCS, NAM,

OAS, OPANAL, UN, UNCTAD, UNESCO, UNIDO, UPU, WHO, WIPO, WMO

Diplomatic representation:

Ambassador Margaret E. McDONALD; Chancery at 2220 Massachusetts Avenue NW, Washington, DC 20008; telephone (202) 319-2660; there are Bahamian Consulates General in Miami and New York;

:The Bahamas Government

US:

Ambassador Chic HECHT; Embassy at Mosmar Building, Queen Street, Nassau (mailing address is P. O. Box N-8197, Nassau); telephone (809) 322-1181 or 328-2206; FAX (809) 328-7838

Diplomatic representation:

*** No entry for this item ***

Flag:

three equal horizontal bands of aquamarine (top), gold, and aquamarine with a black equilateral triangle based on the hoist side

:The Bahamas Economy

Overview:

The Bahamas is a stable, middle-income developing nation whose economy is based primarily on tourism and offshore banking. Tourism alone provides about 50% of GDP and directly or indirectly employs about 50,000 people or 40% of the local work force. The economy has slackened in recent years, as the annual increase in the number of tourists slowed. Nonetheless, the per capita GDP of $9,900 is one of the highest in the region.

GDP:

purchasing power equivalent—$2.5 billion, per capita $9,900; real growth rate 1.0% (1990 est.)

*** No entry for this item ***

Inflation rate (consumer prices):

7.3% (1991 est.)

Unemployment rate: 16.0% (1991)

Budget:

revenues $627.5 million; expenditures $727.5 million, including capital expenditures of $100 million (1992, projected)

*** No entry for this item ***

Exports:

$306 million (f.o.b., 1991 est.);

commodities:

pharmaceuticals, cement, rum, crawfish;

partners:

US 41%, Norway 30%, Denmark 4%

Imports:

$1.14 billion (c.i.f., 1991 est.);

commodities:

foodstuffs, manufactured goods, mineral fuels;

partners:

US 35%, Nigeria 21%, Japan 13%, Angola 11%

External debt: $1.2 billion (December 1990)

Industrial production:

growth rate 3% (1990); accounts for 15% of GDP

Electricity:

368,000 kw capacity; 857 million kWh produced 3,339 kWh per capita (1991)

Industries:

tourism, banking, cement, oil refining and transshipment, salt production, rum, aragonite, pharmaceuticals, spiral welded steel pipe

*** No entry for this item ***

Agriculture:

accounts for less than 5% of GDP; dominated by small-scale producers; principal products—citrus fruit, vegetables, poultry; large net importer of food

*** No entry for this item ***

Illicit drugs:

transshipment point for cocaine

Economic aid:

US commitments, including Ex-Im (FY85-89), $1.0 million; Western (non-US) countries, ODA and OOF bilateral commitments (1970-89), $345 million

Currency:

Bahamian dollar (plural—dollars); 1 Bahamian dollar (B$) = 100 cents

Exchange rates:

Bahamian dollar (B$) per US$1—1.00 (fixed rate)

Fiscal year: calendar year

:The Bahamas Communications

Highways:

2,400 km total; 1,350 km paved, 1,050 km gravel

Ports:

Freeport, Nassau

Merchant marine:

778 ships (1,000 GRT or over) totaling 18,129,173 GRT/30,002,421 DWT; includes 48 passenger, 19 short-sea passenger, 152 cargo, 37 roll-on/roll-off cargo, 42 container, 6 vehicle carrier, 1 railcar carrier, 172 petroleum tanker, 9 liquefied gas, 16 combination ore/oil, 47 chemical tanker, 1 specialized tanker, 143 bulk, 7 combination bulk, 78 refrigerated cargo;

note—a flag of convenience registry

*** No entry for this item ***

Civil air:

11 major transport aircraft

Airports:

59 total, 54 usable; 30 with permanent-surface runways; none with runways over 3,659 m; 3 with runways 2,440-3, 659 m; 26 with runways 1,220-2,439 m

Telecommunications:

highly developed; 99,000 telephones in totally automatic system; tropospheric scatter and submarine cable links to Florida; broadcast stations—3 AM, 2 FM, 1 TV; 3 coaxial submarine cables; 1 Atlantic Ocean INTELSAT earth station

*** No entry for this item ***

:The Bahamas Defense Forces

Branches:
  Royal Bahamas Defense Force (Coast Guard only), Royal Bahamas Police
Branches:
  Force
Manpower availability:
  males 15-49, 68,020; NA fit for military service
Defense expenditures:
  exchange rate conversion—$65 million, 2.7% of GDP (1990)

Bahrain Geography

Total area: 620 km2
Land area: 620 km2
Comparative area: slightly less than 3.5 times the size of Washington, DC
Land boundaries:
  none
Coastline:
  161 km
Maritime claims:
 Continental shelf:
  not specific
 Territorial sea:
  3 nm
Disputes:
  territorial dispute with Qatar over the Hawar Islands; maritime boundary
  with Qatar
Climate:
  arid; mild, pleasant winters; very hot, humid summers
Terrain:
  mostly low desert plain rising gently to low central escarpment
Natural resources:
  oil, associated and nonassociated natural gas, fish
Land use:
  arable land 2%; permanent crops 2%; meadows and pastures 6%; forest and
  woodland 0%; other 90%, includes irrigated NEGL%
Environment:
  subsurface water sources being rapidly depleted (requires development of
  desalination facilities); dust storms; desertification
Note:
  close to primary Middle Eastern crude oil sources; strategic location in
  Persian Gulf through which much of Western world's crude oil must transit to
  reach open ocean

:Bahrain People

Population: 551,513 (July 1992), growth rate 3.1% (1992)
Birth rate: 27 births/1,000 population (1992)
Death rate: 4 deaths/1,000 population (1992)
Net migration rate: 7 migrants/1,000 population (1992)
Infant mortality rate: 21 deaths/1,000 live births (1992)
Life expectancy at birth: 70 years male, 75 years female (1992)

Total fertility rate: 4.0 children born/woman (1992)
Nationality:
  noun - Bahraini(s); adjective - Bahraini
Ethnic divisions:
  Bahraini 63%, Asian 13%, other Arab 10%, Iranian 8%, other 6%
Religions:
  Muslim (Shi`a 70%, Sunni 30%)
Languages:
  Arabic (official); English also widely spoken; Farsi, Urdu
Literacy:
  77% (male 82%, female 69%) age 15 and over can read and write (1990 est.)
Labor force:
  140,000; 42% of labor force is Bahraini; industry and commerce 85%,
  agriculture 5%, services 5%, government 3% (1982)
Organized labor:
  General Committee for Bahrain Workers exists in only eight major designated
  companies

:Bahrain Government

Long-form name:
  State of Bahrain
Type:
  traditional monarchy
Capital: Manama
Administrative divisions:
  12 districts (manatiq, singular - mintaqah); Al Hadd, Al Manamah, Al
  Mintaqah al Gharbiyah, Al Mintaqah al Wusta, Al Mintaqah ash Shamaliyah, Al
  Muharraq, Ar Rifa`wa al Mintaqah al Janubiyah, Jidd Hafs, Madinat Hamad,
  Madinat `Isa, Mintaqat Juzur Hawar, Sitrah
Independence:
  15 August 1971 (from UK)
Constitution:
  26 May 1973, effective 6 December 1973
Legal system:
  based on Islamic law and English common law
National holiday:
  Independence Day, 16 December
Executive branch:
  amir, crown prince and heir apparent, prime minister, Cabinet
Legislative branch:
  unicameral National Assembly was dissolved 26 August 1975 and legislative
  powers were assumed by the Cabinet
Judicial branch:
  High Civil Appeals Court
Leaders:
  Chief of State:
  Amir `ISA bin Salman Al Khalifa (since 2 November 1961); Heir Apparent
HAMAD
  bin `Isa Al Khalifa (son of Amir; born 28 January 1950)
  Head of Government:

Prime Minister KHALIFA bin Salman Al Khalifa (since 19 January 1970)

Political parties and leaders:

  political parties prohibited; several small, clandestine leftist and Islamic
  fundamentalist groups are active

Suffrage:

Elections:

Member of:

  ABEDA, AFESD, AL, AMF, ESCWA, FAO, G-77, GCC, IBRD, ICAO, IDB, ILO,
  IMF,

  IMO, INMARSAT, INTERPOL, IOC, ISO (correspondent), ITU, LORCS, NAM,
  OAPEC,

  OIC, UN, UNCTAD, UNESCO, UNIDO, UPU, WFTU, WHO, WMO

Diplomatic representation:

  Ambassador `Abd al-Rahman Faris Al KHALIFA; Chancery at 3502 International
  Drive NW, Washington, DC 20008; telephone (202) 342-0741 or 342-0742; there
  is a Bahraini Consulate General in New York

 US:

  Ambassador Dr. Charles W. HOSTLER; Embassy at Road No. 3119 (next to Alahli
  Sports Club), Zinj; (mailing address is P. O. 26431, Manama, or FPO AE
  09834-6210); telephone [973] 273-300; FAX (973) 272-594

Flag:

  red with a white serrated band (eight white points) on the hoist side

:Bahrain Economy

Overview:

  Petroleum production and processing account for about 80% of export
  receipts, 60% of government revenues, and 31% of GDP. Economic conditions
  have fluctuated with the changing fortunes of oil since 1985, for example,
  the Gulf crisis of 1990-91. The liberation of Kuwait in early 1991 has
  improved short- to medium-term prospects and has raised investors'
  confidence. Bahrain with its highly developed communication and transport
  facilities is home to numerous multinational firms with business in the
  Gulf. A large share of exports is petroleum products made from imported
  crude.

GDP:

  exchange rate conversion - $4.0 billion, per capita $7,500 (1990); real
  growth rate 6.7% (1988)

Inflation rate (consumer prices):

  1.5% (1989)

Unemployment rate: 8-10% (1989)

Budget:

  revenues $1.2 billion; expenditures $1.32 billion, including capital
  expenditures of $NA (1989)

Exports:

  $3.7 billion (f.o.b., 1990 est.)

 commodities:

  petroleum and petroleum products 80%, aluminum 7%, other 13%

 partners:

UAE 18%, Japan 12%, India 11%, US 6%

Imports:
  $3.7 billion (f.o.b., 1989)
  commodities:
  nonoil 59%, crude oil 41%
  partners:
  Saudi Arabia 41%, US 23%, Japan 8%, UK 8%

External debt: $1.1 billion (December 1989 est.)

Industrial production:
  growth rate 3.8% (1988); accounts for 44% of GDP

Electricity:
  3,600,000 kW capacity; 10,500 million kWh produced, 21,000 kWh per capita
  (1991)

Industries:
  petroleum processing and refining, aluminum smelting, offshore banking, ship
  repairing

Agriculture:
  including fishing, accounts for less than 2% of GDP; not self-sufficient in
  food production; heavily subsidized sector produces fruit, vegetables,
  poultry, dairy products, shrimp, and fish; fish catch 9,000 metric tons in
  1987

Economic aid:
  US commitments, including Ex-Im (FY70-79), $24 million; Western (non-US)
  countries, ODA and OOF bilateral commitments (1970-89), $45 million; OPEC
  bilateral aid (1979-89), $9.8 billion

Currency:
  Bahraini dinar (plural - dinars); 1 Bahraini dinar (BD) = 1,000 fils

Exchange rates:
  Bahraini dinars (BD) per US$1 - 0.3760 (fixed rate)

Fiscal year: calendar year

:Bahrain Communications

Highways:
  200 km bituminous surfaced, including 25 km bridge-causeway to Saudi Arabia
  opened in November 1986; NA km natural surface tracks

Pipelines:
  crude oil 56 km; petroleum products 16 km; natural gas 32 km

Ports:
  Mina' Salman, Manama, Sitrah

Merchant marine:
  9 ships (1,000 GRT or over) totaling 186,367 GRT/249,441 DWT; includes 5
  cargo, 2 container, 1 liquefied gas, 1 bulk

Civil air:
  27 major transport aircraft

Airports:
  3 total, 3 usable; 2 with permanent-surface runways; 2 with runways over
  3,659 m; 1 with runways 1,220-2,439 m

Telecommunications:
  excellent international telecommunications; good domestic services; 98,000
  telephones; broadcast stations - 2 AM, 3 FM, 2 TV; satellite earth stations

- 1 Atlantic Ocean INTELSAT, 1 Indian Ocean INTELSAT, 1 ARABSAT; tropospheric scatter to Qatar, UAE, and microwave to Saudi Arabia; submarine cable to Qatar, UAE, and Saudi Arabia

:Bahrain Defense Forces

Branches:
    Army, Navy, Air Force, Air Defense, Police Force
Manpower availability:
    males 15-49, 190,937; 105,857 fit for military service
Defense expenditures:
    exchange rate conversion - $194 million, 6% of GDP (1990)

Baker Island Geography

Total area: 1.4 km2
Land area: 1.4 km2
Comparative area: about 2.3 times the size of the Mall in Washington, DC
Land boundaries:
    none
Coastline:
    4.8 km
Maritime claims:
  Contiguous zone:
    12 nm
  Continental shelf:
    200 m (depth)
  Exclusive economic zone:
    200 nm
  Territorial sea:
    12 nm
Disputes:
    none
Climate:
    equatorial; scant rainfall, constant wind, burning sun
Terrain:
    low, nearly level coral island surrounded by a narrow fringing reef
Natural resources:
    guano (deposits worked until 1891)
Land use:
    arable land 0%; permanent crops 0%; meadows and pastures 0%; forest and woodland 0%; other 100%
Environment:
    treeless, sparse and scattered vegetation consisting of grasses, prostrate vines, and low growing shrubs; lacks fresh water; primarily a nesting, roosting, and foraging habitat for seabirds, shorebirds, and marine wildlife
Note:
    remote location 2,575 km southwest of Honolulu in the North Pacific Ocean, just north of the Equator, about halfway between Hawaii and Australia

:Baker Island People

Population: uninhabited; American civilians evacuated in 1942 after Japanese air and naval attacks during World War II; occupied by US military during World War

II, but abandoned after the war; public entry is by special-use permit only and generally restricted to scientists and educators

:Baker Island Government

Long-form name:
  none
Type:
  unincorporated territory of the US administered by the Fish and Wildlife Service of the US Department of the Interior as part of the National Wildlife Refuge system
Capital: none; administered from Washington, DC

:Baker Island Economy

Overview: no economic activity

:Baker Island Communications

Ports:
  none; offshore anchorage only, one boat landing area along the middle of the west coast
Airports:
  1 abandoned World War II runway of 1,665 m
Telecommunications:
  there is a day beacon near the middle of the west coast

:Baker Island Defense Forces

Note:
  defense is the responsibility of the US; visited annually by the US Coast Guard

Bangladesh Geography

Total area: 144,000 km2
Land area: 133,910 km2
Comparative area: slightly smaller than Wisconsin
Land boundaries:
  4,246 km total; Burma 193 km, India 4,053 km
Coastline:
  580 km
Maritime claims:
 Contiguous zone:
  18 nm
 Continental shelf:
  up to outer limits of continental margin
 Exclusive economic zone:
  200 nm
 Territorial sea:
  12 nm
Disputes:
  a portion of the boundary with India is in dispute; water sharing problems with upstream riparian India over the Ganges
Climate:
  tropical; cool, dry winter (October to March); hot, humid summer (March to June); cool, rainy monsoon (June to October)

Terrain:
  mostly flat alluvial plain; hilly in southeast
Natural resources:
  natural gas, uranium, arable land, timber
Land use:
  arable land 67%; permanent crops 2%; meadows and pastures 4%; forest and
  woodland 16%; other 11%; includes irrigated 14%
Environment:
  vulnerable to droughts; much of country routinely flooded during summer
  monsoon season; overpopulation; deforestation
Note:
  almost completely surrounded by India

:Bangladesh People

Population: 119,411,711 (July 1992), growth rate 2.4% (1992)
Birth rate: 36 births/1,000 population (1992)
Death rate: 12 deaths/1,000 population (1992)
Net migration rate: 0 migrants/1,000 population (1992)
Infant mortality rate: 112 deaths/1,000 live births (1992)
Life expectancy at birth: 55 years male, 54 years female (1992)
Total fertility rate: 4.6 children born/woman (1992)
Nationality:
  noun - Bangladeshi(s); adjective - Bangladesh
Ethnic divisions:
  Bengali 98%, Biharis 250,000, and tribals less than 1 million
Religions:
  Muslim 83%, Hindu 16%, Buddhist, Christian, and other less than 1%
Languages:
  Bangla (official), English widely used
Literacy:
  35% (male 47%, female 22%) age 15 and over can read and write (1990 est.)
Labor force:
  35,100,000; agriculture 74%, services 15%, industry and commerce 11% (FY86);
  extensive export of labor to Saudi Arabia, UAE, and Oman (1991)
Organized labor:
  3% of labor force belongs to 2,614 registered unions (1986 est.)

:Bangladesh Government

Long-form name:
  People's Republic of Bangladesh
Type:
  republic
Capital: Dhaka
Administrative divisions:
  64 districts (zillagulo, singular - zilla); Bagerhat, Bandarban, Barguna,
  Barisal, Bhola, Bogra, Brahmanbaria, Chandpur, Chapai Nawabganj, Chattagram,
  Chuadanga, Comilla, Cox's Bazar, Dhaka, Dinajpur, Faridpur, Feni, Gaibandha,
  Gazipur, Gopalganj, Habiganj, Jaipurhat, Jamalpur, Jessore, Jhalakati,
  Jhenaidah, Khagrachari, Khulna, Kishorganj, Kurigram, Kushtia, Laksmipur,
  Lalmonirhat, Madaripur, Magura, Manikganj, Meherpur, Moulavibazar,
  Munshiganj, Mymensingh, Naogaon, Narail, Narayanganj, Narsingdi, Nator,

Netrakona, Nilphamari, Noakhali, Pabna, Panchagar, Parbattya Chattagram, Patuakhali, Pirojpur, Rajbari, Rajshahi, Rangpur, Satkhira, Shariyatpur, Sherpur, Sirajganj, Sunamganj, Sylhet, Tangail, Thakurgaon

Independence:
  16 December 1971 (from Pakistan; formerly East Pakistan)

Constitution:
  4 November 1972, effective 16 December 1972, suspended following coup of 24 March 1982, restored 10 November 1986, amended NA March 1991

Legal system:
  based on English common law

National holiday:
  Independence Day, 26 March (1971)

Executive branch:
  president, prime minister, Cabinet

Legislative branch:
  unicameral National Parliament (Jatiya Sangsad)

Judicial branch:
  Supreme Court

Leaders:
  Chief of State:
  President Abdur Rahman BISWAS (since 8 October 1991)
  Head of Government:
  Prime Minister Khaleda ZIAUR Rahman (since 20 March 1991)

Political parties and leaders:
  Bangladesh Nationalist Party (BNP), Khaleda ZIAUR Rahman; Awami League (AL),
  Sheikh Hasina WAZED; Jatiyo Party (JP), Hussain Mohammad ERSHAD; Jamaat-E-Islami (JI), Ali KHAN; Bangladesh Communist Party (BCP), Saifuddin Ahmed MANIK; National Awami Party (Muzaffar); Workers Party, leader NA; Jatiyo Samajtantik Dal (National Socialist Party - SIRAJ), M. A. JALIL; Ganotantri Party, leader NA; Islami Oikya Jote, leader NA; National Democratic Party (NDP), leader NA; Muslim League, Khan A. SABUR; Democratic League, Khondakar MUSHTAQUE Ahmed; United People's Party, Kazi ZAFAR Ahmed

Suffrage:
  universal at age 18

Elections:
  National Parliament:
  last held 27 February 1991 (next to be held NA February 1996); results - percent of vote by party NA; seats - (330 total, 300 elected and 30 seats reserved for women) BNP 168, AL 93, JP 35, JI 20, CBP 5, National Awami Party (Muzaffar) 1, Workers Party 1, SIRAJ 1, Ganotantri Party 1, Islami Oikya Jote 1, NDP 1, independents 3
  President:
  last held 8 October 1991 (next to be held by NA October 1996); results - Abdur Rahman BISWAS received 52.1% of parliamentary vote

:Bangladesh Government

Communists:
  5,000 members (1987 est.)

81

Member of:

AsDB, C, CCC, CP, ESCAP, FAO, G-77, GATT, IAEA, IBRD, ICAO, ICFTU, IDA, IDB,

IFAD, IFC, ILO, IMF, IMO, INTELSAT, INTERPOL, IOC, IOM, ISO, ITU, LORCS,

NAM, OIC, SAARC, UN, UNCTAD, UNESCO, UNIDO, UNIIMOG, UPU, WHO, WFTU, WIPO,

WCL, WMO, WTO

Diplomatic representation:

Ambassador Abul AHSAN; Chancery at 2201 Wisconsin Avenue NW, Washington, DC

20007; telephone (202) 342-8372 through 8376; there is a Bangladesh
Consulate General in New York

US:

Ambassador William B. MILAM; Embassy at Diplomatic Enclave, Madani Avenue, Baridhara, Dhaka (mailing address is G. P. O. Box 323, Dhaka 1212);
telephone [880] (2) 884700-22; FAX [880] (2) 883648

Flag:

green with a large red disk slightly to the hoist side of center; green is
the traditional color of Islam

:Bangladesh Economy

Overview:

Bangladesh is one of the poorest nations in the world. The economy is based
on the output of a narrow range of agricultural products, such as jute,
which is the main cash crop and major source of export earnings, and rice.
Bangladesh is hampered by a relative lack of natural resources, population
growth of more than 2% a year, large-scale unemployment, and a limited
infrastructure; furthermore, it is highly vulnerable to natural disasters.
Despite these constraints, real GDP growth averaged about 3.5% annually
during 1985-89. A strong agricultural performance in FY90 pushed the growth
rate up to 6.2%, and FY91 saw further, though smaller, increases in output.
Alleviation of poverty remains the cornerstone of the government's
development strategy.

GDP:

exchange rate conversion - $23.1 billion, per capita $200; real growth rate
3.2% (FY91)

Inflation rate (consumer prices):

8.9% (FY91 est.)

Unemployment rate: 30%, including underemployment (FY90 est.)

Budget:

revenues $2.24 billion; expenditures $3.7 billion (FY91)

Exports:

$1.7 billion (FY91 est.)

commodities:

garments, jute and jute goods, leather, shrimp

partners:

US 32%, Italy 8.1%, UK 6.2% (FY90)

Imports:

$3.5 billion (FY91 est.)

commodities:
  capital goods, petroleum, food, textiles
partners:
  Japan 9.2%, India 6.2%, Singapore 5.9%, US 5.7%
External debt: $11.1 billion (FY91 est.)
Industrial production:
  growth rate 1% (FY91 est.); accounts for 10% of GDP
Electricity:
  1,990,000 kW capacity; 5,700 million kWh produced, 50 kWh per capita (1990)
Industries:
  jute manufacturing, cotton textiles, food processing, steel, fertilizer
Agriculture:
  accounts for about 40% of GDP, 70% of employment, and one-third of exports;
  imports 10% of food grain requirements; world's largest exporter of jute;
  commercial products - jute, rice, wheat, tea, sugarcane, potatoes, beef,
  milk, poultry; shortages include wheat, vegetable oils and cotton; fish
  catch 778,000 metric tons in 1986
Economic aid:
  US commitments, including Ex-Im (FY70-89), $3.4 billion; Western (non-US)
  countries, ODA and OOF bilateral commitments (1980-89), $11.65 million; OPEC
  bilateral aid (1979-89), $6.52 million; Communist countries (1970-89), $1.5
  billion
Currency:
  taka (plural - taka); 1 taka (Tk) = 100 paise
Exchange rates:
  taka (Tk) per US$1 - 38.800 (January 1992), 36.596 (1991), 34.569 (1990),
  32.270 (1989), 31.733 (1988), 30.950 (1987)
Fiscal year: 1 July - 30 June

:Bangladesh Communications

Railroads:
  2,892 km total (1986); 1,914 km 1.000 meter gauge, 978 km 1.676 meter broad
  gauge
Highways:
  7,240 km total (1985); 3,840 km paved, 3,400 km unpaved
Inland waterways:
  5,150-8,046 km navigable waterways (includes 2,575-3,058 km main cargo
  routes)
Pipelines:
  natural gas 1,220 km
Ports:
  Chittagong, Chalna
Merchant marine:
  44 ships (1,000 GRT or over) totaling 328,382 GRT/479,985 DWT; includes 36
  cargo, 2 petroleum tanker, 3 refrigerated cargo, 3 bulk
Civil air:
  15 major transport aircraft
Airports:
  16 total, 12 usable; 12 with permanent-surface runways; none with runways
  over 3,659 m; 4 with runways 2,440-3,659 m; 6 with runways 1,220-2,439 m

Telecommunications:
  adequate international radio communications and landline service; fair domestic wire and microwave service; fair broadcast service; 241,250 telephones; broadcast stations - 9 AM, 6 FM, 11 TV; 2 Indian Ocean INTELSAT satellite earth stations

:Bangladesh Defense Forces

Branches:
  Army, Navy, Air Force; paramilitary forces - Bangladesh Rifles, Bangladesh Ansars, Armed Police Reserve, Coastal Police
Manpower availability:
  males 15-49, 29,891,224; 17,745,343 fit for military service
Defense expenditures:
  exchange rate conversion - $339 million, 1.5% of GDP (FY92 budget)

Barbados Geography

Total area: 430 km2
Land area: 430 km2
Comparative area: slightly less than 2.5 times the size of Washington, DC
Land boundaries:
  none
Coastline:
  97 km
Maritime claims:
 Exclusive economic zone:
  200 nm
 Territorial sea:
  12 nm
Disputes:
  none
Climate:
  tropical; rainy season (June to October)
Terrain:
  relatively flat; rises gently to central highland region
Natural resources:
  crude oil, fishing, natural gas
Land use:
  arable land 77%; permanent crops 0%; meadows and pastures 9%; forest and woodland 0%; other 14%
Environment:
  subject to hurricanes (especially June to October)
Note:
  easternmost Caribbean island

:Barbados People

Population: 254,934 (July 1992), growth rate 0.1% (1992)
Birth rate: 16 births/1,000 population (1992)
Death rate: 9 deaths/1,000 population (1992)
Net migration rate: —6 migrants/1,000 population (1992)
Infant mortality rate: 22 deaths/1,000 live births (1992)
Life expectancy at birth: 70 years male, 76 years female (1992)

Total fertility rate: 1.8 children born/woman (1992)
Nationality:
  noun - Barbadian(s); adjective - Barbadian
Ethnic divisions:
  African 80%, mixed 16%, European 4%
Religions:
  Protestant 67% (Anglican 40%, Pentecostal 8%, Methodist 7%, other 12%),
  Roman Catholic 4%; none 17%, unknown 3%, other 9% (1980)
Languages:
  English
Literacy:
  99% (male 99%, female 99%) age 15 and over having ever attended school
  (1970)
Labor force:
  120,900 (1991); services and government 37%; commerce 22%; manufacturing and
  construction 22%; transportation, storage, communications, and financial
  institutions 9%; agriculture 8%; utilities 2% (1985 est.)
Organized labor:
  32% of labor force

:Barbados Government

Long-form name:
  none
Type:
  parliamentary democracy
Capital: Bridgetown
Administrative divisions:
  11 parishes; Christ Church, Saint Andrew, Saint George, Saint James, Saint
  John, Saint Joseph, Saint Lucy, Saint Michael, Saint Peter, Saint Philip,
  Saint Thomas; note - there may be a new city of Bridgetown
Independence:
  30 November 1966 (from UK)
Constitution:
  30 November 1966
Legal system:
  English common law; no judicial review of legislative acts
National holiday:
  Independence Day, 30 November (1966)
Executive branch:
  British monarch, governor general, prime minister, deputy prime minister,
  Cabinet
Legislative branch:
  bicameral Parliament consists of an upper house or Senate and a lower house
  or House of Assembly
Judicial branch:
  Supreme Court of Judicature
Leaders:
  Chief of State:
  Queen ELIZABETH II (since 6 February 1952), represented by Governor General
  Dame Nita BARROW (since 6 June 1990)

85

Head of Government:

Prime Minister Lloyd Erskine SANDIFORD (since 2 June 1987)

Political parties and leaders:

Democratic Labor Party (DLP), Erskine SANDIFORD; Barbados Labor Party (BLP),

Henry FORDE; National Democratic Party (NDP), Richie HAYNES

Suffrage:

universal at age 18

Elections:

House of Assembly:

last held 22 January 1991 (next to be held by January 1996); results - DLP 49.8%; seats - (28 total) DLP 18, BLP 10

Other political or pressure groups:

Industrial and General Workers Union, Sir Frank WALCOTT; People's Progressive Movement, Eric SEALY; Workers' Party of Barbados, Dr. George BELLE

Member of:

ACP, C, CARICOM, CDB, ECLAC, FAO, G-77, GATT, IADB, IBRD, ICAO, ICFTU, IFAD,

IFC, ILO, IMF, IMO, INTELSAT, INTERPOL, IOC, ISO (correspondent), ITU, LAES,

LORCS, NAM, OAS, OPANAL, UN, UNCTAD, UNESCO, UNIDO, UPU, WHO, WIPO, WMO

Diplomatic representation:

Ambassador Dr. Rudi WEBSTER; Chancery at 2144 Wyoming Avenue NW, Washington,

DC 20008; telephone (202) 939-9200 through 9202; there is a Barbadian Consulate General in New York and a Consulate in Los Angeles

US:

Ambassador G. Philip HUGHES; Embassy at Canadian Imperial Bank of Commerce Building, Broad Street, Bridgetown (mailing address is P. O. Box 302, Box B, FPO AA 34054); telephone (809) 436-4950 through 4957; FAX (809) 429-5246

:Barbados Government

Flag:

three equal vertical bands of blue (hoist side), yellow, and blue with the head of a black trident centered on the gold band; the trident head represents independence and a break with the past (the colonial coat of arms contained a complete trident)

:Barbados Economy

Overview:

A per capita income of $6,500 gives Barbados one of the highest standards of living of all the small island states of the eastern Caribbean.

Historically, the economy was based on the cultivation of sugarcane and related activities. In recent years, however, the economy has diversified into manufacturing and tourism. The tourist industry is now a major employer of the labor force and a primary source of foreign exchange. The economy slowed in 1990-91, however, and Bridgetown's declining hard currency reserves and inability to finance its deficits have caused it to adopt an austere economic reform program.

GDP:
  purchasing power equivalent - $1.7 billion, per capita $6,500; real growth
  rate—3.1% (1990)
Inflation rate (consumer prices):
  3.4% (1990)
Unemployment rate: 18% (1991)
Budget:
  revenues $514 million; expenditures $615 million (FY91-92)
Exports:
  $210.6 million (f.o.b., 1990)
 commodities:
  sugar and molasses, chemicals, electrical components, clothing, rum,
  machinery and transport equipment
 partners:
  CARICOM 30%, US 20%, UK 20%
Imports:
  $704 million (c.i.f., 1990)
 commodities:
  foodstuffs, consumer durables, raw materials, machinery, crude oil,
  construction materials, chemicals
 partners:
  US 35%, CARICOM 13%, UK 12%, Japan 6%, Canada 8%, Venezuela 4%
External debt: $539.9 million (1990)
Industrial production:
  growth rate—2.7% (1990); accounts for 14% of GDP
Electricity:
  152,100 kW capacity; 539 million kWh produced, 2,117 kWh per capita (1991)
Industries:
  tourism, sugar, light manufacturing, component assembly for export
Agriculture:
  accounts for 10% of GDP; major cash crop is sugarcane; other crops -
  vegetables and cotton; not self-sufficient in food
Economic aid:
  US commitments, including Ex-Im (FY70-89), $15 million; Western (non-US)
  countries, ODA and OOF bilateral commitments (1970-89), $171 million
Currency:
  Barbadian dollars (plural - dollars); 1 Barbadian dollar (Bds$) = 100 cents
Exchange rates:
  Barbadian dollars (Bds$) per US$1 - 2.0113 (fixed rate)
Fiscal year: 1 April - 31 March

:Barbados Communications

Highways:
  1,570 km total; 1,475 km paved, 95 km gravel and earth
Ports:
  Bridgetown
Merchant marine:
  2 cargo ships (1,000 GRT or over) totaling 3,200 GRT/7,338 DWT
Civil air:
  no major transport aircraft

Airports:
  1 with permanent-surface runways 2,440-3,659 m
Telecommunications:
  islandwide automatic telephone system with 89,000 telephones; tropospheric
  scatter link to Trinidad and Saint Lucia; broadcast stations - 3 AM, 2 FM, 2
  (1 is pay) TV; 1 Atlantic Ocean INTELSAT earth station

:Barbados Defense Forces

Branches:
  Royal Barbados Defense Force, Coast Guard, Royal Barbados Police Force
Manpower availability:
  males 15-49, 69,678; 48,803 fit for military service, no conscription
Defense expenditures:
  exchange rate conversion - $10 million, 0.7% of GDP (1989)

Bassas da India Geography

Total area: NA
Land area: undetermined
Comparative area: undetermined
Land boundaries:
  none
Coastline:
  35.2 km
Maritime claims:
 Contiguous zone:
  12 nm
 Continental shelf:
  200 m (depth) or to depth of exploitation
 Exclusive economic zone:
  200 nm
 Territorial sea:
  12 nm
Disputes:
  claimed by Madagascar
Climate:
  tropical
Terrain:
  a volcanic rock 2.4 m high
Natural resources:
  none
Land use:
  arable land 0%; permanent crops 0%; meadows and pastures 0%; forest and
  woodland 0%; other (rock) 100%
Environment:
  surrounded by reefs; subject to periodic cyclones
Note:
  navigational hazard since it is usually under water during high tide;
  located in southern Mozambique Channel about halfway between Africa and
  Madagascar

:Bassas da India People

Population: uninhabited

:Bassas da India Government

Long-form name:
   none
Type:
   French possession administered by Commissioner of the Republic Jacques
   DEWATRE (since July 1991), resident in Reunion
Capital: none; administered by France from Reunion

:Bassas da India Economy

Overview: no economic activity

:Bassas da India Communications

Ports: none; offshore anchorage only

:Bassas da India Defense Forces

Note: defense is the responsibility of France

Belarus Geography

Total area: 207,600 km2
Land area: 207,600 km2
Comparative area: slightly smaller than Kansas
Land boundaries:
   3,098 km total; Latvia 141 km, Lithuania 502 km, Poland 605 km, Russia 959
   km, Ukraine 891 km
Coastline:
   none - landlocked
Maritime claims:
   none - landlocked
Disputes:
   none
Climate:
   mild and moist; transitional between continental and maritime
Terrain:
   generally flat and contains much marshland
Natural resources:
   forest land and peat deposits
Land use:
   arable land NA%; permanent crops NA%; meadows and pastures NA%; forest and
   woodland NA%; other NA%; includes irrigated NA%
Environment:
   southern part of Belarus
   highly contaminated with fallout from 1986 nuclear reactor accident at
   Chernobyl'
Note:
   landlocked

:Belarus People

Population: 10,373,881 (July 1992), growth rate 0.5% (1992)
Birth rate: 15 births/1,000 population (1992)
Death rate: 11 deaths/1,000 population (1992)

Net migration rate: 1 migrant/1,000 population (1992)

Infant mortality rate: 20 deaths/1,000 live births (1992)

Life expectancy at birth: 66 years male, 76 years female (1992)

Total fertility rate: 2.1 children born/woman (1992)

Nationality:
  noun - Belarusian(s); adjective - Belarusian

Ethnic divisions:
  Byelorussian 77.9%, Russian 13.2%, Poles 4.1%, Ukrainian 2.9%, Jews 1.1%,
  other 0.8%

Religions:
  Russian Orthodox NA%, unknown NA%, none NA%, other NA%

Languages:
  Byelorussian NA%, Russian NA%, other NA%

Literacy:
  NA% (male NA%, female NA%) age 15 and over can read and write

Labor force:
  5,418,000; industry and construction 42%, agriculture and forestry 20%,
  other 38% (1990)

Organized labor:
  NA

:Belarus Government

Long-form name:
  Republic of Belarus

Type:
  republic

Capital: Mensk

Administrative divisions:
  6 oblasts (oblastey, singular - oblast'); Brest, Gomel', Grodno, Minsk,
  Mogilev, Vitebsk; note - all oblasts have the same name as their
  administrative center

Independence:
  1 January 1919 Belorussian Republic; 30 December 1922 joined with the USSR;
  25 August 1991 redeclared independence

Constitution:
  adopted April 1978

Legal system:
  based on civil law system

National holiday:
  24 August (1991)

Executive branch:
  NA

Legislative branch:
  unicameral with 360 seats

Judicial branch:
  NA

Leaders:
  Chief of State:
  Chairman of the Supreme Soviet Stanislav S. SHUSHKEVICH (since NA 1991)
  Head of Government:

Prime Minister Vyacheslav F. KEBICH (since NA April 1990), First Deputy
Prime Minister Mikhail MYASNIKOVICH (since early 1991)
Political parties and leaders:
  Belarusian Popular Front, Zenon POZNYAK, chairman; United Democratic Party,
  Stanislav GUSAK, co-chairman; Social Democratic Gramada, Mikhail TKACHEV,
  chairman; Belarus Workers Union, Mikhail SOBOL, Chairman
Suffrage:
  universal at age 18
Elections:
 President:
  NA
 Supreme Soviet:
  last held 4 March 1990 (next to be held NA); results - percent of vote by
  party NA; seats - (360 total) number of seats by party NA; note - 50 seats
  are for public bodies
Communists:
  NA
Other political or pressure groups:
  NA
Member of:
  CE, CIS, CSCE, ECE, IAEA, ILO, INMARSAT, IOC, ITU, NACC, PCA, UN,
UNCTAD,
  UNESCO, UNIDO, UPU, WHO, WIPO, WMO
Diplomatic representation:
  Ambassador Martynov; Chancery at NA NW, Washington, DC 200__; telephone
NA
 US:
  Ambassador (vacant); David SWARTZ, Charge d'Affaires; Embassy at Hotel
  Belarus (telephone 8-011-7-0172-69-08-02) plus 7 hours; (mailing address is
  APO New York is 09862); telephone NA
Flag:
  white, red, and white

:Belarus Economy

Overview:
  In many ways Belarus resembles the three Baltic states, for example, in its
  industrial competence, its higher-than-average standard of living, and its
  critical dependence on the other former Soviet states for fuels and raw
  materials. Belarus ranks fourth in gross output among the former Soviet
  republics, producing 4% of the total GDP and employing 4% of the labor
  force. Once a mainly agricultural area, it now supplies important producer
  and consumer goods - sometimes as the sole producer - to the other states.
  The soil in Belarus is not as fertile as the black earth of Ukraine, but by
  emphasizing favorable crops and livestock (especially pigs and chickens),
  Belarus has become a net exporter to the other republics of meat, milk,
  eggs, flour, and potatoes. Belarus produces only small amounts of oil and
  gas and receives most of its fuel from Russia through the Druzhba oil
  pipeline and the Northern Lights gas pipeline. These pipelines transit
  Belarus enroute to Eastern Europe. Belarus produces petrochemicals,
  plastics, synthetic fibers (nearly 30% of former Soviet output), and

fertilizer (20% of former Soviet output). Raw material resources are limited to potash and peat deposits. The peat (more than one-third of the total for the former Soviet Union) is used in domestic heating as boiler fuel for electric power stations and in the production of chemicals. The potash supports fertilizer production.

GDP:
NA - $NA, per capita $NA; real growth rate —2% (1991)

Inflation rate (consumer prices):
81% (1991)

Unemployment rate: NA%

Budget:
revenues $NA million; expenditures $NA million, including capital expenditures of $NA million

Exports:
$4.3 billion (f.o.b., 1990)
commodities:
machinery and transport equipment, chemicals, foodstuffs
partners:
NA

Imports:
$5.6 billion (c.i.f., 1990)
commodities:
machinery, chemicals, textiles
partners:
NA

External debt: $2.6 billion (end of 1991)

Industrial production:
growth rate —1.5% (1991)

Electricity:
7,500,000 kW capacity; 38,700 million kWh produced, 3,770 kWh per capita (1991)

:Belarus Economy

Industries:
employ about 27% of labor force and produce a wide variety of products essential to the other states; products include (in percent share of total output of former Soviet Union): tractors(12%); metal-cutting machine tools (11%); off-highway dump trucksup to 110-metric- ton load capacity (100%); wheel-type earthmovers for construction and mining (100%); eight-wheel-drive, high-flotation trucks with cargo capacity of 25 metric tons for use in tundra and roadless areas (100%); equipment for animal husbandry and livestock feeding (25%); motorcycles (21.3%); television sets (11%); chemical fibers (28%); fertilizer (18%); linen fabric (11%); wool fabric (7%); radios; refrigerators; and other consumer goods

Agriculture:
accounts for 5.7% of total agricultural output of former Soviet Union; employs 29% of the labor force; in 1988 produced the following (in percent of total Soviet production): grain (3.6%), potatoes (12.2%), vegetables (3.0%), meat (6.0%), milk (7.0%); net exporter of meat, milk, eggs, flour, and potatoes

Illicit drugs:
illicit producer of opium mostly for the domestic market; transshipment point for illicit drugs to Western Europe

Economic aid:
NA

Currency:
as of May 1992, retaining ruble as currency

Exchange rates:
NA

Fiscal year: calendar year

:Belarus Communications

Railroads:
5,570 km (includes NA km electrified); does not include industrial lines (1990)

Highways:
98,200 km total (1990); 66,100 km hard surfaced, 32,100 km earth

Inland waterways:
NA km

Pipelines:
NA

Ports:
none - landlocked

Merchant marine:
none - landlocked

Civil air:
NA major transport aircraft

Airports:
NA

Telecommunications:
telephone network has 1.7 million lines, 15% of which are switched automatically; Minsk has 450,000 lines; telephone density is approximately 17 per 100 persons; as of 31 January 1990, 721,000 applications from households for telephones were still unsatisfied; international connections to other former Soviet republics are by landline or microwave and to other countries by leased connection through the Moscow international gateway switch

:Belarus Defense Forces

Branches:
Republic Security Forces (internal and border troops); CIS Forces (Ground, Air, Air Defense, Strategic Rocket)

Manpower availability:
males 15-49, NA; NA fit for military service; NA reach military age (18) annually

Defense expenditures:
$NA, NA% of GDP

Belgium Geography

Total area: 30,510 km2
Land area: 30,230 km2

Comparative area: slightly larger than Maryland
Land boundaries:
   1,385 km total; France 620 km, Germany 167 km, Luxembourg 148 km,
   Netherlands 450 km
Coastline:
   64 km
Maritime claims:
  Continental shelf:
   not specific
  Exclusive fishing zone:
   equidistant line with neighbors (extends about 68 km from coast)
  Territorial sea:
   12 nm
Disputes:
   none
Climate:
   temperate; mild winters, cool summers; rainy, humid, cloudy
Terrain:
   flat coastal plains in northwest, central rolling hills, rugged mountains of
   Ardennes Forest in southeast
Natural resources:
   coal, natural gas
Land use:
   arable land 24%; permanent crops 1%; meadows and pastures 20%; forest and
   woodland 21%; other 34%, includes irrigated NEGL%
Environment:
   air and water pollution
Note:
   majority of West European capitals within 1,000 km of Brussels; crossroads
   of Western Europe; Brussels is the seat of the EC

:Belgium People

Population: 10,016,623 (July 1992), growth rate 0.3% (1992)
Birth rate: 12 births/1,000 population (1992)
Death rate: 10 deaths/1,000 population (1992)
Net migration rate: 1 migrant/1,000 population (1992)
Infant mortality rate: 8 deaths/1,000 live births (1992)
Life expectancy at birth: 73 years male, 80 years female (1992)
Total fertility rate: 1.6 children born/woman (1992)
Nationality:
   noun - Belgian(s); adjective - Belgian
Ethnic divisions:
   Fleming 55%, Walloon 33%, mixed or other 12%
Religions:
   Roman Catholic 75%, remainder Protestant or other
Languages:
   Flemish (Dutch) 56%, French 32%, German 1%; legally bilingual 11%; divided
   along ethnic lines
Literacy:
   99% (male 99%, female 99%) age 15 and over can read and write (1980 est.)

Labor force:
  4,126,000; services 63.6%, industry 28%, construction 6.1%, agriculture 2.3%
  (1988)
Organized labor:
  70% of labor force

:Belgium Government

Long-form name:
  Kingdom of Belgium
Type:
  constitutional monarchy
Capital: Brussels
Administrative divisions:
  9 provinces (French - provinces, singular - province; Flemish - provincien,
  singular - provincie); Antwerpen, Brabant, Hainaut, Liege, Limburg,
  Luxembourg, Namur, Oost-Vlaanderen, West-Vlaanderen
Independence:
  4 October 1830 (from the Netherlands)
Constitution:
  7 February 1831, last revised 8-9 August 1980; the government is in the
  process of revising the Constitution with the aim of federalizing the
  Belgian state
Legal system:
  civil law system influenced by English constitutional theory; judicial
  review of legislative acts; accepts compulsory ICJ jurisdiction, with
  reservations
National holiday:
  National Day, 21 July (ascension of King Leopold to the throne in 1831)
Executive branch:
  monarch, prime minister, three deputy prime ministers, Cabinet
Legislative branch:
  bicameral Parliament consists of an upper chamber or Senate (Flemish -
  Senaat, French - Senat) and a lower chamber or Chamber of Representatives
  (Flemish - Kamer van Volksvertegenwoordigers, French - Chambre des
  Representants)
Judicial branch:
  Supreme Court of Justice (Flemish - Hof van Cassatie, French - Cour de
  Cassation)
Leaders:
 Chief of State:
  King BAUDOUIN I (since 17 July 1951); Heir Apparent Prince ALBERT of Liege
  (brother of the King; born 6 June 1934)
 Head of Government:
  Prime Minister Jean-Luc DEHAENE (since 6 March 1992)
Political parties and leaders:
  Flemish Social Christian (CVP), Herman van ROMPUY, president; Walloon Social
  Christian (PSC) , Gerard DEPREZ, president; Flemish Socialist (SP), Frank
  VANDENBROUCKE, president; Walloon Socialist (PS), NA; Flemish Liberal
(PVV),
  Guy VERHOF STADT, president; Walloon Liberal (PRL), Antoine DUQUESNE,

president; Francophone Democratic Front (FDF), Georges CLERFAYT, president;
Volksunie (VU), Jaak GABRIELS, president; Communist Party (PCB), Louis van
GEYT, president; Vlaams Blok (VB), Karel DILLEN, chairman; ROSSEM, Jean
Pierre VAN ROSSEM; National Front (FN), Werner van STEEN; Live Differently
(AGALEV), Leo COX; Ecologist (ECOLO), NA; other minor parties

Suffrage:
universal and compulsory at age 18

Elections:
Chamber of Representatives:
last held 24 November 1991 (next to be held by November 1996); results -
percent of vote by party NA; seats - (212 total) number of seats by party NA
Senate:
last held 24 November 1991 (next to be held by November 1996); results -
percent of vote by party NA; seats - (106 total) number of seats by party NA

:Belgium Government

Other political or pressure groups:
Christian and Socialist Trade Unions; Federation of Belgian Industries;
numerous other associations representing bankers, manufacturers,
middle-class artisans, and the legal and medical professions; various
organizations represent the cultural interests of Flanders and Wallonia;
various peace groups such as the Flemish Action Committee Against Nuclear
Weapons and Pax Christi

Member of:
ACCT, AfDB, AG, AsDB, Benelux, BIS, CCC, CE, CERN, COCOM, CSCE,
EBRD, EC,
ECE, EIB, ESA, FAO, G-9, G-10, GATT, IADB, IAEA, IBRD, ICAO, ICC, ICFTU,
IDA, IEA, IFAD, IFC, ILO, IMF, IMO, INMARSAT, INTELSAT, INTERPOL,
IOC, IOM,
ISO, ITU, LORCS, MTCR, NACC, NATO, NEA, OAS (observer), OECD, PCA,
UN,
UNCTAD, UNESCO, UNHCR, UNIDO, UNMOGIP, UNRWA, UNTSO, UPU,
WCL, WEU, WHO,
WIPO, WMO, WTO, ZC

Diplomatic representation:
Ambassador Juan CASSIERS; Chancery at 3330 Garfield Street NW, Washington,
DC 20008; telephone (202) 333-6900; there are Belgian Consulates General in
Atlanta, Chicago, Los Angeles, and New York
US:
Ambassador Bruce S. GELB; Embassy at 27 Boulevard du Regent, B-1000 Brussels
(mailing address is APO AE 09724); telephone [32] (2) 513-3830; FAX [32] (2)
511-2725; there is a US Consulate General in Antwerp

Flag:
three equal vertical bands of black (hoist side), yellow, and red; the
design was based on the flag of France

:Belgium Economy

Overview:
This small private enterprise economy has capitalized on its central
geographic location, highly developed transport network, and diversified
industrial and commercial base. Industry is concentrated mainly in the

populous Flemish area in the north, although the government is encouraging reinvestment in the southern region of Walloon. With few natural resources Belgium must import essential raw materials, making its economy closely dependent on the state of world markets. Over 70% of trade is with other EC countries. During the period 1988-90, Belgium's economic performance was marked by 4% average growth, moderate inflation, and a substantial external surplus. Growth fell to 1.4% in 1991.

GDP:
purchasing power equivalent - $171.8 billion, per capita $17,300; real growth rate 1.4% (1991 est.)

Inflation rate (consumer prices):
3.2% (1991 est.)

Unemployment rate: 9.4% est. (1991 est.)

Budget:
revenues $45.0 billion; expenditures $55.3 billion, including capital expenditures of NA (1989)

Exports:
$118 billion (f.o.b., 1990) Belgium-Luxembourg Economic Union
commodities:
iron and steel, transportation equipment, tractors, diamonds, petroleum products
partners:
EC 74%, US 5%, former Communist countries 2% (1989)

Imports:
$120 billion (c.i.f., 1990) Belgium-Luxembourg Economic Union
commodities:
fuels, grains, chemicals, foodstuffs
partners:
EC 73%, US 4%, oil-exporting less developed countries 4%, former Communist countries 3% (1989)

External debt: $28.8 billion (1990 est.)

Industrial production:
growth rate 1.2% (1991 est.); accounts for almost 30% of GDP

Electricity:
17,400,000 kW capacity; 67,100 million kWh produced, 6,767 kWh per capita (1991)

Industries:
engineering and metal products, processed food and beverages, chemicals, basic metals, textiles, glass, petroleum, coal

Agriculture:
accounts for 2.3% of GDP; emphasis on livestock production - beef, veal, pork, milk; major crops are sugar beets, fresh vegetables, fruits, grain, and tobacco; net importer of farm products

Economic aid:
donor - ODA and OOF commitments (1970-89), $5.8 billion

Currency:
Belgian franc (plural - francs); 1 Belgian franc (BF) = 100 centimes

Exchange rates:
Belgian francs (BF) per US$1 - 32.462 (January 1992), 34.148 (1991), 33.418

(1990), 39.404 (1989), 36.768 (1988), 37.334 (1987)

Fiscal year: calendar year

:Belgium Communications

Railroads:

   Belgian National Railways (SNCB) operates 3,667 km 1.435-meter standard
   gauge, government owned; 2,563 km double track; 1,978 km electrified; 191 km
   1.000-meter gauge, government owned and operated

Highways:

   103,396 km total; 1,317 km limited access, divided autoroute; 11,717 km
   national highway; 1,362 km provincial road; about 38,000 km paved and 51,000
   km unpaved rural roads

Inland waterways:

   2,043 km (1,528 km in regular commercial use)

Pipelines:

   petroleum products 1,167 km; crude oil 161 km; natural gas 3,300 km

Ports:

   Antwerp, Brugge, Gent, Oostende, Zeebrugge

Merchant marine:

   23 ships (1,000 GRT or over) totaling 62,979 GRT/88,738 DWT; includes 10
   cargo, 4 petroleum tanker, 1 liquefied gas, 5 chemical tanker, 1 bulk, 2
   refrigerated cargo

Civil air:

   47 major transport aircraft

Airports:

   42 total, 42 usable; 24 with permanent-surface runways; none with runways
   over 3,659 m; 14 with runways 2,440-3,659 m; 3 with runways 1,220-2,439 m

Telecommunications:

   highly developed, technologically advanced, and completely automated
   domestic and international telephone and telegraph facilities; extensive
   cable network; limited radio relay network; 4,720,000 telephones; broadcast
   stations - 3 AM, 39 FM, 32 TV; 5 submarine cables; 2 satellite earth
   stations - Atlantic Ocean INTELSAT and EUTELSAT systems; nationwide mobile
   phone system

:Belgium Defense Forces

Branches:

   Army, Navy, Air Force, National Gendarmerie

Manpower availability:

   males 15-49, 2,550,088; 2,133,483 fit for military service; 66,249 reach
   military age (19) annually

Defense expenditures:

   exchange rate conversion - $4.2 billion, 2.7% of GDP (1991)

Belize Geography

Total area: 22,960 km2

Land area: 22,800 km2

Comparative area: slightly larger than Massachusetts

Land boundaries:

   516 km total; Guatemala 266 km, Mexico 250 km

Coastline:

386 km
Maritime claims:
  Territorial sea:
    12 nm in the north and 3 nm in the south; note - from the mouth of the
    Sarstoon River to Ranguana Caye, Belize's territorial sea is 3 miles;
    according to Belize's Maritime Areas Act, 1992, the purpose of this
    limitation is to provide a framework for the negotiation of a definitive
    agreement on territorial differences with the Republic of Guatemala"
Disputes:
    claimed by Guatemala, but boundary negotiations to resolve the dispute have
    begun
Climate:
    tropical; very hot and humid; rainy season (May to February)
Terrain:
    flat, swampy coastal plain; low mountains in south
Natural resources:
    arable land potential, timber, fish
Land use:
    arable land 2%; permanent crops NEGL%; meadows and pastures 2%; forest and
    woodland 44%; other 52%, includes irrigated NEGL%
Environment:
    frequent devastating hurricanes (September to December) and coastal flooding
    (especially in south); deforestation
Note:
    national capital moved 80 km inland from Belize City to Belmopan because of
    hurricanes; only country in Central America without a coastline on the North
    Pacific Ocean

:Belize People

Population: 229,143 (July 1992), growth rate 3.0% (1992)
Birth rate: 31 births/1,000 population (1992)
Death rate: 5 deaths/1,000 population (1992)
Net migration rate: 4 migrants/1,000 population (1992)
Infant mortality rate: 30 deaths/1,000 live births (1992)
Life expectancy at birth: 67 years male, 73 years female (1992)
Total fertility rate: 3.8 children born/woman (1992)
Nationality:
    noun - Belizean(s); adjective - Belizean
Ethnic divisions:
    Creole 39.7%, Mestizo 33.1%, Maya 9.5%, Garifuna 7.6%, East Indian 2.1%,
    other 8.0%
Religions:
    Roman Catholic 62%, Protestant 30% (Anglican 12%, Methodist 6%, Mennonite
    4%, Seventh-Day Adventist 3%, Pentecostal 2%, Jehovah's Witnesses 1%, other
    2%), none 2%, unknown 3%, other 3% (1980)
Languages:
    English (official), Spanish, Maya, Garifuna (Carib)
Literacy:
    91% (male 91%, female 91%) age 15 and over having ever attended school
    (1970)

Labor force:
   51,500; agriculture 30.0%, services 16.0%, government 15.4%, commerce 11.2%, manufacturing 10.3%; shortage of skilled labor and all types of technical personnel (1985)
Organized labor:
   12% of labor force; 7 unions currently active

:Belize Government

Long-form name:
   none
Type:
   parliamentary democracy
Capital: Belmopan
Administrative divisions:
   6 districts; Belize, Cayo, Corozal, Orange Walk, Stann Creek, Toledo
Independence:
   21 September 1981 (from UK; formerly British Honduras)
Constitution:
   21 September 1981
Legal system:
   English law
National holiday:
   Independence Day, 21 September
Executive branch:
   British monarch, governor general, prime minister, deputy prime minister, Cabinet
Legislative branch:
   bicameral National Assembly consists of an upper house or Senate and a lower house or House of Representatives
Judicial branch:
   Supreme Court
Leaders:
   Chief of State:
   Queen ELIZABETH II (since 6 February 1952), represented by Governor General Dame Elmira Minita GORDON (since 21 September 1981)
   Head of Government:
   Prime Minister George Cadle PRICE (since 4 September 1989)
Political parties and leaders:
   People's United Party (PUP), George PRICE, Florencio MARIN, Said MUSA; United Democratic Party (UDP), Manuel ESQUIVEL, Dean LINDO, Dean BARROW;
   Belize Popular Party (BPP), Louis SYLVESTRE
Suffrage:
   universal at age 18
Elections:
   National Assembly:
   last held 4 September 1989 (next to be held September 1994); results - percent of vote by party NA; seats - (28 total) PUP 15, UDP 13; note - in January 1990 one member expelled from UDP joined PUP, making the seat count PUP 16, UDP 12

Other political or pressure groups:
 Society for the Promotion of Education and Research (SPEAR) headed by former
 PUP minister; United Workers Front
Member of:
 ACP, C, CARICOM, CDB, ECLAC, FAO, G-77, GATT, IBRD, ICO, IDA, IFAD,
IFC,
 ILO, IMF, IMO, INTERPOL, IOC, IOM (observer), ITU, LORCS, NAM, OAS, UN,
 UNCTAD, UNESCO, UNIDO, UPU, WCL, WMO
Diplomatic representation:
 Ambassador James V. HYDE; Chancery at 2535 Massachusetts Avenue NW,
 Washington, DC 20008; telephone (202) 332-9636
 US:
 Ambassador Eugene L. SCASSA; Embassy at Gabourel Lane and Hutson Street,
 Belize City (mailing address is P. O. Box 286, Belize City); telephone [501]
 (2) 77161; FAX [501] (2) 30802
Flag:
 on a scroll at the bottom, all encircled by a green garland

:Belize Government

        blue with a narrow red stripe along the top and the bottom edges; cen-
        tered is a large white disk bearing the coat of arms; the coat of arms
        features a shield flanked by two workers in front of a mahogany tree
        with the related motto RA FLOREO (I Flourish in the Shade)

:Belize Economy

Overview:
 The economy is based primarily on agriculture, agro-based industry, and
 merchandising, with tourism and construction assuming increasing importance.
 Agriculture accounts for about 30% of GDP and provides 75% of export
 earnings, while sugar, the chief crop, accounts for almost 40% of hard
 currency earnings. The US, Belize's main trading partner, is assisting in
 efforts to reduce dependency on sugar with an agricultural diversification
 program.
GDP:
 exchange rate conversion - $373 million, per capita $1,635; real growth rate
 10% (1990 est.)
Inflation rate (consumer prices):
 3.5% (1990 est.)
Unemployment rate: 12% (1988)
Budget:
 revenues $126.8 million; expenditures $123.1 million, including capital
 expenditures of $44.8 million (FY91 est.)
Exports:
 $134 million (f.o.b., 1991 est.)
 commodities:
 sugar, clothing, seafood, molasses, citrus, wood and wood products
 partners:
 US 47%, UK, Trinidad and Tobago, Canada (1987)
Imports:
 $194 million (c.i.f., 1991 est.)
 commodities:

machinery and transportation equipment, food, manufactured goods, fuels,
chemicals, pharmaceuticals

partners:

US 56%, UK, Netherlands Antilles, Mexico (1991)

External debt: $142 million (December 1991)

Industrial production:

growth rate 9.7% (1989); accounts for 16% of GDP

Electricity:

34,532 kW capacity; 90 million kWh produced, 395 kWh per capita (1991)

Industries:

garment production, citrus concentrates, sugar refining, rum, beverages,
tourism

Agriculture:

accounts for 30% of GDP (including fish and forestry); commercial crops
include sugarcane, bananas, coca, citrus fruits; expanding output of lumber
and cultured shrimp; net importer of basic foods

Illicit drugs:

an illicit producer of cannabis for the international drug trade;
eradication program cut marijuana production from 200 metric tons in 1987 to
about 50 metric tons in 1991; transshipment point for cocaine

Economic aid:

US commitments, including Ex-Im (FY70-89), $104 million; Western (non-US)
countries, ODA and OOF bilateral commitments (1970-89), $215 million

Currency:

Belizean dollar (plural - dollars); 1 Belizean dollar (Bz$) = 100 cents

Exchange rates:

Belizean dollars (Bz$) per US$1 - 2.00 (fixed rate)

Fiscal year: 1 April - 31 March

:Belize Communications

Highways:

2,710 km total; 500 km paved, 1,600 km gravel, 300 km improved earth, and
310 km unimproved earth

Inland waterways:

825 km river network used by shallow-draft craft; seasonally navigable

Ports:

Belize City; additional ports for shallow draught craft include Corozol,
Punta Gorda, Big Creek

Merchant marine:

2 cargo ships (1,000 GRT or over) totaling 3,127 GRT/5,885 DWT

Civil air:

2 major transport aircraft

Airports:

44 total, 34 usable; 3 with permanent-surface runways; none with runways
over 2,439 m; 2 with runways 1,220-2,439 m

Telecommunications:

8,650 telephones; above-average system based on radio relay; broadcast
stations - 6 AM, 5 FM, 1 TV, 1 shortwave; 1 Atlantic Ocean INTELSAT earth
station

:Belize Defense Forces

Branches:

British Forces Belize, Belize Defense Force (including Army, Navy, Air Force, and Volunteer Guard)

Manpower availability:

males 15-49, 55,333; 33,040 fit for military service; 2,509 reach military age (18) annually

Defense expenditures:

exchange rate conversion - $4.8 million, 1.8% of GDP (FY91)

Benin Geography

Total area: 112,620 km2

Land area: 110,620 km2

Comparative area: slightly smaller than Pennsylvania

Land boundaries:

1,989 km total; Burkina 306 km, Niger 266 km, Nigeria 773 km, Togo 644 km

Coastline:

121 km

Maritime claims:

 Territorial sea:

200 nm

Disputes:

Climate:

tropical; hot, humid in south; semiarid in north

Terrain:

mostly flat to undulating plain; some hills and low mountains

Natural resources:

small offshore oil deposits, limestone, marble, timber

Land use:

arable land 12%; permanent crops 4%; meadows and pastures 4%; forest and woodland 35%; other 45%, includes irrigated NEGL%

Environment:

hot, dry, dusty harmattan wind may affect north in winter; deforestation; desertification

Note:

recent droughts have severely affected marginal agriculture in north; no natural harbors

:Benin People

Population: 4,997,599 (July 1992), growth rate 3.3% (1992)

Birth rate: 49 births/1,000 population (1992)

Death rate: 15 deaths/1,000 population (1992)

Net migration rate: 0 migrants/1,000 population (1992)

Infant mortality rate: 115 deaths/1,000 live births (1992)

Life expectancy at birth: 49 years male, 53 years female (1992)

Total fertility rate: 6.9 children born/woman (1992)

Nationality:

noun - Beninese (singular and plural); adjective - Beninese

Ethnic divisions:

African 99% (42 ethnic groups, most important being Fon, Adja, Yoruba, Bariba); Europeans 5,500

Religions:
  indigenous beliefs 70%, Muslim 15%, Christian 15%
Languages:
  French (official); Fon and Yoruba most common vernaculars in south; at least
  six major tribal languages in north
Literacy:
  23% (male 32%, female 16%) age 15 and over can read and write (1990 est.)
Labor force:
  1,900,000 (1987); agriculture 60%, transport, commerce, and public services
  38%, industry less than 2%; 49% of population of working age (1985)
Organized labor:
  about 75% of wage earners

:Benin Government

Long-form name:
  Republic of Benin
Type:
  republic under multiparty democratic rule; dropped Marxism-Leninism December
  1989; democratic reforms adopted February 1990; transition to multiparty
  system completed 4 April 1991
Capital: Porto-Novo
Administrative divisions:
  6 provinces; Atakora, Atlantique, Borgou, Mono, Oueme, Zou
Independence:
  1 August 1960 (from France; formerly Dahomey)
Constitution:
  2 December 1990
Legal system:
  based on French civil law and customary law; has not accepted compulsory ICJ
  jurisdiction
National holiday:
  National Day, 1 August (1990)
Executive branch:
  president, cabinet
Legislative branch:
  unicameral National Assembly (Assemblee Nationale)
Judicial branch:
  Supreme Court (Cour Supreme)
Leaders:
  Chief of State and Head of Government:
  President Nicephore SOGLO (since 4 April 1991)
Political parties and leaders:
  Alliance of the Democratic Union for the Forces of Progress (UDFP), Timothee
  ADANLIN; Movement for Democracy and Social Progress (MDPS), Jean-Roger
  AHOYO; and the Union for Liberty and Development (ULD), Marcellin DEGBE;
  Alliance of the National Party for Democracy and Development (PNDD) and the
  Democratic Renewal Party (PRD), Pascal Chabi KAO; Alliance of the Social
  Democratic Party (PSD) and the National Union for Solidarity and Progress
  (UNSP), Bruno AMOUSSOU; Our Common Cause (NCC), Albert TEVOEDJRE;
National

Rally for Democracy (RND), Joseph KEKE; Alliance of the National Movement
for Democracy and Development (MNDD), Bertin BORNA; Movement for Solidari-
ty,
Union, and Progress (MSUP), Adebo ADENIYI; and Union for Democracy and
National Reconstruction (UDRN), Azaria FAKOREDE; Union for Democracy and
National Solidarity (UDS), Mama Amadou N'DIAYE; Assembly of Liberal
Democrats for National Reconstruction (RDL), Severin ADJOVI; Alliance of the
Alliance for Social Democracy (ASD), Robert DOSSOU, and Bloc for Social
Democracy (BSD), Michel MAGNIDE; Alliance of the Alliance for Democracy and
Progress (ADP), Akindes ADEKPEDJOU, and Democratic Union for Social Renew-
al
(UDRS), Bio Gado Seko N'GOYE; National Union for Democracy and Progress
(UNDP), Robert TAGNON; numerous other small parties

Suffrage:
universal at age 18

Elections:
National Assembly:
last held 10 and 24 March 1991; results - percent of vote by party NA; seats
- (64 total) UDFP-MDPS-ULD 12, PNDD/PRD 9, PSD/UNSP 8, NCC 7, RND 7,
MNDD/MSUP/UDRN 6, UDS 5, RDL 4, ASD/BSD 3, ADP/UDRS 2, UNDP 1
President:
last held 10 and 24 March 1991; results - Nicephore SOGLO 68%, Mathieu
KEREKOU 32%

Communists:
Communist Party of Dahomey (PCD) remains active

:Benin Government

Member of:
ACCT, ACP, AfDB, CEAO, ECA, ECOWAS, Entente, FAO, FZ, G-77, GATT,
IBRD,
ICAO, IDA, IDB, IFAD, IFC, ILO, IMF, IMO, INTELSAT, INTERPOL, IOC, ITU,
LORCS, NAM, OAU, OIC, UN, UNCTAD, UNESCO, UNIDO, UPU, WADB,
WCL, WHO, WIPO,
WMO, WTO

Diplomatic representation:
Ambassador Candide AHOUANSOU; Chancery at 2737 Cathedral Avenue NW,
Washington, DC 20008; telephone (202) 232-6656

US:
Ambassador Harriet W. ISOM; Embassy at Rue Caporal Anani Bernard, Cotonou
(mailing address is B. P. 2012, Cotonou); telephone [229] 30-06-50,
30-05-13, 30-17-92; FAX [229] 30-14-39 and 30-19-74

Flag:
two equal horizontal bands of yellow (top) and red with a vertical green
band on the hoist side

:Benin Economy

Overview:
Benin is one of the least developed countries in the world because of
limited natural resources and a poorly developed infrastructure. Agriculture
accounts for about 35% of GDP, employs about 60% of the labor force, and
generates a major share of foreign exchange earnings. The industrial sector

contributes only about 15% to GDP and employs 2% of the work force. Low prices in recent years have kept down hard currency earnings from Benin's major exports of agricultural products and crude oil.

GDP:
  exchange rate conversion - $2.0 billion, per capita $410; real growth rate 3% (1991)

Inflation rate (consumer prices):
  3.0% (1990)

Unemployment rate: NA%

Budget:
  revenues $194 million; expenditures $390 million, including capital expenditures of $104 million (1990 est.)

Exports:
  $263.3 million (f.o.b., 1990 est.)
  commodities:
  crude oil, cotton, palm products, cocoa
  partners:
  FRG 36%, France 16%, Spain 14%, Italy 8%, UK 4%

Imports:
  $428 million (f.o.b., 1990 est.)
  commodities:
  foodstuffs, beverages, tobacco, petroleum products, intermediate goods, capital goods, light consumer goods
  partners:
  France 34%, Netherlands 10%, Japan 7%, Italy 6%, US 4%

External debt: $1.0 billion (December 1990 est.)

Industrial production:
  growth rate —0.7% (1988); accounts for 15% of GDP

Electricity:
  30,000 kW capacity; 25 million kWh produced, 5 kWh per capita (1991)

Industries:
  textiles, cigarettes, construction materials, beverages, food production, petroleum

Agriculture:
  small farms produce 90% of agricultural output; production is dominated by food crops - corn, sorghum, cassava, beans, and rice; cash crops include cotton, palm oil, and peanuts; poultry and livestock output has not kept up with consumption

Economic aid:
  US commitments, including Ex-Im (FY70-89), $46 million; Western (non-US) countries, ODA and OOF bilateral commitments (1970-89), $1,300 million; OPEC bilateral aid (1979-89), $19 million; Communist countries (1970-89), $101 million

Currency:
  Communaute Financiere Africaine franc (plural - francs); 1 CFA franc (CFAF) = 100 centimes

Exchange rates:
  Communaute Financiere Africaine francs (CFAF) per US$1 - 269.01 (January 1992), 282.11 (1991), 272.26 (1990), 319.01 (1989), 297.85 (1988), 300.54

(1987)
Fiscal year: calendar year

:Benin Communications

Railroads:
  578 km, all 1.000-meter gauge, single track
Highways:
  5,050 km total; 920 km paved, 2,600 laterite, 1,530 km improved earth
Inland waterways:
  navigable along small sections, important only locally
Ports:
  Cotonou
Civil air:
  no major transport aircraft
Airports:
  6 total, 5 usable; 1 with permanent-surface runways; none with runways over
  2,439 m; 4 with runways 1,220-2,439 m
Telecommunications:
  fair system of open wire, submarine cable, and radio relay; broadcast
  stations - 2 AM, 2 FM, 2 TV; 1 Atlantic Ocean INTELSAT earth station

:Benin Defense Forces

Branches:
  Armed Forces (including Army, Navy, Air Force), National Gendarmerie
Manpower availability:
  eligible 15-49, 2,165,515; of the 1,031,738 males 15-49, 528,366 are fit for
  military service; of the 1,133,777 females 15-49, 572,603 are fit for
  military service; about 55,697 males and 53,786 females reach military age
  (18) annually; both sexes are liable for military service
Defense expenditures:
  exchange rate conversion - $29 million, 1.7% of GDP (1988 est.)

Bermuda Geography

Total area: 50 km2
Land area: 50 km2
Comparative area: about 0.3 times the size of Washington, DC
Land boundaries:
  none
Coastline:
  103 km
Maritime claims:
  Exclusive fishing zone:
  200 nm
  Territorial sea:
  12 nm
Climate:
  subtropical; mild, humid; gales, strong winds common in winter
Terrain:
  low hills separated by fertile depressions
Natural resources:
  limestone, pleasant climate fostering tourism

Land use:
   arable land 0%; permanent crops 0%; meadows and pastures 0%; forest and
   woodland 20%; other 80%
Environment:
   ample rainfall, but no rivers or freshwater lakes; consists of about 360
   small coral islands
Note:
   1,050 km east of North Carolina; some reclaimed land leased by US Government
:Bermuda People

Population: 60,213 (July 1992), growth rate 0.8% (1992)
Birth rate: 15 births/1,000 population (1992)
Death rate: 7 deaths/1,000 population (1992)
Net migration rate: NEGL migrants/1,000 population (1992)
Infant mortality rate: 13 deaths/1,000 live births (1992)
Life expectancy at birth: 73 years male, 77 years female (1992)
Total fertility rate: 1.8 children born/woman (1992)
Nationality:
   noun - Bermudian(s); adjective - Bermudian
Ethnic divisions:
   black 61%, white and other 39%
Religions:
   Anglican 37%, Roman Catholic 14%, African Methodist Episcopal (Zion) 10%,
   Methodist 6%, Seventh-Day Adventist 5%, other 28%
Languages:
   English
Literacy:
   98% (male 98%, female 99%) age 15 and over can read and write (1970)
Labor force:
   32,000; clerical 25%, services 22%, laborers 21%, professional and technical
   13%, administrative and managerial 10%, sales 7%, agriculture and fishing 2%
   (1984)
Organized labor:
   8,573 members (1985); largest union is Bermuda Industrial Union

:Bermuda Government

Long-form name:
   none
Type:
   dependent territory of the UK
Capital: Hamilton
Administrative divisions:
   9 parishes and 2 municipalities*; Devonshire, Hamilton, Hamilton*, Paget,
   Pembroke, Saint George*, Saint George's, Sandys, Smiths, Southampton,
   Warwick
Independence:
   none (dependent territory of the UK)
Constitution:
   8 June 1968
Legal system:
   English law

National holiday:
  Bermuda Day, 22 May
Executive branch:
  British monarch, governor, deputy governor, premier, deputy premier,
  Executive Council (cabinet)
Legislative branch:
  bicameral Parliament consists of an upper house or Senate and a lower house
  or House of Assembly
Judicial branch:
  Supreme Court
Leaders:
 Chief of State:
  Queen ELIZABETH II (since 6 February 1952), represented by Governor Lord
  David WADDINGTON
 Head of Government:
  Premier John William David SWAN (since January 1982)
Political parties and leaders:
  United Bermuda Party (UBP), John W. D. SWAN; Progressive Labor Party (PLP),
  Frederick WADE; National Liberal Party (NLP), Gilbert DARRELL
Suffrage:
  universal at age 21
Elections:
 House of Assembly:
  last held 9 February 1989 (next to be held by February 1994); results -
  percent of vote by party NA; seats - (40 total) UBP 23, PLP 15, NLP 1, other
  1
Other political or pressure groups:
  Bermuda Industrial Union (BIU), headed by Ottiwell SIMMONS
Member of:
  CARICOM (observer), CCC, ICFTU, IOC
Diplomatic representation:
  as a dependent territory of the UK, Bermuda's interests in the US are
  represented by the UK
 US:
  Consul General L. Ebersole GAINES; Consulate General at Crown Hill, 16
  Middle Road, Devonshire, Hamilton (mailing address is P. O. Box HM325,
  Hamilton HMBX; PSC 1002, FPO AE 09727-1002); telephone (809) 295-1342;
FAX
  (809) 295-1592
Flag:
  red with the flag of the UK in the upper hoist-side quadrant and the
  Bermudian coat of arms (white and blue shield with a red lion holding a
  scrolled shield showing the sinking of the ship Sea Venture off Bermuda in
  1609) centered on the outer half of the flag

:Bermuda Economy

Overview:
  Bermuda enjoys one of the highest per capita incomes in the world, having
  successfully exploited its location by providing luxury tourist facilities
  and financial services. The tourist industry attracts more than 90% of its

business from North America. The industrial sector is small, and agriculture is severely limited by a lack of suitable land. About 80% of food needs are imported.

GDP:
purchasing power equivalent - $1.3 billion, per capita $22,400; real growth rate 2.0% (1989 est.)

Inflation rate (consumer prices):
5.8% (June 1989, annual rate)

Unemployment rate: 2.0% (1988)

Budget:
revenues $361.6 million; expenditures $396.1 million, including capital expenditures of $74.1 million (FY91 est.)

Exports:
$30 million (f.o.b., FY88)
commodities:
semitropical produce, light manufactures
partners:
US 25%, Italy 25%, UK 14%, Canada 5%, other 31%

Imports:
$420 million (c.i.f., FY88)
commodities:
fuel, foodstuffs, machinery
partners:
US 58%, Netherlands Antilles 9%, UK 8%, Canada 6%, Japan 5%, other 14%

External debt: NA

Industrial production:
growth rate NA%

Electricity:
154,000 kW capacity; 504 million kWh produced, 8,625 kWh per capita (1991)

Industries:
tourism, finance, structural concrete products, paints, pharmaceuticals, ship repairing

Agriculture:
accounts for less than 1% of GDP; most basic foods must be imported; produces bananas, vegetables, citrus fruits, flowers, dairy products

Economic aid:
US commitments, including Ex-Im (FY70-81), $34 million; Western (non-US) countries, ODA and OOF bilateral commitments (1970-89), $277 million

Currency:
Bermudian dollar (plural - dollars); 1 Bermudian dollar (Bd$) = 100 cents

Exchange rates:
Bermudian dollar (Bd$) per US$1 - 1.0000 (fixed rate)

Fiscal year: 1 April - 31 March

:Bermuda Communications

Highways:
210 km public roads, all paved (about 400 km of private roads)

Ports:
Freeport, Hamilton, Saint George

Merchant marine:

73 ships (1,000 GRT or over) totaling 3,511,972 GRT/6,093,321 DWT; includes 4 cargo, 5 refrigerated cargo, 4 container, 7 roll-on/roll-off, 23 petroleum tanker, 12 liquefied gas, 18 bulk; note - a flag of convenience registry

Civil air:

16 major transport aircraft

Airports:

1 with permanent-surface runways 2,440-3,659 m

Telecommunications:

modern with fully automatic telephone system; 52,670 telephones; broadcast stations - 5 AM, 3 FM, 2 TV; 3 submarine cables; 2 Atlantic Ocean INTELSAT earth stations

:Bermuda Defense Forces

Branches:

Bermuda Regiment, Bermuda Police Force, Bermuda Reserve Constabulary

Note:

defense is the responsibility of the UK

Bhutan Geography

Total area: 47,000 km2
Land area: 47,000 km2
Comparative area: slightly more than half the size of Indiana

Land boundaries:

1,075 km; China 470 km, India 605 km

Coastline:

none - landlocked

Maritime claims:

none - landlocked

Disputes:

Climate:

varies; tropical in southern plains; cool winters and hot summers in central valleys; severe winters and cool summers in Himalayas

Terrain:

mostly mountainous with some fertile valleys and savanna

Natural resources:

timber, hydropower, gypsum, calcium carbide, tourism potential

Land use:

arable land 2%; permanent crops NEGL%; meadows and pastures 5%; forest and woodland 70%; other 23%

Environment:

violent storms coming down from the Himalayas were the source of the country name which translates as Land of the Thunder Dragon

Note:

landlocked; strategic location between China and India; controls several key Himalayan mountain passes

:Bhutan People

Population: 1,660,167 (July 1992), growth rate 2.3% (1992)
Birth rate: 40 births/1,000 population (1992)
Death rate: 17 deaths/1,000 population (1992)

Net migration rate: 0 migrants/1,000 population (1992)
Infant mortality rate: 126 deaths/1,000 live births (1992)
Life expectancy at birth: 50 years male, 49 years female (1992)
Total fertility rate: 5.5 children born/woman (1992)
Nationality:
  noun - Bhutanese (singular and plural); adjective - Bhutanese
Ethnic divisions:
  Bhote 60%, ethnic Nepalese 25%, indigenous or migrant tribes 15%
Religions:
  Lamaistic Buddhism 75%, Indian- and Nepalese-influenced Hinduism 25%
Languages:
  Bhotes speak various Tibetan dialects - most widely spoken dialect is
  Dzongkha (official); Nepalese speak various Nepalese dialects
Literacy:
  NA% (male NA%, female NA%)
Labor force:
  NA; agriculture 93%, services 5%, industry and commerce 2%; massive lack of
  skilled labor
Organized labor:
  not permitted

:Bhutan Government

Long-form name:
  Kingdom of Bhutan
Type:
  monarchy; special treaty relationship with India
Capital: Thimphu
Administrative divisions:
  18 districts (dzongkhag, singular and plural); Bumthang, Chhukha, Chirang,
  Daga, Geylegphug, Ha, Lhuntshi, Mongar, Paro, Pemagatsel, Punakha, Samchi,
  Samdrup Jongkhar, Shemgang, Tashigang, Thimphu, Tongsa, Wangdi Phodrang
Independence:
  8 August 1949 (from India)
Constitution:
  no written constitution or bill of rights
Legal system:
  based on Indian law and English common law; has not accepted compulsory ICJ
  jurisdiction
National holiday:
  National Day (Ugyen Wangchuck became first hereditary king), 17 December
  (1907)
Executive branch:
  monarch, chairman of the Royal Advisory Council, Royal Advisory Council
  (Lodoi Tsokde), chairman of the Council of Ministers, Council of Ministers
  (Lhengye Shungtsog)
Legislative branch:
  unicameral National Assembly (Tshogdu)
Judicial branch:
  High Court
Leaders:

Chief of State and Head of Government:
  King Jigme Singye WANGCHUCK (since 24 July 1972)
Political parties and leaders:
  no legal parties
Suffrage:
  each family has one vote in village-level elections
Elections:
  no national elections
Communists:
  no overt Communist presence
Other political or pressure groups:
  Buddhist clergy, Indian merchant community; ethnic Nepalese organizations
  leading militant antigovernment campaign
Member of:
  AsDB, CP, ESCAP, FAO, G-77, IBRD, ICAO, IDA, IFAD, IMF, IOC, ITU, NAM,
  SAARC, UN, UNCTAD, UNESCO, UNIDO, UPU, WHO
Diplomatic representation:
  no formal diplomatic relations, although informal contact is maintained
  between the Bhutanese and US Embassies in New Delhi (India); the Bhutanese
  mission to the UN in New York has consular jurisdiction in the US
Flag:
  divided diagonally from the lower hoist side corner; the upper triangle is
  orange and the lower triangle is red; centered along the dividing line is a
  large black and white dragon facing away from the hoist side

:Bhutan Economy

Overview:
  The economy, one of the world's least developed, is based on agriculture and
  forestry, which provide the main livelihood for 90% of the population and
  account for about 50% of GDP. Rugged mountains dominate the terrain and make
  the building of roads and other infrastructure difficult and expensive. The
  economy is closely aligned with that of India through strong trade and
  monetary links. Low wages in industry lead most Bhutanese to stay in
  agriculture. Most development projects, such as road construction, rely on
  Indian migrant labor. Bhutan's hydropower potential and its attraction for
  tourists are its most important natural resources.
GDP:
  exchange rate conversion - $320 million, per capita $200; real growth rate
  3.1% (1991 est.)
Inflation rate (consumer prices):
  12% (FY90)
Unemployment rate: NA
Budget:
  revenues $112 million; expenditures $121 million, including capital
  expenditures of $58 million (FY91 est.)
Exports:
  $74 million (f.o.b., FY91)
 commodities:
  cardamon, gypsum, timber, handicrafts, cement, fruit
 partners:

India 93%

Imports:

$106.4 million (c.i.f., FY91 est.)

commodities:

fuel and lubricants, grain, machinery and parts, vehicles, fabrics

partners:

India 67%

External debt: $80 million (FY91 est.)

Industrial production:

growth rate NA; accounts for 18% of GDP

Electricity:

353,000 kW capacity; 2,000 million kWh produced, 1,280 kWh per capita (1990)

Industries:

cement, wood products, processed fruits, alcoholic beverages, calcium
carbide

Agriculture:

accounts for 50% of GDP; based on subsistence farming and animal husbandry;
self-sufficient in food except for foodgrains; other production - rice,
corn, root crops, citrus fruit, dairy, and eggs

Economic aid:

Western (non-US) countries, ODA and OOF bilateral commitments (1970-89),
$115 million; OPEC bilateral aid (1979-89), $11 million

Currency:

ngultrum (plural - ngultrum); 1 ngultrum (Nu) = 100 chetrum; note - Indian
currency is also legal tender

Exchange rates:

ngultrum (Nu) per US$1 - 25.927 (January 1992), 22.742 (1991), 17.504
(1990), 16.226 (1989), 13.917 (1988), 12.962 (1987); note - the Bhutanese
ngultrum is at par with the Indian rupee

Fiscal year: 1 July - 30 June

:Bhutan Communications

Highways:

1,304 km total; 418 km surfaced, 515 km improved, 371 km unimproved earth

Civil air:

1 jet, 2 prop

Airports:

2 total, 2 usable; 1 with permanent-surface runways; none with runways over
2,439 m; 2 with runways 1,220-2,439 m

Telecommunications:

inadequate; 1,990 telephones (1988); 22,000 radios (1990 est.); 85 TVs
(1985); broadcast stations - 1 AM, 1 FM, no TV (1990)

:Bhutan Defense Forces

Branches:

Royal Bhutan Army, Palace Guard, Militia

Manpower availability:

males 15-49, 406,360; 217,348 fit for military service; 17,316 reach
military age (18) annually

Defense expenditures:

exchange rate conversion - $NA, NA% of GDP

Bolivia Geography

Total area: 1,098,580 km2
Land area: 1,084,390 km2
Comparative area: slightly less than three times the size of Montana
Land boundaries:
   6,743 km; Argentina 832 km, Brazil 3,400 km, Chile 861 km, Paraguay 750 km,
   Peru 900 km
Coastline:
   none - landlocked
Maritime claims:
   none - landlocked
Disputes:
   has wanted a sovereign corridor to the South Pacific Ocean since the Atacama
   area was lost to Chile in 1884; dispute with Chile over Rio Lauca water
   rights
Climate:
   varies with altitude; humid and tropical to cold and semiarid
Terrain:
   rugged Andes Mountains with a highland plateau (Altiplano), hills, lowland
   plains of the Amazon basin
Natural resources:
   tin, natural gas, crude oil, zinc, tungsten, antimony, silver, iron ore,
   lead, gold, timber
Land use:
   arable land 3%; permanent crops NEGL%; meadows and pastures 25%; forest and
   woodland 52%; other 20%; includes irrigated NEGL%
Environment:
   cold, thin air of high plateau is obstacle to efficient fuel combustion;
   overgrazing; soil erosion; desertification
Note:
   landlocked; shares control of Lago Titicaca, world's highest navigable lake,
   with Peru

:Bolivia People

Population: 7,323,048 (July 1992), growth rate 2.3% (1992)
Birth rate: 33 births/1,000 population (1992)
Death rate: 9 deaths/1,000 population (1992)
Net migration rate: —1 migrant/1,000 population (1992)
Infant mortality rate: 82 deaths/1,000 live births (1992)
Life expectancy at birth: 59 years male, 64 years female (1992)
Total fertility rate: 4.5 children born/woman (1992)
Nationality:
   noun - Bolivian(s); adjective - Bolivian
Ethnic divisions:
   Quechua 30%, Aymara 25%, mixed 25-30%, European 5-15%
Religions:
   Roman Catholic 95%; active Protestant minority, especially Evangelical
   Methodist
Languages:
   Spanish, Quechua, and Aymara (all official)

Literacy:
  78% (male 85%, female 71%) age 15 and over can read and write (1990 est.)
Labor force:
  1,700,000; agriculture 50%, services and utilities 26%, manufacturing 10%,
  mining 4%, other 10% (1983)
Organized labor:
  150,000-200,000, concentrated in mining, industry, construction, and
  transportation; mostly organized under Bolivian Workers' Central (COB) labor
  federation

:Bolivia Government

Long-form name:
  Republic of Bolivia
Type:
  republic
Capital: La Paz (seat of government); Sucre (legal capital and seat of judiciary)
Administrative divisions:
  9 departments (departamentos, singular - departamento); Chuquisaca,
  Cochabamba, Beni, La Paz, Oruro, Pando, Potosi, Santa Cruz, Tarija
Independence:
  6 August 1825 (from Spain)
Constitution:
  2 February 1967
Legal system:
  based on Spanish law and Code Napoleon; has not accepted compulsory ICJ
  jurisdiction
National holiday:
  Independence Day, 6 August (1825)
Executive branch:
  president, vice president, Cabinet
Legislative branch:
  bicameral National Congress (Congreso Nacional) consists of an upper chamber
  or Chamber of Senators (Camara de Senadores) and a lower chamber or Chamber
  of Deputies (Camara de Diputados)
Judicial branch:
  Supreme Court (Corte Suprema)
Leaders:
  Chief of State and Head of Government:
  President Jaime PAZ Zamora (since 6 August 1989); Vice President Luis OSSIO
  Sanjines (since 6 August 1989)
Political parties and leaders:
  Movement of the Revolutionary Left (MIR), Jaime PAZ Zamora; Nationalist
  Democratic Action (ADN), Hugo BANZER Suarez; Nationalist Revolutionary
  Movement (MNR), Gonzalo SANCHEZ de Lozada; Civic Solidarity Union (UCS),
Max
  FERNANDEZ Rojas; Conscience of the Fatherland (CONDEPA), Carlos
PALENQUE
  Aviles; Christian Democratic Party (PDC), Jorge AGREDO; Free Bolivia
  Movement (MBL), led by Antonio ARANIBAR; United Left (IU), a coalition of
  leftist parties that includes Patriotic National Convergency Axis (EJE-P)

led by Walter DELGADILLO, and Bolivian Communist Party (PCB) led by Humberto
RAMIREZ; Revolutionary Vanguard - 9th of April (VR-9), Carlos SERRATE Reich

Suffrage:
universal and compulsory at age 18 (married) or 21 (single)

Elections:
 Chamber of Deputies:
 last held 7 May 1989 (next to be held May 1993); results - percent of vote
 by party NA; note - legislative and presidential candidates run on a unified
 slate, so vote percentages are the same as in section on presidential
 election results; seats - (130 total) MNR 40, ADN 35, MIR 33, IU 10, CONDEPA
 9, PDC 3
 Chamber of Senators:
 last held 7 May 1989 (next to be held May 1993); results - percent of vote
 by party NA; note - legislative and presidential candidates run on a unified
 slate, so vote percentages are the same as in section on presidential
 election results; seats - (27 total) MNR 9, ADN 7, MIR 8, CONDEPA 2, PDC 1

:Bolivia Government

 President:
 last held 7 May 1989 (next to be held May 1993); results - Gonzalo SANCHEZ
 de Lozada (MNR) 23%, Hugo BANZER Suarez (ADN) 22%, Jaime PAZ Zamora
(MIR)
 19%; no candidate received a majority of the popular vote; Jaime PAZ Zamora
 (MIR) formed a coalition with Hugo BANZER (ADN); with ADN support PAZ Zamora
 won the congressional runoff election on 4 August and was inaugurated on 6
 August 1989

Member of:
 AG, ECLAC, FAO, G-11, G-77, IADB, IAEA, IBRD, ICO, IDA, IFAD, IFC, ILO,
IMF,
 IMO, INTELSAT, INTERPOL, IOC, IOM, ITU, LAES, LAIA, LORCS, NAM,
OAS, OPANAL,
 PCA, RG, UN, UNCTAD, UNESCO, UNIDO, UPU, WCL, WFTU, WHO, WMO,
WTO

Diplomatic representation:
 Ambassador Jorge CRESPO; Chancery at 3014 Massachusetts Avenue NW,
 Washington, DC 20008; telephone (202) 483-4410 through 4412; there are
 Bolivian Consulates General in Los Angeles, Miami, New York, and San
 Francisco

 US:
 Ambassador Charles R. BOWERS; Embassy at Banco Popular del Peru Building,
 corner of Calles Mercado y Colon, La Paz (mailing address is P. O. Box 425,
 La Paz, or APO AA 34032); telephone [591] (2) 350251 or 350120; FAX [591]
 (2) 359075

Flag:
 three equal horizontal bands of red (top), yellow, and green with the coat
 of arms centered on the yellow band; similar to the flag of Ghana, which has
 a large black five-pointed star centered in the yellow band

:Bolivia Economy

Overview:

The Bolivian economy steadily deteriorated between 1980 and 1985 as La Paz financed growing budget deficits by expanding the money supply, and inflation spiraled - peaking at 11,700%. An austere orthodox economic program adopted by then President Paz Estenssoro in 1985, however, succeeded in reducing inflation to between 10% and 20% annually since 1987, eventually restarting economic growth. Since August 1989, President Paz Zamora has retained the economic policies of the previous government, keeping inflation down and continuing moderate growth. Nevertheless, Bolivia continues to be one of the poorest countries in Latin America, with widespread poverty and unemployment, and it remains vulnerable to price fluctuations for its limited exports - agricultural products, minerals, and natural gas. Moreover, for many farmers, who constitute half of the country's work force, the main cash crop is coca, which is sold for cocaine processing.

GDP:

exchange rate conversion - $4.6 billion, per capita $630; real growth rate 4% (1991)

Inflation rate (consumer prices):

15% (1991)

Unemployment rate: 7% (1991 est.)

Budget:

revenues $900 million; expenditures $825 million, including capital expenditures of $300 million (1991 est.)

Exports:

$970 million (f.o.b., 1991)

 commodities:

metals 45%, natural gas 25%, other 30% (coffee, soybeans, sugar, cotton, timber)

 partners:

US 15%, Argentina

Imports:

$760 million (c.i.f., 1991)

 commodities:

food, petroleum, consumer goods, capital goods

 partners:

US 22%

External debt: $3.3 billion (December 1991)

Industrial production:

growth rate 6% (1991); accounts for almost 30% of GDP

Electricity:

849,000 kW capacity; 1,798 million kWh produced, 251 kWh per capita (1991)

Industries:

mining, smelting, petroleum, food and beverage, tobacco, handicrafts, clothing; illicit drug industry reportedly produces significant revenues

Agriculture:

accounts for about 20% of GDP (including forestry and fisheries); principal commodities - coffee, coca, cotton, corn, sugarcane, rice, potatoes, timber; self-sufficient in food

Illicit drugs:

world's second-largest producer of coca (after Peru) with an estimated

47,900 hectares under cultivation; voluntary and forced eradication program unable to prevent production from rising to 78,400 metric tons in 1991 from 74,700 tons in 1989; government considers all but 12,000 hectares illicit; intermediate coca products and cocaine exported to or through Colombia and Brazil to the US and other international drug markets

:Bolivia Economy

Economic aid:
US commitments, including Ex-Im (FY70-89), $990 million; Western (non-US) countries, ODA and OOF bilateral commitments (1970-89), $2,025 million; Communist countries (1970-89), $340 million

Currency:
boliviano (plural - bolivianos); 1 boliviano ($B) = 100 centavos

Exchange rates:
bolivianos ($B) per US$1 - 3.7534 (January 1992), 3.5806 (1991), 3.1727 (1990), 2.6917 (1989), 2.3502 (1988), 2.0549 (1987)

Fiscal year: calendar year

:Bolivia Communications

Railroads:
3,684 km total, all narrow gauge; 3,652 km 1.000-meter gauge and 32 km 0.760-meter gauge, all government owned, single track

Highways:
38,836 km total; 1,300 km paved, 6,700 km gravel, 30,836 km improved and unimproved earth

Inland waterways:
10,000 km of commercially navigable waterways

Pipelines:
crude oil 1,800 km; petroleum products 580 km; natural gas 1,495 km

Ports:
none; maritime outlets are Arica and Antofagasta in Chile, Matarani and Ilo in Peru

Merchant marine:
2 cargo and 1 container ships (1,000 GRT or over) totaling 16,951 GRT/26,320 DWT

Civil air:
56 major transport aircraft

Airports:
1,105 total, 943 usable; 9 with permanent-surface runways; 2 with runways over 3,659 m; 7 with runways 2,440-3,659 m; 146 with runways 1,220-2,439 m

Telecommunications:
radio relay system being expanded; improved international services; 144,300 telephones; broadcast stations - 129 AM, no FM, 43 TV, 68 shortwave; 1 Atlantic Ocean INTELSAT earth station

:Bolivia Defense Forces

Branches:
Army, Navy (including Marines), Air Force, National Police Force

Manpower availability:
males 15-49, 1,727,101; 1,122,224 fit for military service; 72,977 reach military age (18) annually

Defense expenditures:
  exchange rate conversion - $80 million, 1.6% of GDP (1990 est).

Bosnia and Herzegovina Geography

Total area: 51,233 km2
Land area: 51,233 km2
Comparative area: slightly larger than Tennessee
Land boundaries:
  1,369 km; Croatia (northwest) 751 km, Croatia (south) 91 km, Serbia and
  Montenegro 527 km
Coastline:
  20 km
Maritime claims:
 Contiguous zone:
  NA nm
 Continental shelf:
  20-meter depth
 Exclusive economic zone:
  12 nm
 Exclusive fishing zone:
  12 nm
 Territorial sea:
  12 nm
Disputes:
  Serbia and Croatia seek to cantonize Bosnia and Herzegovina; Muslim majority
  being forced from many areas
Climate:
  hot summers and cold winters; areas of high elevation have short, cool
  summers and long, severe winters; mild, rainy winters along coast
Terrain:
  mountains and valleys
Natural resources:
  coal, iron, bauxite, manganese, timber, wood products, copper, chromium,
  lead, zinc
Land use:
  20% arable land; 2% permanent crops; 25% meadows and pastures; 36% forest
  and woodland; 16% other; includes 1% irrigated
Environment:
  air pollution from metallurgical plants; water scarce; sites for disposing
  of urban waste are limited; subject to frequent and destructive earthquakes
Note:
  Controls large percentage of important land routes from Western Europe to
  Aegean Sea and Turkish Straits

:Bosnia and Herzegovina People

Population: 4,364,000 (July 1991), growth rate 0.5% (1991)
Birth rate: 14.5 births/1,000 population (1991)
Death rate: 6.5 deaths/1,000 population (1991)
Net migration rate: NA migrants/1,000 population (1991)
Infant mortality rate: 15.2 deaths/1,000 live births (1991)
Life expectancy at birth: 68 years male, 73 years female (1980-82)

Total fertility rate: NA children born/woman (1991)
Nationality:
  noun - Muslim, Serb, Croat (s); adjective - Muslim, Serbian, Croatian
Ethnic divisions:
  Muslim 44%, Serb 33%, Croat 17%
Religions:
  Slavic Muslim 40%, Orthodox 31%, Catholic 15%, Protestant 4%
Languages:
  Serbo-Croatian 99%
Literacy:
  85.5% (male 94.5%, female 76.7%) age 10 and over can read and write (1981
  est.)
Labor force:
  1,026,254; 2% agriculture, industry, mining 45% (1991 est.)
Organized labor:
  NA

:Bosnia and Herzegovina Government

Long-form name:
  none
Type:
  emerging democracy
Capital: Sarajevo
Administrative divisions:
  NA
Independence:
  December 1918; April 1992 from Yugoslavia
Constitution:
  NA
Legal system:
  based on civil law system
National holiday:
  NA
Executive branch:
  president, prime minister, deputy prime minister
Legislative branch:
  NA
Judicial branch:
  NA
Leaders:
 Chief of State:
  President Alija IZETBEGOVIC (since December 1990), Vice President NA
 Head of Government:
  Prime Minister Jore PELIVAN (since January 1991), Deputy Prime Minister
  Muhamed CENGIC and Rusmir MAIIMUTCEHAJIC (since January 1991)
Political parties and leaders:
  Party of Democratic Action, Alija IZETBEGOVIC; Croatian Democratic Union,
  Mate BOBAN; Serbian Democratic Party, Radovah KARADZIC; Muslim Bosnian
  Organization, Muhamed Zulfikar PASIC; Socialist Democratic Party, Nijaz
  DURAKOVIC

Suffrage:
  at age 16 if employed; universal at age 18
Elections:
  NA
Other political or pressure groups:
  NA
Member of:
  CSCE
Diplomatic representation:
  NA
Flag:
  NA

:Bosnia and Herzegovina Economy

Overview:
  Bosnia and Herzegovina ranked next to Macedonia as the poorest component in
  the old Yugoslav federation. Although agriculture has been almost all in
  private hands, farms have been small and inefficient, and the republic
  traditionally has been a net importer of food. Industry has been greatly
  overstaffed, one reflection of the rigidities of Communist central planning
  and management. Tito had pushed the development of military industries in
  the republic with the result that Bosnia hosted a large share of
  Yugoslavia's defense plants. As of April 1992, the newly independent
  republic was being torn apart by bitter interethnic warfare that has caused
  production to plummet, unemployment and inflation to soar, and human misery
  to multiply. The survival of the republic as a political and economic unit
  is in doubt. Both Serbia and Croatia have imposed various economic blockades
  and may permanently take over large areas populated by fellow ethnic groups.
  These areas contain most of the industry. If a much smaller core Muslim
  state survives, it will share many Third World problems of poverty,
  technological backwardness, and dependence on historically soft foreign
  markets for its primary products. In these circumstances, other Muslim
  countries might offer assistance.
GDP:
  $14 billion; real growth rate —37% (1991)
Inflation rate (consumer prices):
  80% per month (1991)
Unemployment rate: 28% (February 1992 est.)
Budget:
  revenues $NA million; expenditures $NA million, including capital
  expenditures of $NA million (19__)
Exports:
  $2,054 million (1990)
 commodities:
  manufactured goods (31%), machinery and transport equipment (20.8%), raw
  materials (18%), miscellaneous manufactured articles (17.3%), chemicals
  (9.4%), fuel and lubricants (1.4%), food and live animals (1.2%)
 partners:
  principally the other former Yugoslav republics
Imports:

$1,891 million (1990)
commodities:
  fuels and lubricants (32%), machinery and transport equipment (23.3%), other
  manufactures (21.3%), chemicals (10%), raw materials (6.7%), food and live
  animals (5.5%), beverages and tobacco (1.9%)
partners:
  principally the other former Yugoslav republics
External debt: NA
Industrial production:
  sharply down because of interethnic and interrepublic warfare (1991-92)
Electricity:
  14,400 million kW capacity; NA million kWh produced, 3,303 kWh per capita
  (1991)
Industries:
  steel production, mining (coal, iron ore, lead, zinc, manganese, and
  bauxite), manufacturing (vehicle assembly, textiles, tobacco products,
  wooden furniture, 40% of former Yugoslavia's armaments including tank and
  aircraft assembly, domestic appliances), oil refining

:Bosnia and Herzegovina Economy

Agriculture:
  accounted for 8.6% of national income in 1989; regularly produces less than
  50% of food needs; the foothills of northern Bosnia support orchards,
  vineyards, livestock, and some wheat and corn; long winters and heavy
  precipitation leach soil fertility reducing agricultural output in the
  mountains; farms are mostly privately held, small, and not very productive
Illicit drugs:
  NA
Economic aid:
  US commitments, including Ex-Im (FY70-87), $NA billion; Western (non-US)
  countries, ODA and OOF bilateral commitments (1970-86), $NA million;
  Communist countries (1971-86), $NA million
Currency:
  none; note - Croatian dinar used in ethnic Croat areas, Yugoslav dinar used
  in all other areas
Exchange rates:
  NA
Fiscal year: calendar year

:Bosnia and Herzegovina Communications

Railroads:
  NA km all 1.000-meter gauge (includes NA km electrified)
Highways:
  21,168 km total (1991); 11,436 km paved, 8,146 km gravel, 1,586 km earth
Inland waterways:
  NA km perennially navigable
Pipelines:
  crude oil 174 km, petroleum products NA km, natural gas NA km
Ports:
  maritime - none; inland - Bosanski Brod
Merchant marine:

NA ships (1,000 GRT or over) totaling NA GRT/NA DWT; includes NA cargo, NA container, NA liquefied gas, NA petroleum tanker

Civil air:

NA major transport aircraft

Airports:

2 main, NA usable; NA with permanent-surface runways; NA with runways over 3,659 m; NA with runways 2,440-3,659 m; NA with runways 1,220-2,439 m

Telecommunications:

Bosnia's telephone and telegraph network is in need of modernization and expansion, many urban areas being below average compared with services in other former Yugoslav republics; 727,000 telephones; broadcast stations - 9 AM, 2 FM, 6 (0 repeaters) TV; 840,000 radios; 1,012,094 TVs; NA submarine coaxial cables; satellite ground stations - none

:Bosnia and Herzegovina Defense Forces

Branches:

Territorial Defense Force

Manpower availability:

males 15-49, NA; NA fit for military service; 39,000 reach military age (18) annually

Defense expenditures:

$NA, NA% of GDP

Botswana Geography

Total area: 600,370 km2
Land area: 585, 370 km2
Comparative area: slightly smaller than Texas
Land boundaries:

4,013 km; Namibia 1,360 km, South Africa 1,840 km, Zimbabwe 813 km

Coastline:

none - landlocked

Maritime claims:

none - landlocked

Disputes:

Climate:

semiarid; warm winters and hot summers

Terrain:

predominately flat to gently rolling tableland; Kalahari Desert in southwest

Natural resources:

diamonds, copper, nickel, salt, soda, ash, potash, coal, iron ore, silver, natural gas

Land use:

urable land 2%; permanent crops 0%; meadows and pastures 75%; forest and woodland 2%; other 21%; includes irrigated NEGL%

Environment:

rains in early 1988 broke six years of drought that had severely affected the important cattle industry; overgazing; desertification

Note:

landlocked

:Botswana People

Population: 1,292,210 (July 1992), growth rate 2.6% (1992)
Birth rate: 35 births/1,000 population (1992)
Death rate: 8 deaths/1,000 population (1992)
Net migration rate: 0 migrants/1,000 population (1992)
Infant mortality rate: 42 deaths/1,000 live births (1992)
Life expectancy at birth: 59 years male, 65 years female (1992)
Total fertility rate: 4.4 children born/woman (1992)
Nationality:
    noun and ajective - Motswana (singular), Batswana (plural)
Ethnic divisions:
    Batswana 95%; Kalanga, Basarwa, and Kgalagadi about 4%; white about 1%
Religions:
    indigenous beliefs 50%, Christian 50%
Languages:
    English (official), Setswana
Literacy:
    23% (male 32%, female 16%) age 15 and over can read and write (1990 est.)
Labor force:
    400,000; 198,500 formal sector employees, most others are engaged in cattle
    raising and subsistence agriculture (1990 est.); 14,600 are employed in
    various mines in South Africa (1990)
Organized labor:
    19 trade unions

:Botswana Government

Long-form name:
    Republic of Botswana
Type:
    parliamentary republic
Capital: Gaborone
Administrative divisions:
    10 districts: Central, Chobe, Ghanzi, Kgalagadi, Kgatleng, Kweneng,
    Ngamiland, North-East, South-East, Southern; note - in addition, there may
    now be 4 town councils named Francistown, Gaborone, Lobaste Selebi-Pikwe
Independence:
    30 September 1966 (from UK; formerly Bechuanaland)
Constitution:
    March 1965, effective 30 September 1966
Legal system:
    based on Roman-Dutch law and local customary law; judicial review limited to
    matters of interpretation; has not accepted compulsory ICJ jurisdiction
National holiday:
    Independence Day, 30 September (1966)
Executive branch:
    president, vice president, Cabinet
Legislative branch:
    bicameral National Assembly consists of an upper house or House of Chiefs
    and a lower house or National Assembly
Judicial branch:

High Court, Court of Appeal

Leaders:

Chief of State and Head of Government:

President Quett K. J. MASIRE (since 13 July 1980); Vice President Peter S. MMUSI (since 3 January 1983)

Political parties and leaders:

Botswana Democratic Party (BDP), Quett MASIRE; Botswana National Front (BNF), Kenneth KOMA; Boswana People's Party (BPP), Knight MARIPE; Botswana Independence Party (BIP), Motsamai MPHO

Suffrage:

universal at age 21

Elections:

National Assembly:

last held 7 October 1989 (next to be held October 1994); results - percent of vote by party NA; seats - (38 total, 34 elected) BDP 35, BNF 3

President:

last held 7 October 1989 (next to be held October 1994); results - President Quett K. J. MASIRE was reelected by the National Assembly

Communists:

no known Communist organization; Kenneth KOMA of BNF has long history of Communist contacts

Member of:

ACP, AfDB, C, CCC, ECA, FAO, FLS, G-77, GATT, IBRD, ICAO, ICFTU, IDA, IFAD, IFC, ILO, IMF, INTERPOL, IOC, ITU, LORCS, NAM, OAU, SACU, SADCC, UN, UNCTAD, UNESCO, UNIDO, UPU, WCL, WHO, WMO

Diplomatic representation:

Ambassador Botsweletse Kingsley SEBELE; Chancery at Suite 7M, 3400 International Drive NW, Washington, DC 20008; telephone (202) 244-4990 or 4991

US:

Ambassador Davie PASSAGE; Embassy at Gaborone (mailing address is P. O. Box 90, Gaborone); telephone [267] 353-982; FAX [267] 356-947

Flag:

light blue with a horizontal white-edged black stripe in the center

:Botswana Economy

Overview:

The economy has historically been based on cattle raising and crops. Agriculture today provides a livelihood for more than 80% of the population, but produces only about 50% of food needs. The driving force behind the rapid economic growth of the 1970s and 1980s has been the mining industry. This sector, mostly on the strength of diamonds, has gone from generating 25% of GDP in 1980 to over 50% in 1989. No other sector has experienced such growth, especially not agriculture, which is plagued by erratic rainfall and poor soils. The unemployment rate remains a problem at 25%. Although diamond production remained level in FY91, substantial gains in coal output and manufacturing helped boost the economy

GDP:
    purchasing power equivalent - $3.6 billion, per capita $2,800; real growth
    rate 6.3% (1991 est.)
Inflation rate (consumer prices):
    12.6% (1991)
Unemployment rate: 25% (1989)
Budget:
    revenues $1,935 million; expenditures $1,885 million, including capital
    expenditures of $658 million (FY93)
Exports:
    $1.8 billion (f.o.b. 1990)
  commodities:
    diamonds 80%, copper and nickel 9%, meat 4%, cattle, animal products
partners:
    Switzerland, UK, SACU (Southern African Customs Union)
Imports:
    $1.6 billion (c.i.f., 1990 est.)
  commodities:
    foodstuffs, vehicles and transport equipment, textiles, petroleum products
partners:
    Switzerland, SACU (Southern African Customs Union), UK, US
External debt: $780 million (December 1990 est.)
Industrial production:
    growth rate 16.8% (FY86); accounts for about 57% of GDP, including mining
Electricity:
    220,000 kW capacity; 630 million kWh produced 858 kWh per capita (1991)
Industries:
    mining of diamonds, copper, nickel, coal, salt, soda ash, potash; livestock
    processing
Agriculture:
    accounts for only 3% of DGP; subsistence farming predominates; cattle
    raising supports 50% of the population; must import large share of food
    needs
Economic aid:
    US commitments, including Ex-Im (FY70-89), $257 million; Western (non-US)
    countries, ODA and OOF bilateral commitments (1970-89), $1,875 million; OPEC
    bilateral aid (1979-89), $43 million; Communist countries (1970-89), $29
    million
Currency:
    pula (plural - pula); 1 pula (P) = 100 thebe
Exchange rates:
    pula (P) per US$1 - 2.1683 (March 1992), 2.0173 (1991), 1.8601 (1990),
    2.0125 (1989), 1.8159 (1988), 1.6779 (1987)
Fiscal year: 1 April - 31 March

:Botswana Communications

Railroads:
    712 km 1.067-meter gauge
Highways:
    11,514 km total; 1,600 km paved; 1,700 km crushed stone or gravel, 5,177 km

improved earth, 3,037 km unimproved earth
Civil air:
  5 major transport aircraft
Airports:
  100 total, 87 unable; 8 with permanent-surface runways; none with runways
  over 3,659 m; 1 with runways 2,440-3,659 m; 27 with runways 1,220-2,439 m
Telecommunications:
  the small system is a combination of open-wire lines, radio relay links, and
  a few radio-communications stations; 26,000 telephones; broadcast stations -
  7 AM, 13 FM, no TV; 1 Indian Ocean INTELSAT earth station

:Botswana Defense Forces

Branches:
  Botswana Defense Force (including Army and Air Wing); Botswana National
  Police
Manpower availability:
  males 15-49, 271,511; 142,947 fit for military service; 14,473 reach
  military age (18) annually
Defense expenditures:
  exchange rate conversion - $136.4 million, 4.4% of GDP (FY92)

Bouvet Island Geography

Total area: 58 km2
Land area: 58 km2
Comparative area: about 0.3 times the size of Washington, DC
Land boundaries:
  none
Coastline:
  29.6 km
Maritime claims:
 Territorial sea:
  4 nm
Disputes:
  none
Climate:
  antarctic
Terrain:
  volcanic; maximum elevation about 800 meters; coast is mostly inacessible
Natural resources:
  none
Land use:
  arable land 0%; permanent crops 0%; meadows and pastures 0%; forest and
  woodland 0%; other 100% (ice)
Environment:
  covered by glacial ice
Note:
  located in the South Atlantic Ocean 2,575 km south-southwest of the Cape of
  Good Hope, South Africa

:Bouvet Island People

Population: uninhabited

:Bouvet Island Government

Long-form name:
　none
Type:
　territory of Norway
Capital:　　none; administered from Oslo, Norway

:Bouvet Island Economy

Overview: no economic activity

:Bouvet Island Communications

Ports:
　none; offshore anchorage only
Telecommunications:
　automatic meteorological station

:Bouvet Island Defense Forces

Note: defense is the responsibility of Norway

Brazil Geography

Total area:　8,511,965 km2
Land area:　8,456,510 km2; includes Arquipelago de Fernando de Noronha, Atol das Rocas,
　Ilha da Trindade, Ilhas Martin Vaz, and Penedos de Sao Pedro e Sao Paulo
Comparative area:　slightly smaller than the US
Land boundaries:
　14,691 km; Argentina 1,224 km, Bolivia 3,400 km, Colombia 1,643 km, French
　Guiana 673 km, Guyana 1,119 km, Paraguay 1,290 km, Peru 1,560 km, Suriname
　597 km, Uruguay 985 km, Venezuela 2,200 km
Coastline:
　7,491 km
Maritime claims:
　Continental shelf:
　200 m (depth) or to depth of exploitation
　Exclusive fishing zone:
　200 nm
　Territorial sea:
　200 nm
Disputes:
　short section of the boundary with Paraguay (just west of Guaira Falls on
　the Rio Parana) is in dispute; two short sections of boundary with Uruguay
　are in dispute (Arroyo de la Invernada area of the Rio Quarai and the
　islands at the confluence of the Rio Quarai and the Uruguay)
Climate:
　mostly tropical, but temperate in south
Terrain:
　mostly flat to rolling lowlands in north; some plains, hills, mountains, and
　narrow coastal belt
Natural resources:
　iron ore, manganese, bauxite, nickel, uranium, phosphates, tin, hydropower,
　gold, platinum, crude oil, timber

Land use:

arable land 7%; permanent crops 1%; meadows and pastures 19%; forest and woodland 67%; other 6%; includes irrigated NEGL%

Environment:

recurrent droughts in northeast; floods and frost in south; deforestation in Amazon basin; air and water pollution in Rio de Janeiro and Sao Paulo

Note:

largest country in South America; shares common boundaries with every South American country except Chile and Ecuador

:Brazil People

Population: 158,202,019 (July 1992), growth rate 1.8% (1992)
Birth rate: 25 births/1,000 population (1992)
Death rate: 7 deaths/1,000 population (1992)
Net migration rate: 0 migrants/1,000 population (1992)
Infant mortality rate: 67 deaths/1,000 live births (1992)
Life expectancy at birth: 62 years male, 69 years female (1992)
Total fertility rate: 3.0 children born/woman (1992)
Nationality:

noun - Brazilian(s); adjective - Brazilian

Ethnic divisions:

Portuguese, Italian, German, Japanese, black, Amerindian; white 55%, mixed 38%, black 6%, other 1%

Religions:

Roman Catholic (nominal) 90%

Languages:

Portuguese (official), Spanish, English, French

Literacy:

81% (male 82%, female 80%) age 15 and over can read and write (1990 est.)

Labor force:

57,000,000 (1989 est.); services 42%, agriculture 31%, industry 27%

Organized labor:

13,000,000 dues paying members (1989 est.)

:Brazil Government

Long-form name:

Federative Republic of Brazil

Type:

federal republic

Capital: Brasilia

Administrative divisions:

26 states (estados, singular - estado) and 1 federal district* (distrito federal); Acre, Alagoas, Amapa, Amazonas, Bahia, Ceara, Distrito Federal*, Espirito Santo, Goias, Maranhao, Mato Grosso, Mato Grosso do Sul, Minas Gerais, Para, Paraiba, Parana, Pernambuco, Piaui, Rio de Janeiro, Rio Grande do Norte, Rio Grande do Sul, Rondonia, Roraima, Santa Catarina, Sao Paulo, Sergipe, Tocantins; note - the former territories of Amapa and Roraima became states in January 1991

Independence:

7 September 1822 (from Portugal)

Constitution:

5 October 1988

Legal system:

based on Latin codes; has not accepted compulsory ICJ jurisdiction

National holiday:

Independence Day, 7 September (1822)

Executive branch:

president, vice president, Cabinet

Legislative branch:

bicameral National Congress (Congresso Nacional) consists of an upper chamber or Federal Senate (Senado Federal) and a lower chamber or Chamber of Deputies (Camara dos Deputados)

Judicial branch:

Supreme Federal Tribunal

Leaders:

Chief of State and Head of Government:

President Fernando Affonso COLLOR de Mello (since 15 March 1990); Vice President Itamar FRANCO (since 15 March 1990)

Political parties and leaders:

National Reconstruction Party (PRN), Daniel TOURINHO, president; Brazilian Democratic Movement Party (PMDB), Orestes QUERCIA, president; Liberal Front Party (PFL), Hugo NAPOLEAO, president; Workers' Party (PT), Luis Ignacio (Lula) da SILVA, president; Brazilian Labor Party (PTB), Luiz GONZAGA de Paiva Muniz, president; Democratic Labor Party (PDT), Leonel BRIZOLA, president; Democratic Social Party (PPS), Paulo MALUF, president; Brazilian Social Democracy Party (PSDB), Tasso JEREISSATI, president; Popular Socialist Party (PPS), Roberto FREIRE, president; Communist Party of Brazil (PCdoB), Joao AMAZONAS, secretary general; Christian Democratic Party (PDC), Siqueira CAMPOS, president

Suffrage:

voluntary at age 16; compulsory between ages 18 and 70; voluntary at age 70

Elections:

Chamber of Deputies:

last held 3 October 1990 (next to be held November 1994); results - PMDB 21%, PFL 17%, PDT 9%, PDS 8%, PRN 7.9%, PTB 7%, PT 7%, other 23.1%; seats

-

(503 total as of 3 February 1991) PMDB 108, PFL 87, PDT 46, PDS 43, PRN 40, PTB 35, PT 35, other 109

Federal Senate:

last held 3 October 1990 (next to be held November 1994); results - percent of vote by party NA; seats - (81 total as of 3 February 1991) PMDB 27, PFL 15, PSDB 10, PTB 8, PDT 5, other 16

:Brazil Government

President:

last held 15 November 1989, with runoff on 17 December 1989 (next to be held November 1994); results - Fernando COLLOR de Mello 53%, Luis Inacio da SILVA 47%; note - first free, direct presidential election since 1960

Communists:

less than 30,000

Other political or pressure groups:

left wing of the Catholic Church and labor unions allied to leftist Worker's
Party are critical of government's social and economic policies
Member of:

AfDB, AG (observer), CCC, ECLAC, FAO, G-11, G-15, G-19, G-24, G-77, GATT,
IADB, IAEA, IBRD, ICAO, ICC, ICFTU, IDA, IFAD, IFC, ILO, IMF, IMO, INMARSAT,
INTELSAT, INTERPOL, IOC, IOM (observer), ISO, ITU, LAES, LAIA, LORCS,
MERCOSUR, NAM (observer), OAS, OPANAL, PCA, RG, UN, UNAVEM, UNCTAD, UNESCO,
UNHCR, UNIDO, UPU, WCL, WHO, WFTU, WIPO, WMO, WTO

Diplomatic representation:

Ambassador Rubens RICUPERO; Chancery at 3006 Massachusetts Avenue NW,
Washington, DC 20008; telephone (202) 745-2700; there are Brazilian
Consulates General in Chicago, Los Angeles, Miami, New Orleans, and New
York, and Consulates in Dallas, Houston, and San Francisco

US:

Ambassador Richard MELTON; Embassy at Avenida das Nacoes, Lote 3, Brasilia,
Distrito Federal (mailing address is APO AA 34030); telephone [55] (61)
321-7272; FAX [55] (61) 225-9136; there are US Consulates General in Rio de
Janeiro and Sao Paulo, and Consulates in PortoAlegre and Recife

Flag:

green with a large yellow diamond in the center bearing a blue celestial
globe with 23 white five-pointed stars (one for each state) arranged in the
same pattern as the night sky over Brazil; the globe has a white equatorial
band with the motto ORDEM E PROGRESSO (Order and Progress)

:Brazil Economy

Overview:

The economy, with large agrarian, mining, and manufacturing sectors, entered
the 1990s with declining real growth, runaway inflation, an unserviceable
foreign debt of $122 billion, and a lack of policy direction. In addition,
the economy remained highly regulated, inward-looking, and protected by
substantial trade and investment barriers. Ownership of major industrial and
mining facilities is divided among private interests - including several
multinationals - and the government. Most large agricultural holdings are
private, with the government channeling financing to this sector. Conflicts
between large landholders and landless peasants have produced intermittent
violence. The Collor government, which assumed office in March 1990, is
embarked on an ambitious reform program that seeks to modernize and
reinvigorate the economy by stabilizing prices, deregulating the economy,
and opening it to increased foreign competition. The government in December
1991 signed a letter of intent with the IMF for a 20-month standby loan.
Having reached an agreement on the repayment of interest arrears accumulated
during 1989 and 1990, Brazilian officials and commercial bankers are engaged
in talks on the reduction of medium- and long-term debt and debt service
payments and on the elimination of remaining interest arrears. A major
long-run strength is Brazil's vast natural resources.

GDP:

exchange rate conversion - $358 billion, per capita $2,300; real growth rate
1.2% (1991)

Inflation rate (consumer prices):
   478.5% (December 1991, annual rate)
Unemployment rate: 4.3% (1991)
Budget:
   revenues $164.3 billion; expenditures $170.6 billion, including capital
   expenditures of $32.9 billion (1990)
Exports:
   $31.6 billion (1991)
 commodities:
   iron ore, soybean bran, orange juice, footwear, coffee
 partners:
   EC 31%, US 24%, Latin America 11%, Japan 8% (1990)
Imports:
   $21.0 billion (1991)
 commodities:
   crude oil, capital goods, chemical products, foodstuffs, coal
 partners:
   Middle East and Africa 22%, US 21%, EC 21%, Latin America 18%, Japan 6%
   (1990)
External debt: $118 billion (December 1991)
Industrial production:
   growth rate—0.5% (1991); accounts for 39% of GDP
Electricity:
   58,500,000 kW capacity; 229,824 million kWh produced, 1,479 kWh per capita
   (1991)
Industries:
   textiles and other consumer goods, shoes, chemicals, cement, lumber, iron
   ore, steel, motor vehicles and auto parts, metalworking, capital goods, tin
Agriculture:
   world's largest producer and exporter of coffee and orange juice concentrate
   and second- largest exporter of soybeans; other products - rice, corn,
   sugarcane, cocoa, beef; self-sufficient in food, except for wheat

:Brazil Economy

Illicit drugs:
   illicit producer of cannabis and coca, mostly for domestic consumption;
   government has a modest eradication program to control cannabis and coca
   cultivation; important transshipment country for Bolivian and Colombian
   cocaine headed for the US and Europe
Economic aid:
   US commitments, including Ex-Im (FY70-89), $2.5 billion; Western (non-US)
   countries, ODA and OOF bilateral commitments (1970-89), $10.2 million; OPEC
   bilateral aid (1979-89), $284 million; former Communist countries (1970-89),
   $1.3 billion
Currency:
   cruzeiro (plural - cruzeiros); 1 cruzeiro (Cr$) = 100 centavos
Exchange rates:
   cruzeiros (Cr$) per US$1 - 1,197.38 (January 1992), 406.61 (1991), 68.300
   (1990), 2.834 (1989), 0.26238 (1988), 0.03923 (1987)
Fiscal year: calendar year

:Brazil Communications

Railroads:
> 28,828 km total; 24,864 km 1.000-meter gauge, 3,877 km 1.600-meter gauge, 74 km mixed 1.600-1.000-meter gauge, 13 km 0.760-meter gauge; 2,360 km electrified

Highways:
> 1,448,000 km total; 48,000 km paved, 1,400,000 km gravel or earth

Inland waterways:
> 50,000 km navigable

Pipelines:
> crude oil 2,000 km; petroleum products 3,804 km; natural gas 1,095 km

Ports:
> Belem, Fortaleza, Ilheus, Manaus, Paranagua, Porto Alegre, Recife, Rio de Janeiro, Rio Grande, Salvador, Santos

Merchant marine:
> 245 ships (1,000 GRT or over) totaling 5,693,500 GRT/9,623,918 DWT; includes 3 passenger-cargo, 49 cargo, 1 refrigerated cargo, 13 container, 9 roll-on/roll-off, 57 petroleum tanker, 15 chemical tanker, 11 liquefied gas, 14 combination ore/oil, 71 bulk, 2 combination bulk; in addition, 2 naval tankers and 4 military transport are sometimes used commercially

Civil air:
> 198 major transport aircraft

Airports:
> 3,563 total, 2,911 usable; 420 with permanent-surface runways; 2 with runways over 3,659 m; 22 with runways 2,240-3,659 m; 550 with runways 1,220-2,439 m

Telecommunications:
> good system; extensive radio relay facilities; 9.86 million telephones; broadcast stations - 1,223 AM, no FM, 112 TV, 151 shortwave; 3 coaxial submarine cables, 3 Atlantic Ocean INTELSAT earth stations and 64 domestic satellite earth stations

:Brazil Defense Forces

Branches:
> Brazilian Army, Navy of Brazil (including Marines), Brazilian Air Force, Military Police (paramilitary)

Manpower availability:
> males 15-49, 41,515,103; 27,987,257 fit for military service; 1,644,571 reach military age (18) annually

Defense expenditures:
> exchange rate conversion - $1.1 billion, 0.3% of GDP (1990)

British Indian Ocean Territory Geography

Total area: 60 km2
Land area: 60 km2; includes the island of Diego Garcia
Comparative area: about 0.3 times the size of Washington, DC
Land boundaries:
> none

Coastline:
> 698 km

Maritime claims:

 Territorial sea:

  UK announced establishment of 200-nm fishery zone in August 1991

Disputes:

  the entire Chagos Archipelago is claimed by Mauritius

Climate:

  tropical marine; hot, humid, moderated by trade winds

Terrain:

  flat and low (up to 4 meters in elevation)

Natural resources:

  coconuts, fish

Land use:

  arable land 0%; permanent crops 0%; meadows and pastures 0%; forest and
  woodland 0%; other 100%

Environment:

  archipelago of 2,300 islands

Note:

  Diego Garcia, largest and southernmost island, occupies strategic location
  in central Indian Ocean; island is site of joint US-UK military facility

:British Indian Ocean Territory People

Population: no permanent civilian population; formerly about 3,000 islanders

Ethnic divisions:

  civilian inhabitants, known as the Ilois, evacuated to Mauritius before
  construction of UK and US defense facilities

:British Indian Ocean Territory Government

Long-form name:

  British Indian Ocean Territory (no short-form name); abbreviated BIOT

Type:

  dependent territory of the UK

Capital: none

Leaders:

 Chief of State:

  Queen ELIZABETH II (since 6 February 1952)

 Head of Government:

  Commissioner Mr. T. G. HARRIS; Administrator Mr. R. G. WELLS (since NA
  1991); note - both reside in the UK

Diplomatic representation:

  none (dependent territory of UK)

Flag:

  white with the flag of the UK in the upper hoist-side quadrant and six blue
  wavy horizontal stripes bearing a palm tree and yellow crown centered on the
  outer half of the flag

:British Indian Ocean Territory Economy

Overview:

  All economic activity is concentrated on the largest island of Diego Garcia,
  where joint UK-US defense facilities are located. Construction projects and
  various services needed to support the military installations are done by
  military and contract employees from the UK and the US. There are no

135

industrial or agricultural activities on the islands.

Electricity:
   provided by the US military

:British Indian Ocean Territory Communications

Highways:
   short stretch of paved road between port and airfield on Diego Garcia
Ports:
   Diego Garcia
Airports:
   1 with permanent-surface runways over 3,659 m on Diego Garcia
Telecommunications:
   minimal facilities; broadcast stations (operated by US Navy) - 1 AM, 1 FM, 1
   TV; 1 Atlantic Ocean INTELSAT earth station

:British Indian Ocean Territory Defense Forces

Note: defense is the responsibility of the UK

British Virgin Islands Geography

Total area: 150 km2
Land area: 150 km2; includes the island of Anegada
Comparative area: about 0.8 times the size of Washington, DC
Coastline:
   80 km
Maritime claims:
  Exclusive fishing zone:
   200 nm
  Territorial sea:
   3 nm
Disputes:
   none
Climate:
   subtropical; humid; temperatures moderated by trade winds
Terrain:
   coral islands relatively flat; volcanic islands steep, hilly
Natural resources:
   negligible
Land use:
   arable land 20%; permanent crops 7%; meadows and pastures 33%; forest and
   woodland 7%; other 33%
Environment:
   subject to hurricanes and tropical storms from July to October
Note:
   strong ties to nearby US Virgin Islands and Puerto Rico

:British Virgin Islands People

Population: 12,555 (July 1992), growth rate 1.2% (1992)
Birth rate: 20 births/1,000 population (1992)
Death rate: 6 deaths/1,000 population (1992)
Net migration rate: —2 migrants/1,000 population (1992)
Infant mortality rate: 20 deaths/1,000 live births (1992)
Life expectancy at birth: 71 years male, 75 years female (1992)

Total fertility rate: 2.3 children born/woman (1992)
Nationality:
   noun - British Virgin Islander(s); adjective - British Virgin Islander
Ethnic divisions:
   over 90% black, remainder of white and Asian origin
Religions:
   Protestant 86% (Methodist 45%, Anglican 21%, Church of God 7%, Seventh-Day
   Adventist 5%, Baptist 4%, Jehovah's Witnesses 2%, other 2%), Roman Catholic
   6%, none 2%, other 6% (1981)
Languages:
   English (official)
Literacy:
   98% (male 98%, female 98%) age 15 and over can read and write (1970)
Labor force:
   4,911 (1980)
Organized labor:
   NA% of labor force

:British Virgin Islands Government

Long-form name:
   none
Type:
   dependent territory of the UK
Capital: Road Town
Administrative divisions:
   none (dependent territory of the UK)
Independence:
   none (dependent territory of the UK)
Constitution:
   1 June 1977
Legal system:
   English law
National holiday:
   Territory Day, 1 July
Executive branch:
   British monarch, governor, chief minister, Executive Council (cabinet)
Legislative branch:
   unicameral Legislative Council
Judicial branch:
   Eastern Caribbean Supreme Court
Leaders:
  Chief of State:
   Queen ELIZABETH II (since 6 February 1952), represented by Governor P. A.
   PENFOLD (since NA 1991)
  Head of Government:
   Chief Minister H. Lavity STOUTT (since NA 1986)
Political parties and leaders:
   United Party (UP), Conrad MADURO; Virgin Islands Party (VIP), H. Lavity
   STOUTT; Independent Progressive Movement (IPM), Cyril B. ROMNEY
Suffrage:

universal at age 18

Elections:

Legislative Council:

last held 12 November 1990 (next to be held by November 1995); results - percent of vote by party NA; seats - (9 total) VIP 6, IPM 1, independents 2

Member of:

CARICOM (associate), CDB, ECLAC (associate), IOC, OECS, UNESCO (associate)

Diplomatic representation:

none (dependent territory of UK)

Flag:

blue with the flag of the UK in the upper hoist-side quadrant and the Virgin Islander coat of arms centered in the outer half of the flag; the coat of arms depicts a woman flanked on either side by a vertical column of six oil lamps above a scroll bearing the Latin word
VIGILATE (Be Watchful)

:British Virgin Islands Economy

Overview:

The economy, one of the most prosperous in the Caribbean area, is highly dependent on the tourist industry, which generates about 21% of the national income. In 1985 the government offered offshore registration to companies wishing to incorporate in the islands, and, in consequence, incorporation fees generated about $2 million in 1987. Livestock raising is the most significant agricultural activity. The islands' crops, limited by poor soils, are unable to meet food requirements.

GDP:

purchasing power equivalent - $130 million, per capita $10,600; real growth rate 6.3% (1990)

Inflation rate (consumer prices):

2.5% (1990 est.)

Unemployment rate: NEGL%

Budget:

revenues $51 million; expenditures $88 million, including capital expenditures of $38 million (1991)

Exports:

$2.7 million (f.o.b., 1988)

commodities:

rum, fresh fish, gravel, sand, fruits, animals

partners:

Virgin Islands (US), Puerto Rico, US

Imports:

$11.5 million (c.i.f., 1988)

commodities:

building materials, automobiles, foodstuffs, machinery

partners:

Virgin Islands (US), Puerto Rico, US

External debt: $4.5 million (1985)

Industrial production:

growth rate—4.0% (1985)

Electricity:
  10,500 kW capacity; 43 million kWh produced, 3,510 kWh per capita (1990)
Industries:
  tourism, light industry, construction, rum, concrete block, offshore
  financial center
Agriculture:
  livestock (including poultry), fish, fruit, vegetables
Economic aid:
  NA
Currency:
  US currency is used
Exchange rates:
  US currency is used
Fiscal year: 1 April - 31 March

:British Virgin Islands Communications

Highways:
  106 km motorable roads (1983)
Ports:
  Road Town
Airports:
  3 total, 3 usable; 2 with permanent-surface runways less than 1,220 m
Telecommunications:
  3,000 telephones; worldwide external telephone service; submarine cable
  communication links to Bermuda; broadcast stations - 1 AM, no FM, 1 TV

:British Virgin Islands Defense Forces

Note: defense is the responsibility of the UK

Brunei Geography

Total area: 5,770 km2
Land area: 5,270 km2
Comparative area: slightly larger than Delaware
Land boundaries:
  381 km; Malaysia 381 km
Coastline:
  161 km
Maritime claims:
 Exclusive fishing zone:
  200 nm
 Territorial sea:
  12 nm
Disputes:
  may wish to purchase the Malaysian salient that divides the country; all of
  the Spratly Islands are claimed by China, Taiwan, and Vietnam; parts of them
  are claimed by Malaysia and the Philippines; in 1984, Brunei established an
  exclusive fishing zone that encompasses Louisa Reef, but has not publicly
  claimed the island
Climate:
  tropical; hot, humid, rainy
Terrain:

flat coastal plain rises to mountains in east; hilly lowland in west

Natural resources:
  crude oil, natural gas, timber

Land use:
  arable land 1%; permanent crops 1%; meadows and pastures 1%; forest and woodland 79%; other 18%; includes irrigated NEGL%

Environment:
  typhoons, earthquakes, and severe flooding are rare

Note:
  close to vital sea lanes through South China Sea linking Indian and Pacific Oceans; two parts physically separated by Malaysia; almost an enclave of Malaysia

:Brunei People

Population: 269,319 (July 1992), growth rate 2.9% (1992)

Birth rate: 27 births/1,000 population (1992)

Death rate: 5 deaths/1,000 population (1992)

Net migration rate: 7 migrants/1,000 population (1992)

Infant mortality rate: 26 deaths/1,000 live births (1992)

Life expectancy at birth: 69 years male, 73 years female (1992)

Total fertility rate: 3.5 children born/woman (1992)

Nationality:
  noun - Bruneian(s); adjective - Bruneian

Ethnic divisions:
  Malay 64%, Chinese 20%, other 16%

Religions:
  Muslim (official) 63%, Buddhism 14%, Christian 8%, indigenous beliefs and other 15% (1981)

Languages:
  Malay (official), English, and Chinese

Literacy:
  77% (male 85%, female 69%) age 15 and over can read and write (1981)

Labor force:
  89,000 (includes members of the Army); 33% of labor force is foreign (1988); government 47.5%; production of oil, natural gas, services, and construction 41.9%; agriculture, forestry, and fishing 3.8% (1986)

Organized labor:
  2% of labor force

:Brunei Government

Long-form name:
  Negara Brunei Darussalam

Type:
  constitutional sultanate

Capital: Bandar Seri Begawan

Administrative divisions:
  4 districts (daerah-daerah, singular - daerah); Belait, Brunei and Muara, Temburong, Tutong

Independence:
  1 January 1984 (from UK)

Constitution:

29 September 1959 (some provisions suspended under a State of Emergency since December 1962, others since independence on 1 January 1984)

Legal system:
  based on Islamic law

National holiday:
  23 February (1984)

Executive branch:
  sultan, prime minister, Council of Cabinet Ministers

Legislative branch:
  unicameral Legislative Council (Majlis Masyuarat Megeri)

Judicial branch:
  Supreme Court

Leaders:
  Chief of State and Head of Government:
  Sultan and Prime Minister His Majesty Paduka Seri Baginda Sultan Haji HASSANAL Bolkiah Mu`izzaddin Waddaulah (since 5 October 1967)

Political parties and leaders:
  Brunei United National Party (inactive), Anak HASANUDDIN, chairman; Brunei National Democratic Party (the first legal political party and now banned), leader NA

Suffrage:
  none

Elections:
  Legislative Council:
  last held in March 1962; in 1970 the Council was changed to an appointive body by decree of the sultan and no elections are planned

Member of:
  APEC, ASEAN, C, ESCAP, G-77, ICAO, IDB, IMO, INTERPOL, IOC, ISO (correspondent), ITU, OIC, UN, UNCTAD, UPU, WHO, WMO

Diplomatic representation:
  Ambassador Mohamed KASSIM bin Haji Mohamed Daud; Chancery at 2600 Virginia Avenue NW, Suite 3000, Washington, DC 20037; telephone (202) 342-0159

US:
  Ambassador (vacant); Embassy at Third Floor, Teck Guan Plaza, Jalan Sultan, American Embassy Box B, APO AP 96440; telephone [673] (2) 229-670; FAX [673] (2) 225-293

Flag:
  yellow with two diagonal bands of white (top, almost double width) and black starting from the upper hoist side; the national emblem in red is superimposed at the center; the emblem includes a swallow-tailed flag on top of a winged column within an upturned crescent above a scroll and flanked by two upraised hands

:Brunei Economy

Overview:
  The economy is a mixture of foreign and domestic entrepreneurship, government regulation and welfare measures, and village tradition. It is almost totally supported by exports of crude oil and natural gas, with revenues from the petroleum sector accounting for more than 50% of GDP. Per

capita GDP of $8,800 is among the highest in the Third World, and substantial income from overseas investment supplements domestic production. The government provides for all medical services and subsidizes food and housing.

GDP:
exchange rate conversion - $3.5 billion, per capita $8,800; real growth rate 1% (1990 est.)

Inflation rate (consumer prices):
1.3% (1989)

Unemployment rate: 3.7%, shortage of skilled labor (1989)

Budget:
revenues $1.3 billion; expenditures $1.5 billion, including capital expenditures of $255 million (1989 est.)

Exports:
$2.2 billion (f.o.b., 1990 est.)
commodities:
crude oil, liquefied natural gas, petroleum products
partners:
Japan 53%, UK 12%, South Korea 9%, Thailand 7%, Singapore 5% (1990)

Imports:
$1.7 billion (c.i.f., 1990 est.)
commodities:
machinery and transport equipment, manufactured goods, food, chemicals
partners:
Singapore 35%, UK 26%, Switzerland 9%, US 9%, Japan 5% (1990)

External debt: none

Industrial production:
growth rate 12.9% (1987); accounts for 52.4% of GDP

Electricity:
310,000 kW capacity; 890 million kWh produced, 2,400 kWh per capita (1990)

Industries:
petroleum, petroleum refining, liquefied natural gas, construction

Agriculture:
imports about 80% of its food needs; principal crops and livestock include rice, cassava, bananas, buffaloes, and pigs

Economic aid:
US commitments, including Ex-Im (FY70-87), $20.6 million; Western (non-US) countries, ODA and OOF bilateral commitments (1970-89), $153 million

Currency:
Bruneian dollar (plural - dollars); 1 Bruneian dollar (B$) = 100 cents

Exchange rates:
Bruneian dollars (B$) per US$1 - 1.7454 (January 1991), 1.8125 (1990), 1.9503 (1989), 2.0124 (1988), 2.1060 (1987), 2.1774 (1986); note - the Bruneian dollar is at par with the Singapore dollar

Fiscal year: calendar year

:Brunei Communications

Railroads:
13 km 0.610-meter narrow-gauge private line

Highways:

1,090 km total; 370 km paved (bituminous treated) and another 52 km under construction, 720 km gravel or unimproved

Inland waterways:
209 km; navigable by craft drawing less than 1.2 meters

Pipelines:
crude oil 135 km; petroleum products 418 km; natural gas 920 km

Ports:
Kuala Belait, Muara

Merchant marine:
7 liquefied gas carriers (1,000 GRT or over) totaling 348,476 GRT/340,635 DWT

Civil air:
4 major transport aircraft (3 Boeing 757-200, 1 Boeing 737-200)

Airports:
2 total, 2 usable; 1 with permanent-surface runways; 1 with runway over 3,659 m; 1 with runway 1,406 m

Telecommunications:
service throughout country is adequate for present needs; international service good to adjacent Malaysia; radiobroadcast coverage good; 33,000 telephones (1987); broadcast stations - 4 AM/FM, 1 TV; 74,000 radio receivers (1987); satellite earth stations - 1 Indian Ocean INTELSAT and 1 Pacific Ocean INTELSAT

:Brunei Defense Forces

Branches:
Ground Forces, Navy, Air Force, and Royal Brunei Police

Manpower availability:
males 15-49, 75,330; 43,969 fit for military service; 2,595 reach military age (18) annually

Defense expenditures:
exchange rate conversion - $233.1 million, 7.1% of GDP (1988)

Bulgaria Geography

Total area: 110,910 km2
Land area: 110,550 km2
Comparative area: slightly larger than Tennessee

Land boundaries:
1,881 km; Greece 494 km, Macedonia 148 km, Romania 608 km, Serbia and Montenegro 318 km, Turkey 240 km

Coastline:
354 km

Maritime claims:
 Contiguous zone:
 24 nm
 Exclusive economic zone:
 200 nm
 Territorial sea:
 12 nm

Disputes:
Macedonia question with Greece and Macedonia

Climate:

temperate; cold, damp winters; hot, dry summers
Terrain:
  mostly mountains with lowlands in north and south
Natural resources:
  bauxite, copper, lead, zinc, coal, timber, arable land
Land use:
  arable land 34%; permanent crops 3%; meadows and pastures 18%; forest and
  woodland 35%; other 10%; includes irrigated 11%
Environment:
  subject to earthquakes, landslides; deforestation; air pollution
Note:
  strategic location near Turkish Straits; controls key land routes from
  Europe to Middle East and Asia

:Bulgaria People

Population: 8,869,161 (July 1992), growth rate —0.5% (1992)
Birth rate: 12 births/1,000 population (1992)
Death rate: 12 deaths/1,000 population (1992)
Net migration rate: —5 migrants/1,000 population (1992)
Infant mortality rate: 13 deaths/1,000 live births (1992)
Life expectancy at birth: 69 years male, 76 years female (1992)
Total fertility rate: 1.7 children born/woman (1992)
Nationality:
  noun - Bulgarian(s); adjective - Bulgarian
Ethnic divisions:
  Bulgarian 85.3%, Turk 8.5%, Gypsy 2.6%, Macedonian 2.5%, Armenian 0.3%,
  Russian 0.2%, other 0.6%
Religions:
  Bulgarian Orthodox 85%; Muslim 13%; Jewish 0.8%; Roman Catholic 0.5%; Uniate
  Catholic 0.2%; Protestant, Gregorian-Armenian, and other 0.5%
Languages:
  Bulgarian; secondary languages closely correspond to ethnic breakdown
Literacy:
  93% (male NA%, female NA%) age 15 and over can read and write (1970 est.)
Labor force:
  4,300,000; industry 33%, agriculture 20%, other 47% (1987)
Organized labor:
  Confederation of Independent Trade Unions of Bulgaria (KNSB); Edinstvo
  (Unity) People's Trade Union (splinter confederation from KNSB); Podkrepa
  (Support) Labor Confederation, legally registered in January 1990

:Bulgaria Government

Long-form name:
  Republic of Bulgaria
Type:
  emerging democracy, diminishing Communist Party influence
Capital: Sofia
Administrative divisions:
  9 provinces (oblasti, singular - oblast); Burgas, Grad Sofiya, Khaskovo,
  Lovech, Mikhaylovgrad, Plovdiv, Razgrad, Sofiya, Varna
Independence:

22 September 1908 (from Ottoman Empire)

Constitution:

adopted 12 July 1991

Legal system:

based on civil law system, with Soviet law influence; has accepted compulsory ICJ jurisdiction

National holiday:

3 March (1878)

Executive branch:

president, chairman of the Council of Ministers (premier), two deputy chairmen of the Council of Ministers, Council of Ministers

Legislative branch:

unicameral National Assembly (Narodno Sobranie)

Judicial branch:

Supreme Court; Constitutional Court

Leaders:

Chief of State:

President Zhelyu ZHELEV (since 1 August 1990)

Head of Government:

Chairman of the Council of Ministers (Premier) Filip DIMITROV (since 8 November 1991); Deputy Chairman of the Council of Ministers (Deputy Prime Minister) Stoyan GANEV (since 8 November 1991); Deputy Chairman of the Council of Ministers Nikolay VASILEV (since 8 November 1991)

Political parties and leaders:

government:

Union of Democratic Forces (UDF), Filip DIMITROV, chairman, consisting of United Democratic Center, Democratic Party, Radical Democratic Party, Christian Democratic Union, Alternative Social Liberal Party, Republican Party, Civic Initiative Movement, Union of the Repressed, and about a dozen other groups; Movement for Rights and Freedoms (pro-Muslim party) (MRF), Ahmed DOGAN, chairman, supports UDF but not officially in coalition with it

opposition:

Bulgarian Socialist Party (BSP), formerly Bulgarian Communist Party (BCP), Zhan VIDENOV, chairman

Suffrage:

universalandcompulsoryatage 18

Elections:

National Assembly:

last held 13 October 1991; results - BSP 33%, UDΓ 34%, MRF 7.5%; seats - (240 total) BSP 106, UDF 110, Movement for Rights and Freedoms 24

President:

last held 12 January 1992; second round held 19 January 1992; results - Zhelyu ZHELEV was elected by popular vote

Communists:

Bulgarian Socialist Party (BSP), formerly Bulgarian Communist Party (BCP), 501,793 members; several small Communist parties

:Bulgaria Government

Other political or pressure groups:

Ecoglasnost; Podkrepa (Support) Labor Confederation; Fatherland Union;

Bulgarian Democratic Youth (formerly Communist Youth Union); Confederation
of Independent Trade Unions of Bulgaria (KNSB); Nationwide Committee for
Defense of National Interests; Peasant Youth League; Bulgarian Agrarian
National Union - United (BZNS); Bulgarian Democratic Center; "Nikola Petkov"
Bulgarian Agrarian National Union; Internal Macedonian Revolutionary
Organization - Union of Macedonian Societies (IMRO-UMS); numerous regional,
ethnic, and national interest groups with various agendas

Member of:

BIS, CCC, CE, CSCE, EBRD, ECE, FAO, G-9, IAEA, IBRD, ICAO, ICFTU, IIB,
ILO,

IMF, IMO, INMARSAT, IOC, ISO, ITU, LORCS, NACC, NSG, PCA, UN,
UNCTAD,

UNESCO, UNIDO, UPU, WHO, WIPO, WMO

Diplomatic representation:

Ambassador Ognyan PISHEV; Chancery at 1621 22nd Street NW, Washington, DC
20008; telephone (202) 387-7969

US:

Ambassador Hugh Kenneth HILL; Embassy at 1 Alexander Stamboliski Boulevard,
Sofia (mailing address is APO AE 09213-5740); telephone [359] (2) 88-48-01
through 05; Embassy has no FAX machine

Flag:

three equal horizontal bands of white (top), green, and red; the national
emblem formerly on the hoist side of the white stripe has been removed - it
contained a rampant lion within a wreath of wheat ears below a red
five-pointed star and above a ribbon bearing the dates 681 (first Bulgarian
state established) and 1944 (liberation from Nazi control)

:Bulgaria Economy

Overview:

Growth in the lackluster Bulgarian economy fell to the 2% annual level in
the 1980s. By 1990, Sofia's foreign debt had skyrocketed to over $10 billion
- giving a debt-service ratio of more than 40% of hard currency earnings and
leading the regime to declare a moratorium on its hard currency payments.
The post-Communist government faces major problems of renovating an aging
industrial plant; coping with worsening energy, food, and consumer goods
shortages; keeping abreast of rapidly unfolding technological developments;
investing in additional energy capacity (the portion of electric power from
nuclear energy reached over one-third in 1990); and motivating workers, in
part by giving them a share in the earnings of their enterprises. Bulgaria's
new government, led by Prime Minister Filip Dimitrov, is strongly committed
to economic reform. The previous government, even though dominated by former
Communists, had taken the first steps toward dismantling the central
planning system, bringing the economy back into balance, and reducing
inflationary pressures. The program produced some encouraging early results,
including eased restrictions on foreign investment, increased support from
international financial institutions, and liberalized currency trading.
Small entrepreneurs have begun to emerge and some privatization of small
enterprises has taken place. The government has passed bills to privatize
large state-owned enterprises and reform the banking system. Negotiations on
an association agreement with the EC began in late 1991.

GNP:
  purchasing power equivalent - $36.4 billion, per capita $4,100; real growth
  rate —22% (1991 est.)
Inflation rate (consumer prices):
  420% (1991 est.)
Unemployment rate: 10% (1991 est.)
Budget:
  revenues NA; expenditures NA, including capital expenditures of $NA billion
  (1991)
Exports:
  $8.4 billion (f.o.b., 1990)
 commodities:
  machinery and equipment 55.3%; agricultural products 15.0%; manufactured
  consumer goods 10.0%; fuels, minerals, raw materials, and metals 18.4%;
  other 1.3% (1990)
 partners:
  former CMEA countries 70.6% (USSR 56.2%, Czechoslovakia 3.9%, Poland 2.5%);
  developed countries 13.6% (Germany 2.1%, Greece 1.2%); less developed
  countries 13.1% (Libya 5.8%, Iran 0.5%) (1990)
Imports:
  $9.6 billion (f.o.b., 1990)
 commodities:
  fuels, minerals, and raw materials 43.7%; machinery and equipment 45.2%;
  manufactured consumer goods 6.7%; agricultural products 3.8%; other 0.6%
 partners:
  former CMEA countries 70.9% (former USSR 52.7%, Poland 4.1%); developed
  countries 20.2% (Germany 5.0%, Austria 2.1%); less developed countries 7.2%
  (Libya 2.0%, Iran 0.7%)
External debt: $11.2 billion (1991)
Industrial production:
  growth rate —14.7% (1990); accounts for about 37% of GNP (1990)
Electricity:
  11,500,000 kW capacity; 45,000 million kWh produced, 5,040 kWh per capita
  (1990)

:Bulgaria Economy

Industries:
  machine building and metal working, food processing, chemicals, textiles,
  building materials, ferrous and nonferrous metals
Agriculture:
  accounts for 22% of GNP (1990); climate and soil conditions support
  livestock raising and the growing of various grain crops, oilseeds,
  vegetables, fruits, and tobacco; more than one-third of the arable land
  devoted to grain; world's fourth-largest tobacco exporter; surplus food
  producer
Illicit drugs:
  transshipment point for southwest Asian heroin transiting the Balkan route
Economic aid:
  donor - $1.6 billion in bilateral aid to non-Communist less developed
  countries (1956-89)

Currency:

lev (plural - leva); 1 lev (Lv) = 100 stotinki

Exchange rates:

leva (Lv) per US$1 - 17.18 (1 January 1992), 16.13 (March 1991), 0.7446 (November 1990), 0.84 (1989), 0.82 (1988), 0.90 (1987); note - floating exchange rate since February 1991

Fiscal year: calendar year

:Bulgaria Communications

Railroads:

4,300 km total, all government owned (1987); 4,055 km 1.435-meter standard gauge, 245 km narrow gauge; 917 km double track; 2,510 km electrified

Highways:

36,908 km total; 33,535 km hard surface (including 242 km superhighways); 3,373 km earth roads (1987)

Inland waterways:

470 km (1987)

Pipelines:

crude oil 193 km; petroleum products 418 km; natural gas 1,400 km (1986)

Ports:

Burgas, Varna, Varna West; river ports are Ruse, Vidin, and Lom on the Danube

Merchant marine:

110 ships (1,000 GRT and over) totaling 1,234,657 GRT/1,847,759 DWT; includes 2 short-sea passenger, 30 cargo, 2 container, 1 passenger-cargo training, 6 roll-on/roll-off, 15 petroleum tanker, 4 chemical carrier, 2 railcar carrier, 48 bulk; Bulgaria owns 1 ship (1,000 GRT or over) totaling 8,717 DWT operating under Liberian registry

Civil air:

86 major transport aircraft

Airports:

380 total, 380 usable; about 120 with permanent-surface runways; 20 with runways 2,440-3,659 m; 20 with runways 1,220-2,439 m

Telecommunications:

extensive radio relay; 2.5 million telephones; direct dialing to 36 countries; phone density is 25 phones per 100 persons; 67% of Sofia households now have a phone (November 1988); broadcast stations - 20 AM, 15 FM, and 29 TV, with 1 Soviet TV repeater in Sofia; 2.1 million TV sets (1990); 92% of country receives No. 1 television program (May 1990); 1 satellite ground station using Intersputnik; INTELSAT is used through a Greek earth station

:Bulgaria Defense Forces

Branches:

Army, Navy, Air and Air Defense Forces, Frontier Troops, Internal Troops

Manpower availability:

males 15-49, 2,181,421; 1,823,678 fit for military service; 65,942 reach military age (19) annually

Defense expenditures:

exchange rate conversion - 4.413 billion leva, 4.4% of GNP (1991); note -

conversion of defense expenditures into US dollars using the current
exchange rate could produce misleading results

Burkina Geography

Total area: 274,200 km2
Land area: 273,800 km2
Comparative area: slightly larger than Colorado
Land boundaries:
 3,192 km; Benin 306 km, Ghana 548 km, Ivory Coast 584 km, Mali 1,000 km,
 Niger 628 km, Togo 126 km
Coastline:
 none - landlocked
Maritime claims:
 none - landlocked
Disputes:
 the disputed international boundary between Burkina and Mali was submitted
 to the International Court of Justice (ICJ) in October 1983 and the ICJ
 issued its final ruling in December 1986, which both sides agreed to accept;
 Burkina and Mali are proceeding with boundary demarcation, including the
 tripoint with Niger
Climate:
 tropical; warm, dry winters; hot, wet summers
Terrain:
 mostly flat to dissected, undulating plains; hills in west and southeast
Natural resources:
 manganese, limestone, marble; small deposits of gold, antimony, copper,
 nickel, bauxite, lead, phosphates, zinc, silver
Land use:
 arable land 10%; permanent crops NEGL%; meadows and pastures 37%; forest and
 woodland 26%; other 27%, includes irrigated NEGL%
Environment:
 recent droughts and desertification severely affecting marginal agricultural
 activities, population distribution, economy; overgrazing; deforestation
Note:
 landlocked

:Burkina People

Population: 9,653,672 (July 1992), growth rate 3.1% (1992)
Birth rate: 49 births/1,000 population (1992)
Death rate: 16 deaths/1,000 population (1992)
Net migration rate: —2 migrants/1,000 population (1992)
Infant mortality rate: 117 deaths/1,000 live births (1992)
Life expectancy at birth: 52 years male, 53 years female (1992)
Total fertility rate: 7.1 children born/woman (1992)
Nationality:
 noun - Burkinabe (singular and plural); adjective - Burkinabe
Ethnic divisions:
 more than 50 tribes; principal tribe is Mossi (about 2.5 million); other
 important groups are Gurunsi, Senufo, Lobi, Bobo, Mande, and Fulani
Religions:
 indigenous beliefs about 65%, Muslim 25%, Christian (mainly Roman Catholic)

10%

Languages:

French (official); tribal languages belong to Sudanic family, spoken by 90% of the population

Literacy:

18% (male 28%, female 9%) age 15 and over can read and write (1990 est.)

Labor force:

3,300,000 residents; 30,000 are wage earners; agriculture 82%, industry 13%, commerce, services, and government 5%; 20% of male labor force migrates annually to neighboring countries for seasonal employment (1984); 44% of population of working age (1985)

Organized labor:

four principal trade union groups represent less than 1% of population

:Burkina Government

Long-form name:

Burkina Faso

Type:

military; established by coup on 4 August 1983

Capital: Ouagadougou

Administrative divisions:

30 provinces; Bam, Bazega, Bougouriba, Boulgou, Boulkiemde, Ganzourgou, Gnagna, Gourma, Houet, Kadiogo, Kenedougou, Komoe, Kossi, Kouritenga, Mouhoun, Namentenga, Naouri, Oubritenga, Oudalan, Passore, Poni, Sanguie, Sanmatenga, Seno, Sissili, Soum, Sourou, Tapoa, Yatenga, Zoundweogo

Independence:

5 August 1960 (from France; formerly Upper Volta)

Constitution:

June 1991

Legal system:

based on French civil law system and customary law

National holiday:

Anniversary of the Revolution, 4 August (1983)

Executive branch:

President, Council of Ministers

Legislative branch:

unicameral National Assembly (Assemblee Nationale) was dissolved on 25 November 1980

Judicial branch:

Appeals Court

Leaders:

 Chief of State and Head of Government:

President Captain Blaise COMPAORE (since 15 October 1987)

Political parties and leaders:

Organization for Popular Democracy (ODP/MT), ruling party; Coordination of Democratic Forces (CFD), composed of opposition parties

Suffrage:

Elections:

the National Assembly was dissolved 25 November 1980; presidential election held December 1991 and legislative election scheduled for 24 May 1992

Communists:

small Communist party front group; some sympathizers

Other political or pressure groups:

committees for the defense of the revolution, watchdog/political action
groups throughout the country in both organizations and communities

Member of:

ACCT, ACP, AfDB, CCC, CEAO, ECA, ECOWAS, Entente, FAO, FZ, G-77,
GATT, IBRD,

ICAO, ICC, ICFTU, IDA, IDB, IFAD, IFC, ILO, IMF, INTELSAT, INTERPOL,
IOC,

ITU, LORCS, NAM, OAU, OIC, PCA, UN, UNCTAD, UNESCO, UNIDO, UPU,
WADB, WCL,

WFTU, WHO, WIPO, WMO, WTO

Diplomatic representation:

Ambassador Paul Desire KABORE; Chancery at 2340 Massachusetts Avenue NW,
Washington, DC 20008; telephone (202) 332-5577 or 6895

US:

Ambassador Edward P. BYRNN; Embassy at Avenue Raoul Follerau, Ouagadougou
(mailing address is 01 B. P. 35, Ouagadougou); telephone [226] 30-67- 23
through 25 and [226] 33-34-22; FAX [226] 31-23-68

Flag:

two equal horizontal bands of red (top) and green with a yellow five-pointed
star in the center; uses the popular pan-African colors of Ethiopia

:Burkina Economy

Overview:

One of the poorest countries in the world, Burkina has a high population
density, few natural resources, and relatively infertile soil. Economic
development is hindered by a poor communications network within a landlocked
country. Agriculture provides about 40% of GDP and is entirely of a
subsistence nature. Industry, dominated by unprofitable
government-controlled corporations, accounts for about 15% of GDP.

GDP:

exchange rate conversion - $2.9 billion, per capita $320 (1988); real growth
rate 1.3% (1990 est.)

Inflation rate (consumer prices):

—0.5% (1989)

Unemployment rate: NA%

Budget:

revenues $275 million; expenditures $287 million, including capital
expenditures of $NA (1989)

Exports:

$262 million (f.o.b., 1989)

commodities:

oilseeds, cotton, live animals, gold

partners:

EC 42% (France 30%, other 12%), Taiwan 17%, Ivory Coast 15% (1985)

Imports:

$619 million (f.o.b., 1989)

commodities:

grain, dairy products, petroleum, machinery

partners:

EC 37% (France 23%, other 14%), Africa 31%, US 15% (1985)

External debt: $962 million (December 1990 est.)

Industrial production:

growth rate 5.7% (1990 est.), accounts for about 15% of GDP (1988)

Electricity:

120,000 kW capacity; 320 million kWh produced, 40 kWh per capita (1991)

Industries:

cotton lint, beverages, agricultural processing, soap, cigarettes, textiles, gold

Agriculture:

accounts for about 40% of GDP; cash crops - peanuts, shea nuts, sesame, cotton; food crops - sorghum, millet, corn, rice; livestock; not self-sufficient in food grains

Economic aid:

US commitments, including Ex-Im (FY70-89), $294 million; Western (non-US) countries, ODA and OOF bilateral commitments (1970-89), $2.9 billion; Communist countries (1970-89), $113 million

Currency:

Communaute Financiere Africaine franc (plural - francs); 1 CFA franc (CFAF) = 100 centimes

Exchange rates:

CFA francs (CFAF) per US$1 - 269.01 (January 1992), 282.11 (1991), 272.26 (1990), 319.01 (1989), 297.85 (1988), 300.54 (1987)

Fiscal year: calendar year

:Burkina Communications

Railroads:

620 km total; 520 km Ouagadougou to Ivory Coast border and 100 km Ouagadougou to Kaya; all 1.00-meter gauge and single track

Highways:

16,500 km total; 1,300 km paved, 7,400 km improved, 7,800 km unimproved (1985)

Civil air:

2 major transport aircraft

Airports:

48 total, 38 usable; 2 with permanent-surface runways; none with runways over 3,659 m; 2 with runways 2,440-3,659 m; 8 with runways 1,220-2,439 m

Telecommunications:

all services only fair; radio relay, wire, and radio communication stations in use; broadcast stations - 2 AM, 1 FM, 2 TV; 1 Atlantic Ocean INTELSAT earth station

:Burkina Defense Forces

Branches:

Army, Air Force, National Gendarmerie, National Police, Peoples' Militia

Manpower availability:

males 15-49, 1,904,647; 971,954 fit for military service; no conscription

Defense expenditures:
  exchange rate conversion - $55 million, 2.7% of GDP (1988 est.)

Burma Geography

Total area: 678,500 km2
Land area: 657,740 km2
Comparative area: slightly smaller than Texas
Land boundaries:
  5,876 km; Bangladesh 193 km, China 2,185 km, India 1,463 km, Laos 235 km,
  Thailand 1,800 km
Coastline:
  1,930 km
Maritime claims:
 Contiguous zone:
  24 nm
 Continental shelf:
  edge of continental margin or 200 nm
 Exclusive economic zone:
  200 nm
 Territorial sea:
  12 nm
Disputes:
  none
Climate:
  tropical monsoon; cloudy, rainy, hot, humid summers (southwest monsoon, June
  to September); less cloudy, scant rainfall, mild temperatures, lower
  humidity during winter (northeast monsoon, December to April)
Terrain:
  central lowlands ringed by steep, rugged highlands
Natural resources:
  crude oil, timber, tin, antimony, zinc, copper, tungsten, lead, coal, some
  marble, limestone, precious stones, natural gas
Land use:
  arable land 15%; permanent crops 1%; meadows and pastures 1%; forest and
  woodland 49%; other 34%; includes irrigated 2%
Environment:
  subject to destructive earthquakes and cyclones; flooding and landslides
  common during rainy season (June to September); deforestation
Note:
  strategic location near major Indian Ocean shipping lanes

:Burma People

Population: 42,642,418 (July 1992), growth rate 1.9% (1992)
Birth rate: 29 births/1,000 population (1992)
Death rate: 10 deaths/1,000 population (1992)
Net migration rate: 0 migrants/1,000 population (1992)
Infant mortality rate: 68 deaths/1,000 live births (1992)
Life expectancy at birth: 57 years male, 61 years female (1992)
Total fertility rate: 3.8 children born/woman (1992)
Nationality:
  noun - Burmese (singular and plural); adjective - Burmese

Ethnic divisions:
   Burman 68%, Shan 9%, Karen 7%, Rakhine 4%, Chinese 3%, Mon 2%, Indian 2%, other 5%
Religions:
   Buddhist 89%, Christian 4% (Baptist 3%, Roman Catholic 1%), Muslim 4%, animist beliefs 1%, other 2%
Languages:
   Burmese; minority ethnic groups have their own languages
Literacy:
   81% (male 89%, female 72%) age 15 and over can read and write (1990 est.)
Labor force:
   16,036,000; agriculture 65.2%, industry 14.3%, trade 10.1%, government 6.3%, other 4.1% (FY89 est.)
Organized labor:
   Workers' Asiayone (association), 1,800,000 members; Peasants' Asiayone, 7,600,000 members

:Burma Government

Long-form name:
   Union of Burma; note - the local official name is Pyidaungzu Myanma Naingngandaw, which has been translated by the US Government as Union of Myanma and by the Burmese as Union of Myanmar
Type:
   military regime
Capital: Rangoon (sometimes translated as Yangon)
Administrative divisions:
   7 divisions* (yin-mya, singular - yin) and 7 states (pyine-mya, singular - pyine); Chin State, Irrawaddy*, Kachin State, Karan State, Kayah State, Magwe*, Mandalay*, Mon State, Pegu*, Rakhine State, Rangoon*, Sagaing*, Shan State, Tenasserim*
Independence:
   4 January 1948 (from UK)
Constitution:
   3 January 1974 (suspended since 18 September 1988)
Legal system:
   martial law in effect throughout most of the country; has not accepted compulsory ICJ jurisdiction
National holiday:
   Independence Day, 4 January (1948)
Executive branch:
   chairman of the State Law and Order Restoration Council, State Law and Order Restoration Council
Legislative branch:
   unicameral People's Assembly (Pyithu Hluttaw) was dissolved after the coup of 18 September 1988
Judicial branch:
   Council of People's Justices was abolished after the coup of 18 September 1988
Leaders:
  Chief of State and Head of Government:

Chairman of the State Law and Order Restoration Council Gen. THAN SHWE (since 23 April 1992)

Political parties and leaders:

National Unity Party (NUP; proregime), THA KYAW; National League for Democracy (NLD), U AUNG SHWE; National Coalition of Union of Burma (NCGUB),

SEIN WIN - consists of individuals legitimately elected but not recognized by military regime; fled to border area and joined with insurgents in December 1990 to form a parallel government

Suffrage:

universal at age 18

Elections:

People's Assembly:

last held 27 May 1990, but Assembly never convened; results - NLD 80%; seats - (485 total) NLD 396, the regime-favored NUP 10, other 79

Communists:

several hundred (est.) in Burma Communist Party (BCP)

Other political or pressure groups:

Kachin Independence Army (KIA), United Wa State Army (UWSA), Karen National Union (KNU) , several Shan factions, including the Shan United Army (SUA) (all ethnically based insurgent groups)

Member of:

AsDB, CP, ESCAP, FAO, G-77, GATT, IAEA, IBRD, ICAO, IDA, IFAD, IFC, ILO,

IMF, IMO, INTERPOL, IOC, ITU, LORCS, UN, UNCTAD, UNESCO, UPU, WHO, WMO

:Burma Government

Diplomatic representation:

Ambassador U THAUNG; Chancery at 2300 S Street NW, Washington, DC 20008; telephone (202) 332-9044 through 9046; there is a Burmese Consulate General in New York

US:

Ambassador (vacant); Deputy Chief of Mission, Charge d'Affaires Franklin P. HUDDLE, Jr.; Embassy at 581 Merchant Street, Rangoon (mailing address is GPO Box 521, AMEMB Box B, APO AP 96546); telephone [95] (1) 82055, 82181; FAX [95] (1) 80409

Flag:

red with a blue rectangle in the upper hoist-side corner bearing, all in white, 14 five-pointed stars encircling a cogwheel containing a stalk of rice; the 14 stars represent the 14 administrative divisions

:Burma Economy

Overview:

Burma is a poor Asian country, with a per capita GDP of about $500. The nation has been unable to achieve any substantial improvement in export earnings because of falling prices for many of its major commodity exports. For rice, traditionally the most important export, the drop in world prices has been accompanied by shrinking markets and a smaller volume of sales. In 1985 teak replaced rice as the largest export and continues to hold this position. The economy is heavily dependent on the agricultural sector, which generates about 40% of GDP and provides employment for 65% of the work force. Burma has been largely isolated from international economic forces and has been trying to encourage foreign investment, so far with little success.

GDP:
  exchange rate conversion - $22.2 billion, per capita $530; real growth rate 5.6% (1991)

Inflation rate (consumer prices):
  40% (1991)

Unemployment rate: 9.6% in urban areas (FY89 est.)

Budget:
  revenues $7.2 billion; expenditures $9.3 billion, including capital expenditures of $6 billion (1991)

Exports:
  $568 million
 commodities:
  teak, rice, oilseed, metals, rubber, gems
 partners:
  Southeast Asia, India, Japan, China, EC, Africa

Imports:
  $1.16 billion
 commodities:
  machinery, transport equipment, chemicals, food products
 partners:
  Japan, EC, China, Southeast Asia

External debt: $4.2 billion (1991)

Industrial production:
  growth rate 2.6% (FY90 est.); accounts for 10% of GDP

Electricity:
  950,000 kW capacity; 2,900 million kWh produced, 70 kWh per capita (1990)

Industries:
  agricultural processing; textiles and footwear; wood and wood products; petroleum refining; mining of copper, tin, tungsten, iron; construction materials; pharmaceuticals; fertilizer

Agriculture:
  accounts for 40% of GDP (including fish and forestry); self-sufficient in food; principal crops - paddy rice, corn, oilseed, sugarcane, pulses; world's largest stand of hardwood trees; rice and teak account for 55% of export revenues; fish catch of 740,000 metric tons (FY90)

Illicit drugs:
  world's largest illicit producer of opium poppy and minor producer of cannabis for the international drug trade; opium production is on the increase as growers respond to the collapse of Rangoon's antinarcotic programs

Economic aid:
  US commitments, including Ex-Im (FY70-89), $158 million; Western (non-US) countries, ODA and OOF bilateral commitments (1970-89), $3.9 billion; Communist countries (1970-89), $424 million

:Burma Economy

Currency:
   kyat (plural - kyats); 1 kyat (K) = 100 pyas
Exchange rates:
   kyats (K) per US$1 - 6.0963 (January 1992), 6.2837 (1991), 6.3386 (1990),
   6.7049 (1989), 6.46 (1988), 6.6535 (1987)
Fiscal year: 1 April - 31 March

:Burma Communications

Railroads:
   3,991 km total, all government owned; 3,878 km 1.000-meter gauge, 113 km
   narrow-gauge industrial lines; 362 km double track
Highways:
   27,000 km total; 3,200 km bituminous, 17,700 km improved earth or gravel,
   6,100 km unimproved earth
Inland waterways:
   12,800 km; 3,200 km navigable by large commercial vessels
Pipelines:
   crude oil 1,343 km; natural gas 330 km
Ports:
   Rangoon, Moulmein, Bassein
Merchant marine:
   71 ships (1,000 GRT or over) totaling 1,036,018 GRT/1,514,121 DWT; includes
   3 passenger-cargo, 19 cargo, 5 refrigerated cargo, 3 vehicle carrier, 3
   container, 2 petroleum tanker, 6 chemical, 1 combination ore/oil, 27 bulk, 1
   combination bulk, 1 roll-on/roll-off
Civil air:
   17 major transport aircraft (including 3 helicopters)
Airports:
   85 total, 82 usable; 27 with permanent-surface runways; none with runways
   over 3,659 m; 3 with runways 2,440-3,659 m; 38 with runways 1,220-2,439 m
Telecommunications:
   meets minimum requirements for local and intercity service; international
   service is good; 53,000 telephones (1986); radiobroadcast coverage is
   limited to the most populous areas; broadcast stations - 2 AM, 1 FM, 1 TV
   (1985); 1 Indian Ocean INTELSAT earth station

:Burma Defense Forces

Branches:
   Army, Navy, Air Force
Manpower availability:
   eligible 15-49, 21,447,878; of the 10,745,530 males 15-49, 5,759,840 are fit
   for military service; of the 10,702,348 females 15-49, 5,721,868 are fit for
   military service; 424,474 males and 410,579 females reach military age (18)
   annually; both sexes are liable for military service
Defense expenditures:
   exchange rate conversion - $1.28 billion, FY(91-92)

Burundi Geography

Total area: 27,830 km2
Land area: 25,650 km2
Comparative area: slightly larger than Maryland

Land boundaries:
  974 km; Rwanda 290 km, Tanzania 451 km, Zaire 233 km
Coastline:
  none - landlocked
Maritime claims:
  none - landlocked
Disputes:
  none
Climate:
  temperate; warm; occasional frost in uplands
Terrain:
  mostly rolling to hilly highland; some plains
Natural resources:
  nickel, uranium, rare earth oxide, peat, cobalt, copper, platinum (not yet
  exploited), vanadium
Land use:
  arable land 43%; permanent crops 8%; meadows and pastures 35%; forest and
  woodland 2%; other 12%; includes irrigated NEGL%
Environment:
  soil exhaustion; soil erosion; deforestation
Note:
  landlocked; straddles crest of the Nile-Congo watershed

:Burundi People

Population: 6,022,341 (July 1992), growth rate 3.2% (1992)
Birth rate: 46 births/1,000 population (1992)
Death rate: 14 deaths/1,000 population (1992)
Net migration rate: 0 migrants/1,000 population (1992)
Infant mortality rate: 106 deaths/1,000 live births (1992)
Life expectancy at birth: 51 years male, 55 years female (1992)
Total fertility rate: 6.8 children born/woman (1992)
Nationality:
  noun - Burundian(s); adjective - Burundi
Ethnic divisions:
  Africans - Hutu (Bantu) 85%, Tutsi (Hamitic) 14%, Twa (Pygmy) 1%; other
  Africans include about 70,000 refugees, mostly Rwandans and Zairians;
  non-Africans include about 3,000 Europeans and 2,000 South Asians
Religions:
  Christian about 67% (Roman Catholic 62%, Protestant 5%), indigenous beliefs
  32%, Muslim 1%
Languages:
  Kirundi and French (official); Swahili (along Lake Tanganyika and in the
  Bujumbura area)
Literacy:
  50% (male 61%, female 40%) age 15 and over can read and write (1990 est.)
Labor force:
  1,900,000 (1983 est.); agriculture 93.0%, government 4.0%, industry and
  commerce 1.5%, services 1.5%; 52% of population of working age (1985)
Organized labor:

sole group is the Union of Burundi Workers (UTB); by charter, membership is extended to all Burundi workers (informally); active membership figures NA

:Burundi Government

Long-form name:
  Republic of Burundi
Type:
  republic
Capital: Bujumbura
Administrative divisions:
  15 provinces; Bubanza, Bujumbura, Bururi, Cankuzo, Cibitoke, Gitega, Karuzi, Kayanza, Kirundo, Makamba, Muramvya, Muyinga, Ngozi, Rutana, Ruyigi
Independence:
  1 July 1962 (from UN trusteeship under Belgian administration)
Constitution:
  20 November 1981; suspended following the coup of 3 September 1987; a constitutional committee was charged with drafting a new constitution created in February 1991; a referendum on the new constitution scheduled for March 1992
Legal system:
  based on German and Belgian civil codes and customary law; has not accepted compulsory ICJ jurisdiction
National holiday:
  Independence Day, 1 July (1962)
Executive branch:
  president; chairman of the Central Committee of the National Party of Unity and Progress (UPRONA), prime minister
Legislative branch:
  unicameral National Assembly (Assemblee Nationale) was dissolved following the coup of 3 September 1987; at an extraordinary party congress held from 27 to 29 December 1990, the Central Committee of the National Party of Unity and Progress (UPRONA) replaced the Military Committee for National Salvation, and became the supreme governing body during the transition to constitutional government
Judicial branch:
  Supreme Court (Cour Supreme)
Leaders:
  Chief of State:
  Major Pierre BUYOYA, President (since 9 September 1987)
  Head of Government:
  Prime Minister Adrien SIBOMANA (since 26 October 1988)
Political parties and leaders:
  only party - National Party of Unity and Progress (UPRONA), Nicolas MAYUGI, secretary general; note - although Burundi is still officially a one-party state, at least four political parties were formed in 1991 in anticipation of proposed constitutional reform in 1992 - Burundi Democratic Front (FRODEBU), Organization of the People of Burundi (RPB), Socialist Party of Burundi (PSB), Movement for Peace and Democracy (MPD) - the Party for the Liberation of the Hutu People (PALIPEHUTU), formed in exile in the early 1980s, is an ethnically based political party dedicated to majority rule;

the government has long accused PALIPEHUTU of practicing devisive ethnic politics and fomenting violence against the state. PALIPEHUTU's exclusivist charter makes it an unlikely candidate for legalization under the new constitution that will require party membership open to all ethnic groups

Suffrage:

universal adult at age NA

Elections:

National Assembly:

dissolved after the coup of 3 September 1987; note - The National Unity Charter outlining the principles for constitutional government was adopted by a national referendum on 5 February 1991

:Burundi Government

Member of:

ACCT, ACP, AfDB, CCC, CEEAC, CEPGL, ECA, FAO, G-77, GATT, IBRD, ICAO, IDA,

IFAD, IFC, ILO, IMF, INTERPOL, ITU, LORCS, NAM, OAU, UN, UNCTAD, UNESCO,

UNIDO, UPU, WHO, WIPO, WMO, WTO

Diplomatic representation:

Ambassador Julien KAVAKURE; Chancery at Suite 212, 2233 Wisconsin Avenue NW,

Washington, DC 20007; telephone (202) 342-2574

US:

Ambassador Cynthia Shepherd PERRY; B. P. 1720, Avenue des Etats-Unis, Bujumbura; telephone [257] (222) 454; FAX [257] (222) 926

Flag:

divided by a white diagonal cross into red panels (top and bottom) and green panels (hoist side and outer side) with a white disk superimposed at the center bearing three red six-pointed stars outlined in green arranged in a triangular design (one star above, two stars below)

:Burundi Economy

Overview:

A landlocked, resource-poor country in an early stage of economic development, Burundi is predominately agricultural with only a few basic industries. Its economic health depends on the coffee crop, which accounts for an average 90% of foreign exchange earnings each year. The ability to pay for imports therefore continues to rest largely on the vagaries of the climate and the international coffee market. As part of its economic reform agenda, launched in February 1991 with IMF and World Bank support, Burundi is trying to diversify its export agriculture capability and attract foreign investment in industry. Several state-owned coffee companies were privatized via public auction in September 1991.

GDP:

exchange rate conversion - $1.13 billion, per capita $200; real growth rate 3.4% (1990 est.)

Inflation rate (consumer prices):

7.1% (1990 est.)

Unemployment rate: NA%

Budget:

revenues $158 million; expenditures $204 million, including capital
expenditures of $131 million (1989 est.)
Exports:
  $74.7 million (f.o.b., 1990)
 commodities:
  coffee 88%, tea, hides, and skins
 partners:
  EC 83%, US 5%, Asia 2%
Imports:
  $234.6 million (c.i.f., 1990)
 commodities:
  capital goods 31%, petroleum products 15%, foodstuffs, consumer goods
 partners:
  EC 57%, Asia 23%, US 3%
External debt: $1.0 billion (1990 est.)
Industrial production:
  real growth rate 5.1% (1986); accounts for about 10% of GDP
Electricity:
  55,000 kW capacity; 105 million kWh produced, 20 kWh per capita (1991)
Industries:
  light consumer goods such as blankets, shoes, soap; assembly of imports;
  public works construction; food processing
Agriculture:
  accounts for 60% of GDP; 90% of population dependent on subsistence farming;
  marginally self-sufficient in food production; cash crops - coffee, cotton,
  tea; food crops - corn, sorghum, sweet potatoes, bananas, manioc; livestock
  - meat, milk, hides, and skins
Economic aid:
  US commitments, including Ex-Im (FY70-89), $71 million; Western (non-US)
  countries, ODA and OOF bilateral commitments (1970-89), $10.2 billion; OPEC
  bilateral aid (1979-89), $32 million; Communist countries (1970-89), $175
  million
Currency:
  Burundi franc (plural - francs); 1 Burundi franc (FBu) = 100 centimes
Exchange rates:
  Burundi francs (FBu) per US$1 - 193.72 (January 1992), 181.51 (1991), 171.26
  (1990), 158.67 (1989), 140.40 (1988), 123. 56 (1987)
Fiscal year: calendar year

:Burundi Communications

Highways:
  5,900 km total; 400 km paved, 2,500 km gravel or laterite, 3,000 km improved
  or unimproved earth
Inland waterways:
  Lake Tanganyika
Ports:
  Bujumbura (lake port) connects to transportation systems of Tanzania and
  Zaire
Civil air:
  no major transport aircraft

Airports:
   6 total, 6 usable; 1 with permanent-surface runways; none with runways over
   3,659 m; 1 with runways 2,440-3,659 m; none with runways 1,220 to 2,439 m
Telecommunications:
   sparse system of wire, radiocommunications, and low-capacity radio relay
   links; 8,000 telephones; broadcast stations - 2 AM, 2 FM, 1 TV; 1 Indian
   Ocean INTELSAT earth station

:Burundi Defense Forces

Branches:
   Army (includes naval and air units); paramilitary Gendarmerie
Manpower availability:
   males 15-49, 1,306,611; 681,050 fit for military service; 59,676 reach
   military age (16) annually
Defense expenditures:
   exchange rate conversion - $28 million, 3.7% of GDP (1989)

Cambodia Geography

Total area: 181,040 km2
Land area: 176,520 km2
Comparative area: slightly smaller than Oklahoma
Land boundaries:
   2,572 km; Laos 541 km, Thailand 803 km, Vietnam 1,228 km
Coastline:
   443 km
Maritime claims:
  Contiguous zone:
   24 nm
  Continental shelf:
   200 nm
  Exclusive economic zone:
   200 nm
  Territorial sea:
   12 nm
Disputes:
   offshore islands and three sections of the boundary with Vietnam are in
   dispute; maritime boundary with Vietnam not defined
Climate:
   tropical; rainy, monsoon season (May to October); dry season (December to
   March); little seasonal temperature variation
Terrain:
   mostly low, flat plains; mountains in southwest and north
Natural resources:
   timber, gemstones, some iron ore, manganese, phosphates, hydropower
   potential
Land use:
   arable land 16%; permanent crops 1%; meadows and pastures 3%; forest and
   woodland 76%; other 4%; includes irrigated 1%
Environment:
   a land of paddies and forests dominated by Mekong River and Tonle Sap

Note:
  buffer between Thailand and Vietnam

:Cambodia People

Population: 7,295,706 (July 1992), growth rate 2.1% (1992)
Birth rate: 37 births/1,000 population (1992)
Death rate: 15 deaths/1,000 population (1992)
Net migration rate: 0 migrants/1,000 population (1992)
Infant mortality rate: 121 deaths/1,000 live births (1992)
Life expectancy at birth: 48 years male, 51 years female (1992)
Total fertility rate: 4.4 children born/woman (1992)
Nationality:
  noun - Cambodian(s); adjective - Cambodian
Ethnic divisions:
  Khmer 90%, Chinese 5%, other 5%
Religions:
  Theravada Buddhism 95%, other 5%
Languages:
  Khmer (official), French
Literacy:
  35% (male 48%, female 22%) age 15 and over can read and write (1990 est.)
Labor force:
  2.5-3.0 million; agriculture 80% (1988 est.)
Organized labor:
  Kampuchea Federation of Trade Unions (FSC); under government control

:Cambodia Government

Long-form name:
  none
Type:
  currently administered by the Supreme National Council (SNC), a body set up
  under United Nations' auspices, in preparation for an internationally
  supervised election in 1993 and including representatives from each of the
  country's four political factions
Capital: Phnom Penh
Administrative divisions:
  19 provinces (khet, singular and plural) and 2 autonomous cities* Banteay
  Meanchey, Batdambang, Kampong Cham, Kampong Chhnang, Kampong Saom
City*,
  Kampong Spoe, Kampong Thum, Kampot, Kandal, Kaoh Kong, Kracheh, Mondol
Kiri,
  Phnom Phen City*, Pouthisat, Preah Vihear, Prey Veng, Rotanokiri,
  Siemreab-Otdar Meanchey, Stoeng Treng, Svay Rieng, Takev
Independence:
  8 November 1949 (from France)
Constitution:
  a new constitution will be drafted after the national election in 1993
National holiday:
  NGC - Independence Day, 17 April (1975); SOC - Liberation Day, 7 January
  (1979)
Executive branch:

a twelve-member Supreme National Council (SNC), chaired by Prince NORODOM
SIHANOUK, composed of representatives from each of the four political
factions; faction names and delegation leaders are: State of Cambodia (SOC)
- HUN SEN; Democratic Kampuchea (DK or Khmer Rouge) - KHIEU SAMPHAN;
Khmer
People's National Liberation Front (KPNLF) - SON SANN; National United Front
for an Independent, Peaceful, Neutral, and Cooperative Cambodia (FUNCINPEC)
- Prince NORODOM RANARIDDH

Legislative branch:
pending a national election in 1993, the incumbent SOC faction's National
Assembly is the only functioning national legislative body

Judicial branch:
pending a national election in 1993, the incumbent SOC faction's Supreme
People's Court is the only functioning national judicial body

Leaders:
 Chief of State:
 SNC - Chairman Prince NORODOM SIHANOUK, under United Nations's supervi-
sion
 Head of Government:
 NGC - vacant, formerly held by SON SANN (since July 1982); will be
 determined following the national election in 1993; SOC - Chairman of the
 Council of Ministers HUN SEN (since 14 January 1985)

Political parties and leaders:
Democratic Kampuchea (DK, also known as the Khmer Rouge) under KHIEU
SAMPHAN; Cambodian Pracheachon Party or Cambodian People's Party (CPP)
(name
changed and HENG SAMRIN replaced in October 1991) under CHEA SIM; Khmer
People's National Liberation Front (KPNLF) under SON SANN; National United
Front for an Independent, Neutral, Peaceful, and Cooperative Cambodia
(FUNCINPEC) under Prince NORODOM RANNARIDH

Suffrage:
universal at age 18

Elections:
UN-supervised election for a 120-member constituent assembly based on
proportional representation within each province will be held nine months
after UN-organized voter registration is complete; the election is not
anticipated before April 1993; the assembly will draft and approve a
constitution and then transform itself into a legislature that will create a
new Cambodian Government

:Cambodia Government

Member of:
AsDB, CP, ESCAP, FAO, G-77, IAEA, IBRD, ICAO, IDA, ILO, IMF, IMO,
INTERPOL,
ITU, LORCS, NAM, PCA, UN, UNCTAD, UNESCO, UPU, WFTU, WHO, WMO,
WTO

Diplomatic representation:
the Supreme National Council (SNC) represents Cambodia in international
organizations - it filled UN seat in September 1991

US:

Charles TWINNING is the US representative to Cambodia

Flag:

SNC - blue background with white map of Cambodia in middle; SOC - two equal horizontal bands of red (top) and blue with a gold stylized five-towered temple representing Angkor Wat in the center

:Cambodia Economy

Overview:

Cambodia is a desperately poor country whose economic development has been stymied by deadly political infighting. The economy is based on agriculture and related industries. Over the past decade Cambodia has been slowly recovering from its near destruction by war and political upheaval. The food situation remains precarious; during the 1980s famine was averted only through international relief. In 1986 the production level of rice, the staple food crop, was able to meet only 80% of domestic needs. The biggest success of the nation's recovery program has been in new rubber plantings and in fishing. Industry, other than rice processing, is almost nonexistent. Foreign trade has been primarily with the former USSR and Vietnam, and both trade and foreign aid are being adversely affected by the breakup of the USSR. Statistical data on the economy continue to be sparse and unreliable. Foreign aid from the former USSR and Eastern Europe has virtually stopped.

GDP:

exchange rate conversion - $930 million, per capita $130; real growth rate NA (1991 est.)

Inflation rate (consumer prices):

53% (1990 est.)

Unemployment rate: NA%

Budget:

revenues $178 million expenditures $NA, including capital expenditures of $NA (1991)

Exports:

$32 million (f.o.b., 1988)

commodities:

natural rubber, rice, pepper, wood

partners:

Vietnam, USSR, Eastern Europe, Japan, India

Imports:

$147 million (c.i.f., 1988)

commodities:

international food aid; fuels, consumer goods, machinery

partners:

Vietnam, USSR, Eastern Europe, Japan, India

External debt: $600 million (1989)

Industrial production:

growth rate NA%

Electricity:

140,000 kW capacity; 200 million kWh produced, 30 kWh per capita (1991)

Industries:

rice milling, fishing, wood and wood products, rubber, cement, gem mining

Agriculture:

mainly subsistence farming except for rubber plantations; main crops - rice, rubber, corn; food shortages - rice, meat, vegetables, dairy products, sugar, flour

Economic aid:
US commitments, including Ex-Im (FY70-89), $725 million; Western (non-US countries) (1970-89), $300 million; Communist countries (1970-89), $1.8 billion

Currency:
riel (plural - riels); 1 riel (CR) = 100 sen

Exchange rates:
riels (CR) per US$1 - 714 (May 1992), 500 (December 1991), 560 (1990), 159.00 (1988), 100.00 (1987)

Fiscal year: calendar year

:Cambodia Communications

Railroads:
612 km 1.000-meter gauge, government owned

Highways:
13,351 km total; 2,622 km bituminous; 7,105 km crushed stone, gravel, or improved earth; 3,624 km unimproved earth; some roads in disrepair

Inland waterways:
3,700 km navigable all year to craft drawing 0.6 meters; 282 km navigable to craft drawing 1.8 meters

Ports:
Kampong Saom, Phnom Penh

Airports:
16 total, 8 usable; 5 with permanent-surface runways; none with runways over 3,659 m; 2 with runways 2,440-3,659 m; 4 with runways 1,220-2,439 m

Telecommunications:
service barely adequate for government requirements and virtually nonexistent for general public; international service limited to Vietnam and other adjacent countries; broadcast stations - 1 AM, no FM, 1 TV

:Cambodia Defense Forces

Branches:
SOC - Cambodian People's Armed Forces (CPAF); Communist resistance forces - National Army of Democratic Kampuchea (Khmer Rouge); non-Communist resistance forces - Armee National Kampuchea Independent (ANKI), which is sometimes anglicized as National Army of Independent Cambodia (NAIC), and Khmer People's National Liberation Armed Forces (KPNLAF) - under the Paris peace agreement of October 1991, all four factions are to observe a cease-fire and prepare for UN-supervised cantonment, disarmament, and 70% demobilization before the election, with the fate of the remaining 30% to be determined by the newly elected government - the United Nations Transitional Authority in Cambodia (UNTAC) will verify the cease-fire and disarm the combatants

Manpower availability:
males 15-49, 1,877,339; 1,032,102 fit for military service; 61,807 reach military age (18) annually

Defense expenditures:
exchange rate conversion - $NA, NA% of GDP

Cameroon Geography

Total area: 475,440 km2
Land area: 469,440 km2
Comparative area: slightly larger than California
Land boundaries:
    4,591 km; Central African Republic 797 km, Chad 1,094 km, Congo 523 km,
    Equatorial Guinea 189 km, Gabon 298 km, Nigeria 1,690 km
Coastline:
    402 km
Maritime claims:
    Territorial sea:
    50 nm
Disputes:
    demarcation of international boundaries in Lake Chad, the lack of which has
    led to border incidents in the past, is completed and awaiting ratification
    by Cameroon, Chad, Niger, and Nigeria; boundary commission created with
    Nigeria to discuss unresolved land and maritime boundaries - has not yet
    convened
Climate:
    varies with terrain from tropical along coast to semiarid and hot in north
Terrain:
    diverse, with coastal plain in southwest, dissected plateau in center,
    mountains in west, plains in north
Natural resources:
    crude oil, bauxite, iron ore, timber, hydropower potential
Land use:
    arable land 13%; permanent crops 2%; meadows and pastures 18%; forest and
    woodland 54%; other 13%; includes irrigated NEGL%
Environment:
    recent volcanic activity with release of poisonous gases; deforestation;
    overgrazing; desertification
Note:
    sometimes referred to as the hinge of Africa

:Cameroon People

Population: 12,658,439 (July 1992), growth rate 3.3% (1992)
Birth rate: 44 births/1,000 population (1992)
Death rate: 11 deaths/1,000 population (1992)
Net migration rate: 0 migrants/1,000 population (1992)
Infant mortality rate: 81 deaths/1,000 live births (1992)
Life expectancy at birth: 55 years male, 60 years female (1992)
Total fertility rate: 6.4 children born/woman (1992)
Nationality:
    noun - Cameroonian(s); adjective - Cameroonian
Ethnic divisions:
    over 200 tribes of widely differing background; Cameroon Highlanders 31%,
    Equatorial Bantu 19%, Kirdi 11%, Fulani 10%, Northwestern Bantu 8%, Eastern
    Nigritic 7%, other African 13%, non-African less than 1%
Religions:
    indigenous beliefs 51%, Christian 33%, Muslim 16%

Languages:

English and French (official), 24 major African language groups

Literacy:

54% (male 66%, female 43%) age 15 and over can read and write (1990 est.)

Labor force:

NA; agriculture 74.4%, industry and transport 11.4%, other services 14.2% (1983); 50% of population of working age (15-64 years) (1985)

Organized labor:

under 45% of wage labor force

:Cameroon Government

Long-form name:

Republic of Cameroon

Type:

unitary republic; multiparty presidential regime (opposition parties legalized 1990)

Capital: Yaounde

Administrative divisions:

10 provinces; Adamaoua, Centre, Est, Extreme-Nord, Littoral, Nord, Nord-Ouest, Ouest, Sud, Sud-Ouest

Independence:

1 January 1960 (from UN trusteeship under French administration; formerly French Cameroon)

Constitution:

20 May 1972

Legal system:

based on French civil law system, with common law influence; has not accepted compulsory ICJ jurisdiction

National holiday:

National Day, 20 May (1972)

Executive branch:

president, Cabinet

Legislative branch:

unicameral National Assembly (Assemblee Nationale)

Judicial branch:

Supreme Court

Leaders:

Chief of State:

President Paul BIYA (since 6 November 1982)

Head of Government:

interim Prime Minister Sadou HAYATOU (since 25 April 1991)

Political parties and leaders:

Cameroon People's Democratic Movement (RDPC), Paul BIYA, president, is government-controlled and was formerly the only party; numerous small parties formed since opposition parties were legalized in 1990

Suffrage:

universal at age 20

Elections:

National Assembly:

next to be held 1 March 1992

President:
last held 24 April 1988 (next to be held April 1993); results - President
Paul BIYA reelected without opposition
Other political or pressure groups:
NA
Member of:
ACCT (associate), ACP, AfDB, BDEAC, CCC, CEEAC, ECA, FAO, FZ, G-19, G-77,
GATT, IAEA, IBRD, ICAO, ICC, IDA, IDB, IFAD, IFC, ILO, IMF, IMO, INMARSAT,
INTELSAT, INTERPOL, IOC, ITU, LORCS, NAM, OAU, OIC, PCA, UDEAC, UN, UNCTAD,
UNESCO, UNIDO, UPU, WCL, WHO, WIPO, WMO, WTO
Diplomatic representation:
Ambassador Paul PONDI; Chancery at 2349 Massachusetts Avenue NW, Washington,
DC 20008; telephone (202) 265-8790 through 8794
US:
Ambassador Frances D. COOK; Embassy at Rue Nachtigal, Yaounde (mailing
address is B. P. 817, Yaounde); telephone [237] 234014; FAX [237] 230753;
there is a US Consulate General in Douala

:Cameroon Government

Flag:
three equal vertical bands of green (hoist side), red, and yellow with a
yellow five-pointed star centered in the red band; uses the popular
pan-African colors of Ethiopia

:Cameroon Economy

Overview:
Because of its offshore oil resources, Cameroon has one of the highest
incomes per capita in tropical Africa. Still, it faces many of the serious
problems facing other underdeveloped countries, such as political
instability, a top-heavy civil service, and a generally unfavorable climate
for business enterprise. The development of the oil sector led rapid
economic growth between 1970 and 1985. Growth came to an abrupt halt in 1986
precipitated by steep declines in the prices of major exports: coffee,
cocoa, and petroleum. Export earnings were cut by almost one-third, and
inefficiencies in fiscal management were exposed. In 1990-92, with support
from the IMF and World Bank, the government has begun to introduce reforms
designed to spur business investment, increase efficiency in agriculture,
and recapitalize the nation's banks. Nationwide strikes organized by
opposition parties in 1991, however, undermined these efforts.
GDP:
exchange rate conversion - $11.5 billion, per capita $1,040; real growth
rate 0.7% (1990 est.)
Inflation rate (consumer prices):
8.6% (FY88)
Unemployment rate: 25% (1990 est.)
Budget:
revenues $1.2 billion; expenditures $1.8 billion, including capital

expenditures of $NA million (FY89)

Exports:
  $2.1 billion (f.o.b., 1990 est.)
  commodities:
  petroleum products 56%, coffee, cocoa, timber, manufactures
  partners:
  EC (particularly France) about 50%, US 10%
Imports:
  $2.1 billion (c.i.f., 1990 est.)
  commodities:
  machines and electrical equipment, transport equipment, chemical products,
  consumer goods
  partners:
  France 41%, Germany 9%, US 4%
External debt: $4.9 billion (December 1989 est.)
Industrial production:
  growth rate - 6.4% (FY87); accounts for 30% of GDP
Electricity:
  755,000 kW capacity; 2,940 million kWh produced, 270 kWh per capita (1991)
Industries:
  crude oil products, food processing, light consumer goods, textiles,
  sawmills
Agriculture:
  the agriculture and forestry sectors provide employment for the majority of
  the population, contributing nearly 25% to GDP and providing a high degree
  of self-sufficiency in staple foods; commercial and food crops include
  coffee, cocoa, timber, cotton, rubber, bananas, oilseed, grains, livestock,
  root starches
Economic aid:
  US commitments, including Ex-Im (FY70-89), $440 million; Western (non-US)
  countries, ODA and OOF bilateral commitments (1970-89), $4.5 billion; OPEC
  bilateral aid (1979-89), $29 million; Communist countries (1970-89), $125
  million

:Cameroon Economy

Currency:
  Communaute Financiere Africaine franc (plural - francs); 1 CFA franc (CFAF)
  = 100 centimes
Exchange rates:
  Communaute Financiere Africaine francs (CFAF) per US$1 - 269.01 (January
  1992), 282.11 (1991), 272.26 (1990), 319.01 (1989), 297.85 (1988), 300.54
  (1987)
Fiscal year: 1 July - 30 June

:Cameroon Communications

Railroads:
  1,003 km total; 858 km 1.000-meter gauge, 145 km 0.600-meter gauge
Highways:
  about 65,000 km total; includes 2,682 km paved, 32,318 km gravel and
  improved earth, and 30,000 km of unimproved earth
Inland waterways:

2,090 km; of decreasing importance
Ports:
  Douala
Merchant marine:
  2 cargo ships (1,000 GRT or over) totaling 24,122 GRT/33,509 DWT
Civil air:
  5 major transport aircraft
Airports:
  56 total, 50 usable; 10 with permanent-surface runways; 1 with runways over
  3,659 m; 5 with runways 2,440-3,659 m; 21 with runways 1,220-2,439 m
Telecommunications:
  good system of open wire, cable, troposcatter, and radio relay; 26,000
  telephones; broadcast stations - 11 AM, 11 FM, 1 TV; 2 Atlantic Ocean
  INTELSAT earth stations

:Cameroon Defense Forces

Branches:
  Army, Navy (including naval infantry), Air Force; National Gendarmerie,
  Presidential Guards
Manpower availability:
  males 15-49, 2,753,059; 1,385,706 fit for military service; 120,011 reach
  military age (18) annually
Defense expenditures:
  exchange rate conversion - $219 million, 1.7% of GDP (1990 est.)

Canada Geography

Total area: 9,976,140 km2
Land area: 9,220,970 km2
Comparative area: slightly larger than US
Land boundaries:
  8,893 km with US (includes 2,477 km with Alaska)
Coastline:
  243,791 km
Maritime claims:
 Continental shelf:
  200 m (depth) or to depth of exploitation
 Exclusive fishing zone:
  200 nm
 Territorial sea:
  12 nm
Disputes:
  maritime boundary disputes with the US
Climate:
  varies from temperate in south to subarctic and arctic in north
Terrain:
  mostly plains with mountains in west and lowlands in southeast
Natural resources:
  nickel, zinc, copper, gold, lead, molybdenum, potash, silver, fish, timber,
  wildlife, coal, crude oil, natural gas
Land use:
  arable land 5%; permanent crops NEGL%; meadows and pastures 3%; forest and

woodland 35%; other 57%; includes NEGL% irrigated

Environment:

80% of population concentrated within 160 km of US border; continuous permafrost in north a serious obstacle to development

Note:

second-largest country in world (after Russia); strategic location between Russia and US via north polar route

:Canada People

Population: 27,351,509 (July 1992), growth rate 1.3% (1992)
Birth rate: 14 births/1,000 population (1992)
Death rate: 7 deaths/1,000 population (1992)
Net migration rate: 6 migrants/1,000 population (1992)
Infant mortality rate: 7 deaths/1,000 live births (1992)
Life expectancy at birth: 74 years male, 81 years female (1992)
Total fertility rate: 1.8 children born/woman (1992)
Nationality:

noun - Canadian(s); adjective - Canadian

Ethnic divisions:

British Isles origin 40%, French origin 27%, other European 20%, indigenous Indian and Eskimo 1.5%

Religions:

Roman Catholic 46%, United Church 16%, Anglican 10%

Languages:

English and French (both official)

Literacy:

99% (male NA%, female NA%) age 15 and over can read and write (1981 est.)

Labor force:

13,380,000; services 75%, manufacturing 14%, agriculture 4%, construction 3%, other 4% (1988)

Organized labor:

30.6% of labor force; 39.6% of nonagricultural paid workers

:Canada Government

Long-form name:

Type:

confederation with parliamentary democracy

Capital: Ottawa

Administrative divisions:

10 provinces and 2 territories*; Alberta, British Columbia, Manitoba, New Brunswick, Newfoundland, Northwest Territories*, Nova Scotia, Ontario, Prince Edward Island, Quebec, Saskatchewan, Yukon Territory*

Independence:

1 July 1867 (from UK)

Constitution:

amended British North America Act 1867 patriated to Canada 17 April 1982; charter of rights and unwritten customs

Legal system:

based on English common law, except in Quebec, where civil law system based on French law prevails; accepts compulsory ICJ jurisdiction, with reservations

National holiday:

Canada Day, 1 July (1867)

Executive branch:

British monarch, governor general, prime minister, deputy prime minister, Cabinet

Legislative branch:

bicameral Parliament (Parlement) consists of an upper house or Senate (Senat) and a lower house or House of Commons (Chambre des Communes)

Judicial branch:

Supreme Court

Leaders:

Chief of State:

Queen ELIZABETH II (since 6 February 1952), represented by Governor General Raymond John HNATSHYN (since 29 January 1990)

Head of Government:

Prime Minister (Martin) Brian MULRONEY (since 4 September 1984); Deputy Prime Minister Donald Frank MAZANKOWSKI (since June 1986)

Political parties and leaders:

Progressive Conservative Party, Brian MULRONEY; Liberal Party, Jean CHRETIEN; New Democratic Party, Audrey McLAUGHLIN

Suffrage:

universal at age 18

Elections:

House of Commons:

last held 21 November 1988 (next to be held by November 1993); results - Progressive Conservative Party 43.0%, Liberal Party 32%, New Democratic Party 20%, other 5%; seats - (295 total) Progressive Conservative Party 159, Liberal Party 80, New Democratic Party 44, independents 12

Communists:

3,000

Member of:

ACCT, AfDB, AG (observer), APEC, AsDB, Australia Group, BIS, C, CCC, CDB, COCOM, CP, CSCE, EBRD, ECE, ECLAC, FAO, G-7, G-8, G-10, GATT, IADB, IAEA,

IBRD, ICAO, ICC, ICFTU, IDA, IEA, IFAD, IFC, ILO, IMF, IMO, INMARSAT, INTELSAT, INTERPOL, IOC, IOM, ISO, ITU, LORCS, MTCR, NACC, NATO, NEA, NSG,

OAS, OECD, PCA, UN, UNCTAD, UNDOF, UNESCO, UNFICYP, UNHCR, UNIDO, UNIIMOG,

UNTSO, UPU, WCL, WHO, WIPO, WMO, WTO, ZC

:Canada Government

Diplomatic representation:

Ambassador Derek BURNEY; Chancery at 501 Pennsylvania Avenue NW, Washington,

DC 20001; telephone (202) 682-1740; there are Canadian Consulates General in Atlanta, Boston, Buffalo, Chicago, Cleveland, Dallas, Detroit, Los Angeles, Minneapolis, New York, Philadelphia, San Francisco, and Seattle

US:

Ambassador Peter TEELEY; Embassy at 100 Wellington Street, K1P 5T1, Ottawa (mailing address is P. O. Box 5000, Ogdensburg, NY 13669-0430); telephone (613) 238-5335 or (613) 238-4470; FAX (613) 238-5720; there are US Consulates General in Calgary, Halifax, Montreal, Quebec, Toronto, and Vancouver

Flag:

three vertical bands of red (hoist side), white (double width, square), and red with a red maple leaf centered in the white band

:Canada Economy

Overview:

As an affluent, high-tech industrial society, Canada today closely resembles the US in per capita output, market-oriented economic system, and pattern of production. Since World War II the impressive growth of the manufacturing, mining, and service sectors has transformed the nation from a largely rural economy into one primarily industrial and urban. In the 1980s, Canada registered one of the highest rates of real growth among the OECD nations, averaging about 3.2%. With its great natural resources, skilled labor force, and modern capital plant, Canada has excellent economic prospects. However, the continuing constitutional impasse between English- and French-speaking areas has observers discussing a possible split in the confederation; foreign investors are becoming edgy.

GDP:

purchasing power equivalent - $521.5 billion, per capita $19,400; real growth rate -1.1% (1991 est.)

Inflation rate (consumer prices):

4.2% (November 1991, annual rate)

Unemployment rate: 10.3% (November 1991)

Budget:

revenues $111.8 billion; expenditures $138.3 billion, including capital expenditures of $NA (FY90 est.)

Exports:

$124.0 billion (f.o.b., 1991)

commodities:

newsprint, wood pulp, timber, crude petroleum, machinery, natural gas, aluminum, motor vehicles and parts; telecommunications equipment

partners:

US, Japan, UK, Germany, South Korea, Netherlands, China

Imports:

$118 billion (c.i.f., 1991)

commodities:

crude petroleum, chemicals, motor vehicles and parts, durable consumer goods, electronic computers; telecommunications equipment and parts

partners:

US, Japan, UK, Germany, France, Mexico, Taiwan, South Korea

External debt: $247 billion (1987)

Industrial production:

growth rate -3.8% (August 1991); accounts for 34% of GDP

Electricity:

106,464,000 kW capacity; 479,600 million kWh produced, 17,872 kWh per capita

(1991)

Industries:

    processed and unprocessed minerals, food products, wood and paper products, transportation equipment, chemicals, fish products, petroleum and natural gas

Agriculture:

    accounts for about 3% of GDP; one of the world's major producers and exporters of grain (wheat and barley); key source of US agricultural imports; large forest resources cover 35% of total land area; commercial fisheries provide annual catch of 1.5 million metric tons, of which 75% is exported

Illicit drugs:

    illicit producer of cannabis for the domestic drug market; use of hydroponics technology permits growers to plant large quantities of high-quality marijuana indoors; growing role as a transit point for heroin and cocaine entering the US market

:Canada Economy

Economic aid:

    donor - ODA and OOF commitments (1970-89), $7.2 billion

Currency:

    Canadian dollar (plural - dollars); 1 Canadian dollar (Can$) = 100 cents

Exchange rates:

    Canadian dollars (Can$) per US$1 - 1.1565 (January 1992), 1.1457 (1991), 1.1668 (1990), 1.1840 (1989), 1.2307 (1988), 1.3260 (1987)

Fiscal year: 1 April - 31 March

:Canada Communications

Railroads:

    93,544 km total; two major transcontinental freight railway systems - Canadian National (government owned) and Canadian Pacific Railway; passenger service - VIA (government operated)

Highways:

    884,272 km total; 712,936 km surfaced (250,023 km paved), 171,336 km earth

Inland waterways:

    3,000 km, including Saint Lawrence Seaway

Pipelines:

    crude and refined oil 23,564 km; natural gas 74,980 km

Ports:

    Halifax, Montreal, Quebec, Saint John (New Brunswick), Saint John's (Newfoundland), Toronto, Vancouver

Merchant marine:

    70 ships (1,000 GRT or over) totaling 500,904 GRT/727,118 DWT; includes 1 passenger, 3 short-sea passenger, 2 passenger-cargo, 10 cargo, 2 railcar carrier, 1 refrigerated cargo, 8 roll-on/roll-off, 1 container, 28 petroleum tanker, 5 chemical tanker, 1 specialized tanker, 8 bulk; note - does not include ships used exclusively in the Great Lakes

Civil air:

    636 major transport aircraft; Air Canada is the major carrier

Airports:

    1,416 total, 1,168 usable; 455 with permanent-surface runways; 4 with runways over 3,659 m; 30 with runways 2,440-3,659 m; 338 with runways 1,220-2,439 m

Telecommunications:
  excellent service provided by modern media; 18.0 million telephones; broadcast stations - 900 AM, 29 FM, 53 (1,400 repeaters) TV; 5 coaxial submarine cables; over 300 earth stations operating in INTELSAT (including 4 Atlantic Ocean and 1 Pacific Ocean) and domestic systems

:Canada Defense Forces

Branches:
  Canadian Armed Forces (including Mobile Command, Maritime Command, Air Command, Communications Command, Canadian Forces Europe, Training Commands),
  Royal Canadian Mounted Police (RCMP)

Manpower availability:
  males 15-49, 7,366,675; 6,387,459 fit for military service; 190,752 reach military age (17) annually

Defense expenditures:
  exchange rate conversion - $11.4 billion, 1.7% of GDP (FY91); $10.5 billion, NA% of GDP (FY 92)

Cape Verde Geography

Total area: 4,030 km2
Land area: 4,030 km2
Comparative area: slightly larger than Rhode Island
Land boundaries:
  none
Coastline:
  965 km
Maritime claims:
  (measured from claimed archipelagic baselines)
 Exclusive economic zone:
  200 nm
 Territorial sea:
  12 nm
Disputes:
  none
Climate:
  temperate; warm, dry, summer; precipitation very erratic
Terrain:
  steep, rugged, rocky, volcanic
Natural resources:
  salt, basalt rock, pozzolana, limestone, kaolin, fish
Land use:
  arable land 9%; permanent crops NEGL%; meadows and pastures 6%; forest and woodland NEGL%; other 85%; includes irrigated 1%
Environment:
  subject to prolonged droughts; harmattan wind can obscure visibility; volcanically and seismically active; deforestation; overgrazing
Note:
  strategic location 500 km from African coast near major north-south sea

routes; important communications station; important sea and air refueling site

:Cape Verde People

Population: 398,276 (July 1992), growth rate 3.0% (1992)
Birth rate: 48 births/1,000 population (1992)
Death rate: 10 deaths/1,000 population (1992)
Net migration rate: - 8 migrants/1,000 population (1992)
Infant mortality rate: 61 deaths/1,000 live births (1992)
Life expectancy at birth: 60 years male, 64 years female (1992)
Total fertility rate: 6.5 children born/woman (1992)
Nationality:
   noun - Cape Verdean(s); adjective - Cape Verdean
Ethnic divisions:
   Creole (mulatto) about 71%, African 28%, European 1%
Religions:
   Roman Catholicism fused with indigenous beliefs
Languages:
   Portuguese and Crioulo, a blend of Portuguese and West African words
Literacy:
   66% (male NA%, female NA%) age 15 and over can read and write (1989 est.)
Labor force:
   102,000 (1985 est.); agriculture (mostly subsistence) 57%, services 29%,
   industry 14% (1981); 51% of population of working age (1985)
Organized labor:
   Trade Unions of Cape Verde Unity Center (UNTC-CS)

:Cape Verde Government

Long-form name:
   Republic of Cape Verde
Type:
   republic
Capital: Praia
Administrative divisions:
   14 districts (concelhos, singular - concelho); Boa Vista, Brava, Fogo, Maio,
   Paul, Praia, Porto Novo, Ribeira Grande, Sal, Santa Catarina, Santa Cruz,
   Sao Nicolau, Sao Vicente, Tarrafal
Independence:
   5 July 1975 (from Portugal)
Constitution:
   7 September 1980; amended 12 February 1981, December 1988, and 28 September
   1990 (legalized opposition parties)
National holiday:
   Independence Day, 5 July (1975)
Executive branch:
   president, prime minister, deputy minister, secretaries of state, Council of
   Ministers (cabinet)
Legislative branch:
   unicameral People's National Assembly (Assembleia Nacional Popular)
Judicial branch:
   Supreme Tribunal of Justice (Supremo Tribunal de Justia)

Leaders:
  Chief of State:
   President Antonio Monteiro MASCARENHAS (since 22 March 1991)
  Head of Government:
   Prime Minister Carlos VEIGA (since 13 January 1991)
Political parties and leaders:
   Movement for Democracy (MPD), Prime Minister Carlos VEIGA, founder and
   chairman; African Party for Independence of Cape Verde (PAICV), Pedro Verona
   Rodrigues PIRES, chairman
Suffrage:
   universal at age 18
Elections:
  People's National Assembly:
   last held 13 January 1991 (next to be held January 1996); results - percent
   of vote by party NA; seats - (79 total) MPD 56, PAICV 23; note - this
   multiparty Assembly election ended 15 years of single-party rule
  President:
   last held 17 February 1991 (next to be held February 1996); results -
   Antonio Monteiro MASCARENHAS (MPD) received 72.6% of vote
Member of:
   ACP, AfDB, ECA, ECOWAS, FAO, G-77, IBRD, ICAO, IDA, IFAD, ILO, IMF,
IMO,
   INTERPOL, IOM (observer), ITU, LORCS, NAM, OAU, UN, UNCTAD,
UNESCO, UNIDO,
   UPU, WCL, WHO, WMO
Diplomatic representation:
   Ambassador Carlos Alberto Santos SILVA; Chancery at 3415 Massachusetts
   Avenue NW, Washington, DC 20007; telephone (202) 965-6820; there is a Cape
   Verdean Consulate General in Boston
  US:
   Ambassador Francis T. (Terry) McNAMARA; Embassy at Rua Hoji Ya Henda Yen-
na
   81, Praia (mailing address is C. P. 201, Praia); telephone [238] 61-43-63 or
   61-42-53; FAX [238] 61-13-55
:Cape Verde Government

Flag:
   two equal horizontal bands of yellow (top) and green with a vertical red
   band on the hoist side; in the upper portion of the red band is a black
   five-pointed star framed by two corn stalks and a yellow clam shell; uses
   the popular pan-African colors of Ethiopia; similar to the flag of
   Guinea-Bissau, which is longer and has an unadorned black star centered in
   the red band

:Cape Verde Economy

Overview:
   Cape Verde's low per capita GDP reflects a poor natural resource base, a
   17-year drought, and a high birthrate. The economy is service oriented, with
   commerce, transport, and public services accounting for 65% of GDP during
   the period 1985-88. Although nearly 70% of the population lives in rural
   areas, agriculture's share of GDP is only 16%; the fishing sector accounts

for 4%. About 90% of food must be imported. The fishing potential, mostly lobster and tuna, is not fully exploited. In 1988 fishing represented only 3.5% of GDP. Cape Verde annually runs a high trade deficit, financed by remittances from emigrants and foreign aid. Economic reforms launched by the new democratic government in February 1991 are aimed at developing the private sector and attracting foreign investment to diversify the economy.

GDP:
exchange rate conversion - $310 million, per capita $800; real growth rate 4% (1990 est.)

Inflation rate (consumer prices):
10% (1990 est.)

Unemployment rate: 25% (1988)

Budget:
revenues $98.3 million; expenditures $138.4 million, including capital expenditures of $NA (1988 est.)

Exports:
$10.9 million (f.o.b., 1989 est.)
commodities:
fish, bananas, salt
partners:
Portugal 40%, Algeria 31%, Angola, Netherlands (1990 est.)

Imports:
$107.8 million (c.i.f., 1989)
commodities:
petroleum, foodstuffs, consumer goods, industrial products
partners:
Sweden 33%, Spain 11%, Germany 5%, Portugal 3%, France 3%, Netherlands, US (1990 est.)

External debt: $150 million (December 1990 est.)

Industrial production:
growth rate 18% (1988 est.); accounts for 7% of GDP

Electricity:
15,000 kW capacity; 15 million kWh produced, 40 kWh per capita (1991)

Industries:
fish processing, salt mining, clothing factories, ship repair, construction materials, food and beverage production

Agriculture:
accounts for 16% of GDP; largely subsistence farming; bananas are the only export crop; other crops - corn, beans, sweet potatoes, coffee; growth potential of agricultural sector limited by poor soils and limited rainfall; annual food imports required; fish catch provides for both domestic consumption and small exports

Economic aid:
US commitments, including Ex-Im (FY75-89), $88 million; Western (non-US) countries, ODA and OOF bilateral commitments (1970-89), $537 million; OPEC bilateral aid (1979-89), $12 million; Communist countries (1970-89), $36 million

Currency:
Cape Verdean escudo (plural - escudos); 1 Cape Verdean escudo (CVEsc) = 100 centavos

:Cape Verde Economy

Exchange rates:
   Cape Verdean escudos (CVEsc) per US$1 - 71.28 (March 1992), 71.41 (1991),
   64.10 (November 1990), 74.86 (December 1989), 72.01 (1988), 72.5 (1987)
Fiscal year: calendar year

:Cape Verde Communications

Ports:
   Mindelo, Praia
Merchant marine:
   7 cargo ships (1,000 GRT or over) totaling 11,717 GRT/19,000 DWT
Civil air:
   3 major transport aircraft
Airports:
   6 total, 6 usable; 6 with permanent-surface runways; none with runways over
   3,659 m; 1 with runways 2,440-3,659 m; 2 with runways 1,220-2,439 m
Telecommunications:
   interisland radio relay system, high-frequency radio to Senegal and
   Guinea-Bissau; over 1,700 telephones; broadcast stations - 1 AM, 6 FM, 1 TV;
   2 coaxial submarine cables; 1 Atlantic Ocean INTELSAT earth station

:Cape Verde Defense Forces

Branches:
   People's Revolutionary Armed Forces (FARP) - Army and Navy are separate
   components of FARP; Security Service
Manpower availability:
   males 15-49, 72,916; 43,010 fit for military service
Defense expenditures:
   exchange rate conversion - $NA, NA% of GDP

Cayman Islands Geography

Total area: 260 km2
Land area: 260 km2
Comparative area: slightly less than 1.5 times the size of Washington, DC
Land boundaries:
   none
Coastline:
   160 km
Maritime claims:
 Exclusive fishing zone:
   200 nm
 Territorial sea:
   3 nm
Disputes:
   none
Climate:
   tropical marine; warm, rainy summers (May to October) and cool, relatively
   dry winters (November to April)
Terrain:
   low-lying limestone base surrounded by coral reefs
Natural resources:

fish, climate and beaches that foster tourism
Land use:
   arable land 0%; permanent crops 0%; meadows and pastures 8%; forest and
   woodland 23%; other 69%
Environment:
   within the Caribbean hurricane belt
Note:
   important location between Cuba and Central America

:Cayman Islands People

Population: 29,139 (July 1992), growth rate 4.4% (1992)
Birth rate: 16 births/1,000 population (1992)
Death rate: 5 deaths/1,000 population (1992)
Net migration rate: 33 migrants/1,000 population (1992)
Infant mortality rate: 8 deaths/1,000 live births (1992)
Life expectancy at birth: 75 years male, 79 years female (1992)
Total fertility rate: 1.5 children born/woman (1992)
Nationality:
   noun - Caymanian(s); adjective - Caymanian
Ethnic divisions:
   40% mixed, 20% white, 20% black, 20% expatriates of various ethnic groups
Religions:
   United Church (Presbyterian and Congregational), Anglican, Baptist, Roman
   Catholic, Church of God, other Protestant denominations
Languages:
   English
Literacy:
   98% (male 98%, female 98%) age 15 and over having ever attended school
   (1970)
Labor force:
   8,061; service workers 18.7%, clerical 18.6%, construction 12.5%, finance
   and investment 6.7%, directors and business managers 5.9% (1979)
Organized labor:
   Global Seaman's Union; Cayman All Trade Union

:Cayman Islands Government

Long-form name:
   none
Type:
   dependent territory of the UK
Capital: George Town
Administrative divisions:
   8 districts; Creek, Eastern, Midland, South Town, Spot Bay, Stake Bay, West
   End, Western
Independence:
   none (dependent territory of the UK)
Constitution:
   1959, revised 1972
Legal system:
   British common law and local statutes
National holiday:

Constitution Day (first Monday in July)
Executive branch:
  British monarch, governor, Executive Council (cabinet)
Legislative branch:
  unicameral Legislative Assembly
Judicial branch:
  Grand Court, Cayman Islands Court of Appeal
Leaders:
  Chief of State:
  Queen ELIZABETH II (since 6 February 1952), represented by Governor Michael
  GORE (since May 1992)
  Head of Government:
  Governor and President of the Executive Council Alan James SCOTT (since NA
  1987)
Political parties and leaders:
  no formal political parties
Suffrage:
  universal at age 18
Elections:
  Legislative Assembly:
  last held November 1988 (next to be held November 1992); results - percent
  of vote by party NA; seats - (15 total, 12 elected)
Member of:
  CARICOM (observer), CDB, IOC
Diplomatic representation:
  as a dependent territory of the UK, Caymanian interests in the US are
  represented by the UK
  US:
  none
Flag:
  blue, with the flag of the UK in the upper hoist-side quadrant and the
  Caymanian coat of arms on a white disk centered on the outer half of the
  flag; the coat of arms includes a pineapple and turtle above a shield with
  three stars (representing the three islands) and a scroll at the bottom
  bearing the motto HE HATH FOUNDED IT UPON THE SEAS
  HE HATH FOUNDED IT UPON THE SEAS

:Cayman Islands Economy

Overview:
  The economy depends heavily on tourism (70% of GDP and 75% of export
  earnings) and offshore financial services, with the tourist industry aimed
  at the luxury market and catering mainly to visitors from North America.
  About 90% of the islands' food and consumer goods needs must be imported.
  The Caymanians enjoy one of the highest standards of living in the region.
GDP:
  exchange rate conversion - $384 million, per capita $14,500 (1989); real
  growth rate 8% (1990)
Inflation rate (consumer prices):
  8% (1990 est.)
Unemployment rate: NA%

Budget:
    revenues $83.6 million; expenditures $98.9 million, including capital
    expenditures of $13.6 million (1990)
Exports:
    $1.5 million (f.o.b., 1987 est.)
  commodities:
    turtle products, manufactured consumer goods
  partners:
    mostly US
Imports:
    $136 million (c.i.f., 1987 est.)
  commodities:
    foodstuffs, manufactured goods
  partners:
    US, Trinidad and Tobago, UK, Netherlands Antilles, Japan
External debt: $15 million (1986)
Industrial production:
    growth rate NA%
Electricity:
    74,000 kW capacity; 256 million kWh produced, 9,313 kWh per capita (1991)
Industries:
    tourism, banking, insurance and finance, construction, building materials,
    furniture making
Agriculture:
    minor production of vegetables, fruit, livestock; turtle farming
Economic aid:
    US commitments, including Ex-Im (FY70-89), $26.7 million; Western (non-US)
    countries, ODA and OOF bilateral commitments (1970-89), $35 million
Currency:
    Caymanian dollar (plural - dollars); 1 Caymanian dollar (CI$) = 100 cents
Exchange rates:
    Caymanian dollars (CI$) per US$1 - 1.20 (fixed rate)
Fiscal year: 1 April - 31 March

:Cayman Islands Communications

Highways:
    160 km of main roads
Ports:
    George Town, Cayman Brac
Merchant marine:
    32 ships (1,000 GRT or over) totaling 364,174 GRT/560,241 DWT; includes 1
    passenger-cargo, 7 cargo, 8 roll-on/roll-off cargo, 6 petroleum tanker, 1
    chemical tanker, 1 specialized tanker, 1 liquefied gas carrier, 5 bulk, 2
    combination bulk; note - a flag of convenience registry
Civil air:
    2 major transport aircraft
Airports:
    3 total; 3 usable; 2 with permanent-surface runways; none with runways over
    2,439 m; 2 with runways 1,220-2,439 m
Telecommunications:

35,000 telephones; telephone system uses 1 submarine coaxial cable and 1
Atlantic Ocean INTELSAT earth station to link islands and access
international services; broadcast stations - 2 AM, 1 FM, no TV

:Cayman Islands Defense Forces

Branches:
Royal Cayman Islands Police Force (RCIPF)
Note:
defense is the responsibility of the UK

Central African Republic Geography

Total area: 622,980 km2
Land area: 622,980 km2
Comparative area: slightly smaller than Texas
Land boundaries:
5,203 km; Cameroon 797 km, Chad 1,197 km, Congo 467 km, Sudan 1,165 km,
Zaire 1,577 km
Coastline:
none - landlocked
Maritime claims:
none - landlocked
Disputes:
none
Climate:
tropical; hot, dry winters; mild to hot, wet summers
Terrain:
vast, flat to rolling, monotonous plateau; scattered hills in northeast and
southwest
Natural resources:
diamonds, uranium, timber, gold, oil
Land use:
arable land 3%; permanent crops NEGL%; meadows and pastures 5%; forest and
woodland 64%; other 28%
Environment:
hot, dry, dusty harmattan winds affect northern areas; poaching has
diminished reputation as one of last great wildlife refuges; desertification
Note:
landlocked; almost the precise center of Africa

:Central African Republic People

Population: 3,029,080 (July 1992), growth rate 2.6% (1992)
Birth rate: 43 births/1,000 population (1992)
Death rate: 18 deaths/1,000 population (1992)
Net migration rate: 0 migrants/1,000 population (1992)
Infant mortality rate: 135 deaths/1,000 live births (1992)
Life expectancy at birth: 46 years male, 49 years female (1992)
Total fertility rate: 5.5 children born/woman (1992)
Nationality:
noun - Central African(s); adjective - Central African
Ethnic divisions:
about 80 ethnic groups, the majority of which have related ethnic and

linguistic characteristics; Baya 34%, Banda 27%, Sara 10%, Mandjia 21%,
Mboum 4%, M'Baka 4%; 6,500 Europeans, of whom 3,600 are French

Religions:

indigenous beliefs 24%, Protestant 25%, Roman Catholic 25%, Muslim 15%,
other 11%; animistic beliefs and practices strongly influence the Christian
majority

Languages:

French (official); Sangho (lingua franca and national language); Arabic,
Hunsa, Swahili

Literacy:

27% (male 33%, female 15%) age 15 and over can read and write (1990 est.)

Labor force:

775,413 (1986 est.); agriculture 85%, commerce and services 9%, industry 3%,
government 3%; about 64,000 salaried workers; 55% of population of working
age (1985)

Organized labor:

1% of labor force

:Central African Republic Government

Long-form name:

Central African Republic (no short-form name); abbreviated CAR

Type:

republic, one-party presidential regime since 1986

Capital: Bangui

Administrative divisions:

14 prefectures (prefectures, singular - prefecture), 2 economic prefectures*
(prefectures economiques, singular - prefecture economique), and 1
commune**; Bamingui-Bangoran, Bangui** Basse-Kotto, Gribingui*, Haute-Kotto,
Haute-Sangha, Haut-Mbomou, Kemo-Gribingui, Lobaye, Mbomou, Nana-Mambere,
Ombella-Mpoko, Ouaka, Ouham, Ouham-Pende, Sangha*, Vakaga

Independence:

13 August 1960 (from France; formerly Central African Empire)

Constitution:

21 November 1986

Legal system:

based on French law

National holiday:

National Day (proclamation of the republic), 1 December (1958)

Executive branch:

president, prime minister, Council of Ministers (cabinet)

Legislative branch:

unicameral National Assembly (Assemblee Nationale) advised by the Economic
and Regional Council (Conseil Economique et Regional); when they sit
together this is known as the Congress (Congros)

Judicial branch:

Supreme Court (Cour Supreme)

Leaders:

Chief of State::

President Andre-Dieudonne KOLINGBA (since 1 September 1981)

Head of Government::

Prime Minister Edouard FRANCK (since 15 March 1991)

Political parties and leaders:

Centrafrican Democratic Rally Party (RDC), Andre-Dieudonne KOLINGBA; note -
as part of political reforms leading to a democratic system announced in
April 1991, 18 opposition parties have been legalized

Suffrage:

universal at age 21

Elections:

National Assembly:

last held 31 July 1987 (next to be held by end of 1992); results - RDC is
the only party; seats - (52 total) RDC 52

President:

last held 21 November 1986 (next to be held by end of 1992); results -
President KOLINGBA was reelected without opposition

Communists:

small number of Communist sympathizers

Member of:

ACCT, ACP, AfDB, BDEAC, CCC, CEEAC, ECA, FAO, FZ, G-77, GATT, IBRD,
ICAO,

ICFTU, IDA, IFAD, ILO, IMF, INTELSAT, INTERPOL, IOC, ITU, LORCS,
NAM, OAU,

UDEAC, UN, UNCTAD, UNESCO, UNIDO, UPU, WCL, WHO, WIPO, WMO

Diplomatic representation:

Ambassador Jean-Pierre SOHAHONG-KOMBET; Chancery at 1618 22nd Street
NW,

Washington, DC 20008; telephone (202) 483-7800 or 7801

US:

Ambassador Daniel H. SIMPSON; Embassy at Avenue du President David Dacko,
Bangui (mailing address is B. P. 924, Bangui); telephone 61-02-00, 61-25-78,
or 61-43-33; FAX [190] (236) 61-44-94

:Central African Republic Government

Flag:

four equal horizontal bands of blue (top), white, green, and yellow with a
vertical red band in center; there is a yellow five-pointed star on the
hoist side of the blue band

:Central African Republic Economy

Overview:

Subsistence agriculture, including forestry, is the backbone of the CAR
economy, with more than 70% of the population living in the countryside. In
1988 the agricultural sector generated about 40% of GDP. Agricultural
products accounted for about 60% of export earnings and the diamond industry
for 30%. The country's 1991 budget deficit was US $70 million and in 1992 is
expected to be about the same. Important constraints to economic development
include the CAR's landlocked position, a poor transportation system, and a
weak human resource base. Multilateral and bilateral development assistance,
particularly from France, plays a major role in providing capital for new
investment.

GDP:

exchange rate conversion - $1.3 billion, per capita $440; real growth rate -

3.0% (1990 est.)

Inflation rate (consumer prices):

-3.0% (1990 est.)

Unemployment rate: 30% in Bangui (1988 est.)

Budget:

revenues $121 million; expenditures $193 million, including capital
expenditures of $NA million (1991 est.)

Exports:

$151.3 million (1990 est.)

commodities:

diamonds, cotton, coffee, timber, tobacco

partners:

France, Belgium, Italy, Japan, US

Imports:

$214.5 million (1990 est.)

commodities:

food, textiles, petroleum products, machinery, electrical equipment, motor
vehicles, chemicals, pharmaceuticals, consumer goods, industrial products

partners:

France, other EC countries, Japan, Algeria, Yugoslavia

External debt: $700 million (1990 est.)

Industrial production:

0.8% (1988); accounts for 12% of GDP

Electricity:

40,000 kW capacity; 95 million kWh produced, 30 kWh per capita (1991)

Industries:

diamond mining, sawmills, breweries, textiles, footwear, assembly of
bicycles and motorcycles

Agriculture:

accounts for 40% of GDP; self-sufficient in food production except for
grain; commercial crops - cotton, coffee, tobacco, timber; food crops -
manioc, yams, millet, corn, bananas

Economic aid:

US commitments, including Ex-Im (FY70-89), $49 million; Western (non-US)
countries, ODA and OOF bilateral commitments (1970-89), $1.5 billion; OPEC
bilateral aid (1979-89), $6 million; Communist countries (1970-89), $38
million

Currency:

Communaute Financiere Africaine franc (plural - francs); 1 CFA franc (CFAF)
= 100 centimes

Exchange rates:

Communaute Financiere Africaine francs (CFAF) per US$1 - 269.01 (January
1992), 282.11 (1991), 272.26 (1990), 319.01 (1989), 297.85 (1988), 300.54
(1987)

:Central African Republic Economy

Fiscal year: calendar year

:Central African Republic Communications

Highways:

22,000 km total; 458 km bituminous, 10,542 km improved earth, 11,000 unimproved earth

Inland waterways:
800 km; traditional trade carried on by means of shallow-draft dugouts;
Oubangui is the most important river

Civil air:
2 major transport aircraft

Airports:
66 total, 52 usable; 4 with permanent-surface runways; none with runways
over 3,659 m; 2 with runways 2,440-3,659 m; 22 with runways 1,220-2,439 m

Telecommunications:
fair system; network relies primarily on radio relay links, with
low-capacity, low-powered radiocommunication also used; broadcast stations -
1 AM, 1 FM, 1 TV; 1 Atlantic Ocean INTELSAT earth station

:Central African Republic Defense Forces

Branches:
Central African Army (including Republican Guard), Air Force, National
Gendarmerie, Police Force

Manpower availability:
males 15-49, 677,889; 354,489 fit for military service

Defense expenditures:
exchange rate conversion - $23 million, 1.8% of GDP (1989 est.)

Chad Geography

Total area: 1,284,000 km2
Land area: 1,259,200 km2
Comparative area: slightly more than three times the size of California
Land boundaries:
5,968 km; Cameroon 1,094 km, Central African Republic 1,197 km, Libya 1,055
km, Niger 1,175 km, Nigeria 87 km, Sudan 1,360 km

Coastline:
none - landlocked

Maritime claims:
none - landlocked

Disputes:
Libya claims and occupies the 100,000 km2 Aozou Strip in the far north;
demarcation of international boundaries in Lake Chad, the lack of which has
led to border incidents in the past, is completed and awaiting ratification
by Cameroon, Chad, Niger, and Nigeria

Climate:
tropical in south, desert in north

Terrain:
broad, arid plains in center, desert in north, mountains in northwest,
lowlands in south

Natural resources:
crude oil (unexploited but exploration under way), uranium, natron, kaolin,
fish (Lake Chad)

Land use:
arable land 2%; permanent crops NEGL%; meadows and pastures 36%; forest and
woodland 11%; other 51%; includes irrigated NEGL%

Environment:

hot, dry, dusty harmattan winds occur in north; drought and desertification adversely affecting south; subject to plagues of locusts

Note:

landlocked; Lake Chad is the most significant water body in the Sahel

:Chad People

Population: 5,238,908 (July 1992), growth rate 2.1% (1992)

Birth rate: 42 births/1,000 population (1992)

Death rate: 21 deaths/1,000 population (1992)

Net migration rate: 0 migrants/1,000 population (1992)

Infant mortality rate: 136 deaths/1,000 live births (1992)

Life expectancy at birth: 39 years male, 41 years female (1992)

Total fertility rate: 5.3 children born/woman (1992)

Nationality:

noun - Chadian(s); adjective - Chadian

Ethnic divisions:

some 200 distinct ethnic groups, most of whom are Muslims (Arabs, Toubou, Hadjerai, Fulbe, Kotoko, Kanembou, Baguirmi, Boulala, Zaghawa, and Maba) in the north and center and non-Muslims (Sara, Ngambaye, Mbaye, Goulaye, Moundang, Moussei, Massa) in the south; some 150,000 nonindigenous, of whom 1,000 are French

Religions:

Muslim 44%, Christian 33%, indigenous beliefs, animism 23%

Languages:

French and Arabic (official); Sara and Sango in south; more than 100 different languages and dialects are spoken

Literacy:

30% (male 42%, female 18%) age 15 and over can read and write French or Arabic (1990 est.)

Labor force:

NA; agriculture (engaged in unpaid subsistence farming, herding, and fishing) 85%

Organized labor:

about 20% of wage labor force

:Chad Government

Long-form name:

Republic of Chad

Type:

republic

Capital: N'Djamena

Administrative divisions:

14 prefectures (prefectures, singular - prefecture); Batha, Biltine, Borkou-Ennedi-Tibesti, Chari-Baguirmi, Guera, Kanem, Lac, Logone Occidental, Logone Oriental, Mayo-Kebbi, Moyen-Chari, Ouaddai, Salamat, Tandjile

Independence:

11 August 1960 (from France)

Constitution:

22 December 1989, suspended 3 December 1990; Provisional National Charter 1 March 1991

Legal system:

based on French civil law system and Chadian customary law; has not accepted compulsory ICJ jurisdiction

National holiday:
  11 August
Executive branch:
  president, Council of State (cabinet)
Legislative branch:
  the National Consultative Council (Conseil National Consultatif) was disbanded 3 December 1990 and replaced by the Provisional Council of the Republic; 30 members appointed by President DEBY on 8 March 1991
Judicial branch:
  Court of Appeal
Leaders:
  Chief of State:
  Col. Idriss DEBY (since 4 December 1990)
  Head of Government:
  Prime Minister Jean ALINGUE Bawoyeu (since 8 March 1991)
Political parties and leaders:
  Patriotic Salvation Movement (MPS; former dissident group), Idriss DEBY, chairman; President DEBY has promised political pluralism, a new constitution, and free elections by September 1993; numerous dissident groups; national conference to be held in 1992
Suffrage:
  universal at age NA
Elections:
  National Consultative Council:
  last held 8 July 1990; disbanded 3 December 1990
  President:
  last held 10 December 1989 (next to be held NA); results - President Hissein HABRE was elected without opposition; note - the government of then President HABRE fell on 1 December 1990, and Idriss DEBY seized power on 3 December 1990; national conference scheduled for mid-1992 and election to follow in 1993
Communists:
  no front organizations or underground party; probably a few Communists and some sympathizers
Other political or pressure groups:
  NA
Member of:
  ACCT, ACP, AfDB, BDEAC, CEEAC, ECA, FAO, FZ, G-77, GATT, IBRD, ICAO, ICFTU,
  IDA, IDB, IFAD, ILO, IMF, INTELSAT, INTERPOL, IOC, ITU, LORCS, NAM, OAU,
  OIC, UDEAC, UN, UNCTAD, UNESCO, UPU, WCL, WHO, WIPO, WMO, WTO
:Chad Government

Diplomatic representation:
  Ambassador ACHEIKH ibn Oumar; Chancery at 2002 R Street NW, Washington, DC
  20009; telephone (202) 462-4009

US:

Ambassador Richard W. BOGOSIAN; Embassy at Avenue Felix Eboue, N'Djamena (mailing address is B. P. 413, N'Djamena); telephone [235] (51) 62-18, 40-09, or 51-62-11; FAX [235] 51-33-72

Flag:

three equal vertical bands of blue (hoist side), yellow, and red; similar to the flag of Romania; also similar to the flag of Andorra, which has a national coat of arms featuring a quartered shield centered in the yellow band; design was based on the flag of France

:Chad Economy

Overview:

The climate, geographic location, and lack of infrastructure and natural resources potential make Chad one of the most underdeveloped countries in the world. Its economy is burdened by the ravages of civil war, conflict with Libya, drought, and food shortages. In 1986 real GDP returned to its 1977 level, with cotton, the major cash crop, accounting for 48% of exports. Over 80% of the work force is employed in subsistence farming and fishing. Industry is based almost entirely on the processing of agricultural products, including cotton, sugarcane, and cattle. Chad is highly dependent on foreign aid, with its economy in trouble and many regions suffering from shortages. Oil companies are exploring areas north of Lake Chad and in the Doba basin in the south. Since coming to power in December 1990, the Deby government has experienced a year of economic chaos.

GDP:

exchange rate conversion - $1.0 billion, per capita $205; real growth rate 0.9% (1989 est.)

Inflation rate (consumer prices):

—4.9% (1989)

Unemployment rate: NA

Budget:

entirely funded by outside donors

Exports:

$174 million (f.o.b., 1990 est.)

commodities:

cotton 48%, cattle 35%, textiles 5%, fish

partners:

France, Nigeria, Cameroon

Imports:

$264 million (c.i.f., 1990 est.)

commodities:

machinery and transportation equipment 39%, industrial goods 20%, petroleum products 13%, foodstuffs 9%; note - excludes military equipment

partners:

US, France, Nigeria, Cameroon

External debt: $530 million (December 1990 est.)

Industrial production:

growth rate 12.9% (1989 est.); accounts for nearly 15% of GDP

Electricity:

40,000 kW capacity; 70 million kWh produced, 15 kWh per capita (1991)

Industries:
   cotton textile mills, slaughterhouses, brewery, natron (sodium carbonate), soap, cigarettes
Agriculture:
   accounts for about 45% of GDP; largely subsistence farming; cotton most important cash crop; food crops include sorghum, millet, peanuts, rice, potatoes, manioc; livestock - cattle, sheep, goats, camels; self-sufficient in food in years of adequate rainfall
Economic aid:
   US commitments, including Ex-Im (FY70-89), $198 million; Western (non-US) countries, ODA and OOF bilateral commitments (1970-89), $1.5 billion; OPEC bilateral aid (1979-89), $28 million; Communist countries (1970-89), $80 million
Currency:
   Communaute Financiere Africaine franc (plural - francs); 1 CFA franc (CFAF) = 100 centimes

:Chad Economy

Exchange rates:
   Communaute Financiere Africaine Francs (CFAF) per US$1 - 269.01 (January 1992), 282.11 (1991), 272.26 (1990), 319.01 (1989), 297.85 (1988), 300.54 (1987)
Fiscal year: calendar year

:Chad Communications

Highways:
   31,322 km total; 32 km bituminous; 7,300 km gravel and laterite; remainder unimproved earth
Inland waterways:
   2,000 km navigable
Civil air:
   3 major transport aircraft
Airports:
   71 total, 55 usable; 4 with permanent-surface runways; none with runways over 3,659 m; 4 with runways 2,440-3,659 m; 25 with runways 1,220-2,439 m
Telecommunications:
   fair system of radiocommunication stations for intercity links; broadcast stations - 6 AM, 1 FM, limited TV service; many facilities are inoperative; 1 Atlantic Ocean INTELSAT earth station

:Chad Defense Forces

Branches:
   Army (includes Ground Forces, Air Force, and Gendarmerie), National Police, Republican Guard
Manpower availability:
   males 15-49, 1,217,728; 632,833 fit for military service; 50,966 reach military age (20) annually
Defense expenditures:
   exchange rate conversion - $39 million, 4.3% of GDP (1988)

   Chile Geography

Total area: 756,950 km2
Land area: 748,800 km2; includes Isla de Pascua (Easter Island) and Isla Sala y Gomez
Comparative area: slightly smaller than twice the size of Montana
Land boundaries:
  6,171 km; Argentina 5,150 km, Bolivia 861 km, Peru 160 km
Coastline:
  6,435 km
Maritime claims:
  Contiguous zone:
   24 nm
  Continental shelf:
   200 nm
  Exclusive economic zone:
   200 nm
  Territorial sea:
   12 nm
Disputes:
   short section of the southern boundary with Argentina is indefinite; Bolivia
   has wanted a sovereign corridor to the South Pacific Ocean since the Atacama
   area was lost to Chile in 1884; dispute with Bolivia over Rio Lauca water
   rights; territorial claim in Antarctica (Chilean Antarctic Territory)
   partially overlaps Argentine claim
Climate:
   temperate; desert in north; cool and damp in south
Terrain:
   low coastal mountains; fertile central valley; rugged Andes in east
Natural resources:
   copper, timber, iron ore, nitrates, precious metals, molybdenum
Land use:
   arable land 7%; permanent crops NEGL%; meadows and pastures 16%; forest and
   woodland 21%; other 56%; includes irrigated 2%
Environment:
   subject to severe earthquakes, active volcanism, tsunami; Atacama Desert one
   of world's driest regions; desertification
Note:
   strategic location relative to sea lanes between Atlantic and Pacific Oceans
   (Strait of Magellan, Beagle Channel, Drake Passage)

:Chile People

Population: 13,528,945 (July 1992), growth rate 1.6% (1992)
Birth rate: 21 births/1,000 population (1992)
Death rate: 6 deaths/1,000 population (1992)
Net migration rate: 0 migrants/1,000 population (1992)
Infant mortality rate: 17 deaths/1,000 live births (1992)
Life expectancy at birth: 71 years male, 77 years female (1992)
Total fertility rate: 2.5 children born/woman (1992)
Nationality:
   noun - Chilean(s); adjective - Chilean
Ethnic divisions:

European and European-Indian 95%, Indian 3%, other 2%

Religions:

Roman Catholic 89%, Protestant 11%, and small Jewish population

Languages:

Spanish

Literacy:

93% (male 94%, female 93%) age 15 and over can read and write (1990 est.)

Labor force:

4,728,000; services 38.3% (includes government 12%); industry and commerce 33.8%; agriculture, forestry, and fishing 19.2%; mining 2.3%; construction 6.4% (1990)

Organized labor:

13% of labor force (1990)

:Chile Government

Long-form name:

Republic of Chile

Type:

republic

Capital: Santiago

Administrative divisions:

13 regions (regiones, singular - region); Aisen del General Carlos Ibanez del Campo, Antofagasta, Araucania, Atacama, Bio-Bio, Coquimbo, Libertador General Bernardo O'Higgins, Los Lagos, Magallanes y de la Antartica Chilena, Maule, Region Metropolitana, Tarapaca, Valparaiso; note - the US does not recognize claims to Antarctica

Independence:

18 September 1810 (from Spain)

Constitution:

11 September 1980, effective 11 March 1981; amended 30 July 1989

Legal system:

based on Code of 1857 derived from Spanish law and subsequent codes influenced by French and Austrian law; judicial review of legislative acts in the Supreme Court; has not accepted compulsory ICJ jurisdiction

National holiday:

Independence Day, 18 September (1810)

Executive branch:

president, Cabinet

Legislative branch:

bicameral National Congress (Congreso Nacional) consisting of an upper house or Senate (Senado) and a lower house or Chamber of Deputies (Camara de Diputados)

Judicial branch:

Supreme Court (Corte Suprema)

Leaders:

 Chief of State and Head of Government:

President Patricio AYLWIN Azocar (since 11 March 1990)

Political parties and leaders:

Concertation of Parties for Democracy now consists mainly of five parties - Christian Democratic Party (PDC), Eduardo FREI Ruiz-Tagle; Party for

Democracy (PPD), Erich SCHNAKE; Radical Party (PR), Carlos GONZALEZ Marquez;
Social Democratic Party (PSP), Roberto MUNOZ Barros; Socialist Party (PS), Ricardo NUNEZ; National Renovation (RN), Andres ALLAMAND; Independent Democratic Union (UDI), Julio DITTBORN; Center-Center Union (UCC), Francisco Juner ERRAZURIZA; Communist Party of Chile (PCCh), Volodia TEITELBOIM; Movement of Revolutionary Left (MIR) is splintered, no single leader

Suffrage:
universal and compulsory at age 18

Elections:
Chamber of Deputies:
last held 14 December 1989 (next to be held December 1993 or January 1994); results - percent of vote by party NA; seats - (120 total) Concertation of Parties for Democracy 72 (PDC 38, PPD 17, PR 5, other 12), RN 29, UDI 11, right-wing independents 8

President:
last held 14 December 1989 (next to be held December 1993 or January 1994); results - Patricio AYLWIN (PDC) 55.2%, Hernan BUCHI 29.4%, other 15.4%

Senate:
last held 14 December 1989 (next to be held December 1993 or January 1994); results - percent of vote by party NA; seats - (46 total, 38 elected) Concertation of Parties for Democracy 22 (PDC 13, PPD 5, PR 2, PSD 1, PRSD 1), RN 6, UDI 2, independents 8

:Chile Government

Communists:
The PCCh has legal party status and has less than 60,000 members

Other political or pressure groups:
revitalized university student federations at all major universities dominated by opposition political groups; labor - United Labor Central (CUT) includes trade unionists from the country's five largest labor confederations; Roman Catholic Church

Member of:
CCC, ECLAC, FAO, G-11, G-77, GATT, IADB, IAEA, IBRD, ICAO, ICFTU, IDA, IFAD,
IFC, ILO, IMF, IMO, INMARSAT, INTELSAT, INTERPOL, IOC, IOM, ISO, ITU, LAES,
LAIA, LORCS, OAS, OPANAL, PCA, RG, UN, UNCTAD, UNESCO, UNIDO, UNMOGIP,
UNTSO, UPU, WCL, WFTV, WHO, WIPO, WMO, WTO

Diplomatic representation:
Ambassador Patricio SILVA Echenique; Chancery at 1732 Massachusetts Avenue NW, Washington, DC 20036; telephone (202) 785-1746; there are Chilean Consulates General in Houston, Los Angeles, Miami, New York, Philadelphia, and San Francisco

US:
Ambassador Curtis KAMMAN; Embassy at Codina Building, 1343 Agustinas, Santiago (mailing address is APO AA 34033); telephone [56] (2) 671-0133; FAX [56] (2) 699-1141

Flag:

two equal horizontal bands of white (top) and red; there is a blue square
the same height as the white band at the hoist-side end of the white band;
the square bears a white five-pointed star in the center; design was based
on the US flag

:Chile Economy

Overview:

The government of President Aylwin, which took power in 1990, has opted to
retain the orthodox economic policies of Pinochet, although the share of
spending for social welfare has risen slightly. In 1991 growth in GDP
recovered to 5.5% (led by consumer spending) after only 2.1% growth in 1990.
The tight monetary policy of 1990 helped cut the rate of inflation from
27.3% in 1990 to 18.7% in 1991. Despite a 12% drop in copper prices, the
trade surplus rose in 1991, and international reserves increased.
Inflationary pressures are not expected to ease much in 1992, and economic
growth is likely to approach 7%.

GDP:

exchange rate conversion - $30.5 billion, per capita $2,300; real growth
rate 5.5% (1991 est.)

Inflation rate (consumer prices):

18.7% (1991)

Unemployment rate: 6.5% (1991)

Budget:

revenues $7.6 billion; expenditures $8.3 billion, including capital
expenditures of $772 million (1991 est.)

Exports:

$8.9 billion (f.o.b., 1991)

commodities:

copper 50%, other metals and minerals 7%, wood products 6.5%, fish and
fishmeal 9%, fruits 5% (1989)

partners:

EC 36%, US 18%, Japan 14%, Brazil 6% (1989)

Imports:

$7.4 billion (f.o.b., 1991)

commodities:

petroleum, wheat, capital goods, spare parts, raw materials

partners:

EC 20%, US 20%, Japan 11%, Brazil 10% (1989)

External debt: $16.2 billion (October 1991)

Industrial production:

growth rate 5.9% (1991 est.); accounts for 36% of GDP

Electricity:

5,502,800 kW capacity; 21,470 million kWh produced, 1,616 kWh per capita
(1991)

Industries:

copper, other minerals, foodstuffs, fish processing, iron and steel, wood
and wood products, transport equipment, cement, textiles

Agriculture:

accounts for about 9% of GDP (including fishing and forestry); major
exporter of fruit, fish, and timber products; major crops - wheat, corn,

grapes, beans, sugar beets, potatoes, deciduous fruit; livestock products -
beef, poultry, wool; self-sufficient in most foods; 1989 fish catch of 6.1
million metric tons; net agricultural importer

Economic aid:

US commitments, including Ex-Im (FY70-89), $521 million; Western (non-US)
countries, ODA and OOF bilateral commitments (1970-89), $1.6 billion;
Communist countries (1970-89), $386 million

Currency:

Chilean peso (plural - pesos); 1 Chilean peso (Ch$) = 100 centavos

Exchange rates:

Chilean pesos (Ch$) per US$1 - 368.66 (January 1992), 349.37 (1991), 305.06
(1990), 267.16 (1989), 245.05 (1988), 219.54 (1987)

:Chile Economy

Fiscal year: calendar year

:Chile Communications

Railroads:

7,766 km total; 3,974 km 1.676-meter gauge, 150 km 1.435-meter standard
gauge, 3,642 km 1.000-meter gauge; electrification, 1,865 km 1.676-meter
gauge, 80 km 1.000-meter gauge

Highways:

79,025 km total; 9,913 km paved, 33,140 km gravel, 35,972 km improved and
unimproved earth (1984)

Inland waterways:

725 km

Pipelines:

crude oil 755 km; petroleum products 785 km; natural gas 320 km

Ports:

Antofagasta, Iquique, Puerto Montt, Punta Arenas, Valparaiso, San Antonio,
Talcahuano, Arica

Merchant marine:

33 ships (1,000 GRT or over) totaling 468,873 GRT/780,932 DWT; includes 11
cargo, 1 refrigerated cargo, 3 roll-on/roll-off cargo, 2 petroleum tanker, 1
chemical tanker, 3 liquefied gas, 3 combination ore/oil, 9 bulk; note - in
addition, 2 naval tanker and 2 military transport are sometimes used
commercially

Civil air:

29 major transport aircraft

Airports:

390 total, 349 usable; 48 with permanent-surface runways; none with runways
over 3,659 m; 12 with runways 2,440-3,659 m; 58 with runways 1,220-2,439 m

Telecommunications:

modern telephone system based on extensive microwave relay facilities;
768,000 telephones; broadcast stations - 159 AM, no FM, 131 TV, 11
shortwave; satellite ground stations - 2 Atlantic Ocean INTELSAT and 3
domestic

:Chile Defense Forces

Branches:

Army of the Nation, National Navy (including Naval Air, Coast Guard, and

Marines), Air Force of the Nation, Carabineros of Chile (National Police), Investigative Police

Manpower availability:

males 15-49, 3,600,654; 2,685,924 fit for military service; 118,480 reach military age (19) annually

Defense expenditures:

exchange rate conversion - $1 billion, 3.4% of GDP (1991 est.)

China Geography

Total area: 9,596,960 km2
Land area: 9,326,410 km2
Comparative area: slightly larger than the US

Land boundaries:

22,143.34 km; Afghanistan 76 km, Bhutan 470 km, Burma 2,185 km, Hong Kong 30 km, India 3,380 km, Kazakhstan 1,533 km, North Korea 1,416 km, Kyrgyzstan 858 km, Laos 423 km, Macau 0.34 km, Mongolia 4,673 km, Nepal 1,236 km, Pakistan 523 km, Russia (northeast) 3,605 km, Russia (northwest) 40 km, Tajikistan 414 km, Vietnam 1,281 km

Coastline:

14,500 km

Maritime claims:

Continental shelf:

claim to shallow areas of East China Sea and Yellow Sea

Territorial sea:

12 nm

Disputes:

boundary with India; bilateral negotiations are under way to resolve disputed sections of the boundary with Russia; boundary with Tajikistan under dispute: a short section of the boundary with North Korea is indefinite; involved in a complex dispute over the Spratly Islands with Malaysia, Philippines, Taiwan, Vietnam, and possibly Brunei; maritime boundary dispute with Vietnam in the Gulf of Tonkin; Paracel Islands occupied by China, but claimed by Vietnam and Taiwan; claims Japanese-administered Senkaku-shoto, as does Taiwan, (Senkaku Islands/Diaoyu Tai)

Climate:

extremely diverse; tropical in south to subarctic in north

Terrain:

mostly mountains, high plateaus, deserts in west; plains, deltas, and hills in east

Natural resources:

coal, iron ore, crude oil, mercury, tin, tungsten, antimony, manganese, molybdenum, vanadium, magnetite, aluminum, lead, zinc, uranium, world's largest hydropower potential

Land use:

arable land 10%; permanent crops NEGL%; meadows and pastures 31%; forest and woodland 14%; other 45%; includes irrigated 5%

Environment:

frequent typhoons (about five times per year along southern and eastern coasts), damaging floods, tsunamis, earthquakes; deforestation; soil

erosion; industrial pollution; water pollution; air pollution;
desertification
Note:
   world's third-largest country (after Russia and Canada)

:China People

Population: 1,169,619,601 (July 1992), growth rate 1.6% (1992)
Birth rate: 22 births/1,000 population (1992)
Death rate: 7 deaths/1,000 population (1992)
Net migration rate: 0 migrants/1,000 population (1992)
Infant mortality rate: 32 deaths/1,000 live births (1992)
Life expectancy at birth: 69 years male, 72 years female (1992)
Total fertility rate: 2.3 children born/woman (1992)
Nationality:
   noun - Chinese (singular and plural); adjective - Chinese
Ethnic divisions:
   Han Chinese 93.3%; Zhuang, Uygur, Hui, Yi, Tibetan, Miao, Manchu, Mongol,
   Buyi, Korean, and other nationalities 6.7%
Religions:
   officially atheist, but traditionally pragmatic and eclectic; most important
   elements of religion are Confucianism, Taoism, and Buddhism; Muslim 2-3%,
   Christian 1% (est.)
Languages:
   Standard Chinese (Putonghua) or Mandarin (based on the Beijing dialect);
   also Yue (Cantonese), Wu (Shanghainese), Minbei (Fuzhou), Minnan
   (Hokkien-Taiwanese), Xiang, Gan, Hakka dialects, and minority languages (see
   ethnic divisions)
Literacy:
   73% (male 84%, female 62%) age 15 and over can read and write (1990 est.)
Labor force:
   567,400,000; agriculture and forestry 60%, industry and commerce 25%,
   construction and mining 5%, social services 5%, other 5% (1990 est.)
Organized labor:
   All-China Federation of Trade Unions (ACFTU) follows the leadership of the
   Chinese Communist Party; membership over 80 million or about 65% of the
   urban work force (1985)

:China Government

Long-form name:
   People's Republic of China; abbreviated PRC
Type:
   Communist Party - led state
Capital: Beijing
Administrative divisions:
   23 provinces (sheng, singular and plural), 5 autonomous regions* (zizhiqu,
   singular and plural), and 3 municipalities** (shi, singular and plural);
   Anhui, Beijing Shi**, Fujian, Gansu, Guangdong, Guangxi*, Guizhou, Hainan,
   Hebei, Heilongjiang, Henan, Hubei, Hunan, Jiangsu, Jiangxi, Jilin, Liaoning,
   Nei Mongol*, Ningxia*, Qinghai, Shaanxi, Shandong, Shanghai Shi**, Shanxi,
   Sichuan, Tianjin Shi**, Xinjiang*, Xizang*, Yunnan, Zhejiang; note - China
   considers Taiwan its 23rd province

Independence:

unification under the Qin (Ch'in) Dynasty 221 BC, Qing (Ch'ing) Dynasty
replaced by the Republic on 12 February 1912, People's Republic established
1 October 1949

Constitution:

most recent promulgated 4 December 1982

Legal system:

a complex amalgam of custom and statute, largely criminal law; rudimentary
civil code in effect since 1 January 1987; new legal codes in effect since 1
January 1980; continuing efforts are being made to improve civil,
administrative, criminal, and commercial law

National holiday:

National Day, 1 October (1949)

Executive branch:

president, vice president, premier, five vice premiers, State Council

Legislative branch:

unicameral National People's Congress (Quanguo Renmin Daibiao Dahui)

Judicial branch:

Supreme People's Court

Leaders:

Chief of State:

President YANG Shangkun (since 8 April 1988); Vice President WANG Zhen
(since 8 April 1988)

Chief of State and Head of Government (de facto):

DENG Xiaoping (since mid-1977)

Head of Government:

Premier LI Peng (Acting Premier since 24 November 1987, Premier since 9
April 1988); Vice Premier YAO Yilin (since 2 July 1979); Vice Premier TIAN
Jiyun (since 20 June 1983); Vice Premier WU Xueqian (since 12 April 1988);
Vice Premier ZOU Jiahua (since 8 April 1991); Vice Premier ZHU Rongji (since
8 April 1991)

Political parties and leaders:

- Chinese Communist Party (CCP), JIANG Zemin, general secretary of the
Central Committee (since 24 June 1989); also, eight registered small parties
controlled by CCP

Suffrage:

universal at age 18

Elections:

National People's Congress:

last held March 1988 (next to be held March 1993); results - CCP is the only
party but there are also independents; seats - (2,976 total) CCP and
independents 2,976 (indirectly elected at county or xian level)

President:

last held 8 April 1988 (next to be held March 1993); results - YANG Shangkun
was nominally elected by the Seventh National People's Congress

:China Government

Communists:

49,000,000 party members (1990 est.)

Other political or pressure groups:

such meaningful opposition as exists consists of loose coalitions, usually
within the party and government organization, that vary by issue

Member of:

AfDB, APEC, AsDB, CCC, ESCAP, FAO, IAEA, IBRD, ICAO, IDA, IFAD, IFC, ILO,

IMF, IMO, INMARSAT, INTELSAT, INTERPOL, IOC, ISO, ITU, LORCS, PCA, UN,

UNCTAD, UNESCO, UNHCR, UNIDO, UN Security Council, UNTSO, UN Trusteeship

Council, UPU, WHO, WIPO, WMO, WTO

Diplomatic representation:

Ambassador ZHU Qizhen; Chancery at 2300 Connecticut Avenue NW, Washington,
DC 20008; telephone (202) 328-2500 through 2502; there are Chinese
Consulates General in Chicago, Houston, Los Angeles, New York, and San
Francisco

US:

Ambassador J. Stapleton ROY; Embassy at Xiu Shui Bei Jie 3, Beijing (mailing
address is 100600, PSC 461, Box 50, Beijing or FPO AP 96521-0002); telephone
[86] (1) 532-3831; FAX [86] (1) 532-3178; there are US Consulates General in
Chengdu, Guangzhou, Shanghai, and Shenyang

Flag:

red with a large yellow five-pointed star and four smaller yellow
five-pointed stars (arranged in a vertical arc toward the middle of the
flag) in the upper hoist-side corner

:China Economy

Overview:

Beginning in late 1978 the Chinese leadership has been trying to move the
economy from the sluggish Soviet-style centrally planned economy to a more
productive and flexible economy with market elements, but still within the
framework of monolithic Communist control. To this end the authorities have
switched to a system of household responsibility in agriculture in place of
the old collectivization, increased the authority of local officials and
plant managers in industry, permitted a wide variety of small-scale
enterprise in services and light manufacturing, and opened the foreign
economic sector to increased trade and joint ventures. The most gratifying
result has been a strong spurt in production, particularly in agriculture in
the early 1980s. Industry also has posted major gains, especially in coastal
areas near Hong Kong and opposite Taiwan, where foreign investment and
modern production methods have helped spur production of both domestic and
export goods. Aggregate output has more than doubled since 1978. On the
darker side, the leadership has often experienced in its hybrid system the
worst results of socialism (bureaucracy, lassitude, corruption) and of
capitalism (windfall gains and stepped-up inflation). Beijing thus has
periodically backtracked, retightening central controls at intervals and
thereby lessening the credibility of the reform process. In 1991 output rose
substantially, particularly in the favored coastal areas. Popular
resistance, changes in central policy, and loss of authority by rural cadres
have weakened China's population control program, which is essential to the
nation's long-term economic viability.

GNP:
  $NA, per capita $NA; real growth rate 6% (1991)
Inflation rate (consumer prices):
  2.1% (1991)
Unemployment rate: 4.0% in urban areas (1991)
Budget:
  deficit $9.5 billion (1990)
Exports:
  $71.9 billion (f.o.b., 1991)
 commodities:
  textiles, garments, telecommunications and recording equipment, petroleum,
  minerals
 partners:
  Hong Kong, Japan, US, USSR, Singapore (1990)
Imports:
  $63.8 billion (c.i.f., 1991)
 commodities:
  specialized industrial machinery, chemicals, manufactured goods, steel,
  textile yarn, fertilizer
 partners:
  Hong Kong, Japan, US, Germany, Taiwan (1990)
External debt: $51 billion (1990 est.)
Industrial production:
  growth rate 14.0% (1991); accounts for 45% of GNP
Electricity:
  138,000,000 kW capacity (1990); 670,000 million kWh produced (1991), 582 kWh
  per capita (1991)
Industries:
  iron, steel, coal, machine building, armaments, textiles, petroleum, cement,
  chemical fertilizers, consumer durables, food processing

:China Economy

Agriculture:
  accounts for 26% of GNP; among the world's largest producers of rice,
  potatoes, sorghum, peanuts, tea, millet, barley, and pork; commercial crops
  include cotton, other fibers, and oilseeds; produces variety of livestock
  products; basically self-sufficient in food; fish catch of 8 million metric
  tons in 1986
Illicit drugs:
  transshipment point for heroin produced in the Golden Triangle
Economic aid:
  donor - to less developed countries (1970-89) $7.0 billion; US commitments,
  including Ex-Im (FY70-87), $220.7 million; Western (non-US) countries, ODA
  and OOF bilateral commitments (1970-87), $13.5 billion
Currency:
  yuan (plural - yuan); 1 yuan (Y) = 10 jiao
Exchange rates:
  yuan (Y) per US$1 - 5.4481 (January 1992), 5.3234 (1991), 4.7832 (1990),
  3.7651 (1989), 3.7221 (1988), 3.7221 (1987)
Fiscal year: calendar year

:China Communications

Railroads:

total about 54,000 km common carrier lines; 53,400 km 1.435-meter standard gauge; 600 km 1.000-meter gauge; of these 11,200 km are double track standard-gauge lines; 6,900 km electrified (1990); 10,000 km dedicated industrial lines (gauges range from 0.762 to 1.067 meters)

Highways:

about 1,029,000 km (1990) all types roads; 170,000 km (est.) paved roads, 648,000 km (est.) gravel/improved earth roads, 211,000 km (est.) unimproved earth roads and tracks

Inland waterways:

138,600 km; about 109,800 km navigable

Pipelines:

crude oil 9,700 km (1990); petroleum products 1,100 km; natural gas 6,200 km

Ports:

Dalian, Guangzhou, Huangpu, Qingdao, Qinhuangdao, Shanghai, Xingang, Zhanjiang, Ningbo, Xiamen, Tanggu, Shantou

Merchant marine:

1,454 ships (1,000 GRT or over) totaling 13,887,312 GRT/20,916,127 DWT; includes 25 passenger, 42 short-sea passenger, 18 passenger-cargo, 6 cargo/training, 801 cargo, 10 refrigerated cargo, 77 container, 19 roll-on/roll-off cargo, 1 multifunction/barge carrier, 177 petroleum tanker, 10 chemical tanker, 254 bulk, 3 liquefied gas, 1 vehicle carrier, 9 combination bulk, 1 barge carrier; note - China beneficially owns an additional 194 ships (1,000 GRT or over) totaling approximately 7,077,089 DWT that operate under Panamanian, British, Hong Kong, Maltese, Liberian, Vanuatu, Cyprus, and Saint Vincent registry

Civil air:

284 major transport aircraft (1988 est.)

Airports:

330 total, 330 usable; 260 with permanent-surface runways; fewer than 10 with runways over 3,500 m; 90 with runways 2,440-3,659 m; 200 with runways 1,220-2,439 m

Telecommunications:

domestic and international services are increasingly available for private use; unevenly distributed internal system serves principal cities, industrial centers, and most townships; 11,000,000 telephones (December 1989); broadcast stations - 274 AM, unknown FM, 202 (2,050 repeaters) TV; more than 215 million radio receivers; 75 million TVs; satellite earth stations - 4 Pacific Ocean INTELSAT, 1 Indian Ocean INTELSAT, 1 INMARSAT, and 55 domestic

:China Defense Forces

Branches;

People's Liberation Army (PLA), PLA Navy (including Marines), PLA Air Force, People's Armed Police

Manpower availability:

males 15-49, 339,554,712; 188,995,620 fit for military service; 11,691,967 reach military age (18) annually

Defense expenditures:
  exchange rate conversion - $12-15 billion, NA of GNP (1991 est.)

Christmas Island Geography

Total area: 135 km2
Land area: 135 km2
Comparative area: about 0.8 times the size of Washington, DC
Land boundaries:
  none
Coastline:
  138.9 km
Maritime claims:
 Contiguous zone:
  12 nm
 Exclusive fishing zone:
  200 nm
 Territorial sea:
  3 nm
Disputes:
  none
Climate:
  tropical; heat and humidity moderated by trade winds
Terrain:
  steep cliffs along coast rise abruptly to central plateau
Natural resources:
  phosphate
Land use:
  arable land 0%; permanent crops 0%; meadows and pastures 0%; forest and
  woodland 0%; other 100%
Environment:
  almost completely surrounded by a reef
Note:
  located along major sea lanes of Indian Ocean

:Christmas Island People

Population: 929 (July 1992), growth rate NA% (1992)
Birth rate: NA births/1,000 population (1992)
Death rate: NA deaths/1,000 population (1992)
Net migration rate: NA migrants/1,000 population (1992)
Infant mortality rate: NA deaths/1,000 live births (1992)
Life expectancy at birth: NA years male, NA years female (1992)
Total fertility rate: NA children born/woman (1992)
Nationality:
  noun - Christmas Islander(s); adjective - Christmas Island
Ethnic divisions:
  Chinese 61%, Malay 25%, European 11%, other 3%; no indigenous population
Religions:
  Buddhist 36.1%, Muslim 25.4%, Christian 17.7% (Roman Catholic 8.2%, Church
  of England 3.2%, Presbyterian 0.9%, Uniting Church 0.4%, Methodist 0.2%,
  Baptist 0.1%, and other 4.7%), none 12.7%, unknown 4.6%, other 3.5% (1981)
Languages:

English

Literacy:
  NA% (male NA%, female NA%)

Labor force:
  NA; all workers are employees of the Phosphate Mining Company of Christmas Island, Ltd.

Organized labor:
  NA

:Christmas Island Government

Long-form name:
  Territory of Christmas Island

Type:
  territory of Australia

Capital: The Settlement

Administrative divisions:
  none (territory of Australia)

Independence:
  none (territory of Australia)

Constitution:
  Christmas Island Act of 1958

Legal system:
  under the authority of the governor general of Australia

National holiday:
  NA

Executive branch:
  British monarch, governor general of Australia, administrator, Advisory Council (cabinet)

Legislative branch:
  none

Judicial branch:
  none

Leaders:
  Chief of State:
  Queen ELIZABETH II (since 6 February 1952)
  Head of Government:
  Administrator W. A. MCKENZIE (since NA)

Member of:
  none

Diplomatic representation:
  none (territory of Australia)

Flag:
  the flag of Australia is used

:Christmas Island Economy

Overview:
  Phosphate mining had been the only significant economic activity, but in December 1987 the Australian Government closed the mine as no longer economically viable. Plans have been under way to reopen the mine and also to build a casino and hotel to develop tourism, with a possible opening date during the first half of 1992.

GDP:
  NA - $NA, per capita $NA; real growth rate NA%
Inflation rate (consumer prices):
  NA%
Unemployment rate: NA%
Budget:
  revenues $NA; expenditures $NA, including capital expenditures of $NA
Exports:
  $NA
 commodities:
  phosphate
 partners:
  Australia, NZ
Imports:
  $NA
 commodities:
  NA
 partners:
  NA
External debt: $NA
Industrial production:
  growth rate NA%
Electricity:
  11,000 kW capacity; 30 million kWh produced, 13,170 kWh per capita (1990)
Industries:
  phosphate extraction (near depletion)
Agriculture:
  NA
Economic aid:
  none
Currency:
  Australian dollar (plural - dollars); 1 Australian dollar ($A) = 100 cents
Exchange rates:
  Australian dollars ($A) per US$1 - 1.3360 (January 1992), 1.2836 (1991),
  1.2799 (1990), 1.2618 (1989), 1.2752 (1988), 1.4267 (1987)
Fiscal year: 1 July - 30 June

:Christmas Island Communications

Ports:
  Flying Fish Cove
Airports:
  1 usable with permanent-surface runway 1,220-2,439 m
Telecommunications:
  4,000 radios (1982)

:Christmas Island Defense Forces

Note: defense is the responsibility of Australia

Clipperton Island Geography

Total area: 7 km2
Land area: 7 km2

Comparative area: about 12 times the size of the Mall in Washington, DC
Land boundaries:
   none
Coastline:
   11.1 km
Maritime claims:
  Exclusive economic zone:
   200 nm
  Territorial sea:
   12 nm
Disputes:
   claimed by Mexico
Climate:
   tropical
Terrain:
   coral atoll
Natural resources:
   none
Land use:
   arable land 0%; permanent crops 0%; meadows and pastures 0%; forest and
   woodland 0%; other (coral) 100%
Environment:
   reef about 8 km in circumference
Note:
   located 1,120 km southwest of Mexico in the North Pacific Ocean; also called
   Ile de la Passion

:Clipperton Island People

Population: uninhabited

:Clipperton Island Government

Long-form name:
   none
Type:
   French possession administered by France from French Polynesia by High
   Commissioner of the Republic Jean MONTPEZAT
Capital: none; administered by France from French Polynesia

:Clipperton Island Economy

Overview:
   The only economic activity is a tuna fishing station.

:Clipperton Island Communications

Ports: none; offshore anchorage only

:Clipperton Island Defense Forces

Note: defense is the responsibility of France

Cocos Islands Geography

Total area: 14 km2
Land area: 14 km2; main islands are West Island and Home Island
Comparative area: about 24 times the size of the Mall in Washington, DC

Land boundaries:
  none
Coastline:
  2.6 km
Maritime claims:
  Exclusive fishing zone:
  200 nm
  Territorial sea:
  3 nm
Disputes:
  none
Climate:
  pleasant, modified by the southeasttrade wind for about nine months of the
  year; moderate rain fall
Terrain:
  flat, low-lying coral atolls
Natural resources:
  fish
Land use:
  arable land 0%; permanent crops 0%; meadows and pastures 0%; forest and
  woodland 0%; other 100%
Environment:
  two coral atolls thickly covered with coconut palms and other vegetation
Note:
  located 1,070 km southwest of Sumatra (Indonesia) in the Indian Ocean about
  halfway between Australia and Sri Lanka

:Cocos Islands People

Population: 597 (July 1992), growth rate - 0.5% (1992)
Birth rate: NA births/1,000 population (1992)
Death rate: NA deaths/1,000 population (1992)
Net migration rate: NA migrants/1,000 population (1992)
Infant mortality rate: NA deaths/1,000 live births (1992)
Life expectancy at birth: NA years male, NA years female (1992)
Total fertility rate: NA children born/woman (1992)
Nationality:
  noun - Cocos Islander(s); adjective - Cocos Islander
Ethnic divisions:
  mostly Europeans on West Island and Cocos Malays on Home Island
Religions:
  almost all Sunni Muslims
Languages:
  English
Literacy:
  NA% (male NA%, female NA%)
Labor force:
  NA
Organized labor:
  none

:Cocos Islands Government

Long-form name:
   Territory of Cocos (Keeling) Islands
Type:
   territory of Australia
Capital: West Island
Administrative divisions:
   none (territory of Australia)
Independence:
   none (territory of Australia)
Constitution:
   Cocos (Keeling) Islands Act of 1955
Legal system:
   based upon the laws of Australia and local laws
National holiday:
   NA
Executive branch:
   British monarch, governor general of Australia, administrator, chairman of
   the Islands Council
Legislative branch:
   unicameral Islands Council
Judicial branch:
   Supreme Court
Leaders:
   Chief of State:
   Queen ELIZABETH II (since 6 February 1952)
   Head of Government:
   Administrator B. CUNNINGHAM (since NA); Chairman of the Islands Council Haji
   Wahin bin BYNIE (since NA)
Suffrage:
   NA
Elections:
   NA
Member of:
   none
Diplomatic representation:
   none (territory of Australia)
Flag:
   the flag of Australia is used

:Cocos Islands Economy

Overview:
   Grown throughout the islands, coconuts are the sole cash crop. Copra and
   fresh coconuts are the major export earners. Small local gardens and fishing
   contribute to the food supply, but additional food and most other
   necessities must be imported from Australia.
GDP:
   $NA, per capita $NA; real growth rate NA%
Inflation rate (consumer prices):
   NA%
Budget:

revenues $NA; expenditures $NA, including capital expenditures of $NA
Exports:
  $NA
 commodities:
  copra
 partners:
  Australia
Imports:
  $NA
 commodities:
  foodstuffs
 partners:
  Australia
External debt: $NA
Industrial production:
  growth rate NA%
Electricity:
  1,000 kW capacity; 2 million kWh produced, 2,980 kWh per capita (1990)
Industries:
  copra products
Agriculture:
  gardens provide vegetables, bananas, pawpaws, coconuts
Economic aid:
  none
Currency:
  Australian dollar (plural - dollars); 1 Australian dollar ($A) = 100 cents
Exchange rates:
  Australian dollars ($A) per US$1 - 1.3360 (January 1992), 1.2836 (1991),
  1.2799 (1990), 1.2618 (1989), 1.2752 (1988), 1.4267 (1987)
Fiscal year: 1 July - 30 June

:Cocos Islands Communications

Ports:
  none; lagoon anchorage only
Airports:
  1 airfield with permanent-surface runway, 1,220-2,439 m; airport on West
  Island is a link in service between Australia and South Africa
Telecommunications:
  250 radios (1985); linked by telephone, telex, and facsimile communications
  via satellite with Australia; broadcast stations - 1 AM, no FM, no TV

:Cocos Islands Defense Forces

Note: defense is the responsibility of Australia

Colombia Geography

Total area: 1,138,910 km2
Land area: 1,038,700 km2; includes Isla de Malpelo, Roncador Cay, Serrana Bank,
and
  Serranilla Bank
Comparative area: slightly less than three times the size of Montana
Land boundaries:

7,408 km; Brazil 1,643 km, Ecuador 590 km, Panama 225 km, Peru 2,900, Venezuela 2,050 km
Coastline:
3,208 km; Caribbean Sea 1,760 km, North Pacific Ocean 1,448 km
Maritime claims:
Continental shelf:
not specified
Exclusive economic zone:
200 nm
Territorial sea:
12 nm
Disputes:
maritime boundary dispute with Venezuela in the Gulf of Venezuela; territorial dispute with Nicaragua over Archipelago de San Andres y Providencia and Quita Sueno Bank
Climate:
tropical along coast and eastern plains; cooler in highlands
Terrain:
flat coastal lowlands, central highlands, high Andes mountains, eastern lowland plains
Natural resources:
crude oil, natural gas, coal, iron ore, nickel, gold, copper, emeralds
Land use:
arable land 4%; permanent crops 2%; meadows and pastures 29%; forest and woodland 49%; other 16%; includes irrigated NEGL%
Environment:
highlands subject to volcanic eruptions; deforestation; soil damage from overuse of pesticides; periodic droughts
Note:
only South American country with coastlines on both North Pacific Ocean and Caribbean Sea

:Colombia People

Population: 34,296,941 (July 1992), growth rate 1.9% (1992)
Birth rate: 24 births/1,000 population (1992)
Death rate: 5 deaths/1,000 population (1992)
Net migration rate: NEGL migrants/1,000 population (1992)
Infant mortality rate: 31 deaths/1,000 live births (1992)
Life expectancy at birth: 69 years male, 74 years female (1992)
Total fertility rate: 2.6 children born/woman (1992)
Nationality:
noun - Colombian(s); adjective - Colombian
Ethnic divisions:
mestizo 58%, white 20%, mulatto 14%, black 4%, mixed black-Indian 3%, Indian 1%
Religions:
Roman Catholic 95%
Languages:
Spanish
Literacy:

87% (male 88%, female 86%) age 15 and over can read and write (1990 est.)
Labor force:
   12,000,000 (1990); services 46%, agriculture 30%, industry 24% (1990)
Organized labor:
   984,000 members (1989), about 8.2% of labor force; the Communist-backed
   Unitary Workers Central or CUT is the largest labor organization, with about
   725,000 members (including all affiliate unions)

:Colombia Government

Long-form name:
   Republic of Colombia
Type:
   republic; executive branch dominates government structure
Capital: Bogota
Administrative divisions:
   23 departments (departamentos, singular - departamento), 5 commissariats*
   (comisarias, singular - comisaria), and 4 intendancies** (intendencias,
   singular - intendencia); Amazonas*, Antioquia, Arauca**, Atlantico, Bolivar,
   Boyaca, Caldas, Caqueta, Casanare**, Cauca, Cesar, Choco, Cordoba,
   Cundinamarca, Guainia*, Guaviare*, Huila, La Guajira, Magdalena, Meta,
   Narino, Norte de Santander, Putumayo**, Quindio, Risaralda, San Andres y
   Providencia**, Santander, Sucre, Tolima, Valle del Cauca, Vaupes*, Vichada*;
   note - there may be a new special district (distrito especial) named Bogota;
   the Constitution of 5 July 1991 states that the commissariats and
   intendancies are to become full departments and a capital district (distrito
   capital) of Santa Fe de Bogota is to be established by 1997
Independence:
   20 July 1810 (from Spain)
Constitution:
   5 July 1991
Legal system:
   based on Spanish law; judicial review of legislative acts in the Supreme
   Court; accepts compulsory ICJ jurisdiction, with reservations
National holiday:
   Independence Day, 20 July (1810)
Executive branch:
   president, presidential designate, Cabinet
Legislative branch:
   bicameral Congress (Congreso) consists of a nationally elected upper chamber
   or Senate (Senado) and a nationally elected lower chamber or House of
   Representatives (Camara de Representantes)
Judicial branch:
   Supreme Court of Justice (Corte Suprema de Justica)
Leaders:
   Chief of State and Head of Government:
   President Cesar GAVIRIA Trujillo (since 7 August 1990)
Political parties and leaders:
   Liberal Party (PL), Cesar GAVIRIA Trujillo, president; Social Conservative
   Party (PCS), Misael PASTRANA Borrero; National Salvation Movement (MSN),
   Alvaro GOMEZ Hurtado; Democratic Alliance M-19 (AD/M-19) is headed by 19th

of April Movement (M-19) leader Antonio NAVARRO Wolf, coalition of small leftist parties and dissident liberals and conservatives; Patriotic Union (UP) is a legal political party formed by Revolutionary Armed Forces of Colombia (FARC) and Colombian Communist Party (PCC), Carlos ROMERO

Suffrage:

universal at age 18

Elections:

President:

last held 27 May 1990 (next to be held May 1994); results - Cesar GAVIRIA Trujillo (Liberal) 47%, Alvaro GOMEZ Hurtado (National Salvation Movement) 24%, Antonio NAVARRO Wolff (M-19) 13%, Rodrigo LLOREDA (Conservative) 12%

Senate:

last held 27 October 1991 (next to be held March 1994); results - percent of vote by party NA; seats - (102 total) Liberal 58, Conservative 22, AD/M-19 9, MSN 5, UP 1, others 7

:Colombia Government

House of Representatives:

last held 27 October 1991 (next to be held March 1994); results - percent of vote by party NA; seats - (161 total) Liberal 87, Conservative 31, AD/M-19 13, MSN 10, UP 3, other 17

Communists:

18,000 members (est.), including Communist Party Youth Organization (JUCO)

Other political or pressure groups:

three insurgent groups are active in Colombia - Revolutionary Armed Forces of Colombia (FARC), led by Manuel MARULANDA and Alfonso CANO; National Liberation Army (ELN), led by Manuel PEREZ; and dissidents of the recently demobilized People's Liberation Army (EPL) led by Francisco CARABALLO

Member of:

AG, CDB, CG, ECLAC, FAO, G-3, G-11, G-24, G-77, GATT, IADB, IAEA, IBRD, ICAO, ICC, ICFTU, IDA, IFAD, IFC, ILO, IMF, IMO, INMARSAT, INTELSAT, INTERPOL, IOC, IOM, ISO, ITU, LAES, LAIA, LORCS, NAM, OAS, OPANAL, PCA, RG, UN, UNCTAD, UNESCO, UNHCR, UNIDO, UPU, WCL, WFTU, WHO, WIPO, WMO, WTO

Diplomatic representation:

Ambassador Jaime GARCIA Parra; Chancery at 2118 Leroy Place NW, Washington, DC 20008; telephone (202) 387-8338; there are Colombian Consulates General in Chicago, Houston, Miami, New Orleans, New York, San Francisco, and San Juan (Puerto Rico), and Consulates in Atlanta, Boston, Detroit, Los Angeles, and Tampa

US:

Ambassador Morris D. BUSBY; Embassy at Calle 38, No. 8-61, Bogota (mailing address is P. O. Box A. A. 3831, Bogota or APO AA 34038); telephone [57] (1) 285-1300 or 1688; FAX [571] 288-5687; there is a US Consulate in Barranquilla

Flag:

three horizontal bands of yellow (top, double-width), blue, and red; similar

to the flag of Ecuador, which is longer and bears the Ecuadorian coat of
arms superimposed in the center

:Colombia Economy

Overview:
Economic development has slowed gradually since 1986, but growth rates
remain high by Latin American standards. Conservative economic policies have
kept inflation and unemployment near 30% and 10%, respectively. The rapid
development of oil, coal, and other nontraditional industries over the past
four years has helped to offset the decline in coffee prices - Colombia's
major export. The collapse of the International Coffee Agreement in the
summer of 1989, a troublesome rural insurgency, and drug-related violence
have dampened growth, but significant economic reforms are likely to
facilitate a resurgent economy in the medium term. These reforms center on
fiscal restraint, trade liberalization, and privatization of state utilities
and commercial banks.

GDP:
exchange rate conversion - $45 billion, per capita $1,300; real growth rate
3.7% (1990 est.)

Inflation rate (consumer prices):
26.8% (1991)

Unemployment rate: 10.5% (1991)

Budget:
revenues $4.39 billion; current expenditures $3.93 billion, capital
expenditures $1.03 billion (1989 est.)

Exports:
$7.5 billion (f.o.b., 1991)
commodities:
petroleum (19%), coffee, coal, bananas, fresh cut flowers
partners:
US 40%, EC 21%, Japan 5%, Netherlands 4%, Sweden 3%

Imports:
$6.1 billion (c.i.f., 1991)
commodities:
industrial equipment, transportation equipment, foodstuffs, chemicals, paper
products
partners:
US 36%, EC 16%, Brazil 4%, Venezuela 3%, Japan 3%

External debt: $17.0 billion (1991)

Industrial production:
growth rate 1% (1991 est.); accounts for 21% of GDP

Electricity:
9,624,000 kW capacity; 38,856 million kWh produced, 1,150 kWh per capita
(1991)

Industries:
textiles, food processing, oil, clothing and footwear, beverages, chemicals,
metal products, cement; mining - gold, coal, emeralds, iron, nickel, silver,
salt

Agriculture:
growth rate 3% (1991 est.) accounts for 22% of GDP; crops make up two-thirds

and livestock one-third of agricultural output; climate and soils permit a
wide variety of crops, such as coffee, rice, tobacco, corn, sugarcane, cocoa
beans, oilseeds, vegetables; forest products and shrimp farming are becoming
more important

Illicit drugs:

illicit producer of cannabis, coca, and opium; about 37,500 hectares of coca
under cultivation; major supplier of cocaine to the US and other
international drug markets

:Colombia Economy

Economic aid:

US commitments, including Ex-Im (FY70-89), $1.6 billion; Western (non-US)
countries, ODA and OOF bilateral commitments (1970-89), $3.3 billion,
Communist countries (1970-89), $399 million

Currency:

Colombian peso (plural - pesos); 1 Colombian peso (Col$) = 100 centavos

Exchange rates:

Colombian pesos (Col$) per US$1 - 711.88 (January 1992), 633.08 (1991),
550.00 (1990), 435.00 (1989), 336.00 (1988), 242.61 (1987)

Fiscal year: calendar year

:Colombia Communications

Railroads:

3,386 km; 3,236 km 0.914-meter gauge, single track (2,611 km in use), 150 km
1. 435-meter gauge

Highways:

75,450 km total; 9,350 km paved, 66,100 km earth and gravel surfaces

Inland waterways:

14,300 km, navigable by river boats

Pipelines:

crude oil 3,585 km; petroleum products 1,350 km; natural gas 830 km; natural
gas liquids 125 km

Ports:

Barranquilla, Buenaventura, Cartagena, Covenas, San Andres, Santa Marta,
Tumaco

Merchant marine:

31 ships (1,000 GRT or over) totaling 289,794 GRT/443,369 DWT; includes 9
cargo, 1 chemical tanker, 3 petroleum tanker, 8 bulk, 10 container; note -
in addition, 2 naval tankers are sometimes used commercially

Civil air:

83 major transport aircraft

Airports:

1,167 total, 1,023 usable; 70 with permanent-surface runways; 1 with runways
over 3,659 m; 8 with runways 2,440-3,659 m; 191 with runways 1,220-2,439 m

Telecommunications:

nationwide radio relay system; 1,890,000 telephones; broadcast stations -
413 AM, no FM, 33 TV, 28 shortwave; 2 Atlantic Ocean INTELSAT earth stations
and 11 domestic satellite earth stations

:Colombia Defense Forces

Branches:
   Army (Ejercito Nacional), Navy (Armada Nacional, including Marines), Air
   Force (Fuerza Aerea de Colombia), National Police (Policia Nacional)
Manpower availability:
   males 15-49, 9,214,691; 6,240,601 fit for military service; 353,691 reach
   military age (18) annually
Defense expenditures:
   exchange rate conversion - $624 million, 1.4% of GDP (1991)

Comoros Geography

Total area: 2,170 km2
Land area: 2,170 km2
Comparative area: slightly more than 12 times the size of Washington, DC
Land boundaries:
   none
Coastline:
   340 km
Maritime claims:
  Exclusive economic zone:
   200 nm
  Territorial sea:
   12 nm
Disputes:
   claims French-administered Mayotte
Climate:
   tropical marine; rainy season (November to May)
Terrain:
   volcanic islands, interiors vary from steep mountains to low hills
Natural resources:
   negligible
Land use:
   arable land 35%; permanent crops 8%; meadows and pastures 7%; forest and
   woodland 16%; other 34%
Environment:
   soil degradation and erosion; deforestation; cyclones possible during rainy
   season
Note:
   important location at northern end of Mozambique Channel

:Comoros People

Population: 493,853 (July 1992), growth rate 3.5% (1992)
Birth rate: 47 births/1,000 population (1992)
Death rate: 12 deaths/1,000 population (1992)
Net migration rate: 0 migrants/1,000 population (1992)
Infant mortality rate: 84 deaths/1,000 live births (1992)
Life expectancy at birth: 55 years male, 59 years female (1992)
Total fertility rate: 6.9 children born/woman (1992)
Nationality:
   noun - Comoran(s); adjective - Comoran
Ethnic divisions:
   Antalote, Cafre, Makoa, Oimatsaha, Sakalava

Religions:

Sunni Muslim 86%, Roman Catholic 14%

Languages:

official languages are Arabic and French but majority of population speak
Comoran, a blend of Swahili and Arabic

Literacy:

48% (male 56%, female 40%) age 15 and over can read and write (1980)

Labor force:

140,000 (1982); agriculture 80%, government 3%; 51% of population of working
age (1985)

Organized labor:

NA

:Comoros Government

Long-form name:

Federal Islamic Republic of the Comoros

Type:

independent republic

Capital: Moroni

Administrative divisions:

three islands; Njazidja, Nzwani, and Mwali, formerly Grand Comore, Anjouan,
and Moheli respectively; note - there are also four municipalities named
Domoni, Fomboni, Moroni, and Mutsamudu

Independence:

31 December 1975 (from France)

Constitution:

1 October 1978, amended October 1982 and January 1985

Legal system:

French and Muslim law in a new consolidated code

National holiday:

Independence Day, 6 July (1975)

Executive branch:

president, Council of Ministers (cabinet)

Legislative branch:

unicameral Federal Assembly (Assemblee Federale)

Judicial branch:

Supreme Court (Cour Supreme)

Leaders:

Chief of State and Head of Government:

President Said Mohamed DJOHAR (since 11 March 1990); coordinator of National
Unity Government (de facto prime minister) - Mohamed Taki ABDULKARIM (1
January 1992)

Suffrage:

universal at age 18

Elections:

Federal Assembly:

last held 22 March 1987 (next to be held March 1992); results - percent of
vote by party NA; seats - (42 total) Udzima 42

President:

last held 11 March 1990 (next to be held March 1996); results - Said Mohamed

DJOHAR (Udzima) 55%, Mohamed TAKI Abdulkarim (UNDC) 45%

Member of:

ACCT, ACP, AfDB, ECA, FAO, FZ, G-77, IBRD, ICAO, IDA, IDB, IFAD, ILO, IMF,

ITU, NAM, OAU, OIC, UN, UNCTAD, UNESCO, UNIDO, UPU, WHO, WMO

Diplomatic representation:

Ambassador Amini Ali MOUMIN; Chancery (temporary) at the Comoran Permanent Mission to the UN, 336 East 45th Street, 2nd Floor, New York, NY 10017; telephone (212) 972-8010

US:

Ambassador Kenneth N. PELTIER; Embassy at address NA, Moroni (mailing address B. P. 1318, Moroni); telephone 73-22-03, 73-29-22

Flag:

green with a white crescent placed diagonally (closed side of the crescent points to the upper hoist-side corner of the flag); there are four white five-pointed stars placed in a line between the points of the crescent; the crescent, stars, and color green are traditional symbols of Islam; the four stars represent the four main islands of the archipelago - Mwali, Njazidja, Nzwani, and Mayotte (which is a territorial collectivity of France, but claimed by the Comoros)

:Comoros Economy

Overview:

One of the world's poorest countries, Comoros is made up of several islands that have poor transportation links, a young and rapidly increasing population, and few natural resources. The low educational level of the labor force contributes to a low level of economic activity, high unemployment, and a heavy dependence on foreign grants and technical assistance. Agriculture, including fishing, hunting, and forestry, is the leading sector of the economy. It contributes about 34% to GDP, employs 80% of the labor force, and provides most of the exports. The country is not self-sufficient in food production, and rice, the main staple, accounts for 90% of imports. During the period 1982-86 the industrial sector grew at an annual average rate of 5.3%, but its contribution to GDP was only 5% in 1988. Despite major investment in the tourist industry, which accounts for about 25% of GDP, growth has stagnated since 1983. A sluggish growth rate of 1.5% during 1985-90 has led to large budget deficits, declining incomes, and balance-of-payments difficulties. Preliminary estimates for 1991 show a moderate increase in the growth rate based on increased exports, tourism, and government investment outlays.

GDP:

exchange rate conversion - $260 million, per capita $540; real growth rate 2.7% (1991 est.)

Inflation rate (consumer prices):

4.0% (1991 est.)

Unemployment rate: over 16% (1988 est.)

Budget:

revenues $88 million; expenditures $92 million, including capital expenditures of $13 million (1990 est.)

Exports:

$16 million (f.o.b., 1990 est.)
commodities:
  vanilla, cloves, perfume oil, copra, ylang-ylang
partners:
  US 53%, France 41%, Africa 4%, FRG 2% (1988)
Imports:
  $41 million (f.o.b., 1990 est.)
commodities:
  rice and other foodstuffs, cement, petroleum products, consumer goods
partners:
  Europe 62% (France 22%), Africa 5%, Pakistan, China (1988)
External debt: $196 million (1991 est.)
Industrial production:
  growth rate 3.4% (1988 est.); accounts for 5% of GDP
Electricity:
  16,000 kW capacity; 25 million kWh produced, 50 kWh per capita (1991)
Industries:
  perfume distillation, textiles, furniture, jewelry, construction materials,
  soft drinks
Agriculture:
  accounts for 34% of GDP; most of population works in subsistence agriculture
  and fishing; plantations produce cash crops for export - vanilla, cloves,
  perfume essences, and copra; principal food crops - coconuts, bananas,
  cassava; world's leading producer of essence of ylang-ylang (for perfumes)
  and second-largest producer of vanilla; large net food importer

:Comoros Economy

Economic aid:
  US commitments, including Ex-Im (FY80-89), $10 million; Western (non-US)
  countries, ODA and OOF bilateral commitments (1970-89), $435 million; OPEC
  bilateral aid (1979-89), $22 million; Communist countries (1970-89), $18
  million
Currency:
  Comoran franc (plural - francs); 1 Comoran franc (CF) = 100 centimes
Exchange rates:
  Comoran francs (CF) per US$1 - 269.01 (January 1992), 282.11 (1991), 272.26
  (1990), 319.01 (1989), 297.85 (1988), 300.54 (1987); note - linked to the
  French franc at 50 to 1 French franc
Fiscal year: calendar year

:Comoros Communications

Highways:
  750 km total; about 210 km bituminous, remainder crushed stone or gravel
Ports:
  Mutsamudu, Moroni
Civil air:
  1 major transport aircraft
Airports:
  4 total, 4 usable; 4 with permanent-surface runways; none with runways over
  3,659 m; 1 with runways 2,440-3,659 m; 3 with runways 1,220-2,439 m
Telecommunications:

sparse system of radio relay and high-frequency radio communication stations for interisland and external communications to Madagascar and Reunion; over 1,800 telephones; broadcast stations - 2 AM, 1 FM, no TV

:Comoros Defense Forces

Branches:
Comoran Security Forces (FCS), Federal Gendarmerie (GFC)
Manpower availability:
males 15-49, 105,022; 62,808 fit for military service
Defense expenditures:
$NA, NA of GDP

Congo Geography

Total area: 342,000 km2
Land area: 341,500 km2
Comparative area: slightly smaller than Montana
Land boundaries:
5,504 km; Angola 201 km, Cameroon 523 km, Central African Republic 467 km, Gabon 1,903 km, Zaire 2,410 km
Coastline:
169 km
Maritime claims:
 Territorial sea:
200 nm
Disputes:
long section with Zaire along the Congo River is indefinite (no division of the river or its islands has been made)
Climate:
tropical; rainy season (March to June); dry season (June to October); constantly high temperatures and humidity; particularly enervating climate astride the Equator
Terrain:
coastal plain, southern basin, central plateau, northern basin
Natural resources:
petroleum, timber, potash, lead, zinc, uranium, copper, phosphates, natural gas
Land use:
arable land 2%; permanent crops NEGL%; meadows and pastures 29%; forest and woodland 62%; other 7%
Environment:
deforestation; about 70% of the population lives in Brazzaville, Pointe Noire, or along the railroad between them

:Congo People

Population: 2,376,687 (July 1992), growth rate 2.9% (1992)
Birth rate: 42 births/1,000 population (1992)
Death rate: 13 deaths/1,000 population (1992)
Net migration rate: 0 migrants/1,000 population (1992)
Infant mortality rate: 109 deaths/1,000 live births (1992)
Life expectancy at birth: 53 years male, 56 years female (1992)
Total fertility rate: 5.7 children born/woman (1992)

Nationality:
  noun - Congolese (singular and plural); adjective - Congolese or Congo
Ethnic divisions:
  about 15 ethnic groups divided into some 75 tribes, almost all Bantu; most
  important ethnic groups are Kongo (48%) in the south, Sangha (20%) and
  M'Bochi (12%) in the north, Teke (17%) in the center; about 8,500 Europeans,
  mostly French
Religions:
  Christian 50%, animist 48%, Muslim 2%
Languages:
  French (official); many African languages with Lingala and Kikongo most
  widely used
Literacy:
  57% (male 70%, female 44%) age 15 and over can read and write (1990 est.)
Labor force:
  79,100 wage earners; agriculture 75%, commerce, industry, and government
  25%; 51% of population of working age; 40% of population economically active
  (1985)
Organized labor:
  20% of labor force (1979 est.)

:Congo Government

Long-form name:
  Republic of the Congo
Type:
  republic
Capital: Brazzaville
Administrative divisions:
  9 regions (regions, singular - region) and 1 commune*; Bouenza,
  Brazzaville*, Cuvette, Kouilou, Lekoumou, Likouala, Niari, Plateaux, Pool,
  Sangha
Independence:
  15 August 1960 (from France; formerly Congo/Brazzaville)
Constitution:
  8 July 1979, currently being modified
Legal system:
  based on French civil law system and customary law
National holiday:
  Congolese National Day, 15 August (1960)
Executive branch:
  president, prime minister, Council of Ministers (cabinet)
Legislative branch:
  a transitional National Assembly
Judicial branch:
  Supreme Court (Cour Supreme)
Leaders:
 Chief of State:
  President Denis SASSOU-NGUESSO (since 8 February 1979); stripped of most
  powers by National Conference in May 1991
 Head of Government:

Prime Minister Andre MILONGO (since May 1991)

Political parties and leaders:

Congolese Labor Party (PCT), President Denis SASSOU-NGUESSO, leader; note - multiparty system legalized, with over 50 parties established

Suffrage:

universal at age 18

Elections:

National Assembly:

transitional body selected by National Conference in May 1991; election for new legislative body to be held spring 1992

President:

last held 26-31 July 1989 (next to be held June 1992); results - President SASSOU-NGUESSO unanimously reelected leader of the PCT by the Party Congress, which automatically made him president

Communists:

small number of Communists and sympathizers

Other political or pressure groups:

Union of Congolese Socialist Youth (UJSC), Congolese Trade Union Congress (CSC), Revolutionary Union of Congolese Women (URFC), General Union of Congolese Pupils and Students (UGEEC)

Member of:

ACCT, ACP, AfDB, BDEAC, CCC, CEEAC, ECA, FAO, FZ, G-77, GATT, IBRD, ICAO,

IDA, IFAD, IFC, ILO, IMF, IMO, INTELSAT, INTERPOL, IOC, ITU, LORCS, NAM,

OAU, UDEAC, UN, UNAVEM, UNCTAD, UNESCO, UNIDO, UPU, WFTU, WHO, WIPO, WMO,

WTO

Diplomatic representation:

Ambassador Roger ISSOMBO; Chancery at 4891 Colorado Avenue NW, Washington,

DC 20011; telephone (202) 726-5500

:Congo Government

US:

Ambassador James Daniel PHILLIPS; Embassy at Avenue Amilcar Cabral, Brazzaville (mailing address is B. P. 1015, Brazzaville, or Box C, APO AE 09828); telephone (242) 83-20-70; FAX [242] 83-63-38

Flag:

red, divided diagonally from the lower hoist side by a yellow band; the upper triangle (hoist side) is green and the lower triangle is red; uses the popular pan-African colors of Ethiopia

:Congo Economy

Overview:

Congo's economy is a mixture of village agriculture and handicrafts, a beginning industrial sector based largely on oil, supporting services, and a government characterized by budget problems and overstaffing. A reform program, supported by the IMF and World Bank, ran into difficulties in 1990-91 because of problems in changing to a democratic political regime and a heavy debt-servicing burden. Oil has supplanted forestry as the mainstay of the economy, providing about two-thirds of government revenues and exports. In the early 1980s rapidly rising oil revenues enabled Congo to finance large-scale development projects with growth averaging 5% annually, one of the highest rates in Africa. During the period 1987-91, however, growth has slowed to an average of roughly 1.5% annually, only half the population growth rate.

GDP:
exchange rate conversion - $2.4 billion, per capita $1,070; real growth rate 0.5% (1990 est.)

Inflation rate (consumer prices):
4.6% (1989 est.)

Unemployment rate: NA%

Budget:
revenues $522 million; expenditures $767 million, including capital expenditures of $141 million (1989)

Exports:
$751 million (f.o.b., 1988)
commodities:
crude petroleum 72%, lumber, plywood, coffee, cocoa, sugar, diamonds
partners:
US, France, other EC

Imports:
$564 million (c.i.f., 1988)
commodities:
foodstuffs, consumer goods, intermediate manufactures, capital equipment
partners:
France, Italy, other EC, US, FRG, Spain, Japan, Brazil

External debt: $4.5 billion (December 1988)

Industrial production:
growth rate 1.2% (1989); accounts for 33% of GDP, including petroleum

Electricity:
140,000 kW capacity; 315 million kWh produced, 135 kWh per capita (1991)

Industries:
crude oil, cement, sawmills, brewery, sugar mill, palm oil, soap, cigarettes

Agriculture:
accounts for 10% of GDP (including fishing and forestry); cassava accounts for 90% of food output; other crops - rice, corn, peanuts, vegetables; cash crops include coffee and cocoa; forest products important export earner; imports over 90% of food needs

Economic aid:
US commitments, including Ex-Im (FY70-89), $60 million; Western (non-US) countries, ODA and OOF bilateral commitments (1970-89), $2.3 billion; OPEC bilateral aid (1979-89), $15 million; Communist countries (1970-89), $338 million

Currency:
Communaute Financiere Africaine franc (plural - francs); 1 CFA franc (CFAF) = 100 centimes

:Congo Economy

Exchange rates:
   Communaute Financiere Africaine francs (CFAF) per US$1 - 269.01 (January
   1992), 282.11 (1991), 272.26 (1990), 319.01 (1989), 297.85 (1988), 300.54
   (1987)
Fiscal year: calendar year

:Congo Communications

Railroads:
   797 km, 1.067-meter gauge, single track (includes 285 km that are privately
   owned)
Highways:
   11,960 km total; 560 km paved; 850 km gravel and laterite; 5,350 km improved
   earth; 5,200 km unimproved earth
Inland waterways:
   the Congo and Ubangi (Oubangui) Rivers provide 1,120 km of commercially
   navigable water transport; the rest are used for local traffic only
Pipelines:
   crude oil 25 km
Ports:
   Pointe-Noire (ocean port), Brazzaville (river port)
Civil air:
   4 major transport aircraft
Airports:
   46 total, 42 usable; 6 with permanent-surface runways; none with runways
   over 3,659 m; 1 with runways 2,440-3,659 m; 17 with runways 1,220-2,439 m
Telecommunications:
   services adequate for government use; primary network is composed of radio
   relay routes and coaxial cables; key centers are Brazzaville, Pointe-Noire,
   and Loubomo; 18,100 telephones; broadcast stations - 4 AM, 1 FM, 4 TV; 1
   Atlantic Ocean satellite earth station

:Congo Defense Forces

Branches:
   Army, Navy (including Naval Infantry), Air Force, National Police
Manpower availability:
   males 15-49, 526,058; 267,393 fit for military service; 23,884 reach
   military age (20) annually
Defense expenditures:
   exchange rate conversion - $100 million, 4.6% of GDP (1987 est.)

Cook Islands Geography

Total area: 240 km2
Land area: 240 km2
Comparative area: slightly less than 1.3 times the size of Washington, DC
Land boundaries:
   none
Coastline:
   120 km
Maritime claims:
 Continental shelf:
   edge of continental margin or minimum of 200 nm

Exclusive economic zone:
   200 nm
Territorial sea:
   12 nm
Disputes:
   none
Climate:
   tropical; moderated by trade winds
Terrain:
   low coral atolls in north; volcanic, hilly islands in south
Natural resources:
   negligible
Land use:
   arable land 4%; permanent crops 22%; meadows and pastures 0%; forest and woodland 0%; other 74%
Environment:
   subject to typhoons from November to March
Note:
   located 4,500 km south of Hawaii in the South Pacific Ocean

:Cook Islands People

Population: 17,977 (July 1992), growth rate 0.5% (1992)
Birth rate: 22 births/1,000 population (1992)
Death rate: 6 deaths/1,000 population (1992)
Net migration rate: -10 migrants/1,000 population (1992)
Infant mortality rate: 25 deaths/1,000 live births (1992)
Life expectancy at birth: 69 years male, 73 years female (1992)
Total fertility rate: 3.0 children born/woman (1992)
Nationality:
   noun - Cook Islander(s); adjective - Cook Islander
Ethnic divisions:
   Polynesian (full blood) 81.3%, Polynesian and European 7.7%, Polynesian and other 7.7%, European 2.4%, other 0.9%
Religions:
   Christian, majority of populace members of Cook Islands Christian Church
Languages:
   English (official); Maori
Literacy:
   NA% (male NA%, female NA%)
Labor force:
   5,810; agriculture 29%, government 27%, services 25%, industry 15%, and other 4% (1981)
Organized labor:
   NA

:Cook Islands Government

Long-form name:
   none
Type:
   self-governing in free association with New Zealand; Cook Islands fully responsible for internal affairs; New Zealand retains responsibility for

external affairs, in consultation with the Cook Islands

Capital: Avarua

Administrative divisions:

Independence:

became self-governing in free association with New Zealand on 4 August 1965 and has the right at any time to move to full independence by unilateral action

Constitution:

4 August 1965

National holiday:

Constitution Day, 4 August

Executive branch:

British monarch, representative of the UK, representative of New Zealand, prime minister, deputy prime minister, Cabinet

Legislative branch:

unicameral Parliament; note - the House of Arikis (chiefs) advises on traditional matters, but has no legislative powers

Judicial branch:

High Court

Leaders:

Chief of State:

Queen ELIZABETH II (since 6 February 1952); Representative of the UK Sir Tangaroa TANGAROA (since NA); Representative of New Zealand Adrian SINCOCK

(since NA)

Head of Government:

Prime Minister Geoffrey HENRY (since 1 February 1989); Deputy Prime Minister Inatio AKARURU (since February 1989)

Political parties and leaders:

Cook Islands Party, Geoffrey HENRY; Democratic Tumu Party, Vincent INGRAM; Democratic Party, Terepai MAOATE; Cook Islands Labor Party, Rena JONASSEN; Cook Islands People's Party, Sadaraka SADARAKA

Suffrage:

universal adult at age NA

Elections:

Parliament:

last held 19 January 1989 (next to be held by January 1994); results - percent of vote by party NA; seats - (24 total) Cook Islands Party 12, Democratic Tumu Party 2, opposition coalition (including Democratic Party) 9, independent 1

Member of:

AsDB, ESCAP (associate), FAO, ICAO, IOC, SPC, SPF, UNESCO, WHO

Diplomatic representation:

none (self-governing in free association with New Zealand)

Flag:

blue, with the flag of the UK in the upper hoist-side quadrant and a large circle of 15 white five-pointed stars (one for every island) centered in the outer half of the flag

:Cook Islands Economy

Overview:
Agriculture provides the economic base. The major export earners are fruit, copra, and clothing. Manufacturing activities are limited to a fruit-processing plant and several clothing factories. Economic development is hindered by the isolation of the islands from foreign markets and a lack of natural resources and good transportation links. A large trade deficit is annually made up for by remittances from emigrants and from foreign aid. Current economic development plans call for exploiting the tourism potential and expanding the fishing industry.

GDP:
exchange rate conversion - $40.0 million, per capita $2,200 (1988 est.); real growth rate 5.3% (1986-88 est.)

Inflation rate (consumer prices):
8.0% (1988)

Unemployment rate: NA%

Budget:
revenues $33.8 million; expenditures $34.4 million, including capital expenditures of $NA (1990 est.)

Exports:
$4.0 million (f.o.b., 1988)
commodities:
copra, fresh and canned fruit, clothing
partners:
NZ 80%, Japan

Imports:
$38.7 million (c.i.f., 1988)
commodities:
foodstuffs, textiles, fuels, timber
partners:
NZ 49%, Japan, Australia, US

External debt: $NA

Industrial production:
growth rate NA%

Electricity:
14,000 kW capacity; 21 million kWh produced, 1,170 kWh per capita (1990)

Industries:
fruit processing, tourism

Agriculture:
export crops - copra, citrus fruits, pineapples, tomatoes, bananas; subsistence crops - yams, taro

Economic aid:
Western (non-US) countries, ODA and OOF bilateral commitments (1970-89), $128 million

Currency:
New Zealand dollar (plural - dollars); 1 New Zealand dollar (NZ$) = 100 cents

Exchange rates:
New Zealand dollars (NZ$) per US$1 - 1.8502 (January 1992), 1.7266 (1991), 1.6750 (1990), 1.6711 (1989), 1.5244 (1988), 1.6886 (1987)

Fiscal year: 1 April - 31 March

:Cook Islands Communications

Highways:
    187 km total (1980); 35 km paved, 35 km gravel, 84 km improved earth, 33 km
    unimproved earth
Ports:
    Avatiu
Merchant marine:
    1 cargo ship (1,000 or over) totaling 1,464 GRT/2,181 DWT
Civil air:
    no major transport aircraft
Airports:
    6 total, 6 usable; 1 with permanent-surface runways; none with runways over
    2,439 m; 4 with runways 1,220-2,439 m
Telecommunications:
    broadcast stations - 2 AM, no FM, no TV; 10,000 radio receivers; 2,052
    telephones; 1 Pacific Ocean INTELSAT earth station

:Cook Islands Defense Forces

Note: defense is the responsibility of New Zealand

Coral Sea Islands Geography

Total area: less than 3 km2
Land area: less than 3 km2; includes numerous small islands and reefs scattered over
a
    sea area of about 1 million km2, with Willis Islets the most important
Comparative area: undetermined
Land boundaries:
    none
Coastline:
    3,095 km
Maritime claims:
  Exclusive fishing zone:
    200 nm
  Territorial sea:
    3 nm
Disputes:
    none
Climate:
    tropical
Terrain:
    sand and coral reefs and islands (or cays)
Natural resources:
    negligible
Land use:
    arable land 0%; permanent crops 0%; meadows and pastures 0%; forest and
    woodland 0%; other, mostly grass or scrub cover 100%; Lihou Reef Reserve and
    Coringa-Herald Reserve were declared National Nature Reserves on 3 August
    1982
Environment:
    subject to occasional tropical cyclones; no permanent fresh water; important

nesting area for birds and turtles

Note:

the islands are located just off the northeast coast of Australia in the Coral Sea

:Coral Sea Islands People

Population: 3 meteorologists (1992)

:Coral Sea Islands Government

Long-form name:

Coral Sea Islands Territory

Type:

territory of Australia administered by the Minister for Arts, Sport, the Environment, Tourism, and Territories Roslyn KELLY

Capital: none; administered from Canberra, Australia

Flag:

the flag of Australia is used

:Coral Sea Islands Economy

Overview: no economic activity

:Coral Sea Islands Communications

Ports: none; offshore anchorages only

:Coral Sea Islands Defense Forces

Note:

defense is the responsibility of Australia; visited regularly by the Royal Australian Navy; Australia has control over the activities of visitors

Costa Rica Geography

Total area: 51,100 km2
Land area: 50,660 km2; includes Isla del Coco
Comparative area: slightly smaller than West Virginia
Land boundaries:
    639 km; Nicaragua 309 km, Panama 330 km
Coastline:
    1,290 km
Maritime claims:
  Continental shelf:
    200 nm
  Exclusive economic zone:
    200 nm
  Territorial sea:
    12 nm
Disputes:
    none
Climate:
    tropical; dry season (December to April); rainy season (May to November)
Terrain:
    coastal plains separated by rugged mountains
Natural resources:
    hydropower potential

Land use:
    arable land 6%; permanent crops 7%; meadows and pastures 45%; forest and
    woodland 34%; other 8%; includes irrigated 1%
Environment:
    subject to occasional earthquakes, hurricanes along Atlantic coast; frequent
    flooding of lowlands at onset of rainy season; active volcanoes;
    deforestation; soil erosion

:Costa Rica People

Population: 3,187,085 (July 1992), growth rate 2.4% (1992)
Birth rate: 27 births/1,000 population (1992)
Death rate: 4 deaths/1,000 population (1992)
Net migration rate: 1 migrant/1,000 population (1992)
Infant mortality rate: 12 deaths/1,000 live births (1992)
Life expectancy at birth: 75 years male, 79 years female (1992)
Total fertility rate: 3.2 children born/woman (1992)
Nationality:
    noun - Costa Rican(s); adjective - Costa Rican
Ethnic divisions:
    white (including mestizo) 96%, black 2%, Indian 1%, Chinese 1%
Religions:
    Roman Catholic 95%
Languages:
    Spanish (official), English spoken around Puerto Limon
Literacy:
    93% (male 93%, female 93%) age 15 and over can read and write (1990 est.)
Labor force:
    868,300; industry and commerce 35.1%, government and services 33%,
    agriculture 27%, other 4.9% (1985 est.)
Organized labor:
    15.1% of labor force

:Costa Rica Government

Long-form name:
    Republic of Costa Rica
Type:
    democratic republic
Capital: San Jose
Administrative divisions:
    7 provinces (provincias, singular - provincia); Alajuela, Cartago,
    Guanacaste, Heredia, Limon, Puntarenas, San Jose
Independence:
    15 September 1821 (from Spain)
Constitution:
    9 November 1949
Legal system:
    based on Spanish civil law system; judicial review of legislative acts in
    the Supreme Court; has not accepted compulsory ICJ jurisdiction
National holiday:
    Independence Day, 15 September (1821)
Executive branch:

president, two vice presidents, Cabinet
Legislative branch:
  unicameral Legislative Assembly (Asamblea Legislativa)
Judicial branch:
  Supreme Court (Corte Suprema)
Leaders:
  Chief of State and Head of Government:
    President Rafael Angel CALDERON Fournier (since 8 May 1990); First Vice
    President German SERRANO Pinto (since 8 May 1990); Second Vice President
    Arnoldo LOPEZ Echandi (since 8 May 1990)
Political parties and leaders:
    National Liberation Party (PLN), Carlos Manuel CASTILLO Morales; Social
    Christian Unity Party (PUSC), Rafael Angel CALDERON Fournier; Marxist
    Popular Vanguard Party (PVP), Humberto VARGAS Carbonell; New Republic
    Movement (MNR), Sergio Erick ARDON Ramirez; Progressive Party (PP), Isaac
    Felipe AZOFEIFA Bolanos; People's Party of Costa Rica (PPC), Lenin CHACON
    Vargas; Radical Democratic Party (PRD), Juan Jose ECHEVERRIA Brealey
Suffrage:
  universal and compulsory at age 18
Elections:
  Legislative Assembly:
    last held 4 February 1990 (next to be held February 1994); results - percent
    of vote by party NA; seats - (57 total) PUSC 29, PLN 25, PVP/PPC 1, regional
    parties 2
  President:
    last held 4 February 1990 (next to be held February 1994); results - Rafael
    Angel CALDERON Fournier 51%, Carlos Manuel CASTILLO 47%
Communists:
  7,500 members and sympathizers
Other political or pressure groups:
    Costa Rican Confederation of Democratic Workers (CCTD; Liberation Party
    affiliate), Confederated Union of Workers (CUT; Communist Party affiliate),
    Authentic Confederation of Democratic Workers (CATD; Communist Party
    affiliate), Chamber of Coffee Growers, National Association for Economic
    Development (ANFE), Free Costa Rica Movement (MCRL; rightwing militants),
    National Association of Educators (ANDE)

:Costa Rica Government

Member of:
  AG (observer), BCIE, CACM, ECLAC, FAO, G-77, IADB, IAEA, IBRD, ICAO,
ICFTU,
  IDA, IFAD, IFC, ILO, IMF, IMO, INTELSAT, INTERPOL, IOC, IOM, ITU,
LAES,
  LORCS, NAM (observer), OAS, OPANAL, UN, UNCTAD, UNESCO, UNIDO,
UPU, WCL,
  WFTU, WHO, WIPO, WMO
Diplomatic representation:
  Ambassador Gonzalo FACIO Segreda; Chancery at Suite 211, 1825 Connecticut
  Avenue NW, Washington, DC 20009; telephone (202) 234-2945 through 2947;
  there are Costa Rican Consulates General at Albuquerque, Houston, Los

Angeles, Miami, New Orleans, New York, San Diego, San Francisco, and San
Juan (Puerto Rico), and a Consulate in Buffalo
US:
Ambassador Luis GUINOT, Jr.; Embassy at Pavas Road, San Jose (mailing
address is APO AA 34020); telephone [506] 20-39-39 FAX (506) 20-2305
Flag:
five horizontal bands of blue (top), white, red (double width), white, and
blue, with the coat of arms in a white disk on the hoist side of the red
band

:Costa Rica Economy

Overview:
In 1991 the economy grew at an estimated 2.5%, down somewhat from the 3.6%
gain of 1990 and below the strong 5.5% gain of 1989. Increases in
agricultural production (on the strength of good coffee and banana crops)
and in construction have been offset by lower rates of growth for industry.
In 1991 consumer prices rose by 27%, about the same as in 1990. The trade
deficit of $270 million was substantially below the 1990 deficit of $677
million. Unemployment is officially reported at 4.6%, but much
underemployment remains. External debt, on a per capita basis, is among the
world's highest.
GDP:
exchange rate conversion - $5.9 billion, per capita $1,900; real growth rate
2.5% (1991 est.)
Inflation rate (consumer prices):
27% (1991 est.)
Unemployment rate: 4.6% (1991)
Budget:
revenues $831 million; expenditures $1.08 billion, including capital
expenditures of $NA (1990 est.)
Exports:
$1.5 billion (f.o.b., 1991 est.)
commodities:
coffee, bananas, textiles, sugar
partners:
US 75%, Germany, Guatemala, Netherlands, UK, Japan
Imports:
$1.8 billion (c.i.f., 1991 est.)
commodities:
petroleum, machinery, consumer durables, chemicals, fertilizer, foodstuffs
partners:
US 40%, Japan, Guatemala, Germany
External debt: $4.5 billion (1990)
Industrial production:
growth rate 2.3% (1990 est.); accounts for 23% of GDP
Electricity:
927,000 kW capacity; 3,408 million kWh produced, 1,095 kWh per capita (1991)
Industries:
food processing, textiles and clothing, construction materials, fertilizer,
plastic products

Agriculture:
    accounts for 20-25% of GDP and 70% of exports; cash commodities - coffee,
    beef, bananas, sugar; other food crops include corn, rice, beans, potatoes;
    normally self-sufficient in food except for grain; depletion of forest
    resources resulting in lower timber output
Illicit drugs:
    illicit production of cannabis on small scattered plots; transshipment
    country for cocaine from South America
Economic aid:
    US commitments, including Ex-Im (FY70-89), $1.4 billion; Western (non-US)
    countries, ODA and OOF bilateral commitments (1970-89), $935 million;
    Communist countries (1971-89), $27 million
Currency:
    Costa Rican colon (plural - colones); 1 Costa Rican colon (C) = 100 centimos
Exchange rates:
    Costa Rican colones (C) per US$1 - 136.35 (January 1992), 122.43 (1991),
    91.58 (1990), 81.504 (1989), 75.805 (1988), 62.776 (1987)

:Costa Rica Economy

Fiscal year: calendar year

:Costa Rica Communications

Railroads:
    950 km total, all 1.067-meter gauge; 260 km electrified
Highways:
    15,400 km total; 7,030 km paved, 7,010 km gravel, 1,360 km unimproved earth
Inland waterways:
    about 730 km, seasonally navigable
Pipelines:
    petroleum products 176 km
Ports:
    Puerto Limon, Caldera, Golfito, Moin, Puntarenas
Merchant marine:
    1 cargo ship (1,000 GRT or over) totaling 2,878 GRT/4,506 DWT
Civil air:
    11 major transport aircraft
Airports:
    164 total, 149 usable; 28 with permanent-surface runways; none with runways
    over 3,659 m; 1 with runways 2,440-3,659 m; 10 with runways 1,220-2,439 m
Telecommunications:
    very good domestic telephone service; 292,000 telephones; connection into
    Central American Microwave System; broadcast stations - 71 AM, no FM, 18 TV,
    13 shortwave; 1 Atlantic Ocean INTELSAT earth station

:Costa Rica Defense Forces

Branches:
    Civil Guard, Rural Assistance Guard; note - Constitution prohibits armed
    forces
Manpower availability:
    males 15-49, 829,576; 559,575 fit for military service; 31,828 reach
    military age (18) annually

Defense expenditures:
  exchange rate conversion - $22 million, 0.5% of GDP (1989)

Croatia Geography

Total area: 56,538 km2
Land area: 56,410 km2
Comparative area: slightly smaller than West Virginia
Land boundaries:
  1,843 km; Bosnia and Hercegovina (east) 751 km, Bosnia and Hercegovina
  (southeast) 91 km, Hungary 292 km, Serbia and Montenegro 254 km, Slovenia
  455 km
Coastline:
  5,790 km; mainland 1,778 km, islands 4,012 km
Maritime claims:
 Contiguous zone:
  NA nm
 Continental shelf:
  200-meter depth or to depth of exploitation
 Exclusive economic zone:
  12 nm
 Exclusive fishing zone:
  12 nm
 Territorial sea:
  12 nm
Disputes:
  Serbian enclaves in eastern Slavonia and along the western Bosnia and
  Hercegovinian border; dispute with Slovenia over fishing rights in Adriatic
Climate:
  Mediterranean and continental; continental climate predominant with hot
  summers and cold winters; mild winters, dry summers along coast
Terrain:
  geographically diverse; flat plains along Hungarian border, low mountains
  and highlands near Adriatic coast, coastline, and islands
Natural resources:
  oil, some coal, bauxite, low-grade iron ore, calcium, natural asphalt,
  silica, mica, clays, salt, fruit, livestock
Land use:
  32% arable land; 20% permanent crops; 18% meadows and pastures; 15% forest
  and woodland; 9% other; includes 5% irrigated
Environment:
  air pollution from metallurgical plants; damaged forest; coastal pollution
  from industrial and domestic waste; subject to frequent and destructive
  earthquakes
Note:
  controls most land routes from Western Europe to Aegean Sea and Turkish
  Straits

:Croatia People

Population: 4,784,000 (July 1991), growth rate 0.39% (for the period 1981-91)
Birth rate: 12.2 births/1,000 population (1991)
Death rate: 11.3 deaths/1,000 population (1991)

Net migration rate: NA migrants/1,000 population (1991)
Infant mortality rate: 10 deaths/1,000 live births (1990)
Life expectancy at birth: 67 years male, 74 years female (1980-82)
Total fertility rate: NA children born/woman (1991)
Nationality:
  noun - Croat(s); adjective - Croatian
Ethnic divisions:
  Croat 78%, Serb 12%, Muslims 0.9%, Hungarian 0.5%, Slovenian 0.5%, others
  7.8%
Religions:
  Catholic 76.5%, Orthodox 11.1%, Slavic Muslim 1.2%, Protestant 1.4%, others
  and unknown 11%
Languages:
  Serbo-Croatian 96%
Literacy:
  96.5% (male 98.6%, female 94.5%) age 10 and over can read and write (1991
  census)
Labor force:
  1,509,489; industry and mining 37%, agriculture 4%, government NA%, other
Organized labor:
  NA

:Croatia Government

Long-form name:
  None
Type:
  parliamentary democracy
Capital: Zagreb
Administrative divisions:
  102 districts (opcine, singular - opcina)
Independence:
  June 1991 from Yugoslavia
Constitution:
  promulgated on 22 December 1990
Legal system:
  based on civil law system; judicial/no judicial review of legislative acts;
  does/does not accept compulsory ICJ jurisdiction
National holiday:
  30 May, Statehood Day (1990)
Executive branch:
  president, prime minister
Legislative branch:
  bicameral
Judicial branch:
  Supreme Court, Constitutional Court
Leaders:
 Chief of State:
  President Franjo TUDJMAN (since April 1990), Vice President NA (since NA)
 Head of Government:
  Prime Minister Franjo GREGURIC (since August 1991), Deputy Prime Minister

Mila RAMLJAK (since NA)

Political parties and leaders:

Christian Democratic Union, TUDJMAN; Croatian Democratic Union (HDZ), Stjepan Mesic; Croatian National Party, Savka DABCEVIC-KUCAR; Croatian Christian Democratic Party (HKDS), Ivan CESAR; Croatian Party of Rights, Dobroslav Paraga; Croatian Social Liberal Party (HSLS), Drazen BUDISA

Suffrage:

at age 16 if employed, universal at age 18

Elections:

Parliament:

last held May 1990 (next to be held NA); results - HDZ won 205 seats; seats - 349 (total)

President:

NA

Other political or pressure groups:

NA

Member of:

CSCE

Diplomatic representation:

Ambassador Dr. Franc Vinko GOLEM, Office of Republic of Croatia, 256 Massachusetts Avenue, NW, Washington, DC 20036; telephone (202) 543-5586

US:

Ambassador NA; Embassy at NA (mailing address is APO New York is 09862); telephone NA

Flag:

red, white, and blue with Croatian coat of arms (red and white checkered)

:Croatia Economy

Overview:

Before the political disintegration of Yugoslavia, the republic of Croatia stood next to Slovenia as the most prosperous and industrialized area, with a per capita output roughly comparable to that of Portugal and perhaps one-third above the Yugoslav average. Serbia and the Serb-dominated army of the old Yugoslavia, however, have seized Croatian territory, and the overriding determinant of Croatia's long-term economic prospects will be the final border settlement. Under the most favorable circumstances, Croatia will retain the Dalmatian coast with its major tourist attractions and Slavonia with its oilfields and rich agricultural land. Even so, Croatia would face monumental problems stemming from: the legacy of longtime Communist mismanagement of the economy; large foreign debt; damage during the fighting to bridges, factories, powerlines, buildings, and houses; and the disruption of economic ties to Serbia and the other former Yugoslav republics. At the minimum, extensive Western aid and investment, especially in the tourist and oil industries, would seem necessary to salvage a desperate economic situation. However, peace and political stability must come first.

GDP:

NA - $26.3 billion, per capita $5,600; real growth rate -25% (1991 est.)

Inflation rate (consumer prices):

14.3% (March 1992)

Unemployment rate: 20% (December 1991)

Budget:

revenues $NA million; expenditures $NA million, including capital expenditures of $NA million

Exports:

$2.9 billion (1990)

commodities:

machinery and transport equipment (30%), other manufacturers (37%), chemicals (11%), food and live animals (9%), raw materials (6.5%), fuels and lubricants (5%)

partners:

principally the other former Yugoslav republics

Imports:

$4.4 billion (1990)

commodities:

machinery and transport equipment (21%), fuels and lubricants (19%), food and live animals (16%), chemicals (14%), manufactured goods (13%), miscellaneous manufactured articles (9%), raw materials (6.5%), beverages and tobacco (1%)

partners:

principally other former Yugoslav republics

External debt: $2.6 billion (may assume some part of foreign debt of former Yugoslavia)

Industrial production:

declined as much as 11% in 1990 and probably another 29% in 1991

Electricity:

3,570,000 kW capacity; 8,830 million kWh produced, 1,855 kWh per capita 1991)

Industries:

chemicals and plastics, machine tools, fabricated metal, electronics, pig iron and rolled steel products, aluminum reduction, paper, wood products (including furniture), building materials (including cement), textiles, shipbuilding, petroleum and petroleum refining, food processing and beverages

:Croatia Economy

Agriculture:

Croatia normally produces a food surplus; most agricultural land in private hands and concentrated in Croat-majority districts in Slavonia and Istria; much of Slavonia's land has been put out of production by fighting; wheat, corn, sugar beets, sunflowers, alfalfa, and clover are main crops in Slavonia; central Croatian highlands are less fertile but support cereal production, orchards, vineyards, livestock breeding, and dairy farming; coastal areas and offshore islands grow olives, citrus fruits, and vegetables

Economic aid:

NA

Currency:

Croatian dinar(s)

Exchange rates:

Croatian dinar per US $1 - 60.00 (April 1992)

Fiscal year: calendar year

:Croatia Communications

Railroads:
2,698 km (34.5% electrified)

Highways:
32,071 km total (1990); 23,305 km paved, 8,439 km gravel, 327 km earth

Inland waterways:
785 km perennially navigable

Pipelines:
crude oil 670 km, petroleum products 20 km, natural gas 310 km

Ports:
maritime - Rijeka, Split, Kardeljevo (Ploce); inland - Vukovar, Osijek, Sisak, Vinkovci

Merchant marine:
11 ships (1,000 GRT or over) totaling 60,802 GRT/65,560 DWT; includes 1 cargo, 3 roll-on/roll-off, 5 passenger ferries, 2 bulk carriers; note - also controlled by Croatian shipowners are 196 ships (1,000 GRT or over) under flags of convenience - primarily Malta and St. Vincent - totaling 2,593,429 GRT/4,101,119 DWT; includes 91 general cargo, 7 roll-on/ roll-off, 6 refrigerated cargo, 13 container ships, 3 multifunction large load carriers, 52 bulk carriers, 3 passenger ships, 11 petroleum tankers, 4 chemical tankers, 6 service vessels

Civil air:
NA major transport aircraft

Airports:
8 total, NA usable; NA with permanent-surface runways; NA with runways over 3,659 m; 7 with runways 2,440-3,659 m; NA with runways 1,220-2,439 m; 1 with runways 900 m

Telecommunications:
350,000 telephones; broadcast stations - 14 AM, 8 FM, 12 (2 repeaters) TV; 1,100,000 radios; 1,027,000 TVs; NA submarine coaxial cables; satellite ground stations - none

:Croatia Defense Forces

Branches:
Ground Forces, Naval Forces, Air and Air Defense Forces, Frontier Guard, Home Guard, Civil Defense

Manpower availability:
males 15-49, 1,188,576; NA fit for military service; 42,664 reach military age (18) annually

Defense expenditures:
$NA, NA% of GDP

Cuba Geography

Total area: 110,860 km2

Land area: 110,860 km2

Comparative area: slightly smaller than Pennsylvania

Land boundaries:
29.1 km; US Naval Base at Guantanamo 29.1 km

note:

Guantanamo is leased and as such remains part of Cuba

Coastline:

3,735 km

Maritime claims:

Exclusive economic zone:

200 nm

Territorial sea:

12 nm

Disputes:

US Naval Base at Guantanamo is leased to US and only mutual agreement or US abandonment of the area can terminate the lease

Climate:

tropical; moderated by trade winds; dry season (November to April); rainy season (May to October)

Terrain:

mostly flat to rolling plains with rugged hills and mountains in the southeast

Natural resources:

cobalt, nickel, iron ore, copper, manganese, salt, timber, silica

Land use:

arable land 23%; permanent crops 6%; meadows and pastures 23%; forest and woodland 17%; other 31%; includes irrigated 10%

Environment:

averages one hurricane every other year

Note:

largest country in Caribbean; 145 km south of Florida

:Cuba People

Population: 10,846,821 (July 1992), growth rate 1.0% (1992)

Birth rate: 17 births/1,000 population (1992)

Death rate: 6 deaths/1,000 population (1992)

Net migration rate: -1 migrant/1,000 population (1992)

Infant mortality rate: 11 deaths/1,000 live births (1992)

Life expectancy at birth: 74 years male, 79 years female (1992)

Total fertility rate: 1.8 children born/woman (1992)

Nationality:

noun - Cuban(s); adjective - Cuban

Ethnic divisions:

mulatto 51%, white 37%, black 11%, Chinese 1%

Religions:

85% nominally Roman Catholic before Castro assumed power

Languages:

Spanish

Literacy:

94% (male 95%, female 93%) age 15 and over can read and write (1990 est.)

Labor force:

3,578,800 in state sector; services and government 30%, industry 22%, agriculture 20%, commerce 11%, construction 10%, transportation and communications 7% (June 1990); economically active population 4,620,800

(1988)
Organized labor:
Workers Central Union of Cuba (CTC), only labor federation approved by government; 2,910,000 members; the CTC is an umbrella organization composed of 17 member unions

:Cuba Government

Long-form name:
Republic of Cuba
Type:
Communist state
Capital: Havana
Administrative divisions:
14 provinces (provincias, singular - provincia) and 1 special municipality* (municipio especial); Camaguey, Ciego de Avila, Cienfuegos, Ciudad de La Habana, Granma, Guantanamo, Holguin, Isla de la Juventud*, La Habana, Las Tunas, Matanzas, Pinar del Rio, Sancti Spiritus, Santiago de Cuba, Villa Clara
Independence:
20 May 1902 (from Spain 10 December 1898); administered by the US from 1898 to 1902
Constitution:
24 February 1976
Legal system:
based on Spanish and American law, with large elements of Communist legal theory; does not accept compulsory ICJ jurisdiction
National holiday:
Rebellion Day, 26 July (1953)
Executive branch:
president of the Council of State, first vice president of the Council of State, Council of State, president of the Council of Ministers, first vice president of the Council of Ministers, Council of Ministers
Legislative branch:
unicameral National Assembly of the People's Power (Asamblea Nacional del Poder Popular)
Judicial branch:
People's Supreme Court (Tribunal Supremo Popular)
Leaders:
 Chief of State and Head of Government:
 President of the Council of State and President of the Council of Ministers Fidel CASTRO Ruz (became Prime Minister in February 1959 and President since 2 December 1976); First Vice President of the Council of State and First Vice President of the Council of Ministers Gen. Raul CASTRO Ruz (since 2 December 1976)
Political parties and leaders:
 only party - Cuban Communist Party (PCC), Fidel CASTRO Ruz, first secretary
Suffrage:
 universal at age 16
Elections:
 National Assembly of the People's Power:

last held December 1986 (next to be held before December 1992); results -
PCC is the only party; seats - (510 total) indirectly elected

Communists:

about 600,000 full and candidate members

Member of:

CCC, ECLAC, FAO, G-77, GATT, IAEA, IBEC, ICAO, IFAD, ILO, IMO,
INTERPOL,

IOC, ISO, ITU, LAES, LORCS, NAM, OAS (excluded from formal participation
since 1962), PCA, UN, UNCTAD, UNESCO, UNIDO, UPU, WCL, WFTU, WHO,
WIPO, WMO,

WTO

Diplomatic representation:

none; protecting power in the US is Switzerland - Cuban Interests Section;
position vacant since March 1992; 2630 and 2639 16th Street NW, Washington,
DC 20009; telephone (202) 797-8518 or 8519, 8520, 8609, 8610

:Cuba Government

US:

protecting power in Cuba is Switzerland - US Interests Section, Swiss
Embassy; Principal Officer Alan H. FLANIGAN; Calzada entre L Y M, Vedado
Seccion, Havana (mailing address is USINT, Swiss Embassy, Havana, Calzada
Entre L Y M, Vedado); telephone 32-0051, 32-0543

Flag:

five equal horizontal bands of blue (top and bottom) alternating with white;
a red equilateral triangle based on the hoist side bears a white
five-pointed star in the center

:Cuba Economy

Overview:

The economy, centrally planned and largely state owned, is highly dependent
on the agricultural sector and foreign trade. Sugar provided about
two-thirds of export revenues in 1991, and over half was exported to the
former Soviet republics. The economy has stagnated since 1985 under policies
that have deemphasized material incentives in the workplace, abolished
farmers' informal produce markets, and raised prices of government-supplied
goods and services. In 1990 the economy probably fell 5% largely as a result
of declining trade with the former Soviet Union and Eastern Europe. Recently
the government has been trying to increase trade with Latin America and
China. Cuba has had difficulty servicing its foreign debt since 1982. The
government currently is encouraging foreign investment in tourist facilities
and in industrial plants idled by falling imports from the former Soviet
Union. Other investment priorities include sugar, basic foods, and nickel.
The annual Soviet subsidy dropped from $4 billion in 1990 to about $1
billion in 1991 because of a lower price paid for Cuban sugar and a sharp
decline in Soviet exports to Cuba. The former Soviet republics have
indicated they will no longer extend aid to Cuba beginning in 1992. Instead
of highly subsidized trade, Cuba has been shifting to trade at market prices
in convertible currencies. Because of increasingly severe shortages of
fuels, industrial raw materials, and spare parts, aggregate output dropped
by one-fifth in 1991.

GNP:

$17 billion, per capita $1,580; real growth rate -20% (1991 est.)
Inflation rate (consumer prices):
  NA%
Budget:
  revenues $12.46 billion; expenditures $14.45 billion, including capital
  expenditures of $NA (1990 est.)
Exports:
  $3.6 billion (f.o.b., 1991 est.)
 commodities:
  sugar, nickel, medical products, shellfish, citrus, tobacco, coffee
 partners:
  former USSR 63%, China 6%, Canada 4%, Japan 4% (1991 est.)
Imports:
  $3.7 billion (c.i.f., 1991 est.)
 commodities:
  petroleum, capital goods, industrial raw materials, food
 partners:
  former USSR 47%, Spain 8%, China 6%, Argentina 5%, Italy 4%, Mexico 3% (1991
  est.)
External debt: $6.8 billion (convertible currency, July 1989)
Industrial production:
  growth rate 0%; accounts for 45% of GDP (1989)
Electricity:
  3,889,000 kW capacity; 16,272 million kWh produced, 1,516 kWh per capita
  (1991)
Industries:
  sugar milling, petroleum refining, food and tobacco processing, textiles,
  chemicals, paper and wood products, metals (particularly nickel), cement,
  fertilizers, consumer goods, agricultural machinery
Agriculture:
  accounts for 11% of GNP (including fishing and forestry); key commercial
  crops - sugarcane, tobacco, and citrus fruits; other products - coffee,
  rice, potatoes, meat, beans; world's largest sugar exporter; not
  self-sufficient in food (excluding sugar)

:Cuba Economy

Economic aid:
  Western (non-US) countries, ODA and OOF bilateral commitments (1970-89),
  $710 million; Communist countries (1970-89), $18.5 billion
Currency:
  Cuban peso (plural - pesos); 1 Cuban peso (Cu$) = 100 centavos
Exchange rates:
  Cuban pesos (Cu$) per US$1 - 1.0000 (linked to the US dollar)
Fiscal year: calendar year

:Cuba Communications

Railroads:
  12,947 km total; Cuban National Railways operates 5,053 km of 1.435-meter
  gauge track; 151.7 km electrified; 7,742 km of sugar plantation lines of
  0.914-m and 1.435-m gauge
Highways:

26,477 km total; 14,477 km paved, 12,000 km gravel and earth surfaced (1989 est.)

Inland waterways:
  240 km

Ports:
  Cienfuegos, Havana, Mariel, Matanzas, Santiago de Cuba; 7 secondary, 35 minor

Merchant marine:
  77 ships (1,000 GRT or over) totaling 537,464 GRT/755,824 DWT; includes 46 cargo, 10 refrigerated cargo, 1 cargo/training, 11 petroleum tanker, 1 chemical tanker, 4 liquefied gas, 4 bulk; note - Cuba beneficially owns an additional 45 ships (1,000 GRT and over) totaling 574,047 DWT under the registry of Panama, Cyprus, and Malta

Civil air:
  88 major transport aircraft

Airports:
  189 total, 167 usable; 73 with permanent-surface runways; 3 with runways over 3,659 m; 12 with runways 2,440-3,659 m; 18 with runways 1,220-2,439 m

Telecommunications:
  broadcast stations - 150 AM, 5 FM, 58 TV; 1,530,000 TVs; 2,140,000 radios; 229,000 telephones; 1 Atlantic Ocean INTELSAT earth station

:Cuba Defense Forces

Branches:
  Revolutionary Armed Forces (including Ground Forces, Revolutionary Navy (MGR), Air and Air Defense Force[DAAFR]), Ministry of Interior and Ministry of Defense Special Troops, Border Guard Troops, Territorial Militia Troops, Youth Labor Army, Civil Defense, National Revolutionary Police

Manpower availability:
  eligible 15-49, 6,130,641; of the 3,076,276 males 15-49, 1,925,648 are fit for military service; of the 3,054,365 females 15-49, 1,907,281 are fit for military service; 97,973 males and 94,514 females reach military age (17) annually

Defense expenditures:
  exchange rate conversion - $1.2-1.4 billion, 6% of GNP (1989 est.)

Cyprus Geography

Total area: 9,250 km2
Land area: 9,240 km2
Comparative area: about 0.7 times the size of Connecticut
Land boundaries:
  none
Coastline:
  648 km
Maritime claims:
 Continental shelf:
  200 m (depth) or to depth of exploitation
 Territorial sea:
  12 nm
Disputes:
  1974 hostilities divided the island into two de facto autonomous areas - a

Greek area controlled by the Cypriot Government (60% of the island's land area) and a Turkish-Cypriot area (35% of the island) that are separated by a narrow UN buffer zone; in addition, there are two UK sovereign base areas (about 5% of the island's land area)

Climate:
temperate, Mediterranean with hot, dry summers and cool, wet winters

Terrain:
central plain with mountains to north and south

Natural resources:
copper, pyrites, asbestos, gypsum, timber, salt, marble, clay earth pigment

Land use:
arable land 40%; permanent crops 7%; meadows and pastures 10%; forest and woodland 18%; other 25%; includes irrigated 10% (most irrigated lands are in the Turkish-Cypriot area of the island)

Environment:
moderate earthquake activity; water resource problems (no natural reservoir catchments, seasonal disparity in rainfall, and most potable resources concentrated in the Turkish-Cypriot area)

:Cyprus People

Population: 716,492 (July 1992), growth rate 1.0% (1992)
Birth rate: 18 births/1,000 population (1992)
Death rate: 8 deaths/1,000 population (1992)
Net migration rate: 0 migrants/1,000 population (1992)
Infant mortality rate: 10 deaths/1,000 live births (1992)
Life expectancy at birth: 74 years male, 78 years female (1992)
Total fertility rate: 2.4 children born/woman (1992)
Nationality:
noun - Cypriot(s); adjective - Cypriot
Ethnic divisions:
Greek 78%; Turkish 18%; other 4%
Religions:
Greek Orthodox 78%, Muslim 18%, Maronite, Armenian, Apostolic, and other 4%
Languages:
Greek, Turkish, English
Literacy:
90% (male 96%, female 85%) age 10 and over can read and write (1976)
Labor force:
Greek area - 278,000; services 45%, industry 35%, agriculture 14%; Turkish area - 71,500 (1990); services 21%, industry 30%, agriculture 27%
Organized labor:
156,000 (1985 est.)

:Cyprus Government

Long-form name:
Republic of Cyprus
Type:
republic; a disaggregation of the two ethnic communities inhabiting the island began after the outbreak of communal strife in 1963; this separation was further solidified following the Turkish invasion of the island in July 1974, which gave the Turkish Cypriots de facto control in the north; Greek

244

Cypriots control the only internationally recognized government; on 15
November 1983 Turkish Cypriot President Rauf DENKTASH declared independence
and the formation of a Turkish Republic of Northern Cyprus (TRNC), which has
been recognized only by Turkey; both sides publicly call for the resolution
of intercommunal differences and creation of a new federal system of
government

Capital: Nicosia

Administrative divisions:
6 districts; Famagusta, Kyrenia, Larnaca, Limassol, Nicosia, Paphos

Independence:
16 August 1960 (from UK)

Constitution:
16 August 1960; negotiations to create the basis for a new or revised
constitution to govern the island and to better relations between Greek and
Turkish Cypriots have been held intermittently; in 1975 Turkish Cypriots
created their own Constitution and governing bodies within the Turkish
Federated State of Cyprus, which was renamed the Turkish Republic of
Northern Cyprus in 1983; a new Constitution for the Turkish area passed by
referendum in May 1985

Legal system:
based on common law, with civil law modifications

National holiday:
Independence Day, 1 October (15 November is celebrated as Independence Day
in the Turkish area)

Executive branch:
president, Council of Ministers (cabinet); note - there is a president,
prime minister, and Council of Ministers (cabinet) in the Turkish area

Legislative branch:
unicameral House of Representatives (Vouli Antiprosopon); note - there is a
unicameral Assembly of the Republic (Cumhuriyet Meclisi) in the Turkish area

Judicial branch:
Supreme Court; note - there is also a Supreme Court in the Turkish area

Leaders:
  Chief of State and Head of Government:
President George VASSILIOU (since February 1988); note - Rauf R. DENKTASH
has been president of the Turkish area since 13 February 1975

Political parties and leaders:
  Greek Cypriot:
Progressive Party of the Working People (AKEL; Communist Party), Dimitrios
CHRISTOFIAS; Democratic Rally (DESY), Glafkos KLERIDES; Democratic Party
(DEKO), Spyros KYPRIANOU; United Democratic Union of the Center (EDEK),
Vassos LYSSARIDES; Socialist Democratic Renewal Movement (ADESOK), Mik-
halis
PAPAPETROU; Liberal Party, Nikos ROLANDIS

:Cyprus Government

  Turkish area:
National Unity Party (UBP), Dervis EROGLU; Communal Liberation Party (TKP),
Mustafa AKINCI; Republican Turkish Party (CTP), Ozker OZGUR; New Cyprus

Party (YKP), Alpay DURDURAN; Social Democratic Party (SDP), Ergun VEHBI; New

Birth Party (YDP), Ali Ozkan ALTINISHIK; Free Democratic Party (HDP), Ismet KOTAK; note - CTP, TKP, and YDP joined in the coalition Democratic Struggle Party (DMP) for the 22 April 1990 legislative election; the CTP and TKP boycotted the byelection of 13 October 1991, which was for 12 seats; the DMP was dissolved after the 1990 election; National Justice Party (MAP), Zorlu TORE; United Sovereignty Party, Arif Salih KIRDAG

Suffrage:

universal at age 18

Elections:

President:

last held 14 February and 21 February 1988 (next to be held February 1993); results - George VASSILIOU 52%, Glafkos KLERIDES 48%

House of Representatives:

last held 19 May 1991; results - DESY 35.8%, AKEL (Communist) 30.6, DEKO 19.5%, EDEK 10. 9%; others 3.2% seats - (56 total) DESY 20, AKEL (Communist) 18, DEKO 11, EDEK 7

Turkish Area: President:

last held 22 April 1990 (next to be held April 1995); results - Rauf R. DENKTASH 66%, Ismail BOZKURT 32.05%

Turkish Area: Assembly of the Republic:

last held 6 May 1990 (next to be held May 1995); results - UBP (conservative) 54.4%, DMP 44.4% YKP .9%; seats - (50 total) UBP (conservative) 45, SDP 1, HDP 2, YDP 2; note - by-election of 13 October 1991 was for 12 seats

Communists:

about 12,000

Other political or pressure groups:

United Democratic Youth Organization (EDON; Communist controlled); Union of Cyprus Farmers (EKA; Communist controlled); Cyprus Farmers Union (PEK; pro-West); Pan-Cyprian Labor Federation (PEO; Communist controlled) ; Confederation of Cypriot Workers (SEK; pro-West); Federation of Turkish Cypriot Labor Unions (Turk-Sen); Confederation of Revolutionary Labor Unions (Dev-Is)

Member of:

C, CCC, CE, CSCE, EBRD, ECE, FAO, G-77, GATT, IAEA, IBRD, ICAO, ICC, ICFTU,

IDA, IFAD, IFC, ILO, IMF, IMO, INTELSAT, INTERPOL, IOC, IOM, ISO, ITU, NAM,

OAS (observer), UN, UNCTAD, UNESCO, UNIDO, UPU, WCL, WFTU, WHO, WIPO, WMO,

WTO; note - the Turkish-Cypriot administered area of Cyprus has observer status in the OIC

Diplomatic representation:

Ambassador Michael E. SHERIFIS; Chancery at 2211 R Street NW, Washington, DC

20008; telephone (202) 462-5772

US:

Ambassador Robert E. LAMB; Embassy at the corner of Therissos Street and

Dositheos Street, Nicosia (mailing address is APO AE 09836); telephone [357] (2) 465151; FAX [357] (2) 459-571

Flag:

white with a copper-colored silhouette of the island (the name Cyprus is derived from the Greek word for copper) above two green crossed olive branches in the center of the flag; the branches symbolize the hope for peace and reconciliation between the Greek and Turkish communities; note - the Turkish cypriot flag has a horizontal red stripe at the top and bottom with a red crescent and red star on a white field

:Cyprus Economy

Overview:

The Greek Cypriot economy is small, diversified, and prosperous. Industry contributes 24% to GDP and employs 35% of the labor force, while the service sector contributes 44% to GDP and employs 45% of the labor force. Rapid growth in exports of agricultural and manufactured products and in tourism have played important roles in the average 6.4% rise in GDP between 1985 and 1990. In mid-1991, the World Bank "graduated" Cyprus off its list of developing countries. In contrast to the bright picture in the south, the Turkish Cypriot economy has less than half the per capita GDP and suffered a series of reverses in 1991. Crippled by the effects of the Gulf war, the collapse of the fruit-to-electronics conglomerate, Polly Peck, Ltd., and a drought, the Turkish area in late 1991 asked for a multibillion-dollar grant from Turkey to help ease the burden of the economic crisis. Turkey normally underwrites a substantial portion of the TRNC economy.

GDP:

purchasing power equivalent - Greek area: $5.5 billion, per capita $9,600; real growth rate 6.0%; Turkish area: $600 million, per capita $4,000; real growth rate 5.9% (1990)

Inflation rate (consumer prices):

Greek area: 4.5%; Turkish area: 69.4% (1990)

Unemployment rate: Greek area: 1.8%; Turkish area: 1.2% (1990)

Budget:

revenues $1.2 billion; expenditures $2.0 billion, including capital expenditures of $250 million (1991)

Exports:

$847 million (f.o.b., 1990)

commodities:

citrus, potatoes, grapes, wine, cement, clothing and shoes

partners:

UK 23%, Greece 10%, Lebanon 10%, Germany 5%

Imports:

$2.3 billion (f.o.b., 1990)

commodities:

consumer goods, petroleum and lubricants, food and feed grains, machinery

partners:

UK 13%, Japan 12%, Italy 10%, Germany 9.1%

External debt: $2.8 billion (1990)

Industrial production:

growth rate 5.6% (1990); accounts for 24% of GDP

Electricity:
   620,000 kW capacity; 1,770 million kWh produced, 2,530 kWh per capita (1991)
Industries:
   food, beverages, textiles, chemicals, metal products, tourism, wood products
Agriculture:
   accounts for 7% of GDP and employs 14% of labor force in the south; major
   crops - potatoes, vegetables, barley, grapes, olives, and citrus fruits;
   vegetables and fruit provide 25% of export revenues
Economic aid:
   US commitments, including Ex-Im (FY70-89), $292 million; Western (non-US)
   countries, ODA and OOF bilateral commitments (1970-89), $250 million; OPEC
   bilateral aid (1979-89), $62 million; Communist countries (1970-89), $24
   million
Currency:
   Cypriot pound (plural - pounds) and in Turkish area, Turkish lira (plural -
   liras); 1 Cypriot pound (#C) = 100 cents and 1 Turkish lira (TL) = 100 kurus

:Cyprus Economy

Exchange rates:
   Cypriot pounds (#C) per US$1 - 0.4683 (March 1992), 0.4615 (1991), 0.4572
   (1990), 0.4933 (1989), 0.4663 (1988), 0.4807 (1987); in Turkish area,
   Turkish liras (TL) per US$1 - 6,098.4 (March 1992), 4,173.9 (1991), 2,608.6
   (1990), 2,121.7 (1989), 1,422.3 (1988), 857.2 (1987)
Fiscal year: calendar year

:Cyprus Communications

Highways:
   10,780 km total; 5,170 km paved; 5,610 km gravel, crushed stone, and earth
Ports:
   Famagusta, Kyrenia, Larnaca, Limassol, Paphos
Merchant marine:
   1,228 ships (1,000 GRT or over) totaling 20,053,213 GRT/35,647,964 DWT;
   includes 8 short-sea passenger, 2 passenger-cargo, 440 cargo, 83
   refrigerated cargo, 22 roll-on/roll-off, 52 container, 5 multifunction large
   load carrier, 107 petroleum tanker, 3 specialized tanker, 3 liquefied gas,
   20 chemical tanker, 32 combination ore/oil, 394 bulk, 3 vehicle carrier, 49
   combination bulk, 2 railcar carrier, 2 passenger, 1 passenger cargo; note -
   a flag of convenience registry; Cuba owns at least 30 of these ships,
   republics of the former USSR own 58, Latvia also has 5 ships, Yugoslavia
   owns 1, and Romania 3
Civil air:
   11 major transport aircraft (Greek Cypriots); 2 (Turkish Cypriots)
Airports:
   14 total, 14 usable; 12 with permanent-surface runways; none with runways
   over 3,659 m; 7 with runways 2,440-3,659 m; 3 with runways 1,220-2,439 m
Telecommunications:
   excellent in both the area controlled by the Cypriot Government (Greek
   area), and in the Turkish-Cypriot administered area; 210,000 telephones;
   largely open-wire and radio relay; broadcast stations - 11 AM, 8 FM, 1 (34
   repeaters) TV in Greek sector and 2 AM, 6 FM and 1 TV in Turkish sector;
   international service by tropospheric scatter, 3 submarine cables, and

satellite earth stations - 1 Atlantic Ocean INTELSAT, 1 Indian Ocean INTELSAT and EUTELSAT earth stations

:Cyprus Defense Forces

Branches:

Greek area - Greek Cypriot National Guard (GCNG; including air and naval elements), Greek Cypriot Police; Turkish area - Turkish Cypriot Security Force

Manpower availability:

males 15-49, 183,899; 126,664 fit for military service; 5,030 reach military age (18) annually

Defense expenditures:

exchange rate conversion - $209 million, 5% of GDP (1990 est.)

Czechoslovakia Geography

Total area: 127,870 km2

Land area: 125,460 km2

Comparative area: slightly larger than New York State

Land boundaries:

3,438 km; Austria 548 km, Germany 815 km, Hungary 676 km, Poland 1,309 km, Ukraine 90 km

Coastline:

none - landlocked

Maritime claims:

none - landlocked

Disputes:

Gabcikovo Nagymaros Dam dispute with Hungary

Climate:

temperate; cool summers; cold, cloudy, humid winters

Terrain:

mixture of hills and mountains separated by plains and basins

Natural resources:

hard coal, timber, lignite, uranium, magnesite, iron ore, copper, zinc

Land use:

arable land 37%; permanent crops 1%; meadows and pastures 13%; forest and woodland 36%; other 13%; includes irrigated 1%

Environment:

infrequent earthquakes; acid rain; water pollution; air pollution

Note:

landlocked; strategically located astride some of oldest and most significant land routes in Europe; Moravian Gate is a traditional military corridor between the North European Plain and the Danube in central Europe

:Czechoslovakia People

Population: 15,725,680 (July 1992), growth rate 0.2% (1992)

Birth rate: 13 births/1,000 population (1992)

Death rate: 11 deaths/1,000 population (1992)

Net migration rate: NEGL migrants/1,000 population (1992)

Infant mortality rate: 11 deaths/1,000 live births (1992)

Life expectancy at birth: 68 years male, 76 years female (1992)

Total fertility rate: 1.9 children born/woman (1992)

249

Nationality:
  noun - Czechoslovak(s); adjective - Czechoslovak
Ethnic divisions:
  Czech 62.9%, Slovak 31.8%, Hungarian 3.8%, Polish 0.5%, German 0.3%,
  Ukrainian 0.3%, Russian 0.1%, other 0.3%
Religions:
  Roman Catholic 50%, Protestant 20%, Orthodox 2%, other 28%
Languages:
  Czech and Slovak (official), Hungarian
Literacy:
  99% (male NA%, female NA%) age 15 and over can read and write (1970 est.)
Labor force:
  8,200,000 (1987); industry 36.9%, agriculture 12.3%, construction,
  communications, and other 50.8% (1982)
Organized labor:
  Czech and Slovak Confederation of Trade Unions (CSKOS); several new
  independent trade unions established

:Czechoslovakia Government

Long-form name:
  Czech and Slovak Federal Republic
Type:
  federal republic in transition
Capital: Prague
Administrative divisions:
  2 republics (republiky, singular - republika); Czech Republic (Ceska
  Republika), Slovak Republic (Slovenska Republika); note - 11 regions (kraj,
  singular); Severocesky, Zapadocesky, Jihocesky, Vychodocesky, Praha,
  Severomoravsky, Jihomoravsky, Bratislava, Zapadoslovensky, Stredoslovensky,
  Vychodoslovensky
Independence:
  28 October 1918 (from Austro-Hungarian Empire)
Constitution:
  11 July 1960; amended in 1968 and 1970; new Czech, Slovak, and federal
  constitutions to be drafted in 1992
Legal system:
  civil law system based on Austro-Hungarian codes, modified by Communist
  legal theory; constitutional court currently being established; has not
  accepted compulsory ICJ jurisdiction; legal code in process of modification
  to bring it in line with Conference on Security and Cooperation in Europe
  (CSCE) obligations and to expunge Marxist-Leninist legal theory
National holiday:
  National Liberation Day, 9 May (1945) and Founding of the Republic, 28
  October (1918)
Executive branch:
  president, prime minister, Cabinet
Legislative branch:
  bicameral Federal Assembly (Federalni Shromazdeni) consists of an upper
  house or Chamber of Nations (Snemovna Narodu) and a lower house or Chamber
  of the People (Snemovna Lidu)

Judicial branch:
  Supreme Court
Leaders:
  Chief of State:
    President Vaclav HAVEL; (interim president from 29 December 1989 and
    president since 5 July 1990)
  Head of Government:
    Prime Minister Marian CALFA (since 10 December 1989); Deputy Prime Minister
    Vaclav KLAUS (since 3 October 1991); Deputy Prime Minister Jiri DIENSTBIER
    (since 28 June 1990); Deputy Prime Minister Jozef MIKLOSKO (since 28 June
    1990); Deputy Prime Minister Pavel RYCHETSKY (since 28 June 1990); Deputy
    Prime Minister Pavel HOFFMAN (since 3 October 1991); note - generally,
    "prime minister" is used at the federal level, "premier" at the republic
    level; Czech Premier - Petr PITHART; Slovak Premier - Jan CARNOGVRSKY

:Czechoslovakia Government

Political parties and leaders:
    note - there are very few federation-wide parties; party affiliation is
    indicted as Czech (C) or Slovak (S); Civic Democratic Party, Vaclav KLAUS,
    chairman, (C/S); Civic Movement, Jiri DIENSTBIER, chairman, (C); Civic
    Democratic Alliance, Jan KALVODA, chairman; Christian Democratic Union
    Public Against Violence, Martin PORUBJAK, chairman, (S); Christian
    Democratic Party, Vaclav BENDA, (C); Christian Democratic Movement, Jan
    CARNOGURSKY,(S); Communist Party of Bohemia and Moravia, Juri
SVOBODA,
    chairman; Movement for a Democratic Slovakia, Vladimir MECIAR, chairman -
    removed from power in November 1989 by massive antiregime demonstrations;
    Czechoslovak Social Democracy, Jiri HORAK, chairman, (C); Czechoslovak
    Socialist Party, Ladislav DVORAK, chairman, (C)(S); Movement for
    Self-Governing Democracy Society for Moravia and Silesia, Jan KRYCER,
    chairman, (C); Party of the Democratic Left, Peter WEISS, chairman
    (Slovakia's renamed Communists) (S); Slovak National Party, Jozef PROKES,
    chairman, (S); Democratic Party, Jan HOLCIK, chairman, (S); Coexistence,
    (C)(S)
Suffrage:
    universal at age 18
Elections:
  Federal Assembly:
    last held 8-9 June 1990 (next to be held 5-6 June 1992); results - Civic
    Forum/Public Against Violence coalition 46%, KSC 13.6%; seats - (300 total)
    Civic Forum/Public Against Violence coalition 170, KSC 47, Christian and
    Democratic Union/Christian Democratic Movement 40, Czech, Slovak, Moravian,
    and Hungarian groups 43
  President:
    last held 5 July 1990 (next to be held 3 July 1992); results - Vaclav HAVEL
    elected by the Federal Assembly
Communists:
    760,000 party members (September 1990); about 1,000,000 members lost since
    November 1989
Other political or pressure groups:

Czechoslovak Socialist Party, Czechoslovak People's Party, Czechoslovak
Social Democracy, Slovak Nationalist Party, Slovak Revival Party, Christian
Democratic Party; over 80 registered political groups fielded candidates in
the 8-9 June 1990 legislative election

Member of:

BIS, CCC, CE, CSCE, EC (associate) ECE, FAO, GATT, HG, IAEA, IBRD, ICAO,
IFCTU, ILO, IMF, IMO, INMARSAT, IOC, ISO, ITU, LORCS, NACC, NSG, PCA,
UN,

UNAVEM, UNCTAD, UNESCO, UNIDO, UPU, WHO, WIPO, WMO, ZC

Diplomatic representation:

Ambassador Rita KLIMOVA; Chancery at 3900 Linnean Avenue NW, Washington,
DC

20008; telephone (202) 363-6315 or 6316

US:

Ambassador Shirley Temple BLACK; Embassy at Trziste 15, 125 48, Prague 1
(mailing address is Unit 25402; APO AE 09213-5630); telephone [42] (2)
536-641/6; FAX [42] (2) 532-457

Flag:

two equal horizontal bands of white (top) and red with a blue isosceles
triangle based on the hoist side

:Czechoslovakia Economy

Overview:

Czechoslovakia is highly industrialized by East European standards and has a
well-educated and skilled labor force. GDP per capita has been the highest
in Eastern Europe. Annual GDP growth slowed to less than 1 percent during
the 1985-90 period. The country is deficient in energy and in many raw
materials. Moreover, its aging capital plant lags well behind West European
standards. In January 1991, Prague launched a sweeping program to convert
its almost entirely state-owned and controlled economy to a market system.
The koruna now enjoys almost full internal convertibility and over 90% of
prices are set by the market. The government is planning to privatize all
small businesses and roughly two-thirds of large enterprises by the end of
1993. New private-sector activity is also expanding. Agriculture - 95%
socialized - is to be privatized by the end of 1992. Reform has taken its
toll on the economy: inflation was roughly 50% in 1991, unemployment was
nearly 70%, and GDP dropped an estimated 15%. In 1992 the government is
anticipating inflation of 10-15%, unemployment of 11-12%, and a drop in GDP
of up to 8%. As of mid-1992, the nation appears to be splitting in two -
into the industrial Czech area and the more agarian Slovak area.

GDP:

purchasing power equivalent - $108.9 billion, per capita $6,900; real growth
rate -15% (1991 est.)

Inflation rate (consumer prices):

52% (1991 est.)

Unemployment rate: officially 6.7% (1991 est.)

Budget:

revenues $4.5 billion; expenditures $4.5 billion, including capital
expenditures of $200 million (1992)

Exports:

$12.0 billion (f.o.b., 1990)
  commodities:
    machinery and equipment 39.2%; fuels, minerals, and metals 8.1%;
    agricultural and forestry products 6.2%, other 46.5%
  partners:
    USSR, Germany, Poland, Austria, Hungary, Yugoslavia, Italy, France, US, UK
Imports:
  $13.3 billion (f.o.b., 1990)
  commodities:
    machinery and equipment 37.3%; fuels, minerals, and metals 22.6%;
    agricultural and forestry products 7.0%; other 33.1%
  partners:
    USSR, Germany, Austria, Poland, Switzerland, Hungary, Yugoslavia, UK, Italy
External debt: $9.1 billion, hard currency indebtedness (December 1991)
Industrial production:
  growth rate -22% (1991 est.); accounts for almost 60% of GNP
Electricity:
  23,000,000 kW capacity; 90,000 million kWh produced, 5,740 kWh per capita
  (1990)
Industries:
  iron and steel, machinery and equipment, cement, sheet glass, motor
  vehicles, armaments, chemicals, ceramics, wood, paper products, footwear
Agriculture:
  accounts for 9% of GDP (includes forestry); largely self-sufficient in food
  production; diversified crop and livestock production, including grains,
  potatoes, sugar beets, hops, fruit, hogs, cattle, and poultry; exporter of
  forest products

:Czechoslovakia Economy

Illicit drugs:
  transshipment point for Southwest Asian heroin and emerging as a
  transshipment point for Latin American cocaine E
Economic aid:
  donor - $4.2 billion in bilateral aid to non-Communist less developed
  countries (1954-89)
Currency:
  koruna (plural - koruny); 1 koruna (Kc) = 100 haleru
Exchange rates:
  koruny (Kcs) per US$1 - 28.36 (January 1992), 29.53 (1991), 17.95 (1990),
  15.05 (1989), 14.36 (1988), 13.69 (1987)
Fiscal year: calendar year

:Czechoslovakia Communications

Railroads:
  13,103 km total; 12,855 km 1.435-meter standard gauge, 102 km 1.520-meter
  broad gauge, 146 km 0.750- and 0.760-meter narrow gauge; 2,861 km double
  track; 3,798 km electrified; government owned (1988)
Highways:
  73,540 km total; including 517 km superhighway (1988)
Inland waterways:
  475 km (1988); the Elbe (Labe) is the principal river

Pipelines:
    crude oil 1,448 km; petroleum products 1,500 km; natural gas 8,100 km
Ports:
    maritime outlets are in Poland (Gdynia, Gdansk, Szczecin), Croatia (Rijeka), Slovenia (Koper), Germany (Hamburg, Rostock); principal river ports are Prague on the Vltava, Decin on the Elbe (Labe), Komarno on the Danube, Bratislava on the Danube
Merchant marine:
    22 ships (1,000 GRT or over) totaling 290,185 GRT/437,291 DWT; includes 13 cargo, 9 bulk
Civil air:
    47 major transport aircraft
Airports:
    158 total, 158 usable; 40 with permanent-surface runways; 19 with runways 2,440-3,659 m; 37 with runways 1,220-2,439 m
Telecommunications:
    inadequate circuit capacity; 4 million telephones; Radrel backbone of network; 25% of households have a telephone; broadcast stations - 32 AM, 15 FM, 41 TV (11 Soviet TV repeaters); 4.4 million TVs (1990); 1 satellite earth station using INTELSAT and Intersputnik

:Czechoslovakia Defense Forces

Branches:
    Army, Air and Air Defense Forces, Civil Defense, Border Guard
Manpower availability:
    males 15-49, 4,110,628; 3,142,457 fit for military service; 142,239 reach military age (18) annually
Defense expenditures:
    exchange rate conversion - 28 billion koruny, NA% of GNP (1991); note - conversion of defense expenditures into US dollars using the current exchange rate would produce misleading results

Denmark Geography

Total area: 43,070 km2
Land area: 42,370 km2; includes the island of Bornholm in the Baltic Sea and the rest of metropolitan Denmark, but excludes the Faroe Islands and Greenland
Comparative area: slightly more than twice the size of Massachusetts
Land boundaries:
    68 km; Germany 68 km
Coastline:
    3,379 km
Maritime claims:
 Contiguous zone:
  4 nm
 Continental shelf:
  200 m (depth) or to depth of exploitation
 Exclusive fishing zone:
  200 nm
 Territorial sea:
  3 nm
Disputes:

Rockall continental shelf dispute involving Iceland, Ireland, and the UK
(Ireland and the UK have signed a boundary agreement in the Rockall area);
Denmark has challenged Norway's maritime claims between Greenland and Jan
Mayen

Climate:
temperate; humid and overcast; mild, windy winters and cool summers

Terrain:
low and flat to gently rolling plains

Natural resources:
crude oil, natural gas, fish, salt, limestone

Land use:
arable land 61%; permanent crops NEGL%; meadows and pastures 6%; forest and
woodland 12%; other 21%; includes irrigated 9%

Environment:
air and water pollution

Note:
controls Danish Straits linking Baltic and North Seas

:Denmark People

Population: 5,163,955 (July 1992), growth rate 0.2% (1992)
Birth rate: 13 births/1,000 population (1992)
Death rate: 12 deaths/1,000 population (1992)
Net migration rate: 1 migrant/1,000 population (1992)
Infant mortality rate: 7 deaths/1,000 live births (1992)
Life expectancy at birth: 72 years male, 78 years female (1992)
Total fertility rate: 1.7 children born/woman (1992)
Nationality:
noun - Dane(s); adjective - Danish
Ethnic divisions:
Scandinavian, Eskimo, Faroese, German
Religions:
Evangelical Lutheran 91%, other Protestant and Roman Catholic 2%, other 7%
(1988)
Languages:
Danish, Faroese, Greenlandic (an Eskimo dialect); small German-speaking
minority
Literacy:
99% (male NA%, female NA%) age 15 and over can read and write (1980 est.)
Labor force:
2,581,400; private services 36.4%; government services 30.2%; manufacturing
and mining 20%; construction 6.8%; agriculture, forestry, and fishing 5.9%;
electricity/gas/water 0.7% (1990)
Organized labor:
65% of labor force

:Denmark Government

Long-form name:
Kingdom of Denmark
Type:
constitutional monarchy
Capital: Copenhagen

Administrative divisions:
  metropolitan Denmark - 14 counties (amter, singular - amt) and 1 city*
  (stad); Arhus, Bornholm, Frederiksborg, Fyn, Kbenhavn, Nordjylland, Ribe,
  Ringkbing, Roskilde, Snderjylland, Staden Kbenhavn*, Storstrm, Vejle,
  Vestsjaelland, Viborg; note - see separate entries for the Faroe Islands and
  Greenland, which are part of the Danish realm and self-governing
  administrative divisions
Independence:
  became a constitutional monarchy in 1849
Constitution:
  5 June 1953
Legal system:
  civil law system; judicial review of legislative acts; accepts compulsory
  ICJ jurisdiction, with reservations
National holiday:
  Birthday of the Queen, 16 April (1940)
Executive branch:
  monarch, heir apparent, prime minister, Cabinet
Legislative branch:
  unicameral parliament (Folketing)
Judicial branch:
  Supreme Court
Leaders:
 Chief of State:
  Queen MARGRETHE II (since January 1972); Heir Apparent Crown Prince
  FREDERIK, elder son of the Queen (born 26 May 1968)
 Head of Government:
  Prime Minister Poul SCHLUTER (since 10 September 1982)
Political parties and leaders:
  Social Democratic Party, Paul Nyrup RASMUSSEN; Conservative Party, Poul
  SCHLUTER; Liberal Party, Uffe ELLEMANN-JENSEN; Socialist People's Party,
  Holger K. NIELSEN; Progress Party, Pia KJAERSGAARD; Center Democratic Par-
ty,
  Mimi Stilling JAKOBSEN; Radical Liberal Party, Marianne JELVED; Christian
  People's Party, Jam SJURSEN; Left Socialist Party, Elizabeth BRUN-OLESEN;
  Justice Party, Poul Gerhard KRISTIANSEN; Socialist Workers Party, leader NA;
  Communist Workers' Party (KAP), leader NA; Common Course, Preben Meller
  HANSEN; Green Party, Inger BORLEHMANN
Suffrage:
  universal at age 21
Elections:
 Parliament:
  last held 12 December 1990 (next to be held by December 1994); results -
  Social Democratic Party 37.4%, Conservative Party 16.0%, Liberal 15.8%,
  Socialist People's Party 8.3%, Progress Party 6.4%, Center Democratic Party
  5.1%, Radical Liberal Party 3.5%, Christian People's Party 2.3%, other 5.2%;
  seats - (179 total; includes 2 from Greenland and 2 from the Faroe Islands)
  Social Democratic 69, Conservative 30, Liberal 29, Socialist People's 15,
  Progress Party 12, Center Democratic 9, Radical Liberal 7, Christian
  People's 4

:Denmark Government

Member of:
AfDB, AG (observer), AsDB, Australia Group, BIS, CCC, CE, CERN, COCOM, CSCE,
EBRD, EC, ECE, EIB, ESA, FAO, G-9, GATT, IADB, IAEA, IBRD, ICAO, ICC, ICFTU,
IDA, IEA, IFAD, IFC, ILO, IMF, IMO, INMARSAT, INTELSAT, INTERPOL, IOC, IOM,
ISO, ITU, LORCS, MTCR, NACC, NATO, NC, NEA, NIB, NSG, OECD, PCA, UN, UNCTAD,
UNESCO, UNFICYP, UNHCR, UNIDO, UNIIMOG, UNMOGIP, UNTSO, UPU, WHO, WIPO, WM,
ZC

Diplomatic representation:
Ambassador Peter Pedersen DYVIG; Chancery at 3200 Whitehaven Street NW, Washington, DC 20008; telephone (202) 234-4300; there are Danish Consulates General in Chicago, Los Angeles, and New York

US:
Ambassador Richard B. STONE; Embassy at Dag Hammarskjolds Alle 24, 2100 Copenhagen O (mailing address is APO AE 09716); telephone [45] (31) 42-31-44; FAX [45] (35) 43-0223

Flag:
red with a white cross that extends to the edges of the flag; the vertical part of the cross is shifted to the hoist side, and that design element of the (Danish flag) was subsequently adopted by the other Nordic countries of Finland, Iceland, Norway, and Sweden

:Denmark Economy

Overview:
This modern economy features high-tech agriculture, up-to-date small-scale and corporate industry, extensive government welfare measures, comfortable living standards, and high dependence on foreign trade. Denmark probably will continue its successful economic recovery in 1992 with tight fiscal and monetary policies and export- oriented growth. Prime Minister Schluter's main priorities are to maintain a current account surplus in order to pay off extensive external debt and to continue to freeze public-sector expenditures in order to reduce the budget deficit. The rate of growth by 1993 - boosted by increased investment and domestic demand - may be sufficient to start to cut Denmark's high unemployment rate, which is expected to remain at about 11% in 1992. Low inflation, low wage increases, and the current account surplus put Denmark in a good competitive position for the EC's anticipated single market, although Denmark must cut its VAT and income taxes.

GDP:
purchasing power equivalent - $91.1 billion, per capita $17,700; real growth rate 2.0% (1991)

Inflation rate (consumer prices):
2.4% (1991)

Unemployment rate: 10.6% (1991)

Budget:

revenues $44.1 billion; expenditures $50 billion, including capital
expenditures of $NA billion (1991 est.)
Exports:
  $37.8 billion (f.o.b., 1991)
  commodities:
  meat and meat products, dairy products, transport equipment (shipbuilding),
  fish, chemicals, industrial machinery
  partners:
  EC 54.2% (Germany 22.5%, UK 10.3%, France 5.9%), Sweden 11.5%, Norway
  5.8%,
  US 5.0%, Japan 3.6% (1991)
Imports:
  $31.6 billion (c.i.f., 1991)
  commodities:
  petroleum, machinery and equipment, chemicals, grain and foodstuffs,
  textiles, paper
  partners:
  EC 52.8% (Germany 22.5%, UK 8.1%), Sweden 10.8%, US 6.3% (1991)
External debt: $45 billion (1991)
Industrial production:
  growth rate 0% (1991 est.)
Electricity:
  11,215,000 kW capacity; 31,000 million kWh produced, 6,030 kWh per capita
  (1991)
Industries:
  food processing, machinery and equipment, textiles and clothing, chemical
  products, electronics, construction, furniture, and other wood products
Agriculture:
  accounts for 4.5% of GDP and employs 6% of labor force (includes fishing and
  forestry); farm products account for nearly 15% of export revenues;
  principal products - meat, dairy, grain, potatoes, rape, sugar beets, fish;
  self-sufficient in food production
Economic aid:
  donor - ODA and OOF commitments (1970-89) $5.9 billion
Currency:
  Danish krone (plural - kroner); 1 Danish krone (DKr) = 100 re

:Denmark Economy

Exchange rates:
  Danish kroner (DKr) per US$1 - 6.116 (January 1992), 6.396 (1991), 6.189
  (1990), 7.310 (1989), 6.732 (1988), 6.840 (1987)
Fiscal year: calendar year

:Denmark Communications

Railroads:
  2,675 km 1.435-meter standard gauge; Danish State Railways (DSB) operate
  2,120 km (1,999 km rail line and 121 km rail ferry services); 188 km
  electrified, 730 km double tracked; 650 km of standard- gauge lines are
  privately owned and operated
Highways:
  66,482 km total; 64,551 km concrete, bitumen, or stone block; 1,931 km

gravel, crushed stone, improved earth
Inland waterways:
  417 km
Pipelines:
  crude oil 110 km; petroleum products 578 km; natural gas 700 km
Ports:
  Alborg, Arhus, Copenhagen, Esbjerg, Fredericia; numerous secondary and minor
  ports
Merchant marine:
  317 ships (1,000 GRT or over) totaling 5,367,063 GRT/7,921,891 DWT; includes
  13 short-sea passenger, 94 cargo, 21 refrigerated cargo, 38 container, 39
  roll-on/roll-off, 1 railcar carrier, 42 petroleum tanker, 14 chemical
  tanker, 33 liquefied gas, 4 livestock carrier, 17 bulk, 1 combination bulk;
  note - Denmark has created its own internal register, called the Danish
  International Ship register (DIS); DIS ships do not have to meet Danish
  manning regulations, and they amount to a flag of convenience within the
  Danish register; by the end of 1990, 258 of the Danish-flag ships belonged
  to the DIS
Civil air:
  69 major transport aircraft
Airports:
  121 total, 108 usable; 27 with permanent-surface runways; none with runways
  over 3,659 m; 9 with runways 2,440-3,659 m; 6 with runways 1,220-2,439 m
Telecommunications:
  excellent telephone, telegraph, and broadcast services; 4,509,000
  telephones; buried and submarine cables and radio relay support trunk
  network; broadcast stations - 3 AM, 2 FM, 50 TV; 19 submarine coaxial
  cables; 7 earth stations operating in INTELSAT, EUTELSAT, and INMARSAT

:Denmark Defense Forces

Branches:
  Royal Danish Army, Royal Danish Navy, Royal Danish Air Force, Home Guard
Manpower availability:
  males 15-49, 1,372,878; 1,181,857 fit for military service; 38,221 reach
  military age (20) annually
Defense expenditures:
  exchange rate conversion - $2.5 billion, 2% of GDP (1991)

Djibouti Geography

Total area: 22,000 km2
Land area: 21,980 km2
Comparative area: slightly larger than Massachusetts
Land boundaries:
  517 km; Ethiopia 459 km, Somalia 58 km
Coastline:
  314 km
Maritime claims:
 Contiguous zone:
  24 nm
 Exclusive economic zone:
  200 nm

Territorial sea:
  12 nm
Disputes:
  possible claim by Somalia based on unification of ethnic Somalis
Climate:
  desert; torrid, dry
Terrain:
  coastal plain and plateau separated by central mountains
Natural resources:
  geothermal areas
Land use:
  arable land 0%; permanent crops 0%; meadows and pastures 9%; forest and
  woodland NEGL%; other 91%
Environment:
  vast wasteland
Note:
  strategic location near world's busiest shipping lanes and close to Arabian
  oilfields; terminus of rail traffic into Ethiopia

:Djibouti People

Population: 390,906 (July 1992), growth rate 2.7% (1992)
Birth rate: 43 births/1,000 population (1992)
Death rate: 16 deaths/1,000 population (1992)
Net migration rate: 0 migrants/1,000 population (1992)
Infant mortality rate: 115 deaths/1,000 live births (1992)
Life expectancy at birth: 47 years male, 50 years female (1992)
Total fertility rate: 6.3 children born/woman (1992)
Nationality:
  noun - Djiboutian(s); adjective - Djiboutian
Ethnic divisions:
  Somali 60%, Afar 35%, French, Arab, Ethiopian, and Italian 5%
Religions:
  Muslim 94%, Christian 6%
Languages:
  French and Arabic (both official); Somali and Afar widely used
Literacy:
  48% (male 63%, female 34%) age 15 and over can read and write (1990)
Labor force:
  NA, but a small number of semiskilled laborers at the port and 3,000 railway
  workers; 52% of population of working age (1983)
Organized labor:
  3,000 railway workers, General Union of Djiboutian Workers (UGTD),
  government affiliated; some smaller unions

:Djibouti Government

Long-form name:
  Republic of Djibouti
Type:
  republic
Capital: Djibouti
Administrative divisions:

5 districts (cercles, singular - cercle); `Ali Sabih, Dikhil, Djibouti, Obock, Tadjoura

Independence:
27 June 1977 (from France; formerly French Territory of the Afars and Issas)

Constitution:
partial constitution ratified January 1981 by the National Assembly

Legal system:
based on French civil law system, traditional practices, and Islamic law

National holiday:
Independence Day, 27 June (1977)

Executive branch:
president, prime minister, Council of Ministers

Legislative branch:
National Assembly (Assemblee Nationale)

Judicial branch:
Supreme Court (Cour Supreme)

Leaders:
Chief of State:
President Hassan GOULED Aptidon (since 24 June 1977)
Head of Government:
Prime Minister BARKAT Gourad Hamadou (since 30 September 1978)

Political parties and leaders:
only party - People's Progress Assembly (RPP), Hassan GOULED Aptidon

Suffrage:
universal adult at age NA

Elections:
National Assembly:
last held 24 April 1987 (next scheduled for May 1992 but post- poned); results - RPP is the only party; seats - (65 total) RPP 65
President:
last held 24 April 1987 (next to be held April 1993); results - President Hassan GOULED Aptidon was reelected without opposition

Other political or pressure groups:
Front for the Restoration of Unity and Democracy and affiliates

Member of:
ACCT, ACP, AfDB, AFESD, AL, ECA, FAO, G-77, IBRD, ICAO, IDA, IDB, IFAD, IFC,
IGADD, ILO, IMF, IMO, INTERPOL, IOC, ITU, LORCS, NAM, OAU, OIC, UN, UNESCO,
UNCTAD, UPU, WHO, WMO

Diplomatic representation:
Ambassador Roble OLHAYE; Chancery at Suite 515, 1156 15th Street NW, Washington, DC 20005; telephone (202) 331-0270
US:
Ambassador Charles R. BAQUET III; Embassy at Villa Plateau du Serpent, Boulevard Marechal Joffre, Djibouti (mailing address is B. P. 185, Djibouti); telephone [253] 35-39-95; FAX [253] 35-39-40

Flag:
two equal horizontal bands of light blue (top) and light green with a white

isosceles triangle based on the hoist side bearing a red five-pointed star in the center

:Djibouti Economy

Overview:

The economy is based on service activities connected with the country's strategic location and status as a free trade zone in northeast Africa. Djibouti provides services as both a transit port for the region and an international transshipment and refueling center. It has few natural resources and little industry. The nation is, therefore, heavily dependent on foreign assistance to help support its balance of payments and to finance development projects. An unemployment rate of over 30% continues to be a major problem. Per capita consumption dropped an estimated 35% over the last five years because of recession and a high population growth rate (including immigrants and refugees).

GDP:

exchange rate conversion - $340 million, $1,000 per capita; real growth rate -1.0% (1989 est.)

Inflation rate (consumer prices):

3.7% (1989)

Unemployment rate: over 30% (1989)

Budget:

revenues $131 million; expenditures $154 million, including capital expenditures of $25 million (1990 est.)

Exports:

$190 million (f.o.b., 1990 est.)

commodities:

hides and skins, coffee (in transit)

partners:

Middle East 50%, Africa 43%, Western Europe 7%

Imports:

$311 million (f.o.b., 1990 est.)

commodities:

foods, beverages, transport equipment, chemicals, petroleum products

partners:

EC 36%, Africa 21%, Asia 12%, US 2%

External debt: $355 million (December 1990)

Industrial production:

growth rate 0.1% (1989); manufacturing accounts for 4% of GDP

Electricity:

115,000 kW capacity; 200 million kWh produced, 580 kWh per capita (1991)

Industries:

limited to a few small-scale enterprises, such as dairy products and mineral-water bottling

Agriculture:

accounts for only 5% of GDP; scanty rainfall limits crop production to mostly fruit and vegetables; half of population pastoral nomads herding goats, sheep, and camels; imports bulk of food needs

Economic aid:

US commitments, including Ex-Im (FY78-89), $39 million; Western (non-US)

countries, including ODA and OOF bilateral commitments (1970-89), $1.1 billion; OPEC bilateral aid (1979-89), $149 million; Communist countries (1970-89), $35 million

Currency:
Djiboutian franc (plural - francs); 1 Djiboutian franc (DF) = 100 centimes

Exchange rates:
Djiboutian francs (DF) per US$1 - 177.721 (fixed rate since 1973)

Fiscal year: calendar year

:Djibouti Communications

Railroads:
the Ethiopian-Djibouti railroad extends for 97 km through Djibouti

Highways:
2,900 km total; 280 km paved; 2,620 km improved or unimproved earth (1982)

Ports:
Djibouti

Civil air:
1 major transport aircraft

Airports:
13 total, 11 usable; 2 with permanent-surface runways; none with runways over 3,659 m; 2 with runways 2,440-3,659 m; 5 with runways 1,220-2,439 m

Telecommunications:
fair system of urban facilities in Djibouti and radio relay stations at outlying places; broadcast stations - 2 AM, 1 FM, 1 TV; 1 Indian Ocean INTELSAT earth station and 1 ARABSAT; 1 submarine cable to Saudi Arabia

:Djibouti Defense Forces

Branches:
Djibouti National Army (including Navy and Air Force), National Security Force (Force Nationale de Securite), National Police Force

Manpower availability:
males 15-49, 96,150; 56,077 fit for military service

Defense expenditures:
exchange rate conversion - $29.9 million, NA% of GDP (1986)

Dominica Geography

Total area: 750 km2
Land area: 750 km2
Comparative area: slightly more than four times the size of Washington, DC
Land boundaries:
none
Coastline:
148 km
Maritime claims:
 Contiguous zone:
 24 nm
 Exclusive economic zone:
 200 nm
 Territorial sea:
 12 nm
Disputes:

Climate:
  tropical; moderated by northeast trade winds; heavy rainfall
Terrain:
  rugged mountains of volcanic origin
Natural resources:
  timber
Land use:
  arable land 9%; permanent crops 13%; meadows and pastures 3%; forest and woodland 41%; other 34%
Environment:
  flash floods a constant hazard; occasional hurricanes
Note:
  located 550 km southeast of Puerto Rico in the Caribbean Sea

:Dominica People

Population: 87,035 (July 1992), growth rate 1.6% (1992)
Birth rate: 24 births/1,000 population (1992)
Death rate: 5 deaths/1,000 population (1992)
Net migration rate: -3 migrants/1,000 population (1992)
Infant mortality rate: 11 deaths/1,000 live births (1992)
Life expectancy at birth: 74 years male, 79 years female (1992)
Total fertility rate: 2.4 children born/woman (1992)
Nationality:
  noun - Dominican(s); adjective - Dominican
Ethnic divisions:
  mostly black; some Carib Indians
Religions:
  Roman Catholic 77%, Protestant 15% (Methodist 5%, Pentecostal 3%, Seventh-Day Adventist 3%, Baptist 2%, other 2%), none 2%, unknown 1%, other 5%
Languages:
  English (official); French patois widely spoken
Literacy:
  94% (male 94%, female 94%) age 15 and over having ever attended school (1970)
Labor force:
  25,000; agriculture 40%, industry and commerce 32%, services 28% (1984)
Organized labor:
  25% of labor force

:Dominica Government

Long-form name:
  Commonwealth of Dominica
Type:
  parliamentary democracy
Capital: Roseau
Administrative divisions:
  10 parishes; Saint Andrew, Saint David, Saint George, Saint John, Saint Joseph, Saint Luke, Saint Mark, Saint Patrick, Saint Paul, Saint Peter
Independence:

3 November 1978 (from UK)
Constitution:
   3 November 1978
Legal system:
   based on English common law
National holiday:
   Independence Day, 3 November (1978)
Executive branch:
   president, prime minister, Cabinet
Legislative branch:
   unicameral House of Assembly
Judicial branch:
   Eastern Caribbean Supreme Court
Leaders:
  Chief of State:
   President Sir Clarence Augustus SEIGNORET (since 19 December 1983)
  Head of Government:
   Prime Minister (Mary) Eugenia CHARLES (since 21 July 1980, elected for a
   third term 28 May 1990)
Political parties and leaders:
   Dominica Freedom Party (DFP), (Mary) Eugenia CHARLES; Dominica Labor Party
   (DLP), Pierre CHARLES; United Workers Party (UWP), Edison JAMES
Suffrage:
   universal at age 18
Elections:
  House of Assembly:
   last held 28 May 1990 (next to be held May 1995); results - percent of vote
   by party NA; seats - (30 total; 9 appointed senators and 21 elected
   representatives) DFP 11, UWP 6, DLP 4
  President:
   last held 20 December 1988 (next to be held December 1993); results -
   President Sir Clarence Augustus SEIGNORET was reelected by the House of
   Assembly
Other political or pressure groups:
   Dominica Liberation Movement (DLM), a small leftist group
Member of:
   ACCT, ACP, C, CARICOM, CDB, ECLAC, FAO, G-77, IBRD, ICFTU, IDA,
IFAD, IFC,
   ILO, IMF, IMO, INTERPOL, LORCS, NAM (observer), OAS, OECS, UN,
UNCTAD,
   UNESCO, UNIDO, UPU, WCL, WHO, WMO
Diplomatic representation:
   there is no Chancery in the US
  US:
   no official presence since the Ambassador resides in Bridgetown (Barbados),
   but travels frequently to Dominica

:Dominica Government

Flag:
   green with a centered cross of three equal bands - the vertical part is

265

yellow (hoist side), black, and white - the horizontal part is yellow (top), black, and white; superimposed in the center of the cross is a red disk bearing a sisserou parrot encircled by 10 green five-pointed stars edged in yellow; the 10 stars represent the 10 administrative divisions (parishes)

:Dominica Economy

Overview:

The economy is dependent on agriculture and thus is highly vulnerable to climatic conditions. Agriculture accounts for about 30% of GDP and employs 40% of the labor force. Principal products include bananas, citrus, mangoes, root crops, and coconuts. In 1990, GDP grew by 7%, bouncing back from the 1.6% decline of 1989. The tourist industry remains undeveloped because of a rugged coastline and the lack of an international airport.

GDP:

purchasing power equivalent - $170 million, per capita $2,000; real growth rate 7.0% (1990 est.)

Inflation rate (consumer prices):

4.7% (1990)

Unemployment rate: 10% (1989 est.)

Budget:

revenues $48 million; expenditures $85 million, including capital expenditures of $41 million (FY90)

Exports:

$59.9 million (f.o.b., 1990)

commodities:

bananas, coconuts, grapefruit, soap, galvanized sheets

partners:

UK 72%, Jamaica 10%, OECS 6%, US 3%, other 9%

Imports:

$103.9 million (c.i.f., 1990)

commodities:

food, oils and fats, chemicals, fuels and lubricants, manufactured goods, machinery and equipment

partners:

US 23%, UK 18%, CARICOM 15%, OECS 15%, Japan 5%, Canada 3%, other 21%

External debt: $73 million (1990 est.)

Industrial production:

growth rate 4.5% in manufacturing (1988 est.); accounts for 11% of GDP

Electricity:

7,000 kW capacity; 16 million kWh produced, 185 kWh per capita (1991)

Industries:

soap, beverages, tourism, food processing, furniture, cement blocks, shoes

Agriculture:

accounts for 30% of GDP; principal crops - bananas, citrus, mangoes, root crops, and coconuts; bananas provide the bulk of export earnings; forestry and fisheries potential not exploited

Economic aid:

Western (non-US) countries, ODA and OOF bilateral commitments (1970-89), $120 million

Currency:

266

East Caribbean dollar (plural - dollars); 1 EC dollar (EC$) = 100 cents
Exchange rates:
  East Caribbean dollars (EC$) per US$1 - 2.70 (fixed rate since 1976)
Fiscal year: 1 July - 30 June

:Dominica Communications

Highways:
  750 km total; 370 km paved, 380 km gravel and earth
Ports:
  Roseau, Portsmouth
Civil air:
  NA
Airports:
  2 total, 2 usable; 2 with permanent-surface runways; none with runways over
  2,439 m; 1 with runways 1,220-2,439 m
Telecommunications:
  4,600 telephones in fully automatic network; VHF and UHF link to Saint
  Lucia; new SHF links to Martinique and Guadeloupe; broadcast stations - 3
  AM, 2 FM, 1 cable TV

:Dominica Defense Forces

Branches:
  Commonwealth of Dominica Police Force (including Coast Guard)
Manpower availability:
  NA
Defense expenditures:
  exchange rate conversion - $NA, NA% of GDP

Dominican Republic Geography

Total area: 48,730 km2
Land area: 48,380 km2
Comparative area: slightly more than twice the size of New Hampshire
Land boundaries:
  275 km; Haiti 275 km
Coastline:
  1,288 km
Maritime claims:
 Contiguous zone:
  24 nm
 Continental shelf:
  outer edge of continental margin or 200 nm
 Exclusive economic zone:
  200 nm
 Territorial sea:
  6 nm
Disputes:
  none
Climate:
  tropical maritime; little seasonal temperature variation
Terrain:
  rugged highlands and mountains with fertile valleys interspersed

Natural resources:
  nickel, bauxite, gold, silver
Land use:
  arable land 23%; permanent crops 7%; meadows and pastures 43%; forest and woodland 13%; other 14%; includes irrigated 4%
Environment:
  subject to occasional hurricanes (July to October); deforestation
Note:
  shares island of Hispaniola with Haiti (western one-third is Haiti, eastern two-thirds is the Dominican Republic)

:Dominican Republic People

Population: 7,515,892 (July 1992), growth rate 1.9% (1992)
Birth rate: 26 births/1,000 population (1992)
Death rate: 7 deaths/1,000 population (1992)
Net migration rate: -1 migrant/1,000 population (1992)
Infant mortality rate: 56 deaths/1,000 live births (1992)
Life expectancy at birth: 66 years male, 70 years female (1992)
Total fertility rate: 3.0 children born/woman (1992)
Nationality:
  noun - Dominican(s); adjective - Dominican
Ethnic divisions:
  mixed 73%, white 16%, black 11%
Religions:
  Roman Catholic 95%
Languages:
  Spanish
Literacy:
  83% (male 85%, female 82%) age 15 and over can read and write (1990 est.)
Labor force:
  2,300,000 to 2,600,000; agriculture 49%, services 33%, industry 18% (1986)
Organized labor:
  12% of labor force (1989 est.)

:Dominican Republic Government

Long-form name:
  Dominican Republic (no short-form name)
Type:
  republic
Capital: Santo Domingo
Administrative divisions:
  29 provinces (provincias, singular - provincia) and 1 district* (distrito); Azua, Baoruco, Barahona, Dajabon, Distrito Nacional*, Duarte, Elias Pina, El Seibo, Espaillat, Hato Mayor, Independencia, La Altagracia, La Romana, La Vega, Maria Trinidad Sanchez, Monsenor Nouel, Monte Cristi, Monte Plata, Pedernales, Peravia, Puerto Plata, Salcedo, Samana, Sanchez Ramirez, San Cristobal, San Juan, San Pedro De Macoris, Santiago, Santiago Rodriguez, Valverde
Independence:
  27 February 1844 (from Haiti)
Constitution:

28 November 1966

Legal system:

based on French civil codes

National holiday:

Independence Day, 27 February (1844)

Executive branch:

president, vice president, Cabinet

Legislative branch:

bicameral National Congress (Congreso Nacional) consists of an upper chamber or Senate (Senado) and lower chamber or Chamber of Deputies (Camara de Diputados)

Judicial branch:

Supreme Court (Corte Suprema)

Leaders:

Chief of State and Head of Government:

President Joaquin BALAGUER Ricardo (since 16 August 1986, fifth elected term began 16 August 1990); Vice President Carlos A. MORALES Troncoso (since 16 August 1986)

Political parties and leaders:

Major parties:

Social Christian Reformist Party (PRSC), Joaquin BALAGUER Ricardo; Dominican Revolutionary Party (PRD), Jose Franciso PENA Gomez; Dominican Liberation Party (PLD), Juan BOSCH Gavino; Independent Revolutionary Party (PRI), Jacobo MAJLUTA

Minor parties:

National Veterans and Civilian Party (PNVC), Juan Rene BEAUCHAMPS Javier; Liberal Party of the Dominican Republic (PLRD), Andres Van Der HORST; Democratic Quisqueyan Party (PQD), Elias WESSIN Chavez; National Progressive Force (FNP), Marino VINICIO Castillo; Popular Christian Party (PPC), Rogelio DELGADO Bogaert; Dominican Communist Party (PCD) Narciso ISA Conde; Dominican Workers' Party (PTD), Ivan RODRIGUEZ; Anti-Imperialist Patriotic Union (UPA), Ignacio RODRIGUEZ Chiappini

Note:

in 1983 several leftist parties, including the PCD, joined to form the Dominican Leftist Front (FID); however, they still retain individual party structures

Suffrage:

universal and compulsory at age 18 or if married; members of the armed forces and police cannot vote

:Dominican Republic Government

Elections:

Chamber of Deputies:

last held 16 May 1990 (next to be held May 1994); results - percent of vote by party NA; seats - (120 total) PLD 44, PRSC 41, PRD 33, PRI 2

President:

last held 16 May 1990 (next to be held May 1994); results - Joaquin BALAGUER (PRSC) 35.7%, Juan BOSCH Gavino (PLD) 34.4%

Senate:

last held 16 May 1990 (next to be held May 1994); results - percent of vote by party NA; seats - (30 total) PRSC 16, PLD 12, PRD 2

Communists:

an estimated 8,000 to 10,000 members in several legal and illegal factions; effectiveness limited by ideological differences, organizational inadequacies, and severe funding shortages

Member of:

ACP, CARICOM (observer), ECLAC, FAO, G-11, G-77, GATT, IADB, IAEA, IBRD,

ICAO, ICFTU, IDA, IFAD, IFC, ILO, IMF, IMO, INTELSAT, INTERPOL, IOC, IOM,

ITU, LAES, LORCS, NAM (guest), OAS, OPANAL, PCA, UN, UNCTAD, UNESCO, UNIDO,

UPU, WCL, WFTU, WHO, WMO, WTO

Diplomatic representation:

Ambassador Jose del Carmen ARIZA Gomez; Chancery at 1715 22nd Street NW, Washington, DC 20008; telephone (202) 332-6280; there are Dominican Consulates General in Boston, Chicago, Los Angeles, Mayaguez (Puerto Rico), Miami, New Orleans, New York, Philadelphia, San Juan (Puerto Rico), and Consulates in Charlotte Amalie (Virgin Islands), Detroit, Houston, Jacksonville, Minneapolis, Mobile, Ponce (Puerto Rico), and San Francisco

US:

Ambassador Robert S. PASTORINO; Embassy at the corner of Calle Cesar Nicolas Penson and Calle Leopoldo Navarro, Santo Domingo (mailing address is APO AA 34041-0008); telephone (809) 5412171

Flag:

a centered white cross that extends to the edges, divides the flag into four rectangles - the top ones are blue (hoist side) and red, the bottom ones are red (hoist side) and blue; a small coat of arms is at the center of the cross

:Dominican Republic Economy

Overview:

The economy is largely dependent on trade; imported components average 60% of the value of goods consumed in the domestic market. Rapid growth of free trade zones has established a significant expansion of manufacturing for export, especially wearing apparel. Over the past decade, tourism has also increased in importance and is a major earner of foreign exchange and a source of new jobs. Agriculture remains a key sector of the economy. The principal commercial crop is sugarcane, followed by coffee, cotton, cocoa, and tobacco. Domestic industry is based on the processing of agricultural products, durable consumer goods, minerals, and chemicals. Unemployment is officially reported at about 30%, but there is considerable underemployment. A fiscal austerity program has brought inflation under control, but in 1991 the economy contracted for a second straight year.

GDP:

exchange rate conversion - $7 billion, per capita $950; real growth rate -2% (1991 est.)

Inflation rate (consumer prices):

9% (1991 est.)

Unemployment rate: 30% (1991 est.)

Budget:
  revenues NA; expenditures $1.1 billion, including capital expenditures of NA
  (1992 est.)
Exports:
  $775 million (f.o.b., 1991 est.)
  commodities:
  sugar, coffee, cocoa, gold, ferronickel
  partners:
  US 60%, EC 19%, Puerto Rico 8% (1990)
Imports:
  $1.8 billion (c.i.f., 1991 est.)
  commodities:
  foodstuffs, petroleum, cotton and fabrics, chemicals and pharmaceuticals
  partners:
  US 50%
External debt: $4.7 billion (1991 est.)
Industrial production:
  growth rate NA; accounts for 20% of GDP
Electricity:
  2,133,000 kW capacity; 4,410 million kWh produced, 597 kWh per capita (1991)
Industries:
  tourism, sugar processing, ferronickel and gold mining, textiles, cement,
  tobacco
Agriculture:
  accounts for 15% of GDP and employs 49% of labor force; sugarcane is the
  most important commercial crop, followed by coffee, cotton, cocoa, and
  tobacco; food crops - rice, beans, potatoes, corn, bananas; animal output -
  cattle, hogs, dairy products, meat, eggs; not self-sufficient in food
Economic aid:
  US commitments, including Ex-Im (FY85-89), $575 million; Western (non-US)
  countries, ODA and OOF bilateral commitments (1970-89), $655 million
Currency:
  Dominican peso (plural - pesos); 1 Dominican peso (RD$) = 100 centavos
Exchange rates:
  Dominican pesos (RD$) per US$1 - 12.609 (January 1992), 12.692 (1991), 8.525
  (1990), 6.340 (1989), 6.113 (1988), 3.845 (1987)
Fiscal year: calendar year

:Dominican Republic Communications

Railroads:
  1,655 km total in numerous segments; 4 different gauges from 0.558 m to
  1.435 m
Highways:
  12,000 km total; 5,800 km paved, 5,600 km gravel and improved earth, 600 km
  unimproved
Pipelines:
  crude oil 96 km; petroleum products 8 km
Ports:
  Santo Domingo, Haina, San Pedro de Macoris, Puerto Plata
Merchant marine:

1 cargo ship (1,000 GRT or over) totaling 1,587 GRT/1,165 DWT

Civil air:

23 major transport aircraft

Airports:

36 total, 30 usable; 12 with permanent-surface runways; none with runways over 3,659 m; 3 with runways 2,440-3,659 m; 9 with runways 1,220-2,439 m

Telecommunications:

relatively efficient domestic system based on islandwide microwave relay network; 190,000 telephones; broadcast stations - 120 AM, no FM, 18 TV, 6 shortwave; 1 coaxial submarine cable; 1 Atlantic Ocean INTELSAT earth station

:Dominican Republic Defense Forces

Branches:

Army, Navy, Air Force, National Police

Manpower availability:

males 15-49, 2,013,294; 1,271,772 fit for military service; 80,117 reach military age (18) annually

Defense expenditures:

exchange rate conversion - $70 million, 1% of GDP (1990)

Ecuador Geography

Total area: 283,560 km2

Land area: 276,840 km2; includes Galapagos Islands

Comparative area: slightly smaller than Nevada

Land boundaries:

2,010 km; Colombia 590 km, Peru 1,420 km

Coastline:

2,237 km

Maritime claims:

 Continental shelf:

 claims continental shelf between mainland and Galapagos Islands

 Territorial sea:

 200 nm

Disputes:

three sections of the boundary with Peru are in dispute

Climate:

tropical along coast becoming cooler inland

Terrain:

coastal plain (Costa), inter-Andean central highlands (Sierra), and flat to rolling eastern jungle (Oriente)

Natural resources:

petroleum, fish, timber

Land use:

arable land 6%; permanent crops 3%; meadows and pastures 17%; forest and woodland 51%; other 23%; includes irrigated 2%

Environment:

subject to frequent earthquakes, landslides, volcanic activity; deforestation; desertification; soil erosion; periodic droughts

Note:

Cotopaxi in Andes is highest active volcano in world

:Ecuador People

Population: 10,933,143 (July 1992), growth rate 2.2% (1992)
Birth rate: 28 births/1,000 population (1992)
Death rate: 6 deaths/1,000 population (1992)
Net migration rate: 0 migrants/1,000 population (1992)
Infant mortality rate: 42 deaths/1,000 live births (1992)
Life expectancy at birth: 67 years male, 72 years female (1992)
Total fertility rate: 3.5 children born/woman (1992)
Nationality:
  noun - Ecuadorian(s); adjective - Ecuadorian
Ethnic divisions:
  mestizo (mixed Indian and Spanish) 55%, Indian 25%, Spanish 10%, black 10%
Religions:
  Roman Catholic 95%
Languages:
  Spanish (official); Indian languages, especially Quechua
Literacy:
  86% (male 88%, female 84%) age 15 and over can read and write (1990 est.)
Labor force:
  2,800,000; agriculture 35%, manufacturing 21%, commerce 16%, services and
  other activities 28% (1982)
Organized labor:
  less than 15% of labor force

:Ecuador Government

Long-form name:
  Republic of Ecuador
Type:
  republic
Capital: Quito
Administrative divisions:
  21 provinces (provincias, singular - provincia); Azuay, Bolivar, Canar,
  Carchi, Chimborazo, Cotopaxi, El Oro, Esmeraldas, Galapagos, Guayas,
  Imbabura, Loja, Los Rios, Manabi, Morona-Santiago, Napo, Pastaza, Pichincha,
  Sucumbios, Tungurahua, Zamora-Chinchipe
Independence:
  24 May 1822 (from Spain; Battle of Pichincha)
Constitution:
  10 August 1979
Legal system:
  based on civil law system; has not accepted compulsory ICJ jurisdiction
National holiday:
  Independence Day, 10 August (1809, independence of Quito)
Executive branch:
  president, vice president, Cabinet
Legislative branch:
  unicameral National Congress (Congreso Nacional)
Judicial branch:
  Supreme Court (Corte Suprema)
Leaders:

Chief of State and Head of Government:

President Rodrigo BORJA Cevallos (since 10 August 1988); Vice President Luis PARODI Valverde (since 10 August 1988)

Suffrage:

universal at age 18; compulsory for literate persons ages 18-65, optional for other eligible voters

Elections:

National Congress:

last held 17 June 1990 (next to be held 17 May 1992); results - percent of vote by party NA; seats - (72 total) PSC 16, ID 14, PRE 13, PSE 8, DP 7, CFP 3, PC 3, PLR 3, FADI 2, FRA 2, MPD 1

President:

runoff election held 5 July 1992; results - Sixto DURAN elected as president and Alberto DAHIK elected as vice president

Communists:

Communist Party of Ecuador (PCE, pro-Moscow), Rene Mauge MOSQUERA, secretary

general, 5,000 members; Communist Party of Ecuador/Marxist-Leninist (PCMLE, Maoist), 3,000 members; Socialist Party of Ecuador (PSE, pro-Cuba), 5,000 members (est.); National Liberation Party (PLN, Communist), less than 5,000 members (est.)

Member of:

AG, ECLAC, FAO, G-11, G-77, IADB, IAEA, IBRD, ICAO, ICC, ICFTU, IDA, IFAD,

IFC, ILO, IMF, IMO, INTELSAT, INTERPOL, IOC, IOM, ITU, LAES, LAIA, LORCS,

NAM, OAS, OPANAL, OPEC, PCA, RG, UN, UNCTAD, UNESCO, UNIDO, UPU, WCL, WFTU,

WHO, WIPO, WMO, WTO

Diplomatic representation:

Ambassador Jaime MONCAYO; Chancery at 2535 15th Street NW, Washington, DC

20009; telephone (202) 234-7200; there are Ecuadorian Consulates General in Chicago, Houston, Los Angeles, Miami, New Orleans, New York, and San Francisco, and a Consulate in San Diego

:Ecuador Government

US:

Ambassador vacant; Embassy at Avenida 12 de Octubre y Avenida Patria; Quito (mailing address is P. O. Box 538, Quito, or APO AA 34039); telephone [593] (2) 562-890; FAX [593] (2) 502-052; there is a US Consulate General in Guayaquil

Flag:

three horizontal bands of yellow (top, double width), blue, and red with the coat of arms superimposed at the center of the flag; similar to the flag of Colombia that is shorter and does not bear a coat of arms

:Ecuador Economy

Overview:

Ecuador has substantial oil resources and rich agricultural areas. Growth has been uneven because of natural disasters (for example, a major earthquake in 1987), fluctuations in global oil prices, and government policies designed to curb inflation. The government has not taken a supportive attitude toward either domestic or foreign investment, although its agreement to enter the Andean free trade zone is an encouraging move. As 1991 ended, Ecuador received a standby IMF loan of $105 million, which will permit the country to proceed with the rescheduling of Paris Club debt.

GDP:
exchange rate conversion - $11.5 billion, per capita $1,070; real growth rate 2.5% (1991)

Inflation rate (consumer prices):
49% (1991)

Unemployment rate: 8.0% (1990)

Budget:
revenues $2.2 billion; expenditures $2.2 billion, including capital expenditures of $375 million (1991)

Exports:
$2.9 billion (f.o.b., 1991)
commodities:
petroleum 47%, coffee, bananas, cocoa products, shrimp, fish products
partners:
US 60%, Latin America, Caribbean, EC countries

Imports:
$1.95 billion (f.o.b., 1991)
commodities:
transport equipment, vehicles, machinery, chemicals
partners:
US 34%, Latin America, Caribbean, EC, Japan

External debt: $12.4 billion (December 1991)

Industrial production:
growth rate -3.8% (1989); accounts for almost 40% of GDP, including petroleum

Electricity:
2,344,000 kW capacity; 6,430 million kWh produced, 598 kWh per capita (1991)

Industries:
petroleum, food processing, textiles, metal works, paper products, wood products, chemicals, plastics, fishing, timber

Agriculture:
accounts for 18% of GDP and 35% of labor force (including fishing and forestry); leading producer and exporter of bananas and balsawood; other exports - coffee, cocoa, fish, shrimp; crop production - rice, potatoes, manioc, plantains, sugarcane; livestock sector - cattle, sheep, hogs, beef, pork, dairy products; net importer of foodgrains, dairy products, and sugar

Illicit drugs:
minor illicit producer of coca following the successful eradication campaign of 1985-87; significant transit country, however, for derivatives of coca originating in Colombia, Bolivia, and Peru

Economic aid:
US commitments, including Ex-Im (FY70-89), $498 million; Western (non-US) countries, ODA and OOF bilateral commitments (1970-89), $2.15 billion; Communist countries (1970-89), $64 million

Currency:
  sucre (plural - sucres); 1 sucre (S/) = 100 centavos

:Ecuador Economy

Exchange rates:
  sucres (S/) per US$1 - 1,046.25 (1991), 869.54 (December 1990), 767.75
  (1990), 526.35 (1989), 301.61 (1988), 170.46 (1987)
Fiscal year: calendar year

:Ecuador Communications

Railroads:
  965 km total; all 1.067-meter-gauge single track
Highways:
  28,000 km total; 3,600 km paved, 17,400 km gravel and improved earth, 7,000
  km unimproved earth
Inland waterways:
  1,500 km
Pipelines:
  crude oil 800 km; petroleum products 1,358 km
Ports:
  Guayaquil, Manta, Puerto Bolivar, Esmeraldas
Merchant marine:
  46 ships (1,000 GRT or over) totaling 337,999 GRT/491,996 DWT; includes 2
  passenger, 4 cargo, 17 refrigerated cargo, 4 container, 1 roll-on/roll-off,
  15 petroleum tanker, 1 liquefied gas, 2 bulk
Civil air:
  23 major transport aircraft
Airports:
  143 total, 142 usable; 43 with permanent-surface runways; 1 with runway over
  3,659 m; 6 with runways 2,440-3,659 m; 23 with runways 1,220-2,439 m
Telecommunications:
  domestic facilities generally adequate; 318,000 telephones; broadcast
  stations - 272 AM, no FM, 33 TV, 39 shortwave; 1 Atlantic Ocean INTELSAT
  earth station

:Ecuador Defense Forces

Branches:
  Army (Ejercito Ecuatoriano), Navy (Armada Ecuatoriana), Air Force (Fuerza
  Aerea Ecuatoriana), National Police
Manpower availability:
  males 15-49, 2,804,260; 1,898,401 fit for military service; 115,139 reach
  military age (20) annually
Defense expenditures:
  exchange rate conversion - $NA, NA% of GDP

Egypt Geography

Total area: 1,001,450 km2
Land area: 995,450 km2
Comparative area: slightly more than three times the size of New Mexico
Land boundaries:
  2,689 km; Gaza Strip 11 km, Israel 255 km, Libya 1,150 km, Sudan 1,273 km
Coastline:

2,450 km
Maritime claims:
 Contiguous zone:
  24 nm
 Continental shelf:
  200 m (depth) or to depth of exploitation
 Exclusive economic zone:
  undefined
 Territorial sea:
  12 nm
Disputes:
   Administrative boundary with Sudan does not coincide with international
   boundary
Climate:
   desert; hot, dry summers with moderate winters
Terrain:
   vast desert plateau interrupted by Nile valley and delta
Natural resources:
   crude oil, natural gas, iron ore, phosphates, manganese, limestone, gypsum,
   talc, asbestos, lead, zinc
Land use:
   arable land 3%; permanent crops 2%; meadows and pastures 0%; forest and
   woodland NEGL%; other 95%; includes irrigated 5%
Environment:
   Nile is only perennial water source; increasing soil salinization below
   Aswan High Dam; hot, driving windstorm called khamsin occurs in spring;
   water pollution; desertification
Note:
   controls Sinai Peninsula, only land bridge between Africa and remainder of
   Eastern Hemisphere; controls Suez Canal, shortest sea link between Indian
   Ocean and Mediterranean; size and juxtaposition to Israel establish its
   major role in Middle Eastern geopolitics

:Egypt People

Population: 56,368,950 (July 1992), growth rate 2.3% (1992)
Birth rate: 33 births/1,000 population (1992)
Death rate: 9 deaths/1,000 population (1992)
Net migration rate: NEGL migrants/1,000 population (1992)
Infant mortality rate: 80 deaths/1,000 live births (1992)
Life expectancy at birth: 58 years male, 62 years female (1992)
Total fertility rate: 4.4 children born/woman (1992)
Nationality:
   noun - Egyptian(s); adjective - Egyptian
Ethnic divisions:
   Eastern Hamitic stock 90%; Greek, Italian, Syro-Lebanese 10%
Religions:
   (official estimate) Muslim (mostly Sunni) 94%; Coptic Christian and other 6%
Languages:
   Arabic (official); English and French widely understood by educated classes
Literacy:

48% (male 63%, female 34%) age 15 and over can read and write (1990 est.)
Labor force:
  15,000,000 (1989 est.); government, public sector enterprises, and armed
  forces 36%; agriculture 34%; privately owned service and manufacturing
  enterprises 20% (1984); shortage of skilled labor; 2,500,000 Egyptians work
  abroad, mostly in Iraq and the Gulf Arab states (1988 est.)
Organized labor:
  2,500,000 (est.)

:Egypt Government

Long-form name:
  Arab Republic of Egypt
Type:
  republic
Capital: Cairo
Administrative divisions:
  26 governorates (muhafazah, singular - muhafazah); Ad Daqahliyah, Al Bahr al
  Ahmar, Al Buchayrah, Al Fayyum, Al Gharbiyah, Al Iskandariyah, Al
  Isma`iliyah, Al Jizah, Al Minufiyah, Al Minya, Al Qahirah, Al Qalyubiyah, Al
  Wadi al Jadid, Ash Sharqiyah, As Suways, Aswan, Asyu`t, Bani Suwayf, Bur
  Sa`id, Dumyat, Janub Sina, Kafr ash Shaykh, Matruh, Qina, Shamal Sina, Suhaj
Independence:
  28 February 1922 (from UK); formerly United Arab Republic
Constitution:
  11 September 1971
Legal system:
  based on English common law, Islamic law, and Napoleonic codes; judicial
  review by Supreme Court and Council of State (oversees validity of
  administrative decisions); accepts compulsory ICJ jurisdiction, with
  reservations
National holiday:
  Anniversary of the Revolution, 23 July (1952)
Executive branch:
  president, prime minister, Cabinet
Legislative branch:
  unicameral People's Assembly (Majlis al-Cha'b); note - there is an Advisory
  Council (Majlis al-Shura) that functions in a consultative role
Judicial branch:
  Supreme Constitutional Court
Leaders:
  Chief of State:
  President Mohammed Hosni MUBARAK (was made acting President on 6 October
  1981 upon the assassination of President SADAT and sworn in as President on
  14 October 1981)
  Head of Government:
  Prime Minister Atef Mohammed Najib SEDKY (since 12 November 1986)
Political parties and leaders:
  formation of political parties must be approved by government; National
  Democratic Party (NDP), President Mohammed Hosni MUBARAK, leader, is the
  dominant party; legal opposition parties are Socialist Liberal Party (SLP),

Kamal MURAD; Socialist Labor Party, Ibrahim SHUKRI; National Progressive
Unionist Grouping (NPUG), Khalid MUHYI-AL-DIN; Umma Party, Ahmad al-
SABAHI;

New Wafd Party (NWP), Fu'd SIRAJ AL-DIN; Misr al-Fatah Party (Young Egypt
Party), Ali al-Din SALIH; The Greens Party, Hasan RAJAB; Nasserist Arab
Democratic Party, Dia' AL-DIN DAWOUD

Suffrage:
universal and compulsory at age 18

Elections:
Advisory Council:
last held 8 June 1989 (next to be held June 1995); results - NDP 100%; seats
- (258 total, 172 elected) NDP 172

People's Assembly:
last held 29 November 1990 (next to be held November 1995); results - NDP
78.4%, NPUG 1.4%, independents 18.7%; seats - (437 total, 444 elected) -
including NDP 348, NPUG 6, independents 83; note - most opposition parties
boycotted

:Egypt Government

President:
last held 5 October 1987 (next to be held October 1993); results - President
Hosni MUBARAK was reelected

Communists:
about 500 party members

Other political or pressure groups:
Islamic groups are illegal, but the largest one, the Muslim Brotherhood, is
tolerated by the government; trade unions and professional associations are
officially sanctioned

Member of:
ACC, ACCT (associate), AfDB, AFESD, AG (observer), AL, AMF, CAEU, CCC,
EBRD,
ECA, ESCWA, FAO, G-15, G-19, G-24, G-77, GATT, IAEA, IBRD, ICAO, ICC,
IDA,
IDB, IFAD, IFC, ILO, IMF, IMO, INMARSAT, INTELSAT, INTERPOL, IOC,
IOM
(observer), ISO, ITU, LORCS, NAM, OAPEC, OAS (observer), OAU, OIC, PCA,
UN,
UNCTAD, UNESCO, UNIDO, UNRWA, UPU, WHO, WIPO, WMO, WTO

Diplomatic representation:
Ambassador El Sayed Abdel Raouf EL REEDY; Chancery at 2310 Decatur Place
NW,
Washington, DC 20008; telephone (202) 232-5400; there are Egyptian
Consulates General in Chicago, Houston, New York, and San Francisco

US:
Ambassador Robert PELLETREAU; Embassy at Lazougi Street, Garden City, Cairo
(mailing address is APO AE 09839); telephone [20] (2) 355-7371; FAX [20] (2)
355-7375; there is a US Consulate General in Alexandria

Flag:
three equal horizontal bands of red (top), white, and black with the
national emblem (a shield superimposed on a golden eagle facing the hoist

side above a scroll bearing the name of the country in Arabic) centered in the white band; similar to the flag of Yemen, which has a plain white band; also similar to the flag of Syria that has two green stars and to the flag of Iraq, which has three green stars (plus an Arabic inscription) in a horizontal line centered in the white band

:Egypt Economy

Overview:

Egypt has one of the largest public sectors of all the Third World economies, most industrial plants being owned by the government. Overregulation holds back technical modernization and foreign investment. Even so, the economy grew rapidly during the late 1970s and early 1980s, but in 1986 the collapse of world oil prices and an increasingly heavy burden of debt servicing led Egypt to begin negotiations with the IMF for balance-of-payments support. As part of the 1987 agreement with the IMF, the government agreed to institute a reform program to reduce inflation, promote economic growth, and improve its external position. The reforms have been slow in coming, however, and the economy has been largely stagnant for the past four years. The addition of 1 million people every seven months to Egypt's population exerts enormous pressure on the 5% of the total land area available for agriculture.

GDP:

exchange rate conversion - $39.2 billion, per capita $720; real growth rate 2% (1991 est.)

Inflation rate (consumer prices):

17% (1991 est.)

Unemployment rate: 15% (1991 est.)

Budget:

revenues $9.4 billion; expenditures $15.9 billion, including capital expenditures of $6 billion (FY90 est.)

Exports:

$4.5 billion (f.o.b., 1991 est.)

commodities:

crude oil and petroleum products, cotton yarn, raw cotton, textiles, metal products, chemicals

partners:

EC, Eastern Europe, US, Japan

Imports:

$11.7 billion (f.o.b., 1991 est.)

commodities:

machinery and equipment, foods, fertilizers, wood products, durable consumer goods, capital goods

partners:

EC, US, Japan, Eastern Europe

External debt: $38 billion (December 1991 est.)

Industrial production:

growth rate 7.3% (FY89 est.); accounts for 18% of GDP

Electricity:

13,500,000 kW capacity; 45,000 million kWh produced, 820 kWh per capita (1991)

Industries:

textiles, food processing, tourism, chemicals, petroleum, construction, cement, metals

Agriculture:

accounts for 20% of GDP and employs more than one-third of labor force; dependent on irrigation water from the Nile; world's sixth-largest cotton exporter; other crops produced include rice, corn, wheat, beans, fruit, vegetables; not self-sufficient in food; livestock - cattle, water buffalo, sheep, and goats; annual fish catch about 140,000 metric tons

Economic aid:

US commitments, including Ex-Im (FY70-89), $15.7 billion; Western (non-US) countries, ODA and OOF bilateral commitments (1970-88), $10.1 billion; OPEC bilateral aid (1979-89), $2.9 billion; Communist countries (1970-89), $2.4 billion

:Egypt Economy

Currency:

Egyptian pound (plural - pounds); 1 Egyptian pound (#E) = 100 piasters

Exchange rates:

Egyptian pounds (#E) per US$1 - 3.3310 (January 1992), 2.7072 (1990), 2.5171 (1989), 2.2233 (1988), 1.5183 (1987)

Fiscal year: 1 July - 30 June

:Egypt Communications

Railroads:

5,110 km total; 4,763 km 1,435-meter standard gauge, 347 km 0.750-meter gauge; 951 km double track; 25 km electrified

Highways:

51,925 km total; 17,900 km paved, 2,500 km gravel, 13,500 km improved earth, 18,025 km unimproved earth

Inland waterways:

3,500 km (including the Nile, Lake Nasser, Alexandria-Cairo Waterway, and numerous smaller canals in the delta); Suez Canal, 193.5 km long (including approaches), used by oceangoing vessels drawing up to 16.1 meters of water

Pipelines:

crude oil 1,171 km; petroleum products 596 km; natural gas 460 km

Ports:

Alexandria, Port Said, Suez, Bur Safajah, Damietta

Merchant marine:

150 ships (1,000 GRT or over) totaling 1,019,182 GRT/1,499,880 DWT; includes 11 passenger, 5 short-sea passenger, 2 passenger-cargo, 86 cargo, 3 refrigerated cargo, 15 roll-on/roll-off, 12 petroleum tanker, 15 bulk, 1 container

Civil air:

50 major transport aircraft

Airports:

92 total, 82 usable; 66 with permanent-surface runways; 2 with runways over 3,659 m; 44 with runways 2,440-3,659 m; 24 with runways 1,220-2,439 m

Telecommunications:

system is large but still inadequate for needs; principal centers are Alexandria, Cairo, Al Mansurah, Ismailia, Suez and Tanta; intercity connections by coaxial cable and microwave; extensive upgrading in progress; 600,000 telephones (est.); broadcast stations - 39 AM, 6 FM, 41 TV; satellite earth stations - 1 Atlantic Ocean INTELSAT, 1 Indian Ocean INTELSAT, 1 INMARSAT, 1 ARABSAT; 5 submarine coaxial cables; tropospheric scatter to Sudan; radio relay to Libya, Israel, and Jordan

:Egypt Defense Forces

Branches:
  Army, Navy, Air Force, Air Defense Command
Manpower availability:
  males 15-49, 13,911,006; 9,044,425 fit for military service; 563,321 reach military age (20) annually
Defense expenditures:
  exchange rate conversion - $2.5 billion, 6.4% of GDP (1991)

El Salvador Geography

Total area: 21,040 km2
Land area: 20,720 km2
Comparative area: slightly smaller than Massachusetts
Land boundaries:
  545 km; Guatemala 203 km, Honduras 342 km
Coastline:
  307 km
Maritime claims:
  Territorial sea:
  200 nm (overflight and navigation permitted beyond 12 nm)
Disputes:
  dispute with Honduras over several sections of the land boundary; dispute over Golfo de Fonseca maritime boundary because of disputed sovereignty of islands
Climate:
  tropical; rainy season (May to October); dry season (November to April)
Terrain:
  mostly mountains with narrow coastal belt and central plateau
Natural resources:
  hydropower, geothermal power, crude oil
Land use:
  arable land 27%; permanent crops 8%; meadows and pastures 29%; forest and woodland 6%; other 30%; includes irrigated 5%
Environment:
  The Land of Volcanoes; subject to frequent and sometimes very destructive earthquakes; deforestation; soil erosion; water pollution
Note:
  smallest Central American country and only one without a coastline on Caribbean Sea

:El Salvador People

Population: 5,574,279 (July 1992), growth rate 2.2% (1992)
Birth rate: 33 births/1,000 population (1992)
Death rate: 5 deaths/1,000 population (1992)
Net migration rate: - 6 migrants/1,000 population (1992)

Infant mortality rate: 26 deaths/1,000 live births (1992)
Life expectancy at birth: 68 years male, 75 years female (1992)
Total fertility rate: 4.0 children born/woman (1992)
Nationality:
noun - Salvadoran(s); adjective - Salvadoran
Ethnic divisions:
mestizo 89%, Indian 10%, white 1%
Religions:
Roman Catholic about 75%, with extensive activity by Protestant groups
throughout the country (more than 1 million Protestant evangelicals in El
Salvador at the end of 1990)
Languages:
Spanish, Nahua (among some Indians)
Literacy:
73% (male 76%, female 70%) age 15 and over can read and write (1990 est.)
Labor force:
1,700,000 (1982 est.); agriculture 40%, commerce 16%, manufacturing 15%,
government 13%, financial services 9%, transportation 6%, other 1%; shortage
of skilled labor and a large pool of unskilled labor, but manpower training
programs improving situation (1984 est.)
Organized labor:
total labor force 15%; agricultural labor force 10%; urban labor force 7%
(1987 est.)

:El Salvador Government

Long-form name:
Republic of El Salvador
Type:
republic
Capital: San Salvador
Administrative divisions:
14 departments (departamentos, singular - departamento); Ahuachapan,
Cabanas, Chalatenango, Cuscatlan, La Libertad, La Paz, La Union, Morazan,
San Miguel, San Salvador, Santa Ana, San Vicente, Sonsonate, Usulutan
Independence:
15 September 1821 (from Spain)
Constitution:
20 December 1983
Legal system:
based on civil and Roman law, with traces of common law; judicial review of
legislative acts in the Supreme Court; accepts compulsory ICJ jurisdiction,
with reservations
National holiday:
Independence Day, 15 September (1821)
Executive branch:
president, vice president, Council of Ministers (cabinet)
Legislative branch:
unicameral Legislative Assembly (Asamblea Legislativa)
Judicial branch:
Supreme Court (Corte Suprema)

Leaders:
  Chief of State and Head of Government:
    President Alfredo CRISTIANI Buchard (since 1 June 1989); Vice President Jose
    Francisco MERINO (since 1 June 1989)
Political parties and leaders:
    National Republican Alliance (ARENA), Armando CALDERON Sol; Christian
    Democratic Party (PDC), Fidel CHAVEZ Mena; National Conciliation Party
    (PCN), Ciro CRUZ Zepeda; National Democratic Union (UDN), Mario
AGUINADA
    Carranza; the Democratic Convergence (CD) is a coalition of three parties -
    the Social Democratic Party (PSD), Wilfredo BARILLAS; the National
    Revolutionary Movement (MNR), Victor VALLE; and the Popular Social Christian
    Movement (MPSC), Ruben ZAMORA; Authentic Christian Movement (MAC), Ju-
lio REY
    PRENDES; Democratic Action (AD), Ricardo GONZALEZ Camacho
Suffrage:
    universal at age 18
Elections:
  Legislative Assembly:
    last held 10 March 1991 (next to be held March 1994); results - ARENA 44.3%,
    PDC 27.96%, CD 12.16%, PCN 8.99%, MAC 3.23%, UDN 2.68%; seats - (84 total)
    ARENA 39, PDC 26, PCN 9, CD 8, UDN 1, MAC 1
  President:
    last held 19 March 1989 (next to be held March 1994); results - Alfredo
    CRISTIANI (ARENA) 53.8%, Fidel CHAVEZ Mena (PDC) 36.6%, other 9.6%
Other political or pressure groups:
  Business organizations:
    National Association of Private Enterprise (ANEP), conservative; Productive
    Alliance (AP), conservative; National Federation of Salvadoran Small
    Businessmen (FENAPES), conservative

:El Salvador Government

  FMLN front organizations:
    Labor fronts include - National Union of Salvadoran Workers (UNTS), leftist
    umbrella front group, leads FMLN front network; National Federation of
    Salvadoran Workers (FENASTRAS), best organized of front groups and
    controlled by FMLN's National Resistance (RN); Social Security Institute
    Workers Union (STISSS), one of the most militant fronts, is controlled by
    FMLN's Armed Forces of National Resistance (FARN) and RN; Association of
    Telecommunications Workers (ASTTEL); Centralized Union Federation of El
    Salvador (FUSS); Treasury Ministry Employees (AGEMHA); Nonlabor fronts
    include - Committee of Mothers and Families of Political Prisoners,
    Disappeared Persons, and Assassinated of El Salvador (COMADRES);
    Nongovernmental Human Rights Commission (CDHES); Committee of Dismissed
and
    Unemployed of El Salvador (CODYDES); General Association of Salvadoran
    University Students (AGEUS); National Association of Salvadoran Educators
    (ANDES-21 DE JUNIO); Salvadoran Revolutionary Student Front (FERS),
    associated with the Popular Forces of Liberation (FPL); Association of
    National University Educators (ADUES); Salvadoran University Students Front

(FEUS); Christian Committee for the Displaced of El Salvador (CRIPDES), an FPL front; The Association for Communal Development in El Salvador (PADECOES), controlled by the People's Revolutionary Army (ERP); Confederation of Cooperative Associations of El Salvador (COACES)

Other political or pressure groups:

Labor organizations:

Federation of Construction and Transport Workers Unions (FESINCONSTRANS), independent; Salvadoran Communal Union (UCS), peasant association; Unitary Federation of Salvadoran Unions (FUSS), leftist; National Federation of Salvadoran Workers (FENASTRAS), leftist; Democratic Workers Central (CTD), moderate; General Confederation of Workers (CGT), moderate; National Unity of Salvadoran Workers (UNTS), leftist; National Union of Workers and Peasants (UNOC), moderate labor coalition of democratic labor organizations; United Workers Front (FUT)

Leftist political parties:

National Democratic Union (UDN), National Revolutionary Movement (MNR), and Popular Social Movement (MPSC)

Leftist revolutionary movement:

Farabundo Marti National Liberation Front (FMLN), leadership body of the insurgency, five factions - Popular Liberation Forces (FPL), Armed Forces of National Resistance (FARN), People's Revolutionary Army (ERP), Salvadoran Communist Party/Armed Forces of Liberation (PCES/FAL), and Central American Workers' Revolutionary Party (PRTC)/Popular Liberation Revolutionary Armed Forces (FARLP)

Member of:

BCIE, CACM, ECLAC, FAO, G-77, IADB, IAEA, IBRD, ICAO, ICFTU, IDA, IFAD, IFC,

ILO, IMF, IMO, INTELSAT, IOC, IOM, ITU, LAES, LORCS, NAM (observer), OAS,

OPANAL, PCA, UN, UNCTAD, UNESCO, UNIDO, UPU, WCL, WFTU, WHO, WIPO, WMO

Diplomatic representation:

Ambassador Miguel Angel SALAVERRIA; Chancery at 2308 California Street NW, Washington, DC 20008; telephone (202) 265-9671 through 3482; there are Salvadoran Consulates General in Houston, Los Angeles, Miami, New Orleans, New York, and San Francisco

US:

Ambassador William G. WALKER; Embassy at 25 Avenida Norte No. 1230, San Salvador (mailing address is APO AA 34023); telephone [503] 26-7100; FAX [503] (26) 5839

:El Salvador Government

Flag:

three equal horizontal bands of blue (top), white, and blue with the national coat of arms centered in the white band; the coat of arms features a round emblem encircled by the words REPUBLICA DE EL SALVADOR EN LA AMERICA CENTRAL; similar to the flag of Nicaragua, which has a different coat of arms centered in the white band - it features a triangle encircled by the words REPUBLICA DE NICARAGUA on top and AMERICA CENTRAL on the bottom; also

similar to the flag of Honduras, which has five blue stars arranged in an X pattern centered in the white band

:El Salvador Economy

Overview:

The agricultural sector accounts for 25% of GDP, employs about 40% of the labor force, and contributes about 66% to total exports. Coffee is the major commercial crop, accounting for 45% of export earnings. The manufacturing sector, based largely on food and beverage processing, accounts for 18% of GDP and 15% of employment. Economic losses because of guerrilla sabotage total more than $2 billion since 1979. The costs of maintaining a large military seriously constrain the government's efforts to provide essential social services. Nevertheless, growth in national output during the period 1990-91 exceeded growth in population for the first time since 1987.

GDP:

exchange rate conversion - $5.5 billion, per capita $1,010; real growth rate 3% (1991 est.)

Inflation rate (consumer prices):

19% (1990)

Unemployment rate: 10% (1989)

Budget:

revenues $751 million; expenditures $790 million, including capital expenditures of $NA (1990 est.)

Exports:

$580 million (f.o.b., 1990 est.)

commodities:

coffee 45%, sugar, cotton, shrimp

partners:

US 49%, Germany 24%, Guatemala 7%, Costa Rica 4%, Japan 4%

Imports:

$1.2 billion (c.i.f., 1990 est.)

commodities:

petroleum products, consumer goods, foodstuffs, machinery, construction materials, fertilizer

partners:

US 40%, Guatemala 12%, Venezuela 7%, Mexico 7%, Germany 5%, Japan 4%

External debt: $2.0 billion (December 1990 est.)

Industrial production:

growth rate 2.4% (1990); accounts for 22% of GDP

Electricity:

682,000 kW capacity; 1,927 million kWh produced, 356 kWh per capita (1991)

Industries:

food processing, textiles, clothing, beverages, petroleum, tobacco products, chemicals, furniture

Agriculture:

accounts for 25% of GDP and 40% of labor force (including fishing and forestry); coffee most important commercial crop; other products - sugarcane, corn, rice, beans, oilseeds, beef, dairy products, shrimp; not self-sufficient in food

Illicit drugs:

transshipment point for cocaine

Economic aid:

US commitments, including Ex-Im (FY70-90), $2.95 billion; Western (non-US) countries, ODA and OOF bilateral commitments (1970-89), $525 million

Currency:

Salvadoran colon (plural - colones); 1 Salvadoran colon (C) = 100 centavos

Exchange rates:

Salvadoran colones (C) per US$1 - 8.1 (January 1992), floating rate since mid-1990); 5.0000 (fixed rate 1986 to mid-1990)

Fiscal year: calendar year

:El Salvador Communications

Railroads:

602 km 0.914-meter gauge, single track

Highways:

10,000 km total; 1,500 km paved, 4,100 km gravel, 4,400 km improved and unimproved earth

Inland waterways:

Rio Lempa partially navigable

Ports:

Acajutla, Cutuco

Civil air:

7 major transport aircraft

Airports:

107 total, 77 usable; 5 with permanent-surface runways; none with runways over 3,659 m; 1 with runways 2,440-3,659 m; 4 with runways 1,220-2,439 m

Telecommunications:

nationwide trunk radio relay system; connection into Central American Microwave System; 116,000 telephones; broadcast stations - 77 AM, no FM, 5 TV, 2 shortwave; 1 Atlantic Ocean INTELSAT earth station

:El Salvador Defense Forces

Branches:

Army, Navy, Air Force, National Guard, National Police, Treasury Police

Manpower availability:

males 15-49, 1,265,149; 809,419 fit for military service; 68,445 reach military age (18) annually

Defense expenditures:

exchange rate conversion - $220 million, 3.6% of GDP (1991)

Equatorial Guinea Geography

Total area: 28,050 km2

Land area: 28,050 km2

Comparative area: slightly larger than Maryland

Land boundaries:

539 km; Cameroon 189 km, Gabon 350 km

Coastline:

296 km

Maritime claims:

 Exclusive economic zone:

200 nm
  Territorial sea:
  12 nm
Disputes:
  maritime boundary dispute with Gabon because of disputed sovereignty over
  islands in Corisco Bay
Climate:
  tropical; always hot, humid
Terrain:
  coastal plains rise to interior hills; islands are volcanic
Natural resources:
  timber, crude oil, small unexploited deposits of gold, manganese, uranium
Land use:
  arable land 8%; permanent crops 4%; meadows and pastures 4%; forest and
  woodland 51%; other 33%
Environment:
  subject to violent windstorms
Note:
  insular and continental regions rather widely separated

:Equatorial Guinea People

Population: 388,799 (July 1992), growth rate 2.6% (1992)
Birth rate: 42 births/1,000 population (1992)
Death rate: 15 deaths/1,000 population (1992)
Net migration rate: 0 migrants/1,000 population (1992)
Infant mortality rate: 107 deaths/1,000 live births (1992)
Life expectancy at birth: 49 years male, 53 years female (1992)
Total fertility rate: 5.4 children born/woman (1992)
Nationality:
  noun - Equatorial Guinean(s) or Equatoguinean(s); adjective - Equatorial
  Guinean or Equatoguinean
Ethnic divisions:
  indigenous population of Bioko, primarily Bubi, some Fernandinos; Rio Muni,
  primarily Fang; less than 1,000 Europeans, mostly Spanish
Religions:
  natives all nominally Christian and predominantly Roman Catholic; some pagan
  practices retained
Languages:
  Spanish (official), pidgin English, Fang, Bubi, Ibo
Literacy:
  50% (male 64%, female 37%) age 15 and over can read and write (1990 est.)
Labor force:
  172,000 (1986 est.); agriculture 66%, services 23%, industry 11% (1980);
  labor shortages on plantations; 58% of population of working age (1985)
Organized labor:
  no formal trade unions

:Equatorial Guinea Government

Long-form name:
  Republic of Equatorial Guinea
Type:

republic in transition to multiparty democracy

Capital: Malabo

Administrative divisions:

7 provinces (provincias, singular - provincia); Annobon, Bioko Norte, Bioko
Sur, Centro Sur, Kie-Ntem, Litoral, Wele-Nzas

Independence:

12 October 1968 (from Spain; formerly Spanish Guinea)

Constitution:

new constitution 17 November 1991

Legal system:

partly based on Spanish civil law and tribal custom

National holiday:

Independence Day, 12 October (1968)

Executive branch:

president, prime minister, deputy prime minister, Council of Ministers
(cabinet)

Legislative branch:

unicameral House of Representatives of the People (Camara de Representantes
del Pueblo)

Judicial branch:

Supreme Tribunal

Leaders:

Chief of State:

President Brig. Gen. (Ret.) Teodoro OBIANG NGUEMA MBASOGO (since 3 August

1979)

Head of Government:

Prime Minister Cristino SERICHE BIOKO MALABO (since 15 August 1982);
Deputy

Prime Minister Isidoro Eyi MONSUY ANDEME (since 15 August 1989)

Political parties and leaders:

only party - Democratic Party for Equatorial Guinea (PDGE), Brig. Gen.

(Ret.) Teodoro OBIANG NGUEMA MBASOGO, party leader; multipartyism legalized

in new constitution of November 1991, promulgated January 1992

Suffrage:

universal adult at age NA

Elections:

Chamber of People's Representatives:

last held 10 July 1988 (next to be held 10 July 1993); results - PDGE is the
only party; seats - (41 total) PDGE 41

President:

last held 25 June 1989 (next to be held 25 June 1996); results - President

Brig. Gen. (Ret.) Teodoro OBIANG NGUEMA MBASOGO was reelected without
opposition

Member of:

ACP, AfDB, BDEAC, CEEAC, ECA, FAO, FZ, G-77, IBRD, ICAO, IDA, IFAD,
ILO,

IMF, IMO, INTERPOL, IOC, ITU, LORCS (associate), NAM, OAS (observer),
OAU,

UDEAC, UN, UNCTAD, UNESCO, UNIDO, UPU, WHO

Diplomatic representation:

Ambassador Damaso OBIANG NDONG; Chancery (temporary) 57 Magnolia Avenue,

Mount Vernon, NY 10553; telephone (914) 667-9664

US:

Ambassador John E. BENNETT; Embassy at Calle de Los Ministros, Malabo (mailing address is P.O. Box 597, Malabo); telephone [240] (9) 2185, 2406, 2507; FAX [240] (9) 2164

:Equatorial Guinea Government

Flag:

three equal horizontal bands of green (top), white, and red with a blue isosceles triangle based on the hoist side and the coat of arms centered in the white band; the coat of arms has six yellow six-pointed stars (representing the mainland and five offshore islands) above a gray shield bearing a silk-cotton tree and below which is a scroll with the motto UNIDAD, PAZ, JUSTICIA (Unity, Peace, Justice)

:Equatorial Guinea Economy

Overview:

The economy, destroyed during the regime of former President Macias NGUEMA, is now based on agriculture, forestry, and fishing, which account for about half of GDP and nearly all exports. Subsistence agriculture predominates, with cocoa, coffee, and wood products providing income, foreign exchange, and government revenues. There is little industry. Commerce accounts for about 8% of GDP and the construction, public works, and service sectors for about 38%. Undeveloped natural resources include titanium, iron ore, manganese, uranium, and alluvial gold. Oil exploration, taking place under concessions offered to US, French, and Spanish firms, has been moderately successful.

GDP:

exchange rate conversion - $156 million, per capita $400; real growth rate 1.6% (1988 est.)

Inflation rate (consumer prices):

3.6% (1990 est.)

Unemployment rate: NA%

Budget:

revenues $27 million; expenditures $29 million, including capital expenditures of NA (1990 est.)

Exports:

$37 million (f.o.b., 1990 est.)

commodities:

coffee, timber, cocoa beans

partners:

Spain 38.2%, Italy 12.2%, Netherlands 11.4%, FRG 6.9%, Nigeria 12.4 (1988)

Imports:

$68.3 million (c.i.f., 1990)

commodities:

petroleum, food, beverages, clothing, machinery

partners:

France 25.9%, Spain 21.0%, Italy 16%, US 12.8%, Netherlands 8%, Germany 3.1%, Gabon 2.9%, Nigeria 1.8 (1988)

External debt: $213 million (1990)

Industrial production:
growth rate - 6.8% (1990 est.)

Electricity:
23,000 kW capacity; 60 million kWh produced, 160 kWh per capita (1991)

Industries:
fishing, sawmilling

Agriculture:
cash crops - timber and coffee from Rio Muni, cocoa from Bioko; food crops - rice, yams, cassava, bananas, oil palm nuts, manioc, livestock

Illicit drugs:
transshipment point for illicit drugs from Central and Southwest Asia to Western Europe

Economic aid:
US commitments, including Ex-Im (FY81-89), $14 million; Western (non-US) countries, ODA and OOF bilateral commitments (1970-89) $130 million; Communist countries (1970-89), $55 million

Currency:
Communaute Financiere Africaine franc (plural - francs); 1 CFA franc (CFAF) = 100 centimes

Exchange rates:
Communaute Financiere Africaine francs (CFAF) per US$1 - 269.01 (January 1992), 282.11 (1991), 272.26 (1990), 319.01 (1989), 297.85 (1988), 300.54 (1987)

:Equatorial Guinea Economy

Fiscal year: 1 April - 31 March

:Equatorial Guinea Communications

Highways:
Rio Muni - 2,460 km; Bioko - 300 km

Ports:
Malabo, Bata

Merchant marine:
2 ships (1,000 GRT or over) totaling 6,413 GRT/6,699 DWT; includes 1 cargo and 1 passenger-cargo

Civil air:
1 major transport aircraft

Airports:
3 total, 3 usable; 2 with permanent-surface runways; none with runways over 3,659 m; 1 with runways 2,440-3,659 m; 1 with runways 1,220-2,439 m

Telecommunications:
poor system with adequate government services; international communications from Bata and Malabo to African and European countries; 2,000 telephones; broadcast stations - 2 AM, no FM, 1 TV; 1 Indian Ocean INTELSAT earth station

:Equatorial Guinea Defense Forces

Branches:
   Army, Navy, Air Force, National Guard, National Police
Manpower availability:
   males 15-49, 81,850; 41,528 fit for military service
Defense expenditures:
   exchange rate conversion - $NA, NA% of GNP

Estonia Geography

Total area: 45,100 km2
Land area: 43,200 km2; (includes 1,520 islands in the Baltic Sea)
Comparative area: slightly larger than New Hampshire and Vermont combined
Land boundaries:
   557 km; Latvia 267 km, Russia 290 km
Coastline:
   1,393 km
Maritime claims:
  Contiguous zone:
   NA nm
  Continental shelf:
   NA meter depth
  Exclusive economic zone:
   NA nm
  Exclusive fishing zone:
   NA nm
  Territorial sea:
   NA nm
Disputes:
   international small border strips along the northern (Narva) and southern
   (Petseri) sections of eastern border with Russia ceded to Russia in 1945 by
   the Estonian SSR
Climate:
   maritime, wet, moderate winters
Terrain:
   marshy, lowlands
Natural resources:
   shale oil, peat, phosphorite, amber
Land use:
   22% arable land; NA% permanent crops; 11% meadows and pastures; 31% forest
   and woodland; 21% other; includes NA% irrigated; 15% swamps and lakes
Environment:
   coastal waters largely polluted

:Estonia People

Population: 1,607,349 (July 1992), growth rate 0.7% (1992)
Birth rate: 16 births/1,000 population (1992)
Death rate: 12 deaths/1,000 population (1992)
Net migration rate: 3 migrants/1,000 population (1992)
Infant mortality rate: 25 deaths/1,000 live births (1992)
Life expectancy at birth: 65 years male, 74 years female (1992)
Total fertility rate: 2.3 children born/woman (1992)
Nationality:

noun - Estonian(s); adjective - Estonian
Ethnic divisions:
   Estonian 61.5%, Russian 30.3%, Ukrainian 3.17%, Byelorussian 1.8%, Finn
   1.1%, other 2.13% (1989)
Religions:
   Lutheran is primary denomination
Languages:
   Estonian NA% (official), Latvian NA%, Lithuanian NA%, Russian NA%, other
NA%
Literacy:
   NA% (male NA%, female NA%)
Labor force:
   796,000; industry and construction 42%, agriculture and forestry 13%, other
   45% (1990)
Organized labor:
   NA

:Estonia Government

Long-form name:
   Republic of Estonia
Type:
   republic
Capital: Tallinn
Administrative divisions:
   none - all districts are under direct republic jurisdiction
Independence:
   8 November 1917; occupied by Germany in March 1918 and restored to power in
   November 1918; annexed by USSR 6 August 1940; declared independence 20
   August 1991 and regained independence from USSR 6 September 1991
Constitution:
   currently rewriting constitution, but readopted the constitution of 1938
Legal system:
   based on civil law system; no judicial review of legislative acts
National holiday:
   Independence Day, 24 February (1918)
Executive branch:
   prime minister
Legislative branch:
   unicameral Supreme Council
Judicial branch:
   Supreme Court
Leaders:
  Chief of State:
   Chairman, Supreme Council Arnold R'UTEL (since April 1983)
  Head of Government:
   Prime Minister Tiit VAHI (since January 1992)
Political parties and leaders:
   Popular Front of Estonia (Rahvarinne), NA chairman; Estonian Christian
   Democratic Party, Aivar KALA, chairman; Estonian Christian Democratic Union,
   Illar HALLASTE, chairman; Estonian Heritage Society (EMS), Trivimi VELLISTE,

chairman; Estonian National Independence Party (ERSP), Lagle PAREK, chairman; Estonian Social Democratic Party, Marju LAURISTIN, chairman; Estonian Green Party, Tonu OJA; Independent Estonian Communist Party, Vaino VALJAS; People's Centrist Party, Edgar SAVISAAR, chairman

Suffrage:
universal at age 18

Elections:

Congress of Estonia:
last held March 1990 (next to be held NA); note - Congress of Estonia is a quasi-governmental structure; results - percent of vote by party NA; seats - (495 total) number of seats by party NA

President:
last held NA 1990; (next to be held NA); results - NA

Supreme Council:
last held 18 March 1990; (next to be held NA); results - percent of vote by party NA; seats - (105 total) number of seats by party NA

Other political or pressure groups:
NA

Member of:
CSCE, IAEA, ICFTU, NACC, UN, UNCTAD

Diplomatic representation:
Ambassador Ernst JAAKSON, Legation of Estonia, Office of Consulate General, 9 Rockefeller Plaza, Suite 1421, New York, NY 10020; telephone (212) 247-1450

:Estonia Government

US:
Ambassador Robert C. FRASURE; Embassy at Kentmanni 20, Tallin EE 0001; telephone 011-[358] (49) 303-182 (cellular); FAX [358] (49) 306-817 (cellular); note - dialing to Baltics still requires use of an international operator unless you use the cellular phone lines

Flag:
pre-1940 flag restored by Supreme Soviet in May 1990; flag is three equal horizontal bands of blue, black, and white

:Estonia Economy

Overview:
Starting in July 1991, under a new law on private ownership, small enterprises, such as retail shops and restaurants, were sold to private owners. The auctioning of large-scale enterprises is now in progress with the proceeds being held in escrow until the prior ownership (that is, Estonian or the Commonwealth of Independent States) can be established. Estonia ranks first in per capita consumption among the former Soviet republics. Agriculture is well developed, especially meat production, and provides a surplus for export. Only about one-fifth of the work force is in agriculture. The major share of the work force engages in manufacturing both capital and consumer goods based on raw materials and intermediate products from the other former Soviet republics. These manufactures are of high quality by ex-Soviet standards and are exported to the other republics. Estonia's mineral resources are limited to major deposits of shale oil (60% of old Soviet total) and phosphorites (400 million tons). Estonia has a

large, relatively modern port and produces more than half of its own energy needs at highly polluting shale oil power plants. Like the other 14 successor republics, Estonia is suffering through a difficult transitional period - between a collapsed command economic structure and a still-to-be-built market structure. It has advantages in the transition, not having suffered so long under the Soviet yoke and having better chances of developing profitable ties to the Nordic and West European countries.

GDP:
$NA billion, per capita $NA; real growth rate -11% (1992)

Inflation rate (consumer prices):
approximately 200% (1991)

Unemployment rate: NA%

Budget:
revenues $NA million; expenditures $NA million, including capital expenditures of $NA million

Exports:
$186 million (f.o.b., 1990)
commodities:
machinery 30%, food 17%, chemicals 11%, electric power 9%
partners:
Russia 50%, other former Soviet republics 30%, Ukraine 15%, West 5%

Imports:
$1.2 billion (c.i.f., 1990)
commodities:
machinery 45%, oil 13%, chemicals 12%
partners:
NA

External debt: $650 million (end of 1991)

Industrial production:
growth rate -9% (1991)

Electricity:
3,305,000 kW capacity; 17,200 million kWh produced, 10,865 kWh per capita (1990)

Industries:
accounts for 30% of labor force; oil shale, shipbuilding, phosphates, electric motors, excavators, cement, furniture, clothing, textiles, paper, shoes, apparel

Agriculture:
employs 20% of work force; very efficient; net exports of meat, fish, dairy products, and potatoes; imports feedgrains for livestock; fruits and vegetables

:Estonia Economy

Illicit drugs:
transshipment point for illicit drugs from Central and Southwest Asia to Western Europe

Economic aid:
US commitments, including Ex-Im (1992), $10 million; Western (non-US) countries, ODA and OOF bilateral commitments (1970-86), $NA million; Communist countries (1971-86), $NA million

Currency:
  kroon; to be introduced in 1992
Exchange rates:
  NA
Fiscal year: calendar year

:Estonia Communications

Railroads:
  1,030 km (includes NA km electrified); does not include industrial lines
  (1990)
Highways:
  30,300 km total (1990); 29,200 km hard surfaced; 1,100 km earth
Inland waterways:
  500 km perennially navigable
Pipelines:
  crude oil NA km, refined products NA km, natural gas NA km
Ports:
  maritime - Tallinn, Parnu; inland - Narva
Merchant marine:
  65 ships (1,000 GRT or over) totaling 386,634 GRT/516,866 DWT; includes 51
  cargo, 6 roll-on/roll-off, 2 short-sea passenger, 6 bulk
Civil air:
  NA major transport aircraft
Airports:
  NA total, NA usable; NA with permanent-surface runways; NA with runways over
  3,659 m; NA with runways 2,440-3,659 m; NA with runways 1,220-2,439 m
Telecommunications:
  telephone diversity - NA; broadcast stations - 3 TV (provide Estonian
  programs as well as Moscow Ostenkino's first and second programs);
  international traffic is carried to the other former USSR republics by
  landline or microwave and to other countries by leased connection to the
  Moscow international gateway switch, by the Finnish cellular net, and by an
  old copper submarine cable to Finland

:Estonia Defense Forces

Branches:
  Republic Security Forces (internal and border troops), National Guard;
  Russian Forces (Ground, Navy, Air, Air Defense, and Border Guard)
Manpower availability:
  males 15-49, total mobilized force projected 120,000-130,000; NA fit for
  military service; between 10,000-12,000 reach military age (18) annually
Defense expenditures:
  $NA, NA% of GDP

Ethiopia Geography

Total area: 1,221,900 km2
Land area: 1,101,000 km2
Comparative area: slightly less than twice the size of Texas
Land boundaries:
  5,141 km; Djibouti 459 km, Kenya 861 km, Somalia 1,600 km, Sudan 2,221 km
Coastline:

1,094 km
Maritime claims:
 Territorial sea:
  12 nm
Disputes:
    southern half of the boundary with Somalia is a Provisional Administrative
    Line; possible claim by Somalia based on unification of ethnic Somalis;
    territorial dispute with Somalia over the Ogaden; independence referendum in
    Eritrea scheduled for April 1992
Climate:
    tropical monsoon with wide topographic-induced variation; some areas prone
    to extended droughts
Terrain:
    high plateau with central mountain range divided by Great Rift Valley
Natural resources:
    small reserves of gold, platinum, copper, potash
Land use:
    arable land 12%; permanent crops 1%; meadows and pastures 41%; forest and
    woodland 24%; other 22%; includes irrigated NEGL%
Environment:
    geologically active Great Rift Valley susceptible to earthquakes, volcanic
    eruptions; deforestation; overgrazing; soil erosion; desertification;
    frequent droughts; famine
Note:
    strategic geopolitical position along world's busiest shipping lanes and
    close to Arabian oilfields

:Ethiopia People

Population: 54,270,464 (July 1992), growth rate 3.2% (1992)
Birth rate: 45 births/1,000 population (1992)
Death rate: 14 deaths/1,000 population (1992)
Net migration rate: 2 migrants/1,000 population (1992)
Infant mortality rate: 112 deaths/1,000 live births (1992)
Life expectancy at birth: 50 years male, 53 years female (1992)
Total fertility rate: 6.9 children born/woman (1992)
Nationality:
    noun - Ethiopian(s); adjective - Ethiopian
Ethnic divisions:
    Oromo 40%, Amhara and Tigrean 32%, Sidamo 9%, Shankella 6%, Somali 6%, Afar
    4%, Gurage 2%, other 1%
Religions:
    Muslim 40-45%, Ethiopian Orthodox 35-40%, animist 15-20%, other 5%
Languages:
    Amharic (official), Tigrinya, Orominga, Guaraginga, Somali, Arabic, English
    (major foreign language taught in schools)
Literacy:
    62% (male NA%, female NA%) age 10 and over can read and write (1983 est.)
Labor force:
    18,000,000; agriculture and animal husbandry 80%, government and services
    12%, industry and construction 8% (1985)

Organized labor:
  All Ethiopian Trade Union formed by the government in January 1977 to
  represent 273,000 registered trade union members; was dissolved when the TGE
  came to power; labor code of 1975 is being redrafted

:Ethiopia Government

Long-form name:
  none

Type:
  on 28 May 1991 the Ethiopian People's Revolutionary Democratic Front (EPRDF)
  toppled the authoritarian government of MENGISTU Haile-Mariam and took
  control in Addis Ababa; the Transitional Government of Ethiopia (TGE),
  announced as a two-year transitional period; on 29 May 1991, Issayas
  AFEWORKE, secretary general of the Eritrean People's Liberation Front
  (EPLF), announced the formation of the Provisional Government in Eritrea
  (PGE), in preparation for an eventual referendum on independence for the
  province

Capital: Addis Ababa

Administrative divisions:
  14 administrative regions (astedader akababiwach, singular - astedader
  akababi) and 1 autonomous region* (rasgez akababi); Addis Ababa (Addis
  Ababa), Afar, Agew, Amhara, Benishangul, Ertra (Eritrea)*, Gambela,
  Gurage-Hadiya-Wolayta, Harer, Kefa, Omo, Oromo, Sidamo, Somali, Tigray

Independence:
  oldest independent country in Africa and one of the oldest in the world - at
  least 2,000 years

Constitution:
  to be redrafted by 1993

Legal system:
  NA

National holiday:
  National Revolution Day 12 September (1974)

Executive branch:
  president, prime minister, Council of Ministers

Legislative branch:
  Council of Representatives

Judicial branch:
  Supreme Court

Leaders:
 Chief of State:
  Interim President Meles ZENAWI (since 1 June 1991); transitional government
 Head of Government:
  Acting Prime Minister Tamirat LAYNE (since 6 June 1991)

Political parties and leaders:
  NA

Suffrage:
  universal at age 18

Elections:
 Council of Representatives:
  last held 14 June 1987 (next to be held after new constitution drafted)

President:

last held 10 September 1987; next election planned after new constitution drafted; results - MENGISTU Haile-Mariam elected by the now defunct National Assembly, but resigned and left Ethiopia on 21 May 1991

Other political or pressure groups:

Oromo Liberation Front (OLF); Ethiopian People's Revolutionary Party (EPRP); numerous small, ethnic-based groups have formed since Mengistu's resignation

Member of:

ACP, AfDB, CCC, ECA, FAO, G-24, G-77, IAEA, IBRD, ICAO, IDA, IFAD, IFC, IGADD, ILO, IMF, IMO, INTELSAT, INTERPOL, IOC, ISO, ITU, LORCS, NAM, OAU,

UN, UNCTAD, UNESCO, UNIDO, UPU, WFTU, WHO, WMO, WTO

Diplomatic representation:

Counselor, Charge d'Affaires ad interim Girma AMARE; Chancery at 2134 Kalorama Road NW, Washington, DC 20008; telephone (202) 234-2281 or 2282

:Ethiopia Government

US:

Charge d'Affaires Marc A. BAAS; Embassy at Entoto Street, Addis Ababa (mailing address is P. O. Box 1014, Addis Ababa); telephone [251] (01) 550666; FAX [251] (1) 551-166

Flag:

three equal horizontal bands of green (top), yellow, and red; Ethiopia is the oldest independent country in Africa, and the colors of her flag were so often adopted by other African countries upon independence that they became known as the pan-African colors

:Ethiopia Economy

Overview:

Ethiopia is one of the poorest and least developed countries in Africa. Its economy is based on subsistence agriculture, which accounts for about 45% of GDP, 90% of exports, and 80% of total employment; coffee generates 60% of export earnings. The manufacturing sector is heavily dependent on inputs from the agricultural sector. Over 90% of large-scale industry, but less than 10% of agriculture, is state run; the government is considering selling off a portion of state-owned plants. Favorable agricultural weather largely explains the 4.5% growth in output in FY89, whereas drought and deteriorating internal security conditions prevented growth in FY90. In 1991 the lack of law and order, particularly in the south, interfered with economic development and growth.

GDP:

exchange rate conversion - $6.6 billion, per capita $130, real growth rate-0.4% (FY90 est.)

Inflation rate (consumer prices):

5.2% (1989)

Unemployment rate: NA

Budget:

revenues $1.8 billion; expenditures $1.7 billion, including capital expenditures of $842 million (FY88)

Exports:

$429 million (f.o.b., FY88)

commodities:
  coffee 60%, hides
partners:
  US, FRG, Djibouti, Japan, PDRY, France, Italy, Saudi Arabia
Imports:
  $1.1 billion (c.i.f., FY88)
commodities:
  food, fuels, capital goods
partners:
  USSR, Italy, FRG, Japan, UK, US, France
External debt: $2.6 billion (1988)
Industrial production:
  growth rate 2.3% (FY89 est.); accounts for 13% of GDP
Electricity:
  330,000 kW capacity; 650 million kWh produced, 10 kWh per capita (1991)
Industries:
  food processing, beverages, textiles, chemicals, metals processing, cement
Agriculture:
  accounts for 45% of GDP and is the most important sector of the economy even
  though frequent droughts and poor cultivation practices keep farm output
  low; famines not uncommon; export crops of coffee and oilseeds grown partly
  on state farms; estimated 50% of agricultural production at subsistence
  level; principal crops and livestock - cereals, pulses, coffee, oilseeds,
  sugarcane, potatoes and other vegetables, hides and skins, cattle, sheep,
  goats
Economic aid:
  US commitments, including Ex-Im (FY70-89), $504 million; Western (non-US)
  countries, ODA and OOF bilateral commitments (1970-89), $3.4 billion; OPEC
  bilateral aid (1979-89), $8 million; Communist countries (1970-89), $2.0
  billion
Currency:
  birr (plural - birr); 1 birr (Br) = 100 cents
Exchange rates:
  birr (Br) per US$1 - 2.0700 (fixed rate)

:Ethiopia Economy

Fiscal year: 8 July - 7 July

:Ethiopia Communications

Railroads:
  988 km total; 681 km 1.000-meter gauge; 307 km 0.950-meter gauge
  (nonoperational)
Highways:
  44,300 km total; 3,650 km paved, 9,650 km gravel, 3,000 km improved earth,
  28,000 km unimproved earth
Ports:
  Aseb, Mitsiwa
Merchant marine:
  12 ships (1,000 GRT or over) totaling 62,627 GRT/88,909 DWT; includes 8
  cargo, 1 roll-on/roll off, 1 livestock carrier, 2 petroleum tanker
Civil air:

25 major transport aircraft

Airports:

123 total, 86 usable; 9 with permanent-surface runways; 1 with runways over 3,659 m; 13 with runways 2,440-3,659 m; 38 with runways 1,220-2,439 m

Telecommunications:

open-wire and radio relay system adequate for government use; open-wire to Sudan and Djibouti; radio relay to Kenya and Djibouti; broadcast stations - 4 AM, no FM, 1 TV; 100,000 TV sets; 9,000,000 radios; 1 Atlantic Ocean INTELSAT earth station

:Ethiopia Defense Forces

Branches:

Army, Navy, Air Force, Police Force

Manpower availability:

males 15-49, 12,015,589; 6,230,680 fit for military service; 572,982 reach military age (18) annually

Defense expenditures:

exchange rate conversion - $760 million, 12.8% of GDP (1989)

Europa Island Geography

Total area: 28 km2

Land area: 28 km2

Comparative area: about 0.2 times the size of Washington, DC

Land boundaries:

Coastline:

22.2 km

Maritime claims:

 Exclusive economic zone:

200 nm

 Territorial sea:

12 nm

Disputes:

claimed by Madagascar

Climate:

tropical

Terrain:

NA

Natural resources:

negligible

Land use:

arable land NA%; permanent crops NA%; meadows and pastures NA%; forest and woodland NA%; other NA%; heavily wooded

Environment:

wildlife sanctuary

Note:

located in the Mozambique Channel 340 km west of Madagascar

:Europa Island People

Population: uninhabited

:Europa Island Government

Long-form name:
   none
Type:
   French possession administered by Commissioner of the Republic Jacques
   DEWATRE (as of July 1991); resident in Reunion
Capital: none; administered by France from Reunion

:Europa Island Economy

Overview: no economic activity

:Europa Island Communications

Ports:
   none; offshore anchorage only
Airports:
   1 with runways 1,220 to 2,439 m
Telecommunications:
   1 meteorological station

:Europa Island Defense Forces

Note: defense is the responsibility of France

Falkland Islands (Islas Malvinas) Geography

Total area: 12,170 km2
Land area: 12,170 km2; includes the two main islands of East and West Falkland and
   about 200 small islands
Comparative area: slightly smaller than Connecticut
Land boundaries:
   none
Coastline:
   1,288 km
Maritime claims:
 Continental shelf:
   100 meter depth
 Exclusive fishing zone:
   150 nm
 Territorial sea:
   12 nm
Disputes:
   administered by the UK, claimed by Argentina
Climate:
   cold marine; strong westerly winds, cloudy, humid; rain occurs on more than
   half of days in year; occasional snow all year, except in January and
   February, but does not accumulate
Terrain:
   rocky, hilly, mountainous with some boggy, undulating plains
Natural resources:
   fish and wildlife
Land use:
   arable land 0%; permanent crops 0%; meadows and pastures 99%; forest and
   woodland 0%; other 1%
Environment:
   poor soil fertility and a short growing season

Note:

   deeply indented coast provides good natural harbors

:Falkland Islands (Islas Malvinas) People

Population: 1,900 (July 1992), growth rate 0.2% (1992)
Birth rate: NA births/1,000 population (1992)
Death rate: NA deaths/1,000 population (1992)
Net migration rate: NA migrants/1,000 population (1992)
Infant mortality rate: NA deaths/1,000 live births (1992)
Life expectancy at birth: NA years male, NA years female (1992)
Total fertility rate: NA children born/woman (1992)
Nationality:

   noun - Falkland Islander(s); adjective - Falkland Island
Ethnic divisions:

   almost totally British
Religions:

   primarily Anglican, Roman Catholic, and United Free Church; Evangelist
   Church, Jehovah's Witnesses, Lutheran, Seventh-Day Adventist
Languages:

   English
Literacy:

   NA% (male NA%, female NA%) but compulsory education age 5 to 15 (1988)
Labor force:

   1,100 (est.); agriculture, mostly sheepherding about 95%
Organized labor:

   Falkland Islands General Employees Union, 400 members

:Falkland Islands (Islas Malvinas) Government

Long-form name:

   Colony of the Falkland Islands
Type:

   dependent territory of the UK
Capital: Stanley
Administrative divisions:

   none (dependent territory of the UK)
Independence:

   none (dependent territory of the UK)
Constitution:

   3 October 1985
Legal system:

   English common law
National holiday:

   Liberation Day, 14 June (1982)
Executive branch:

   British monarch, governor, Executive Council
Legislative branch:

   unicameral Legislative Council
Judicial branch:

   Supreme Court
Leaders:

  Chief of State:

Queen ELIZABETH II (since 6 February 1952)
Head of Government:
Governor William Hugh FULLERTON (since NA 1988)
Suffrage:
universal at age 18
Elections:
Legislative Council:
last held 11 October 1989 (next to be held October 1994); results - percent
of vote by party NA; seats - (10 total, 8 elected) number of seats by party
NA
Member of:
ICFTU
Diplomatic representation:
none (dependent territory of the UK)
Flag:
blue with the flag of the UK in the upper hoist-side quadrant and the
Falkland Island coat of arms in a white disk centered on the outer half of
the flag; the coat of arms contains a white ram (sheep raising is the major
economic activity) above the sailing ship Desire (whose crew discovered the
islands) with a scroll at the bottom bearing the motto DESIRE THE RIGHT

:Falkland Islands (Islas Malvinas) Economy

Overview:
The economy is based on sheep farming, which directly or indirectly employs
most of the work force. A few dairy herds are kept to meet domestic
consumption of milk and milk products, and crops grown are primarily those
for providing winter fodder. Exports feature shipments of high-grade wool to
the UK and the sale of postage stamps and coins. Rich stocks of fish in the
surrounding waters are not presently exploited by the islanders. So far,
efforts to establish a domestic fishing industry have been unsuccessful. In
1987 the government began selling fishing licenses to foreign trawlers
operating within the Falklands exclusive fishing zone. These license fees
amount to more than $40 million per year and are a primary source of income
for the government. To encourage tourism, the Falkland Islands Development
Corporation has built three lodges for visitors attracted by the abundant
wildlife and trout fishing.
GDP:
$NA, per capita $NA; real growth rate NA%
Inflation rate (consumer prices):
7.4% (1980-87 average)
Unemployment rate: NA%; labor shortage
Budget:
revenues $62.7 million; expenditures $41.8 million, excluding capital
expenditures of $NA (FY90)
Exports:
at least $14.7 million
commodities:
wool, hides and skins, and other
partners:
UK, Netherlands, Japan (1987 est.)

Imports:

at least $13.9 million

commodities:

food, clothing, fuels, and machinery

partners:

UK, Netherlands Antilles (Curacao), Japan (1987 est.)

External debt: $NA

Industrial production:

growth rate NA%

Electricity:

9,200 kW capacity; 17 million kWh produced, 8,638 kWh per capita (1991)

Industries:

wool and fish processing

Agriculture:

predominantly sheep farming; small dairy herds; some fodder and vegetable crops

Economic aid:

Western (non-US) countries, ODA and OOF bilateral commitments (1970-89), $277 million

Currency:

Falkland pound (plural - pounds); 1 Falkland pound (#F) = 100 pence

Exchange rates:

Falkland pound (#F) per US$1 - 0.5519 (January 1992), 0.5652 (1991), 0.5604 (1990), 0.6099 (1989), 0.5614 (1988), 0.6102 (1987); note - the Falkland pound is at par with the British pound

Fiscal year: 1 April - 31 March

:Falkland Islands (Islas Malvinas) Communications

Highways:

510 km total; 30 km paved, 80 km gravel, and 400 km unimproved earth

Ports:

Port Stanley

Civil air:

no major transport aircraft

Airports:

5 total, 5 usable; 2 with permanent-surface runways; none with runways over 3,659 m; 1 with runways 2,440-3,659 m; none with runways 1,220 to 2,439 m

Telecommunications:

government-operated radiotelephone and private VHF/CB radio networks provide effective service to almost all points on both islands; 590 telephones; broadcast stations - 2 AM, 3 FM, no TV; 1 Atlantic Ocean INTELSAT earth station with links through London to other countries

:Falkland Islands (Islas Malvinas) Defense Forces

Branches:

British Forces Falkland Islands (including Army, Royal Air Force, Royal Navy, and Royal Marines); Police Force

Note:

defense is the responsibility of the UK

Faroe Islands Geography

Total area: 1,400 km2
Land area: 1,400 km2
Comparative area: slightly less than eight times the size of Washington, DC
Land boundaries:
  none
Coastline:
  764 km
Maritime claims:
  Exclusive fishing zone:
  200 nm
  Territorial sea:
  3 nm
Disputes:
  none
Climate:
  mild winters, cool summers; usually overcast; foggy, windy
Terrain:
  rugged, rocky, some low peaks; cliffs along most of coast
Natural resources:
  fish
Land use:
  arable land 2%; permanent crops 0%; meadows and pastures 0%; forest and
  woodland 0%; other 98%
Environment:
  precipitous terrain limits habitation to small coastal lowlands; archipelago
  of 18 inhabited islands and a few uninhabited islets
Note:
  strategically located along important sea lanes in northeastern Atlantic
  about midway between Iceland and Shetland Islands

:Faroe Islands People

Population: 48,588 (July 1992), growth rate 0.9% (1992)
Birth rate: 17 births/1,000 population (1992)
Death rate: 8 deaths/1,000 population (1992)
Net migration rate: 0 migrants/1,000 population (1992)
Infant mortality rate: 7 deaths/1,000 live births (1992)
Life expectancy at birth: 75 years male, 81 years female (1992)
Total fertility rate: 2.2 children born/woman (1992)
Nationality:
  noun - Faroese (singular and plural); adjective - Faroese
Ethnic divisions:
  homogeneous Scandinavian population
Religions:
  Evangelical Lutheran
Languages:
  Faroese (derived from Old Norse), Danish
Literacy:
  NA% (male NA%, female NA%)
Labor force:
  17,585; largely engaged in fishing, manufacturing, transportation, and

commerce

Organized labor:

  NA

:Faroe Islands Government

Long-form name:

Type:

  part of the Danish realm; self-governing overseas administrative division of
  Denmark

Capital: Torshavn

Administrative divisions:

  none (self-governing overseas administrative division of Denmark)

Independence:

  part of the Danish realm; self-governing overseas administrative division of
  Denmark

Constitution:

  Danish

Legal system:

  Danish

National holiday:

  Birthday of the Queen, 16 April (1940)

Executive branch:

  Danish monarch, high commissioner, prime minister, deputy prime minister,
  Cabinet (Landsstyri)

Legislative branch:

  unicameral Parliament (Lgting)

Judicial branch:

Leaders:

 Chief of State:

  Queen MARGRETHE II (since 14 January 1972), represented by High Commissioner

  Bent KLINTE (since NA)

 Head of Government:

  Prime Minister Atli P. DAM (since 15 January 1991)

Political parties and leaders:

 opposition:

  Cooperation Coalition Party, Pauli ELLEFSEN; Republican Party, Signer
  HANSEN; Progressive and Fishing Industry Party-Christian People's Party
  (PFIP-CPP), leader NA; Progress Party, leader NA; Home Rule Party, Hilmar
  KASS

 two-party ruling coalition:

  Social Democratic Party, Atli P. DAM; People's Party, Jogvan SUND- STEIN

Suffrage:

  universal at age 20

Elections:

 Danish Parliament:

  last held on 12 December 1990 (next to be held by December 1994); results -
  percent of vote by party NA; seats - (2 total) Social Democratic 1, People's

Party 1; note - the Faroe Islands elects two representatives to the Danish Parliament

Faroese Parliament:

last held 17 November 1990 (next to be held November 1994); results - Social Democratic 27.4%, People's Party 21.9%, Cooperation Coalition Party 18.9%, Republican Party 14.7%, Home Rule 8.8%, PFIP-CPP 5.9%, other 2.4%; seats - (32 total) two-party coalition 17 (Social Democratic 10, People's Party 7), Cooperation Coalition Party 6, Republican Party 4, Home Rule 3, PFIP-CPP 2

Diplomatic representation:

none (self-governing overseas administrative division of Denmark)

Flag:

white with a red cross outlined in blue that extends to the edges of the flag; the vertical part of the cross is shifted to the hoist side in the style of the DANNEBROG (Danish flag)

:Faroe Islands Economy

Overview:

The Faroese, who have long been enjoying the affluent living standards of the Danes and other Scandinavians, now must cope with the decline of the all-important fishing industry and with an external debt twice the size of annual income. When the nations of the world extended their fishing zones to 200 nautical miles in the early 1970s, the Faroese no longer could continue their traditional long-distance fishing and subsequently depleted their own nearby fishing areas. The government's tight controls on fish stocks and its austerity measures have caused a recession, and subsidy cuts will force further reductions in the fishing industry, which has already been plagued with bankrupcies. An annual Danish subsidy of $140 million continues to provide roughly one-third of the islands' budget revenues.

GDP:

purchasing power equivalent - $662 million, per capita $14,000; real growth rate 3% (1989 est.)

Inflation rate (consumer prices):

2.0% (1988)

Unemployment rate: 5-6% (1991 est.)

Budget:

revenues $425 million; expenditures $480 million, including capital expenditures of NA (1991 est.)

Exports:

$386 million (f.o.b., 1990 est.)

commodities:

fish and fish products 88%, animal feedstuffs, transport equipment (1989)

partners:

Denmark 20%, Germany 18.3%, UK 14.2%, France 11.2%, Spain 7.9%, US 4.5%

Imports:

$322 million (c.i.f., 1990 est.)

commodities:

machinery and transport equipment 24.4%, manufactures 24%, food and livestock 19%, fuels 12%, chemicals 6.5%

partners:

Denmark 43.8%, Norway 19.8%, Sweden 4.9%, Germany 4.2%, US 1.3%

External debt: $1.3 billion (1989)
Industrial production:
  growth rate NA%
Electricity:
  80,000 kW capacity; 280 million kWh produced, 5,910 kWh per capita (1991)
Industries:
  fishing, shipbuilding, handicrafts
Agriculture:
  accounts for 27% of GDP and employs 27% of labor force; principal crops -
  potatoes and vegetables; livestock - sheep; annual fish catch about 360,000
  metric tons
Economic aid:
  none
Currency:
  Danish krone (plural - kroner); 1 Danish krone (DKr) = 100 ore
Exchange rates:
  Danish kroner (DKr) per US$1 - 6.116 (January 1992), 6.396 (1991), 6.189
  (1990), 7.310 (1989), 6.732 (1988), 6.840 (1987)
Fiscal year: 1 April - 31 March

:Faroe Islands Communications

Highways:
  200 km
Ports:
  Torshavn, Tvoroyri
Merchant marine:
  10 ships (1,000 GRT or over) totaling 22,015 GRT/24,007 DWT; includes 1
  short-sea passenger, 5 cargo, 2 roll-on/roll-off, 2 refrigerated cargo; note
  - a subset of the Danish register
Airports:
  1 with permanent surface runways 1,220-2,439 m
Telecommunications:
  good international communications; fair domestic facilities; 27,900
  telephones; broadcast stations - 1 AM, 3 (10 repeaters) FM, 3 (29 repeaters)
  TV; 3 coaxial submarine cables

:Faroe Islands Defense Forces

Branches:
  no organized native military forces; only a small Police Force is maintained
Note:
  defense is the responsibility of Denmark

  Fiji Geography

Total area: 18,270 km2
Land area: 18,270 km2
Comparative area: slightly smaller than New Jersey
Land boundaries:
  none
Coastline:
  1,129 km
Maritime claims:

(measured from claimed archipelagic baselines)
Continental shelf:
  200 m (depth) or to depth of exploitation; rectilinear shelf claim added
Exclusive economic zone:
  200 nm
Territorial sea:
  12 nm
Disputes:
  none
Climate:
  tropical marine; only slight seasonal temperature variation
Terrain:
  mostly mountains of volcanic origin
Natural resources:
  timber, fish, gold, copper; offshore oil potential
Land use:
  arable land 8%; permanent crops 5%; meadows and pastures 3%; forest and
  woodland 65%; other 19%; includes irrigated NEGL%
Environment:
  subject to hurricanes from November to January; includes 332 islands of
  which approximately 110 are inhabited
Note:
  located 2,500 km north of New Zealand in the South Pacific Ocean

:Fiji People

Population: 749,946 (July 1992), growth rate 0.9% (1992)
Birth rate: 25 births/1,000 population (1992)
Death rate: 7 deaths/1,000 population (1992)
Net migration rate: -10 migrants/1,000 population (1992)
Infant mortality rate: 19 deaths/1,000 live births (1992)
Life expectancy at birth: 62 years male, 67 years female (1992)
Total fertility rate: 3.0 children born/woman (1992)
Nationality:
  noun - Fijian(s); adjective - Fijian
Ethnic divisions:
  Indian 49%, Fijian 46%, European, other Pacific Islanders, overseas Chinese,
  and other 5%
Religions:
  Christian 52% (Methodist 37%, Roman Catholic 9%), Hindu 38%, Muslim 8%,
  other 2%; note - Fijians are mainly Christian, Indians are Hindu, and there
  is a Muslim minority (1986)
Languages:
  English (official); Fijian; Hindustani
Literacy:
  86% (male 90%, female 81%) age 15 and over can read and write (1985 est.)
Labor force:
  235,000; subsistence agriculture 67%, wage earners 18%, salary earners 15%
  (1987)
Organized labor:

about 45,000 employees belong to some 46 trade unions, which are organized along lines of work and ethnic origin (1983)

:Fiji Government

Long-form name:
  Republic of Fiji
Type:
  military coup leader Maj. Gen. Sitiveni RABUKA formally declared Fiji a republic on 6 October 1987
Capital: Suva
Administrative divisions:
  4 divisions and 1 dependency*; Central, Eastern, Northern, Rotuma*, Western
Independence:
  10 October 1970 (from UK)
Constitution:
  10 October 1970 (suspended 1 October 1987); a new Constitution was proposed on 23 September 1988 and promulgated on 25 July 1990
Legal system:
  based on British system
National holiday:
  Independence Day, 10 October (1970)
Executive branch:
  president, prime minister, Cabinet Great Councils of Chiefs (highest ranking members of the traditional chiefly system)
Legislative branch:
  the bicameral Parliament, consisting of an upper house or Senate and a lower house or House of Representatives, was dissolved following the coup of 14 May 1987; the Constitution of 23 September 1988 provides for a bicameral Parliament
Judicial branch:
  Supreme Court
Leaders:
  Chief of State:
  President Ratu Sir Penaia Kanatabatu GANILAU (since 5 December 1987)
  Head of Government:
  Prime Minister Ratu Sir Kamisese MARA (since 5 December 1987); Deputy Prime Minister Josefata KAMIKAMICA (since October 1991); note - Ratu Sir Kamisese MARA served as prime minister from 10 October 1970 until the 5-11 April 1987 election; after a second coup led by Maj. Gen. Sitiveni RABUKA on 25 September 1987, Ratu Sir Kamisese MARA was reappointed as prime minister
Political parties and leaders:
  Fijian Political Party (primarily Fijian), leader Maj. Gen. Sitivini RABUKA; National Federation Party (NFP; primarily Indian), Siddiq KOYA; Christian Fijian Nationalist Party (CFNP), Sakeasi BUTADROKA; Fiji Labor Party (FLP), Jokapeci KOROI; All National Congress (ANC), Apisai TORA; General Voters Party (GVP), Max OLSSON; Fiji Conservative Party (FCP), Isireli VUIBAU; Conservative Party of Fiji (CPF), Jolale ULUDOLE and Viliame SAVU; Fiji Indian Liberal Party, Swami MAHARAJ; Fiji Indian Congress Party, Ishwari BAJPAI; Fiji Independent Labor (Muslim), leader NA; Four Corners Party, David TULVANUAVOU

Suffrage:
  none
Elections:
  House of Representatives:
    last held 14 May 1987 (next to be held 23-29 May 1992); results - percent of
    vote by party NA; seats - (70 total, with ethnic Fijians allocated 37 seats,
    ethnic Indians 27 seats, and independents and other 6 seats) number of seats
    by party NA
Member of:
  ACP, AsDB, CP, ESCAP, FAO, G-77, IBRD, ICAO, ICFTU, IDA, IFAD, IFC, ILO,
  IMF, IMO, INTELSAT, INTERPOL, IOC, ITU, LORCS, PCA, SPC, SPF, UN,
UNCTAD,
  UNESCO, UNIDO, UNIFIL, UPU, WHO, WIPO, WMO

:Fiji Government

Diplomatic representation:
  Ambassador Pita Kewa NACUVA; Chancery at Suite 240, 2233 Wisconsin Avenue
  NW, Washington, DC 20007; telephone (202) 337-8320; there is a Fijian
  Consulate in New York
  US:
  Ambassador Evelyn I. H. TEEGEN; Embassy at 31 Loftus Street, Suva (mailing
  address is P. O. Box 218, Suva); telephone [679] 314-466; FAX [679] 300-081
Flag:
  light blue with the flag of the UK in the upper hoist-side quadrant and the
  Fijian shield centered on the outer half of the flag; the shield depicts a
  yellow lion above a white field quartered by the cross of Saint George
  featuring stalks of sugarcane, a palm tree, bananas, and a white dove

:Fiji Economy

Overview:
  Fiji's economy is primarily agricultural, with a large subsistence sector.
  Sugar exports are a major source of foreign exchange, and sugar processing
  accounts for one-third of industrial output. Industry, including sugar
  milling, contributes 13% to GDP. Fiji traditionally had earned considerable
  sums of hard currency from the 250,000 tourists who visited each year. In
  1987, however, after two military coups, the economy went into decline. GDP
  dropped by 7.8% in 1987 and by another 2.5% in 1988; political uncertainty
  created a drop in tourism, and the worst drought of the century caused sugar
  production to fall sharply. In contrast, sugar and tourism turned in strong
  performances in 1989, and the economy rebounded vigorously. In 1990 the
  economy received a setback from cyclone Sina, which cut sugar output by an
  estimated 21%.
GDP:
  exchange rate conversion - $1.3 billion, per capita $1,700; real growth rate
  3.5% (1991 est.)
Inflation rate (consumer prices):
  7.0% (1991)
Unemployment rate: 5.9% (1991 est.)
Budget:
  revenues $413 million; expenditures $464 million, including capital
  expenditures of NA (1992 est.)

Exports:
   $646 million (f.o.b., 1991 est.)
   commodities:
   sugar 40%, gold, clothing, copra, processed fish, lumber
   partners:
   EC 31%, Australia 21%, Japan 8%, US 6%
Imports:
   $840 million (c.i.f., 1991 est.)
   commodities:
   machinery and transport equipment 32%, food 15%, petroleum products,
   consumer goods, chemicals
   partners:
   Australia 30%, NZ 17%, Japan 13%, EC 6%, US 6%
External debt: $428 million (December 1990 est.)
Industrial production:
   growth rate 8.4% (1991 est.); accounts for 13% of GDP
Electricity:
   215,000 kW capacity; 330 million kWh produced, 430 kWh per capita (1990)
Industries:
   sugar, tourism, copra, gold, silver, fishing, clothing, lumber, small
   cottage industries
Agriculture:
   accounts for 23% of GDP; principal cash crop is sugarcane; coconuts,
   cassava, rice, sweet potatoes, and bananas; small livestock sector includes
   cattle, pigs, horses, and goats
Economic aid:
   Western (non-US) countries, ODA and OOF bilateral commitments (1980-89),
   $815 million
Currency:
   Fijian dollar (plural - dollars); 1 Fijian dollar (F$) = 100 cents
Exchange rates:
   Fijian dollars (F$) per US$1 - 1.4855 (January 1992), 1.4756 (1991), 1.4809
   (1990), 1.4833 (1989), 1.4303 (1988), 1.2439 (1987)
Fiscal year: calendar year

:Fiji Communications

Railroads:
   644 km 0.610-meter narrow gauge, belonging to the government-owned Fiji
   Sugar Corporation
Highways:
   3,300 km total (1984) - 1,590 km paved; 1,290 km gravel, crushed stone, or
   stabilized soil surface; 420 unimproved earth
Inland waterways:
   203 km; 122 km navigable by motorized craft and 200-metric-ton barges
Ports:
   Lambasa, Lautoka, Savusavu, Suva
Merchant marine:
   7 ships (1,000 GRT or over) totaling 40,072 GRT/47,187 DWT; includes 2
   roll-on/roll-off, 2 container, 1 petroleum tanker, 1 chemical tanker, 1
   cargo

Civil air:
  1 DC-3 and 1 light aircraft
Airports:
  25 total, 22 usable; 2 with permanent-surface runways; none with runways
  over 3,659 m; 1 with runways 2,440-3,659 m; 2 with runways 1,220-2,439 m
Telecommunications:
  modern local, interisland, and international (wire/radio integrated) public
  and special-purpose telephone, telegraph, and teleprinter facilities;
  regional radio center; important COMPAC cable link between US-Canada and New
  Zealand-Australia; 53,228 telephones; broadcast stations - 7 AM, 1 FM, no
  TV; 1 Pacific Ocean INTELSAT earth station
:Fiji Defense Forces

Branches:
  Fiji Military Force (FMF; including a naval division, Police)
Manpower availability:
  males 15-49, 192,056; 105,898 fit for military service; 7,564 reach military
  age (18) annually
Defense expenditures:
  exchange rate conversion - $22.4 million, 1.7% of GDP (FY 91)

Finland Geography

Total area: 337,030 km2
Land area: 305,470 km2
Comparative area: slightly smaller than Montana
Land boundaries:
  2,628 km; Norway 729 km, Sweden 586 km, Russia 1,313 km
Coastline:
  1,126 km; excludes islands and coastal indentations
Maritime claims:
 Contiguous zone:
  6 nm
 Continental shelf:
  200 m (depth) or to depth of exploitation
 Exclusive fishing zone:
  12 nm
 Territorial sea:
  4 nm
Disputes:
  none
Climate:
  cold temperate; potentially subarctic, but comparatively mild because of
  moderating influence of the North Atlantic Current, Baltic Sea, and more
  than 60,000 lakes
Terrain:
  mostly low, flat to rolling plains interspersed with lakes and low hills
Natural resources:
  timber, copper, zinc, iron ore, silver
Land use:
  arable land 8%; permanent crops 0%; meadows and pastures NEGL%; forest and
  woodland 76%; other 16%; includes irrigated NEGL%

Environment:
    permanently wet ground covers about 30% of land; population concentrated on
    small southwestern coastal plain
Note:
    long boundary with Russia; Helsinki is northernmost national capital on
    European continent

:Finland People

Population: 5,004,273 (July 1992), growth rate 0.3% (1992)
Birth rate: 12 births/1,000 population (1992)
Death rate: 10 deaths/1,000 population (1992)
Net migration rate: NEGL migrants/1,000 population (1992)
Infant mortality rate: 6 deaths/1,000 live births (1992)
Life expectancy at birth: 72 years male, 80 years female (1992)
Total fertility rate: 1.7 children born/woman (1992)
Nationality:
    noun - Finn(s); adjective - Finnish
Ethnic divisions:
    Finn, Swede, Lapp, Gypsy, Tatar
Religions:
    Evangelical Lutheran 89%, Greek Orthodox 1%, none 9%, other 1%
Languages:
    Finnish 93.5%, Swedish (both official) 6.3%; small Lapp- and
    Russian-speaking minorities
Literacy:
    100% (male NA%, female NA%) age 15 and over can read and write (1980 est.)
Labor force:
    2,533,000; public services 30.4%; industry 20.9%; commerce 15.0%; finance,
    insurance, and business services 10.2%; agriculture and forestry 8.6%;
    transport and communications 7.7%; construction 7.2%
Organized labor:
    80% of labor force

:Finland Government

Long-form name:
    Republic of Finland
Type:
    republic
Capital: Helsinki
Administrative divisions:
    12 provinces (laanit, singular - laani); Ahvenanmaa, Hame, Keski-Suomi,
    Kuopio, Kymi, Lappi, Mikkeli, Oulu, Pohjois-Karjala, Turku ja Pori, Uusimaa,
    Vaasa
Independence:
    6 December 1917 (from Soviet Union)
Constitution:
    17 July 1919
Legal system:
    civil law system based on Swedish law; Supreme Court may request legislation
    interpreting or modifying laws; accepts compulsory ICJ jurisdiction, with
    reservations

National holiday:
   Independence Day, 6 December (1917)
Executive branch:
   president, prime minister, deputy prime minister, Council of State
   (Valtioneuvosto)
Legislative branch:
   unicameral Parliament (Eduskunta)
Judicial branch:
   Supreme Court (Korkein Oikeus)
Leaders:
  Chief of State:
   President Mauno KOIVISTO (since 27 January 1982)
  Head of Government:
   Prime Minister Esko AHO (since 26 April 1991); Deputy Prime Minister Ilkka
   KANERVA (since 26 April 1991)
Suffrage:
   universal at age 18
Elections:
  Parliament:
   last held 17 March 1991 (next to be held March 1995); results - Center Party
   24.8%, Social Democratic Party 22.1%, National Coalition (Conservative)
   Party 19.3%, Leftist Alliance (Communist) 10.1%, Green League 6.8%, Swedish
   People's Party 5.5%, Rural 4.8%, Finnish Christian League 3.1%, Liberal
   People's Party 0.8%; seats - (200 total) Center Party 55, Social Democratic
   Party 48, National Coalition (Conservative) Party 40, Leftist Alliance
   (Communist) 19, Swedish People's Party 12, Green League 10, Finnish
   Christian League 8, Rural 7, Liberal People's Party 1
  President:
   last held 31 January - 1 February and 15 February 1988 (next to be held
   January 1994); results - Mauno KOIVISTO 48%, Paavo VAYRYNEN 20%, Harri
   HOLKERI 18%
Communists:
   28,000 registered members; an additional 45,000 persons belong to People's
   Democratic League
Other political or pressure groups:
   Finnish Communist Party-Unity, Yrjo HAKANEN; Constitutional Rightist Party;
   Finnish Pensioners Party; Communist Workers Party, Timo LAHDENMAKI

:Finland Government

Member of:
   AfDB, AG (observer), AsDB, Australia Group, BIS, CCC, CE, CERN, CSCE,
EBRD,
   ECE, EFTA, ESA (associate), FAO, G-9, GATT, IADB, IAEA, IBRD, ICAO, ICC,
   ICFTU, IDA, IFAD, IFC, ILO, IMF, IMO, INMARSAT, INTELSAT, INTERPOL,
IOC, IOM
   (observer), ISO, ITU, LORCS, MTCR, NAM (guest), NC, NEA, NIB, NSG, OAS
   (observer), OECD, PCA, UN, UNCTAD, UNDOF, UNESCO, UNFICYP, UNHCR,
UNIDO,
   UNIFIL, UNIIMOG, UNMOGIP, UNTSO, UPU, WHO, WIPO, WMO, WTO, ZC
Diplomatic representation:

Ambassador Jukka VALTASAARI; Chancery at 3216 New Mexico Avenue NW, Washington, DC 20016; telephone (202) 363-2430; there are Finnish Consulates General in Los Angeles and New York, and Consulates in Chicago and Houston

US:

Ambassador John H. KELLY (as of December 1991); Embassy at Itainen Puistotie 14A, SF-00140, Helsinki (mailing address is APO AE 09723); telephone [358] (0) 171931; FAX [358] (0) 174681

Flag:

white with a blue cross that extends to the edges of the flag; the vertical part of the cross is shifted to the hoist side in the style of the DANNEBROG (Danish flag)

:Finland Economy

Overview:

Finland has a highly industrialized, largely free market economy, with per capita output nearly three-fourths the US figure. Its main economic force is the manufacturing sector - principally the wood, metals, and engineering industries. Trade is important, with the export of goods representing about 30% of GDP. Except for timber and several minerals, Finland depends on imported raw materials, energy, and some components of manufactured goods. Because of the climate, agricultural development is limited to maintaining self-sufficiency in basic commodities. The economy, which experienced an average of 4.9% annual growth between 1987 and 1989, sank into a deep recession in 1991 as growth contracted by 6.2%. The recession - which is expected to bottom out in late 1992 - has been caused by economic overheating, depressed foreign markets, and the dismantling of the barter system between Finland and the former Soviet Union in which Soviet oil and gas had been exchanged for Finnish manufactured goods. The Finnish Government has proposed efforts to increase industrial competitiveness and efficiency by an increase in exports to Western markets, cuts in public expenditures, partial privatization of state enterprises, and foreign investment and exchange liberalization. Helsinki tied the markkaa to the EC's European Currency Unit to promote stability but was forced to devalue the markkaa by about 12% in November 1991. The devaluation should improve industrial competitiveness and business confidence in 1992. Finland, as a member of EFTA, negotiated a European Economic Area arrangement with the EC that allows for free movement of capital, goods, services, and labor within the organization as of January 1993. Finland applied for full EC membership in March 1992.

GDP:

purchasing power equivalent - $80.6 billion, per capita $16,200; real growth rate - 6.2% (1991)

Inflation rate (consumer prices):

2.9% (1991)

Unemployment rate: 7.6% (1991)

Budget:

revenues $35.8 billion; expenditures $41.5 billion, including capital expenditures of NA billion (1991)

Exports:

$22.9 billion (f.o.b., 1991)

commodities:
    timber, paper and pulp, ships, machinery, clothing and footwear
    partners:
    EC 50.25%, Germany 15.5%, UK 10.4%, EFTA 20.7%, Sweden 14%, US 6.1%,
Japan
    1.5%, USSR/EE 6.71% (1991)
Imports:
    $21.6 billion (c.i.f., 1991)
    commodities:
    foodstuffs, petroleum and petroleum products, chemicals, transport
    equipment, iron and steel, machinery, textile yarn and fabrics, fodder
    grains
    partners:
    EC 45.9% (Germany 16.9%), UK 7.7%, EFTA 19.9%, Sweden 12.3%, US 6.9%,
Japan
    6%, USSR/EE 10.7%
External debt: $5.3 billion (1989)
Industrial production:
    growth rate - 8.6% (1991 est.)
Electricity:
    13,324,000 kW capacity; 49,330 million kWh produced, 9,857 kWh per capita
    (1991)

:Finland Economy

Industries:
    metal products, shipbuilding, forestry and wood processing (pulp, paper),
    copper refining, foodstuffs, chemicals, textiles, clothing
Agriculture:
    accounts for 8% of GDP (including forestry); livestock production,
    especially dairy cattle, predominates; forestry is an important export
    earner and a secondary occupation for the rural population; main crops -
    cereals, sugar beets, potatoes; 85% self-sufficient, but short of foodgrains
    and fodder grains; annual fish catch about 160,000 metric tons
Economic aid:
    donor - ODA and OOF commitments (1970-89), $2.7 billion
Currency:
    markka (plural - markkaa); 1 markka (FMk) or Finmark = 100 pennia
Exchange rates:
    markkaa (FMk) per US$1 - 4.2967 (January 1992), 4.0440 (1991), 3.8235
    (1990), 4.2912 (1989), 4.1828 (1988), 4.3956 (1987)
Fiscal year: calendar year

:Finland Communications

Railroads:
    5,924 km total; Finnish State Railways (VR) operate a total of 5,863 km
    1.524-meter gauge, of which 480 km are multiple track and 1,445 km are
    electrified
Highways:
    about 103,000 km total, including 35,000 km paved (bituminous, concrete,
    bituminous-treated surface) and 38,000 km unpaved (stabilized gravel,
    gravel, earth); additional 30,000 km of private (state-subsidized) roads

Inland waterways:
  6,675 km total (including Saimaa Canal); 3,700 km suitable for steamers
Pipelines:
  natural gas 580 km
Ports:
  Helsinki, Oulu, Pori, Rauma, Turku; 6 secondary, numerous minor ports
Merchant marine:
  80 ships (1,000 GRT or over) totaling 794,094 GRT/732,585 DWT; includes 1
  passenger, 9 short-sea passenger, 16 cargo, 1 refrigerated cargo, 26
  roll-on/roll-off, 12 petroleum tanker, 6 chemical tanker, 2 liquefied gas, 7
  bulk
Civil air:
  42 major transport
Airports:
  159 total, 156 usable; 58 with permanent-surface runways; none with runways
  over 3,659 m; 23 with runways 2,440-3,659 m; 22 with runways 1,220-2,439 m
Telecommunications:
  good service from cable and radio relay network; 3,140,000 telephones;
  broadcast stations - 6 AM, 105 FM, 235 TV; 1 submarine cable; INTELSAT
  satellite transmission service via Swedish earth station and a receive-only
  INTELSAT earth station near Helsinki

:Finland Defense Forces

Branches:
  Army, Navy, Air Force, Frontier Guard (including Coast Guard)
Manpower availability:
  males 15-49, 1,314,305; 1,087,286 fit for military service; 33,053 reach
  military age (17) annually
Defense expenditures:
  exchange rate conversion - $1.8 billion, 1.6% of GDP (1989 est.)

France Geography

Total area: 547,030 km2
Land area: 545,630 km2; includes Corsica and the rest of metropolitan France, but
  excludes the overseas administrative divisions
Comparative area: slightly more than twice the size of Colorado
Land boundaries:
  2,892.4 km; Andorra 60 km, Belgium 620 km, Germany 451 km, Italy 488 km,
  Luxembourg 73 km, Monaco 4.4 km, Spain 623 km, Switzerland 573 km
Coastline:
  3,427 km; mainland 2,783 km, Corsica 644 km
Maritime claims:
 Contiguous zone:
  12-24 nm
 Exclusive economic zone:
  200 nm
 Territorial sea:
  12 nm
Disputes:
  Madagascar claims Bassas da India, Europa Island, Glorioso Islands, Juan de
  Nova Island, and Tromelin Island; Comoros claims Mayotte; Mauritius claims

Tromelin Island; Seychelles claims Tromelin Island; Suriname claims part of French Guiana; Mexico claims Clipperton Island; territorial claim in Antarctica (Adelie Land)

Climate:
generally cool winters and mild summers, but mild winters and hot summers along the Mediterranean

Terrain:
mostly flat plains or gently rolling hills in north and west; remainder is mountainous, especially Pyrenees in south, Alps in east

Natural resources:
coal, iron ore, bauxite, fish, timber, zinc, potash

Land use:
arable land 32%; permanent crops 2%; meadows and pastures 23%; forest and woodland 27%; other 16%; includes irrigated 2%

Environment:
most of large urban areas and industrial centers in Rhone, Garonne, Seine, or Loire River basins; occasional warm tropical wind known as mistral

Note:
largest West European nation

:France People

Population: 57,287,258 (July 1992), growth rate 0.5% (1992)
Birth rate: 13 births/1,000 population (1992)
Death rate: 9 deaths/1,000 population (1992)
Net migration rate: 1 migrant/1,000 population (1992)
Infant mortality rate: 7 deaths/1,000 live births (1992)
Life expectancy at birth: 74 years male, 82 years female (1992)
Total fertility rate: 1.8 children born/woman (1992)

Nationality:
noun - Frenchman(men), Frenchwoman(women); adjective - French

Ethnic divisions:
Celtic and Latin with Teutonic, Slavic, North African, Indochinese, and Basque minorities

Religions:
Roman Catholic 90%, Protestant 2%, Jewish 1%, Muslim (North African workers) 1%, unaffiliated 6%

Languages:
French (100% of population); rapidly declining regional dialects (Provencal, Breton, Alsatian, Corsican, Catalan, Basque, Flemish)

Literacy:
99% (male NA%, female NA%) age 15 and over can read and write (1980 est.)

Labor force:
24,170,000; services 61.5%, industry 31.3%, agriculture 7.3% (1987)

Organized labor:
20% of labor force (est.)

:France Government

Long-form name:
French Republic

Type:
republic

Capital: Paris
Administrative divisions:

metropolitan France - 22 regions (regions, singular - region); Alsace, Aquitaine, Auvergne, Basse-Normandie, Bourgogne, Bretagne, Centre, Champagne-Ardenne, Corse, Franche-Comte, Haute-Normandie, Ile-de-France, Languedoc-Roussillon, Limousin, Lorraine, Midi-Pyrenees, Nord-Pas-de-Calais, Pays de la Loire, Picardie, Poitou-Charentes, Provence-Alpes-Cote d'Azur, Rhone-Alpes; note - the 22 regions are subdivided into 96 departments; see separate entries for the overseas departments (French Guiana, Guadeloupe, Martinique, Reunion) and the territorial collectivities (Mayotte, Saint Pierre and Miquelon)

Independence:

unified by Clovis in 486, First Republic proclaimed in 1792

Constitution:

28 September 1958, amended concerning election of president in 1962

Dependent areas:

Bassas da India, Clipperton Island, Europa Island, French Polynesia, French Southern and Antarctic Lands, Glorioso Islands, Juan de Nova Island, New Caledonia, Tromelin Island, Wallis and Futuna

note:

the US does not recognize claims to Antarctica

Legal system:

civil law system with indigenous concepts; review of administrative but not legislative acts

National holiday:

Taking of the Bastille, 14 July (1789)

Executive branch:

president, prime minister, Council of Ministers (cabinet)

Legislative branch:

bicameral Parliament (Parlement) consists of an upper house or Senate (Senat) and a lower house or National Assembly (Assemblee Nationale)

Judicial branch:

Constitutional Court (Cour Constitutionnelle)

Leaders:

Chief of State:

President Francois MITTERRAND (since 21 May 1981)

Head of Government:

Prime Minister Pierre BEREGOVOY (since 2 April 1992)

Political parties and leaders:

Rally for the Republic (RPR, formerly UDR), Jacques CHIRAC; Union for French Democracy (UDF, federation of PR, CDS, and RAD), Valery Giscard d'ESTAING; Republican Party (PR), Gerard LONGUET; Center for Social Democrats (CDS), Pierre MEHAIGNERIE; Radical (RAD), Yves GALLAND; Socialist Party (PS), Laurent FABIUS; Left Radical Movement (MRG), Emile ZUCCARELLI; Communist
Party (PCF), Georges MARCHAIS; National Front (FN), Jean-Marie LE PEN

Suffrage:

universal at age 18

Elections:

National Assembly:

last held 5 and 12 June 1988 (next to be held June 1993); results - Second
Ballot PS-MRG 48. 7%, RPR 23.1%, UDF 21%, PCF 3.4%, other 3.8%; seats - (577
total) PS 272, RPR 127, UDF 91, UDC 40, PCF 26, independents 21

:France Government

President:
last held 8 May 1988 (next to be held May 1995); results - Second Ballot
Francois MITTERRAND 54%, Jacques CHIRAC 46%

Elections:
Senate:
last held 24 September 1989 (next to be held September 1992); results -
percent of vote by party NA; seats - (321 total; 296 metropolitan France, 13
for overseas departments and territories, and 12 for French nationals
abroad) RPR 91, UDF 143 (PR 52, CDS 68, RAD 23), PS 66, PCF 16, independents
2, unknown 3

Communists:
700,000 claimed but probably closer to 150,000; Communist voters, 2.8
million in 1988 election

Other political or pressure groups:
Communist-controlled labor union (Confederation Generale du Travail) nearly
2.4 million members (claimed); Socialist-leaning labor union (Confederation
Francaise Democratique du Travail or CFDT) about 800,000 members est.;
independent labor union (Force Ouvriere) 1 million members (est.);
independent white-collar union (Confederation Generale des Cadres) 340,000
members (claimed); National Council of French Employers (Conseil National du
Patronat Francais - CNPF or Patronat)

Member of:
ACCT, AfDB, AG (observer), AsDB, Australia Group, BDEAC, BIS, CCC, CDB,
CE,
CERN, COCOM, CSCE, EBRD, EC, ECE, ECLAC, EIB, ESA, ESCAP, FAO, FZ,
GATT,
G-5, G-7, G-10, IABD, IAEA, IBRD, ICAO, ICC, ICFTU, IDA, IFAD, IFC, ILO,
IMF, IMO, INMARSAT, INTELSAT, INTERPOL, IOC, IOM (observer), ISO, ITU,
LORCS, MTCR, NACC, NATO, NEA, NSG, OAS (observer), OECD, PCA, SPC,
UN,
UNCTAD, UNESCO, UNHCR, UNIDO, UNIFIL, UNRWA, UN Security Council,
UN
Trusteeship Council, UNTSO, UPU, WCL, WEU, WFTU, WHO, WIPO, WMO,
WTO

Diplomatic representation:
Ambassador Jacques ANDREANI; Chancery at 4101 Reservoir Road NW, Wash-
ington,
DC 20007; telephone (202) 944-6000; there are French Consulates General in
Boston, Chicago, Detroit, Houston, Los Angeles, New Orleans, Miami, New
York, San Francisco, and San Juan (Puerto Rico)

US:
Ambassador Walter J. P. CURLEY; Embassy at 2 Avenue Gabriel, 75382 Paris
Cedex 08, Unit 21551 (mailing address is APO AE 09777); telephone [33] (1)
42-96-12-02 or 42-61-80-75; FAX [33] (1) 42-66-97-83; there are US
Consulates General in Bordeaux, Marseille, and Strasbourg

Flag:
  three equal vertical bands of blue (hoist side), white, and red; known as
  the French Tricouleur (Tricolor); the design and colors have been the basis
  for a number of other flags, including those of Belgium, Chad, Ireland,
  Ivory Coast, and Luxembourg; the official flag for all French dependent
  areas

:France Economy

Overview:
  One of the world's most developed economies, France has substantial
  agricultural resources and a highly diversified modern industrial sector.
  Large tracts of fertile land, the application of modern technology, and
  subsidies have combined to make it the leading agricultural producer in
  Western Europe. France is largely self-sufficient in agricultural products
  and is a major exporter of wheat and dairy products. The industrial sector
  generates about one-quarter of GDP, and the growing services sector has
  become crucial to the economy. After expanding at a rapid 3.8% pace during
  the period 1988-89, the economy slowed down in 1990, with growth of 1.5% in
  1990 and 1.4% in 1991; growth in 1992 is expected to be about 2%. The
  economy has had difficulty generating enough jobs for new entrants into the
  labor force, resulting in a high unemployment rate, which rose to almost 10%
  in 1991. The steadily advancing economic integration within the European
  Community is a major force affecting the fortunes of the various economic
  sectors.

GDP:
  purchasing power equivalent - $1,033.7 billion, per capita $18,300; real
  growth rate 1.4% (1991 est.)

Inflation rate (consumer prices):
  3.3% (1991 est.)

Unemployment rate: 9.8% (end 1991)

Budget:
  revenues $229.8 billion; expenditures $246.4 billion, including capital
  expenditures of $36 billion (1992 budget)

Exports:
  $209.5 billion (f.o.b., 1990)
  commodities:
  machinery and transportation equipment, chemicals, foodstuffs, agricultural
  products, iron and steel products, textiles and clothing
  partners:
  FRG 17.3%, Italy 11.4%, UK 9.2%, Spain 10.3%, Netherlands 9.0%,
  Belgium-Luxembourg 9.4%, US 6.1%, Japan 1.9%, former USSR 0.7% (1989 est.)

Imports:
  $232.5 billion (c.i.f., 1990)
  commodities:
  crude oil, machinery and equipment, agricultural products, chemicals, iron
  and steel products
  partners:
  FRG 18.9%, Italy 11.6%, Belgium-Luxembourg 8.8%, Netherlands 8.6%, US 8.0%,
  Spain 7.9%, UK 7.2%, Japan 4.0%, former USSR 1.4% (1989 est.)

External debt: $59.3 billion (December 1987)

Industrial production:
   growth rate 1.2% (1990); accounts for 26% of GDP
Electricity:
   109,972,000 kW capacity; 399,318 million kWh produced, 7,200 kWh per capita
   (1991)
Industries:
   steel, machinery, chemicals, automobiles, metallurgy, aircraft, electronics,
   mining, textiles, food processing, and tourism
Agriculture:
   accounts for 4% of GDP (including fishing and forestry); one of the world's
   top five wheat producers; other principal products - beef, dairy products,
   cereals, sugar beets, potatoes, wine grapes; self-sufficient for most
   temperate-zone foods; shortages include fats and oils and tropical produce,
   but overall net exporter of farm products; fish catch of 850,000 metric tons
   ranks among world's top 20 countries and is all used domestically

:France Economy

Economic aid:
   donor - ODA and OOF commitments (1970-89), $75.1 billion
Currency:
   French franc (plural - francs); 1 French franc (F) = 100 centimes
Exchange rates:
   French francs (F) per US$1 - 5.3801 (January 1992), 5.6421 (1991), 5.4453
   (1990), 6.3801 (1989), 5.9569 (1988), 6.0107 (1987)
Fiscal year: calendar year

:France Communications

Railroads:
   French National Railways (SNCF) operates 34,568 km 1.435-meter standard
   gauge; 11,674 km electrified, 15,132 km double or multiple track; 2,138 km
   of various gauges (1.000-meter to 1.440-meter), privately owned and operated
Highways:
   1,551,400 km total; 33,400 km national highway; 347,000 km departmental
   highway; 421,000 km community roads; 750,000 km rural roads; 5,401 km of
   controlled-access divided autoroutes; about 803,000 km paved
Inland waterways:
   14,932 km; 6,969 km heavily traveled
Pipelines:
   crude oil 3,059 km; petroleum products 4,487 km; natural gas 24,746 km
Ports:
   maritime - Bordeaux, Boulogne, Brest, Cherbourg, Dunkerque, Fos-Sur-Mer, Le
   Havre, Marseille, Nantes, Rouen, Sete, Toulon; inland - 42
Merchant marine:
   128 ships (1,000 GRT or over) totaling 3,222,539 GRT/5,117,091 DWT; includes
   6 short-sea passenger, 11 cargo, 18 container, 1 multifunction large-load
   carrier, 30 roll-on/roll-off, 34 petroleum tanker, 8 chemical tanker, 6
   liquefied gas, 2 specialized tanker, 11 bulk, 1 refrigerated cargo; note -
   France also maintains a captive register for French-owned ships in the
   Kerguelen Islands (French Southern and Antarctic Lands) and French Polynesia
Civil air:
   195 major transport aircraft (1989 est.)

Airports:

472 total, 460 usable; 251 with permanent-surface runways; 3 with runways over 3,659 m; 36 with runways 2,440-3,659 m; 136 with runways 1,220-2,439 m

Telecommunications:

highly developed; extensive cable and radio relay networks; large-scale introduction of optical-fiber systems; satellite systems for domestic traffic; 39,200,000 telephones; broadcast stations - 41 AM, 800 (mostly repeaters) FM, 846 (mostly repeaters) TV; 24 submarine coaxial cables; 2 INTELSAT earth stations (with total of 5 antennas - 2 for the Indian Ocean INTELSAT and 3 for the Atlantic Ocean INTELSAT); HF radio communications with more than 20 countries; INMARSAT service; EUTELSAT TV service

:France Defense Forces

Branches:

Army, Navy (including Naval Air), Air Force, National Gendarmerie

Manpower availability:

males 15-49, 14,599,636; 12,225,969 fit for military service; 411,211 reach military age (18) annually

Defense expenditures:

exchange rate conversion - $33.1 billion, 3.4% of GDP (1991)

French Guiana Geography

Total area: 91,000 km2
Land area: 89,150 km2
Comparative area: slightly smaller than Indiana
Land boundaries:

1,183 km; Brazil 673 km, Suriname 510 km

Coastline:

378 km

Maritime claims:

Exclusive economic zone:

200 nm

Territorial sea:

12 nm

Disputes:

Suriname claims area between Riviere Litani and Riviere Marouini (both headwaters of the Lawa)

Climate:

tropical; hot, humid; little seasonal temperature variation

Terrain:

low-lying coastal plains rising to hills and small mountains

Natural resources:

bauxite, timber, gold (widely scattered), cinnabar, kaolin, fish

Land use:

arable land NEGL%; permanent crops NEGL%; meadows and pastures NEGL%; forest
and woodland 82%; other 18%

Environment:

mostly an unsettled wilderness

:French Guiana People

Population: 127,505 (July 1992), growth rate 4.6% (1992)
Birth rate: 27 births/1,000 population (1992)
Death rate: 5 deaths/1,000 population (1992)
Net migration rate: 24 migrants/1,000 population (1992)
Infant mortality rate: 17 deaths/1,000 live births (1992)
Life expectancy at birth: 71 years male, 78 years female (1992)
Total fertility rate: 3.6 children born/woman (1992)
Nationality:
    noun - French Guianese (singular and plural); adjective - French Guianese;
    note - they are a colony/department; they hold French passports
Ethnic divisions:
    black or mulatto 66%; Caucasian 12%; East Indian, Chinese, Amerindian 12%;
    other 10%
Religions:
    predominantly Roman Catholic
Languages:
    French
Literacy:
    82% (male 81%, female 83%) age 15 and over can read and write (1982)
Labor force:
    23,265; services, government, and commerce 60.6%, industry 21.2%,
    agriculture 18.2% (1980)
Organized labor:
    7% of labor force

:French Guiana Government

Long-form name:
    Department of Guiana
Type:
    overseas department of France
Capital: Cayenne
Administrative divisions:
    none (overseas department of France)
Independence:
    none (overseas department of France)
Constitution:
    28 September 1958 (French Constitution)
Legal system:
    French legal system
National holiday:
    Taking of the Bastille, 14 July (1789)
Executive branch:
    French president, commissioner of the republic
Legislative branch:
    unicameral General Council and a unicameral Regional Council
Judicial branch:
    highest local court is the Court of Appeals based in Martinique with
    jurisdiction over Martinique, Guadeloupe, and French Guiana
Leaders:
  Chief of State:

President Francois MITTERRAND (since 21 May 1981)
  Head of Government:
  Commissioner of the Republic Jean-Francois DICHIARA (since NA 1990)
Political parties and leaders:
  Guianese Socialist Party (PSG), Gerard HOLDER; Rally for the Republic (RPR),
  Paulin BRUNE; Guianese Democratic Action (ADG), Andre LECANTE; Union for
  French Democracy (UDF), Claude Ho A CHUCK; National Front (FN), Guy
MALON;
  Popular and National Party of Guiana (PNPG), Claude ROBO; National
  Anti-Colonist Guianese Party (PANGA), Michel KAPEL
Suffrage:
  universal at age 18
Elections:
  French National Assembly:
  last held 24 September 1989 (next to be held September 1992); results -
  percent of vote by party NA; seats - (2 total) PSG 1, RPR 1
  French Senate:
  last held 24 September 1989 (next to be held September 1992); results -
  percent of vote by party NA; seats - (1 total) PSG 1
  Regional Council:
  last held 16 March 1986 (next to be held NA 1991); results - PSG 43%, RPR
  27.7%, ADG 12.2%, UDF 8. 9%, FN 3.7%, PNPG 1.4%, other 3.1%; seats - (31
  total) PSG 15, RPR 9, ADG 4, UDF 3
Member of:
  FZ, WCL, WFTU
Diplomatic representation:
  as an overseas department of France, the interests of French Guiana are
  represented in the US by France
Flag:
  the flag of France is used

:French Guiana Economy

Overview:
  The economy is tied closely to that of France through subsidies and imports.
  Besides the French space center at Kourou, fishing and forestry are the most
  important economic activities, with exports of fish and fish products
  (mostly shrimp) accounting for more than 60% of total revenue in 1987. The
  large reserves of tropical hardwoods, not fully exploited, support an
  expanding sawmill industry that provides sawn logs for export. Cultivation
  of crops - rice, cassava, bananas, and sugarcane - are limited to the
  coastal area, where the population is largely concentrated. French Guiana is
  heavily dependent on imports of food and energy. Unemployment is a serious
  problem, particularly among younger workers.
GDP:
  exchange rate conversion - $186 million, per capita $2,240; real growth rate
  NA% (1985)
Inflation rate (consumer prices):
  4.1% (1987)
Unemployment rate: 15% (1987)
Budget:

revenues $735 million; expenditures $735 million, including capital
expenditures of NA (1987)

Exports:
  $54.0 million (f.o.b., 1987)
 commodities:
  shrimp, timber, rum, rosewood essence
 partners:
  France 31%, US 22%, Japan 10% (1987)
Imports:
  $394.0 million (c.i.f., 1987)
 commodities:
  food (grains, processed meat), other consumer goods, producer goods,
  petroleum
 partners:
  France 62%, Trinidad and Tobago 9%, US 4%, FRG 3% (1987)
External debt: $1.2 billion (1988)
Industrial production:
  growth rate NA%
Electricity:
  92,000 kW capacity; 185 million kWh produced, 1,821 kWh per capita (1991)
Industries:
  construction, shrimp processing, forestry products, rum, gold mining
Agriculture:
  some vegetables for local consumption; rice, corn, manioc, cocoa, bananas,
  sugar; livestock - cattle, pigs, poultry
Economic aid:
  Western (non-US) countries, ODA and OOF bilateral commitments (1970-89),
  $1.51 billion
Currency:
  French franc (plural - francs); 1 French franc (F) = 100 centimes
Exchange rates:
  French francs (F) per US$1 - 5.3801 (January 1992), 5.6421 (1991), 5.4453
  (1990), 6.3801 (1989), 5.9569 (1988), 6.0107 (1987)
Fiscal year: calendar year

:French Guiana Communications

Highways:
  680 km total; 510 km paved, 170 km improved and unimproved earth
Inland waterways:
  460 km, navigable by small oceangoing vessels and river and coastal
  steamers; 3,300 km navigable by native craft
Ports:
  Cayenne
Civil air:
  no major transport aircraft
Airports:
  10 total, 10 usable; 4 with permanent-surface runways; none with runways
  over 3,659 m; 1 with runways 2,440-3,659 m; 1 with runways 1,220-2,439 m
Telecommunications:

fair open-wire and radio relay system; 18,100 telephones; broadcast stations
- 5 AM, 7 FM, 9 TV; 1 Atlantic Ocean INTELSAT earth station

:French Guiana Defense Forces

Branches:
French Forces, Gendarmerie
Manpower availability:
males 15-49 37,467; 24,534 fit for military service
Note:
defense is the responsibility of France

French Polynesia Geography

Total area: 3,941 km2
Land area: 3,660 km2
Comparative area: slightly less than one-third the size of Connecticut
Land boundaries:
none
Coastline:
2,525 km
Maritime claims:
 Exclusive economic zone:
200 nm
 Territorial sea:
12 nm
Disputes:
none
Climate:
tropical, but moderate
Terrain:
mixture of rugged high islands and low islands with reefs
Natural resources:
timber, fish, cobalt
Land use:
arable land 1%; permanent crops 19%; meadows and pastures 5%; forest and
woodland 31%; other 44%
Environment:
occasional cyclonic storm in January; includes five archipelagoes
Note:
Makatea in French Polynesia is one of the three great phosphate rock islands
in the Pacific Ocean - the others are Banaba (Ocean Island) in Kiribati and
Nauru

:French Polynesia People

Population: 205,620 (July 1992), growth rate 2.3% (1992)
Birth rate: 28 births/1,000 population (1992)
Death rate: 5 deaths/1,000 population (1992)
Net migration rate: 0 migrants/1,000 population (1992)
Infant mortality rate: 15 deaths/1,000 live births (1992)
Life expectancy at birth: 68 years male, 73 years female (1992)
Total fertility rate: 3.3 children born/woman (1992)
Nationality:

noun - French Polynesian(s); adjective - French Polynesian
Ethnic divisions:
  Polynesian 78%, Chinese 12%, local French 6%, metropolitan French 4%
Religions:
  mainly Christian; Protestant 54%, Roman Catholic 30%, other 16%
Languages:
  French and Tahitian (both official)
Literacy:
  98% (male 98%, female 98%) age 14 and over but definition of literacy not
  available (1977)
Labor force:
  76,630 employed (1988)
Organized labor:
  NA

:French Polynesia Government

Long-form name:
  Territory of French Polynesia
Type:
  overseas territory of France since 1946
Capital: Papeete
Administrative divisions:
  none (overseas territory of France); there are no first-order administrative
  divisions as defined by the US Government, but there are 5 archipelagic
  divisions named Archipel des Marquises, Archipel des Tuamotu, Archipel des
  Tubuai, Iles du Vent, and Iles Sous-le-Vent; note - Clipperton Island is
  administered by France from French Polynesia
Independence:
  none (overseas territory of France)
Constitution:
  28 September 1958 (French Constitution)
Legal system:
  based on French system
National holiday:
  Taking of the Bastille, 14 July (1789)
Executive branch:
  French president, high commissioner of the republic, president of the
  Council of Ministers, vice president of the Council of Ministers, Council of
  Ministers
Legislative branch:
  unicameral Territorial Assembly
Judicial branch:
  Court of Appeal
Leaders:
 Chief of State:
  President Francois MITTERRAND (since 21 May 1981); High Commissioner of the
  Republic Jean MONTPEZAT (since November 1987)
 Head of Government:
  President of the Council of Ministers Gaston FLOSSE (since 10 May 1991);
  Vice President of the Council of Ministers Joel BUILLARD (since 12 September

1991)

Political parties and leaders:

People's Rally (Tahoeraa Huiraatira; Gaullist), Gaston FLOSSE; Polynesian Union Party (Te Tiarama; centrist), Alexandre LEONTIEFF; New Fatherland Party (Ai'a Api), Emile VERNAUDON; Polynesian Liberation Front (Tavini Huiraatira), Oscar TEMARU; other small parties

Suffrage:

universal at age 18

Elections:

National Assembly last held 5 and 12 June 1988 (next to be held June 1993); results - percent of vote by party NA; seats - (2 total) People's Rally (Gaullist) 1, New Fatherland Party 1

French Senate:

last held 24 September 1989 (next to be held September 1992); results - percent of vote by party NA; seats - (1 total) party NA

Territorial Assembly:

last held 17 March 1991 (next to be held March 1996); results - percent of vote by party NA; seats - (41 total) People's Rally (Gaullist) 18, Polynesian Union Party 14, New Fatherland Party 5, other 4

Member of:

FZ, ICFTU, SPC, WMO

Diplomatic representation:

as an overseas territory of France, French Polynesian interests are represented in the US by France

:French Polynesia Government

Flag: the flag of France is used

:French Polynesia Economy

Overview:

Since 1962, when France stationed military personnel in the region, French Polynesia has changed from a subsistence economy to one in which a high proportion of the work force is either employed by the military or supports the tourist industry. Tourism accounts for about 20% of GDP and is a primary source of hard currency earnings.

GDP:

exchange rate conversion - $1.2 billion, per capita $6,000; real growth rate NA% (1991 est.)

Inflation rate (consumer prices):

2.9% (1989)

Unemployment rate: 14.9% (1988 est.)

Budget:

revenues $614 million; expenditures $957 million, including capital expenditures of $NA (1988)

Exports:

$88.9 million (f.o.b., 1989)

commodities:

coconut products 79%, mother-of-pearl 14%, vanilla, shark meat

partners:

France 54%, US 17%, Japan 17%

Imports:

$765 million (c.i.f., 1989)
  commodities:
  fuels, foodstuffs, equipment
  partners:
  France 53%, US 11%, Australia 6%, NZ 5%
External debt: $NA
Industrial production:
  growth rate NA%
Electricity:
  72,000 kW capacity; 265 million kWh produced, 1,390 kWh per capita (1990)
Industries:
  tourism, pearls, agricultural processing, handicrafts
Agriculture:
  coconut and vanilla plantations; vegetables and fruit; poultry, beef, dairy
  products
Economic aid:
  Western (non-US) countries, ODA and OOF bilateral commitments (1970-88),
  $3.95 billion
Currency:
  Comptoirs Francais du Pacifique franc (plural - francs); 1 CFP franc (CFPF)
  = 100 centimes
Exchange rates:
  Comptoirs Francais du Pacifique francs (CFPF) per US$1 - 97.81 (January
  1992), 102.57 (1991), 99.00 (1990), 115.99 (1989), 108.30 (1988), 109.27
  (1987); note - linked at the rate of 18.18 to the French franc
Fiscal year: calendar year

:French Polynesia Communications

Highways:
  600 km (1982)
Ports:
  Papeete, Bora-bora
Merchant marine:
  3 ships (1,000 GRT or over) totaling 4,128 GRT/6,710 DWT; includes 2
  passenger-cargo, 1 refrigerated cargo; note - a captive subset of the French
  register
Civil air:
  about 6 major transport aircraft
Airports:
  43 total, 41 usable; 23 with permanent-surface runways; none with runways
  over 3,659 m; 2 with runways 2,440-3,659 m; 12 with runways 1,220-2,439 m
Telecommunications:
  33,200 telephones; 84,000 radio receivers; 26,400 TV sets; broadcast
  stations - 5 AM, 2 FM, 6 TV; 1 Pacific Ocean INTELSAT earth station

:French Polynesia Defense Forces

Branches:
  French forces (including Army, Navy, Air Force), Gendarmerie
Manpower availability:
  males 15-49, 50,844; NA fit for military service

defense is responsibility of France

French Southern and Antarctic Lands Geography

Total area: 7,781 km2
Land area: 7,781 km2; includes Ile Amsterdam, Ile Saint-Paul, Iles Kerguelen, and Iles
   Crozet; excludes Terre Adelie claim of about 500,000 km2 in Antarctica that
   is not recognized by the US
Comparative area: slightly less than 1.5 times the size of Delaware
Land boundaries:
   none
Coastline:
   1,232 km
Maritime claims:
  Exclusive economic zone:
   200 nm (Iles Kerguelen only)
  Territorial sea:
   12 nm
Disputes:
   Terre Adelie claim in Antarctica is not recognized by the US
Climate:
   antarctic
Terrain:
   volcanic
Natural resources:
   fish, crayfish
Land use:
   arable land 0%; permanent crops 0%; meadows and pastures 0%; forest and
   woodland 0%; other 100%
Environment:
   Ile Amsterdam and Ile Saint-Paul are extinct volcanoes
Note:
   located in the southern Indian Ocean about equidistant between Africa,
   Antarctica, and Australia

:French Southern and Antarctic Lands People

Population: summer (January 1991) - 200, winter (July 1992) - 150, growth rate 0.0%
   (1992); note - mostly researchers

:French Southern and Antarctic Lands Government

Long-form name:
   Territory of the French Southern and Antarctic Lands
Type:
   overseas territory of France since 1955; governed by High Administrator
   Bernard de GOUTTES (since May 1990), who is assisted by a 7-member
   Consultative Council and a 12-member Scientific Council
Capital: none; administered from Paris, France
Administrative divisions:
   none (overseas territory of France); there are no first-order administrative
   divisions as defined by the US Government, but there are 3 districts named

Ile Crozet, Iles Kerguelen, and Iles Saint-Paul et Amsterdam; excludes Terre
Adelie claim in Antarctica that is not recognized by the US

Flag:
the flag of France is used

:French Southern and Antarctic Lands Economy

Overview:
Economic activity is limited to servicing meteorological and geophysical
research stations and French and other fishing fleets. The fishing catches
landed on Iles Kerguelen by foreign ships are exported to France and
Reunion.

Budget:
$33.6 million (1990)

:French Southern and Antarctic Lands Communications

Ports:
none; offshore anchorage only

Merchant marine:
12 ships (1,000 GRT or over) totaling 192,752 GRT/334,400 DWT; includes 1
cargo, 3 refrigerated cargo, 2 roll-on/roll-off cargo, 2 petroleum tanker, 1
liquefied gas, 2 bulk, 1 multifunction large load carrier; note - a captive
subset of the French register

Telecommunications:
NA

:French Southern and Antarctic Lands Defense Forces

Branches:
French Forces (including Army, Navy, Air Force)

Note:
defense is the responsibility of France

Gabon Geography

Total area: 267,670 km2
Land area: 257,670 km2
Comparative area: slightly smaller than Colorado
Land boundaries:
2,551 km; Cameroon 298 km, Congo 1,903 km, Equatorial Guinea 350 km
Coastline:
885 km
Maritime claims:
 Contiguous zone:
 24 nm
 Exclusive economic zone:
 200 nm
 Territorial sea:
 12 nm
Disputes:
maritime boundary dispute with Equatorial Guinea because of disputed
sovereignty over islands in Corisco Bay
Climate:
tropical; always hot, humid
Terrain:

narrow coastal plain; hilly interior; savanna in east and south
Natural resources:
   crude oil, manganese, uranium, gold, timber, iron ore
Land use:
   arable land 1%; permanent crops 1%; meadows and pastures 18%; forest and
   woodland 78%; other 2%
Environment:
   deforestation

:Gabon People

Population: 1,106,355 (July 1992), growth rate 1.5% (1992)
Birth rate: 29 births/1,000 population (1992)
Death rate: 14 deaths/1,000 population (1992)
Net migration rate: 0 migrants/1,000 population (1992)
Infant mortality rate: 100 deaths/1,000 live births (1992)
Life expectancy at birth: 51 years male, 56 years female (1992)
Total fertility rate: 4.1 children born/woman (1992)
Nationality:
   noun - Gabonese (singular and plural); adjective - Gabonese
Ethnic divisions:
   about 40 Bantu tribes, including four major tribal groupings (Fang, Eshira,
   Bapounou, Bateke); about 100,000 expatriate Africans and Europeans,
   including 27,000 French
Religions:
   Christian 55-75%, Muslim less than 1%, remainder animist
Languages:
   French (official), Fang, Myene, Bateke, Bapounou/Eschira, Bandjabi
Literacy:
   61% (male 74%, female 48%) age 15 and over can read and write (1990 est.)
Labor force:
   120,000 salaried; agriculture 65.0%, industry and commerce 30.0%, services
   2.5%, government 2.5%; 58% of population of working age (1983)
Organized labor:
   there are 38,000 members of the national trade union, the Gabonese Trade
   Union Confederation (COSYGA)

:Gabon Government

Long-form name:
   Gabonese Republic
Type:
   republic; multiparty presidential regime (opposition parties legalized 1990)
Capital: Libreville
Administrative divisions:
   9 provinces; Estuaire, Haut-Ogooue, Moyen-Ogooue, Ngounie, Nyanga,
   Ogooue-Ivindo, Ogooue-Lolo, Ogooue-Maritime, Woleu-Ntem
Independence:
   17 August 1960 (from France)
Constitution:
   21 February 1961, revised 15 April 1975
Legal system:
   based on French civil law system and customary law; judicial review of

legislative acts in Constitutional Chamber of the Supreme Court; compulsory ICJ jurisdiction not accepted

National holiday:
Renovation Day (Gabonese Democratic Party established), 12 March (1968)

Executive branch:
president, prime minister, Cabinet

Legislative branch:
unicameral National Assembly (Assemblee Nationale)

Judicial branch:
Supreme Court (Cour Supreme)

Leaders:
Chief of State:
President El Hadj Omar BONGO (since 2 December 1967)
Head of Government:
Prime Minister Casimir OYE-MBA (since 3 May 1990)

Political parties and leaders:
Gabonese Democratic Party (PDG, former sole party), El Hadj Omar BONGO, president; National Recovery Movement - Lumberjacks (Morena-Bucherons); Gabonese Party for Progress (PGP); National Recovery Movement (Morena-Original); Association for Socialism in Gabon (APSG); Gabonese Socialist Union (USG); Circle for Renewal and Progress (CRP); Union for Democracy and Development (UDD)

Suffrage:
universal at age 21

Elections:
National Assembly:
last held on 28 October 1990 (next to be held by NA); results - percent of vote NA; seats - (120 total, 111 elected) PDG 62, National Recovery Movement - Lumberjacks (Morena-Bucherons) 19, PGP 18, National Recovery Movement (Morena-Original) 7, APSG 6, USG 4, CRP 1, independents 3
President:
last held on 9 November 1986 (next to be held December 1993); results - President Omar BONGO was reelected without opposition

Member of:
ACCT, ACP, AfDB, BDEAC, CCC, CEEAC, ECA, FAO, FZ, G-24, G-77, GATT, IAEA,
IBRD, ICAO, ICC, IDA, IDB, IFAD, IFC, ILO, IMF, IMO, INMARSAT, INTELSAT,
INTERPOL, IOC, ITU, LORCS (associate), NAM, OAU, OIC, OPEC, UDEAC, UN,
UNCTAD, UNESCO, UNIDO, UPU, WCL, WHO, WIPO, WMO, WTO

Diplomatic representation:
Ambassador-designate Alexandre SAMBAT; Chancery at 2034 20th Street NW, Washington, DC 20009; telephone (202) 797-1000

:Gabon Government

US:
Ambassador Keith L. WAUCHOPE; Embassy at Boulevard de la Mer, Libreville (mailing address is B. P. 4000, Libreville); telephone (241) 762003/4, or 743492

Flag:
  three equal horizontal bands of green (top), yellow, and blue

:Gabon Economy

Overview:
  The economy, dependent on timber and manganese until the early 1970s, is now
  dominated by the oil sector. During the period 1981-85, oil accounted for
  about 46% of GDP, 83% of export earnings, and 65% of government revenues on
  average. The high oil prices of the early 1980s contributed to a substantial
  increase in per capita income, stimulated domestic demand, reinforced
  migration from rural to urban areas, and raised the level of real wages to
  among the highest in Sub-Saharan Africa. The three-year slide of Gabon's
  economy, which began with falling oil prices in 1985, was reversed in 1989
  because of a near doubling of oil prices over their 1988 lows. In 1990 the
  economy posted strong growth despite serious strikes, but debt servicing
  problems are hindering economic advancement. The agricultural and industrial
  sectors are relatively underdeveloped, except for oil.

GDP:
  exchange rate conversion - $3.3 billion, per capita $3,090; real growth rate
  13% (1990 est.)

Inflation rate (consumer prices):
  3% (1989 est.)

Unemployment rate: NA%

Budget:
  revenues $1.1 billion; expenditures $1.5 billion, including capital
  expenditures of $277 million (1990 est.)

Exports:
  $1.16 billion (f.o.b., 1989)
 commodities:
  crude oil 70%, manganese 11%, wood 12%, uranium 6%
 partners:
  France 53%, US 22%, FRG, Japan

Imports:
  $0.78 billion (c.i.f., 1989)
 commodities:
  foodstuffs, chemical products, petroleum products, construction materials,
  manufactures, machinery
 partners:
  France 48%, US 2.6%, FRG, Japan, UK

External debt: $3.4 billion (December 1990 est.)

Industrial production:
  growth rate -10% (1988 est.)

Electricity:
  315,000 kW capacity; 995 million kWh produced, 920 kWh per capita (1991)

Industries:
  petroleum, food and beverages, timber, cement, plywood, textiles, mining -
  manganese, uranium, gold

Agriculture:
  accounts for 10% of GDP (including fishing and forestry); cash crops -
  cocoa, coffee, palm oil; livestock not developed; importer of food; small

337

fishing operations provide a catch of about 20,000 metric tons; okoume (a tropical softwood) is the most important timber product

Economic aid:

US commitments, including Ex-Im (FY70-89), $66 million; Western (non-US) countries, ODA and OOF bilateral commitments (1970-89), $2,225 million; Communist countries (1970-89), $27 million

Currency:

Communaute Financiere Africaine franc (plural - francs); 1 CFA franc (CFAF) = 100 centimes

:Gabon Economy

Exchange rates:

Communaute Financiere Africaine francs (CFAF) per US$1 - 269.01 (January 1992), 282.11 (1991), 272.26 (1990), 319.01 (1989), 297.85 (1988), 300.54 (1987)

Fiscal year: calendar year

:Gabon Communications

Railroads:

649 km 1.437-meter standard-gauge single track (Transgabonese Railroad)

Highways:

7,500 km total; 560 km paved, 960 km laterite, 5,980 km earth

Inland waterways:

1,600 km perennially navigable

Pipelines:

crude oil 270 km; petroleum products 14 km

Ports:

Owendo, Port-Gentil, Libreville

Merchant marine:

2 cargo ships (1,000 GRT or over) totaling 18,563 GRT/25,330 DWT

Civil air:

15 major transport aircraft

Airports:

70 total, 59 usable; 10 with permanent-surface runways; none with runways over 3,659 m; 2 with runways 2,440-3,659 m; 22 with runways 1,220-2,439 m

Telecommunications:

adequate system of cable, radio relay, tropospheric scatter links and radiocommunication stations; 15,000 telephones; broadcast stations - 6 AM, 6 FM, 3 (5 repeaters) TV; satellite earth stations - 3 Atlantic Ocean INTELSAT and 12 domestic satellite

:Gabon Defense Forces

Branches:

Army, Navy, Air Force, Presidential Guard, National Gendarmerie, National Police

Manpower availability:

males 15-49, 267,580; 134,665 fit for military service; 9,262 reach military age (20) annually

Defense expenditures:

exchange rate conversion - $102 million, 3.2% of GDP (1990 est.)

The Gambia Geography

Total area: 11,300 km2
Land area: 10,000 km2
Comparative area: slightly more than twice the size of Delaware
Land boundaries:
  740 km; Senegal 740 km
Coastline:
  80 km
Maritime claims:
  Contiguous zone:
  18 nm
  Continental shelf:
  not specific
  Exclusive fishing zone:
  200 nm
  Territorial sea:
  12 nm
Disputes:
  short section of boundary with Senegal is indefinite
Climate:
  tropical; hot, rainy season (June to November); cooler, dry season (November to May)
Terrain:
  flood plain of the Gambia River flanked by some low hills
Natural resources:
  fish
Land use:
  arable land 16%; permanent crops 0%; meadows and pastures 9%; forest and woodland 20%; other 55%; includes irrigated 3%
Environment:
  deforestation
Note:
  almost an enclave of Senegal; smallest country on the continent of Africa

:The Gambia People

Population: 902,089 (July 1992), growth rate 3.1% (1992)
Birth rate: 47 births/1,000 population (1992)
Death rate: 17 deaths/1,000 population (1992)
Net migration rate: 0 migrants/1,000 population (1992)
Infant mortality rate: 129 deaths/1,000 live births (1992)
Life expectancy at birth: 47 years male, 51 years female (1992)
Total fertility rate: 6.4 children born/woman (1992)
Nationality:
  noun - Gambian(s); adjective - Gambian
Ethnic divisions:
  African 99% (Mandinka 42%, Fula 18%, Wolof 16%, Jola 10%, Serahuli 9%, other 4%); non-Gambian 1%
Religions:
  Muslim 90%, Christian 9%, indigenous beliefs 1%
Languages:
  English (official); Mandinka, Wolof, Fula, other indigenous vernaculars

Literacy:
  27% (male 39%, female 16%) age 15 and over can read and write (1990 est.)
Labor force:
  400,000 (1986 est.); agriculture 75.0%, industry, commerce, and services
  18.9%, government 6.1%; 55% population of working age (1983)
Organized labor:
  25-30% of wage labor force

:The Gambia Government

Long-form name:
  Republic of The Gambia
Type:
  republic under multiparty democratic rule
Capital: Banjul
Administrative divisions:
  5 divisions and 1 city*; Banjul*, Lower River, MacCarthy Island, North Bank,
  Upper River, Western
Independence:
  18 February 1965 (from UK); The Gambia and Senegal signed an agreement on 12
  December 1981 (effective 1 February 1982) that called for the creation of a
  loose confederation to be known as Senegambia, but the agreement was
  dissolved on 30 September 1989
Constitution:
  24 April 1970
Legal system:
  based on a composite of English common law, Koranic law, and customary law;
  accepts compulsory ICJ jurisdiction, with reservations
National holiday:
  Independence Day, 18 February (1965)
Executive branch:
  president, vice president, Cabinet
Legislative branch:
  unicameral House of Representatives
Judicial branch:
  Supreme Court
Leaders:
  Chief of State and Head of Government:
    President Alhaji Sir Dawda Kairaba JAWARA (since 24 April 1970); Vice
    President Bakary Bunja DARBO (since 12 May 1982)
Political parties and leaders:
  People's Progressive Party (PPP), Dawda K. JAWARA, secretary general;
  National Convention Party (NCP), Sheriff DIBBA; Gambian People's Party
  (GPP), Hassan Musa CAMARA; United Party (UP), leader NA; People's Democratic
  Organization of Independence and Socialism (PDOIS), leader NA; People's
  Democratic Party (PDP), Jabel SALLAH
Suffrage:
  universal at age 21
Elections:
  House of Representatives:
    last held on 11 March 1987 (next to be held by March 1992); results - PPP

56.6%, NCP 27.6%, GPP 14.7%, PDOIS 1%; seats - (43 total, 36 elected) PPP
31, NCP 5

President:

last held on 11 March 1987 (next to be held March 1992); results - Sir Dawda
JAWARA (PPP) 61.1%, Sherif Mustapha DIBBA (NCP) 25.2%, Assan Musa
CAMARA
(GPP) 13.7%

Member of:

ACP, AfDB, C, CCC, ECA, ECOWAS, FAO, G-77, GATT, IBRD, ICAO, ICFTU,
IDA,
IDB, IFAD, IFC, IMF, IMO, INTERPOL, IOC, ITU, LORCS, NAM, OAU, OIC,
UN,
UNCTAD, UNESCO, UNIDO, UPU, WCL, WFTU, WHO, WIPO, WMO, WTO

Diplomatic representation:

Ambassador Ousman A. SALLAH; Chancery at Suite 720, 1030 15th Street NW,
Washington, DC 20005; telephone (202) 842-1356 or 842-1359

US:

Ambassador Arlene RENDER; Embassy at Pipeline Road (Kairaba Avenue), Fajara,
Banjul (mailing address is P. M. B. No. 19, Banjul); telephone Serrekunda
[220] 92856 or 92858, 91970, 91971

:The Gambia Government

Flag: three equal horizontal bands of red (top), blue with white edges, and green

:The Gambia Economy

Overview:

The Gambia has no important mineral or other natural resources and has a
limited agricultural base. It is one of the world's poorest countries with a
per capita income of about $230. About 75% of the population is engaged in
crop production and livestock raising, which contribute 30% to GDP.
Small-scale manufacturing activity - processing peanuts, fish, and hides -
accounts for less than 10% of GDP. Tourism is a growing industry. The Gambia
imports one-third of its food, all fuel, and most manufactured goods.
Exports are concentrated on peanut products (about 75% of total value).

GDP:

exchange rate conversion - $207 million, per capita $235; real growth rate
3% (FY91 est.)

Inflation rate (consumer prices):

6.0% (FY91)

Unemployment rate: NA%

Budget:

revenues $79 million; expenditures $84 million, including capital
expenditures of $21 million (FY90)

Exports:

$116 million (f o b , FY90)

commodities:

peanuts and peanut products, fish, cotton lint, palm kernels

partners:

Japan 60%, Europe 29%, Africa 5%, US 1, other 5% (1989)

Imports:

$147 million (f.o.b., FY90)

commodities:

foodstuffs, manufactures, raw materials, fuel, machinery and transport equipment

partners:

Europe 57%, Asia 25%, USSR/EE 9%, US 6%, other 3% (1989)

External debt: $336 million (December 1990 est.)

Industrial production:

growth rate 6.7%; accounts for 5.8% of GDP (FY90)

Electricity:

30,000 kW capacity; 65 million kWh produced, 75 kWh per capita (1991)

Industries:

peanut processing, tourism, beverages, agricultural machinery assembly, woodworking, metalworking, clothing

Agriculture:

accounts for 30% of GDP and employs about 75% of the population; imports one-third of food requirements; major export crop is peanuts; the other principal crops - millet, sorghum, rice, corn, cassava, palm kernels; livestock - cattle, sheep, and goats; forestry and fishing resources not fully exploited

Economic aid:

US commitments, including Ex-Im (FY70-89), $93 million; Western (non-US) countries, ODA and OOF bilateral commitments (1970-89), $535 million; Communist countries (1970-89), $39 million

Currency:

dalasi (plural - dalasi); 1 dalasi (D) = 100 bututs

Exchange rates:

dalasi (D) per US$1 - 8.790 (March 1992), 8.803 (1991), 7.883 (1990), 7.5846 (1989), 6.7086 (1988), 7.0744 (1987)

Fiscal year: 1 July - 30 June

:The Gambia Communications

Highways:

3,083 km total; 431 km paved, 501 km gravel/laterite, and 2,151 km unimproved earth

Inland waterways:

400 km

Ports:

Banjul

Civil air:

4 major transport aircraft

Airports:

1 with permanent-surface runway 2,440-3,659 m

Telecommunications:

adequate network of radio relay and wire; 3,500 telephones; broadcast stations - 3 AM, 2 FM; 1 Atlantic Ocean INTELSAT earth station

:The Gambia Defense Forces

Branches: Army, Navy, National Gendarmerie, National Police Manpower availability: males 15-49, 194,480; 98,271 fit for military service Defense expenditures: exchange rate conversion - more than $1 million, 0.7% of GDP (1989) \

Gaza Strip Geography

Total area: 380 km2
Land area: 380 km2
Comparative area: slightly more than twice the size of Washington, DC
Land boundaries:
   62 km; Egypt 11 km, Israel 51 km
Coastline:
   40 km
Maritime claims:
   Israeli occupied with status to be determined
Disputes:
   Israeli occupied with status to be determined
Climate:
   temperate, mild winters, dry and warm to hot summers
Terrain:
   flat to rolling, sand- and dune- covered coastal plain
Natural resources:
   negligible
Land use:
   arable land 13%, permanent crops 32%, meadows and pastures 0%, forest and
   woodland 0%, other 55%
Environment:
   desertification
Note:
   The war between Israel and the Arab states in June 1967 ended with Israel in
   control of the West Bank and the Gaza Strip, the Sinai, and the Golan
   Heights. As stated in the 1978 Camp David accords and reaffirmed by
   President Bush's post - Gulf crisis peace initiative, the final status of
   the West Bank and the Gaza Strip, their relationship with their neighbors,
   and a peace treaty be-tween Israel and Jordan are to be negotiated among the
   concerned parties. Camp David further specifies that these negotiations will
   resolve the respective boundaries. Pending the completion of this process,
   it is US policy that the final status of the West Bank and the Gaza Strip
   has yet to be determined. In the US view, the term West Bank describes all
   of the area west of the Jordan River under Jordanian administration before
   the 1967 Arab-Israeli war. With respect to negotiations envisaged in the
   framework agreement, however, it is US policy that a distinction must be
   made between Jerusalem and the rest of the West Bank because of the city's
   special status and circumstances. Therefore, a negotiated solution for the
   final status of Jerusalem could be different in character from that of the
   rest of the West Bank.
   The Gaza Strip is currently governed by Israeli military authorities and
   Israeli civil administration; it is US policy that the final status of the
   Gaza Strip will be determined by negotiations among the concerned parties;
   these negotiations will determine how this area is to be governed.
   There are 18 Jewish settlements in the Gaza Strip.

:Gaza Strip People

Population: 681,026 (July 1992), growth rate 3.6% (1992); in addition, there are
4,000

Jewish settlers in the Gaza Strip (1992 est.)

Birth rate: 46 births/1,000 population (1992)

Death rate: 6 deaths/1,000 population (1992)

Net migration rate: - 4 migrants/1,000 population (1992)

Infant mortality rate: 41 deaths/1,000 live births (1992)

Life expectancy at birth: 66 years male, 68 years female (1992)

Total fertility rate: 6.9 children born/woman (1992)

Nationality:

NA

Ethnic divisions:

Palestinian Arab and other 99.8%, Jewish 0.2%

Religions:

Muslim (predominantly Sunni) 99%, Christian 0.7%, Jewish 0.3%

Languages:

Arabic, Israeli settlers speak Hebrew; English widely understood

Literacy:

NA% (male NA%, female NA%)

Labor force:

(excluding Israeli Jewish settlers) small industry, commerce and business 32.0%, construction 24.4%, service and other 25.5%, and agriculture 18.1% (1984)

Organized labor:

NA

:Gaza Strip Government

Long-form name: none

:Gaza Strip Economy

Overview:

In 1990 roughly 40% of Gaza Strip workers were employed across the border by Israeli industrial, construction, and agricultural enterprises, with worker remittances accounting for about one-third of GNP. The construction, agricultural, and industrial sectors account for about 15%, 12%, and 8% of GNP, respectively. Gaza depends upon Israel for some 90% of its external trade. Unrest in the territory in 1988-92 (intifadah) has raised unemployment and substantially lowered the standard of living of Gazans. The Persian Gulf crisis and its aftershocks also have dealt severe blows to Gaza since August 1990. Worker remittances from the Gulf states have plunged, unemployment has increased, and exports have fallen dramatically. The area's economic outlook remains bleak.

GNP:

exchange rate conversion - $380 million, per capita $590; real growth rate - 30% (1991 est.)

Inflation rate (consumer prices):

9% (1991 est.)

Unemployment rate: 20% (1990 est.)

Budget:

revenues $33.8 million; expenditures $33.3 million, including capital expenditures of $NA (FY88)

Exports:

$30 million (f.o.b., 1989)

commodities:
  citrus
partners:
  Israel, Egypt
Imports:
  $255 million (c.i.f., 1989)
commodities:
  food, consumer goods, construction materials
partners:
  Israel, Egypt
External debt: $NA
Industrial production:
  growth rate 10% (1989); accounts for about 8% of GNP
Electricity:
  power supplied by Israel
Industries:
  generally small family businesses that produce textiles, soap, olive-wood
  carvings, and mother-of-pearl souvenirs; the Israelis have established some
  small-scale modern industries in an industrial center
Agriculture:
  accounts for about 12% of GNP; olives, citrus and other fruits, vegetables,
  beef, dairy products
Economic aid:
  NA
Currency:
  new Israeli shekel (plural - shekels); 1 new Israeli shekel (NIS) = 100 new
  agorot
Exchange rates:
  new Israeli shekels (NIS) per US$1 - 2.2984 (January 1992), 2.2792 (1991),
  2.0162 (1990), 1.9164 (1989), 1.5989 (1988), 1.5946 (1987)
Fiscal year: previously 1 April - 31 March; FY91 was 1 April - 31 December, and
since 1
  January 1992 the fiscal year has conformed to the calendar year

:Gaza Strip Communications

Railroads:
  one line, abandoned and in disrepair, some trackage remains
Highways:
  small, poorly developed indigenous road network
Ports:
  facilities for small boats to service the city of Gaza
Airports:
  1 with permanent-surface runway less than 1,220 m
Telecommunications:
  broadcast stations - no AM, no FM, no TV

:Gaza Strip Defense Forces

Branches:
  NA
Manpower availability:
  males 15-49, 136,311; NA fit for military service

Defense expenditures:
exchange rate conversion - $NA, NA% of GDP

Georgia Geography

Total area: 69,700 km2
Land area: 69,700 km2
Comparative area: slightly larger than South Carolina
Land boundaries:
1,461 km; Armenia 164 km, Azerbaijan 322 km, Russia 723 km, Turkey 252 km
Coastline:
310 km
Maritime claims:
Contiguous zone:
NA nm
Continental Shelf:
NA meter depth
Exclusive economic zone:
NA nm
Exclusive fishing zone:
NA nm
Territorial sea:
NA nm, Georgian claims unknown; 12 nm in 1973 USSR-Turkish Protocol
concerning the sea boundary between the two states in the Black Sea
Disputes:
none
Climate:
warm and pleasant; Mediterranean-like on Black Sea coast
Terrain:
largely mountainous with Great Caucasus Mountains in the north and Lesser
Caucasus Mountains in the south; Colchis lowland opens to the Black Sea in
the west; Kura River Basin in the east; good soils in river valley flood
plains, foothills of Colchis lowland
Natural resources:
forest lands, hydropower, manganese deposits, iron ores, copper, minor coal
and oil deposits; coastal climate and soils allow for important tea and
citrus growth
Land use:
NA% arable land; NA% permanent crops; NA% meadows and pastures; NA% forest
and woodland; NA% other; includes 200,000 hectares irrigated
Environment:
air pollution, particularly in Rustavi; heavy pollution of Kura River, Black
Sea

:Georgia People

Population: 5,570,978 (July 1992), growth rate 0.8% (1992)
Birth rate: 17 births/1,000 population (1992)
Death rate: 9 deaths/1,000 population (1992)
Net migration rate: 1 migrant/1,000 population (1992)
Infant mortality rate: 34 deaths/1,000 live births (1992)
Life expectancy at birth: 67 years male, 75 years female (1992)
Total fertility rate: 2.2 children born/woman (1992)

Nationality:
noun - Georgian(s); adjective - Georgian
Ethnic divisions:
Georgian 68.8%, Armenian 9.0%, Russian Azari 5.1%, Ossetian 3.2%, Abkhaz
1.7%, other 4.8%
Religions:
Russian Orthodox 10%, Georgian Orthodox 65%, Armenian Orthodox 8%, Muslim
11%, unknown 6%
Languages:
Georgian (official language) 71%, Russian 9%, other 20% - Armenian 7%,
Azerbaijani 6%
Literacy:
NA% (male NA%, female NA%) age 15 and over can read and write
Labor force:
2,834,000; agriculture 29.1% (1988), government NA%, industry 17.8%, other
53.1%
Organized labor:
NA

:Georgia Government

Long-form name:
Republic of Georgia
Type:
republic
Capital: T'bilisi (Tbilisi)
Administrative divisions:
2 autonomous republics (avtomnoy respubliki, singular - avtom respublika);
Abkhazia (Sukhumi), Ajaria (Batumi); note - the administrative centers of
the autonomous republics are included in parentheses; there are no oblasts -
the rayons around T'bilisi are under direct republic jurisdiction; also
included is the South Ossetia Autonomous Oblast
Independence:
9 April 1991 (from Soviet Union); formerly Georgian Soviet Socialist
Republic
Constitution:
adopted NA, effective NA
Legal system:
NA
National holiday:
Independence Day, 9 April 1991
Executive branch:
State Council, chairman of State Council, Council of Ministers, prime
minister
Legislative branch:
unicameral Supreme Soviet
Judicial branch:
Supreme Court
Leaders:
 Chief of State:
Chairman of State Council Eduard SHEVARDNADZE (since March 1992)

Head of Government:

Acting Prime Minister Tengiz SIGUA (since January 1992); First Deputy Prime Minister Otar KVILITAYA (since January 1992); First Deputy Prime Minister Tengiz KITOVANI (since March 1992)

Political parties and leaders:

All-Georgian Merab Kostava Society, Vazha ADAMIA, chairman; All-Georgian Tradionalists' Union, Akakiy ASATIANI, chairman; Georgian National Front - Radical Union, Ruslan GONGADZE, chairman; Social-Democratic Party, Guram MUCHAIDZE, chairman; All-Georgian Rustaveli Society, Akakiy BAKRADZE, chairman; Georgian Monarchists' Party, Teymur JORJOLIANI, chairman; Georgian Popular Front, Nodar NATADZE, chairman; National Democratic Party, Georgiy CHANTURIA, chairman; National Independence Party, Irakliy TSERETELI, chairman; Charter 1991 Party, Tedo PAATASHVILI, chairman; Democratic Georgia Party, Georgiy SHENGELAYA, Chairman

Suffrage:

universal at age 18

Elections:

Georgian Parliament:

last held November 1990; results - 7-party coalition Round Table - Free Georgia 62%, other 38%; seats - (250) Round Table - Free Georgia 155, other 95

President:

Zviad GAMSAKHURDIYA, 87% of vote

Other political or pressure groups:

NA

Member of:

CSCE, IMF, World Bank

:Georgia Government

Diplomatic representation:

Ambassador NA, Chancery at NA NW, Washington, DC 200__; telephone (202) NA

US:

Ambassador NA; Embassy at NA (mailing address is APO New York 09862)

Flag:

maroon field with small rectangle in upper left corner; rectangle divided horizontally with black on top, white below

:Georgia Economy

Overview:

Among the former Soviet republics, Georgia is noted for its Black Sea tourist industry, its large output of citrus fruits and tea, and the amazing diversity of an industrial sector that accounted, however, for less than 2% of the USSR's output. Another salient characteristic of the economy has been a flourishing private sector (compared with the other republics). Almost 30% of the labor force is employed in agriculture and 18% in industry. Mineral resources consist of manganese and copper, and, to a lesser extent, molybdenum, arsenic, tungsten, and mercury. Except for very small quantities of domestic oil, gas, and coal, fuel must be imported from neighboring republics. Oil and its products are delivered by pipeline from Azerbaijan to the port of Batumi for export and local refining. Gas is supplied in pipelines from Krasnodar and Stavropol'. Georgia is nearly self-sufficient in electric power, thanks to abundant hydropower stations as well as some thermal power stations. The dismantling of central economic controls is being delayed by political factionalism, marked by armed struggles between the elected government and the opposition, and industrial output seems to have fallen more steeply in Georgia in 1991 than in any other of the former Soviet republics. To prevent further economic decline, Georgia must establish domestic peace and must maintain economic ties to the other former Soviet republics while developing new links to the West.

GDP:

purchasing power equivalent - $NA; per capita $NA; real growth rate - 23% (1991)

Inflation rate (consumer prices):

approximately 90% (1991)

Unemployment rate: NA%

Budget:

revenues $NA; expenditures $NA, including capital expenditures of $NA million (1991)

Exports:

$176 million (f.o.b., 1990)

commodities:

citrus fruits, tea, other agricultural products; diverse types of machinery; ferrous and nonferrous metals; textiles

partners:

NA

Imports:

$1.5 billion (c.i.f., 1990)

commodities:

machinery and parts, fuel, transport equipment, textiles

partners:

NA

External debt: $650 million (1991 est.)

Industrial production:

growth rate - 19% (1991)

Electricity:

4,575,000 kW capacity; 15,300 million kWh produced, about 2,600 kWh per capita (1991)

Industries:

Heavy industrial products include raw steel, rolled steel, cement, lumber; machine tools, foundry equipment, electric mining locomotives, tower cranes, electric welding equipment, machinery for food preparation, meat packing, dairy, and fishing industries; air-conditioning electric motors up to 100 kW in size, electric motors for cranes, magnetic starters for motors; devices for control of industrial processes; trucks, tractors, and other farm machinery; light industrial products, including cloth, hosiery, and shoes

:Georgia Economy

Agriculture:

accounted for 97% of former USSR citrus fruits and 93% of former USSR tea; berries and grapes; sugar; vegetables, grains, and potatoes; cattle, pigs, sheep, goats, and poultry

Illicit drugs:
    illicit producers of cannabis and opium; mostly for domestic consumption;
    status of government eradication programs unknown; used as transshipment
    points for illicit drugs to Western Europe
Economic aid:
    US commitments, including Ex-Im (FY70-87), $NA billion; Western (non-US)
    countries, ODA and OOF bilateral commitments (1970-86), $NA million;
    Communist countries (1971-86), $NA million
Currency:
    as of May 1992, retaining ruble as currency
Exchange rates:
    NA
Fiscal year: calendar year

:Georgia Communications

Railroads:
    1,570 km, does not include industrial lines (1990)
Highways:
    33,900 km total; 29,500 km hard surfaced, 4,400 km earth (1990)
Inland waterways:
    NA km perennially navigable
Pipelines:
    crude oil NA km, refined products NA km, natural gas NA km
Ports:
    maritime - Batumi, Poti; inland - NA
Merchant marine:
    54 ships (1,000 GRT or over) totaling 715,802 GRT/1,108,068 DWT; includes 16
    bulk cargo, 34 oil tanker, 2 chemical tanker, and 2 specialized liquid
    carrier
Civil air:
    NA major transport aircraft
Airports:
    NA total, NA usable; NA with permanent-surface runways; NA with runways over
    3,659 m; NA with runways 2,440-3,659 m; NA with runways 1,220-2,439 m
Telecommunications:
    poor telephone service; 339,000 unsatisfied applications for telephones (31
    January 1992); international links via landline to CIS members and Turkey;
    low capacity satellite earth station and leased international connections
    via the Moscow international gateway switch

:Georgia Defense Forces

Branches:
    Republic Security Forces (internal and border troops), National Guard; CIS
    Forces (Ground, Navy, Air, and Air Defense)
Manpower availability:
    males 15-49, NA fit for military service; NA reach military age (18)
    annually
Defense expenditures:
    $NA, NA% of GNP

Germany Geography

Total area: 356,910 km2
Land area: 349,520 km2; comprises the formerly separate Federal Republic of Germany,
  the German Democratic Republic, and Berlin following formal unification on 3
  October 1990
Comparative area: slightly smaller than Montana
Land boundaries:
  3,790 km; Austria 784 km, Belgium 167 km, Czechoslovakia 815 km, Denmark 68
  km, France 451 km, Luxembourg 138 km, Netherlands 577 km, Poland 456 km,
  Switzerland 334 km
Coastline:
  2,389 km
Maritime claims:
 Continental shelf:
  200 m (depth) or to depth of exploitation
 Exclusive fishing zone:
  200 nm
 Territorial sea:
  North Sea and Schleswig-Holstein coast of Baltic Sea - 3 nm (extends, at one
  point, to 16 nm in the Helgolander Bucht); remainder of Baltic Sea - 12 nm
Disputes:
  the boundaries of Germany were set by the Treaty on the Final Settlement
  With Respect to Germany signed 12 September 1990 in Moscow by the Federal
  Republic of Germany, the German Democratic Republic, France, the United
  Kingdom, the United States, and the Soviet Union; this Treaty entered into
  force on 15 March 1991; a subsequent Treaty between Germany and Poland,
  reaffirming the German-Polish boundary, was signed on 14 November 1990 and
  took effect on 16 January 1992
Climate:
  temperate and marine; cool, cloudy, wet winters and summers; occasional
  warm, tropical foehn wind; high relative humidity
Terrain:
  lowlands in north, uplands in center, Bavarian Alps in south
Natural resources:
  iron ore, coal, potash, timber, lignite, uranium, copper, natural gas, salt,
  nickel
Land use:
  arable land 34%; permanent crops 1%; meadows and pastures 16%; forest and
  woodland 30%; other 19%; includes irrigated 1%
Environment:
  air and water pollution; groundwater, lakes, and air quality in eastern
  Germany are especially bad; significant deforestation in the eastern
  mountains caused by air pollution and acid rain
Note:
  strategic location on North European Plain and along the entrance to the
  Baltic Sea

:Germany People

Population: 80,387,283 (July 1992), growth rate 0.5% (1992)
Birth rate: 11 births/1,000 population (1992)

Death rate: 11 deaths/1,000 population (1992)

Net migration rate: 5 migrants/1,000 population (1992)

Infant mortality rate: 7 deaths/1,000 live births (1992)

Life expectancy at birth: 73 years male, 79 years female (1992)

Total fertility rate: 1.4 children born/woman (1992)

Nationality:

noun - German(s); adjective - German

Ethnic divisions:

primarily German; small Danish and Slavic minorities

Religions:

Protestant 45%, Roman Catholic 37%, unaffiliated or other 18%

Languages:

German

Literacy:

99% (male NA%, female NA%) age 15 and over can read and write (1970 est.)

Labor force:

36,750,000; industry 41%, agriculture 6%, other 53% (1987)

Organized labor:

47% of labor force (1986 est.)

:Germany Government

Long-form name:

Federal Republic of Germany

Type:

federal republic

Capital: Berlin; note - the shift from Bonn to Berlin will take place over a period
of years with Bonn retaining many administrative functions and several
ministries

Administrative divisions:

16 states (lander, singular - land); Baden-Wurttemberg, Bayern, Berlin,
Brandenburg, Bremen, Hamburg, Hessen, Mecklenburg-Vorpommern, Niedersach-
sen,
Nordrhein-Westfalen, Rheinland-Pfalz, Saarland, Sachsen, Sachsen-Anhalt,
Schleswig-Holstein, Thuringen

Independence:

18 January 1871 (German Empire unification); divided into four zones of
occupation (UK, US, USSR, and later, France) in 1945 following World War II;
Federal Republic of Germany (FRG or West Germany) proclaimed 23 May 1949 and
included the former UK, US, and French zones; German Democratic Republic
(GDR or East Germany) proclaimed 7 October 1949 and included the former USSR
zone; unification of West Germany and East Germany took place 3 October
1990; all four power rights formally relinquished 15 March 1991

Constitution:

23 May 1949, provisional constitution known as Basic Law

Legal system:

civil law system with indigenous concepts; judicial review of legislative
acts in the Federal Constitutional Court; has not accepted compulsory ICJ
jurisdiction

National holiday:

German Unity Day, 3 October (1990)

Executive branch:

president, chancellor, Cabinet

Legislative branch:

bicameral parliament (no official name for the two chambers as a whole) consists of an upper chamber or Federal Council (Bundesrat) and a lower chamber or Federal Diet (Bundestag)

Judicial branch:

Federal Constitutional Court (Bundesverfassungsgericht)

Leaders:

Chief of State:

President Dr. Richard von WEIZSACKER (since 1 July 1984)

Head of Government:

Chancellor Dr. Helmut KOHL (since 4 October 1982)

*** No entry for this item ***

Political parties and leaders:

Christian Democratic Union (CDU), Helmut KOHL, chairman; Christian Social Union (CSU), Theo WAIGEL; Free Democratic Party (FDP), Otto Count LAMBSDORFF, chairman; Social Democratic Party (SPD), Bjoern ENGHOLM, - chairman; - Green - Party - Ludger VOLMER, Christine WEISKE, co-chairmen (after the 2 December 1990 election the East and West German Green Parties united); Alliance 90 united to form one party in September 1991, Petra MORAWE, chairwoman; Republikaner, Franz SCHOENHUBER; National Democratic

Party (NPD), Walter BACHMANN; Communist Party (DKP), Rolf PRIEMER

Suffrage:

universal at age 18

:Germany Government

Elections:

Federal Diet:

last held 2 December 1990 (next to be held October 1994); results - CDU 36.7%, SPD 33.5%, FDP 11.0%, CSU 7.1%, Green Party (West Germany) 3.9%, PDS

2.4%, Republikaner 2.1%, Alliance 90/Green Party (East Germany) 1.2%, other 2.1%; seats - (662 total, 656 statutory with special rules to allow for slight expansion) CDU 268, SPD 239, FDP 79, CSU 51, PDS 17, Alliance 90/Green Party (East Germany) 8; note - special rules for this election allowed former East German parties to win seats if they received at least 5% of vote in eastern Germany

*** No entry for this item ***

Communists:

West - about 40,000 members and supporters; East - about 200,000 party members (December 1991)

Other political or pressure groups:

expellee, refugee, and veterans groups

Member of:

AfDB, AG (observer), AsDB, BDEAC, BIS, CCC, CE, CERN, COCOM, CSCE, EBRD, EC,

ECE, EIB, ESA, FAO, G-5, G-7, G-10, GATT, IADB, IAEA, IBRD, ICAO, ICC, ICFTU, IDA, IEA, IFAD, IFC, ILO, IMF, IMO, INMARSAT, INTELSAT,

INTERPOL,

IOC, IOM, ISO, ITU, LORCS, NATO, NEA, OAS (observer), OECD, PCA, UN, UNCTAD,

UNESCO, UNIDO, UNHCR, UPU, WEU, WFTU, WHO, WIPO, WMO, WTO

Diplomatic representation:

Ambassador Dr. Immo STABREIT will become Ambassador in late summer/early fall 1992; Chancery at 4645 Reservoir Road NW, Washington, DC 20007; telephone (202) 298-4000; there are German Consulates General in Atlanta, Boston, Chicago, Detroit, Houston, Los Angeles, San Francisco, Seattle, and New York, and Consulates in Miami and New Orleans

US:

Ambassador Robert M. KIMMITT; Embassy at Deichmanns Avenue, 5300 Bonn 2 (mailing address is APO AE 09080); telephone [49] (228) 3391; there is a US Branch Office in Berlin and US Consulates General in Frankfurt, Hamburg, Leipzig, Munich, and Stuttgart

Flag:

three equal horizontal bands of black (top), red, and yellow

:Germany Economy

Overview:

The Federal Republic of Germany is making substantial progress in integrating and modernizing eastern Germany, but at a heavy economic cost. Western Germany's growth in 1991 slowed to 3.1% - the lowest rate since 1987 - because of slack world growth and higher interest rates and taxes required by the unification process. While western Germany's economy was in recession in the last half of 1991, eastern Germany's economy bottomed out after a nearly two-year freefall and shows signs of recovery, particularly in the construction, transportation, and service sectors. Eastern Germany could begin a fragile recovery later, concentrated in 1992 in construction, transportation, and services. The two regions remain vastly different, however, despite eastern Germany's progress. Western Germany has an advanced market economy and is a world leader in exports. It has a highly urbanized and skilled population that enjoys excellent living standards, abundant leisure time, and comprehensive social welfare benefits. Western Germany is relatively poor in natural resources, coal being the most important mineral. Western Germany's world-class companies manufacture technologically advanced goods. The region's economy is mature: services and manufacturing account for the dominant share of economic activity, and raw materials and semimanufactured goods constitute a large portion of imports. In recent years, manufacturing has accounted for about 31% of GDP, with other sectors contributing lesser amounts. Gross fixed investment in 1990 accounted for about 21% of GDP. In 1991, GDP in the western region was an estimated $19,200 per capita. In contrast, eastern Germany's economy is shedding the obsolete heavy industries that dominated the economy during the Communist era. Eastern Germany's share of all-German GDP is only about 7%, and eastern productivity is just 30% that of the west. The privatization agency for eastern Germany, the Treuhand, is rapidly selling many of the 11,500 firms under its control. The pace of private investment is starting to pick up, but questions about property rights and environmental liabilities remain. Eastern Germany has one of the world's largest reserves of low-grade lignite coal but little else in the way of mineral resources. The quality of statistics from eastern Germany is improving, yet many gaps remain; the federal government began producing all-German data for select economic statistics at the start of 1992. The most challenging economic problem is promoting eastern Germany's economic reconstruction - specifically, finding the right mix of fiscal, monetary, regulatory, and tax policies that will spur investment in eastern Germany - without destabilizing western Germany's economy or damaging relations with West European partners. The biggest danger is that excessive wage settlements and heavy federal borrowing could fuel inflation and prompt the German Central Bank, the Bundesbank, to keep a tight monetary policy to choke off a wage-price spiral. Meanwhile, the FRG has been providing billions of dollars to help the former Soviet republics and the reformist economies of Eastern Europe.

GDP:
  purchasing power equivalent - Federal Republic of Germany: $1,331.4 billion, per capita $16,700; real growth rate 0.7%; western Germany: $1,235.8 billion, per capita $19,200; real growth rate 3.1%; eastern Germany $95.6 billion, per capita $5,870; real growth rate - 30% (1991 est.)

Inflation rate (consumer prices):
  West - 3.5% (1991); East - NA%

Unemployment rate: West - 6.3% (1991); East - 11% (1991)

Budget:
  West (federal, state, local) - revenues $684 billion; expenditures $704 billion, including capital expenditures $NA (1990), East - NA

Exports:
  West - $324.3 billion (f.o.b., 1989)

:Germany Economy

  commodities:
  manufactures 86.6% (including machines and machine tools, chemicals, motor vehicles, iron and steel products), agricultural products 4.9%, raw materials 2.3%, fuels 1.3%

Exports:
  partners:
  EC 53.3% (France 12.7%, Netherlands 8.3%, Italy 9.1%, UK 8.3%, Belgium-Luxembourg 7.3%), other Western Europe 15.9%, US 7.1%, Eastern Europe 4.1%, OPEC 2.7% (1990)

Imports:
  West - $346.5 billion (f.o.b., 1989)
  commodities:
  manufactures 68.5%, agricultural products 12.0%, fuels 9.7%, raw materials 7.1%
  partners:
  EC 51.7% (France 11.7%, Netherlands 10.1%, Italy 9.3%, UK 6.7%, Belgium-Luxembourg 7.2%), other Western Europe 13.4%, US 6.6%, Eastern Europe 3.8%, OPEC 2.5% (1990)

External debt: West - $500 million (June 1988); East - $20.6 billion (1989)

Industrial production:
  growth rates, West - 5.4% (1990); East - 30% (1991 est.)

Electricity:

133,000,000 kW capacity; 580,000 million kWh produced, 7,390 kWh per capita (1991)

Industries:

West - among world's largest producers of iron, steel, coal, cement, chemicals, machinery, vehicles, machine tools, electronics; food and beverages; East - metal fabrication, chemicals, brown coal, shipbuilding, machine building, food and beverages, textiles, petroleum refining

Agriculture:

West - accounts for about 2% of GDP (including fishing and forestry); diversified crop and livestock farming; principal crops and livestock include potatoes, wheat, barley, sugar beets, fruit, cabbage, cattle, pigs, poultry; net importer of food; fish catch of 202,000 metric tons in 1987; East - accounts for about 10% of GDP (including fishing and forestry); principal crops - wheat, rye, barley, potatoes, sugar beets, fruit; livestock products include pork, beef, chicken, milk, hides and skins; net importer of food; fish catch of 193,600 metric tons in 1987

Economic aid:

West - donor - ODA and OOF commitments (1970-89), $75.5 billion; East - donor - $4.0 billion extended bilaterally to non-Communist less developed countries (1956-89)

Currency:

deutsche mark (plural - deutsche marks); 1 deutsche mark (DM) = 100 pfennige

Exchange rates:

deutsche marks (DM) per US$1 - 1.6611 (March 1992), 1.6595 (1991), 1.6157 (1990), 1.8800 (1989), 1.7562 (1988), 1.7974 (1987)

Fiscal year: calendar year

:Germany Communications

Railroads:

West - 31,443 km total; 27,421 km government owned, 1.435-meter standard gauge (12,491 km double track, 11,501 km electrified); 4,022 km nongovernment owned, including 3,598 km 1.435-meter standard gauge (214 km electrified) and 424 km 1.000-meter gauge (186 km electrified); East - 14,025 km total; 13,750 km 1.435-meter standard gauge, 275 km 1.000-meter or other narrow gauge; 3,830 (est.) km 1.435-meter standard gauge double-track; 3,475 km overhead electrified (1988)

Highways:

West - 466,305 km total; 169,568 km primary, includes 6,435 km autobahn, 32,460 km national highways (Bundesstrassen), 65,425 km state highways (Landesstrassen), 65,248 km county roads (Kreisstrassen); 296,737 km of secondary communal roads (Gemeindestrassen); East - 124,604 km total; 47,203 km concrete, asphalt, stone block, of which 1,855 km are autobahn and limited access roads, 11,326 are trunk roads, and 34,022 are regional roads; 77,401 municipal roads (1988)

Inland waterways:

West - 5,222 km, of which almost 70% are usable by craft of 1,000-metric ton capacity or larger; major rivers include the Rhine and Elbe; Kiel Canal is an important connection between the Baltic Sea and North Sea; East - 2,319 km (1988)

Pipelines:

crude oil 3,644 km; petroleum products 3,946 km; natural gas 97,564 km
(1988)

Ports:

maritime - Bremerhaven, Brunsbuttel, Cuxhaven, Emden, Bremen, Hamburg, Kiel,
Lubeck, Wilhelmshaven, Rostock, Wismar, Stralsund, Sassnitz; inland - 31
major

Merchant marine:

607 ships (1,000 GRT or over) totaling 5,210,060 GRT/6,626,333 DWT; includes
3 passenger, 5 short-sea passenger, 324 cargo, 10 refrigerated cargo, 135
container, 31 roll-on/roll-off cargo, 5 railcar carrier, 6 barge carrier, 11
oil tanker, 21 chemical tanker, 22 liquefied gas tanker, 5 combination
ore/oil, 14 combination bulk, 15 bulk; note - the German register includes
ships of the former East and West Germany; during 1991 the fleet underwent
major restructuring as surplus ships were sold off

Civil air:

239 major transport aircraft

Airports:

462 total, 455 usable; 242 with permanent-surface runways; 4 with runways
over 3,659 m; 40 with runways 2,440-3,659 m; 55 with runways 1,220-2,439 m

Telecommunications:

West - highly developed, modern telecommunication service to all parts of
the country; fully adequate in all respects; 40,300,000 telephones;
intensively developed, highly redundant cable and radio relay networks, all
completely automatic; broadcast stations - 80 AM, 470 FM, 225 (6,000
repeaters) TV; 6 submarine coaxial cables; satellite earth stations - 12
Atlantic Ocean INTELSAT antennas, 2 Indian Ocean INTELSAT antennas,
EUTELSAT, and domestic systems; 2 HF radiocommunication centers;
tropospheric links East - badly needs modernization; 3,970,000 telephones;
broadcast stations - 23 AM, 17 FM, 21 TV (15 Soviet TV repeaters); 6,181,860
TVs; 6,700,000 radios; 1 satellite earth station operating in INTELSAT and
Intersputnik systems

:Germany Defense Forces

Branches:

Army, Navy, Air Force, Federal Border Police

Manpower availability:

males 15-49, 20,300,359; 17,612,677 fit for military service; 414,330 reach
military age (18) annually

Defense expenditures:

exchange rate conversion - $39.5 billion, 2.5% of GDP (1991)

Ghana Geography

Total area: 238,540 km2

Land area: 230,020 km2

Comparative area: slightly smaller than Oregon

Land boundaries:

2,093 km; Burkina 548 km, Ivory Coast 668 km, Togo 877 km

Coastline:

539 km

Maritime claims:

Contiguous zone:

24 nm

Continental shelf:

200 nm

Exclusive economic zone:

200 nm

Territorial sea:

12 nm

Disputes:

Climate:

tropical; warm and comparatively dry along southeast coast; hot and humid in
southwest; hot and dry in north

Terrain:

mostly low plains with dissected plateau in south-central area

Natural resources:

gold, timber, industrial diamonds, bauxite, manganese, fish, rubber

Land use:

arable land 5%; permanent crops 7%; meadows and pastures 15%; forest and
woodland 37%; other 36%; includes irrigated NEGL%

Environment:

recent drought in north severely affecting marginal agricultural activities;
deforestation; overgrazing; soil erosion; dry, northeasterly harmattan wind
(January to March)

Note:

Lake Volta is the world's largest artificial lake

:Ghana People

Population: 16,185,351 (July 1992), growth rate 3.1% (1992)

Birth rate: 45 births/1,000 population (1992)

Death rate: 13 deaths/1,000 population (1992)

Net migration rate: - 1 migrant/1,000 population (1992)

Infant mortality rate: 86 deaths/1,000 live births (1992)

Life expectancy at birth: 53 years male, 57 years female (1992)

Total fertility rate: 6.3 children born/woman (1992)

Nationality:

noun - Ghanaian(s); adjective - Ghanaian

Ethnic divisions:

black African 99.8% (major tribes - Akan 44%, Moshi-Dagomba 16%, Ewe 13%, Ga
8%), European and other 0.2%

Religions:

indigenous beliefs 38%, Muslim 30%, Christian 24%, other 8%

Languages:

English (official); African languages include Akan, Moshi-Dagomba, Ewe, and
Ga

Literacy:

60% (male 70%, female 51%) age 15 and over can read and write (1990 est.)

Labor force:

3,700,000; agriculture and fishing 54.7%, industry 18.7%, sales and clerical
15.2%, services, transportation, and communications 7.7%, professional 3.7%;
48% of population of working age (1983)

Organized labor:
  467,000 (about 13% of labor force)

:Ghana Government

Long-form name:
  Republic of Ghana
Type:
  military
Capital: Accra
Administrative divisions:
  10 regions; Ashanti, Brong-Ahafo, Central, Eastern, Greater Accra, Northern,
  Upper East, Upper West, Volta, Western
Independence:
  6 March 1957 (from UK, formerly Gold Coast)
Constitution:
  24 September 1979; suspended 31 December 1981
Legal system:
  based on English common law and customary law; has not accepted compulsory
  ICJ jurisdiction
National holiday:
  Independence Day, 6 March (1957)
Executive branch:
  chairman of the Provisional National Defense Council (PNDC), PNDC, Cabinet
Legislative branch:
  unicameral National Assembly dissolved after 31 December 1981 coup, and
  legislative powers were assumed by the Provisional National Defense Council
Judicial branch:
  Supreme Court
Leaders:
  Chief of State and Head of Government:
  Chairman of the Provisional National Defense Council Flt. Lt. (Ret.) Jerry
  John RAWLINGS (since 31 December 1981)
Political parties and leaders:
  none; political parties outlawed after 31 December 1981 coup
Suffrage:
  none
Elections:
  no national elections; district assembly elections held in 1988-89
Member of:
  ACP, AfDB, C, CCC, ECA, ECOWAS, FAO, G-24, G-77, GATT, IAEA, IBRD,
  ICAO,
  IDA, IFAD, IFC, ILO, IMF, IMO, INTELSAT, INTERPOL, IOC, IOM (observer),
  ISO,
  ITU, LORCS, NAM, OAU, UN, UNCTAD, UNESCO, UNIDO, UNIFIL,
  UNIIMOG, UPU, WCL,
  WHO, WIPO, WMO, WTO
Diplomatic representation:
  Ambassador Dr. Joseph ABBEY; Chancery at 3512 International Drive NW,
  Washington, DC 20008; telephone (202) 686-4520; there is a Ghanaian
  Consulate General in New York

US:

Ambassador Raymond C. EWING; Embassy at Ring Road East, East of Danquah Circle, Accra (mailing address is P. O. Box 194, Accra); telephone [233] (21) 775348, 775349

Flag:

three equal horizontal bands of red (top), yellow, and green with a large black five-pointed star centered in the gold band; uses the popular pan-African colors of Ethiopia; similar to the flag of Bolivia, which has a coat of arms centered in the yellow band

:Ghana Economy

Overview:

Supported by substantial international assistance, Ghana has been implementing a steady economic rebuilding program since 1983, including moves toward privatization and relaxation of government controls. Heavily dependent on cocoa, gold, and timber exports, economic growth so far has not spread substantially to other areas of the economy. The costs of sending peacekeeping forces to Liberia and preparing for the transition to a democratic government have been boosting government expenditures and undercutting structural adjustment reforms. Ghana opened a stock exchange in 1990. Much of the economic improvement in 1991 was caused by favorable weather (following a severe drought the previous year) that led to plentiful harvests in Ghana's agriculturally based economy.

GDP:

$6.2 billion; per capita $400; real growth rate 5% (1991 est.)

Inflation rate (consumer prices):

10% (1991 est.)

Unemployment rate: 10% (1991)

Budget:

revenues $821 million; expenditures $782 million, including capital expenditures of $151 million (1990 est.)

Exports:

$843 million (f.o.b., 1991 est.)

commodities:

cocoa 45%, gold, timber, tuna, bauxite, and aluminum

partners:

US 23%, UK, other EC

Imports:

$1.2 billion (c.i.f., 1991 est.)

commodities:

petroleum 16%, consumer goods, foods, intermediate goods, capital equipment

partners:

US 10%, UK, FRG, France, Japan, South Korea, GDR

External debt: $3.1 billion (1990 est.)

Industrial production:

growth rate 7.4% in manufacturing (1989); accounts for almost 1.5% of GDP

Electricity:

1,180,000 kW capacity; 4,140 million kWh produced, 265 kWh per capita (1991)

Industries:

mining, lumbering, light manufacturing, fishing, aluminum, food processing

Agriculture:
accounts for more than 50% of GDP (including fishing and forestry); the major cash crop is cocoa; other principal crops - rice, coffee, cassava, peanuts, corn, shea nuts, timber; normally self-sufficient in food

Illicit drugs:
illicit producer of cannabis for the international drug trade

Economic aid:
US commitments, including Ex-Im (FY70-89), $455 million; Western (non-US) countries, ODA and OOF bilateral commitments (1970-89), $2.6 billion; OPEC bilateral aid (1979-89), $78 million; Communist countries (1970-89), $106 million

Currency:
cedi (plural - cedis); 1 cedi (C) = 100 pesewas

Fiscal year: calendar year

:Ghana Communications

Railroads:
953 km, all 1.067-meter gauge; 32 km double track; railroads undergoing major renovation

Highways:
32,250 km total; 6,084 km concrete or bituminous surface, 26,166 km gravel, laterite, and improved earth surfaces

Inland waterways:
Volta, Ankobra, and Tano Rivers provide 168 km of perennial navigation for launches and lighters; Lake Volta provides 1,125 km of arterial and feeder waterways

Pipelines:
none

Ports:
Tema, Takoradi

Merchant marine:
5 cargo and 1 refrigerated cargo (1,000 GRT or over) totaling 53,435 GRT/69,167 DWT

Civil air:
8 major transport aircraft

Airports:
10 total, 9 usable; 5 with permanent-surface runways; none with runways over 3,659 m; 1 with runways 2,440-3,659 m; 7 with runways 1,220-2,439 m

Telecommunications:
poor to fair system handled primarily by microwave links; 42,300 telephones; broadcast stations - 4 AM, 1 FM, 4 (8 translators) TV; 1 Atlantic Ocean INTELSAT earth station

:Ghana Defense Forces

Branches:
Army, Navy, Air Force, National Police Force, National Civil Defense

Manpower availability:
males 15-49, 3,661,558; 2,049,842 fit for military service; 170,742 reach military age (18) annually

Defense expenditures:
exchange rate conversion - $30 million, less than 1% of GNP (1989 est.)

Gibraltar Geography

Total area: 6.5 km2
Land area: 6.5 km2
Comparative area: about 11 times the size of the Mall in Washington, DC
Land boundaries:
   1.2 km; Spain 1.2 km
Coastline:
   12 km
Maritime claims:
 Exclusive fishing zone:
   3 nm
 Territorial sea:
   3 nm
Disputes:
   source of occasional friction between Spain and the UK
Climate:
   Mediterranean with mild winters and warm summers
Terrain:
   a narrow coastal lowland borders The Rock
Natural resources:
   negligible
Land use:
   arable land 0%; permanent crops 0%; meadows and pastures 0%; forest and
   woodland 0%; other 100%
Environment:
   natural freshwater sources are meager, so large water catchments (concrete
   or natural rock) collect rain water
Note:
   strategic location on Strait of Gibraltar that links the North Atlantic
   Ocean and Mediterranean Sea

:Gibraltar People

Population: 29,651 (July 1992), growth rate 0.1% (1992)
Birth rate: 18 births/1,000 population (1992)
Death rate: 8 deaths/1,000 population (1992)
Net migration rate: - 9 migrants/1,000 population (1992)
Infant mortality rate: 6 deaths/1,000 live births (1992)
Life expectancy at birth: 72 years male, 79 years female (1992)
Total fertility rate: 2.5 children born/woman (1992)
Nationality:
   noun - Gibraltarian(s); adjective - Gibraltar
Ethnic divisions:
   mostly Italian, English, Maltese, Portuguese, and Spanish descent
Religions:
   Roman Catholic 74%, Protestant 11% (Church of England 8%, other 3%), Moslem
   8%, Jewish 2%, none or other 5% (1981)
Languages:
   English and Spanish are primary languages; Italian, Portuguese, and Russian
   also spoken; English used in the schools and for official purposes
Literacy:

NA% (male NA%, female NA%)

Labor force:

about 14,800 (including non-Gibraltar laborers); UK military establishments and civil government employ nearly 50% of the labor force

Organized labor:

over 6,000

:Gibraltar Government

Long-form name:

Digraph:

f Assembly *** last held on 24 March 1988 (next to be held March 1992); results - percent of vote by party NA; seats - (18 total, 15 elected) SL 8, GCL/AACR 7

Type:

dependent territory of the UK

Capital: Gibraltar

Administrative divisions:

none (dependent territory of the UK)

Independence:

none (dependent territory of the UK)

Constitution:

30 May 1969

Legal system:

English law

National holiday:

Commonwealth Day (second Monday of March)

Executive branch:

British monarch, governor, chief minister, Gibraltar Council, Council of Ministers (cabinet)

Legislative branch:

unicameral House of Assembly

Judicial branch:

Supreme Court, Court of Appeal

Leaders:

Chief of State:

Queen ELIZABETH II (since 6 February 1952), represented by Governor and Commander in Chief Adm. Sir Derek REFFELL (since NA 1989)

Head of Government:

Chief Minister Joe BOSSANO (since 25 March 1988)

Political parties and leaders:

Socialist Labor Party (SL), Joe BOSSANO; Gibraltar Labor Party/Association for the Advancement of Civil Rights (GCL/AACR), leader NA; Gibraltar Social Democrats, Peter CARUANA; Gibraltar National Party, Joe GARCIA

Suffrage:

universal at age 18, plus other UK subjects resident six months or more

Elections:

House of Assembly:

last held on 24 March 1988 (next to be held March 1992); results - percent of vote by party NA; seats - (18 total, 15 elected) SL 8, GCL/AACR 7

Other political or pressure groups:
  Housewives Association, Chamber of Commerce, Gibraltar Representatives
  Organization
Diplomatic representation:
  none (dependent territory of the UK)
Flag:
  two horizontal bands of white (top, double width) and red with a
  three-towered red castle in the center of the white band; hanging from the
  castle gate is a gold key centered in the red band

:Gibraltar Economy

Overview:
  The economy depends heavily on British defense expenditures, revenue from
  tourists, fees for services to shipping, and revenues from banking and
  finance activities. Because more than 70% of the economy is in the public
  sector, changes in government spending have a major impact on the level of
  employment. Construction workers are particularly affected when government
  expenditures are cut.
GNP:
  exchange rate conversion - $182 million, per capita $4,600; real growth rate
  5% (FY87)
Inflation rate (consumer prices):
  3.6% (1988)
Unemployment rate: NA%
Budget:
  revenues $136 million; expenditures $139 million, including capital
  expenditures of NA (FY88)
Exports:
  $82 million (f.o.b., 1988)
 commodities:
  (principally reexports) petroleum 51%, manufactured goods 41%, other 8%
 partners:
  UK, Morocco, Portugal, Netherlands, Spain, US, FRG
Imports:
  $258 million (c.i.f., 1988)
 commodities:
  fuels, manufactured goods, and foodstuffs
 partners:
  UK, Spain, Japan, Netherlands
External debt: $318 million (1987)
Industrial production:
  growth rate NA%
Electricity:
  47,000 kW capacity; 200 million kWh produced, 6,670 kWh per capita (1991)
Industries:
  tourism, banking and finance, construction, commerce; support to large UK
  naval and air bases; transit trade and supply depot in the port; light
  manufacturing of tobacco, roasted coffee, ice, mineral waters, candy, beer,
  and canned fish
Agriculture:

364

Economic aid:
   US commitments, including Ex-Im (FY70-88), $0.8 million; Western (non-US)
   countries, ODA and OOF bilateral commitments (1970-89), $188 million
Currency:
   Gibraltar pound (plural - pounds); 1 Gibraltar pound (#G) = 100 pence
Exchange rates:
   Gibraltar pounds (#G) per US$1 - 0.5799 (March 1992), 0.5652 (1991), 0.5603
   (1990), 0.6099 (1989), 0.5614 (1988), 0.6102 (1987); note - the Gibraltar
   pound is at par with the British pound
Fiscal year: 1 July - 30 June

:Gibraltar Communications

Railroads:
   1.000-meter-gauge system in dockyard area only
Highways:
   50 km, mostly good bitumen and concrete
Pipelines:
   none
Ports:
   Gibraltar
Merchant marine:
   21 ships (1,000 GRT or over) totaling 795,356 GRT/1,490,737 DWT; includes 5
   cargo, 2 refrigerated cargo, 1 container, 6 petroleum tanker, 1 chemical
   tanker, 6 bulk; note - a flag of convenience registry
Civil air:
   1 major transport aircraft
Airports:
   1 with permanent-surface runways 1,220-2,439 m
Telecommunications:
   adequate, automatic domestic system and adequate international
   radiocommunication and microwave facilities; 9,400 telephones; broadcast
   stations - 1 AM, 6 FM, 4 TV; 1 Atlantic Ocean INTELSAT earth station

:Gibraltar Defense Forces

Branches:
   British Army, Royal Navy, Royal Air Force
Note:
   defense is the responsibility of the UK

Glorioso Islands Geography

Total area: 5 km2
Land area: 5 km2; includes Ile Glorieuse, Ile du Lys, Verte Rocks, Wreck Rock, and
   South Rock
Comparative area: about 8.5 times the size of the Mall in Washington, DC
Land boundaries:
   none
Coastline:
   35.2 km
Maritime claims:
  Contiguous zone:

12 nm
  Exclusive economic zone:
  200 nm
  Territorial sea:
  12 nm
Disputes:
  claimed by Madagascar
Climate:
  tropical
Terrain:
  undetermined
Natural resources:
  guano, coconuts
Land use:
  arable land 0%; permanent crops 0%; meadows and pastures 0%; forest and
  woodland 0%; other - lush vegetation and coconut palms 100%
Environment:
  subject to periodic cyclones
Note:
  located in the Indian Ocean just north of the Mozambique Channel between
  Africa and Madagascar

:Glorioso Islands People

Population: uninhabited

:Glorioso Islands Government

Long-form name:
  none
Type:
  French possession administered by Commissioner of the Republic Jacques
  DEWATRE, resident in Reunion
Capital: none; administered by France from Reunion

:Glorioso Islands Economy

Overview: no economic activity

:Glorioso Islands Communications

Ports:
  none; offshore anchorage only
Airports:
  1 with runways 1,220-2,439 m

:Glorioso Islands Defense Forces

Note: defense is the responsibility of France

Greece Geography

Total area: 131,940 km2
Land area: 130,800 km2
Comparative area: slightly smaller than Alabama
Land boundaries:
  1,210 km; Albania 282 km, Bulgaria 494 km, Turkey 206 km, Macedonia 228 km
Coastline:

13,676 km
Maritime claims:
 Continental shelf:
 200 m (depth) or to depth of exploitation
 Territorial sea:
 6 nm, but Greece has threatened to claim 12 nm
Disputes:
 air, continental shelf, and territorial water disputes with Turkey in Aegean
 Sea; Cyprus question
Climate:
 temperate; mild, wet winters; hot, dry summers
Terrain:
 mostly mountains with ranges extending into sea as peninsulas or chains of
 islands
Natural resources:
 bauxite, lignite, magnesite, crude oil, marble
Land use:
 arable land 23%; permanent crops 8%; meadows and pastures 40%; forest and
 woodland 20%; other 9%; includes irrigated 7%
Environment:
 subject to severe earthquakes; air pollution; archipelago of 2,000 islands
Note:
 strategic location dominating the Aegean Sea and southern approach to
 Turkish Straits

:Greece People

Population: 10,064,250 (July 1992), growth rate 0.2% (1992)
Birth rate: 11 births/1,000 population (1992)
Death rate: 9 deaths/1,000 population (1992)
Net migration rate: 0 migrants/1,000 population (1992)
Infant mortality rate: 10 deaths/1,000 live births (1992)
Life expectancy at birth: 75 years male, 81 years female (1992)
Total fertility rate: 1.5 children born/woman (1992)
Nationality:
 noun - Greek(s); adjective - Greek
Ethnic divisions:
 Greek 98%, other 2%; note - the Greek Government states there are no ethnic
 divisions in Greece
Religions:
 Greek Orthodox 98%, Muslim 1.3%, other 0.7%
Languages:
 Greek (official); English and French widely understood
Literacy:
 93% (male 98%, female 89%) age 15 and over can read and write (1990 est.)
Labor force:
 3,657,000; services 44%, agriculture 27%, manufacturing and mining 20%,
 construction 6% (1988)
Organized labor:
 10-15% of total labor force, 20-25% of urban labor force

:Greece Government

Long-form name:
  Hellenic Republic
Type:
  presidential parliamentary government; monarchy rejected by referendum 8
  December 1974
Capital: Athens
Administrative divisions:
  52 departments (nomoi, singular - nomos); Aitolia kai Akarnania, Akhaia,
  Argolis, Arkadhia, Arta, Attiki, Dhodhekanisos, Dhrama, Evritania, Evros,
  Evvoia, Florina, Fokis, Fthiotis, Grevena, Ilia, Imathia, Ioannina,
  Iraklion, Kardhitsa, Kastoria, Kavala, Kefallinia, Kerkira, Khalkidhiki,
  Khania, Khios, Kikladhes, Kilkis, Korinthia, Kozani, Lakonia, Larisa,
  Lasithi, Lesvos, Levkas, Magnisia, Messinia, Pella, Pieria, Piraievs,
  Preveza, Rethimni, Rodhopi, Samos, Serrai, Thesprotia, Thessaloniki,
  Trikala, Voiotia, Xanthi, Zakinthos, autonomous region: Agios Oros (Mt.
  Athos)
Independence:
  1829 (from the Ottoman Empire)
Constitution:
  11 June 1975
Legal system:
  based on codified Roman law; judiciary divided into civil, criminal, and
  administrative courts
National holiday:
  Independence Day (proclamation of the war of independence), 25 March (1821)
Executive branch:
  president, prime minister, Cabinet
Legislative branch:
  unicameral Greek Chamber of Deputies (Vouli ton Ellinon)
Judicial branch:
  Supreme Court
Leaders:
 Chief of State:
  President Konstantinos KARAMANLIS (since 5 May 1990); -
 Head of Government:
  Prime Minister Konstantinos MITSOTAKIS (since 11 April 1990)
Political parties and leaders:
  New Democracy (ND; conservative), Konstantinos MITSOTAKIS; Panhellenic
  Socialist Movement (PASOK), Andreas PAPANDREOU; Left Alliance, Maria
  DAMANAKI; Democratic Renewal (DEANA), Konstantinos STEFANOPOULOS;
Communist
  Party (KKE), Aleka PAPARIGA; Ecologist-Alternative List, leader rotates
Suffrage:
  universal and compulsory at age 18
Elections:
 Chamber of Deputies:
  last held 8 April 1990 (next to be held April 1994); results - ND 46.89%,
  PASOK 38.62%, Left Alliance 10.27%, PASOK/Left Alliance 1.02%,
  Ecologist-Alternative List 0.77%, DEANA 0.67%, Muslim independents 0.5%;
  seats - (300 total) ND 150, PASOK 123, Left Alliance 19, PASOK-Left Alliance

4, Muslim independents 2, DEANA 1, Ecologist-Alternative List 1; note - one DEANA deputy joined ND in July, giving ND 151 seats; in November, a special electoral court ruled in favor of ND on a contested seat, at PASOK'S expense; PASOK and the Left Alliance divided their four joint mandates evenly, and the seven KKE deputies split off from the Left Alliance; new configuration: ND 152, PASOK 124, Left Alliance 14, KKE 7, others unchanged

President:
last held 4 May 1990 (next to be held May 1995); results - Konstantinos KARAMANLIS was elected by Parliament

:Greece Government

Communists:
an estimated 60,000 members and sympathizers

Member of:
AG, BIS, CCC, CE, CERN, COCOM, CSCE, EBRD, EC, ECE, EIB, FAO, G-6, GATT,
IAEA, IBRD, ICAO, ICC, ICFTU, IDA, IEA, IFAD, IFC, ILO, IMF, IMO, INMARSAT,
INTELSAT, INTERPOL, IOC, IOM, ISO, ITU, LORCS, NACC, NAM (guest), NATO, NEA,
NSG, OAS (observer), OECD, PCA, UN, UNCTAD, UNESCO, UNHCR, UNIDO, UPU, WHO,
WIPO, WMO, WTO, ZC

Diplomatic representation:
Ambassador Christos ZACHARAKIS; Chancery at 2221 Massachusetts Avenue NW,
Washington, DC 20008; telephone (202) 939-5800; there are Greek Consulates General in Atlanta, Boston, Chicago, Los Angeles, New York, and San Francisco, and a Consulate in New Orleans

US:
Ambassador Michael G. SOTIRHOS; Embassy at 91 Vasilissis Sophias Boulevard, 10160 Athens (mailing address is APO AE 09842; telephone [30] (1) 721-2951 or 721-8401; there is a US Consulate General in Thessaloniki

Flag:
nine equal horizontal stripes of blue alternating with white; there is a blue square in the upper hoist-side corner bearing a white cross; the cross symbolizes Greek Orthodoxy, the established religion of the country

:Greece Economy

Overview:
Greece has a mixed capitalistic economy with the basic entrepreneurial system overlaid in 1981-89 by a socialist government that enlarged the public sector from 55% of GDP in 1981 to about 70% when Prime Minister Mitsotakis took office. Tourism continues as a major industry, and agriculture - although handicapped by geographic limitations and fragmented, small farms - is self-sufficient except for meat, dairy products, and animal feedstuffs. The Mitsotakis government inherited several severe economic problems from the preceding socialist and caretaker administrations, which had neglected the runaway budget deficit, a ballooning current account deficit, and accelerating inflation. In early 1991, the government secured a $2.5 billion assistance package from the EC under the strictest terms yet

369

imposed on a member country, as the EC finally ran out of patience with Greece's failure to put its financial affairs in order. Over the next three years, Athens must bring inflation down to 7%, cut the current account deficit and central government borrowing as a percentage of GDP, slash public-sector employment by 10%, curb public-sector pay raises, and broaden the tax base.

GDP:
purchasing power equivalent - $77.6 billion, per capita $7,730; real growth rate 1.0% (1991)

Inflation rate (consumer prices):
17.8% (1991)

Unemployment rate: 8.6% (1991)

Budget:
revenues $24.0 billion; expenditures $33.0 billion, including capital expenditures of $3.3 billion (1991)

Exports:
$6.4 billion (f.o.b., 1990)
commodities:
manufactured goods 48%, food and beverages 22%, fuels and lubricants 6%
partners:
Germany 22%, Italy 17%, France 10%, UK 7%, US 6%

Imports:
$18.7 billion (c.i.f., 1990)
commodities:
consumer goods 33%, machinery 17%, foodstuffs 12%, fuels and lubricants 8%
partners:
Germany 21%, Italy 15%, Netherlands 11%, France 8%, UK 5%

External debt: $25.5 billion (1990)

Industrial production:
growth rate - 2.4% (1990); accounts for 22% of GDP

Electricity:
10,500,000 kW capacity; 36,420 million kWh produced, 3,630 kWh per capita (1991)

Industries:
food and tobacco processing, textiles, chemicals, metal products, tourism, mining, petroleum

Agriculture:
including fishing and forestry, accounts for 17% of GDP and 27% of the labor force; principal products - wheat, corn, barley, sugar beets, olives, tomatoes, wine, tobacco, potatoes; self-sufficient in food except meat, dairy products, and animal feedstuffs; fish catch of 115,000 metric tons in 1988

Economic aid:
US commitments, including Ex-Im (FY70-81), $525 million; Western (non-US) countries, ODA and OOF bilateral commitments (1970-89), $1,390 million

:Greece Economy

Currency:
drachma (plural - drachmas); 1 drachma (Dr) = 100 lepta

Exchange rates:

drachma (Dr) per US$1 - 182.33 (January 1992), 182.27 (1991), 158.51 (1990), 162.42 (1989), 141.86 (1988), 135.43 (1987)

Fiscal year: calendar year

:Greece Communications

Railroads:

2,479 km total; 1,565 km 1.435-meter standard gauge, of which 36 km electrified and 100 km double track, 892 km 1.000-meter gauge; 22 km 0.750-meter narrow gauge; all government owned

Highways:

38,938 km total; 16,090 km paved, 13,676 km crushed stone and gravel, 5,632 km improved earth, 3,540 km unimproved earth

Inland waterways:

80 km; system consists of three coastal canals and three unconnected rivers

Pipelines:

crude oil 26 km; petroleum products 547 km

Ports:

Piraievs, Thessaloniki

Merchant marine:

977 ships (1,000 GRT or over) totaling 23,450,910 GRT/42,934,863 DWT; includes 15 passenger, 66 short-sea passenger, 2 passenger-cargo, 136 cargo, 24 container, 15 roll-on/roll-off cargo, 18 refrigerated cargo, 1 vehicle carrier, 196 petroleum tanker, 18 chemical tanker, 9 liquefied gas, 37 combination ore/oil, 3 specialized tanker, 417 bulk, 19 combination bulk, 1 livestock carrier; note - ethnic Greeks also own large numbers of ships under the registry of Liberia, Panama, Cyprus, Malta, and The Bahamas

Civil air:

39 major transport aircraft

Airports:

77 total, 77 usable; 77 with permanent-surface runways; none with runways over 3,659 m; 19 with runways 2,440-3,659 m; 23 with runways 1,220-2,439 m

Telecommunications:

adequate, modern networks reach all areas; 4,080,000 telephones; microwave carries most traffic; extensive open-wire network; submarine cables to off-shore islands; broadcast stations - 29 AM, 17 (20 repeaters) FM, 361 TV; tropospheric links, 8 submarine cables; 1 satellite earth station operating in INTELSAT (1 Atlantic Ocean and 1 Indian Ocean antenna), and EUTELSAT systems

:Greece Defense Forces

Branches:

Hellenic Army, Hellenic Navy, Hellenic Air Force, Police

Manpower availability:

males 15-49, 2,453,756; 1,883,152 fit for military service; 73,913 reach military age (21) annually

Defense expenditures:

exchange rate conversion - $3.8 billion, 5.6% of GDP (1991)

Greenland Geography

Total area: 2,175,600 km2
Land area: 341,700 km2 (ice free)

Comparative area: slightly more than three times the size of Texas

Land boundaries:
  none

Coastline:
  44,087 km

Maritime claims:
 Exclusive fishing zone:
  200 nm
 Territorial sea:
  3 nm

Disputes:
  Denmark has challenged Norway's maritime claims between Greenland and Jan
  Mayen

Climate:
  arctic to subarctic; cool summers, cold winters

Terrain:
  flat to gradually sloping icecap covers all but a narrow, mountainous,
  barren, rocky coast

Natural resources:
  zinc, lead, iron ore, coal, molybdenum, cryolite, uranium, fish

Land use:
  arable land 0%; permanent crops 0%; meadows and pastures 1%; forest and
  woodland NEGL%; other 99%

Environment:
  sparse population confined to small settlements along coast; continuous
  permafrost over northern two-thirds of the island

Note:
  dominates North Atlantic Ocean between North America and Europe

:Greenland People

Population: 57,407 (July 1992), growth rate 1.1% (1992)
Birth rate: 19 births/1,000 population (1992)
Death rate: 8 deaths/1,000 population (1992)
Net migration rate: 0 migrants/1,000 population (1992)
Infant mortality rate: 27 deaths/1,000 live births (1992)
Life expectancy at birth: 63 years male, 69 years female (1992)
Total fertility rate: 2.2 children born/woman (1992)
Nationality:
  noun - Greenlander(s); adjective - Greenlandic
Ethnic divisions:
  Greenlander (Eskimos and Greenland-born Caucasians) 86%, Danish 14%
Religions:
  Evangelical Lutheran
Languages:
  Eskimo dialects, Danish
Literacy:
  NA% (male NA%, female NA%)
Labor force:
  22,800; largely engaged in fishing, hunting, sheep breeding

Organized labor:
  NA

:Greenland Government

Long-form name:
  none
Type:
  part of the Danish realm; self-governing overseas administrative division
Capital: Nuuk (Godthab)
Administrative divisions:
  3 municipalities (kommuner, - singular - kommun); - Nordgronland,
  Ostgrnland, Vestgronland
Independence:
  part of the Danish realm; self-governing overseas administrative division
Constitution:
  Danish
Legal system:
  Danish
National holiday:
  Birthday of the Queen, 16 April (1940)
Executive branch:
  Danish monarch, high commissioner, home rule chairman, prime minister,
  Cabinet (Landsstyre)
Legislative branch:
  unicameral Parliament (Landsting)
Judicial branch:
  High Court (Landsret)
Leaders:
 Chief of State:
  Queen MARGRETHE II (since 14 January 1972), represented by High Commission-
er
  Bent KLINTE (since NA)
 Head of Government:
  Home Rule Chairman Lars Emil JOHANSEN (since 15 March 1991)
Political parties and leaders:
  two-party ruling coalition - Siumut (a moderate socialist party that
  advocates more distinct Greenlandic identity and greater autonomy from
  Denmark), Lars Emil JOHANSEN, chairman; - Inuit - Ataqatigiit - (IA; - a -
  Marxist-Leninist party that favors complete independence from Denmark rather
  than home rule), leader NA; Atassut Party (a more conservative party that
  favors continuing close relations with Denmark), leader NA; Polar Party
  (conservative-Greenland nationalist), leader NA; Center Party (a new
  nonsocialist protest party), leader NA
Suffrage:
  universal at age 18
Elections:
 Danish Folketing:
  last held on 12 December 1990 (next to be held by December 1994); Greenland
  elects two representatives to the Folketing; results - percent of vote by
  party NA; seats - (2 total) Siumut 1, Atassut 1

Landsting:

last held on 5 March 1991 (next to be held 5 March 1995); results - percent of vote by party NA; seats - (27 total) Siumut 11, Atassut Party 8, Inuit Ataqatigiit 5, Center Party 2, Polar Party 1

Member of:

NC

Diplomatic representation:

none (self-governing overseas administrative division of Denmark)

Flag:

two equal horizontal bands of white (top) and red with a large disk slightly to the hoist side of center - the top half of the disk is red, the bottom half is white

:Greenland Economy

Overview:

Over the past 25 years, the economy has changed from one based on subsistence whaling, hunting, and fishing to one dependent on foreign trade. Fishing is still the most important industry, accounting for over 75% of exports and about 25% of the population's income. Maintenance of a social welfare system similar to Denmark's has given the public sector a dominant role in the economy. In 1990, the economy became critically dependent on shrimp exports and on an annual subsidy (now about $500 million) from the Danish Government because cod exports dropped off and commercial mineral production stopped. As of 1992, the government also has taken control of the health sector from Denmark. The new Home Rule government installed in March 1991 has decided to end much of the central control of the economy and to open it wider to competitive forces.

GNP:

purchasing power equivalent - $500 million, per capita $9,000; real growth rate 5% (1988)

Inflation rate (consumer prices):

1.6% (1991)

Unemployment rate: 9% (1990 est.)

Budget:

revenues $381 million; expenditures $381 million, including capital expenditures of $36 million (1989)

Exports:

$435 million (f.o.b., 1990 est.)

commodities:

fish and fish products 83%, metallic ores and concentrates 13%

partners:

Denmark 79%, Benelux 9%, Germany 5%

Imports:

$420 million (c.i.f., 1990 est.)

commodities:

manufactured goods 28%, machinery and transport equipment 24%, food and live animals 12.4%, petroleum and petroleum products 12%

partners:

Denmark 65%, Norway 8.8%, US 4.6%, Germany 3.8%, Japan 3.8%, Sweden 2.4%

External debt: $480 million (1990 est.)

Industrial production:
  growth rate NA%
Electricity:
  84,000 kW capacity; 176 million kWh produced, 3,180 kWh per capita (1991)
Industries:
  fish processing (mainly shrimp), potential for platinum and gold mining,
  handicrafts, shipyards
Agriculture:
  sector dominated by fishing and sheep raising; crops limited to forage and
  small garden vegetables; 1988 fish catch of 133,500 metric tons
Economic aid:
  none
Currency:
  Danish krone (plural - kroner); 1 Danish krone (DKr) = 100 re
Exchange rates:
  Danish kroner (DKr) per US$1 - 6.447 (March 1992), 6.396 (1991), 6.189
  (1990), 7.310 (1989), 6.732 (1988), 6.840 (1987)
Fiscal year: calendar year

:Greenland Communications

Highways:
  80 km
Ports:
  Kangerluarsoruseq (Faeringehavn), Paamiut (Frederikshaab), Nuuk (Godthaab),
  Sisimiut (Holsteinsborg), Julianehaab, Maarmorilik, North Star Bay
Merchant marine:
  1 refrigerated cargo (1,000 GRT or over) totaling 1,021 GRT/1,778 DWT; note
  - operates under the registry of Denmark
Civil air:
  2 major transport aircraft
Airports:
  11 total, 8 usable; 5 with permanent-surface runways; none with runways over
  3,659 m; 2 with runways 2,440-3,659 m; 2 with runways 1,220-2,439 m
Telecommunications:
  adequate domestic and international service provided by cables and
  microwave; 17,900 telephones; broadcast stations - 5 AM, 7 (35 repeaters)
  FM, 4 (9 repeaters) TV; 2 coaxial submarine cables; 1 Atlantic Ocean
  INTELSAT earth station

:Greenland Defense Forces

Note: defensc is responsibility of Denmark

Grenada Geography

Total area: 340 km2
Land area: 340 km2
Comparative area: slightly less than twice the size of Washington, DC
Land boundaries:
  none
Coastline:
  121 km
Maritime claims:

Exclusive economic zone:
  200 nm
 Territorial sea:
  12 nm
Disputes:
  none
Climate:
  tropical; tempered by northeast trade winds
Terrain:
  volcanic in origin with central mountains
Natural resources:
  timber, tropical fruit, deepwater harbors
Land use:
  arable land 15%; permanent crops 26%; meadows and pastures 3%; forest and woodland 9%; other 47%
Environment:
  lies on edge of hurricane belt; hurricane season lasts from June to November
Note:
  islands of the Grenadines group are divided politically with Saint Vincent and the Grenadines

:Grenada People

Population: 83,556 (July 1992), growth rate - 0.3% (1992)
Birth rate: 34 births/1,000 population (1992)
Death rate: 7 deaths/1,000 population (1992)
Net migration rate: - 30 migrants/1,000 population (1992)
Infant mortality rate: 28 deaths/1,000 live births (1992)
Life expectancy at birth: 69 years male, 74 years female (1992)
Total fertility rate: 4.6 children born/woman (1992)
Nationality:
  noun - Grenadian(s); adjective - Grenadian
Ethnic divisions:
  mainly of black African descent
Religions:
  largely Roman Catholic; Anglican; other Protestant sects
Languages:
  English (official); some French patois
Literacy:
  98% (male 98%, female 98%) age 15 and over having ever attended school (1970)
Labor force:
  36,000; services 31%, agriculture 24%, construction 8%, manufacturing 5%, other 32% (1985)
Organized labor:
  20% of labor force

:Grenada Government

Long-form name:
  none
Type:
  parliamentary democracy

Capital: Saint George's
Administrative divisions:
  6 parishes and 1 dependency*; Carriacou and Little Martinique*, Saint
  Andrew, Saint David, Saint George, Saint John, Saint Mark, Saint Patrick
Independence:
  7 February 1974 (from UK)
Constitution:
  19 December 1973
Legal system:
  based on English common law
National holiday:
  Independence Day, 7 February (1974)
Executive branch:
  British monarch, governor general, prime minister, Ministers of Government
  (cabinet)
Legislative branch:
  bicameral Parliament consists of an upper house or Senate and a lower house
  or House of Representatives
Judicial branch:
  Supreme Court
Leaders:
 Chief of State:
  Queen ELIZABETH II (since 6 February 1952), represented by Governor General
  Sir Paul SCOON (since 30 September 1978)
 Head of Government:
  Prime Minister Nicholas BRATHWAITE (since 13 March 1990)
Political parties and leaders:
  National Democratic Congress (NDC), Nicholas BRATHWAITE; Grenada United
  Labor Party (GULP), Sir Eric GAIRY; The National Party (TNP), Ben JONES; New
  National Party (NNP), Keith MITCHELL; Maurice Bishop Patriotic Movement
  (MBPM), Terrence MARRYSHOW; New Jewel Movement (NJM), Bernard
COARD
Suffrage:
  universal at age 18
Elections:
 House of Representatives:
  last held on 13 March 1990 (next to be held by NA March 1996); results -
  percent of vote by party NA; seats - (15 total) NDC 8, GULP 3, TNP 2, NNP 2
Member of:
  ACP, C, CARICOM, CDB, ECLAC, FAO, G-77, IBRD, ICAO, ICFTU, IDA,
IFAD, IFC,
  ILO, IMF, INTERPOL, IOC, ITU, LAES, LORCS, NAM, OAS, OECS, OPANAL,
UN,
  UNCTAD, UNESCO, UNIDO, UPU, WCL, WHO, WTO
Diplomatic representation:
  Ambassador Denneth MODESTE; Chancery at 1701 New Hampshire Avenue NW,
  Washington, DC 20009; telephone (202) 265-2561; there is a Grenadian
  Consulate General in New York
 US:
  Charge d'Affaires Annette VELER; Embassy at Ross Point Inn, Saint George's

(mailing address is P. O. Box 54, Saint George's); telephone (809) 444-1173 through 1178

:Grenada Government

Flag:

a rectangle divided diagonally into yellow triangles (top and bottom) and green triangles (hoist side and outer side) with a red border around the flag; there are seven yellow five-pointed stars with three centered in the top red border, three centered in the bottom red border, and one on a red disk superimposed at the center of the flag; there is also a symbolic nutmeg pod on the hoist-side triangle (Grenada is the world's second-largest producer of nutmeg, after Indonesia); the seven stars represent the seven administrative divisions

:Grenada Economy

Overview:

The economy is essentially agricultural and centers on the traditional production of spices and tropical plants. Agriculture accounts for about 16% of GDP and 80% of exports and employs 24% of the labor force. Tourism is the leading foreign exchange earner, followed by agricultural exports. Manufacturing remains relatively undeveloped, but is expected to grow, given a more favorable private investment climate since 1983. Despite an impressive average annual growth rate for the economy of 5.5% during the period 1986-91, unemployment remains high at about 25%.

GDP:

purchasing power equivalent - $238 million, per capita $2,800 (1989); real growth rate 5.2% (1990 est.)

Inflation rate (consumer prices):

7.0% (1990)

Unemployment rate: 25% (1990 est.)

Budget:

revenues $54.9 million; expenditures $77.6 million, including capital expenditures of $16.6 million (1990 est.)

Exports:

$26.0 million (f.o.b., 1990 est.)

commodities:

nutmeg 36%, cocoa beans 9%, bananas 14%, mace 8%, textiles 5%

partners:

US 12%, UK, FRG, Netherlands, Trinidad and Tobago (1989)

Imports:

$105.0 million (f.o.b., 1989 est.)

commodities:

food 25%, manufactured goods 22%, machinery 20%, chemicals 10%, fuel 6% (1989)

partners:

US 29%, UK, Trinidad and Tobago, Japan, Canada (1989)

External debt: $90 million (1990 est.)

Industrial production:

growth rate 5.8% (1989 est.); accounts for 6% of GDP

Electricity:

12,500 kW capacity; 26 million kWh produced, 310 kWh per capita (1991)

Industries:

food and beverage, textile, light assembly operations, tourism, construction

Agriculture:

accounts for 16% of GDP and 80% of exports; bananas, cocoa, nutmeg, and mace account for two-thirds of total crop production; world's second-largest producer and fourth-largest exporter of nutmeg and mace; small-size farms predominate, growing a variety of citrus fruits, avocados, root crops, sugarcane, corn, and vegetables

Economic aid:

US commitments, including Ex-Im (FY84-89), $60 million; Western (non-US) countries, ODA and OOF bilateral commitments (1970-89), $70 million; Communist countries (1970-89), $32 million

Currency:

East Caribbean dollar (plural - dollars); 1 EC dollar (EC$) = 100 cents

Exchange rates:

East Caribbean dollars (EC$) per US$1 - 2.70 (fixed rate since 1976)

Fiscal year: calendar year

:Grenada Communications

Highways:

1,000 km total; 600 km paved, 300 km otherwise improved; 100 km unimproved

Ports:

Saint George's

Civil air:

no major transport aircraft

Airports:

3 total, 3 usable; 2 with permanent-surface runways; none with runways over 3,659 m; 1 with runways 2,440-3,659 m; 1 with runways 1,220-2,439 m

Telecommunications:

automatic, islandwide telephone system with 5,650 telephones; new SHF radio links to Trinidad and Tobago and Saint Vincent; VHF and UHF radio links to Trinidad and Carriacou; broadcast stations - 1 AM, no FM, 1 TV

:Grenada Defense Forces

Branches:

Royal Grenada Police Force, Coast Guard

Manpower availability:

NA

Defense expenditures:

$NA, NA% of GDP

Guadeloupe Geography

Total area: 1,780 km2
Land area: 1,760 km2
Comparative area: 10 times the size of Washington, DC
Land boundaries:

Coastline:

306 km

Maritime claims:

Continental shelf:

200 m (depth) or to depth of exploitation
Exclusive economic zone:
  200 nm
 Territorial sea:
  12 nm
Disputes:
  none
Climate:
  subtropical tempered by trade winds; relatively high humidity
Terrain:
  Basse-Terre is volcanic in origin with interior mountains; Grand-Terre is
  low limestone formation
Natural resources:
  cultivable land, beaches, and climate that foster tourism
Land use:
  arable land 18%; permanent crops 5%; meadows and pastures 13%; forest and
  woodland 40%; other 24%; includes irrigated 1%
Environment:
  subject to hurricanes (June to October); La Soufriere is an active volcano
Note:
  located 500 km southeast of Puerto Rico in the Caribbean Sea

:Guadeloupe People

Population: 409,132 (July 1992), growth rate 2.1% (1992)
Birth rate: 19 births/1,000 population (1992)
Death rate: 6 deaths/1,000 population (1992)
Net migration rate: 8 migrants/1,000 population (1992)
Infant mortality rate: 10 deaths/1,000 live births (1992)
Life expectancy at birth: 74 years male, 80 years female (1992)
Total fertility rate: 2.0 children born/woman (1992)
Nationality:
  noun - Guadeloupian(s); adjective - Guadeloupe
Ethnic divisions:
  black or mulatto 90%; white 5%; East Indian, Lebanese, Chinese less than 5%
Religions:
  Roman Catholic 95%, Hindu and pagan African 5%
Languages:
  French, creole patois
Literacy:
  90% (male 90%, female 91%) age 15 and over can read and write (1982)
Labor force:
  120,000; 53.0% services, government, and commerce, 25.8% industry, 21.2%
  agriculture
Organized labor:
  11% of labor force

:Guadeloupe Government

Long-form name:
  Department of Guadeloupe
Type:
  overseas department of France

Capital: Basse-Terre

Administrative divisions:
  none (overseas department of France)

Independence:
  none (overseas department of France)

Constitution:
  28 September 1958 (French Constitution)

Legal system:
  French legal system

National holiday:
  Taking of the Bastille, 14 July (1789)

Executive branch:
  government commissioner

Legislative branch:
  unicameral General Council and unicameral Regional Council

Judicial branch:
  Court of Appeal (Cour d'Appel) with jurisdiction over Guadeloupe, French Guiana, and Martinique

Leaders:
 Chief of State:
  President Francois MITTERRAND (since 21 May 1981)
 Head of Government:
  Commissioner of the Republic Jean-Paul PROUST (since November 1989)

Political parties and leaders:
  Rally for the Republic (RPR), Marlene CAPTANT; Communist Party of Guadeloupe (PCG), Christian Medard CELESTE; Socialist Party (PSG), Dominique LARIFLA; Popular Union for the Liberation of Guadeloupe (UPLG); Independent Republicans; Union for French Democracy (UDF); Union for a New Majority (UNM)

Suffrage:
  universal at age 18

Elections:
 French National Assembly:
  last held on 5 and 12 June 1988 (next to be held June 1994); Guadeloupe elects four representatives; results - percent of vote by party NA; seats - (4 total) PS 2 seats, RPR 1 seat, PCG 1 seat
 French Senate:
  last held on 5 and 12 June 1988 (next to be held June 1994); Guadeloupe elects two representatives; results - percent of vote by party NA; seats - (2 total) PCG 1, PS 1
 General Council:
  last held NA 1986 (next to be held by NA 1992); results - percent of vote by party NA; seats - (42 total) number of seats by party NA
 Regional Council:
  last held on 16 March 1992 (next to be held by 16 March 1998); results - RPR 33.1%, PSG 28.7%, PCG 23.8%, UDF 10.7%, other 3.7%; seats - (41 total) RPR 15, PSG 12, PCG 10, UDF 4

Communists:
  3,000 est.

Other political or pressure groups:

381

Popular Union for the Liberation of Guadeloupe (UPLG); Popular Movement for Independent Guadeloupe (MPGI); General Union of Guadeloupe Workers (UGTG); General Federation of Guadeloupe Workers (CGT-G); Christian Movement for the Liberation of Guadeloupe (KLPG)

:Guadeloupe Government

Member of:
  FZ, WCL
Diplomatic representation:
  as an overseas department of France, the interests of Guadeloupe are represented in the US by France
Flag:
  the flag of France is used

:Guadeloupe Economy

Overview:
  The economy depends on agriculture, tourism, light industry, and services. It is also dependent upon France for large subsidies and imports. Tourism is a key industry, with most tourists from the US. In addition, an increasingly large number of cruise ships visit the islands. The traditionally important sugarcane crop is slowly being replaced by other crops, such as bananas (which now supply about 50% of export earnings), eggplant, and flowers. Other vegetables and root crops are cultivated for local consumption, although Guadeloupe is still dependent on imported food, which comes mainly from France. Light industry consists mostly of sugar and rum production. Most manufactured goods and fuel are imported. Unemployment is especially high among the young.
GDP:
  exchange rate conversion - $1.1 billion, per capita $3,300; real growth rate NA% (1987)
Inflation rate (consumer prices):
  2.3% (1988)
Unemployment rate: 38% (1987)
Budget:
  revenues $254 million; expenditures $254 million, including capital expenditures of NA (1989)
Exports:
  $153 million (f.o.b., 1988)
  commodities:
  bananas, sugar, rum
  partners:
  France 68%, Martinique 22% (1987)
Imports:
  $1.2 billion (c.i.f., 1988)
  commodities:
  vehicles, foodstuffs, clothing and other consumer goods, construction materials, petroleum products
  partners:
  France 64%, Italy, FRG, US (1987)
External debt: $NA
Industrial production:

growth rate NA%

Electricity:

171,500 kW capacity; 441 million kWh produced, 1,279 kWh per capita (1991)

Industries:

construction, cement, rum, sugar, tourism

Agriculture:

cash crops - bananas and sugarcane; other products include tropical fruits and vegetables; livestock - cattle, pigs, and goats; not self-sufficient in food

Economic aid:

US commitments, including Ex-Im (FY70-88), $4 million; Western (non-US) countries, ODA and OOF bilateral commitments (1970-89), $8.235 billion

Currency:

French franc (plural - francs); 1 French franc (F) = 100 centimes

Exchange rates:

French francs (F) per US$1 - 5.6397 (March 1992), 5.6421 (1991), 5.4453 (1990), 6.3801 (1989), 5.9569 (1988), 6.0107 (1987)

Fiscal year: calendar year

:Guadeloupe Communications

Railroads:

privately owned, narrow-gauge plantation lines

Highways:

1,940 km total; 1,600 km paved, 340 km gravel and earth

Ports:

Pointe-a-Pitre, Basse-Terre

Civil air:

2 major transport aircraft

Airports:

9 total, 9 usable, 8 with permanent-surface runways; none with runways over 3,659 m; 1 with runways 2,440-3,659 m; 1 with runways 1,220-2,439 m

Telecommunications:

domestic facilities inadequate; 57,300 telephones; interisland radio relay to Antigua and Barbuda, Dominica, and Martinique; broadcast stations - 2 AM, 8 FM (30 private stations licensed to broadcast FM), 9 TV; 1 Atlantic Ocean INTELSAT ground station

:Guadeloupe Defense Forces

Branches:

French Forces, Gendarmerie

Manpower availability:

males 15-49, 98,069; NA fit for military service

Note:

defense is responsibility of France

Guam Geography

Total area: 541.3 km2

Land area: 541.3 km2

Comparative area: slightly more than three times the size of Washington, DC

Land boundaries:

Coastline:
   125.5 km
Maritime claims:
  Contiguous zone:
   12 nm
  Continental shelf:
   200 m (depth)
  Exclusive economic zone:
   200 nm
  Territorial sea:
   12 nm
Disputes:
   none
Climate:
   tropical marine; generally warm and humid, moderated by northeast trade
   winds; dry season from January to June, rainy season from July to December;
   little seasonal temperature variation
Terrain:
   volcanic origin, surrounded by coral reefs; relatively flat coraline
   limestone plateau (source of most fresh water) with steep coastal cliffs and
   narrow coastal plains in north, low-rising hills in center, mountains in
   south
Natural resources:
   fishing (largely undeveloped), tourism (especially from Japan)
Land use:
   arable land 11%; permanent crops 11%; meadows and pastures 15%; forest and
   woodland 18%; other 45%
Environment:
   frequent squalls during rainy season; subject to relatively rare, but
   potentially very destructive typhoons (especially in August)
Note:
   largest and southernmost island in the Mariana Islands archipelago;
   strategic location in western North Pacific Ocean 5,955 km west-southwest of
   Honolulu about three-quarters of the way between Hawaii and the Philippines

:Guam People

Population: 142,271 (July 1992), growth rate 2.6% (1992)
Birth rate: 27 births/1,000 population (1992)
Death rate: 4 deaths/1,000 population (1992)
Net migration rate: 3 migrants/1,000 population (1992)
Infant mortality rate: 15 deaths/1,000 live births (1992)
Life expectancy at birth: 72 years male, 76 years female (1992)
Total fertility rate: 2.5 children born/woman (1992)
Nationality:
   noun - Guamanian(s); adjective - Guamanian; note - Guamanians are US
   citizens
Ethnic divisions:
   Chamorro 47%, Filipino 25%, Caucasian 10%, Chinese, Japanese, Korean, and
   other 18%
Religions:

Roman Catholic 98%, other 2%

Languages:

English and Chamorro, most residents bilingual; Japanese also widely spoken

Literacy:

96% (male 96%, female 96%) age 15 and over can read and write (1980)

Labor force:

46,930; federal and territorial government 40%, private 60% (trade 18%, services 15.6%, construction 13.8%, other 12.6%) (1990)

Organized labor:

13% of labor force

:Guam Government

Long-form name:

Territory of Guam

Type:

organized, unincorporated territory of the US; policy relations between Guam and the US are under the jurisdiction of the Office of Territorial and International Affairs, US Department of the Interior

Capital: Agana

Administrative divisions:

none (territory of the US)

Independence:

none (territory of the US)

Constitution:

Organic Act of 1 August 1950

Legal system:

NA

National holiday:

Guam Discovery Day (first Monday in March), Liberation Day (July 21), US Government holidays

Executive branch:

President of the US, governor, lieutenant governor, Cabinet

Legislative branch:

unicameral Legislature

Judicial branch:

Federal District Court of Guam, Territorial Superior Court of Guam

Leaders:

Chief of State:

President George BUSH (since 20 January 1989)

Head of Government:

Governor Joseph A. ADA (since November 1986); Lieutenant Governor Frank F. BLAS

Political parties and leaders:

Democratic Party (controls the legislature); Republican Party (party of the Governor)

Suffrage:

universal at age 18; US citizens, but do not vote in US presidential elections

Elections:

Governor:

last held on 6 November 1990 (next to be held November 1994); results -
Joseph F. ADA reelected

Legislature:

last held on 6 November 1990 (next to be held November 1992); a byelection
was held in April 1991 to replace a deceased legislator, results - percent
of vote by party NA; seats - (21 total) Democratic 11, Republican 10

US House of Representatives:

last held 6 November 1990 (next to be held 3 November 1992); Guam elects one
nonvoting delegate; results - Ben BLAZ was elected as the nonacting
delegate; seats - (1 total) Republican 1

Member of:

ESCAP (associate), IOC, SPC

Diplomatic representation:

none (territory of the US)

Flag:

territorial flag is dark blue with a narrow red border on all four sides;
centered is a red-bordered, pointed, vertical ellipse containing a beach
scene, outrigger canoe with sail, and a palm tree with the word GUAM
superimposed in bold red letters; US flag is the national flag

:Guam Economy

Overview:

The economy is based on US military spending and on revenues from tourism.
Over the past 20 years the tourist industry has grown rapidly, creating a
construction boom for new hotels and the expansion of older ones. Visitors
numbered about 900,000 in 1990. The small manufacturing sector includes
textiles and clothing, beverage, food, and watch production. About 60% of
the labor force works for the private sector and the rest for government.
Most food and industrial goods are imported, with about 75% from the US. In
1991 the unemployment rate was about 4.1%.

GNP:

purchasing power equivalent - $2.0 billion, per capita $14,000; real growth
rate NA% (1991 est.)

Inflation rate (consumer prices):

12.6% (1991)

Unemployment rate: 4.1% (1991 est.)

Budget:

revenues $525 million; expenditures $395 million, including capital
expenditures of $NA.

Exports:

$34 million (f.o.b., 1984)

commodities:

mostly transshipments of refined petroleum products, construction materials,
fish, food and beverage products

partners:

US 25%, Trust Territory of the Pacific Islands 63%, other 12%

Imports:

$493 million (c.i.f., 1984)

commodities:

petroleum and petroleum products, food, manufactured goods

partners:
US 23%, Japan 19%, other 58%
External debt: $NA
Industrial production:
growth rate NA%
Electricity:
500,000 kW capacity; 2,300 million kWh produced, 16,300 kWh per capita
(1990)
Industries:
US military, tourism, construction, transshipment services, concrete
products, printing and publishing, food processing, textiles
Agriculture:
relatively undeveloped with most food imported; fruits, vegetables, eggs,
pork, poultry, beef, copra
Economic aid:
although Guam receives no foreign aid, it does receive large transfer
payments from the general revenues of the US Federal Treasury into which
Guamanians pay no income or excise taxes; under the provisions of a special
law of Congress, the Guamanian Treasury, rather than the US Treasury,
receives federal income taxes paid by military and civilian Federal
employees stationed in Guam
Currency:
US currency is used
Exchange rates:
US currency is used
Fiscal year: 1 October - 30 September

:Guam Communications

Highways:
674 km all-weather roads
Ports:
Apra Harbor
Airports:
5 total, 4 usable; 3 with permanent-surface runways; none with runways over
3,659 m; 3 with runways 2,440-3,659 m; none with runways 1,220-2,439 m
Telecommunications:
26,317 telephones (1989); broadcast stations - 3 AM, 3 FM, 3 TV; 2 Pacific
Ocean INTELSAT ground stations

:Guam Defense Forces

Note: defense is the responsibility of the US

Guatemala Geography

Total area: 108,890 km2
Land area: 108,430 km2
Comparative area: slightly smaller than Tennessee
Land boundaries:
1,687 km; Belize 266 km, El Salvador 203 km, Honduras 256 km, Mexico 962 km
Coastline:
400 km
Maritime claims:

Continental shelf:
  not specific
Exclusive economic zone:
  200 nm
Territorial sea:
  12 nm
Disputes:
  claims Belize, but boundary negotiations to resolve the dispute have begun
Climate:
  tropical; hot, humid in lowlands; cooler in highlands
Terrain:
  mostly mountains with narrow coastal plains and rolling limestone plateau
  (Peten)
Natural resources:
  crude oil, nickel, rare woods, fish, chicle
Land use:
  arable land 12%; permanent crops 4%; meadows and pastures 12%; forest and
  woodland 40%; other 32%; includes irrigated 1%
Environment:
  numerous volcanoes in mountains, with frequent violent earthquakes;
  Caribbean coast subject to hurricanes and other tropical storms;
  deforestation; soil erosion; water pollution
Note:
  no natural harbors on west coast

:Guatemala People

Population: 9,784,275 (July 1992), growth rate 2.4% (1992)
Birth rate: 34 births/1,000 population (1992)
Death rate: 8 deaths/1,000 population (1992)
Net migration rate: -2 migrants/1,000 population (1992)
Infant mortality rate: 56 deaths/1,000 live births (1992)
Life expectancy at birth: 61 years male, 66 years female (1992)
Total fertility rate: 4.6 children born/woman (1992)
Nationality:
  noun - Guatemalan(s); adjective - Guatemalan
Ethnic divisions:
  Ladino (mestizo - mixed Indian and European ancestry) 56%, Indian 44%
Religions:
  predominantly Roman Catholic; also Protestant, traditional Mayan
Languages:
  Spanish, but over 40% of the population speaks an Indian language as a
  primary tongue (18 Indian dialects, including Quiche, Cakchiquel, Kekchi)
Literacy:
  55% (male 63%, female 47%) age 15 and over can read and write (1990 est.)
Labor force:
  2,500,000; agriculture 60%, services 13%, manufacturing 12%, commerce 7%,
  construction 4%, transport 3%, utilities 0.8%, mining 0.4% (1985)
Organized labor:
  8% of labor force (1988 est.)

:Guatemala Government

388

Long-form name:
Republic of Guatemala
Type:
republic
Capital: Guatemala
Administrative divisions:
22 departments (departamentos, singular - departamento); Alta Verapaz, Baja
Verapaz, Chimaltenango, Chiquimula, El Progreso, Escuintla, Guatemala,
Huehuetenango, Izabal, Jalapa, Jutiapa, Peten, Quetzaltenango, Quiche,
Retalhuleu, Sacatepequez, San Marcos, Santa Rosa, Solola, Suchitepequez,
Totonicapan, Zacapa
Independence:
15 September 1821 (from Spain)
Constitution:
31 May 1985, effective 14 January 1986
Legal system:
civil law system; judicial review of legislative acts; has not accepted
compulsory ICJ jurisdiction
National holiday:
Independence Day, 15 September (1821)
Executive branch:
president, vice president, Council of Ministers (cabinet)
Legislative branch:
unicameral Congress of the Republic (Congreso de la Republica)
Judicial branch:
Supreme Court of Justice (Corte Suprema de Justicia)
Leaders:
  Chief of State and Head of Government:
    President Jorge SERRANO Elias (since 14 January 1991); Vice President
    Gustavo ESPINA Salguero (since 14 January 1991)
Political parties and leaders:
National Centrist Union (UCN), Jorge CARPIO Nicolle; Solidarity Action
Movement (MAS), Jorge SERRANO Elias; Christian Democratic Party (DCG),
Alfonso CABRERA Hidalgo; National Advancement Party (PAN), Alvaro ARZU
Irigoyen; National Liberation Movement (MLN), Mario SANDOVAL Alarcon; So-
cial
Democratic Party (PSD), Mario SOLARZANO Martinez; Popular Alliance 5 (AP-5),
Max ORLANDO Molina; Revolutionary Party (PR), Carlos CHAVARRIA; National
Authentic Center (CAN), Hector MAYORA Dawe; Democratic Institutional Party
(PID), Oscar RIVAS; Nationalist United Front (FUN), Gabriel GIRON;
Guatemalan Republican Front (FRG), Efrain RIOS Montt
Suffrage:
universal at age 18
Elections:
  Congress:
    last held on 11 November 1990 (next to be held 11 November 1995); results -
    UCN 25.6%, MAS 24.3%, DCG 17. 5%, PAN 17.3%, MLN 4.8%, PSD/AP-5 3.6%,
PR
    2.1%; seats - (116 total) UCN 38, DCG 27, MAS 18, PAN 12, Pro - Rios Montt
    10, MLN 4, PR 1, PSD/AP-5 1, independent 5

President:
  runoff held on 11 January 1991 (next to be held 11 November 1995); results -
  Jorge SERRANO Elias (MAS) 68.1%, Jorge CARPIO Nicolle (UCN) 31.9%
Communists:
  Guatemalan Labor Party (PGT); main radical left guerrilla groups - Guerrilla
  Army of the Poor (EGP), Revolutionary Organization of the People in Arms
  (ORPA), Rebel Armed Forces (FAR), and PGT dissidents

:Guatemala Government

Other political or pressure groups:
  Federated Chambers of Commerce and Industry (CACIF), Mutual Support Group
  (GAM), Unity for Popular and Labor Action (UASP), Agrarian Owners Group
  (UNAGRO), Committee for Campesino Unity (CUC)
Member of:
  BCIE, CACM, CCC, ECLAC, FAO, G-24, G-77, GATT, IADB, IAEA, IBRD,
  ICAO,
  ICFTU, IDA, IFAD, IFC, ILO, IMF, IMO, INTELSAT, INTERPOL, IOC, IOM,
  ITU,
  LAES, LAIA, LORCS, OAS, OPANAL, PCA, UN, UNCTAD, UNESCO, UNIDO,
  UPU, WCL,
  WFTU, WHO, WIPO, WMO
Diplomatic representation:
  Ambassador Juan Jose CASO-FANJUL; Chancery at 2220 R Street NW, Washing-
ton,
  DC 20008; telephone (202) 745-4952 through 4954; there are Guatemalan
  Consulates General in Chicago, Houston, Los Angeles, Miami, New Orleans, New
  York, and San Francisco
  US:
  Ambassador Thomas F. STROOCK; Embassy at 7-01 Avenida de la Reforma, Zone
  10, Guatemala City (mailing address is APO AA 34024); telephone [502] (2)
  31-15-41
Flag:
  three equal vertical bands of light blue (hoist side), white, and light blue
  with the coat of arms centered in the white band; the coat of arms includes
  a green and red quetzal (the national bird) and a scroll bearing the
  inscription LIBERTAD 15 DE SEPTIEMBRE DE 1821 (the original date of
  independence from Spain) all superimposed on a pair of crossed rifles and a
  pair of crossed swords and framed by a wreath

:Guatemala Economy

Overview:
  The economy is based on family and corporate agriculture, which accounts for
  26% of GDP, employs about 60% of the labor force, and supplies two-thirds of
  exports. Manufacturing, predominantly in private hands, accounts for about
  18% of GDP and 12% of the labor force. In both 1990 and 1991, the economy
  grew by 3%, the fourth and fifth consecutive years of mild growth. Inflation
  at 40% in 1990-91 was more than double the 1987-89 level.
GDP:
  exchange rate conversion - $11.7 billion, per capita $1,260; real growth
  rate 3% (1991 est.)
Inflation rate (consumer prices):

40% (1991 est.)

Unemployment rate: 6.7%, with 30-40% underemployment (1989 est.)

Budget:

revenues $1.05 billion; expenditures $1.3 billion, including capital
expenditures of $270 million (1989 est.)

Exports:

$1.16 billion (f.o.b., 1990)

commodities:

coffee 26%, sugar 13%, bananas 7%, beef 2%

partners:

US 39%, El Salvador, Costa Rica, Germany, Honduras

Imports:

$1.66 billion (c.i.f., 1990)

commodities:

fuel and petroleum products, machinery, grain, fertilizers, motor vehicles

partners:

US 40%, Mexico, Venezuela, Japan, Germany

External debt: $2.6 billion (December 1990 est.)

Industrial production:

growth rate NA; accounts for 18% of GDP

Electricity:

802,600 kW capacity; 2,461 million kWh produced, 266 kWh per capita (1991)

Industries:

sugar, textiles and clothing, furniture, chemicals, petroleum, metals,
rubber, tourism

Agriculture:

accounts for 26% of GDP; most important sector of economy and contributes
two-thirds of export earnings; principal crops - sugarcane, corn, bananas,
coffee, beans, cardamom; livestock - cattle, sheep, pigs, chickens; food
importer

Illicit drugs:

illicit producer of opium poppy and cannabis for the international drug
trade; the government has an active eradication program for cannabis and
opium poppy; transit country for cocaine shipments

Economic aid:

US commitments, including Ex-Im (FY70-90), $1.1 billion; Western (non-US)
countries, ODA and OOF bilateral commitments (1970-89), $7.92 billion

Currency:

quetzal (plural - quetzales); 1 quetzal (Q) = 100 centavos

Exchange rates:

free market quetzales (Q) per US$1 - 5.0854 (January 1992), 5.0289 (1991),
2.8161 (1989), 2.6196 (1988), 2.500 (1987); note - black-market rate 2.800
(May 1989)

Fiscal year: calendar year

:Guatemala Communications

Railroads:

884 km 0.914-meter gauge, single track; 782 km government owned, 102 km
privately owned

Highways:

26,429 km total; 2,868 km paved, 11,421 km gravel, and 12,140 unimproved

Inland waterways:

260 km navigable year round; additional 730 km navigable during high-water season

Pipelines:

crude oil 275 km

Ports:

Puerto Barrios, Puerto Quetzal, Santo Tomas de Castilla

Merchant marine:

1 cargo ship (1,000 GRT or over) totaling 4,129 GRT/6,450 DWT

Civil air:

8 major transport aircraft

Airports:

448 total, 400 usable; 11 with permanent-surface runways; none with runways over 3,659 m; 3 with runways 2,440-3,659 m; 19 with runways 1,220-2,439 m

Telecommunications:

fairly modern network centered in Guatemala [city]; 97,670 telephones; broadcast stations - 91 AM, no FM, 25 TV, 15 shortwave; connection into Central American Microwave System; 1 Atlantic Ocean INTELSAT earth station

:Guatemala Defense Forces

Branches:

Army, Navy, Air Force

Manpower availability:

males 15-49, 2,169,073; 1,420,116 fit for military service; 107,239 reach military age (18) annually

Defense expenditures:

exchange rate conversion - $113 million, 1% of GDP (1990)

Guernsey Geography

Total area: 194 km2

Land area: 194 km2; includes Alderney, Guernsey, Herm, Sark, and some other smaller

islands

Comparative area: slightly larger than Washington, DC

Land boundaries:

Coastline:

50 km

Maritime claims:

 Exclusive fishing zone:

 200 nm

 Territorial sea:

 3 nm

Disputes:

Climate:

temperate with mild winters and cool summers; about 50% of days are overcast

Terrain:

mostly level with low hills in southwest

Natural resources:

cropland
Land use:
    arable land NA%; permanent crops NA%; meadows and pastures NA%; forest and woodland NA%; other NA%; cultivated about 50%
Environment:
    large, deepwater harbor at Saint Peter Port
Note:
    52 km west of France

:Guernsey People

Population: 57,949 (July 1992), growth rate 0.6% (1992)
Birth rate: 12 births/1,000 population (1992)
Death rate: 11 deaths/1,000 population (1992)
Net migration rate: 5 migrants/1,000 population (1992)
Infant mortality rate: 6 deaths/1,000 live births (1992)
Life expectancy at birth: 72 years male, 78 years female (1992)
Total fertility rate: 1.6 children born/woman (1992)
Nationality:
    noun - Channel Islander(s); adjective - Channel Islander
Ethnic divisions:
    UK and Norman-French descent
Religions:
    Anglican, Roman Catholic, Presbyterian, Baptist, Congregational, Methodist
Languages:
    English, French; Norman-French dialect spoken in country districts
Literacy:
    NA% (male NA%, female NA%) but compulsory education age 5 to 16
Labor force:
    NA
Organized labor:
    NA

:Guernsey Government

Long-form name:
    Bailiwick of Guernsey
Type:
    British crown dependency
Capital: Saint Peter Port
Administrative divisions:
    none (British crown dependency)
Independence:
    none (British crown dependency)
Constitution:
    unwritten; partly statutes, partly common law and practice
Legal system:
    English law and local statute; justice is administered by the Royal Court
National holiday:
    Liberation Day, 9 May (1945)
Executive branch:
    British monarch, lieutenant governor, bailiff, deputy bailiff
Legislative branch:

unicameral Assembly of the States
Judicial branch:
  Royal Court
Leaders:
 Chief of State:
  Queen ELIZABETH II (since 6 February 1952)
 Head of Government:
  Lieutenant Governor Lt. Gen. Sir Michael WILKINS (since NA 1990); Bailiff
  Mr. Graham Martyn DOREY (since February 1992)
Political parties and leaders:
  none; all independents
Suffrage:
  universal at age 18
Elections:
 Assembly of the States:
  last held NA (next to be held NA); results - no percent of vote by party
  since all are independents; seats - (60 total, 33 elected), all independents
Member of:
  none
Diplomatic representation:
  none (British crown dependency)
Flag:
  white with the red cross of Saint George (patron saint of England) extending
  to the edges of the flag

:Guernsey Economy

Overview:
  Tourism is a major source of revenue. Other economic activity includes
  financial services, breeding the world-famous Guernsey cattle, and growing
  tomatoes and flowers for export.
GDP:
  $NA, per capita $NA; real growth rate 9% (1987)
Inflation rate (consumer prices):
  7% (1988)
Unemployment rate: NA%
Budget:
  revenues $208.9 million; expenditures $173.9 million, including capital
  expenditures of NA (1988)
Exports:
 $NA
 commodities:
  tomatoes, flowers and ferns, sweet peppers, eggplant, other vegetables
 partners:
  UK (regarded as internal trade)
Imports:
 $NA
 commodities:
  coal, gasoline, and oil
 partners:
  UK (regarded as internal trade)

External debt: $NA
Industrial production:
  growth rate NA%
Electricity:
  173,000 kW capacity; 525 million kWh produced, 9,340 kWh per capita (1989)
Industries:
  tourism, banking
Agriculture:
  tomatoes, flowers (mostly grown in greenhouses), sweet peppers, eggplant,
  other vegetables and fruit; Guernsey cattle
Economic aid:
  none
Currency:
  Guernsey pound (plural - pounds); 1 Guernsey (#G) pound = 100 pence
Exchange rates:
  Guernsey pounds (#G) per US$1 - 0.5799 (March 1992), 0.5652 (1991), 0.5603
  (1990), 0.6099 (1989), 0.5614 (1988), 0.6102 (1987); note - the Guernsey
  pound is at par with the British pound
Fiscal year: calendar year

:Guernsey Communications

Ports:
  Saint Peter Port, Saint Sampson
Telecommunications:
  broadcast stations - 1 AM, no FM, 1 TV; 41,900 telephones; 1 submarine cable

:Guernsey Defense Forces

Note: defense is the responsibility of the UK

Guinea Geography

Total area: 245,860 km2
Land area: 245,860 km2
Comparative area: slightly smaller than Oregon
Land boundaries:
  3,399 km; Guinea-Bissau 386 km, Ivory Coast 610 km, Liberia 563 km, Mali 858
  km, Senegal 330 km, Sierra Leone 652 km
Coastline:
  320 km
Maritime claims:
 Exclusive economic zone:
  200 nm
 Territorial sea:
  12 nm
Disputes:
  none
Climate:
  generally hot and humid; monsoonal-type rainy season (June to November) with
  southwesterly winds; dry season (December to May) with northeasterly
  harmattan winds
Terrain:
  generally flat coastal plain, hilly to mountainous interior

Natural resources:

bauxite, iron ore, diamonds, gold, uranium, hydropower, fish

Land use:

arable land 6%; permanent crops NEGL%; meadows and pastures 12%; forest and woodland 42%; other 40%; includes irrigated NEGL%

Environment:

hot, dry, dusty harmattan haze may reduce visibility during dry season; deforestation

:Guinea People

Population: 7,783,926 (July 1992), growth rate - 1.5% (1992)

Birth rate: 46 births/1,000 population (1992)

Death rate: 21 deaths/1,000 population (1992)

Net migration rate: -40 migrants/1,000 population (1992)

Infant mortality rate: 143 deaths/1,000 live births (1992)

Life expectancy at birth: 41 years male, 45 years female (1992)

Total fertility rate: 6.0 children born/woman (1992)

Nationality:

noun - Guinean(s); adjective - Guinean

Ethnic divisions:

Fulani 35%, Malinke 30%, Soussou 20%, small indigenous tribes 15%

Religions:

Muslim 85%, Christian 8%, indigenous beliefs 7%

Languages:

French (official); each tribe has its own language

Literacy:

24% (male 35%, female 13%) age 15 and over can read and write (1990 est.)

Labor force:

2,400,000 (1983); agriculture 82.0%, industry and commerce 11.0%, services 5.4%; 88,112 civil servants (1987); 52% of population of working age (1985)

Organized labor:

virtually 100% of wage earners loosely affiliated with the National Confederation of Guinean Workers

:Guinea Government

Long-form name:

Republic of Guinea

Type:

republic

Capital: Conakry

Administrative divisions:

33 administrative regions (regions administratives, singular - region administrative); Beyla, Boffa, Boke, Conakry, Coyah, Dabola, Dalaba, Dinguiraye, Faranah, Forecariah, Fria, Gaoual, Gueckedou, Kankan, Kerouane, Kindia, Kissidougou, Koubia, Koundara, Kouroussa, Labe, Lelouma, Lola, Macenta, Mali, Mamou, Mandiana, Nzerekore, Pita, Siguiri, Telimele, Tougue, Yomou

Independence:

2 October 1958 (from France; formerly French Guinea)

Constitution:

23 December 1990 (Loi Fundamentale)

Legal system:

based on French civil law system, customary law, and decree; legal codes currently being revised; has not accepted compulsory ICJ jurisdiction

National holiday:

Anniversary of the Second Republic, 3 April (1984)

Executive branch:

president, Transitional Committee for National Recovery (Comite Transitionale de Redressement National or CTRN) replaced the Military Committee for National Recovery (Comite Militaire de Redressement National or CMRN); Council of Ministers (cabinet)

Legislative branch:

People's National Assembly (Assemblee Nationale Populaire) was dissolved after the 3 April 1984 coup; note: framework for a new National Assembly established in December 1991 (will have 114 seats)

Judicial branch:

Court of Appeal (Cour d'Appel)

Leaders:

Chief of State and Head of Government:

Gen. Lansana CONTE (since 5 April 1984)

Political parties and leaders:

none; following the 3 April 1984 coup, all political activity was banned

Suffrage:

Elections:

Member of:

ACCT, ACP, AfDB, CEAO, ECA, ECOWAS, FAO, FZ, G-77, IBRD, ICAO, IDA, IDB,

IFAD, IFC, ILO, IMF, IMO, INTELSAT, INTERPOL, IOC, ISO (correspondent), ITU,

LORCS, NAM, OAU, OIC, UN, UNCTAD, UNESCO, UNIDO, UPU, WCL, WHO, WIPO, WMO,

WTO

Diplomatic representation:

Ambassador (vacant); Charge d'Affaires ad interim Ansoumane CAMARA; Chancery

at 2112 Leroy Place NW, Washington, DC 20008; telephone (202) 483-9420

US:

Ambassador Dane F. SMITH, Jr.; Embassy at 2nd Boulevard and 9th Avenue, Conakry (mailing address is B. P. 603, Conakry); telephone (224) 44-15-20 through 24

Flag:

three equal vertical bands of red (hoist side), yellow, and green; uses the popular pan-African colors of Ethiopia; similar to the flag of Rwanda, which has a large black letter R centered in the yellow band

:Guinea Economy

Overview:

Although possessing many natural resources and considerable potential for agricultural development, Guinea is one of the poorest countries in the world. The agricultural sector contributes about 40% to GDP and employs more than 80% of the work force, while industry accounts for 27% of GDP. Guinea possesses over 25% of the world's bauxite reserves; exports of bauxite and alumina accounted for about 70% of total exports in 1989.

GDP:
exchange rate conversion - $3.0 billion, per capita $410; real growth rate 4.3% (1990 est.)

Inflation rate (consumer prices):
19.6% (1990 est.)

Unemployment rate: NA%

Budget:
revenues $449 million; expenditures $708 million, including capital expenditures of $361 million (1990 est.)

Exports:
$788 million (f.o.b., 1990 est.)
commodities:
alumina, bauxite, diamonds, coffee, pineapples, bananas, palm kernels
partners:
US 33%, EC 33%, USSR and Eastern Europe 20%, Canada

Imports:
$692 million (c.i.f., 1990 est.)
commodities:
petroleum products, metals, machinery, transport equipment, foodstuffs, textiles, and other grain
partners:
US 16%, France, Brazil

External debt: $2.6 billion (1990 est.)

Industrial production:
growth rate NA%; accounts for 27% of GDP

Electricity:
113,000 kW capacity; 300 million kWh produced, 40 kWh per capita (1989)

Industries:
bauxite mining, alumina, gold, diamond mining, light manufacturing and agricultural processing industries

Agriculture:
accounts for 40% of GDP (includes fishing and forestry); mostly subsistence farming; principal products - rice, coffee, pineapples, palm kernels, cassava, bananas, sweet potatoes, timber; livestock - cattle, sheep and goats; not self-sufficient in food grains

Economic aid:
US commitments, including Ex-Im (FY70-89), $227 million; Western (non-US) countries, ODA and OOF bilateral commitments (1970-89), $1,465 million; OPEC bilateral aid (1979-89), $120 million; Communist countries (1970-89), $446 million

Currency:
Guinean franc (plural - francs); 1 Guinean franc (FG) = 100 centimes

Exchange rates:
Guinean francs (FG) per US$1 - 675 (1990), 618 (1989), 515 (1988), 440 (1987), 383 (1986)

Fiscal year: calendar year

:Guinea Communications

Railroads:
   1,045 km; 806 km 1.000-meter gauge, 239 km 1.435-meter standard gauge
Highways:
   30,100 km total; 1,145 km paved, 12,955 km gravel or laterite (of which
   barely 4,500 km are currently all-weather roads), 16,000 km unimproved earth
   (1987)
Inland waterways:
   1,295 km navigable by shallow-draft native craft
Ports:
   Conakry, Kamsar
Civil air:
   10 major transport aircraft
Airports:
   15 total, 15 usable; 4 with permanent-surface runways; none with runways
   over 3,659 m; 3 with runways 2,440-3,659 m; 10 with runways 1,220-2,439 m
Telecommunications:
   poor to fair system of open-wire lines, small radiocommunication stations,
   and new radio relay system; 15,000 telephones; broadcast stations - 3 AM 1
   FM, 1 TV; 65,000 TV sets; 200,000 radio receivers; 1 Atlantic Ocean INTELSAT
   earth station

:Guinea Defense Forces

Branches:
   Army, Navy (acts primarily as a coast guard), Air Force, Republican Guard,
   paramilitary National Gendarmerie, National Police Force
Manpower availability:
   males 15-49, 1,759,811; 888,968 fit for military service (1989)
Defense expenditures:
   exchange rate conversion - $29 million, 1.2% of GDP (1988)

Guinea-Bissau Geography

Total area: 36,120 km2
Land area: 28,000 km2
Comparative area: slightly less than three times the size of Connecticut
Land boundaries:
   724 km; Guinea 386, Senegal 338 km
Coastline:
   350 km
Maritime claims:
 Exclusive economic zone:
   200 nm
 Territorial sea:
   12 nm
Disputes:
   the International Court of Justice (ICJ) on 12 November 1991 rendered its
   decision on the Guinea-Bissau/Senegal maritime boundary in favor of Senegal
Climate:
   tropical; generally hot and humid; monsoon-type rainy season (June to
   November) with southwesterly winds; dry season (December to May) with

northeasterly harmattan winds

Terrain:
  mostly low coastal plain rising to savanna in east

Natural resources:
  unexploited deposits of petroleum, bauxite, phosphates; fish, timber

Land use:
  arable land 11%; permanent crops 1%; meadows and pastures 43%; forest and woodland 38%; other 7%

Environment:
  hot, dry, dusty harmattan haze may reduce visibility during dry season

:Guinea-Bissau People

Population: 1,047,137 (July 1992), growth rate 2.4% (1992)
Birth rate: 42 births/1,000 population (1992)
Death rate: 18 deaths/1,000 population (1992)
Net migration rate: 0 migrants/1,000 population (1992)
Infant mortality rate: 124 deaths/1,000 live births (1992)
Life expectancy at birth: 45 years male, 48 years female (1992)
Total fertility rate: 5.7 children born/woman (1992)

Nationality:
  noun - Guinea-Bissauan(s); adjective - Guinea-Bissauan

Ethnic divisions:
  African about 99% (Balanta 30%, Fula 20%, Manjaca 14%, Mandinga 13%, Papel 7%); European and mulatto less than 1%

Religions:
  indigenous beliefs 65%, Muslim 30%, Christian 5%

Languages:
  Portuguese (official); Criolo and numerous African languages

Literacy:
  36% (male 50%, female 24%) age 15 and over can read and write (1990 est.)

Labor force:
  403,000 (est.); agriculture 90%, industry, services, and commerce 5%, government 5%; population of working age 53% (1983)

Organized labor:
  only one trade union - the National Union of Workers of Guinea-Bissau (UNTG)

:Guinea-Bissau Government

Long-form name:
  Republic of Guinea-Bissau

Type:
  republic; highly centralized multiparty since mid-1991; the African Party for the Independence of Guinea-Bissau and Cape Verde (PAIGC) held an extraordinary party congress in December 1990 and established a two-year transition program during which the constitution will be revised, allowing for multiple political parties and a presidential election in 1993

Capital: Bissau

Administrative divisions:
  9 regions (regioes, singular - regiao); Bafata, Biombo, Bissau, Bolama, Cacheu, Gabu, Oio, Quinara, Tombali

Independence:
  10 September 1974 (from Portugal; formerly Portuguese Guinea)

Constitution:
  16 May 1984
Legal system:
  NA
National holiday:
  Independence Day, 10 September (1974)
Executive branch:
  president of the Council of State, vice presidents of the Council of State,
  Council of State, Council of Ministers (cabinet)
Legislative branch:
  unicameral National People's Assembly (Assembleia Nacional Popular)
Judicial branch:
  none; there is a Ministry of Justice in the Council of Ministers
Leaders:
 Chief of State and Head of Government:
  President of the Council of State Brig. Gen. Joao Bernardo VIEIRA (assumed
  power 14 November 1980 and elected President of Council of State on 16 May
  1984)
Political parties and leaders:
  3 parties - African Party for the Independence of Guinea-Bissau and Cape
  Verde (PAIGC), President Joao Bernardo VIEIRA, leader; PAIGC is still the
  major party and controls all aspects of the Government, but 2 opposition
  parties registered in late 1991; Democratic Social Front (FDS), Rafael
  BARBOSA, leader; Bafata Movement, Domingos Fernandes GARNER, leader;
  Democratic Front, Aristides MENEZES, leader; other parties forming
Suffrage:
  universal at age 15
Elections:
 National People's Assembly:
  last held 15 June 1989 (next to be held 15 June 1994); results - PAIGC is
  the only party; seats - (150 total) PAIGC 150, appointed by Regional
  Councils
 President of Council of State:
  last held 19 June 1989 (next to be held NA 1993); results - Brig. Gen. Joao
  Bernardo VIEIRA was reelected without opposition by the National People's
  Assembly
Member of:
  ACCT (associate), ACP, AfDB, ECA, ECOWAS, FAO, G-77, IBRD, ICAO, IDA,
IDB,
  IFAD, IFC, ILO, IMF, IMO, IOM (observer), ITU, LORCS, NAM, OAU, OIC, UN,
  UNCTAD, UNESCO, UNIDO, UPU, WFTU, WHO, WIPO, WMO
Diplomatic representation:
  Ambassador Alfredo Lopes CABRAL; Chancery at 918 16th Street NW, Mezzanine
  Suite, Washington, DC 20006; telephone (202) 872-4222,

:Guinea-Bissau Government

 US:
  Ambassador William L. JACOBSEN, Jr.; Embassy at 17 Avenida Domingos Ramos,
  Bissau (mailing address is 1067 Bissau Codex, Bissau, Guinea-Bissau);
  telephone [245] 20-1139, 20-1145, 20-1113

Flag:
   two equal horizontal bands of yellow (top) and green with a vertical red
   band on the hoist side; there is a black five-pointed star centered in the
   red band; uses the popular pan-African colors of Ethiopia; similar to the
   flag of Cape Verde, which has the black star raised above the center of the
   red band and is framed by two corn stalks and a yellow clam shell

:Guinea-Bissau Economy

Overview:
   Guinea-Bissau ranks among the poorest countries in the world, with a per
   capita GDP below $200. Agriculture and fishing are the main economic
   activities. Cashew nuts, peanuts, and palm kernels are the primary exports.
   Exploitation of known mineral deposits is unlikely at present because of a
   weak infrastructure and the high cost of development. The government's
   four-year plan (1988-91) has targeted agricultural development as the top
   priority.

GDP:
   exchange rate conversion - $162 million, per capita $160; real growth rate
   5.0% (1989)

Inflation rate (consumer prices):
   25% (1990 est.)

Unemployment rate: NA%

Budget:
   revenues $22.7 million; expenditures $30.8 million, including capital
   expenditures of $18.0 million (1989 est.)

Exports:
   $14.2 million (f.o.b., 1989 est.)
   commodities:
   cashews, fish, peanuts, palm kernels
   partners:
   Portugal, Senegal, France, The Gambia, Netherlands, Spain

Imports:
   $68.9 million (f.o.b., 1989 est.)
   commodities:
   capital equipment, consumer goods, semiprocessed goods, foods, petroleum
   partners:
   Portugal, Netherlands, Senegal, USSR, Germany

External debt: $462 million (December 1990 est.)

Industrial production:
   growth rate - 1.0% (1989 est.); accounts for 10% of GDP (1989 est.)

Electricity:
   22,000 kW capacity; 30 million kWh produced, 30 kWh per capita (1991)

Industries:
   agricultural processing, beer, soft drinks

Agriculture:
   accounts for over 50% of GDP, nearly 100% of exports, and 90% of employment;
   rice is the staple food; other crops include corn, beans, cassava, cashew
   nuts, peanuts, palm kernels, and cotton; not self-sufficient in food;
   fishing and forestry potential not fully exploited

Economic aid:

US commitments, including Ex-Im (FY70-89), $49 million; Western (non-US) countries, ODA and OOF bilateral commitments (1970-89), $615 million; OPEC bilateral aid (1979-89), $41 million; Communist countries (1970-89), $68 million

Currency:

Guinea-Bissauan peso (plural - pesos); 1 Guinea-Bissauan peso (PG) = 100 centavos

Exchange rates:

Guinea-Bissauan pesos (PG) per US$1 - 1987.2 (1989), 1363.6 (1988), 851.65 (1987), 238.98 (1986)

Fiscal year: calendar year

:Guinea-Bissau Communications

Highways:

3,218 km; 2,698 km bituminous, remainder earth

Inland waterways:

scattered stretches are important to coastal commerce

Ports:

Bissau

Civil air:

2 major transport aircraft

Airports:

34 total, 15 usable; 4 with permanent-surface runways; none with runways over 3,659 m; 1 with runways 2,440-3,659 m; 5 with runways 1,220-2,439 m

Telecommunications:

poor system of radio relay, open-wire lines, and radiocommunications; 3,000 telephones; broadcast stations - 2 AM, 3 FM, 1 TV

:Guinea-Bissau Defense Forces

Branches:

People's Revolutionary Armed Force (FARP; including Army, Navy, Air Force), paramilitary force

Manpower availability:

males 15-49, 228,856; 130,580 fit for military service

Defense expenditures:

exchange rate conversion - $9.3 million, 5-6% of GDP (1987)

Guyana Geography

Total area: 214,970 km2
Land area: 196,850 km2
Comparative area: slightly smaller than Idaho
Land boundaries:
2,462 km; Brazil 1,119 km, Suriname 600 km, Venezuela 743 km
Coastline:
459 km
Maritime claims:
Continental shelf:
outer edge of continental margin or 200 nm
Exclusive fishing zone:
200 nm
Territorial sea:

12 nm

Disputes:

all of the area west of the Essequibo River claimed by Venezuela; Suriname claims area between New (Upper Courantyne) and Courantyne/Kutari Rivers (all headwaters of the Courantyne)

Climate:

tropical; hot, humid, moderated by northeast trade winds; two rainy seasons (May to mid-August, mid-November to mid-January)

Terrain:

mostly rolling highlands; low coastal plain; savanna in south

Natural resources:

bauxite, gold, diamonds, hardwood timber, shrimp, fish

Land use:

arable land 3%; permanent crops NEGL%; meadows and pastures 6%; forest and woodland 83%; other 8%; includes irrigated 1%

Environment:

flash floods a constant threat during rainy seasons; water pollution

:Guyana People

Population: 739,431 (July 1992), growth rate - 0.6% (1992)

Birth rate: 21 births/1,000 population (1992)

Death rate: 7 deaths/1,000 population (1992)

Net migration rate: -20 migrants/1,000 population (1992)

Infant mortality rate: 50 deaths/1,000 live births (1992)

Life expectancy at birth: 61 years male, 68 years female (1992)

Total fertility rate: 2.4 children born/woman (1992)

Nationality:

noun - Guyanese (singular and plural); adjective - Guyanese

Ethnic divisions:

East Indian 51%, black and mixed 43%, Amerindian 4%, European and Chinese 2%

Religions:

Christian 57%, Hindu 33%, Muslim 9%, other 1%

Languages:

English, Amerindian dialects

Literacy:

95% (male 98%, female 96%) age 15 and over having ever attended school (1990 est.)

Labor force:

268,000; industry and commerce 44.5%, agriculture 33.8%, services 21.7%; public-sector employment amounts to 60-80% of the total labor force (1985)

Organized labor:

34% of labor force

:Guyana Government

Long-form name:

Co-operative Republic of Guyana

Type:

republic

Capital: Georgetown

Administrative divisions:

10 regions; Barima-Waini, Cuyuni-Mazaruni, Demerara-Mahaica, East

Berbice-Corentyne, Essequibo Islands-West Demerara, Mahaica-Berbice, Pomeroon-Supenaam, Potaro-Siparuni, Upper Demerara-Berbice, Upper Takutu-Upper Essequibo

Independence:
  26 May 1966 (from UK; formerly British Guiana)

Constitution:
  6 October 1980

Legal system:
  based on English common law with certain admixtures of Roman-Dutch law; has not accepted compulsory ICJ jurisdiction

National holiday:
  Republic Day, 23 February (1970)

Executive branch:
  executive president, first vice president, prime minister, first deputy prime minister, Cabinet

Legislative branch:
  unicameral National Assembly

Judicial branch:
  Supreme Court of Judicature

Leaders:
 Chief of State:
  Executive President Hugh Desmond HOYTE (since 6 August 1985); First Vice President Hamilton GREEN (since 6 August 1985)
 Head of Government:
  Prime Minister Hamilton GREEN (since NA August 1985)

Political parties and leaders:
  People's National Congress (PNC), Hugh Desmond HOYTE; People's Progressive Party (PPP), Cheddi JAGAN; Working People's Alliance (WPA), Eusi KWAYANA, Rupert ROOPNARINE; Democratic Labor Movement (DLM), Paul TENNASSEE; People's
  Democratic Movement (PDM), Llewellyn JOHN; National Democratic Front (NDF), Joseph BACCHUS; United Force (UF), Manzoor NADIR; United Republican Party (URP), Leslie RAMSAMMY; National Republican Party (NRP), Robert GANGADEEN;
  Guyanese Labor Party (GLP), Nanda GOPAUL

Suffrage:
  universal at age 18

Elections:
 Executive President:
  last held on 9 December 1985 (next to be held 1992); results - Hugh Desmond HOYTE was elected president since he was leader of the party with the most votes in the National Assembly elections
 National Assembly:
  last held on 9 December 1985 (next to be held mid-1992); results - PNC 78%, PPP 16%, UF 4%, WPA 2%; seats - (65 total, 53 elected) PNC 42, PPP 8, UF 2, WPA 1

Other political or pressure groups:
  Trades Union Congress (TUC); Guyana Council of Indian Organizations (GCIO); Civil Liberties Action Committee (CLAC); the latter two organizations are small and active but not well organized; Guyanese Action for Reform and

Democracy (GUARD) includes various labor groups, as well as several of the
smaller political parties

:Guyana Government

Member of:
  ACP, C, CARICOM, CCC, CDB, ECLAC, FAO, G-77, GATT, IADB, IBRD,
  ICAO, ICFTU,
  IDA, IFAD, IFC, ILO, IMF, IMO, INTERPOL, IOC, ITU, LAES, LORCS, NAM,
  OAS,
  UN, UNCTAD, UNESCO, UNIDO, UPU, WCL, WFTU, WHO, WMO
Diplomatic representation:
  Ambassador Dr. Cedric Hilburn GRANT; Chancery at 2490 Tracy Place NW,
  Washington, DC 20008; telephone (202) 265-6900; there is a Guyanese
  Consulate General in New York
  US:
  Ambassador George JONES; Embassy at 99-100 Young and Duke Streets,
  Georgetown; telephone [592] (2) 54900 through 54909
Flag:
  green with a red isosceles triangle (based on the hoist side) superimposed
  on a long yellow arrowhead; there is a narrow black border between the red
  and yellow, and a narrow white border between the yellow and the green

:Guyana Economy

Overview:
  Guyana is one of the world's poorest countries with a per capita income less
  than one-fifth the South American average. After growing on average at less
  than 1% a year in 1986-87, GDP dropped by 5% a year in 1988-90. The decline
  resulted from bad weather, labor trouble in the canefields, and flooding and
  equipment problems in the bauxite industry. Consumer prices rose about 100%
  in 1989 and 75% in 1990, and the current account deficit widened
  substantially as sugar and bauxite exports fell. Moreover, electric power is
  in short supply and constitutes a major barrier to future gains in national
  output. The government, in association with international financial
  agencies, seeks to reduce its payment arrears and to raise new funds. The
  government's stabilization program - aimed at establishing realistic
  exchange rates, reasonable price stability, and a resumption of growth -
  requires considerable public administrative abilities and continued patience
  by consumers during a long incubation period. In 1991, buoyed by a recovery
  in mining and agriculture, the economy posted 6% growth, according to
  official figures. A large volume of illegal and quasi- legal economic
  activity is not captured in estimates of the country's total output.
GDP:
  exchange rate conversion - $250 million, per capita $300; real growth rate
  6% (1991 est.)
Inflation rate (consumer prices):
  75% (1990)
Unemployment rate: 12-15% (1990 est.)
Budget:
  revenues $126 million; expenditures $250 million (1990 est.)
Exports:
  $189 million (f.o.b., 1990 est.)

commodities:

bauxite, sugar, gold, rice, shrimp, molasses, timber, rum

partners:

UK 31%, US 23%, CARICOM 7%, Canada 6% (1988)

Imports:

$246 million (c.i.f., 1991)

commodities:

manufactures, machinery, food, petroleum

partners:

US 33%, CARICOM 10%, UK 9%, Canada 2% (1989)

External debt: $2.0 billion, including arrears (1990)

Industrial production:

growth rate - 12.0% (1990 est.); accounts for about 11% of GDP

Electricity:

252,500 kW capacity; 647 million kWh produced, 863 kWh per capita (1991)

Industries:

bauxite mining, sugar, rice milling, timber, fishing (shrimp), textiles, gold mining

Agriculture:

most important sector, accounting for 24% of GDP and about half of exports; sugar and rice are key crops; development potential exists for fishing and forestry; not self-sufficient in food, especially wheat, vegetable oils, and animal products

Economic aid:

US commitments, including Ex-Im (FY70-89), $116 million; Western (non-US) countries, ODA and OOF bilateral commitments (1970-89), $325 million; Communist countries 1970-89, $242 million

Currency:

Guyanese dollar (plural - dollars); 1 Guyanese dollar (G$) = 100 cents

:Guyana Economy

Exchange rates:

Guyanese dollars (G$) per US$1 - 124.1 (March 1992) 111.8 (1991), 39.533 (1990), 27.159 (1989), 10.000 (1988), 9.756 (1987)

Fiscal year: calendar year

:Guyana Communications

Railroads:

187 km total, all single track 0.914-meter gauge

Highways:

7,665 km total; 550 km paved, 5,000 km gravel, 1,525 km earth, 590 km unimproved

Inland waterways:

6,000 km total of navigable waterways; Berbice, Demerara, and Essequibo Rivers are navigable by oceangoing vessels for 150 km, 100 km, and 80 km, respectively

Ports:

Georgetown

Civil air:

3 major transport aircraft

Airports:

54 total, 49 usable; 5 with permanent-surface runways; none with runways over 3,659 m; none with runways 2,440-3,659 m; 13 with runways 1,220-2,439 m

Telecommunications:

fair system with radio relay network; over 27,000 telephones; tropospheric scatter link to Trinidad; broadcast stations - 4 AM, 3 FM, no TV, 1 shortwave; 1 Atlantic Ocean INTELSAT earth station

:Guyana Defense Forces

Branches:

Guyana Defense Force (GDF; includes Coast Guard and Air Corps), Guyana Police Force (GPF), Guyana People's Militia (GPM), Guyana National Service (GNS)

Manpower availability:

males 15-49, 196,066; 149,045 fit for military service

Defense expenditures:

exchange rate conversion - $5.5 million, 6% of GDP (1989 est.)

Haiti Geography

Total area: 27,750 km2
Land area: 27,560 km2
Comparative area: slightly larger than Maryland
Land boundaries:

275 km; Dominican Republic 275 km

Coastline:

1,771 km

Maritime claims:

Contiguous zone:

24 nm

Continental shelf:

to depth of exploitation

Exclusive economic zone:

200 nm

Territorial sea:

12 nm

Disputes:

claims US-administered Navassa Island

Climate:

tropical; semiarid where mountains in east cut off trade winds

Terrain:

mostly rough and mountainous

Natural resources:

bauxite

Land use:

arable land 20%; permanent crops 13%; meadows and pastures 18%; forest and woodland 4%; other 45%; includes irrigated 3%

Environment:

lies in the middle of the hurricane belt and subject to severe storms from June to October; occasional flooding and earthquakes; deforestation; soil erosion

Note:

shares island of Hispaniola with Dominican Republic

:Haiti People

Population: 6,431,977 (July 1992), growth rate 2.3% (1992)
Birth rate: 42 births/1,000 population (1992)
Death rate: 15 deaths/1,000 population (1992)
Net migration rate: -5 migrants/1,000 population (1992)
Infant mortality rate: 104 deaths/1,000 live births (1992)
Life expectancy at birth: 53 years male, 55 years female (1992)
Total fertility rate: 6.2 children born/woman (1992)
Nationality:
   noun - Haitian(s); adjective - Haitian
Ethnic divisions:
   black 95%, mulatto and European 5%
Religions:
   Roman Catholic is the official religion; Roman Catholic 80% (of which an
   overwhelming majority also practice Voodoo), Protestant 16% (Baptist 10%,
   Pentecostal 4%, Adventist 1%, other 1%), none 1%, other 3% (1982)
Languages:
   French (official) spoken by only 10% of population; all speak Creole
Literacy:
   53% (male 59%, female 47%) age 15 and over can read and write (1990 est.)
Labor force:
   2,300,000; agriculture 66%, services 25%, industry 9%; shortage of skilled
   labor, unskilled labor abundant (1982)
Organized labor:
   NA

:Haiti Government

Long-form name:
   Republic of Haiti
Type:
   republic
Capital: Port-au-Prince
Administrative divisions:
   9 departments, (departements, singular - departement); Artibonite, Centre,
   Grand'Anse, Nord, Nord-Est, Nord-Ouest, Ouest, Sud, Sud-Est
Independence:
   1 January 1804 (from France)
Constitution:
   27 August 1983, suspended February 1986; draft constitution approved March
   1987, suspended June 1988, most articles reinstated March 1989; October
   1991, government claims to be observing the Constitution
Legal system:
   based on Roman civil law system; accepts compulsory ICJ jurisdiction
National holiday:
   Independence Day, 1 January (1804)
Executive branch:
   president, Council of Ministers (cabinet)
Legislative branch:
   bicameral National Assembly (Assemblee Nationale) consisting of an upper
   house or Senate and a lower house or Chamber of Deputies

Judicial branch:

Court of Appeal (Cour de Cassation)

Leaders:

Chief of State:

President Jean-Bertrand ARISTIDE (since 7 February 1991), ousted in a coup in September 1991, but still recognized by international community as Chief of State; President Joseph NERETTE installed by military on 7 October 1991

Head of Government:

de facto Prime Minister Marc BAZIN (since June 1992)

Political parties and leaders:

National Front for Change and Democracy (FNCD) led by Jean-Bertrand ARISTIDE, including Congress of Democratic Movements (CONACOM), Victor BENOIT; National Konbite Movement (MKN), Volvick Remy JOSEPH; National Alliance for Democracy and Progress (ANDP), a coalition - that broke up following elections - consisting of Movement for the Installation of Democracy in Haiti (MIDH), Marc BAZIN; National Progressive Revolutionary Party (PANPRA), Serge GILLES; and National Patriotic Movement of November 28 (MNP-28), Dejean BELIZAIRE; National Agricultural and Industrial Party (PAIN), Louis DEJOIE; Movement for National Reconstruction (MRN), Rene THEODORE; Haitian Christian Democratic Party (PDCH), Joseph DOUZE; As-

sembly

of Progressive National Democrats (RDNP), Leslie MANIGAT; National Party of Labor (PNT), Thomas DESULME; Mobilization for National Development (MDN), Hubert DE RONCERAY; Democratic Movement for the Liberation of Haiti (MODELH), Francois LATORTUE; Haitian Social Christian Party (PSCH), Gre-

goire

EUGENE; Movement for the Organization of the Country (MOP), Gesner

COMEAU

Suffrage:

universal at age 18

Elections:

Chamber of Deputies:

last held 16 December 1990, with runoff held 20 January 1991 (next to be held by December 1994); results - percent of vote NA; seats - (83 total) FNCD 27, ANDP 17, PDCH 7, PAIN 6, RDNP 6, MDN 5, PNT 3, MKN 2,

MODELH 2, MRN

1, independents 5, other 2

:Haiti Government

President:

last held 16 December 1990 (next election to be held by December 1995); results - Rev. Jean-Bertrand ARISTIDE 67.5%, Marc BAZIN 14.2%, Louis DEJOIE 4.9%

Elections:

Senate:

last held 16 December 1990, with runoff held 20 January 1991 (next to be held December 1992); results - percent of vote NA; seats - (27 total) FNCD 13, ANDP 6, PAIN 2, MRN 2, PDCH 1, RDNP 1, PNT 1, independent 1

Communists:

United Party of Haitian Communists (PUCH), Rene THEODORE (roughly 2,000 members)

Other political or pressure groups:

Democratic Unity Confederation (KID), Roman Catholic Church, Confederation of Haitian Workers (CTH), Federation of Workers Trade Unions (FOS), Autonomous Haitian Workers (CATH), National Popular Assembly (APN)

Member of:

ACCT, CARICOM (observer), CCC, ECLAC, FAO, G-77, GATT, IADB, IAEA, IBRD, ICAO, IDA, IFAD, IFC, ILO, IMF, IMO, INTELSAT, INTERPOL, IOC, ITU, LAES, LORCS, OAS, OPANAL, PCA, UN, UNCTAD, UNESCO, UNIDO, UPU, WCL, WFTU, WHO, WIPO, WMO, WTO

Diplomatic representation:

Ambassador Jean CASIMIR; Chancery at 2311 Massachusetts Avenue NW, Washington, DC 20008; telephone (202) 332-4090 through 4092; there are Haitian Consulates General in Boston, Chicago, Miami, New York, and San Juan (Puerto Rico)

US:

Ambassador Alvin P. ADAMS, Jr.; Embassy at Harry Truman Boulevard, Port-au-Prince (mailing address is P. O. Box 1761, Port-au-Prince), telephone [509] 22-0354 or 22-0368, 22-0200, 22-0612

Flag:

two equal horizontal bands of blue (top) and red with a centered white rectangle bearing the coat of arms, which contains a palm tree flanked by flags and two cannons above a scroll bearing the motto L'UNION FAIT LA FORCE (Union Makes Strength)

:Haiti Economy

Overview:

About 75% of the population live in abject poverty. Agriculture is mainly small-scale subsistence farming and employs nearly three-fourths of the work force. The majority of the population does not have ready access to safe drinking water, adequate medical care, or sufficient food. Few social assistance programs exist, and the lack of employment opportunities remains one of the most critical problems facing the economy, along with soil erosion and political instability. Trade sanctions applied by the Organization of American States in response to the September 1991 coup against President Aristide have further damaged the economy.

GDP:

exchange rate conversion - $2.7 billion, per capita $440; real growth rate - 3.0% (1990 est.)

Inflation rate (consumer prices):

20% (1990 est.)

Unemployment rate: 25-50% (1990 est.)

Budget:

revenues $300 million; expenditures $416 million, including capital expenditures of $145 million (1990 est.)

Exports:

$169 million (f.o.b., 1990 est.)

commodities:
  light manufactures 65%, coffee 19%, other agriculture 8%, other 8%
partners:
  US 84%, Italy 4%, France 3%, other industrial countries 6%, less developed
  countries 3% (1987)
Imports:
  $348 million (c.i.f., 1990 est.)
commodities:
  machines and manufactures 34%, food and beverages 22%, petroleum products
  14%, chemicals 10%, fats and oils 9%
partners:
  US 64%, Netherlands Antilles 5%, Japan 5%, France 4%, Canada 3%, Germany 3%
  (1987)
External debt: $838 million (December 1990)
Industrial production:
  growth rate 0.3% (FY88); accounts for 15% of GDP
Electricity:
  217,000 kW capacity; 468 million kWh produced, 74 kWh per capita (1991)
Industries:
  sugar refining, textiles, flour milling, cement manufacturing, tourism,
  light assembly industries based on imported parts
Agriculture:
  accounts for 28% of GDP and employs 74% of work force; mostly small-scale
  subsistence farms; commercial crops - coffee, mangoes, sugarcane and wood;
  staple crops - rice, corn, sorghum; shortage of wheat flour
Illicit drugs:
  transshipment point for cocaine
Economic aid:
  US commitments, including Ex-Im (1970-89), $700 million; Western (non-US)
  countries, ODA and OOF bilateral commitments (1970-89), $770 million
Currency:
  gourde (plural - gourdes); 1 gourde (G) = 100 centimes
Exchange rates:
  gourdes (G) per US$1 - 5.0 (fixed rate)
Fiscal year: 1 October - 30 September

:Haiti Communications

Railroads:
  40 km 0.760-meter narrow gauge, single-track, privately owned industrial
  line
Highways:
  4,000 km total; 950 km paved, 900 km otherwise improved, 2,150 km unimproved
Inland waterways:
  negligible; less than 100 km navigable
Ports:
  Port-au-Prince, Cap-Haitien
Civil air:
  12 major transport aircraft
Airports:
  13 total, 10 usable; 3 with permanent-surface runways; none with runways

over 3,659 m; 1 with runways 2,440-3,659 m; 3 with runways 1,220-2,439 m
Telecommunications:
domestic facilities barely adequate, international facilities slightly
better; 36,000 telephones; broadcast stations - 33 AM, no FM, 4 TV, 2
shortwave; 1 Atlantic Ocean INTELSAT earth station

:Haiti Defense Forces

Branches:
Army (including Police), Navy, Air Force
Manpower availability:
males 15-49, 1,313,044; 706,221 fit for military service; 59,060 reach
military age (18) annually
Defense expenditures:
exchange rate conversion - $34 million, 1.5% of GDP (1988 est.)

Heard Island and McDonald Islands Geography

Total area: 412 km2
Land area: 412 km2
Comparative area: slightly less than 2.5 times the size of Washington, DC
Land boundaries:
none
Coastline:
101.9 km
Maritime claims:
 Exclusive fishing zone:
200 nm
 Territorial sea:
3 nm
Disputes:
none
Climate:
antarctic
Terrain:
Heard Island - bleak and mountainous, with an extinct volcano; McDonald
Islands - small and rocky
Land use:
arable land 0%; permanent crops 0%; meadows and pastures 0%; forest and
woodland 0%; other 100%
Environment:
primarily used as research stations
Note:
located 4,100 km southwest of Australia in the southern Indian Ocean

:Heard Island and McDonald Islands People

Population: uninhabited

:Heard Island and McDonald Islands Government

Long-form name:
Territory of Heard Island and McDonald Islands
Type:
territory of Australia administered by the Antarctic Division of the

Department of Science in Canberra (Australia)
Capital: none; administered from Canberra, Australia

:Heard Island and McDonald Islands Economy

Overview: no economic activity

:Heard Island and McDonald Islands Communications

Ports: none; offshore anchorage only

:Heard Island and McDonald Islands Defense Forces

Note: defense is the responsibility of Australia

Holy See (Vatican City) Geography

Total area: 0.438 km2
Land area: 0.438 km2
Comparative area: about 0.7 times the size of The Mall in Washington, DC
Land boundaries:
  3.2 km; Italy 3.2 km
Coastline:
  none - landlocked
Maritime claims:
  none - landlocked
Disputes:
  none
Climate:
  temperate; mild, rainy winters (September to mid-May) with hot, dry summers
  (May to September)
Terrain:
  low hill
Natural resources:
  none
Land use:
  arable land 0%; permanent crops 0%; meadows and pastures 0%; forest and
  woodland 0%; other 100%
Environment:
  urban
Note:
  landlocked; enclave of Rome, Italy; world's smallest state; outside the
  Vatican City, 13 buildings in Rome and Castel Gandolfo (the pope's summer
  residence) enjoy extraterritorial rights

:Holy See (Vatican City) People

Population: 802 (July 1992), growth rate 1.2% (1992)
Nationality:
  no noun or adjectival forms
Ethnic divisions:
  primarily Italians but also Swiss and other nationalities
Religions:
  Roman Catholic
Languages:
  Italian, Latin, and various other languages
Literacy:

100% (male NA%, female NA%)
Labor force:
   high dignitaries, priests, nuns, guards, and 3,000 lay workers who live
   outside the Vatican
Organized labor:
   Association of Vatican Lay Workers, 1,800 members (1987)

:Holy See (Vatican City) Government

Long-form name:
   State of the Vatican City; note - the Vatican City is the physical seat of
   the Holy See, which is the central government of the Roman Catholic Church
Type:
   monarchical-sacerdotal state
Capital: Vatican City
Independence:
   11 February 1929 (from Italy)
Constitution:
   Apostolic Constitution of 1967 (effective 1 March 1968)
National holiday:
   Installation Day of the Pope (John Paul II), 22 October (1978); note - Pope
   John Paul II was elected on 16 October 1978
Executive branch:
   pope
Legislative branch:
   unicameral Pontifical Commission
Judicial branch:
   none; normally handled by Italy
Leaders:
  Chief of State:
   Pope JOHN PAUL II (Karol WOJTYA; since 16 October 1978)
  Head of Government:
   Secretary of State Archbishop Angelo SODANO
Political parties and leaders:
   none
Suffrage:
   limited to cardinals less than 80 years old
Elections:
  Pope:
   last held 16 October 1978 (next to be held after the death of the current
   pope); results - Karol WOJTYA was elected for life by the College of
   Cardinals
Other political or pressure groups:
   none (exclusive of influence exercised by church officers)
Member of:
   CSCE, IAEA, ICFTU, IMF (observer), INTELSAT, IOM (observer), ITU, OAS
   (observer), UN (observer), UNCTAD, UNHCR, UPU, WIPO, WTO (observer)
Diplomatic representation:
   Apostolic Pro-Nuncio Archbishop Agostino CACCIAVILLAN; 3339 Massachusetts
   Avenue NW, Washington, DC 20008; telephone (202) 333-7121
   US:

Ambassador Thomas P. MELADY; Embassy at Villino Pacelli, Via Aurelia 294, 00165 Rome (mailing address is APO AE 09624); telephone [396] 639-0558

Flag:
two vertical bands of yellow (hoist side) and white with the crossed keys of Saint Peter and the papal tiara centered in the white band

:Holy See (Vatican City) Economy

Overview:
This unique, noncommercial economy is supported financially by contributions (known as Peter's Pence) from Roman Catholics throughout the world, the sale of postage stamps and tourist mementos, fees for admission to museums, and the sale of publications. The incomes and living standards of lay workers are comparable to, or somewhat better than, those of counterparts who work in the city of Rome.

Budget:
revenues $92 million; expenditures $178 million, including capital expenditures of $NA (1992)

Electricity:
5,000 kW standby capacity (1990); power supplied by Italy

Industries:
printing and production of a small amount of mosaics and staff uniforms; worldwide banking and financial activities

Currency:
Vatican lira (plural - lire); 1 Vatican lira (VLit) = 100 centesimi

Exchange rates:
Vatican lire (VLit) per US$1 - 1,248.4 (March 1992), 1,240.6 (1991), 1,198.1 (1990), 1,372.1 (1989), 1,301.6 (1988), 1,296.1 (1987); note - the Vatican lira is at par with the Italian lira which circulates freely

Fiscal year: calendar year

:Holy See (Vatican City) Communications

Railroads:
850 m, 750 mm gauge (links with Italian network near the Rome station of Saint Peter's)

Highways:
none; all city streets

Telecommunications:
broadcast stations - 3 AM, 4 FM, no TV; 2,000-line automatic telephone exchange; no communications satellite systems

:Holy See (Vatican City) Defense Forces

Note:
defense is the responsibility of Italy; Swiss Papal Guards are posted at entrances to the Vatican City

Honduras Geography

Total area: 112,090 km2
Land area: 111,890 km2
Comparative area: slightly larger than Tennessee
Land boundaries:
1,520 km; Guatemala 256 km, El Salvador 342 km, Nicaragua 922 km
Coastline:

820 km
Maritime claims:
 Contiguous zone:
 24 nm
 Continental shelf:
 200 m (depth) or to depth of exploitation
 Exclusive economic zone:
 200 nm
 Territorial sea:
 12 nm
Disputes:
 dispute with El Salvador over several sections of the land boundary; dispute
 over Golfo de Fonseca maritime boundary because of disputed sovereignty of
 islands; unresolved maritime boundary with Nicaragua
Climate:
 subtropical in lowlands, temperate in mountains
Terrain:
 mostly mountains in interior, narrow coastal plains
Natural resources:
 timber, gold, silver, copper, lead, zinc, iron ore, antimony, coal, fish
Land use:
 arable land 14%; permanent crops 2%; meadows and pastures 30%; forest and
 woodland 34%; other 20%; includes irrigated 1%
Environment:
 subject to frequent, but generally mild, earthquakes; damaging hurricanes
 and floods along Caribbean coast; deforestation; soil erosion

:Honduras People

Population: 5,092,776 (July 1992), growth rate 2.8% (1992)
Birth rate: 37 births/1,000 population (1992)
Death rate: 7 deaths/1,000 population (1992)
Net migration rate: -2 migrants/1,000 population (1992)
Infant mortality rate: 54 deaths/1,000 live births (1992)
Life expectancy at birth: 65 years male, 68 years female (1992)
Total fertility rate: 4.8 children born/woman (1992)
Nationality:
 noun - Honduran(s); adjective - Honduran
Ethnic divisions:
 mestizo (mixed Indian and European) 90%, Indian 7%, black 2%, white 1%
Religions:
 Roman Catholic about 97%; small Protestant minority
Languages:
 Spanish, Indian dialects
Literacy:
 73% (male 76%, female 71%) age 15 and over can read and write (1990 cst.)
Labor force:
 1,300,000; agriculture 62%, services 20%, manufacturing 9%, construction 3%,
 other 6% (1985)
Organized labor:
 40% of urban labor force, 20% of rural work force (1985)

:Honduras Government

Long-form name:
Republic of Honduras
Type:
republic
Capital: Tegucigalpa
Administrative divisions:
18 departments (departamentos, singular - departamento); Atlantida,
Choluteca, Colon, Comayagua, Copan, Cortes, El Paraiso, Francisco Morazan,
Gracias a Dios, Intibuca, Islas de la Bahia, La Paz, Lempira, Ocotepeque,
Olancho, Santa Barbara, Valle, Yoro
Independence:
15 September 1821 (from Spain)
Constitution:
11 January 1982, effective 20 January 1982
Legal system:
rooted in Roman and Spanish civil law; some influence of English common law;
accepts ICJ jurisdiction, with reservations
National holiday:
Independence Day, 15 September (1821)
Executive branch:
president, Council of Ministers (cabinet)
Legislative branch:
unicameral National Congress (Congreso Nacional)
Judicial branch:
Supreme Court of Justice (Corte Suprema de Justica)
Leaders:
 Chief of State and Head of Government:
 President Rafael Leonardo CALLEJAS Romero (since 26 January 1990)
Political parties and leaders:
Liberal Party (PLH) - faction leaders, Carlos FLORES Facusse (leader of
Florista Liberal Movement), Carlos MONTOYA (Azconista subfaction), Ramon
VILLEDA Bermudez and Jorge Arturo REINA (M-Lider faction); National Party
(PNH), Jose Celin DISCUA, party president; PNH faction leaders - Oswaldo
RAMOS Soto and Rafael Leonardo CALLEJAS Romero (Monarca faction); Nation-
al
Innovation and Unity Party - Social Democrats (PINU-SD), Enrique AGUILAR
Cerrato Paz; Christian Democratic Party (PDCH), Jorge ILLESCAS; Democratic
Action (AD), Walter LOPEZ Reyes
Suffrage:
universal and compulsory at age 18
Elections:
 National Congress:
 last held on 26 November 1989 (next to be held November 1993); results - PNH
 51%, PLH 43%, PDCH 1.9%, PINU-SD 1.5%, other 2.6%; seats - (128 total) PNH
 71, PLH 55, PINU-SD 2
 President:
 last held on 26 November 1989 (next to be held November 1993); results -
 Rafael Leonardo CALLEJAS (PNH) 51%, Carlos FLORES Facusse (PLH) 43.3%,
other

418

5.7%

Other political or pressure groups:
National Association of Honduran Campesinos (ANACH), Honduran Council of Private Enterprise (COHEP), Confederation of Honduran Workers (CTH), National Union of Campesinos (UNC), General Workers Confederation (CGT), United Federation of Honduran Workers (FUTH), Committee for the Defense of Human Rights in Honduras (CODEH), Coordinating Committee of Popular Organizations (CCOP)

:Honduras Government

Member of:
BCIE, CACM, ECLAC, FAO, G-77, IADB, IBRD, ICAO, ICFTU, IDA, IFAD, IFC, ILO,
IMF, IMO, INTELSAT, INTERPOL, IOC, IOM, ITU, LAES, LAIA, LORCS, OAS, OPANAL,
PCA, UN, UNCTAD, UNESCO, UNIDO, UPU, WCL, WFTU, WHO, WIPO, WMO

Diplomatic representation:
Ambassador Jorge Ramon HERNANDEZ Alcerro; Chancery at 3007 Tilden Street NW,
Washington, DC 20008; telephone (202) 966-7702; there are Honduran Consulates General in Chicago, Los Angeles, Miami, New Orleans, New York, and San Francisco, and Consulates in Baton Rouge, Boston, Detroit, Houston, and Jacksonville

US:
Ambassador S. Crescencio ARCOS; Embassy at Avenida La Paz, Tegucigalpa (mailing address is APO AA 34022); telephone [504] 32-3120

Flag:
three equal horizontal bands of blue (top), white, and blue with five blue five-pointed stars arranged in an X pattern centered in the white band; the stars represent the members of the former Federal Republic of Central America - Costa Rica, El Salvador, Guatemala, Honduras, and Nicaragua; similar to the flag of El Salvador, which features a round emblem encircled by the words REPUBLICA DE EL SALVADOR EN LA AMERICA CENTRAL centered in the
white band; also similar to the flag of Nicaragua, which features a triangle encircled by the word REPUBLICA DE NICARAGUA on top and AMERICA CENTRAL on
the bottom, centered in the white band

:Honduras Economy

Overview:
Honduras is one of the poorest countries in the Western Hemisphere. Agriculture, the most important sector of the economy, accounts for more than 25% of GDP, employs 62% of the labor force, and produces two-thirds of exports. Productivity remains low. Industry, still in its early stages, employs nearly 9% of the labor force, accounts for 15% of GDP, and generates 20% of exports. The service sectors, including public administration, account for 50% of GDP and employ nearly 20% of the labor force. Basic problems facing the economy include rapid population growth, high unemployment, sharply increased inflation, a lack of basic services, a large

419

and inefficient public sector, and the dependence of the export sector mostly on coffee and bananas, which are subject to sharp price fluctuations. Despite government efforts at reform and large-scale foreign assistance, the economy still is unable to take advantage of its sizable natural resources.

GDP:
exchange rate conversion - $5.2 billion, per capita $1,050; real growth rate - 0.3% (1991 est.)

Inflation rate (consumer prices):
26% (1991 est.)

Unemployment rate: 15% unemployed, 30-40% underemployed (1989)

Budget:
revenues $1.4 billion; expenditures $1.9 billion, including capital expenditures of $511 million (1990 est.)

Exports:
$1.0 billion (f.o.b., 1991)
commodities:
bananas, coffee, shrimp, lobster, minerals, lumber
partners:
US 52%, Germany 11%, Japan, Italy, Belgium

Imports:
$1.3 billion (c.i.f. 1991)
commodities:
machinery and transport equipment, chemical products, manufactured goods, fuel and oil, foodstuffs
partners:
US 39%, Japan 9%, CACM, Venezuela, Mexico

External debt: $2.8 billion (1990)

Industrial production:
growth rate 2.9% (1989); accounts for 15% of GDP

Electricity:
575,000 kW capacity; 1,850 million kWh produced, 374 kWh per capita (1991)

Industries:
agricultural processing (sugar and coffee), textiles, clothing, wood products

Agriculture:
most important sector, accounting for more than 25% of GDP, over 60% of the labor force, and two-thirds of exports; principal products include bananas, coffee, timber, beef, citrus fruit, shrimp; importer of wheat

Illicit drugs:
illicit producer of cannabis, cultivated on small plots and used principally for local consumption; transshipment point for cocaine

Economic aid:
US commitments, including Ex-Im (FY70-89), $1.4 billion; Western (non-US) countries, ODA and OOF bilateral commitments (1970-89), $1.1 billion

Currency:
lempira (plural - lempiras); 1 lempira (L) = 100 centavos

:Honduras Economy

Exchange rates:
lempiras (L) per US$1 - 5.4 (fixed rate); 5.70 parallel black-market rate

(November 1990)

Fiscal year: calendar year

:Honduras Communications

Railroads:

785 km total; 508 km 1.067-meter gauge, 277 km 0.914-meter gauge

Highways:

8,950 km total; 1,700 km paved, 5,000 km otherwise improved, 2,250 km unimproved earth

Inland waterways:

465 km navigable by small craft

Ports:

Puerto Castilla, Puerto Cortes, San Lorenzo

Merchant marine:

201 ships (1,000 GRT or over) totaling 629,134 GRT/939,289 DWT; includes 2 passenger-cargo, 127 cargo, 17 refrigerated - cargo, - 7 - container, - 2 - roll-on/roll-off cargo, 19 petroleum tanker, 2 chemical tanker, 3 specialized tanker, 1 vehicle carrier, 18 bulk, 2 passenger, 1 short-sea passenger; note - a flag of convenience registry; Republics of the former USSR own 10 ships under the Honduran flag

Civil air:

6 major transport aircraft

Airports:

171 total, 133 usable; 8 with permanent-surface runways; none with runways over 3,659 m; 4 with runways 2,440-3,659 m; 12 with runways 1,220-2,439 m

Telecommunications:

improved, but still inadequate; connection into Central American Microwave System; 35,100 telephones; broadcast stations - 176 AM, no FM, 28 TV, 7 shortwave; 2 Atlantic Ocean INTELSAT earth stations

:Honduras Defense Forces

Branches:

Army, Navy (including Marines), Air Force, Public Security Forces (FUSEP)

Manpower availability:

males 15-49, 1,148,376; 684,375 fit for military service; 57,028 reach military age (18) annually

Defense expenditures:

exchange rate conversion - $43.4 million, about 1% of GDP (1992 est.)

Hong Kong Geography

Total area: 1,040 km2

Land area: 990 km2

Comparative area: slightly less than six times the size of Washington, DC

Land boundaries:

30 km; China 30 km

Coastline:

733 km

Maritime claims:

 Exclusive fishing zone:

 3 nm

 Territorial sea:

3 nm
Disputes:
  none
Climate:
  tropical monsoon; cool and humid in winter, hot and rainy from spring
  through summer, warm and sunny in fall
Terrain:
  hilly to mountainous with steep slopes; lowlands in north
Natural resources:
  outstanding deepwater harbor, feldspar
Land use:
  arable land 7%; permanent crops 1%; meadows and pastures 1%; forest and
  woodland 12%; other 79%; includes irrigated 3%
Environment:
  more than 200 islands; occasional typhoons

:Hong Kong People

Population: 5,889,095 (July 1992), growth rate 0.6% (1992)
Birth rate: 13 births/1,000 population (1992)
Death rate: 5 deaths/1,000 population (1992)
Net migration rate: - 2 migrants/1,000 population (1992)
Infant mortality rate: 7 deaths/1,000 live births (1992)
Life expectancy at birth: 76 years male, 83 years female (1992)
Total fertility rate: 1.4 children born/woman (1992)
Nationality:
  adjective - Hong Kong
Ethnic divisions:
  Chinese 98%, other 2%
Religions:
  eclectic mixture of local religions 90%, Christian 10%
Languages:
  Chinese (Cantonese), English
Literacy:
  77% (male 90%, female 64%) age 15 and over having ever attended school
  (1971)
Labor force:
  2,800,000 (1990); manufacturing 28.5%, wholesale and retail trade,
  restaurants, and hotels 27.9%, services 17.7%, financing, insurance, and
  real estate 9.2%, transport and communications 4.5%, construction 2.5%,
  other 9.7% (1989)
Organized labor:
  16% of labor force (1990)

:Hong Kong Government

Long-form name:
  none; abbreviated HK
Type:
  dependent territory of the UK; scheduled to revert to China in 1997
Capital: Victoria
Administrative divisions:
  none (dependent territory of the UK)

Independence:
  none (dependent territory of the UK); the UK signed an agreement with China
  on 19 December 1984 to return Hong Kong to China on 1 July 1997; in the
  joint declaration, China promises to respect Hong Kong's existing social and
  economic systems and lifestyle for 50 years after transition
Constitution:
  unwritten; partly statutes, partly common law and practice; new Basic Law
  approved in March 1990 in preparation for 1997
Legal system:
  based on English common law
National holiday:
  Liberation Day, 29 August (1945)
Executive branch:
  British monarch, governor, chief secretary of the Executive Council
Legislative branch:
  Legislative Council
Judicial branch:
  Supreme Court
Leaders:
 Chief of State:
  Queen ELIZABETH II (since 6 February 1952)
 Head of Government:
  Governor-designate Chris PATTEN (since July 1992); Chief Secretary Sir David
  Robert FORD (since February 1987)
Suffrage:
  direct election - universal at age 21 as a permanent resident living in the
  territory of Hong Kong for the past seven years; indirect election - limited
  to about 100,000 professionals of electoral college and functional
  constituencies
Elections:
 Legislative Council:
  indirect elections last held 12 September 1991 and direct elections were
  held 15 September 1991 (next to be held for the first time in September
  1995); results - percent of vote by party NA; seats - (60 total; 21
  indirectly elected by functional constituencies, 18 directly elected, 18
  appointed by governor, 3 ex officio members); indirect elections - number of
  seats by functional constituency NA; direct elections - UDHK 12, Meeting
  Point 3, ADPL 1, other 2
Communists:
  5,000 (est.) cadres affiliated with Communist Party of China
Other political or pressure groups:
  Federation of Trade Unions (pro-China), Hong Kong and Kowloon Trade Union
  Council (pro-Taiwan), Confederation of Trade Unions (prodemocracy), Hong
  Kong General Chamber of Commerce, Chinese General Chamber of Commerce
  (pro-China), Federation of Hong Kong Industries, Chinese Manufacturers'
  Association of Hong Kong, Hong Kong Professional Teachers' Union, Hong Kong
  Alliance in Support of the Patriotic Democratic Movement in China
Member of:
  APEC, AsDB, CCC, ESCAP (associate), GATT, ICFTU, IMO (associate), IOC, ISO
  (correspondent), WCL, WMO

:Hong Kong Government

Diplomatic representation:
as a dependent territory of the UK, the interests of Hong Kong in the US are represented by the UK

US:
Consul General Richard L. WILLIAMS; Consulate General at 26 Garden Road, Hong Kong (mailing address is Box 30, Hong Kong, or FPO AP 96522-0002); telephone [852] 239-011

Flag:
blue with the flag of the UK in the upper hoist-side quadrant with the Hong Kong coat of arms on a white disk centered on the outer half of the flag; the coat of arms contains a shield (bearing two junks below a crown) held by a lion (representing the UK) and a dragon (representing China) with another lion above the shield and a banner bearing the words HONG KONG below the shield

:Hong Kong Economy

Overview:
Hong Kong has a bustling free market economy with few tariffs or nontariff barriers. Natural resources are limited, and food and raw materials must be imported. Manufacturing accounts for about 18% of GDP, employs 28% of the labor force, and exports about 90% of its output. Real GDP growth averaged a remarkable 8% in 1987-88, then slowed to 2.5-3.0% in 1989-90. Unemployment, which has been declining since the mid-1980s, is now about 2%. A shortage of labor continues to put upward pressure on prices and the cost of living. Short-term prospects remain solid so long as major trading partners continue to be reasonably prosperous. The crackdown in China in 1989-91 casts a shadow over the longer term economic outlook.

GDP:
exchange rate conversion - $80.9 billion, per capita $13,800; real growth rate 3.8% (1991 est.)

Inflation rate (consumer prices):
12.0% (1991 est.)

Unemployment rate: 2.0% (1991 est.)

Budget:
$8.8 billion (FY90)

Exports:
$82.0 billion (f.o.b., 1990), including reexports of $53.1 billion
commodities:
clothing, textiles, yarn and fabric, footwear, electrical appliances, watches and clocks, toys
partners:
China 25%, US 24%, Germany 7%, Japan 6%, UK 2%, (1990)

Imports:
$82.4 billion (c.i.f., 1990)
commodities:
foodstuffs, transport equipment, raw materials, semimanufactures, petroleum
partners:
China 37%, Japan 16%, Taiwan 9%, US 8% (1990)

External debt: $9.5 billion (December 1990 est.)

Industrial production:
  growth rate 4% 1991 (est)
Electricity:
  8,600,000 kW capacity; 25,637 million kWh produced, 4,378 kWh per capita
  (1991)
Industries:
  textiles, clothing, tourism, electronics, plastics, toys, watches, clocks
Agriculture:
  minor role in the economy; rice, vegetables, dairy products; less than 20%
  self-sufficient; shortages of rice, wheat, water
Illicit drugs:
  a hub for Southeast Asian heroin trade; transshipment and major financial
  and money-laundering center
Economic aid:
  US commitments, including Ex-Im (FY70-87), $152 million; Western (non-US)
  countries, ODA and OOF bilateral commitments (1970-89), $923 million
Currency:
  Hong Kong dollar (plural - dollars); 1 Hong Kong dollar (HK$) = 100 cents
Exchange rates:
  Hong Kong dollars (HK$) per US$ - 7.800 (1991), 7.790 (1990), 7.800 (1989),
  7.810 (1988), 7.760 (1987); note - linked to the US dollar at the rate of
  about 7.8 HK$ per 1 US$ since 1985
Fiscal year: 1 April - 31 March

:Hong Kong Communications

Railroads:
  35 km 1.435-meter standard gauge, government owned
Highways:
  1,484 km total; 794 km paved, 306 km gravel, crushed stone, or earth
Ports:
  Hong Kong
Merchant marine:
  142 ships (1,000 GRT or over), totaling 5,035,223 GRT/8,598,134 DWT;
  includes 1 passenger, 1 short-sea passenger, 15 cargo, 5 refrigerated cargo,
  26 container, 13 petroleum tanker, 1 chemical tanker, 6 combination ore/oil,
  5 liquefied gas, 68 bulk, 1 combination bulk; note - a flag of convenience
  registry; ships registered in Hong Kong fly the UK flag, and an estimated
  500 Hong Kong - owned ships are registered elsewhere
Civil air:
  16 major transport aircraft
Airports:
  2 total; 2 usable; 2 with permanent-surface runways; none with runways over
  3,659 m; 1 with runways 2,440-3,659 m; none with runways 1,220-2,439 m
Telecommunications:
  modern facilities provide excellent domestic and international services;
  3,000,000 telephones; microwave transmission links and extensive optical
  fiber transmission network; broadcast stations - 6 AM, 6 FM, 4 TV; 1 British
  Broadcasting Corporation (BBC) repeater station and 1 British Forces
  Broadcasting Service repeater station; 2,500,000 radio receivers; 1,312,000
  TV sets (1,224,000 color TV sets); satellite earth stations - 1 Pacific

Ocean INTELSAT and 2 Indian Ocean INTELSAT; coaxial cable to Guangzhou, China; links to 5 international submarine cables providing access to ASEAN member nations, Japan, Taiwan, Australia, Middle East, and Western Europe

:Hong Kong Defense Forces

Branches:
Headquarters of British Forces, Royal Navy, Royal Air Force, Royal Hong Kong Auxiliary Air Force, Royal Hong Kong Police Force

Manpower availability:
males 15-49, 1,732,360; 1,334,923 fit for military service; 46,285 reach military age (18) annually

Defense expenditures:
exchange rate conversion - $300 million, 0.5% of GDP (1989 est.); this represents one-fourth of the total cost of defending itself, the remainder being paid by the UK

Note:
defense is the responsibility of the UK

Howland Island Geography

Total area: 1.6 km2
Land area: 1.6 km2
Comparative area: about 2.7 times the size of the Mall in Washington, DC
Land boundaries:
none
Coastline:
6.4 km
Maritime claims:
Contiguous zone:
12 nm
Continental shelf:
200 m (depth)
Exclusive economic zone:
200 nm
Territorial sea:
12 nm
Disputes:
none
Climate:
equatorial; scant rainfall, constant wind, burning sun
Terrain:
low-lying, nearly level, sandy, coral island surrounded by a narrow fringing reef; depressed central area
Natural resources:
guano (deposits worked until late 1800s)
Land use:
arable land 0%; permanent crops 0%; meadows and pastures 0%; forest and woodland 5%; other 95%
Environment:
almost totally covered with grasses, prostrate vines, and low-growing shrubs; small area of trees in the center; lacks fresh water; primarily a nesting, roosting, and foraging habitat for seabirds, shorebirds, and marine

wildlife; feral cats

Note:

remote location 2,575 km southwest of Honolulu in the North Pacific Ocean, just north of the Equator, about halfway between Hawaii and Australia

:Howland Island People

Population: uninhabited

Population: note:

American civilians evacuated in 1942 after Japanese air and naval attacks during World War II; occupied by US military during World War II, but abandoned after the war; public entry is by special-use permit only and generally restricted to scientists and educators

:Howland Island Government

Long-form name:

Type:

unincorporated territory of the US administered by the Fish and Wildlife Service of the US Department of the Interior as part of the National Wildlife Refuge System

Capital: none; administered from Washington, DC

:Howland Island Economy

Overview: no economic activity

:Howland Island Communications

Ports:

none; offshore anchorage only, one boat landing area along the middle of the west coast

Airports:

airstrip constructed in 1937 for scheduled refueling stop on the round-the-world flight of Amelia Earhart and Fred Noonan - they left Lae, New Guinea, for Howland Island, but were never seen again; the airstrip is no longer serviceable

Note:

Earhart Light is a day beacon near the middle of the west coast that was partially destroyed during World War II, but has since been rebuilt in memory of famed aviatrix Amelia Earhart

:Howland Island Defense Forces

Note:

defense is the responsibility of the US; visited annually by the US Coast Guard

Hungary Geography

Total area: 93,030 km2
Land area: 92,340 km2
Comparative area: slightly smaller than Indiana
Land boundaries:

2,113 km; Austria 366 km, Slovenia 82 km, Czechoslovakia 676 km, Romania 443 km, Croatia 292 km, Serbia and Montenegro 151 km, Ukraine 103 km

Coastline:

none - landlocked
Maritime claims:
  none - landlocked
Disputes:
  Gabcikovo Dam dispute with Czechoslovakia
Climate:
  temperate; cold, cloudy, humid winters; warm summers
Terrain:
  mostly flat to rolling plains
Natural resources:
  bauxite, coal, natural gas, fertile soils
Land use:
  arable land 54%; permanent crops 3%; meadows and pastures 14%; forest and woodland 18%; other 11%; includes irrigated 2%
Environment:
  levees are common along many streams, but flooding occurs almost every year
Note:
  landlocked; strategic location astride main land routes between Western Europe and Balkan Peninsula as well as between Ukraine and Mediterranean basin

:Hungary People

Population: 10,333,327 (July 1992), growth rate - 0.1% (1992)
Birth rate: 12 births/1,000 population (1992)
Death rate: 13 deaths/1,000 population (1992)
Net migration rate: 0 migrants/1,000 population (1992)
Infant mortality rate: 14 deaths/1,000 live births (1992)
Life expectancy at birth: 66 years male, 75 years female (1992)
Total fertility rate: 1.8 children born/woman (1992)
Nationality:
  noun - Hungarian(s); adjective - Hungarian
Ethnic divisions:
  Hungarian 96.6%, Gypsy 5.8%, German 1.6%, Slovak 1.1%, Southern Slav 0.3%, Romanian 0.2%
Religions:
  Roman Catholic 67.5%, Calvinist 20.0%, Lutheran 5.0%, atheist and other 7.5%
Languages:
  Hungarian 98.2%, other 1.8%
Literacy:
  99% (male 99%, female 98%) age 15 and over can read and write (1980)
Labor force:
  5.4 million; services, trade, government, and other 43.2%, industry 30.9%, agriculture 18.8%, construction 7.1% (1991)
Organized labor:
  45-55% of labor force; Central Council of Hungarian Trade Unions (SZOT) includes 19 affiliated unions, all controlled by the government; independent unions legal; may be as many as 12 small independent unions in operation

:Hungary Government

Long-form name:
  Republic of Hungary

Type:
  republic
Capital: Budapest
Administrative divisions:
  19 counties (megyek, singular - megye) and 1 capital city* (fovaros);
  Bacs-Kiskun, Baranya, Bekes, Borsod-Abauj-Zemplen, Budapest*, Csongrad,
  Fejer, Gyor-Moson-Sopron, Hajdu-Bihar, Heves, Jasz-Nagykun-Szolnok,
  Komarom-Esztergom, Nograd, Pest, Somogy, Szabolcs-Szatmar-Bereg, Tolna, Vas,
  Veszprem, Zala
Independence:
  1001, unification by King Stephen I
Constitution:
  18 August 1949, effective 20 August 1949, revised 19 April 1972; 18 October
  1989 revision ensured legal rights for individuals and constitutional checks
  on the authority of the prime minister and also established the principle of
  parliamentary oversight
Legal system:
  in process of revision, moving toward rule of law based on Western model
National holiday:
  October 23 (1956); commemorates the Hungarian uprising
Executive branch:
  president, prime minister
Legislative branch:
  unicameral National Assembly (Orszaggyules)
Judicial branch:
  Supreme Court, may be restructured as part of ongoing government overhaul
Leaders:
 Chief of State:
  President Arpad GONCZ (since 3 August 1990; previously interim President
  from 2 May 1990)
 Head of Government:
  Prime Minister Jozsef ANTALL (since 23 May 1990)
Political parties and leaders:
  Democratic Forum, Jozsef ANTALL, chairman; Dr. Lajos FUR, acting president;
  Free Democrats, Peter TOLGYESSY, chairman; Independent Smallholders, Jozsef
  TORGYAN, president; Hungarian Socialist Party (MSP), Gyula HORN, chairman;
  Young Democrats, Gabor FODOR, head; Christian Democrats, Dr. Lazlo SURJAN,
  president; note - the Hungarian Socialist (Communist) Workers' Party (MSZMP)
  renounced Communism and became the Hungarian Socialist Party (MSP) in
  October 1989; there is still a small (fringe) MSZMP
Suffrage:
  universal at age 18
Elections:
 President:
  last held 3 August 1990 (next to be held August 1994); results - President
  GONCZ elected by popular vote; note - President GONCZ was elected by the
  National Assembly with a total of 294 votes out of 304 as interim President
  from 2 May 1990 until elected President
 National Assembly:
  last held on 25 March 1990 (first round, with the second round held 8 April
  429

1990); results - percent of vote by party NA; seats - (386 total) Democratic
Forum 162, Free Democrats 90, Independent Smallholders 45, Hungarian
Socialist Party (MSP) 33, Young Democrats 22, Christian Democrats 21,
independents or jointly sponsored candidates 13

Communists:
fewer than 100,000 (December 1989)

:Hungary Government

Member of:
BIS, CCC, CE, CSCE, ECE, FAO, G-9, GATT, HG, IAEA, IBRD, ICAO, IDA, IFC,
ILO, IMF, IMO, INTERPOL, IOC, IOM (observer), ISO, ITU, LORCS, NACC,
NSG,
PCA, UN, UNCTAD, UNESCO, UNIDO, UNIIMOG, UPU, WHO, WIPO, WMO,
WTO, ZC

Diplomatic representation:
Ambassador Pal TAR; Chancery at 3910 Shoemaker Street NW, Washington, DC
20008; telephone (202) 362-6730; there is a Hungarian Consulate General in
New York

US:
Ambassador Charles THOMAS; Embassy at V. Szabadsag Ter 12, Budapest (mail-ing
address is APO AE 09213-5270); telephone [36] (1) 112-6450; FAX 132-8934

Flag:
three equal horizontal bands of red (top), white, and green

:Hungary Economy

Overview:
Hungary is in the midst of a difficult transition between a command and a
market economy. Agriculture is an important sector, providing sizable export
earnings and meeting domestic food needs. Industry accounts for about 40% of
GDP and 30% of employment. Hungary claims that less than 20% of foreign
trade is now with former CEMA countries, while about 70% is with OECD
members. Hungary's economic reform programs during the Communist era gave it
a head start in creating a market economy and attracting foreign investment.
In 1990, Hungary received half of all foreign investment in Eastern Europe
and in 1991 received the largest single share. The growing private sector
accounts for one-quarter to one-third of national output according to
unofficial estimates. Privatization of state enterprises is progressing,
although excessive redtape, bureaucratic oversight, and uncertainties about
pricing have slowed the process. Escalating unemployment and high rates of
inflation may impede efforts to speed up privatization and budget reform,
while Hungary's heavy foreign debt will make the government reluctant to
introduce full convertability of the forint before 1993.

GDP:
purchasing power equivalent - $60.1 billion, per capita $5,700; real growth
rate - 7% (1991 est.)

Inflation rate (consumer prices):
34% (1991 est.)

Unemployment rate: 8.0% (1991)

Budget:
revenues $12.7 billion; expenditures $13.6 billion (1992 planned)

Exports:
  $10.2 billion (f.o.b. 1991)
  commodities:
  capital goods 25.9%, foods 23%, consumer goods 16.5%, fuels 2.4%, other
  32.2%
  partners:
  USSR and Eastern Europe 31.9%, EC 32.2%, EFTA 12% (1990)
Imports:
  $11.7 billion (f.o.b., 1991)
  commodities:
  capital goods 31.6%, fuels 13.8%, manufactured consumer goods 14.6%,
  agriculture 6%, other 34.0%
  partners:
  USSR and Eastern Europe 34%, EC 31%, EFTA 15.4%
External debt: $22.7 billion (January 1991)
Industrial production:
  growth rate - 20% (1991 est.)
Electricity:
  6,967,000 kW capacity; 28,376 million kWh produced, 2,750 kWh per capita
  (1990)
Industries:
  mining, metallurgy, engineering industries, processed foods, textiles,
  chemicals (especially pharmaceuticals), trucks, buses
Agriculture:
  including forestry, accounts for about 15% of GDP and 19% of employment;
  highly diversified crop-livestock farming; principal crops - wheat, corn,
  sunflowers, potatoes, sugar beets; livestock - hogs, cattle, poultry, dairy
  products; self-sufficient in food output
Illicit drugs:
  transshipment point for Southeast Asia heroin transiting the Balkan route

:Hungary Economy

Economic aid:
  recipient - $9.1 billion in assistance from OECD countries (from 1st quarter
  1990 to end of 2nd quarter 1991)
Currency:
  forint (plural - forints); 1 forint (Ft) = 100 filler
Fiscal year: calendar year

:Hungary Communications

Railroads:
  7,765 km total; 7,508 km 1.435-meter standard gauge, 222 km narrow gauge
  (mostly 0.760-meter), 35 km 1.520-meter broad gauge; 1,147 km double track,
  2,161 km electrified; all government owned (1991)
Highways:
  130,014 km total; 29,715 km national highway system - 26,834 km asphalt, 142
  km concrete, 51 km stone and road brick, 2,276 km macadam, 412 km unpaved;
  58,495 km country roads (66% unpaved), and 41,804 km (est.) other roads (70%
  unpaved) (1988)
Inland waterways:
  1,622 km (1988)

Pipelines:
    crude oil 1,204 km; petroleum products 630 km; natural gas 3,895 km (1986)
Ports:
    Budapest and Dunaujvaros are river ports on the Danube; maritime outlets are
    Rostock (Germany), Gdansk (Poland), Gdynia (Poland), Szczecin (Poland),
    Galati (Romania), and Braila (Romania)
Merchant marine:
    14 cargo ships (1,000 GRT or over) and 1 bulk totaling 85,489 GRT/119,520
    DWT
Civil air:
    28 major transport aircraft
Airports:
    90 total, 90 usable; 20 with permanent-surface runways; 2 with runways over
    3,659 m; 10 with runways 2,440-3,659 m; 15 with runways 1,220-2,439 m
Telecommunications:
    automatic telephone network based on radio relay system; 1.9 million phones;
    telephone density is at 17 per 100 inhabitants; 49% of all phones are in
    Budapest; 12-15 year wait for a phone; 16,000 telex lines (June 1990);
    broadcast stations - 32 AM, 15 FM, 41 TV (8 Soviet TV repeaters); 4.2
    million TVs (1990); 1 satellite ground station using INTELSAT and
    Intersputnik

:Hungary Defense Forces

Branches:
    Ground Forces, Air and Air Defense Forces, Border Guard, Territorial Defense
Manpower availability:
    males 15-49, 2,619,277; 2,092,867 fit for military service; 87,469 reach
    military age (18) annually
Defense expenditures:
    exchange rate conversion - 60.8 billion forints, 1.7% of GNP (1992 est.);
    note - conversion of defense expenditures into US dollars using the current
    exchange rate would produce misleading results

Iceland Geography

Total area: 103,000 km2
Land area: 100,250 km2
Comparative area: slightly smaller than Kentucky
Land boundaries:
    none
Coastline:
    4,988 km
Maritime claims:
 Continental shelf:
  edge of continental margin or 200 nm
 Exclusive economic zone:
  200 nm
 Territorial sea:
  12 nm
Disputes:
    Rockall continental shelf dispute involving Denmark, Ireland, and the UK
    (Ireland and the UK have signed a boundary agreement in the Rockall area)

Climate:

    temperate; moderated by North Atlantic Current; mild, windy winters; damp,
    cool summers
Terrain:

    mostly plateau interspersed with mountain peaks, icefields; coast deeply
    indented by bays and fiords
Natural resources:

    fish, hydroelectric and geothermal power, diatomite
Land use:

    arable land NEGL%; permanent crops 0%; meadows and pastures 23%; forest and
    woodland 1%; other 76%
Environment:

    subject to earthquakes and volcanic activity
Note:

    strategic location between Greenland and Europe; westernmost European
    country

:Iceland People

Population: 259,012 (July 1992), growth rate 0.9% (1992)
Birth rate: 18 births/1,000 population (1992)
Death rate: 7 deaths/1,000 population (1992)
Net migration rate: -2 migrants/1,000 population (1992)
Infant mortality rate: 4 deaths/1,000 live births (1992)
Life expectancy at birth: 76 years male, 81 years female (1992)
Total fertility rate: 2.2 children born/woman (1992)
Nationality:

    noun - Icelander(s); adjective - Icelandic
Ethnic divisions:

    homogeneous mixture of descendants of Norwegians and Celts
Religions:

    Evangelical Lutheran 96%, other Protestant and Roman Catholic 3%, none 1%
    (1988)
Languages:

    Icelandic
Literacy:

    100% (male NA%, female NA%) age 15 and over can read and write (1976 est.)
Labor force:

    134,429; commerce, finance, and services 55.4%, other manufacturing 14.3%.,
    agriculture 5.8%, fish processing 7.9%, fishing 5.0% (1986)
Organized labor:

    60% of labor force

:Iceland Government

Long-form name:

    Republic of Iceland
Type:

    republic
Capital: Reykjavik
Administrative divisions:

    23 counties (syslar, singular - sysla) and 14 independent towns*
    (kaupstadhir, singular - kaupstadhur); Akranes*, Akureyri*, Arnessysla,

Austur-Bardhastrandarsysla, Austur-Hunavatnssysla, Austur-Skaftafellssysla, Borgarfjardharsysla, Dalasysla, Eyjafjardharsysla, Gullbringusysla, Hafnarfjordhur*, Husavik*, Isafjordhur*, Keflavik*, Kjosarsysla, Kopavogur*, Myrasysla, Neskaupstadhur*, Nordhur-Isafjardharsysla, Nordhur-Mulasys-la, Nordhur-Thingeyjarsysla, Olafsfjordhur*, Rangarvallasysla, Reykjavik*, Saudharkrokur*, Seydhisfjordhur*, Siglufjordhur*, Skagafjardharsysla, Snaefellsnes-og Hnappadalssysla, Strandasysla, Sudhur-Mulasysla, Sudhur-Thingeyjarsysla, Vesttmannaeyjar*, Vestur-Bardhastrandarsysla, Vestur-Hunavatnssysla, Vestur-Isafjardharsysla, Vestur-Skaftafellssysla

Independence:

17 June 1944 (from Denmark)

Constitution:

16 June 1944, effective 17 June 1944

Legal system:

civil law system based on Danish law; does not accept compulsory ICJ jurisdiction

National holiday:

Anniversary of the Establishment of the Republic, 17 June (1944)

Executive branch:

president, prime minister, Cabinet

Legislative branch:

unicameral Parliament (Althing)

Judicial branch:

Supreme Court (Haestirettur)

Leaders:

Chief of State:

President Vigdis FINNBOGADOTTIR (since 1 August 1980)

Head of Government:

Prime Minister David ODDSSON (since 30 April 1991)

Political parties and leaders:

Independence Party (conservative), David ODDSSON; Progressive Party, Steingrimur HERMANNSSON; Social Democratic Party, Jon Baldvin HANNIBALSSON;

People's Alliance (left socialist), Olafur Ragnar GRIMSSON; Citizens Party (conservative nationalist), Julius SOLNES; Women's List

Suffrage:

universal at age 20

Elections:

President:

last held on 29 June 1980 (next scheduled for June 1992); results - there were no elections in 1984 and 1988 as President Vigdis FINNBOGADOTTIR was unopposed

Althing:

last held on 20 April 1991 (next to be held by April 1995); results - Independence Party 38.6%, Progressive Party 18.9%, Social Democratic Party 15.5%, People's Alliance 14.4%, Womens List 8.13%, Liberals 1.2%, other 3.27% seats - (63 total) Independence 26, Progressive 13, Social Democratic 10, People's Alliance 9, Womens List 5

:Iceland Government

Member of:
  BIS, CCC, CE, CSCE, EBRD, ECE, EFTA, FAO, GATT, IAEA, IBRD, ICAO, ICC,
  ICFTU, IDA, IFC, ILO, IMF, IMO, INTELSAT, INTERPOL, IOC, ISO
  (correspondent), ITU, LORCS, NACC, NATO, NC, NEA, NIB, OECD, PCA, UN,
  UNCTAD, UNESCO, UPU, WHO, WIPO, WMO
Diplomatic representation:
  Ambassador Tomas A. TOMASSON; Chancery at 2022 Connecticut Avenue NW,
  Washington, DC 20008; telephone (202) 265-6653 through 6655; there is an
  Icelandic Consulate General in New York
  US:
  Ambassador Charles E. COBB, Jr.; Embassy at Laufasvegur 21, Box 40,
  Reykjavik (mailing address is FPO AE 09728-0340); telephone [354] (1) 29100
Flag:
  blue with a red cross outlined in white that extends to the edges of the
  flag; the vertical part of the cross is shifted to the hoist side in the
  style of the Dannebrog (Danish flag)

:Iceland Economy

Overview:
  Iceland's prosperous Scandinavian-type economy is basically capitalistic,
  but with extensive welfare measures, low unemployment, and comparatively
  even distribution of income. The economy is heavily dependent on the fishing
  industry, which provides nearly 75% of export earnings. In the absence of
  other natural resources, Iceland's economy is vulnerable to changing world
  fish prices. The economic improvements resulting from climbing fish prices
  in 1990 and a noninflationary labor agreement probably will be reversed by
  tighter fish quotas and a delay in the construction of an aluminum smelting
  plant. The conservative government's economic priorities include reducing
  the budget and current account deficits, containing inflation, revising
  agricultural and fishing policies, diversifying the economy, and tying the
  krona to the EC's European currency unit in 1993. The fishing industries -
  notably the shrimp industry - are experiencing a series of bankruptcies and
  mergers. Inflation has continued to drop sharply from 20% in 1989 to about
  7.5% in 1991 and possibly 3% in 1992, while unemployment is expected to
  increase to 2.5%. GDP is expected to contract by nearly 4% in 1992.
GDP:
  purchasing power equivalent - $4.2 billion, per capita $16,200; real growth
  rate 0.3% (1991)
Inflation rate (consumer prices):
  7.5% (1991)
Unemployment rate: 1.8% (1991)
Budget:
  revenues $1.7 billion; expenditures $1.9 billion, including capital
  expenditures of $NA million (1991 est.)
Exports:
  $1.6 billion (f.o.b., 1991)
  commodities:
  fish and fish products, animal products, aluminum, diatomite
  partners:
  EC 67.7% (UK 25.3%, FRG 12.7%), US 9.9%, Japan 6% (1990)

Imports:

$1.7 billion (c.i.f., 1991)

commodities:

machinery and transportation equipment, petroleum, foodstuffs, textiles

partners:

EC 49.8% (FRG 12.4%, Denmark 8.6%, UK 8.1%), US 14.4%, Japan 5.6% (1990)

External debt: $3 billion (1990)

Industrial production:

growth rate 1.75% (1991 est.)

Electricity:

1,063,000 kW capacity; 5,165 million kWh produced, 20,780 kWh per capita (1991)

Industries:

fish processing, aluminum smelting, ferro-silicon production, hydropower

Agriculture:

accounts for about 25% of GDP (including fishing); fishing is most important economic activity, contributing nearly 75% to export earnings; principal crops - potatoes and turnips; livestock - cattle, sheep; self-sufficient in crops; fish catch of about 1.4 million metric tons in 1989

Economic aid:

US commitments, including Ex-Im (FY70-81), $19.1 million

Currency:

krona (plural - kronur); 1 Icelandic krona (IKr) = 100 aurar

:Iceland Economy

Exchange rates:

Icelandic kronur (IKr) per US$1 - 57.277 (January 1992), 58.996 (1991), 58.284 (1990), 57.042 (1989), 43.014 (1988), 38.677 (1987)

Fiscal year: calendar year

:Iceland Communications

Highways:

12,343 km total; 166 km bitumen and concrete; 1,284 km bituminous treated and gravel; 10,893 km earth

Ports:

Reykjavik, Akureyri, Hafnarfjordhur, Keflavik, Seydhisfjordhur, Siglufjordhur, Vestmannaeyjar

Merchant marine:

12 ships (1,000 GRT or over) totaling 37,969 GRT/57,060 DWT; includes 5 cargo, 3 refrigerated cargo, 2 roll-on/roll-off cargo, 1 petroleum tanker, 1 chemical tanker

Civil air:

20 major transport aircraft

Airports:

94 total, 89 usable; 4 with permanent-surface runways; none with runways over 3,659 m; 1 with runways 2,440-3,659 m; 12 with runways 1,220-2,439 m

Telecommunications:

adequate domestic service; coaxial and fiber-optical cables and radio relay for trunk network; 135,000 telephones; broadcast stations - 19 AM, 30 (43 repeaters) FM, 13 (132 repeaters) TV; 2 submarine cables; 1 Atlantic Ocean INTELSAT earth station carries majority of international traffic

:Iceland Defense Forces

Branches:

no armed forces; Police, Coast Guard; Iceland's defense is provided by the
US-manned Icelandic Defense Force (IDF) headquartered at Keflavik

Manpower availability:

males 15-49, 69,072; 61,556 fit for military service; no conscription or
compulsory military service

Defense expenditures:

India Geography

Total area: 3,287,590 km2
Land area: 2,973,190 km2
Comparative area: slightly more than one-third the size of the US
Land boundaries:

14,103 km; Bangladesh 4,053 km, Bhutan 605 km, Burma 1,463 km, China 3,380,
Nepal 1,690 km, Pakistan 2,912 km

Coastline:

7,000 km

Maritime claims:

Contiguous zone:

24 nm

Continental shelf:

edge of continental margin or 200 nm

Exclusive economic zone:

200 nm

Territorial sea:

12 nm

Disputes:

boundaries with Bangladesh, China, and Pakistan; water sharing problems with
downstream riparians, Bangladesh over the Ganges and Pakistan over the Indus

Climate:

varies from tropical monsoon in south to temperate in north

Terrain:

upland plain (Deccan Plateau) in south, flat to rolling plain along the
Ganges, deserts in west, Himalayas in north

Natural resources:

coal (fourth-largest reserves in the world), iron ore, manganese, mica,
bauxite, titanium ore, chromite, natural gas, diamonds, crude oil, limestone

Land use:

arable land 55%; permanent crops 1%; meadows and pastures 4%; forest and
woodland 23%; other 17%; includes irrigated 13%

Environment:

droughts, flash floods, severe thunderstorms common; deforestation; soil
erosion; overgrazing; air and water pollution; desertification

Note:

dominates South Asian subcontinent; near important Indian Ocean trade routes

:India People

Population: 886,362,180 (July 1992), growth rate 1.9% (1992)
Birth rate: 30 births/1,000 population (1992)
Death rate: 11 deaths/1,000 population (1992)
Net migration rate: 0 migrants/1,000 population (1992)
Infant mortality rate: 81 deaths/1,000 live births (1992)
Life expectancy at birth: 57 years male, 58 years female (1992)
Total fertility rate: 3.7 children born/woman (1992)
Nationality:
  noun - Indian(s); adjective - Indian
Ethnic divisions:
  Indo-Aryan 72%, Dravidian 25%, Mongoloid and other 3%
Religions:
  Hindu 82.6%, Muslim 11.4%, Christian 2.4%, Sikh 2.0%, Buddhist 0.7%, Jains
  0.5%, other 0.4%
Languages:
  Hindi, English, and 14 other official languages - Bengali, Telugu, Marathi,
  Tamil, Urdu, Gujarati, Malayalam, Kannada, Oriya, Punjabi, Assamese,
  Kashmiri, Sindhi, and Sanskrit; 24 languages spoken by a million or more
  persons each; numerous other languages and dialects, for the most part
  mutually unintelligible; Hindi is the national language and primary tongue
  of 30% of the people; English enjoys associate status but is the most
  important language for national, political, and commercial communication;
  Hindustani, a popular variant of Hindi/Urdu, is spoken widely throughout
  northern India
Literacy:
  48% (male 62%, female 34%) age 15 and over can read and write (1990 est.)
Labor force:
  284,400,000; 67% agriculture (FY85)
Organized labor:
  less than 5% of the labor force

:India Government

Long-form name:
  Republic of India
Type:
  federal republic
Capital: New Delhi
Administrative divisions:
  25 states and 7 union territories*; Andaman and Nicobar Islands*, Andhra
  Pradesh, Arunachal Pradesh, Assam, Bihar, Chandigarh*, Dadra and Nagar
  Haveli*, Daman and Diu*, Delhi*, Goa, Gujarat, Haryana, Himachal Pradesh,
  Jammu and Kashmir, Karnataka, Kerala, Lakshadweep*, Madhya Pradesh,
  Maharashtra, Manipur, Meghalaya, Mizoram, Nagaland, Orissa, Pondicherry*,
  Punjab, Rajasthan, Sikkim, Tamil Nadu, Tripura, Uttar Pradesh, West Bengal
Independence:
  15 August 1947 (from UK)
Constitution:
  26 January 1950
Legal system:
  based on English common law; limited judicial review of legislative acts;

accepts compulsory ICJ jurisdiction, with reservations

National holiday:

Anniversary of the Proclamation of the Republic, 26 January (1950)

Executive branch:

president, vice president, prime minister, Council of Ministers

Legislative branch:

bicameral Parliament (Sansad) consists of an upper house or Council of
States (Rajya Sabha) and a lower house or People's Assembly (Lok Sabha)

Judicial branch:

Supreme Court

Leaders:

Chief of State:

President Ramaswamy Iyer VENKATARAMAN (since 25 July 1987); Vice President
Dr. Shankar Dayal SHARMA (since 3 September 1987)

Head of Government:

Prime Minister P. V. Narasimha RAO (since 21 June 1991)

Political parties and leaders:

Congress (I) Party, P. V. Narasimha RAO, president; Bharatiya Janata Party,
L. K. ADVANI; Janata Dal Party, V. P. SINGH; Communist Party of
India/Marxist (CPI/M), Harkishan Singh SURJEET; Communist Party of India
(CPI), C. Rajeswara RAO; Telugu Desam (a regional party in Andhra Pradesh),
N. T. Rama RAO; All-India Anna Dravida Munnetra Kazagham (AIADMK; a regional
party in Tamil Nadu), JAYALALITHA; Samajwadi Janata Party, CHANDRA
SHEKHAR;
Shiv Sena, Bal THACKERAY; Revolutionary Socialist Party (RSP), Tridip
CHOWDHURY; Bahujana Samaj Party (BSP), Kanshi RAM; Congress (S) Party,
leader NA; Communist Party of India/Marxist-Leninist (CPI/ML), Satyanarayan
SINGH; Dravida Munnetra Kazagham (a regional party in Tamil Nadu), M.
KARUNANIDHI; Akali Dal factions representing Sikh religious community in the
Punjab; National Conference (NC; a regional party in Jammu and Kashmir),
Farooq ABDULLAH; Asom Gana Parishad (a regional party in Assam), Prafulla
MAHANTA

Suffrage:

universal at age 18

:India Government

Elections:

People's Assembly:

last held 21 May, 12 and 15 June 1991 (next to be held by November 1996);
results - percent of vote by party NA; seats - (545 total), 520 elected -
Congress (I) Party 231, Bharatiya Janata Party 119, Janata Dal Party 59,
CPI/M 35, CPI 14, Telugu Desam 13, AIADMK 11, Samajwadi Janata Party 5, Shiv
Sena 4, RSP 4, BSP 1, Congress (S) Party 1, other 23; note - second and
third rounds of voting were delayed because of the assassination of Congress
President Rajiv GANDHI on 21 May 1991

Communists:

466,000 members claimed by CPI, 361,000 members claimed by CPI/M; Communist
extremist groups, about 15,000 members

Other political or pressure groups:
    various separatist groups seeking greater communal and/or regional autonomy;
    numerous religious or militant/chauvinistic organizations, including Adam
    Sena, Ananda Marg, Vishwa Hindu Parishad, and Rashtriya Swayamsevak Sangh
Member of:
    AfDB, AG (observer), AsDB, C, CCC, CP, ESCAP, FAO, G-6, G-15, G-19, G-24,
    G-77, GATT, IAEA, IBRD, ICAO, ICC, ICFTU, IDA, IFAD, IFC, ILO, IMF, IMO,
    INMARSAT, INTELSAT, INTERPOL, IOC, ISO, ITU, LORCS, NAM, PCA,
SAARC, UN,
    UNAVEM, UNCTAD, UNESCO, UNIDO, UNIIMOG, UPU, WFTU, WHO,
WIPO, WMO, WTO
Diplomatic representation:
    Ambassador Abid HUSSEIN; Chancery at 2107 Massachusetts Avenue NW,
    Washington, DC 20008; telephone (202) 939-7000; there are Indian Consulates
    General in Chicago, New York, and San Francisco
    US:
    Ambassador William CLARK, Jr.; Embassy at Shanti Path, Chanakyapuri 110021,
    New Delhi; telephone [91] (11) 600651; FAX [91] (11) 687-2028, 687-2391;
    there are US Consulates General in Bombay, Calcutta, and Madras
Flag:
    three equal horizontal bands of orange (top), white, and green with a blue
    chakra (24-spoked wheel) centered in the white band; similar to the flag of
    Niger, which has a small orange disk centered in the white band

:India Economy

Overview:
    India's economy is a mixture of traditional village farming and handicrafts,
    modern agriculture, old and new branches of industry, and a multitude of
    support services. It presents both the entrepreneurial skills and drives of
    the capitalist system and widespread government intervention of the
    socialist mold. Growth of 4-5% annually in the 1980s has softened the impact
    of population growth on unemployment, social tranquility, and the
    environment. Agricultural output has continued to expand, reflecting the
    greater use of modern farming techniques and improved seed that have helped
    to make India self-sufficient in food grains and a net agricultural
    exporter. However, tens of millions of villagers, particularly in the south,
    have not benefited from the green revolution and live in abject poverty, and
    great numbers of urban residents lack the basic essentials of life. Industry
    has benefited from a partial liberalization of controls. The growth rate of
    the service sector has also been strong. India, however, has been challenged
    more recently by much lower foreign exchange reserves, higher inflation, and
    a large debt service burden.
GDP:
    exchange rate conversion - $328 billion, per capita $380; real growth rate
    2.5% (FY92 est.)
Inflation rate (consumer prices):
    12.0% (1991)
Unemployment rate: 20% (1991 est.)
Budget:
    revenues $38.5 billion; expenditures $53.4 billion, including capital

expenditures of $11.1 billion (FY92)

Exports:

$20.2 billion (f.o.b., FY91)

commodities:

gems and jewelry, engineering goods, clothing, textiles, chemicals, tea, coffee, fish products

partners:

EC 25%, US 16%, USSR and Eastern Europe 19%, Japan 10% (1989)

Imports:

$25.2 billion (c.i.f., FY91)

commodities:

petroleum products, capital goods, uncut gems, gems, jewelry, chemicals, iron and steel, edible oils

partners:

EC 33%, Middle East 19%, US 12%, Japan 8%, USSR and Eastern Europe 8% (1989)

External debt: $72.0 billion (1991 est.)

Industrial production:

growth rate 8.4% (1990); accounts for about 25% of GDP

Electricity:

80,000,000 kW capacity; 290,000 million kWh produced, 330 kWh per capita (1991)

Industries:

textiles, food processing, steel, machinery, transportation equipment, cement, jute manufactures, mining, petroleum, power, chemicals, pharmaceuticals, electronics

Agriculture:

accounts for about 30% of GDP and employs 67% of labor force; self-sufficient in food grains; principal crops - rice, wheat, oilseeds, cotton, jute, tea, sugarcane, potatoes; livestock - cattle, buffaloes, sheep, goats and poultry; fish catch of about 3 million metric tons ranks India among the world's top 10 fishing nations

:India Economy

Illicit drugs:

licit producer of opium poppy for the pharmaceutical trade, but some opium is diverted to illicit international drug markets; major transit country for illicit narcotics produced in neighboring countries; illicit producer of hashish

Economic aid:

US commitments, including Ex-Im (FY70-89), $4.4 billion; Western (non-US) countries, ODA and OOF bilateral commitments (1980-89), $31.7 billion; OPEC bilateral aid (1979-89), $315 million; USSR (1970-89), $11.6 billion; Eastern Europe (1970-89), $105 million

Currency:

Indian rupee (plural - rupees); 1 Indian rupee (Re) = 100 paise

Exchange rates:

Indian rupees (Rs) per US$1 - 25.917 (January 1992), 22.742 (1991), 17.504 (1990), 16.226 (1989), 13.917 (1988), 12.962 (1987)

Fiscal year: 1 April - 31 March

:India Communications

Railroads:
  61,850 km total (1986); 33,553 km 1.676-meter broad gauge, 24,051 km
  1.000-meter gauge, 4,246 km narrow gauge (0.762 meter and 0.610 meter);
  12,617 km is double track; 6,500 km is electrified
Highways:
  1,970,000 km total (1989); 960,000 km surfaced and 1,010,000 km gravel,
  crushed stone, or earth
Inland waterways:
  16,180 km; 3,631 km navigable by large vessels
Pipelines:
  crude oil 3,497 km; petroleum products 1,703 km; natural gas 902 km (1989)
Ports:
  Bombay, Calcutta, Cochin, Kandla, Madras, New Mangalore, Port Blair (Andaman
  Islands)
Merchant marine:
  299 ships (1,000 GRT or over) totaling 5,991,278 GRT/9,935,463 DWT; includes
  1 short-sea passenger, 7 passenger-cargo, 91 cargo, 1 roll-on/roll-off, 8
  container, 54 oil tanker, 10 chemical tanker, 8 combination ore/oil, 111
  bulk, 2 combination bulk, 6 liquefied gas
Civil air:
  93 major transport aircraft
Airports:
  341 total, 288 usable; 203 with permanent-surface runways; 2 with runways
  over 3,659 m; 59 with runways 2,440-3,659 m; 87 with runways 1,220-2,439 m
Telecommunications:
  poor domestic telephone service, international radio communications
  adequate; 4,700,000 telephones; broadcast stations - 96 AM, 4 FM, 274 TV
  (government controlled); domestic satellite system for communications and
  TV; 3 Indian Ocean INTELSAT earth stations; submarine cables to Malaysia and
  United Arab Emirates

:India Defense Forces

Branches:
  Army, Navy, Air Force, Security or Paramilitary Forces, Border Security
  Force, Coast Guard, Assam Rifles
Manpower availability:
  males 15-49, 237,803,153; 140,140,736 fit for military service; about
  9,474,290 reach military age (17) annually
Defense expenditures:
  exchange rate conversion - $NA, NA% of GNP (FY91)

Indian Ocean Geography

Total area: 73,600,000 km2
Land area: 73,600,000 km2; Arabian Sea, Bass Strait, Bay of Bengal, Java Sea, Persian
  Gulf, Red Sea, Strait of Malacca, Timor Sea, and other tributary water
  bodies
Comparative area: slightly less than eight times the size of the US; third-largest ocean
  (after the Pacific Ocean and Atlantic Ocean, but larger than the Arctic

Ocean)

Coastline:

66,526 km

Disputes:

some maritime disputes (see littoral states)

Climate:

northeast monsoon (December to April), southwest monsoon (June to October); tropical cyclones occur during May/June and October/November in the north Indian Ocean and January/February in the south Indian Ocean

Terrain:

surface dominated by counterclockwise gyre (broad, circular system of currents) in the south Indian Ocean; unique reversal of surface currents in the north Indian Ocean - low pressure over southwest Asia from hot, rising, summer air results in the southwest monsoon and southwest-to-northeast winds and currents, while high pressure over northern Asia from cold, falling, winter air results in the northeast monsoon and northeast-to-southwest winds and currents; ocean floor is dominated by the Mid-Indian Ocean Ridge and subdivided by the Southeast Indian Ocean Ridge, Southwest Indian Ocean Ridge, and Ninety East Ridge; maximum depth is 7,258 meters in the Java Trench

Natural resources:

oil and gas fields, fish, shrimp, sand and gravel aggregates, placer deposits, polymetallic nodules

Environment:

endangered marine species include the dugong, seals, turtles, and whales; oil pollution in the Arabian Sea, Persian Gulf, and Red Sea

Note:

major chokepoints include Bab el Mandeb, Strait of Hormuz, Strait of Malacca, southern access to the Suez Canal, and the Lombok Strait; ships subject to superstructure icing in extreme south near Antarctica from May to October

:Indian Ocean Economy

Overview:

The Indian Ocean provides a major highway for the movement of petroleum products from the Middle East to Europe and North and South American countries. Fish from the ocean are of growing economic importance to many of the bordering countries as a source of both food and exports. Fishing fleets from Russia, Japan, Korea, and Taiwan also exploit the Indian Ocean, mainly for shrimp and tuna. Large reserves of hydrocarbons are being tapped in the offshore areas of Saudi Arabia, Iran, India, and Western Australia. An estimated 40% of the world's offshore oil production comes from the Indian Ocean. Beach sands rich in heavy minerals and offshore placer deposits are actively exploited by bordering countries, particularly India, South Africa, Indonesia, Sri Lanka, and Thailand.

Industries:

based on exploitation of natural resources, particularly marine life, minerals, oil and gas production, fishing, sand and gravel aggregates, placer deposits

:Indian Ocean Communications

Ports:
  Bombay (India), Calcutta (India), Madras (India), Colombo (Sri Lanka),
  Durban (South Africa), Fremantle (Australia), Jakarta (Indonesia), Melbourne
  (Australia), Richard's Bay (South Africa)
Telecommunications:
  submarine cables from India to United Arab Emirates and Malaysia

Indonesia Geography

Total area: 1,919,440 km2
Land area: 1,826,440 km2
Comparative area: slightly less than three times the size of Texas
Land boundaries:
  2,602 km; Malaysia 1,782 km, Papua New Guinea 820 km
Coastline:
  54,716 km
Maritime claims:
  (measured from claimed archipelagic baselines)
 Exclusive economic zone:
  200 nm
 Territorial sea:
  12 nm
Disputes:
  sovereignty over Timor Timur (East Timor Province) disputed with Portugal
Climate:
  tropical; hot, humid; more moderate in highlands
Terrain:
  mostly coastal lowlands; larger islands have interior mountains
Natural resources:
  crude oil, tin, natural gas liquids, nickel, timber, bauxite, copper,
  fertile soils, coal, gold, silver
Land use:
  arable land 8%; permanent crops 3%; meadows and pastures 7%; forest and
  woodland 67%; other 15%; includes irrigated 3%
Environment:
  archipelago of 13,500 islands (6,000 inhabited); occasional floods, severe
  droughts, and tsunamis; deforestation
Note:
  straddles Equator; strategic location astride or along major sea lanes from
  Indian Ocean to Pacific Ocean

:Indonesia People

Population: 195,683,531 (July 1992), growth rate 1.7% (1992)
Birth rate: 25 births/1,000 population (1992)
Death rate: 8 deaths/1,000 population (1992)
Net migration rate: 0 migrants/1,000 population (1992)
Infant mortality rate: 70 deaths/1,000 live births (1992)
Life expectancy at birth: 59 years male, 64 years female (1992)
Total fertility rate: 2.8 children born/woman (1992)
Nationality:
  noun - Indonesian(s); adjective - Indonesian
Ethnic divisions:

majority of Malay stock comprising Javanese 45.0%, Sundanese 14.0%, Madurese 7.5%, coastal Malays 7.5%, other 26.0%

Religions:

Muslim 87%, Protestant 6%, Roman Catholic 3%, Hindu 2%, Buddhist 1%, other 1% (1985)

Languages:

Bahasa Indonesia (modified form of Malay; official); English and Dutch leading foreign languages; local dialects, the most widely spoken of which is Javanese

Literacy:

77% (male 84%, female 68%) age 15 and over can read and write (1990 est.)

Labor force:

67,000,000; agriculture 55%, manufacturing 10%, construction 4%, transport and communications 3% (1985 est.)

Organized labor:

3,000,000 members (claimed); about 5% of labor force

:Indonesia Government

Long-form name:

Republic of Indonesia

Type:

republic

Capital: Jakarta

Administrative divisions:

24 provinces (propinsi-propinsi, singular - propinsi), 2 special regions* (daerah-daerah istimewa, singular - daerah istimewa), and 1 special capital city district** (daerah khusus ibukota); Aceh*, Bali, Bengkulu, Irian Jaya, Jakarta Raya**, Jambi, Jawa Barat, Jawa Tengah, Jawa Timur, Kalimantan Barat, Kalimantan Selatan, Kalimantan Tengah, Kalimantan Timur, Lampung, Maluku, Nusa Tenggara Barat, Nusa Tenggara Timur, Riau, Sulawesi Selatan, Sulawesi Tengah, Sulawesi Tenggara, Sulawesi Utara, Sumatera Barat, Sumatera Selatan, Sumatera Utara, Timor Timur, Yogyakarta*

Independence:

17 August 1945 (proclaimed independence; on 27 December 1949, Indonesia became legally independent from the Netherlands)

Constitution:

August 1945, abrogated by Federal Constitution of 1949 and Provisional Constitution of 1950, restored 5 July 1959

Legal system:

based on Roman-Dutch law, substantially modified by indigenous concepts and by new criminal procedures code; has not accepted compulsory ICJ jurisdiction

National holiday:

Independence Day, 17 August (1945)

Executive branch:

president, vice president, Cabinet

Legislative branch:

unicameral House of Representatives (Dewan Perwakilan Rakyat or DPR); note - the People's Consultative Assembly (Majelis Permusyawaratan Rakyat or MPR) includes the DPR plus 500 indirectly elected members who meet every five years to elect the president and vice president and, theoretically, to determine national policy

Judicial branch:

Supreme Court (Mahkamah Agung)

Leaders:

Chief of State and Head of Government:

President Gen. (Ret.) SOEHARTO (since 27 March 1968); Vice President Lt. Gen. (Ret.) SUDHARMONO (since 11 March 1988)

Political parties and leaders:

GOLKAR (quasi-official party based on functional groups), Lt. Gen. (Ret.) WAHONO, general chairman; Indonesia Democracy Party (PDI - federation of former Nationalist and Christian Parties), SOERYADI, chairman; Development Unity Party (PPP, federation of former Islamic parties), Ismail Hasan METAREUM, chairman

Suffrage:

universal at age 17 and married persons regardless of age

Elections:

House of Representatives:

last held on 23 April 1987 (next to be held 8 June 1992); results - Golkar 73%, UDP 16%, PDI 11%; seats - (500 total - 400 elected, 100 appointed) Golkar 299, UDP 61, PDI 40

Communists:

Communist Party (PKI) was officially banned in March 1966; current strength about 1,000-3,000, with less than 10% engaged in organized activity; pre-October 1965 hardcore membership about 1.5 million

:Indonesia Government

Member of:

APEC, AsDB, ASEAN, CCC, CP, ESCAP, FAO, G-15, G-19, G-77, GATT, IAEA, IBRD,

ICAO, ICC, ICFTU, IDA, IDB, IFAD, IFC, ILO, IMF, IMO, INMARSAT, INTELSAT,

INTERPOL, IOC, ISO, ITU, LORCS, NAM, OIC, OPEC, UN, UNCTAD, UNESCO, UNIDO,

UNIIMOG, UPU, WCL, WFTU, WHO, WIPO, WMO, WTO

Diplomatic representation:

Ambassador Abdul Rachman RAMLY; Chancery at 2020 Massachusetts Avenue NW,

Washington, DC 20036; telephone (202) 775-5200; there are Indonesian Consulates General in Houston, New York, and Los Angeles, and Consulates in Chicago and San Francisco

US:

Ambassador John C. MONJO; Embassy at Medan Merdeka Selatan 5, Jakarta (mailing address is APO AP 96520); telephone [62] (21) 360-360; FAX [62] (21) 360-644; there are US Consulates in Medan and Surabaya

Flag:

two equal horizontal bands of red (top) and white; similar to the flag of Monaco, which is shorter; also similar to the flag of Poland, which is white (top) and red

:Indonesia Economy

Overview:

Indonesia is a mixed economy with many socialist institutions and central planning but with a recent emphasis on deregulation and private enterprise. Indonesia has extensive natural wealth, yet, with a large and rapidly increasing population, it remains a poor country. GDP growth in 1985-91 averaged about 6%, quite impressive, but not sufficient to both slash underemployment and absorb the 2.3 million workers annually entering the labor force. Agriculture, including forestry and fishing, is an important sector, accounting for 23% of GDP and over 50% of the labor force. The staple crop is rice. Once the world's largest rice importer, Indonesia is now nearly self-sufficient. Plantation crops - rubber and palm oil - and textiles and plywood are being encouraged for both export and job generation. Industrial output now accounts for 30% of GDP and is based on a supply of diverse natural resources, including crude oil, natural gas, timber, metals, and coal. Of these, the oil sector dominates the external economy, generating more than 20% of the government's revenues and 40% of export earnings in 1989. However, the economy's growth is highly dependent on the continuing expansion of nonoil exports. Japan is Indonesia's most important customer and supplier of aid. In 1991, rapid growth in the money supply prompted Jakarta to implement a tight monetary policy, forcing the private sector to go to foreign banks for investment financing. Real interest rates remained above 10%, off-shore commercial debt grew, and real GDP growth dropped slightly from the 7% of 1990.

GDP:

exchange rate conversion - $122 billion, per capita $630; real growth rate 6.0% (1991 est.)

Inflation rate (consumer prices):

10% (1991 est.)

Unemployment rate: 3%; underemployment 45% (1991 est.)

Budget:

revenues $17.2 billion; expenditures $23.4 billion, including capital expenditures of $8.9 billion (FY91)

Exports:

$25.7 billion (f.o.b., 1990)

commodities:

petroleum and liquefied natural gas 40%, timber 15%, textiles 7%, rubber 5%, coffee 3%

partners:

Japan 40%, US 14%, Singapore 7%, Europe 16% (1990)

Imports:

$21.8 billion (f.o.b., 1990)

commodities:

machinery 39%, chemical products 19%, manufactured goods 16%

partners:

Japan 23%, US 13%, EC, Singapore

External debt: $58.5 billion (1990 est.)

Industrial production:

growth rate 11.6% (1989 est.); accounts for 30% of GDP

Electricity:

11,600,000 kW capacity; 38,000 million kWh produced, 200 kWh per capita

(1990)

Industries:

petroleum, textiles, mining, cement, chemical fertilizers, plywood, food, rubber

:Indonesia Economy

Agriculture:

accounts for 23% of GDP; subsistence food production; small-holder and plantation production for export; main products are rice, cassava, peanuts, rubber, cocoa, coffee, palm oil, copra, other tropical products, poultry, beef, pork, eggs

Illicit drugs:

illicit producer of cannabis for the international drug trade, but not a major player; government actively eradicating plantings and prosecuting traffickers

Economic aid:

US commitments, including Ex-Im (FY70-89), $4.4 billion; Western (non-US) countries, ODA and OOF bilateral commitments (1970-89), $25.9 billion; OPEC bilateral aid (1979-89), $213 million; Communist countries (1970-89), $175 million

Currency:

Indonesian rupiah (plural - rupiahs); 1 Indonesian rupiah (Rp) = 100 sen (sen no longer used)

Exchange rates:

Indonesian rupiahs (Rp) per US$1 - 1,998.2 (January 1992), 1,950.3 (1991), 1,842.8 (1990), 1,770.1 (1989), 1,685.7 (1988), 1,643.8 (1987)

Fiscal year: 1 April - 31 March

:Indonesia Communications

Railroads:

6,964 km total; 6,389 km 1.067-meter gauge, 497 km 0.750-meter gauge, 78 km 0.600-meter gauge; 211 km double track; 101 km electrified; all government owned

Highways:

119,500 km total; 11,812 km state, 34,180 km provincial, and 73,508 km district roads

Inland waterways:

21,579 km total; Sumatra 5,471 km, Java and Madura 820 km, Kalimantan 10,460 km, Celebes 241 km, Irian Jaya 4,587 km

Pipelines:

crude oil 2,505 km; petroleum products 456 km; natural gas 1,703 km (1989)

Ports:

Cilacap, Cirebon, Jakarta, Kupang, Palembang, Ujungpandang, Semarang, Surabaya

Merchant marine:

387 ships (1,000 GRT or over) totaling 1,698,946 GRT/2,560,414 DWT; includes 5 short-sea passenger, 13 passenger-cargo, 231 cargo, 8 container, 3 roll-on/roll-off cargo, 3 vehicle carrier, 79 petroleum tanker, 5 chemical tanker, 6 liquefied gas, 7 specialized tanker, 1 livestock carrier, 25 bulk, 1 passenger

Civil air:

about 216 commercial transport aircraft

Airports:
437 total, 410 usable; 114 with permanent-surface runways; 1 with runways
over 3,659 m; 12 with runways 2,440-3,659 m; 64 with runways 1,220-2,439 m

Telecommunications:
interisland microwave system and HF police net; domestic service fair,
international service good; radiobroadcast coverage good; 763,000 telephones
(1986); broadcast stations - 618 AM, 38 FM, 9 TV; satellite earth stations -
1 Indian Ocean INTELSAT earth station and 1 Pacific Ocean INTELSAT earth
station; and 1 domestic satellite communications system

:Indonesia Defense Forces

Branches:
Army, Navy, Air Force, National Police

Manpower availability:
males 15-49, 51,906,415; 30,668,815 fit for military service; 2,095,698
reach military age (18) annually

Defense expenditures:
exchange rate conversion - $1.7 billion, 2% of GNP (FY91)

Iran Geography

Total area: 1,648,000 km2
Land area: 1,636,000 km2
Comparative area: slightly larger than Alaska
Land boundaries:
5,440 km; Afghanistan 936 km, Armenia 35 km, Azerbaijan (north) 432 km,
Azerbaijan (northwest) 179 km, Iraq 1,458 km, Pakistan 909 km, Turkey 499
km, Turkmenistan 992 km

Coastline:
2,440 km
note:
Iran also borders the Caspian Sea (740 km)

Maritime claims:
Continental shelf:
not specific
Exclusive fishing zone:
50 nm in the Sea of Oman; continental shelf limit, continental shelf
boundaries, or median lines in the Persian Gulf
Territorial sea:
12 nm

Disputes:
Iran and Iraq restored diplomatic relations in 1990 but are still trying to
work out written agreements settling outstanding disputes from their
eight-year war concerning border demarcation, prisoners-of-war, and freedom
of navigation and sovereignty over the Shatt-al-Arab waterway; Iran occupies
two islands in the Persian Gulf claimed by the UAE: Tunb as Sughra (Arabic),
Jazireh-ye Tonb-e Kuchek (Persian) or Lesser Tunb, and Tunb al Kubra
(Arabic), Jazireh-ye Tonb-e Bozorg (Persian) or Greater Tunb; it jointly
administers with the UAE an island in the Persian Gulf claimed by the UAE,
Abu Musa (Arabic) or Jazireh-ye Abu Musa (Persian)

Climate:

mostly arid or semiarid, subtropical along Caspian coast
Terrain:
   rugged, mountainous rim; high, central basin with deserts, mountains; small,
   discontinuous plains along both coasts
Natural resources:
   petroleum, natural gas, coal, chromium, copper, iron ore, lead, manganese,
   zinc, sulfur
Land use:
   arable land 8%; permanent crops NEGL%; meadows and pastures 27%; forest and
   woodland 11%; other 54%; includes irrigated 2%
Environment:
   deforestation; overgrazing; desertification

:Iran People

Population: 61,183,138 (July 1992), growth rate 3.5% (1992)
Birth rate: 44 births/1,000 population (1992)
Death rate: 8 deaths/1,000 population (1992)
Net migration rate: 0 migrants/1,000 population (1992)
Infant mortality rate: 64 deaths/1,000 live births (1992)
Life expectancy at birth: 64 years male, 66 years female (1992)
Total fertility rate: 6.5 children born/woman (1992)
Nationality:
   noun - Iranian(s); adjective - Iranian
Ethnic divisions:
   Persian 51%, Azerbaijani 25%, Kurd 9%, Gilaki and Mazandarani 8%, Lur 2%,
   Baloch 1%, Arab 1%, other 3%
Religions:
   Shi`a Muslim 95%, Sunni Muslim 4%, Zoroastrian, Jewish, Christian, and
   Baha'i 1%
Languages:
   58% Persian and Persian dialects, 26% Turkic and Turkic dialects, 9%
   Kurdish, 2% Luri, 1% Baloch, 1% Arabic, 1% Turkish, 2% other
Literacy:
   54% (male 64%, female 43%) age 15 and over can read and write (1990 est.)
Labor force:
   15,400,000; agriculture 33%, manufacturing 21%; shortage of skilled labor
   (1988 est.)
Organized labor:
   none

:Iran Government

Long-form name:
   Islamic Republic of Iran
Type:
   theocratic republic
Capital: Tehran
Administrative divisions:
   24 provinces (ostanha, singular - ostan); Azarbayjan-e Bakhtari,
   Azarbayjan-e Khavari, Bakhtaran, Bushehr, Chahar Machall va Bakhtiari,
   Ecsfahan, Fars, Gilan, Hamadan, Hormozgan, Ilam, Kerman, Khorasan,
   Khuzestan, Kohkiluyeh va Buyer Achmadi, Kordestan, Lorestan, Markazi,

Mazandaran, Semnan, Sistan va Baluchestan, Tehran, Yazd, Zanjan

Independence:

1 April 1979, Islamic Republic of Iran proclaimed

Constitution:

2-3 December 1979; revised 1989 to expand powers of the presidency and eliminate the prime ministership

Legal system:

the Constitution codifies Islamic principles of government

National holiday:

Islamic Republic Day, 1 April (1979)

Executive branch:

cleric (faqih), president, Council of Ministers

Legislative branch:

unicameral Islamic Consultative Assembly (Majles-e-Shura-ye-Eslami)

Judicial branch:

Supreme Court

Leaders:

Cleric and functional Chief of State:

Leader of the Islamic Revolution Ayatollah Ali HOSEINI-KHAMENEI (since 4 June 1989)

Head of Government:

President Ali Akbar HASHEMI-RAFSANJANI (since 3 August 1989)

Political parties and leaders:

there are at least 18 licensed parties; the three most important are -
Tehran Militant Clergy Association, Mohammad Reza MAHDAVI-KANI; Militant Clerics Association, Mehdi MAHDAVI-KARUBI and Mohammad Asqar MUSAVI-KHOINIHA; Fedaiyin Islam Organization, Sadeq KHALKHALI

Suffrage:

universal at age 15

Elections:

President:

last held July 1989 (next to be held April 1993); results - Ali Akbar HASHEMI-RAFSANJANI was elected with only token opposition

Islamic Consultative Assembly:

last held 8 April 1992 (next to be held April 1996); results - percent of vote by party NA; seats - (270 seats total) number of seats by party NA

Communists:

1,000 to 2,000 est. hardcore; 15,000 to 20,000 est. sympathizers; crackdown in 1983 crippled the party; trials of captured leaders began in late 1983

Other political or pressure groups:

groups that generally support the Islamic Republic include Hizballah, Hojjatiyeh Society, Mojahedin of the Islamic Revolution, Muslim Students Following the Line of the Imam; armed political groups that have been almost completely repressed by the government include Mojahedin-e Khalq Organization (MEK), People's Fedayeen, Kurdish Democratic Party; the Society for the Defense of Freedom

:Iran Government

Member of:

CCC, CP, ESCAP, FAO, G-19, G-24, G-77, IAEA, IBRD, ICAO, ICC, IDA, IDB,

IFAD, IFC, ILO, IMF, IMO, INMARSAT, INTELSAT, INTERPOL, IOC, ISO, ITU,

LORCS, NAM, OIC, OPEC, PCA, UN, UNCTAD, UNESCO, UNHCR, UNIDO, UPU, WFTU,

WHO, WMO, WTO

Diplomatic representation:

none; protecting power in the US is Pakistan - Iranian Interests Section,

2315 Massachusetts Avenue NW, Washington, DC 20008; telephone (202) 939-6200

US:

protecting power in Iran is Switzerland

Flag:

three equal horizontal bands of green (top), white, and red; the national emblem (a stylized representation of the word Allah) in red is centered in the white band; Allah Alkbar (God is Great) in white Arabic script is repeated 11 times along the bottom edge of the green band and 11 times along the top edge of the red band

:Iran Economy

Overview:

Iran's economy is a mixture of central planning, state ownership of oil and other large enterprises, village agriculture, and small-scale private trading and service ventures. After a decade of economic decline, Iran's GNP grew roughly 4% in FY90 and 10% in FY91. An oil windfall in 1990 combined with a substantial increase in imports contributed to Iran's recent economic growth. Iran has also begun implementing a number of economic reforms to reduce government intervention (including subsidies) and has allocated substantial resources to development projects in the hope of stimulating the economy. Nevertheless, lower oil revenues in 1991 - oil accounts for more than 90% of export revenues and provides roughly 65% of the financing for the five-year economic development plan - and dramatic increases in external debt are threatening development plans and could prompt Iran to cut imports, thus limiting economic growth in the medium term.

GNP:

exchange rate conversion - $90 billion, per capita $1,500; real growth rate 10% (FY91 est.)

Inflation rate (consumer prices):

18% (FY91 est.)

Unemployment rate: 30% (1989)

Budget:

revenues $63 billion; expenditures $80 billion, including capital expenditures of $23 billion (FY90 est.)

Exports:

$17.8 billion (f.o.b., 1990)

commodities:

petroleum 90%, carpets, fruits, nuts, hides

partners:

Japan, Italy, France, Netherlands, Belgium/Luxembourg, Spain, and Germany

Imports:

$15.9 billion (c.i.f., 1990)

commodities:

machinery, military supplies, metal works, foodstuffs, pharmaceuticals,
technical services, refined oil products
 partners:
Germany, Japan, Italy, UK, France
External debt: $10 billion (1990 est.)
Industrial production:
  growth rate NA%
Electricity:
  14,579,000 kW capacity; 40,000 million kWh produced, 740 kWh per capita
  (1989)
Industries:
  petroleum, petrochemicals, textiles, cement and other building materials,
  food processing (particularly sugar refining and vegetable oil production),
  metal fabricating (steel and copper)
Agriculture:
  principal products - wheat, rice, other grains, sugar beets, fruits, nuts,
  cotton, dairy products, wool, caviar; not self-sufficient in food
Illicit drugs:
  illicit producer of opium poppy for the domestic and international drug
  trade
Economic aid:
  US commitments, including Ex-Im (FY70-80), $1.0 billion; Western (non-US)
  countries, ODA and OOF bilateral commitments (1970-89), $1.675 billion;
  Communist countries (1970-89), $976 million; note - aid fell sharply
  following the 1979 revolution

:Iran Economy

Currency:
  Iranian rial (plural - rials); 1 Iranian rial (IR) = 100 dinars; note -
  domestic figures are generally referred to in terms of the toman (plural -
  tomans), which equals 10 rials
Exchange rates:
  Iranian rials (IR) per US$1 - 65.515 (January 1992), 67.505 (1991), 68.096
  (1990), 72.015 (1989), 68.683 (1988), 71.460 (1987); note - black-market
  rate 1,400 (January 1991)
Fiscal year: 21 March - 20 March

:Iran Communications

Railroads:
  4,850 km total; 4,760 km 1.432-meter gauge, 92 km 1.676-meter gauge; 480 km
  under construction from Bafq to Bandar Abbas, rail construction from Bafq to
  Sirjan has been completed and is operational
Highways:
  140,072 km total; 42,694 km paved surfaces; 46,866 km gravel and crushed
  stone; 49,440 km improved earth; 1,200 km (est.) rural road network
Inland waterways:
  904 km; the Shatt-al-Arab is usually navigable by maritime traffic for about
  130 km, but closed since September 1980 because of Iran-Iraq war
Pipelines:
  crude oil 5,900 km; petroleum products 3,900 km; natural gas 4,550 km
Ports:

Abadan (largely destroyed in fighting during 1980-88 war), Bandar Beheshti, Bandar-e Abbas, Bandar-e Bushehr, Bandar-e Khomeyni, Bandar-e Shahid Raja, Khorramshahr (largely destroyed in fighting during 1980-88 war)

Merchant marine:

134 ships (1,000 GRT or over) totaling 4,466,395 GRT/8,329,760 DWT; includes 38 cargo, 6 roll-on/roll-off cargo, 32 oil tanker, 4 chemical tanker, 3 refrigerated cargo, 47 bulk, 2 combination bulk, 1 liquefied gas

Civil air:

48 major transport aircraft

Airports:

214 total, 188 usable; 81 with permanent-surface runways; 16 with runways over 3,659 m; 16 with runways 2,440-3,659 m; 71 with runways 1,220-2,439 m

Telecommunications:

radio relay extends throughout country; system centered in Tehran; 2,143,000 telephones; broadcast stations - 77 AM, 3 FM, 28 TV; satellite earth stations - 2 Atlantic Ocean INTELSAT and 1 Indian Ocean INTELSAT; HF radio and radio relay to Turkey, Pakistan, Syria, Kuwait, Tajikistan, and Uzbekistan

:Iran Defense Forces

Branches:

Islamic Republic of Iran Ground Forces, Navy, Air Force, and Revolutionary Guard Corps (includes Basij militia and own ground, air, and naval forces); Law Enforcement Forces

Manpower availability:

males 15-49, 13,267,810; 7,895,591 fit for military service; 552,408 reach military age (21) annually

Defense expenditures:

exchange rate conversion - $13 billion, 14-15% of GNP (1991 est.)

Iraq Geography

Total area: 436,245 km2
Land area: 435,292 km2 (est.)
Comparative area: slightly more than twice the size of Idaho

Land boundaries:

3,576 km; Iran 1,458 km, Jordan 134 km, Kuwait 240 km, Saudi Arabia 808 km, Syria 605 km, Turkey 331 km

Coastline:

58 km

Maritime claims:

 Continental shelf:
 not specific
 Territorial sea:
 12 nm

Disputes:

Iran and Iraq restored diplomatic relations in 1990 but are still trying to work out written agreements settling outstanding disputes from their eight-year war concerning border demarcation, prisoners-of-war, and freedom of navigation and sovereignty over the Shatt-al-Arab waterway; in April 1991 official Iraqi acceptance of UN Security Council Resolution 687, which demands that Iraq accept the inviolability of the boundary set forth in its

1963 agreement with Kuwait, ending earlier claims to Bubiyan and Warbah Islands or to all of Kuwait; a United Nations Boundary Demarcation Commission is demarcating the Iraq-Kuwait boundary persuant to Resolution 687, and, on 17 June 1992, the UN Security Council reaffirmed the finality of the Boundary Demarcation Commission's decisions; periodic disputes with upstream riparian Syria over Euphrates water rights; potential dispute over water development plans by Turkey for the Tigris and Euphrates Rivers

Climate:
mostly desert; mild to cool winters with dry, hot, cloudless summers; northernmost regions along Iranian and Turkish borders experience cold winters with occasionally heavy snows

Terrain:
mostly broad plains; reedy marshes in southeast; mountains along borders with Iran and Turkey

Natural resources:
crude oil, natural gas, phosphates, sulfur

Land use:
arable land 12%; permanent crops 1%; meadows and pastures 9%; forest and woodland 3%; other 75%; includes irrigated 4%

Environment:
development of Tigris-Euphrates Rivers system contingent upon agreements with upstream riparians (Syria, Turkey); air and water pollution; soil degradation (salinization) and erosion; desertification

:Iraq People

Population: 18,445,847 (July 1992), growth rate 3.7% (1992)
Birth rate: 45 births/1,000 population (1992)
Death rate: 9 deaths/1,000 population (1992)
Net migration rate: NEGL migrants/1,000 population (1992)
Infant mortality rate: 84 deaths/1,000 live births (1992)
Life expectancy at birth: 62 years male, 64 years female (1992)
Total fertility rate: 7.0 children born/woman (1992)

Nationality:
noun - Iraqi(s); adjective - Iraqi

Ethnic divisions:
Arab 75-80%, Kurdish 15-20%, Turkoman, Assyrian or other 5%

Religions:
Muslim 97%, (Shi`a 60-65%, Sunni 32-37%), Christian or other 3%

Languages:
Arabic (official), Kurdish (official in Kurdish regions), Assyrian, Armenian

Literacy:
60% (male 70%, female 49%) age 15 and over can read and write (1990 est.)

Labor force:
4,400,000 (1989); services 48%, agriculture 30%, industry 22%, severe labor shortage, expatriate labor force about 1,600,000 (July 1990)

Organized labor:
less than 10% of the labor force

:Iraq Government

Long-form name:
Republic of Iraq

455

Type:

republic

Capital: Baghdad

Administrative divisions:

18 provinces (muhafazat, singular - muhafazah); Al Anbar, Al Basrah, Al Muthanna, Al Qadisiyah, An Najaf, Arbil, As Sulaymaniyah, At Ta'im, Babil, Baghdad, Dahuk, Dhi Qar, Diyala, Karbala, Maysan, Ninawa, Salah ad Din, Wasit

Independence:

3 October 1932 (from League of Nations mandate under British administration)

Constitution:

22 September 1968, effective 16 July 1970 (interim Constitution); new constitution drafted in 1990 but not adopted

Legal system:

based on Islamic law in special religious courts, civil law system elsewhere; has not accepted compulsory ICJ jurisdiction

National holiday:

Anniversary of the Revolution, 17 July (1968)

Executive branch:

president, vice president, chairman of the Revolutionary Command Council, vice chairman of the Revolutionary Command Council, prime minister, first deputy prime minister, Council of Ministers

Legislative branch:

unicameral National Assembly (Majlis al-Watani)

Judicial branch:

Court of Cassation

Leaders:

 Chief of State:

President SADDAM Husayn (since 16 July 1979); Vice President Taha Muhyi al-Din MA'RUF (since 21 April 1974); Vice President Taha Yasin RAMADAN (since 23 March 1991)

 Head of Government:

Prime Minister Muhammad Hamza al-ZUBAYDI (since 13 September 1991); Deputy

Prime Minister Tariq `AZIZ (since NA 1979)

Suffrage:

universal adult at age 18

Elections:

 National Assembly:

last held on 1 April 1989 (next to be held NA); results - Sunni Arabs 53%, Shi`a Arabs 30%, Kurds 15%, Christians 2% est.; seats - (250 total) number of seats by party NA

Other political or pressure groups:

political parties and activity severely restricted; possibly some opposition to regime from disaffected members of the regime, Army officers, and Shi`a religious and Kurdish ethnic dissidents

Member of:

ABEDA, ACC, AFESD, AL, AMF, CAEU, CCC, ESCWA, FAO, G-19, G-77, IAEA, IBRD,

ICAO, IDA, IDB, IFAD, IFC, ILO, IMF, IMO, INMARSAT, INTELSAT,

INTERPOL, IOC,

ISO, ITU, LORCS, NAM, OAPEC, OIC, OPEC, PCA, UN, UNCTAD, UNESCO, UNIDO, UPU,

WFTU, WHO, WIPO, WMO, WTO

Diplomatic representation:

Iraq has an Interest Section in the Algerian Embassy in Washington, DC; Chancery at 1801 P Street NW, Washington, DC 20036; telephone (202) 483-7500

:Iraq Government

US:

no US representative in Baghdad since mid-January 1991; Embassy in Masbah Quarter (opposite the Foreign Ministry Club), Baghdad (mailing address is P. O. Box 2447 Alwiyah, Baghdad); telephone [964] (1) 719-6138 or 719-6139, 718-1840, 719-3791

Flag:

three equal horizontal bands of red (top), white, and black with three green five-pointed stars in a horizontal line centered in the white band; the phrase Allahu Akbar (God is Great) in green Arabic script - Allahu to the right of the middle star and Akbar to the left of the middle star - was added in January 1991 during the Persian Gulf crisis; similar to the flag of Syria that has two stars but no script and the flag of Yemen that has a plain white band; also similar to the flag of Egypt that has a symbolic eagle centered in the white band

:Iraq Economy

Overview:

The Ba`thist regime engages in extensive central planning and management of industrial production and foreign trade while leaving some small-scale industry and services and most agriculture to private enterprise. The economy has been dominated by the oil sector, which has provided about 95% of foreign exchange earnings. In the 1980s financial problems, caused by massive expenditures in the eight-year war with Iran and damage to oil export facilities by Iran, led the government to implement austerity measures and to borrow heavily and later reschedule foreign debt payments. After the end of hostilities in 1988, oil exports gradually increased with the construction of new pipelines and restoration of damaged facilities. Agricultural development remained hampered by labor shortages, salinization, and dislocations caused by previous land reform and collectivization programs. The industrial sector, although accorded high priority by the government, also was under financial constraints. Iraq's seizure of Kuwait in August 1990, subsequent international economic embargoes, and military actions by an international coalition beginning in January 1991 drastically changed the economic picture. Oil exports were cut to near zero, and industrial and transportation facilities were severely damaged. Throughout 1991, the UN's economic embargo worked to reduce exports and imports and to increase prices for most goods. The government's policy to allocate goods to key supporters of the regime exacerbated shortages.

GNP:

$35 billion, per capita $1,940; real growth rate 10% (1989 est.)

Inflation rate (consumer prices):

45% (1989)

457

Unemployment rate: less than 5% (1989 est.)
Budget:
   revenues $NA billion; expenditures $NA billion, including capital
   expenditures of NA (1989)
Exports:
   $10.4 billion (f.o.b., 1990)
  commodities:
   crude oil and refined products, fertilizer, sulfur
  partners:
   US, Brazil, Turkey, Japan, Netherlands, Spain (1990)
Imports:
   $6.6 billion (c.i.f., 1990)
  commodities:
   manufactures, food
  partners:
   FRG, US, Turkey, France, UK (1990)
External debt: $45 billion (1989 est.), excluding debt of about $35 billion owed to Arab
   Gulf states
Industrial production:
   NA%; manufacturing accounts for 10% of GNP (1989)
Electricity:
   3,800,000 kW available out of 9,902,000 kw capacity due to Gulf war; 7,700
   million kWh produced, 430 kWh per capita (1991)
Industries:
   petroleum production and refining, chemicals, textiles, construction
   materials, food processing
Agriculture:
   accounts for 11% of GNP but 30% of labor force; principal products - wheat,
   barley, rice, vegetables, dates, other fruit, cotton, wool; livestock -
   cattle, sheep; not self-sufficient in food output

:Iraq Economy

Economic aid:
   US commitments, including Ex-Im (FY70-80), $3 million; Western (non-US)
   countries, ODA and OOF bilateral commitments (1970-89), $647 million;
   Communist countries (1970-89), $3.9 billion
Currency:
   Iraqi dinar (plural - dinars); 1 Iraqi dinar (ID) = 1,000 fils
Exchange rates:
   Iraqi dinars (ID) per US$1 - 3.1 (fixed official rate since 1982);
   black-market rate (December 1991) US$1 = 12 Iraqi dinars
Fiscal year: calendar year

:Iraq Communications

Railroads:
   2,457 km 1.435-meter standard gauge
Highways:
   34,700 km total; 17,500 km paved, 5,500 km improved earth, 11,700 km
   unimproved earth
Inland waterways:

1,015 km; Shatt-al-Arab usually navigable by maritime traffic for about 130 km, but closed since September 1980 because of Iran-Iraq war; Tigris and Euphrates Rivers have navigable sections for shallow-draft watercraft; Shatt-al-Basrah canal was navigable by shallow-draft craft before closing in 1991 because of the Persian Gulf war

Pipelines:
  crude oil 4,350 km; petroleum products 725 km; natural gas 1,360 km
Ports:
  Umm Qasr, Khawr az Zubayr, Al Basrah (closed since 1980)
Merchant marine:
  42 ships (1,000 GRT or over) totaling 936,665 GRT/1,683,212 DWT; includes 1 passenger, 1 passenger-cargo, 16 cargo, 1 refrigerated cargo, 3 roll-on/roll-off cargo, 19 petroleum tanker, 1 chemical tanker; note - since the 2 August 1990 invasion of Kuwait by Iraqi forces, Iraq has sought to register at least part of its merchant fleet under convenience flags; none of the Iraqi flag merchant fleet was trading internationally as of 1 January 1992
Civil air:
  34 major transport aircraft (including 7 grounded in Iran; excluding 12 IL-76s and 7 Kuwait Airlines)
Airports:
  113 total, 98 usable; 73 with permanent-surface runways; 8 with runways over 3,659 m; 52 with runways 2,440-3,659 m; 12 with runways 1,220-2,439 m
Telecommunications:
  reconstitution of damaged telecommunication infrastructure began after Desert Storm; the network consists of coaxial cables and microwave links; 632,000 telephones; the network is operational; broadcast stations - 16 AM, 1 FM, 13 TV; satellite earth stations - 1 Atlantic Ocean INTELSAT, 1 Indian Ocean INTELSAT, 1 GORIZONT Atlantic Ocean in the Intersputnik system and 1 ARABSAT; coaxial cable and microwave to Jordan, Kuwait, Syria, and Turkey

:Iraq Defense Forces

Branches:
  Army and Republican Guard, Navy, Air Force, Border Guard Force, Internal Security Forces
Manpower availability:
  males 15-49, 4,042,374; 2,272,578 fit for military service; 213,788 reach military age (18) annually
Defense expenditures:
  exchange rate conversion - $NA, NA% of GNP

Ireland Geography

Total area: 70,280 km2
Land area: 68,890 km2
Comparative area: slightly larger than West Virginia
Land boundaries:
  360 km; UK 360 km
Coastline:
  1,448 km
Maritime claims:
  Continental shelf:

459

no precise definition
Exclusive fishing zone:
  200 nm
Territorial sea:
  12 nm
Disputes:
  Northern Ireland question with the UK; Rockall continental shelf dispute
  involving Denmark, Iceland, and the UK (Ireland and the UK have signed a
  boundary agreement in the Rockall area)
Climate:
  temperate maritime; modified by North Atlantic Current; mild winters, cool
  summers; consistently humid; overcast about half the time
Terrain:
  mostly level to rolling interior plain surrounded by rugged hills and low
  mountains; sea cliffs on west coast
Natural resources:
  zinc, lead, natural gas, crude oil, barite, copper, gypsum, limestone,
  dolomite, peat, silver
Land use:
  arable land 14%; permanent crops NEGL%; meadows and pastures 71%; forest and
  woodland 5%; other 10%
Environment:
  deforestation

:Ireland People

Population: 3,521,207 (July 1992), growth rate 0.2% (1992)
Birth rate: 15 births/1,000 population (1992)
Death rate: 9 deaths/1,000 population (1992)
Net migration rate: -4 migrants/1,000 population (1992)
Infant mortality rate: 8 deaths/1,000 live births (1992)
Life expectancy at birth: 72 years male, 78 years female (1992)
Total fertility rate: 2.0 children born/woman (1992)
Nationality:
  noun - Irishman(men), Irish (collective pl.); adjective - Irish
Ethnic divisions:
  Celtic, with English minority
Religions:
  Roman Catholic 93%, Anglican 3%, none 1%, unknown 2%, other 1% (1981)
Languages:
  Irish (Gaelic) and English; English is the language generally used, with
  Gaelic spoken in a few areas, mostly along the western seaboard
Literacy:
  98% (male NA%, female NA%) age 15 and over can read and write (1981)
Labor force:
  1,333,000; services 57.0%, manufacturing and construction 26.1%,
  agriculture, forestry, and fishing 15.0%, energy and mining 1.9% (1991)
Organized labor:
  58% of labor force (1991)

:Ireland Government

Long-form name:
  none
Type:
  republic
Capital: Dublin
Administrative divisions:
  26 counties; Carlow, Cavan, Clare, Cork, Donegal, Dublin, Galway, Kerry,
  Kildare, Kilkenny, Laois, Leitrim, Limerick, Longford, Louth, Mayo, Meath,
  Monaghan, Offaly, Roscommon, Sligo, Tipperary, Waterford, Westmeath,
  Wexford, Wicklow
Independence:
  6 December 1921 (from UK)
Constitution:
  29 December 1937; adopted 1937
Legal system:
  based on English common law, substantially modified by indigenous concepts;
  judicial review of legislative acts in Supreme Court; has not accepted
  compulsory ICJ jurisdiction
National holiday:
  Saint Patrick's Day, 17 March
Executive branch:
  president, prime minister, deputy prime minister, Cabinet
Legislative branch:
  bicameral Parliament (Oireachtas) consists of an upper house or Senate
  (Seanad Eireann) and a lower house or House of Representatives (Dail
  Eireann)
Judicial branch:
  Supreme Court
Leaders:
 Chief of State:
  President Mary Bourke ROBINSON (since 9 November 1990)
 Head of Government:
  Prime Minister Albert REYNOLDS (since 11 February 1992)
Political parties and leaders:
  Fianna Fail, Albert REYNOLDS; Labor Party, Richard SPRING; Fine Gael, John
  BRUTON; Communist Party of Ireland, Michael O'RIORDAN; Workers' Party
  (vacant); Sinn Fein, Gerry ADAMS; Progressive Democrats, Desmond O'MALLEY;
  note - Prime Minister REYNOLDS heads a coalition consisting of the Fianna
  Fail and the Progressive Democrats
Suffrage:
  universal at age 18
Elections:
 President:
  last held 9 November 1990 (next to be held November 1997); results - Mary
  Bourke ROBINSON 52.8%, Brian LENIHAN 47.2%
 Senate:
  last held on 17 February 1987 (next to be held February 1992); results -
  percent of vote by party NA; seats - (60 total, 49 elected) Fianna Fail 30,
  Fine Gael 16, Labor 3, independents 11
 House of Representatives:

461

last held on 12 July 1989 (next to be held June 1994); results - Fianna Fail
44.0%, Fine Gael 29.4%, Labor Party 9.3%, Progressive Democrats 5.4%,
Workers' Party 4.9%, Sinn Fein 1.1%, independents 5.9%; seats - (166 total)
Fianna Fail 77, Fine Gael 55, Labor Party 15, Workers' Party 7, Progressive
Democrats 6, independents 6

Communists:
    under 500

:Ireland Government

Member of:
    AG, BIS, CCC, CE, CSCE, EBRD, EC, ECE, EIB, ESA, FAO, GATT, IAEA,
IBRD,
    ICAO, ICC, IDA, IEA, IFAD, IFC, ILO, IMF, IMO, INTELSAT, INTERPOL, IOC,
ISO,
    ITU, LORCS, NEA, NSG, OECD, UN, UNCTAD, UNESCO, UNFICYP, UNIDO,
UNIFIL,
    UNIIMOG, UNTSO, UPU, WHO, WIPO, WMO, ZC

Diplomatic representation:
    Ambassador Dermot GALLAGHER; Chancery at 2234 Massachusetts Avenue NW,
    Washington, DC 20008; telephone (202) 462-3939; there are Irish Consulates
    General in Boston, Chicago, New York, and San Francisco
    US:
    Ambassador Richard A. MOORE; Embassy at 42 Elgin Road, Ballsbridge, Dublin;
    telephone [353] (1) 688777; FAX [353] (1) 689-946

Flag:
    three equal vertical bands of green (hoist side), white, and orange; similar
    to the flag of the Ivory Coast, which is shorter and has the colors reversed
    - orange (hoist side), white, and green; also similar to the flag of Italy,
    which is shorter and has colors of green (hoist side), white, and red

:Ireland Economy

Overview:
    The economy is small, open, and trade dependent. Agriculture, once the most
    important sector, is now dwarfed by industry, which accounts for 37% of GDP
    and about 80% of exports and employs 26% of the labor force. The government
    has successfully reduced the rate of inflation from double-digit figures in
    the late 1970s to 3.8% in 1991. In 1987, after years of deficits, the
    balance of payments was brought into the black. Unemployment, however,
    remains a serious problem. A 1991 unemployment rate of 20.4% placed Ireland
    along with Spain as the countries with the worst jobless records in Western
    Europe.

GDP:
    purchasing power equivalent - $39.2 billion, per capita $11,200; real growth
    rate 1.3% (1991 est.)

Inflation rate (consumer prices):
    3.8% (1991)

Unemployment rate: 20.4% (1991)

Budget:
    revenues $11.4 billion; expenditures $12.6 billion, including capital
    expenditures of $1.6 billion (1992 est.)

Exports:

$27.8 billion (f.o.b., 1991)

commodities:

chemicals, data processing equipment, industrial machinery, live animals, animal products

partners:

EC 74% (UK 34%, Germany 11%, France 10%), US 8%

Imports:

$24.5 billion (c.i.f., 1991)

commodities:

food, animal feed, chemicals, petroleum and petroleum products, machinery, textiles, clothing

partners:

EC 66% (UK 41%, Germany 9%, France 4%), US 14%

External debt: $14.8 billion (1990)

Industrial production:

growth rate 3.0% (1991); accounts for 37% of GDP

Electricity:

4,957,000 kW capacity; 14,480 million kWh produced, 4,080 kWh per capita (1991)

Industries:

food products, brewing, textiles, clothing, chemicals, pharmaceuticals, machinery, transportation equipment, glass and crystal

Agriculture:

accounts for 11% of GDP and 15% of the labor force; principal crops - turnips, barley, potatoes, sugar beets, wheat; livestock - meat and dairy products; 85% self-sufficient in food; food shortages include bread grain, fruits, vegetables

Economic aid:

donor - ODA commitments (1980-89), $90 million

Currency:

Irish pound (plural - pounds); 1 Irish pound (#Ir) = 100 pence

Exchange rates:

Irish pounds (#Ir) per US$1 - 0.6227 (March 1992), 0.6190 (1991), 0.6030 (1990), 0.7472 (1989), 0.6553 (1988), 0.6720 (1987)

Fiscal year: calendar year

:Ireland Communications

Railroads:

Irish National Railways (CIE) operates 1,947 km 1.602-meter gauge, government owned; 485 km double track; 38 km electrified

Highways:

92,294 km total; 87,422 km paved, 4,872 km gravel or crushed stone

Inland waterways:

limited for commercial traffic

Pipelines:

natural gas 225 km

Ports:

Cork, Dublin, Shannon Estuary, Waterford

Merchant marine:

55 ships (1,000 GRT or over) totaling 146,081 GRT/177,058 DWT; includes 4

short-sea passenger, 32 cargo, 2 refrigerated cargo, 3 container, 3
petroleum tanker, 3 specialized tanker, 2 chemical tanker, 6 bulk

Civil air:

23 major transport aircraft

Airports:

36 total, 35 usable; 17 with permanent-surface runways; none with runways
over 3,659 m; 2 with runways 2,440-3,659 m; 6 with runways 1,220-2,439 m

Telecommunications:

small, modern system using cable and digital microwave circuits; 900,000
telephones; broadcast stations - 9 AM, 45 FM, 86 TV; 2 coaxial submarine
cables; 1 Atlantic Ocean INTELSAT earth station

:Ireland Defense Forces

Branches:

Army (including Naval Service and Air Corps), National Police (GARDA)

Manpower availability:

males 15-49, 894,421; 724,262 fit for military service; 34,182 reach
military age (17) annually

Defense expenditures:

exchange rate conversion - $566 million, 1-2% of GDP (1992 est.)

:Israel Header

Note:

The Arab territories occupied by Israel since the 1967 war are not included
in the data below. As stated in the 1978 Camp David Accords and reaffirmed
by President Bush's post-Gulf crisis peace initiative, the final status of
the West Bank and Gaza Strip, their relationship with their neighbors, and a
peace treaty between Israel and Jordan are to be negotiated among the
concerned parties. The Camp David Accords further specify that these
negotiations will resolve the location of the respective boundaries. Pending
the completion of this process, it is US policy that the final status of the
West Bank and Gaza Strip has yet to be determined (see West Bank and Gaza
Strip entries). On 25 April 1982 Israel relinquished control of the Sinai to
Egypt. Statistics for the Israeli-occupied Golan Heights are included in the
Syria entry.

Israel Geography

Total area: 20,770 km2
Land area: 20,330 km2
Comparative area: slightly larger than New Jersey

Land boundaries:

1,006 km; Egypt 255 km, Jordan 238 km, Lebanon 79 km, Syria 76 km, West Bank
307, Gaza Strip 51 km

Coastline:

273 km

Maritime claims:

 Continental shelf:

  to depth of exploitation

 Territorial sea:

  6 nm

Disputes:

separated from Lebanon, Syria, and the West Bank by the 1949 Armistice Line; differences with Jordan over the location of the 1949 Armistice Line that separates the two countries; West Bank and Gaza Strip are Israeli occupied with status to be determined; Golan Heights is Israeli occupied; Israeli troops in southern Lebanon since June 1982; water-sharing issues with Jordan

Climate:
temperate; hot and dry in desert areas

Terrain:
Negev desert in the south; low coastal plain; central mountains; Jordan Rift Valley

Natural resources:
copper, phosphates, bromide, potash, clay, sand, sulfur, asphalt, manganese, small amounts of natural gas and crude oil

Land use:
arable land 17%; permanent crops 5%; meadows and pastures 40%; forest and woodland 6%; other 32%; includes irrigated 11%

Environment:
sandstorms may occur during spring and summer; limited arable land and natural water resources pose serious constraints; deforestation

Note:
there are 175 Jewish settlements in the West Bank, 38 in the Israeli-occupied Golan Heights, 18 in the Gaza Strip, and 14 Israeli-built Jewish neighborhoods in East Jerusalem

:Israel People

Population: 4,748,059 (July 1992), growth rate 4.0% (1992); includes 95,000 Jewish settlers in the West Bank, 14,000 in the Israeli-occupied Golan Heights, 4,000 in the Gaza Strip, and 132,000 in East Jerusalem (1992 est.)

Birth rate: 21 births/1,000 population (1992)

Death rate: 6 deaths/1,000 population (1992)

Net migration rate: 26 migrants/1,000 population (1992)

Infant mortality rate: 9 deaths/1,000 live births (1992)

Life expectancy at birth: 76 years male, 80 years female (1992)

Total fertility rate: 2.9 children born/woman (1992)

Nationality:
noun - Israeli(s); adjective - Israeli

Ethnic divisions:
Jewish 83%, non-Jewish (mostly Arab) 17%

Religions:
Judaism 82%, Islam (mostly Sunni Muslim) 14%, Christian 2%, Druze and other 2%

Languages:
Hebrew (official); Arabic used officially for Arab minority; English most commonly used foreign language

Literacy:
92% (male 95%, female 89%) age 15 and over can read and write (1983)

Labor force:
1,400,000 (1984 est.); public services 29.3%; industry, mining, and manufacturing 22.8%; commerce 12.8%; finance and business 9.5%; transport, storage, and communications 6.8%; construction and public works 6.5%;

personal and other services 5.8%; agriculture, forestry, and fishing 5.5%;
electricity and water 1.0% (1983)

Organized labor:
90% of labor force

:Israel Government

Long-form name:
State of Israel

Type:
republic

Capital: Israel proclaimed Jerusalem its capital in 1950, but the US, like nearly all
other countries, maintains its Embassy in Tel Aviv

Administrative divisions:
6 districts (mehozot, singular - mehoz); Central, Haifa, Jerusalem,
Northern, Southern, Tel Aviv

Independence:
14 May 1948 (from League of Nations mandate under British administration)

Constitution:
no formal constitution; some of the functions of a constitution are filled
by the Declaration of Establishment (1948), the basic laws of the parliament
(Knesset), and the Israeli citizenship law

Legal system:
mixture of English common law, British Mandate regulations, and, in personal
matters, Jewish, Christian, and Muslim legal systems; in December 1985,
Israel informed the UN Secretariat that it would no longer accept compulsory
ICJ jurisdiction

National holiday:
Independence Day; Israel declared independence on 14 May 1948, but the
Jewish calendar is lunar and the holiday may occur in April or May

Executive branch:
president, prime minister, vice prime minister, Cabinet

Legislative branch:
unicameral parliament (Knesset)

Judicial branch:
Supreme Court

Leaders:
 Chief of State:
 President Chaim HERZOG (since 5 May 1983)
 Head of Government:
 Prime Minister Yitzhak SHAMIR (since 20 October 1986)

Political parties and leaders:
Israel currently has a coalition government comprising 12 parties that hold
66 of the Knesset's 120 seats; currently in state of flux; election held 23
June 1992
 Members of the government:
 Likud bloc, Prime Minister Yitzhak SHAMIR; Sephardic Torah Guardians (SHAS),
 Minister of Interior Arieh DER'I; National Religious Party, Minister of
 Education Shulamit ALONI; Agudat Israel, Avraham SHAPIRA; Degel HaTorah,
 Avraham RAVITZ; Moriya, Minister of Immigrant Absorption, Yair TZABAN;
 Ge'ulat Israel, Eliezer MIZRAHI; New Liberal Party, Minister of Finance,

Avraham SHOCHAT; Tehiya Party, Minister of Science Technology, Yuval
NEEMAN;
Tzomet Party Unity for Peace and Aliyah, Rafael EITAN; Moledet Party,
Rehavam ZEEVI
Opposition parties:
Labor Party, Shimon PERES; Citizens' Rights Movement, Shulamit ALONI; United
Workers' Party (MAPAM), Yair TZABAN; Center Movement-Shinui, Amnon
RUBENSTEIN; New Israeli Communist Party (MAKI), Meir WILNER; Progressive
List for Peace, Muhammad MI'ARI; Arab Democratic Party, `Abd Al Wahab
DARAWSHAH; Black Panthers, Charlie BITON
Suffrage:
universal at age 18

:Israel Government

Elections:
President:
last held 23 February 1988 (next to be held February 1994); results - Chaim
HERZOG reelected by Knesset
Knesset:
last held June 1992 (next to be held by NA; results - percent of vote by
party NA; seats - (120 total) Labor Party 44, Likud bloc 12, SHAS 6,
National Religious Party 6, Meretz 12, Agudat Yisrael 4, PAZI 3, MAKI 3,
Tehiya Party 3, Tzomet Party 8, Moledet Party 3, Degel HaTorah 4, Center
Movement Progressive List for Peace 1, Arab Democratic Party 2; Black
Panthers 1, Moriya 1, Ge'ulat Yisrael 1, Unity for Peace and Aliyah 1
Communists:
Hadash (predominantly Arab but with Jews in its leadership) has some 1,500
members
Other political or pressure groups:
Gush Emunim, Jewish nationalists advocating Jewish settlement on the West
Bank and Gaza Strip; Peace Now, critical of government's West Bank/Gaza
Strip and Lebanon policies
Member of:
AG (observer), CCC, EBRD, FAO, GATT, IADB, IAEA, IBRD, ICAO, ICC,
ICFTU,
IDA, IFAD, IFC, ILO, IMF, IMO, INMARSAT, INTELSAT, INTERPOL, IOC,
IOM, ISO,
ITU, OAS (observer), PCA, UN, UNCTAD, UNESCO, UNHCR, UNIDO, UPU,
WHO, WIPO,
WMO, WTO
Diplomatic representation:
Ambassador Zalman SHOVAL; Chancery at 3514 International Drive NW,
Washington, DC 20008; telephone (202) 364-5500; there are Israeli Consulates
General in Atlanta, Boston, Chicago, Houston, Los Angeles, Miami, New York,
Philadelphia, and San Francisco
US:
Ambassador William HARROP; Embassy at 71 Hayarkon Street, Tel Aviv (mailing
address is APO AE 09830; telephone [972] (3) 654338; FAX [972] (3) 663449;
there is a US Consulate General in Jerusalem
Flag:

white with a blue hexagram (six-pointed linear star) known as the Magen
David (Shield of David) centered between two equal horizontal blue bands
near the top and bottom edges of the flag

:Israel Economy

Overview:

Israel has a market economy with substantial government participation. It
depends on imports of crude oil, grains, raw materials, and military
equipment. Despite limited natural resources, Israel has intensively
developed its agricultural and industrial sectors over the past 20 years.
Industry employs about 20% of Israeli workers, agriculture 5%, and services
most of the rest. Diamonds, high-technology equipment, and agricultural
products (fruits and vegetables) are leading exports. Israel usually posts
balance-of-payments deficits, which are covered by large transfer payments
from abroad and by foreign loans. Roughly half of the government's $17
billion external debt is owed to the United States, which is its major
source of economic and military aid. To earn needed foreign exchange, Israel
has been targeting high-technology niches in international markets, such as
medical scanning equipment. Iraq's invasion of Kuwait in August 1990 dealt a
blow to Israel's economy. Higher world oil prices added an estimated $300
million to the oil import bill that year and helped keep annual inflation at
18%. Regional tension and the continuing Palestinian uprising (intifadah)
have contributed to a sharp drop in tourism - a key foreign exchange earner
- to the lowest level since the 1973 Arab-Israeli war. The influx of Jewish
immigrants from the former USSR, which topped 330,000 during the period
1990-91, will increase unemployment, intensify housing problems, widen the
government budget deficit, and fuel inflation.

GDP:

purchasing power equivalent - $54.6 billion, per capita $12,000; real growth
rate 5% (1991 est.)

Inflation rate (consumer prices):

18% (1991 est.)

Unemployment rate: 11% (1991 est.)

Budget:

revenues $41.7 billion; expenditures $47.6 billion, including capital
expenditures of $NA (FY92)

Exports:

$12.1 billion (f.o.b., 1991 est.)

commodities:

polished diamonds, citrus and other fruits, textiles and clothing, processed
foods, fertilizer and chemical products, military hardware, electronics

partners:

US, EC, Japan, Hong Kong, Switzerland

Imports:

$18.1 billion (c.i.f., 1991 est.)

commodities:

military equipment, rough diamonds, oil, chemicals, machinery, iron and
steel, cereals, textiles, vehicles, ships, aircraft

partners:

US, EC, Switzerland, Japan, South Africa, Canada, Hong Kong

External debt: $24 billion, of which government debt is $17 billion (December 1991 est.)

Industrial production:
growth rate - 7% (1991 est.); accounts for about 20% of GDP

Electricity:
5,300,000 kWh capacity; 21,000 million kWh produced, 4,800 kWh per capita (1991)

Industries:
food processing, diamond cutting and polishing, textiles, clothing, chemicals, metal products, military equipment, transport equipment, electrical equipment, miscellaneous machinery, potash mining, high-technology electronics, tourism

:Israel Economy

Agriculture:
accounts for about 3% of GDP; largely self-sufficient in food production, except for grains; principal products - citrus and other fruits, vegetables, cotton; livestock products - beef, dairy, and poultry

Economic aid:
US commitments, including Ex-Im (FY70-90), $18.2 billion; Western (non-US) countries, ODA and OOF bilateral commitments (1970-89), $2.8 billion

Currency:
new Israeli shekel (plural - shekels); 1 new Israeli shekel (NIS) = 100 new agorot

Exchange rates:
new Israeli shekels (NIS) per US$1 - 2.4019 (March 1992), 2.2791 (1991), 2.0162 (1990), 1.9164 (1989), 1.5989 (1988), 1.5946 (1987)

Fiscal year: previously 1 April - 31 March; FY91 was 1 April - 31 December, and since 1
January 1992 the fiscal year has conformed to the calendar year

:Israel Communications

Railroads:
600 km 1.435-meter gauge, single track; diesel operated

Highways:
4,750 km; majority is bituminous surfaced

Pipelines:
crude oil 708 km; petroleum products 290 km; natural gas 89 km

Ports:
Ashdod, Haifa

Merchant marine:
34 ships (1,000 GRT or over) totaling 629,966 GRT/721,106 DWT; includes 8 cargo, 23 container, 2 refrigerated cargo, 1 roll-on/roll-off; note - Israel also maintains a significant flag of convenience fleet, which is normally at least as large as the Israeli flag fleet; the Israeli flag of convenience fleet typically includes all of its petroleum tankers

Civil air:
32 major transport aircraft

Airports:
51 total, 44 usable; 26 with permanent-surface runways; none with runways over 3,659 m; 6 with runways 2,440-3,659 m; 11 with runways 1,220-2,439 m

Telecommunications:

most highly developed in the Middle East although not the largest; good
system of coaxial cable and radio relay; 1,800,000 telephones; broadcast
stations - 14 AM, 21 FM, 20 TV; 3 submarine cables; satellite earth stations
- 2 Atlantic Ocean INTELSAT and 1 Indian Ocean INTELSAT

:Israel Defense Forces

Branches:

Israel Defense Forces, including ground, naval, and air components;
historically, there have been no separate Israeli military services

Manpower availability:

eligible 15-49, 2,357,195; of the 1,189,275 males 15-49, 977,332 are fit for
military service; of the 1,167,920 females 15-49, 955,928 are fit for
military service; 44,624 males and 42,705 females reach military age (18)
annually; both sexes are liable for military service; Nahal or Pioneer
Fighting Youth, Frontier Guard, Chen

Defense expenditures:

$7.5 billion, 12.1% of GNP (1992 budget); note - does not include pay for
reserve soldiers and other defense-related categories; actual outlays would
therefore be higher

Italy Geography

Total area: 301,230 km2

Land area: 294, 020 km2; includes Sardinia and Sicily

Comparative area: slightly larger than Arizona

Land boundaries:

1,899.2 km; Austria 430 km, France 488 km, San Marino 39 km, Slovenia 199
km, Switzerland 740 km, Vatican City 3.2 km

Coastline:

4,996 km

Maritime claims:

Continental shelf:

200 m (depth) or to depth of exploitation

Territorial sea:

12 nm

Disputes:

Climate:

predominantly Mediterranean; Alpine in far north; hot, dry in south

Terrain:

mostly rugged and mountainous; some plains, coastal lowlands

Natural resources:

mercury, potash, marble, sulfur, dwindling natural gas and crude oil
reserves, fish, coal

Land use:

arable land 32%; permanent crops 10%; meadows and pastures 17%; forest and
woodland 22%; other 19%; includes irrigated 10%

Environment:

regional risks include land-slides, mudflows, snowslides, earthquakes,
volcanic eruptions, flooding, pollution; land sinkage in Venice

Note:

strategic location dominating central Mediterranean as well as southern sea and air approaches to Western Europe

:Italy People

Population: 57,904,628 (July 1992), growth rate 0.2% (1992)
Birth rate: 10 births/1,000 population (1992)
Death rate: 10 deaths/1,000 population (1992)
Net migration rate: 1 migrant/1,000 population (1992)
Infant mortality rate: 8 deaths/1,000 live births (1992)
Life expectancy at birth: 74 years male, 81 years female (1992)
Total fertility rate: 1.4 children born/woman (1992)
Nationality:
    noun - Italian(s); adjective - Italian
Ethnic divisions:
    primarily Italian but population includes small clusters of German-,
    French-, and Slovene-Italians in the north and Albanian-Italians and
    Greek-Italians in the south; Sicilians; Sardinians
Religions:
    virtually 100% Roman Catholic
Languages:
    Italian; parts of Trentino-Alto Adige region are predominantly German
    speaking; small French-speaking minority in Valle d'Aosta region;
    Slovene-speaking minority in the Trieste-Gorizia area
Literacy:
    97% (male 98%, female 96%) age 15 and over can read and write (1990 est.)
Labor force:
    23,988,000; services 58%, industry 32.2%, agriculture 9.8% (1988)
Organized labor:
    40-45% of labor force (est.)

:Italy Government

Long-form name:
    Italian Republic
Type:
    republic
Capital: Rome
Administrative divisions:
    20 regions (regioni, singular - regione); Abruzzi, Basilicata, Calabria,
    Campania, Emilia-Romagna, Friuli-Venezia Giulia, Lazio, Liguria, Lombardia,
    Marche, Molise, Piemonte, Puglia, Sardegna, Sicilia, Toscana, Trentino-Alto
    Adige, Umbria, Valle d'Aosta, Veneto
Independence:
    17 March 1861, Kingdom of Italy proclaimed
Constitution:
    1 January 1948
Legal system:
    based on civil law system, with ecclesiastical law influence; appeals
    treated as trials de novo; judicial review under certain conditions in
    Constitutional Court; has not accepted compulsory ICJ jurisdiction
National holiday:
    Anniversary of the Republic, 2 June (1946)

Executive branch:
    president, prime minister (president of the Council of Ministers)
Legislative branch:
    bicameral Parliament (Parlamento) consists of an upper chamber or Senate of
    the Republic (Senato della Repubblica) and a lower chamber or Chamber of
    Deputies (Camera dei Deputati)
Judicial branch:
    Constitutional Court (Corte Costituzionale)
Leaders:
  Chief of State:
  President Oscar Luigi SCALFARO (since 28 May 1992)
  Head of Government:
  Prime Minister Guiliano AMATO (since 28 June 1992); Deputy Prime Minister
Political parties and leaders:
    Christian Democratic Party (DC), Arnaldo FORLANI (general secretary),
    Ciriaco De MITA (president); Socialist Party (PSI), Bettino CRAXI (party
    secretary); Social Democratic Party (PSDI), Carlo VIZZINI (party secretary);
    Liberal Party (PLI), Renato ALTISSIMO (secretary general); Democratic Party
    of the Left (PDS - was Communist Party, or PCI, until January 1991), Achille
    OCCHETTO (secretary general); Italian Social Movement (MSI), Gianfranco FINI
    (national secretary); Republican Party (PRI), Giorgio La MALFA (political
    secretary); Lega Nord (Northern League), Umberto BOSSI, president
Suffrage:
    universal at age 18 (except in senatorial elections, where minimum age is
    25)
Elections:
  Senate:
    last held 5-6 April 1992 (next to be held by April 1997); results - DC
    33.9%, PCI 28.3%, PSI 10.7%, other 27.1%; seats - (326 total, 315 elected)
    DC 107, PDS 64, PSI 49, Leagues 25, other 70
  Chamber of Deputies:
    last held 5-6 April 1992 (next to be held April 1997); results - DC 29.7%,
    PDS 26.6%, PSI 13.6%, Leagues 8.7%, Communist Renewal 5.6%, MSI 5.4%, PRI
    4.4%, PLI 2.8%, PSDI 2.7%, other 11%

:Italy Government

Other political or pressure groups:
    the Roman Catholic Church; three major trade union confederations (CGIL -
    Communist dominated, CISL - Christian Democratic, and UIL - Social
    Democratic, Socialist, and Republican); Italian manufacturers association
    (Confindustria); organized farm groups (Confcoltivatori, Confagricoltura)
Member of:
    AfDB, AG (observer), Australia Group, AsDB, BIS, CCC, CDB (nonregional
    member), CE, CERN, COCOM, CSCE, EBRD, EC, ECE, EIB, ESA, FAO, G-7, G-
10,
    GATT, IADB, IAEA, IBRD, ICAO, ICC, ICFTU, IDA, IFAD, IEA, IFC, ILO, IMF,
    IMO, INMARSAT, INTELSAT, INTERPOL, IOC, IOM, ISO, ITU, LORCS,
MTCR, NACC,
    NATO, NEA, NSG, OAS (observer), OECD, PCA, MTCR, UN, UNCTAD,
UNESCO, UNHCR,

UNIDO, UNIFIL, UNIIMOG, UNMOGIP, UNTSO, UPU, WCL, WEU, WHO, WIPO, WMO, WTO, ZC

Diplomatic representation:

Ambassador Boris BIANCHERI CHIAPPORI; Chancery at 1601 Fuller Street NW, Washington, DC 20009; telephone (202) 328-5500; there are Italian Consulates General in Boston, Chicago, Houston, New Orleans, Los Angeles, Philadelphia, San Francisco, and Consulates in Detroit and Newark (New Jersey)

US:

Ambassador Peter F. SECCHIA; Embassy at Via Veneto 119/A, 00187, Rome (mailing address is APO AE 09624); telephone [39] (6) 46741, FAX [39] (6) 467-2356; there are US Consulates General in Florence, Genoa, Milan, Naples, and Palermo (Sicily)

Flag:

three equal vertical bands of green (hoist side), white, and red; similar to the flag of Ireland, which is longer and is green (hoist side), white, and orange; also similar to the flag of the Ivory Coast, which has the colors reversed - orange (hoist side), white, and green

:Italy Economy

Overview:

Since World War II the economy has changed from one based on agriculture into a ranking industrial economy, with approximately the same total and per capita output as France and the UK. The country is still divided into a developed industrial north, dominated by small private companies, and an undeveloped agricultural south, dominated by large public enterprises. Services account for 48% of GDP, industry about 35%, agriculture 4%, and public administration 13%. Most raw materials needed by industry and over 75% of energy requirements must be imported. After growing at an annual average rate of 3% during the period 1983-90, growth slowed to about 1% in 1991. For the 1990s, Italy faces the problems of refurbishing a tottering communications system, curbing pollution in major industrial centers, and adjusting to the new competitive forces accompanying the ongoing economic integration of the European Community.

GDP:

purchasing power equivalent - $965.0 billion, per capita $16,700; real growth rate 1.0% (1991 est.)

Inflation rate (consumer prices):

6.5% (1991)

Unemployment rate: 11.0% (1991 est.)

Budget:

revenues $431 billion; expenditures $565 billion, including capital expenditures of $48 billion (1991)

Exports:

$209 billion (f.o.b., 1991)

commodities:

textiles, wearing apparel, metals, transportation equipment, chemicals

partners:

EC 58.5%, US 8%, OPEC 4%

Imports:

$222 billion (c.i.f., 1991)
commodities:
petroleum, industrial machinery, chemicals, metals, food, agricultural
products
partners:
EC 58%, OPEC 7%, US 5%
External debt: NA
Industrial production:
growth rate - 2.0% (1991); accounts for almost 35% of GDP
Electricity:
57,500,000 kW capacity; 235,000 million kWh produced, 4,072 kWh per capita
(1991)
Industries:
machinery, iron and steel, chemicals, food processing, textiles, motor
vehicles, clothing, footwear, ceramics
Agriculture:
accounts for about 4% of GDP and 10% of the work force; self-sufficient in
foods other than meat and dairy products; principal crops - fruits,
vegetables, grapes, potatoes, sugar beets, soybeans, grain, olives; fish
catch of 388,200 metric tons in 1988
Economic aid:
donor - ODA and OOF commitments (1970-89), $25.9 billion
Currency:
Italian lira (plural - lire); 1 Italian lira (Lit) = 100 centesimi
Exchange rates:
Italian lire (Lit) per US$1 - 1,248.4 (March 1992), 1,240.6 (January 1991),
1,198.1 (1990), 1,372.1 (1989), 1,301.6 (1988), 1,296.1 (1987)

:Italy Economy

Fiscal year: calendar year

:Italy Communications

Railroads:
20,011 km total; 16,066 km 1.435-meter government-owned standard gauge
(8,999 km electrified); 3,945 km privately owned - 2,100 km 1.435-meter
standard gauge (1,155 km electrified) and 1,845 km 0.950-meter narrow gauge
(380 km electrified)
Highways:
294,410 km total; autostrada (expressway) 5,900 km, state highways 45,170
km, provincial highways 101,680 km, communal highways 141,660 km; 260,500 km
paved, 26,900 km gravel and crushed stone, 7,010 km earth
Inland waterways:
2,400 km for various types of commercial traffic, although of limited
overall value
Pipelines:
crude oil 1,703 km; petroleum products 2,148 km; natural gas 19,400 km
Ports:
Cagliari (Sardinia), Genoa, La Spezia, Livorno, Naples, Palermo (Sicily),
Taranto, Trieste, Venice
Merchant marine:
546 ships (1,000 GRT or over) totaling 7,004,462 GRT/10,265,132 DWT;

includes 17 passenger, 39 short-sea passenger, 94 cargo, 4 refrigerated cargo, 24 container, 66 roll-on/roll-off cargo, 9 vehicle carrier, 1 multifunction large-load carrier, 1 livestock carrier, 142 petroleum tanker, 33 chemical tanker, 39 liquefied gas, 10 specialized tanker, 10 combination ore/oil, 55 bulk, 2 combination bulk

Civil air:

125 major transport aircraft

Airports:

137 total, 134 usable; 91 with permanent-surface runways; 2 with runways over 3,659 m; 36 with runways 2,440-3,659 m; 39 with runways 1,220-2,439 m

Telecommunications:

modern, well-developed, fast; 25,600,000 telephones; fully automated telephone, telex, and data services; high-capacity cable and radio relay trunks; very good broadcast service by stations - 135 AM, 28 (1,840 repeaters) FM, 83 (1,000 repeaters) TV; international service by 21 submarine cables; 3 satellite earth stations operating in INTELSAT with 3 Atlantic Ocean antennas and 2 Indian Ocean antennas; also participates in INMARSAT and EUTELSAT systems

:Italy Defense Forces

Branches:

Army, Navy, Air Force, Carabinieri

Manpower availability:

males 15-49, 14,864,191; 12,980,362 fit for military service; 441,768 reach military age (18) annually

Defense expenditures:

exchange rate conversion - $22.7 billion, 2.2% of GDP (1991)

Ivory Coast Geography

Total area: 322,460 km2
Land area: 318,000 km2
Comparative area: slightly larger than New Mexico
Land boundaries:

3,110 km; Burkina 584 km, Ghana 668 km, Guinea 610 km, Liberia 716 km, Mali 532 km

Coastline:

515 km

Maritime claims:

Continental shelf:

200 m (depth)

Exclusive economic zone:

200 nm

Territorial sea:

12 nm

Disputes:

Climate:

tropical along coast, semiarid in far north; three seasons - warm and dry (November to March), hot and dry (March to May), hot and wet (June to October)

Terrain:

mostly flat to undulating plains; mountains in northwest
Natural resources:
  crude oil, diamonds, manganese, iron ore, cobalt, bauxite, copper
Land use:
  arable land 9%; permanent crops 4%; meadows and pastures 9%; forest and
  woodland 26%; other 52%; includes irrigated NEGL%
Environment:
  coast has heavy surf and no natural harbors; severe deforestation

:Ivory Coast People

Population: 13,497,153 (July 1992), growth rate 3.9% (1992)
Birth rate: 47 births/1,000 population (1992)
Death rate: 12 deaths/1,000 population (1992)
Net migration rate: 3 migrants/1,000 population (1992)
Infant mortality rate: 94 deaths/1,000 live births (1992)
Life expectancy at birth: 53 years male, 57 years female (1992)
Total fertility rate: 6.8 children born/woman (1992)
Nationality:
  noun - Ivorian(s); adjective - Ivorian
Ethnic divisions:
  over 60 ethnic groups; most important are the Baoule 23%, Bete 18%, Senoufou
  15%, Malinke 11%, and Agni; foreign Africans, mostly Burkinabe about 2
  million; non-Africans about 130,000 to 330,000 (French 30,000 and Lebanese
  100,000 to 300,000)
Religions:
  indigenous 63%, Muslim 25%, Christian 12%,
Languages:
  French (official), over 60 native dialects; Dioula most widely spoken
Literacy:
  54% (male 67%, female 40%) age 15 and over can read and write (1990 est.)
Labor force:
  5,718,000; over 85% of population engaged in agriculture, forestry,
  livestock raising; about 11% of labor force are wage earners, nearly half in
  agriculture and the remainder in government, industry, commerce, and
  professions; 54% of population of working age (1985)
Organized labor:
  20% of wage labor force

:Ivory Coast Government

Long-form name:
  Republic of the Ivory Coast; note - the local official name is Republique de
  Cote d'Ivoire
Type:
  republic; multiparty presidential regime established 1960
Capital: Yamoussoukro (although Yamoussoukro has been the capital since 1983,
Adibjan
  remains the administrative center; foreign governments, including the United
  States, maintain presence in Abidjan)
Administrative divisions:
  49 departments (departements, singular - (departement); Abengourou, Abidjan,
  Aboisso, Adzope, Agboville, Bangolo, Beoumi, Biankouma, Bondoukou,

Bongouanou, Bouafle, Bouake, Bouna, Boundiali, Dabakala, Daloa, Danane, Daoukro, Dimbokro, Divo, Duekoue, Ferkessedougou, Gagnoa, Grand-Lahou, Guiglo, Issia, Katiola, Korhogo, Lakota, Man, Mankono, Mbahiakro, Odienne, Oume, Sakassou, San-Pedro, Sassandra, Seguela, Sinfra, Soubre, Tabou, Tanda, Tingrela, Tiassale, Touba, Toumodi, Vavoua, Yamoussoukro, Zuenoula

Independence:

7 August 1960 (from France)

Constitution:

3 November 1960

Legal system:

based on French civil law system and customary law; judicial review in the Constitutional Chamber of the Supreme Court; has not accepted compulsory ICJ jurisdiction

National holiday:

National Day, 7 December

Executive branch:

president, Council of Ministers (cabinet)

Legislative branch:

unicameral National Assembly (Assemblee Nationale)

Judicial branch:

Supreme Court (Cour Supreme)

Leaders:

Chief of State and Head of Government:

President Dr. Felix HOUPHOUET-BOIGNY (since 27 November 1960); Prime Minister Alassane OUATTARA (since 7 November 1990)

Political parties and leaders:

Democratic Party of the Ivory Coast (PDCI), Dr. Felix HOUPHOUET-BOIGNY; Ivorian Popular Front (FPI), Laurent GBAGBO; Ivorian Worker's Party (PIT), Francis WODIE; Ivorian Socialist Party (PSI), Morifere BAMBA; over 20 smaller parties

Suffrage:

universal at age 21

Elections:

President:

last held 28 October 1990 (next to be held October 1995); results - President Felix HOUPHOUET-BOIGNY received 81% of the vote in his first contested election; he is currently serving his seventh consecutive five-year term

National Assembly:

last held 25 November 1990 (next to be held November 1995); results - percent of vote by party NA; seats - (175 total) PDCI 163, FPI 9, PIT 1, independents 2

Member of:

ACCT, ACP, AfDB, CCC, CEAO, ECA, ECOWAS, Entente, FAO, FZ, G-24, G-77, GATT,
IAEA, IBRD, ICAO, ICC, IDA, IFAD, IFC, ILO, IMF, IMO, INTELSAT, INTERPOL,
IOC, ISO, ITU, LORCS, NAM, OAU, UN, UNCTAD, UNESCO, UNIDO, UPU, WADB, WCL,
WHO, WIPO, WMO, WTO

:Ivory Coast Government

Diplomatic representation:
Ambassador Charles GOMIS; Chancery at 2424 Massachusetts Avenue NW, Washington, DC 20008; telephone (202) 797-0300
US:
Ambassador Kenneth L. BROWN; Embassy at 5 Rue Jesse Owens, Abidjan (mailing address is 01 B. P. 1712, Abidjan); telephone [225] 21-09-79 or 21-46-72, FAX [225] 22-32-59

Flag:
three equal vertical bands of orange (hoist side), white, and green; similar to the flag of Ireland, which is longer and has the colors reversed - green (hoist side), white, and orange; also similar to the flag of Italy, which is green (hoist side), white, and red; design was based on the flag of France

:Ivory Coast Economy

Overview:
Ivory Coast is among the world's largest producers and exporters of coffee, cocoa beans, and palm-kernel oil. Consequently, the economy is highly sensitive to fluctuations in international prices for coffee and cocoa and to weather conditions. Despite attempts by the government to diversify, the economy is still largely dependent on agriculture and related industries. The agricultural sector accounts for over one-third of GDP and about 80% of export earnings and employs about 85% of the labor force. A collapse of world cocoa and coffee prices in 1986 threw the economy into a recession, from which the country had not recovered by 1990. Continuing poor prices for commodity exports, an overvalued exchange rate, a bloated public-sector wage bill, and a large foreign debt hindered economic recovery in 1991.

GDP:
exchange rate conversion - $10 billion, per capita $800; real growth rate -2.9% (1990)

Inflation rate (consumer prices):
-0.8% (1990 est.)

Unemployment rate: 14% (1985)

Budget:
revenues $2.8 billion (1989 est.); expenditures $4.1 billion, including capital expenditures of $NA (1989 est.)

Exports:
$2.5 billion (f.o.b., 1989)
commodities:
cocoa 30%, coffee 20%, tropical woods 11%, cotton, bananas, pineapples, palm oil, cotton
partners:
France, FRG, Netherlands, US, Belgium, Spain (1985)

Imports:
$1.4 billion (f.o.b., 1989)
commodities:
manufactured goods and semifinished products 50%, consumer goods 40%, raw materials and fuels 10%
partners:
France, other EC, Nigeria, US, Japan (1985)

External debt: $15.0 billion (1990 est.)
Industrial production:
  growth rate - 6% (1989); accounts for 17% of GDP
Electricity:
  1,210,000 kW capacity; 2,680 million kWh produced, 210 kWh per capita (1991)
Industries:
  foodstuffs, wood processing, oil refinery, automobile assembly, textiles,
  fertilizer, beverage
Agriculture:
  most important sector, contributing one-third to GDP and 80% to exports;
  cash crops include coffee, cocoa beans, timber, bananas, palm kernels,
  rubber; food crops - corn, rice, manioc, sweet potatoes; not self-sufficient
  in bread grain and dairy products
Illicit drugs:
  illicit producer of cannabis on a small scale for the international drug
  trade
Economic aid:
  US commitments, including Ex-Im (FY70-89), $356 million; Western (non-US)
  countries, ODA and OOF bilateral commitments (1970-88), $5.2 billion
Currency:
  Communaute Financiere Africaine franc (plural - francs); 1 CFA franc (CFAF)
  = 100 centimes

:Ivory Coast Economy

Exchange rates:
  Communaute Financiere Africaine francs (CFAF) per US$1 - 269.01 (January
  1992), 282.11 (1991), 272.26 (1990), 319.01 (1989), 297.85 (1988), 300.54
  (1987), 346.30 (1986)
Fiscal year: calendar year

:Ivory Coast Communications

Railroads:
  660 km (Burkina border to Abidjan, 1.00-meter gauge, single track, except 25
  km Abidjan-Anyama section is double track)
Highways:
  46,600 km total; 3,600 km paved; 32,000 km gravel, crushed stone, laterite,
  and improved earth; 11,000 km unimproved
Inland waterways:
  980 km navigable rivers, canals, and numerous coastal lagoons
Ports:
  Abidjan, San-Pedro
Merchant marine:
  7 ships (1,000 GRT or over) totaling 70,957 GRT/ 91,782 DWT; includes 5
  cargo, 1 petroleum tanker, 1 chemical tanker
Civil air:
  14 major transport aircraft, including multinationally owned Air Afrique
  fleet
Airports:
  45 total, 39 usable; 7 with permanent-surface runways; none with runways
  over 3,659 m; 3 with runways 2,440-3,659 m; 15 with runways 1,220-2,439 m
Telecommunications:

well-developed by African standards but operating well below capacity; consists of open-wire lines and radio relay links; 87,700 telephones; broadcast stations - 3 AM, 17 FM, 13 TV, 1 Atlantic Ocean and 1 Indian Ocean INTELSAT earth station; 2 coaxial submarine cables

:Ivory Coast Defense Forces

Branches:
Army, Navy, Air Force, paramilitary Gendarmerie, Republican Guard, Military Fire Group
Manpower availability:
males 15-49, 3,083,765; 1,597,108 fit for military service; 141,259 males reach military age (18) annually
Defense expenditures:
exchange rate conversion - $200 million, 2.3% of GDP (1988)

Jamaica Geography

Total area: 10,990 km2
Land area: 10,830 km2
Comparative area: slightly smaller than Connecticut
Land boundaries:
none
Coastline:
1,022 km
Maritime claims:
 Territorial sea:
12 nm
Disputes:
none
Climate:
tropical; hot, humid; temperate interior
Terrain:
mostly mountains with narrow, discontinuous coastal plain
Natural resources:
bauxite, gypsum, limestone
Land use:
arable land 19%; permanent crops 6%; meadows and pastures 18%; forest and woodland 28%; other 29%; includes irrigated 3%
Environment:
subject to hurricanes (especially July to November); deforestation; water pollution
Note:
strategic location between Cayman Trench and Jamaica Channel, the main sea lanes for Panama Canal

:Jamaica People

Population: 2,506,701 (July 1992), growth rate 0.9% (1992)
Birth rate: 23 births/1,000 population (1992)
Death rate: 6 deaths/1,000 population (1992)
Net migration rate: -8 migrants/1,000 population (1992)
Infant mortality rate: 18 deaths/1,000 live births (1992)
Life expectancy at birth: 72 years male, 76 years female (1992)

Total fertility rate: 2.5 children born/woman (1992)
Nationality:
  noun - Jamaican(s); adjective - Jamaican
Ethnic divisions:
  African 76.3%, Afro-European 15.1%, East Indian and Afro-East Indian 3.0%,
  white 3.2%, Chinese and Afro-Chinese 1.2%, other 1.2%
Religions:
  predominantly Protestant 55.9% (Church of God 18.4%, Baptist 10%, Anglican
  7.1%, Seventh-Day Adventist 6.9%, Pentecostal 5.2%, Methodist 3.1%, United
  Church 2.7%, other 2.5%), Roman Catholic 5%, other 39.1%, including some
  spiritualist cults (1982)
Languages:
  English, Creole
Literacy:
  98% (male 98%, female 99%) age 15 and over having ever attended school (1990
  est.)
Labor force:
  1,062,100; services 41%, agriculture 22.5%, industry 19%; unemployed 17.5%
  (1989)
Organized labor:
  24% of labor force (1989)

:Jamaica Government

Long-form name:
  none
Type:
  parliamentary democracy
Capital: Kingston
Administrative divisions:
  14 parishes; Clarendon, Hanover, Kingston, Manchester, Portland, Saint
  Andrew, Saint Ann, Saint Catherine, Saint Elizabeth, Saint James, Saint
  Mary, Saint Thomas, Trelawny, Westmoreland
Independence:
  6 August 1962 (from UK)
Constitution:
  6 August 1962
Legal system:
  based on English common law; has not accepted compulsory ICJ jurisdiction
National holiday:
  Independence Day (first Monday in August)
Executive branch:
  British monarch, governor general, prime minister, Cabinet
Legislative branch:
  bicameral Parliament consists of an upper house or Senate and a lower house
  or House of Representatives
Judicial branch:
  Supreme Court
Leaders:
  Chief of State:
    Queen ELIZABETH II (since 6 February 1952), represented by Governor General

Howard COOKE (since 1 August 1991)

Head of Government:

Prime Minister P. J. Patterson (since 30 March 1992)

Political parties and leaders:

People's National Party (PNP) P. J. Patterson; Jamaica Labor Party (JLP), Edward SEAGA

Suffrage:

universal at age 18

Elections:

House of Representatives:

last held 9 February 1989 (next to be held by February 1994); results - PNP 57%, JLP 43%; seats - (60 total) PNP 45, JLP 15

Other political or pressure groups:

Rastafarians (black religious/racial cultists, pan-Africanists)

Member of:

ACP, C, CARICOM, CCC, CDB, ECLAC, FAO, G-15, G-19, G-77, GATT, G-15, IADB,

IAEA, IBRD, ICAO, ICFTU, IFAD, IFC, ILO, IMF, IMO, INTELSAT, INTERPOL, IOC,

ISO, ITU, LAES, LORCS, NAM, OAS, OPANAL, UN, UNCTAD, UNESCO, UNIDO, UPU,

WCL, WFTU, WHO, WIPO, WMO, WTO

Diplomatic representation:

Ambassador Richard BERNAL; Chancery at Suite 355, 1850 K Street NW, Washington, DC 20006; telephone (202) 452-0660; there are Jamaican Consulates General in Miami and New York

US:

Ambassador Glen A. HOLDEN; Embassy at 3rd Floor, Jamaica Mutual Life Center, 2 Oxford Road, Kingston; telephone (809) 929-4850 through 4859, FAX (809) 926-6743

Flag:

diagonal yellow cross divides the flag into four triangles - green (top and bottom) and black (hoist side and fly side)

:Jamaica Economy

Overview:

The economy is based on sugar, bauxite, and tourism. In 1985 it suffered a setback with the closure of some facilities in the bauxite and alumina industry, a major source of hard currency earnings. Since 1986 an economic recovery has been under way. In 1987 conditions began to improve for the bauxite and alumina industry because of increases in world metal prices. The recovery has also been supported by growth in the manufacturing and tourism sectors. In September 1988, Hurricane Gilbert inflicted severe damage on crops and the electric power system, a sharp but temporary setback to the economy. By October 1989 the economic recovery from the hurricane was largely complete, and real growth was up about 3% for 1989. In 1991, however, growth dropped to 1.0% as a result of the US recession, lower world bauxite prices, and monetary instability.

GDP:

exchange rate conversion - $3.6 billion, per capita $1,400; real growth rate

1.0% (1991 est.)

Inflation rate (consumer prices):
  80% (1991 projected)

Unemployment rate: 15.1% (1991)

Budget:
  revenues $600 million; expenditures $736 million (FY91 est.)

Exports:
  $1.2 billion (f.o.b., 1991, projected)
  commodities:
  bauxite, alumina, sugar, bananas
  partners:
  US 36%, UK, Canada, Norway, Trinidad and Tobago

Imports:
  $1.8 billion (c.i.f., 1991 projected)
  commodities:
  petroleum, machinery, food, consumer goods, construction goods
  partners:
  US 48%, UK, Venezuela, Canada, Japan, Trinidad and Tobago

External debt: $3.8 billion (1991 est.)

Industrial production:
  growth rate - 2.0% (1990); accounts for almost 25% of GDP

Electricity:
  1,122,000 kW capacity; 2,520 million kWh produced, 1,012 kWh per capita
  (1991)

Industries:
  tourism, bauxite mining, textiles, food processing, light manufactures

Agriculture:
  accounts for about 9% of GDP, 22% of work force, and 17% of exports;
  commercial crops - sugarcane, bananas, coffee, citrus, potatoes, and
  vegetables; live-stock and livestock products include poultry, goats, milk;
  not self-sufficient in grain, meat, and dairy products

Illicit drugs:
  illicit cultivation of cannabis; transshipment point for cocaine from
  Central and South America to North America; government has an active
  cannabis eradication program

Economic aid:
  US commitments, including Ex-Im (FY70-89), $1.2 billion; other countries,
  ODA and OOF bilateral commitments (1970-89), $1.6 billion

Currency:
  Jamaican dollar (plural - dollars); 1 Jamaican dollar (J$) = 100 cents

:Jamaica Economy

Exchange rates:
  Jamaican dollars (J$) per US$1 - 21.946 (January 1992), 12.116 (1991), 7.184
  (1990), 5.7446 (1989), 5.4886 (1988), 5.4867 (1987), 5.4778 (1986)

Fiscal year: 1 April - 31 March

:Jamaica Communications

Railroads:
  294 km, all 1.435-meter standard gauge, single track

Highways:

483

18,200 km total; 12,600 km paved, 3,200 km gravel, 2,400 km improved earth
Pipelines:
  petroleum products 10 km
Ports:
  Kingston, Montego Bay
Merchant marine:
  4 ships (1,000 GRT or over) totaling 9,619 GRT/16,302 DWT; includes 1
  roll-on/roll-off cargo, 1 petroleum tanker, 2 bulk
Civil air:
  8 major transport aircraft
Airports:
  36 total, 23 usable; 13 with permanent-surface runways; none with runways
  over 3,659 m; 2 with runways 2,440-3,659 m; 1 with runways 1,220-2,439 m
Telecommunications:
  fully automatic domestic telephone network; 127,000 telephones; broadcast
  stations - 10 AM, 17 FM, 8 TV; 2 Atlantic Ocean INTELSAT earth stations; 3
  coaxial submarine cables

:Jamaica Defense Forces

Branches:
  Jamaica Defense Force (including Coast Guard and Air Wing), Jamaica
  Constabulary Force
Manpower availability:
  males 15-49, 640,058; 454,131 fit for military service; no conscription;
  26,785 reach minimum volunteer age (18) annually
Defense expenditures:
  exchange rate conversion - $20 million, less than 1% of GDP (FY91)

Jan Mayen Geography

Total area: 373 km2
Land area: 373 km2
Comparative area: slightly more than twice the size of Washington, DC
Land boundaries:
  none
Coastline:
  124.1 km
Maritime claims:
 Contiguous zone:
  10 nm
 Continental shelf:
  200 m (depth) or to depth of exploitation
 Exclusive fishing zone:
  200 nm
 Territorial sea:
  4 nm
Disputes:
  Denmark has challenged Norway's maritime claims beween Greenland and Jan
  Mayen
Climate:
  arctic maritime with frequent storms and persistent fog
Terrain:

volcanic island, partly covered by glaciers; Beerenberg is the highest peak, with an elevation of 2,277 meters

Natural resources:
none

Land use:
arable land 0%; permanent crops 0%; meadows and pastures 0%; forest and woodland 0%; other 100%

Environment:
barren volcanic island with some moss and grass; volcanic activity resumed in 1970

Note:
located north of the Arctic Circle about 590 km north-northeast of Iceland between the Greenland Sea and the Norwegian Sea

:Jan Mayen People

Population: no permanent inhabitants

:Jan Mayen Government

Long-form name:
none

Type:
territory of Norway

Capital: none; administered from Oslo, Norway, through a governor (sysselmann) resident in Longyearbyen (Svalbard)

:Jan Mayen Economy

Overview:
Jan Mayen is a volcanic island with no exploitable natural resources. Economic activity is limited to providing services for employees of Norway's radio and meteorological stations located on the island.

Electricity:
15,000 kW capacity; 40 million kWh produced, NA kWh per capita (1989)

:Jan Mayen Communications

Ports:
none; offshore anchorage only

Airports:
1 with runways 1,220 to 2,439 m

Telecommunications:
radio and meteorological station

:Jan Mayen Defense Forces

Note: defense is the responsibility of Norway

Japan Geography

Total area: 377,835 km2

Land area: 374,744 km2; includes Bonin Islands (Ogasawara-gunto), Daito-shoto, Minami-jima, Okinotori-shima, Ryukyu Islands (Nansei-shoto), and Volcano Islands (Kazan-retto)

Comparative area: slightly smaller than California

Land boundaries:

Coastline:
  29,751 km
Maritime claims:
  Exclusive fishing zone:
    200 nm
  Territorial sea:
    12 nm (3 nm in international straits - La Perouse or Soya, Tsugaru, Osumi,
    and Eastern and Western channels of the Korea or Tsushima Strait)
Disputes:
  Etorofu, Kunashiri, and Shikotan Islands and the Habomai island group
  occupied by the Soviet Union in 1945, now administered by Russia, claimed by
  Japan; Liancourt Rocks disputed with South Korea; Senkaku-shoto (Senkaku
  Islands) claimed by China and Taiwan
Climate:
  varies from tropical in south to cool temperate in north
Terrain:
  mostly rugged and mountainous
Natural resources:
  negligible mineral resources, fish
Land use:
  arable land 13%; permanent crops 1%; meadows and pastures 1%; forest and
  woodland 67%; other 18%; includes irrigated 9%
Environment:
  many dormant and some active volcanoes; about 1,500 seismic occurrences
  (mostly tremors) every year; subject to tsunamis
Note:
  strategic location in northeast Asia

:Japan People

Population: 124,460,481 (July 1992), growth rate 0.4% (1992)
Birth rate: 10 births/1,000 population (1992)
Death rate: 7 deaths/1,000 population (1992)
Net migration rate: 0 migrants/1,000 population (1992)
Infant mortality rate: 4 deaths/1,000 live births (1992)
Life expectancy at birth: 77 years male, 82 years female (1992)
Total fertility rate: 1.6 children born/woman (1992)
Nationality:
  noun - Japanese (singular and plural); adjective - Japanese
Ethnic divisions:
  Japanese 99.4%, other (mostly Korean) 0.6%
Religions:
  most Japanese observe both Shinto and Buddhist rites so the percentages add
  to more than 100% - Shinto 95.8%, Buddhist 76.3%, Christian 1.4%, other 12%
  (1985)
Languages:
  Japanese
Literacy:
  99% (male NA%, female NA%) age 15 and over can read and write (1970 est.)
Labor force:
  63,330,000; trade and services 54%; manufacturing, mining, and construction

33%; agriculture, forestry, and fishing 7%; government 3% (1988)

Organized labor:

about 29% of employed workers; public service 76.4%, transportation and telecommunications 57.9%, mining 48.7%, manufacturing 33.7%, services 18.2%, wholesale, retail, and restaurant 9.3%

:Japan Government

Long-form name:

Type:

constitutional monarchy

Capital: Tokyo

Administrative divisions:

47 prefectures; Aichi, Akita, Aomori, Chiba, Ehime, Fukui, Fukuoka, Fukushima, Gifu, Gumma, Hiroshima, Hokkaido, Hyogo, Ibaraki, Ishikawa, Iwate, Kagawa, Kagoshima, Kanagawa, Kochi, Kumamoto, Kyoto, Mie, Miyagi, Miyazaki, Nagano, Nagasaki, Nara, Niigata, Oita, Okayama, Okinawa, Osaka, Saga, Saitama, Shiga, Shimane, Shizuoka, Tochigi, Tokushima, Tokyo, Tottori, Toyama, Wakayama, Yamagata, Yamaguchi, Yamanashi

Independence:

660 BC, traditional founding by Emperor Jimmu

Constitution:

3 May 1947

Legal system:

civil law system with English-American influence; judicial review of legislative acts in the Supreme Court; accepts compulsory ICJ jurisdiction, with reservations

National holiday:

Birthday of the Emperor, 23 December (1933)

Executive branch:

Emperor, prime minister, Cabinet

Legislative branch:

bicameral Diet (Kokkai) consists of an upper house or House of Councillors (Sangi-in) and a lower house or House of Representatives (Shugi-in)

Judicial branch:

Supreme Court

Leaders:

 Chief of State:

 Emperor AKIHITO (since 7 January 1989)

 Head of Government:

 Prime Minister Kiichi MIYAZAWA (since 5 November 1991)

Political parties and leaders:

Liberal Democratic Party (LDP), Kiichi MIYAZAWA, president; Tamisuke WATANUKI, secretary general; Social Democratic Party of Japan (SDPJ), Makoto TANABE, Chairman; Democratic Socialist Party (DSP), Keizo OUCHI, chairman; Japan Communist Party (JCP), Tetsuzo FUWA, Presidium chairman; Komeito (Clean Government Party, CGP), Koshiro ISHIDA, chairman

Suffrage:

universal at age 20

Elections:

487

House of Councillors:

last held on 23 July 1989 (next to be held 26 July 1992); results - percent
of vote by party NA; seats - (263 total) LDP 114, SDPJ 71, CGP 20, JCP 14,
other 33

House of Representatives:

last held on 18 February 1990 (next to be held by February 1993); results -
percent of vote by party NA; seats - (512 total) LDP 278, SDPJ 137, CGP 46,
JCP 16, DSP 13, others 5, independents 6, vacant 11

Communists:

about 490,000 registered Communist party members

:Japan Government

Member of:

AfDB, AG (observer), Australia Group, APEC, AsDB, BIS, CCC, COCOM, CP,
EBRD,
ESCAP, FAO, G-2, G-5, G-7, G-8, G-10, GATT, IADB, IAEA, IBRD, ICAO, ICC,
ICFTU, IDA, IEA, IFAD, IFC, ILO, IMF, IMO, INMARSAT, INTELSAT,
INTERPOL,
IOC, IOM (observer), ISO, ITU, LORCS, MTCR, NEA, NSG, OAS (observer),
OECD,
PCA, UN, UNCTAD, UNESCO, UNHCR, UNIDO, UNRWA, UPU, WFTU, WHO,
WIPO, WMO,
WTO, ZC

Diplomatic representation:

Ambassador Takakazu KURIYAMA; Chancery at 2520 Massachusetts Avenue NW,
Washington, DC 20008; telephone (202) 939-6700; there are Japanese
Consulates General in Agana (Guam), Anchorage, Atlanta, Boston, Chicago,
Honolulu, Houston, Kansas City (Missouri), Los Angeles, New Orleans, New
York, San Francisco, Seattle, and Portland (Oregon), and a Consulate in
Saipan (Northern Mariana Islands)

US:

Ambassador Michael H. ARMACOST; Embassy at 10-5, Akasaka 1-chome, Minato-
ku
(107), Tokyo (mailing address is APO AP 96337-0001); telephone [81] (3)
3224-5000; FAX [81] (3) 3505-1862; there are US Consulates General in Naha
(Okinawa), Osaka-Kobe, and Sapporo and a Consulate in Fukuoka

Flag:

white with a large red disk (representing the sun without rays) in the
center

:Japan Economy

Overview:

Government-industry cooperation, a strong work ethic, and a comparatively
small defense allocation have helped Japan advance with extraordinary
rapidity, notably in high-technology fields. Industry, the most important
sector of the economy, is heavily dependent on imported raw materials and
fuels. Self-suffcent in rice, Japan must import 50% of its requirements for
other grain and fodder crops. Japan maintains one of the world's largest
fishing fleets and accounts for nearly 15% of the global catch. Overall
economic growth has been spectacular: a 10% average in the 1960s, a 5%
average in the 1970s and 1980s. A major contributor to overall growth of

4.5% in 1991 was net exports, which cushioned the effect of slower growth in domestic demand. Inflation remains low at 3.3% and is easing due to lower oil prices and a stronger yen. Japan continues to run a huge trade surplus, $80 billion in 1991, which supports extensive investment in foreign assets. The increased crowding of its habitable land area and the aging of its population are two major long-run problems.

GDP:
    purchasing power equivalent - $2,360.7 billion, per capita $19,000; real growth rate 4.5% (1991)

Inflation rate (consumer prices):
    3.3% (1991)

Unemployment rate: 2.1% (1991)

Budget:
    revenues $481 billion; expenditures $531 billion, including capital expenditures (public works only) of about $60 billion (FY91)

Exports:
    $314.3 billion (f.o.b., 1991)
  commodities:
    manufactures 97% (including machinery 40%, motor vehicles 18%, consumer electronics 10%)
  partners:
    Southeast Asia 31%, US 29%, Western Europe 23%, Communist countries 4%, Middle East 3%

Imports:
    $236.6 billion (c.i.f., 1991)
  commodities:
    manufactures 50%, fossil fuels 21%, foodstuffs and raw materials 25%
  partners:
    Southeast Asia 25%, US 22%, Western Europe 17%, Middle East 12%, Communist countries 8%

External debt: $NA

Industrial production:
    growth rate 2.1% (1991); accounts for 30% of GDP (mining and manufacturing)

Electricity:
    196,000,000 kW capacity; 823,000 million kWh produced, 6,640 kWh per capita (1991)

Industries:
    metallurgy, engineering, electrical and electronic, textiles, chemicals, automobiles, fishing, telecommunications, machine tools, construction equipment

Agriculture:
    accounts for only 2% of GDP; highly subsidized and protected sector, with crop yields among highest in world; principal crops - rice, sugar beets, vegetables, fruit; animal products include pork, poultry, dairy and eggs, about 50% self-sufficient in food production; shortages of wheat, corn, soybeans; world's largest fish catch of 11.9 million metric tons in 1988

:Japan Economy

Economic aid:
    donor - ODA and OOF commitments (1970-89), $83.2 billion; ODA outlay of $9.1

billion in 1990 (est.)

Currency:
    yen (plural - yen); 1 yen (Y) = 100 sen

Exchange rates:
    yen (Y) per US$1 - 132.70 (March 1992), 134.71 (1991), 144.79 (1990), 137.96 (1989), 128.15 (1988), 144.64 (1987)

Fiscal year: 1 April - 31 March

:Japan Communications

Railroads:
    27,327 km total; 2,012 km 1.435-meter standard gauge and 25,315 km predominantly 1.067-meter narrow gauge; 5,724 km doubletrack and multitrack sections, 9,038 km 1.067-meter narrow-gauge electrified, 2,012 km 1.435-meter standard-gauge electrified (1987)

Highways:
    1,111,974 km total; 754,102 km paved, 357,872 km gravel, crushed stone, or unpaved; 4,400 km national expressways; 46,805 km national highways; 128,539 km prefectural roads; and 930,230 km city, town, and village roads

Inland waterways:
    about 1,770 km; seagoing craft ply all coastal inland seas

Pipelines:
    crude oil 84 km; petroleum products 322 km; natural gas 1,800 km

Ports:
    Chiba, Muroran, Kitakyushu, Kobe, Tomakomai, Nagoya, Osaka, Tokyo, Yokkaichi, Yokohama, Kawasaki, Niigata, Fushiki-Toyama, Shimizu, Himeji, Wakayama-Shimozu, Shimonoseki, Tokuyama-Shimomatsu

Merchant marine:
    976 ships (1,000 GRT or over) totaling 21,684,459 GRT/34,683,035 DWT; includes 10 passenger, 40 short-sea passenger, 3 passenger cargo, 89 cargo, 44 container, 36 roll-on/roll-off cargo, 111 refrigerated cargo, 93 vehicle carrier, 227 petroleum tanker, 11 chemical tanker, 40 liquefied gas, 9 combination ore/oil, 3 specialized tanker, 260 bulk; note - Japan also owns a large flag of convenience fleet, including up to 55% of the total number of ships under the Panamanian flag

Civil air:
    360 major transport aircraft

Airports:
    163 total, 158 usable; 131 with permanent-surface runways; 2 with runways over 3,659 m; 31 with runways 2,440-3,659 m; 51 with runways 1,220-2,439 m

Telecommunications:
    excellent domestic and international service; 64,000,000 telephones; broadcast stations - 318 AM, 58 FM, 12,350 TV (196 major - 1 kw or greater); satellite earth stations - 4 Pacific Ocean INTELSAT and 1 Indian Ocean INTELSAT; submarine cables to US (via Guam), Philippines, China, and Russia

:Japan Defense Forces

Branches:
    Japan Ground Self-Defense Force (Army), Japan Maritime Self-Defense Force (Navy), Japan Air Self-Defense Force (Air Force), Maritime Safety Agency (Coast Guard)

Manpower availability:

males 15-49, 32,219,754; 27,767,280 fit for military service; 1,042,493 reach military age (18) annually

Defense expenditures:
exchange rate conversion - $36.7 billion, 0.94% of GDP (FY92 est.)

Jarvis Island Geography

Total area: 4.5 km2
Land area: 4.5 km2
Comparative area: about 7.5 times the size of the Mall in Washington, DC
Land boundaries:
none
Coastline:
8 km
Maritime claims:
 Contiguous zone:
 12 nm
 Continental shelf:
 200 m (depth)
 Exclusive economic zone:
 200 nm
 Territorial sea:
 12 nm
Disputes:
none
Climate:
tropical; scant rainfall, constant wind, burning sun
Terrain:
sandy, coral island surrounded by a narrow fringing reef
Natural resources:
guano (deposits worked until late 1800s)
Land use:
arable land 0%; permanent crops 0%; meadows and pastures 0%; forest and woodland 0%; other 100%
Environment:
sparse bunch grass, prostrate vines, and low-growing shrubs; lacks fresh water; primarily a nesting, roosting, and foraging habitat for seabirds, shorebirds, and marine wildlife; feral cats
Note:
2,090 km south of Honolulu in the South Pacific Ocean, just south of the Equator, about halfway between Hawaii and the Cook Islands

:Jarvis Island People

Population: uninhabited
Population: note:
Millersville settlement on western side of island occasionally used as a weather station from 1935 until World War II, when it was abandoned; reoccupied in 1957 during the International Geophysical Year by scientists who left in 1958; public entry is by special-use permit only and generally restricted to scientists and educators

:Jarvis Island Government

Long-form name:
  none (territory of the US)
Type:
  unincorporated territory of the US administered by the Fish and Wildlife
  Service of the US Department of the Interior as part of the National
  Wildlife Refuge System
Capital: none; administered from Washington, DC

:Jarvis Island Economy

Overview: no economic activity

:Jarvis Island Communications

Ports:
  none; offshore anchorage only - one boat landing area in the middle of the
  west coast and another near the southwest corner of the island
Note:
  there is a day beacon near the middle of the west coast

:Jarvis Island Defense Forces

Note:
  defense is the responsibility of the US; visited annually by the US Coast
  Guard

Jersey Geography

Total area: 117 km2
Land area: 117 km2
Comparative area: about 0.7 times the size of Washington, DC
Land boundaries:
  none
Coastline:
  70 km
Maritime claims:
  Exclusive fishing zone:
  200 nm
  Territorial sea:
  3 nm
Disputes:
  none
Climate:
  temperate; mild winters and cool summers
Terrain:
  gently rolling plain with low, rugged hills along north coast
Natural resources:
  agricultural land
Land use:
  arable land NA%; permanent crops NA%; meadows and pastures NA%; forest and
  woodland NA%; other NA%; about 58% of land under cultivation
Environment:
  about 30% of population concentrated in Saint Helier
Note:
  largest and southernmost of Channel Islands; 27 km from France

:Jersey People

Population: 85,026 (July 1992), growth rate 0.8% (1992)
Birth rate: 12 births/1,000 population (1992)
Death rate: 10 deaths/1,000 population (1992)
Net migration rate: 6 migrants/1,000 population (1992)
Infant mortality rate: 6 deaths/1,000 live births (1992)
Life expectancy at birth: 72 years male, 78 years female (1992)
Total fertility rate: 1.3 children born/woman (1992)
Nationality:
   noun - Channel Islander(s); adjective - Channel Islander
Ethnic divisions:
   UK and Norman-French descent
Religions:
   Anglican, Roman Catholic, Baptist, Congregational New Church, Methodist,
   Presbyterian
Languages:
   English and French (official), with the Norman-French dialect spoken in
   country districts
Literacy:
   NA% (male NA%, female NA%) but compulsory education age 5 to 16
Labor force:
   NA
Organized labor:
   none

:Jersey Government

Long-form name:
   Bailiwick of Jersey
Type:
   British crown dependency
Capital: Saint Helier
Administrative divisions:
   none (British crown dependency)
Independence:
   none (British crown dependency)
Constitution:
   unwritten; partly statutes, partly common law and practice
Legal system:
   English law and local statute
National holiday:
   Liberation Day, 9 May (1945)
Executive branch:
   British monarch, lieutenant governor, bailiff
Legislative branch:
   unicameral Assembly of the States
Judicial branch:
   Royal Court
Leaders:
 Chief of State:
   Queen ELIZABETH II (since 6 February 1952)

Head of Government:

Lieutenant Governor and Commander in Chief Air Marshal Sir John SUTTON (since NA 1990); Bailiff Peter CRILL (since NA)

Political parties and leaders:

none; all independents

Suffrage:

universal adult at age NA

Elections:

Assembly of the States:

last held NA (next to be held NA); results - no percent of vote by party since all are independents; seats - (56 total, 52 elected) 52 independents

Member of:

Diplomatic representation:

none (British crown dependency)

Flag:

white with the diagonal red cross of Saint Patrick (patron saint of Ireland) extending to the corners of the flag

:Jersey Economy

Overview:

The economy is based largely on financial services, agriculture, and tourism. Potatoes, cauliflower, tomatoes, and especially flowers are important export crops, shipped mostly to the UK. The Jersey breed of dairy cattle is known worldwide and represents an important export earner. Milk products go to the UK and other EC countries. In 1986 the finance sector overtook tourism as the main contributor to GDP, accounting for 40% of the island's output. In recent years the government has encouraged light industry to locate in Jersey, with the result that an electronics industry has developed alongside the traditional manufacturing of knitwear. All raw material and energy requirements are imported, as well as a large share of Jersey's food needs.

GDP:

$NA, per capita $NA; real growth rate 8% (1987 est.)

Inflation rate (consumer prices):

8% (1988 est.)

Unemployment rate: NA%

Budget:

revenues $308.0 million; expenditures $284.4 million, including capital expenditures of NA (1985)

Exports:

$NA

commodities:

light industrial and electrical goods, foodstuffs, textiles

partners:

UK

Imports:

$NA

commodities:

machinery and transport equipment, manufactured goods, foodstuffs, mineral

fuels, chemicals
partners:
  UK
External debt: $NA
Industrial production:
  growth rate NA%
Electricity:
  50,000 kW standby capacity (1990); power supplied by France
Industries:
  tourism, banking and finance, dairy
Agriculture:
  potatoes, cauliflowers, tomatoes; dairy and cattle farming
Economic aid:
  none
Currency:
  Jersey pound (plural - pounds); 1 Jersey pound (#J) = 100 pence
Exchange rates:
  Jersey pounds (#J) per US$1 - 0.5799 (March 1992), 0.5652 (1991), 0.5603
  (1990), 0.6099 (1989), 0.5614 (1988), 0.6102 (1987), 0.6817 (1986); the
  Jersey pound is at par with the British pound
Fiscal year: 1 April - 31 March

:Jersey Communications

Ports:
  Saint Helier, Gorey, Saint Aubin
Airports:
  1 with permanent-surface runway 1,220-2,439 m (Saint Peter)
Telecommunications:
  63,700 telephones; broadcast stations - 1 AM, no FM, 1 TV; 3 submarine
  cables

:Jersey Defense Forces

Note: defense is the responsibility of the UK

Johnston Atoll Geography

Total area: 2.8 km2
Land area: 2.8 km2
Comparative area: about 4.7 times the size of the Mall in Washington, DC
Land boundaries:
  none
Coastline:
  10 km
Maritime claims:
 Contiguous zone:
  12 nm
 Continental shelf:
  200 m (depth)
 Exclusive economic zone:
  200 nm
 Territorial sea:
  12 nm

Disputes:

Climate:

  tropical, but generally dry; consistent northeast trade winds with little
  seasonal temperature variation

Terrain:

  mostly flat with a maximum elevation of 4 meters

Natural resources:

  guano (deposits worked until about 1890)

Land use:

  arable land 0%; permanent crops 0%; meadows and pastures 0%; forest and
  woodland 0%; other 100%

Environment:

  some low-growing vegetation

Note:

  strategic location 717 nautical miles west-southwest of Honolulu in the
  North Pacific Ocean, about one-third of the way between Hawaii and the
  Marshall Islands; Johnston Island and Sand Island are natural islands; North
  Island (Akau) and East Island (Hikina) are manmade islands formed from coral
  dredging; closed to the public; former nuclear weapons test site; site of
  Johnston Atoll Chemical Agent Disposal System (JACADS)

:Johnston Atoll People

Population: 1,375 (December 1991); all US government personnel and contractors

:Johnston Atoll Government

Long-form name:

  none (territory of the US)

Type:

  unincorporated territory of the US administered by the US Defense Nuclear
  Agency (DNA) and managed cooperatively by DNA and the Fish and Wildlife
  Service of the US Department of the Interior as part of the National
  Wildlife Refuge system

Capital:

none; administered from Washington, DC Diplomatic representation: none (territory of
the US) Flag: the flag of the US is used

:Johnston Atoll Economy

Overview:

  Economic activity is limited to providing services to US military personnel
  and contractors located on the island. All food and manufactured goods must
  be imported.

Electricity:

  supplied by the management and operations contractor

:Johnston Atoll Communications

Ports:

  Johnston Island

Airports:

  1 with permanent-surface runways 2,743 m

Telecommunications:

excellent system including 60-channel submarine cable, Autodin/SRT terminal, digital telephone switch, Military Affiliated Radio System (MARS station), commercial satellite television system, and UHF/VHF air-ground radio, marine VHF/FM Channel 16

Note:

US Coast Guard operates a LORAN transmitting station (estimated closing date for LORAN is December 1992)

:Johnston Atoll Defense Forces

Note: defense is the responsibility of the US

Jordan Geography

Total area: 91,880 km2
Land area: 91,540 km2
Comparative area: slightly smaller than Indiana
Land boundaries:

1,586 km; Iraq 134 km, Israel 238 km, Saudi Arabia 742 km, Syria 375 km, West Bank 97 km

Coastline:

26 km

Maritime claims:

 Territorial sea:

 3 nm

Disputes:

differences with Israel over the location of the 1949 Armistice Line that separates the two countries

Climate:

mostly arid desert; rainy season in west (November to April)

Terrain:

mostly desert plateau in east, highland area in west; Great Rift Valley separates East and West Banks of the Jordan River

Natural resources:

phosphates, potash, shale oil

Land use:

arable land 4%; permanent crops 0.5%; meadows and pastures 1%; forest and woodland 0.5%; other 94%; includes irrigated 0.5%

Environment:

lack of natural water resources; deforestation; overgrazing; soil erosion; desertification

Note:

The war between Israel and the Arab states in June 1967 ended with Israel in control of the West Bank. As stated in the 1978 Camp David accords and reaffirmed by President Bush's post - Gulf crisis peace initiative, the final status of the West Bank and Gaza Strip, their relationship with their neighbors, and a peace treaty between Israel and Jordan are to be negotiated among the concerned parties. The Camp David accords also specify that these negotiations will resolve the location of the respective boundaries. Pending the completion of this process, it is US policy that the final status of the West Bank and Gaza Strip has yet to be determined.

:Jordan People

Population: 3,557,304 (July 1992), growth rate 4.1% (1992); Palestinians now consti-
tute
  roughly two-thirds of the population; most are Jordanian citizens
Birth rate: 45 births/1,000 population (1992)
Death rate: 5 deaths/1,000 population (1992)
Net migration rate: 1 migrant/1,000 population (1992)
Infant mortality rate: 38 deaths/1,000 live births (1992)
Life expectancy at birth: 70 years male, 73 years female (1992)
Total fertility rate: 7.0 children born/woman (1992)
Nationality:
  noun - Jordanian(s); adjective - Jordanian
Ethnic divisions:
  Arab 98%, Circassian 1%, Armenian 1%
Religions:
  Sunni Muslim 92%, Christian 8%
Languages:
  Arabic (official); English widely understood among upper and middle classes
Literacy:
  80% (male 89%, female 70%) age 15 and over can read and write (1990 est.)
Labor force:
  572,000 (1988); agriculture 20%, manufacturing and mining 20% (1987 est.)
Organized labor:
  about 10% of labor force

:Jordan Government

Long-form name:
  Hashemite Kingdom of Jordan
Type:
  constitutional monarchy
Capital: Amman
Administrative divisions:
  8 governorates (muhafazat, singular - muhafazah); Al Balqa', Al Karak, Al
  Mafraq, `Amman, At Tafilah, Az Zarqa', Irbid, Ma`an
Independence:
  25 May 1946 (from League of Nations mandate under British administration;
  formerly Transjordan)
Constitution:
  8 January 1952
Legal system:
  based on Islamic law and French codes; judicial review of legislative acts
  in a specially provided High Tribunal; has not accepted compulsory ICJ
  jurisdiction
National holiday:
  Independence Day, 25 May (1946)
Executive branch:
  monarch, prime minister, deputy prime minister, Cabinet
Legislative branch:
  bicameral National Assembly (Majlis al-`Umma) consists of an upper house or
  House of Notables (Majlis al-A`ayan) and a lower house or House of
  Representatives (Majlis al-Nuwaab); note - the House of Representatives has

been convened and dissolved by the King several times since 1974 and in
November 1989 the first parliamentary elections in 22 years were held

Judicial branch:

Court of Cassation

Leaders:

 Chief of State:

 King HUSSEIN Ibn Talal Al Hashemi (since 11 August 1952)

 Head of Government:

 Prime Minister Zayd bin SHAKIR (since 21 November 1991)

Political parties and leaders:

approximately 24 parties have been formed since the National Charter, but
the number fluctuates; after the 1989 parliamentary elections, King Hussein
promised to allow the formation of political parties; a national charter
that sets forth the ground rules for democracy in Jordan - including the
creation of political parties - was approved in principle by the special
National Conference on 9 June 1991, but its specific provisions have yet to
be passed by National Assembly

Suffrage:

universal at age 20

Elections:

 House of Representatives:

last held 8 November 1989 (next to be held November 1993); results - percent
of vote by party NA; seats - (80 total) Muslim Brotherhood (fundamentalist)
22, Independent Islamic bloc (generally traditionalist) 6, Democratic bloc
(mostly leftist) 9, Constitutionalist bloc (traditionalist) 17, Nationalist
bloc (traditionalist) 16, independent 10

Member of:

 ABEDA, ACC, AFESD, AL, AMF, CAEU, CCC, ESCWA, FAO, G-77, IAEA,
IBRD, ICAO,

 ICC, IDA, IDB, IFAD, IFC, ILO, IMF, IMO, INTELSAT, INTERPOL, IOC, ISO
 (correspondent), ITU, LORCS, NAM, OIC, UN, UNAVEM, UNCTAD, UNESCO,
UNIDO,

 UNRWA, UPU, WFTU, WHO, WIPO, WMO, WTO

:Jordan Government

Diplomatic representation:

Ambassador Hussein A. HAMMAMI; Chancery at 3504 International Drive NW,
Washington, DC 20008; telephone (202) 966-2664

 US:

Ambassador Roger Gram HARRISON; Embassy on Jebel Amman, Amman (mailing
address is P. O. Box 354, Amman, or APO AE 09892); telephone [962] (6)
644-371

Flag:

three equal horizontal bands of black (top), white, and green with a red
isosceles triangle based on the hoist side bearing a small white
seven-pointed star; the seven points on the star represent the seven
fundamental laws of the Koran

:Jordan Economy

Overview:

Jordan benefited from increased Arab aid during the oil boom of the late

1970s and early 1980s, when its annual GNP growth averaged more than 10%. In the remainder of the 1980s, however, reductions in both Arab aid and worker remittances slowed economic growth to an average of roughly 2% per year. Imports - mainly oil, capital goods, consumer durables, and food - have been outstripping exports, with the difference covered by aid, remittances, and borrowing. In mid-1989, the Jordanian Government began debt-rescheduling negotiations and agreed to implement an IMF program designed to gradually reduce the budget deficit and implement badly needed structural reforms. The Persian Gulf crisis that began in August 1990, however, aggravated Jordan's already serious economic problems, forcing the government to shelve the IMF program, stop most debt payments, and suspend rescheduling negotiations. Aid from Gulf Arab states and worker remittances have plunged, and refugees have flooded the country, straining government resources. Economic recovery is unlikely without substantial foreign aid, debt relief, and economic reform.

GDP:
  exchange rate conversion - $3.6 billion, per capita $1,100; real growth rate 3% (1991 est.)
Inflation rate (consumer prices):
  9% (1991 est.)
Unemployment rate: 40% (1991 est.)
Budget:
  revenues $1.7 billion; expenditures $1.9 billion, including capital expenditures of $NA (1992)
Exports:
  $1.0 billion (f.o.b., 1991 est.)
  commodities:
  phosphates, fertilizers, potash, agricultural products, manufactures
  partners:
  India, Iraq, Saudi Arabia, Indonesia, Ethiopia, UAE, China
Imports:
  $2.3 billion (c.i.f., 1991 est.)
  commodities:
  crude oil, machinery, transport equipment, food, live animals, manufactured goods
  partners:
  EC, US, Iraq, Saudi Arabia, Japan, Turkey
External debt: $9 billion (December 1991 est.)
Industrial production:
  growth rate 1% (1991 est.); accounts for 20% of GDP
Electricity:
  1,025,000 kW capacity; 3,900 million kWh produced, 1,150 kWh per capita (1991)
Industries:
  phosphate mining, petroleum refining, cement, potash, light manufacturing
Agriculture:
  accounts for about 7% of GDP; principal products are wheat, barley, citrus fruit, tomatoes, melons, olives; livestock - sheep, goats, poultry; large net importer of food
Economic aid:
  US commitments, including Ex-Im (FY70-89), $1.7 billion; Western (non-US)

countries, ODA and OOF bilateral commitments (1970-89), $1.5 billion; OPEC bilateral aid (1979-89), $9.5 billion; Communist countries (1970-89), $44 million

Currency:
  Jordanian dinar (plural - dinars); 1 Jordanian dinar (JD) = 1,000 fils

:Jordan Economy

Exchange rates:
  Jordanian dinars (JD) per US$1 - 0.6861 (March 1992), 0.6807 1991), 0.6636 (1990), 0.5704 (1989), 0.3709 (1988), 0.3387 (1987)

Fiscal year: calendar year

:Jordan Communications

Railroads:
  619 km 1.050-meter gauge, single track

Highways:
  7,500 km; 5,500 km asphalt, 2,000 km gravel and crushed stone

Pipelines:
  crude oil 209 km

Ports:
  Al `Aqabah

Merchant marine:
  2 ships (1,000 GRT or over) totaling 60,378 GRT/113,557 DWT; includes 1 cargo and 1 petroleum tanker

Civil air:
  23 major transport aircraft

Airports:
  19 total, 15 usable; 14 with permanent-surface runways; 1 with runways over 3,659 m; 13 with runways 2,440-3,659 m; none with runways 1,220-2,439 m

Telecommunications:
  adequate telephone system of microwave, cable, and radio links; 81,500 telephones; broadcast stations - 5 AM, 7 FM, 8 TV; satellite earth stations - 1 Atlantic Ocean INTELSAT, 1 Indian Ocean INTELSAT, 1 ARABSAT, 1 domestic
  TV receive-only; coaxial cable and microwave to Iraq, Saudi Arabia, and Syria; microwave link to Lebanon is inactive; participates in a microwave network linking Syria, Jordan, Egypt, Libya, Tunisia, Algeria, and Morocco

:Jordan Defense Forces

Branches:
  Jordan Arab Army, Royal Jordanian Air Force, Royal Jordanian Navy, Public Security Force

Manpower availability:
  males 15-49, 808,725; 576,934 fit for military service; 39,310 reach military age (18) annually

Defense expenditures:
  exchange rate conversion - $404 million, 9.5% of GDP (1990)

Juan de Nova Island Geography

Total area: 4.4 km2
Land area: 4.4 km2
Comparative area: about 7.5 times the size of the Mall in Washington, DC

Land boundaries:
    none
Coastline:
    24.1 km
Maritime claims:
  Contiguous zone:
    12 nm
  Continental shelf:
    200 m (depth) or to depth of exploitation
  Exclusive economic zone:
    200 nm
  Territorial sea:
    12 nm
Disputes:
    claimed by Madagascar
Climate:
    tropical
Terrain:
    undetermined
Natural resources:
    guano deposits and other fertilizers
Land use:
    arable land 0%; permanent crops 0%; meadows and pastures 0%; forest and
    woodland 90%; other 10%
Environment:
    subject to periodic cyclones; wildlife sanctuary
Note:
    located in the central Mozambique Channel about halfway between Africa and
    Madagascar

:Juan de Nova Island People

Population: uninhabited

:Juan de Nova Island Government

Long-form name:
    none
Type:
    French possession administered by Commissioner of the Republic Jacques
    DEWATRE, resident in Reunion
Capital: none; administered by France from Reunion

:Juan de Nova Island Economy

Overview: no economic activity

:Juan de Nova Island Communications

Railroads:
    short line going to a jetty
Ports:
    none; offshore anchorage only
Airports:
    1 with non-permanent-surface runways 1,220-2,439 m

:Juan de Nova Island Defense Forces

Note: defense is the responsibility of France

Kazakhstan Geography

Total area: 2,717,300 km2
Land area: 2,669,800 km2
Comparative area: slightly less than four times the size of Texas
Land boundaries:
   12,012 km; China 1,533 km, Kyrgyzstan 1,051 km, Russia 6,846 km,
   Turkmenistan 379 km, Uzbekistan 2,203 km
Coastline:
   0 km
   note:
   Kazakhstan does border the Aral Sea (1,015 km) and the Caspian Sea (1,894
   km)
Maritime claims:
   none - landlocked
Disputes:
   none
Climate:
   dry continental, about half is desert
Terrain:
   extends from the Volga to the Altai mountains and from the plains in western
   Siberia to oasis and desert in Central Asia
Natural resources:
   petroleum, coal, iron, manganese, chrome, nickel, cobalt, copper,
   molybdenum, lead, zinc, bauxite, gold, uranium, iron
Land use:
   NA% arable land; NA% permanent crops; NA% meadows and pastures; NA% forest
   and woodland; NA% other; includes NA% irrigated
Environment:
   drying up of Aral Sea is causing increased concentrations of chemical
   pesticides and natural salts; industrial pollution

:Kazakhstan People

Population: 17,103,927 (July 1992), growth rate 1.0% (1992)
Birth rate: 23 births/1,000 population (1992)
Death rate: 8 deaths/1,000 population (1992)
Net migration rate: -6.1 migrants/1,000 population (1991)
Infant mortality rate: 25.9 deaths/1,000 live births (1992)
Life expectancy at birth: 63 years male, 72 years female (1992)
Total fertility rate: 2.9 children born/woman (1992)
Nationality:
   noun - Kazakh(s); adjective - Kazakhstani
Ethnic divisions:
   Kazakh (Qazaq) 40%, Russian 38%, other Slavs 7%, Germans 6%, other 9%
Religions:
   Muslim 47% Russian Orthodox NA%, Lutheran NA%
Languages:
   Kazakh (Qazaq; official language), Russian

Literacy:
 NA% (male NA%, female NA%) age 15 and over can read and write
Labor force:
 8,267,000 (1989)
Organized labor:
 official trade unions, independent coal miners' union

:Kazakhstan Government

Long-form name:
 Republic of Kazakhstan
Type:
 republic
Capital: Alma-Ata (Almaty)
Administrative divisions:
 19 oblasts (oblastey, singular - oblast'); Aktyubinsk, Alma-Ata, Atyrau,
 Chimkent, Dzhambul, Dzhezkazgan, Karaganda, Kokchetav, Kustanay, Kzyl-Orda,
 Mangistauz (Aqtau), Pavlodar, Semipalatinsk, Severo-Kazakhstan
 (Petropavlovsk), Taldy-Kurgan, Tselinograd, Turgay (Arkalyk), Ural'sk,
 Vostochno-Kazakhstan (Ust'-Kamenogorsk); note - an oblast has the same name
 as its administrative center (exceptions have the administrative center name
 following in parentheses)
Independence:
 16 December 1991; from the Soviet Union (formerly the Kazakh Soviet
 Socialist Republic)
Constitution:
 new postindependence constitution under preparation
Legal system:
 NA
National holiday:
 NA
Executive branch:
 president with presidential appointed cabinet of ministers
Legislative branch:
 Supreme Soviet
Judicial branch:
 NA
Leaders:
 Chief of State:
 President Nursultan A. NAZARBAYEV (since April 1990), Vice President Yerik
 ASANBAYEV (since 1 December 1991)
 Head of Government:
 Prime Minister Sergey TERESHCHENKO (since 14 October 1991), Deputy Prime
 Minister Davlat SEMBAYEV (since November 1990)
Political parties and leaders:
 Peoples Forum Party, Olzhas SULEIMENOV and Mukhtar SHAKHANOV, co-
chairmen;
 Socialist Party (former Communist Party), Anuar ALIJANOV, chairman;
 ZHOLTOKSAN, Hasan KOJAKHETOV, chairmen; AZAT Party, Sabitkazi
AKETAEV,
 chairman

Suffrage:
  universal at age 18
Elections:
 President:
  last held 1 December 1991 (next to be held NA); percent of vote by party NA;
  seats - (NA total) percent of seats by party NA
Communists:
  party disbanded 6 September 1992
Member of:
  CIS, CSCE, IMF, NACC, OIC, UN, UNCTAD
Diplomatic representation:
  Ambassador NA; Chancery at NA NW, Washington, DC 200__; telephone NA;
there
  are NA Consulates General
 US:
  Ambassador-designate William Courtney; Embassy at Hotel Kazakhstan,
  Alma-Ata, (mailing address is APO AE 09862); telephone 8-011-7-3272-61-90-56
Flag:
  no national flag yet adopted

:Kazakhstan Economy

Overview:
  The second-largest in area of the 15 former Soviet republics, Kazakhstan has
  vast oil, coal, and agricultural resources. Kazakhstan is highly dependent
  on trade with Russia, exchanging its natural resources for finished consumer
  and industrial goods. Kazakhstan now finds itself with serious pollution
  problems, backward technology, and little experience in foreign markets. The
  government in 1991 pushed privatization of the economy at a faster pace than
  Russia's program. The ongoing transitional period - marked by sharp
  inflation in wages and prices, lower output, lost jobs, and disruption of
  time-honored channels of supply - has brought considerable social unrest.
  Kazakhstan lacks the funds, technology, and managerial skills for a quick
  recovery of output. US firms have been enlisted to increase oil output but
  face formidable obstacles; for example, oil can now reach Western markets
  only through pipelines that run across independent (and sometimes
  unfriendly) former Soviet republics. Finally, the end of monolithic
  Communist control has brought ethnic grievances into the open. The 6 million
  Russians in the republic, formerly the favored class, now face the hostility
  of a society dominated by Muslims. Ethnic rivalry will be just one of the
  formidable obstacles to the creation of a productive, technologically
  advancing society.
GDP:
  purchasing power equivalent - $NA; per capita NA; real growth rate - 7%
  (1991 est.)
Inflation rate (consumer prices).
  83% (1991)
Unemployment rate: NA%
Budget:
  revenues $NA million; expenditures $NA million, including capital
  expenditures of $1.76 billion (1991)

Exports:
  $4.2 billion (f.o.b., 1991)
  commodities:
  oil, ferrous and nonferrous metals, chemicals, grain, wool, meat (1991)
  partners:
  Russia, Ukraine, Uzbekistan
Imports:
  $NA million (c.i.f., 1990)
  commodities:
  machinery and parts, industrial materials
  partners:
  Russia and other former Soviet republics
External debt: $2.6 billion (1991 est.)
Industrial production:
  growth rate 0.7% (1991)
Electricity:
  17,900,000 kW capacity; 79,100 million kWh produced, 4,735 kWh per capita
  (1991)
Industries:
  extractive industries (oil, coal, iron ore, manganese, chromite, lead, zinc,
  copper, titanium, bauxite, gold, silver, phosphates, sulfur) iron and steel,
  nonferrous metal, tractors and other agricultural machinery, electric
  motors, construction materials
Agriculture:
  employs 30% of the labor force; grain, mostly spring wheat; meat, cotton,
  wool

:Kazakhstan Economy

Illicit drugs:
  illicit producers of cannabis and opium; mostly for domestic consumption;
  status of government eradication programs unknown; used as transshipment
  points for illicit drugs to Western Europe
Economic aid:
  US commitments, including Ex-Im (FY70-87), $NA billion; Western (non-US)
  countries, ODA and OOF bilateral commitments (1970-86), $NA million;
  Communist countries (1971-86), $NA million
Currency:
  as of May 1992, retaining ruble as currency
Exchange rates:
  NA
Fiscal year: calendar year

:Kazakhstan Communications

Railroads:
  14,460 km (all 1.520-meter gauge); does not include industrial lines (1990)
Highways:
  189,000 km total (1990); 188,900 km hard surfaced (paved or gravel), 80,900
  km earth
Inland waterways:
  NA km perennially navigable
Pipelines:

crude oil NA km, refined products NA km, natural gas NA

Ports:

none - landlocked; inland - Guryev

Civil air:

NA major transport aircraft

Airports:

NA

Telecommunications:

telephone service is poor, with only about 6 telephones for each 100
persons; of the approximately 1 million telephones, Alma-Ata has 184,000;
international traffic with other former USSR republics and China carried by
landline and microwave, and with other countries by satellite and through
the Moscow international gateway switch; satellite earth stations - INTELSAT
and Orbita

:Kazakhstan Defense Forces

Branches:

Republic Security Forces (internal and border troops), National Guard; CIS
Forces (Ground, Air, Air Defense, and Strategic Rocket)

Manpower availability:

males 15-49, NA fit for military service; NA reach military age (18)
annually

Defense expenditures:

$NA, NA% of GDP

Kenya Geography

Total area: 582,650 km2

Land area: 569,250 km2

Comparative area: slightly more than twice the size of Nevada

Land boundaries:

3,477 km; Ethiopia 861 km, Somalia 682 km, Sudan 232 km, Tanzania 769 km,
Uganda 933 km

Coastline:

536 km

Maritime claims:

 Exclusive economic zone:

200 nm

 Territorial sea:

12 nm

Disputes:

administrative boundary with Sudan does not coincide with international
boundary; possible claim by Somalia based on unification of ethnic Somalis

Climate:

varies from tropical along coast to arid in interior

Terrain:

low plains rise to central highlands bisected by Great Rift Valley; fertile
plateau in west

Natural resources:

gold, limestone, soda ash, salt barytes, rubies, fluorspar, garnets,
wildlife

Land use:

507

arable land 3%; permanent crops 1%; meadows and pastures 7%; forest and woodland 4%; other 85%; includes irrigated NEGL%

Environment:

unique physiography supports abundant and varied wildlife of scientific and economic value; deforestation; soil erosion; desertification; glaciers on Mt. Kenya

Note:

the Kenyan Highlands comprise one of the most successful agricultural production regions in Africa

:Kenya People

Population: 26,164,473 (July 1992), growth rate 3.6% (1992)

Birth rate: 44 births/1,000 population (1992)

Death rate: 8 deaths/1,000 population (1992)

Net migration rate: 0 migrants/1,000 population (1992)

Infant mortality rate: 68 deaths/1,000 live births (1992)

Life expectancy at birth: 60 years male, 64 years female (1992)

Total fertility rate: 6.2 children born/woman (1992)

Nationality:

noun - Kenyan(s); adjective - Kenyan

Ethnic divisions:

Kikuyu 21%, Luhya 14%, Luo 13%, Kalenjin 11%, Kamba 11%, Kisii 6%, Meru 6%,

Asian, European, and Arab 1%

Religions:

Protestant 38%, Roman Catholic 28%, indigenous beliefs 26%, Muslim 6%

Languages:

English and Swahili (official); numerous indigenous languages

Literacy:

69% (male 80%, female 58%) age 15 and over can read and write (1990 est.)

Labor force:

9.2 million (includes unemployed); the total employed is 1.37 million (14.8% of the labor force); services 54.8%, industry 26.2%, agriculture 19.0% (1989)

Organized labor:

390,000 (est.)

:Kenya Government

Long-form name:

Republic of Kenya

Type:

republic

Capital: Nairobi

Administrative divisions:

7 provinces and 1 area*; Central, Coast, Eastern, Nairobi Area*, North Eastern, Nyanza, Rift Valley, Western

Independence:

12 December 1963 (from UK; formerly British East Africa)

Constitution:

12 December 1963, amended as a republic 1964; reissued with amendments 1979, 1983, 1986, 1988, and 1991

Legal system:

based on English common law, tribal law, and Islamic law; judicial review in High Court; accepts compulsory ICJ jurisdiction, with reservations; constitutional amendment of 1982 making Kenya a de jure one-party state repealed in 1991

National holiday:

Independence Day, 12 December (1963)

Executive branch:

president, vice president, Cabinet

Legislative branch:

unicameral National Assembly (Bunge)

Judicial branch:

Court of Appeal, High Court

Leaders:

Chief of State and Head of Government:

President Daniel Teroitich arap MOI (since 14 October 1978); Vice President George SAITOTI (since 10 May 1989)

Political parties and leaders:

ruling party is Kenya African National Union (KANU), Daniel T. arap MOI, president; opposition parties include Forum for the Restoration of Democracy (FORD), Oginga ODINJA; Democratic Party of Kenya (DP), KIBAKI; note - some dozen other opposition parties

Suffrage:

universal at age 18

Elections:

President:

last held on 21 March 1988 (next to be held before March 1993); results - President Daniel T. arap MOI was reelected

National Assembly:

last held on 21 March 1988 (next to be held before March 1993); will be first multiparty election since repeal of one-party state law

Other political or pressure groups:

labor unions; exile opposition - Mwakenya and other groups

Member of:

ACP, AfDB, C, CCC, EADB, ECA, FAO, G-77, GATT, IAEA, IBRD, ICAO, IDA, IFAD,

IFC, IGADD, ILO, IMF, IMO, INTELSAT, INTERPOL, IOC, IOM, ISO, ITU, LORCS,

NAM, OAU, UN, UNCTAD, UNESCO, UNIDO, UNIIMOG, UPU, WCL, WHO, WIPO, WMO, WTO

Diplomatic representation:

Ambassador Denis Daudi AFANDE; Chancery at 2249 R Street NW, Washington, DC

20008; telephone (202) 387-6101; there are Kenyan Consulates General in Los Angeles and New York

:Kenya Government

US:

Ambassador Smith HEMPSTONE, Jr.; Embassy at the corner of Moi Avenue and Haile Selassie Avenue, Nairobi (mailing address is P. O. Box 30137, Nairobi

or APO AE 09831); telephone [254] (2) 334141; FAX [254] (2) 340838; there is
a US Consulate in Mombasa

Flag:
three equal horizontal bands of black (top), red, and green; the red band is
edged in white; a large warrior's shield covering crossed spears is
superimposed at the center

:Kenya Economy

Overview:
Kenya's 3.6% annual population growth rate - one of the highest in the world
- presents a serious problem for the country's economy. In the meantime, GDP
growth in the near term has kept slightly ahead of population - annually
averaging 4.9% in the 1986-90 period. Undependable weather conditions and a
shortage of arable land hamper long-term growth in agriculture, the leading
economic sector. In 1991, deficient rainfall, stagnant export volume, and
sagging export prices held economic growth below the all-important
population growth figure.

GDP:
exchange rate conversion - $9.7 billion, per capita $385 (1989 est.); real
growth rate 2.3% (1991 est.)

Inflation rate (consumer prices):
14.3% (1991 est.)

Unemployment rate: NA%, but there is a high level of unemployment and underemployment

Budget:
revenues $2.4 billion; expenditures $2.8 billion, including capital
expenditures of $0.74 billion (FY90)

Exports:
$1.0 billion (f.o.b., 1991 est.)
commodities:
tea 25%, coffee 21%, petroleum products 7% (1989)
partners:
EC 44%, Africa 25%, Asia 5%, US 5%, Middle East 4% (1988)

Imports:
$1.9 billion (f.o.b., 1991 est.)
commodities:
machinery and transportation equipment 29%, petroleum and petroleum products
15%, iron and steel 7%, raw materials, food and consumer goods (1989)
partners:
EC 45%, Asia 11%, Middle East 12%, US 5% (1988)

External debt: $6.0 billion (December 1991 est.)

Industrial production:
growth rate 5.4% (1989 est.); accounts for 17% of GDP

Electricity:
730,000 kW capacity; 2,700 million kWh produced, 110 kWh per capita (1990)

Industries:
small-scale consumer goods (plastic, furniture, batteries, textiles, soap,
cigarettes, flour), agricultural processing, oil refining, cement, tourism

Agriculture:
most important sector, accounting for 29% of GDP, about 19% of the work

force, and over 50% of exports; cash crops - coffee, tea, sisal, pineapple;
food products - corn, wheat, sugarcane, fruit, vegetables, dairy products;
food output not keeping pace with population growth

Illicit drugs:

illicit producer of cannabis used mostly for domestic consumption;
widespread cultivation of cannabis and qat on small plots; transit country
for heroin and methaqualone en route from Southwest Asia to West Africa,
Western Europe, and the US

Economic aid:

US commitments, including Ex-Im (FY70-89), $839 million; Western (non-US)
countries, ODA and OOF bilateral commitments (1970-89), $7,490 million; OPEC
bilateral aid (1979-89), $74 million; Communist countries (1970-89), $83
million

Currency:

Kenyan shilling (plural - shillings); 1 Kenyan shilling (KSh) = 100 cents

:Kenya Economy

Exchange rates:

Kenyan shillings (KSh) per US$1 - 28.466 (January 1992), 27.508 (1991),
22.915 (1990), 20.572 (1989), 17.747 (1988), 16.454 (1987)

Fiscal year: 1 July - 30 June

:Kenya Communications

Railroads:

2,040 km 1.000-meter gauge

Highways:

64,590 km total; 7,000 km paved, 4,150 km gravel, remainder improved earth

Inland waterways:

part of Lake Victoria system is within boundaries of Kenya; principal inland
port is at Kisumu

Pipelines:

petroleum products 483 km

Ports:

Mombasa, Lamu

Merchant marine:

1 petroleum tanker ship (1,000 GRT or over) totaling 7,727 GRT/5,558 DWT

Civil air:

19 major transport aircraft

Airports:

249 total, 214 usable; 21 with permanent-surface runways; 2 with runways
over 3,659 m; 2 with runways 2,440-3,659 m; 46 with runways 1,220-2,439 m

Telecommunications:

in top group of African systems; consists primarily of radio relay links;
over 260,000 telephones; broadcast stations - 16 AM; 4 FM, 6 TV; satellite
earth stations   1 Atlantic Ocean INTELSAT and 1 Indian Ocean INTELSA i

:Kenya Defense Forces

Branches:

Army, Navy, Air Force, paramilitary General Service Unit of the Police

Manpower availability:

males 15-49, 5,688,543; 3,513,611 fit for military service; no conscription

Defense expenditures:
  exchange rate conversion - $100 million, 1% of GDP (1989 est.)

Kingman Reef Geography

Total area: 1 km2
Land area: 1 km2
Comparative area: about 1.7 times the size of the Mall in Washington, DC
Land boundaries:
  none
Coastline:
  3 km
Maritime claims:
 Contiguous zone:
  12 nm
 Continental shelf:
  200 m (depth)
 Exclusive economic zone:
  200 nm
 Territorial sea:
  12 nm
Disputes:
  none
Climate:
  tropical, but moderated by prevailing winds
Terrain:
  low and nearly level with a maximum elevation of about 1 meter
Natural resources:
  none
Land use:
  arable land 0%; permanent crops 0%; meadows and pastures 0%; forest and
  woodland 0%; other 100%
Environment:
  barren coral atoll with deep interior lagoon; wet or awash most of the time
Note:
  located 1,600 km south-southwest of Honolulu in the North Pacific Ocean,
  about halfway between Hawaii and American Samoa; maximum elevation of about
  1 meter makes this a navigational hazard; closed to the public

:Kingman Reef People

Population: uninhabited

:Kingman Reef Government

Long-form name:
  none
Type:
  unincorporated territory of the US administered by the US Navy
Capital: none; administered from Washington, DC

:Kingman Reef Economy

Overview: no economic activity

:Kingman Reef Communications

Ports:

none; offshore anchorage only

Airports:

lagoon was used as a halfway station between Hawaii and American Samoa by Pan American Airways for flying boats in 1937 and 1938

:Kingman Reef Defense Forces

Note: defense is the responsibility of the US

Kiribati Geography

Total area: 717 km2

Land area: 717 km2; includes three island groups - Gilbert Islands, Line Islands, Phoenix Islands

Comparative area: slightly more than four times the size of Washington, DC

Land boundaries:

Coastline:

1,143 km

Maritime claims:

 Exclusive economic zone:

 200 nm

 Territorial sea:

 12 nm

Disputes:

Climate:

tropical; marine, hot and humid, moderated by trade winds

Terrain:

mostly low-lying coral atolls surrounded by extensive reefs

Natural resources:

phosphate (production discontinued in 1979)

Land use:

arable land NEGL%; permanent crops 51%; meadows and pastures 0%; forest and woodland 3%; other 46%

Environment:

typhoons can occur any time, but usually November to March; 20 of the 33 islands are inhabited

Note:

Banaba (Ocean Island) in Kiribati is one of the three great phosphate rock islands in the Pacific Ocean - the others are Makatea in French Polynesia and Nauru

:Kiribati People

Population: 74,788 (July 1992), growth rate 2.1% (1992)

Birth rate: 33 births/1,000 population (1992)

Death rate: 12 deaths/1,000 population (1992)

Net migration rate: 1 migrant/1,000 population (1992)

Infant mortality rate: 99 deaths/1,000 live births (1992)

Life expectancy at birth: 52 years male, 56 years female (1992)

Total fertility rate: 3.9 children born/woman (1992)

Nationality:

noun - I-Kiribati (singular and plural); adjective - I-Kiribati
Ethnic divisions:
  Micronesian
Religions:
  Roman Catholic 52.6%, Protestant (Congregational) 40.9%, Seventh-Day
  Adventist, Baha'i, Church of God, Mormon 6% (1985)
Languages:
  English (official), Gilbertese
Literacy:
  NA% (male NA%, female NA%)
Labor force:
  7,870 economically active, not including subsistence farmers (1985 est.)
Organized labor:
  Kiribati Trades Union Congress - 2,500 members

:Kiribati Government

Long-form name:
  Republic of Kiribati; note - pronounced Kiribas
Type:
  republic
Capital: Tarawa
Administrative divisions:
  3 units; Gilbert Islands, Line Islands, Phoenix Islands; note - a new
  administrative structure of 6 districts (Banaba, Central Gilberts, Line
  Islands, Northern Gilberts, Southern Gilberts, Tarawa) may have been changed
  to 21 island councils (one for each of the inhabited islands) named Abaiang,
  Abemama, Aranuka, Arorae, Banaba, Beru, Butaritari, Canton, Kiritimati,
  Kuria, Maiana, Makin, Marakei, Nikunau, Nonouti, Onotoa, Tabiteuea,
  Tabuaeran, Tamana, Tarawa, Teraina
Independence:
  12 July 1979 (from UK; formerly Gilbert Islands)
Constitution:
  12 July 1979
National holiday:
  Independence Day, 12 July (1979)
Executive branch:
  president (Beretitenti), vice president (Kauoman-ni-Beretitenti), Cabinet
Legislative branch:
  unicameral House of Assembly (Maneaba Ni Maungatabu)
Judicial branch:
  Court of Appeal, High Court
Leaders:
  Chief of State and Head of Government:
  President Teatao TEANNAKI (since 8 July 1991); Vice President Taomati IUTA
  (since 8 July 1991)
Political parties and leaders:
  National Progressive Party, Teatao TEANNAKI; Christian Democratic Party,
  Teburoro TITO; New Movement Party, leader NA; Liberal Party, Tewareka
  TENTOA; note - there is no tradition of formally organized political parties
  in Kiribati; they more closely resemble factions or interest groups because

514

they have no party headquarters, formal platforms, or party structures
Suffrage:
  universal at age 18
Elections:
 President:
  last held on 8 July 1991 (next to be held May 1995); results - Teatao
  TEANNAKI 52%, Roniti TEIWAKI 28%
 House of Assembly:
  last held on 8 May 1991 (next to be held May 1995); results - percent of
  vote by party NA; seats - (40 total; 39 elected) percent of seats by party
  NA
Member of:
  ACP, AsDB, C, ESCAP (associate), IBRD, ICAO, ICFTU, IDA, IFC, IMF,
INTERPOL,
  ITU, SPC, SPF, UNESCO, UPU, WHO, WTO
Diplomatic representation:
  Ambassador (vacant) lives in Tarawa (Kiribati)
 US:
  the ambassador to Fiji is accredited to Kiribati
Flag:
  the upper half is red with a yellow frigate bird flying over a yellow rising
  sun, and the lower half is blue with three horizontal wavy white stripes to
  represent the ocean

:Kiribati Economy

Overview:
  The country has few national resources. Commercially viable phosphate
  deposits were exhausted at the time of independence in 1979. Copra and fish
  now represent the bulk of production and exports. The economy has fluctuated
  widely in recent years. Real GDP declined about 8% in 1987, as the fish
  catch fell sharply to only one-fourth the level of 1986 and copra production
  was hampered by repeated rains. Output rebounded strongly in 1988, with real
  GDP growing by 17%. The upturn in economic growth came from an increase in
  copra production and a good fish catch. Following the strong surge in output
  in 1988, GNP increased 1% in both 1989 and 1990.
GDP:
  exchange rate conversion - $36.8 million, per capita $525; real growth rate
  1.0% (1990 est.)
Inflation rate (consumer prices):
  4.0% (1990 cst.)
Unemployment rate: 2% (1985); considerable underemployment
Budget:
  revenues $29.9 million; expenditures $16.3 million, including capital
  expenditures of $14.0 million (1990 est.)
Exports:
  $5.8 million (f.o.b., 1990 est.)
 commodities:
  fish 55%, copra 42%
 partners:
  EC 20%, Marshall Islands 12%, US 8%, American Samoa 4% (1985)

Imports:
  $26.7 million (c.i.f., 1990 est.)
  commodities:
  foodstuffs, fuel, transportation equipment
  partners:
  Australia 39%, Japan 21%, NZ 6%, UK 6%, US 3% (1985)
External debt: $2.0 million (December 1989 est.)
Industrial production:
  growth rate 0% (1988 est.); accounts for less than 4% of GDP
Electricity:
  5,000 kW capacity; 13 million kWh produced, 190 kWh per capita (1990)
Industries:
  fishing, handicrafts
Agriculture:
  accounts for 30% of GDP (including fishing); copra and fish contribute about
  95% to exports; subsistence farming predominates; food crops - taro,
  breadfruit, sweet potatoes, vegetables; not self-sufficient in food
Economic aid:
  Western (non-US) countries, ODA and OOF bilateral commitments (1970-89),
  $273 million
Currency:
  Australian dollar (plural - dollars); 1 Australian dollar ($A) = 100 cents
Exchange rates:
  Australian dollars ($A) per US$1 - 1.3177 (March 1992), 1.2835 (1991),
  1.2799 (1990), 1.2618 (1989), 1.2752 (1988), 1.4267 (1987), 1.4905 (1986)
Fiscal year: NA

:Kiribati Communications

Highways:
  640 km of motorable roads
Inland waterways:
  small network of canals, totaling 5 km, in Line Islands
Ports:
  Banaba and Betio (Tarawa)
Civil air:
  2 Trislanders; no major transport aircraft
Airports:
  21 total; 20 usable; 4 with permanent-surface runways; none with runways
  over 2,439 m; 5 with runways 1,220-2,439 m
Telecommunications:
  1,400 telephones; broadcast stations - 1 AM, no FM, no TV; 1 Pacific Ocean
  INTELSAT earth station

:Kiribati Defense Forces

Branches:
  no military force maintained; the Police Force carries out law enforcement
  functions and paramilitary duties; there are small police posts on all
  islands
Manpower availability:
  NA

Defense expenditures:
$NA, NA% of GDP

Korea, North Geography

Total area: 120,540 km2
Land area: 120,410 km2
Comparative area: slightly smaller than Mississippi
Land boundaries:
    1,673 km; China 1,416 km, South Korea 238 km, Russia 19 km
Coastline:
    2,495 km
Maritime claims:
  Exclusive economic zone:
    200 nm
  Military boundary line:
    50 nm in the Sea of Japan and the exclusive economic zone limit in the
    Yellow Sea (all foreign vessels and aircraft without permission are banned)
  Territorial sea:
    12 nm
Disputes:
    short section of boundary with China is indefinite; Demarcation Line with
    South Korea
Climate:
    temperate with rainfall concentrated in summer
Terrain:
    mostly hills and mountains separated by deep, narrow valleys; coastal plains
    wide in west, discontinuous in east
Natural resources:
    coal, lead, tungsten, zinc, graphite, magnesite, iron ore, copper, gold,
    pyrites, salt, fluorspar, hydropower
Land use:
    arable land 18%; permanent crops 1%; meadows and pastures NEGL%; forest and
    woodland 74%; other 7%; includes irrigated 9%
Environment:
    mountainous interior is isolated, nearly inaccessible, and sparsely
    populated; late spring droughts often followed by severe flooding
Note:
    strategic location bordering China, South Korea, and Russia

:Korea, North People

Population: 22,227,303 (July 1992), growth rate 1.9% (1992)
Birth rate: 24 births/1,000 population (1992)
Death rate: 6 deaths/1,000 population (1992)
Net migration rate: 0 migrants/1,000 population (1992)
Infant mortality rate: 30 deaths/1,000 live births (1992)
Life expectancy at birth: 66 years male, 72 years female (1992)
Total fertility rate: 2.4 children born/woman (1992)
Nationality:
    noun - Korean(s);adjective - Korean
Ethnic divisions:
    racially homogeneous

Religions:

Buddhism and Confucianism; some Christianity and syncretic Chondogyo; autonomous religious activities now almost nonexistent; government-sponsored religious groups exist to provide illusion of religious freedom

Languages:

Korean

Literacy:

99%, (male 99%, female 99%); note - presumed to be virtually universal among population under age 60

Labor force:

9,615,000; agricultural 36%, nonagricultural 64%; shortage of skilled and unskilled labor (mid-1987 est.)

Organized labor:

1,600,000 members; single-trade union system coordinated by the General Federation of Trade Unions of Korea under the Central Committee

:Korea, North Government

Long-form name:

Democratic People's Republic of Korea; abbreviated DPRK

Type:

Communist state; Stalinist dictatorship

Capital: P'yongyang

Administrative divisions:

9 provinces (do, singular and plural) and 3 special cities* (jikhalsi, singular and plural); Chagang-do, Hamgyong-namdo, Hamgyong-bukto, Hwanghae-namdo, Hwanghae-bukto, Kaesong-si*, Kangwon-do, Namp'o-si*, P'yongan-bukto, P'yongan-namdo,P'yongyang-si*, Yanggang-do

Independence:

9 September 1948

Constitution:

adopted 1948, revised 27 December 1972

Legal system:

based on German civil law system with Japanese influences and Communist legal theory; no judicial review of legislative acts; has not accepted compulsory ICJ jurisdiction

National holiday:

Independence Day, 9 September (1948)

Executive branch:

president, two vice presidents, premier, eleven vice premiers, State Administration Council (cabinet)

Legislative branch:

unicameral Supreme People's Assembly (Ch'oego Inmin Hoeui)

Judicial branch:

Central Court

Leaders:

Chief of State:

President KIM Il-song (national leader since 1945, formally President since 28 December 1972); designated Successor KIM Chong-il (son of President, born 16 February 1942)

Head of Government:

518

Premier YON Hyong-muk (since December 1988)

Political parties and leaders:

major party - Korean Workers' Party (KWP), KIM Il-song, general secretary, and his son, KIM Chong-il, secretary, Central Committee; Korean Social Democratic Party, YI Kye-paek, chairman; Chondoist Chongu Party, CHONG Sin-hyok, chairman

Suffrage:

universal at age 17

Elections:

President:

last held 24 May 1990 (next to be held NA 1994); results - President KIM Il-song was reelected without opposition

Supreme People's Assembly:

last held on 24 May 1990 (next to be held NA 1994); results - percent of vote by party NA; seats - (687 total) the KWP approves a single list of candidates who are elected without opposition; minor parties hold a few seats

Communists:

KWP claims membership of about 3 million

Member of:

ESCAP, FAO, G-77, IAEA, ICAO, IFAD, IMF (observer), IMO, IOC, ISO, ITU, LORCS, NAM, UN, UNCTAD, UNESCO, UNIDO, UPU, WFTU, WHO, WIPO, WMO, WTO

Diplomatic representation:

:Korea, North Government

Flag:

three horizontal bands of blue (top), red (triple width), and blue; the red band is edged in white; on the hoist side of the red band is a white disk with a red five-pointed star

:Korea, North Economy

Overview:

More than 90% of this command economy is socialized; agricultural land is collectivized; and state-owned industry produces 95% of manufactured goods. State control of economic affairs is unusually tight even for a Communist country because of the small size and homogeneity of the society and the strict rule of KIM Il-song and his son, KIM Chong-il. Economic growth during the period 1984-89 averaged 2-3%, but output declined by 2-4% annually during 1990-91, largely because of disruptions in economic relations with the USSR. Abundant natural resources and hydropower form the basis of industrial development. Output of the extractive industries includes coal, iron ore, magnesite, graphite, copper, zinc, lead, and precious metals. Manufacturing is centered on heavy industry, with light industry lagging far behind. Despite the use of improved seed varieties, expansion of irrigation, and the heavy use of fertilizers, North Korea has not yet become self-sufficient in food production. Four consecutive years of poor harvests, coupled with distribution problems, have led to chronic food shortages. North Korea remains far behind South Korea in economic development and living standards.

GNP:
   purchasing power equivalent - $23.3 billion, per capita $1,100; real growth
   rate -2% (1991 est.)
Inflation rate (consumer prices):
   NA%
Unemployment rate: officially none
Budget:
   revenues $17.3 billion; expenditures $17.7 billion, including capital
   expenditures of $NA (1990)
Exports:
   $2.02 billion (f.o.b., 1990)
  commodities:
   minerals, metallurgical products, agricultural products, manufactures
  partners:
   USSR, China, Japan, Hong Kong, Germany, Singapore
Imports:
   $2.62 billion (f.o.b., 1990 est.)
  commodities:
   petroleum, machinery and equipment, coking coal, grain
  partners:
   USSR, Japan, China, Hong Kong, FRG, Singapore
External debt: $7 billion (1991)
Industrial production:
   growth rate NA%
Electricity:
   7,140,000 kW capacity; 36,000 million kWh produced, 1,650 kWh per capita
   (1991)
Industries:
   machine building, military products, electric power, chemicals, mining,
   metallurgy, textiles, food processing
Agriculture:
   accounts for about 25% of GNP and 36% of work force; principal crops - rice,
   corn, potatoes, soybeans, pulses; livestock and livestock products - cattle,
   hogs, pork, eggs; not self-sufficient in grain; fish catch estimated at 1.7
   million metric tons in 1987
Economic aid:
   Communist countries, $1.4 billion a year in the 1980s
Currency:
   North Korean won (plural - won); 1 North Korean won (Wn) = 100 chon

:Korea, North Economy

Exchange rates:
   North Korean won (Wn) per US$1 - 2.13 (May 1992), 2.14 (September 1991), 2.1
   (January 1990), 2.3 (December 1989), 2.13 (December 1988), 0.94 (March 1987)
Fiscal year: calendar year

:Korea, North Communications

Railroads:
   4,915 km total; 4,250 km 1.435-meter standard gauge, 665 km 0.762-meter
   narrow gauge; 159 km double track; 3,084 km electrified; government owned
   (1989)

Highways:

about 30,000 km (1989); 98.5% gravel, crushed stone, or earth surface; 1.5% paved

Inland waterways:

2,253 km; mostly navigable by small craft only

Pipelines:

crude oil 37 km

Ports:

Ch'ongjin, Haeju, Hungnam, Namp'o, Wonsan, Songnim, Najin, Sonbong (formerly Unggi), Kim Chaek

Merchant marine:

78 ships (1,000 GRT and over) totaling 543,033 GRT/804,507 DWT; includes 1 passenger, 1 short-sea passenger, 1 passenger-cargo, 67 cargo, 2 petroleum tanker, 4 bulk, 1 combination bulk, 1 container

Airports:

55 total, 55 usable (est.); about 30 with permanent-surface runways; fewer than 5 with runways over 3,659 m; 20 with runways 2,440-3,659 m; 30 with runways 1,220-2,439 m

Telecommunications:

broadcast stations - 18 AM, no FM, 11 TV; 200,000 TV sets; 3,500,000 radio receivers; 1 Indian Ocean INTELSAT earth station

:Korea, North Defense Forces

Branches:

Korean People's Army (including the Army, Navy, Air Force), Civil Security Forces

Manpower availability:

males 15-49, 6,476,839; 3,949,568 fit for military service; 227,154 reach military age (18) annually

Defense expenditures:

exchange rate conversion - about $5 billion, 20-25% of GNP (1991 est.); note - the officially announced but suspect figure is $1.9 billion (1991) 8% of GNP (1991 est.)

Korea, South Geography

Total area: 98,480 km2
Land area: 98,190 km2
Comparative area: slightly larger than Indiana
Land boundaries:

238 km; North Korea 238 km

Coastline:

2,413 km

Maritime claims:

 Continental shelf:

  not specific

 Territorial sea:

 12 nm (3 nm in the Korea Strait)

Disputes:

Demarcation Line with North Korea; Liancourt Rocks claimed by Japan

Climate:

temperate, with rainfall heavier in summer than winter

Terrain:
  mostly hills and mountains; wide coastal plains in west and south
Natural resources:
  coal, tungsten, graphite, molybdenum, lead, hydropower
Land use:
  arable land 21%; permanent crops 1%; meadows and pastures 1%; forest and
  woodland 67%; other 10%; includes irrigated 12%
Environment:
  occasional typhoons bring high winds and floods; earthquakes in southwest;
  air pollution in large cities

:Korea, South People

Population: 44,149,199 (July 1992), growth rate 1.1% (1992)
Birth rate: 16 births/1,000 population (1992)
Death rate: 6 deaths/1,000 population (1992)
Net migration rate: 1 migrant/1,000 population (1992)
Infant mortality rate: 23 deaths/1,000 live births (1992)
Life expectancy at birth: 67 years male, 73 years female (1992)
Total fertility rate: 1.6 children born/woman (1992)
Nationality:
  noun - Korean(s);adjective - Korean
Ethnic divisions:
  homogeneous; small Chinese minority (about 20,000)
Religions:
  strong Confucian tradition; vigorous Christian minority (24.3% of the total
  population); Buddhism; pervasive folk religion (Shamanism); Chondogyo
  (religion of the heavenly way), eclectic religion with nationalist overtones
  founded in 19th century, about 0.1% of population
Languages:
  Korean; English widely taught in high school
Literacy:
  96% (male 99%, female 94%) age 15 and over can read and write (1990 est.)
Labor force:
  16,900,000; 52% services and other; 27% mining and manufacturing; 21%
  agriculture, fishing, forestry (1987)
Organized labor:
  23.4% (1989) of labor force in government-sanctioned unions

:Korea, South Government

Long-form name:
  Republic of Korea; abbreviated ROK
Type:
  republic
Capital: Seoul
Administrative divisions:
  9 provinces (do, singular and plural) and 6 special cities* (jikhalsi,
  singular and plural); Cheju-do, Cholla-bukto, Cholla-namdo,
  Ch'ungch'ong-bukto, Ch'ungch'ong-namdo, Inch'on-jikhalsi*, Kangwon-do,
  Kwangju-jikhalsi*, Kyonggi-do, Kyongsang-bukto, Kyongsang-namdo,
  Pusan-jikhalsi*, Soul-t'ukpyolsi*, Taegu-jikhalsi*, Taejon-jikhalsi*
Independence:

15 August 1948

Constitution:

25 February 1988

Legal system:

combines elements of continental European civil law systems, Anglo-American law, and Chinese classical thought

National holiday:

Independence Day, 15 August (1948)

Executive branch:

president, prime minister, two deputy prime ministers, State Council (cabinet)

Legislative branch:

unicameral National Assembly (Kuk Hoe)

Judicial branch:

Supreme Court

Leaders:

Chief of State:

President ROH Tae Woo (since 25 February 1988)

Head of Government:

Prime Minister CHUNG Won Shik (since 24 May 1991); Deputy Prime Minister CHOI Gak Kyu (since 19 February 1991)

Political parties and leaders:

ruling party:

Democratic Liberal Party (DLP), ROH Tae Woo, president, KIM Young Sam, chairman; KIM Chong Pil and PAK Tae Chun, co-chairmen; note - the DLP resulted from a merger of the Democratic Justice Party (DJP), Reunification Democratic Party (RDP), and New Democratic Republican Party (NDRP) on 9 February 1990

opposition:

Democratic Party (DP), result of a merger of the New Democratic Party and the Democratic Party formalized 16 September 1991; KIM Dae Jung, executive chairman; LEE Ki Taek, executive chairman; several smaller parties

Suffrage:

universal at age 20

Elections:

President:

last held on 16 December 1987 (next to be held December 1992); results - ROH Tae Woo (DJP) 35.9%, KIM Young Sam (RDP) 27.5%, KIM Dae Jung (PPD) 26.5%,

other 10.1%

National Assembly:

last held on 26 April 1988 (next to be held around March 1992); results - DJP 34%, RDP 24%, PPD 19%, NDRP 15%, other 8%; seats - (296 total) DJP 125, PPD 70, RDP 59, NDRP 35, other 10; note - on 9 February 1990 the DJP, RDP, and NDRP merged to form the DLP; also the PPD, later renamed the NDP, merged with another party to form the DP in September 1991. The distribution of seats as of December 1991 was DLP 214, DP 72, independent 9, vacant 1

:Korea, South Government

Other political or pressure groups:

Korean National Council of Churches; National Democratic Alliance of Korea; National Council of College Student Representatives; National Federation of Farmers' Associations; National Council of Labor Unions; Federation of Korean Trade Unions; Korean Veterans' Association; Federation of Korean Industries; Korean Traders Association

Member of:

AfDB, APEC, AsDB, CCC, COCOM, CP, EBRD, ESCAP, FAO, G-77, GATT, IAEA, IBRD,

ICAO, ICC, ICFTU, IDA, IFAD, IFC, IMF, ILO, IMF, INMARSAT, INTELSAT, INTERPOL, IOC, IOM, ISO, ITU, LORCS, OAS, UN, UNCTAD, UNESCO, UNIDO, UPU,

WHO, WIPO, WMO, WTO

Diplomatic representation:

Ambassador HYUN Hong Joo; Chancery at 2370 Massachusetts Avenue NW, Washington, DC 20008; telephone (202) 939-5600; there are Korean Consulates General in Agana (Guam), Anchorage, Atlanta, Chicago, Honolulu, Houston, Los Angeles, New York, San Francisco, and Seattle

US:

Ambassador Donald P. GREGG; Embassy at 82 Sejong-Ro, Chongro-ku, Seoul, AMEMB, Unit 15550 (mailing address is APO AP 96205-0001); telephone [82] (2) 732-2601 through 2618; FAX [82] (2) 738-8845; there is a US Consulate in Pusan

Flag:

white with a red (top) and blue yin-yang symbol in the center; there is a different black trigram from the ancient I Ching (Book of Changes) in each corner of the white field

:Korea, South Economy

Overview:

The driving force behind the economy's dynamic growth has been the planned development of an export-oriented economy in a vigorously entrepreneurial society. Real GNP has increased more than 10% annually over the past six years. This growth has led to an overheated situation characterized by a tight labor market, strong inflationary pressures, and a rapidly rising current account deficit. Policymakers have stated they will focus attention on slowing inflation. In any event, the economy will remain the envy of the great majority of the world's peoples.

GNP:

purchasing power equivalent - $273 billion, per capita $6,300; real growth rate 8.7% (1991 est.)

Inflation rate (consumer prices):

9.7% (1991)

Unemployment rate: 2.4% (1991)

Budget:

revenues $44 billion; expenditures $44 billion, including capital expenditures of $NA (1992)

Exports:

$71.9 billion (f.o.b., 1991)

commodities:

textiles, clothing, electronic and electrical equipment, footwear,
machinery, steel, automobiles, ships, fish
partners:
US 26%, Japan 18% (1991)
Imports:
$81.6 billion (c.i.f., 1991)
commodities:
machinery, electronics and electronic equipment, oil, steel, transport
equipment, textiles, organic chemicals, grains
partners:
Japan 26%, US 23% (1991)
External debt: $38.2 billion (1991)
Industrial production:
growth rate 7.5% (1991 est.); accounts for about 45% of GNP
Electricity:
24,000,000 kW capacity; 106,000 million kWh produced, 2,460 kWh per capita
(1991)
Industries:
textiles, clothing, footwear, food processing, chemicals, steel,
electronics, automobile production, shipbuilding
Agriculture:
accounts for 8% of GNP and employs 21% of work force (including fishing and
forestry); principal crops - rice, root crops, barley, vegetables, fruit;
livestock and livestock products - cattle, hogs, chickens, milk, eggs;
self-sufficient in food, except for wheat; fish catch of 2.9 million metric
tons, seventh-largest in world
Economic aid:
US commitments, including Ex-Im (FY70-89), $3.9 billion; non-US countries
(1970-89), $3.0 billion
Currency:
South Korean won (plural - won); 1 South Korean won (W) = 100 chon
(theoretical)
Exchange rates:
South Korean won (W) per US$1 - 766.66 (January 1992), 733.35 (1991), 707.76
(1990), 671.46 (1989), 731.47 (1988), 822.57 (1987)

:Korea, South Economy

Fiscal year: calendar year

:Korea, South Communications

Railroads:
3,106 km operating in 1983; 3,059 km 1.435-meter standard gauge, 47 km
0.610-meter narrow gauge, 712 km double track, 418 km electrified;
government owned
Highways:
62,936 km total (1982); 13,476 km national highway, 49,460 km provincial and
local roads
Inland waterways:
1,609 km; use restricted to small native craft
Pipelines:
petroleum products 455 km

Ports:

Pusan, Inchon, Kunsan, Mokpo, Ulsan

Merchant marine:

435 ships (1,000 GRT or over) totaling 6,924,818 GRT/11,389,397 DWT; includes 2 short-sea passenger, 140 cargo, 53 container, 11 refrigerated cargo, 9 vehicle carrier, 42 petroleum tanker, 10 chemical tanker, 14 liquefied gas, 5 combination ore/oil, 145 bulk, 3 combination bulk, 1 multifunction large-load carrier

Civil air:

93 major transport aircraft

Airports:

105 total, 97 usable; 60 with permanent-surface runways; none with runways over 3,659 m; 23 with runways 2,440-3,659 m; 16 with runways 1,220-2,439 m

Telecommunications:

adequate domestic and international services; 4,800,000 telephones; broadcast stations - 79 AM, 46 FM, 256 TV (57 of 1 kW or greater); satellite earth stations - 2 Pacific Ocean INTELSAT and 1 Indian Ocean INTELSAT

:Korea, South Defense Forces

Branches:

Army, Navy, Marines Corps, Air Force

Manpower availability:

males 15-49, 13,131,113; 8,456,428 fit for military service; 448,450 reach military age (18) annually

Defense expenditures:

exchange rate conversion - $12.6 billion, 4.5% of GNP (1992 budget)

Kuwait Geography

Total area: 17,820 km2
Land area: 17,820 km2
Comparative area: slightly smaller than New Jersey
Land boundaries:

462 km; Iraq 240 km, Saudi Arabia 222 km

Coastline:

499 km

Maritime claims:

Continental shelf:

not specific

Territorial sea:

12 nm

Disputes:

in April 1991 official Iraqi acceptance of UN Security Council Resolution 687, which demands that Iraq accept the inviolability of the boundary set forth in its 1963 agreement with Kuwait, ending earlier claims to Bubiyan and Warbah Islands or to all of Kuwait; a UN Boundary Demarcation Commission is demarcating the Iraq-Kuwait boundary persuant to Resolution 687, and, on 17 June 1992, the UN Security Council reaffirmed the finality of the Boundary Demarcation Commission's decisions; ownership of Qaruh and Umm al Maradim Islands disputed by Saudi Arabia

Climate:

dry desert; intensely hot summers; short, cool winters

Terrain:
   flat to slightly undulating desert plain
Natural resources:
   petroleum, fish, shrimp, natural gas
Land use:
   arable land NEGL%; permanent crops 0%; meadows and pastures 8%; forest and
   woodland NEGL%; other 92%; includes irrigated NEGL%
Environment:
   some of world's largest and most sophisticated desalination facilities
   provide most of water; air and water pollution; desertification
Note:
   strategic location at head of Persian Gulf

:Kuwait People

Population: 1,378,613 (July 1992), growth rate NA (1992)
Birth rate: 32 births/1,000 population (1992)
Death rate: 2 deaths/1,000 population (1992)
Net migration rate: NA migrants/1,000 population (1992)
Infant mortality rate: 14 deaths/1,000 live births (1992)
Life expectancy at birth: 72 years male, 76 years female (1992)
Total fertility rate: 4.4 children born/woman (1992)
Nationality:
   noun - Kuwaiti(s); adjective - Kuwaiti
Ethnic divisions:
   Kuwaiti 50%, other Arab 35%, South Asian 9%, Iranian 4%, other 2%
Religions:
   Muslim 85% (Shi`a 30%, Sunni 45%, other 10%), Christian, Hindu, Parsi, and
   other 15%
Languages:
   Arabic (official); English widely spoken
Literacy:
   74% (male 78%, female 69%) age 15 and over can read and write (1985)
Labor force:
   566,000 (1986); services 45.0%, construction 20.0%, trade 12.0%,
   manufacturing 8.6%, finance and real estate 2.6%, agriculture 1.9%, power
   and water 1.7%, mining and quarrying 1.4%; 70% of labor force was
   non-Kuwaiti
Organized labor:
   labor unions exist in oil industry and among government personnel

:Kuwait Government

Long-form name:
   State of Kuwait
Type:
   nominal constitutional monarchy
Capital: Kuwait
Administrative divisions:
   5 governorates (mu'hafaz'at, singular - muh'afaz'ah); Al Ah'madi, Al Jahrah,
   Al Kuwayt, 'Hawalli; Farwaniyah
Independence:
   19 June 1961 (from UK)

Constitution:

16 November 1962 (some provisions suspended since 29 August 1962)

Legal system:

civil law system with Islamic law significant in personal matters; has not accepted compulsory ICJ jurisdiction

National holiday:

National Day, 25 February

Executive branch:

amir, prime minister, deputy prime minister, Council of Ministers (cabinet)

Legislative branch:

National Assembly (Majlis al `umma) dissolved 3 July 1986; elections for new Assembly scheduled for October 1992

Judicial branch:

High Court of Appeal

Leaders:

Chief of State:

Amir Shaykh JABIR al-Ahmad al-Jabir al-Sabah (since 31 December 1977)

Head of Government:

Prime Minister and Crown Prince SA`UD al-`Abdallah al-Salim al-Sabah (since 8 February 1978); Deputy Prime Minister SALIM al-Sabah al-Salim al-Sabah

Political parties and leaders:

Suffrage:

adult males who resided in Kuwait before 1920 and their male descendants at age 21; note - out of all citizens, only 10% are eligible to vote and only 5% actually vote

Elections:

National Assembly:

dissolved 3 July 1986; new elections are scheduled for October 1992

Other political or pressure groups:

40,000 Palestinian community; small, clandestine leftist and Shi`a fundamentalist groups are active; several groups critical of government policies are active

Member of:

ABEDA, AfDB, AFESD, AL, AMF, BDEAC, CAEU, ESCWA, FAO, G-77, GATT, GCC, IAEA,

IBRD, ICAO, IDA, IDB, IFAD, IFC, ILO, IMF, IMO, INMARSAT, INTELSAT, INTERPOL, IOC, ISO (correspondent), ITU, LORCS, NAM, OAPEC, OIC, OPEC, UN,

UNCTAD, UNESCO, UNIDO, UPU, WFTU, WHO, WMO, WTO

Diplomatic representation:

Ambassador Shaykh Sa`ud Nasir al-SABAH; Chancery at 2940 Tilden Street NW, Washington, DC 20008; telephone (202) 966-0702

US:

Ambassador Edward (Skip) GNEHM, Jr.; Embassy at Bneid al-Gar (opposite the Kuwait International Hotel), Kuwait City (mailing address is P.O. Box 77 SAFAT, 13001 SAFAT, Kuwait; APO AE 09880); telephone [965] 242-4151 through

4159; FAX [956] 244-2855

:Kuwait Government

Flag:
   three equal horizontal bands of green (top), white, and red with a black
   trapezoid based on the hoist side

:Kuwait Economy

Overview:
   Up to the invasion by Iraq in August 1990, the oil sector had dominated the
   economy. Kuwait has the third-largest oil reserves in the world after Saudi
   Arabia and Iraq. Earnings from hydrocarbons have generated over 90% of both
   export and government revenues and contributed about 40% to GDP. Most of the
   nonoil sector has traditionally been dependent upon oil-derived government
   revenues. Iraq's destruction of Kuwait's oil industry during the Gulf war
   has devastated the economy. Iraq destroyed or damaged more than 80% of
   Kuwait's 950 operating oil wells, as well as sabotaged key surface
   facilities. Firefighters brought all of the roughly 750 oil well fires and
   blowouts under control by November 1991. By yearend, production had been
   brought back to 400,000 barrels per day; it could take two to three years to
   restore Kuwait's oil production to its prewar level of about 2.0 million
   barrels per day. Meanwhile, population had been greatly reduced because of
   the war, from 2.1 million to 1.4 million.

GDP:
   exchange rate conversion - $8.75 billion, per capita $6,200; real growth
   rate -50% (1991 est.)

Inflation rate (consumer prices):
   NA

Unemployment rate: NA

Budget:
   revenues $7.1 billion; expenditures $10.5 billion, including capital
   expenditures of $3.1 billion (FY88)

Exports:
   $11.4 billion (f.o.b., 1989)
  commodities:
   oil 90%
  partners:
   Japan 19%, Netherlands 9%, US 8%, Pakistan 6%

Imports:
   $6.6 billion (f.o.b., 1989)
  commodities:
   food, construction materials, vehicles and parts, clothing
  partners:
   US 15%, Japan 12%, FRG 8%, UK 7%

External debt: $7.2 billion (December 1989 est.)

Industrial production:
   growth rate 3% (1988); accounts for 52% of GDP

Electricity:
   3,100,000 kW available out of 8,290,000 kW capacity due to Persian Gulf war;
   7,300 million kWh produced, 3,311 kWh per capita (1991)

Industries:
   petroleum, petrochemicals, desalination, food processing, building
   materials, salt, construction

Agriculture:
 virtually none; dependent on imports for food; about 75% of potable water
 must be distilled or imported
Economic aid:
 donor - pledged $18.3 billion in bilateral aid to less developed countries
 (1979-89)
Currency:
 Kuwaiti dinar (plural - dinars); 1 Kuwaiti dinar (KD) = 1,000 fils
Exchange rates:
 Kuwaiti dinars (KD) per US$1 - 0.2950 (March 1992), 0.2843 (1991), 0.2915
 (1990), 0.2937 (1989), 0.2790 (1988), 0.2786 (1987)

:Kuwait Economy

Fiscal year: 1 July - 30 June

:Kuwait Communications

Railroads:
 6,456 km total track length (1990); over 700 km double track; government
 owned
Highways:
 3,900 km total; 3,000 km bituminous; 900 km earth, sand, light gravel
Pipelines:
 crude oil 877 km; petroleum products 40 km; natural gas 165 km
Ports:
 Ash Shu`aybah, Ash Shuwaykh, Mina' al 'Ahmadi
Merchant marine:
 29 ships (1,000 GRT or over), totaling 1,196,435 GRT/1,957,216 DWT; includes
 2 cargo, 4 livestock carrier, 18 oil tanker, 4 liquefied gas; note - all
 Kuwaiti ships greater than 1,000 GRT were outside Kuwaiti waters at the time
 of the Iraqi invasion; many of these ships transferred to the Liberian flag
 or to the flags of other Persian Gulf states; only 1 has returned to Kuwaiti
 flag since the liberation of Kuwait
Civil air:
 9 major transport aircraft
Airports:
 7 total, 4 usable; 4 with permanent-surface runways; none with runways over
 3,659 m; 4 with runways 2,440-3,659 m; none with runways 1,220-2,439 m
Telecommunications:
 civil network suffered extensive damage as a result of Desert Storm;
 reconstruction is under way with some restored international and domestic
 capabilities; broadcast stations - 3 AM, 0 FM, 3 TV; satellite earth
 stations - destroyed during Persian Gulf war; temporary mobile satellite
 ground stations provide international telecommunications; coaxial cable and
 radio relay to Saudi Arabia; service to Iraq is nonoperational

:Kuwait Defense Forces

Branches:
 Army, Navy, Air Force, National Police Force, National Guard
Manpower availability:
 males 15-49, 389,770; 234,609 fit for military service; 12,773 reach
 military age (18) annually

Defense expenditures:
  exchange rate conversion - $9.17 billion, 20.4% of GDP (1992 budget)

Kyrgyzstan Geography

Total area: 198,500 km2
Land area: 191,300 km2
Comparative area: slightly smaller than South Dakota
Land boundaries:
  3,878 km; China 858 km, Kazakhstan 1,051 km, Tajikistan 870 km, Uzbekistan
  1,099 km
Coastline:
  none - landlocked
Maritime claims:
  none - landlocked
Disputes:
  territorial dispute with Tajikistan on southern boundary in Isfara Valley
  area
Climate:
  dry continental to polar in high Tien Shan; subtropical in south (Fergana
  Valley)
Terrain:
  peaks of Tien Shan rise to 7,000 meters, and associated valleys and basins
  encompass entire nation
Natural resources:
  small amounts of coal, natural gas, oil; also nepheline, rare earth metals,
  mercury, bismuth, gold, uranium, lead, zinc, hydroelectric power
Land use:
  NA% arable land; NA% permanent crops; NA% meadows and pastures; NA% forest
  and woodland; NA% other; includes NA% irrigated
Environment:
  NA

:Kyrgyzstan People

Population: 4,567,875 (July 1992), growth rate 1.9% (1992)
Birth rate: 31 births/1,000 population (1992)
Death rate: 8 deaths/1,000 population (1992)
Net migration rate: - 8.5 migrants/1,000 population (1992)
Infant mortality rate: 56 deaths/1,000 live births (1991)
Life expectancy at birth: 62 years male, 71 years female (1992)
Total fertility rate: 4.0 children born/woman (1992)
Nationality:
  noun - Kirghiz(s); adjective - Kirghiz
Ethnic divisions:
  Kirghiz 52%, Russian 21%, Uzbek 13%, other 14%
Religions:
  Muslim 70%, Russian Orthodox NA%
Languages:
  Kirghiz (Kyrgyz)
Literacy:
  NA% (male NA%, female NA%) age 15 and over can read and write
Labor force:

1,894,000 (1989); agriculture 33%, other 49%, industry 18%, other NA% (1988)
Organized labor:
  NA

:Kyrgyzstan Government

Long-form name:
  Republic of Kyrgyzstan
Type:
  republic
Capital: Bishkek (formerly Frunze)
Administrative divisions:
  6 oblasts (oblastey, singular - oblast'); Chu, Dzhalal-Abad, Issyk-Kul',
  Naryn, Osh, Talas; note - an oblast has the same name as its administrative
  center
Independence:
  31 August 1991 (from Soviet Union; formerly Kirghiz Soviet Socialist
  Republic)
Constitution:
  adopted NA, effective 20 April 1978, amended 23 September 1989; note - new
  constitution is being drafted
Legal system:
  NA
National holiday:
  NA
Executive branch:
  president, Cabinet of Ministers
Legislative branch:
  unicameral body or bicameral
Judicial branch:
  Supreme Court
Leaders:
  President Askar AKAYEV; Vice President Felix KULOV; Chairman, Supreme
  Soviet, Medetkav SHERIMKULOV; Spiritual leader of Kyrgyz Muslims, Sadyk-
zhav
  KAMALOV
 Chief of State:
  President Askar AKAYEV (since 28 October 1990), Vice President Felix KULOV
  (since 2 March 1992)
 Head of Government:
  Prime Minister Tursenbek CHYNGYSHEV (since 2 March 1992)
Political parties and leaders:
  Kyrgyzstan Democratic Movement, Zhypur ZHEKSHEYEV, Kazat AKMAKOV,
and
  Toshubek TURGANALIEV, co-chairmen of popular front coalition of 40 informal
  groups for Democratic Renewal and Civic Accord, 117-man pro-Akayev
  parliamentary faction; Civic Accord, Coalition representing nonnative
  minority groups; National Revived Asaba (Banner) Party, Asan ORMUSHEV,
  chairman; Communist Party now banned
Suffrage:
  universal at age 18

Elections:

President:

last held 12 October 1991 (next to be held NA 1996); results - AKAYEV won in uncontested election with 95% of vote with 90% of electorate voting; note - Republic Supreme Soviet elections held 25 February 1990; presidential elections held first by Supreme Soviet 28 October 1990, then by popular vote 12 October 1991

Supreme Soviet:

note - last held 25 February 1990 (next to be held no later than November 1994); results - Commnunists (310) 90%, seats - (350 total)

Other political or pressure groups:

National Unity Democratic Movement; Peasant Party; Council of Free Trade Union; Union of Entrepreneurs

Member of:

CIS, CSCE, IMF, UN, UNCTAD

:Kyrgyzstan Government

Diplomatic representation:

Ambassador NA; Chancery at NW, Washington, DC 200__; telephone (202) NA; there are Consulates General in NA;

US:

Charge Ralph Bresler; Interim Chancery at #66 Derzhinskiy Prospekt; Residence: Hotel Pishpek (mailing address is APO AE 09862); telephone 8-011-7-3312-22-22-70

Flag:

red-orange field with yellow sun in center with folk motif medallion inscribed

:Kyrgyzstan Economy

Overview:

Kyrgyzstan's small economy (less than 1% of the total for the former Soviet Union) is oriented toward agriculture, producing mainly livestock such as goats and sheep, as well as cotton, grain, and tobacco. Industry, concentrated around Bishkek, produces small quantities of electric motors, livestock feeding equipment, washing machines, furniture, cement, paper, and bricks. Mineral extraction is small, the most important minerals being rare earth metals and gold. Kyrgyzstan is a net importer of most types of food and fuel but is a net exporter of electricity. By early 1991, the Kirghiz leadership had accelerated reform, primarily by privatizing business and granting life-long tenure to farmers. In 1991 overall industrial and livestock output declined substantially.

GDP:

purchasing power equivalent - $NA billion, per capita $NA; real growth rate -5% (1991)

Inflation rate (consumer prices):

88% (1991)

Unemployment rate: NA%

Budget:

revenues $NA million; expenditures $NA million

Exports:

$115 million (1990)

commodities:
  wool, chemicals, cotton, ferrous and nonferrous metals, shoes, machinery,
  tobacco
partners:
  Russia 70%, Ukraine, Uzbekistan, Kazakhstan, and others
Imports:
  $1.5 million (c.i.f., 1990)
 commodities:
  lumber, industrial products, ferrous metals, fuel, machinery, textiles,
  footwear
External debt: $650 million (1991)
Industrial production:
  growth rate 0.1% (1991)
Electricity:
  NA kW capacity; 13,900 million kWh produced, 3,232 kWh per capita (1991)
Industries:
  small machinery, textiles, food-processing industries, cement, shoes, sawn
  logs, steel, refrigerators, furniture, electric motors, gold, and rare earth
  metals
Agriculture:
  wool, tobacco, cotton, livestock (sheep and goats) and cattle, vegetables,
  meat, grapes, fruits and berries, eggs, milk, potatoes
Illicit drugs:
  poppy cultivation legal
Economic aid:
  US commitments, including Ex-Im (FY70-87), $NA billion; Western (non-US)
  countries, ODA and OOF bilateral commitments (1970-86), $NA million;
  Communist countries (1971-86), $NA million
Currency:
  as of May 1992, retaining ruble as currency
Fiscal year: calendar year

:Kyrgyzstan Communications

Railroads:
  370 km; does not include industrial lines (1990)
Highways:
  30,300 km total; 22,600 km paved or graveled, 7,700 km earth(1990)
Inland waterways:
  NA km perennially navigable
Pipelines:
  NA
Ports:
  none - landlocked
Civil air:
  NA
Airports:
  NA
Telecommunications:
  poorly developed; connections with other CIS countries by landline or
  microwave and with other countries by leased connections with Moscow

international gateway switch; satellite earth stations - Orbita and INTELSAT (TV receive only)

:Kyrgyzstan Defense Forces

Branches:
Republic Security Forces (internal and border troops); National Guard, Civil Defense; CIS Forces (Ground, Air, and Air Defense)
Manpower availability:
males 15-49, NA fit for military service; NA reach military age (18) annually
Defense expenditures:
$NA, NA% of GDP

Laos Geography

Total area: 236,800 km2
Land area: 230,800 km2
Comparative area: slightly larger than Utah
Land boundaries:
5,083 km; Burma 235 km, Cambodia 541 km, China 423 km, Thailand 1,754 km, Vietnam 2,130 km
Coastline:
none - landlocked
Maritime claims:
none - landlocked
Disputes:
boundary dispute with Thailand
Climate:
tropical monsoon; rainy season (May to November); dry season (December to April)
Terrain:
mostly rugged mountains; some plains and plateaus
Natural resources:
timber, hydropower, gypsum, tin, gold, gemstones
Land use:
arable land 4%; permanent crops NEGL%; meadows and pastures 3%; forest and woodland 58%; other 35%; includes irrigated 1%
Environment:
deforestation; soil erosion; subject to floods
Note:
landlocked

:Laos People

Population: 4,440,213 (July 1992), growth rate 2.9% (1992)
Birth rate: 44 births/1,000 population (1992)
Death rate: 16 deaths/1,000 population (1992)
Net migration rate: 0 migrants/1,000 population (1992)
Infant mortality rate: 107 deaths/1,000 live births (1992)
Life expectancy at birth: 49 years male, 52 years female (1992)
Total fertility rate: 6.3 children born/woman (1992)
Nationality:
noun - Lao(s) or Laotian(s); adjective - Lao or Laotian

Ethnic divisions:

Lao 50%, Phoutheung (Kha) 15%, tribal Thai 20%, Meo, Hmong, Yao, and other 15%

Religions:

Buddhist 85%, animist and other 15%

Languages:

Lao (official), French, and English

Literacy:

84% (male 92%, female 76%) age 15 to 45 can read and write (1985 est.)

Labor force:

1-1.5 million; 85-90% in agriculture (est.)

Organized labor:

Lao Federation of Trade Unions is subordinate to the Communist party

:Laos Government

Long-form name:

Lao People's Democratic Republic

Type:

Communist state

Capital: Vientiane

Administrative divisions:

16 provinces (khoueng, singular and plural) and 1 municipality* (kampheng nakhon, singular and plural); Attapu, Bokeo, Bolikhamsai, Champasak, Houaphan, Khammouan, Louang Namtha, Louangphrabang, Oudomxai, Phongsali, Saravan, Savannakhet, Sekong, Vientiane, Vientiane*, Xaignabouri, Xiangkhoang

Independence:

19 July 1949 (from France)

Constitution:

promulgated August 1991

Legal system:

based on civil law system; has not accepted compulsory ICJ jurisdiction

National holiday:

National Day (proclamation of the Lao People's Democratic Republic), 2 December (1975)

Executive branch:

president, chairman and two vice chairmen of the Council of Ministers, Council of Ministers (cabinet)

Legislative branch:

Supreme People's Assembly

Judicial branch:

People's Supreme Court

Leaders:

Chief of State:

President KAYSONE PHOMVIHAN (since 15 August 1991)

Head of Government:

Chairman of the Council of Ministers Gen. KHAMTAI SIPHANDON (since 15 August
1991)

Political parties and leaders:

Lao People's Revolutionary Party (LPRP), KAYSONE PHOMVIHAN, party chairman;

includes Lao Patriotic Front and Alliance Committee of Patriotic Neutralist Forces; other parties moribund

Suffrage:

universal at age 18

Elections:

Supreme People's Assembly:

last held on 26 March 1989 (next to be held NA); results - percent of vote by party NA; seats - (79 total) number of seats by party NA

Other political or pressure groups:

non-Communist political groups moribund; most leaders have fled the country

Member of:

ACCT (associate), AsDB, CP, ESCAP, FAO, G-77, IBRD, ICAO, IDA, IFAD, ILO, IMF, INTERPOL, IOC, ITU, LORCS, NAM, PCA, UN, UNCTAD, UNESCO, UNIDO, UPU,

WFTU, WHO, WMO, WTO

Diplomatic representation:

Charge d'Affaires LINTHONG PHETSAVAN; Chancery at 2222 S Street NW, Washington, DC 20008; telephone (202) 332-6416 or 6417

US:

Charge d'Affaires Charles B. SALMON, Jr.; Embassy at Rue Bartholonie, Vientiane (mailing address is B. P. 114, Vientiane, or AMEMB, Box V, APO AP 96546); telephone (856) 2220, 2357, 2384; FAX (856) 4675

:Laos Government

Flag:

three horizontal bands of red (top), blue (double width), and red with a large white disk centered in the blue band

:Laos Economy

Overview:

One of the world's poorest nations, Laos has had a Communist centrally planned economy with government ownership and control of productive enterprises of any size. In recent years, however, the government has been decentralizing control and encouraging private enterprise. Laos is a landlocked country with a primitive infrastructure; that is, it has no railroads, a rudimentary road system, limited external and internal telecommunications, and electricity available in only a limited area. Subsistence agriculture is the main occupation, accounting for over 60% of GDP and providing about 85-90% of total employment. The predominant crop is rice. For the foreseeable future the economy will continue to depend for its survival on foreign aid from the IMF and other international sources; aid from the former USSR and Eastern Europe has been cut sharply.

GDP:

exchange rate conversion - $800 million, per capita $200; real growth rate 4% (1991)

Inflation rate (consumer prices):

10.4% (December 1991)

Unemployment rate: 21% (1989 est.)

Budget:

revenues $83 million; expenditures $188.5 million, including capital
expenditures of $94 million (1990 est.)
Exports:
$72 million (f.o.b., 1990 est.)
commodities:
electricity, wood products, coffee, tin
partners:
Thailand, Malaysia, Vietnam, USSR, US, China
Imports:
$238 million (c.i.f., 1990 est.)
commodities:
food, fuel oil, consumer goods, manufactures
partners:
Thailand, USSR, Japan, France, Vietnam, China
External debt: $1.1 billion (1990 est.)
Industrial production:
growth rate 12% (1991 est.); accounts for about 18% of GDP (1991 est.)
Electricity:
226,000 kW capacity; 1,100 million kWh produced, 270 kWh per capita (1991)
Industries:
tin and gypsum mining, timber, electric power, agricultural processing,
construction
Agriculture:
accounts for 60% of GDP and employs most of the work force; subsistence
farming predominates; normally self-sufficient in nondrought years;
principal crops - rice (80% of cultivated land), sweet potatoes, vegetables,
corn, coffee, sugarcane, cotton; livestock - buffaloes, hogs, cattle,
chicken
Illicit drugs:
illicit producer of cannabis, opium poppy for the international drug trade,
third-largest opium producer
Economic aid:
US commitments, including Ex-Im (FY70-79), $276 million; Western (non-US)
countries, ODA and OOF bilateral commitments (1970-89), $605 million;
Communist countries (1970-89), $995 million
Currency:
new kip (plural - kips); 1 new kip (NK) = 100 at

:Laos Economy

Exchange rates:
new kips (NK) per US$1 - 710 (May 1992), 710 (December 1991), 700 (September
1990), 576 (1989), 385 (1988), 200 (1987)
Fiscal year: 1 July - 30 June

:Laos Communications

Railroads:
none
Highways:
about 27,527 km total; 1,856 km bituminous or bituminous treated; 7,451 km
gravel, crushed stone, or improved earth; 18,220 km unimproved earth and
often impassable during rainy season mid-May to mid-September

Inland waterways:
   about 4,587 km, primarily Mekong and tributaries; 2,897 additional
   kilometers are sectionally navigable by craft drawing less than 0.5 m
Pipelines:
   petroleum products 136 km
Ports:
   none
Airports:
   57 total, 47 usable; 8 with permanent-surface runways; none with runways
   over 3,659 m; 1 with runways 2,440-3,659 m; 14 with runways 1,220-2,439 m
Telecommunications:
   service to general public considered poor; radio communications network
   provides generally erratic service to government users; 7,390 telephones
   (1986); broadcast stations - 10 AM, no FM, 1 TV; 1 satellite earth station

:Laos Defense Forces

Branches:
   Lao People's Army (LPA; including naval, aviation, and militia elements),
   Air Force, National Police Department
Manpower availability:
   males 15-49, 946,289; 509,931 fit for military service; 45,232 reach
   military age (18) annually; conscription age NA
Defense expenditures:
   exchange rate conversion - $NA, NA% of GDP

Latvia Geography

Total area: 64,100 km2
Land area: 64,100 km2
Comparative area: slightly larger than West Virginia
Land boundaries:
   1,078 km; Belarus 141 km, Estonia 267 km, Lithuania 453 km, Russia 217 km
Coastline:
   531 km
Maritime claims:
 Contiguous zone:
  NA nm
 Continental shelf:
  NA meter depth
 Exclusive fishing zone:
  NA nm
 Exclusive economic zone:
  NA nm
 Territorial sea:
  NA nm
Disputes:
   the Abrene section of border ceded by the Latvian Soviet Socialist Republic
   to Russia in 1944
Climate:
   maritime; wet, moderate winters
Terrain:
   low plain

Natural resources:
  minimal; amber, peat, limestone, dolomite
Land use:
  27% arable land; NA% permanent crops; 13% meadows and pastures; 39% forest
  and woodland; 21% other; includes NA% irrigated
Environment:
  heightened levels of air and water pollution because of a lack of waste
  conversion equipment; Gulf of Riga heavily polluted

:Latvia People

Population: 2,728,937 (July 1992), growth rate 0.6% (1992)
Birth rate: 15 births/1,000 population (1992)
Death rate: 12 deaths/1,000 population (1992)
Net migration rate: 4 migrants/1,000 population (1992)
Infant mortality rate: 19 deaths/1,000 live births (1992)
Life expectancy at birth: 65 years male, 75 years female (1992)
Total fertility rate: 2.1 children born/woman (1992)
Nationality:
  noun - Latvian(s);adjective - Latvian
Ethnic divisions:
  Latvian 51.8%, Russian 33.8%, Byelorussian 4.5%, Ukrainian 3.4%, Polish
  2.3%, other 4.2%
Religions:
  Lutheran, Roman Catholic, Russian Orthodox
Languages:
  Latvian NA% (official), Lithuanian NA%, Russian NA%, other NA%
Literacy:
  NA% (male NA%, female NA%) age 15 and over can read and write
Labor force:
  1,407,000; industry and construction 41%, agriculture and forestry 16%,
  other 43% (1990)
Organized labor:
  NA

:Latvia Government

Long-form name:
  Republic of Latvia
Type:
  republic
Capital: Riga
Administrative divisions:
  none - all districts are under direct republic jurisdiction
Independence:
  18 November 1918; annexed by the USSR 21 July 1940, the Latvian Soviet
  Socialist Republic declared independence 6 September 1991 from USSR
Constitution:
  April 1978, currently rewriting constitution, but readopted the 1922
  Constitution
Legal system:
  based on civil law system
National holiday:

Independence Day, 18 November (1918)

Executive branch:

Prime Minister

Legislative branch:

unicameral Supreme Council

Judicial branch:

Supreme Court

Leaders:

Chief of State:

Chairman, Supreme Council, Anatolijs GORBUNOVS (since October 1988);
Chairmen, Andrejs KRASTINS, Valdis BIRKAVS (since NA 1992)

Head of Government:

Prime Minister Ivars GODMANIS (since May 1990)

Political parties and leaders:

Democratic Labor Party of Latvia, Juris BOJARS, chairman; Inter-Front of the
Working People of Latvia, Igor LOPATIN, chairman; note - Inter-Front was
banned after the coup; Latvian National Movement for Independence, Eduards
BERKLAVS, chairman; Latvian Social Democratic Party, Janis DINEVICS,
chairman; Social Democratic Party of Latvia, Uldis BERZINS, chairman;
Latvian People's Front, Romualdas RAZUKAS, chairman; Latvian Liberal Party,
Georg LANSMANIS, chairman

Suffrage:

universal at age 18

Elections:

President:

last held October 1988 (next to be held NA; note - elected by Parliament;
new elections have not been scheduled; results - percent of vote by party NA

Supreme Council:

last held 18 March 1990 (next to be held NA); results - undetermined; seats
- (234 total) Latvian Communist Party 59, Latvian Democratic Workers Party
31, Social Democratic Party of Latvia 4, Green Party of Latvia 7, Latvian
Farmers Union 7, 126 supported by the Latvia Popular Front

Congress of Latvia:

last held April 1990 (next to be held NA); note - the Congress of Latvia is
a quasi-governmental structure; results - percent of vote by party NA%;
seats - (231 total) number of seats by party NA

Member of:

CSCE, IAEA, UN

Diplomatic representation:

Ambassador Dr. Anatol DINBERGS; Chancery at 4325 17th St. NW, Washington,
DC

20011; telephone (202) 726-8213 and 8214

:Latvia Government

US:

Ambassador Ints SILINS; (mailing address is APO AE 09862); telephone [358]
(49) 306-067 (cellular), (7) (01-32) 325-968/185; FAX [358] (49) 308-326
(cellular), (7) (01-32) 220-502

Flag:

541

two horizontal bands of maroon (top), white (middle, narrower than other two bands) and maroon (bottom)

:Latvia Economy

Overview:

Latvia is in the process of reforming the centrally planned economy inherited from the former USSR into a market economy. Prices have been freed, and privatization of shops and farms has begun. Latvia lacks natural resources, aside from its arable land and small forests. Its most valuable economic asset is its work force, which is better educated and disciplined than in most of the former Soviet republics. Industrial production is highly diversified, with products ranging from agricultural machinery to consumer electronics. One conspicuous vulnerability: Latvia produces only 10% of its electric power needs. Latvia in the near term must retain key commercial ties to Russia, Belarus, and Ukraine while moving in the long run toward joint ventures, technological support, and trade ties to the West. Because of the efficiency of its mostly individual farms, Latvians enjoy a diet that is higher in meat, vegetables, and dairy products and lower in grain and potatoes than diets in the 12 non-Baltic republics of the USSR. Good relations with Russia are threatened by animosity between ethnic Russians (34% of the population) and native Latvians.

GDP:

purchasing power equivalent - $NA; per capital NA; real growth rate - 8% (1991)

Inflation rate (consumer prices):

approximately 200% (1991)

Unemployment rate: NA%

Budget:

revenues $NA; expenditures $NA, including capital expenditures of $NA (1991)

Exports:

$239 million (f.o.b., 1990)

commodities:

food 14%, railroad cars 13%, chemicals 12%

partners:

Russia 50%, Ukraine 15%, other former Soviet republics 30%, West 5%

Imports:

$9.0 billion (c.i.f., 1989)

commodities:

machinery 35%, petroleum products 13%, chemicals 9%

partners:

NA

External debt: $650 million (1991 est.)

Industrial production:

growth rate 0% (1991)

Electricity:

1,975,000 kW capacity; 6,500 million kWh produced, 2,381 kWh per capita (1990)

Industries:

employs 33.2% of labor force; highly diversified; dependent on imports for energy, raw materials, and intermediate products; produces buses, vans,

street and railroad cars, synthetic fibers, agricultural machinery,
fertilizers, washing machines, radios, electronics, pharmaceuticals,
processed foods, textiles

Agriculture:
employs 23% of labor force; principally dairy farming and livestock feeding;
products - meat, milk, eggs, grain, sugar beets, potatoes, and vegetables;
fishing and fish packing

Illicit drugs:
transshipment point for illicit drugs from Central and Southwest Asia to
Western Europe

:Latvia Economy

Economic aid:
US commitments, including Ex-Im (FY70-87), $NA billion; Western (non-US)
countries, ODA and OOF bilateral commitments (1970-86), $NA million;
Communist countries (1971-86), $NA million

Currency:
as of May 1992, retaining ruble as currency but planning early introduction
of ``lat"

Exchange rates:
NA

Fiscal year: calendar year

:Latvia Communications

Railroads:
2,400 km (includes NA km electrified) does not include industrial lines
(1990)

Highways:
59,500 km total (1990); 33,000 km hard surfaced 26,500 km earth

Inland waterways:
300 km perennially navigable

Pipelines:
crude oil NA km, refined products NA km, natural gas NA km

Ports:
maritime - Riga, Ventspils, Liepaja; inland - Daugavpils

Merchant marine:
96 ships (1,000 GRT or over) totaling 917,979 GRT/1,194,666 DWT; includes 14
cargo, 29 refrigerated cargo, 2 container, 9 roll-on/roll-off, 42 petroleum
tanker

Civil air:
NA major transport aircraft

Airports:
NA total, NA usable; NA with permanent-surface runways; NA with runways over
3,659 m; NA with runways 2,440-3,659 m; NA with runways 1,220-2,439 m

Telecommunications:
broadcast stations - NA; international traffic carried by leased connection
to the Moscow international gateway switch and the Finnish cellular net

:Latvia Defense Forces

Branches:
Republic Security Forces (internal and border troops), National Guard,

Russian Forces (Ground, Navy, Air, Air Defense, Border Guard
Manpower availability:
  males 15-49, NA; NA fit for military service; NA reach military age (18)
  annually
Defense expenditures:
  NA% of GDP; 3-5% of Latvia's budget (1992)

Lebanon Geography

Total area: 10,400 km2
Land area: 10,230 km2
Comparative area: about 0.8 times the size of Connecticut
Land boundaries:
  454 km; Israel 79 km, Syria 375 km
Coastline:
  225 km
Maritime claims:
  Territorial sea:
    12 nm
Disputes:
  separated from Israel by the 1949 Armistice Line; Israeli troops in southern
  Lebanon since June 1982; Syrian troops in northern Lebanon since October
  1976
Climate:
  Mediterranean; mild to cool, wet winters with hot, dry summers
Terrain:
  narrow coastal plain; Al Biqa` (Bekaa Valley) separates Lebanon and
  Anti-Lebanon Mountains
Natural resources:
  limestone, iron ore, salt; water-surplus state in a water-deficit region
Land use:
  arable land 21%; permanent crops 9%; meadows and pastures 1%; forest and
  woodland 8%; other 61%; includes irrigated 7%
Environment:
  rugged terrain historically helped isolate, protect, and develop numerous
  factional groups based on religion, clan, ethnicity; deforestation; soil
  erosion; air and water pollution; desertification
Note:
  Nahr al Litani only major river in Near East not crossing an international
  boundary

:Lebanon People

Population: 3,439,115 (July 1992), growth rate 1.6% (1992)
Birth rate: 28 births/1,000 population (1992)
Death rate: 7 deaths/1,000 population (1992)
Net migration rate: -5 migrants/1,000 population (1992)
Infant mortality rate: 43 deaths/1,000 live births (1992)
Life expectancy at birth: 66 years male, 71 years female (1992)
Total fertility rate: 3.6 children born/woman (1992)
Nationality:
  noun - Lebanese (singular and plural); adjective - Lebanese
Ethnic divisions:

Arab 95%, Armenian 4%, other 1%

Religions:

Islam 75%, Christian 25%, Judaism NEGL%; 17 legally recognized groups - 5 Islam (Alawite or Nusayri, Druze, Isma`ilite, Shi`a, Sunni); 11 Christian, consisting of 4 Orthodox Christian (Armenian Orthodox, Greek Orthodox, Nestorean, Syriac Orthodox), 6 Catholic (Armenian Catholic, Caldean, Greek Catholic, Maronite, Roman Catholic, and Syrian Catholic) and the Protestants; 1 Jewish

Languages:

Arabic and French (both official); Armenian, English

Literacy:

80% (male 88%, female 73%) age 15 and over can read and write (1990 est.)

Labor force:

650,000; industry, commerce, and services 79%, agriculture 11%, government 10% (1985)

Organized labor:

250,000 members (est.)

:Lebanon Government

Long-form name:

Republic of Lebanon; note - may be changed to Lebanese Republic

Type:

republic

Capital: Beirut

Administrative divisions:

5 governorates (muhafazat, singular - muhafazah); Al Biqa, `Al Janub, Ash Shamal, Bayrut, Jabal Lubnan

Independence:

22 November 1943 (from League of Nations mandate under French administration)

Constitution:

26 May 1926 (amended)

Legal system:

mixture of Ottoman law, canon law, Napoleonic code, and civil law; no judicial review of legislative acts; has not accepted compulsory ICJ jurisdiction

National holiday:

Independence Day, 22 November (1943)

Executive branch:

president, prime minister, Cabinet; note - by custom, the president is a Maronite Christian, the prime minister is a Sunni Muslim, and the speaker of the legislature is a Shi`a Muslim

Legislative branch:

unicameral National Assembly (Arabic - Majlis Alnuwah, French - Assemblee Nationale)

Judicial branch:

four Courts of Cassation (three courts for civil and commercial cases and one court for criminal cases)

Leaders:

Chief of State:

President Ilyas HARAWI (since 24 November 1989)
 Head of Government:
 Prime Minister Rashid SULH (since 13 May 1992)
Political parties and leaders:
   political party activity is organized along largely sectarian lines;
   numerous political groupings exist, consisting of individual political
   figures and followers motivated by religious, clan, and economic
   considerations; most parties have well-armed militias, which are still
   involved in occasional clashes
Suffrage:
   compulsory for all males at age 21; authorized for women at age 21 with
   elementary education
Elections:
 National Assembly:
   elections should be held every four years, but security conditions have
   prevented elections since May 1972; in June 1991, the Cabinet appointed 40
   new deputies to fill vacancies and balance Christian and Muslim
   representation; the legislature's mandate expires in 1994
Communists:
   the Lebanese Communist Party was legalized in 1970; members and sympathizers
   estimated at 2,000-3,000
Member of:
   ABEDA, ACCT, AFESD, AL, AMF, CCC, ESCWA, FAO, G-24, G-77, IAEA,
IBRD, ICAO,
   ICC, ICFTU, IDA, IDB, IFAD, IFC, ILO, IMF, IMO, INTELSAT, INTERPOL,
IOC,
   ITU, LORCS, NAM, OIC, PCA, UN, UNCTAD, UNESCO, UNHCR, UNIDO,
UNRWA, UPU,
   WFTU, WHO, WIPO, WMO, WTO

:Lebanon Government

Diplomatic representation:
   Ambassador - no ambassador at present; Mission is headed by Charge; Chancery
   at 2560 28th Street NW, Washington, DC 20008; telephone (202) 939-6300;
   there are Lebanese Consulates General in Detroit, New York, and Los Angeles
 US:
   Ambassador Ryan C. CROCKER; Embassy at Antelias, Beirut (mailing address is
   P. O. Box 70-840, Beirut, or Box B, FPO AE 09836); telephone [961] 417774 or
   415802, 415803, 402200, 403300
Flag:
   three horizontal bands of red (top), white (double width), and red with a
   green and brown cedar tree centered in the white band

:Lebanon Government

Note: Between early 1975 and late 1976 Lebanon was torn by civil war between its
Christians - then aided by Syrian troops - and its Muslims and their Palestinian allies.
The cease-fire established in October 1976 between the domestic political groups generally held for about six years, despite occasional fighting. Syrian troops constituted as
the Arab Deterrent Force by the Arab League have remained in Lebanon. Syria's move
toward supporting the Lebanese Muslims, and the Palestinians and Israel's growing
support for Lebanese Christians, brought the two sides into rough equilibrium, but no

progress was made toward national reconciliation or political reforms - the original cause of the war. Continuing Israeli concern about the Palestinian presence in Lebanon led to the Israeli invasion of Lebanon in June 1982. Israeli forces occupied all of the southern portion of the country and mounted a summer-long siege of Beirut, which resulted in the evacuation of the PLO from Beirut in September under the supervision of a multinational force (MNF) made up of US, French, and Italian troops. Within days of the departure of the MNF, Lebanon's newly elected president, Bashir Gemayel, was assassinated; his elder brother Amin was elected to succeed him. In the immediate wake of Bashir's death, however, Christian militiamen massacred hundreds of Palestinian refugees in two Beirut camps. This prompted the return of the MNF to ease the security burden on Lebanon's weak Army and security forces. In late March 1984 the last MNF units withdrew. In 1988, President Gemayel completed his term of office. Because parliamentarians failed to elect a presidential successor, Gemayel appointed then Lebanese Armed Forces (LAF) Commander Gen. Michel Awn acting president. Lebanese parliamentarians met in Ta'if, Saudi Arabia, in late 1989 and concluded a national reconciliation pact that codified a new power-sharing formula, specifying reduced powers for the Christian president and giving Muslims more authority. Rene MUAWAD was subsequently elected president on 4 November 1989, ending a 13-month period during which Lebanon had no president and rival Muslim and Christian governments. MUAWAD was assassinated 17 days later, on 22 November; on 24 November, Ilyas Harawi was elected to succeed MUAWAD. In October 1990, the civil war was apparently brought to a conclusion when Syrian and Lebanese forces ousted renegade Christian General Awn from his stronghold in East Beirut. Awn had defied the legitimate government and established a separate ministate within East Beirut after being appointed acting Prime Minister by outgoing President Gemayel in 1988. Awn and his supporters feared Ta'if would diminish Christian power in Lebanon and increase the influence of Syria. Awn was granted amnesty and allowed to travel in France in August 1991. Since the removal of Awn, the Lebanese Government has made substantial progress in strengthening the central government, rebuilding government institutions, and extending its authority throughout the nation. The LAF has deployed from Beirut north along the coast road to Tripoli, southeast into the Shuf mountains, and south to Sidon and Tyre. Many militiamen from Christian and Muslim groups have evacuated Beirut for their strongholds in the north, south, and east of the country. Some heavy weapons possessed by the militias have been turned over to the government, or sold outside the country, which has begun a plan to integrate some militiamen into the military and the internal security forces. Lebanon and Syria signed a treaty of friendship and cooperation in May 1991. Lebanon continues to be partially occupied by Syrian troops, which are deployed in Beirut, its southern suburbs, the Bekaa Valley, and northern Lebanon. Iran also maintains a small contingent of revolutionary guards in the Bekaa Valley to support Lebanese Islamic fundamentalist groups. Israel withdrew the bulk of its forces from the south in 1985, although it still retains troops in a 10-km-deep security zone north of its border with Lebanon. Israel arms and trains the Army of South Lebanon (ASL), which also occupies the security zone and is Israel's first line of defense against attacks on its northern border. The following description is based on the present constitutional and customary practices of the Lebanese system.

:Lebanon Economy

Overview:

Since 1975 civil war has seriously damaged Lebanon's economic infrastructure, cut national output by half, and all but ended Lebanon's

547

position as a Middle Eastern entrepot and banking hub. Following October 1990, however, a tentative peace has enabled the central government to begin restoring control in Beirut, collect taxes, and regain access to key port and government facilities. The battered economy has also been propped up by a financially sound banking system and resilient small- and medium-scale manufacturers. Family remittances, banking transactions, manufactured and farm exports, the narcotics trade, and international emergency aid are main sources of foreign exchange. In the relatively settled year of 1991, industrial production, agricultural output, and exports showed substantial gains. The further rebuilding of the war-ravaged country could provide a major stimulus to the economy in 1992, provided that the political and military situation remains reasonably calm.

GDP:

exchange rate conversion - $4.8 billion, per capita $1,400; real growth rate NA (1991 est.)

Inflation rate (consumer prices):

30% (1991)

Unemployment rate: 35% (1991 est.)

Budget:

revenues $533 million; expenditures $1.3 billion, including capital expenditures of $NA (1991 est.)

Exports:

$700 million (f.o.b., 1990 est.)

commodities:

agricultural products, chemicals, textiles, precious and semiprecious metals and jewelry, metals and metal products

partners:

Saudi Arabia 16%, Switzerland 8%, Jordan 6%, Kuwait 6%, US 5%

Imports:

$1.8 billion (c.i.f., 1990 est.)

commodities:

NA

partners:

Italy 14%, France 12%, US 6%, Turkey 5%, Saudi Arabia 3%

External debt: $900 million (1990 est.)

Industrial production:

growth rate NA%

Electricity:

1,381,000 kW capacity; 3,870 million kWh produced, 1,170 kWh per capita (1989)

Industries:

banking, food processing, textiles, cement, oil refining, chemicals, jewelry, some metal fabricating

Agriculture:

accounts for about one-third of GDP; principal products - citrus fruits, vegetables, potatoes, olives, tobacco, hemp (hashish), sheep, and goats; not self-sufficient in grain

Illicit drugs:

illicit producer of opium and hashish for the international drug trade;

opium poppy production in Al Biqa` is increasing; hashish production is shipped to Western Europe, Israel, US, and the Middle East

:Lebanon Economy

Economic aid:
US commitments, including Ex-Im (FY70-88), $356 million; Western (non-US) countries, ODA and OOF bilateral commitments (1970-89), $664 million; OPEC bilateral aid (1979-89), $962 million; Communist countries (1970-89), $9 million

Currency:
Lebanese pound (plural - pounds); 1 Lebanese pound (#L) = 100 piasters

Exchange rates:
Lebanese pounds (#L) per US$1 - 879.00 (January 1992), 928.23 (1991), 695.09 (1990), 496.69 (1989), 409.23 (1988), 224.60 (1987)

Fiscal year: calendar year

:Lebanon Communications

Railroads:
system in disrepair, considered inoperable

Highways:
7,300 km total; 6,200 km paved, 450 km gravel and crushed stone, 650 km improved earth

Pipelines:
crude oil 72 km (none in operation)

Ports:
Beirut, Tripoli, Ra'Sil`ata, Juniyah, Sidon, Az Zahrani, Tyre

Merchant marine:
56 ships (1,000 GRT or over) totaling 236,196 GRT/346,760 DWT; includes 36 cargo, 1 refrigerated cargo, 2 vehicle carrier, 2 roll-on/roll-off, 1 container, 8 livestock carrier, 1 chemical tanker, 1 specialized tanker, 3 bulk, 1 combination bulk

Civil air:
19 major transport aircraft

Airports:
9 total, 8 usable; 6 with permanent-surface runways; none with runways over 3,659 m; 3 with runways 2,440-3,659 m; 2 with runways 1,220-2,439 m; none under the direct control of the Lebanese Government

Telecommunications:
rebuilding program disrupted; had fair system of microwave relay, cable; 325,000 telephones; broadcast stations - 5 AM, 3 FM (numerous AM and FM radio stations are operated inconsistently by various factions), 13 TV; 1 Indian Ocean INTELSAT and 1 Atlantic Ocean INTELSAT satellite earth station, erratic operations; 3 submarine coaxial cables; radio relay to Jordan inoperable, but operational to Syria, coaxial cable to Syria

:Lebanon Defense Forces

Branches:
Lebanese Armed Forces (LAF) (including Army, Navy, and Air Force)

Manpower availability:
males 15-49, 750,319; 465,938 fit for military service

Defense expenditures:
   exchange rate conversion - $271 million, 8.2% of GDP (1992 budget)

Lesotho Geography

Total area: 30,350 km2
Land area: 30,350 km2
Comparative area: slightly larger than Maryland
Land boundaries:
   909 km; South Africa 909 km
Coastline:
   none - landlocked
Maritime claims:
   none - landlocked
Disputes:
   none
Climate:
   temperate; cool to cold, dry winters; hot, wet summers
Terrain:
   mostly highland with some plateaus, hills, and mountains
Natural resources:
   some diamonds and other minerals, water, agricultural and grazing land
Land use:
   arable land 10%; permanent crops 0%; meadows and pastures 66%; forest and
   woodland 0%; other 24%
Environment:
   population pressure forcing settlement in marginal areas results in
   overgrazing, severe soil erosion, soil exhaustion; desertification
Note:
   landlocked; surrounded by South Africa; Highlands Water Project will
   control, store, and redirect water to South Africa

:Lesotho People

Population: 1,848,925 (July 1992), growth rate 2.6% (1992)
Birth rate: 35 births/1,000 population (1992)
Death rate: 10 deaths/1,000 population (1992)
Net migration rate: 0 migrants/1,000 population (1992)
Infant mortality rate: 74 deaths/1,000 live births (1992)
Life expectancy at birth: 60 years male, 63 years female (1992)
Total fertility rate: 4.7 children born/woman (1992)
Nationality:
   noun - Mosotho (singular), Basotho (plural); adjective - Basotho
Ethnic divisions:
   Sotho 99.7%; Europeans 1,600, Asians 800
Religions:
   Christian 80%, rest indigenous beliefs
Languages:
   Sesotho (southern Sotho) and English (official); also Zulu and Xhosa
Literacy:
   59% (male 44%, female 68%) age 15 and over can read and write (1966)
Labor force:
   689,000 economically active; 86.2% of resident population engaged in

subsistence agriculture; roughly 60% of active male labor force works in
South Africa

Organized labor:
there are two trade union federations; the government favors formation of a
single, umbrella trade union confederation

:Lesotho Government

Long-form name:
Kingdom of Lesotho

Type:
constitutional monarchy

Capital: Maseru

Administrative divisions:
10 districts; Berea, Butha-Buthe, Leribe, Mafeteng, Maseru, Mohale's Hoek,
Mokhotlong, Qacha's Nek, Quthing, Thaba-Tseka

Independence:
4 October 1966 (from UK; formerly Basutoland)

Constitution:
4 October 1966, suspended January 1970

Legal system:
based on English common law and Roman-Dutch law; judicial review of
legislative acts in High Court and Court of Appeal; has not accepted
compulsory ICJ jurisdiction

National holiday:
Independence Day, 4 October (1966)

Executive branch:
monarch, chairman of the Military Council, Military Council, Council of
Ministers (cabinet)

Legislative branch:
none - the bicameral Parliament was dissolved following the military coup in
January 1986; note - a National Constituent Assembly convened in June 1990
to rewrite the constitution and debate issues of national importance, but it
has no legislative authority

Judicial branch:
High Court, Court of Appeal

Leaders:
Chief of State:
King LETSIE III (since 12 November 1990 following dismissal of his father,
exiled King MOSHOESHOE II, by Maj. Gen. LEKHANYA)

Head of Government:
Chairman of the Military Council Col. Elias Phisoana RAMAEMA (since 30 April
1991)

Political parties and leaders:
Basotho National Party (BNP), Evaristus SEKHONYANA; Basutoland Congress
Party (BCP), Ntsu MOKHEHLE; National Independent Party (NIP), A. C.
MANYELI;
Marematlou Freedom Party (MFP), Bernard M. KHAKETLA; United Democratic
Party, Charles MOFELI; Communist Party of Lesotho (CPL), J. M. KENA

Suffrage:
universal at age 21

Elections:

National Assembly:

dissolved following the military coup in January 1986; military has pledged
elections will take place in June 1992

Member of:

ACP, AfDB, C, CCC, ECA, FAO, G-77, GATT, IBRD, ICAO, ICFTU, IDA, IFAD,
IFC,

ILO, IMF, INTERPOL, IOC, ITU, LORCS, NAM, OAU, SACU, SADCC, UN,
UNCTAD,

UNESCO, UNHCR, UNIDO, UPU, WCL, WHO, WIPO, WMO, WTO

Diplomatic representation:

Ambassador Tseliso THAMAE; Chancery at 2511 Massachusetts Avenue NW,
Washington, DC 20008; telephone (202) 797-5534

US:

Ambassador Leonard H.O. SPEARMAN, Sr.; Embassy at address NA, Maseru
(mailing address is P. O. Box 333, Maseru 100 Lesotho); telephone [266]
312-666; FAX (266) 310-116

:Lesotho Government

Flag:

divided diagonally from the lower hoist side corner; the upper half is white
bearing the brown silhouette of a large shield with crossed spear and club;
the lower half is a diagonal blue band with a green triangle in the corner

:Lesotho Economy

Overview:

Small, landlocked, and mountainous, Lesotho has no important natural
resources other than water. Its economy is based on agriculture, light
manufacturing, and remittances from laborers employed in South Africa ($153
million in 1989). The great majority of households gain their livelihoods
from subsistence farming and migrant labor. Manufacturing depends largely on
farm products to support the milling, canning, leather, and jute industries;
other industries include textile, clothing, and light engineering.
Industry's share of GDP rose from 6% in 1982 to 15% in 1989. Political and
economic instability in South Africa raises uncertainty for Lesotho's
economy, especially with respect to migrant worker remittances - typically
about 40% of GDP.

GDP:

exchange rate conversion - $420 million, per capita $240; real growth rate
4.0% (1990 est.)

Inflation rate (consumer prices):

15% (1990 est.)

Unemployment rate: at least 55% among adult males (1991 est.)

Budget:

expenditures $399 million, including capital expenditures of $132 million
(FY92-93)

Exports:

$59 million (f.o.b., 1990)

commodities:

wool, mohair, wheat, cattle, peas, beans, corn, hides, skins, baskets

partners:

South Africa 53%, EC 30%, North and South America 13% (1989)
Imports:
  $604 million (f.o.b., 1990)
  commodities:
  mainly corn, building materials, clothing, vehicles, machinery, medicines,
  petroleum
  partners:
  South Africa 95%, EC 2% (1989)
External debt: $370 million (December 1990 est.)
Industrial production:
  growth rate 7.8% (1989 est.); accounts for 15% of GDP
Electricity:
  power supplied by South Africa
Industries:
  food, beverages, textiles, handicrafts, tourism
Agriculture:
  accounts for 18% of GDP and employs 60-70% of all households; exceedingly
  primitive, mostly subsistence farming and livestock; principal crops are
  corn, wheat, pulses, sorghum, barley
Economic aid:
  US commitments, including Ex-Im (FY70-89), $268 million; Western (non-US)
  countries, ODA and OOF bilateral commitments (1970-89), $819 million; OPEC
  bilateral aid (1979-89), $4 million; Communist countries (1970-89), $14
  million
Currency:
  loti (plural - maloti); 1 loti (L) = 100 lisente
Exchange rates:
  maloti (M) per US$1 - 2.8809 (March 1992), 2.7563 (1991), 2.5863 (1990),
  2.6166 (1989), 2.2611 (1988), 2.0350 (1987); note - the Basotho loti is at
  par with the South African rand

:Lesotho Economy

Fiscal year: 1 April - 31 March

:Lesotho Communications

Railroads:
  2.6 km; owned, operated by, and included in the statistics of South Africa
Highways:
  7,215 km total; 572 km paved; 2,337 km crushed stone, gravel, or stabilized
  soil; 1,806 km improved earth, 2,500 km unimproved earth (1988)
Civil air:
  1 major transport aircraft
Airports:
  28 total, 28 usable; 3 with permanent surface runways; none with runways
  over 3,659 m; 1 with runways 2,440-3,659 m; 2 with runways 1,220-2,439 m
Telecommunications:
  rudimentary system consisting of a few landlines, a small microwave system,
  and minor radio communications stations; 5,920 telephones; broadcast
  stations - 3 AM, 2 FM, 1 TV; 1 Atlantic Ocean INTELSAT earth station

:Lesotho Defense Forces

Branches:

Royal Lesotho Defense Force (RLDF; including Army, Air Wing), Royal Lesotho Mounted Police

Manpower availability:

males 15-49, 408,003; 220,129 fit for military service

Defense expenditures:

exchange rate conversion - $55 million, 13.1% of GDP (1990 est.)

Liberia Geography

Total area: 111,370 km2

Land area: 96,320 km2

Comparative area: slightly larger than Tennessee

Land boundaries:

1,585 km; Guinea 563 km, Ivory Coast 716 km, Sierra Leone 306 km

Coastline:

579 km

Maritime claims:

Continental shelf:

200 m (depth) or to depth of exploitation

Territorial sea:

200 nm

Disputes:

Climate:

tropical; hot, humid; dry winters with hot days and cool to cold nights; wet, cloudy summers with frequent heavy showers

Terrain:

mostly flat to rolling coastal plains rising to rolling plateau and low mountains in northeast

Natural resources:

iron ore, timber, diamonds, gold

Land use:

arable land 1%; permanent crops 3%; meadows and pastures 2%; forest and woodland 39%; other 55%; includes irrigated NEGL%

Environment:

West Africa's largest tropical rain forest, subject to deforestation

:Liberia People

Population: 2,462,276 (July 1992), growth rate 29.6% (1992)

Birth rate: 44 births/1,000 population (1992)

Death rate: 13 deaths/1,000 population (1992)

Net migration rate: 265 migrants/1,000 population (1992)

Infant mortality rate: 119 deaths/1,000 live births (1992)

Life expectancy at birth: 54 years male, 59 years female (1992)

Total fertility rate: 6.5 children born/woman (1992)

Nationality:

noun - Liberian(s); adjective - Liberian

Ethnic divisions:

indigenous African tribes, including Kpelle, Bassa, Gio, Kru, Grebo, Mano, Krahn, Gola, Gbandi, Loma, Kissi, Vai, and Bella 95%; descendants of repatriated slaves known as Americo-Liberians 5%

Religions:

traditional 70%, Muslim 20%, Christian 10%

Languages:

English (official); more than 20 local languages of the Niger-Congo language group; English used by about 20%

Literacy:

40% (male 50%, female 29%) age 15 and over can read and write (1990 est.)

Labor force:

510,000, including 220,000 in the monetary economy; agriculture 70.5%, services 10.8%, industry and commerce 4.5%, other 14.2%; non-African foreigners hold about 95% of the top-level management and engineering jobs; 52% of population of working age

Organized labor:

2% of labor force

:Liberia Government

Long-form name:

Republic of Liberia

Type:

republic

Capital: Monrovia

Administrative divisions:

13 counties; Bomi, Bong, Grand Bassa, Cape Mount, Grand Gedeh, Grand Kru, Lofa, Margibi, Maryland, Montserrado, Nimba, River Cess, Sinoe

Independence:

26 July 1847

Constitution:

6 January 1986

Legal system:

dual system of statutory law based on Anglo-American common law for the modern sector and customary law based on unwritten tribal practices for indigenous sector

National holiday:

Independence Day, 26 July (1847)

Executive branch:

president, vice president, Cabinet

Legislative branch:

bicameral National Assembly consists of an upper house or Senate and a lower house or House of Representatives

Judicial branch:

People's Supreme Court

Leaders:

Chief of State and Head of Government:

interim President Dr. Amos SAWYER (since 15 November 1990); Vice President, vacant (since August 1991); note - this is an interim government appointed by the Economic Community of West African States (ECOWAS) that will be replaced after elections are held under a West African - brokered peace plan; rival rebel factions led by Prince Y. JOHNSON and Charles TAYLOR are challenging the SAWYER government's legitimacy while observing a tenuous cease-fire; the former president, Gen. Dr. Samuel Kanyon DOE, was killed on

9 September 1990 by Prince Y. JOHNSON

Political parties and leaders:

National Democratic Party of Liberia (NDPL), Augustus CAINE, chairman; Liberian Action Party (LAP), Emmanuel KOROMAH, chairman; Unity Party (UP), Carlos SMITH, chairman; United People's Party (UPP), Gabriel Baccus MATTHEWS, chairman

Suffrage:

universal at age 18

Elections:

President:

last held on 15 October 1985 (next to be held NA); results - Gen. Dr. Samuel Kanyon DOE (NDPL) 50.9%, Jackson DOE (LAP) 26.4%, other 22.7%; note - President Doe was killed by rebel forces on 9 September 1990

Senate:

last held on 15 October 1985 (next to be held NA); results - percent of vote by party NA; seats - (26 total) NDPL 21, LAP 3, UP 1, UPP 1

House of Representatives:

last held on 15 October 1985 (next to be held NA); results - percent of vote by party NA; seats - (64 total) NDPL 51, LAP 8, UP 3, UPP 2

Member of:

ACP, AfDB, CCC, ECA, ECOWAS, FAO, G-77, IAEA, IBRD, ICAO, ICFTU, IDA, IFAD,

IFC, ILO, IMF, IMO, INMARSAT, INTERPOL, IOC, ITU, LORCS, NAM, OAU, UN,

UNCTAD, UNESCO, UPU, WCL, WHO, WIPO, WMO

:Liberia Government

Diplomatic representation:

Ambassador Eugenia A. WORDSWORTH-STEVENSON; Chancery at 5201 16th Street NW,

Washington, DC 20011; telephone (202) 723-0437 through 0440; there is a Liberian Consulate General in New York

US:

Ambassador Peter J. de VOS; Embassy at 111 United Nations Drive, Monrovia (mailing address is P. O. Box 98, Monrovia, or APO AE 09813; telephone [231] 222991 through 222994; FAX (231) 223-710

Flag:

11 equal horizontal stripes of red (top and bottom) alternating with white; there is a white five-pointed star on a blue square in the upper hoist-side corner; the design was based on the US flag

:Liberia Economy

Overview:

Civil war during 1990 destroyed much of Liberia's economy, especially the infrastructure in and around Monrovia. Expatriate businessmen fled the country, taking capital and expertise with them. Many will not return. Richly endowed with water, mineral resources, forests, and a climate favorable to agriculture, Liberia had been a producer and exporter of basic products, while local manufacturing, mainly foreign owned, had been small in scope. Political instability threatens prospects for economic reconstruction and repatriation of some 750,000 Liberian refugees who fled to neighboring

556

countries. In 1991, the political impasse between the interim government and the rebel leader Charles Taylor prevented restoration of normal economic life.

GDP:
exchange rate conversion - $988 million, per capita $400; real growth rate 1.5% (1988)

Inflation rate (consumer prices):
12% (1989)

Unemployment rate: 43% urban (1988)

Budget:
revenues $242.1 million; expenditures $435.4 million, including capital expenditures of $29.5 million (1989)

Exports:
$505 million (f.o.b., 1989 est.)

commodities:
iron ore 61%, rubber 20%, timber 11%, coffee

partners:
US, EC, Netherlands

Imports:
$394 million (c.i.f., 1989 est.)

commodities:
rice, mineral fuels, chemicals, machinery, transportation equipment, other foodstuffs

partners:
US, EC, Japan, China, Netherlands, ECOWAS

External debt: $1.6 billion (December 1990 est.)

Industrial production:
growth rate 1.5% in manufacturing (1987); accounts for 22% of GDP

Electricity:
410,000 kW capacity; 750 million kWh produced, 275 kWh per capita (1991)

Industries:
rubber processing, food processing, construction materials, furniture, palm oil processing, mining (iron ore, diamonds)

Agriculture:
accounts for about 40% of GDP (including fishing and forestry); principal products - rubber, timber, coffee, cocoa, rice, cassava, palm oil, sugarcane, bananas, sheep, and goats; not self-sufficient in food, imports 25% of rice consumption

Economic aid:
US commitments, including Ex-Im (FY70-89), $665 million; Western (non-US) countries, ODA and OOF bilateral commitments (1970-89), $870 million; OPEC bilateral aid (1979-89), $25 million; Communist countries (1970-89), $77 million

Currency:
Liberian dollar (plural - dollars); 1 Liberian dollar (L$) = 100 cents

Exchange rates:
Liberian dollars (L$) per US$1 - 1.00 (fixed rate since 1940); unofficial parallel exchange rate of L$7 = US$1, January 1992

:Liberia Economy

Fiscal year: calendar year

:Liberia Communications

Railroads:

480 km total; 328 km 1.435-meter standard gauge, 152 km 1.067-meter narrow
gauge; all lines single track; rail systems owned and operated by foreign
steel and financial interests in conjunction with Liberian Government

Highways:

10,087 km total; 603 km bituminous treated, 2,848 km all weather, 4,313 km
dry weather; there are also 2,323 km of private, laterite-surfaced roads
open to public use, owned by rubber and timber companies

Ports:

Monrovia, Buchanan, Greenville, Harper (or Cape Palmas)

Merchant marine:

1,564 ships (1,000 GRT or over) totaling 54,049,124 DWT/ 95,338,925 DWT;
includes 19 passenger, 1 short-sea passenger, 145 cargo, 51 refrigerated
cargo, 22 roll-on/roll-off, 62 vehicle carrier, 89 container, 4 barge
carrier, 460 petroleum tanker, 105 chemical, 57 combination ore/oil, 50
liquefied gas, 6 specialized tanker, 465 bulk, 1 multifunction large-load
carrier, 27 combination bulk; note - a flag of convenience registry; all
ships are foreign owned; the top 4 owning flags are US 18%, Japan 16%, Hong
Kong 10%, and Norway 9%

Civil air:

1 major transport aircraft

Airports:

66 total, 49 usable; 2 with permanent-surface runways; none with runways
over 3,659 m; 1 with runways 2,440-3,659 m; 4 with runways 1,220-2,439 m

Telecommunications:

telephone and telegraph service via radio relay network; main center is
Monrovia; broadcast stations - 3 AM, 4 FM, 5 TV; 1 Atlantic Ocean INTELSAT
earth stations; most telecommunications services inoperable due to
insurgency movement

:Liberia Defense Forces

Branches:

Monrovia-based Armed Forces of Liberia (Army only) along with a police
force; rest of country controlled by the army of the National Patriotic
Front of Liberia (NPFL) insurgent group

Manpower availability:

males 15-49, 585,224; 312,420 fit for military service; no conscription

Defense expenditures:

exchange rate conversion - $NA, NA% of GDP

Libya Geography

Total area: 1,759,540 km2

Land area: 1,759,540 km2

Comparative area: slightly larger than Alaska

Land boundaries:

4,383 km; Algeria 982 km, Chad 1,055 km, Egypt 1,150 km, Niger 354 km, Sudan
383 km, Tunisia 459 km

Coastline:

1,770 km
Maritime claims:
 Territorial sea:
  12 nm
 Gulf of Sidra closing line:
  32 degrees 30 minutes N
Disputes:
 claims and occupies the 100,000 km2 Aozou Strip in northern Chad; maritime
 boundary dispute with Tunisia; Libya claims about 19,400 km2 in northern
 Niger; Libya claims about 19,400 km2 in southeastern Algeria
Climate:
 Mediterranean along coast; dry, extreme desert interior
Terrain:
 mostly barren, flat to undulating plains, plateaus, depressions
Natural resources:
 crude oil, natural gas, gypsum
Land use:
 arable land 1%; permanent crops 0%; meadows and pastures 8%; forest and
 woodland 0%; other 91%; includes irrigated NEGL%
Environment:
 hot, dry, dust-laden ghibli is a southern wind lasting one to four days in
 spring and fall; desertification; sparse natural surface-water resources
Note:
 the Great Manmade River Project, the largest water development scheme in the
 world, is being built to bring water from large aquifers under the Sahara to
 coastal cities

:Libya People

Population: 4,484,795 (July 1992), growth rate 3.0% (1992)
Birth rate: 36 births/1,000 population (1992)
Death rate: 6 deaths/1,000 population (1992)
Net migration rate: 0 migrants/1,000 population (1992)
Infant mortality rate: 60 deaths/1,000 live births (1992)
Life expectancy at birth: 66 years male, 71 years female (1992)
Total fertility rate: 4.9 children born/woman (1992)
Nationality:
 noun - Libyan(s); adjective - Libyan
Ethnic divisions:
 Berber and Arab 97%; some Greeks, Maltese, Italians, Egyptians, Pakistanis,
 Turks, Indians, and Tunisians
Religions:
 Sunni Muslim 97%
Languages:
 Arabic; Italian and English widely understood in major cities
Literacy:
 64% (male 75%, female 50%) age 15 and over can read and write (1990 est.)
Labor force:
 1,000,000, includes about 280,000 resident foreigners; industry 31%,
 services 27%, government 24%, agriculture 18%
Organized labor:

National Trade Unions' Federation, 275,000 members; General Union for Oil and Petrochemicals; Pan-Africa Federation of Petroleum Energy and Allied Workers

:Libya Government

Long-form name:
  Socialist People's Libyan Arab Jamahiriya
Digraph:
  Tripoli Administration divisions *** 25 municipalities (baladiyah, singular - baladiyat; Ajdabiya, Al `Aziziyah, Al Fatih, Al Jabal al Akhdar, Al Jufrah, Al Khums, Al Kufrah, An Nuqat al Khams, Ash Shati', Awbari, Az Zawiyah, Banghazi, Darnah, Ghadamis, Gharyan, Misratah, Murzuq, Sabha, Sawfajjin, Surt, Tarabulus, Tarhunah, Tubruq, Yafran, Zlitan
Type:
  Jamahiriya (a state of the masses); in theory, governed by the populace through local councils; in fact, a military dictatorship
Capital: Tripoli Administration divisions
Administrative divisions:
  25 municipalities (baladiyah, singular - baladiyat; Ajdabiya, Al 'Aziziyah, Al Fatih, Al Jabal al Akhdar, Al Jufrah, Al Khums, Al Kufrah, An Nuqat al Khams, Ash Shati', Awbari, Az Zawiyah, Banghazi, Darnah, Ghadamis, Gharyan, Misratah, Murzuq Sabha, Sawfajjin, Surt, Tarabulus, Tarhunah, Tubruq, Yafran, Zlitan
Independence:
  24 December 1951 (from Italy)
Constitution:
  11 December 1969, amended 2 March 1977
Legal system:
  based on Italian civil law system and Islamic law; separate religious courts; no constitutional provision for judicial review of legislative acts; has not accepted compulsory ICJ jurisdiction
National holiday:
  Revolution Day, 1 September (1969)
Executive branch:
  revolutionary leader, chairman of the General People's Committee (premier), General People's Committee (cabinet)
Legislative branch:
  unicameral General People's Congress
Judicial branch:
  Supreme Court
Leaders:
 Chief of State:
  Revolutionary Leader Col. Mu`ammar Abu Minyar al-QADHAFI (since 1 September 1969)
 Head of Government:
  Chairman of the General People's Committee (Premier) Abu Zayd `umar DURDA (since 7 October 1990)
Political parties and leaders:

Suffrage:

universal and compulsory at age 18

Elections:

national elections are indirect through a hierarchy of peoples' committees

Other political or pressure groups:

various Arab nationalist movements and the Arab Socialist Resurrection
(Ba'th) party with almost negligible memberships may be functioning
clandestinely, as well as some Islamic elements

Member of:

ABEDA, AfDB, AFESD, AL, AMF, AMU, CAEU, CCC, ECA, FAO, G-77, IAEA,
IBRD,

ICAO, IDA, IDB, IFAD, IFC, ILO, IMF, IMO, INTELSAT, INTERPOL, IOC, ITU,
LORCS, NAM, OAPEC, OAU, OIC, OPEC, UN, UNCTAD, UNESCO, UNIDO,
UPU, WHO,

WIPO, WMO, WTO

:Libya Government

Diplomatic representation:

Flag:

plain green; green is the traditional color of Islam (the state religion)

:Libya Economy

Overview:

The socialist-oriented economy depends primarily upon revenues from the oil
sector, which contributes practically all export earnings and about
one-third of GDP. Since 1980, however, the sharp drop in oil prices and the
resulting decline in export revenues have adversely affected economic
development. In 1988 per capita GDP was the highest in Africa at $5,410, but
GDP growth rates have slowed and fluctuate sharply in response to changes in
the world oil market. Import restrictions and inefficient resource
allocations have led to shortages of basic goods and foodstuffs, although
the reopening of the Libyan-Tunisian border in April 1988 and the
Libyan-Egyptian border in December 1989 have somewhat eased shortages.
Austerity budgets and a lack of trained technicians have undermined the
government's ability to implement a number of planned infrastructure
development projects. Windfall revenues from the hike in world oil prices in
late 1990 improved the foreign payments position and resulted in a current
account surplus for the first time in five years. The nonoil manufacturing
and construction sectors, which account for about 22% of GDP, have expanded
from processing mostly agricultural products to include petrochemicals,
iron, steel, and aluminum. Although agriculture accounts for about 5% of
GDP, it employs about 20% of the labor force. Climatic conditions and poor
soils severely limit farm output, and Libya imports about 75% of its food
requirements.

GDP:

exchange rate conversion - $28.9 billion, per capita $6,800; real growth
rate 9% (1990 est.)

Inflation rate (consumer prices):

7% (1991 est.)

Unemployment rate: 2% (1988 est.)

Budget:
  revenues $8.1 billion; expenditures $9.8 billion, including capital
  expenditures of $3.1 billion (1989 est.)
Exports:
  $11 billion (f.o.b., 1990 est.)
  commodities:
  petroleum, peanuts, hides
  partners:
  Italy, USSR, Germany, Spain, France, Belgium/Luxembourg, Turkey
Imports:
  $7.6 billion (f.o.b., 1990 est.)
  commodities:
  machinery, transport equipment, food, manufactured goods
  partners:
  Italy, USSR, Germany, UK, Japan
External debt: $3.5 billion, excluding military debt (1991 est.)
Industrial production:
  growth rate - 4%; accounts for 22% of GDP (not including oil) (1989)
Electricity:
  4,700,000 kW capacity; 13,700 million kWh produced, 3,100 kWh per capita
  (1991)
Industries:
  petroleum, food processing, textiles, handicrafts, cement
Agriculture:
  5% of GNP; cash crops - wheat, barley, olives, dates, citrus fruits,
  peanuts; 75% of food is imported
Economic aid:
  Western (non-US) countries, ODA and OOF bilateral commitments (1970-87),
  $242 million; no longer a recipient

:Libya Economy

Currency:
  Libyan dinar (plural - dinars); 1 Libyan dinar (LD) = 1,000 dirhams
Exchange rates:
  Libyan dinars (LD) per US$1 - 0.2743 (March 1992), 0.2669 (1991), 0.2699
  (1990), 0.2922 (1989), 0.2853 (1988), 0.2706 (1987)
Fiscal year: calendar year

:Libya Communications

Pipelines:
  crude oil 4,383 km; natural gas 1,947 km; petroleum products 443 km
  (includes liquid petroleum gas 256 km)
Ports:
  Tobruk, Tripoli, Banghazi, Misratah, Marsa al Burayqah, Ra's Lanuf
Merchant marine:
  30 ships (1,000 GRT or over) totaling 684,969 GRT/1,209,084 DWT; includes 3
  short-sea passenger, 11 cargo, 4 roll-on/roll-off, 10 petroleum tanker, 1
  chemical tanker, 1 liquefied gas
Civil air:
  59 major transport aircraft
Airports:

133 total, 120 usable; 53 with permanent-surface runways; 9 with runways
over 3,659 m; 28 with runways 2,440-3,659 m; 46 with runways 1,220-2,439 m
Telecommunications:
modern telecommunications system using radio relay, coaxial cable,
tropospheric scatter, and domestic satellite stations; 370,000 telephones;
broadcast stations - 17 AM, 3 FM, 12 TV; satellite earth stations - 1
Atlantic Ocean INTELSAT, 1 Indian Ocean INTELSAT, and 14 domestic; submarine
cables to France and Italy; radio relay to Tunisia and Egypt; tropospheric
scatter to Greece; planned ARABSAT and Intersputnik satellite stations

:Libya Defense Forces

Branches:
Armed Peoples of the Libyan Arab Jamahiriya (including Army, Navy, Air and
Air Defense Command), National Police
Manpower availability:
males 15-49, 1,056,686; 624,027 fit for military service; 50,916 reach
military age (17) annually; conscription now being implemented
Defense expenditures:
exchange rate conversion - $NA, 11.1% of GDP (1987)

Liechtenstein Geography

Total area: 160 km2
Land area: 160 km2
Comparative area: about 0.9 times the size of Washington, DC
Land boundaries:
78 km; Austria 37 km, Switzerland 41 km
Coastline:
none - landlocked
Maritime claims:
none - landlocked
Disputes:
none
Climate:
continental; cold, cloudy winters with frequent snow or rain; cool to
moderately warm, cloudy, humid summers
Terrain:
mostly mountainous (Alps) with Rhine Valley in western third
Natural resources:
hydroelectric potential
Land use:
arable land 25%; permanent crops 0%; meadows and pastures 38%; forest and
woodland 19%; other 18%
Environment:
variety of microclimatic variations based on elevation
Note:
landlocked

:Liechtenstein People

Population: 28,642 (July 1992), growth rate 0.6% (1992)
Birth rate: 13 births/1,000 population (1992)

Death rate: 7 deaths/1,000 population (1992)
Net migration rate: 0 migrants/1,000 population (1992)
Infant mortality rate: 5 deaths/1,000 live births (1992)
Life expectancy at birth: 74 years male, 81 years female (1992)
Total fertility rate: 1.5 children born/woman (1992)
Nationality:
  noun - Liechtensteiner(s); adjective - Liechtenstein
Ethnic divisions:
  Alemannic 95%, Italian and other 5%
Religions:
  Roman Catholic 87.3%, Protestant 8.3%, unknown 1.6%, other 2.8% (1988)
Languages:
  German (official), Alemannic dialect
Literacy:
  100% (male 100%, female 100%) age 10 and over can read and write (1981)
Labor force:
  19,905, of which 11,933 are foreigners; 6,885 commute from Austria and
  Switzerland to work each day; industry, trade, and building 53.2%, services
  45%, agriculture, fishing, forestry, and horticulture 1.8% (1990)
Organized labor:
  NA

:Liechtenstein Government

Long-form name:
  Principality of Liechtenstein
Type:
  hereditary constitutional monarchy
Capital: Vaduz
Administrative divisions:
  11 communes (gemeinden, singular - gemeinde); Balzers, Eschen, Gamprin,
  Mauren, Planken, Ruggell, Schaan, Schellenberg, Triesen, Triesenberg, Vaduz
Independence:
  23 January 1719, Imperial Principality of Liechtenstein established
Constitution:
  5 October 1921
Legal system:
  local civil and penal codes; accepts compulsory ICJ jurisdiction, with
  reservations
National holiday:
  Assumption Day, 15 August
Executive branch:
  reigning prince, hereditary prince, head of government, deputy head of
  government
Legislative branch:
  unicameral Diet (Landtag)
Judicial branch:
  Supreme Court (Oberster Gerichtshof) for criminal cases and Superior Court
  (Obergericht) for civil cases
Leaders:
  Chief of State:

Prince Hans ADAM II (since 13 November 1989; assumed executive powers 26 August 1984); Heir Apparent Prince ALOIS von und zu Liechtenstein (born 11 June 1968)

Head of Government:

Hans BRUNHART (since 26 April 1978); Deputy Head of Government Dr. Herbert WILLE (since 2 February 1986)

Political parties and leaders:

Fatherland Union (VU), Dr. Otto HASLER; Progressive Citizens' Party (FBP), Emanuel VOGT; Free Electoral List (FW)

Suffrage:

universal at age 18

Elections:

Diet:

last held on 5 March 1989 (next to be held by March 1993); results - percent of vote by party NA; seats - (25 total) VU 13, FBP 12

Member of:

CE, CSCE, EBRD, IAEA, INTELSAT, INTERPOL, IOC, ITU, LORCS, UN, UNCTAD, UPU,

WIPO

Diplomatic representation:

in routine diplomatic matters, Liechtenstein is represented in the US by the Swiss Embassy

US:

the US has no diplomatic or consular mission in Liechtenstein, but the US Consul General at Zurich (Switzerland) has consular accreditation at Vaduz

Flag:

two equal horizontal bands of blue (top) and red with a gold crown on the hoist side of the blue band

:Liechtenstein Economy

Overview:

The prosperous economy is based primarily on small-scale light industry and tourism. Industry accounts for 53% of total employment, the service sector 45% (mostly based on tourism), and agriculture and forestry 2%. The sale of postage stamps to collectors is estimated at $10 million annually. Low business taxes (the maximum tax rate is 20%) and easy incorporation rules have induced about 25,000 holding or so-called letter box companies to establish nominal offices in Liechtenstein. Such companies, incorporated solely for tax purposes, provide 30% of state revenues. The economy is tied closely to that of Switzerland in a customs union, and incomes and living standards parallel those of the more prosperous Swiss groups.

GDP:

purchasing power equivalent - $630 million, per capita $22,300; real growth rate NA% (1990 est.)

Inflation rate (consumer prices):

5.4% (1990)

Unemployment rate: 1.5% (1990)

Budget:

revenues $259 million; expenditures $292 million, including capital expenditures of NA (1990)

Exports:
  $1.6 billion
  commodities:
  small specialty machinery, dental products, stamps, hardware, pottery
  partners:
  EFTA countries 20.9% (Switzerland 15.4%), EC countries 42.7%, other 36.4%
  (1990)
Imports:
  $NA
  commodities:
  machinery, metal goods, textiles, foodstuffs, motor vehicles
  partners:
  NA
External debt: $NA
Industrial production:
  growth rate NA%
Electricity:
  23,000 kW capacity; 150 million kWh produced, 5,340 kWh per capita (1989)
Industries:
  electronics, metal manufacturing, textiles, ceramics, pharmaceuticals, food
  products, precision instruments, tourism
Agriculture:
  livestock, vegetables, corn, wheat, potatoes, grapes
Economic aid:
  none
Currency:
  Swiss franc, franken, or franco (plural - francs, franken, or franchi); 1
  Swiss franc, franken, or franco (SwF) = 100 centimes, rappen, or centesimi
Exchange rates:
  Swiss francs, franken, or franchi (SwF) per US$1 - 1.5079 (March 1992),
  1.4340 (1991), 1.3892 (1990), 1.6359 (1989), 1.4633 (1988), 1.4912 (1987)
Fiscal year: calendar year

:Liechtenstein Communications

Railroads:
  18.5 km 1.435-meter standard gauge, electrified; owned, operated, and
  included in statistics of Austrian Federal Railways
Highways:
  130.66 km main roads, 192.27 km byroads
Civil air:
  no transport aircraft
Airports:
  none
Telecommunications:
  limited, but sufficient automatic telephone system; 25,400 telephones;
  linked to Swiss networks by cable and radio relay for international
  telephone, radio, and TV services

:Liechtenstein Defense Forces

Branches:
  Police Department

Note:
defense is responsibility of Switzerland

Lithuania Geography

Total area: 65,200 km2
Land area: 65,200 km2
Comparative area: slightly larger than West Virginia
Land boundaries:
   1,273 km; Belarus 502 km, Latvia 453 km, Poland 91 km, Russia (Kaliningrad)
   227 km
Coastline:
   108 km
Maritime claims:
  Contiguous zone:
   NA nm
  Continental shelf:
   NA meter depth
  Exclusive fishing zone:
   NA nm
  Exclusive economic zone:
   NA nm
  Territorial sea:
   NA nm
Disputes:
   dispute with Russia (Kaliningrad Oblast) over the position of the Neman
   River border presently located on the Lithuanian bank and not in midriver as
   by international standards
Climate:
   maritime; wet, moderate winters
Terrain:
   lowland, many scattered small lakes, fertile soil
Natural resources:
   peat
Land use:
   49.1% arable land; NA% permanent crops; 22.2% meadows and pastures; 16.3%
   forest and woodland; 12.4% other; includes NA% irrigated
Environment:
   NA

:Lithuania People

Population: 3,788,542 (July 1992), growth rate 0.8% (1992)
Birth rate: 15 births/1,000 population (1992)
Death rate: 11 deaths/1,000 population (1992)
Net migration rate: 4 migrants/1,000 population (1992)
Infant mortality rate: 18 deaths/1,000 live births (1992)
Life expectancy at birth: 66 years male, 76 years female (1992)
Total fertility rate: 2.1 children born/woman (1992)
Nationality:
   noun - Lithuanian(s); adjective - Lithuanian
Ethnic divisions:
   Lithuanian 80.1%, Russian 8.6%, Poles 7.7%, Byelorussian 1.5%, other 2.1%

Religions:
    Catholic NA%, Lutheran NA%, unknown NA%, none NA%, other NA%
Languages:
    Lithuanian (official), Polish NA%, Russian NA%
Literacy:
    NA% (male NA%, female NA%) age 15 and over can read and write
Labor force:
    1,836,000; industry and construction 42%, agriculture and forestry 18%,
    other 40% (1990)
Organized labor:
    Lithuanian Trade Union Association; Labor Federation of Lithuania; Union of
    Workers

:Lithuania Government

Long-form name:
    Republic of Lithuania
Type:
    republic
Capital: Vilnius
Administrative divisions:
    none - all rayons are under direct republic jurisdiction
Independence:
    1918; annexed by the Soviet Union 3 August 1940; restored independence 11
    March 1990; and regained indpendence from the USSR 6 September 1991
Constitution:
    NA; Constitutional Commission has drafted a new constitution that will be
    sent to Parliament for ratification
Legal system:
    based on civil law system; no judicial review of legislative acts
National holiday:
    Independence Day, 16 February; Defenders of Freedom Day, 13 January
Executive branch:
    prime minister, Council of Ministers, Government,
Legislative branch:
    unicameral Supreme Council, Parliament
Judicial branch:
    Supreme Court; Court of Appeals; district and city courts; Procurator
    General of Lithuania
Leaders:
  Chief of State:
    Chairman, Supreme Council Vytautas LANDSBERGIS (since March 1990), Deputy
    Chairmen Bronius KUZMICKAS (since March 1990), Ceslovas STANKEVICIUS
(since
    March 1990)
  Head of Government:
    Prime Minister Gediminas VAGNORIUS (since January 1991); Deputy Prime
    Ministers Algis DOBROVOLSKAS (since January 1991), Vytantas PAKALNISKIS
    (since January 1991), Zigmas VAISVILA (since January 1991)
Political parties and leaders:
    Christian Democratic Party, FNU KATILIUS, chairman; Democratic Labor Party

of Lithuania, Algirdas Mykolas BRAZAUSKAS, chairman; Lithuanian Democratic Party, Sauluis PECELIUNAS, chairman; Lithuanian Green Party, Irena IGNATAVICIENE, chairwoman; Lithuanian Humanism Party, Vytautas KAZLAUSKAS,
chairman; Lithuanian Independence Party, Virgilijus CEPAITIS, chairman; Lithuanian Liberty League, Antanas TERLECKAS; Lithuanian Liberals Union, Vytautus RADZVILAS, chairman; Lithuanian Nationalist Union, Rimantas SMETONA, chairman; Lithuania Social Democratic Party, Aloizas SAKALAS, chairman

Suffrage:
universal at age 18

Elections:
President:
last held March 1990 (elected by Parliament); results - LANDSBERGIS, BRAZAUSKAS
Supreme Council:
last held 24 February 1990; results - Sajudis (nationalist movement won a large majority) (90) 63%; seats - (141 total)

Other political or pressure groups:
Sajudis; Lithuanian Future Forum; Farmers Union

Member of:
CSCE, IAEA, ILO, NACC, UN, UNCTAD

:Lithuania Government

Diplomatic representation:
Ambassador Stasys LOZORAITIS, Jr.; Embassy at 2622 16th St. NW, Washington, DC 20009; telephone (202) 234-5860, 2639
US:
Ambassador Darryl JOHNSON; Embassy at Mykolaicio putino 4, Vilnius; (mailing address is APO AE 09862); telephone [7] (01-22) 628-049

Flag:
yellow, green, and red horizontal stripes

:Lithuania Economy

Overview:
Lithuania is striving to become a small, independent, largely privatized economy rather than a segment of a huge, centrally planned economy. Although substantially above average in living standards and technology in the old USSR, Lithuania historically lagged behind Latvia and Estonia in economic development. It is ahead of its Baltic neighbors, however, in implementing market reform. The country has no important natural resources aside from its arable land and strategic location. Industry depends entirely on imported materials that have come from the republics of the former USSR. Lithuania benefits from its ice-free port at Klaipeda on the Baltic Sea and its rail and highway hub at Vilnius, which provides land communication between Eastern Europe and Russia, Latvia, Estonia, and Belarus. Industry produces a small assortment of high-quality products, ranging from complex machine tools to sophisticated consumer electronics. Thanks to nuclear power, Lithuania is presently self-sufficient in electricity, exporting its surplus to Latvia and Belarus; the nuclear facilities inherited from the USSR, however, have come under world scrutiny as seriously deficient in safety

standards. Agriculture is efficient compared with most of the former Soviet Union. Lithuania holds first place in per capita consumption of meat, second place for eggs and potatoes, and fourth place for milk and dairy products. Grain must be imported to support the meat and dairy industries. As to economic reforms, Lithuania is pressing ahead with plans to privatize at least 60% of state-owned property (industry, agriculture, and housing) having already sold many small enterprises using a voucher system. Other government priorities include stimulating foreign investment by protecting the property rights of foreign firms and redirecting foreign trade away from Eastern markets to the more competitive Western markets. For the moment, Lithuania will remain highly dependent on Russia for energy, raw materials, grains, and markets for its products.

GDP:
purchasing power equivalent - $NA; per capita NA; real growth rate -13% (1991)

Inflation rate (consumer prices):
200% (1991)

Unemployment rate: NA%

Budget:
revenues 4.8 billion rubles; expenditures 4.7 billion rubles (1989 economic survey); note - budget revenues and expenditures are not given for other former Soviet republics; implied deficit from these figures does not have a clear interpretation

Exports:
700 million rubles (f.o.b., 1990)
commodities:
electronics 18%, petroleum products 16%, food 10%, chemicals 6% (1989)
partners:
Russia 60%, Ukraine 15%, other former Soviet republics 20%, West 5%

Imports:
2.2 billion rubles (c.i.f., 1990)
commodities:
oil 24%, machinery 14%, chemicals 8%, grain NA%
partners:
NA

External debt: $650 million (1991 est.)

Industrial production:
growth rate -1.3% (1991)

Electricity:
5,875,000 kW capacity; 25,500 million kWh produced, NA kWh per capita (1991)

:Lithuania Economy

Industries:
employs 25% of the labor force; its shares in the total production of the former USSR are metal-cutting machine tools 6.6%; electric motors 4.6%; television sets 6.2%; refrigerators and freezers 5.4%; other production includes petroleum refining, shipbuilding (small ships), furniture making, textiles, food processing, fertilizers, agricultural machinery, optical equipment, electronic components, computers, and amber

Agriculture:

employs 29% of labor force; sugar, grain, potatoes, sugarbeets, vegetables, meat, milk, dairy products, eggs, and fish; most developed are the livestock and dairy branches - these depend on imported grain; Lithuania is a net exporter of meat, milk, and eggs

Illicit drugs:

transshipment point for illicit drugs from Central and Southwest Asia to Western Europe

Economic aid:

US commitments, including Ex-Im (1992), $10 million; Western (non-US) countries, ODA and OOF bilateral commitments (1970-86), $NA million; Communist countries (1971-86), $NA million

Currency:

as of May 1992, retaining ruble as currency but planning early introduction of ``litas"

Exchange rates:

NA

Fiscal year: calendar year

:Lithuania Communications

Railroads:

2,010 km (includes NA km electrified); does not include industrial lines (1990)

Highways:

44,200 km total (1990); 35,500 km hard surfaced, 8,700 km earth

Inland waterways:

600 km perennially navigable

Pipelines:

NA

Ports:

maritime - Klaipeda; inland - Kaunas

Merchant marine:

66 ships (1,000 GRT or over) totaling 268,854 GRT/315,690 DWT; includes 27 cargo, 24 timber carrier, 1 container, 3 railcar carrier, 11 combination bulk

Civil air:

NA

Airports:

NA

Telecommunications:

better developed than in most other former USSR republics; 22.4 telephones per 100 persons; broadcast stations - 13 AM, 26 FM, 1 SW, 1 LW, 3 TV; landlines or microwave to former USSR republics; leased connection to the Moscow international switch for traffic with other countries; satellite earth stations (8 channels to Norway)

:Lithuania Defense Forces

Branches:

Ground Forces, Republic Security Forces (internal and border troops), National Guard/Volunteers; Russian Forces (Ground, Navy, Air, and Air Defense)

Manpower availability:
  NA

Luxembourg Geography

Total area: 2,586 km
Land area: 2,586 km
Comparative area: slightly smaller than Rhode Island
Land boundaries:
  359 km; Belgium 148 km, France 73 km, Germany 138 km
Coastline:
  none - landlocked
Maritime claims:
  none - landlocked
Disputes:
  none
Climate:
  modified continental with mild winters, cool summers
Terrain:
  mostly gently rolling uplands with broad, shallow valleys; uplands to
  slightly mountainous in the north; steep slope down to Moselle floodplain in
  the southeast
Natural resources:
  iron ore (no longer exploited)
Land use:
  arable land 24%; permanent crops 1%; meadows and pastures 20%; forest and
  woodland 21%; other 34%
Environment:
  deforestation
Note:
  landlocked

:Luxembourg People

Population: 392,405 (July 1992), growth rate 1.0% (1992)
Birth rate: 12 births/1,000 population (1992)
Death rate: 10 deaths/1,000 population (1992)
Net migration rate: 7 migrants/1,000 population (1992)
Infant mortality rate: 8 deaths/1,000 live births (1992)
Life expectancy at birth: 73 years male, 80 years female (1992)
Total fertility rate: 1.6 children born/woman (1992)
Nationality:
  noun - Luxembourger(s); adjective - Luxembourg
Ethnic divisions:
  Celtic base, with French and German blend; also guest and worker residents
  from Portugal, Italy, and European countries
Religions:
  Roman Catholic 97%, Protestant and Jewish 3%
Languages:
  Luxembourgisch, German, French; many also speak English
Literacy:
  100% (male 100%, female 100%) age 15 and over can read and write (1980 est.)
Labor force:

177,300; one-third of labor force is foreign workers, mostly from Portugal, Italy, France, Belgium, and FRG; services 65%, industry 31.6%, agriculture 3.4% (1988)

Organized labor:

100,000 (est.) members of four confederated trade unions

:Luxembourg Government

Long-form name:

Grand Duchy of Luxembourg

Type:

constitutional monarchy

Capital: Luxembourg

Administrative divisions:

3 districts; Diekirch, Grevenmacher, Luxembourg

Independence:

1839

Constitution:

17 October 1868, occasional revisions

Legal system:

based on civil law system; accepts compulsory ICJ jurisdiction

National holiday:

National Day (public celebration of the Grand Duke's birthday), 23 June (1921)

Executive branch:

grand duke, prime minister, vice prime minister, Council of Ministers (cabinet)

Legislative branch:

unicameral Chamber of Deputies (Chambre des Deputes); note - the Council of State (Conseil d'Etat) is an advisory body whose views are considered by the Chamber of Deputies

Judicial branch:

Superior Court of Justice (Cour Superieure de Justice)

Leaders:

Chief of State:

Grand Duke JEAN (since 12 November 1964); Heir Apparent Prince HENRI (son of Grand Duke Jean, born 16 April 1955)

Head of Government:

Prime Minister Jacques SANTER (since 21 July 1984); Vice Prime Minister Jacques F. POOS (since 21 July 1984)

Political parties and leaders:

Christian Social Party (CSV), Jacques SANTER; Socialist Workers Party (LSAP), Jacques POOS; Liberal (DP), Colette FLESCH; Communist (KPL), Andre HOFFMANN; Green Alternative (GAP), Jean HUSS

Suffrage:

universal and compulsory at age 18

Elections:

Chamber of Deputies:

last held on 18 June 1989 (next to be held by June 1994); results - CSV 31.7%, LSAP 27.2%, DP 16.2%, Greens 8.4%, PAC 7.3%, KPL 5.1%, other 4.1%; seats - (60 total) CSV 22, LSAP 18, DP 11, Greens 4, PAC 4, KPL 1

573

Other political or pressure groups:
  group of steel industries representing iron and steel industry, Centrale
  Paysanne representing agricultural producers; Christian and Socialist labor
  unions; Federation of Industrialists; Artisans and Shopkeepers Federation
Member of:
  ACCT, Australia Group, Benelux, CCC, CE, COCOM, CSCE, EBRD, EC, ECE,
EIB,
  EMS, FAO, GATT, IAEA, IBRD, ICAO, ICC, ICFTU, IDA, IEA, IFAD, IFC, ILO,
IMF,
  IMO, INTELSAT, INTERPOL, IOC, IOM, ITU, LORCS, MTCR, NACC, NATO,
NEA, NSG,
  OECD, PCA, UN, UNCTAD, UNESCO, UNIDO, UPU, WCL, WEU, WHO, WIPO,
WMO, ZC
Diplomatic representation:
  Ambassador Alphonse BERNS; Chancery at 2200 Massachusetts Avenue NW,
  Washington, DC 20008; telephone (202) 265-4171; there are Luxembourg
  Consulates General in New York and San Francisco

:Luxembourg Government

US:
  Ambassador Edward M. ROWELL; Embassy at 22 Boulevard Emmanuel-Servais,
2535
  Luxembourg City; PSC 11 (mailing address is APO AE 09132-5380); telephone
  [352] 460123; FAX [352] 461401
Flag:
  three equal horizontal bands of red (top), white, and light blue; similar to
  the flag of the Netherlands, which uses a darker blue and is shorter; design
  was based on the flag of France

:Luxembourg Economy

Overview:
  The stable economy features moderate growth, low inflation, and negligible
  unemployment. Agriculture is based on small but highly productive
  family-owned farms. The industrial sector, until recently dominated by
  steel, has become increasingly more diversified, particularly toward
  high-technology firms. During the past decade, growth in the financial
  sector has more than compensated for the decline in steel. Services,
  especially banking, account for a growing proportion of the economy.
  Luxembourg participates in an economic union with Belgium on trade and most
  financial matters and is also closely connected economically to the
  Netherlands.
GDP:
  purchasing power equivalent - $7.83 billion, per capita $20,200; real growth
  rate 2.5% (1991 est.)
Inflation rate (consumer prices):
  3.7% (1990)
Unemployment rate: 1.3% (1990)
Budget:
  revenues $2.5 billion; expenditures $2.3 billion, including capital
  expenditures of NA (1988)
Exports:

$6.3 billion (f.o.b., 1990)
  commodities:
  finished steel products, chemicals, rubber products, glass, aluminum, other
  industrial products
  partners:
  EC 75%, US 5%
Imports:
  $7.5 billion (c.i.f., 1990)
  commodities:
  minerals, metals, foodstuffs, quality consumer goods
  partners:
  Belgium 37%, FRG 31%, France 12%, US 2%
External debt: $131.6 million (1989 est.)
Industrial production:
  growth rate - 0.5% (1990); accounts for 25% of GDP
Electricity:
  1,500,000 kW capacity; 1,163 million kWh produced, 3,170 kWh per capita
  (1991)
Industries:
  banking, iron and steel, food processing, chemicals, metal products,
  engineering, tires, glass, aluminum
Agriculture:
  accounts for less than 3% of GDP (including forestry); principal products -
  barley, oats, potatoes, wheat, fruits, wine grapes; cattle raising
  widespread
Economic aid:
  none
Currency:
  Luxembourg franc (plural - francs); 1 Luxembourg franc (LuxF) = 100 centimes
Exchange rates:
  Luxembourg francs (LuxF) per US$1 - 32.462 (January 1992), 34.148 (1991),
  33.418 (1990), 39.404 (1989), 36.768 (1988), 37.334 (1987); note - the
  Luxembourg franc is at par with the Belgian franc, which circulates freely
  in Luxembourg
Fiscal year: calendar year

:Luxembourg Communications

Railroads:
  Luxembourg National Railways (CFL) operates 270 km 1.435-meter standard
  gauge; 162 km double track; 162 km electrified
Highways:
  5,108 km total; 4,995 km paved, 57 km gravel, 56 km earth; about 80 km
  limited access divided highway
Inland waterways:
  37 km; Moselle River
Pipelines:
  petroleum products 48 km
Ports:
  Mertert (river port)
Merchant marine:

49 ships (1,000 GRT or over) totaling 1,592,985 GRT/2,642,249 DWT; includes 3 cargo, 5 container, 5 roll-on/roll-off, 6 petroleum tanker, 4 chemical tanker, 3 combination ore/oil, 8 liquefied gas, 1 passenger, 8 bulk, 6 combination bulk

Civil air:

13 major transport aircraft

Airports:

2 total, 2 usable; 1 with permanent-surface runways; 1 with runways over 3,659 m; 1 with runways less than 1,220 m

Telecommunications:

highly developed, completely automated and efficient system, mainly buried cables; 230,000 telephones; broadcast stations - 2 AM, 3 FM, 3 TV; 3 channels leased on TAT-6 coaxial submarine cable; 1 direct-broadcast satellite earth station; nationwide mobile phone system

:Luxembourg Defense Forces

Branches:

Army, National Gendarmerie

Manpower availability:

males 15-49, 100,994; 83,957 fit for military service; 2,320 reach military age (19) annually

Defense expenditures:

exchange rate conversion - $100 million, 1.4% of GDP (1991)

Macau Geography

Total area: 16 km2
Land area: 16 km2
Comparative area: about 0.1 times the size of Washington, DC
Land boundaries:

0.34 km; China 0.34 km

Coastline:

40 km

Maritime claims:

not known

Disputes:

Climate:

subtropical; marine with cool winters, warm summers

Terrain:

generally flat

Natural resources:

negligible

Land use:

arable land 0%; permanent crops 0%; meadows and pastures 0%; forest and woodland 0%; other 100%

Environment:

essentially urban; one causeway and one bridge connect the two islands to the peninsula on mainland

Note:

27 km west-southwest of Hong Kong on the southeast coast of China

:Macau People

Population: 473,333 (July 1992), growth rate 1.7% (1992)
Birth rate: 17 births/1,000 population (1992)
Death rate: 4 deaths/1,000 population (1992)
Net migration rate: 4 migrants/1,000 population (1992)
Infant mortality rate: 8 deaths/1,000 live births (1992)
Life expectancy at birth: 78 years male, 84 years female (1992)
Total fertility rate: 1.6 children born/woman (1992)
Nationality:
   noun - Macanese (singular and plural); adjective - Macau
Ethnic divisions:
   Chinese 95%, Portuguese 3%, other 2%
Religions:
   Buddhist 45%, Roman Catholic 7%, Protestant 1%, none 45.8%, other 1.2%
   (1981)
Languages:
   Portuguese (official); Cantonese is the language of commerce
Literacy:
   90% (male 93%, female 86%) age 15 and over can read and write (1981)
Labor force:
   180,000 (1986)
Organized labor:
   none

:Macau Government

Long-form name:
   none
Type:
   overseas territory of Portugal; scheduled to revert to China in 1999
Capital: Macau
Administrative divisions:
   2 districts (concelhos, singular - concelho); Ilhas, Macau
Independence:
   none (territory of Portugal); Portugal signed an agreement with China on 13
   April 1987 to return Macau to China on 20 December 1999; in the joint
   declaration, China promises to respect Macau's existing social and economic
   systems and lifestyle for 50 years after transition
Constitution:
   17 February 1976, Organic Law of Macau; basic law drafted primarily by
   Beijing awaiting final approval
Legal system:
   Portuguese civil law system
National holiday:
   Day of Portugal, 10 June
Executive branch:
   President of Portugal, governor, Consultative Council (cabinet)
Legislative branch:
   Legislative Assembly
Judicial branch:
   Supreme Court

Leaders:
  Chief of State:
  President (of Portugal) Mario Alberto SOARES (since 9 March 1986)
  Head of Government:
  Governor Gen. Vasco Joachim Rocha VIEIRA (since 20 March 1991)
Political parties and leaders:
  Association to Defend the Interests of Macau; Macau Democratic Center; Group
  to Study the Development of Macau; Macau Independent Group
Suffrage:
  universal at age 18
Elections:
  Legislative Assembly:
  last held on 10 March 1991; results - percent of vote by party NA; seats -
  (23 total; 8 elected by universal suffrage, 8 by indirect suffrage, and 7
  appointed by the governor) number of seats by party NA
Other political or pressure groups:
  wealthy Macanese and Chinese representing local interests, wealthy
  pro-Communist merchants representing China's interests; in January 1967 the
  Macau Government acceded to Chinese demands that gave China veto power over
  administration
Member of:
  IMO (associate), WTO (associate)
Diplomatic representation:
  as Chinese territory under Portuguese administration, Macanese interests in
  the US are represented by Portugal
  US:
  the US has no offices in Macau, and US interests are monitored by the US
  Consulate General in Hong Kong
Flag:
  the flag of Portugal is used

:Macau Economy

Overview:
  The economy is based largely on tourism (including gambling) and textile and
  fireworks manufacturing. Efforts to diversify have spawned other small
  industries - toys, artificial flowers, and electronics. The tourist sector
  has accounted for roughly 25% of GDP, and the clothing industry has provided
  about two-thirds of export earnings; the gambling industry represented 36%
  of GDP in 1991. Macau depends on China for most of its food, fresh water,
  and energy imports. Japan and Hong Kong are the main suppliers of raw
  materials and capital goods.
GDP:
  exchange rate conversion - $3.1 billion, per capita $6,900; real growth rate
  6% (1991 est.)
Inflation rate (consumer prices):
  8.8% (1990 est.)
Unemployment rate: 2% (1989 est.)
Budget:
  revenues $305 million; expenditures $298 million, including capital
  expenditures of $NA (1989)

Exports:
  $1.5 billion (1990 est.)
 commodities:
  textiles, clothing, toys
 partners:
  US 33%, Hong Kong 15%, FRG 12%, France 10% (1987)
Imports:
  $1.8 billion (1990 est.)
 commodities:
  raw materials, foodstuffs, capital goods
 partners:
  Hong Kong 39%, China 21%, Japan 10% (1987)
External debt: $91 million (1985)
Industrial production:
  NA
Electricity:
  220,000 kW capacity; 520 million kWh produced, 1,165 kWh per capita (1991)
Industries:
  clothing, textiles, toys, plastic products, furniture, tourism
Agriculture:
  rice, vegetables; food shortages - rice, vegetables, meat; depends mostly on
  imports for food requirements
Economic aid:
  none
Currency:
  pataca (plural - patacas); 1 pataca (P) = 100 avos
Exchange rates:
  patacas (P) per US$1 - 8.034 (1991), 8.024 (1990), 8.030 (1989), 8.044
  (1988), 7.993 (1987); note - linked to the Hong Kong dollar at the rate of
  1.03 patacas per Hong Kong dollar
Fiscal year: calendar year

:Macau Communications

Highways:
  42 km paved
Ports:
  Macau
Civil air:
  no major transport aircraft
Airports:
  none useable, 1 under construction; 1 seaplane station
Telecommunications:
  fairly modern communication facilities maintained for domestic and
  international services; 52,000 telephones; broadcast stations - 4 AM, 3 FM,
  no TV; 75,000 radio receivers (est.); international high-frequency radio
  communication facility; access to international communications carriers
  provided via Hong Kong and China; 1 Indian Ocean INTELSAT earth station

:Macau Defense Forces

Manpower availability:
  males 15-49, 135,923; 76,414 fit for military service

Note:
  defense is responsibility of Portugal

:Macedonia Header

Note:
  Macedonia has proclaimed independent statehood but has not been formally
  recognized as a state by the United States.

Macedonia Geography

Total area: 25,333 km2
Land area: 24,856 km2
Comparative area: slightly larger than Vermont
Land boundaries:
  748 km; Albania 151 km, Bulgaria 148 km, Greece 228 km, Serbia and
  Montenegro 221 km
Coastline:
  none - landlocked
Disputes:
  Greece claims republic's name implies territorial claims against Aegean
  Macedonia
Climate:
  hot, dry summers and autumns and relatively cold winters with heavy snowfall
Terrain:
  territory covered with deep basins and valleys; there are three large lakes,
  each divided by a frontier line
Natural resources:
  chromium, lead, zinc, manganese, tungsten, nickel, low-grade iron ore,
  asbestos, sulphur, timber
Land use:
  arable land 5%; permanent crops 5%; meadows and pastures 20%; forest and
  woodland 30%; other 40%; includes irrigated NA%
Environment:
  Macedonia suffers from high seismic hazard; air pollution from metallurgical
  plants
Note:
  major transportation corridor from Western and Central Europe to Aegean Sea

:Macedonia People

Population: 2,174,000 (July 1992), growth rate NA% (1992)
Birth rate: NA births/1,000 population (1992)
Death rate: NA deaths/1,000 population (1992)
Net migration rate: NA migrants/1,000 population (1992)
Infant mortality rate: NA deaths/1,000 live births (1992)
Life expectancy at birth: 71 years male, 75 years female (1992)
Total fertility rate: NA children born/woman (1992)
Ethnic divisions:
  Macedonian 67%, Albanian 20%, Turkish 4%, Serb 2%, other 7%
Religions:
  Eastern Orthodox 59%, Muslim 26%, Catholic 4%, Protestant 1%, unknown 10%
Languages:
  Macedonian 70%, Albanian 21%, Turkish 3%, Serbo-Croatian 3%, other 3%

580

Literacy:
  89.1% (male 94.2%, female 83.8%) age 10 and over can read and write (1992 est.)
Labor force:
  507,324; agriculture 8%, manufacturing and mining 40% (1990)
Organized labor:
  NA

:Macedonia Government

Long-form name:
  Republic of Macedonia
Type:
  emerging democracy
Capital: Skopje
Administrative divisions:
  NA
Independence:
  20 November 1991 from Yugoslavia
Constitution:
  adopted 17 November 1991, effective 20 November 1991
Legal system:
  based on civil law system; judicial review of legislative acts
National holiday:
  NA
Executive branch:
  presidency, Council of Ministers, prime minister
Legislative branch:
  unicameral Assembly
Judicial branch:
  Constitutional Court, Judicial Court of the Republic
Leaders:
 Chief of State:
  President Kiro GLIGOROV (since 27 January 1991)
 Head of Government:
  Prime Minister Nikola KLJUSEV (since March 1991), Deputy Prime Ministers Jovan ANDONOV (since March 1991), Blaze RISTOVSKI (since March 1991), and Bezir ZUTA (since March 1991)
Political parties and leaders:
  Social Democratic Alliance (SDA; former Communist Party), Branko CRVENKOVSKI, chairman; Party of Democratic Prosperity, (PDP), Nevzat HALILI,
  chairman; National Democratic Party, Iliaz HALIMI, chairman; Alliance of Reform Forces of Macedonia (MARF), Sojan ANDOV, chairman; Socialist Party, chairman NA; Internal Macedonian Revolutionary Organization - Democratic Party for Macedonian National Unity (IMRO-DPMNU), Ljupco GEORGIEVSKI, chairman
Suffrage:
  universal at age 18
Elections:
 President:

last held 27 January 1991 (next to be held NA); results - Kiro GLIGOREV won

Assembly:

last held 11 November 1990 (next to be held NA);results - percent of vote by
party NA; seats - (120 total) IMRO-DPMNU 37, SDA 31, PDP 25, MARF 17, Party
of Yugoslavs 1, Socialists 5, others 4

Communists:

NA

Other political or pressure groups:

Movement for All Macedonian Action (MAAK), IMRU-Democratic Party, League
for

Democracy, Albanian Democratic Union-Liberal Party

Member of:

Diplomatic representation:

has not been formerly recognized by the US

Flag:

NA

:Macedonia Economy

Overview:

Macedonia, although the poorest among the six republics of a disintegrated
Yugoslav federation, can meet basic food and energy needs through its own
agricultural and coal resources. As a breakaway republic, however, it will
move down toward a bare subsistence level of life unless economic ties are
reforged or enlarged with its neighbors Serbia, Albania, Greece, and
Bulgaria. The economy depends on outside sources for all of its oil and gas
and its modern machinery and parts. Continued political turmoil, both
internally and in the region as a whole, prevents any swift readjustments of
trade patterns and economic rules of the game. Inflation in early 1992 was
out of control, the result of fracturing trade links, the decline in
economic activity, and general uncertainties about the future status of the
country; prices rose 38% in March 1992 alone. Macedonia's geographical
isolation, technological backwardness, and political instability place it
far down the list of countries of interest to Western investors. Recognition
of Macedonia by the EC and an internal commitment to economic reform would
help to encourage foreign investment over the long run.

GDP:

$7.1 billion, per capita $3,110; real growth rate -18% (1991 est.)

Unemployment rate: 20% (1991 est.)

Exports:

$578 million (1990)

commodities:

manufactured goods 40%, machinery and transport equipment 14%, miscellaneous
manufactured articles 23%, raw materials 7.6%, food (rice) and live animals
5.7%, beverages and tobacco 4.5%, chemicals 4.7%

partners:

principally Serbia and the other former Yugoslav republics, Germany, Greece,
Albania

Imports:

$1,112 million (1990)

commodities:
  fuels and lubricants 19%, manufactured goods 18%, machinery and transport equipment 15%, food and live animals 14%, chemicals 11.4%, raw materials 10%, miscellaneous manufactured articles 8.0%, beverages and tobacco 3.5%
partners:
  other former Yugoslav republics, Greece, Albania, Germany, Bulgaria
External debt: $NA
Industrial production:
  growth rate -18% (1991 est.)
Electricity:
  1,600,000 kw capacity; 6,300 million kWh produced, 3,103 kWh per capita (1991)
Industries:
  low levels of technology predominate, such as, oil refining by distillation only; produces basic fuels; mining and manufacturing processes result in the extraction and production of coal as well as metallic chromium, lead, zinc, and ferronickel; light industry produces basic textiles, wood products, and tobacco
Agriculture:
  provides 12% of Macedonia's GDP and meets the basic need for food; principal crops are rice, tobacco, wheat, corn, and millet; also grown are cotton, sesame, mulberry leaves, citrus fruit, and vegetables; Macedonia is one of the seven legal cultivators of the opium poppy for the world pharmaceutical industry, including some exports to the US; agricultural production is highly labor intensive

:Macedonia Economy

Illicit drugs:
  NA
Economic aid:
  $NA
Currency:
  denar (plural - denars); 1 denar (NA) = 100 NA
Exchange rates:
  denar (NA) per US$1 - 240 (January 1991)
Fiscal year: calendar year

:Macedonia Communications

Railroads:
  NA
Highways:
  10,591 km total (1991); 5,091 km paved, 1,404 km gravel, 4,096 km earth
Inland waterways:
  NA km
Pipelines:
  none
Ports:
  none - landlocked
Airports:
  2 main
Telecommunications:

125,000 telephones; broadcast stations - 6 AM, 2 FM, 5 (2 relays) TV; 370,000 radios, 325,000 TV; satellite communications ground stations - none

:Macedonia Defense Forces

Branches:
  Army, Air and Air Defense Force
Manpower availability:
  males 15-49, 590,613; NA fit for military service; 22,913 reach military age (18) annually
Defense expenditures:
  exchange rate conversion - 7.0 billion dinars (est.), NA% of GDP (1992); note - conversion of the military budget into US dollars using the current exchange rate could produce misleading results

Madagascar Geography

Total area: 587,040 km2
Land area: 581,540 km2
Comparative area: slightly less than twice the size of Arizona
Land boundaries:
  none
Coastline:
  4,828 km
Maritime claims:
 Exclusive economic zone:
  200 nm
 Territorial sea:
  12 nm
Disputes:
  claims Bassas da India, Europa Island, Glorioso Islands, Juan de Nova Island, and Tromelin Island (all administered by France)
Climate:
  tropical along coast, temperate inland, arid in south
Terrain:
  narrow coastal plain, high plateau and mountains in center
Natural resources:
  graphite, chromite, coal, bauxite, salt, quartz, tar sands, semiprecious stones, mica, fish
Land use:
  arable land 4%; permanent crops 1%; meadows and pastures 58%; forest and woodland 26%; other 11%; includes irrigated 2%
Environment:
  subject to periodic cyclones; deforestation; overgrazing; soil erosion; desertification
Note:
  world's fourth-largest island; strategic location along Mozambique Channel

:Madagascar People

Population: 12,596,263 (July 1992), growth rate 3.2% (1992)
Birth rate: 46 births/1,000 population (1992)
Death rate: 14 deaths/1,000 population (1992)
Net migration rate: 0 migrants/1,000 population (1992)

Infant mortality rate: 93 deaths/1,000 live births (1992)
Life expectancy at birth: 51 years male, 55 years female (1992)
Total fertility rate: 6.8 children born/woman (1992)
Nationality:
  noun - Malagasy (singular and plural); adjective - Malagasy
Ethnic divisions:
  basic split between highlanders of predominantly Malayo-Indonesian origin
  (Merina and related Betsileo) on the one hand and coastal tribes,
  collectively termed the Cotiers, with mixed African, Malayo-Indonesian, and
  Arab ancestry (Betsimisaraka, Tsimihety, Antaisaka, Sakalava), on the other;
  there are also small French, Indian, Creole, and Comoran communities; no
  current, accurate assessment of tribal numbers is available
Religions:
  indigenous beliefs 52%, Christian about 41%, Muslim 7%
Languages:
  French and Malagasy (official)
Literacy:
  80% (male 88%, female 73%) age 15 and over can read and write (1990 est.)
Labor force:
  4,900,000; 90% nonsalaried family workers engaged in subsistence
  agriculture; 175,000 wage earners - agriculture 26%, domestic service 17%,
  industry 15%, commerce 14%, construction 11%, services 9%, transportation
  6%, other 2%; 51% of population of working age (1985)
Organized labor:
  4% of labor force

:Madagascar Government

Long-form name:
  Democratic Republic of Madagascar
Type:
  republic
Capital: Antananarivo
Administrative divisions:
  6 provinces (plural - NA, singular - faritanin'); Antananarivo, Antsiranana,
  Fianarantsoa, Mahajanga, Toamasina, Toliary
Independence:
  26 June 1960 (from France; formerly Malagasy Republic)
Constitution:
  21 December 1975; note - a new constitution is to be in place before 1993
Legal system:
  based on French civil law system and traditional Malagasy law; has not
  accepted compulsory ICJ jurisdiction
National holiday:
  Independence Day, 26 June (1960)
Executive branch:
  president, prime minister, Council of Ministers
Legislative branch:
  unicameral Popular National Assembly (Assemblee Nationale Populaire); note -
  the National Assembly has suspended its operations during 1992 in
  preparation for new legislative and presidential elections. In its place, an

interim High Authority of State and a Social and Economic Recovery Council
have been established

Judicial branch:

Supreme Court (Cour Supreme), High Constitutional Court (Haute Cour
Constitutionnelle)

Leaders:

Chief of State:

President Adm. Didier RATSIRAKA (since 15 June 1975)

Head of Government:

Prime Minister Guy RASANAMAZY (since 8 August 1991)

Political parties and leaders:

some 30 political parties now exist in Madagascar, the most important of
which are the Advance Guard of the Malagasy Revolution (AREMA), Didier
RATSIRAKA; Congress Party for Malagasy Independence (AKFM),
RAKOTOVAO-ANDRIATIANA; Congress Party for Malagasy Independence-
Revival
(AKFM-R), Pastor Richard ANDRIAMANJATO; Movement for National Unity
(VONJY),
Dr. Marojama RAZANABAHINY; Malagasy Christian Democratic Union
(UDECMA),
Norbert ANDRIAMORASATA; Militants for the Establishment of a Proletarian
Regime (MFM), Manandafy RAKOTONIRINA; National Movement for the Inde-
pendence
of Madagascar (MONIMA), Monja JAONA; National Union for the Defense of
Democracy (UNDD), Albert ZAFY

Suffrage:

universal at age 18

Elections:

President:

last held on 12 March 1989 (next to be held NA 1992); results - Didier
RATSIRAKA (AREMA) 62%, Manandafy RAKOTONIRINA (MFM/MFT) 20%,
Dr. Jerome
Marojama RAZANABAHINY (VONJY) 15%, Monja JAONA (MONIMA) 3%

Popular National Assembly:

last held on 28 May 1989 (next to be held 1992); results - AREMA 88.2%, MFM
5.1%, AKFM 3.7%, VONJY 2.2%, other 0.8%; seats - (137 total) AREMA 120,
MFM
7, AKFM 5, VONJY 4, MONIMA 1

:Madagascar Government

Member of:

ACCT, ACP, AfDB, CCC, ECA, FAO, G-77, GATT, IAEA, IBRD, ICAO, ICC,
ICFTU,
IDA, IFAD, IFC, ILO, IMF, IMO, INTELSAT, INTERPOL, IOC, ITU, LORCS,
NAM,
OAU, UN, UNCTAD, UNESCO, UNHCR, UNIDO, UPU, WCL, WFTU, WHO,
WIPO, WMO, WTO

Diplomatic representation:

Ambassador Pierrot Jocelyn RAJAONARIVELO; Chancery at 2374 Massachusetts
Avenue NW, Washington, DC 20008; telephone (202) 265-5525 or 5526; there is

a Malagasy Consulate General in New York

US:

Ambassador Howard K. WALKER; Embassy at 14 and 16 Rue Rainitovo, Antsahavola, Antananarivo (mailing address is B. P. 620, Antananarivo); telephone [261] (2) 212-57, 209-56, 200-89, 207-18

Flag:

two equal horizontal bands of red (top) and green with a vertical white band of the same width on hoist side

:Madagascar Economy

Overview:

Madagascar is one of the poorest countries in the world. Agriculture, including fishing and forestry, is the mainstay of the economy, accounting for over 40% of GDP, employing about 80% of the labor force, and contributing to more than 70% of total export earnings. Industry is largely confined to the processing of agricultural products and textile manufacturing; in 1990 it accounted for only 16% of GDP and employed almost 5% of the labor force. In 1986 the government introduced a five-year development plan that stressed self-sufficiency in food (mainly rice) by 1990, increased production for exports, and reduced energy imports. After mid-1991, however, output dropped sharply because of protracted antigovernment strikes and demonstrations for political reform.

GDP:

exchange rate conversion - $2.4 billion, per capita $200; real growth rate -3.8% (1991 est.)

Inflation rate (consumer prices):

10% (1991)

Unemployment rate: NA%

Budget:

revenues $390 million; expenditures $525 million, including capital expenditures of $240 million (1990 est.)

Exports:

$290 million (f.o.b., 1990 est.)

commodities:

coffee 45%, vanilla 15%, cloves 11%, sugar, petroleum products

partners:

France, Japan, Italy, Germany, US

Imports:

$436 million (f.o.b., 1990 est.)

commodities:

intermediate manufactures 30%, capital goods 28%, petroleum 15%, consumer goods 14%, food 13%

partners:

France, Germany, UK, other EC, US

External debt: $4.4 billion (1991)

Industrial production:

growth rate 5.2% (1990 est.); accounts for 16% of GDP

Electricity:

125,000 kW capacity; 450 million kWh produced, 35 kWh per capita (1991)

Industries:

agricultural processing (meat canneries, soap factories, breweries, tanneries, sugar refining plants), light consumer goods industries (textiles, glassware), cement, automobile assembly plant, paper, petroleum

Agriculture:
accounts for 40% of GDP; cash crops - coffee, vanilla, sugarcane, cloves, cocoa; food crops - rice, cassava, beans, bananas, peanuts; cattle raising widespread; almost self-sufficient in rice

Illicit drugs:
illicit producer of cannabis (cultivated and wild varieties) used mostly for domestic consumption

Economic aid:
US commitments, including Ex-Im (FY70-89), $136 million; Western (non-US) countries, ODA and OOF bilateral commitments (1970-89), $3,125 million; Communist countries (1970-89), $491 million

Currency:
Malagasy franc (plural - francs); 1 Malagasy franc (FMG) = 100 centimes

:Madagascar Economy

Exchange rates:
Malagasy francs (FMG) per US$1 - 1,943.4 (March 1992), 1,835.4 (1991), 1,454.6 (December 1990), 1,603.4 (1989) , 1,407.1 (1988), 1,069.2 (1987)

Fiscal year: calendar year

:Madagascar Communications

Railroads:
1,020 km 1.000-meter gauge

Highways:
40,000 km total; 4,694 km paved, 811 km crushed stone, gravel, or stabilized soil, 34,495 km improved and unimproved earth (est.)

Inland waterways:
of local importance only; isolated streams and small portions of Canal des Pangalanes

Ports:
Toamasina, Antsiranana, Mahajanga, Toliara

Merchant marine:
14 ships (1,000 GRT or over) totaling 59,255 GRT/81,509 DWT; includes 9 cargo, 2 roll-on/roll-off cargo, 1 petroleum tanker, 1 chemical tanker, 1 liquefied gas

Civil air:
8 major transport aircraft

Airports:
148 total, 103 usable; 30 with permanent-surface runways; none with runways over 3,659 m; 3 with runways 2,440-3,659 m; 34 with runways 1,220-2,439 m

Telecommunications:
above average system includes open-wire lines, coaxial cables, radio relay, and troposcatter links; submarine cable to Bahrain; satellite earth stations - 1 Indian Ocean INTELSAT and broadcast stations - 17 AM, 3 FM, 1 (36 repeaters) TV

:Madagascar Defense Forces

Branches:

Popular Armed Forces (including Intervention Forces, Development Forces, Aeronaval Forces - including Navy and Air Force), Gendarmerie, Presidential Security Regiment

Manpower availability:

males 15-49, 2,730,713; 1,625,335 fit for military service; 114,687 reach military age (20) annually

Defense expenditures:

exchange rate conversion - $37 million, 2.2% of GDP (1989 est.)

Malawi Geography

Total area: 118,480 km2

Land area: 94,080 km2

Comparative area: slightly larger than Pennsylvania

Land boundaries:

2,881 km; Mozambique 1,569 km, Tanzania 475 km, Zambia 837 km

Coastline:

none - landlocked

Maritime claims:

none - landlocked

Disputes:

dispute with Tanzania over the boundary in Lake Nyasa (Lake Malawi)

Climate:

tropical; rainy season (November to May); dry season (May to November)

Terrain:

narrow elongated plateau with rolling plains, rounded hills, some mountains

Natural resources:

limestone; unexploited deposits of uranium, coal, and bauxite

Land use:

arable land 25%; permanent crops NEGL%; meadows and pastures 20%; forest and woodland 50%; other 5%; includes irrigated NEGL%

Environment:

deforestation

Note:

landlocked

:Malawi People

Population: 9,605,342 (July 1992), growth rate 1.8% (1992); note - 900,000 Mozambican

refugees in Malawi (1990 est.)

Birth rate: 52 births/1,000 population (1992)

Death rate: 17 deaths/1,000 population (1992)

Net migration rate: -17 migrants/1,000 population (1992)

Infant mortality rate: 134 deaths/1,000 live births (1992)

Life expectancy at birth: 48 years male, 51 years female (1992)

Total fertility rate: 7.6 children born/woman (1992)

Nationality:

noun - Malawian(s); adjective - Malawian

Ethnic divisions:

Chewa, Nyanja, Tumbuko, Yao, Lomwe, Sena, Tonga, Ngoni, Ngonde, Asian, European

Religions:

Protestant 55%, Roman Catholic 20%, Muslim 20%; traditional indigenous beliefs are also practiced

Languages:

English and Chichewa (official); other languages important regionally

Literacy:

22% (male 34%, female 12%) age 15 and over can read and write (1966)

Labor force:

428,000 wage earners; agriculture 43%, manufacturing 16%, personal services 15%, commerce 9%, construction 7%, miscellaneous services 4%, other permanently employed 6% (1986)

Organized labor:

small minority of wage earners are unionized

:Malawi Government

Long-form name:

Republic of Malawi

Type:

one-party state

Capital: Lilongwe

Administrative divisions:

24 districts; Blantyre, Chikwawa, Chiradzulu, Chitipa, Dedza, Dowa, Karonga, Kasungu, Lilongwe, Machinga (Kasupe), Mangochi, Mchinji, Mulanje, Mwanza, Mzimba, Ntcheu, Nkhata Bay, Nkhotakota, Nsanje, Ntchisi, Rumphi, Salima, Thyolo, Zomba

Independence:

6 July 1964 (from UK; formerly Nyasaland)

Constitution:

6 July 1964; republished as amended January 1974

Legal system:

based on English common law and customary law; judicial review of legislative acts in the Supreme Court of Appeal; has not accepted compulsory ICJ jurisdiction

National holiday:

Independence Day, 6 July (1964)

Executive branch:

president, Cabinet

Legislative branch:

unicameral National Assembly

Judicial branch:

High Court, Supreme Court of Appeal

Leaders:

Chief of State and Head of Government:

President Dr. Hastings Kamuzu BANDA (since 6 July 1966; sworn in as President for Life 6 July 1971)

Political parties and leaders:

only party - Malawi Congress Party (MCP), Wadson DELEZA, administrative secretary; John TEMBO, treasurer general; top party position of secretary general vacant since 1983

Suffrage:

universal at age 21

Elections:

President:

President BANDA sworn in as President for Life on 6 July 1971

National Assembly:

last held 27-28 May 1987 (next to be held by May 1992); results - MCP is the
only party; seats - (133 total, 112 elected) MCP 133

Member of:

ACP, AfDB, C, CCC, ECA, FAO, G-77, GATT, IBRD, ICAO, ICFTU, IDA, IFAD,
IFC,

ILO, IMF, IMO, INTELSAT, INTERPOL, IOC, ISO (correspondent), ITU, LORCS,
NAM, OAU, SADCC, UN, UNCTAD, UNESCO, UNIDO, UPU, WHO, WIPO,
WMO, WTO

Diplomatic representation:

Ambassador Robert B. MBAYA; Chancery at 2408 Massachusetts Avenue NW,
Washington, DC 20008; telephone (202) 797-1007

US:

Ambassador Michael T. F. PISTOR; Embassy in new capital city development
area, address NA (mailing address is P. O. Box 30016, Lilongwe); telephone
[265] 730-166; FAX [265] 732-282

Flag:

three equal horizontal bands of black (top), red, and green with a radiant,
rising, red sun centered in the black band; similar to the flag of
Afghanistan, which is longer and has the national coat of arms superimposed
on the hoist side of the black and red bands

:Malawi Economy

Overview:

Landlocked Malawi ranks among the world's least developed countries. The
economy is predominately agricultural, with about 90% of the population
living in rural areas. Agriculture accounts for 40% of GDP and 90% of export
revenues. After two years of weak performance, economic growth improved
significantly in 1988-91 as a result of good weather and a broadly based
economic adjustment effort by the government. The economy depends on
substantial inflows of economic assistance from the IMF, the World Bank, and
individual donor nations.

GDP:

exchange rate conversion - $1.9 billion, per capita $200; growth rate 4.2%
(1991 est.)

Inflation rate (consumer prices):

9% (1991 est.)

Unemployment rate: NA%

Budget:

revenues $398 million; expenditures $510 million, including capital
expenditures of $154 million (FY91 est.)

Exports:

$390 million (f.o.b., 1990 est.)

commodities:

tobacco, tea, sugar, coffee, peanuts

partners:

US, UK, Zambia, South Africa, Germany

Imports:
  $560 million (c.i.f., 1990 est.)
  commodities:
  food, petroleum, semimanufactures, consumer goods, transportation equipment
  partners:
  South Africa, Japan, US, UK, Zimbabwe

External debt: $1.8 billion (December 1991 est.)

Industrial production:
  growth rate 4.0% (1990 est.); accounts for about 18% of GDP (1988)

Electricity:
  185,000 kW capacity; 550 million kWh produced, 60 kWh per capita (1991)

Industries:
  agricultural processing (tea, tobacco, sugar), sawmilling, cement, consumer
  goods

Agriculture:
  accounts for 40% of GDP; cash crops - tobacco, sugarcane, cotton, tea, and
  corn; subsistence crops - potatoes, cassava, sorghum, pulses; livestock -
  cattle and goats

Economic aid:
  US commitments, including Ex-Im (FY70-89), $215 million; Western (non-US)
  countries, ODA and OOF bilateral commitments (1970-89), $2,150 million

Currency:
  Malawian kwacha (plural - kwacha); 1 Malawian kwacha (MK) = 100 tambala

Exchange rates:
  Malawian kwacha (MK) per US$1 - 2.7200 (January 1992), 2.8033 (1991), 2.7289
  (1990), 2.7595 (1989), 2.5613 (1988), 2.2087 (1987)

Fiscal year: 1 April - 31 March

:Malawi Communications

Railroads:
  789 km 1.067-meter gauge

Highways:
  13,135 km total; 2,364 km paved; 251 km crushed stone, gravel, or stabilized
  soil; 10,520 km earth and improved earth

Inland waterways:
  Lake Nyasa (Lake Malawi); Shire River, 144 km

Ports:
  Chipoka, Monkey Bay, Nkhata Bay, and Nkotakota - all on Lake Nyasa (Lake
  Malawi)

Civil air:
  5 major transport aircraft

Airports:
  48 total, 43 usable; 6 with permanent-surface runways; none with runways
  over 3,659 m; 1 with runways 2,440-3,659 m; 9 with runways 1,220-2,439 m

Telecommunications:
  fair system of open-wire lines, radio relay links, and radio communications
  stations; 42,250 telephones; broadcast stations - 10 AM, 17 FM, no TV;
  satellite earth stations - 1 Indian Ocean INTELSAT and 1 Atlantic Ocean
  INTELSAT

Note:

a majority of exports would normally go through Mozambique on the Beira or Nacala railroads, but now most go through South Africa because of insurgent activity and damage to rail lines

:Malawi Defense Forces

Branches:

Army (including Air Wing and Naval Detachment), Police (including paramilitary Mobile Force Unit), paramilitary Malawi Young Pioneers

Manpower availability:

males 15-49, 2,000,406; 1,016,901 fit for military service

Defense expenditures:

exchange rate conversion - $22 million, 1.6% of GDP (1989 est.)

Malaysia Geography

Total area: 329,750 km2
Land area: 328,550 km2
Comparative area: slightly larger than New Mexico
Land boundaries:

2,669 km; Brunei 381 km, Indonesia 1,782, Thailand 506 km

Coastline:

4,675 km; Peninsular Malaysia 2,068 km, East Malaysia 2,607 km

Maritime claims:

Continental shelf:

200 m (depth) or to depth of exploitation, specified boundary in the South China Sea

Exclusive fishing zone:

200 nm

Exclusive economic zone:

200 nm

Territorial sea:

12 nm

Disputes:

involved in a complex dispute over the Spratly Islands with China, Philippines, Taiwan, Vietnam, and possibly Brunei; State of Sabah claimed by the Philippines; Brunei may wish to purchase the Malaysian salient that divides Brunei into two parts; two islands in dispute with Singapore

Climate:

tropical; annual southwest (April to October) and northeast (October to February) monsoons

Terrain:

coastal plains rising to hills and mountains

Natural resources:

tin, crude oil, timber, copper, iron ore, natural gas, bauxite

Land use:

arable land 3%; permanent crops 10%; meadows and pastures NEGL%; forest and woodland 63%; other 24%; includes irrigated 1%

Environment:

subject to flooding; air and water pollution

Note:

strategic location along Strait of Malacca and southern South China Sea

:Malaysia People

Population: 18,410,920 (July 1992), growth rate 2.4% (1992)
Birth rate: 29 births/1,000 population (1992)
Death rate: 6 deaths/1,000 population (1992)
Net migration rate: 0 migrants/1,000 population (1992)
Infant mortality rate: 27 deaths/1,000 live births (1992)
Life expectancy at birth: 66 years male, 71 years female (1992)
Total fertility rate: 3.6 children born/woman (1992)
Nationality:
  noun - Malaysian(s); adjective - Malaysian
Ethnic divisions:
  Malay and other indigenous 59%, Chinese 32%, Indian 9%
Religions:
  Peninsular Malaysia - Malays nearly all Muslim, Chinese predominantly
  Buddhists, Indians predominantly Hindu; Sabah - Muslim 38%, Christian 17%,
  other 45%; Sarawak - tribal religion 35%, Buddhist and Confucianist 24%,
  Muslim 20%, Christian 16%, other 5%
Languages:
  Peninsular Malaysia - Malay (official); English, Chinese dialects, Tamil;
  Sabah - English, Malay, numerous tribal dialects, Mandarin and Hakka
  dialects predominate among Chinese; Sarawak - English, Malay, Mandarin,
  numerous tribal languages
Literacy:
  78% (male 86%, female 70%) age 15 and over can read and write (1990 est.)
Labor force:
  7,258,000 (1991 est.)
Organized labor:
  640,000; 10% of total labor force (1990)

:Malaysia Government

Long-form name:
  none
Type:
  Federation of Malaysia formed 9 July 1963; constitutional monarchy nominally
  headed by the paramount ruler (king) and a bicameral Parliament; Peninsular
  Malaysian states - hereditary rulers in all but Melaka, where governors are
  appointed by Malaysian Pulau Pinang Government; powers of state governments
  are limited by federal Constitution; Sabah - self-governing state, holds 20
  seats in House of Representatives, with foreign affairs, defense, internal
  security, and other powers delegated to federal government; Sarawak -
  self-governing state within Malaysia, holds 27 seats in House of
  Representatives, with foreign affairs, defense, internal security, and other
  powers delegated to federal government
Capital: Kuala Lumpur
Administrative divisions:
  13 states (negeri-negeri, singular - negeri) and 2 federal territories*
  (wilayah-wilayah persekutuan, singular - wilayah persekutuan); Johor, Kedah,
  Kelantan, Labuan*, Melaka, Negeri Sembilan, Pahang, Perak, Perlis, Pulau
  Pinang, Sabah, Sarawak, Selangor, Terengganu, Wilayah Persekutuan*
Independence:

31 August 1957 (from UK)

Constitution:

31 August 1957, amended 16 September 1963 when Federation of Malaya became Federation of Malaysia

Legal system:

based on English common law; judicial review of legislative acts in the Supreme Court at request of supreme head of the federation; has not accepted compulsory ICJ jurisdiction

National holiday:

National Day, 31 August (1957)

Executive branch:

paramount ruler, deputy paramount ruler, prime minister, deputy prime minister, Cabinet

Legislative branch:

bicameral Parliament (Parlimen) consists of an upper house or Senate (Dewan Negara) and a lower house or House of Representatives (Dewan Rakyat)

Judicial branch:

Supreme Court

Leaders:

Chief of State:

Paramount Ruler AZLAN Muhibbuddin Shah ibni Sultan Yusof Izzudin (since 26 April 1989); Deputy Paramount Ruler JA'AFAR ibni Abdul Rahman (since 26 April 1989)

Head of Government:

Prime Minister Dr. MAHATHIR bin Mohamad (since 16 July 1981); Deputy Prime Minister Abdul GHAFAR Bin Baba (since 7 May 1986)

Political parties and leaders:

Peninsular Malaysia:

National Front, a confederation of 13 political parties dominated by United Malays National Organization Baru (UMNO Baru), MAHATHIR bin Mohamad; Malaysian Chinese Association (MCA), LING Liong Sik; Gerakan Rakyat Malaysia, Datuk LIM Keng Yaik; Malaysian Indian Congress (MIC), Datuk S. Samy VELLU

Sabah:

Berjaya Party, Datuk Haji Mohammed NOOR Mansor; Bersatu Sabah (PBS), Joseph Pairin KITINGAN; United Sabah National Organizaton (USNO), leader NA

:Malaysia Government

Sarawak:

coalition Sarawak National Front composed of the Party Pesaka Bumiputra Bersatu (PBB), Datuk Patinggi Amar Haji Abdul TAIB Mahmud; Sarawak United People's Party (SUPP), Datuk Amar James WONG Soon Kai; Sarawak National Party (SNAP), Datuk Amar James WONG; Parti Bansa Dayak Sarawak (PBDS), Datuk

Leo MOGGIE; major opposition parties are Democratic Action Party (DAP), LIM Kit Siang and Pan-Malaysian Islamic Party (PAS), Fadzil NOOR

Suffrage:

universal at age 21

Elections:

House of Representatives:

last held 21 October 1990 (next to be held by August 1995); results - National Front 52%, other 48%; seats - (180 total) National Front 127, DAP 20, PAS 7, independents 4, other 22; note - within the National Front, UMNO got 71 seats and MCA 18 seats

Member of:

APEC, AsDB, ASEAN, C, CCC, CP, ESCAP, FAO, G-15, G-77, GATT, IAEA, IBRD,

ICAO, ICFTU, IDA, IDB, IFAD, IFC, ILO, IMF, IMO, INMARSAT, INTELSAT, INTERPOL, IOC, ISO, ITU, LORCS, NAM, OIC, UN, UNCTAD, UNESCO, UNIDO,

UNIIMOG, UPU, WCL, WHO, WIPO, WMO

Diplomatic representation:

Ambassador Abdul MAJID Mohamed; Chancery at 2401 Massachusetts Avenue NW,

Washington, DC 20008; telephone (202) 328-2700; there are Malaysian Consulates General in Los Angeles and New York

US:

Ambassador Paul M. CLEVELAND; Embassy at 376 Jalan Tun Razak, 50400 Kuala Lumpur (mailing address is P. O. Box No. 10035, 50700 Kuala Lumpur); telephone [60] (3) 248-9011; FAX [60] (3) 242-2207

Flag:

fourteen equal horizontal stripes of red (top) alternating with white (bottom); there is a blue rectangle in the upper hoist-side corner bearing a yellow crescent and a yellow fourteen-pointed star; the crescent and the star are traditional symbols of Islam; the design was based on the flag of the US

:Malaysia Economy

Overview:

During the period 1988-91 booming exports helped Malaysia continue to recover from the severe 1985-86 recession. Real output grew by 8.8% in 1989, 10% in 1990, and 8.6% in 1991, helped by vigorous growth in manufacturing output, further increases in foreign direct investment - particularly from Japanese and Taiwanese firms facing higher costs at home - and increased oil production. Malaysia has become the world's third-largest producer of semiconductor devices (after the US and Japan) and the world's largest exporter of semiconductor devices. Inflation has remained low; unemployment has stood at 6% of the labor force; and the government has followed prudent fiscal/monetary policies. The country is not self-sufficient in food, and some of the rural population subsist at the poverty level. Malaysia's high export dependence leaves it vulnerable to a recession in the OECD countries or a fall in world commodity prices.

GDP:

exchange rate conversion - $48.0 billion, per capita $2,670; real growth rate 8.6% (1991 est.)

Inflation rate (consumer prices):

4.5% (1991 est.)

Unemployment rate: 5.8% (1991 est.)

Budget:

revenues $12.2 billion; expenditures $14.4 billion, including capital

expenditures of $3.2 billion (1991 est.)

Exports:

$35.4 billion (f.o.b., 1991)

commodities:

electrical manufactures, crude petroleum, timber, rubber, palm oil, textiles

partners:

Singapore, US, Japan, EC

Imports:

$38.7 billion (c.i.f., 1991)

commodities:

food, crude oil, consumer goods, intermediate goods, capital equipment, chemicals

partners:

Japan, US, Singapore, Germany, UK

External debt: $21.3 billion (1991 est.)

Industrial production:

growth rate 18% (1990); accounts for 40% of GDP

Electricity:

5,600,000 kW capacity; 16,500 million kWh produced, 940 kWh per capita (1990)

Industries:

Peninsular Malaysia:

rubber and oil palm processing and manufacturing, light manufacturing industry, electronics, tin mining and smelting, logging and processing timber

Sabah:

logging, petroleum production

Sarawak:

agriculture processing, petroleum production and refining, logging

Agriculture:

Peninsular Malaysia:

natural rubber, palm oil, rice

Sabah:

mainly subsistence, but also rubber, timber, coconut, rice

:Malaysia Economy

Sarawak:

rubber, timber, pepper; there is a deficit of rice in all areas; fish catch of 608,000 metric tons in 1987

Illicit drugs:

transit point for Golden Triangle heroin going to the US, Western Europe, and the Third World

Economic aid:

US commitments, including Ex-Im (FY70-84), $170 million; Western (non-US) countries, ODA and OOF bilateral commitments (1970-89), $4.7 million; OPEC bilateral aid (1979-89), $42 million

Currency:

ringgit (plural - ringgits); 1 ringgit (M$) = 100 sen

Exchange rates:

ringgits (M$) per US$1 - 2.6930 (January 1992), 2.7501 (1991), 1.7048

(1990), 2.7088 (1989), 2.6188 (1988), 2.5196 (1987)

Fiscal year: calendar year

:Malaysia Communications

Railroads:
 Peninsular Malaysia:
 1,665 km 1.04-meter gauge; 13 km double track, government owned
Railroads:
 Sabah:
 136 km 1.000-meter gauge
Highways:
 Peninsular Malaysia:
 23,600 km (19,352 km hard surfaced, mostly bituminous-surface treatment, and
 4,248 km unpaved)
 Sabah:
 3,782 km
 Sarawak:
 1,644 km
Inland waterways:
 Peninsular Malaysia:
 3,209 km
 Sabah:
 1,569 km
 Sarawak:
 2,518 km
Pipelines:
 crude oil 1,307 km; natural gas 379 km
Ports:
 Tanjong Kidurong, Kota Kinabalu, Kuching, Pasir Gudang, Penang, Port Kelang,
 Sandakan, Tawau
Merchant marine:
 167 ships (1,000 GRT or over) totaling 1,653,633 GRT/2,444,393 DWT; includes
 1 passenger-cargo, 1 short-sea passenger, 64 cargo, 27 container, 2 vehicle
 carrier, 2 roll-on/roll-off, 1 livestock carrier, 37 petroleum tanker, 5
 chemical tanker, 6 liquefied gas, 21 bulk
Civil air:
 53 major transport aircraft
Airports:
 115 total, 108 usable; 33 with permanent-surface runways; 1 with runways
 over 3,659 m; 7 with runways 2,440-3,659 m; 18 with runways 1,220-2,439 m
Telecommunications:
 good intercity service provided to Peninsular Malaysia mainly by radio
 relay; adequate intercity radio relay network between Sabah and Sarawak via
 Brunei; international service good; good coverage by radio and television
 broadcasts; 994,860 telephones (1984); broadcast stations - 28 AM, 3 FM, 33
 TV; submarine cables extend to India and Sarawak; SEACOM submarine cable
 links to Hong Kong and Singapore; satellite earth stations - 1 Indian Ocean
 INTELSAT and 1 Pacific Ocean INTELSAT, and 2 domestic

:Malaysia Defense Forces

Branches:
  Royal Malaysian Army, Royal Malaysian Navy, Royal Malaysian Air Force, Royal
  Malaysian Police Force, Marine Police, Sarawak Border Scouts
Manpower availability:
  males 15-49, 4,728,103; 2,878,574 fit for military service; 179,486 reach
  military age (21) annually
Defense expenditures:
  exchange rate conversion - $2.4 billion, about 5% of GDP (1992 budget)

Maldives Geography

Total area: 300 km2
Land area: 300 km2
Comparative area: slightly more than 1.5 times the size of Washington, DC
Land boundaries:
  none
Coastline:
  644 km
Maritime claims:
 Exclusive economic zone:
  35-310 nm (defined by geographic coordinates; segment of zone coincides with
  maritime boundary with India)
 Territorial sea:
  12 nm
Disputes:
  none
Climate:
  tropical; hot, humid; dry, northeast monsoon (November to March); rainy,
  southwest monsoon (June to August)
Terrain:
  flat with elevations only as high as 2.5 meters
Natural resources:
  fish
Land use:
  arable land 10%; permanent crops 0%; meadows and pastures 3%; forest and
  woodland 3%; other 84%
Environment:
  1,200 coral islands grouped into 19 atolls
Note:
  archipelago of strategic location astride and along major sea lanes in
  Indian Ocean

:Maldives People

Population: 234,371 (July 1992), growth rate 3.7% (1992)
Birth rate: 45 births/1,000 population (1992)
Death rate: 8 deaths/1,000 population (1992)
Net migration rate: 0 migrants/1,000 population (1992)
Infant mortality rate: 61 deaths/1,000 live births (1992)
Life expectancy at birth: 62 years male, 64 years female (1992)
Total fertility rate: 6.5 children born/woman (1992)
Nationality:
  noun - Maldivian(s); adjective - Maldivian
599

Ethnic divisions:
  Maldivians are a generally homogenous admixture of Sinhalese, Dravidian, Arab, Austrolasian, and African
Religions:
  Sunni Muslim
Languages:
  Divehi (dialect of Sinhala; script derived from Arabic); English spoken by most government officials
Literacy:
  92% (male 92%, female 92%) age 15 and over can read and write (1985)
Labor force:
  66,000 (est.); 25% engaged in fishing industry
Organized labor:
  none

:Maldives Government

Long-form name:
  Republic of Maldives
Type:
  republic
Capital: Male
Administrative divisions:
  19 district (atolls); Aliff, Baa, Daalu, Faafu, Gaafu Aliff, Gaafu Daalu, Haa Aliff, Haa Daalu, Kaafu, Laamu, Laviyani, Meemu, Naviyani, Noonu, Raa, Seenu, Shaviyani, Thaa, Waavu
Independence:
  26 July 1965 (from UK)
Constitution:
  4 June 1964
Legal system:
  based on Islamic law with admixtures of English common law primarily in commercial matters; has not accepted compulsory ICJ jurisdiction
National holiday:
  Independence Day, 26 July (1965)
Executive branch:
  president, Cabinet
Legislative branch:
  unicameral Citizens' Council (Majlis)
Judicial branch:
  High Court
Leaders:
  Chief of State and Head of Government:
  President Maumoon Abdul GAYOOM (since 11 November 1978)
Political parties and leaders:
  no organized political parties; country governed by the Didi clan for the past eight centuries
Suffrage:
  universal at age 21
Elections:
  President:

last held 23 September 1988 (next to be held September 1994); results -
President Maumoon Abdul GAYOOM reelected
Citizens' Council:
last held on 7 December 1989 (next to be held 7 December 1994); results -
percent of vote NA; seats - (48 total, 40 elected)
Member of:
AsDB, C, CP, ESCAP, FAO, G-77, GATT, IBRD, ICAO, IDA, IDB, IFAD, IFC,
IMF,
IMO, INTERPOL, IOC, ITU, NAM, OIC, SAARC, UN, UNCTAD, UNESCO,
UNIDO, UPU,
WHO, WMO, WTO
Diplomatic representation:
Maldives does not maintain an embassy in the US, but does have a UN mission
in New York
US:
the US Ambassador to Sri Lanka is accredited to Maldives and makes periodic
visits there; US Consular Agency, Midhath Hilmy, Male; telephone 2581
Flag:
red with a large green rectangle in the center bearing a vertical white
crescent; the closed side of the crescent is on the hoist side of the flag

:Maldives Economy

Overview:
The economy is based on fishing, tourism, and shipping. Agriculture is
limited to the production of a few subsistence crops that provide only 10%
of food requirements. Fishing is the largest industry, employing 25% of the
work force and accounting for over 60% of exports; it is also an important
source of government revenue. During the 1980s tourism has become one of the
most important and highest growth sectors of the economy. In 1988 industry
accounted for about 5% of GDP. Real GDP is officially estimated to have
increased by about 10% annually during the period 1974-90.
GDP:
exchange rate conversion - $174 million, per capita $770 (1988); real growth
rate 10.1% (1990 est.)
Inflation rate (consumer prices):
10.7% (1990 est.)
Unemployment rate: NEGL%
Budget:
revenues $67 million; expenditures $82 million, including capital
expenditures of $45 million (1990 est.)
Exports:
$52.0 million (f.o.b., 1990)
commodities:
fish 57%, clothing 25%
partners:
US, UK, Sri Lanka
Imports:
$128.9 million (c.i.f., 1990)
commodities:
consumer goods 54%, intermediate and capital goods 33%, petroleum products

13%
  partners:
   Singapore, Germany, Sri Lanka, India
External debt: $70 million (December 1989)
Industrial production:
   growth rate -5.0% (1988); accounts for 6% of GDP
Electricity:
   5,000 kW capacity; 11 million kWh produced, 50 kWh per capita (1990)
Industries:
   fishing and fish processing, tourism, shipping, boat building, some coconut
   processing, garments, woven mats, coir (rope), handicrafts
Agriculture:
   accounts for almost 30% of GDP (including fishing); fishing more important
   than farming; limited production of coconuts, corn, sweet potatoes; most
   staple foods must be imported; fish catch of 67,000 tons (1990 est.)
Economic aid:
   US commitments, including Ex-Im (FY70-88), $28 million; Western (non-US)
   countries, ODA and OOF bilateral commitments (1970-89), $125 million; OPEC
   bilateral aid (1979-89), $14 million
Currency:
   rufiyaa (plural - rufiyaa); 1 rufiyaa (Rf) = 100 laaris
Exchange rates:
   rufiyaa (Rf) per US$1 - 10.234 (January 1992), 10.253 (1991), 9.509 (1990),
   9.0408 (1989), 8.7846 (1988), 9.2230 (1987)
Fiscal year: calendar year

:Maldives Communications

Highways:
   Male has 9.6 km of coral highways within the city
Ports:
   Male, Gan
Merchant marine:
   13 ships (1,000 GRT or over) totaling 37,293 GRT/56,246 DWT; includes 11
   cargo, 1 container, 1 petroleum tanker
Civil air:
   1 major transport aircraft
Airports:
   2 with permanent-surface runways 2,440-3,659 m
Telecommunications:
   minimal domestic and international facilities; 2,804 telephones; broadcast
   stations - 2 AM, 1 FM, 1 TV; 1 Indian Ocean INTELSAT earth station

:Maldives Defense Forces

Branches:
   National Security Service (paramilitary police force)
Manpower availability:
   males 15-49, 52,195; 29,162 fit for military service
Defense expenditures:
   exchange rate conversion - $1.8 million, NA% of GDP (1984 est.)

   Mali Geography

Total area: 1,240,000 km2
Land area: 1,220,000 km2
Comparative area: slightly less than twice the size of Texas
Land boundaries:
  7,243 km; Algeria 1,376 km, Burkina 1,000 km, Guinea 858 km, Ivory Coast 532
  km, Mauritania 2,237 km, Niger 821 km, Senegal 419 km
Coastline:
  none - landlocked
Maritime claims:
  none - landlocked
Disputes:
  the disputed international boundary between Burkina and Mali was submitted
  to the International Court of Justice (ICJ) in October 1983 and the ICJ
  issued its final ruling in December 1986, which both sides agreed to accept;
  Burkina and Mali are proceeding with boundary demarcation, including the
  tripoint with Niger
Climate:
  subtropical to arid; hot and dry February to June; rainy, humid, and mild
  June to November; cool and dry November to February
Terrain:
  mostly flat to rolling northern plains covered by sand; savanna in south,
  rugged hills in northeast
Natural resources:
  gold, phosphates, kaolin, salt, limestone, uranium; bauxite, iron ore,
  manganese, tin, and copper deposits are known but not exploited
Land use:
  arable land 2%; permanent crops NEGL%; meadows and pastures 25%; forest and
  woodland 7%; other 66%; includes irrigated NEGL%
Environment:
  hot, dust-laden harmattan; haze common during dry seasons; desertification
Note:
  landlocked

:Mali People

Population: 8,641,178 (July 1992), growth rate 2.5% (1992)
Birth rate: 52 births/1,000 population (1992)
Death rate: 21 deaths/1,000 population (1992)
Net migration rate: -5 migrants/1,000 population (1992)
Infant mortality rate: 110 deaths/1,000 live births (1992)
Life expectancy at birth: 43 years male, 47 years female (1992)
Total fertility rate: 7.3 children born/woman (1992)
Nationality:
  noun - Malian(s); adjective - Malian
Ethnic divisions:
  Mando (Bambara, Malinke, Sarakole) 50%, Peul 17%, Voltaic 12%, Songhai 6%,
  Tuareg and Moor 5%, other 10%
Religions:
  Muslim 90%, indigenous beliefs 9%, Christian 1%
Languages:
  French (official); Bambara spoken by about 80% of the population; numerous

African languages
Literacy:
  32% (male 41%, female 24%) age 15 and over can read and write (1990 est.)
Labor force:
  2,666,000 (1986 est.); agriculture 80%, services 19%, industry and commerce
  1% (1981); 50% of population of working age (1985)
Organized labor:
  National Union of Malian Workers (UNTM) is umbrella organization for over 13
  national unions

:Mali Government

Long-form name:
  Republic of Mali
Type:
  republic; an interim government appointed by the national reform conference
  has organized a series of democratic elections and is scheduled to hand over
  power to an elected government on 26 March 1992
Capital: Bamako
Administrative divisions:
  8 regions (regions, singular - region); Gao, Kayes, Kidal, Koulikoro, Mopti,
  Segou, Sikasso, Tombouctou
Independence:
  22 September 1960 (from France; formerly French Sudan)
Constitution:
  2 June 1974, effective 19 June 1979; amended September 1981 and March 1985;
  new constitution presented during national reform conference in August 1991;
  a constitutional referendum is scheduled for 16 January 1992
Legal system:
  based on French civil law system and customary law; judicial review of
  legislative acts in Constitutional Section of Court of State; has not
  accepted compulsory ICJ jurisdiction
National holiday:
  Anniversary of the Proclamation of the Republic, 22 September (1960)
Executive branch:
  Transition Committee for the Salvation of the People (CTSP) composed of 25
  members, predominantly civilian
Legislative branch:
  Transition Committee for the Salvation of the People (CTSP)
Judicial branch:
  Supreme Court (Cour Supreme)
Leaders:
  Chief of State:
  Lt. Col. Amadou Toumani TOURE
  Head of Government:
  Prime Minister Soumana SAKO (since 2 April 1991)
Political parties and leaders:
  formerly the only party, the Democratic Union of Malian People (UDPM), was
  disbanded after the coup of 26 March 1991, and the new regime legalized the
  formation of political parties on 5 April 1991; new political parties are
  Union of Democratic Forces (UFD), Demba DIALLO; Union for Democracy and

Development (UDD), Moussa Bala COULIBALY; Sudanese Union/African Democratic
Rally (US-RDA), Mamadou Madeira KEITA; African Party for Solidarity and
Justice (ADEMA), Alpha Oumar KONARE; Party for Democracy and Progress (PDP),
Idrissa TRAORE; Democratic Party for Justice (PDJ), Abdul BA; Rally for
Democracy and Progress (RDP), Almany SYLLA; Party for the Unity of Malian
People (PUPM), Nock AGATTIA; Hisboulah al Islamiya, Hamidou DRAMERA; Union
of Progressive Forces (UFP), Yacouba SIDIBE; National Congress of Democratic
Initiative (CNID), Mountaga TALL; Assembly for Justice and Progress, Kady
DRAME; Sudanese Progressive Party (PPS), Sekene Mody SISSOKO; numerous small
parties formed in 1991; 46 total parties

Suffrage:
universal at age 21

Elections:
President:
last held on 9 June 1985 (next to be held March 1992); results - Gen. Moussa
TRAORE was reelected without opposition

:Mali Government

National Assembly:
last held on 26 June 1988 (next to be held NA 1992); results - UDPM was the
only party; seats - (82 total) UDPM 82; note - following the military coup
of 26 March 1991, President TRAORE was deposed and the UDPM was disbanded;
the 25-member CTSP has instituted a multiparty system, and presidential
elections are to be held on 26 March 1992 and legislative elections on 9
February 1992 (new National Assembly to have 116 seats)

Member of:
ACCT, ACP, AfDB, CCC, CEAO, ECA, ECOWAS, FAO, FZ, G-77, IAEA, IBRD, ICAO,
IDA, IDB, IFAD, IFC, ILO, IMF, INTELSAT, INTERPOL, IOC, ITU, LORCS, NAM,
OAU, OIC, UN, UNCTAD, UNESCO, UNIDO, UPU, WADB, WCL, WHO, WIPO, WMO, WTO

Diplomatic representation:
Ambassador Mohamed Alhousseyni TOURE; Chancery at 2130 R Street NW,
Washington, DC 20008; telephone (202) 332-2249 or 939-8950
US:
Ambassador Herbert D. GELBER; Embassy at Rue Rochester NY and Rue Mohamed
V., Bamako (mailing address is B. P. 34, Bamako); telephone [223] 225470;
FAX [233] 22-80-59

Flag:
three equal vertical bands of green (hoist side), yellow, and red; uses the
popular pan-African colors of Ethiopia

:Mali Economy

Overview:
Mali is among the poorest countries in the world, with about 70% of its land

area desert or semidesert. Economic activity is largely confined to the riverine area irrigated by the Niger. About 10% of the population live as nomads and some 80% of the labor force is engaged in agriculture and fishing. Industrial activity is concentrated on processing farm commodities.

GDP:
exchange rate conversion - $2.2 billion, per capita $265; real growth rate 2.2% (1990 est.)

Inflation rate (consumer prices):
-1.6% (1990)

Unemployment rate: NA%

Budget:
revenues $329 million; expenditures $519 million, including capital expenditures of $178 (1989 est.)

Exports:
$285 million (f.o.b., 1989 est.)
commodities:
livestock, peanuts, dried fish, cotton, skins
partners:
mostly franc zone and Western Europe

Imports:
$513 million (f.o.b., 1989 est.)
commodities:
textiles, vehicles, petroleum products, machinery, sugar, cereals
partners:
mostly franc zone and Western Europe

External debt: $2.2 billion (1989 est.)

Industrial production:
growth rate 19.9% (1989 est.); accounts for 7% of GDP

Electricity:
260,000 kW capacity; 750 million kWh produced, 90 kWh per capita (1991)

Industries:
small local consumer goods and processing, construction, phosphate, gold, fishing

Agriculture:
accounts for 50% of GDP; most production based on small subsistence farms; cotton and livestock products account for over 70% of exports; other crops - millet, rice, corn, vegetables, peanuts; livestock - cattle, sheep, and goats

Economic aid:
US commitments, including Ex-Im (FY70-89), $349 million; Western (non-US) countries, ODA and OOF bilateral commitments (1970-89), $3,020 million; OPEC bilateral aid (1979-89), $92 million; Communist countries (1970-89), $190 million

Currency:
Communaute Financiere Africaine franc (plural - francs); 1 CFA franc (CFAF) = 100 centimes

Exchange rates:
Communaute Financiere Africaine francs (CFAF) per US$1 - 269.01 (January 1992), 282.11 (1991), 272.26 (1990), 319.01 (1989), 297.85 (1988), 300.54

(1987)

Fiscal year: calendar year

:Mali Communications

Railroads:
  642 km 1.000-meter gauge; linked to Senegal's rail system through Kayes
Highways:
  about 15,700 km total; 1,670 km paved, 3,670 km gravel and improved earth,
  10,360 km unimproved earth
Inland waterways:
  1,815 km navigable
Civil air:
  no major transport aircraft
Airports:
  35 total, 27 usable; 8 with permanent-surface runways; none with runways
  over 3,659 m; 5 with runways 2,440-3,659 m; 10 with runways 1,220-2,439 m
Telecommunications:
  domestic system poor but improving; provides only minimal service with radio
  relay, wire, and radio communications stations; expansion of radio relay in
  progress; 11,000 telephones; broadcast stations - 2 AM, 2 FM, 2 TV;
  satellite earth stations - 1 Atlantic Ocean INTELSAT and 1 Indian Ocean
  INTELSAT

:Mali Defense Forces

Branches:
  Army, Air Force, Gendarmerie, Republican Guard, National Guard, National
  Police, Surete Nationale
Manpower availability:
  males 15-49, 1,701,050; 966,293 fit for military service; no conscription
Defense expenditures:
  exchange rate conversion - $41 million, 2% of GDP (1989)

Malta Geography

Total area: 320 km2
Land area: 320 km2
Comparative area: slightly less than twice the size of Washington, DC
Land boundaries:
  none
Coastline:
  140 km
Maritime claims:
  Contiguous zone:
  24 nm
  Continental shelf:
  200 m (depth) or to depth of exploitation
  Exclusive fishing zone:
  25 nm
  Territorial sea:
  12 nm
Disputes:
  none

607

Climate:
  Mediterranean with mild, rainy winters and hot, dry summers
Terrain:
  mostly low, rocky, flat to dissected plains; many coastal cliffs
Natural resources:
  limestone, salt
Land use:
  arable land 38%; permanent crops 3%; meadows and pastures 0%; forest and
  woodland 0%; other 59%; includes irrigated 3%
Environment:
  numerous bays provide good harbors; fresh water very scarce - increasing
  reliance on desalination
Note:
  strategic location in central Mediterranean, 93 km south of Sicily, 290 km
  north of Libya

:Malta People

Population: 359,231 (July 1992), growth rate 0.8% (1992)
Birth rate: 14 births/1,000 population (1992)
Death rate: 8 deaths/1,000 population (1992)
Net migration rate: 1 migrant/1,000 population (1992)
Infant mortality rate: 7 deaths/1,000 live births (1992)
Life expectancy at birth: 74 years male, 79 years female (1992)
Total fertility rate: 2.0 children born/woman (1992)
Nationality:
  noun - Maltese (singular and plural); adjective - Maltese
Ethnic divisions:
  mixture of Arab, Sicilian, Norman, Spanish, Italian, English
Religions:
  Roman Catholic 98%
Languages:
  Maltese and English (official)
Literacy:
  84% (male 86%, female 82%) age 15 and over can read and write (1985)
Labor force:
  127,200; government (excluding job corps) 37%, services 26%, manufacturing
  22%, training programs 9%, construction 4%, agriculture 2% (1990)
Organized labor:
  about 40% of labor force

:Malta Government

Long-form name:
  Republic of Malta
Type:
  parliamentary democracy
Capital: Valletta
Administrative divisions:
  none (administration directly from Valletta)
Independence:
  21 September 1964 (from UK)
Constitution:

26 April 1974, effective 2 June 1974

Legal system:
  based on English common law and Roman civil law; has accepted compulsory ICJ
  jurisdiction, with reservations

National holiday:
  Independence Day, 21 September

Executive branch:
  president, prime minister, deputy prime minister, Cabinet

Legislative branch:
  unicameral House of Representatives

Judicial branch:
  Constitutional Court and Court of Appeal

Leaders:
  Chief of State:
  President Vincent (Censu) TABONE (since 4 April 1989)
  Head of Government:
  Prime Minister Dr. Edward (Eddie) FENECH ADAMI (since 12 May 1987); Deputy
  Prime Minister Dr. Guido DE MARCO (since 14 May 1987)

Political parties and leaders:
  Nationalist Party (NP), Edward FENECH ADAMI; Malta Labor Party (MLP), Al-
fred
  SANT

Suffrage:
  universal at age 18

Elections:
  House of Representatives:
  last held on 22 February 1992 (next to be held by February 1997); results -
  NP 51.8%, MLP 46.5%; seats - (usually 65 total) MLP 36, NP 29; note -
  additional seats are given to the party with the largest popular vote to
  ensure a legislative majority; current total 69 (MLP 33, NP 36 after
  adjustment)

Member of:
  C, CCC, CE, CSCE, EBRD, ECE, FAO, G-77, GATT, IBRD, ICAO, ICFTU, IFAD,
ILO,
  IMF, IMO, INTERPOL, IOC, ITU, NAM, PCA, UN, UNCTAD, UNESCO,
UNIDO, UPU, WCL,
  WHO, WIPO, WMO, WTO

Diplomatic representation:
  Ambassador Albert BORG OLIVIER DE PUGET; Chancery at 2017 Connecticut
Avenue
  NW, Washington, DC 20008; telephone (202) 462-3611 or 3612; there is a
  Maltese Consulate General in New York
  US:
  Ambassador Sally J. NOVETZKE; Embassy at 2nd Floor, Development House,
Saint
  Anne Street, Floriana, Valletta (mailing address is P. O. Box 535,
  Valletta); telephone [356] 240424, 240425, 243216, 243217, 243653, 223654;
  FAX same as phone numbers

Flag:

609

two equal vertical bands of white (hoist side) and red; in the upper
hoist-side corner is a representation of the George Cross, edged in red

:Malta Economy

Overview:

Significant resources are limestone, a favorable geographic location, and a
productive labor force. Malta produces only about 20% of its food needs, has
limited freshwater supplies, and has no domestic energy sources.
Consequently, the economy is highly dependent on foreign trade and services.
Manufacturing and tourism are the largest contributors to the economy.
Manufacturing accounts for about 27% of GDP, with the electronics and
textile industries major contributors. In 1990 inflation was held to a low
3.0%. Per capita GDP at $7,000 places Malta in the middle-income range of
the world's nations.

GDP:

exchange rate conversion - $2.5 billion, per capita $7,000 (1991 est.); real
growth rate 5.5% (1990)

Inflation rate (consumer prices):

3.0% (1990)

Unemployment rate: 3.8% (1990)

Budget:

revenues $1.3 billion; expenditures $1.3 billion, including capital
expenditures of $380 million (1992 plan)

Exports:

$1.1 billion (f.o.b., 1990)

commodities:

clothing, textiles, footwear, ships

partners:

Italy 30%, Germany 22%, UK 11%

Imports:

$2.0 billion (f.o.b., 1990)

commodities:

food, petroleum, machinery and semimanufactured goods

partners:

Italy 30%, UK 16%, Germany 13%, US 4%

External debt: $90 million, medium and long term (December 1987)

Industrial production:

growth rate 19.0% (1990); accounts for 27% of GDP

Electricity:

328,000 kW capacity; 1,110 million kWh produced, 2,990 kWh per capita (1991)

Industries:

tourism, electronics, ship repair yard, construction, food manufacturing,
textiles, footwear, clothing, beverages, tobacco

Agriculture:

accounts for 3% of GDP; overall, 20% self-sufficient; main products -
potatoes, cauliflower, grapes, wheat, barley, tomatoes, citrus, cut flowers,
green peppers, hogs, poultry, eggs; generally adequate supplies of
vegetables, poultry, milk, pork products; seasonal or periodic shortages in
grain, animal fodder, fruits, other basic foodstuffs

Economic aid:

US commitments, including Ex-Im (FY70-81), $172 million; Western (non-US) countries, ODA and OOF bilateral commitments (1970-89), $336 million; OPEC bilateral aid (1979-89), $76 million; Communist countries (1970-88), $48 million

Currency:

Maltese lira (plural - liri); 1 Maltese lira (LM) = 100 cents

Exchange rates:

Maltese liri (LM) per US$1 - 0.3257 (March 1992), 0.3004 (1991), 0.3172 (1990), 0.3483 (1989), 0.3306 (1988), 0.3451 (1987)

Fiscal year: 1 April - 31 March

:Malta Communications

Highways:

1,291 km total; 1,179 km paved (asphalt), 77 km crushed stone or gravel, 35 km improved and unimproved earth

Ports:

Valletta, Marsaxlokk

Merchant marine:

658 ships (1,000 GRT or over) totaling 9,003,001 GRT/15,332,287 DWT; includes 3 passenger, 13 short-sea passenger, 241 cargo, 14 container, 2 passenger-cargo, 16 roll-on/roll-off, 2 vehicle carrier, 1 barge carrier, 15 refrigerated cargo, 11 chemical tanker, 12 combination ore/oil, 2 specialized tanker, 3 liquefied gas, 124 petroleum tanker, 176 bulk, 23 combination bulk; note - a flag of convenience registry; China owns 2 ships, former republics of the USSR own 52 ships, Cuba owns 10, Vietnam owns 6, Yugoslavia owns 9, Romania owns 4

Civil air:

7 major transport aircraft

Airports:

1 with permanent-surface runways 2,440-3,659 m

Telecommunications:

automatic system satisfies normal requirements; 153,000 telephones; excellent service by broadcast stations - 8 AM, 4 FM, and 2 TV; submarine cable and radio relay between islands; international service by 1 submarine cable; 1 Atlantic Ocean INTELSAT earth station

:Malta Defense Forces

Branches:

Armed Forces, Maltese Police Force

Manpower availability:

males 15-49, 95,661; 76,267 fit for military service

Defense expenditures:

exchange rate conversion - $21.9 million, 1.3% of GDP (1989 est.)

Man, Isle of Geography

Total area: 588 km2

Land area: 588 km2

Comparative area: slightly less than 3.5 times the size of Washington, DC

Land boundaries:

Coastline:

113 km
Maritime claims:
  Exclusive fishing zone:
  200 nm
  Territorial sea:
  3 nm
Disputes:
  none
Climate:
  cool summers and mild winters; humid; overcast about half the time
Terrain:
  hills in north and south bisected by central valley
Natural resources:
  lead, iron ore
Land use:
  arable land NA%; permanent crops NA%; meadows and pastures NA%; forest and
  woodland NA%; other NA%; extensive arable land and forests
Environment:
  strong westerly winds prevail
Note:
  located in Irish Sea equidistant from England, Scotland, and Ireland

:Man, Isle of People

Population: 64,068 (July 1992), growth rate 0.1% (1992)
Birth rate: 11 births/1,000 population (1992)
Death rate: 14 deaths/1,000 population (1992)
Net migration rate: 4 migrants/1,000 population (1992)
Infant mortality rate: 9 deaths/1,000 live births (1992)
Life expectancy at birth: 72 years male, 78 years female (1992)
Total fertility rate: 1.8 children born/woman (1992)
Nationality:
  noun - Manxman, Manxwoman; adjective - Manx
Ethnic divisions:
  native Manx of Norse-Celtic descent; British
Religions:
  Anglican, Roman Catholic, Methodist, Baptist, Presbyterian, Society of
  Friends
Languages:
  English, Manx Gaelic
Literacy:
  NA% (male NA%, female NA%) but compulsory education ages 5 to 16
Labor force:
  25,864 (1981)
Organized labor:
  22 labor unions patterned along British lines

:Man, Isle of Government

Long-form name:
  none
Type:
  British crown dependency

Capital: Douglas
Administrative divisions:
  none (British crown dependency)
Independence:
  none (British crown dependency)
Constitution:
  1961, Isle of Man Constitution Act
Legal system:
  English law and local statute
National holiday:
  Tynwald Day, 5 July
Executive branch:
  British monarch, lieutenant governor, prime minister, Executive Council
  (cabinet)
Legislative branch:
  bicameral Tynwald consists of an upper house or Legislative Council and a
  lower house or House of Keys
Judicial branch:
  High Court of Justice
Leaders:
  Chief of State:
    Lord of Mann Queen ELIZABETH II (since 6 February 1952), represented by
    Lieutenant Governor Air Marshal Sir Laurence JONES (since NA 1990)
  Head of Government:
    President of the Legislative Council Sir Charles KERRUISH (since NA 1990)
Political parties and leaders:
  there is no party system and members sit as independents
Suffrage:
  universal at age 21
Elections:
  House of Keys:
    last held in 1991 (next to be held NA 1996); results - percent of vote NA;
    no party system; seats - (24 total) independents 24
Member of:
  none
Diplomatic representation:
  none (British crown dependency)
Flag:
  red with the Three Legs of Man emblem (Trinacria), in the center; the three
  legs are joined at the thigh and bent at the knee; in order to have the toes
  pointing clockwise on both sides of the flag, a two-sided emblem is used
  ria), in the center; the three legs are joined at the thigh and bent at the
  knee; in order to have the toes pointing clockwise on both sides of the
  flag, a two-sided emblem is used

:Man, Isle of Economy

Overview:
  Offshore banking, manufacturing, and tourism are key sectors of the economy.
  The government's policy of offering incentives to high-technology companies
  and financial institutions to locate on the island has paid off in expanding

employment opportunities in high-income industries. As a result, agriculture and fishing, once the mainstays of the economy, have declined in their shares of GNP. Banking now contributes over 20% to GNP and manufacturing about 15%. Trade is mostly with the UK.

GNP:
exchange rate conversion - $490 million, per capita $7,573; real growth rate NA% (1988)

Inflation rate (consumer prices):
NA%

Unemployment rate: 1.5% (1988)

Budget:
revenues $130.4 million; expenditures $114.4 million, including capital expenditures of $18.1 million (FY85 est.)

Exports:
$NA
commodities:
tweeds, herring, processed shellfish, meat
partners:
UK

Imports:
$NA
commodities:
timber, fertilizers, fish
partners:
UK

External debt: $NA

Industrial production:
growth rate NA%

Electricity:
61,000 kW capacity; 190 million kWh produced, 2,930 kWh per capita (1989)

Industries:
an important offshore financial center; financial services, light manufacturing, tourism

Agriculture:
cereals and vegetables; cattle, sheep, pigs, poultry

Economic aid:
NA

Currency:
Manx pound (plural - pounds); 1 Manx pound (#M) = 100 pence

Exchange rates:
Manx pounds (#M) per US$1 - 0.5799 (March 1992), 0.5652 (1991), 0.5603 (1990), 0.6099 (1989), 0.5614 (1988), 0. 6102 (1987); the Manx pound is at par with the British pound

Fiscal year: 1 April - 31 March

:Man, Isle of Communications

Railroads:
36 km electric track, 24 km steam track

Highways:
640 km motorable roads

Ports:

Douglas, Ramsey, Peel

Merchant marine:

79 ships (1,000 GRT or over) totaling 1,436,196 GRT/2,479,432 DWT; includes 12 cargo, 7 container, 10 roll-on/roll-off, 30 petroleum tanker, 4 chemical tanker, 5 liquefied gas, 11 bulk; note - a captive register of the United Kingdom, although not all ships on the register are British owned

Airports:

1 total; 1 usable with permanent-surface runway 1,220-2,439 m

Telecommunications:

24,435 telephones; broadcast stations - 1 AM, 4 FM, 4 TV

:Man, Isle of Defense Forces

Note: defense is the responsibility of the UK

Marshall Islands Geography

Total area: 181.3 km2

Land area: 181.3 km2; includes the atolls of Bikini, Eniwetok, and Kwajalein

Comparative area: slightly larger than Washington, DC

Land boundaries:

Coastline:

370.4 km

Maritime claims:

Contiguous zone:

24 nm

Exclusive economic zone:

200 nm

Territorial sea:

12 nm

Disputes:

claims US territory of Wake Island

Climate:

wet season May to November; hot and humid; islands border typhoon belt

Terrain:

low coral limestone and sand islands

Natural resources:

phosphate deposits, marine products, deep seabed minerals

Land use:

arable land 0%; permanent crops 60%; meadows and pastures 0%; forest and woodland 0%; other 40%

Environment:

occasionally subject to typhoons; two archipelagic island chains of 30 atolls and 1,152 islands

Note:

located 3,825 km southwest of Honolulu in the North Pacific Ocean, about two-thirds of the way between Hawaii and Papua New Guinea; Bikini and Eniwetok are former US nuclear test sites; Kwajalein, the famous World War II battleground, is now used as a US missile test range

:Marshall Islands People

Population: 50,004 (July 1992), growth rate 3.9% (1992)
Birth rate: 47 births/1,000 population (1992)
Death rate: 8 deaths/1,000 population (1992)
Net migration rate: 0 migrants/1,000 population (1992)
Infant mortality rate: 52 deaths/1,000 live births (1992)
Life expectancy at birth: 61 years male, 64 years female (1992)
Total fertility rate: 7.0 children born/woman (1992)
Nationality:
   noun - Marshallese (singular and plural); adjective - Marshallese
Ethnic divisions:
   almost entirely Micronesian
Religions:
   predominantly Christian, mostly Protestant
Languages:
   English universally spoken and is the official language; two major
   Marshallese dialects from Malayo-Polynesian family; Japanese
Literacy:
   93% (male 100%, female 88%) age 15 and over can read and write (1980)
Labor force:
   4,800 (1986)
Organized labor:
   none

:Marshall Islands Government

Long-form name:
   Republic of the Marshall Islands
Type:
   constitutional government in free association with the US; the Compact of
   Free Association entered into force 21 October 1986
Capital: Majuro
Administrative divisions:
   none
Independence:
   21 October 1986 (from the US-administered UN trusteeship; formerly the
   Marshall Islands District of the Trust Territory of the Pacific Islands)
Constitution:
   1 May 1979
Legal system:
   based on adapted Trust Territory laws, acts of the legislature, municipal,
   common, and customary laws
National holiday:
   Proclamation of the Republic of the Marshall Islands, 1 May (1979)
Executive branch:
   president, Cabinet
Legislative branch:
   unicameral Nitijela (parliament)
Judicial branch:
   Supreme Court
Leaders:
   Chief of State and Head of Government:

President Amata KABUA (since 1979)

Political parties and leaders:

no formal parties; President KABUA is chief political (and traditional)
leader

Suffrage:

universal at age 18

Elections:

President:

last held 6 January 1992 (next to be held NA; results - President Amata
KABUA was reelected

Parliament:

last held 18 November 1991 (next to be held November 1995); results -
percent of vote NA; seats - (33 total)

Member of:

AsDB, ESCAP (associate), ICAO, SPC, SPF, UN, UNCTAD

Diplomatic representation:

Ambassador Wilfred I. KENDALL; Chancery at 2433 Massachusetts Avenue, NW,
Washington, DC 20008; telephone (202) 234-5414

US:

Ambassador William BODDE, Jr.; Embassy at NA address (mailing address is P.
O. Box 1379, Majuro, Republic of the Marshall Islands 96960-1379); telephone
(011) 692-4011; FAX (011) 692-4012

Flag:

blue with two stripes radiating from the lower hoist-side corner - orange
(top) and white; there is a white star with four large rays and 20 small
rays on the hoist side above the two stripes

:Marshall Islands Economy

Overview:

Agriculture and tourism are the mainstays of the economy. Agricultural
production is concentrated on small farms, and the most important commercial
crops are coconuts, tomatoes, melons, and breadfruit. A few cattle ranches
supply the domestic meat market. Small-scale industry is limited to
handicrafts, fish processing, and copra. The tourist industry is the primary
source of foreign exchange and employs about 10% of the labor force. The
islands have few natural resources, and imports far exceed exports. In 1987
the US Government provided grants of $40 million out of the Marshallese
budget of $55 million.

GDP:

exchange rate conversion - $63 million, per capita $1,500; real growth rate
NA% (1989 est.)

Inflation rate (consumer prices):

NA

Unemployment rate: NA%

Budget:

revenues $55 million; expenditures NA, including capital expenditures of NA
(1987 est.)

Exports:

$2.5 million (f.o.b., 1985)

commodities:

copra, copra oil, agricultural products, handicrafts
partners:
NA
Imports:
$29.2 million (c.i.f., 1985)
commodities:
foodstuffs, beverages, building materials
partners:
NA
External debt: $NA
Industrial production:
growth rate NA%
Electricity:
42,000 kW capacity; 80 million kWh produced, 1,840 kWh per capita (1990)
Industries:
copra, fish, tourism; craft items from shell, wood, and pearls; offshore
banking (embryonic)
Agriculture:
coconuts, cacao, taro, breadfruit, fruits, copra; pigs, chickens
Economic aid:
under the terms of the Compact of Free Association, the US is to provide
approximately $40 million in aid annually
Currency:
US currency is used
Exchange rates:
US currency is used
Fiscal year: 1 October - 30 September

:Marshall Islands Communications

Highways:
paved roads on major islands (Majuro, Kwajalein), otherwise stone-, coral-,
or laterite-surfaced roads and tracks
Ports:
Majuro
Merchant marine:
32 ships (1,000 GRT or over) totaling 2,347,312 GRT/4,630,172 DWT; includes
2 cargo, 1 container, 9 petroleum tanker, 18 bulk carrier, 2 combination
ore/oil; note - a flag of convenience registry
Airports:
17 total, 16 usable; 4 with permanent-surface runways; 8 with runways
1,220-2,439 m
Telecommunications:
telephone network - 570 lines (Majuro) and 186 (Ebeye); telex services;
islands interconnected by shortwave radio (used mostly for government
purposes); broadcast stations - 1 AM, 2 FM, 1 TV, 1 shortwave; 2 Pacific
Ocean INTELSAT earth stations; US Government satellite communications system
on Kwajalein

:Marshall Islands Defense Forces

Note: defense is the responsibility of the US

618

Martinique Geography

Total area: 1,100 km2
Land area: 1,060 km2
Comparative area: slightly more than six times the size of Washington, DC
Land boundaries:
  none
Coastline:
  290 km
Maritime claims:
 Exclusive economic zone:
  200 nm
 Territorial sea:
  12 nm
Disputes:
  none
Climate:
  tropical; moderated by trade winds; rainy season (June to October)
Terrain:
  mountainous with indented coastline; dormant volcano
Natural resources:
  coastal scenery and beaches, cultivable land
Land use:
  arable land 10%; permanent crops 8%; meadows and pastures 30%; forest and
  woodland 26%; other 26%; includes irrigated 5%
Environment:
  subject to hurricanes, flooding, and volcanic activity that result in an
  average of one major natural disaster every five years
Note:
  located 625 km southeast of Puerto Rico in the Caribbean Sea

:Martinique People

Population: 371,803 (July 1992), growth rate 1.4% (1992)
Birth rate: 19 births/1,000 population (1992)
Death rate: 6 deaths/1,000 population (1992)
Net migration rate: 1 migrant/1,000 population (1992)
Infant mortality rate: 11 deaths/1,000 live births (1992)
Life expectancy at birth: 75 years male, 81 years female (1992)
Total fertility rate: 1.9 children born/woman (1992)
Nationality:
  noun - Martiniquais (singular and plural); adjective - Martiniquais
Ethnic divisions:
  African and African-Caucasian-Indian mixture 90%, Caucasian 5%, East Indian,
  Lebanese, Chinese less than 5%
Religions.
  Roman Catholic 95%, Hindu and pagan African 5%
Languages:
  French, Creole patois
Literacy:
  93% (male 92%, female 93%) age 15 and over can read and write (1982)
Labor force:

100,000; service industry 31.7%, construction and public works 29.4%, agriculture 13.1%, industry 7.3%, fisheries 2.2%, other 16.3%

Organized labor:
  11% of labor force

:Martinique Government

Long-form name:
  Department of Martinique
Type:
  overseas department of France
Capital: Fort-de-France
Administrative divisions:
  none (overseas department of France)
Independence:
  none (overseas department of France)
Constitution:
  28 September 1958 (French Constitution)
Legal system:
  French legal system
National holiday:
  Taking of the Bastille, 14 July (1789)
Executive branch:
  government commissioner
Legislative branch:
  unicameral General Council
Judicial branch:
  Supreme Court
Leaders:
  Chief of State:
  President Francois MITTERRAND (since 21 May 1981)
  Head of Government:
  Government Commissioner Jean Claude ROURE (since 5 May 1989); President of the General Council Emile MAURICE (since NA 1988)
Suffrage:
  universal at age 18
Elections:
  General Council:
  last held in October 1988 (next to be held by March 1991); results - percent of vote by party NA; seats - (44 total) number of seats by party NA
  Regional Assembly:
  last held on 16 March 1986 (next to be held by March 1992); results - UDF/RPR coalition 49.8%, PPM/FSM/PCM coalition 41.3%, other 8.9%; seats - (41 total) PPM/FSM/PCM coalition 21, UDF/RPR coalition 20
  French Senate:
  last held 24 September 1989 (next to be held September 1992); results - percent of vote by party NA; seats - (2 total) UDF 1, PPM 1
  French National Assembly:
  last held on 5 and 12 June 1988 (next to be held June 1993); results - percent of vote by party NA; seats - (4 total) PPM 1, FSM 1, RPR 1, UDF 1
Communists:

1,000 (est.)

Other political or pressure groups:

Proletarian Action Group (GAP); Alhed Marie-Jeanne Socialist Revolution Group (GRS); Martinique Independence Movement (MIM); Caribbean Revolutionary Alliance (ARC); Central Union for Martinique Workers (CSTM), Marc Pulvar; Frantz Fanon Circle; League of Workers and Peasants

Member of:

FZ, WCL

Diplomatic representation:

as an overseas department of France, Martiniquais interests are represented in the US by France

:Martinique Government

US:

Consul General Raymond G. ROBINSON; Consulate General at 14 Rue Blenac, Fort-de-France (mailing address is B. P. 561, Fort-de-France 97206); telephone [596] 63-13-03

Flag:

the flag of France is used

:Martinique Economy

Overview:

The economy is based on sugarcane, bananas, tourism, and light industry. Agriculture accounts for about 12% of GDP and the small industrial sector for 10%. Sugar production has declined, with most of the sugarcane now used for the production of rum. Banana exports are increasing, going mostly to France. The bulk of meat, vegetable, and grain requirements must be imported, contributing to a chronic trade deficit that requires large annual transfers of aid from France. Tourism has become more important than agricultural exports as a source of foreign exchange. The majority of the work force is employed in the service sector and in administration. In 1986 per capita GDP was relatively high at $6,000. During 1986 the unemployment rate was 30% and was particularly severe among younger workers.

GDP:

exchange rate conversion - $2.0 billion, per capita $6,000; real growth rate NA% (1986)

Inflation rate (consumer prices):

2.9% (1989)

Unemployment rate: 30% (1986)

Budget:

revenues $268 million; expenditures $268 million, including capital expenditures of $NA (1989 est.)

Exports:

$196 million (f.o.b., 1988)

commodities:

refined petroleum products, bananas, rum, pineapples

partners:

France 65%, Guadeloupe 24%, Germany (1987)

Imports:

$1.3 billion (c.i.f., 1988)

commodities:
  petroleum products, foodstuffs, construction materials, vehicles, clothing
  and other consumer goods
partners:
  France 65%, UK, Italy, Germany, Japan, US (1987)
External debt: $NA
Industrial production:
  growth rate NA%
Electricity:
  113,100 kW capacity; 588 million kWh produced, 1,703 kWh per capita (1991)
Industries:
  construction, rum, cement, oil refining, sugar, tourism
Agriculture:
  including fishing and forestry, accounts for about 12% of GDP; principal
  crops - pineapples, avocados, bananas, flowers, vegetables, and sugarcane
  for rum; dependent on imported food, particularly meat and vegetables
Economic aid:
  Western (non-US) countries, ODA and OOF bilateral commitments (1970-89),
  $10.1 billion
Currency:
  French franc (plural - francs); 1 French franc (F) = 100 centimes
Exchange rates:
  French francs (F) per US$1 - 5.3801 (January 1992), 5.6421 (1991), 5.4453
  (1990), 6.3801 (1989), 5.9569 (1988), 6.0107 (1987)
Fiscal year: calendar year

:Martinique Communications

Highways:
  1,680 km total; 1,300 km paved, 380 km gravel and earth
Ports:
  Fort-de-France
Civil air:
  no major transport aircraft
Airports:
  2 total; 2 usable; 1 with permanent-surface runways; 1 with runway
  2,440-3,659 m; 1 with runways less than 2,439 m
Telecommunications:
  domestic facilities are adequate; 68,900 telephones; interisland radio relay
  links to Guadeloupe, Dominica, and Saint Lucia; broadcast stations - 1 AM, 6
  FM, 10 TV; 2 Atlantic Ocean INTELSAT earth stations

:Martinique Defense Forces

Branches:
  French Forces, Gendarmerie
Manpower availability:
  males 15-49, 95,235; NA fit for military service
Note:
  defense is the responsibility of France

Mauritania Geography

Total area:　1,030,700 km2
Land area:　1,030,400 km2
Comparative area:　slightly larger than three times the size of New Mexico
Land boundaries:
　5,074 km; Algeria 463 km, Mali 2,237 km, Senegal 813 km, Western Sahara
　1,561 km
Coastline:
　754 km
Maritime claims:
　Continental shelf:
　edge of continental margin or 200 nm
　Exclusive economic zone:
　200 nm
　Territorial sea:
　12 nm
Disputes:
　boundary with Senegal
Climate:
　desert; constantly hot, dry, dusty
Terrain:
　mostly barren, flat plains of the Sahara; some central hills
Natural resources:
　iron ore, gypsum, fish, copper, phosphate
Land use:
　arable land 1%; permanent crops NEGL%; meadows and pastures 38%; forest and
　woodland 5%; other 56%; includes irrigated NEGL%
Environment:
　hot, dry, dust/sand-laden sirocco wind blows primarily in March and April;
　desertification; only perennial river is the Senegal

:Mauritania People

Population:　2,059,187 (July 1992), growth rate 3.1% (1992)
Birth rate:　48 births/1,000 population (1992)
Death rate:　17 deaths/1,000 population (1992)
Net migration rate:　0 migrants/1,000 population (1992)
Infant mortality rate:　89 deaths/1,000 live births (1992)
Life expectancy at birth:　44 years male, 50 years female (1992)
Total fertility rate:　7.1 children born/woman (1992)
Nationality:
　noun - Mauritanian(s); adjective - Mauritanian
Ethnic divisions:
　mixed Maur/black 40%, Maur 30%, black 30%
Religions:
　Muslim, nearly 100%
Languages:
　Hasaniya Arabic (official); Hasaniya Arabic, Pular, Soninke, Wolof
　(official)
Literacy:
　34% (male 47%, female 21%) age 10 and over can read and write (1990 est.)
Labor force:

465,000 (1981 est.); 45,000 wage earners (1980); agriculture 47%, services 29%, industry and commerce 14%, government 10%; 53% of population of working age (1985)

Organized labor:
30,000 members claimed by single union, Mauritanian Workers' Union

:Mauritania Government

Long-form name:
Islamic Republic of Mauritania

Type:
republic; military first seized power in bloodless coup 10 July 1978; a palace coup that took place on 12 December 1984 brought President Taya to power; he was elected in 1992

Capital: Nouakchott

Administrative divisions:
12 regions(regions, singular - region); Adrar, Assaba, Brakna, Dakhlet Nouadhibou, Gorgol, Guidimaka, Hodh ech Chargui, Hodh el Gharbi, Inchiri, Tagant, Tiris Zemmour, Trarza; note - there may be a new capital district of Nouakchott

Independence:
28 November 1960 (from France)

Constitution:
currently 12 July 1991; 20 May 1961 Constitution abrogated after coup of 10 July 1978; provisional constitution published 17 December 1980 but abandoned in 1981; constitutional charter published 27 February 1985 after Taya came to power; latest constitution approved after general referendum 12 July 1991

Legal system:
based on Islamic law

National holiday:
Independence Day, 28 November (1960)

Executive branch:
president

Legislative branch:
National Assembly (Assemblee Nationale) and Senate

Judicial branch:
Supreme Court (Cour Supreme)

Leaders:
 Chief of State and Head of Government:
President Col. Maaouya Ould Sid`Ahmed TAYA (since 12 December 1984)

Political parties and leaders:
legalized by constitution passed 12 July 1991; emerging parties include Democratic and Social Republican Party (PRDS), led by President Col. Maaouya Ould Sid`Ahmed TAYA; Union of Democratic Forces (UDF), coalition of seven opposition factions, three leaders: Mohameden Ould BABAH, Diop Mamadou AMADOU, and Messoud Ould BOULKHEIR; Assembly for Democracy (RDU), Mohamed
Ould SIDI BABA; Rally for Democracy and Unity (RDUN), Mohamed Ould Sidi BABA; Popular Social and Democratic Union (UPSD), Mohamed Mahmoud Ould MAH;
Progressive Popular Alliance (APP), Taleb Ould Jiddou Ould Mohamed

LAGHDAF;
  Mauritanian Party for Renewal (PMR), Moulaye El Hassan Ould JEYID; National
  Avant-Garde Party (PAN or PAGN), Khattry Ould Taleb JIDDOU; Mauritanian
  Party of the Democratic Center (PCDM), Bamba Ould SIDI BADI; Union for
  Planning and Construction (UPC), Mohamed Ould EYAHA; Democratic Justice
  Party (PJD), Mohamed Abdallahi Ould EL BANE; Party for Liberty, Equality,
  and Justice (PLEJ), Ba Mamadou ALASSANE; Labor and National Unity Party
  (PTUN), Ali Bouna Ould OUENINA
Suffrage:
  universal at age 18
Elections:
 President:
  last held January 1992 (next to be held NA)
 results:
  President Col. Maabuya Ould Sid`Ahmed TAYA elected
 Senate:
  last held 3 and 10 April 1992 (next to be held April 1998)

:Mauritania Government

 National Assembly:
  last held 6 and 13 March 1992 (next to be held NA 1997)
Member of:
  ABEDA, ACCT (associate), ACP, AfDB, AFESD, AL, AMF, AMU, CAEU, CCC,
CEAO,
  ECA, ECOWAS, FAO, G-77, GATT, IBRD, ICAO, IDA, IDB, IFAD, IFC, ILO,
IMF,
  IMO, INTELSAT, INTERPOL, IOC, ITU, LORCS, NAM, OAU, OIC, UN,
UNCTAD, UNESCO,
  UNIDO, UPU, WHO, WIPO, WMO, WTO
Diplomatic representation:
  Ambassador Mohamed Fall OULD AININA; Chancery at 2129 Leroy Place NW,
  Washington, DC 20008; telephone (202) 232-5700
 US:
  Ambassador Gordon S. BROWN; Embassy at address NA, Nouakchott (mailing
  address is B. P. 222, Nouakchott); telephone [222] (2) 526-60 or 526-63; FAX
  [222] (2) 515-92
Flag:
  green with a yellow five-pointed star above a yellow, horizontal crescent;
  the closed side of the crescent is down; the crescent, star, and color green
  are traditional symbols of Islam

:Mauritania Economy

Overview:
  A majority of the population still depends on agriculture and livestock for
  a livelihood, even though most of the nomads and many subsistence farmers
  were forced into the cities by recurrent droughts in the 1970s and 1980s.
  Mauritania has extensive deposits of iron ore, which account for almost 50%
  of total exports. The decline in world demand for this ore, however, has led
  to cutbacks in production. The nation's coastal waters are among the richest
  fishing areas in the world, but overexploitation by foreigners threatens
  this key source of revenue. The country's first deepwater port opened near

Nouakchott in 1986. In recent years, the droughts, the endemic conflict with Senegal, rising energy costs, and economic mismanagement have resulted in a substantial buildup of foreign debt. The government has begun the second stage of an economic reform program in consultation with the World Bank, the IMF, and major donor countries. But the reform process suffered a major setback following the Gulf war of early 1991. Because of Mauritania's support of Saddam Husayn, bilateral aid from its two top donors, Saudi Arabia and Kuwait, was suspended, and multilateral aid was reduced.

GDP:
exchange rate conversion - $1.1 billion, per capita $535; real growth rate 3% (1991 est.)

Inflation rate (consumer prices):
6.5% (1990 est.)

Unemployment rate: 20% (1991 est.)

Budget:
revenues $280 million; expenditures $346 million, including capital expenditures of $61 million (1989 est.)

Exports:
$436 million (f.o.b., 1990)
commodities:
iron ore, processed fish, small amounts of gum arabic and gypsum; unrecorded but numerically significant cattle exports to Senegal
partners:
EC 43%, Japan 27%, USSR 11%, Ivory Coast 3%

Imports:
$389 million (c.i.f., 1990)
commodities:
foodstuffs, consumer goods, petroleum products, capital goods
partners:
EC 60%, Algeria 15%, China 6%, US 3%

External debt: $1.9 billion (1990)

Industrial production:
growth rate 4.4% (1988 est.); accounts for almost 20% of GDP

Electricity:
190,000 kW capacity; 135 million kWh produced, 70 kWh per capita (1991)

Industries:
fishing, fish processing, mining of iron ore and gypsum

Agriculture:
accounts for 29% of GDP (including fishing); largely subsistence farming and nomadic cattle and sheep herding except in Senegal river valley; crops - dates, millet, sorghum, root crops; fish products number-one export; large food deficit in years of drought

Economic aid:
US commitments, including Ex-Im (FY70-89), $168 million; Western (non-US) countries, ODA and OOF bilateral commitments (1970-89), $1.3 billion; OPEC bilateral aid (1979-89), $490 million; Communist countries (1970-89), $277 million; Arab Development Bank (1991), $20 million

:Mauritania Economy

Currency:
  ouguiya (plural - ouguiya); 1 ouguiya (UM) = 5 khoums
Exchange rates:
  ouguiya (UM) per US$1 - 79.300 (January 1992), 81.946 (1991), 80.609 (1990),
  83.051 (1989), 75.261 (1988), 73.878 (1987)
Fiscal year: calendar year

:Mauritania Communications

Railroads:
  690 km 1.435-meter (standard) gauge, single track, owned and operated by
  government mining company
Highways:
  7,525 km total; 1,685 km paved; 1,040 km gravel, crushed stone, or otherwise
  improved; 4,800 km unimproved roads, trails, tracks
Inland waterways:
  mostly ferry traffic on the Senegal River
Ports:
  Nouadhibou, Nouakchott
Merchant marine:
  1 cargo ship (1,000 GRT or over) totaling 1,290 GRT/1,840 DWT
Civil air:
  3 major transport aircraft
Airports:
  28 total, 28 usable; 9 with permanent-surface runways; none with runways
  over 3,659 m; 5 with runways 2,440-3,659 m; 16 with runways 1,220-2,439 m
Telecommunications:
  poor system of cable and open-wire lines, minor radio relay links, and radio
  communications stations (improvements being made); broadcast stations - 2
  AM, no FM, 1 TV; satellite earth stations - 1 Atlantic Ocean INTELSAT and 2
  ARABSAT, with six planned

:Mauritania Defense Forces

Branches:
  Army, Navy, Air Force, National Gendarmerie, National Guard, National
  Police, Presidential Guard
Manpower availability:
  males 15-49, 436,897; 213,307 fit for military service; conscription law not
  implemented
Defense expenditures:
  exchange rate conversion - $40 million, 4.2% of GDP (1989)

Mauritius Geography

Total area: 1,860 km2
Land area: 1,850 km2; includes Agalega Islands, Cargados Carajos Shoals (Saint
  Brandon), and Rodrigues
Comparative area: slightly less than 10.5 times the size of Washington, DC
Land boundaries:
  none
Coastline:
  177 km
Maritime claims:

Continental shelf:
  edge of continental margin or 200 nm
Exclusive economic zone:
  200 nm
Territorial sea:
  12 nm
Disputes:
  claims UK-administered Chagos Archipelago, which includes the island of
  Diego Garcia in UK-administered British Indian Ocean Territory; claims
  French-administered Tromelin Island
Climate:
  tropical modified by southeast trade winds; warm, dry winter (May to
  November); hot, wet, humid summer (November to May)
Terrain:
  small coastal plain rising to discontinuous mountains encircling central
  plateau
Natural resources:
  arable land, fish
Land use:
  arable land 54%; permanent crops 4%; meadows and pastures 4%; forest and
  woodland 31%; other 7%; includes irrigated 9%
Environment:
  subject to cyclones (November to April); almost completely surrounded by
  reefs
Note:
  located 900 km east of Madagascar in the Indian Ocean

:Mauritius People

Population: 1,092,130 (July 1992), growth rate 0.8% (1992)
Birth rate: 19 births/1,000 population (1992)
Death rate: 7 deaths/1,000 population (1992)
Net migration rate: -4 migrants/1,000 population (1992)
Infant mortality rate: 22 deaths/1,000 live births (1992)
Life expectancy at birth: 66 years male, 73 years female (1992)
Total fertility rate: 2.1 children born/woman (1992)
Nationality:
  noun - Mauritian(s); adjective - Mauritian
Ethnic divisions:
  Indo-Mauritian 68%, Creole 27%, Sino-Mauritian 3%, Franco-Mauritian 2%
Religions:
  Hindu 52%, Christian (Roman Catholic 26%, Protestant 2.3%) 28.3%, Muslim
  16.6%, other 3.1%
Languages:
  English (official), Creole, French, Hindi, Urdu, Hakka, Bojpoori
Literacy:
  82.8 % (male 88.7%, female 77.1%) age 13 and over can read and write (1985
  UNESCO estimate)
Labor force:
  335,000; government services 29%, agriculture and fishing 27%, manufacturing
  22%, other 22%; 43% of population of working age (1985)

Organized labor:
  35% of labor force in more than 270 unions

:Mauritius Government

Long-form name:
  none
Type:
  parliamentary democracy
Capital: Port Louis
Administrative divisions:
  9 districts and 3 dependencies*; Agalega Islands*, Black River, Cargados
  Carajos*, Flacq, Grand Port, Moka, Pamplemousses, Plaines Wilhems, Port
  Louis, Riviere du Rempart, Rodrigues*, Savanne
Independence:
  12 March 1968 (from UK)
Constitution:
  12 March 1968
Legal system:
  based on French civil law system with elements of English common law in
  certain areas
National holiday:
  Independence Day, 12 March (1968)
Executive branch:
  British monarch, governor general, prime minister, deputy prime minister,
  Council of Ministers (cabinet)
Legislative branch:
  unicameral Legislative Assembly
Judicial branch:
  Supreme Court
Leaders:
  Chief of State:
  Queen ELIZABETH II (since 6 February 1952), represented by Governor General
  Sir Veerasamy RINGADOO (since 17 January 1986)
  Head of Government:
  Prime Minister Sir Anerood JUGNAUTH (since 12 June 1982); Deputy Prime
  Minister Prem NABABSING (since 26 September 1990)
Political parties and leaders:
  government coalition:
  Militant Socialist Movement (MSM), A. JUGNAUTH; Mauritian Militant Move-
ment
  (MMM), Paul BERENGER; Organization of the People of Rodrigues (OPR), Louis
  Serge CLAIR; Democratic Labor Movement (MTD), Anil BAICHOO
  opposition:
  Mauritian Labor Party (MLP), Navin RAMGOOLMAN; Socialist Workers Front,
  Sylvio MICHEL; Mauritian Social Democratic Party (PMSD), G. DUVAL
Elections:
  Legislative Assembly:
  last held on 15 September 1991 (next to be held by 15 September 1996);
  results - MSM/MMM 53%, MLP/PMSD 38%; seats - (70 total, 62 elected)
MSM/MMM

alliance 59 (MSM 29, MMM 26, OPR 2, MTD 2); MLP/PMSD 3
Communists:
   may be 2,000 sympathizers
Other political or pressure groups:
   various labor unions
Member of:
   ACCT, ACP, AfDB, C, CCC, ECA, FAO, G-77, GATT, IAEA, IBRD, ICAO, ICFTU, IDA,
   IFAD, IFC, ILO, IMF, IMO, INTELSAT, INTERPOL, IOC, ISO (correspondent), ITU,
   LORCS, NAM, OAU, PCA, UN, UNCTAD, UNESCO, UNIDO, UPU, WCL, WFTU, WHO, WIPO,
   WMO, WTO
Diplomatic representation:
   Ambassador Chitmansing JESSERAMSING; Chancery at Suite 134, 4301 Connecticut
   Avenue NW, Washington, DC 20008; telephone (202) 244-1491 or 1492

:Mauritius Government

   US:
   Ambassador Penne Percy KORTH; Embassy at 4th Floor, Rogers House, John
   Kennedy Street, Port Louis; telephone [230] 208-9763 through 208-9767; FAX
   [230] 208-9534
Flag:
   four equal horizontal bands of red (top), blue, yellow, and green

:Mauritius Economy

Overview:
   The economy is based on sugar, manufacturing (mainly textiles), and tourism.
   Sugarcane is grown on about 90% of the cultivated land area and accounts for
   40% of export earnings. The government's development strategy is centered on
   industrialization (with a view to exports), agricultural diversification,
   and tourism. Economic performance in FY91 was impressive, with 6% real
   growth and low unemployment.
GDP:
   exchange rate conversion - $2.5 billion, per capita $2,300; real growth rate
   6.1% (FY91 est.)
Inflation rate (consumer prices):
   13.2% (FY91 est.)
Unemployment rate: 2.4% (1991 est.)
Budget:
   revenues $557 million; expenditures $607 million, including capital
   expenditures of $111 million (FY90)
Exports:
   $1.2 billion (f.o.b., 1990)
  commodities:
   textiles 44%, sugar 40%, light manufactures 10%
  partners:
   EC and US have preferential treatment, EC 77%, US 15%
Imports:
   $1.6 billion (f.o.b., 1990)

commodities:

manufactured goods 50%, capital equipment 17%, foodstuffs 13%, petroleum
products 8%, chemicals 7%

partners:

EC, US, South Africa, Japan

External debt: $869 million (1991 est.)

Industrial production:

growth rate 12.9% (FY87); accounts for 25% of GDP

Electricity:

235,000 kW capacity; 425 million kWh produced, 395 kWh per capita (1991)

Industries:

food processing (largely sugar milling), textiles, wearing apparel,
chemicals, metal products, transport equipment, nonelectrical machinery,
tourism

Agriculture:

accounts for 10% of GDP; about 90% of cultivated land in sugarcane; other
products - tea, corn, potatoes, bananas, pulses, cattle, goats, fish; net
food importer, especially rice and fish

Illicit drugs:

illicit producer of cannabis for the international drug trade

Economic aid:

US commitments, including Ex-Im (FY70-89), $76 million; Western (non-US)
countries (1970-89), $709 million; Communist countries (1970-89), $54
million

Currency:

Mauritian rupee (plural - rupees); 1 Mauritian rupee (MauR) = 100 cents

Exchange rates:

Mauritian rupees (MauRs) per US$1 - 15.198 (January 1992), 15.652 (1991),
14.839 (1990), 15.250 (1989), 13.438 (1988), 12.878 (1987)

Fiscal year: 1 July - 30 June

:Mauritius Communications

Highways:

1,800 km total; 1,640 km paved, 160 km earth

Ports:

Port Louis

Merchant marine:

9 ships (1,000 GRT or over) totaling 94,710 GRT/150,345 DWT; includes 1
passenger-cargo, 3 cargo, 1 roll-on/roll-off, 1 liquefied gas, 3 bulk

Civil air:

7 major transport aircraft

Airports:

5 total, 4 usable; 2 with permanent-surface runways; none with runways over
3,659 m; 1 with runways 2,440-3,659 m; none with runways 1,220-2,439 m

Telecommunications:

small system with good service utilizing primarily radio relay; new
microwave link to Reunion; high-frequency radio links to several countries;
over 48,000 telephones; broadcast stations - 2 AM, no FM, 4 TV; 1 Indian
Ocean INTELSAT earth station

:Mauritius Defense Forces

Branches:
   paramilitary Special Mobile Force, Special Support Unit, National Police
   Force, National Coast Guard
Manpower availability:
   males 15-49, 307,237; 157,246 fit for military service
Defense expenditures:
   exchange rate conversion - $5 million, 0.2% of GDP (FY89)

Mayotte Geography

Total area: 375 km2
Land area: 375 km2
Comparative area: slightly more than twice the size of Washington, DC
Land boundaries:
   none
Coastline:
   185.2 km
Maritime claims:
  Exclusive economic zone:
   200 nm
  Territorial sea:
   12 nm
Disputes:
   claimed by Comoros
Climate:
   tropical; marine; hot, humid, rainy season during northeastern monsoon
   (November to May); dry season is cooler (May to November)
Terrain:
   generally undulating with ancient volcanic peaks, deep ravines
Natural resources:
   negligible
Land use:
   arable land NA%; permanent crops NA%; meadows and pastures NA%; forest and
   woodland NA%; other NA%
Environment:
   subject to cyclones during rainy season
Note:
   part of Comoro Archipelago; located in the Mozambique Channel about halfway
   between Africa and Madagascar

:Mayotte People

Population: 86,628 (July 1992), growth rate 3.8% (1992)
Birth rate: 50 births/1,000 population (1992)
Death rate: 12 deaths/1,000 population (1992)
Net migration rate: 0 migrants/1,000 population (1992)
Infant mortality rate: 84 deaths/1,000 live births (1992)
Life expectancy at birth: 55 years male, 59 years female (1992)
Total fertility rate: 6.9 children born/woman (1992)
Nationality:
   noun - Mahorais (singular and plural); adjective - Mahoran
Religions:
   Muslim 99%; remainder Christian, mostly Roman Catholic

Languages:
  Mahorian (a Swahili dialect), French
Literacy:
  NA% (male NA%, female NA%)
Labor force:
  NA
Organized labor:
  NA

:Mayotte Government

Long-form name:
  Territorial Collectivity of Mayotte
Type:
  territorial collectivity of France
Capital: Mamoutzou
Administrative divisions:
  none (territorial collectivity of France)
Independence:
  none (territorial collectivity of France)
Constitution:
  28 September 1958 (French Constitution)
Legal system:
  French law
National holiday:
  Taking of the Bastille, 14 July (1789)
Executive branch:
  government commissioner
Legislative branch:
  unicameral General Council (Conseil General)
Judicial branch:
  Supreme Court (Tribunal Superieur d'Appel)
Leaders:
 Chief of State:
  President Francois MITTERRAND (since 21 May 1981)
 Head of Government:
  Commissioner, Representative of the French Government Jean-Paul COSTE (since
  NA 1991); President of the General Council Youssouf BAMANA (since NA 1976)
Political parties and leaders:
  Mahoran Popular Movement (MPM), Younoussa BAMANA; Party for the Mahoran
  Democratic Rally (PRDM), Daroueche MAOULIDA; Mahoran Rally for the Repub-
lic
  (RMPR), Mansour KAMARDINE; Union of the Center (UDC)
Suffrage:
  universal at age 18
Elections:
 General Council:
  last held June 1988 (next to be held June 1993); results - percent of vote
  by party NA; seats - (17 total) MPM 9, RPR 6, other 2
 French Senate:
  last held on 24 September 1989 (next to be held September 1992); results -

percent of vote by party NA; seats - (1 total) MPM 1
French National Assembly:
last held 5 and 12 June 1988 (next to be held June 1993); results - percent
of vote by party NA; seats - (1 total) UDC 1
Member of:
FZ
Diplomatic representation:
as a territorial collectivity of France, Mahoran interests are represented
in the US by France
Flag:
the flag of France is used

:Mayotte Economy

Overview:
Economic activity is based primarily on the agricultural sector, including
fishing and livestock raising. Mayotte is not self-sufficient and must
import a large portion of its food requirements, mainly from France. The
economy and future development of the island is heavily dependent on French
financial assistance.
GDP:
exchange rate conversion - $NA, per capita $NA; real growth rate NA%
Inflation rate (consumer prices):
NA%
Unemployment rate: NA%
Budget:
revenues $NA; expenditures $37.3 million, including capital expenditures of
$NA (1985)
Exports:
$4.0 million (f.o.b., 1984)
commodities:
ylang-ylang, vanilla
partners:
France 79%, Comoros 10%, Reunion 9%
Imports:
$21.8 million (f.o.b., 1984)
commodities:
building materials, transportation equipment, rice, clothing, flour
partners:
France 57%, Kenya 16%, South Africa 11%, Pakistan 8%
External debt: $NA
Industrial production:
growth rate NA%
Electricity:
NA kW capacity; NA million kWh produced, NA kWh per capita
Industries:
newly created lobster and shrimp industry
Agriculture:
most important sector; provides all export earnings; crops - vanilla,
ylang-ylang, coffee, copra; imports major share of food needs
Economic aid:

Western (non-US) countries, ODA and OOF bilateral commitments (1970-89), $402 million

Currency:
French franc (plural - francs); 1 French franc (F) = 100 centimes

Exchange rates:
French francs (F) per US$1 - 5.3801 (January 1992), 5.6421 (1991), 5.4453 (1990), 6.3801 (1989), 5.9569 (1988), 6.0107 (1987)

Fiscal year: calendar year

:Mayotte Communications

Highways:
42 km total; 18 km bituminous

Ports:
Dzaoudzi

Civil air:
no major transport aircraft

Airports:
1 with permanent-surface runways 1,220-2,439 m

Telecommunications:
small system administered by French Department of Posts and Telecommunications; includes radio relay and high-frequency radio communications for links to Comoros and international communications; 450 telephones; broadcast stations - 1 AM, no FM, no TV

:Mayotte Defense Forces

Note: defense is the responsibility of France

Mexico Geography

Total area: 1,972,550 km2
Land area: 1,923,040 km2
Comparative area: slightly less than three times the size of Texas
Land boundaries:
4,538 km; Belize 250 km, Guatemala 962 km, US 3,326 km
Coastline:
9,330 km
Maritime claims:
 Contiguous zone:
 24 nm
 Continental shelf:
 natural prolongation of continental margin or 200 nm
 Exclusive economic zone:
 200 nm
 Territorial sea:
 12 nm
Disputes:
claims Clipperton Island (French possession)
Climate:
varies from tropical to desert
Terrain:
high, rugged mountains, low coastal plains, high plateaus, and desert
Natural resources:

crude oil, silver, copper, gold, lead, zinc, natural gas, timber

Land use:

arable land 12%; permanent crops 1%; meadows and pastures 39%; forest and woodland 24%; other 24%; includes irrigated 3%

Environment:

subject to tsunamis along the Pacific coast and destructive earthquakes in the center and south; natural water resources scarce and polluted in north, inaccessible and poor quality in center and extreme southeast; deforestation; erosion widespread; desertification; serious air pollution in Mexico City and urban centers along US-Mexico border

Note:

strategic location on southern border of US

:Mexico People

Population: 92,380,721 (July 1992), growth rate 2.3% (1992)

Birth rate: 29 births/1,000 population (1992)

Death rate: 5 deaths/1,000 population (1992)

Net migration rate: -1 migrant/1,000 population (1992)

Infant mortality rate: 30 deaths/1,000 live births (1992)

Life expectancy at birth: 69 years male, 76 years female (1992)

Total fertility rate: 3.3 children born/woman (1992)

Nationality:

noun - Mexican(s); adjective - Mexican

Ethnic divisions:

mestizo (Indian-Spanish) 60%, Amerindian or predominantly Amerindian 30%, Caucasian or predominantly Caucasian 9%, other 1%

Religions:

nominally Roman Catholic 89%, Protestant 6%

Languages:

Spanish; various Mayan dialects

Literacy:

87% (male 90%, female 85%) age 15 and over can read and write (1985 est.)

Labor force:

26,100,000 (1988); services 31.4%, agriculture, forestry, hunting, and fishing 26%, commerce 13.9%, manufacturing 12.8%, construction 9.5%, transportation 4.8%, mining and quarrying 1.3%, electricity 0.3% (1986)

Organized labor:

35% of labor force

:Mexico Government

Long-form name:

United Mexican States

Type:

federal republic operating under a centralized government

Capital: Mexico

Administrative divisions:

31 states (estados, singular - estado) and 1 federal district* (distrito federal); Aguascalientes, Baja California, Baja California Sur, Campeche, Chiapas, Chihuahua, Coahuila, Colima, Distrito Federal*, Durango, Guanajuato, Guerrero, Hidalgo, Jalisco, Mexico, Michoacan, Morelos, Nayarit, Nuevo Leon, Oaxaca, Puebla, Queretaro, Quintana Roo, San Luis Potosi,

Sinaloa, Sonora, Tabasco, Tamaulipas, Tlaxcala, Veracruz, Yucatan, Zacatecas
Independence:
16 September 1810 (from Spain)
Constitution:
5 February 1917
Legal system:
mixture of US constitutional theory and civil law system; judicial review of legislative acts; accepts compulsory ICJ jurisdiction, with reservations
National holiday:
Independence Day, 16 September (1810)
Executive branch:
president, Cabinet
Legislative branch:
bicameral National Congress (Congreso de la Union) consists of an upper chamber or Senate (Camara de Senadores) and a lower chamber or Chamber of Deputies (Camara de Diputados)
Judicial branch:
Supreme Court of Justice (Corte Suprema de Justicia)
Leaders:
 Chief of State and Head of Government:
President Carlos SALINAS de Gortari (since 1 December 1988)
Political parties and leaders:
(recognized parties) Institutional Revolutionary Party (PRI), Genaro BORREGO Estrada; National Action Party (PAN), Luis ALVAREZ; Popular Socialist Party (PPS), Indalecio SAYAGO Herrera; Democratic Revolutionary Party (PRD), Cuauhtemoc CARDENAS Solorzano; Cardenist Front for the National Reconstruction Party (PFCRN), Rafael AGUILAR Talamantes; Authentic Party of the Mexican Revolution (PARM), Carlos Enrique CANTU Rosas
Suffrage:
universal and compulsory (but not enforced) at age 18
Elections:
 President:
last held on 6 July 1988 (next to be held September 1994); results - Carlos SALINAS de Gortari (PRI) 50.74%, Cuauhtemoc CARDENAS Solorzano (FDN) 31.06%,
Manuel CLOUTHIER (PAN) 16.81%; other 1.39%; note - several of the smaller parties ran a common candidate under a coalition called the National Democratic Front (FDN)
 Senate:
last held on 18 August 1988 (next to be held midyear 1994); results - percent of vote by party NA; seats in full Senate - (64 total) number of seats by party; PRI 61, PRD 2, PAN 1
 Chamber of Deputies:
last held on 18 August 1991 (next to be held midyear 1994); results - PRI 53%, PAN 20%, PFCRN 10%, PPS 6%, PARM 7%, PMS (now part of PRD) 4%; seats -
(500 total) PRI 320, PAN 89, PRD 41, PFCRN 23, PARM 15, PPS 12
:Mexico Government

Other political or pressure groups:
   Roman Catholic Church, Confederation of Mexican Workers (CTM), Confederation
   of Industrial Chambers (CONCAMIN), Confederation of National Chambers of
   Commerce (CONCANACO), National Peasant Confederation (CNC), UNE (no
   expansion), Revolutionary Workers Party (PRT), Mexican Democratic Party
   (PDM), Revolutionary Confederation of Workers and Peasants (CROC), Regional
   Confederation of Mexican Workers (CROM), Confederation of Employers of the
   Mexican Republic (COPARMEX), National Chamber of Transformation Industries
   (CANACINTRA), Coordinator for Foreign Trade Business Organizations (COECE)
Member of:
   AG (observer), CARICOM (observer) CCC, CDB, CG, EBRD, ECLAC, FAO, G-3,
G-6,
   G-11, G-15, G-19, G-24, G-77, GATT, IADB, IAEA, IBRD, ICAO, ICC, ICFTU,
IDA,
   IFAD, IFC, ILO, IMF, IMO, INTELSAT, INTERPOL, IOC, IOM (observer), ISO,
ITU,
   LAES, LAIA, LORCS, NAM (observer), OAS, OPANAL, PCA, RG, UN,
UNCTAD, UNESCO,
   UNIDO, UPU, WCL, WHO, WIPO, WMO, WTO
Diplomatic representation:
   Ambassador Gustavo PETRICIOLI Iturbide; Chancery at 1911 Pennsylvania Ave-
nue
   NW, Washington, DC 20006; telephone (202) 728-1600; there are Mexican
   Consulates General in Chicago, Dallas, Denver, El Paso, Houston, Los
   Angeles, New Orleans, New York, San Francisco, San Antonio, San Diego, and
   Consulates in Albuquerque, Atlanta, Austin, Boston, Brownsville (Texas),
   Calexico (California), Corpus Christi, Del Rio (Texas), Detroit, Douglas
   (Arizona), Eagle Pass (Texas), Fresno (California), Kansas City (Missouri),
   Laredo, McAllen (Texas), Miami, Nogales (Arizona), Oxnard (California),
   Philadelphia, Phoenix, Presidio (Texas), Sacramento, St. Louis, St. Paul
   (Minneapolis), Salt Lake City, San Bernardino, San Jose, San Juan (Puerto
   Rico), and Seattle
US:
   Ambassador John D. NEGROPONTE, Jr.; Embassy at Paseo de la Reforma 305,
   06500 Mexico, D.F. (mailing address is P. O. Box 3087, Laredo, TX
   78044-3087); telephone [52] (5) 211-0042; FAX [52] (5) 511-9980, 208-3373;
   there are US Consulates General in Ciudad Juarez, Guadalajara, Monterrey,
   and Tijuana, and Consulates in Hermosillo, Matamoros, Mazatlan, Merida, and
   Nuevo Laredo
Flag:
   three equal vertical bands of green (hoist side), white, and red; the coat
   of arms (an eagle perched on a cactus with a snake in its beak) is centered
   in the white band

:Mexico Economy

Overview:
   Mexico's economy is a mixture of state-owned industrial plants (notably
   oil), private manufacturing and services, and both large-scale and
   traditional agriculture. In the 1980s, Mexico experienced severe economic
   difficulties: the nation accumulated large external debts as world petroleum

prices fell; rapid population growth outstripped the domestic food supply; and inflation, unemployment, and pressures to emigrate became more acute. Growth in national output, however, is recovering, rising from 1.4% in 1988 to 4% in 1990 and again in 1991. The US is Mexico's major trading partner, accounting for two-thirds of its exports and imports. After petroleum, border assembly plants and tourism are the largest earners of foreign exchange. The government, in consultation with international economic agencies, is implementing programs to stabilize the economy and foster growth. In 1991 the government began negotiations with the US and Canada on a free trade agreement.

GDP:
exchange rate conversion - $289 billion, per capita $3,200; real growth rate 4% (1991 est.)

Inflation rate (consumer prices):
18.8% (1991 est.)

Unemployment rate: 14-17% (1991 est.)

Budget:
revenues $41.0 billion; expenditures $47.9 billion, including capital expenditures of $6.3 billion (1990)

Exports:
$27.4 billion (f.o.b., 1991 est.)
commodities:
crude oil, oil products, coffee, shrimp, engines, motor vehicles, cotton, consumer electronics
partners:
US 68%, EC 14%, Japan 6% (1990 est.)

Imports:
$36.7 billion (c.i.f., 1991)
commodities:
grain, metal manufactures, agricultural machinery, electrical equipment
partners:
US 69%, EC 13%, Japan 6% (1990)

External debt: $98.4 billion (1991)

Industrial production:
growth rate 5.5% (1991 est.); accounts for 28% of GDP

Electricity:
26,150,000 kW capacity; 114,277 million kWh produced, 1,270 kWh per capita (1991)

Industries:
food and beverages, tobacco, chemicals, iron and steel, petroleum, mining, textiles, clothing, transportation equipment, tourism

Agriculture:
accounts for 9% of GDP and over 25% of work force; large number of small farms at subsistence level; major food crops - corn, wheat, rice, beans; cash crops - cotton, coffee, fruit, tomatoes; fish catch of 1.4 million metric tons among top 20 nations (1987)

Illicit drugs:
illicit cultivation of opium poppy and cannabis continues in spite of active government eradication program; major supplier to the US market; continues as the primary transshipment country for US-bound cocaine from South America

:Mexico Economy

Economic aid:
   US commitments, including Ex-Im (FY70-89), $3.1 billion; Western (non-US)
   countries, ODA and OOF bilateral commitments (1970-89), $7.7 billion;
   Communist countries (1970-89), $110 million

Currency:
   Mexican peso (plural - pesos); 1 Mexican peso (Mex$) = 100 centavos

Exchange rates:
   market rate of Mexican pesos (Mex$) per US$1 - 3,068.5 (January 1992),
   3,018.4 (1991) 2,940.9 (January 1991), 2,812.6 (1990), 2,461.3 (1989),
   2,273.1 (1988), 1,378.2 (1987)

Fiscal year: calendar year

:Mexico Communications

Railroads:
   24,500 km total; breakdown NA

Highways:
   212,000 km total; 65,000 km paved, 30,000 km semipaved or cobblestone,
   62,000 km rural roads (improved earth) or roads under construction, 55,000
   km unimproved earth roads

Inland waterways:
   2,900 km navigable rivers and coastal canals

Pipelines:
   crude oil 28,200 km; petroleum products 10,150 km; natural gas 13,254 km;
   petrochemical 1,400 km

Ports:
   Acapulco, Coatzacoalcos, Ensenada, Guaymas, Manzanillo, Mazatlan, Progreso,
   Puerto Vallarta, Salina Cruz, Tampico, Veracruz

Merchant marine:
   58 ships (1,000 GRT or over) totaling 875,239 GRT/1,301,355 DWT; includes 4
   short-sea passenger, 3 cargo, 2 refrigerated cargo, 2 roll-on/roll-off, 30
   petroleum tanker, 4 chemical tanker, 7 liquefied gas, 1 bulk, 1 combination
   bulk, 4 container

Civil air:
   186 major transport aircraft

Airports:
   1,815 total, 1,505 usable; 200 with permanent-surface runways; 3 with
   runways over 3,659 m; 33 with runways 2,440-3,659 m; 284 with runways
   1,220-2,439 m

Telecommunications:
   highly developed system with extensive radio relay links; privatized in
   December 1990; connected into Central America Microwave System; 6,410,000
   telephones; broadcast stations - 679 AM, no FM, 238 TV, 22 shortwave; 120
   domestic satellite terminals; earth stations - 4 Atlantic Ocean INTELSAT and
   1 Pacific Ocean INTELSAT

:Mexico Defense Forces

Branches:
   National Defense (including Army and Air Force), Navy (including Marines)

Manpower availability:

males 15-49, 23,023,871; 16,852,513 fit for military service; 1,138,455 reach military age (18) annually

Defense expenditures:

exchange rate conversion - $1.6 billion, less than 1% of GDP (1982 budget)

Micronesia, Federated States of Geography

Total area: 702 km2

Land area: 702 km2; includes Pohnpei, Truk, Yap, and Kosrae

Comparative area: slightly less than four times the size of Washington, DC

Land boundaries:

Coastline:

6,112 km

Maritime claims:

Exclusive economic zone:

200 nm

Territorial sea:

12 nm

Disputes:

Climate:

tropical; heavy year-round rainfall, especially in the eastern islands; located on southern edge of the typhoon belt with occasional severe damage

Terrain:

islands vary geologically from high mountainous islands to low, coral atolls; volcanic outcroppings on Pohnpei, Kosrae, and Truk

Natural resources:

forests, marine products, deep-seabed minerals

Land use:

arable land NA%; permanent crops NA%; meadows and pastures NA%; forest and woodland NA%; other NA%

Environment:

subject to typhoons from June to December; four major island groups totaling 607 islands

Note:

located 5,150 km west-southwest of Honolulu in the North Pacific Ocean, about three-quarters of the way between Hawaii and Indonesia

:Micronesia, Federated States of People

Population: 114,694 (July 1992), growth rate 3.4% (1992)

Birth rate: 29 births/1,000 population (1992)

Death rate: 7 deaths/1,000 population (1992)

Net migration rate: 12 migrants/1,000 population (1992)

Infant mortality rate: 39 deaths/1,000 live births (1992)

Life expectancy at birth: 65 years male, 69 years female (1992)

Total fertility rate: 4.1 children born/woman (1992)

Nationality:

noun - Micronesian(s); adjective - Micronesian; Kosrae(s), Pohnpeian(s), Trukese (singular and plural), Yapese (singular and plural)

Ethnic divisions:

nine ethnic Micronesian and Polynesian groups

Religions:

predominantly Christian, divided between Roman Catholic and Protestant; other churches include Assembly of God, Jehovah's Witnesses, Seventh-Day Adventist, Latter-Day Saints, and the Baha'i Faith

Languages:

English is the official and common language; most indigenous languages fall within the Austronesian language family, the exceptions are the Polynesian languages; major indigenous languages are Trukese, Pohnpeian, Yapese, and Kosrean

Literacy:

90% (male 90%, female 85%) age 15 and over can read and write (1980)

Labor force:

NA; two-thirds are government employees; 45,000 people are between the ages of 15 and 65

Organized labor:

NA

:Micronesia, Federated States of Government

Long-form name:

Federated States of Micronesia (no short-form name)

Type:

constitutional government in free association with the US; the Compact of Free Association entered into force 3 November 1986

Capital: Kolonia (on the island of Pohnpei); note - a new capital is being built about 10 km southwest in the Palikir valley

Administrative divisions:

4 states; Kosrae, Pohnpei, Chuuk, Yap

Independence:

3 November 1986 (from the US-administered UN Trusteeship; formerly the Kosrae, Pohnpei, Truk, and Yap districts of the Trust Territory of the Pacific Islands)

Constitution:

10 May 1979

Legal system:

based on adapted Trust Territory laws, acts of the legislature, municipal, common, and customary laws

National holiday:

Proclamation of the Federated States of Micronesia, 10 May (1979)

Executive branch:

president, vice president, Cabinet

Legislative branch:

unicameral Congress

Judicial branch:

Supreme Court

Leaders:

Chief of State and Head of Government:

President Bailey OLTER (since 21 May 1991); Vice President Jacob NENA (since 21 May 1991)

Political parties and leaders:

no formal parties

Suffrage:
  universal at age 18
Elections:
 President:
  last held ll May 1991 (next to be held March 1995); results - President
  Bailey OLTER elected president; Vice-President Jacob NENA
 Congress:
  last held on 5 March 1991 (next to be held March 1993); results - percent of
  vote NA; seats - (14 total)
Member of:
  ESCAP (associate), ICAO, SPC, SPF, UN, UNCTAD
Diplomatic representation:
  Ambassador Jesse B. MAREHALAU; Embassy at 1725 N St., NW, Washington, DC
  20036; telephone (202) 223-4383
 US:
  Ambassador Aurelia BRAZEAL; Embassy at address NA, Kolonia (mailing address
  is P. O. Box 1286, Pohnpei, Federated States of Micronesia 96941); telephone
  691-320-2187; FAX 691-320-2186
Flag:
  light blue with four white five-pointed stars centered; the stars are
  arranged in a diamond pattern

:Micronesia, Federated States of Economy

Overview:
  Economic activity consists primarily of subsistence farming and fishing. The
  islands have few mineral deposits worth exploiting, except for high-grade
  phosphate. The potential for a tourist industry exists, but the remoteness
  of the location and a lack of adequate facilities hinder development.
  Financial assistance from the US is the primary source of revenue, with the
  US pledged to spend $1 billion in the islands in the l990s. Geographical
  isolation and a poorly developed infrastructure are major impediments to
  long-term growth.
GNP:
  purchasing power equivalent - $150 million, per capita $1,500; real growth
  rate NA% (1989 est.); note - GNP numbers reflect US spending
Inflation rate (consumer prices):
  NA%
Unemployment rate: NA
Budget:
  revenues $165 million; expenditures $115 million, including capital
  expenditures of $20 million (1988)
Exports:
  $2.3 million (f.o.b., 1988)
 commodities:
  copra
 partners:
  NA
Imports:
  $67.7 million (c.i.f., 1988)
 commodities:

NA

  partners:

  NA

External debt: $NA

Industrial production:

  growth rate NA%

Electricity:

  18,000 kW capacity; 40 million kWh produced, 380 kWh per capita (1990)

Industries:

  tourism, construction, fish processing, craft items from shell, wood, and
  pearls

Agriculture:

  mainly a subsistence economy; copra, black pepper; tropical fruits and
  vegetables, coconuts, cassava, sweet potatoes, pigs, chickens

Economic aid:

  under terms of the Compact of Free Association, the US will provide $1.3
  billion in grant aid during the period 1986-2001

Currency:

  US currency is used

Exchange rates:

  US currency is used

Fiscal year: 1 October - 30 September

:Micronesia, Federated States of Communications

Highways:

  39 km of paved roads on major islands; also 187 km stone-, coral-, or
  laterite-surfaced roads

Ports:

  Colonia (Yap), Truk (Kosrae), Okat (Kosrae)

Airports:

  6 total, 5 usable; 4 with permanent-surface runways; none with runways over
  2,439 m; 4 with runways 1,220-2,439

Telecommunications:

  telephone network - 960 telephone lines total at Kolonia and Truk; islands
  interconnected by shortwave radio (used mostly for government purposes);
  16,000 radio receivers, 1,125 TV sets (est. 1987); broadcast stations - 5
  AM, 1 FM, 6 TV, 1 shortwave; 4 Pacific Ocean INTELSAT earth stations

:Micronesia, Federated States of Defense Forces

Note: defense is the responsibility of the US

Midway Islands Geography

Total area: 5.2 km2

Land area: 5.2 km2; includes Eastern Island and Sand Island

Comparative area: about nine times the size of the Mall in Washington, DC

Land boundaries:

  none

Coastline:

  15 km

Maritime claims:

  Contiguous zone:

12 nm
  Continental shelf:
    200 m (depth)
  Exclusive economic zone:
    200 nm
  Territorial sea:
    12 nm
Disputes:
  none
Climate:
  tropical, but moderated by prevailing easterly winds
Terrain:
  low, nearly level
Natural resources:
  fish and wildlife
Land use:
  arable land 0%; permanent crops 0%; meadows and pastures 0%; forest and woodland 0%; other 100%
Environment:
  coral atoll
Note:
  located 2,350 km west-northwest of Honolulu at the western end of Hawaiian Islands group, about one-third of the way between Honolulu and Tokyo; closed to the public

:Midway Islands People

Population: 453 US military personnel (1992)

:Midway Islands Government

Long-form name:
  none
Type:
  unincorporated territory of the US administered by the US Navy, under command of the Barbers Point Naval Air Station in Hawaii and managed cooperatively by the US Navy and the Fish and Wildlife Service of the US Department of the Interior as part of the National Wildlife Refuge System; legislation before Congress in 1990 proposed inclusion of territory within the State of Hawaii
Capital: none; administered from Washington, DC
Diplomatic representation:
  none (territory of the US)
Flag:
  the US flag is used

:Midway Islands Economy

Overview:
  The economy is based on providing support services for US naval operations located on the islands. All food and manufactured goods must be imported.
Electricity:
  supplied by US Military

:Midway Islands Communications

Highways:
  32 km total
Pipelines:
  7.8 km
Ports:
  Sand Island
Airports:
  3 total; 2 usable; 1 with permanent-surface runways; none with runways over
  2,439 m; 2 with runways 1,220-2,439 m

:Midway Islands Defense Forces

Note: defense is the responsibility of the US

Moldova Geography

Total area: 33,700 km2
Land area: 33,700 km2
Comparative area: slightly more than twice the size of Hawaii
Land boundaries:
  1,389 km; Romania 450 km, Ukraine 939 km
Coastline:
  none - landlocked
Maritime claims:
  none - landlocked
Disputes:
  potential dispute with Ukraine over former southern Bessarabian areas;
  northern Bukovina ceded to Ukraine upon Moldova's incorporation into USSR;
  internal with ethnic Russians in the Trans-Dnestr and Gagauz Muslims in the
  South
Climate:
  mild winters, warm summers
Terrain:
  rolling steppe, gradual slope south to Black Sea
Natural resources:
  lignite, phosphorites, gypsum
Land use:
  NA% arable land; NA% permanent crops; NA% meadows and pastures; NA% forest
  and woodland; NA% other; includes NA% irrigated
Environment:
  NA

:Moldova People

Population: 4,458,435 (July 1992), growth rate 0.7% (1992)
Birth rate: 19 births/1,000 population (1992)
Death rate: 10 deaths/1,000 population (1992)
Net migration rate: -2 migrants/1,000 population (1992)
Infant mortality rate: 35 deaths/1,000 live births (1992)
Life expectancy at birth: 64 years male, 71 years female (1992)
Total fertility rate: 2.6 children born/woman (1992)
Nationality:
  noun - Moldovan(s); adjective - Moldovan
Ethnic divisions:

Moldavian (Moldovan) 64.5%, Ukrainian 13.8%, Russian 13.0%, Gagauz 3.5%, Jews 1.5%, Bulgarian 2.0%, other 1.0% (1989 figures)
Religions:
Eastern Orthodox 98.5%, Jewish 1.5%, Baptist only about 1,000 members, other 1.0%; note - almost all churchgoers are ethnic Moldovan; the Slavic population are not churchgoers (1991 figures)
Languages:
Romanian; (Moldovan official), Russian
Literacy:
NA% (male NA%, female NA%) age 15 and over can read and write
Labor force:
2,095,000; agriculture 34.4%, industry 20.1%, other 45.5% (1985 figures)
Organized labor:
NA

:Moldova Government

Long-form name:
Republic of Moldova
Type:
republic
Capital: Chisinau (Kishinev)
Administrative divisions:
previously divided into 40 rayons; now to be divided into 7-9 larger districts at some future point
Independence:
27 August 1991 (from Soviet Union; formerly Soviet Socialist Republic of Moldova)
Constitution:
formulating a new constitution; old constitution is still in effect but has been heavily amended during the past few years
Legal system:
based on civil law system; no judicial review of legislative acts; does not accept compulsory ICJ jurisdiction but accepts many UN and CSCE documents
National holiday:
Independence Day, 27 August 1991
Executive branch:
president, prime minister, Cabinet of Ministers
Legislative branch:
Moldovan Supreme Soviet
Judicial branch:
Supreme Court (highest civil court in Moldova)
Leaders:
Chief of State and Head of Government:
Prime Minister Valeriy MURAVSKY (since 28 May 1991), 1st Deputy Prime Minister Constantin OBOROC (since June 1990); 1st Deputy Prime Minister Constantin TAMPIZA (since June 1990); 1st Deputy Prime Minister Andrei SANGHELI (since June 1990)
Chief of State:
President Mircea SNEGUR (since 3 September 1990)
Head of Legislature:

Chairman of the Supreme Soviet (Premier) Valeriy MURAVSKIY (since May 1991);

1st Deputy Prime Minister Ian HADIRCA (since 11 May 1990); Deputy Prime Minister Victor PUSCASU, 21 November 1989; Deputy Prime Minister Mihial PLASICHUK, NA

Political parties and leaders:

Moldovan Popular Front, Yuriy ROSHKA, chairman (since summer 1990); Unitatea-Yedinstvo Intermovement, V. YAKOVLEV, chairman; Bulgarian Rebirth Society, Ivan ZABUNOV, chairman; Democratic Group, five cochairmen

Suffrage:

universal at age 18

Elections:

President:

last held 8 December 1991; results - Mircea SNEGUR won 98.17% of vote

Moldovan Supreme Soviet:

last held 25 February 1990; results - Moldovan Popular Front 33%, Intermovement 34%, Communist Party 32%; seats - (366 total) Popular Front Club 35; Sovereignty Club 35; Club of Independent Deputies 25; Agrarian Club 110; Club Bujak 15; Reality Club 25; Soviet Moldova 80; remaining 41 seats probably belong to Onestr region deputies who usually boycott Moldovan legislative proceedings

:Moldova Government

Other political or pressure groups:

United Council of Labor Collectives (UCLC), Igor SMIRNOV, chairman; Social Democratic Party of Moldova (SDPM), V. CHIOBATARU, leader; The Ecology Movement of Moldova (EMM), G. MALARCHUK, chairman; The Christian Democratic

League of Women of Moldova (CDLWM), L. LARI, chairman; National Christian Party of Moldova (NCPM), D. TODIKE, M. BARAGA, V. NIKU, leaders; The
Peoples

Movement Gagauz Khalky (GKh), S. GULGAR, leader; The Democratic Party of Gagauzia (DPG), G. SAVOSTIN, chairman; The Alliance of Working People of Moldova (AWPM), G. POLOGOV, president

Member of:

CSCE, UN

Diplomatic representation:

Ambassador vacant

US:

Charge Howard Steers; Interim Chancery at #103 Strada Alexei Mateevich, Kishinev (mailing address is APO AE 09862); telephone 8-011-7-0422-23-28-94 at Hotel Seabeco in Kishinev

Flag:

same color scheme as Romania - 3 equal vertical bands of blue (hoist side), yellow, and red; emblem in center of flag is of a Roman eagle carrying a cross in its beak and an olive branch in its claws

:Moldova Economy

Overview:

Moldova, the next-to-smallest of the former Soviet republics in area, is the most densely inhabited. Moldova has a little more than 1% of the population, labor force, capital stock, and output of the former Soviet Union. Living standards have been below average for the European USSR. The country enjoys a favorable climate, and economic development has been primarily based on agriculture, featuring fruits, vegetables, wine, and tobacco. Industry accounts for 20% of the labor force, whereas agriculture employs more than one-third. Moldova has no major mineral resources and has depended on the former Soviet republics for coal, oil, gas, steel, most electronic equipment, machine tools, and major consumer durables such as automobiles. Its industrial and agricultural products, in turn, have been exported to the other former Soviet republics. Moldova has freed prices on most goods and has legalized private ownership of property, including agricultural land. Moldova's economic prospects are dimmed by the difficulties of moving toward a market economy and the political problems of redefining ties to the other former Soviet republics and Romania.

GDP:
NA; per capita NA; real growth rate -12% (1991)

Inflation rate (consumer prices):
97% (1991)

Unemployment rate: NA%

Budget:
revenues $NA million; expenditures $NA million, including capital expenditures of $NA million (1992)

Exports:
$400 million rubles (f.o.b., 1990)
commodities:
foodstuffs, wine, tobacco, textiles and footwear, machinery, chemicals (1991)
partners:
NA

Imports:
$1.9 billion rubles (c.i.f., 1990)
commodities:
oil, gas, coal, steel machinery, foodstuffs, automobiles, and other consumer durables
partners:
NA

External debt: $650 million (1991 est.)

Industrial production:
growth rate -7% (1991)

Electricity:
3,000,000 kW capacity; 13,000 million kWh produced, 2,806 kWh per capita (1991)

Industries:
key products (with share of total former Soviet output in parentheses where known): agricultural machinery, foundry equipment, refrigerators and freezers (2.7%), washing machines (5.0%), hosiery (2.0%), refined sugar (3.1%), vegetable oil (3.7%), canned food (8.6%), shoes, textiles

Agriculture:
Moldova's principal economic activity; products (shown in share of total output of the former Soviet republics): Grain (1.6%), sugar beets (2.6%),

sunflower seed (4.4%), vegetables (4.4%), fruits and berries (9.7%), grapes
(20.1%), meat (1.7%), milk (1.4%), and eggs (1.4%)
Illicit drugs:
transshipment point for illicit drugs to Western Europe

:Moldova Economy

Economic aid:
US commitments, including Ex-Im (1991), $NA, Western (non-US) countries, ODA
and OOF bilateral commitments (1991), $NA million
Currency:
as of May 1992, retaining ruble as currency
Fiscal year: calendar year

:Moldova Communications

Railroads:
1,150 km (includes NA km electrified) (1990); does not include industrial
lines
Highways:
20,000 km total (1990); 13,900 km hard-surfaced, 6,100 km earth
Inland waterways:
NA km perennially navigable
Pipelines:
NA
Ports:
none - landlocked
Merchant marine:
NA
Civil air:
NA major transport aircraft
Airports:
NA
Telecommunications:
poorly supplied with telephones; 215,000 unsatisfied applications for
telephone installations (31 January 1990); connected to Ukraine by landline
and countries beyond the former USSR through the switching center in Moscow

:Moldova Defense Forces

Branches:
Republic Security Forces (internal and border troops); Russian Forces
(Ground, Navy, Air, and Air Defense)
Manpower availability:
NA
Defense expenditures:
$NA, NA% of GDP

Monaco Geography

Total area: 1.9 km2
Land area: 1.9 km2
Comparative area: about three times the size of the Mall in Washington, DC
Land boundaries:
4.4 km; France 4.4 km
Coastline:

4.1 km
Maritime claims:
 Territorial sea:
  12 nm
Disputes:
  none
Climate:
  Mediterranean with mild, wet winters and hot, dry summers
Terrain:
  hilly, rugged, rocky
Natural resources:
  none
Land use:
  arable land 0%; permanent crops 0%; meadows and pastures 0%; forest and
  woodland 0%; other 100%
Environment:
  almost entirely urban
Note:
  second-smallest independent state in world (after Vatican City)

:Monaco People

Population: 29,965 (July 1992), growth rate 0.9% (1992)
Birth rate: 7 births/1,000 population (1992)
Death rate: 7 deaths/1,000 population (1992)
Net migration rate: 9 migrants/1,000 population (1992)
Infant mortality rate: 8 deaths/1,000 live births (1992)
Life expectancy at birth: 72 years male, 80 years female (1992)
Total fertility rate: 1.1 children born/woman (1992)
Nationality:
  noun - Monacan(s) or Monegasque(s); adjective - Monacan or Monegasque
Ethnic divisions:
  French 47%, Monegasque 16%, Italian 16%, other 21%
Religions:
  Roman Catholic 95%
Languages:
  French (official), English, Italian, Monegasque
Literacy:
  NA% (male NA%, female NA%)
Labor force:
  NA
Organized labor:
  4,000 members in 35 unions

:Monaco Government

Long-form name.
  Principality of Monaco
Type:
  constitutional monarchy
Capital: Monaco
Administrative divisions:
  4 quarters (quartiers, singular - quartier); Fontvieille, La Condamine,

651

Monaco-Ville, Monte-Carlo
Independence:
  1419, rule by the House of Grimaldi
Constitution:
  17 December 1962
Legal system:
  based on French law; has not accepted compulsory ICJ jurisdiction
National holiday:
  National Day, 19 November
Executive branch:
  prince, minister of state, Council of Government (cabinet)
Legislative branch:
  National Council (Conseil National)
Judicial branch:
  Supreme Tribunal (Tribunal Supreme)
Leaders:
  Chief of State:
  Prince RAINIER III (since November 1949); Heir Apparent Prince ALBERT
  Alexandre Louis Pierre (born 14 March 1958)
  Head of Government:
  Minister of State Jean AUSSEIL (since 16 September 1985)
Political parties and leaders:
  National and Democratic Union (UND), Democratic Union Movement (MUD), Mo-
naco
  Action, Monegasque Socialist Party (PSM)
Suffrage:
  universal adult at age 25
Elections:
  National Council:
  last held on 24 January 1988 (next to be held 24 January 1993); results -
  percent of vote by party NA; seats - (18 total) UND 18
Member of:
  ACCT, CSCE, IAEA, ICAO, IMF (observer), IMO, INMARSAT, INTELSAT,
INTERPOL,
  IOC, ITU, LORCS, UN (observer), UNCTAD, UNESCO, UPU, WHO, WIPO
Diplomatic representation:
  Monaco maintains honorary consulates general in Boston, Chicago, Los
  Angeles, New Orleans, New York, and San Francisco, and honorary consulates
  in Dallas, Honolulu, Palm Beach, Philadelphia, and Washington
  US:
  no mission in Monaco, but the US Consul General in Marseille, France, is
  accredited to Monaco; Consul General R. Susan WOOD; Consulate General at 12
  Boulevard Paul Peytral, 13286 Marseille Cedex (mailing address APO AE
  09777); telephone [33] (91) 549-200
Flag:
  two equal horizontal bands of red (top) and white; similar to the flag of
  Indonesia which is longer and the flag of Poland which is white (top) and
  red

:Monaco Economy

Overview:

Monaco, situated on the French Mediterranean coast, is a popular resort, attracting tourists to its casino and pleasant climate. The Principality has successfully sought to diversify into services and small, high-value-added, nonpolluting industries. The state has no income tax and low business taxes and thrives as a tax haven both for individuals who have established residence and for foreign companies that have set up businesses and offices. About 50% of Monaco's annual revenue comes from value-added taxes on hotels, banks, and the industrial sector; about 25% of revenue comes from tourism. Living standards are high, that is, roughly comparable to those in prosperous French metropolitan suburbs.

GDP:

exchange rate conversion - $475 million, per capita $16,000; real growth rate NA% (1991 est.)

Inflation rate (consumer prices):

NA%

Unemployment rate: full employment (1989)

Budget:

revenues $424 million; expenditures $376 million, including capital expenditures of $NA (1991)

Exports:

$NA; full customs integration with France, which collects and rebates Monacan trade duties; also participates in EC market system through customs union with France

Imports:

$NA; full customs integration with France, which collects and rebates Monacan trade duties; also participates in EC market system through customs union with France

External debt: $NA

Industrial production:

growth rate NA%

Electricity:

10,000 kW standby capacity (1991); power supplied by France Indus

Agriculture:

NA

Economic aid:

NA

Currency:

French franc (plural   francs); 1 French franc (F) = 100 centimes

Exchange rates:

French francs (F) per US$1 - 5.3801 (January 1992), 5.6421 (1991), 5.4453 (1990), 6.3801 (1989), 5.9569 (1988), 6.0107 (1987)

Fiscal year: calendar year

:Monaco Communications

Railroads:

1.6 km 1.435-meter gauge

Highways:

none; city streets

Ports:

Monaco
Merchant marine:
   1 petroleum tanker (1,000 GRT or over) totaling 3,268 GRT/4,959 DWT
Civil air:
   no major transport aircraft
Airports:
   1 usable airfield with permanent-surface runways
Telecommunications:
   served by cable into the French communications system; automatic telephone
   system; 38,200 telephones; broadcast stations - 3 AM, 4 FM, 5 TV; no
   communication satellite earth stations

:Monaco Defense Forces

Note: defense is the responsibility of France

Mongolia Geography

Total area: 1,565,000 km2
Land area: 1,565,000 km2
Comparative area: slightly larger than Alaska
Land boundaries:
   8,114 km; China 4,673 km, Russia 3,441 km
Coastline:
   none - landlocked
Maritime claims:
   none - landlocked
Disputes:
   none
Climate:
   desert; continental (large daily and seasonal temperature ranges)
Terrain:
   vast semidesert and desert plains; mountains in west and southwest; Gobi
   Desert in southeast
Natural resources:
   oil, coal, copper, molybdenum, tungsten, phosphates, tin, nickel, zinc,
   wolfram, fluorspar, gold
Land use:
   arable land 1%; permanent crops 0%; meadows and pastures 79%; forest and
   woodland 10%; other 10%; includes irrigated NEGL%
Environment:
   harsh and rugged
Note:
   landlocked; strategic location between China and Russia

:Mongolia People

Population: 2,305,516 (July 1992), growth rate 2.6% (1992)
Birth rate: 34 births/1,000 population (1992)
Death rate: 7 deaths/1,000 population (1992)
Net migration rate: 0 migrants/1,000 population (1992)
Infant mortality rate: 47 deaths/1,000 live births (1992)
Life expectancy at birth: 63 years male, 68 years female (1992)
Total fertility rate: 4.5 children born/woman (1992)

Nationality:
  noun - Mongolian(s); adjective - Mongolian
Ethnic divisions:
  Mongol 90%, Kazakh 4%, Chinese 2%, Russian 2%, other 2%
Religions:
  predominantly Tibetan Buddhist, Muslim (about 4%); previously limited
  religious activity because of Communist regime
Languages:
  Khalkha Mongol used by over 90% of population; minor languages include
  Turkic, Russian, and Chinese
Literacy:
  90% (male NA%, female NA%) (1989 est.)
Labor force:
  NA, but primarily herding/agricultural; over half the adult population is in
  the labor force, including a large percentage of women; shortage of skilled
  labor
Organized labor:
  425,000 members of the Central Council of Mongolian Trade Unions (CCMTU)
  controlled by the government (1984); independent labor organizations now
  being formed

:Mongolia Government

Long-form name:
  Mongolia
Type:
  in transition from Communist state to republic
Capital: Ulaanbaatar
Administrative divisions:
  18 provinces (aymguud, singular - aymag) and 3 municipalities* (hotuud,
  singular - hot); Arhangay, Bayanhongor, Bayan-Olgiy, Bulgan, Darhan*,
  Dornod, Dornogovi, Dundgovi, Dzavhan, Erdenet*, Govi-Altay, Hentiy, Hovd,
  Hovsgol, Omnogovi, Ovorhangay, Selenge, Suhbaatar, Tov, Ulaanbaatar*, Uvs
Independence:
  13 March 1921 (from China; formerly Outer Mongolia)
Constitution:
  12 February 1992
Legal system:
  blend of Russian, Chinese, and Turkish systems of law; no constitutional
  provision for judicial review of legislative acts; has not accepted
  compulsory ICJ jurisdiction
National holiday:
  Mongolian People's Revolution (NAADAM) 11-13 July; observed 13 July
Executive branch:
  premier, deputy premiers, Cabinet, president, vice president
Legislative branch:
  State Great Hural
Judicial branch:
  High Court; serves as appeals court for people's and provincial courts, but
  to date rarely overturns verdicts of lower courts
Leaders:

Chief of State:

President Punsalmaagiyn OCHIRBAT (since 3 September 1990); Vice President Radnaasumbereliyn GONCHIGDORJ (since 7 September 1990)

Head of Government:

Premier Dashiyn BYAMBASUREN (since 11 September 1990)

Political parties and leaders:

ruling party:

Mongolian People's Revolutionary Party (MPRP), Budragchagiin DASH-YONDON, general secretary

opposition:

Social Democratic Party (SDP), BATBAYAR; Mongolian Democratic Association, Ts. ELBEGDORJ, chief coordinator; Mongolian Party of National Progress, GANBOLD

other:

Mongolian Democratic Party (MDP), BATUUL; Free Labor Party, C. DUL; note - opposition parties were legalized in May 1990; additional parties exist: The Green Party, The Buddhist Party, The Republican Party, Mongolian People's Party, and Mongolian Revival Party; these were formed but may not be officially registered because of low rates of membership

Suffrage:

universal at age 18

Elections:

President:

last held 3 September 1990 (next to be held NA July 1994); results - Punsalmaagiyn OCHIRBAT elected by the People's Great Hural

State Great Hural:

first time held June 1992; note - according to the new present Constitution, the two parliamentary bodies are to be combined into a single popularly elected house consisting of 76 members; results - NA

:Mongolia Government

People's Small Hural:

last held on 29 July 1990 (next to be held June 1992); results - MPRP 62.3%, MDP 24.5%, SDP 7. 5%, PNP 5.7%; seats - (50 total) MPRP 33, other 17; note - People's Small Hural will not exist after State Great Hural is assembled

Communists:

MPRP membership 90,000 (1990 est.)

Member of:

AsDB, ESCAP, FAO, GATT, G-77, IAEA, IBEC, IBRD, ICAO, ILO, IMF, IOC, ISO,
ITU, LORCS, NAM, UN, UNCTAD, UNESCO, UNIDO, UPU, WFTU, WHO, WIPO, WMO, WTO

Diplomatic representation:

Ambassador Luvsandorj DAWAGIV; Chancery, (202) 983-1962

US:

Ambassador Joseph E. LAKE; Deputy Chief of Mission Thomas E. DOWLING; Embassy at Ulaanbaatar, c/o American Embassy Beijing; PSC 461, Box 300, FPO AP 06521-0002; telephone (800) 29095 and 29639

Flag:

a new flag of unknown description reportedly has been adopted

:Mongolia Economy

Overview:

Mongolia's severe climate, scattered population, and wide expanses of unproductive land have constrained economic development. Economic activity traditionally has been based on agriculture and the breeding of livestock - Mongolia has the highest number of livestock per person in the world. In recent years extensive mineral resources have been developed with Soviet support. The mining and processing of coal, copper, molybdenum, tin, tungsten, and gold account for a large part of industrial production. Timber and fishing are also important sectors. In 1991-92 Mongolian leadership is struggling with severe economic dislocations, mainly attributable to the economic crumbling of the USSR, by far Mongolia's leading trade and development partner. Moscow almost certainly cut aid in 1991, and the dissolution of the USSR at yearend 1991 makes prospects for aid quite bleak for 1992. Industry in 1991-92 has been hit hard by energy shortages, mainly due to disruptions in coal production and shortfalls in petroleum imports. The government is moving away from the Soviet-style centrally planned economy through privatization and price reform.

GDP:

exchange rate conversion - $2.1 billion, per capita $900; real growth rate -3% (1991 est.)

Inflation rate (consumer prices):

100% (1991 est.)

Unemployment rate: 15% (1991 est.)

Budget:

deficit of $67 million (1991)

Exports:

$279 million (f.o.b., 1991)

commodities:

copper, livestock, animal products, cashmere, wool, hides, fluorspar, other nonferrous metals

partners:

USSR 75%, China 10%, Japan 4%

Imports:

$360 million (f.o.b., 1991)

commodities:

machinery and equipment, fuels, food products, industrial consumer goods, chemicals, building materials, sugar, tea

partners:

USSR 75%, Austria 5%, China 5%

External debt: $16.8 billion (yearend 1990); 98.6% with USSR

Industrial production:

growth rate -12% (1991 est.)

Electricity:

1,238,000 kW capacity; 3,700 million kWh produced, 1,692 kWh per capita (1990)

Industries:

copper, processing of animal products, building materials, food and beverage, mining (particularly coal)

Agriculture:

657

accounts for about 20% of GDP and provides livelihood for about 50% of the population; livestock raising predominates (primarily sheep and goats, but also cattle, camels, and horses); crops - wheat, barley, potatoes, forage

:Mongolia Economy

Economic aid:
about $300 million in trade credits and $34 million in grant aid from USSR and other CEMA countries, plus $7.4 million from UNDP (1990); in 1991, $170 million in grants and technical assistance from Western donor countries, including $30 million from World Bank and $30 million from the IMF; over $200 million from donor countries projected in 1992

Currency:
tughrik (plural - tughriks); 1 tughrik (Tug) = 100 mongos

Exchange rates:
tughriks (Tug) per US$1 - 7.1 (1991), 5.63 (1990), 3.00 (1989)

Fiscal year: calendar year

:Mongolia Communications

Railroads:
1,750 km 1.524-meter broad gauge (1988)

Highways:
46,700 km total; 1,000 km hard surface; 45,700 km other surfaces (1988)

Inland waterways:
397 km of principal routes (1988)

Civil air:
25 major transport aircraft

Airports:
81 total, 31 usable; 11 with permanent-surface runways; fewer than 5 with runways over 3,659 m; fewer than 20 with runways 2,440-3,659 m; 12 with runways 1,220-2,439 m

Telecommunications:
63,000 telephones (1989); broadcast stations - 12 AM, 1 FM, 1 TV (with 18 provincial repeaters); repeat of Russian TV; 120,000 TVs; 220,000 radios; at least 1 earth station

:Mongolia Defense Forces

Branches:
Mongolian People's Army (includes Border Guards), Air Force

Manpower availability:
males 15-49, 551,548; 359,904 fit for military service; 25,275 reach military age (18) annually

Defense expenditures:
exchange rate conversion - $22.8 million of GDP (1992 budget)

Montserrat Geography

Total area: 100 km2
Land area: 100 km2
Comparative area: about 0.6 times the size of Washington, DC
Land boundaries:
none
Coastline:
40 km

Maritime claims:
 Exclusive fishing zone:
  200 nm
 Territorial sea:
  3 nm
Disputes:
 none
Climate:
 tropical; little daily or seasonal temperature variation
Terrain:
 volcanic islands, mostly mountainous, with small coastal lowland
Natural resources:
 negligible
Land use:
 arable land 20%; permanent crops 0%; meadows and pastures 10%; forest and
 woodland 40%; other 30%
Environment:
 subject to severe hurricanes from June to November
Note:
 located 400 km southeast of Puerto Rico in the Caribbean Sea

:Montserrat People

Population: 12,617 (July 1992), growth rate 0.4 (1992)
Birth rate: 17 births/1,000 population (1992)
Death rate: 10 deaths/1,000 population (1992)
Net migration rate: -3 migrants/1,000 population (1992)
Infant mortality rate: 11 deaths/1,000 live births (1992)
Life expectancy at birth: 74 years male, 78 years female (1992)
Total fertility rate: 2.2 children born/woman (1992)
Nationality:
 noun - Montserratian(s); adjective - Montserratian
Ethnic divisions:
 mostly black with a few Europeans
Religions:
 Anglican, Methodist, Roman Catholic, Pentecostal, Seventh-Day Adventist,
 other Christian denominations
Languages:
 English
Literacy:
 97% (male 97%, female 97%) age 15 and over having ever attended school
 (1970)
Labor force:
 5,100; community, social, and personal services 40.5%, construction 13.5%,
 trade, restaurants, and hotels 12.3%, manufacturing 10.5%, agriculture,
 forestry, and fishing 8.8%, other 14.4% (1983 est.)
Organized labor:
 30% of labor force, three trade unions with 1,500 members (1984 est.)

:Montserrat Government

Long-form name:

Type:
   dependent territory of the UK
Capital: Plymouth
Administrative divisions:
   3 parishes; Saint Anthony, Saint Georges, Saint Peter
Independence:
   none (dependent territory of the UK)
Constitution:
   1 January 1960
Legal system:
   English common law and statute law
National holiday:
   Celebration of the Birthday of the Queen (second Saturday of June)
Executive branch:
   monarch, governor, Executive Council (cabinet), chief minister
Legislative branch:
   unicameral Legislative Council
Judicial branch:
   Supreme Court
Leaders:
  Chief of State:
   Queen ELIZABETH II (since 6 February 1952), represented by Governor David
   TAYLOR (since NA 1990)
  Head of Government:
   Chief Minister Reuben T. MEADE (since October 1991)
Political parties and leaders:
   National Progressive Party (NPP) Reuben T. MEADE; People's Liberation
   Movement (PLM), Noel TUITT; National Development Party (NDP), Bertrand
   OSBORNE; Independent (IND), Ruby BRAMBLE
Suffrage:
   universal at age 18
Elections:
  Legislative Council:
   last held on 8 October 1991; results - percent of vote by party NA; seats -
   (11 total, 7 elected) NPP 4, NDP 1, PLM 1, independent 1
Member of:
   CARICOM, CDB, ECLAC (associate), ICFTU, OECS, WCL
Diplomatic representation:
   none (dependent territory of the UK)
Flag:
   blue with the flag of the UK in the upper hoist-side quadrant and the
   Montserratian coat of arms centered in the outer half of the flag; the coat
   of arms features a woman standing beside a yellow harp with her arm around a
   black cross

:Montserrat Economy

Overview:
   The economy is small and open with economic activity centered on tourism and
   construction. Tourism is the most important sector and accounted for 20% of
   GDP in 1986. Agriculture accounted for about 4% of GDP and industry 10%. The

economy is heavily dependent on imports, making it vulnerable to fluctuations in world prices. Exports consist mainly of electronic parts sold to the US.

GDP:
  exchange rate conversion - $54.2 million, per capita $4,500 (1988); real growth rate 10% (1990 est.)
Inflation rate (consumer prices):
  6.8% (1990)
Unemployment rate: 3.0% (1987)
Budget:
  revenues $12.1 million; expenditures $14.3 million, including capital expenditures of $3.2 million (1988)
Exports:
  $2.3 million (f.o.b., 1988 est.)
  commodities:
  electronic parts, plastic bags, apparel, hot peppers, live plants, cattle
  partners:
  NA
Imports:
  $30 million (c.i.f., 1988 est.)
  commodities:
  machinery and transportation equipment, foodstuffs, manufactured goods, fuels, lubricants, and related materials
  partners:
  NA
External debt: $2.05 million (1987)
Industrial production:
  growth rate 8.1% (1986); accounts for 10% of GDP
Electricity:
  5,271 kW capacity; 12 million kWh produced, 960 kWh per capita (1991)
Industries:
  tourism; light manufacturing - rum, textiles, electronic appliances
Agriculture:
  accounts for 4% of GDP; small-scale farming; food crops - tomatoes, onions, peppers; not self-sufficient in food, especially livestock products
Economic aid:
  Western (non-US) countries, ODA and OOF bilateral commitments (1970-89), $90 million
Currency:
  East Caribbean dollar (plural - dollars); 1 EC dollar (EC$) = 100 cents
Exchange rates:
  East Caribbean dollars (EC$) per US$1 - 2.70 (fixed rate since 1976)
Fiscal year: 1 April - 31 March

:Montserrat Communications

Highways:
  280 km total; about 200 km paved, 80 km gravel and earth
Ports:
  Plymouth
Airports:

1 with permanent-surface runways 1,036 m
Telecommunications:
  3,000 telephones; broadcast stations - 8 AM, 4 FM, 1 TV
:Montserrat Defense Forces

Branches:
  Police Force
Note:
  defense is the responsibility of the UK

Morocco Geography

Total area: 446,550 km2
Land area: 446,300 km2
Comparative area: slightly larger than California
Land boundaries:
  2,002 km; Algeria 1,559 km, Western Sahara 443 km
Coastline:
  1,835 km
Maritime claims:
 Contiguous zone:
  24 nm
 Continental shelf:
  200 m (depth) or to depth of exploitation
 Exclusive economic zone:
  200 nm
 Territorial sea:
  12 nm
Disputes:
  claims and administers Western Sahara, but sovereignty is unresolved; the UN
  is attempting to hold a referendum; the UN-administered cease-fire has been
  currently in effect since September 1991 Spain controls five places of
  sovereignty (plazas de soberania) on and off the coast of Morocco - the
  coastal enclaves of Ceuta and Melilla which Morocco contests as well as the
  islands of Penon de Alhucemas, Penon de Velez de la Gomera, and Islas
  Chafarinas
Climate:
  Mediterranean, becoming more extreme in the interior
Terrain:
  mostly mountains with rich coastal plains
Natural resources:
  phosphates, iron ore, manganese, lead, zinc, fish, salt
Land use:
  arable land 18%; permanent crops 1%; meadows and pastures 28%; forest and
  woodland 12%; other 41%; includes irrigated 1%
Environment:
  northern mountains geologically unstable and subject to earthquakes;
  desertification
Note:
  strategic location along Strait of Gibraltar
:Morocco People

Population: 26,708,587 (July 1992), growth rate 2.1% (1992)
Birth rate: 29 births/1,000 population (1992)
Death rate: 8 deaths/1,000 population (1992)
Net migration rate: - 1 migrant/1,000 population (1992)
Infant mortality rate: 56 deaths/1,000 live births (1992)
Life expectancy at birth: 63 years male, 67 years female (1992)
Total fertility rate: 3.7 children born/woman (1992)
Nationality:
    noun - Moroccan(s); adjective - Moroccan
Ethnic divisions:
    Arab-Berber 99.1%, non-Moroccan 0.7%, Jewish 0.2%
Religions:
    Muslim 98.7%, Christian 1.1%, Jewish 0.2%
Languages:
    Arabic (official); several Berber dialects; French is often the language of
    business, government, and diplomacy
Literacy:
    50% (male 61%, female 38%) age 15 and over can read and write (1990 est.)
Labor force:
    7,400,000; agriculture 50%, services 26%, industry 15%, other 9% (1985)
Organized labor:
    about 5% of the labor force, mainly in the Union of Moroccan Workers (UMT)
    and the Democratic Confederation of Labor (CDT)

:Morocco Government

Long-form name:
    Kingdom of Morocco
Type:
    constitutional monarchy
Capital: Rabat
Administrative divisions:
    37 provinces and 5 municipalities* (wilayas, singular - wilaya); Agadir, Al
    Hoceima, Azilal, Beni Mellal, Ben Slimane, Boulemane, Casablanca*, Chaouen,
    El Jadida, El Kelaa des Srarhna, Er Rachidia, Essaouira, Fes, Fes*, Figuig,
    Guelmim, Ifrane, Kenitra, Khemisset, Khenifra, Khouribga, Laayoune, Larache,
    Marrakech, Marrakech*, Meknes, Meknes*, Nador, Ouarzazate, Oujda,
    Rabat-Sale*, Safi, Settat, Sidi Kacem, Tanger, Tan-Tan, Taounate,
    Taroudannt, Tata, Taza, Tetouan, Tiznit
Independence:
    2 March 1956 (from France)
Constitution:
    10 March 1972
Legal system:
    based on Islamic law and French and Spanish civil law system; judicial
    review of legislative acts in Constitutional Chamber of Supreme Court
National holiday:
    National Day (anniversary of King Hassan II's accession to the throne), 3
    March (1961)
Executive branch:
    monarch, prime minister, Council of Ministers (cabinet)

Legislative branch:

unicameral Chamber of Representatives (Majlis Nawab)

Judicial branch:

Supreme Court

Leaders:

Chief of State:

King HASSAN II (since 3 March 1961)

Head of Government:

Prime Minister Dr. Azzedine LARAKI (since 30 September 1986)

Political parties and leaders:

Morocco has 15 political parties; the major ones are Istiqlal, M'Hamed BOUCETTA; Socialist Union of Popular Forces (USFP); Popular Movement (MP), Secretariat General; National Assembly of Independents (RNI), Ahmed OSMAN; National Democratic Party (PND), Mohamed Arsalane EL-JADIDI; Party for Progress and Socialism (PPS); Constitutional Union (UC), Maati BOUABID

Suffrage:

universal at age 21

Elections:

Chamber of Representatives:

last held on 14 September 1984 (were scheduled for September 1990, but postponed until NA 1992); results - percent of vote by party NA; seats - (306 total, 206 elected) CU 83, RNI 61, MP 47, Istiqlal 41, USFP 36, PND 24, other 14

Communists:

about 2,000

Member of:

ABEDA, ACCT (associate), AfDB, AFESD, AL, AMF, AMU, CCC, EBRD, ECA, FAO,

G-77, GATT, IAEA, IBRD, ICAO, ICC, ICFTU, IDA, IDB, IFAD, IFC, IIB, ILO, IMF, IMO, INTELSAT, INTERPOL, IOC, ISO, ITU, LORCS, OAS (observer), NAM,

OIC, UN, UNCTAD, UNESCO, UNHCR, UNIDO, UPU, WHO, WIPO, WMO, WTO

:Morocco Government

Diplomatic representation:

Ambassador Mohamed BELKHAYAT; Chancery at 1601 21st Street NW, Washington,

DC 20009; telephone (202) 462-7979; there is a Moroccan Consulate General in New York

US:

Ambassador Frederick VREELAND; Embassy at 2 Avenue de Marrakech, Rabat (mailing address is P. O. Box 120, Rabat, or PSC 74, APO AE 09718; telephone [212] (7) 76-22-65; FAX [212] (7) 76-56-61; there is a US Consulate General in Casablanca

Flag:

red with a green pentacle (five-pointed, linear star) known as Solomon's seal in the center of the flag; green is the traditional color of Islam

:Morocco Economy

Overview:

The economy had recovered moderately in 1990 because of: the resolution of a trade dispute with India over phosphoric acid sales, a rebound in textile sales to the EC, lower prices for food imports, a sharp increase in worker remittances, increased Arab donor aid, and generous debt rescheduling agreements. Economic performance in 1991 was mixed. A record harvest helped real GDP advance by 4.2%, although nonagricultural output grew by less than 1%. Inflation accelerated slightly as easier financial policies triggered rapid credit and monetary growth. Despite recovery of domestic demand, import volume growth slowed while export volume was adversely affected by phosphate marketing difficulties. In January 1992, Morocco reached a new 12-month standby arrangement for $129 million with the IMF. In February 1992, the Paris Club rescheduled $1.4 billion of Morocco's commercial debt. This is thought to be Morocco's last rescheduling. By 1993 the Moroccan authorities hope to be in a position to meet all debt service obligations without additional rescheduling. Servicing this large debt, high unemployment, and Morocco's vulnerability to external economic forces remain severe long-term problems.

GDP:

exchange rate conversion - $27.3 billion, per capita $1,060; real growth rate 4.2% (1991)

Inflation rate (consumer prices):

8.1% (1991)

Unemployment rate: 16% (1991)

Budget:

revenues $7.5 billion; expenditures $7.7 billion, including capital expenditures of $1.9 billion (1992)

Exports:

$4.1 billion (f.o.b., 1991)

commodities:

food and beverages 30%, semiprocessed goods 23%, consumer goods 21%, phosphates 17%

partners:

EC 58%, India 7%, Japan 5%, USSR 3%, US 2%

Imports:

$6.0 billion (f.o.b., 1991)

commodities:

capital goods 24%, semiprocessed goods 22%, raw materials 16%, fuel and lubricants 16%, food and beverages 13%, consumer goods 9%

partners:

EC 53%, US 11%, Canada 4%, Iraq 3%, USSR 3%, Japan 2%

External debt: $20 billion (1991)

Industrial production:

growth rate 4% (1989 est.); accounts for an estimated 20% of GDP

Electricity:

2,270,000 kW capacity; 8,170 million kWh produced, 310 kWh per capita (1991)

Industries:

phosphate rock mining and processing, food processing, leather goods, textiles, construction, tourism

Agriculture:

50% of employment and 30% of export value; not self-sufficient in food; cereal farming and livestock raising predominate; barley, wheat, citrus fruit, wine, vegetables, olives; fishing catch of 491,000 metric tons in 1987

:Morocco Economy

Illicit drugs:
illicit producer of hashish; trafficking on the increase for both domestic and international drug markets; shipments of hashish mostly directed to Western Europe; occasional transit point for cocaine from South America destined for Western Europe.

Economic aid:
US commitments, including Ex-Im (FY70-89), $1.3 billion; Western (non-US) countries, ODA and OOF bilateral commitments (1970-89), $7.5 billion; OPEC bilateral aid (1979-89), $4.8 billion; Communist countries (1970-89), $2.5 billion; $2.8 billion debt canceled by Saudi Arabia (1991); IMF standby agreement worth $13 million; World Bank, $450 million (1991)

Currency:
Moroccan dirham (plural - dirhams); 1 Moroccan dirham (DH) = 100 centimes

Exchange rates:
Moroccan dirhams (DH) per US$1 - 8.889 (March 1992), 8.707 (1991), 8.242 (1990), 8.488 (1989), 8.209 (1988), 8.359 (1987)

Fiscal year: calendar year

:Morocco Communications

Railroads:
1,893 km 1.435-meter standard gauge (246 km double track, 974 km electrified)

Highways:
59,198 km total; 27,740 km paved, 31,458 km gravel, crushed stone, improved earth, and unimproved earth

Pipelines:
crude oil 362 km; petroleum products (abandoned) 491 km; natural gas 241 km

Ports:
Agadir, Casablanca, El Jorf Lasfar, Kenitra, Mohammedia, Nador, Safi, Tangier; also Spanish-controlled Ceuta and Melilla

Merchant marine:
51 ships (1,000 GRT or over) totaling 315,249 GRT/487,479 DWT; includes 10 cargo, 2 container, 12 refrigerated cargo, 6 roll-on/roll-off, 3 petroleum tanker, 11 chemical tanker, 4 bulk, 3 short-sea passenger

Civil air:
28 major transport aircraft

Airports:
75 total, 67 usable; 26 with permanent-surface runways; 2 with runways over 3,659 m; 13 with runways 2,440-3,659 m; 27 with runways 1,220-2,439 m

Telecommunications:
good system composed of wire lines, cables, and radio relay links; principal centers are Casablanca and Rabat; secondary centers are Fes, Marrakech, Oujda, Tangier, and Tetouan; 280,000 telephones; broadcast stations - 20 AM, 7 FM, 26 TV and 26 additional rebroadcast sites; 5 submarine cables; satellite earth stations - 2 Atlantic Ocean INTELSAT and 1 ARABSAT; radio

relay to Gibraltar, Spain, and Western Sahara; coaxial cable and microwave to Algeria; microwave network linking Syria, Jordan, Egypt, Libya, Tunisia, Algeria, and Morocco

:Morocco Defense Forces

Branches:
Royal Moroccan Army, Royal Moroccan Navy, Royal Moroccan Air Force, Royal Gendarmerie, Auxiliary Forces
Manpower availability:
males 15-49, 6,604,712; 4,196,449 fit for military service; 293,204 reach military age (18) annually; limited conscription
Defense expenditures:
exchange rate conversion - $1.1 billion, 4.2% of GDP (1992 budget)

Mozambique Geography

Total area: 801,590 km2
Land area: 784,090 km2
Comparative area: slightly less than twice the size of California
Land boundaries:
4,571 km total; Malawi 1,569 km, South Africa 491 km, Swaziland 105 km, Tanzania 756 km, Zambia 419 km, Zimbabwe 1,231 km
Coastline:
2,470 km
Maritime claims:
 Exclusive economic zone:
 200 nm
 Territorial sea:
 12 nm
Disputes:
none
Climate:
tropical to subtropical
Terrain:
mostly coastal lowlands, uplands in center, high plateaus in northwest, mountains in west
Natural resources:
coal, titanium
Land use:
arable land 4%; permanent crops NEGL%; meadows and pastures 56%; forest and woodland 20%; other 20%; includes irrigated NEGL%
Environment:
severe drought and floods occur in south; desertification

:Mozambique People

Population: 15,469,150 (July 1992), growth rate 4.1% (1992); note - 1.5 million Mozambican refugees; 900,000 in Malawi (1991 est.)
Birth rate: 46 births/1,000 population (1992)
Death rate: 17 deaths/1,000 population (1992)
Net migration rate: 12 migrants/1,000 population (1992)
Infant mortality rate: 134 deaths/1,000 live births (1992)
Life expectancy at birth: 46 years male, 49 years female (1992)

Total fertility rate: 6.4 children born/woman (1992)
Nationality:
  noun - Mozambican(s); adjective - Mozambican
Ethnic divisions:
  majority from indigenous tribal groups; Europeans about 10,000,
  Euro-Africans 35,000, Indians 15,000
Religions:
  indigenous beliefs 60%, Christian 30%, Muslim 10%
Languages:
  Portuguese (official); many indigenous dialects
Literacy:
  33% (male 45%, female 21%) age 15 and over can read and write (1990 est.)
Labor force:
  NA, but 90% engaged in agriculture
Organized labor:
  225,000 workers belong to a single union, the Mozambique Workers'
  Organization (OTM)

:Mozambique Government

Long-form name:
  Republic of Mozambique
Type:
  republic
Capital: Maputo
Administrative divisions:
  10 provinces (provincias, singular - provincia); Cabo Delgado, Gaza,
  Inhambane, Manica, Maputo, Nampula, Niassa, Sofala, Tete, Zambezia
Independence:
  25 June 1975 (from Portugal)
Constitution:
  30 November 1990
Legal system:
  based on Portuguese civil law system and customary law
National holiday:
  Independence Day, 25 June (1975)
Executive branch:
  president, prime minister, Cabinet
Legislative branch:
  unicameral Assembly of the Republic (Assembleia da Republica)
Judicial branch:
  People's Courts at all levels
Leaders:
 Chief of State:
  President Joaquim Alberto CHISSANO (since 6 November 1986)
 Head of Government:
  Prime Minister Mario da Graca MACHUNGO (since 17 July 1986)
Political parties and leaders:
  Front for the Liberation of Mozambique (FRELIMO) - formerly a Marxist
  organization with close ties to the USSR - was the only legal party before
  30 November 1990 when the new Constitution went into effect establishing a

multiparty system; note - the government plans multiparty elections as early
as 1993; 14 parties, including the Liberal Democratic Party of Mozambique
(PALMO), the Mozambique National Union (UNAMO), and the Mozambique National
Movement (MONAMO) have already emerged

Suffrage:
universal adult at age 18

Elections:
draft electoral law provides for periodic, direct presidential and Assembly
elections

Communists:
about 200,000 FRELIMO members; note - FRELIMO no longer considers itself a
Communist party

Member of:
ACP, AfDB, CCC, ECA, FAO, FLS, G-77, IBRD, ICAO, IDA, IFAD, IFC, ILO, IMF,
INMARSAT, IMO, INTELSAT, INTERPOL, IOC, ITU, LORCS, NAM, OAU, SADCC, UN,
UNCTAD, UNESCO, UNIDO, UPU, WHO, WMO

Diplomatic representation:
Ambassador Hipolito PATRICIO; Chancery at Suite 570, 1990 M Street NW,
Washington, DC 20036; telephone (202) 293-7146

US:
Ambassador Townsend B. FRIEDMAN, Jr.; Embassy at Avenida Kenneth Kuanda, 193
Maputo (mailing address is P. O. Box 783, Maputo); telephone [258] (1)
49-27-97, 49-01-67, 49-03-50; FAX [258] (1) 49-01-14

:Mozambique Government

Flag:
three equal horizontal bands of green (top), black, and yellow with a red
isosceles triangle based on the hoist side; the black band is edged in
white; centered in the triangle is a yellow five-pointed star bearing a
crossed rifle and hoe in black superimposed on an open white book

:Mozambique Economy

Overview:
One of Africa's poorest countries, Mozambique has failed to exploit the
economic potential of its sizable agricultural, hydropower, and
transportation resources. Indeed, national output, consumption, and
investment declined throughout the first half of the 1980s because of
internal disorders, lack of government administrative control, and a growing
foreign debt. A sharp increase in foreign aid, attracted by an economic
reform policy, has resulted in successive years of economic growth since
1985. Agricultural output, nevertheless, is at about only 75% of its 1981
level, and grain has to be imported. Industry operates at only 20-40% of
capacity. The economy depends heavily on foreign assistance to keep afloat.
The continuation of civil strife through 1991 has dimmed chances of foreign
investment, and growth was a mere 1%. Living standards, already abysmally
low, dropped by 3-4% in both 1990 and 1991.

GDP:

exchange rate conversion - $1.7 billion, per capita $120; real growth rate 1.0% (1991 est.)

Inflation rate (consumer prices):
40.5% (1990 est.)

Unemployment rate: 50% (1989 est.)

Budget:
revenues $369 million; expenditures $860 million, including capital expenditures of $432 million (1989 est.)

Exports:
$117 million (f.o.b., 1990 est.)
commodities:
shrimp 48%, cashews 21%, sugar 10%, copra 3%, citrus 3%
partners:
US, Western Europe, GDR, Japan

Imports:
$870 million (c.i.f., 1990 est.), including aid
commodities:
food, clothing, farm equipment, petroleum
partners:
US, Western Europe, USSR

External debt: $4.9 billion (1991 est.)

Industrial production:
growth rate 5% (1989 est.)

Electricity:
2,270,000 kW capacity; 1,745 million kWh produced, 115 kWh per capita (1991)

Industries:
food, beverages, chemicals (fertilizer, soap, paints), petroleum products, textiles, nonmetallic mineral products (cement, glass, asbestos), tobacco

Agriculture:
accounts for 80% of the labor force, 50% of GDP, and about 90% of exports; cash crops - cotton, cashew nuts, sugarcane, tea, shrimp; other crops - cassava, corn, rice, tropical fruits; not self-sufficient in food

Economic aid:
US commitments, including Ex-Im (FY70-89), $350 million; Western (non-US) countries, ODA and OOF bilateral commitments (1970-89), $4.4 billion; OPEC bilateral aid (1979-89), $37 million; Communist countries (1970-89), $890 million

Currency:
metical (plural - meticais); 1 metical (Mt) = 100 centavos

Exchange rates:
meticais (Mt) per US$1 - 2,358 (1 May 1992), 1,811.18 (1991), 929.00 (1990), 800.00 (1989), 528.60 (1988), 289.44 (1987)

:Mozambique Economy

Fiscal year: calendar year

:Mozambique Communications

Railroads:
3,288 km total; 3,140 km 1.067-meter gauge; 148 km 0.762-meter narrow gauge; Malawi-Nacala, Malawi-Beira, and Zimbabwe-Maputo lines are subject to closure because of insurgency

Highways:
    26,498 km total; 4,593 km paved; 829 km gravel, crushed stone, stabilized
    soil; 21,076 km unimproved earth
Inland waterways:
    about 3,750 km of navigable routes
Pipelines:
    crude oil (not operating) 306 km; petroleum products 289 km
Ports:
    Maputo, Beira, Nacala
Merchant marine:
    5 cargo ships (1,000 GRT or over) totaling 7,806 GRT/12,873 DWT
Civil air:
    7 major transport aircraft
Airports:
    195 total, 137 usable; 27 with permanent-surface runways; 1 with runways
    over 3,659 m; 5 with runways 2,440-3,659 m; 26 with runways 1,220-2,439 m
Telecommunications:
    fair system of troposcatter, open-wire lines, and radio relay; broadcast
    stations - 29 AM, 4 FM, 1 TV; earth stations - 2 Atlantic Ocean INTELSAT and
    3 domestic Indian Ocean INTELSAT

:Mozambique Defense Forces

Branches:
    Army, Naval Command, Air and Air Defense Forces, Border Guards, Militia
Manpower availability:
    males 15-49, 3,490,554; 2,004,913 fit for military service
Defense expenditures:
    exchange rate conversion - $107 million, 6-7% of GDP (1989)

Namibia Geography

Total area: 824,290 km2
Land area: 823,290 km2
Comparative area: slightly more than half the size of Alaska
Land boundaries:
    3,935 km total; Angola 1,376 km, Botswana 1,360 km, South Africa 966 km,
    Zambia 233 km
Coastline:
    1,489 km
Maritime claims:
  Exclusive economic zone:
    200 nm
  Territorial sea:
    12 nm
Disputes:
    short section of boundary with Botswana is indefinite; disputed island with
    Botswana in the Chobe River; quadripoint with Botswana, Zambia, and Zimbabwe
    is in disagreement; claim by Namibia to Walvis Bay and 12 offshore islands
    administered by South Africa; Namibia and South Africa have agreed to
    jointly administer the area for an interim period; the terms and dates to be
    covered by joint administration arrangements have not been established at
    this time, and Namibia will continue to maintain a claim to sovereignty over

the entire area; recent dispute with Botswana over uninhabited Sidudu Island in the Linyanti River

Climate:

desert; hot, dry; rainfall sparse and erratic

Terrain:

mostly high plateau; Namib Desert along coast; Kalahari Desert in east

Natural resources:

diamonds, copper, uranium, gold, lead, tin, lithium, cadmium, zinc, salt, vanadium, natural gas, fish; suspected deposits of oil, natural gas, coal, and iron ore

Land use:

arable land 1%; permanent crops NEGL%; meadows and pastures 64%; forest and woodland 22%; other 13%; includes irrigated NEGL%

Environment:

inhospitable with very limited natural water resources; desertification

Note:

Walvis Bay area is an exclave of South Africa in Namibia

:Namibia People

Population: 1,574,927 (July 1992), growth rate 3.5% (1992)
Birth rate: 45 births/1,000 population (1992)
Death rate: 9 deaths/1,000 population (1992)
Net migration rate: 0 migrants/1,000 population (1992)
Infant mortality rate: 66 deaths/1,000 live births (1992)
Life expectancy at birth: 58 years male, 63 years female (1992)
Total fertility rate: 6.5 children born/woman (1992)
Nationality:

noun - Namibian(s); adjective - Namibian

Ethnic divisions:

black 86%, white 6.6%, mixed 7.4%; about 50% of the population belong to the Ovambo tribe and 9% from the Kavangos tribe

Religions:

predominantly Christian

Languages:

English is official language; Afrikaans is common language of most of population and about 60% of white population, German 32%, English 7%; several indigenous languages

Literacy:

38% (male 45%, female 31%) age 15 and over can read and write (1960)

Labor force:

500,000; agriculture 60%, industry and commerce 19%, services 8%, government 7%, mining 6% (1981 est.)

Organized labor:

20 trade unions representing about 90,000 workers

:Namibia Government

Long-form name:

Republic of Namibia

Type:

republic

Capital: Windhoek

Administrative divisions:

the former administrative structure of 26 districts has been abolished and 14 temporary regions are still being determined; note - the 26 districts were Bethanien, Boesmanland, Caprivi Oos, Damaraland, Gobabis, Grootfontein, Hereroland Oos, Hereroland Wes, Kaokoland, Karasburg, Karibib, Kavango, Keetmanshoop, Luderitz, Maltahohe, Mariental, Namaland, Okahandja, Omaruru, Otjiwarongo, Outjo, Owambo, Rehoboth, Swakopmund, Tsumeb, Windhoek

Independence:

21 March 1990 (from South African mandate)

Constitution:

ratified 9 February 1990

Legal system:

based on Roman-Dutch law and 1990 constitution

National holiday:

Independence Day, 21 March (1990)

Executive branch:

president, Cabinet

Legislative branch:

bicameral; House of Review (upper house, to be established with elections in late 1992 by planned new regional authorities); National Assembly (lower house elected by universal suffrage)

Judicial branch:

Supreme Court

Leaders:

Chief of State and Head of Government:

President Sam NUJOMA (since 21 March 1990)

Political parties and leaders:

South-West Africa People's Organization (SWAPO), Sam NUJOMA; Democratic Turnhalle Alliance (DTA), Dirk MUDGE; United Democratic Front (UDF), Justus GAROEB; Action Christian National (ACN), Kosie PRETORIUS; National Patriotic Front (NPF), Moses KATJIUONGUA; Federal Convention of Namibia (FCN), Hans DIERGAARDT; Namibia National Front (NNF), Vekuii RUKORO

Suffrage:

universal at age 18

Elections:

President:

last held 16 February 1990 (next to be held March 1995); results - Sam NUJOMA was elected president by the Constituent Assembly (now the National Assembly)

National Assembly:

last held on 7-11 November 1989 (next to be held by November 1994); results - percent of vote by party NA; seats - (72 total) SWAPO 41, DTA 21, UDF 4, ACN 3, NNF 1, FCN 1, NPF 1

Other political or pressure groups:

NA

Member of:

ACP, AfDB, CECA (associate), ECA, FAO, FLS, G-77, IAEA, IBRD, ICAO, ILO, IMF, ITU, NAM, SACU, SADCC, UN, UNCTAD, UNESCO, UNHCR, UNIDO, WCL, WFTU, WHO

Diplomatic representation:

Ambassador Tuliameni KALOMOH; Chancery at 1605 New Hampshire Ave. NW, Washington, DC 20009 (mailing address is PO Box 34738, Washington, DC 20043); telephone (202) 986-0540

:Namibia Government

US:

Ambassador Genta Hawkins HOLMES; Embassy at Ausplan Building, 14 Lossen St.,

Windhoek (mailing address is P. O. Box 9890, Windhoek 9000, Namibia); telephone [264] (61) 221-601, 222-675, 222-680; FAX [264] (61) 229-792

Flag:

a large blue triangle with a yellow sunburst fills the upper left section, and an equal green triangle (solid) fills the lower right section; the triangles are separated by a red stripe that is contrasted by two narrow white-edge borders

:Namibia Economy

Overview:

The economy is heavily dependent on the mining industry to extract and process minerals for export. Mining accounts for almost 25% of GDP. Namibia is the fourth-largest exporter of nonfuel minerals in Africa and the world's fifth-largest producer of uranium. Alluvial diamond deposits are among the richest in the world, making Namibia a primary source for gem-quality diamonds. Namibia also produces large quantities of lead, zinc, tin, silver, and tungsten, and it has substantial resources of coal. More than half the population depends on agriculture (largely subsistence agriculture) for its livelihood.

GDP:

exchange rate conversion - $2 billion, per capita $1,400; real growth rate 5.1% (1991 est.)

Inflation rate (consumer prices):

17% (1991 - Windhoek)

Unemployment rate: over 25% (1991)

Budget:

revenues $864 million; expenditures $1,112 million, including capital expenditures of $144 million (FY 92)

Exports:

$1,021 million (f.o.b., 1989)

commodities:

uranium, diamonds, zinc, copper, cattle, processed fish, karakul skins

partners:

Switzerland, South Africa, FRG, Japan

Imports:

$894 million (f.o.b., 1989)

commodities:

foodstuffs, petroleum products and fuel, machinery and equipment

partners:

South Africa, FRG, US, Switzerland

External debt: about $250 million; under a 1971 International Court of Justice (ICJ) ruling, Namibia may not be liable for debt incurred during its colonial period

Industrial production:
  growth rate - 6% (1990 est.); accounts for 35% of GDP, including mining
Electricity:
  490,000 kW capacity; 1,290 million kWh produced, 850 kWh per capita (1991)
Industries:
  meatpacking, fish processing, dairy products, mining (copper, lead, zinc,
  diamond, uranium)
Agriculture:
  mostly subsistence farming; livestock raising major source of cash income;
  crops - millet, sorghum, peanuts; fish catch potential of over 1 million
  metric tons not being fulfilled, 1988 catch reaching only 384,000 metric
  tons; not self-sufficient in food
Economic aid:
  Western (non-US) countries, ODA and OOF bilateral commitments (1970-87),
  $47.2 million
Currency:
  South African rand (plural - rand); 1 South African rand (R) = 100 cents
Exchange rates:
  South African rand (R) per US$1 - 2.8809 (March 1992), 2.7653 (1991), 2.5863
  (1990), 2.6166 (1989), 2.2611 (1988), 2.0350 (1987), 2.2685 (1986)
Fiscal year: 1 April - 31 March

:Namibia Communications

Railroads:
  2,341 km 1.067-meter gauge, single track
Highways:
  54,500 km; 4,079 km paved, 2,540 km gravel, 47,881 km earth roads and tracks
Ports:
  Luderitz; primary maritime outlet is Walvis Bay (South Africa)
Civil air:
  NA major transport aircraft
Airports:
  137 total, 112 usable; 21 with permanent-surface runways; 1 with runways
  over 3,659 m; 4 with runways 2,440-3,659 m; 63 with runways 1,220-2,439 m
Telecommunications:
  good urban, fair rural services; radio relay connects major towns, wires
  extend to other population centers; 62,800 telephones; broadcast stations -
  4 AM, 40 FM, 3 TV

:Namibia Defense Forces

Branches:
  National Defense Force (Army), Police
Manpower availability:
  males 15-49, 320,277; 189,997 fit for military service
Defense expenditures:
  exchange rate conversion - $66 million, 3.4% of GDP (FY 92)

Nauru Geography

Total area: 21 km2
Land area: 21 km2
Comparative area: about one-tenth the size of Washington, DC

Land boundaries:
  none
Coastline:
  30 km
Maritime claims:
  Exclusive fishing zone:
  200 nm
  Territorial sea:
  12 nm
Disputes:
  none
Climate:
  tropical; monsoonal; rainy season (November to February)
Terrain:
  sandy beach rises to fertile ring around raised coral reefs with phosphate
  plateau in center
Natural resources:
  phosphates
Land use:
  arable land 0%; permanent crops 0%; meadows and pastures 0%; forest and
  woodland 0%; other 100%
Environment:
  only 53 km south of Equator
Note:
  located 500 km north-northeast of Papua New Guinea, Nauru is one of the
  three great phosphate rock islands in the Pacific Ocean - the others are
  Banaba (Ocean Island) in Kiribati and Makatea in French Polynesia

:Nauru People

Population: 9,460 (July 1992), growth rate 1.3% (1992)
Birth rate: 18 births/1,000 population (1992)
Death rate: 5 deaths/1,000 population (1992)
Net migration rate: NEGL migrants/1,000 population (1992)
Infant mortality rate: 41 deaths/1,000 live births (1992)
Life expectancy at birth: 64 years male, 69 years female (1992)
Total fertility rate: 2.1 children born/woman (1992)
Nationality:
  noun - Nauruan(s); adjective - Nauruan
Ethnic divisions:
  Nauruan 58%, other Pacific Islander 26%, Chinese 8%, European 8%
Religions:
  Christian (two-thirds Protestant, one-third Roman Catholic)
Languages:
  Nauruan, a distinct Pacific Island language (official); English widely
  understood, spoken, and used for most government and commercial purposes
Literacy:
  NA% (male NA%, female NA%)
Labor force:
  NA

Organized labor:
  NA

:Nauru Government

Long-form name:
  Republic of Nauru
Type:
  republic
Capital: no capital city as such; government offices in Yaren District
Administrative divisions:
  14 districts; Aiwo, Anabar, Anetan, Anibare, Baiti, Boe, Buada, Denigomodu,
  Ewa, Ijuw, Meneng, Nibok, Uaboe, Yaren
Independence:
  31 January 1968 (from UN trusteeship under Australia, New Zealand, and UK);
  formerly Pleasant Island
Constitution:
  29 January 1968
Legal system:
  own Acts of Parliament and British common law
National holiday:
  Independence Day, 31 January (1968)
Executive branch:
  president, Cabinet
Legislative branch:
  unicameral Parliament
Judicial branch:
  Supreme Court
Leaders:
 Chief of State and Head of Government:
  President Bernard DOWIYOGO (since 12 December 1989)
Political parties and leaders:
  none
Suffrage:
  universal and compulsory at age 20
Elections:
 President:
  last held 9 December 1989 (next to be held December 1992); results - Bernard
  DOWIYOGO elected by Parliament
 Parliament:
  last held on 9 December 1989 (next to be held December 1992); results -
  percent of vote NA; seats - (18 total) independents 18
Member of:
  C (special), ESCAP, ICAO, INTERPOL, ITU, SPC, SPF, UPU
Diplomatic representation:
  Ambassador-designate Theodore Conrad MOSES resident in Melbourne
  (Australia); there is a Nauruan Consulate in Agana (Guam)
 US:
  the US Ambassador to Australia is accredited to Nauru
Flag:
  blue with a narrow, horizontal, yellow stripe across the center and a large

white 12-pointed star below the stripe on the hoist side; the star indicates the country's location in relation to the Equator (the yellow stripe) and the 12 points symbolize the 12 original tribes of Nauru

:Nauru Economy

Overview:
Revenues come from the export of phosphates, the reserves of which are expected to be exhausted by the year 2000. Phosphates have given Nauruans one of the highest per capita incomes in the Third World - $10,000 annually. Few other resources exist, so most necessities must be imported, including fresh water from Australia. The rehabilitation of mined land and the replacement of income from phosphates are serious long-term problems. Substantial amounts of phosphate income are invested in trust funds to help cushion the transition.

GNP:
exchange rate conversion - over $90 million, per capita $10,000; real growth rate NA% (1989)

Inflation rate (consumer prices):
NA%

Unemployment rate: 0%

Budget:
revenues $69.7 million; expenditures $51.5 million, including capital expenditures of $NA (FY86 est.)

Exports:
$93 million (f.o.b., 1984)
commodities:
phosphates
partners:
Australia, NZ

Imports:
$73 million (c.i.f., 1984)
commodities:
food, fuel, manufactures, building materials, machinery
partners:
Australia, UK, NZ, Japan

External debt: $33.3 million

Industrial production:
growth rate NA%

Electricity:
14,000 kW capacity; 50 million kWh produced, 5,430 kWh per capita (1990)

Industries:
phosphate mining, financial services, coconuts

Agriculture:
negligible; almost completely dependent on imports for food and water

Economic aid:
Western (non-US) countries (1970-89), $2 million

Currency:
Australian dollar (plural - dollars); 1 Australian dollar ($A) = 100 cents

Exchange rates:
Australian dollars ($A) per US$1 - 1.3177 (March 1992), 1.2834 (1991),

1.2799 (1990), 1.2618 (1989), 1.2752 (1988), 1.4267 (1987)

Fiscal year: 1 July - 30 June

:Nauru Communications

Railroads:

3.9 km; used to haul phosphates from the center of the island to processing facilities on the southwest coast

Highways:

about 27 km total; 21 km paved, 6 km improved earth

Ports:

Nauru

Merchant marine:

1 bulk ship (1,000 GRT or over) totaling 4,426 GRT/5,750 DWT

Civil air:

3 major transport aircraft, one on order

Airports:

1 with permanent-surface runway 1,220-2,439 m

Telecommunications:

adequate local and international radio communications provided via Australian facilities; 1,600 telephones; 4,000 radios; broadcast stations - 1 AM, no FM, no TV; 1 Pacific Ocean INTELSAT earth station

:Nauru Defense Forces

Branches:

no regular armed forces; Directorate of the Nauru Police Force

Manpower availability:

males 15-49, NA; NA fit for military service

Defense expenditures:

$NA - no formal defense structure

Navassa Island Geography

Total area: 5.2 km2

Land area: 5.2 km2

Comparative area: about nine times the size of the Mall in Washington, DC

Land boundaries:

Coastline:

8 km

Maritime claims:

Contiguous zone:

12 nm

Continental shelf:

200 m (depth)

Exclusive economic zone:

200 nm

Territorial sea:

12 nm

Disputes:

claimed by Haiti

Climate:

marine, tropical

Terrain:

raised coral and limestone plateau, flat to undulating; ringed by vertical white cliffs (9 to 15 meters high)

Natural resources:

guano

Land use:

arable land 0%; permanent crops 0%; meadows and pastures 10%; forest and woodland 0%; other 90%

Environment:

mostly exposed rock, but enough grassland to support goat herds; dense stands of fig-like trees, scattered cactus

Note:

strategic location between Cuba, Haiti, and Jamaica in the Caribbean Sea; 160 km south of the US Naval Base at Guantanamo, Cuba

:Navassa Island People

Population: uninhabited; transient Haitian fishermen and others camp on the island

:Navassa Island Government

Long-form name:

none (territory of the US)

Type:

unincorporated territory of the US administered by the US Coast Guard

Capital: none; administered from Washington, DC

:Navassa Island Economy

Overview: no economic activity

:Navassa Island Communications

Ports: none; offshore anchorage only

:Navassa Island Defense Forces

Note: defense is the responsibility of the US

Nepal Geography

Total area: 140,800 km2
Land area: 136,800 km2
Comparative area: slightly larger than Arkansas
Land boundaries:

2,926 km total; China 1,236 km, India 1,690 km

Coastline:

none - landlocked

Maritime claims:

none - landlocked

Disputes:

Climate:

varies from cool summers and severe winters in north to subtropical summers and mild winters in south

Terrain:

Terai or flat river plain of the Ganges in south, central hill region, rugged Himalayas in north

Natural resources:
    quartz, water, timber, hydroelectric potential, scenic beauty; small
    deposits of lignite, copper, cobalt, iron ore
Land use:
    arable land 17%; permanent crops NEGL%; meadows and pastures 13%; forest and
    woodland 33%; other 37%; includes irrigated 2%
Environment:
    contains eight of world's 10 highest peaks; deforestation; soil erosion;
    water pollution
Note:
    landlocked; strategic location between China and India

:Nepal People

Population: 20,086,455 (July 1992), growth rate 2.4% (1992)
Birth rate: 38 births/1,000 population (1992)
Death rate: 14 deaths/1,000 population (1992)
Net migration rate: 0 migrants/1,000 population (1992)
Infant mortality rate: 90 deaths/1,000 live births (1992)
Life expectancy at birth: 51 years male, 51 years female (1992)
Total fertility rate: 5.4 children born/woman (1992)
Nationality:
    noun - Nepalese (singular and plural); adjective - Nepalese
Ethnic divisions:
    Newars, Indians, Tibetans, Gurungs, Magars, Tamangs, Bhotias, Rais, Limbus,
    Sherpas, as well as many smaller groups
Religions:
    only official Hindu state in world, although no sharp distinction between
    many Hindu (about 90% of population) and Buddhist groups (about 5% of
    population); Muslims 3%, other 2% (1981)
Languages:
    Nepali (official); 20 languages divided into numerous dialects
Literacy:
    26% (male 38%, female 13%) age 15 and over can read and write (1990 est.)
Labor force:
    8,500,000 (1991 est.); agriculture 93%, services 5%, industry 2%; severe
    lack of skilled labor
Organized labor:
    Teachers' Union and many other nonofficially recognized unions

:Nepal Government

Long-form name:
    Kingdom of Nepal
Type:
    parliamentary democracy as of 12 May 1991
Capital: Kathmandu
Administrative divisions:
    14 zones (anchal, singular and plural); Bagmati, Bheri, Dhawalagiri,
    Gandaki, Janakpur, Karnali, Kosi, Lumbini, Mahakali, Mechi, Narayani, Rapti,
    Sagarmatha, Seti
Independence:
    1768, unified by Prithyi Narayan Shah

Constitution:
   9 November 1990
Legal system:
   based on Hindu legal concepts and English common law; has not accepted
   compulsory ICJ jurisdiction
National holiday:
   Birthday of His Majesty the King, 28 December (1945)
Executive branch:
   monarch, prime minister, Council of Ministers
Legislative branch:
   bicameral Parliament consists of an upper house or National Council and a
   lower house or House of Representatives
Judicial branch:
   Supreme Court (Sarbochha Adalat)
Leaders:
   Chief of State:
   King BIRENDRA Bir Bikram Shah Dev (since 31 January 1972, crowned King 24
   February 1985); Heir Apparent Crown Prince DIPENDRA Bir Bikram Shah Dev,
son
   of the King (born 21 June 1971)
   Head of Government:
   Prime Minister Girija Prasad KOIRALA (since 29 May 1991)
Political parties and leaders:
   ruling party:
   Nepali Congress Party (NCP), Girija Prasad KOIRALA, Ganesh Man SINGH,
   Krishna Prasad BHATTARAI
   center:
   the NDP has two factions: National Democratic Party/Chand (NDP/Chand),
   Lokinra Bahadur CHAND, and National Democratic Party/Thapa (NDP/Thapa),
   Surya Bahadur THAPA - the two factions announced a merger in late 1991;
   Terai Rights Sadbhavana (Goodwill) Party, G. N. Naryan SINGH
   Communist:
   Communist Party of Nepal/United Marxist and Leninist (CPN/UML), Man Mohan
   ADIKHARY; United People's Front (UPF), N. K. PRASAI, Lila Mani POKHAREL;
   Nepal Workers and Peasants Party, leader NA; Rohit Party, N. M. BIJUKCHHE;
   Democratic Party, leader NA
Suffrage:
   universal at age 18
Elections:
   House of Representatives:
   last held on 12 May 1991 (next to be held May 1996); results - NCP 38%,
   CPN/UML 28%, NDP/Chand 6%, UPF 5%, NDP/Thapa 5%, Terai Rights Sadbha-
vana
   Party 4%, Rohit 2%, CPN (Democratic) 1%, independents 4%, other 7%; seats -
   (205 total) NCP 110, CPN/UML 69, UPF 9, Terai Rights Sadbhavana Party 6,
   NDP/Chand 3, Rohit 2, CPN (Democratic) 2, NDP/Thapa 1, independents 3; note
   the new Constitution of 9 November 1990 gives Nepal a multiparty democracy
   system for the first time in 32 years
:Nepal Government

Communists:
    Communist Party of Nepal (CPN)
Other political or pressure groups:
    numerous small, left-leaning student groups in the capital; several small,
    radical Nepalese antimonarchist groups
Member of:
    AsDB, CCC, CP, ESCAP, FAO, G-77, IBRD, ICAO, IDA, IFAD, IFC, ILO, IMF, IMO,
    INTELSAT, INTERPOL, IOC, ITU, LORCS, NAM, SAARC, UN, UNCTAD, UNESCO, UNIDO,
    UNIFIL, UPU, WFTU, WHO, WMO, WTO
Diplomatic representation:
    Ambassador Yog Prasad UPADHYAYA; Chancery at 2131 Leroy Place NW,
    Washington, DC 20008; telephone (202) 667-4550; there is a Nepalese
    Consulate General in New York
US:
    Ambassador Julia Chang BLOCH; Embassy at Pani Pokhari, Kathmandu; telephone
    [977] (1) 411179 or 412718, 411604, 411613, 413890; FAX [977] (1) 419963
Flag:
    red with a blue border around the unique shape of two overlapping right
    triangles; the smaller, upper triangle bears a white stylized moon and the
    larger, lower triangle bears a white 12-pointed sun

:Nepal Economy

Overview:
    Nepal is among the poorest and least developed countries in the world.
    Agriculture is the mainstay of the economy, providing a livelihood for over
    90% of the population and accounting for 60% of GDP. Industrial activity is
    limited, mainly involving the processing of agricultural produce (jute,
    sugarcane, tobacco, and grain). Production of textiles and carpets has
    expanded recently and accounted for 87% of foreign exchange earnings in
    FY89. Apart from agricultural land and forests, the only other exploitable
    natural resources are mica, hydropower, and tourism. Agricultural production
    in the late 1980s grew by about 5%, as compared with annual population
    growth of 2.6%. Forty percent or more of the population is undernourished
    partly because of poor distribution. Since May 1991, the government has been
    encouraging privatization and foreign investment. It has introduced policies
    to eliminate many business licenses and registration requirements in order
    to simplify domestic and foreign investment procedures. Economic prospects
    for the 1990s remain poor because the economy starts from such a low base.
GDP:
    exchange rate conversion - $3.2 billion, per capita $165; real growth rate
    3.5% (FY91)
Inflation rate (consumer prices):
    15.0% (December 1991)
Unemployment rate: 5%; underemployment estimated at 25-40% (1987)
Budget:
    revenues $294.0 million; expenditures $624.0 million, including capital
    expenditures of $396 (FY92 est.)
Exports:

$180 million (f.o.b., FY91) but does not include unrecorded border trade with India
  commodities:
  clothing, carpets, leather goods, grain
  partners:
  US, India, Germany, UK
Imports:
  $545 million (c.i.f., FY91 est.)
  commodities:
  petroleum products 20%, fertilizer 11%, machinery 10%
  partners:
  India, Singapore, Japan, Germany
External debt: $2.5 billion (April 1990 est.)
Industrial production:
  growth rate 6% (FY91 est.); accounts for 7% of GDP
Electricity:
  280,000 kW capacity; 540 million kWh produced, 30 kWh per capita (1990)
Industries:
  small rice, jute, sugar, and oilseed mills; cigarette, textile, carpet,
  cement, and brick production; tourism
Agriculture:
  accounts for 60% of GDP and 90% of work force; farm products - rice, corn,
  wheat, sugarcane, root crops, milk, buffalo meat; not self-sufficient in
  food, particularly in drought years
Illicit drugs:
  illicit producer of cannabis for the domestic and international drug markets
Economic aid:
  US commitments, including Ex-Im (FY70-89), $304 million; Western (non-US)
  countries, ODA and OOF bilateral commitments (1980-89), $2,230 million; OPEC
  bilateral aid (1979-89), $30 million; Communist countries (1970-89), $286
  million

:Nepal Economy

Currency:
  Nepalese rupee (plural - rupees); 1 Nepalese rupee (NR) = 100 paisa
Exchange rates:
  Nepalese rupees (NRs) per US$1 - 42.7 (January 1992), 37.255 (1991), 29.370
  (1990), 27.189 (1989), 23.289 (1988), 21.819 (1987)
Fiscal year: 16 July - 15 July

:Nepal Communications

Railroads:
  52 km (1990), all 0.762-meter narrow gauge; all in Terai close to Indian
  border; 10 km from Raxaul to Birganj is government owned
Highways:
  7,080 km total (1990); 2,898 km paved, 1,660 km gravel or crushed stone;
  also 2,522 km of seasonally motorable tracks
Civil air:
  5 major and 11 minor transport aircraft
Airports:
  37 total, 37 usable; 5 with permanent-surface runways; none with runways

over 3,659 m; 1 with runways 2,440-3,659 m; 8 with runways 1,220-2,439 m
Telecommunications:
poor telephone and telegraph service; fair radio communication and broadcast service; international radio communication service is poor; 50,000 telephones (1990); broadcast stations - 88 AM, no FM, 1 TV; 1 Indian Ocean INTELSAT earth station

:Nepal Defense Forces

Branches:
Royal Nepalese Army, Royal Nepalese Army Air Service, Nepalese Police Force
Manpower availability:
males 15-49, 4,798,984; 2,488,749 fit for military service; 225,873 reach military age (17) annually
Defense expenditures:
exchange rate conversion - $34 million, 2% of GDP (FY92)

Netherlands Geography

Total area: 37,330 km2
Land area: 33,920 km2
Comparative area: slightly less than twice the size of New Jersey
Land boundaries:
1,027 km total; Belgium 450 km, Germany 577 km
Coastline:
451 km
Maritime claims:
 Continental shelf:
 not specific
 Territorial sea:
 12 nm
Disputes:
none
Climate:
temperate; marine; cool summers and mild winters
Terrain:
mostly coastal lowland and reclaimed land (polders); some hills in southeast
Natural resources:
natural gas, crude oil, fertile soil
Land use:
arable land 26%; permanent crops 1%; meadows and pastures 32%; forest and woodland 9%; other 32%; includes irrigated 16%
Environment:
27% of the land area is below sea level and protected from the North Sea by dikes
Note:
located at mouths of three major European rivers (Rhine, Maas or Meuse, Schelde)

:Netherlands People

Population: 15,112,064 (July 1992), growth rate 0.6% (1992)
Birth rate: 13 births/1,000 population (1992)
Death rate: 8 deaths/1,000 population (1992)

Net migration rate: 1 migrant/1,000 population (1992)
Infant mortality rate: 7 deaths/1,000 live births (1992)
Life expectancy at birth: 75 years male, 81 years female (1992)
Total fertility rate: 1.6 children born/woman (1992)
Nationality:
  noun - Dutchman(men), Dutchwoman(women); adjective - Dutch
Ethnic divisions:
  Dutch 96%, Moroccans, Turks, and other 4% (1988)
Religions:
  Roman Catholic 36%, Protestant 27%, other 6%, unaffiliated 31% (1988)
Languages:
  Dutch
Literacy:
  99% (male NA%, female NA%) age 15 and over can read and write (1979 est.)
Labor force:
  5,300,000; services 50.1%, manufacturing and construction 28.2%, government
  15.9%, agriculture 5.8% (1986)
Organized labor:
  29% of labor force

:Netherlands Government

Long-form name:
  Kingdom of the Netherlands
Type:
  constitutional monarchy
Capital: Amsterdam; The Hague is the seat of government
Administrative divisions:
  12 provinces (provincien, singular - provincie); Drenthe, Flevoland,
  Friesland, Gelderland, Groningen, Limburg, Noord-Brabant, Noord-Holland,
  Overijssel, Utrecht, Zeeland, Zuid-Holland
Independence:
  1579 (from Spain)
Constitution:
  17 February 1983
Dependent areas:
  Aruba, Netherlands Antilles
Legal system:
  civil law system incorporating French penal theory; judicial review in the
  Supreme Court of legislation of lower order rather than Acts of the States
  General; accepts compulsory ICJ jurisdiction, with reservations
National holiday:
  Queen's Day, 30 April (1938)
Executive branch:
  monarch, prime minister, vice prime minister, Cabinet, Cabinet of Ministers
Legislative branch:
  bicameral legislature (Staten Generaal) consists of an upper chamber or
  First Chamber (Eerste Kamer) and a lower chamber or Second Chamber (Tweede
  Kamer)
Judicial branch:
  Supreme Court (De Hoge Raad)

Leaders:

  Chief of State:

    Queen BEATRIX Wilhelmina Armgard (since 30 April 1980); Heir Apparent
    WILLEM-ALEXANDER, Prince of Orange, son of Queen Beatrix (born 27 April
    1967)

  Head of Government:

    Prime Minister Ruud (Rudolph) F. M. LUBBERS (since 4 November 1982); Vice
    Prime Minister Wim KOK (since 2 November 1989)

Political parties and leaders:

    Christian Democratic Appeal (CDA), Willem van VELZEN; Labor (PvdA), Wim
KOK;

    Liberal (VVD), Joris VOORHOEVE; Democrats '66 (D'66), Hans van MIERIO; a
    host of minor parties

Suffrage:

    universal at age 18

Elections:

  First Chamber:

    last held on 9 June 1991 (next to be held 9 June 1995); results - elected by
    the country's 12 provincial councils; seats - (75 total) percent of seats by
    party NA

  Second Chamber:

    last held on 6 September 1989 (next to be held by September 1993); results -
    CDA 35.3%, PvdA 31. 9%, VVD 14.6%, D'66 7.9%, other 10.3%; seats - (150
    total) CDA 54, PvdA 49, VVD 22, D'66 12, other 13

Communists:

    about 6,000

:Netherlands Government

Other political or pressure groups:

    large multinational firms; Federation of Netherlands Trade Union Movement
    (comprising Socialist and Catholic trade unions) and a Protestant trade
    union; Federation of Catholic and Protestant Employers Associations; the
    nondenominational Federation of Netherlands Enterprises; and IKV -
    Interchurch Peace Council

Member of:

    AfDB, AG (observer), AsDB, Australia Group, Benelux, BIS, CCC, CE, CERN,
    COCOM, CSCE, EBRD, EC, ECE, ECLAC, EIB, EMS, ESA, ESCAP, FAO, G-10,
GATT,

    IADB, IAEA, IBRD, ICAO, ICC, ICFTU, IDA, IEA, IFAD, IFC, ILO, IMF, IMO,
    INMARSAT, INTELSAT, INTERPOL, IOC, IOM, ISO, ITU, LORCS, MTCR,
NACC, NATO,

    NEA, NSG, OAS (observer), OECD, PCA, UN, UNCTAD, UNESCO, UNHCR,
UNIDO,

    UNTSO, UPU, WCL, WEU, WHO, WIPO, WMO, WTO, ZC

Diplomatic representation:

    Ambassador Johan Hendrick MEESMAN; Chancery at 4200 Linnean Avenue NW,
    Washington, DC 20008; telephone (202) 244-5300; there are Dutch Consulates
    General in Chicago, Houston, Los Angeles, New York, and San Francisco

  US:

    Ambassador C. Howard WILKINS, Jr.; Embassy at Lange Voorhout 102, The Hague (mailing address PSC 71, Box 1000, APO AE 09715); telephone [31] (70) 310-9209; FAX [31] (70) 361-4688; there is a US Consulate General in Amsterdam

Flag:

three equal horizontal bands of red (top), white, and blue; similar to the flag of Luxembourg, which uses a lighter blue and is longer

:Netherlands Economy

Overview:

This highly developed and affluent economy is based on private enterprise. The government makes its presence felt, however, through many regulations, permit requirements, and welfare programs affecting most aspects of economic activity. The trade and financial services sector contributes over 50% of GDP. Industrial activity provides about 25% of GDP and is led by the food-processing, oil-refining, and metalworking industries. The highly mechanized agricultural sector employs only 5% of the labor force, but provides large surpluses for export and the domestic food-processing industry. An unemployment rate of 6.2% and a sizable budget deficit are currently the most serious economic problems.

GDP:

purchasing power equivalent - $249.6 billion, per capita $16,600; real growth rate 2.2% (1991 est.)

Inflation rate (consumer prices):

3.6% (1991 est.)

Unemployment rate: 6.2% (1991 est.)

Budget:

revenues $98.7 billion; expenditures $110.8 billion, including capital expenditures of $NA (1991)

Exports:

$131.5 billion (f.o.b., 1990)

commodities:

agricultural products, processed foods and tobacco, natural gas, chemicals, metal products, textiles, clothing

partners:

EC 74.9% (FRG 28.3%, Belgium-Luxembourg 14.2%, France 10.7%, UK 10.2%), US

4.7% (1988)

Imports:

$125.9 billion (c.i.f., 1990)

commodities:

raw materials and semifinished products, consumer goods, transportation equipment, crude oil, food products

partners:

EC 63.8% (FRG 26.5%, Belgium-Luxembourg 23.1%, UK 8.1%), US 7.9% (1988)

External debt: none

Industrial production:

growth rate 1.7% (1991 est.); accounts for 25% of GDP

Electricity:

22,216,000 kW capacity; 63,570 million kWh produced, 4,300 kWh per capita (1991)

Industries:

agroindustries, metal and engineering products, electrical machinery and
equipment, chemicals, petroleum, fishing, construction, microelectronics

Agriculture:

accounts for 4% of GDP; animal production predominates; crops - grains,
potatoes, sugar beets, fruits, vegetables; shortages of grain, fats, and
oils

Illicit drugs:

European producer of illicit amphetamines and other synethic drugs

Economic aid:

donor - ODA and OOF commitments (1970-89), $19.4 billion

Currency:

Netherlands guilder, gulden, or florin (plural - guilders, gulden, or
florins); 1 Netherlands guilder, gulden, or florin (f.) = 100 cents

:Netherlands Economy

Exchange rates:

Netherlands guilders, gulden, or florins (f.) per US$1 - 1.7753 (January
1992), 1.8697 (1991), 1.8209 (1990), 2.1207 (1989), 1.9766 (1988), 2.0257
(1987)

Fiscal year: calendar year

:Netherlands Communications

Railroads:

3,037 km track (includes 1,871 km electrified and 1,800 km double track);
2,871 km 1.435-meter standard gauge operated by Netherlands Railways (NS);
166 km privately owned

Highways:

108,360 km total; 92,525 km paved (including 2,185 km of limited access,
divided highways); 15,835 km gravel, crushed stone

Inland waterways:

6,340 km, of which 35% is usable by craft of 1,000 metric ton capacity or
larger

Pipelines:

crude oil 418 km; petroleum products 965 km; natural gas 10,230 km

Ports:

maritime - Amsterdam, Delfzijl, Den Helder, Dordrecht, Eemshaven, Ijmuiden,
Rotterdam, Scheveningen, Terneuzen, Vlissingen; inland - 29 ports

Merchant marine:

345 ships (1,000 GRT or over) totaling 2,630,962 GRT/3,687,598 DWT; includes
3 short-sea passenger, 191 cargo, 30 refrigerated cargo, 24 container, 12
roll-on/roll-off, 2 livestock carrier, 10 multifunction large-load carrier,
22 oil tanker, 27 chemical tanker, 10 liquefied gas, 2 specialized tanker, 9
bulk, 3 combination bulk; note - many Dutch-owned ships are also registered
on the captive Netherlands Antilles register

Civil air:

98 major transport aircraft

Airports:

28 total, 28 usable; 19 with permanent-surface runways; none with runways
over 3,659 m; 11 with runways 2,440-3,659 m; 6 with runways 1,220-2,439 m

Telecommunications:

highly developed, well maintained, and integrated; extensive redundant system of multiconductor cables, supplemented by radio relay links; 9,418,000 telephones; broadcast stations - 3 (3 relays) AM, 12 (39 repeaters) FM, 8 (7 repeaters) TV; 5 submarine cables; 1 communication satellite earth station operating in INTELSAT (1 Indian Ocean and 2 Atlantic Ocean antenna) and EUTELSAT systems; nationwide mobile phone system

:Netherlands Defense Forces

Branches:
  Royal Netherlands Army, Royal Netherlands Navy (including Naval Air Service and Marine Corps), Royal Netherlands Air Force, Royal Constabulary
Manpower availability:
  males 15-49, 4,144,477; 3,649,746 fit for military service; 111,952 reach military age (20) annually
Defense expenditures:
  exchange rate conversion - $7.2 billion, 2.9% of GDP (1991)

Netherlands Antilles Geography

Total area: 960 km2
Land area: 960 km2; includes Bonaire, Curacao, Saba, Sint Eustatius, and Sint Maarten
  (Dutch part of the island of Saint Martin)
Comparative area: slightly less than 5.5 times the size of Washington, DC
Land boundaries:
  none
Coastline:
  364 km
Maritime claims:
 Exclusive fishing zone:
  12 nm
 Territorial sea:
  12 nm
Disputes:
  none
Climate:
  tropical; ameliorated by northeast trade winds
Terrain:
  generally hilly, volcanic interiors
Natural resources:
  phosphates (Curacao only), salt (Bonaire only)
Land use:
  arable land 8%; permanent crops 0%; meadows and pastures 0%; forest and woodland 0%; other 92%
Environment:
  Curacao and Bonaire are south of Caribbean hurricane belt, so rarely threatened; Sint Maarten, Saba, and Sint Eustatius are subject to hurricanes from July to October
Note.
  consists of two island groups - Curacao and Bonaire are located off the coast of Venezuela, and Sint Maarten, Saba, and Sint Eustatius lie 800 km to the north

:Netherlands Antilles People

Population: 184,325 (July 1992), growth rate 0.3% (1992)
Birth rate: 18 births/1,000 population (1992)
Death rate: 6 deaths/1,000 population (1992)
Net migration rate: -9 migrants/1,000 population (1992)
Infant mortality rate: 11 deaths/1,000 live births (1992)
Life expectancy at birth: 73 years male, 77 years female (1992)
Total fertility rate: 2.0 children born/woman (1992)
Nationality:
    noun - Netherlands Antillean(s); adjective - Netherlands Antillean
Ethnic divisions:
    mixed African 85%; remainder Carib Indian, European, Latin, and Oriental
Religions:
    predominantly Roman Catholic; Protestant, Jewish, Seventh-Day Adventist
Languages:
    Dutch (official); Papiamento, a Spanish-Portuguese-Dutch-English dialect
    predominates; English widely spoken; Spanish
Literacy:
    94% (male 94%, female 93%) age 15 and over can read and write (1981)
Labor force:
    89,000; government 65%, industry and commerce 28% (1983)
Organized labor:
    60-70% of labor force

:Netherlands Antilles Government

Long-form name:
    none
Digraph:
    political parties are indigenous to each island ***
Type:
    part of the Dutch realm - full autonomy in internal affairs granted in 1954
Capital: Willemstad
Administrative divisions:
    none (part of the Dutch realm)
Independence:
    none (part of the Dutch realm)
Constitution:
    29 December 1954, Statute of the Realm of the Netherlands, as amended
Legal system:
    based on Dutch civil law system, with some English common law influence
National holiday:
    Queen's Day, 30 April (1938)
Executive branch:
    Dutch monarch, governor, prime minister, vice prime minister, Council of
    Ministers (cabinet)
Legislative branch:
    legislature (Staten)
Judicial branch:
    Joint High Court of Justice
Leaders:

Chief of State:
  Queen BEATRIX Wilhelmina Armgard (since 30 April 1980), represented by
  Governor General Jaime SALEH (since October 1989)
Head of Government:
  Prime Minister Maria LIBERIA-PETERS (since 17 May 1988, previously served
  from September 1984 to November 1985)
Political parties and leaders:
  political parties are indigenous to each island
  Bonaire:
  Patriotic Union of Bonaire (UPB), Rudy ELLIS; Democratic Party of Bonaire
  (PDB), Franklin CRESTIAN
  Curacao:
  National People's Party (PNP), Maria LIBERIA-PETERS; New Antilles Movement
  (MAN), Domenico Felip Don MARTINA; Workers' Liberation Front (FOL), Wilson
  (Papa) GODETT; Socialist Independent (SI), George HUECK and Nelson MONTE;
  Democratic Party of Curacao (DP), Augustin DIAZ; Nos Patria, Chin BEHILIA
  Saba:
  Windward Islands People's Movement (WIPM Saba), Will JOHNSON; Saba
  Democratic Labor Movement, Vernon HASSELL; Saba Unity Party, Carmen
SIMMONDS
  Sint Eustatius:
  Democratic Party of Sint Eustatius (DP-St.E), K. Van PUTTEN; Windward
  Islands People's Movement (WIPM); St. Eustatius Alliance (SEA), Ralph BERKEL
  Sint Maarten:
  Democratic Party of Sint Maarten (DP-St.M), Claude WATHEY; Patriotic
  Movement of Sint Maarten (SPA), Vance JAMES
Suffrage:
  universal at age 18

:Netherlands Antilles Government

Elections:
  Staten:
    last held on 16 March 1990 (next to be held March 1994); results - percent
    of vote by party NA; seats - (22 total) PNP 7, FOL-SI 3, UPB 3, MAN 2,
    DP-St. M 2, DP 1, SPM 1, WIPM 1, DP-St. E 1, Nos Patria 1; note - the
    government of Prime Minister Maria LIBERIA-PETERS is a coalition of several
    parties
Member of:
  CARICOM (observer), ECLAC (associate), ICFTU, INTERPOL, IOC, UNESCO
  (associate), UPU, WCL, WMO, WTO (associate)
Diplomatic representation:
  as an autonomous part of the Netherlands, Netherlands Antillean interests in
  the US are represented by the Netherlands
  US:
  Consul General Sharon P. WILKINSON; Consulate General at Sint Anna Boulevard
  19, Willemstad, Curacao (mailing address P. O. Box 158, Willemstad,
  Curacao); telephone [599] (9) 613066; FAX [599] (9) 616489
Flag:
  white with a horizontal blue stripe in the center superimposed on a vertical
  red band also centered; five white five-pointed stars are arranged in an

oval pattern in the center of the blue band; the five stars represent the five main islands of Bonaire, Curacao, Saba, Sint Eustatius, and Sint Maarten

:Netherlands Antilles Economy

Overview:

Tourism, petroleum refining, and offshore finance are the mainstays of the economy. The islands enjoy a high per capita income and a well-developed infrastructure as compared with other countries in the region. Unlike many Latin American countries, the Netherlands Antilles has avoided large international debt. Almost all consumer and capital goods are imported, with the US being the major supplier.

GDP:

exchange rate conversion - $1.4 billion, per capita $7,600; real growth rate 1.5% (1990 est.)

Inflation rate (consumer prices):

5% (1990 est.)

Unemployment rate: 21% (1991)

Budget:

revenues $454 million; expenditures $525 million, including capital expenditures of $42 million (1989 est.)

Exports:

$1.1 billion (f.o.b., 1988)

commodities:

petroleum products 98%

partners:

US 40%, Italy 6%, The Bahamas 5%

Imports:

$1.4 billion (c.i.f., 1988)

commodities:

crude petroleum 64%, food, manufactures

partners:

Venezuela 42%, US 18%, Netherlands 6%

External debt: $701.2 million (December 1987)

Industrial production:

growth rate NA%

Electricity:

125,000 kW capacity; 365 million kWh produced, 1,985 kWh per capita (1991)

Industries:

tourism (Curacao and Sint Maarten), petroleum refining (Curacao), petroleum transshipment facilities (Curacao and Bonaire), light manufacturing (Curacao)

Agriculture:

hampered by poor soils and scarcity of water; chief products - aloes, sorghum, peanuts, fresh vegetables, tropical fruit; not self-sufficient in food

Economic aid:

Western (non-US) countries, ODA and OOF bilateral commitments (1970-89), $513 million

Currency:

Netherlands Antillean guilder, gulden, or florin (plural - guilders, gulden, or florins); 1 Netherlands Antillean guilder, gulden, or florin (NAf.) = 100 cents

Exchange rates:

Netherlands Antillean guilders, gulden, or florins (NAf.) per US$1 - 1.79 (fixed rate since 1989; 1.80 fixed rate 1971-88)

Fiscal year: calendar year

:Netherlands Antilles Communications

Highways:

950 km total; 300 km paved, 650 km gravel and earth

Ports:

Willemstad, Philipsburg, Kralendijk

Merchant marine:

80 ships (1,000 GRT or over) totaling 607,010 GRT/695,864 DWT; includes 4 passenger, 27 cargo, 13 refrigerated cargo, 7 container, 9 roll-on/roll-off, 11 multifunction large-load carrier, 4 chemical tanker, 3 liquefied gas, 1 bulk, 1 oil tanker; note - all but a few are foreign owned, mostly in the Netherlands

Civil air:

8 major transport aircraft

Airports:

7 total, 6 usable; 6 with permanent-surface runways; none with runways over 3,659 m; 2 with runways 2,440-3,659 m; 2 with runways 1,220-2,439 m

Telecommunications:

generally adequate facilities; extensive interisland radio relay links; broadcast stations - 9 AM, 4 FM, 1 TV; 2 submarine cables; 2 Atlantic Ocean INTELSAT earth stations

:Netherlands Antilles Defense Forces

Branches:

Royal Netherlands Navy, Marine Corps, Royal Netherlands Air Force, National Guard, Police Force

Manpower availability:

males 15-49 49,082; 27,656 fit for military service; 1,673 reach military age (20) annually

Note:

defense is responsibility of the Netherlands

New Caledonia Geography

Total area: 19,060 km2
Land area: 18,760 km2
Comparative area: slightly smaller than New Jersey
Land boundaries:

Coastline:

2,254 km

Maritime claims:

 Exclusive economic zone:

 200 nm

 Territorial sea:

12 nm
Disputes:
  none
Climate:
  tropical; modified by southeast trade winds; hot, humid
Terrain:
  coastal plains with interior mountains
Natural resources:
  nickel, chrome, iron, cobalt, manganese, silver, gold, lead, copper
Land use:
  arable land NEGL%; permanent crops NEGL%; meadows and pastures 14%; forest
  and woodland 51%; other 35%
Environment:
  typhoons most frequent from November to March
Note:
  located 1,750 km east of Australia in the South Pacific Ocean

:New Caledonia People

Population: 174,805 (July 1992), growth rate 1.9% (1992)
Birth rate: 23 births/1,000 population (1992)
Death rate: 5 deaths/1,000 population (1992)
Net migration rate: 1 migrant/1,000 population (1992)
Infant mortality rate: 17 deaths/1,000 live births (1992)
Life expectancy at birth: 70 years male, 76 years female (1992)
Total fertility rate: 2.7 children born/woman (1992)
Nationality:
  noun - New Caledonian(s); adjective - New Caledonian
Ethnic divisions:
  Melanesian 42.5%, European 37.1%, Wallisian 8.4%, Polynesian 3.8%,
  Indonesian 3.6%, Vietnamese 1.6%, other 3.0%
Religions:
  Roman Catholic 60%, Protestant 30%, other 10%
Languages:
  French; 28 Melanesian-Polynesian dialects
Literacy:
  91% (male 91%, female 90%) age 15 and over can read and write (1976)
Labor force:
  50,469; foreign workers for plantations and mines from Wallis and Futuna,
  Vanuatu, and French Polynesia (1980 est.)
Organized labor:
  NA

:New Caledonia Government

Long-form name:
  Territory of New Caledonia and Dependencies
Type:
  overseas territory of France since 1956
Capital: Noumea
Administrative divisions:
  none (overseas territory of France); there are no first-order administrative
  divisions as defined by the US Government, but there are 3 provinces named

Iles Loyaute, Nord, and Sud

Independence:
    none (overseas territory of France); note - a referendum on independence
    will be held in 1998, with a review of the issue in 1992

Constitution:
    28 September 1958 (French Constitution)

Legal system:
    the 1988 Matignon Accords grant substantial autonomy to the islands;
    formerly under French law

National holiday:
    Taking of the Bastille, 14 July (1789)

Executive branch:
    French President, high commissioner, Consultative Committee (cabinet)

Legislative branch:
    unicameral Territorial Assembly

Judicial branch:
    Court of Appeal

Leaders:
  Chief of State:
    President Francois MITTERRAND (since 21 May 1981)
  Head of Government:
    High Commissioner and President of the Council of Government Alain
    CHRISTNACHT (since 15 January 1991)

Suffrage:
    universal adult at age 18

Elections:
  Territorial Assembly:
    last held 11 June 1989 (next to be held 1993); results - RPCR 44.5%, FLNKS
    28.5%, FN 7%, CD 5%, UO 4%, other 11%; seats - (54 total) RPCR 27, FLNKS 19,
    FN 3, other 5; note - election boycotted by FULK
  French Senate:
    last held 24 September 1989 (next to be held September 1992); results -
    percent of vote by party NA; seats - (1 total) RPCR 1
  French National Assembly:
    last held 5 and 12 June 1988 (next to be held June 1993); results - RPR
    83.5%, FN 13.5%, other 3%; seats - (2 total) RPCR 2

Member of:
    FZ, ICFTU, SPC, WMO

Diplomatic representation:
    as an overseas territory of France, New Caledonian interests are represented
    in the US by France

Flag:
    the flag of France is used

:New Caledonia Economy

Overview:
    New Caledonia has more than 25% of the world's known nickel resources. In
    recent years the economy has suffered because of depressed international
    demand for nickel, the principal source of export earnings. Only a
    negligible amount of the land is suitable for cultivation, and food accounts

for about 25% of imports.

GNP:
exchange rate conversion - $1.0 billion, per capita $6,000 (1991 est.); real growth rate 2.4% (1988)

Inflation rate (consumer prices):
4.1% (1989)

Unemployment rate: 16.0% (1989)

Budget:
revenues $224.0 million; expenditures $211.0 million, including capital expenditures of NA (1985)

Exports:
$671 million (f.o.b., 1989)

commodities:
nickel metal 87%, nickel ore

partners:
France 52.3%, Japan 15.8%, US 6.4%

Imports:
$764 million (c.i.f., 1989)

commodities:
foods, fuels, minerals, machines, electrical equipment

partners:
France 44.0%, US 10%, Australia 9%

External debt: $NA

Industrial production:
growth rate NA%

Electricity:
400,000 kW capacity; 2,200 million kWh produced, 12,790 kWh per capita (1990)

Industries:
nickel mining

Agriculture:
large areas devoted to cattle grazing; coffee, corn, wheat, vegetables; 60% self-sufficient in beef

Illicit drugs:
illicit cannabis cultivation is becoming a principal source of income for some families

Economic aid:
Western (non-US) countries, ODA and OOF bilateral commitments (1970-89), $4,185 million

Currency:
Comptoirs Francais du Pacifique franc (plural - francs); 1 CFP franc (CFPF) = 100 centimes

Exchange rates:
Comptoirs Francais duPacifique francs (CFPF) per US$1 - 97.81 (January 1992), 102.57 (1991), 99.00 (1990), 115.99 (1989), 108.30 (1988), 109.27 (1987); note - linked at the rate of 18.18 to the French franc

Fiscal year: calendar year

:New Caledonia Communications

Highways:
  6,340 km total; only about 10% paved (1987)
Ports:
  Noumea, Nepoui, Poro, Thio
Civil air:
  1 major transport aircraft
Airports:
  29 total, 27 usable; 1 with permanent-surface runways; none with runways
  over 3,659 m; 1 with runways 2,440-3,659 m; 2 with runways 1,220-2,439 m
Telecommunications:
  32,578 telephones (1987); broadcast stations - 5 AM, 3 FM, 7 TV; 1 Pacific
  Ocean INTELSAT earth station

:New Caledonia Defense Forces

Branches:
  Gendarmerie, Police Force
Manpower availability:
  males 15-49, 46,388; NA fit for military service
Note:
  defense is the responsibility of France

New Zealand Geography

Total area: 268,680 km2
Land area: 268,670 km2; includes Antipodes Islands, Auckland Islands, Bounty Islands,
  Campbell Island, Chatham Islands, and Kermadec Islands
Comparative area: about the size of Colorado
Land boundaries:
  none
Coastline:
  15,134 km
Maritime claims:
 Continental shelf:
  edge of continental margin or 200 nm
 Exclusive economic zone:
  200 nm
 Territorial sea:
  12 nm
Disputes:
  territorial claim in Antarctica (Ross Dependency)
Climate:
  temperate with sharp regional contrasts
Terrain:
  predominately mountainous with some large coastal plains
Natural resources:
  natural gas, iron ore, sand, coal, timber, hydropower, gold, limestone
Land use:
  arable land 2%; permanent crops 0%; meadows and pastures 53%; forest and
  woodland 38%; other 7%; includes irrigated 1%
Environment:
  earthquakes are common, though usually not severe

:New Zealand People

Population: 3,347,369 (July 1992), growth rate 0.7% (1992)
Birth rate: 16 births/1,000 population (1992)
Death rate: 8 deaths/1,000 population (1992)
Net migration rate: -2 migrants/1,000 population (1992)
Infant mortality rate: 9 deaths/1,000 live births (1992)
Life expectancy at birth: 72 years male, 80 years female (1992)
Total fertility rate: 2.1 children born/woman (1992)
Nationality:
  noun - New Zealander(s); adjective - New Zealand
Ethnic divisions:
  European 88%, Maori 8.9%, Pacific Islander 2.9%, other 0.2%
Religions:
  Anglican 24%, Presbyterian 18%, Roman Catholic 15%, Methodist 5%, Baptist
  2%, other Protestant 3%, unspecified or none 9% (1986)
Languages:
  English (official), Maori
Literacy:
  99% (male NA%, female NA%) age 15 and over can read and write (1970)
Labor force:
  1,603,500 (June 1991); services 67.4%, manufacturing 19.8%, primary
  production 9.3% (1987)
Organized labor:
  681,000 members; 43% of labor force (1986)

:New Zealand Government

Long-form name:
  none; abbreviated NZ
Type:
  parliamentary democracy
Capital: Wellington
Administrative divisions:
  93 counties, 9 districts*, and 3 town districts**; Akaroa, Amuri, Ashburton,
  Bay of Islands, Bruce, Buller, Chatham Islands, Cheviot, Clifton, Clutha,
  Cook, Dannevirke, Egmont, Eketahuna, Ellesmere, Eltham, Eyre, Featherston,
  Franklin, Golden Bay, Great Barrier Island, Grey, Hauraki Plains, Hawera*,
  Hawke's Bay, Heathcote, Hikurangi**, Hobson, Hokianga, Horowhenua, Hurunui,
  Hutt, Inangahua, Inglewood, Kaikoura, Kairanga, Kiwitea, Lake, Mackenzie,
  Malvern, Manaia**, Manawatu, Mangonui, Maniototo, Marlborough, Masterton,
  Matamata, Mount Herbert, Ohinemuri, Opotiki, Oroua, Otamatea, Otorohanga*,
  Oxford, Pahiatua, Paparua, Patea, Piako, Pohangina, Raglan, Rangiora*,
  Rangitikei, Rodney, Rotorua*, Runanga, Saint Kilda, Silverpeaks, Southland,
  Stewart Island, Stratford, Strathallan, Taranaki, Taumarunui, Taupo,
  Tauranga, Thames-Coromandel*, Tuapeka, Vincent, Waiapu, Waiheke, Waihemo,
  Waikato, Waikohu, Waimairi, Waimarino, Waimate, Waimate West, Waimea, Wai-
pa,
  Waipawa*, Waipukurau*, Wairarapa South, Wairewa, Wairoa, Waitaki, Waitomo*,
  Waitotara, Wallace, Wanganui, Waverley**, Westland, Whakatane*, Whangarei,
  Whangaroa, Woodville
Independence:

699

26 September 1907 (from UK)

Constitution:

no formal, written constitution; consists of various documents, including certain acts of the UK and New Zealand Parliaments; Constitution Act 1986 was to have come into force 1 January 1987, but has not been enacted

Dependent areas:

Cook Islands, Niue, Tokelau

Legal system:

based on English law, with special land legislation and land courts for Maoris; accepts compulsory ICJ jurisdiction, with reservations

National holiday:

Waitangi Day (Treaty of Waitangi established British sovereignty), 6 February (1840)

Executive branch:

British monarch, governor general, prime minister, deputy prime minister, Cabinet

Legislative branch:

unicameral House of Representatives (commonly called Parliament)

Judicial branch:

High Court, Court of Appeal

Leaders:

Chief of State:

Queen ELIZABETH II (since 6 February 1952), represented by Governor General Dame Catherine TIZARD (since 12 December 1990)

Head of Government:

Prime Minister James BOLGER (since 29 October 1990); Deputy Prime Minister Donald McKINNON (since 2 November 1990)

Political parties and leaders:

National Party (NP; government), James BOLGER; New Zealand Labor Party (NZLP; opposition), Michael MOORE; NewLabor Party (NLP), Jim ANDERTON; Democratic Party, Dick RYAN; New Zealand Liberal Party, Hanmish MACINTYRE

and Gilbert MYLES; Green Party, no official leader; Mana Motuhake, Martin RATA; Socialist Unity Party (SUP; pro-Soviet), Kenneth DOUGLAS; note - the New Labor, Democratic, and Mana Motuhake parties formed a coalition in September 1991; the Green Party joined the coalition in May 1992

:New Zealand Government

Suffrage:

universal at age 18

Elections:

House of Representatives:

last held on 27 October 1990 (next to be held October 1993); results - NP 49%, NZLP 35%, Green Party 7%, NLP 5%; seats - (97 total) NP 67, NZLP 29, NLP 1

Member of:

ANZUS (US suspended security obligations to NZ on 11 August 1986), APEC, AsDB, Australia Group, C, CCC, CP, COCOM, (cooperating country), EBRD, ESCAP, FAO, GATT, IAEA, IBRD, ICAO, ICFTU, IDA, IEA, IFAD, IFC, ILO, IMF,

IMO, INMARSAT, INTELSAT, INTERPOL, IOC, IOM (observer), ISO, ITU, LORCS,

MTCR, OECD, PCA, SPC, SPF, UN, UNCTAD, UNESCO, UNIDO, UNIIMOG, UNTSO, UPU,

WHO, WIPO, WMO

Diplomatic representation:

Ambassador - Denis Bazely Gordon McLEAN; Chancery at 37 Observatory Circle NW, Washington, DC 20008; telephone (202) 328-4800; there are New Zealand Consulates General in Los Angeles and New York

US:

Ambassador Della M. NEWMAN; Embassy at 29 Fitzherbert Terrace, Thorndon, Wellington (mailing address is P. O. Box 1190, Wellington; PSC 467, Box 1, FPO AP 96531-1001); telephone [64] (4) 722-068; FAX [64] (4) 723-537; there is a US Consulate General in Auckland

Flag:

blue with the flag of the UK in the upper hoist-side quadrant with four red five-pointed stars edged in white centered in the outer half of the flag; the stars represent the Southern Cross constellation

:New Zealand Economy

Overview:

Since 1984 the government has been reorienting an agrarian economy dependent on a guaranteed British market to an open free market economy that can compete on the global scene. The government has hoped that dynamic growth would boost real incomes, reduce inflationary pressures, and permit the expansion of welfare benefits. The results have been mixed: inflation is down from double-digit levels, but growth has been sluggish and unemployment, always a highly sensitive issue, has exceeded 10% since May 1991. In 1988, GDP fell by 1%, in 1989 grew by a moderate 2.4%, and was flat in 1990-91.

GDP:

purchasing power equivalent - $46.2 billion, per capita $14,000; real growth rate - 0.4% (1991 est.)

Inflation rate (consumer prices):

1.0% (1991)

Unemployment rate: 10.7% (September 1991)

Budget:

revenues $17.6 billion; expenditures $18.3 billion, including capital expenditures of $NA (FY91 est.)

Exports:

$9.4 billion (f.o.b., FY91)

commodities:

wool, lamb, mutton, beef, fruit, fish, cheese, manufactures, chemicals, forestry products

partners:

EC 18.3%, Japan 17.9%, Australia 17.5%, US 13.5%, China 3.6%, South Korea 3.1%

Imports:

$8.4 billion (f.o.b., FY91)

commodities:

petroleum, consumer goods, motor vehicles, industrial equipment
partners:
    Australia 19.7%, Japan 16.9%, EC 16.9%, US 15.3%, Taiwan 3.0%
External debt: $17.4 billion (1989)
Industrial production:
    growth rate 1.9% (1990); accounts for about 20% of GDP
Electricity:
    7,800,000 kW capacity; 28,000 million kWh produced, 8,500 kWh per capita
    (1990)
Industries:
    food processing, wood and paper products, textiles, machinery,
    transportation equipment, banking and insurance, tourism, mining
Agriculture:
    accounts for about 9% of GDP and 10% of the work force; livestock
    predominates - wool, meat, dairy products all export earners; crops - wheat,
    barley, potatoes, pulses, fruits, and vegetables; surplus producer of farm
    products; fish catch reached a record 503,000 metric tons in 1988
Economic aid:
    donor - ODA and OOF commitments (1970-89), $526 million
Currency:
    New Zealand dollar (plural - dollars); 1 New Zealand dollar (NZ$) = 100
    cents
Exchange rates:
    New Zealand dollars (NZ$) per US$1 - 1.8245 (March 1992), 1.7265 (1991),
    1.6750 (1990), 1.6711 (1989), 1.5244 (1988), 1.6886 (1987)
Fiscal year: 1 July - 30 June

:New Zealand Communications

Railroads:
    4,716 km total; all 1.067-meter gauge; 274 km double track; 113 km
    electrified; over 99% government owned
Highways:
    92,648 km total; 49,547 km paved, 43,101 km gravel or crushed stone
Inland waterways:
    1,609 km; of little importance to transportation
Pipelines:
    natural gas 1,000 km; petroleum products 160 km; condensate 150 km
Ports:
    Auckland, Christchurch, Dunedin, Wellington, Tauranga
Merchant marine:
    18 ships (1,000 GRT or over) totaling 182,206 GRT/246,446 DWT; includes 2
    cargo, 5 roll-on/roll-off, 1 railcar carrier, 4 oil tanker, 1 liquefied gas,
    5 bulk
Civil air:
    about 40 major transport aircraft
Airports:
    118 total, 118 usable; 34 with permanent-surface runways; none with runways
    over 3,659 m; 2 with runways 2,440-3,659 m; 43 with runways 1,220-2,439 m
Telecommunications:
    excellent international and domestic systems; 2,110,000 telephones;

broadcast stations - 64 AM, 2 FM, 14 TV; submarine cables extend to
Australia and Fiji; 2 Pacific Ocean INTELSAT earth stations

:New Zealand Defense Forces

Branches:
New Zealand Army, Royal New Zealand Navy, Royal New Zealand Air Force
Manpower availability:
males 15-49, 874,703; 739,923 fit for military service; 30,297 reach
military age (20) annually
Defense expenditures:
exchange rate conversion - $792 million, 2% of GDP (FY92)

Nicaragua Geography

Total area: 129,494 km2
Land area: 120,254 km2
Comparative area: slightly larger than New York State
Land boundaries:
1,231 km total; Costa Rica 309 km, Honduras 922 km
Coastline:
910 km
Maritime claims:
 Contiguous zone:
25 nm security zone (status of claim uncertain)
 Continental shelf:
not specified
 Territorial sea:
200 nm
Disputes:
territorial disputes with Colombia over the Archipelago de San Andres y
Providencia and Quita Sueno Bank; unresolved maritime boundary in Golfo de
Fonseca
Climate:
tropical in lowlands, cooler in highlands
Terrain:
extensive Atlantic coastal plains rising to central interior mountains;
narrow Pacific coastal plain interrupted by volcanoes
Natural resources:
gold, silver, copper, tungsten, lead, zinc, timber, fish
Land use:
arable land 9%; permanent crops 1%; meadows and pastures 43%; forest and
woodland 35%; other 12%; including irrigated 1%
Environment:
subject to destructive earthquakes, volcanoes, landslides, and occasional
severe hurricanes; deforestation; soil erosion; water pollution

:Nicaragua People

Population: 3,878,150 (July 1992), growth rate 2.8% (1992)
Birth rate: 37 births/1,000 population (1992)
Death rate: 7 deaths/1,000 population (1992)
Net migration rate: -1 migrant/1,000 population (1992)
Infant mortality rate: 57 deaths/1,000 live births (1992)

Life expectancy at birth: 60 years male, 66 years female (1992)
Total fertility rate: 4.6 children born/woman (1992)
Nationality:
  noun - Nicaraguan(s); adjective - Nicaraguan
Ethnic divisions:
  mestizo 69%, white 17%, black 9%, Indian 5%
Religions:
  Roman Catholic 95%, Protestant 5%
Languages:
  Spanish (official); English- and Indian-speaking minorities on Atlantic
  coast
Literacy:
  57% (male 57%, female 57%) age 15 and over can read and write (1971)
Labor force:
  1,086,000; service 43%, agriculture 44%, industry 13% (1986)
Organized labor:
  35% of labor force

:Nicaragua Government

Long-form name:
  Republic of Nicaragua
Type:
  republic
Capital: Managua
Administrative divisions:
  9 administrative regions encompassing 17 departments (departamentos,
  singular - departamento); Boaco, Carazo, Chinandega, Chontales, Esteli,
  Granada, Jinotega, Leon, Madriz, Managua, Masaya, Matagalpa, North Atlantic
  Coast Autonomous Zone (RAAN), Nueva Segovia, Rio San Juan, Rivas, South
  Atlantic Coast Autonomous Zone (RAAS)
Independence:
  15 September 1821 (from Spain)
Constitution:
  January 1987
Legal system:
  civil law system; Supreme Court may review administrative acts
National holiday:
  Independence Day, 15 September (1821)
Executive branch:
  president, vice president, Cabinet
Legislative branch:
  National Assembly (Asamblea Nacional)
Judicial branch:
  Supreme Court (Corte Suprema) and municipal courts
Leaders:
  Chief of State and Head of Government:
  President Violeta Barrios de CHAMORRO (since 25 April 1990); Vice President
  Virgilio GODOY (since 25 April 1990)
Political parties and leaders:
  ruling coalition:

National Opposition Union (UNO) is a 14-party alliance - National
Conservative Party (PNC), Silviano MATAMOROS; Conservative Popular Alliance
Party (PAPC), Myriam ARGUELLO; National Conservative Action Party (PANC),
Hernaldo ZUNIGA; National Democratic Confidence Party (PDCN), Augustin
JARQUIN; Independent Liberal Party (PLI), Wilfredo NAVARRO; Neo-Liberal
Party (PALI), Andres ZUNIGA; Liberal Constitutionalist Party (PLC), Jose
Ernesto SOMARRIBA; National Action Party (PAN), Eduardo RIVAS; Nicaraguan
Socialist Party (PSN), Gustavo TABLADA; Communist Party of Nicaragua
(PCdeN), Eli ALTIMIRANO; Popular Social Christian Party (PPSC), Luis
Humberto GUZMAN; Nicaraguan Democratic Movement (MDN), Roberto
URROZ; Social
Democratic Party (PSD), Guillermo POTOY; Central American Integrationist
Party (PIAC), Alejandro PEREZ

opposition parties:
Sandinista National Liberation Front (FSLN), Daniel ORTEGA; Central American
Unionist Party (PUCA), Blanca ROJAS; Democratic Conservative Party of
Nicaragua (PCDN), Jose BRENES; Liberal Party of National Unity (PLUIN),
Eduardo CORONADO; Movement of Revolutionary Unity (MUR), Francisco
SAMPER;
Social Christian Party (PSC), Erick RAMIREZ; Revolutionary Workers' Party
(PRT), Bonifacio MIRANDA; Social Conservative Party (PSOC), Fernando
AGUERRO; Popular Action Movement - Marxist-Leninist (MAP-ML), Isidro
TELLEZ;
Popular Social Christian Party (PPSC), Mauricio DIAZ

Suffrage:
universal at age 16

:Nicaragua Government

Elections:
President:
last held on 25 February 1990 (next to be held February 1996); results -
Violeta Barrios de CHAMORRO (UNO) 54.7%, Daniel ORTEGA Saavedra (FSLN)
40.8%, other 4.5%
National Assembly:
last held on 25 February 1990 (next to be held February 1996); results - UNO
53.9%, FSLN 40.8%, PSC 1.6%, MUR 1.0%; seats - (92 total) UNO 51, FSLN 39,
PSC 1, MUR 1

Communists:
15,000-20,000

Other political or pressure groups:
National Workers Front (FNT) is a Sandinista umbrella group of eight labor
unions: Sandinista Workers' Central (CST), Farm Workers Association (ATC),
Health Workers Federation (FETASALUD), National Union of Employees (UNE),
National Association of Educators of Nicaragua (ANDEN), Union of Journalists
of Nicaragua (UPN), Heroes and Martyrs Confederation of Professional
Associations (CONAPRO), and the National Union of Farmers and Ranchers
(UNAG); Permanent Congress of Workers (CPT) is an umbrella group of four
non-Sandinista labor unions: Confederation of Labor Unification (CUS),
Autonomous Nicaraguan Workers' Central (CTN-A), Independent General
Confederation of Labor (CGT-I), and Labor Action and Unity Central (CAUS);

Nicaraguan Workers' Central (CTN) is an independent labor union; Superior
Council of Private Enterprise (COSEP) is a confederation of business groups
Member of:
BCIE, CACM, ECLAC, FAO, G-77, GATT, IADB, IAEA, IBRD, ICAO, ICFTU,
IDA,
IFAD, IFC, ILO, IMF, IMO, INTELSAT, INTERPOL, IOC, IOM, ITU, LAES,
LORCS,
NAM, OAS, OPANAL, PCA, UN, UNCTAD, UNESCO, UNHCR, UNIDO, UPU,
WCL, WFTU,
WHO, WIPO, WMO
Diplomatic representation:
Ambassador Ernesto PALAZIO; Chancery at 1627 New Hampshire Avenue NW,
Washington, DC 20009; telephone (202) 939-6570
US:
Ambassador Harry W. SHLAUDEMAN; Embassy at Kilometer 4.5 Carretera Sur.,
Managua (mailing address is APO AA 34021); telephone [505] (2) 666010 or
666013, 666015 through 18, 666026, 666027, 666032 through 34; FAX [505] (2)
666046
Flag:
three equal horizontal bands of blue (top), white, and blue with the
national coat of arms centered in the white band; the coat of arms features
a triangle encircled by the words REPUBLICA DE NICARAGUA on the top and
AMERICA CENTRAL on the bottom; similar to the flag of El Salvador, which
features a round emblem encircled by the words REPUBLICA DE EL SALVADOR
EN
LA AMERICA CENTRAL centered in the white band; also similar to the flag of
Honduras, which has five blue stars arranged in an X pattern centered in the
white band

:Nicaragua Economy

Overview:
Government control of the economy historically has been extensive, although
the CHAMORRO government has pledged to greatly reduce intervention. Four
private banks have been licensed, and the government has liberalized foreign
trade and abolished price controls on most goods. Over 50% of the
agricultural and industrial firms remain state owned. Sandinista economic
policies and the war had produced a severe economic crisis. The foundation
of the economy continues to be the export of agricultural commodities,
largely coffee and cotton. Farm production fell by roughly 7% in 1989 and 4%
in 1990, and remained about even in 1991. The agricultural sector employs
44% of the work force and accounts for 15% of GDP and 80% of export
earnings. Industry, which employs 13% of the work force and contributes
about 25% to GDP, showed a drop of 7% in 1989, fell slightly in 1990, and
remained flat in 1991; output still is below pre-1979 levels. External debt
is one of the highest in the world on a per capita basis. In 1991 the
inflation rate was 766%, down sharply from the 13,490% of 1990.
GDP:
exchange rate conversion - $1.6 billion, per capita $425; real growth rate
-1.0% (1991 est.)
Inflation rate (consumer prices):

766% (1991)

Unemployment rate: 13%; underemployment 50% (1991)

Budget:

revenues $347 million; expenditures $499 million, including capital
expenditures of $NA million (1991)

Exports:

$342 million (f.o.b., 1991 est.)

commodities:

coffee, cotton, sugar, bananas, seafood, meat, chemicals

partners:

OECD 75%, USSR and Eastern Europe 15%, other 10%

Imports:

$738 million (c.i.f., 1991 est.)

commodities:

petroleum, food, chemicals, machinery, clothing

partners:

Latin America 30%, US 25%, EC 20%, USSR and Eastern Europe 10%, other 15%
(1990 est.)

External debt: $10 billion (December 1991)

Industrial production:

growth rate NA; accounts for about 25% of GDP

Electricity:

423,000 kW capacity; 1,409 million kWh produced, 376 kWh per capita (1991)

Industries:

food processing, chemicals, metal products, textiles, clothing, petroleum
refining and distribution, beverages, footwear

Agriculture:

accounts for 15% of GDP and 44% of work force; cash crops - coffee, bananas,
sugarcane, cotton; food crops - rice, corn, cassava, citrus fruit, beans;
variety of animal products - beef, veal, pork, poultry, dairy; normally
self-sufficient in food

Economic aid:

US commitments, including Ex-Im (FY70-89), $294 million; Western (non-US)
countries, ODA and OOF bilateral commitments (1970-89), $1,381 million;
Communist countries (1970-89), $3.5 billion

Currency:

cordoba (plural - cordobas); 1 cordoba (C$) = 100 centavos

:Nicaragua Economy

Exchange rates:

cordobas (C$) per US$1 - 25,000,000 (March 1992), 21,354,000 (1991), 15,655
(1989), 270 (1988), 102.60 (1987)

Fiscal year: calendar year

:Nicaragua Communications

Railroads:

373 km 1.067-meter narrow gauge, government owned; majority of system not
operating; 3 km 1.435-meter gauge line at Puerto Cabezas (does not connect
with mainline)

Highways:

25,930 km total; 4,000 km paved, 2,170 km gravel or crushed stone, 5,425 km

earth or graded earth, 14,335 km unimproved; Pan-American highway 368.5 km
Inland waterways:
  2,220 km, including 2 large lakes
Pipelines:
  crude oil 56 km
Ports:
  Corinto, El Bluff, Puerto Cabezas, Puerto Sandino, Rama
Merchant marine:
  2 cargo ships (1,000 GRT or over) totaling 2,161 GRT/2,500 DWT
Civil air:
  9 major transport aircraft
Airports:
  228 total, 155 usable; 11 with permanent-surface runways; none with runways
  over 3,659 m; 2 with runways 2,440-3,659 m; 12 with runways 1,220-2,439 m
Telecommunications:
  low-capacity radio relay and wire system being expanded; connection into
  Central American Microwave System; 60,000 telephones; broadcast stations -
  45 AM, no FM, 7 TV, 3 shortwave; earth stations - 1 Intersputnik and 1
  Atlantic Ocean INTELSAT

:Nicaragua Defense Forces

Branches:
  Ground Forces, Navy, Air Force
Manpower availability:
  males 15-49, 878,066; 541,090 fit for military service; 42,997 reach
  military age (18) annually
Defense expenditures:
  exchange rate conversion - $70 million, 3.8% of GDP (1991 budget)

Niger Geography

Total area: 1,267,000 km2
Land area: 1,266,700 km2
Comparative area: slightly less than twice the size of Texas
Land boundaries:
  5,697 km total; Algeria 956 km, Benin 266 km, Burkina 628 km, Chad 1,175 km,
  Libya 354 km, Mali 821 km, Nigeria 1,497 km
Coastline:
  none - landlocked
Maritime claims:
  none - landlocked
Disputes:
  Libya claims about 19,400 km2 in northern Niger; demarcation of
  international boundaries in Lake Chad, the lack of which has led to border
  incidents in the past, is completed and awaiting ratification by Cameroon,
  Chad, Niger, and Nigeria; Burkina and Mali are proceeding with boundary
  demarcation, including the tripoint with Niger
Climate:
  desert; mostly hot, dry, dusty; tropical in extreme south
Terrain:
  predominately desert plains and sand dunes; flat to rolling plains in south;
  hills in north

Natural resources:
  uranium, coal, iron ore, tin, phosphates
Land use:
  arable land 3%; permanent crops 0%; meadows and pastures 7%; forest and
  woodland 2%; other 88%; includes irrigated NEGL%
Environment:
  recurrent drought and desertification severely affecting marginal
  agricultural activities; overgrazing; soil erosion
Note:
  landlocked

:Niger People

Population: 8,052,945 (July 1992), growth rate 3.5% (1992)
Birth rate: 58 births/1,000 population (1992)
Death rate: 23 deaths/1,000 population (1992)
Net migration rate: 0 migrants/1,000 population (1992)
Infant mortality rate: 115 deaths/1,000 live births (1992)
Life expectancy at birth: 42 years male, 45 years female (1992)
Total fertility rate: 7.4 children born/woman (1992)
Nationality:
  noun - Nigerien(s); adjective - Nigerien
Ethnic divisions:
  Hausa 56%; Djerma 22%; Fula 8.5%; Tuareg 8%; Beri Beri (Kanouri) 4.3%; Arab,
  Toubou, and Gourmantche 1.2%; about 4,000 French expatriates
Religions:
  Muslim 80%, remainder indigenous beliefs and Christians
Languages:
  French (official); Hausa, Djerma
Literacy:
  28% (male 40%, female 17%) age 15 and over can read and write (1990 est.)
Labor force:
  2,500,000 wage earners (1982); agriculture 90%, industry and commerce 6%,
  government 4%; 51% of population of working age (1985)
Organized labor:
  negligible

:Niger Government

Long-form name:
  Republic of Niger
Type:
  as of November 1991, transition government appointed by national reform
  conference; scheduled to turn over power to democratically elected
  government in January 1993
Capital: Niamey
Administrative divisions:
  7 departments (departements, singular - departement); Agadez, Diffa, Dosso,
  Maradi, Niamey, Tahoua, Zinder
Independence:
  3 August 1960 (from France)
Constitution:
  December 1989 constitution revised November 1991 by National Democratic

Reform Conference

Legal system:

based on French civil law system and customary law; has not accepted compulsory ICJ jurisdiction

National holiday:

Republic Day, 18 December (1958)

Executive branch:

president (ceremonial), prime minister (interim), Cabinet

Legislative branch:

National Assembly

Judicial branch:

State Court (Cour d'Etat), Court of Appeal (Cour d'Apel)

Leaders:

Chief of State:

President Brig. Gen. Ali SAIBOU (since 14 November 1987); ceremonial post since national conference (1991)

Head of Government:

Interim Prime Minister Amadou CHEIFFOU (since November 1991)

Political parties and leaders:

National Movement of the Development Society (MNSD-NASSARA), Tanda MAMADOU;

Niger Progressive Party - African Democratic Rally (PPN-RDA), Harou KOUKA; Union of Popular Forces for Democracy and Progress (UDFP-SAWABA), Djibo BAKARY; Niger Democratic Union (UDN-SAWABA), Mamoudou PASCAL; Union of

Patriots, Democrats, and Progressives (UPDP), Andre SALIFOU; Niger Social Democrat Party (PSDN-ALHERI), Mallam Adji WAZIRI; Niger Party for Democracy

and Socialism (PNDS-TARAYA), Issoufou MAHAMADOU; Democratic and Social

Convention (CDS-RAHAMA), Mahamane OUSMANE; Union for Democracy and Progress

(UDP), Bello TCHIOUSSO; Union for Democracy and Social Progress (UDPS-AMANA), Akoli DAOUEL; Masses Union for Democratic Action (UMAD-AIKI),

Belko GARBA; Worker's Liberation Party (PLT), Idi Ango OUMAROU; Convention

for Social Rehabilitation (CRS), Abdoul Karim SEYNI; Popular Movement for Democracy in Niger (MPDN), Abdou SANDA; Popular Front for National Liberation (FPLN), Diallo SABO; Republican Party for Freedom and Progress in Niger (PRLPN), Alka ALMOU; other parties forming

Suffrage:

universal adult at age 18

Elections:

President:

President Ali SAIBOU has been in office since December 1989, but the presidency is now a largely ceremonial position

:Niger Government

710

National Assembly:
last held 10 December 1989 (next to be held NA); results - MNSD was the only
party; seats - (150 total) MNSD 150 (indirectly elected); note - Niger held
a national conference from July to November 1991 to decide upon a
transitional government and an agenda for multiparty elections
Member of:
ACCT, ACP, AfDB, CCC, CEAO, ECA, ECOWAS, Entente, FAO, FZ, G-77,
GATT, IAEA,
IBRD, ICAO, IDA, IDB, IFAD, IFC, ILO, IMF, INTELSAT, INTERPOL, IOC,
ITU,
LORCS, NAM, OAU, OIC, UN, UNCTAD, UNESCO, UNIDO, UPU, WADB,
WCL, WHO, WIPO,
WMO, WTO
Diplomatic representation:
Ambassador Moumouni Adamou DJERMAKOYE; Chancery at 2204 R Street NW,
Washington, DC 20008; telephone (202) 483-4224 through 4227
US:
Ambassador Jennifer C. WARD; Embassy at Avenue des Ambassades, Niamey
(mailing address is B. P. 11201, Niamey); telephone [227] 72-26-61 through
64
Flag:
three equal horizontal bands of orange (top), white, and green with a small
orange disk (representing the sun) centered in the white band; similar to
the flag of India, which has a blue spoked wheel centered in the white band

:Niger Economy

Overview:
About 90% of the population is engaged in farming and stock raising,
activities that generate almost half the national income. The economy also
depends heavily on exploitation of large uranium deposits. Uranium
production grew rapidly in the mid-1970s, but tapered off in the early 1980s
when world prices declined. France is a major customer, while Germany,
Japan, and Spain also make regular purchases. The depressed demand for
uranium has contributed to an overall sluggishness in the economy, a severe
trade imbalance, and a mounting external debt.
GDP:
exchange rate conversion - $2.4 billion, per capita $300; real growth rate
-3.4% (1991)
Inflation rate (consumer prices):
NA
Unemployment rate: NA%
Budget:
revenues $220 million; expenditures $446 million, including capital
expenditures of $190 million (FY89 est.)
Exports:
$320 million (f.o.b., 1990)
commodities:
uranium 75%, livestock products, cowpeas, onions
partners:
France 65%, Nigeria 11%, Ivory Coast, Italy

Imports:
    $439 million (c.i.f., 1990)
    commodities:
    petroleum products, primary materials, machinery, vehicles and parts,
    electronic equipment, pharmaceuticals, chemical products, cereals,
    foodstuffs
    partners:
    France 32%, Ivory Coast 11%, Germany 5%, Italy 4%, Nigeria 4%
External debt: $1.8 billion (December 1990 est.)
Industrial production:
    growth rate 0% (1989); accounts for 18% of GDP
Electricity:
    105,000 kW capacity; 230 million kWh produced, 30 kWh per capita (1991)
Industries:
    cement, brick, textiles, food processing, chemicals, slaughterhouses, and a
    few other small light industries; uranium production began in 1971
Agriculture:
    accounts for roughly 40% of GDP and 90% of labor force; cash crops -
    cowpeas, cotton, peanuts; food crops - millet, sorghum, cassava, rice;
    livestock - cattle, sheep, goats; self-sufficient in food except in drought
    years
Economic aid:
    US commitments, including Ex-Im (FY70-89), $380 million; Western (non-US)
    countries, ODA and OOF bilateral commitments (1970-89), $3,165 million; OPEC
    bilateral aid (1979-89), $504 million; Communist countries (1970-89), $61
    million
Currency:
    Communaute Financiere Africaine franc (plural - francs); 1 CFA franc (CFAF)
    = 100 centimes
Exchange rates:
    Communaute Financiere Africaine francs (CFAF) per US$1 - 269.01 (January
    1992), 282.11 (1991), 272.26 (1990), 319.01 (1989), 297.85 (1988), 300.54
    (1987)

:Niger Economy

Fiscal year: 1 October - 30 September

:Niger Communications

Highways:
    39,970 km total; 3,170 km bituminous, 10,330 km gravel and laterite, 3,470
    km earthen, 23,000 km tracks
Inland waterways:
    Niger River is navigable 300 km from Niamey to Gaya on the Benin frontier
    from mid-December through March
Civil air:
    2 major transport aircraft
Airports:
    29 total, 27 usable; 8 with permanent-surface runways; none with runways
    over 3,659 m; 2 with runways 2,440-3,659 m; 13 with runways 1,220-2,439 m
Telecommunications:
    small system of wire, radiocommunications, and radio relay links

concentrated in southwestern area; 14,260 telephones; broadcast stations -
15 AM, 5 FM, 18 TV; satellite earth stations - 1 Atlantic Ocean INTELSAT, 1
Indian Ocean INTELSAT, and 3 domestic, with 1 planned

:Niger Defense Forces

Branches:
  Army, Air Force, Gendarmerie, Republican National Guard, National police
Manpower availability:
  males 15-49, 1,724,293; 928,177 fit for military service; 83,528 reach
  military age (18) annually
Defense expenditures:
  exchange rate conversion - $27 million, 1.3% of GDP (1989)

Nigeria Geography

Total area: 923,770 km2
Land area: 910,770 km2
Comparative area: slightly more than twice the size of California
Land boundaries:
  4,047 km total; Benin 773 km, Cameroon 1,690 km, Chad 87 km, Niger 1,497 km
Coastline:
  853 km
Maritime claims:
 Continental shelf:
  200 m (depth) or to depth of exploitation
 Exclusive economic zone:
  200 nm
 Territorial sea:
  30 nm
Disputes:
  demarcation of international boundaries in Lake Chad, the lack of which has
  led to border incidents in the past, is completed and awaiting ratification
  by Cameroon, Chad, Niger, and Nigeria; boundary commission created with
  Cameroon to discuss unresolved land and maritime boundaries - has not yet
  convened
Climate:
  varies - equatorial in south, tropical in center, arid in north
Terrain:
  southern lowlands merge into central hills and plateaus; mountains in
  southeast, plains in north
Natural resources:
  crude oil, tin, columbite, iron ore, coal, limestone, lead, zinc, natural
  gas
Land use:
  arable land 31%; permanent crops 3%; meadows and pastures 23%; forest and
  woodland 15%; other 28%; includes irrigated NEGL%
Environment:
  recent droughts in north severely affecting marginal agricultural
  activities; desertification; soil degradation, rapid deforestation

:Nigeria People

Population: 126,274,589 (July 1992), growth rate 3.0% (1992); note - a new population
   figure of 88.5 million is in the process of being incorporated into revised
   Census Bureau figures (April 1992)
Birth rate: 46 births/1,000 population (1992)
Death rate: 16 deaths/1,000 population (1992)
Net migration rate: NEGL migrants/1,000 population (1992)
Infant mortality rate: 110 deaths/1,000 live births (1992)
Life expectancy at birth: 48 years male, 50 years female (1992)
Total fertility rate: 6.5 children born/woman (1992)
Nationality:
   noun - Nigerian(s); adjective - Nigerian
Ethnic divisions:
   more than 250 tribal groups; Hausa and Fulani of the north, Yoruba of the
   southwest, and Ibos of the southeast make up 65% of the population; about
   27,000 non-Africans
Religions:
   Muslim 50%, Christian 40%, indigenous beliefs 10%
Languages:
   English (official); Hausa, Yoruba, Ibo, Fulani, and several other languages
   also widely used
Literacy:
   51% (male 62%, female 40%) age 15 and over can read and write (1990 est.)
Labor force:
   42,844,000; agriculture 54%, industry, commerce, and services 19%,
   government 15%; 49% of population of working age (1985)
Organized labor:
   3,520,000 wage earners belong to 42 recognized trade unions, which come
   under a single national labor federation - the Nigerian Labor Congress (NLC)

:Nigeria Government

Long-form name:
   Federal Republic of Nigeria
Type:
   military government since 31 December 1983
Capital: Abuja; note - on 12 December 1991 the capital was officially moved from
   Lagos to Abuja; many government offices remain in Lagos pending completion
   of facilities in Abuja
Administrative divisions:
   30 states and 1 territory*; Abia, Abuja Capital Territory*, Adamawa, Akwa
   Ibom, Anambra, Bauchi, Benue, Borno, Cross River, Delta, Edo, Enugu, Imo,
   Jigawa, Kaduna, Kano, Katsina, Kebbi, Kogi, Kwara, Lagos, Niger, Ogun, Ondo,
   Osun, Oyo, Plateau, Rivers, Sokoto, Taraba, Yobe
Independence:
   1 October 1960 (from UK)
Constitution:
   1 October 1979, amended 9 February 1984, revised 1989
Legal system:
   based on English common law, Islamic law, and tribal law
National holiday:

Independence Day, 1 October (1960)

Executive branch:

president of the Armed Forces Ruling Council, Armed Forces Ruling Council, National Council of State, Council of Ministers (cabinet)

Legislative branch:

National Assembly was dissolved after the military coup of 31 December 1983

Judicial branch:

Supreme Court, Federal Court of Appeal

Leaders:

Chief of State and Head of Government:

President and Commander in Chief of Armed Forces Gen. Ibrahim BABANGIDA (since 27 August 1985)

Political parties and leaders:

two political parties established by the government in 1989 - Social Democratic Party (SDP) and National Republican Convention (NRC)

Suffrage:

universal at age 21

Elections:

President:

first presidential elections since the 31 December 1983 coup scheduled for late 1992

National Assembly:

first elections since it was dissolved after the 31 December 1983 coup scheduled for 4 July 1992

Communists:

the pro-Communist underground consists of a small fraction of the Nigerian left; leftist leaders are prominent in the country's central labor organization but have little influence on the government

Member of:

ACP, AfDB, C, CCC, ECA, ECOWAS, FAO, G-15, G-19, G-24, G-77, GATT, IAEA,

IBRD, ICAO, ICC, IDA, IFAD, IFC, ILO, IMO, IMF, INMARSAT, INTELSAT, INTERPOL, IOC, ISO, ITU, LORCS, NAM, OAU, OIC, OPEC, PCA, UN, UNCTAD,

UNESCO, UNHCR, UNIDO, UNIIMOG, UPU, WCL, WHO, WMO, WTO

Diplomatic representation:

Ambassador Zubair Mahmud KAZAURE; Chancery at 2201 M Street NW, Washington,

DC 20037; telephone (202) 822-1500; there is a Nigerian Consulate General in New York

:Nigeria Government

US:

Ambassador Lannon WALKER; Embassy at 2 Eleke Crescent, Lagos (mailing address is P. O. Box 554, Lagos); telephone [234] (1) 610097; FAX [234] (1) 610257; there is a US Consulate General in Kaduna; note - the US Government has requested Nigerian Government permission to open an Embassy Branch Office in Abuja; the US Embassy will remain in Lagos until a later date, when the Branch Office in Abuja will become the Embassy and the Embassy in Lagos will become a Consulate General

Flag:
three equal vertical bands of green (hoist side), white, and green

:Nigeria Economy

Overview:
Although Nigeria is Africa's leading oil-producing country, it remains poor with a $250 per capita GDP. In 1991 massive government spending, much of it to help ensure a smooth transition to civilian rule, ballooned the budget deficit and caused inflation and interest rates to rise. The lack of fiscal discipline forced the IMF to declare Nigeria not in compliance with an 18-month standby facility started in January 1991. Lagos has set ambitious targets for expanding oil production capacity and is offering foreign companies more attractive investment incentives. Government efforts to reduce Nigeria's dependence on oil exports and to sustain noninflationary growth, however, have fallen short because of inadequate new investment funds and endemic corruption. Living standards continue to deteriorate from the higher level of the early 1980s oil boom.

GDP:
exchange rate conversion - $30 billion, per capita $250; real growth rate 5.2% (1990 est.)

Inflation rate (consumer prices):
40% (1991)

Unemployment rate: NA%

Budget:
revenues $10 billion; expenditures $10 billion, including capital expenditures of $NA (1992 est.)

Exports:
$13.6 billion (f.o.b., 1990)
commodities:
oil 95%, cocoa, rubber
partners:
EC 51%, US 32%

Imports:
$6.9 billion (c.i.f., 1990)
commodities:
consumer goods, capital equipment, chemicals, raw materials
partners:
EC, US

External debt: $32 billion (December 1991 est.)

Industrial production:
growth rate 7.2% (1990); accounts for 8.5% of GDP

Electricity:
4,740,000 kW capacity; 11,280 million kWh produced, 90 kWh per capita (1991)

Industries:
crude oil and mining - coal, tin, columbite; primary processing industries - palm oil, peanut, cotton, rubber, wood, hides and skins; manufacturing industries - textiles, cement, building materials, food products, footwear, chemical, printing, ceramics, steel

Agriculture:
accounts for 32% of GDP and half of labor force; inefficient small-scale

farming dominates; once a large net exporter of food and now an importer; cash crops - cocoa, peanuts, palm oil, rubber; food crops - corn, rice, sorghum, millet, cassava, yams; livestock - cattle, sheep, goats, pigs; fishing and forestry resources extensively exploited

Illicit drugs:

illicit heroin and some cocaine trafficking; marijuana cultivation for domestic consumption and export; major transit country for heroin en route from southeast and southwest Asia via Africa to Western Europe and the US; growing transit route for cocaine from South America via West Africa to Western Europe and the US

:Nigeria Economy

Economic aid:

US commitments, including Ex-Im (FY70-89), $705 million; Western (non-US) countries, ODA and OOF bilateral commitments (1970-89), $3.0 billion; Communist countries (1970-89), $2.2 billion

Currency:

naira (plural - naira); 1 naira (N) = 100 kobo

Exchange rates:

naira (N) per US$1 - 10.226 (February 1992), 9.909 (1991), 8.038 (1990), 7.3647 (1989), 4.5370 (1988), 4.0160 (1987)

Fiscal year: calendar year

:Nigeria Communications

Railroads:

3,505 km 1.067-meter gauge

Highways:

107,990 km total 30,019 km paved (mostly bituminous-surface treatment); 25,411 km laterite, gravel, crushed stone, improved earth; 52,560 km unimproved

Inland waterways:

8,575 km consisting of Niger and Benue Rivers and smaller rivers and creeks

Pipelines:

crude oil 2,042 km; natural gas 500 km; petroleum products 3,000 km

Ports:

Lagos, Port Harcourt, Calabar, Warri, Onne, Sapele

Merchant marine:

28 ships (1,000 GRT or over) totaling 418,046 GRT/664,949 DWT; includes 17 cargo, 1 refrigerated cargo, 1 roll-on/roll-off, 7 petroleum tanker, 1 chemical tanker, 1 bulk

Civil air:

57 major transport aircraft

Airports:

76 total, 64 usable; 33 with permanent-surface runways; 1 with runways over 3,659 m; 15 with runways 2,440-3,659 m; 22 with runways 1,220-2,439 m

Telecommunications:

above-average system limited by poor maintenance; major expansion in progress; radio relay and cable routes; broadcast stations - 35 AM, 17 FM, 28 TV; satellite earth stations - 2 Atlantic Ocean INTELSAT, 1 Indian Ocean INTELSAT, 20 domestic stations; 1 coaxial submarine cable

:Nigeria Defense Forces

Branches:
   Army, Navy, Air Force, paramilitary Police Force
Manpower availability:
   males 15-49, 28,778,532; 16,451,582 fit for military service; 1,256,440
   reach military age (18) annually
Defense expenditures:
   exchange rate conversion - $300 million, 1% of GDP (1990 est.)
\

Niue Geography

Total area: 260 km2
Land area: 260 km2
Comparative area: slightly less than 1.5 times the size of Washington, DC
Land boundaries:
   none
Coastline:
   64 km
Maritime claims:
 Exclusive economic zone:
   200 nm
 Territorial sea:
   12 nm
Disputes:
   none
Climate:
   tropical; modified by southeast trade winds
Terrain:
   steep limestone cliffs along coast, central plateau
Natural resources:
   fish, arable land
Land use:
   arable land 61%; permanent crops 4%; meadows and pastures 4%; forest and
   woodland 19%; other 12%
Environment:
   subject to typhoons
Note:
   one of world's largest coral islands; located about 460 km east of Tonga
:Niue People

Population: 1,751 (July 1992), growth rate - 6.4% (1992)
Birth rate: NA births/1,000 population (1992)
Death rate: NA deaths/1,000 population (1992)
Net migration rate: NA migrants/1,000 population (1992)
Infant mortality rate: NA deaths/1,000 live births (1992)
Life expectancy at birth: NA years male, NA years female (1992)
Total fertility rate: NA children born/woman (1992)
Nationality:
   noun - Niuean(s); adjective - Niuean
Ethnic divisions:

Polynesian, with some 200 Europeans, Samoans, and Tongans
Religions:
 Ekalesia Nieue (Niuean Church) - a Protestant church closely related to the London Missionary Society 75%, Mormon 10%, Roman Catholic, Jehovah's Witnesses, Seventh-Day Adventist 5%
Languages:
 Polynesian tongue closely related to Tongan and Samoan; English
Literacy:
 NA% (male NA%, female NA%) but compulsory education age 5 to 14
Labor force:
 1,000 (1981 est.); most work on family plantations; paid work exists only in government service, small industry, and the Niue Development Board
Organized labor:
 NA

:Niue Government

Long-form name:
 none
Type:
 self-governing territory in free association with New Zealand; Niue fully responsible for internal affairs; New Zealand retains responsibility for external affairs
Capital: Alofi
Administrative divisions:
 none
Independence:
 became a self-governing territory in free association with New Zealand on 19 October 1974
Constitution:
 19 October 1974 (Niue Constitution Act)
Legal system:
 English common law
National holiday:
 Waitangi Day (Treaty of Waitangi established British sovereignty), 6 February (1840)
Executive branch:
 British monarch, premier, Cabinet
Legislative branch:
 Legislative Assembly
Judicial branch:
 Appeal Court of New Zealand, High Court
Leaders:
 Chief of State:
 Queen ELIZABETH II (since 6 February 1952), represented by New Zealand Representative John SPRINGFORD (since 1974)
 Head of Government:
 Premier Sir Robert R. REX (since October 1974)
Political parties and leaders:
 Niue Island Party (NIP), Young VIVIAN
Suffrage:

universal adult at age 18

Elections:

Legislative Assembly:

last held on 8 April 1990 (next to be held March 1993); results - percent of vote NA; seats - (20 total, 6 elected) NIP 1, independents 5

Member of:

ESCAP (associate), SPC, SPF

Diplomatic representation:

none (self-governing territory in free association with New Zealand)

Flag:

yellow with the flag of the UK in the upper hoist-side quadrant; the flag of the UK bears five yellow five-pointed stars - a large one on a blue disk in the center and a smaller one on each arm of the bold red cross

:Niue Economy

Overview:

The economy is heavily dependent on aid from New Zealand. Government expenditures regularly exceed revenues, with the shortfall made up by grants from New Zealand - the grants are used to pay wages to public employees. The agricultural sector consists mainly of subsistence gardening, although some cash crops are grown for export. Industry consists primarily of small factories to process passion fruit, lime oil, honey, and coconut cream. The sale of postage stamps to foreign collectors is an important source of revenue. The island in recent years has suffered a serious loss of population because of migration of Niueans to New Zealand.

GNP:

exchange rate conversion - $2.1 million, per capita $1,000; real growth rate NA% (1989 est.)

Inflation rate (consumer prices):

9.6% (1984)

Unemployment rate: NA%

Budget:

revenues $5.5 million; expenditures $6.3 million, including capital expenditures of $NA (FY85 est.)

Exports:

$175,274 (f.o.b., 1985)

commodities:

canned coconut cream, copra, honey, passion fruit products, pawpaw, root crops, limes, footballs, stamps, handicrafts

partners:

NZ 89%, Fiji, Cook Islands, Australia

Imports:

$3.8 million (c.i.f., 1985)

commodities:

food, live animals, manufactured goods, machinery, fuels, lubricants, chemicals, drugs

partners:

NZ 59%, Fiji 20%, Japan 13%, Western Samoa, Australia, US

External debt: $NA

Industrial production:

growth rate NA%

Electricity:

1,500 kW capacity; 3 million kWh produced, 1,490 kWh per capita (1990)

Industries:

tourist, handicrafts

Agriculture:

copra, coconuts, passion fruit, honey, limes; subsistence crops - taro, yams, cassava (tapioca), sweet potatoes; pigs, poultry, beef cattle

Economic aid:

Western (non-US) countries, ODA and OOF bilateral commitments (1970-89), $62 million

Currency:

New Zealand dollar (plural - dollars); 1 New Zealand dollar (NZ$) = 100 cents

Exchange rates:

New Zealand dollars (NZ$) per US$1 - 1.8245 (March 1992), 1.7265 (1991), 1.6750 (1990), 1.6711 (1989), 1.5244 (1988), 1.6886 (1987)

Fiscal year: 1 April - 31 March

:Niue Communications

Highways:

123 km all-weather roads, 106 km access and plantation roads

Ports:

none; offshore anchorage only

Airports:

1 with permanent-surface runway of 1,650 m

Telecommunications:

single-line telephone system connects all villages on island; 383 telephones; 1,000 radio receivers (1987 est.); broadcast stations - 1 AM, 1 FM, no TV

:Niue Defense Forces

Branches:

Police Force

Note:

defense is the responsibility of New Zealand

Norfolk Island Geography

Total area: 34.6 km2
Land area: 34.6 km2
Comparative area: about 0.2 times the size of Washington, DC
Land boundaries:

Coastline:

32 km

Maritime claims:

 Exclusive fishing zone:

 200 nm

 Territorial sea:

 3 nm

Disputes:

Climate:
  subtropical, mild, little seasonal temperature variation
Terrain:
  volcanic formation with mostly rolling plains
Natural resources:
  fish
Land use:
  arable land 0%; permanent crops 0%; meadows and pastures 25%; forest and woodland 0%; other 75%
Environment:
  subject to typhoons (especially May to July)
Note:
  located 1,575 km east of Australia in the South Pacific Ocean

:Norfolk Island People

Population: 2,620 (July 1992), growth rate 1.7% (1992)
Birth rate: NA births/1,000 population (1992)
Death rate: NA deaths/1,000 population (1992)
Net migration rate: NA migrants/1,000 population (1992)
Infant mortality rate: NA deaths/1,000 live births (1992)
Life expectancy at birth: NA years male, NA years female (1992)
Total fertility rate: NA children born/woman (1992)
Nationality:
  noun - Norfolk Islander(s); adjective - Norfolk Islander(s)
Ethnic divisions:
  descendants of the Bounty mutiny; more recently, Australian and New Zealand settlers
Religions:
  Anglican 39%, Roman Catholic 11.7%, Uniting Church in Australia 16.4%, Seventh-Day Adventist 4.4%, none 9.2%, unknown 16.9%, other 2.4% (1986)
Languages:
  English (official) and Norfolk - a mixture of 18th century English and ancient Tahitian
Literacy:
  NA% (male NA%, female NA%)
Labor force:
  NA
Organized labor:
  NA

:Norfolk Island Government

Long-form name:
  Territory of Norfolk Island
Type:
  territory of Australia
Capital: Kingston (administrative center), Burnt Pine (commercial center)
Administrative divisions:
  none (territory of Australia)
Independence.
  none (territory of Australia)

Constitution:
  Norfolk Island Act of 1957
Legal system:
  wide legislative and executive responsibility under the Norfolk Island Act
  of 1979; Supreme Court
National holiday:
  Pitcairners Arrival Day Anniversary, 8 June (1856)
Executive branch:
  British monarch, governor general of Australia, administrator, Executive
  Council (cabinet)
Legislative branch:
  unicameral Legislative Assembly
Judicial branch:
  Supreme Court
Leaders:
 Chief of State:
  Queen ELIZABETH II (since 6 February 1952), represented by Administrator H.
  B. MACDONALD (since NA 1989), who is appointed by the Governor General of
  Australia
 Head of Government:
  Assembly President and Chief Minister John Terence BROWN (since NA)
Political parties and leaders:
  NA
Suffrage:
  universal at age 18
Elections:
 Legislative Assembly:
  last held 1989 (held every three years); results - percent of vote by party
  NA; seats - (9 total) percent of seats by party NA
Member of:
  none
Diplomatic representation:
  none (territory of Australia)
Flag:
  three vertical bands of green (hoist side), white, and green with a large
  green Norfolk Island pine tree centered in the slightly wider white band

:Norfolk Island Economy

Overview:
  The primary economic activity is tourism, which has brought a level of
  prosperity unusual among inhabitants of the Pacific Islands. The number of
  visitors has increased steadily over the years and reached 29,000 in FY89.
  Revenues from tourism have given the island a favorable balance of trade and
  helped the agricultural sector to become self-sufficient in the production
  of beef, poultry, and eggs.
GDP:
  exchange rate conversion - $NA, per capita $NA; real growth rate NA%
Inflation rate (consumer prices):
  NA%
Unemployment rate: NA%

Budget:
  revenues $NA; expenditures $4.2 million, including capital expenditures of
  $400,000 (FY89)
Exports:
  $1.7 million (f.o.b., FY86)
  commodities:
  postage stamps, seeds of the Norfolk Island pine and Kentia Palm, small
  quantities of avocados
  partners:
  Australia, Pacific Islands, NZ, Asia, Europe
Imports:
  $15.6 million (c.i.f., FY86)
  commodities:
  NA
  partners:
  Australia, Pacific Islands, NZ, Asia, Europe
External debt: NA
Industrial production:
  growth rate NA%
Electricity:
  7,000 kW capacity; 8 million kWh produced, 3,160 kWh per capita (1990)
Industries:
  tourism
Agriculture:
  Norfolk Island pine seed, Kentia palm seed, cereals, vegetables, fruit,
  cattle, poultry
Economic aid:
  none
Currency:
  Australian dollar (plural - dollars); 1 Australian dollar ($A) = 100 cents
Exchange rates:
  Australian dollars ($A) per US$1 - 1.3177 (March 1992), 1.2835 (1991),
  1.2799 (1990), 1.2618 (1989), 1.2752 (1988), 1.4267 (1987)
Fiscal year: 1 July - 30 June

:Norfolk Island Communications

Highways:
  80 km of roads, including 53 km paved; remainder are earth formed or coral
  surfaced
Ports:
  none; loading jetties at Kingston and Cascade
Airports:
  1 with permanent-surface runways 1,220-2,439 m (Australian owned)
Telecommunications:
  1,500 radio receivers (1982); radio link service with Sydney; 987 telephones
  (1983); broadcast stations - 1 AM, no FM, no TV

:Norfolk Island Defense Forces

Note: defense is the responsibility of Australia

Northern Mariana Islands Geography

Total area: 477 km2
Land area: 477 km2; comprises 16 islands including Saipan, Rota, and Tinian
Comparative area: slightly more than 2.5 times the size of Washington, DC
Land boundaries:
   none
Coastline:
   1,482 km
Maritime claims:
  Contiguous zone:
   12 nm
  Continental shelf:
   200 m (depth)
  Exclusive economic zone:
   200 nm
  Territorial sea:
   3 nm
Disputes:
   none
Climate:
   tropical marine; moderated by northeast trade winds, little seasonal
   temperature variation; dry season December to July, rainy season July to
   October
Terrain:
   southern islands are limestone with level terraces and fringing coral reefs;
   northern islands are volcanic; highest elevation is 471 meters (Mt. Tagpochu
   on Saipan)
Natural resources:
   arable land, fish
Land use:
   arable land 1%; permanent crops NA%; meadows and pastures 19%; forest and
   woodland NA%; other NA%
Environment:
   active volcanos on Pagan and Agrihan; subject to typhoons during the rainy
   season
Note:
   strategic location 5,635 km west-southwest of Honolulu in the North Pacific
   Ocean, about three-quarters of the way between Hawaii and the Philippines

:Northern Mariana Islands People

Population: 47,168 (July 1992), growth rate 3.0% (1992)
Birth rate: 35 births/1,000 population (1992)
Death rate: 5 deaths/1,000 population (1992)
Net migration rate: 0 migrants/1,000 population (1992)
Infant mortality rate: 38 deaths/1,000 live births (1992)
Life expectancy at birth: 66 years male, 69 years female (1992)
Total fertility rate: 2.7 children born/woman (1992)
Nationality:
   undetermined
Ethnic divisions:
   Chamorro majority; Carolinians and other Micronesians; Spanish, German,

725

Japanese admixtures

Religions:

Christian with a Roman Catholic majority, although traditional beliefs and taboos may still be found

Languages:

English, but Chamorro and Carolinian are also spoken in the home and taught in school

Literacy:

96% (male 97%, female 96%) age 15 and over can read and write (1980)

Labor force:

12,788 local; 18,799 foreign workers (1990 est.)

Organized labor:

NA

:Northern Mariana Islands Government

Long-form name:

Commonwealth of the Northern Mariana Islands

Type:

commonwealth in political union with the US and administered by the Office of Territorial and International Affairs, US Department of the Interior

Capital: Saipan

Administrative divisions:

Independence:

none (commonwealth in political union with the US)

Constitution:

Covenant Agreement effective 3 November 1986

Legal system:

based on US system except for customs, wages, immigration laws, and taxation

National holiday:

Commonwealth Day, 8 January (1978)

Executive branch:

US President; governor, lieutenant governor

Legislative branch:

bicameral Legislature consists of an upper house or Senate and a lower house or House of Representatives

Judicial branch:

Commonwealth Court and the Federal District Court

Leaders:

Chief of State:

President George BUSH (since 20 January 1989); Vice President Dan QUAYLE (since 20 January 1989)

Head of Government:

Governor Lorenzo I. DeLeon GUERRERO (since 9 January 1990); Lieutenant Governor Benjamin T. MANGLONA (since 9 January 1990)

Political parties and leaders:

Republican Party, Alonzo IGISOMAR; Democratic Party, Felicidad OGUMORO

Suffrage:

universal at age 18; indigenous inhabitants are US citizens but do not vote in US presidential elections

Elections:
  Governor:
    last held in November 1989 (next to be held November 1993); results -
    Lorenzo I. DeLeon GUERRERO, Republican Party, was elected governor
  Senate:
    last held on November 1991 (next to be held November 1993); results -
    percent of vote by party NA; seats - (9 total) Republications 6, Democrats 3
  House of Representatives:
    last held in November 1991 (next to be held November 1993); results -
    percent of vote by party NA; seats - (15 total) Republicans 5, Democrats 10
  US House of Representatives:
    the Commonwealth does not have a nonvoting delegate in Congress; instead, it
    has an elected official ``resident representative'' located in Washington,
    DC; seats - (1 total) Republican (Juan N. BABAUTA)
Member of:
  ESCAP (associate), SPC
Diplomatic representation:
  none
Flag:
  blue with a white five-pointed star superimposed on the gray silhouette of a
  latte stone (a traditional foundation stone used in building) in the center

:Northern Mariana Islands Economy

Overview:
  The economy benefits substantially from financial assistance from the US. An
  agreement for the years 1986 to 1992 entitles the islands to $228 million
  for capital development, government operations, and special programs.
  Another major source of income is the tourist industry, which employs about
  10% of the work force. Japanese tourists predominate. The agricultural
  sector is made up of cattle ranches and small farms producing coconuts,
  breadfruit, tomatoes, and melons. Industry is small scale in nature - mostly
  handicrafts and fish processing.
GNP:
  purchasing power equivalent - $165 million, per capita $3,498; real growth
  rate NA% (1982); note - GNP numbers reflect US spending
Inflation rate (consumer prices):
  NA%
Unemployment rate: NA%
Budget:
  revenues $NA; expenditures $112.2 million, including capital expenditures of
  $NA (February 1990)
Exports:
  $153.9 million (1989)
  commodities:
   manufactured goods, garments, vegetables, beef, pork
  partners:
   NA
Imports:
  $313.7 million, a 43% increase over previous year (1989)
  commodities:

NA
  partners:
  NA
External debt: none
Industrial production:
  growth rate NA%
Electricity:
  25,000 kW capacity; 35 million kWh produced, 740 kWh per capita (1990)
Industries:
  tourism, construction, light industry, handicrafts
Agriculture:
  coffee, coconuts, fruits, tobacco, cattle
Economic aid:
  none
Currency:
  US currency is used
Exchange rates:
  US currency is used
Fiscal year: 1 October - 30 September

:Northern Mariana Islands Communications

Highways:
  381.5 km total (134.5 km first-grade primary, 55 km secondary, 192 km local)
  (1991)
Ports:
  Saipan, Rota, Tinian
Airports:
  6 total, 4 usable; 3 with permanent-surface runways; none with runways over
  3,659 m; 1 with runways 2,440-3,659 m; 2 with runways 1,220-2,439 m
Telecommunications:
  broadcast stations - 2 AM, 1 FM (1984), 1 TV; 2 Pacific Ocean INTELSAT earth
  stations

:Northern Mariana Islands Defense Forces

Note: defense is the responsibility of the US

Norway Geography

Total area: 324,220 km2
Land area: 307,860 km2
Comparative area: slightly larger than New Mexico
Land boundaries:
  2,515 km total; Finland 729 km, Sweden 1,619 km, Russia 167 km
Coastline:
  21,925 km; includes mainland 3,419 km, large islands 2,413 km, long fjords,
  numerous small islands, and minor indentations 16,093 km
Maritime claims:
 Contiguous zone:
  10 nm
 Continental shelf:
  to depth of exploitation
 Exclusive economic zone:

200 nm

Territorial sea:

4 nm

Disputes:

territorial claim in Antarctica (Queen Maud Land); Denmark has challenged
Norway's maritime claims between Greenland and Jan Mayen; maritime boundary
dispute with Russia over portion of Barents Sea

Climate:

temperate along coast, modified by North Atlantic Current; colder interior;
rainy year-round on west coast

Terrain:

glaciated; mostly high plateaus and rugged mountains broken by fertile
valleys; small, scattered plains; coastline deeply indented by fjords;
arctic tundra in north

Natural resources:

crude oil, copper, natural gas, pyrites, nickel, iron ore, zinc, lead, fish,
timber, hydropower

Land use:

arable land 3%; permanent crops 0%; meadows and pastures NEGL%; forest and
woodland 27%; other 70%; includes irrigated NEGL%

Environment:

air and water pollution; acid rain; note - strategic location adjacent to
sea lanes and air routes in North Atlantic; one of most rugged and longest
coastlines in world; Norway and Turkey only NATO members having a land
boundary with Russia

:Norway People

Population: 4,294,876 (July 1992), growth rate 0.5% (1992)

Birth rate: 14 births/1,000 population (1992)

Death rate: 10 deaths/1,000 population (1992)

Net migration rate: 2 migrants/1,000 population (1992)

Infant mortality rate: 7 deaths/1,000 live births (1992)

Life expectancy at birth: 74 years male, 81 years female (1992)

Total fertility rate: 1.8 children born/woman (1992)

Nationality:

noun - Norwegian(s); adjective - Norwegian

Ethnic divisions:

Germanic (Nordic, Alpine, Baltic) and racial-cultural minority of 20,000
Lapps

Religions:

Evangelical Lutheran (state church) 87.8%, other Protestant and Roman
Catholic 3.8%, none 3.2%, unknown 5.2% (1980)

Languages:

Norwegian (official); small Lapp- and Finnish-speaking minorities

Literacy:

99% (male NA%, female NA%) age 15 and over can read and write (1976 est.)

Labor force:

2,167,000 (September 1990); services 34.7%, commerce 18%, mining and
manufacturing 16.6%, banking and financial services 7.5%, transportation and
communications 7.2%, construction 7.2%, agriculture, forestry, and fishing

6.4% (1989)
Organized labor:
  66% of labor force (1985)

:Norway Government

Long-form name:
  Kingdom of Norway
Type:
  constitutional monarchy
Capital: Oslo
Administrative divisions:
  19 provinces (fylker, singular - fylke); Akershus, Aust-Agder, Buskerud,
  Finnmark, Hedmark, Hordaland, More og Romsdal, Nordland, Nord-Trondelag,
  Oppland, Oslo, OCstfold, Rogaland, Sogn og Fjordane, Sor-Trondelag,
  Telemark, Troms, Vest-Agder, Vestfold
Independence:
  26 October 1905 (from Sweden)
Constitution:
  17 May 1814, modified in 1884
Dependent areas:
  Bouvet Island, Jan Mayen, Svalbard
Legal system:
  mixture of customary law, civil law system, and common law traditions;
  Supreme Court renders advisory opinions to legislature when asked; accepts
  compulsory ICJ jurisdiction, with reservations
National holiday:
  Constitution Day, 17 May (1814)
Executive branch:
  monarch, prime minister, State Council (cabinet)
Legislative branch:
  unicameral Parliament (Storting) with an Upper Chamber (Lagting) and a Lower
  Chamber (Odelsting)
Judicial branch:
  Supreme Court (Hoiesterett)
Leaders:
 Chief of State:
  King HARALD V (since 17 January 1991); Heir Apparent Crown Prince HAAKON
  MAGNUS (born 20 July 1973)
 Head of Government:
  Prime Minister Gro Harlem BRUNDTLAND (since 3 November 1990)
Political parties and leaders:
  Labor, Gro Harlem BRUNDTLAND; Conservative, Kaci Kullmann FIVE; Center
  Party, Anne Enger LAHNSTEIN; Christian People's, Kjell Magne BONDEVIK;
  Socialist Left, Erick SOLHEIM; Norwegian Communist, Kare Andre NILSEN;
  Progress, Carl I. HAGEN; Liberal, Odd Einar DORUM; Finnmark List, leader NA
Suffrage:
  universal at age 18
Elections:
 Storting:
  last held on 11 September 1989 (next to be held 6 September 1993); results -

730

Labor 34.3%, Conservative 22.2%, Progress 13.0%, Socialist Left 10.1%,
Christian People's 8.5%, Center Party 6.6%, Finnmark List 0.3%, other 5%;
seats - (165 total) Labor 63, Conservative 37, Progress 22, Socialist Left
17, Christian People's 14, Center Party 11, Finnmark List 1

Communists:

15,500 est.; 5,500 Norwegian Communist Party (NKP); 10,000 Workers Communist
Party Marxist-Leninist (AKP-ML, pro-Chinese)

Member of:

AfDB, AsDB, Australia Group, BIS, CCC, CE, CERN, COCOM, CSCE, EBRD, ECE,

EFTA, ESA, FAO, GATT, IADB, IAEA, IBRD, ICAO, ICC, ICFTU, IDA, IEA, IFAD,

IFC, ILO, IMF, IMO, INMARSAT, INTELSAT, INTERPOL, IOC, IOM, ISO, ITU, LORCS,

MTCR, NACC, NATO, NC, NEA, NIB, NSG, OECD, PCA, UN, UNAVEM, UNCTAD, UNESCO,

UNHCR, UNIDO, UNIFIL, UNIIMOG, UNMOGIP, UNTSO, UPU, WHO, WIPO, WMO, ZC

:Norway Government

Diplomatic representation:

Ambassador Kjeld VIBE; Chancery at 2720 34th Street NW, Washington, DC
20008; telephone (202) 333-6000; there are Norwegian Consulates General in
Houston, Los Angeles, Minneapolis, New York, and San Francisco, and
Consulates in Miami and New Orleans

US:

Ambassador Loret Miller RUPPE; Embassy at Drammensveien 18, 0244 Oslo 2
(mailing address is APO AE 09707); telephone [47] (2) 44-85-50; FAX [47] (2)
43-07-77

Flag:

red with a blue cross outlined in white that extends to the edges of the
flag; the vertical part of the cross is shifted to the hoist side in the
style of the Dannebrog (Danish flag)

:Norway Economy

Overview:

Norway has a mixed economy involving a combination of free market activity
and government intervention. The government controls key areas, such as the
vital petroleum sector, through large-scale state enterprises and
extensively subsidizes agricultural, fishing, and other sectors. Norway also
maintains an extensive welfare system that helps propel public-sector
expenditures to slightly more than 50% of the GDP and results in one of the
highest average tax burdens in the world (54%). A small country with a high
dependence on international trade, Norway is basically an exporter of raw
materials and semiprocessed goods, with an abundance of small- and
medium-sized firms, and is ranked among the major shipping nations. The
country is richly endowed with natural resources - petroleum, hydropower,
fish, forests, and minerals - and is highly dependent on its oil sector to
keep its economy afloat. Although one of the government's main priorities is
to reduce this dependency, this situation is not likely to improve for years
to come. The government also hopes to reduce unemployment and strengthen and

diversify the economy through tax reform and an expansionary 1992 budget. Forecasters predict that economic growth will rise slightly in 1992 because of public-sector expansion and moderate improvements in private investment and demand. Inflation will remain about 3%, while unemployment continues at record levels of over 5% because of the weakness of the economy outside the oil sector. Oslo, a member of the European Free Trade Area, is continuing to deregulate and harmonize with EC regulations to prepare for the European Economic Area (EEA) - which creates a EC/EFTA market with free movement of capital, goods, services, and labor - which takes effect in 1993.

GDP:
purchasing power equivalent - $72.9 billion, per capita $17,100; real growth rate 4.1% (1991 est.)

Inflation rate (consumer prices):
3.5% (1991)

Unemployment rate: 5.4% (1991, excluding people in job-training programs)

Budget:
revenues $47.9 billion; expenditures $52.7 billion, including capital expenditures of $NA (1991)

Exports:
$34.2 billion (f.o.b., 1991)
 commodities:
petroleum and petroleum products 36.5%, natural gas 7.5%, fish 7%, aluminum 6%, ships 6.2%, pulp and paper
 partners:
EC 66.5%, Nordic countries 19.5%, developing countries 7.8%, US 4.6%, Japan 1.9% (1991)

Imports:
$25.1 billion (c.i.f., 1991)
 commodities:
machinery, fuels and lubricants, transportation equipment, chemicals, foodstuffs, clothing, ships
 partners:
EC 46.8%, Nordic countries 26.1%, developing countries 12.3%, US 7.8%, Japan 4.7% (1991)

External debt: $10.2 billion (1991)

Industrial production:
growth rate 4.7% (1991)

Electricity:
26,735,000 kW capacity; 121,685 million kWh produced, 28,950 kWh per capita (1991)

:Norway Economy

Industries:
petroleum and gas, food processing, shipbuilding, pulp and paper products, metals, chemicals, timber, mining, textiles, fishing

Agriculture:
accounts for 2.8% of GDP and 6.4% of labor force; among world's top 10 fishing nations; livestock output exceeds value of crops; over half of food needs imported; fish catch of 1.76 million metric tons in 1989

Economic aid:

donor - ODA and OOF commitments (1970-89), $4.4 billion
Currency:
   Norwegian krone (plural - kroner); 1 Norwegian krone (NKr) = 100 re
Exchange rates:
   Norwegian kroner (NKr) per US$1 - 6.1956 (January 1992), 6.4829 (1991),
   6.2597 (1990), 6.9045 (1989), 6.5170 (1988), 6.7375 (1987)
Fiscal year: calendar year

:Norway Communications

Railroads:
   4,223 km 1.435-meter standard gauge; Norwegian State Railways (NSB) operates
   4,219 km (2,450 km electrified and 96 km double track); 4 km other
Highways:
   79,540 km total; 38,580 km paved; 40,960 km gravel, crushed stone, and earth
Inland waterways:
   1,577 km along west coast; 2.4 m draft vessels maximum
Pipelines:
   refined products 53 km
Ports:
   Oslo, Bergen, Fredrikstad, Kristiansand, Stavanger, Trondheim
Merchant marine:
   864 ships (1,000 GRT or over) totaling 22,978,202 GRT/40,128,177 DWT;
   includes 12 passenger, 20 short-sea passenger, 118 cargo, 2 passenger-cargo,
   19 refrigerated cargo, 16 container, 49 roll-on/roll-off, 22 vehicle
   carrier, 1 railcar carrier, 180 oil tanker, 93 chemical tanker, 83 liquefied
   gas, 28 combination ore/oil, 211 bulk, 10 combination bulk; note - the
   government has created a captive register, the Norwegian International Ship
   Register (NIS), as a subset of the Norwegian register; ships on the NIS
   enjoy many benefits of flags of convenience and do not have to be crewed by
   Norwegians; the majority of ships (777) under the Norwegian flag are now
   registered with the NIS
Civil air:
   76 major transport aircraft
Airports:
   103 total, 102 usable; 64 with permanent-surface runways; none with runways
   over 3,659 m; 12 with runways 2,440-3,659 m; 16 with runways 1,220-2,439 m
Telecommunications:
   high-quality domestic and international telephone, telegraph, and telex
   services; 2 buried coaxial cable systems; 3,102,000 telephones; broadcast
   stations - 46 AM, 350 private and 143 government FM, 54 (2,100 repeaters)
   TV; 4 coaxial submarine cables; 3 communications satellite earth stations
   operating in the EUTELSAT, INTELSAT (1 Atlantic Ocean), MARISAT, and
   domestic systems

:Norway Defense Forces

Branches:
   Norwegian Army, Royal Norwegian Navy, Royal Norwegian Air Force, Home
Guard
Manpower availability:
   males 15-49, 1,129,871; 944,290 fit for military service; 33,175 reach
   military age (20) annually

Defense expenditures:
  exchange rate conversion - $3.8 billion, 3.8% of GDP (1991)

Oman Geography

Total area: 212,460 km2
Land area: 212,460 km2
Comparative area: slightly smaller than Kansas
Land boundaries:
  1,374 km total; Saudi Arabia 676 km, UAE 410 km, Yemen 288 km
Coastline:
  2,092 km
Maritime claims:
 Continental shelf:
  to be defined
 Exclusive economic zone:
  200 nm
 Territorial sea:
  12 nm
Disputes:
  no defined boundary with most of UAE; Administrative Line with UAE in far
  north; there is a proposed treaty with Yemen (which has not yet been
  formally accepted) to settle the Omani-Yemeni boundary
Climate:
  dry desert; hot, humid along coast; hot, dry interior; strong southwest
  summer monsoon (May to September) in far south
Terrain:
  vast central desert plain, rugged mountains in north and south
Natural resources:
  crude oil, copper, asbestos, some marble, limestone, chromium, gypsum,
  natural gas
Land use:
  arable land NEGL%; permanent crops NEGL%; meadows and pastures 5%; forest
  and woodland NEGL%; other 95%; includes irrigated NEGL%
Environment:
  summer winds often raise large sandstorms and duststorms in interior; sparse
  natural freshwater resources
Note:
  strategic location with small foothold on Musandam Peninsula controlling
  Strait of Hormuz (17% of world's oil production transits this point going
  from Persian Gulf to Arabian Sea)

:Oman People

Population: 1,587,581 (July 1992), growth rate 3.5% (1992)
Birth rate: 41 births/1,000 population (1992)
Death rate: 6 deaths/1,000 population (1992)
Net migration rate: 0 migrants/1,000 population (1992)
Infant mortality rate: 40 deaths/1,000 live births (1992)
Life expectancy at birth: 65 years male, 69 years female (1992)
Total fertility rate: 6.6 children born/woman (1992)
Nationality:
  noun - Omani(s); adjective - Omani

Ethnic divisions:

mostly Arab, with small Balochi, Zanzibari, and South Asian (Indian, Pakistani, Bangladeshi) groups

Religions:

Ibadhi Muslim 75%; remainder Sunni Muslim, Shi`a Muslim, some Hindu

Languages:

Arabic (official); English, Balochi, Urdu, Indian dialects

Literacy:

NA% (male NA%, female NA%)

Labor force:

430,000; agriculture 60% (est.); 58% are non-Omani

Organized labor:

trade unions are illegal

:Oman Government

Long-form name:

Sultanate of Oman

Type:

absolute monarchy; independent, with residual UK influence

Capital: Muscat

Administrative divisions:

there are no first-order administrative divisions as defined by the US Government, but there are 3 governorates (muhafazah, singular - muhafazat); Musqat, Musandam, Zufar

Independence:

1650, expulsion of the Portuguese

Constitution:

Legal system:

based on English common law and Islamic law; ultimate appeal to the sultan; has not accepted compulsory ICJ jurisdiction

National holiday:

National Day, 18 November

Executive branch:

sultan, Cabinet

Legislative branch:

National Assembly

Judicial branch:

none; traditional Islamic judges and a nascent civil court system

Leaders:

Chief of State and Head of Government:

Sultan and Prime Minister QABOOS bin Sa`id Al Sa`id (since 23 July 1970)

Suffrage:

Elections:

elections scheduled for October 1992

Other political or pressure groups:

outlawed Popular Front for the Liberation of Oman (PFLO), based in Yemen

Member of:

ABEDA, AFESD, AL, AMF, ESCWA, FAO, G-77, GCC, IBRD, ICAO, IDA, IDB,

IFAD,
IFC, IMF, IMO, INMARSAT, INTELSAT, INTERPOL, IOC, ISO (correspondent), ITU,
NAM, OIC, UN, UNCTAD, UNESCO, UNIDO, UPU, WFTU, WHO, WMO

Diplomatic representation:
Ambassador Awadh bin Badr AL-SHANFARI; Chancery at 2342 Massachusetts Avenue
NW, Washington, DC 20008; telephone (202) 387-1980 through 1982
US:
Ambassador Richard W. BOEHM; Embassy at address NA, Muscat (mailing address
is P. O. Box 50202 Madinat Qaboos, Muscat); telephone [968] 698-989; FAX
[968] 604-316

Flag:
three horizontal bands of white (top, double width), red, and green (double
width) with a broad, vertical, red band on the hoist side; the national
emblem (a khanjar dagger in its sheath superimposed on two crossed swords in
scabbards) in white is centered at the top of the vertical band

:Oman Economy

Overview:
Economic performance is closely tied to the fortunes of the oil industry.
Petroleum accounts for more than 90% of export earnings, about 80% of
government revenues, and roughly 40% of GDP. Oman has proved oil reserves of
4 billion barrels, equivalent to about 20 years' supply at the current rate
of extraction. Although agriculture employs a majority of the population,
urban centers depend on imported food.

GDP:
exchange rate conversion - $10.6 billion, per capita $6,925 (1990); real
growth rate 0.5% (1989)

Inflation rate (consumer prices):
1.3% (1989)

Unemployment rate: NA%

Budget:
revenues $4.9 billion; expenditures $4.9 billion, including capital
expenditures of $825 million (1990)

Exports:
$5.5 billion (f.o.b., 1990)
commodities:
petroleum, reexports, fish, processed copper, fruits and vegetables
partners:
Japan 35%, South Korea 21%, Singapore 7%, US 6%

Imports:
$2.5 billion (f.o.b, 1990)
commodities:
machinery, transportation equipment, manufactured goods, food, livestock,
lubricants
partners:
UK 20%, UAE 20%, Japan 17%, US 7%

External debt: $3.1 billion (December 1989 est.)

Industrial production:

growth rate 10% (1989), including petroleum sector

Electricity:

1,120,000 kW capacity; 5,000 million kWh produced, 3,800 kWh per capita (1991)

Industries:

crude oil production and refining, natural gas production, construction, cement, copper

Agriculture:

accounts for 6% of GDP and 60% of the labor force (including fishing); less than 2% of land cultivated; largely subsistence farming (dates, limes, bananas, alfalfa, vegetables, camels, cattle); not self-sufficient in food; annual fish catch averages 100,000 metric tons

Economic aid:

US commitments, including Ex-Im (FY70-89), $137 million; Western (non-US) countries, ODA and OOF bilateral commitments (1970-89), $148 million; OPEC bilateral aid (1979-89), $797 million

Currency:

Omani rial (plural - rials); 1 Omani rial (RO) = 1,000 baiza

Exchange rates:

Omani rials (RO) per US$1 - 0.3845 (fixed rate since 1986)

Fiscal year: calendar year

:Oman Communications

Highways:

26,000 km total; 6,000 km paved, 20,000 km motorable track

Pipelines:

crude oil 1,300 km; natural gas 1,030 km

Ports:

Mina' Qabus, Mina' Raysut

Merchant marine:

1 passenger ship (1,000 GRT or over) totaling 4,442 GRT/1,320 DWT

Civil air:

19 major transport aircraft

Airports:

134 total, 127 usable; 6 with permanent-surface runways; 1 with runways over 3,659 m; 8 with runways 2,440-3,659 m; 73 with runways 1,220-2,439 m

Telecommunications:

fair system of open-wire, microwave, and radio communications stations; limited coaxial cable 50,000 telephones; broadcast stations - 2 AM, 3 FM, 7 TV; satellite earth stations - 2 Indian Ocean INTELSAT, 1 ARABSAT, and 8 domestic

:Oman Defense Forces

Branches:

Army, Navy, Air Force, Royal Oman Police

Manpower availability:

males 15-49, 359,394; 204,006 fit for military service

Defense expenditures:

exchange rate conversion - $1.73 billion, 16% of GDP (1992 budget)

Pacific Islands, Trust Territory of the Geography

Total area: 458 km2
Land area: 458 km2
Comparative area: slightly more than 2.5 times the size of Washington, DC
Land boundaries:
   none
Coastline:
   1,519 km
Maritime claims:
  Contiguous zone:
   12 nm
  Continental shelf:
   200 m (depth)
  Exclusive fishing zone:
   200 nm
  Territorial sea:
   3 nm
Disputes:
   none
Climate:
   wet season May to November; hot and humid
Terrain:
   about 200 islands varying geologically from the high, mountainous main
   island of Babelthuap to low, coral islands usually fringed by large barrier
   reefs
Natural resources:
   forests, minerals (especially gold), marine products; deep-seabed minerals
Land use:
   arable land NA%; permanent crops NA%; meadows and pastures NA%; forest and
   woodland NA%; other NA%
Environment:
   subject to typhoons from June to December; archipelago of six island groups
   totaling over 200 islands in the Caroline chain
Note:
   important location 850 km southeast of the Philippines; includes World War
   II battleground of Peleliu and world-famous rock islands

:Pacific Islands, Trust Territory of the People

Population: 15,775 (July 1992), growth rate 1.9% (1992)
Birth rate: 23 births/1,000 population (1992)
Death rate: 7 deaths/1,000 population (1992)
Net migration rate: 2 migrants/1,000 population (1992)
Infant mortality rate: 25 deaths/1,000 live births (1992)
Life expectancy at birth: 69 years male, 73 years female (1992)
Total fertility rate: 3.0 children born/woman (1992)
Nationality:
   noun - Palauan(s); adjective - Palauan
Ethnic divisions:
   Palauans are a composite of Polynesian, Malayan, and Melanesian races
Religions:
   predominantly Christian, including Catholics, Seventh-Day Adventists,

Jehovah's Witnesses, the Assembly of God, the Liebenzell Mission, and Latter-Day Saints; a third of the population observes the Modekngei religion, indigenous to Palau

Languages:
English is an official language, though Palauan is also official in 13 of Palau's 16 states, and Tobi and Sonsorolese are official in the 3 other states

Literacy:
92% (male 93%, female 91%) age 15 and over can read and write (1980)

Labor force:
NA

Organized labor:
NA

:Pacific Islands, Trust Territory of the Government

Long-form name:
Trust Territory of the Pacific Islands (no short-form name); may change to Republic of Palau after independence; note - Belau, the native form of Palau, is sometimes used

Type:
UN trusteeship administered by the US; constitutional government signed a Compact of Free Association with the US on 10 January 1986, which was never approved in a series of UN-observed plebiscites; until the UN trusteeship is terminated with entry into force of the Compact, Palau remains under US administration as the Palau District of the Trust Territory of the Pacific Islands

Capital: Koror; a new capital is being built about 20 km northeast in eastern Babelthuap

Administrative divisions:
there are no first-order administrative divisions as defined by the US Government, but there are 16 states; Aimeliik, Airai, Angaur, Kayangel, Koror, Melekeok, Ngaraard, Ngardmau, Ngaremlengui, Ngatpang, Ngchesar, Ngerchelong, Ngiwal, Peleliu, Sonsorol, Tobi

Independence:
still part of the US-administered UN trusteeship (the last polity remaining under the trusteeship; the Republic of the Marshall Islands, Federated States of Micronesia, and Commonwealth of the Northern Marianas have left); administered by the Office of Territorial and International Affairs, US Department of Interior

Constitution:
1 January 1981

Legal system:
based on Trust Territory laws, acts of the legislature, municipal, common, and customary laws

National holiday:
Constitution Day, 9 July (1979)

Executive branch:
US president, US vice president, national president, national vice president

Legislative branch:
bicameral Parliament (Olbiil Era Kelulau or OEK) consists of an upper house

or Senate and a lower house or House of Delegates

Judicial branch:
  Supreme Court, National Court, and Court of Common Pleas

Leaders:
  Chief of State:
  President George BUSH (since 20 January 1989); represented by the Assistant
  Secretary for Territorial Affairs, US Department of the Interior, Stella
  GUERRA (since 21 July 1989) and J. Victor HOBSON Jr., Director (since 16
  December 1990)
  Head of Government:
  President Ngiratkel ETPISON (since 2 November 1988), Vice-President Kuniwo
  NAKAMURA (since 2 November 1988)

Suffrage:
  universal at age 18

Elections:
  House of Delegates:
  last held 2 November 1988 (next to be held NA November 1992); results -
  percent of vote NA; seats - (16 total); number of seats by party NA
  President:
  last held on 2 November 1988 (next to be held NA November 1992); results -
  Ngiratkel ETPISON 26.3%, Roman TMETUCHL 25.9%, Thomas REMENGESAU
19.5%,
  other 28.3%

:Pacific Islands, Trust Territory of the Government

  Senate:
  last held 2 November 1988 (next to be held NA November 1992); results -
  percent of vote NA; seats - (14 total); number of seats by party NA

Member of:
  ESCAP (associate), SPC, SPF (observer)

Diplomatic representation:
  none
  US:
  US Liaison Officer Lloyed W. MOSS; US Liaison Office at Top Side, Neeriyas,
  Koror (mailing address: P. O. Box 6028, Koror, PW 96940); telephone (680)
  488-2920; (680) 488-2911

Flag:
  light blue with a large yellow disk (representing the moon) shifted slightly
  to the hoist side

:Pacific Islands, Trust Territory of the Economy

Overview:
  The economy consists primarily of subsistence agriculture and fishing.
  Tourism provides some foreign exchange, although the remote location of
  Palau and a shortage of suitable facilities has hindered development. The
  government is the major employer of the work force, relying heavily on
  financial assistance from the US.

GDP:
  purchasing power equivalent - $31.6 million, per capita $2,260; real growth
  rate NA% (1986); note - GDP numbers reflect US spending

Inflation rate (consumer prices):

NA%

Unemployment rate: 20% (1986)

Budget:

revenues $6.0 million; expenditures NA, including capital expenditures of NA
(1986)

Exports:

$0.5 million (f.o.b., 1986)

commodities:

NA

partners:

US, Japan

Imports:

$27.2 million (c.i.f., 1986)

commodities:

NA

partners:

US

External debt: about $100 million (1989)

Industrial production:

growth rate NA%

Electricity:

16,000 kW capacity; 22 million kWh produced, 1,540 kWh per capita (1990)

Industries:

tourism, craft items (shell, wood, pearl), some commercial fishing and
agriculture

Agriculture:

subsistence-level production of coconut, copra, cassava, sweet potatoes

Economic aid:

US commitments, including Ex-Im (FY70-89), $2,560 million; Western (non-US)
countries, ODA and OOF bilateral commitments (1970-89), $92 million

Currency:

US currency is used

Exchange rates:

US currency is used

Fiscal year: 1 October - 30 September

:Pacific Islands, Trust Territory of the Communications

Highways:

22.3 km paved, some stone-, coral-, or laterite-surfaced roads (1991)

Ports:

Koror

Airports:

2 with permanent-surface runways 1,220-2,439 m

Telecommunications:

broadcast stations - 1 AM, 1 FM, 2 TV; 1 Pacific Ocean INTELSAT earth
station

:Pacific Islands, Trust Territory of the Defense Forces

Note:

defense is the responsibility of the US and that will not change when the UN

trusteeship terminates if the Compact of Free Association with the US goes
into effect

Pacific Ocean Geography

Total area: 165,384,000 km2
Land area: 165,384,000 km2; includes Arafura Sea, Banda Sea, Bellingshausen Sea,
Bering
   Sea, Bering Strait, Coral Sea, East China Sea, Gulf of Alaska, Makassar
   Strait, Philippine Sea, Ross Sea, Sea of Japan, Sea of Okhotsk, South China
   Sea, Tasman Sea, and other tributary water bodies
Comparative area: slightly less than 18 times the size of the US; the largest ocean
(followed
   by the Atlantic Ocean, the Indian Ocean, and the Arctic Ocean); covers about
   one-third of the global surface; larger than the total land area of the
   world
Coastline:
   135,663 km
Disputes:
   some maritime disputes (see littoral states)
Climate:
   the western Pacific is monsoonal - a rainy season occurs during the summer
   months, when moisture-laden winds blow from the ocean over the land, and a
   dry season during the winter months, when dry winds blow from the Asian land
   mass back to the ocean
Terrain:
   surface in the northern Pacific dominated by a clockwise, warm-water gyre
   (broad, circular system of currents) and in the southern Pacific by a
   counterclockwise, cool-water gyre; sea ice occurs in the Bering Sea and Sea
   of Okhotsk during winter and reaches maximum northern extent from Antarctica
   in October; the ocean floor in the eastern Pacific is dominated by the East
   Pacific Rise, while the western Pacific is dissected by deep trenches; the
   world's greatest depth is 10,924 meters in the Marianas Trench
Natural resources:
   oil and gas fields, polymetallic nodules, sand and gravel aggregates, placer
   deposits, fish
Environment:
   endangered marine species include the dugong, sea lion, sea otter, seals,
   turtles, and whales; oil pollution in Philippine Sea and South China Sea;
   dotted with low coral islands and rugged volcanic islands in the
   southwestern Pacific Ocean; subject to tropical cyclones (typhoons) in
   southeast and east Asia from May to December (most frequent from July to
   October); tropical cyclones (hurricanes) may form south of Mexico and strike
   Central America and Mexico from June to October (most common in August and
   September); southern shipping lanes subject to icebergs from Antarctica;
   occasional El Nino phenomenon occurs off the coast of Peru when the trade
   winds slacken and the warm Equatorial Countercurrent moves south, killing
   the plankton that is the primary food source for anchovies; consequently,
   the anchovies move to better feeding grounds, causing resident marine birds
   to starve by the thousands because of their lost food source
Note:

the major choke points are the Bering Strait, Panama Canal, Luzon Strait, and the Singapore Strait; the Equator divides the Pacific Ocean into the North Pacific Ocean and the South Pacific Ocean; ships subject to superstructure icing in extreme north from October to May and in extreme south from May to October; persistent fog in the northern Pacific from June to December is a hazard to shipping; surrounded by a zone of violent volcanic and earthquake activity sometimes referred to as the Pacific Ring of Fire

:Pacific Ocean Economy

Overview:

The Pacific Ocean is a major contributor to the world economy and particularly to those nations its waters directly touch. It provides cheap sea transportation between East and West, extensive fishing grounds, offshore oil and gas fields, minerals, and sand and gravel for the construction industry. In 1985 over half (54%) of the world's total fish catch came from the Pacific Ocean, which is the only ocean where the fish catch has increased every year since 1978. Exploitation of offshore oil and gas reserves is playing an ever-increasing role in the energy supplies of Australia, New Zealand, China, US, and Peru. The high cost of recovering offshore oil and gas, combined with the wide swings in world prices for oil since 1985, has slowed but not stopped new drillings.

Industries:

fishing, oil and gas production

:Pacific Ocean Communications

Ports:

Bangkok (Thailand), Hong Kong, Los Angeles (US), Manila (Philippines), Pusan (South Korea), San Francisco (US), Seattle (US), Shanghai (China), Singapore, Sydney (Australia), Vladivostok (Russia), Wellington (NZ), Yokohama (Japan)

Telecommunications:

several submarine cables with network focused on Guam and Hawaii

Pakistan Geography

Total area: 803,940 km2
Land area: 778,720 km2
Comparative area: slightly less than twice the size of California
Land boundaries:

6,774 km total; Afghanistan 2,430 km, China 523 km, India 2,912 km, Iran 909 km

Coastline:

1,046 km

Maritime claims:

 Contiguous zone:

  24 nm

 Continental shelf:

  edge of continental margin or 200 nm

 Exclusive economic zone:

  200 nm

 Territorial sea:

12 nm

Disputes:

boundary with India; border question (Durand line); water sharing problems with upstream riparian India over the Indus

Climate:

mostly hot, dry desert; temperate in northwest; arctic in north

Terrain:

flat Indus plain in east; mountains in north and northwest; Balochistan plateau in west

Natural resources:

land, extensive natural gas reserves, limited crude oil, poor quality coal, iron ore, copper, salt, limestone

Land use:

arable land 26%; permanent crops NEGL%; meadows and pastures 6%; forest and woodland 4%; other 64%; includes irrigated 19%

Environment:

frequent earthquakes, occasionally severe especially in north and west; flooding along the Indus after heavy rains (July and August); deforestation; soil erosion; desertification; water logging

Note:

controls Khyber Pass and Malakand Pass, traditional invasion routes between Central Asia and the Indian Subcontinent

:Pakistan People

Population: 121,664,539 (July 1992), growth rate 2.9% (1992)

Birth rate: 43 births/1,000 population (1992)

Death rate: 13 deaths/1,000 population (1992)

Net migration rate: -1 migrant/1,000 population (1992)

Infant mortality rate: 105 deaths/1,000 live births (1992)

Life expectancy at birth: 56 years male, 57 years female (1992)

Total fertility rate: 6.6 children born/woman (1992)

Nationality:

noun - Pakistani(s); adjective - Pakistani

Ethnic divisions:

Punjabi, Sindhi, Pashtun (Pathan), Baloch, Muhajir (immigrants from India and their descendents)

Religions:

Muslim 97% (Sunni 77%, Shi`a 20%), Christian, Hindu, and other 3%

Languages:

Urdu and English (both official); total spoken languages - Punjabi 64%, Sindhi 12%, Pashtu 8%, Urdu 7%, Balochi and other 9%; English is lingua franca of Pakistani elite and most government ministries, but official policies are promoting its gradual replacement by Urdu

Literacy:

35% (male 47%, female 21%) age 15 and over can read and write (1990 est.)

Labor force:

28,900,000; agriculture 54%, mining and manufacturing 13%, services 33%; extensive export of labor (1987 est.)

Organized labor:

about 10% of industrial work force

:Pakistan Government

Long-form name:
Islamic Republic of Pakistan
Type:
parliamentary with strong executive, federal republic
Capital: Islamabad
Administrative divisions:
4 provinces, 1 territory*, and 1 capital territory**; Balochistan, Federally
Administered Tribal Areas*, Islamabad Capital Territory**, North-West
Frontier, Punjab, Sindh; note - the Pakistani-administered portion of the
disputed Jammu and Kashmir region includes Azad Kashmir and the Northern
Areas
Independence:
14 August 1947 (from UK; formerly West Pakistan)
Constitution:
10 April 1973, suspended 5 July 1977, restored with amendments, 30 December
1985
Legal system:
based on English common law with provisions to accommodate Pakistan's
stature as an Islamic state; accepts compulsory ICJ jurisdiction, with
reservations
National holiday:
Pakistan Day (proclamation of the republic), 23 March (1956)
Executive branch:
president, prime minister, Cabinet
Legislative branch:
bicameral Parliament (Majlis-e-Shoora) consists of an upper house or Senate
and a lower house or National Assembly
Judicial branch:
Supreme Court, Federal Islamic (Shari`at) Court
Leaders:
 Chief of State:
President GHULAM ISHAQ Khan (since 13 December 1988)
 Head of Government:
Prime Minister Mian Nawaz SHARIF (since 6 November 1990)
Political parties and leaders:
Islamic Democratic Alliance (Islami Jamuri Ittehad or IJI) - the Pakistan
Muslim League (PML) led by Mohammed Khan JUNEJO is the main party in the
IJI; Pakistan People's Party (PPP), Benazir BHUTTO; note - in September 1990
the PPP announced the formation of the People's Democratic Alliance (PDA),
an electoral alliance including the following four parties - PPP, Solidarity
Movement (Tehrik Istiqlal), Movement for the Implementation of Shi`a
Jurisprudence (Tehrik-i-Nifaz Fiqh Jafariya or TNFJ), and the PML (Malik
faction); Muhajir Qaumi Movement (MQM), Altaf HUSSAIN; Awami National Par-
ty
(ANP), Khan Abdul Wali KHAN; Jamiat-ul-Ulema-i-Islam (JUI), Fazlur
RAHMAN;
Jamhoori Watan Party (JWP), Mohammad Akbar Khan BUGTI; Pakistan National
Party (PNP), Mir Ghaus Bakhsh BIZENJO; Pakistan Khawa Milli Party (PKMP),
leader NA; Assembly of Pakistani Clergy (Jamiat-ul-Ulema-e-Pakistan or JUP),
745

Maulana Shah Ahmed NOORANI; Jamaat-i-Islami (JI), Qazi Hussain AHMED

Suffrage:

universal at age 21

Elections:

President:

last held on 12 December 1988 (next to be held NA December 1993); results - Ghulam Ishaq KHAN was elected by Parliament and the four provincial assemblies

:Pakistan Government

Senate:

last held March 1991 (next to be held NA March 1994); seats - (87 total) IJI 57, Tribal Area Representatives (nonparty) 8, PPP 5, ANP 5, JWP 4, MQM 3, PNP 2, PKMP 1, JUI 1, independent 1

Elections:

National Assembly:

last held on 24 October 1990 (next to be held by NA October 1995); results - percent of vote by party NA; seats - (217 total) IJI 107, PDA 45, MQM 15, ANP 6, JUI 2, JWP 2, PNP 2, PKMP 1, independents 14, religious minorities 10, Tribal Area Representatives (nonparty) 8, vacant 1

Communists:

the Communist party is officially banned but is allowed to operate openly

Other political or pressure groups:

military remains dominant political force; ulema (clergy), industrialists, and small merchants also influential

Member of:

AsDB, C, CCC, CP, ESCAP, FAO, G-19, G-24, G-77, GATT, IAEA, IBRD, ICAO, ICC,

ICFTU, IDA, IDB, IFAD, IFC, ILO, IMF, IMO, INMARSAT, INTELSAT, INTERPOL,

IOC, ISO, ITU, LORCS, NAM, OAS (observer), OIC, PCA, SAARC, UN, UNCTAD,

UNESCO, UNHCR, UNIDO, UPU, WCL, WFTU, WHO, WIPO, WMO, WTO

Diplomatic representation:

Ambassador Abida HUSSAIN; Chancery at 2315 Massachusetts Avenue NW, Washington, DC 20008; telephone (202) 939-6200; there is a Pakistani Consulate General in New York

US:

Ambassador Nicholas PLATT; Embassy at Diplomatic Enclave, Ramna 5, Islamabad (mailing address is P. O. Box 1048, PSC 1212, Box 2000, Islamabad or APO AE 09812-2000); telephone [92] (51) 826161 through 79; FAX [92] (51) 822004; there are US Consulates General in Karachi and Lahore and a Consulate in Peshawar

Flag:

green with a vertical white band on the hoist side; a large white crescent and star are centered in the green field; the crescent, star, and color green are traditional symbols of Islam

:Pakistan Economy

Overview:

Pakistan is a poor Third World country faced with the usual problems of rapidly increasing population, sizable government deficits, and heavy dependence on foreign aid. In addition, the economy must support a large military establishment and provide for the needs of 4 million Afghan refugees. A real economic growth rate averaging 5-6% in recent years has enabled the country to cope with these problems. Almost all agriculture and small-scale industry is in private hands. In 1990, Pakistan embarked on a sweeping economic liberalization program to boost foreign and domestic private investment and lower foreign aid dependence. The SHARIF government has denationalized several state-owned firms and has attracted some foreign investment. Pakistan likely will have difficulty raising living standards because of its rapidly expanding population. At the current rate of growth, population would double in 25 years.

GNP:
    exchange rate conversion - $45.4 billion, per capita $380; real growth rate 4.8% (FY91 est.)

Inflation rate (consumer prices):
    12.3% (FY91)

Unemployment rate: 10% (FY91 est.)

Budget:
    revenues $6.4 billion; expenditures $10 billion, including capital expenditures of $2.6 billion (FY92 est.)

Exports:
    $6.0 billion (f.o.b., FY91)
    commodities:
    cotton, textiles, clothing, rice
    partners:
    EC 31%, Japan 9%, US 13% (FY90)

Imports:
    $7.9 billion (f.o.b., FY91)
    commodities:
    petroleum, petroleum products, machinery, transportation, equipment, vegetable oils, animal fats, chemicals
    partners:
    EC 21%, US 14%, Japan 13% (FY90)

External debt: $20.1 billion (1990 est.)

Industrial production:
    growth rate 5.7% (FY91); accounts for almost 20% of GNP

Electricity:
    8,500,000 kW capacity; 35,000 million kWh produced, 300 kWh per capita (1991)

Industries:
    textiles, food processing, beverages, construction materials, clothing, paper products, shrimp

Agriculture:
    25% of GNP, over 50% of labor force; world's largest contiguous irrigation system; major crops - cotton, wheat, rice, sugarcane, fruits, and vegetables; live-stock products - milk, beef, mutton, eggs; self-sufficient in food grain

Illicit drugs:

illicit producer of opium and hashish for the international drug trade; government eradication efforts on poppy cultivation of limited success

:Pakistan Economy

Economic aid:
(including Bangladesh only before 1972) US commitments, including Ex-Im (FY70-89), $4.5 billion; Western (non-US) countries, ODA and OOF bilateral commitments (1980-89), $9.1 billion; OPEC bilateral aid (1979-89), $2.3 billion; Communist countries (1970-89), $3.2 billion
Currency:
Pakistani rupee (plural - rupees); 1 Pakistani rupee (PRe) = 100 paisa
Exchange rates:
Pakistani rupees (PRs) per US$1 - 24.980 (March 1992), 23.801 (1991), 21.707 (1990), 20.541 (1989), 18.003 (1988), 17.399 (1987)
Fiscal year: 1 July - 30 June

:Pakistan Communications

Railroads:
8,773 km total; 7,718 km broad gauge, 445 km 1-meter gauge, and 610 km less than 1-meter gauge; 1,037 km broad-gauge double track; 286 km electrified; all government owned (1985)
Highways:
101,315 km total (1987); 40,155 km paved, 23,000 km gravel, 29,000 km improved earth, and 9,160 km unimproved earth or sand tracks (1985)
Pipelines:
crude oil 250 km; natural gas 4,044 km; petroleum products 885 km (1987)
Ports:
Gwadar, Karachi, Port Muhammad bin Qasim
Merchant marine:
28 ships (1,000 GRT or over) totaling 334,227 GRT/495,425 DWT; includes 3 passenger-cargo, 24 cargo, 1 petroleum tanker
Civil air:
40 major transport aircraft
Airports:
112 total, 104 usable; 75 with permanent-surface runways; 1 with runways over 3,659 m; 31 with runways 2,440-3,659 m; 43 with runways 1,220-2,439 m
Telecommunications:
good international communication service over microwave and INTELSAT satellite; domestic communications poor; 813,000 telephones (1990); broadcast service good; broadcast stations - 19 AM, 8 FM, 29 TV; satellite earth stations - 1 Atlantic Ocean INTELSAT and 2 Indian Ocean INTELSAT

:Pakistan Defense Forces

Branches:
Army, Navy, Air Force, Civil Armed Forces, National Guard
Manpower availability:
males 15-49, 27,811,099; 17,064,073 fit for military service; 1,287,041 reach military age (17) annually
Defense expenditures:
exchange rate conversion - $2.9 billion, 6% of GNP (1992 budget)

Palmyra Atoll Geography

Total area: 11.9 km2
Land area: 11.9 km2
Comparative area: about 20 times the size of The Mall in Washington, DC
Land boundaries:
  none
Coastline:
  14.5 km
Maritime claims:
 Contiguous zone:
  12 nm
 Continental shelf:
  200 m (depth)
 Exclusive economic zone:
  200 nm
 Territorial sea:
  12 nm
Disputes:
  none
Climate:
  equatorial, hot, and very rainy
Terrain:
  low, with maximum elevations of about 2 meters
Natural resources:
  none
Land use:
  arable land 0%; permanent crops 0%; meadows and pastures 0%; forest and
  woodland 100%; other 0%
Environment:
  about 50 islets covered with dense vegetation, coconut trees, and balsa-like
  trees up to 30 meters tall
Note:
  located 1,600 km south-southwest of Honolulu in the North Pacific Ocean,
  almost halfway between Hawaii and American Samoa

:Palmyra Atoll People

Population: uninhabited

:Palmyra Atoll Government

Long-form name:
  none
Type:
  unincorporated territory of the US; privately owned, but administered by the
  Office of Territorial and International Affairs, US Department of the
  Interior
Capital: none; administered from Washington, DC

:Palmyra Atoll Economy

Overview: no economic activity

:Palmyra Atoll Communications

Ports:
  the main harbor is West Lagoon, which is entered by a channel on the

southwest side of the atoll; both the channel and harbor will accommodate
vessels drawing 4 meters of water; much of the road and many causeways built
during the war are unserviceable and overgrown

Airports:
1 with permanent-surface runway 1,220-2,439 m

:Palmyra Atoll Defense Forces

Branches:
Note:
defense is the responsibility of the US

Panama Geography

Total area: 78,200 km2
Land area: 75,990 km2
Comparative area: slightly smaller than South Carolina
Land boundaries:
555 km total; Colombia 225 km, Costa Rica 330 km
Coastline:
2,490 km
Maritime claims:
Territorial sea:
200 nm
Disputes:
none
Climate:
tropical; hot, humid, cloudy; prolonged rainy season (May to January), short
dry season (January to May)
Terrain:
interior mostly steep, rugged mountains and dissected, upland plains;
coastal areas largely plains and rolling hills
Natural resources:
copper, mahogany forests, shrimp
Land use:
arable land 6%; permanent crops 2%; meadows and pastures 15%; forest and
woodland 54%; other 23%; includes irrigated NEGL%
Environment:
dense tropical forest in east and northwest
Note:
strategic location on eastern end of isthmus forming land bridge connecting
North and South America; controls Panama Canal that links North Atlantic
Ocean via Caribbean Sea with North Pacific Ocean

:Panama People

Population: 2,529,902 (July 1992), growth rate 2.0% (1992)
Birth rate: 25 births/1,000 population (1992)
Death rate: 5 deaths/1,000 population (1992)
Net migration rate: NEGL migrants/1,000 population (1992)
Infant mortality rate: 17 deaths/1,000 live births (1992)
Life expectancy at birth: 73 years male, 77 years female (1992)
Total fertility rate: 3.0 children born/woman (1992)
Nationality:

noun - Panamanian(s); adjective - Panamanian
Ethnic divisions:
  mestizo (mixed Indian and European ancestry) 70%, West Indian 14%, white
  10%, Indian 6%
Religions:
  Roman Catholic over 93%, Protestant 6%
Languages:
  Spanish (official); English as native tongue 14%; many Panamanians bilingual
Literacy:
  88% (male 88%, female 88%) age 15 and over can read and write (1990 est.)
Labor force:
  770,472 (1987); government and community services 27.9%; agriculture,
  hunting, and fishing 26.2%; commerce, restaurants, and hotels 16%;
  manufacturing and mining 10.5%; construction 5.3%; transportation and
  communications 5.3%; finance, insurance, and real estate 4.2%; Canal Zone
  2.4%; shortage of skilled labor, but an oversupply of unskilled labor
Organized labor:
  17% of labor force (1986)

:Panama Government

Long-form name:
  Republic of Panama
Type:
  centralized republic
Capital: Panama
Administrative divisions:
  9 provinces (provincias, singular - provincia) and 1 territory* (comarca);
  Bocas del Toro, Chiriqui, Cocle, Colon, Darien, Herrera, Los Santos, Panama,
  San Blas*, Veraguas
Independence:
  3 November 1903 (from Colombia; became independent from Spain 28 November
  1821)
Constitution:
  11 October 1972; major reforms adopted April 1983
Legal system:
  based on civil law system; judicial review of legislative acts in the
  Supreme Court of Justice; accepts compulsory ICJ jurisdiction, with
  reservations
National holiday:
  Independence Day, 3 November (1903)
Executive branch:
  president, two vice presidents, Cabinet
Legislative branch:
  unicameral Legislative Assembly (Asamblea Legislativa)
Judicial branch:
  Supreme Court of Justice (Corte Suprema de Justicia) currently being
  reorganized
Leaders:
  Chief of State and Head of Government:
  President Guillermo ENDARA (since 20 December 1989, elected 7 May 1989);

First Vice President Ricardo ARIAS Calderon (since 20 December 1989, elected 7 May 1989); Second Vice President Guillermo FORD Boyd (since 20 December 1989, elected 7 May 1989)

Political parties and leaders:

government alliance:

Nationalist Republican Liberal Movement (MOLIRENA), Alfredo RAMIREZ; Authentic Liberal Party (PLA), Arnulfo ESCALONA; Arnulfista Party (PA), Mireya MOSCOSO DE GRUBER;

opposition parties:

Christian Democratic Party (PDC), Ricardo ARIAS Calderon; Democratic Revolutionary Party (PRD, ex-official government party), Gerardo GONZALEZ; Agrarian Labor Party (PALA), Carlos LOPEZ Guevara; Liberal Party (PL), Roderick ESQUIVEL; Popular Action Party (PAPO); Socialist Workers Party (PST, leftist), Jose CAMBRA; Revolutionary Workers Party (PRT, leftist), Graciela DIXON

Suffrage:

universal and compulsory at age 18

Elections:

President:

last held on 7 May 1989, annulled but later upheld (next to be held NA May 1994); results - anti-NORIEGA coalition believed to have won about 75% of the total votes cast

Legislative Assembly:

last held on 27 January 1991 (next to be held NA May 1994); results - percent of vote by party NA; seats - (67 total)

progovernment parties:

PDC 28, MOLIRENA 16, PA 7, PLA 4

:Panama Government

opposition parties:

PRD 10, PALA 1, PL 1; note - the PDC went into opposition after President Guillermo ENDARA ousted the PDC from the coalition government in April 1991

Communists:

People's Party (PdP), mainline Communist party, did not obtain the necessary 3% of the total vote in the 1984 election to retain its legal status; about 3,000 members

Other political or pressure groups:

National Council of Organized Workers (CONATO); National Council of Private Enterprise (CONEP); Panamanian Association of Business Executives (APEDE); National Civic Crusade; National Committee for the Right to Life

Member of:

AG (associate), CG, ECLAC, FAO, G-77, IADB, IAEA, IBRD, ICAO, ICFTU, IDA,

IFAD, IFC, ILO, IMF, IMO, INMARSAT, INTELSAT, INTERPOL, IOC, IOM, ITU, LAES,

LAIA (observer), LORCS, NAM, OAS, OPANAL, PCA, UN, UNCTAD, UNESCO, UNIDO,

UPU, WCL, WFTU, WHO, WIPO, WMO, WTO

Diplomatic representation:

Ambassador Jaime FORD; Chancery at 2862 McGill Terrace NW, Washington, DC

20008; telephone (202) 483-1407; the status of the Consulates General and Consulates has not yet been determined

US:

Ambassador Deane R. HINTON; Embassy at Avenida Balboa and Calle 38, Apartado

6959, Panama City 5 (mailing address is Box E, APO AA 34002); telephone (507) 27-1777; FAX (507) 27-1964

Flag:

divided into four, equal rectangles; the top quadrants are white with a blue five-pointed star in the center (hoist side) and plain red, the bottom quadrants are plain blue (hoist side) and white with a red five-pointed star in the center

:Panama Economy

Overview:

GDP expanded by roughly 9.3% in 1991, following growth of 4.6% in 1990 and a 0.4% contraction in 1989. Delay in coming to terms with the international financial institutions on policies to implement structural reform in Panama generated uncertainty in the private sector and tempered the pace of business expansion in 1991. Public investment was limited as the administration kept the fiscal deficit below 3% of GDP. Unemployment and economic reform are the two major issues the government must face in 1992-93.

GDP:

exchange rate conversion - $5.0 billion, per capita $2,040; real growth rate 9.3% (1991 est.)

Inflation rate (consumer prices):

2.0% (1991 est.)

Unemployment rate: 17% (1991 est.)

Budget:

revenues $1.5 billion; expenditures $1.7 billion, including capital expenditures of $140 million (1991 est.)

Exports:

$380 million (f.o.b., 1991 est.)

commodities:

bananas 28%, shrimp 14%, sugar 12%, clothing 5%, coffee 4%

partners:

US 44%, Central America and Caribbean, EC (1991 est.)

Imports:

$1.5 billion (f.o.b., 1991 est.)

commodities:

capital goods 13%, crude oil 12%, foodstuffs 10%, consumer goods, chemicals (1990)

partners:

US 37%, Japan, EC, Central America and Caribbean, Mexico, Venezuela (1989 est.)

External debt: $5.4 billion (December 1991 est.)

Industrial production:

growth rate 7.2% (1991 est.); accounts for almost 9.4% of GDP

Electricity:

1,135,000 kW capacity; 3,397 million kWh produced, 1,372 kWh per capita (1991)

Industries:

manufacturing and construction activities, petroleum refining, brewing, cement and other construction material, sugar mills

Agriculture:

accounts for 12% of GDP (1991 est.), 25% of labor force (1989); crops - bananas, rice, corn, coffee, sugarcane; livestock; fishing; importer of food grain, vegetables

Economic aid:

US commitments, including Ex-Im (FY70-89), $516 million; Western (non-US) countries, ODA and OOF bilateral commitments (1970-89), $582 million; Communist countries (1970-89), $4 million

Currency:

balboa (plural - balboas); 1 balboa (B) = 100 centesimos

Exchange rates:

balboas (B) per US$1 - 1.000 (fixed rate)

Fiscal year: calendar year

:Panama Communications

Railroads:

238 km total; 78 km 1.524-meter gauge, 160 km 0.914-meter gauge

Highways:

8,530 km total; 2,745 km paved, 3,270 km gravel or crushed stone, 2,515 km improved and unimproved earth

Inland waterways:

800 km navigable by shallow draft vessels; 82 km Panama Canal

Pipelines:

crude oil 130 km

Ports:

Cristobal, Balboa, Puerto de La Bahia de Las Minas

Merchant marine:

3,004 ships (1,000 GRT or over) totaling 41,314,623 GRT/73,325,176 DWT; includes 20 passenger, 22 short-sea passenger, 3 passenger-cargo, 1,046 cargo, 205 refrigerated cargo, 175 container, 65 roll-on/roll-off cargo, 111 vehicle carrier, 9 livestock carrier, 4 multifunction large-load carrier, 340 petroleum tanker, 177 chemical tanker, 23 combination ore/oil, 101 liquefied gas, 8 specialized tanker, 659 bulk, 35 combination bulk, 1 barge carrier; note - all but 5 are foreign owned and operated; the top 4 foreign owners are Japan 36%, Greece 8%, Hong Kong 8%, and the US 7%; (China owns at least 128 ships, Vietnam 4, former Yugoslavia 4, Cuba 4, Cyprus 5, and the republics of the former USSR 12)

Civil air:

5 major transport aircraft

Airports:

112 total, 102 usable; 39 with permanent-surface runways; none with runways over 3,659 m; 2 with runways 2,440-3,659 m; 15 with runways 1,220-2,439 m

Telecommunications:

domestic and international facilities well developed; connection into Central American Microwave System; 220,000 telephones; broadcast stations -

91 AM, no FM, 23 TV; 1 coaxial submarine cable; satellite ground stations - 2 Atlantic Ocean INTELSAT

:Panama Defense Forces

Branches:

note - the Panamanian Defense Forces (PDF) ceased to exist as a military institution shortly after the United States invaded Panama on 20 December 1989; President ENDARA has restructured the forces into a civilian police service under the new name of Panamanian Public Forces (PPF); a Council of Public Security and National Defense under Menalco SOLIS in the office of the president coordinates the activities of the security forces; the Institutional Protection Service under Carlos BARES is attached to the presidency

Manpower availability:

males 15-49, 661,101; 455,412 fit for military service; no conscription

Defense expenditures:

exchange rate conversion - $75.5 million, 1.5% of GDP (1990)

Papua New Guinea Geography

Total area: 461,690 km2
Land area: 451,710 km2
Comparative area: slightly larger than California
Land boundaries:

820 km; Indonesia 820 km

Coastline:

5,152 km

Maritime claims:

(measured from claimed archipelagic baselines)

Continental shelf:

200 m (depth) or to depth of exploitation

Exclusive economic zone:

200 nm

Territorial sea:

12 nm

Disputes:

Climate:

tropical; northwest monsoon (December to March), southeast monsoon (May to October); slight seasonal temperature variation

Terrain:

mostly mountains with coastal lowlands and rolling foothills

Natural resources:

gold, copper, silver, natural gas, timber, oil potential

Land use:

arable land NEGL%; permanent crops 1%; meadows and pastures NEGL%; forest and woodland 71%; other 28%

Environment:

one of world's largest swamps along southwest coast; some active volcanos; frequent earthquakes

Note:

shares island of New Guinea with Indonesia

:Papua New Guinea People

Population: 4,006,509 (July 1992), growth rate 2.3% (1992)
Birth rate: 34 births/1,000 population (1992)
Death rate: 11 deaths/1,000 population (1992)
Net migration rate: 0 migrants/1,000 population (1992)
Infant mortality rate: 67 deaths/1,000 live births (1992)
Life expectancy at birth: 55 years male, 56 years female (1992)
Total fertility rate: 4.9 children born/woman (1992)
Nationality:
  noun - Papua New Guinean(s); adjective - Papua New Guinean
Ethnic divisions:
  predominantly Melanesian and Papuan; some Negrito, Micronesian, and
  Polynesian
Religions:
  Roman Catholic 22%, Lutheran 16%, Presbyterian/Methodist/London Missionary
  Society 8%, Anglican 5%, Evangelical Alliance 4%, Seventh-Day Adventist 1%,
  other Protestant sects 10%; indigenous beliefs 34%
Languages:
  715 indigenous languages; English spoken by 1-2%, pidgin English widespread,
  Motu spoken in Papua region
Literacy:
  52% (male 65%, female 38%) age 15 and over can read and write (1990 est.)
Labor force:
  NA
Organized labor:
  more than 50 trade unions, some with fewer than 20 members

:Papua New Guinea Government

Long-form name:
  Independent State of Papua New Guinea
Type:
  parliamentary democracy
Capital: Port Moresby
Administrative divisions:
  20 provinces; Central, Chimbu, Eastern Highlands, East New Britain, East
  Sepik, Enga, Gulf, Madang, Manus, Milne Bay, Morobe, National Capital, New
  Ireland, Northern, North Solomons, Sandaun, Southern Highlands, Western,
  Western Highlands, West New Britain
Independence:
  16 September 1975 (from UN trusteeship under Australian administration)
Constitution:
  16 September 1975
Legal system:
  based on English common law
National holiday:
  Independence Day, 16 September (1975)
Executive branch:
  British monarch, governor general, prime minister, deputy prime minister,
  National Executive Council (cabinet)
Legislative branch:

unicameral National Parliament (sometimes referred to as the House of
Assembly)

Judicial branch:

Supreme Court

Leaders:

Chief of State:

Queen Elizabeth II (since 6 February 1952), represented by Governor General
Wiwa KOROWI (since NA November 1991)

Head of Government:

Prime Minister Paias WINGTI (since 17 July 1992)

Political parties and leaders:

Papua New Guinea United Party (Pangu Party), Rabbie NAMALIU; People's
Democratic Movement (PDM), Paias WINGTI; People's Action Party (PAP), Akoka
DOI; People's Progress Party (PPP), Sir Julius CHAN; United Party (UP), Paul
TORATO; Papua Party (PP), Galeva KWARARA; National Party (NP), Paul PORA;
Melanesian Alliance (MA), Fr. John MOMIS

Suffrage:

universal at age 18

Elections:

National Parliament:

last held 13-26 June 1992 (next to be held NA 1997); results - percent by
party NA; seats - (109 total) Pangu Party 24, PDM 17, PPP 10, PAP 10,
independents 30, others 18

Member of:

ACP, AsDB, ASEAN (observer), C, CP, ESCAP, FAO, G-77, IBRD, ICAO, ICFTU,
IDA, IFAD, IFC, ILO, IMF, IMO, INTELSAT, INTERPOL, IOC, ISO, ITU,
LORCS, NAM

(observer), SPC, SPF, UN, UNCTAD, UNESCO, UNIDO, UPU, WHO, WMO

Diplomatic representation:

Ambassador Margaret TAYLOR; Chancery at 3rd floor, 1615 New Hampshire Avenue

NW, Washington, DC 20009; telephone (202) 745-3680

US:

Ambassador Robert W. FARRAND; Embassy at Armit Street, Port Moresby (mailing

address is P. O. Box 1492, Port Moresby, or APO AE 96553); telephone [675]
211-455 or 594, 654; FAX [675] 213-423

:Papua New Guinea Government

Flag:

divided diagonally from upper hoist-side corner; the upper triangle is red
with a soaring yellow bird of paradise centered; the lower triangle is black
with five white five-pointed stars of the Southern Cross constellation
centered

:Papua New Guinea Economy

Overview:

Papua New Guinea is richly endowed with natural resources, but exploitation
has been hampered by the rugged terrain and the high cost of developing an
infrastructure. Agriculture provides a subsistence livelihood for 85% of the
population. Mining of numerous deposits, including copper and gold, accounts

for about 60% of export earnings. Budgetary support from Australia and development aid under World Bank auspices have helped sustain the economy. Robust growth in 1991 was led by the mining sector; the opening of a large new gold mine featured in the advance.

GDP:
exchange rate conversion - $3.1 billion, per capita $800; real growth rate 9% (1991)

Inflation rate (consumer prices):
6.8% (first half 1991)

Unemployment rate: 5% (1988)

Budget:
revenues $1.26 billion; expenditures $1.46 billion, including capital expenditures of $273 million (1992 est.)

Exports:
$1.14 billion (f.o.b., 1990)
commodities:
copper ore, gold, coffee, logs, palm oil, cocoa, lobster
partners:
FRG, Japan, Australia, UK, Spain, US

Imports:
$1.18 billion (c.i.f., 1990)
commodities:
machinery and transport equipment, food, fuels, chemicals, consumer goods
partners:
Australia, Singapore, Japan, US, New Zealand, UK

External debt: $2.2 billion (April 1991)

Industrial production:
growth rate 2.4% (1990 est.); accounts for 25% of GDP

Electricity:
397,000 kW capacity; 1,510 million kWh produced, 400 kWh per capita (1990)

Industries:
copra crushing, oil palm processing, plywood processing, wood chip production, gold, silver, copper, construction, tourism

Agriculture:
one-third of GDP; livelihood for 85% of population; fertile soils and favorable climate permits cultivating a wide variety of crops; cash crops - coffee, cocoa, coconuts, palm kernels; other products - tea, rubber, sweet potatoes, fruit, vegetables, poultry, pork; net importer of food for urban centers

Economic aid:
US commitments, including Ex-Im (FY70-89), $40.6 million; Western (non-US) countries, ODA and OOF bilateral commitments (1970-89), $6.5 billion; OPEC bilateral aid (1979-89), $17 million

Currency:
kina (plural - kina); 1 kina (K) = 100 toea

Exchange rates:
kina (K) per US$1 - 1.0413 (March 1992), 1.0508 (1991), 1.0467 (1990), 1.1685 (1989), 1.1538 (1988), 1.1012 (1987)

Fiscal year: calendar year

:Papua New Guinea Communications

Railroads:
  none
Highways:
  19,200 km total; 640 km paved, 10,960 km gravel, crushed stone, or
  stabilized-soil surface, 7,600 km unimproved earth
Inland waterways:
  10,940 km
Ports:
  Anewa Bay, Lae, Madang, Port Moresby, Rabaul
Merchant marine:
  8 ships (1,000 GRT or over) totaling 14,102 GRT/16,016 DWT; includes 2
  cargo, 1 roll-on/roll-off cargo, 3 combination ore/oil, 1 bulk, 1 container
Civil air:
  about 15 major transport aircraft
Airports:
  503 total, 460 usable; 18 with permanent-surface runways; none with runways
  over 3,659 m; 1 with runways 2,440-3,659 m; 39 with runways 1,220-2,439 m
Telecommunications:
  services are adequate and being improved; facilities provide radiobroadcast,
  radiotelephone and telegraph, coastal radio, aeronautical radio, and
  international radiocommunication services; submarine cables extend to
  Australia and Guam; 51,700 telephones (1985); broadcast stations - 31 AM, 2
  FM, 2 TV (1987); 1 Pacific Ocean INTELSAT earth station

:Papua New Guinea Defense Forces

Branches:
  Papua New Guinea Defense Force (including Army, Navy, Air Force)
Manpower availability:
  males 15-49, 1,013,812; 564,081 fit for military service
Defense expenditures:
  exchange rate conversion - $42 million, 1.3% of GDP (1989 est.)

Paracel Islands Geography

Total area: NA
Land area: undetermined
Comparative area: undetermined
Land boundaries:
  none
Coastline:
  518 km
Maritime claims:
  undetermined
Disputes:
  occupied by China, but claimed by Taiwan and Vietnam
Climate:
  tropical
Terrain:
  undetermined
Natural resources:
  none
Land use:

arable land 0%; permanent crops 0%; meadows and pastures 0%; forest and woodland 0%; other 100%
Environment:
 subject to typhoons
Note:
 located 400 km east of Vietnam in the South China Sea about one-third of the way between Vietnam and the Philippines

:Paracel Islands People

Population: no permanent inhabitants

:Paracel Islands Government

Long-form name: none

:Paracel Islands Economy

Overview: no economic activity

:Paracel Islands Communications

Ports:
 small Chinese port facilities on Woody Island and Duncan Island currently under expansion
Airports:
 1 on Woody Island

:Paracel Islands Defense Forces

Note: occupied by China

Paraguay Geography

Total area: 406,750 km2
Land area: 397,300 km2
Comparative area: slightly smaller than California
Land boundaries:
 3,920 km total; Argentina 1,880 km, Bolivia 750 km, Brazil 1,290 km
Coastline:
 none - landlocked
Maritime claims:
 none - landlocked
Disputes:
 short section of the boundary with Brazil (just west of Guaira Falls on the Rio Parana) has not been determined
Climate:
 varies from temperate in east to semiarid in far west
Terrain:
 grassy plains and wooded hills east of Rio Paraguay; Gran Chaco region west of Rio Paraguay mostly low, marshy plain near the river, and dry forest and thorny scrub elsewhere
Natural resources:
 iron ore, manganese, limestone, hydropower, timber
Land use:
 arable land 20%; permanent crops 1%; meadows and pastures 39%; forest and woodland 35%; other 5%; includes irrigated NEGL%
Environment:

local flooding in southeast (early September to June); poorly drained plains
may become boggy (early October to June)
Note:
   landlocked; buffer between Argentina and Brazil

:Paraguay People

Population: 4,929,446 (July 1992), growth rate 2.9% (1992)
Birth rate: 33 births/1,000 population (1992)
Death rate: 5 deaths/1,000 population (1992)
Net migration rate: 0 migrants/1,000 population (1992)
Infant mortality rate: 28 deaths/1,000 live births (1992)
Life expectancy at birth: 71 years male, 74 years female (1992)
Total fertility rate: 4.4 children born/woman (1992)
Nationality:
   noun - Paraguayan(s); adjective - Paraguayan
Ethnic divisions:
   mestizo (Spanish and Indian) 95%, white and Indian 5%
Religions:
   Roman Catholic 90%; Mennonite and other Protestant denominations
Languages:
   Spanish (official) and Guarani
Literacy:
   90% (male 92%, female 88%) age 15 and over can read and write (1990 est.)
Labor force:
   1,418,000 (1991 est.); agriculture, industry and commerce, services,
   government (1986)
Organized labor:
   about 2% of labor force

:Paraguay Government

Long-form name:
   Republic of Paraguay
Type:
   republic
Capital: Asuncion
Administrative divisions:
   19 departments (departamentos, singular - departamento); Alto Paraguay, Alto
   Parana, Amambay, Boqueron, Caaguazu, Caazapa, Canindeyu, Central, Chaco,
   Concepcion, Cordillera, Guaira, Itapua, Misiones, Neembucu, Nueva Asuncion,
   Paraguari, Presidente Hayes, San Pedro
Independence:
   14 May 1811 (from Spain)
Constitution:
   25 August 1967; Constituent Assembly rewrote the Constitution that was
   promulgated on 20 June 1992
Legal system:
   based on Argentine codes, Roman law, and French codes; judicial review of
   legislative acts in Supreme Court of Justice; does not accept compulsory ICJ
   jurisdiction
National holiday:
   Independence Days, 14-15 May (1811)

761

Executive branch:
   president, Council of Ministers (cabinet), Council of State
Legislative branch:
   bicameral Congress (Congreso) consists of an upper chamber or Chamber of
   Senators (Camara de Senadores) and a lower chamber or Chamber of Deputies
   (Camara de Diputados)
Judicial branch:
   Supreme Court of Justice (Corte Suprema de Justicia)
Leaders:
   Chief of State and Head of Government:
   President Gen. Andres RODRIGUEZ Pedotti (since 15 May 1989)
Political parties and leaders:
   Colorado Party, Luis Maria ARGANA, acting president; Authentic Radical
   Liberal Party (PLRA), Juan Manuel BENITEZ Florentin; Christian Democratic
   Party (PDC), Jose Angel BURRO; Febrerista Revolutionary Party (PRF), Victor
   BAREIRO; Popular Democratic Party (PDP), Hugo RICHER
Suffrage:
   universal and compulsory at age 18 and up to age 60
Elections:
   President:
   last held 1 May 1989 (next to be held NA February 1993); results - Gen.
   RODRIGUEZ 75.8%, Domingo LAINO 19.4%
   Chamber of Senators:
   last held 1 May 1989 (next to be held by NA May 1993); results - percent of
   vote by party NA; seats - (36 total) Colorado Party 24, PLRA 10, PLR 1, PRF
   1
   Chamber of Deputies:
   last held on 1 May 1989 (next to be held by NA May 1994); results - percent
   of vote by party NA; seats - (72 total) Colorado Party 48, PLRA 19, PRF 2,
   PDC 1, other 2
Communists:
   Oscar CREYDT faction and Miguel Angel SOLER faction (both illegal); 3,000 to
   4,000 (est.) party members and sympathizers in Paraguay, very few are hard
   core; party beginning to return from exile is small and deeply divided
Other political or pressure groups:
   Confederation of Workers (CUT); Roman Catholic Church

:Paraguay Government

Member of:
   AG (observer), CCC, ECLAC, FAO, G-77, IADB, IAEA, IBRD, ICAO, IDA, IFAD,
   IFC, ILO, IMF, INTELSAT, INTERPOL, IOC, IOM, ITU, LAES, LAIA, LORCS,
OAS,
   OPANAL, PCA, RG, UN, UNCTAD, UNESCO, UNIDO, UPU, WCL, WHO,
WIPO, WMO
Diplomatic representation:
   Ambassador Juan Esteban Aguirre MARTINEZ; Chancery at 2400 Massachusetts
   Avenue NW, Washington, DC 20008; telephone (202) 483-6960 through 6962;
   there are Paraguayan Consulates General in New Orleans and New York, and a
   Consulate in Houston
US:

Ambassador Jon D. GLASSMAN; Embassy at 1776 Avenida Mariscal Lopez, Asuncion

(mailing address is C. P. 402, Asuncion, or APO AA 34036-0001); telephone [595] (21) 213-715; FAX [595] (21) 213-728

Flag:

three equal, horizontal bands of red (top), white, and blue with an emblem centered in the white band; unusual flag in that the emblem is different on each side; the obverse (hoist side at the left) bears the national coat of arms (a yellow five-pointed star within a green wreath capped by the words REPUBLICA DEL PARAGUAY, all within two circles); the reverse (hoist side at the right) bears the seal of the treasury (a yellow lion below a red Cap of Liberty and the words Paz y Justicia (Peace and Justice) capped by the words REPUBLICA DEL PARAGUAY, all within two circles)

:Paraguay Economy

Overview:

Agriculture, including forestry, accounts for about 25% of GDP, employs about 45% of the labor force, and provides the bulk of exports. Paraguay has no known significant mineral or petroleum resources but does have a large hydropower potential. Since 1981 economic performance has declined compared with the boom period of 1976-81, when real GDP grew at an average annual rate of nearly 11%. During the period 1982-86 real GDP fell in three of five years, inflation jumped to an annual rate of 32%, and foreign debt rose. Factors responsible for the erratic behavior of the economy were the completion of the Itaipu hydroelectric dam, bad weather for crops, and weak international commodity prices for agricultural exports. In 1987 the economy experienced a minor recovery because of improved weather conditions and stronger international prices for key agricultural exports. The recovery continued through 1990, on the strength of bumper crops in 1988-89. In a major step to increase its economic activity in the region, Paraguay in March 1991 joined the Southern Cone Common Market (MERCOSUR), which includes

Brazil, Argentina, and Uruguay. During 1991 the government began to more seriously address its arrearages with international creditors and its domestic fiscal problems. Inflation was cut in third, but the foreign trade deficit widened to more than $1 billion. For the long run, the government must press forward with general market-oriented economic reforms.

GDP:

exchange rate conversion - $7.0 billion, per capita $1,460; real growth rate 3.0% (1991 est.)

Inflation rate (consumer prices):

15% (1991 est.)

Unemployment rate: 14% (1991 est.)

Budget:

revenues $1.2 billion; expenditures $1.2 billion, including capital expenditures of $487 million (1991)

Exports:

$642 million (f.o.b., 1991)

commodities:

cotton, soybean, timber, vegetable oils, coffee, tung oil, meat products

partners:
  EC 37%, Brazil 25%, Argentina 10%, Chile 6%, US 6%
Imports:
  $1.85 billion (c.i.f., 1991)
  commodities:
  capital goods 35%, consumer goods 20%, fuels and lubricants 19%, raw
  materials 16%, foodstuffs, beverages, and tobacco 10%
  partners:
  Brazil 30%, EC 20%, US 18%, Argentina 8%, Japan 7%
External debt: $1.7 billion (1991 est.)
Industrial production:
  growth rate 5.9% (1989 est.); accounts for 16% of GDP
Electricity:
  5,578,000 kW capacity; 15,447 million kWh produced, 3,219 kWh per capita
  (1991)
Industries:
  meat packing, oilseed crushing, milling, brewing, textiles, other light
  consumer goods, cement, construction
Agriculture:
  accounts for 25% of GDP and 44% of labor force; cash crops - cotton,
  sugarcane; other crops - corn, wheat, tobacco, soybeans, cassava, fruits,
  and vegetables; animal products - beef, pork, eggs, milk; surplus producer
  of timber; self-sufficient in most foods

:Paraguay Economy

Illicit drugs:
  illicit producer of cannabis for the international drug trade; important
  transshipment point for Bolivian cocaine headed for the US and Europe
Economic aid:
  US commitments, including Ex-Im (FY70-89), $172 million; Western (non-US)
  countries, ODA and OOF bilateral commitments (1970-89), $1.1 billion
Currency:
  guarani (plural - guaranies); 1 guarani (G) = 100 centimos
Exchange rates:
  guaranies (G) per US$ - 1,447.5 (March 1992), 1,325.2 (1991), 1,229.8
  (1990), 1,056.2 (1989), 550.00 (fixed rate 1986-February 1989),
Fiscal year: calendar year

:Paraguay Communications

Railroads:
  970 km total; 440 km 1.435-meter standard gauge, 60 km 1.000-meter gauge,
  470 km various narrow gauge (privately owned)
Highways:
  21,960 km total; 1,788 km paved, 474 km gravel, and 19,698 km earth
Inland waterways:
  3,100 km
Ports:
  Asuncion
Merchant marine:
  13 ships (1,000 GRT or over) totaling 16,747 GRT/19,865 DWT; includes 11
  cargo, 2 petroleum tanker; note - 1 naval cargo ship is sometimes used

commercially

Civil air:

9 major transport aircraft

Airports:

845 total, 716 usable; 7 with permanent-surface runways; 0 with runways over 3,659 m; 3 with runways 2,440-3,659 m; 66 with runways 1,220-2,439 m

Telecommunications:

principal center in Asuncion; fair intercity microwave net; 78,300 telephones; broadcast stations - 40 AM, no FM, 5 TV, 7 shortwave; 1 Atlantic Ocean INTELSAT earth station

:Paraguay Defense Forces

Branches:

Army, Navy (including Naval Air and Marines), Air Force

Manpower availability:

males 15-49, 1,172,813; 853,129 fit for military service; 49,917 reach military age (17) annually

Defense expenditures:

exchange rate conversion - $84 million, 1.4% of GDP (1988 est.)

Peru Geography

Total area: 1,285,220 km2

Land area: 1,280,000 km2

Comparative area: slightly smaller than Alaska

Land boundaries:

6,940 km total; Bolivia 900 km, Brazil 1,560 km, Chile 160 km, Colombia 2,900 km, Ecuador 1,420 km

Coastline:

2,414 km

Maritime claims:

Territorial sea:

200 nm

Disputes:

three sections of the boundary with Ecuador are in dispute

Climate:

varies from tropical in east to dry desert in west

Terrain:

western coastal plain (costa), high and rugged Andes in center (sierra), eastern lowland jungle of Amazon Basin (selva)

Natural resources:

copper, silver, gold, petroleum, timber, fish, iron ore, coal, phosphate, potash

Land use:

arable land 3%; permanent crops NEGL%; meadows and pastures 21%; forest and woodland 55%; other 21%; includes irrigated 1%

Environment:

subject to earthquakes, tsunamis, landslides, mild volcanic activity; deforestation; overgrazing; soil erosion; desertification; air pollution in Lima

Note:

shares control of Lago Titicaca, world's highest navigable lake, with
Bolivia

:Peru People

Population: 22,767,543 (July 1992), growth rate 2.0% (1992)
Birth rate: 27 births/1,000 population (1992)
Death rate: 7 deaths/1,000 population (1992)
Net migration rate: 0 migrants/1,000 population (1992)
Infant mortality rate: 59 deaths/1,000 live births (1992)
Life expectancy at birth: 63 years male, 67 years female (1992)
Total fertility rate: 3.3 children born/woman (1992)
Nationality:
  noun - Peruvian(s); adjective - Peruvian
Ethnic divisions:
  Indian 45%; mestizo (mixed Indian and European ancestry) 37%; white 15%;
  black, Japanese, Chinese, and other 3%
Religions:
  predominantly Roman Catholic
Languages:
  Spanish and Quechua (both official), Aymara
Literacy:
  85% (male 92%, female 29%) age 15 and over can read and write (1990 est.)
Labor force:
  6,800,000 (1986); government and other services 44%, agriculture 37%,
  industry 19% (1988 est.)
Organized labor:
  about 40% of salaried workers (1983 est.)

:Peru Government

Long-form name:
  Republic of Peru
Type:
  in transition, President FUJIMORI on 5 April 1992 suspended the constitution
  and dissolved the legislative and judicial branches
Capital: Lima
Administrative divisions:
  24 departments (departamentos, singular - departamento) and 1 constitutional
  province* (provincia constitucional); Amazonas, Ancash, Apurimac, Arequipa,
  Ayacucho, Cajamarca, Callao*, Cusco, Huancavelica, Huanuco, Ica, Junin, La
  Libertad, Lambayeque, Lima, Loreto, Madre de Dios, Moquegua, Pasco, Piura,
  Puno, San Martin, Tacna, Tumbes, Ucayali; note - the 1979 Constitution and
  legislation enacted from 1987 to 1990 mandate the creation of regions
  (regiones, singular - region) intended to function eventually as autonomous
  economic and administrative entities; so far, 12 regions have been
  constituted from 23 existing departments - Amazonas (from Loreto), Andres
  Avelino Caceres (from Huanuco, Pasco, Junin), Arequipa (from Arequipa),
  Chavin (from Ancash), Grau (from Tumbes, Piura), Inca (from Cusco, Madre de
  Dios, Apurimac), La Libertad (from La Libertad), Los Libertadores-Huari
  (from Ica, Ayacucho, Huancavelica), Mariategui (from Moquegua, Tacna, Puno),
  Nor Oriental del Maranon (from Lambayeque, Cajamarca, Amazonas), San Martin
  (from San Martin), Ucayali (from Ucayali); formation of another region has

been delayed by the reluctance of the constitutional province of Callao to merge with the department of Lima; because of inadequate funding from the central government, the regions have yet to assume their responsibilities and at the moment coexist with the departmental structure

Independence:

28 July 1821 (from Spain)

Constitution:

28 July 1980 (often referred to as the 1979 Constitution because the Constituent Assembly met in 1979, but the Constitution actually took effect the following year); suspended 5 April 1992

Legal system:

based on civil law system; has not accepted compulsory ICJ jurisdiction

National holiday:

Independence Day, 28 July (1821)

Executive branch:

president, two vice presidents (vacant as of 19 May 1992), prime minister, Council of Ministers (cabinet)

Legislative branch:

bicameral Congress (Congreso) consists of an upper chamber or Senate (Senado) and a lower chamber or Chamber of Deputies (Camara de Diputados); note - dissolved on 5 April 1992; being reconstituted

Judicial branch:

Supreme Court of Justice (Corte Suprema de Justicia)

Leaders:

Chief of State:

President Alberto FUJIMORI (since 28 July 1990); note - slots for first and second Vice Presidents vacant as of 19 May 1992

Head of Government:

Prime Minister Oscar DE LA PUENTE Raygada (since 6 April 1992)

:Peru Government

Political parties and leaders:

Change 90 (Cambio 90), Alberto FUJIMORI; Popular Christian Party (PPC), Luis BEDOYA Reyes; Popular Action Party (AP), Eduardo CALMELL del Solar; Liberty Movement (ML), Luis BUSTAMANTE; American Popular Revolutionary Alliance (APRA), Luis ALVA Castro, Alan GARCIA; National Front of Workers and Peasants (FNTC), Roger CACERES; United Left (IU), leader NA; Independent Moralizing Front (FIM), Fernando OLIVERA Vega; Socialist Left (IS), leader NA; note - Democratic Front (FREDEMO) was a loosely organized coalition of the PPC, AP, and ML during the 8 April 1990 elections, but the parties no longer maintain a formal alliance

Suffrage:

universal at age 18

Elections:

President:

last held on 10 June 1990 (next to be held NA April 1995); results - Alberto FUJIMORI 56.53%, Mario VARGAS Llosa 33.92%, other 9.55%

Senate:

last held on 8 April 1990; dissolved on 5 April 1992; because of suspension of constitutional role, next election not yet scheduled; results - percent of vote by party NA; seats - (62 total; 60 elected, 2 ex-presidents who are senators for life) FREDEMO 20, APRA 16, Change 90 14, IU 6, IS 3, FNTC 1; note - as a result of the dissolution of FREDEMO and defections and expulsions from the various parties, the seats have been reallocated: APRA 17, Change 90 13, AP 8, IU 6, PPC 5, ML 4, IS 3, FNTC 1, independents 4, other 1 (January 1992)

Chamber of Deputies:

last held 8 April 1990 dissolved on 5 April 1992; because of suspension of constitutional role, next election not yet scheduled; results - percent of vote by party NA; seats - (180 total) FREDEMO 62, APRA 53, Change 90 32, IU 16, IS 4, FNTC 3, other 10; note - as a result of the dissolution of FREDEMO and defections and expulsions from the various parties, the seats have been reallocated: APRA 53, AP 25, Change 90 25, PPC 23, IU 16, ML 7, FIM 3, IS 4, FNTC 3, independents 15, other 4, and 2 currently nonvoting deputies

Communists:

Peruvian Communist Party-Unity (PCP-U), 2,000; other minor Communist parties

Other political or pressure groups:

leftist guerrilla groups:

Shining Path, Abimael GUZMAN; Tupac Amaru Revolutionary Movement, Nestor SERPA and Victor POLAY

Member of:

AG, CCC, ECLAC, FAO, G-11, G-19, G-24, G-77, GATT, IADB, IAEA, IBRD, ICAO,

ICFTU, IDA, IFAD, IFC, ILO, IMF, IMO, INMARSAT, INTELSAT, INTERPOL, IOC,

IOM, ISO, ITU, LAES, LAIA, LORCS, NAM, OAS, OPANAL, PCA, RG, UN, UNCTAD,

UNESCO, UNIDO, UNIIMOG, UPU, WCL, WFTU, WHO, WIPO, WMO, WTO

Diplomatic representation:

Ambassador vacant; Chancery at 1700 Massachusetts Avenue NW, Washington, DC 20036; telephone (202) 833-9860 through 9869); Peruvian Consulates General are located in Chicago, Houston, Los Angeles, Miami, New York, Paterson (New Jersey), San Francisco, and San Juan (Puerto Rico)

US:

Ambassador Anthony C. E. QUAINTON; Embassy at the corner of Avenida Inca Garcilaso de la Vega and Avenida Espana, Lima (mailing address is P. O. Box 1991, Lima 1, or APO AA 34031); telephone [51] (14) 33-8000; FAX [51] (14) 316682

Flag:

three equal, vertical bands of red (hoist side), white, and red with the coat of arms centered in the white band; the coat of arms features a shield bearing a llama, cinchona tree (the source of quinine), and a yellow cornucopia spilling out gold coins, all framed by a green wreath

:Peru Economy

Overview:

The Peruvian economy is becoming increasingly market oriented, with a large dose of government ownership remaining in mining, energy, and banking. In the 1980s the economy suffered from hyperinflation, declining per capita output, and mounting external debt. Peru was shut off from IMF and World

Bank support in the mid-1980s because of its huge debt arrears. An austerity program implemented shortly after the FUJIMORI government took office in July 1990 contributed to a third consecutive yearly contraction of economic activity, but the slide halted late in the year, and output rose 2.4% in 1991. After a burst of inflation as the austerity program eliminated government price subsidies, monthly price increases eased to the single-digit level and by December 1991 dropped to the lowest increase since mid-1987. Lima obtained a financial rescue package from multilateral lenders in September 1991, and, although it faces $14 billion in arrears on its external debt, is working to pay some $1.8 billion of these to the IMF and World Bank by 1993.

GDP:
exchange rate conversion - $20.6 billion, per capita $920; real growth rate 2.4% (1991 est.)

Inflation rate (consumer prices):
139% (1991)

Unemployment rate: 15.0%; underemployment 65% (1991 est.)

Budget:
revenues $1.7 billion; expenditures $1.8 billion, including capital expenditures of $250 million (1991 est.)

Exports:
$3.3 billion (f.o.b., 1991 est.)
commodities:
copper, fishmeal, zinc, crude petroleum and byproducts, lead, refined silver, coffee, cotton
partners:
EC 28%, US 22%, Japan 13%, Latin America 12%, former USSR 2%

Imports:
$3.5 billion (f.o.b., 1991 est.)
commodities:
foodstuffs, machinery, transport equipment, iron and steel semimanufactures, chemicals, pharmaceuticals
partners:
US 32%, Latin America 22%, EC 17%, Switzerland 6%, Japan 3%

External debt: $19.4 billion (December 1991 est.)

Industrial production:
growth rate 1.0% (1991 est.); accounts for almost 24% of GDP

Electricity:
4,896,000 kW capacity; 15,851 million kWh produced, 709 kWh per capita (1991)

Industries:
mining of metals, petroleum, fishing, textiles, clothing, food processing, cement, auto assembly, steel, shipbuilding, metal fabrication

Agriculture:
accounts for 10% of GDP, about 35% of labor force; commercial crops - coffee, cotton, sugarcane; other crops - rice, wheat, potatoes, plantains, coca; animal products - poultry, red meats, dairy, wool; not self-sufficient in grain or vegetable oil; fish catch of 6.9 million metric tons (1990)

:Peru Economy

Illicit drugs:
    world's largest coca leaf producer with about 121,000 hectares under
    cultivation; source of supply for most of the world's coca paste and cocaine
    base; at least 85% of coca cultivation is for illicit production; most of
    cocaine base is shipped to Colombian drug dealers for processing into
    cocaine for the international drug market
Economic aid:
    US commitments, including Ex-Im (FY70-89), $1.7 billion; Western (non-US)
    countries, ODA and OOF bilateral commitments (1970-89), $4.3 billion;
    Communist countries (1970-89), $577 million
Currency:
    (S/.) nuevo sol (plural - nuevos soles); 1 nuevo sol (S/.) = 100 centavos
Exchange rates:
    nuevo sol (S/. per US$1 - 0.960 (March 1992), 0.772 (1991), 0.187 (1990),
    2.666 (1989), 0.129 (1988), 0.017 (1987)
Fiscal year: calendar year

:Peru Communications

Railroads:
    1,801 km total; 1,501 km 1.435-meter gauge, 300 km 0.914-meter gauge
Highways:
    69,942 km total; 7,459 km paved, 13,538 km improved, 48,945 km unimproved
    earth
Inland waterways:
    8,600 km of navigable tributaries of Amazon system and 208 km Lago Titicaca
Pipelines:
    crude oil 800 km, natural gas and natural gas liquids 64 km
Ports:
    Callao, Ilo, Iquitos, Matarani, Talara
Merchant marine:
    26 ships (1,000 GRT or over) totaling 286,313 GRT/461,233 DWT; includes 14
    cargo, 1 refrigerated cargo, 1 roll-on/roll-off cargo, 3 petroleum tanker, 7
    bulk; note - in addition, 8 naval tankers and 1 naval cargo are sometimes
    used commercially
Civil air:
    44 major transport aircraft
Airports:
    221 total, 201 usable; 36 with permanent-surface runways; 2 with runways
    over 3,659 m; 23 with runways 2,440-3,659 m; 43 with runways 1,220-2,439 m
Telecommunications:
    fairly adequate for most requirements; nationwide microwave system; 544,000
    telephones; broadcast stations - 273 AM, no FM, 140 TV, 144 shortwave;
    satellite earth stations - 2 Atlantic Ocean INTELSAT, 12 domestic

:Peru Defense Forces

Branches:
    Army (Ejercito Peruano), Navy (Marina de Guerra del Peru), Air Force (Fuerza
    Aerea del Peru), National Police
Manpower availability:
    males 15-49, 5,863,227; 3,964,930 fit for military service; 236,484 reach
    military age (20) annually

Defense expenditures:

exchange rate conversion - $430 million, 2.4% of GDP (1991)

Philippines Geography

Total area: 300,000 km2

Land area: 298,170 km2

Comparative area: slightly larger than Arizona

Land boundaries:

Coastline:

36,289 km

Maritime claims:

(measured from claimed archipelagic baselines)

Continental shelf:

to depth of exploitation

Exclusive economic zone:

200 nm

Territorial sea:

irregular polygon extending up to 100 nm from coastline as defined by 1898
treaty; since late 1970s has also claimed polygonal-shaped area in South
China Sea up to 285 nm in breadth

Disputes:

involved in a complex dispute over the Spratly Islands with China, Malaysia,
Taiwan, Vietnam, and possibly Brunei; claims Malaysian state of Sabah

Climate:

tropical marine; northeast monsoon (November to April); southwest monsoon
(May to October)

Terrain:

mostly mountains with narrow to extensive coastal lowlands

Natural resources:

timber, crude oil, nickel, cobalt, silver, gold, salt, copper

Land use:

arable land 26%; permanent crops 11%; meadows and pastures 4%; forest and
woodland 40%; other 19%; includes irrigated 5%

Environment:

astride typhoon belt, usually affected by 15 and struck by five to six
cyclonic storms per year; subject to landslides, active volcanoes,
destructive earthquakes, tsunami; deforestation; soil erosion; water
pollution

:Philippines People

Population: 67,114,060 (July 1992), growth rate 2.0% (1992)

Birth rate: 28 births/1,000 population (1992)

Death rate: 7 deaths/1,000 population (1992)

Net migration rate: -1 migrant/1,000 population (1992)

Infant mortality rate: 53 deaths/1,000 live births (1992)

Life expectancy at birth: 62 years male, 68 years female (1992)

Total fertility rate: 3.5 children born/woman (1992)

Nationality:

noun - Filipino(s); adjective - Philippine

Ethnic divisions:

Christian Malay 91.5%, Muslim Malay 4%, Chinese 1.5%, other 3%
Religions:
  Roman Catholic 83%, Protestant 9%, Muslim 5%, Buddhist and other 3%
Languages:
  Pilipino (based on Tagalog) and English; both official
Literacy:
  90% (male 90%, female 90%) age 15 and over can read and write (1990 est.)
Labor force:
  24,120,000; agriculture 46%, industry and commerce 16%, services 18.5%,
  government 10%, other 9.5% (1989)
Organized labor:
  3,945 registered unions; total membership 5.7 million (includes 2.8 million
  members of the National Congress of Farmers Organizations)

:Philippines Government

Long-form name:
  Republic of the Philippines
Type:
  republic
Capital: Manila
Administrative divisions:
  72 provinces and 61 chartered cities*; Abra, Agusan del Norte, Agusan del
  Sur, Aklan, Albay, Angeles*, Antique, Aurora, Bacolod*, Bago*, Baguio*,
  Bais*, Basilan, Basilan City*, Bataan, Batanes, Batangas, Batangas City*,
  Benguet, Bohol, Bukidnon, Bulacan, Butuan*, Cabanatuan*, Cadiz*, Cagayan,
  Cagayan de Oro*, Calbayog*, Caloocan*, Camarines Norte, Camarines Sur,
  Camiguin, Canlaon*, Capiz, Catanduanes, Cavite, Cavite City*, Cebu, Cebu
  City*, Cotabato*, Dagupan*, Danao*, Dapitan*, Davao City* Davao, Davao del
  Sur, Davao Oriental, Dipolog*, Dumaguete*, Eastern Samar, General Santos*,
  Gingoog*, Ifugao, Iligan*, Ilocos Norte, Ilocos Sur, Iloilo, Iloilo City*,
  Iriga*, Isabela, Kalinga-Apayao, La Carlota*, Laguna, Lanao del Norte, Lanao
  del Sur, Laoag*, Lapu-Lapu*, La Union, Legaspi*, Leyte, Lipa*, Lucena*,
  Maguindanao, Mandaue*, Manila*, Marawi*, Marinduque, Masbate, Mindoro
  Occidental, Mindoro Oriental, Misamis Occidental, Misamis Oriental,
  Mountain, Naga*, Negros Occidental, Negros Oriental, North Cotabato,
  Northern Samar, Nueva Ecija, Nueva Vizcaya, Olongapo*, Ormoc*, Oroquieta*,
  Ozamis*, Pagadian*, Palawan, Palayan*, Pampanga, Pangasinan, Pasay*, Puerto
  Princesa*, Quezon, Quezon City*, Quirino, Rizal, Romblon, Roxas*, Samar, San
  Carlos* (in Negros Occidental), San Carlos* (in Pangasinan), San Jose*, San
  Pablo*, Silay*, Siquijor, Sorsogon, South Cotabato, Southern Leyte, Sultan
  Kudarat, Sulu, Surigao*, Surigao del Norte, Surigao del Sur, Tacloban*,
  Tagaytay*, Tagbilaran*, Tangub*, Tarlac, Tawitawi, Toledo*, Trece Martires*,
  Zambales, Zamboanga*, Zamboanga del Norte, Zamboanga del Sur
Independence:
  4 July 1946 (from US)
Constitution:
  2 February 1987, effective 11 February 1987
Legal system:
  based on Spanish and Anglo-American law; accepts compulsory ICJ
  jurisdiction, with reservations

National holiday:

Independence Day (from Spain), 12 June (1898)

Executive branch:

president, vice president, Cabinet

Legislative branch:

bicameral Congress (Kongreso) consists of an upper house or Senate (Senado) and a lower house or House of Representatives (Kapulungan Ng Mga Kinatawan)

Judicial branch:

Supreme Court

Leaders:

Chief of State and Head of Government:

President Corazon C. AQUINO (since 25 February 1986); Vice President Salvador H. LAUREL (since 25 February 1986)

Political parties and leaders:

Alliance of Philippine Democrats (LDP), Neptali GONZALES and Jose (Peping) COJUANGCO; Nationalist People's Coalition (NPC), Fidel Valdes RAMOS; Liberal Party, Jovito SALONGA; New Society Movement (KBL), Amelda MARCOS

Suffrage:

universal at age 15

Elections:

President:

last held 11 May 1992 (next election to be held NA May 1998);results - Fidel Valdes RAMOS won 23.6% of votes, a narrow plurality

:Philippines Government

Senate:

last held 11 May 1992 (next election to be held NA May 1998); results - LDP 66%, NPC 20%, Lakas-NUCD 8%, Liberal 6%; seats - (24 total) LDP 24, NPC 5, Lakas-NUCD 2, Liberal 1

Elections:

House of Representatives:

last held 11 May 1992 (next election to be held NA May 1998); results - LDP 43.5%; Lakas-NUCD 25%, NPC 23.5%, Liberal 5%, KBL 3%;seats - (200 total) LDP 87, Lakas-NUCD 51, NPC 47, Liberal 10, KBL 5

Communists:

the Communist Party of the Philippines (CPP) controls about 15,500-16,500 full-time insurgents and is not recognized as a legal party; a second Communist party, Philippine Communist Party (PKP), has quasi-legal status

Member of:

APEC, AsDB, ASEAN, CCC, CP, ESCAP, FAO, G-24, G-77, GATT, IAEA, IBRD, ICAO, ICFTU, IDA, IFAD, IFC, ILO, IMF, IMO, INMARSAT, INTELSAT, INTERPOL, IOC, IOM, ISO, ITU, LORCS, NAM (observer), UN, UNCTAD, UNESCO, UNIDO, UPU, WCL, WFTU, WHO, WIPO, WMO

Diplomatic representation:

Ambassador Emmanuel PELAEZ; Chancery at 1617 Massachusetts Avenue NW, Washington, DC 20036; telephone (202) 483-1414; there are Philippine

Consulates General in Agana (Guam), Chicago, Honolulu, Houston, Los Angeles, New York, San Francisco, and Seattle

US:

Ambassador Frank G. WISNER II; Embassy at 1201 Roxas Boulevard, Manila (mailing address is APO AP 96440); telephone [63] (2) 521-7116; FAX [63] (2) 522-4361; there is a US Consulate in Cebu

Flag:

two equal horizontal bands of blue (top) and red with a white equilateral triangle based on the hoist side; in the center of the triangle is a yellow sun with eight primary rays (each containing three individual rays) and in each corner of the triangle is a small yellow five-pointed star

:Philippines Economy

Overview:

Following the recession of 1984-85, the Philippine economy grew on the average of 5.0% per year during 1986-89. It slowed again during the period 1990-91. The agricultural sector together with forestry and fishing, plays an important role in the economy, employing about 45% of the work force and providing almost 30% of GDP. The Philippines is the world's largest exporter of coconuts and coconut products. Manufacturing contributes about 35% of GDP. Major industries include food processing, chemicals, and textiles.

GNP:

exchange rate conversion - $47 billion, per capita $720; real growth rate 0.1% (1991 est.)

Inflation rate (consumer prices):

17.6% (1991 est.)

Unemployment rate: 10.0% (1991 est.)

Budget:

$8.4 billion; expenditures $9.36 billion, including capital expenditures of $1.8 billion (1991 est.)

Exports:

$8.7 billion (f.o.b., 1991 est.)

commodities:

electrical equipment 19%, textiles 16%, minerals and ores 11%, farm products 10%, coconut 10%, chemicals 5%, fish 5%, forest products 4%

partners:

US 36%, EC 19%, Japan 18%, ESCAP 9%, ASEAN 7%

Imports:

$12.3 billion (c.i.f., 1991)

commodities:

raw materials 53%, capital goods 17%, petroleum products 17%

partners:

US 25%, Japan 17%, ESCAP 13%, EC 11%, ASEAN 10%, Middle East 10%

External debt: $28.9 billion (1991)

Industrial production:

growth rate - 5% (1991 est.); accounts for 35% of GNP

Electricity:

7,500,000 kW capacity; 31,000 million kWh produced, 470 kWh per capita (1991)

Industries:

textiles, pharmaceuticals, chemicals, wood products, food processing, electronics assembly, petroleum refining, fishing

Agriculture:
accounts for about one-third of GNP and 45% of labor force; major crops - rice, coconut, corn, sugarcane, bananas, pineapple, mango; animal products - pork, eggs, beef; net exporter of farm products; fish catch of 2 million metric tons annually

Illicit drugs:
illicit producer of cannabis for the international drug trade; growers are producing more and better quality cannabis despite government eradication efforts

Economic aid:
US commitments, including Ex-Im (FY70-89), $3.6 billion; Western (non-US) countries, ODA and OOF bilateral commitments (1970-88), $7.9 billion; OPEC bilateral aid (1979-89), $5 million; Communist countries (1975-89), $123 million

Currency:
Philippine peso (plural - pesos); 1 Philippine peso (P) = 100 centavos

:Philippines Economy

Exchange rates:
Philippine pesos (P) per US$1 - 25.810 (March 1992), 27.479 (1991), 24.311 (1990), 21.737 (1989), 21.095 (1988), 20.568 (1987)

Fiscal year: calendar year

:Philippines Communications

Railroads:
378 km operable on Luzon, 34% government owned (1982)

Highways:
156,000 km total (1984); 29,000 km paved; 77,000 km gravel, crushed-stone, or stabilized-soil surface; 50,000 km unimproved earth

Inland waterways:
3,219 km; limited to shallow-draft (less than 1.5 m) vessels

Pipelines:
petroleum products 357 km

Ports:
Cagayan de Oro, Cebu, Davao, Guimaras, Iloilo, Legaspi, Manila, Subic Bay

Merchant marine:
552 ships (1,000 GRT or over) totaling 8,150,425 GRT/13,624,527 DWT; includes 1 passenger, 11 short-sea passenger, 13 passenger-cargo, 155 cargo, 22 refrigerated cargo, 23 vehicle carrier, 8 livestock carrier, 13 roll-on/roll-off cargo, 8 container, 35 petroleum tanker, 1 chemical tanker, 6 liquefied gas, 2 combination ore/oil, 247 bulk, 7 combination bulk; note - many Philippine flag ships are foreign owned and are on the register for the purpose of long-term bare-boat charter back to their original owners who are principally in Japan and Germany

Civil air:
53 major transport aircraft

Airports:
278 total, 244 usable; 72 with permanent-surface runways; none with runways over 3,659 m; 9 with runways 2,440-3,659 m; 53 with runways 1,220-2,439 m

Telecommunications:

good international radio and submarine cable services; domestic and interisland service adequate; 872,900 telephones; broadcast stations - 267 AM (including 6 US), 55 FM, 33 TV (including 4 US); submarine cables extended to Hong Kong, Guam, Singapore, Taiwan, and Japan; satellite earth stations - 1 Indian Ocean INTELSAT, 2 Pacific Ocean INTELSAT, and 11 domestic

:Philippines Defense Forces

Branches:

Army, Navy (including Coast Guard and Marine Corps), Air Force

Manpower availability:

males 15-49, 16,719,421; 11,816,366 fit for military service; 698,683 reach military age (20) annually

Defense expenditures:

exchange rate conversion - $915 million, 1.9% of GNP (1991)

Pitcairn Islands Geography

Total area: 47 km2
Land area: 47 km2
Comparative area: about 0.3 times the size of Washington, DC
Land boundaries:

Coastline:

51 km

Maritime claims:

 Exclusive fishing zone:

200 nm

 Territorial sea:

3 nm

Disputes:

Climate:

tropical, hot, humid, modified by southeast trade winds; rainy season (November to March)

Terrain:

rugged volcanic formation; rocky coastline with cliffs

Natural resources:

miro trees (used for handicrafts), fish

Land use:

arable land NA%; permanent crops NA%; meadows and pastures NA%; forest and woodland NA%; other NA%

Environment:

subject to typhoons (especially November to March)

Note:

located in the South Pacific Ocean about halfway between Peru and New Zealand

:Pitcairn Islands People

Population: 52 (July 1992), growth rate 0.0% (1992)
Birth rate: NA births/1,000 population (1992)

Death rate: NA deaths/1,000 population (1992)
Net migration rate: NA migrants/1,000 population (1992)
Infant mortality rate: NA deaths/1,000 live births (1992)
Life expectancy at birth: NA years male, NA years female (1992)
Total fertility rate: NA children born/woman (1992)
Nationality:
  noun - Pitcairn Islander(s); adjective - Pitcairn Islander
Ethnic divisions:
  descendants of Bounty mutineers
Religions:
  Seventh-Day Adventist 100%
Languages:
  English (official); also a Tahitian/English dialect
Literacy:
  NA% (male NA%, female NA%)
Labor force:
  NA; no business community in the usual sense; some public works; subsistence
  farming and fishing
Organized labor:
  NA

:Pitcairn Islands Government

Long-form name:
  Pitcairn, Henderson, Ducie, and Oeno Islands
Type:
  dependent territory of the UK
Capital: Adamstown
Administrative divisions:
  none (dependent territory of the UK)
Independence:
  none (dependent territory of the UK)
Constitution:
  Local Government Ordinance of 1964
Legal system:
  local island by-laws
National holiday:
  Celebration of the Birthday of the Queen (second Saturday in June), 10 June
  1989
Executive branch:
  British monarch, governor, island magistrate
Legislative branch:
  unicameral Island Council
Judicial branch:
  Island Court
Leaders:
 Chief of State:
  Queen ELIZABETH II (since 6 February 1952), represented by the Governor and
  UK High Commissioner to New Zealand David Joseph MOSS (since NA 1990)
 Head of Government:
  Island Magistrate and Chairman of the Island Council Brian YOUNG (since NA

777

1985)
Political parties and leaders:
NA
Suffrage:
universal at age 18 with three years residency
Elections:
 Island Council:
 last held NA (next to be held NA); results - percent of vote by party NA;
 seats - (11 total, 5 elected) number of seats by party NA
Other political or pressure groups:
NA
Member of:
SPC
Diplomatic representation:
none (dependent territory of the UK)
Flag:
blue with the flag of the UK in the upper hoist-side quadrant and the
Pitcairn Islander coat of arms centered on the outer half of the flag; the
coat of arms is yellow, green, and light blue with a shield featuring a
yellow anchor

:Pitcairn Islands Economy

Overview:
The inhabitants exist on fishing and subsistence farming. The fertile soil
of the valleys produces a wide variety of fruits and vegetables, including
citrus, sugarcane, watermelons, bananas, yams, and beans. Bartering is an
important part of the economy. The major sources of revenue are the sale of
postage stamps to collectors and the sale of handicrafts to passing ships.
GDP:
$NA, per capita $NA; real growth rate NA%
Inflation rate (consumer prices):
NA%
Unemployment rate: NA%
Budget:
revenues $430,440; expenditures $429,983, including capital expenditures of
$NA (FY87 est.)
Exports:
$NA
 commodities:
 fruits, vegetables, curios
 partners:
NA
Imports:
$NA
 commodities:
 fuel oil, machinery, building materials, flour, sugar, other foodstuffs
 partners:
NA
External debt: $NA
Industrial production:

growth rate NA%

Electricity:

110 kW capacity; 0.30 million kWh produced, 5,360 kWh per capita (1990)

Industries:

postage stamp sales, handicrafts

Agriculture:

based on subsistence fishing and farming; wide variety of fruits and
vegetables grown; must import grain products

Economic aid:

Currency:

New Zealand dollar (plural - dollars); 1 New Zealand dollar (NZ$) = 100
cents

Exchange rates:

New Zealand dollars (NZ$) per US$1 - 1.8245 (March 1992), 1.7265 (1991),
1.6750 (1990), 1.6711 (1989), 1.5244 (1988), 1.6866 (1987)

Fiscal year: 1 April - 31 March

:Pitcairn Islands Communications

Railroads:

Highways:

6.4 km dirt roads

Ports:

Bounty Bay

Airports:

Telecommunications:

24 telephones; party line telephone service on the island; broadcast
stations - 1 AM, no FM, no TV; diesel generator provides electricity

:Pitcairn Islands Defense Forces

Note: defense is the responsibility of the UK

Poland Geography

Total area: 312,680 km2
Land area: 304,510 km2
Comparative area: slightly smaller than New Mexico
Land boundaries:

3,321 km total; Belarus 605 km, Czechoslovakia 1,309 km, Germany 456 km,
Lithuania 91 km, Russia (Kaliningrad Oblast) 432 km, Ukraine 428 km

Coastline:

491 km

Maritime claims:

Exclusive economic zone:

200 nm

Territorial sea:

12 nm

Disputes:

Climate:

temperate with cold, cloudy, moderately severe winters with frequent
precipitation; mild summers with frequent showers and thundershowers
Terrain:
  mostly flat plain; mountains along southern border
Natural resources:
  coal, sulfur, copper, natural gas, silver, lead, salt
Land use:
  arable land 46%; permanent crops 1%; meadows and pastures 13%; forest and
  woodland 28%; other 12%; includes irrigated NEGL%
Environment:
  plain crossed by a few north flowing, meandering streams; severe air and
  water pollution in south
Note:
  historically, an area of conflict because of flat terrain and the lack of
  natural barriers on the North European Plain

:Poland People

Population: 38,385,617 (July 1992), growth rate 0.4% (1992)
Birth rate: 14 births/1,000 population (1992)
Death rate: 10 deaths/1,000 population (1992)
Net migration rate: -1 migrant/1,000 population (1992)
Infant mortality rate: 14 deaths/1,000 live births (1992)
Life expectancy at birth: 68 years male, 76 years female (1992)
Total fertility rate: 2.0 children born/woman(1992)
Nationality:
  noun - Pole(s); adjective - Polish
Ethnic divisions:
  Polish 97.6%, German 1.3%, Ukrainian 0.6%, Belorussian 0.5% (1990 est.)
Religions:
  Roman Catholic 95% (about 75% practicing), Russian Orthodox, Protestant, and
  other 5%
Languages:
  Polish
Literacy:
  98% (male 99%, female 98%) age 15 and over can read and write (1978)
Labor force:
  17,104,000; industry and construction 36.1%; agriculture 27.3%; trade,
  transport, and communications 14.8%; government and other 21.8% (1989)
Organized labor:
  trade union pluralism

:Poland Government

Long-form name:
  Republic of Poland
Type:
  democratic state
Capital: Warsaw
Administrative divisions:
  49 provinces (wojewodztwa, singular - wojewodztwo); Biaa Podlaska, Biaystok,
  Bielsko, Bydgoszcz, Chem, Ciechanow, Czestochowa, Elblag, Gdansk, Gorzow,
  Jelenia Gora, Kalisz, Katowice, Kielce, Konin, Koszalin, Krakow, Krosno,

Legnica, Leszno, odz, omza, Lublin, Nowy Sacz, Olsztyn, Opole, Ostroteka, Pia, Piotrkow, Pock, Poznan, Przemysl, Radom, Rzeszow, Siedlce, Sieradz, Skierniewice, Supsk, Suwaki, Szczecin, Tarnobrzeg, Tarnow, Torun, Wabrzych, Warszawa, Wocawek, Wrocaw, Zamosc, Zielona Gora

Independence:

11 November 1918, independent republic proclaimed

Constitution:

Communist-imposed Constitution of 22 July 1952; developing a democratic Constitution

Legal system:

mixture of Continental (Napoleonic) civil law and holdover Communist legal theory; changes being gradually introduced as part of broader democratization process; no judicial review of legislative acts; has not accepted compulsory ICJ jurisdiction

National holiday:

Constitution Day, 3 May (1794)

Executive branch:

president, prime minister, Council of Ministers (cabinet)

Legislative branch:

bicameral National Assembly (Zgromadzenie Narodowe) consists of an upper house or Senate (Senat) and a lower house or Diet (Sejm)

Judicial branch:

Supreme Court

Leaders:

Chief of State:

President Lech WALESA (since 22 December 1990)

Head of Government:

Prime Minister Hanna SUCHOCKA (since 10 July 1992)

Political parties and leaders:

Solidarity Bloc:

Democratic Union (UD), Tadeusz MAZOWIECKI; Christian-National Union (ZCHN),

Wieslaw CHRZANOWSKI; Centrum (PC), Jaroslaw KACZYNSKI; Liberal-Democratic

Congress, Donald TUSK; Peasant Alliance (PL), Gabriel JANOWSKI; Solidarity Trade Union (NSZZ), Marian KRZAKLEWSKI; Solidarity Labor (SP), Ryszard BUGAJ; Christian-Democratic Party (PCHD), Pawel LACZKOWSKI; Democratic-Social Movement (RDS), Zbigniew BUJAK; Kracow Coalition in Solidarity with the President, Mieczyslaw GIL; Solidarity 80, Marian JURCZYK

Non-Communist, Non-Solidarity:

Confederation for an Independent Poland (KPN), Leszek MOCZULSKI; Beer Lovers' Party (PPPP), Janusz REWINSKI; Christian Democrats (CHD), Andrzej OWSINSKI; German Minority (MN), Henryk KROL; Western Union (KPN Front), Damian JAKUBOWSKI; RealPolitik (UPR), Janusz KORWIN-MIKKE; Democratic Party

(SD), Antoni MACKIEWICZ

Communist origin or linked:

Social Democracy (SDRP, or SLD), Wlodzimierz Cimoszewicz; Polish Peasants' Party (PSL), Waldermar PAWLAK; Party X, Stanislaw Tyminski

Suffrage:
  universal at age 18

:Poland Government

Elections:
 President:
  first round held 25 November 1990, second round held 9 December 1990 (next
  to be held NA November 1995); results - second round Lech WALESA 74.7%,
  Stanislaw TYMINSKI 25.3%
 Senate:
  last held 27 October 1991 (next to be held no later than NA October 1995);
  results -
 Solidarity Bloc:
  UD 21%, NSZZ 11%, ZCHN 9%, PC 9%, Liberal-Democratic Congress 6%, PL 7%,
  PCHD 3%, other local candidates 11%
 Non-Communist, Non-Solidarity:
  KPN 4%, CHD 1%, MN 1%, local candidates 5%
 Communist origin or linked:
  PSL 8%, SLD 4%; seats - (100 total)
 Solidarity Bloc:
  UD 21, NSZZ 11, ZCHN 9, Liberal-Democratic Congress 6, PL 7, PCHD 3, other
  local candidates 11;
 Non-Communist, Non-Solidarity:
  KPN 4, CHD 1, MN 1 local candidates 5
 Communist origin or linked:
  PSL 8, SLD 4
 Sejm:
  last held 27 October 1991 (next to be held no later than NA October 1995);
  results -
 Solidarity Bloc:
  UD 12.31%, ZCHN 8.73%, PL 8.71%, Liberal-Democratic Congress 7.48%, PL
  5.46%, NSZZ 5.05%, SP 2.05%, PCHD 1.11%
 Non-Communist, Non-Solidarity:
  KPN 7.50%, PPPP 3.27%, CHD 2.36%, UPR 2.25%, MN 1.70%
 Communist origin or linked:
  SLD 11.98%, PSL 8.67%; seats - (460 total)
 Solidarity Bloc:
  UD 62, ZCHN 9, PC 44, Liberal-Democratic Congress 37, PL 28, NSZZ 27, SP 4,
  PCHD 4, RDS 1, Krackow Coalition in Solidarity with the President 1, Piast
  Agreement 1, Bydgoszcz Peasant List 1, Solidarity 80 1
 Non-Communist, Non-Solidarity:
  KPN 46, PPPP 16, MN 7, CHD 5, Western Union 4, UPR 3, Autonomous Silesia 2,
  SD 1, Orthodox Election Committee 1, Committee of Women Against Hardships 1,
  Podhale Union 1, Wielkopolska Group 1, Wielkopolska and Lubuski Inhabitants
  1
 Communist origin or linked:
  SLD 60, PSL 48, Party X 3
Communists:
  70,000 members in the Communist successor parties (1990)
Other political or pressure groups:

powerful Roman Catholic Church; Confederation for an Independent Poland
(KPN), a nationalist group; Solidarity (trade union); All Poland Trade Union
Alliance (OPZZ), populist program; Clubs of Catholic Intellectuals (KIKs)
Member of:
 BIS, CCC, CE, CERN, CSCE, ECE, FAO, GATT, Hexagonale, IAEA, IBEC, IBRD,
 ICAO, ICFTU, IDA, IIB, ILO, IMF, IMO, INMARSAT, IOC, ISO, ITU, LORCS,
PCA,
 UN, UNCTAD, UNESCO, UNDOF, UNIDO, UNIIMOG, UPU, WCL, WHO,
WIPO
Diplomatic representation:
 Ambassador Kazimierz DZIEWANOWSKI; Chancery at 2640 16th Street NW,
 Washington, DC 20009; telephone (202) 234-3800 through 3802; there are
 Polish Consulates General in Chicago, Los Angeles, and New York

:Poland Government

 US:
 Ambassador Thomas W. SIMONS, Jr.; Embassy at Aleje Ujazdowskie 29/31, Warsaw
 (mailing address is American Embassy Warsaw, Box 5010, or APO AE
 09213-5010); telephone [48] (2) 628-8298; FAX [48] (2) 628-9326; there is a
 US Consulate General in Krakow and a Consulate in Poznan
Flag:
 two equal horizontal bands of white (top) and red; similar to the flags of
 Indonesia and Monaco which are red (top) and white

:Poland Economy

Overview:
 Poland is undergoing a difficult transition from a Soviet-style economy -
 with state ownership and control of productive assets - to a market economy.
 On January 1, 1990, the new Solidarity-led government implemented shock
 therapy by slashing subsidies, decontrolling prices, tightening the money
 supply, stabilizing the foreign exchange rate, lowering import barriers, and
 restraining state sector wages. As a result, consumer goods shortages and
 lines disappeared, and inflation fell from 640% in 1989 to 60% in 1991.
 Western governments, which hold two-thirds of Poland's $48 billion external
 debt, pledged in 1991 to forgive half of Poland's official debt by 1994, and
 the private sector grew, accounting for 22% of industrial production and 40%
 of nonagricultural output by 1991. Production fell in state enterprises,
 however, and the unemployment rate climbed steadily from virtually nothing
 in 1989 to 11.4% in December 1991. Poland fell out of compliance with its
 IMF program by mid-1991, and talks with commercial creditors stalled. The
 increase in unemployment and the decline in living standards led to popular
 discontent and a change in government in January 1991 and again in December.
 The new government has promised selective industrial intervention, some
 relaxation in monetary policy, and an improved social safety net, but will
 be constrained by the decline in output and the growing budget deficit.
GDP:
 purchasing power equivalent - $162.7 billion, per capita $4,300; real growth
 rate -5% (1991 est.)
Inflation rate (consumer prices):
 60% (1991 est.)

Unemployment rate: 11.4% (end December 1991)

Budget:

   revenues $19.5 billion; expenditures $22.4 billion, including capital
   expenditures of $1.5 billion (1991 est.)

Exports:

   $12.8 billion (f.o.b., 1991 est.)

  commodities:

   machinery 23%, metals 17%, chemicals 13%, fuels 11%, food 10% (1991 est.)

  partners:

   FRG 25.1%, former USSR 15.3%, UK 7.1%, Switzerland 4.7% (1990)

Imports:

   $12.9 billion (f.o.b., 1991 est.)

  commodities:

   machinery 35%, fuels 20%, chemicals 13%, food 11%, light industry 7% (1991
   est.)

  partners:

   FRG 20.1%, former USSR 19.8%, Italy 7.5%, Switzerland 6.4% (1990)

External debt: $48.5 billion (January 1992); note - Poland's Western government
creditors

   promised in 1991 to forgive 30% of Warsaw's official debt - currently $33
   billion - immediately and to forgive another 20% by 1994, if Poland adheres
   to its IMF program

Industrial production:

   growth rate -14% (State sector 1991 est.)

Electricity:

   31,530,000 kW capacity; 136,300 million kWh produced, 3,610 kWh per capita
   (1990)

Industries:

   machine building, iron and steel, extractive industries, chemicals,
   shipbuilding, food processing, glass, beverages, textiles

:Poland Economy

Agriculture:

   accounts for 15% of GDP and 27% of labor force; 75% of output from private
   farms, 25% from state farms; productivity remains low by European standards;
   leading European producer of rye, rapeseed, and potatoes; wide variety of
   other crops and livestock; major exporter of pork products; normally
   self-sufficient in food

Illicit drugs:

   illicit producers of opium for domestic consumption and amphetamines for the
   international market; emerging as a transshipment point for illicit drugs to
   Western Europe

Economic aid:

   donor - bilateral aid to non-Communist less developed countries, $2.2
   billion (1954-89); note - the G-24 has pledged $8 billion in grants and
   credit guarantees to Poland

Currency:

   Zoty (plural - Zotych); 1 Zoty (Z) = 100 groszy

Exchange rates:

   Zotych (z) per US$1 - 13,443 (March 1992), 10,576 (1991), 9,500 (1990),

1,439.18 (1989), 430.55 (1988), 265.08 (1987)
Fiscal year: calendar year

:Poland Communications

Railroads:

27,041 km total; 24,287 km 1.435-meter gauge, 397 km 1.520-meter gauge, 2,357 km narrow gauge; 8,987 km double track; 11,016 km electrified; government owned (1989)

Highways:

299,887 km total; 130,000 km improved hard surface (concrete, asphalt, stone block); 24,000 km unimproved hard surface (crushed stone, gravel); 100,000 km earth; 45,887 km other urban roads (1985)

Inland waterways:

3,997 km navigable rivers and canals (1989)

Pipelines:

natural gas 4,500 km, crude oil 1,986 km, petroleum products 360 km (1987)

Ports:

Gdansk, Gdynia, Szczecin, Swinoujscie; principal inland ports are Gliwice on Kana Gliwice, Wrocaw on the Oder, and Warsaw on the Vistula

Merchant marine:

222 ships (1,000 GRT or over) totaling 2,851,016 GRT/4,019,531 DWT; includes 5 short-sea passenger, 79 cargo, 4 refrigerated cargo, 14 roll-on/roll-off cargo, 12 container, 1 petroleum tanker, 4 chemical tanker, 102 bulk, 1 passenger; Poland owns 1 ship of 6,333 DWT operating under Liberian registry

Civil air:

48 major transport aircraft

Airports:

160 total, 160 usable; 85 with permanent-surface runways; 1 with runway over 3,659 m; 35 with runways 2,440-3,659 m; 65 with runways 1,220-2,439 m

Telecommunications:

severely underdeveloped and outmoded system; cable, open wire and microwave; phone density is 10.5 phones per 100 residents (October 1990); 3.1 million subscribers; exchanges are 86% automatic (February 1990); broadcast stations - 27 AM, 27 FM, 40 (5 Soviet repeaters) TV; 9.6 million TVs; 1 satellite earth station using INTELSAT, EUTELSAT, INMARSAT and Intersputnik

:Poland Defense Forces

Branches:

Army, Navy, Air and Air Defense Force

Manpower availability:

males 15-49, 9,785,823; 7,696,425 fit for military service; 294,191 reach military age (19) annually

Defense expenditures:

exchange rate conversion - 19.2 trillion zotych, NA% of GDP (1991); note - conversion of defense expenditures into US dollars using the current exchange rate could produce misleading results

Portugal Geography

Total area: 92,080 km2
Land area: 91,640 km2; includes Azores and Madeira Islands
Comparative area: slightly smaller than Indiana

Land boundaries:
   1,214 km; Spain 1,214 km
Coastline:
   1,793 km
Maritime claims:
  Continental shelf:
   200 m (depth) or to depth of exploitation
  Exclusive economic zone:
   200 nm
  Territorial sea:
   12 nm
Disputes:
   sovereignty over Timor Timur (East Timor Province) disputed with Indonesia
Climate:
   maritime temperate; cool and rainy in north, warmer and drier in south
Terrain:
   mountainous north of the Tagus, rolling plains in south
Natural resources:
   fish, forests (cork), tungsten, iron ore, uranium ore, marble
Land use:
   arable land 32%; permanent crops 6%; meadows and pastures 6%; forest and
   woodland 40%; other 16%; includes irrigated 7%
Environment:
   Azores subject to severe earthquakes
Note:
   Azores and Madeira Islands occupy strategic locations along western sea
   approaches to Strait of Gibraltar

:Portugal People

Population: 10,448,509 (July 1992), growth rate 0.4% (1992)
Birth rate: 12 births/1,000 population (1992)
Death rate: 10 deaths/1,000 population (1992)
Net migration rate: 2 migrants/1,000 population (1992)
Infant mortality rate: 10 deaths/1,000 live births (1992)
Life expectancy at birth: 71 years male, 78 years female (1992)
Total fertility rate: 1.4 children born/woman (1992)
Nationality:
   noun - Portuguese (singular and plural); adjective - Portuguese
Ethnic divisions:
   homogeneous Mediterranean stock in mainland, Azores, Madeira Islands;
   citizens of black African descent who immigrated to mainland during
   decolonization number less than 100,000
Religions:
   Roman Catholic 97%, Protestant denominations 1%, other 2%
Languages:
   Portuguese
Literacy:
   85% (male 89%, female 82%) age 15 and over can read and write (1990 est.)
Labor force:
   4,605,700; services 45%, industry 35%, agriculture 20% (1988)

Organized labor:

about 55% of the labor force; the Communist-dominated General Confederation of Portuguese Workers - Intersindical (CGTP-IN) represents more than half of the unionized labor force; its main competition, the General Workers Union (UGT), is organized by the Socialists and Social Democrats and represents less than half of unionized labor

:Portugal Government

Long-form name:

Portuguese Republic

Type:

republic

Capital: Lisbon

Administrative divisions:

18 districts (distritos, singular - distrito) and 2 autonomous regions* (regioes autonomas, singular - regiao autonoma); Aveiro, Acores (Azores)*, Beja, Braga, Braganca, Castelo Branco, Coimbra, Evora, Faro, Guarda, Leiria, Lisboa, Madeira*, Portalegre, Porto, Santarem, Setubal, Viana do Castelo, Vila Real, Viseu

Independence:

1140; independent republic proclaimed 5 October 1910

Constitution:

25 April 1976, revised 30 October 1982 and 1 June 1989

Legal system:

civil law system; the Constitutional Tribunal reviews the constitutionality of legislation; accepts compulsory ICJ jurisdiction, with reservations

National holiday:

Day of Portugal, 10 June

Executive branch:

president, Council of State, prime minister, deputy prime minister, Council of Ministers (cabinet)

Legislative branch:

unicameral Assembly of the Republic (Assembleia da Republica)

Judicial branch:

Supreme Tribunal of Justice (Supremo Tribunal de Justica)

Leaders:

Chief of State:

President Dr. Mario Alberto Nobre Lopes SOARES (since 9 March 1986)

Head of Government:

Prime Minister Anibal CAVACO SILVA (since 6 November 1985)

Political parties and leaders:

Social Democratic Party (PSD), Anibal CAVACO Silva; Portuguese Socialist Party (PS), Jorge SAMPAIO; Party of Democratic Renewal (PRD), Herminio MARTINHO; Portuguese Communist Party (PCP), Alvaro CUNHAL; Social Democratic

Center (CDS), Andriano MORREIRA (interim); National Solidarity Party, Manuel SERGIO; Center Democratic Party; United Democratic Coalition (CDU; Communists)

Suffrage:

universal at age 18

Elections:
  President:
    last held 13 February 1991 (next to be held NA February 1996); results - Dr.
    Mario Lopes SOARES 70%, Basilio HORTA 14%, Carlos CARVALHAS 13%,
Carlos
    MARQUES 3%
  Assembly of the Republic:
    last held 6 October 1991 (next to be held NA October 1995); results - PSD
    50.4%, PS 29.3%, CDU 8.8%, Center Democrats 4.4%, National Solidarity Party
    1.7%, PRD 0.6%, other 4.8%; seats - (230 total) PSD 135, PS 72, CDU 17,
    Center Democrats 5, National Solidarity Party 1
Communists:
  Portuguese Communist Party claims membership of 200,753 (December 1983)

:Portugal Government

Member of:
  AfDB, BIS, CCC, CE, CERN, COCOM, CSCE, EBRD, EC, ECE, ECLAC, EIB,
FAO, GATT,
  IADB, IAEA, IBRD, ICAO, ICC, ICFTU, IEA, IFAD, IFC, ILO, IMF, IMO,
INMARSAT,
  INTELSAT, INTERPOL, IOC, IOM, ISO, ITU, LAIA (observer), LORCS, NAM
(guest),
  NATO, NEA, OAS (observer), OECD, PCA, UN, UNCTAD, UNESCO, UNIDO,
UPU, WCL,
  WEU, WHO, WIPO, WMO, WTO
Diplomatic representation:
  Ambassador Joao Eduardo M. PEREIRA BASTOS; Chancery at 2125 Kalorama
Road
  NW, Washington, DC 20008; telephone (202) 328-8610; there are Portuguese
  Consulates General in Boston, New York, and San Francisco, and Consulates in
  Los Angeles, Newark (New Jersey), New Bedford (Massachusetts), and
  Providence (Rhode Island)
  US:
  Ambassador Everett E. BRIGGS; Embassy at Avenida das Forcas Armadas, 1600
  Lisbon (mailing address is PSC 83, APO AE 09726); telephone [351] (1)
  726-6600 or 6659, 8670, 8880; FAX [351] (1) 726-9109; there is a US
  Consulate in Oporto and Ponta Delgada (Azores)
Flag:
  two vertical bands of green (hoist side, two-fifths) and red (three-fifths)
  with the Portuguese coat of arms centered on the dividing line

:Portugal Economy

Overview:
  Although Portugal has experienced strong growth since joining the EC in 1986
  - at least 4% each year through 1990 - it remains one of the poorest
  members. To prepare for the European single market, the government is
  restructuring and modernizing the economy and in 1989 embarked on a major
  privatization program. The global slowdown and tight monetary policies to
  counter inflation caused growth to slow in 1991, but it is likely to recover
  in 1992.
GDP:

purchasing power equivalent - $87.3 billion, per capita $8,400; real growth rate 2.7% (1991 est.)

Inflation rate (consumer prices):
12.0% (1991 est.)

Unemployment rate: 4.0% (1991 est.)

Budget:
revenues $27.0 billion; expenditures $33.9 billion, including capital expenditures of $6.7 billion (1991 est.)

Exports:
$16.4 billion (f.o.b., 1990)
commodities:
cotton textiles, cork and paper products, canned fish, wine, timber and timber products, resin, machinery, appliances
partners:
EC 74%, other developed countries 13.2%, US 4.8%

Imports:
$25.1 billion (c.i.f., 1990)
commodities:
machinery and transport equipment, agricultural products, chemicals, petroleum, textiles
partners:
EC 69.1%, other developed countries 11.4% less developed countries 15.1%, US 3.9%

External debt: $15.0 billion (1991 est.)

Industrial production:
growth rate 9.1% (1990); accounts for 40% of GDP

Electricity:
6,729,000 kW capacity; 16,000 million kWh produced, 1,530 kWh per capita (1991)

Industries:
textiles and footwear; wood pulp, paper, and cork; metalworking; oil refining; chemicals; fish canning; wine; tourism

Agriculture:
accounts for 6.1% of GDP and about 20% of labor force; small, inefficient farms; imports more than half of food needs; major crops - grain, potatoes, olives, grapes; livestock sector - sheep, cattle, goats, poultry, meat, dairy products

Illicit drugs:
increasingly import gateway country for Latin American cocaine entering the European market

Economic aid:
US commitments, including Ex-Im (FY70-89), $1.8 billion; Western (non-US) countries, ODA and OOF bilateral commitments (1970-89), $1.2 billion

Currency:
Portuguese escudo (plural - escudos); 1 Portuguese escudo (Esc) = 100 centavos

:Portugal Economy

Exchange rates:
Portuguese escudos (Esc) per US$1 - 143.09 (March 1992), 144.48 (1991),

142.55 (1990), 157.46 (1989), 143.95 (1988), 140.88 (1987)

Fiscal year: calendar year

:Portugal Communications

Railroads:

3,613 km total; state-owned Portuguese Railroad Co. (CP) operates 2,858 km 1.665-meter gauge (434 km electrified and 426 km double track), 755 km 1.000-meter gauge; 12 km (1.435-meter gauge) electrified, double track, privately owned

Highways:

73,661 km total; 61,599 km surfaced (bituminous, gravel, and crushed stone), including 140 km of limited-access divided highway; 7,962 km improved earth; 4,100 km unimproved earth (motorable tracks)

Inland waterways:

820 km navigable; relatively unimportant to national economy, used by shallow-draft craft limited to 300-metric-ton cargo capacity

Pipelines:

crude oil 11 km; petroleum products 58 km

Ports:

Leixoes, Lisbon, Porto, Ponta Delgada (Azores), Velas (Azores), Setubal, Sines

Merchant marine:

53 ships (1,000 GRT or over) totaling 738,774 GRT/1,300,787 DWT; includes 1 short-sea passenger, 20 cargo, 3 refrigerated cargo, 3 container, 1 roll-on/roll-off cargo, 13 petroleum tanker, 2 chemical tanker, 8 bulk, 2 vehicle carrier; note - Portugal has created a captive register on Madeira (MAR) for Portuguese-owned ships that will have the taxation and crewing benefits of a flag of convenience; although only one ship currently is known to fly the Portuguese flag on the MAR register, it is likely that a majority of Portuguese flag ships will transfer to this subregister in a few years

Civil air:

43 major transport aircraft

Airports:

65 total, 62 usable; 36 with permanent-surface runways; 1 with runways over 3,659 m; 12 with runways 2,440-3,659 m; 8 with runways 1,220-2,439 m

Telecommunications:

generally adequate integrated network of coaxial cables, open wire and radio relay; 2,690,000 telephones; broadcast stations - 57 AM, 66 (22 repeaters) FM, 66 (23 repeaters) TV; 6 submarine cables; 3 INTELSAT earth stations (2 Atlantic Ocean, 1 Indian Ocean), EUTELSAT, domestic satellite systems (mainland and Azores); tropospheric link to Azores

:Portugal Defense Forces

Branches:

Army, Navy (including Marines), Air Force, National Republican Guard, Fiscal Guard, Public Security Police

Manpower availability:

males 15-49, 2,666,450; 2,166,341 fit for military service; 88,826 reach military age (20) annually

Defense expenditures:

exchange rate conversion - $1.7 billion, 2.8% of GDP (1991)

Puerto Rico Geography

Total area: 9,104 km2
Land area: 8,959 km2
Comparative area: slightly less than three times the size of Rhode Island
Land boundaries:
  none
Coastline:
  501 km
Maritime claims:
 Contiguous zone:
  12 nm
 Continental shelf:
  200 m (depth)
 Exclusive economic zone:
  200 nm
 Territorial sea:
  12 nm
Disputes:
  none
Climate:
  tropical marine, mild, little seasonal temperature variation
Terrain:
  mostly mountains with coastal plain belt in north; mountains precipitous to
  sea on west coast
Natural resources:
  some copper and nickel; potential for onshore and offshore crude oil
Land use:
  arable land 8%; permanent crops 9%; meadows and pastures 41%; forest and
  woodland 20%; other 22%
Environment:
  many small rivers and high central mountains ensure land is well watered;
  south coast relatively dry; fertile coastal plain belt in north
Note:
  important location between the Dominican Republic and the Virgin Islands
  group along the Mona Passage - a key shipping lane to the Panama Canal; San
  Juan is one of the biggest and best natural harbors in the Caribbean

:Puerto Rico People

Population: 3,776,654 (July 1992), growth rate 1.0% (1992)
Birth rate: 17 births/1,000 population (1992)
Death rate: 8 deaths/1,000 population (1992)
Net migration rate: 0 migrants/1,000 population (1992)
Infant mortality rate: 14 deaths/1,000 live births (1992)
Life expectancy at birth: 70 years male, 78 years female (1992)
Total fertility rate: 2.1 children born/woman (1992)
Nationality:
  noun - Puerto Rican(s); adjective - Puerto Rican
Ethnic divisions:
  almost entirely Hispanic
Religions:

Roman Catholic 85%, Protestant denominations and other 15%
Languages:
  Spanish (official); English is widely understood
Literacy:
  89% (male 90%, female 88%) age 15 and over can read and write (1980)
Labor force:
  1,068,000; government 28%, manufacturing 15%, trade 14%, agriculture 3%,
  other 40% (1990)
Organized labor:
  115,000 members in 4 unions; the largest is the General Confederation of
  Puerto Rican Workers with 35,000 members (1983)

:Puerto Rico Government

Long-form name:
  Commonwealth of Puerto Rico
Type:
  commonwealth associated with the US
Capital: San Juan
Administrative divisions:
  none (commonwealth associated with the US)
Independence:
  none (commonwealth associated with the US)
Constitution:
  ratified 3 March 1952; approved by US Congress 3 July 1952; effective 25
  July 1952
Legal system:
  based on Spanish civil code
National holiday:
  Constitution Day, 25 July (1952)
Executive branch:
  US president, US vice president, governor
Legislative branch:
  bicameral Legislative Assembly consists of an upper house or Senate and a
  lower house or House of Representatives
Judicial branch:
  Supreme Court
Leaders:
  Chief of State:
  President George BUSH (since 20 January 1989); Vice President Dan QUAYLE
  (since 20 January 1989)
  Head of Government:
  Governor Rafael HERNANDEZ Colon (since 2 January 1989)
Political parties and leaders:
  National Republican Party of Puerto Rico, Freddy VALENTIN; Popular
  Democratic Party (PPD), Rafael HERNANDEZ Colon; New Progressive Party
(PNP),
  Carlos ROMERO Barcelo; Puerto Rican Socialist Party (PSP), Juan MARI Bras
  and Carlos GALLISA; Puerto Rican Independence Party (PIP), Ruben BERRIOS
  Martinez; Puerto Rican Communist Party (PCP), leader(s) unknown; Puerto
  Rican Renewal Party (PRP, breakaway group from PNP), leader (vacant), Puerto

Rico Democratic Party, Richard MACHADO
Suffrage:
universal at age 18; citizens of Puerto Rico are also US citizens, but do
not vote in US presidential elections
Elections:
Governor:
last held 8 November 1988 (next to be held 3 November 1992); results -
Rafael HERNANDEZ Colon (PPD) 48.7%, Baltasar CORRADA Del Rio (PNP)
45.8%,
Ruben BERRIOS Martinez (PIP) 5.5%
Senate:
last held 8 November 1988 (next to be held 3 November 1992); results -
percent of vote by party NA; seats - (27 total) PPD 18, PNP 8, PIP 1
US House of Representatives:
last held 8 November 1988 (next to be held 3 November 1992); results -
percent of vote by party NA; seats - (1 total) seats by party NA; note -
Puerto Rico elects one nonvoting representative to the US House of
Representatives, Jaime B. FUSTER
House of Representatives:
last held 8 November 1988 (next to be held 3 November 1992); results -
percent of vote by party NA; seats - (53 total) PPD 36, PNP 15, PIP 2

:Puerto Rico Government

Other political or pressure groups:
all have engaged in terrorist activities - Armed Forces for National
Liberation (FALN), Volunteers of the Puerto Rican Revolution, Boricua
Popular Army (also known as the Macheteros), Armed Forces of Popular
Resistance
Member of:
CARICOM (observer), ECLAC, ICFTU, IOC, WCL, WFTU, WTO (associate)
Diplomatic representation:
none (commonwealth associated with the US)
Flag:
five equal horizontal bands of red (top and bottom) alternating with white;
a blue isosceles triangle based on the hoist side bears a large white
five-pointed star in the center; design based on the US flag

:Puerto Rico Economy

Overview:
Puerto Rico has one of the most dynamic economies in the Caribbean region.
Industry has surpassed agriculture as the primary sector of economic
activity and income. Encouraged by duty free access to the US and by tax
incentives, US firms have invested heavily in Puerto Rico since the 1950s.
Important new industries include pharmaceuticals, electronics, textiles,
petrochemicals, and processed foods. Sugar production has lost out to dairy
production and other livestock products as the main source of income in the
agricultural sector. Tourism has traditionally been an important source of
income for the island. The economy has largely recovered from the
disruptions caused by Hurricane Hugo in September 1989. The tourism
infrastructure has been especially hard hit.
GNP:

purchasing power equivalent - $21.6 billion, per capita $6,600; real growth
rate 2.2% (FY90)

Inflation rate (consumer prices):
1.3% (October 1990-91)

Unemployment rate: 15.5% (October 1991)

Budget:
revenues $5.8 billion; expenditures $5.8 billion, including capital
expenditures of $258 million (FY89)

Exports:
NA

commodities:
pharmaceuticals, electronics, apparel, canned tuna, rum, beverage
concentrates, medical equipment, instruments

partners:
US 87% (FY90)

Imports:
NA

commodities:
chemicals, clothing, food, fish, petroleum products

partners:
US 68% (FY90)

External debt: $NA

Industrial production:
growth rate 3.8% (FY90)

Electricity:
4,149,000 kW capacity; 14,844 million kWh produced, 4,510 kWh per capita
(1990)

Industries:
manufacturing of pharmaceuticals, electronics, apparel, food products,
instruments; tourism

Agriculture:
accounts for 3% of labor force; crops - sugarcane, coffee, pineapples,
plantains, bananas; livestock - cattle, chickens; imports a large share of
food needs

Economic aid:
none

Currency:
US currency is used

Exchange rates:
US currency is used

Fiscal year: 1 July - 30 June

:Puerto Rico Communications

Railroads:
96 km rural narrow-gauge system for hauling sugarcane; no passenger
railroads

Highways:
13,762 km paved (1982)

Ports:
San Juan, Ponce, Mayaguez, Areclbo

Airports:

30 total; 24 usable; 19 with permanent-surface runways; none with runways over 3,659 m; 3 with runways 2,440-3,659 m; 5 with runways 1,220-2,439 m

Telecommunications:

900,000 or 99% of total households have TV; 1,067,787 telephones (1988); broadcast stations - 50 AM, 63 FM, 9 TV (1990)

:Puerto Rico Defense Forces

Branches:

paramilitary National Guard, Police Force

Manpower availability:

males 15-49, 830,133; NA fit for military service

Note:

defense is the responsibility of the US

Qatar Geography

Total area: 11,000 km2

Land area: 11,000 km2

Comparative area: slightly smaller than Connecticut

Land boundaries:

60 km total; Saudi Arabia 40 km, UAE 20 km

Coastline:

563 km

Maritime claims:

*** No entry for this item ***

Continental shelf:

not specific

Exclusive economic zone:

200 nm

Territorial sea:

12 nm

Disputes:

location and status of Qatar's southern boundaries with Saudi Arabia and UAE are unresolved; territorial dispute with Bahrain over the Hawar Islands; maritime boundary with Bahrain

Climate:

desert; hot, dry; humid and sultry in summer

Terrain:

mostly flat and barren desert covered with loose sand and gravel

Natural resources:

crude oil, natural gas, fish

Land use:

arable land NEGL%; permanent crops 0%; meadows and pastures 5%; forest and woodland 0%; other 95%

Environment:

haze, duststorms, sandstorms common; limited freshwater resources mean increasing dependence on large-scale desalination facilities

Note:

strategic location in central Persian Gulf near major crude oil sources

:Qatar People

Population: 484,387 (July 1992), growth rate 3.2% (1992)
Birth rate: 21 births/1,000 population (1992)
Death rate: 4 deaths/1,000 population (1992)
Net migration rate: 15 migrants/1,000 population (1992)
Infant mortality rate: 24 deaths/1,000 live births (1992)
Life expectancy at birth: 69 years male, 74 years female (1992)
Total fertility rate: 4.0 children born/woman (1992)
Nationality:
    noun - Qatari(s); adjective - Qatari
Ethnic divisions:
    Arab 40%, Pakistani 18%, Indian 18%, Iranian 10%, other 14%
Religions:
    Muslim 95%
Languages:
    Arabic (official); English is commonly used as second language
Literacy:
    76% (male 77%, female 72%) age 15 and over can read and write (1986)
Labor force:
    104,000; 85% non-Qatari in private sector (1983)
Organized labor:
    trade unions are illegal

:Qatar Government

Long-form name:
    State of Qatar
Type:
    traditional monarchy
Capital: Doha
Administrative divisions:
    there are no first-order administrative divisions as defined by the US
    Government, but there are 9 municipalities (baladiyat, singular -
    baladiyah); Ad Dawhah, Al Ghuwayriyah, Al Jumayliyah, Al Khawr, Al Rayyan,
    Al Wakrah, Ash Shamal, Jarayan al Batnah, Umm Salal
Independence:
    3 September 1971 (from UK)
Constitution:
    provisional constitution enacted 2 April 1970
Legal system:
    discretionary system of law controlled by the amir, although civil codes are
    being implemented; Islamic law is significant in personal matters
National holiday:
    Independence Day, 3 September (1971)
Executive branch:
    amir, Council of Ministers (cabinet)
Legislative branch:
    unicameral Advisory Council (Majlis al-Shura)
Judicial branch:
    Court of Appeal
Leaders:
    Chief of State and Head of Government:

796

Amir and Prime Minister KHALIFA bin Hamad Al Thani (since 22 February 1972);
Heir Apparent HAMAD bin Khalifa Al Thani (appointed 31 May 1977; son of
Amir)

Political parties and leaders:
 none

Suffrage:
 none

Elections:
 Advisory Council:
 constitution calls for elections for part of this consultative body, but no
 elections have been held; seats - (30 total)

Member of:
 ABEDA, AFESD, AL, AMF, ESCWA, FAO, G-77, GCC, IAEA, IBRD, ICAO,
 IDB, IFAD,
 ILO, IMF, IMO, INMARSAT, INTELSAT, INTERPOL, IOC, ITU, LORCS, NAM,
 OAPEC,
 OIC, OPEC, UN, UNCTAD, UNESCO, UNIDO, UPU, WHO, WIPO, WMO

Diplomatic representation:
 Ambassador Hamad `Abd al-`Aziz AL-KAWARI, Chancery at Suite 1180, 600 New
 Hampshire Avenue NW, Washington, DC 20037; telephone (202) 338-0111
 US:
 Ambassador Kenton W. KEITH; Embassy at 149 Ali Bin Ahmed St., Farig Bin
 Omran (opposite the television station), Doha (mailing address is P. O. Box
 2399, Doha); telephone (0974) 864701 through 864703; FAX (0974) 861669

Flag:
 maroon with a broad white serrated band (nine white points) on the hoist
 side

:Qatar Economy

Overview:
 Oil is the backbone of the economy and accounts for more than 85% of export
 earnings and roughly 75% of government revenues. Proved oil reserves of 3.3
 billion barrels should ensure continued output at current levels for about
 25 years. Oil has given Qatar a per capita GDP of about $15,000, comparable
 to the leading industrial countries. Production and export of natural gas is
 becoming increasingly important.

GDP:
 exchange rate conversion - $7.4 billion, per capita $15,000; real growth
 rate NA (1990)

Inflation rate (consumer prices):
 4.9% (1988 est.)

Unemployment rate: NA%

Budget:
 revenues $2.1 billion; expenditures $3.2 billion, including capital
 expenditures of $490 million (FY91 est.)

Exports:
 $3.2 billion (f.o.b., 1990 est.)
 commodities:
 petroleum products 85%, steel, fertilizers
 partners:

Japan 61%, Brazil 9%, UAE 3%, Singapore 3%
Imports:
    $1.5 billion (f.o.b., 1990 est.)
  commodities:
    foodstuffs, beverages, animal and vegetable oils, chemicals, machinery and
    equipment
  partners:
    UK 13%, Japan 11%, US 8%, Italy 8%
External debt: $1.1 billion (December 1989 est.)
Industrial production:
    growth rate 0.6% (1987); accounts for 64% of GDP, including oil
Electricity:
    1,520,000 kW capacity; 4,200 million kWh produced, 8,080 kWh per capita
    (1991)
Industries:
    crude oil production and refining, fertilizers, petrochemicals, steel,
    cement
Agriculture:
    farming and grazing on small scale, less than 2% of GDP; commercial fishing
    increasing in importance; most food imported
Economic aid:
    donor - pledged $2.7 billion in ODA to less developed countries (1979-88)
Currency:
    Qatari riyal (plural - riyals); 1 Qatari riyal (QR) = 100 dirhams
Exchange rates:
    Qatari riyals (QR) per US$1 - 3.6400 riyals (fixed rate)
Fiscal year: 1 April - 31 March

:Qatar Communications

Highways:
    1,500 km total; 1,000 km paved, 500 km gravel or natural surface (est.)
Pipelines:
    crude oil 235 km, natural gas 400 km
Ports:
    Doha, Umm Sa'id, Halul Island
Merchant marine:
    23 ships (1,000 GRT or over) totaling 473,042 GRT/716,039 DWT; includes 14
    cargo, 5 container, 3 petroleum tanker, 1 refrigerated cargo
Civil air:
    3 major transport aircraft
Airports:
    4 total, 4 usable; 1 with permanent-surface runways; 1 with runways over
    3,659 m; none with runways 2,440-3,659 m; 2 with runways 1,220-2,439 m
Telecommunications:
    modern system centered in Doha; 110,000 telephones; tropospheric scatter to
    Bahrain; radio relay to Saudi Arabia and UAE; submarine cable to Bahrain and
    UAE; broadcast stations - 2 AM, 3 FM, 3 TV; satellite earth stations - 1
    Atlantic Ocean INTELSAT, 1 Indian Ocean INTELSAT, 1 ARABSAT

:Qatar Defense Forces

Branches:
  Army, Navy, Air Force, Public Security
Manpower availability:
  males 15-49, 211,812; 112,250 fit for military service; 3,414 reach military age (18) annually
Defense expenditures:
  exchange rate conversion - $NA, NA%, of GDP

Reunion Geography

Total area: 2,510 km2
Land area: 2,500 km2
Comparative area: slightly smaller than Rhode Island
Land boundaries:
  none
Coastline:
  201 km
Maritime claims:
 Exclusive economic zone:
  200 nm
 Territorial sea:
  12 nm
Disputes:
  none
Climate:
  tropical, but moderates with elevation; cool and dry from May to November, hot and rainy from November to April
Terrain:
  mostly rugged and mountainous; fertile lowlands along coast
Natural resources:
  fish, arable land
Land use:
  arable land 20%; permanent crops 2%; meadows and pastures 4%; forest and woodland 35%; other 39%; includes irrigated 2%
Environment:
  periodic devastating cyclones
Note:
  located 750 km east of Madagascar in the Indian Ocean

:Reunion People

Population: 626,414 (July 1992), growth rate 2.1% (1992)
Birth rate: 26 births/1,000 population (1992)
Death rate: 5 deaths/1,000 population (1992)
Net migration rate;   0 migrants/1,000 population (1992)
Infant mortality rate: 8 deaths/1,000 live births (1992)
Life expectancy at birth: 70 years male, 77 years female (1992)
Total fertility rate: 2.8 children born/woman (1992)
Nationality:
  noun - Reunionese (singular and plural); adjective - Reunionese
Ethnic divisions:
  most of the population is of intermixed French, African, Malagasy, Chinese, Pakistani, and Indian ancestry

Religions:
  Roman Catholic 94%
Languages:
  French (official); Creole widely used
Literacy:
  69% (male 67%, female 74%) age 15 and over can read and write (1982)
Labor force:
  NA; agriculture 30%, industry 21%, services 49% (1981); 63% of population of
  working age (1983)
Organized labor:
  General Confederation of Workers of Reunion (CGTR)

:Reunion Government

Long-form name:
  Department of Reunion
Type:
  overseas department of France
Capital: Saint-Denis
Administrative divisions:
  none (overseas department of France)
Independence:
  none (overseas department of France)
Constitution:
  28 September 1958 (French Constitution)
Legal system:
  French law
National holiday:
  Taking of the Bastille, 14 July (1789)
Executive branch:
  French president, commissioner of the Republic
Legislative branch:
  General Council, Regional Council
Judicial branch:
  Court of Appeals (Cour d'Appel)
Leaders:
 Chief of State:
  President Francois MITTERRAND (since 21 May 1981)
 Head of Government:
  Commissioner of the Republic Jacques DEWATRE (since July 1991)
Political parties and leaders:
  Rally for the Republic (RPR), Francois MAS; Union for French Democracy
  (UDF), Gilbert GERARD; Communist Party of Reunion (PCR), Paul VERGES;
  France-Reunion Future (FRA), Andre THIEN AH KOON; Socialist Party (PS),
  Jean-Claude FRUTEAU; Social Democrats (CDS); other small parties
Suffrage:
  universal at age 18
Elections:
 General Council:
  last held September/October 1988 (next to be held NA 1994); results -
  percent of vote by party NA; seats - (44 total) PCR 9, PS 4, UDF 6, other

left-wing 2, RPR 4, right-wing 19

Regional Council:
last held 16 March 1986 (next to be held NA March 1992); results - RPR/UDF
36.8%, PCR 28.2%, FRA and other right wing 17.3%, PS 14.1%, other 3.6%;
seats - (45 total) RPR/UDF 18, PCR 13, FRA and other right wing 8, PS 6

French Senate:
last held 24 September 1989 (next to be held NA September 1992); results -
percent of vote by party NA; seats - (3 total) RPR-UDF 1, PS 1, independent
1

French National Assembly:
last held 5 and 12 June 1988 (next to be held NA June 1993); results -
percent of vote by party NA; seats - (5 total) PCR 2, RPR 1, UDF-CDS 1, FRA
1; note - Reunion elects 3 members to the French Senate and 5 members to the
French National Assembly who are voting members

Communists:
Communist party small but has support among sugarcane cutters, the minuscule
Popular Movement for the Liberation of Reunion (MPLR), and in the district
of Le Port

Member of:
FZ, WFTU

:Reunion Government

Diplomatic representation:
as an overseas department of France, Reunionese interests are represented in
the US by France

Flag:
the flag of France is used

:Reunion Economy

Overview:
The economy has traditionally been based on agriculture. Sugarcane has been
the primary crop for more than a century, and in some years it accounts for
85% of exports. The government has been pushing the development of a tourist
industry to relieve high unemployment, which recently amounted to one-third
of the labor force. The gap in Reunion between the well-off and the poor is
extraordinary and accounts for the persistent social tensions. The white and
Indian communities are substantially better off than other segments of the
population, often approaching European standards, whereas indigenous groups
suffer the poverty and unemployment typical of the poorer nations of the
African continent. The outbreak of severe rioting in February 1991
illustrates the seriousness of socioeconomic tensions. The economic
well-being of Reunion depends heavily on continued financial assistance from
France.

GDP:
exchange rate conversion - $3.37 billion, per capita $6,000 (1987 est.);
real growth rate 9% (1987 est.)

Inflation rate (consumer prices):
1.3% (1988)

Unemployment rate: 35% (February 1991)

Budget:
revenues $358 million; expenditures $914 million, including capital

expenditures of $NA (1986)

Exports:
  $166 million (f.o.b., 1988)
  commodities:
  sugar 75%, rum and molasses 4%, perfume essences 4%, lobster 3%, vanilla and
  tea 1%
  partners:
  France, Mauritius, Bahrain, South Africa, Italy
Imports:
  $1.7 billion (c.i.f., 1988)
  commodities:
  manufactured goods, food, beverages, tobacco, machinery and transportation
  equipment, raw materials, and petroleum products
  partners:
  France, Mauritius, Bahrain, South Africa, Italy
External debt: $NA
Industrial production:
  growth rate NA%; about 25% of GDP
Electricity:
  245,000 kW capacity; 546 million kWh produced, 965 kWh per capita (1989)
Industries:
  sugar, rum, cigarettes, several small shops producing handicraft items
Agriculture:
  accounts for 30% of labor force; dominant sector of economy; cash crops -
  sugarcane, vanilla, tobacco; food crops - tropical fruits, vegetables, corn;
  imports large share of food needs
Economic aid:
  Western (non-US) countries, ODA and OOF bilateral commitments (1970-89),
  $14.8 billion
Currency:
  French franc (plural - francs); 1 French franc (F) = 100 centimes
Exchange rates:
  French francs (F) per US$1 - 5.6397 (March 1992), 5.6421 (1991), 5.4453
  (1990), 6.3801 (1989), 5.9569 (1988), 6.0107 (1987)

:Reunion Economy

Fiscal year: calendar year

:Reunion Communications

Highways:
  2,800 km total; 2,200 km paved, 600 km gravel, crushed stone, or stabilized
  earth
Ports:
  Pointe des Galets
Civil air:
  3 major transport aircraft
Airports:
  2 total, 2 usable; 2 with permanent surface runways; none with runways over
  3,659 m; 1 with runway 2,440-3,659 m; 1 with runway 1,220-2,439 m
Telecommunications:
  adequate system; modern open-wire and microwave network; principal center

Saint-Denis; radiocommunication to Comoros, France, Madagascar; new microwave route to Mauritius; 85,900 telephones; broadcast stations - 3 AM, 13 FM, 1 (18 repeaters) TV; 1 Indian Ocean INTELSAT earth station

:Reunion Defense Forces

Branches:
French Forces (including Army, Navy, Air Force, Gendarmerie)
Manpower availability:
males 15-49, 164,974; 85,370 fit for military service; 6,083 reach military age (18) annually
Note:
defense is the responsibility of France

Romania Geography

Total area: 237,500 km2
Land area: 230,340 km2
Comparative area: slightly smaller than Oregon
Land boundaries:
2,508 km total; Bulgaria 608 km, Hungary 443 km, Moldova 450 km, Serbia and Montenegro 476 km, Ukraine (north) 362 km, Ukraine (south) 169 km
Coastline:
225 km
Maritime claims:
 Continental shelf:
 200 m (depth) or to depth of exploitation
 Exclusive economic zone:
 200 nm
 Territorial sea:
 12 nm
Disputes:
none
Climate:
temperate; cold, cloudy winters with frequent snow and fog; sunny summers with frequent showers and thunderstorms
Terrain:
central Transylvanian Basin is separated from the plain of Moldavia on the east by the Carpathian Mountains and separated from the Walachian Plain on the south by the Transylvanian Alps
Natural resources:
crude oil (reserves being exhausted), timber, natural gas, coal, iron ore, salt
Land use:
arable land 43%; permanent crops 3%; meadows and pastures 19%; forest and woodland 28%; other 7%; includes irrigated 11%
Environment:
frequent earthquakes most severe in south and southwest; geologic structure and climate promote landslides; air pollution in south
Note:
controls most easily traversable land route between the Balkans, Moldova, and the Ukraine

:Romania People

Population: 23,169,914 (July 1992), growth rate 0.0% (1992)
Birth rate: 14 births/1,000 population (1992)
Death rate: 10 deaths/1,000 population (1992)
Net migration rate: -3 migrants/1,000 population (1992)
Infant mortality rate: 22 deaths/1,000 live births (1992)
Life expectancy at birth: 68 years male, 74 years female (1992)
Total fertility rate: 1.8 children born/woman (1992)
Nationality:
  noun - Romanian(s); adjective - Romanian
Ethnic divisions:
  Romanian 89.1%, Hungarian 8.9%, German 0.4%, Ukrainian, Serb, Croat,
  Russian, Turk, and Gypsy 1.6%
Religions:
  Romanian Orthodox 70%, Roman Catholic 6%, Greek Catholic (Uniate) 3%,
  Protestant 6%, unaffiliated 15%
Languages:
  Romanian, Hungarian, German
Literacy:
  96% (male NA%, female NA%) age 15 and over can read and write (1970 est.)
Labor force:
  10,945,700; industry 38%, agriculture 28%, other 34% (1989)
Organized labor:
  until December 1989, a single trade union system organized by the General
  Confederation of Romanian Trade Unions (UGSR) under control of the Communist
  Party; since CEAUSESCU'S overthrow, newly created trade and professional
  trade unions are joining umbrella organizations, including the Organization
  of Free Trade Unions, Fratia (Brotherhood), and the Alfa Cartel; many other
  trade unions have been formed

:Romania Government

Long-form name:
  none
Type:
  republic
Capital: Bucharest
Administrative divisions:
  40 counties (judete, singular - judet) and 1 municipality* (municipiu);
  Alba, Arad, Arges, Bacau, Bihor, Bistrita-Nasaud, Botosani, Braila, Brasov,
  Bucuresti*, Buzau, Calarasi, Caras-Severin, Cluj, Constanta, Covasna,
  Dimbovita, Dolj, Galati, Gorj, Giurgiu, Harghita, Hunedoara, Ialomita, Iasi,
  Maramures, Mehedinti, Mures, Neamt, Olt, Prahova, Salaj, Satu Mare, Sibiu,
  Suceava, Teleorman, Timis, Tulcea, Vaslui, Vilcea, Vrancea
Independence:
  1881 (from Turkey); republic proclaimed 30 December 1947
Constitution:
  8 December 1991
Legal system:
  former mixture of civil law system and Communist legal theory that
  increasingly reflected Romanian traditions is being revised

National holiday:
National Day of Romania, 1 December (1990)
Executive branch:
*** No entry for this item ***
president, prime minister, Council of Ministers (cabinet)
Legislative branch:
bicameral Parliament consists of an upper house or Senate (Senat) and a
lower house or House of Deputies (Adunarea Deputatilor)
Judicial branch:
Supreme Court of Justice
Leaders:
Chief of State:
President Ion ILIESCU (since 20 June 1990, previously President of
Provisional Council of National Unity since 23 December 1989)
Head of Government:
Prime Minister Teodor STOLOJAN (since 2 October 1991)
Political parties and leaders:
National Salvation Front (FSN), Petre ROMAN; Democratuc National Salvation
Front (DNSF), Olivia GHERMAN; Magyar Democratic Union (UDMR), Geza
DOMOKOS;
National Liberal Party (PNL), Radu CAMPEANU; National Peasants' Christian
and Democratic Party (PNTCD), Corneliu COPOSU; Ecology Movement (MER),
Toma
Gheorghe MAIORESCU; Romanian National Unity Party (PUNR), Radu
CEONTEA;
there are now more than 100 other parties; note - although the Communist
Party has ceased to exist, small proto-Communist parties, notably the
Socialist Labor Party, have been formed
Suffrage:
universal at age 18
Elections:
President:
last held 20 May 1990 (next to be held NA 1992); results - Ion ILIESCU 85%,
Radu CAMPEANU 10.5%, Ion RATIU 3.8%
Senate:
last held 20 May 1990 (next to be held NA 1992); results - FSN 67%, other
33%; seats - (118 total) FSN 92, UDMR 12, PNL 9, PUNR 2, PNTCD 1, MER 1,
other 1
House of Deputies:
last held 20 May 1990 (next to be held NA 1992); results - FSN 66%, UDMR 7%,
PNL 6%, MER 2%, PNTCD 2%, PUNR 2%, other 15%; seats - (387 total) FSN 263,
UDMR 29, PNL 29, PNTCD 12, MER 12, PUNR 9, other 33

:Romania Government

Member of:
BIS, CCC, CSCE, ECE, FAO, G-9, G-77, GATT, IAEA, IBEC, IBRD, ICAO,
IFAD,
IFC, IIB, ILO, IMF, IMO, INTERPOL, IOC, ITU, LORCS, NAM (guest), PCA,
UN,
UNCTAD, UNESCO, UNIDO, UPU, WFTU, WHO, WIPO, WMO, WTO

Diplomatic representation:

Ambassador Aurel MUNTEANU; Chancery at 1607 23rd Street NW, Washington, DC

20008; telephone (202) 232-4747

US:

Ambassador John R. DAVIS; Embassy at Strada Tudor Arghezi 7-9, Bucharest (mailing address is APO AE 09213-5260); telephone [40] (0) 10-40-40; FAX [40] (0) 12-03-95

Flag:

three equal vertical bands of blue (hoist side), yellow, and red; the national coat of arms that used to be centered in the yellow band has been removed; now similar to the flags of Andorra and Chad

:Romania Economy

Overview:

Industry, which accounts for about one-third of the labor force and generates over half the GDP, suffers from an aging capital plant and persistent shortages of energy. The year 1991 witnessed about a 17% drop in industrial production because of energy and input shortages and labor unrest. In recent years the agricultural sector has had to contend with flooding, mismanagement, shortages of inputs, and disarray caused by the dismantling of cooperatives. A shortage of fuel and equipment in 1991 contributed to a lackluster harvest, a problem compounded by corruption and a poor distribution system. The new government is loosening the tight central controls of CEAUSESCU'S command economy. It has instituted moderate land reforms, with more than one-half of cropland now in private hands, and it has liberalized private agricultural output. Also, the new regime is permitting the establishment of private enterprises, largely in services, handicrafts, and small-scale industry. A law providing for the privatization of large state firms has been passed. Most of the large state firms have been converted into joint-stock companies, but the selling of shares and assets to private owners has been delayed. While the government has halted the old policy of diverting food from domestic consumption to hard currency export markets, supplies remain scarce in some areas. Furthermore, real wages in Romania fell about 20% in 1991, contributing to the unrest which forced the resignation of ROMAN in September. The new government continues to impose price ceilings on key consumer items.

GDP:

purchasing power equivalent - $71.9 billion, per capita $3,100; real growth rate - 12% (1991 est.)

Inflation rate (consumer prices):

215% (1991 est.)

Unemployment rate: 4% (1991 est.)

Budget:

revenues $19 billion; expenditures $20 billion, including capital expenditures of $2.1 billion (1991 est.)

Exports:

$4.0 billion (f.o.b., 1991 est.)

commodities:

machinery and equipment 29.3%, fuels, minerals and metals 32.1%,

manufactured consumer goods 18.1%, agricultural materials and forestry
products 9.0%, other 11.5% (1989)
partners:
USSR 27%, Eastern Europe 23%, EC 15%, US 5%, China 4% (1987)
Imports:
$5.4 billion (f.o.b., 1991 est.)
commodities:
fuels, minerals, and metals 56.0%, machinery and equipment 25.5%,
agricultural and forestry products 8.6%, manufactured consumer goods 3.4%,
other 6.5% (1989)
partners:
Communist countries 60%, non-Communist countries 40% (1987)
External debt: $2 billion (1991)
Industrial production:
growth rate -17% (1991 est.)
Electricity:
22,700,000 kW capacity; 64,200 million kWh produced, 2,760 kWh per capita
(1990)
Industries:
mining, timber, construction materials, metallurgy, chemicals, machine
building, food processing, petroleum

:Romania Economy

Agriculture:
accounts for 15% of GDP and 28% of labor force; major wheat and corn
producer; other products - sugar beets, sunflower seed, potatoes, milk,
eggs, meat, grapes
Illicit drugs:
transshipment point for southwest Asian heroin transiting the Balkan route
Economic aid:
donor - $4.4 billion in bilateral aid to non-Communist less developed
countries (1956-89)
Currency:
leu (plural - lei); 1 leu (L) = 100 bani
Exchange rates:
lei (L) per US$1 - 198.00 (March 1992), 76.39 (1991), 22.432 (1990), 14.922
(1989), 14.277 (1988), 14.557 (1987)
Fiscal year: calendar year

:Romania Communications

Railroads:
11,275 km total; 10,860 km 1.435-meter gauge, 370 km narrow gauge, 45 km
broad gauge; 3,411 km electrified, 3,060 km double track; government owned
(1987)
Highways:
72,799 km total; 35,970 km paved; 27,729 km gravel, crushed stone, and other
stabilized surfaces; 9,100 km unsurfaced roads (1985)
Inland waterways:
1,724 km (1984)
Pipelines:
crude oil 2,800 km, petroleum products 1,429 km, natural gas 6,400 km

Ports:
  Constanta, Galati, Braila, Mangalia; inland ports are Giurgiu, Drobeta-Turnu Severin, Orsova
Merchant marine:
  262 ships (1,000 GRT or over) totaling 3,320,373 GRT/5,207,580 DWT; includes 1 passenger-cargo, 174 cargo, 2 container, 1 rail-car carrier, 9 roll-on/roll-off cargo, 13 petroleum tanker, 60 bulk, 2 combination ore/oil
Civil air:
  59 major transport aircraft
Airports:
  165 total, 165 usable; 25 with permanent-surface runways; 15 with runways 2,440-3,659 m; 15 with runways 1,220-2,439 m
Telecommunications:
  poor service; about 2.3 million telephone customers; 89% of phone network is automatic; cable and open wire; trunk network is microwave; present phone density is 9.85 per 100 residents; roughly 3,300 villages with no service (February 1990); broadcast stations - 12 AM, 5 FM, 13 TV (1990); 1 satellite ground station using INTELSAT

:Romania Defense Forces

Branches:
  Army, Navy, Air and Air Defense Forces, Paramilitary Forces, Civil Defense
Manpower availability:
  males 15-49, 5,799,837; 4,909,642 fit for military service; 184,913 reach military age (20) annually
Defense expenditures:
  exchange rate conversion - 50 billion lei (unofficial), NA% of GDP (1991); note - conversion of defense expenditures into US dollars using the current exchange rate could produce misleading results

Russia Geography

Total area: 17,075,200 km2
Land area: 16,995,800 km2
Comparative area: slightly more than 1.8 times the size of the US
Land boundaries:
  20,139 km total; Azerbaijan 284 km, Belarus 959 km, China (southeast) 3,605 km, China (south) 40 km, Estonia 290 km, Finland 1,313 km, Georgia 723 km, Kazakhstan 6,846 km, North Korea 19 km, Latvia 217 km, Lithuania (Kaliningrad Oblast) 227 km, Mongolia 3,441 km, Norway 167 km, Poland (Kaliningrad Oblast) 432 km, Ukraine 1,576 km
Coastline:
  37,653 km
Maritime claims:
 Contiguous zone:
  NA nm
 Continental shelf:
  200-meter depth or to depth of exploitation
 Exclusive economic zone:
  200 nm
 Exclusive fishing zone:
  NA nm

Territorial sea:
  12 nm
Disputes:
  inherited disputes from former USSR including: sections of the boundary with
  China, a section of the boundary with Tajikistan; boundary with Latvia,
  Lithuania, and Estonia; Etorofu, Kunashiri, and Shikotan Islands and the
  Habomai island group occupied by the Soviet Union in 1945, claimed by Japan;
  maritime dispute with Norway over portion of the Barents Sea; has made no
  territorial claim in Antarctica (but has reserved the right to do so) and
  does not recognize the claims of any other nation
Climate:
  ranges from steppes in the south through humid continental in much of
  European Russia; subarctic in Siberia to tundra climate in the polar north;
  winters vary from cool along Black Sea coast to frigid in Siberia; summers
  vary from warm in the steppes to cool along Arctic coast
Terrain:
  broad plain with low hills west of Urals; vast coniferous forest and tundra
  in Siberia; uplands and mountains along southern border regions
Natural resources:
  wide natural resource base including major deposits of oil, natural gas,
  coal, and many strategic minerals; timber; note - formidable obstacles of
  climate, terrain, and distance hinder exploitation of natural resources
Land use:
  NA% arable land; NA% permanent crops; NA% meadows and pastures; NA% forest
  and woodland; NA% other; includes NA% irrigated
Environment:
  despite its size, only a small percentage of land is arable and much is too
  far north; permafrost over much of Siberia is a major impediment to
  development; catastrophic pollution of land, air, water, including both
  inland waterways and sea coasts
Note:
  largest country in the world in terms of area but unfavorably located in
  relation to major sea lanes of the world

:Russia People

Population: 149,527,479 (July 1992), growth rate 0.4% (1992)
Birth rate: 15 births/1,000 population (1992)
Death rate: 11 deaths/1,000 population (1992)
Net migration rate: 1 migrant/1,000 population (1992)
Infant mortality rate: 31 deaths/1,000 live births (1992)
Life expectancy at birth: 63 years male, 74 years female (1992)
Total fertility rate: 2.1 children born/woman (1992)
Nationality:
  noun - Russian(s); adjective - Russian
Ethnic divisions:
  Estonian NA%, Latvian NA%, Lithuanian NA%, Russian NA%, other NA%
Religions:
  Russian Orthodox NA%, unknown NA%, none NA%, other NA%
Languages:
  Estonian NA%, Latvian NA%, Lithuanian NA%, Russian NA%, other NA%

Literacy:
NA% (male NA%, female NA%) age 15 and over can read and write
Labor force:
78,682,000 (1989); industry and construction 43.0%, agriculture and forestry
13.0%, transport and communication 7.9%, trade and distribution 7.9%, other
28.2%
Organized labor:
NA

:Russia Government

Long-form name:
Russian Federation
Type:
federation
Capital: Moscow
Administrative divisions:
20 autonomous republics (avtomnykh respublik, singular - automnaya
respublika); Adygea (Maykop), Bashkortostan (Ufa), Buryatia (Ulan-Ude),
Checheno-Ingushetia (Groznyy), Chuvashia (Cheboksary), Dagestan
(Makhachkala), Gorno-Altay (Gorno-Altaysk), Kabardino-Balkaria (Nal`chik),
Kalmykia (Elista), Karachay-Cherkessia (Cherkessk), Karelia (Petrozavodsk),
Khakassia (Abakan), Komi (Syktyvkar), Mari El (Yoshkar-Ola), Mordvinia
(Saransk), North Ossetia (Vladikavkaz; formerly Ordzhonikidze), Tatarstan
(Kazan'), Tuva (Kyzyl), Udmurtia (Izhevsk), Yakutia (Yakutsk); 49 oblasts
(oblastey, singular - oblast'); Amur (Blagoveshchensk), Arkhangel'sk,
Astrakhan', Belgorod, Bryansk, Chelyabinsk, Chita, Irkutsk, Ivanovo,
Kaliningrad, Kaluga, Kamchata (Petropavlovsk-Kamchatskiy), Kemerovo, Kirov,
Kostroma, Kurgan, Kursk, Leningrad (St. Petersburg), Lipetsk, Magadan,
Moscow, Murmansk, Nizhegorod (Nizhniy Novgorod; formerly Gor'kiy), Novgorod,
Novosibirsk, Omsk, Orel, Orenburg, Penza, Perm', Pskov, Rostov, Ryazan',
Sakhalin (Yuzhno-Sakhalinsk), Samara (formerly Kuybyshev), Saratov,
Smolensk, Sverdlovsk (Yekaterinburg), Tambov, Tomsk, Tula, Tver' (formerly
Kalinin), Tyumen', Ul'yanovsk, Vladmir, Volgograd, Vologda, Voronezh,
Yaroslavl'; 6 krays (krayer, singular - kray); Altay (Barnaul), Khabarovsk,
Krasnodar, Krasnoyarsk, Primorskiy (Vladivostok), Stavropol; note - the
cities of Moscow and St. Petersburg have oblast status; an administrative
division has the same name as its administrative center (exceptions have the
administrative center name following in parentheses); it is possible that 4
more administrative divisions will be added
Independence:
24 August 1991, declared by Supreme Council (from Soviet Union; formerly
Russian Soviet Federative Socialist Republic); 1 December 1991 referendum on
independence passed
Constitution:
a new constitution is in the process of being drafted
Legal system:
based on civil law system; judicial review of legislative acts; does not
accept compulsory ICJ jurisdiction
National holiday:
NA

Executive branch:
    president, vice president, Security Council, President's Administration,
    Council of Ministers
Legislative branch:
    Congress of People's Deputies, Supreme Soviet
Judicial branch:
    Constitutional Court
Leaders:
  Chief of State and Head of Government:
    *** No entry for this item ***
    President Boris YEL'TSIN (since 12 June 1991), Vice President Aleksandr
    RUTSKOY (since 12 June 1991), State Secretary Gennadiy BURBULIS (since July
    1991); 1st Deputy Chairman of the Council of Ministers Yegor GAYDAR (since
    March 1992), 2nd Deputy Chairman of the Council of Ministers Aleksandr
    SHOKHIN (since 7 November 1991)

:Russia Government

Political parties and leaders:
    Democratic Russia, A. Lev PONOMAREV and Gleb YAKUNIN, cochairmen;
Democratic
    Party of Russia, Nikolay TRAVKIN, chairman; People's Party of Free Russia,
    Aleksandr RUTSKOY, chairman; Russian Movement for Democratic Reforms,
    Gavriil POPOV, chairman
Suffrage:
    universal at age 18
Elections:
  President:
    last held 12 June 1991 (next to be held 1996); results - percent of vote by
    party NA%
  Congress of People's Deputies:
    last held March 1990 (next to be held 1995); results - percent of vote by
    party NA%; seats - (1,063 total) number of seats by party NA
  Supreme Soviet:
    last held May 1990 (next to be held 1995); results - percent of vote by
    party NA%; seats - (252 total) number of seats by party NA
Communists:
    NA
Other political or pressure groups:
    NA
Member of:
    CIS, CSCE, ESCAP, ECE, IAEA, IBRD, ICAO, ICFTU, IMF, INTERPOL, IMO,
    INMARSAT, IOC, ISO, ITU, LORCS, NACC, NSG, PCA, UN, UNCTAD,
UNESCO, UNTSO,
    UPU, WFTU, WHO, WIPO, WMO, WTO, ZG
Diplomatic representation:
    Ambassador LUKIN; Chancery at 1125 16th Street NW, Washington, DC 20036;
    telephone (202) 628-7551
  US:
    Ambassador Robert S. STRAUSS; Embassy at Ulitsa Chaykovskogo 19/21/23,
    Moscow (mailing address is APO AE 09721); telephone [7] (095) 252-2450

through 59; there is a consulate at St. Petersburg (formerly Leningrad); future consulates will be in Yekaterinburg and Vladivostok

Flag:
  tricolor; three equal bands of white (top), blue, red (bottom)

:Russia Economy

Overview:
  Russia, one of the world's largest economies, possesses a wealth of natural resources and a diverse industrial base. Within the now-dismantled USSR, it had produced 60% of total output, with 55% of the total labor force and 60% of the total capital stock. Russia depends on its world-class deposits of oil and gas not only for its own needs but also for vital hard currency earnings. Self-sufficient in coal and iron ore, it has a crude steel production capacity of about 95 million tons, second only to Japan. Russia's machine-building sector - 60% of the old USSR's - lags behind world standards of efficiency and quality of product. Other major industrial sectors - chemicals, construction materials, light industry, and food processing - also suffer from quality problems, obsolescent capital equipment, and pollution. Consumer goods have had lower priority, and the product mix has not mirrored household preferences. Furthermore, the transition to a more market-oriented economy has disrupted channels of supply to factories and distribution outlets; substantial imports of foods and medical supplies have helped maintain minimum standards of consumption. Russia inherited 70% of the former USSR's defense production facilities and is experiencing major social problems during conversion of many of these plants to civilian production. Russia produces almost half of the old USSR's farm products, but most warm-climate crops must be imported. Under the old USSR, production of industrial and agricultural goods often was concentrated in a single firm or a single republic. Today, producing units often have lost their major customers and their major sources of supply, and the market institutions and incentives for adjusting to the new political and economic situations are only slowly emerging. Rank-and-file Russians will continue to suffer major deprivations in 1992 and beyond before the country begins to realize its great economic potential. The comprehensive economic reform program enacted in January 1992 faces many economic and political hurdles before it will lead to sustained economic growth.

GDP:
  purchasing power equivalent - $NA, per capita $NA; real growth rate - 9% (1991)

Inflation rate (consumer prices):
  89% (1991)

Unemployment rate: NA%

Budget:
  NA

Exports:
  $58.7 billion (f.o.b., 1991)
  commodities:
    petroleum and petroleum products, natural gas, wood and wood products, coal, nonferrous metals, chemicals, and a wide variety of civilian and military manufactures

partners:

  Western Europe, Japan, Eastern Europe

Imports:

  $43.5 billion (c.i.f., 1991)

  commodities:

  machinery and equipment, chemicals, consumer goods, grain, meat,
  semifinished metal products

  partners:

  Western and Eastern Europe, Japan, Third World countries, Cuba

External debt: $40 billion (end of 1991 est.)

Industrial production:

  -8% after adjustment for inflation due to shift to more expensive products,
  -2% before this adjustment (1991)

:Russia Economy

Electricity:

  42,500 MW capacity; 1,100 billion kWh produced, 7,430 kWh per capita (1991)

Industries:

  complete range of mining and extractive industries producing coal, oil, gas,
  chemicals, and metals; all forms of machine building from rolling mills to
  high-performance aircraft and space vehicles; ship- building; road and rail
  transportation equipment; communications equipment; agricultural machinery,
  tractors, and construction equipment; electric power generating and
  transmitting equipment; medical and scientific instruments; consumer
  durables

Agriculture:

  grain, meat, milk, vegetables, fruits; because of its northern location
  Russia does not grow citrus, cotton, tea, and other warm climate products

Illicit drugs:

  illicit producers of cannabis and opium; mostly for domestic consumption;
  government has active eradication program; used as transshipment point for
  illicit drugs to Western Europe

Economic aid:

  US commitments, including Ex-Im (FY70-87), $NA; Western (non-US) countries,
  ODA and OOF bilateral commitments (1970-86), $NA; Communist countries
  (1971-86), $NA million

Currency:

  ruble (plural - rubles); 1 ruble (R) = 100 kopeks

Exchange rates:

  150 rubles per US$1 (20 July 1992) but subject to wide fluctuations

Fiscal year: calendar year

:Russia Communications

Railroads:

  87,180 km all 1.520-meter broad gauge (includes NA km electrified); does not
  include industrial lines (1990)

Highways:

  879,100 km total (1990); 652,500 km hard-surfaced, 226,600 km earth

Inland waterways:

  NA km perennially navigable

Pipelines:

crude oil and petroleum products 68,400 km, natural gas NA km

Ports:

maritime - St. Petersburg (Leningrad), Kaliningrad, Murmansk, Arkhangel'sk, Novorossiysk, Vladivostok, Nakhodka, Kholmsk, Korsakov, Magadan, Tiksi, Tuapse, Vanino, Vostochnyy, Vyborg; inland - Astrakhan', Nizhniy Novgorod (Gor'kiy), Kazan', Khabarovsk, Krasnoyarsk, Samara (Kuybyshev), Moscow, Rostov, Volgograd

Merchant marine:

842 ships (1,000 GRT or over) totaling 8,151,393 GRT/11,308,812 DWT; includes 494 cargo, 39 container, 2 barge carrier, 3 roll-on/float-off, 69 roll-on/roll-off, 131 petroleum tanker, 53 bulk cargo, 9 chemical tanker, 2 specialized liquid carriers, 17 combination ore/oil, 23 passenger

Civil air:

NA major transport aircraft

Airports:

NA total, NA usable; NA with permanent-surface runways; NA with runways over 3,659 m; NA with runways 2,440-3,659 m; NA with runways 1,220-2,439 m

Telecommunications:

the telephone system is inadequate for a large industrial country, consisting of about 36 million lines of which only about 3% are switched automatically; as of 31 January 1990, 10.8 million applications for telephones for household use could not be satisfied; telephone density is 11 per 100 persons; international connections are made via satellite, land line, microwave, and outdated submarine cables, and are generally unsatisfactory; the international gateway switch in Moscow handles international traffic for the other former Soviet republics as well as for Russia; broadcast stations - 1,050 AM/FM/SW (reach 98.6% of population), 310 TV (580 repeaters) (reach 98% of population); satellite ground stations - INTELSAT, Intersputnik, INMARSAT, Orbita

:Russia Defense Forces

Branches:

Russian defence forces will be comprised of those ground-, air-, and sea-based conventional assets currently on Russian soil and those scheduled to be withdrawn from other countries; strategic forces will remain under CIS control

Manpower availability:

males 15-49, 36,288,000; 27,216,000 fit for military service; 1,020,341 reach military age (18) annually

Defense expenditures:

$NA, NA% of GDP

Rwanda Geography

Total area: 26,340 km2

Land area: 24,950 km2

Comparative area: slightly smaller than Maryland

Land boundaries:

893 km total; Burundi 290 km, Tanzania 217 km, Uganda 169 km, Zaire 217 km

Coastline:

none - landlocked

Maritime claims:

none - landlocked
Disputes:
  none
Climate:
  temperate; two rainy seasons (February to April, November to January); mild
  in mountains with frost and snow possible
Terrain:
  mostly grassy uplands and hills; mountains in west
Natural resources:
  gold, cassiterite (tin ore), wolframite (tungsten ore), natural gas,
  hydropower
Land use:
  arable land 29%; permanent crops 11%; meadows and pastures 18%; forest and
  woodland 10%; other 32%; includes irrigated NEGL%
Environment:
  deforestation; overgrazing; soil exhaustion; soil erosion; periodic droughts
Note:
  landlocked

:Rwanda People

Population: 8,206,446 (July 1992), growth rate 3.8% (1992)
Birth rate: 52 births/1,000 population (1992)
Death rate: 14 deaths/1,000 population (1992)
Net migration rate: 0 migrants/1,000 population (1992)
Infant mortality rate: 108 deaths/1,000 live births (1992)
Life expectancy at birth: 51 years male, 55 years female (1992)
Total fertility rate: 8.3 children born/woman (1992)
Nationality:
  noun - Rwandan(s); adjective - Rwandan
Ethnic divisions:
  Hutu 90%, Tutsi 9%, Twa (Pygmoid) 1%
Religions:
  Roman Catholic 65%, Protestant 9%, Muslim 1%, indigenous beliefs and other
  25%
Languages:
  Kinyarwanda, French (official); Kiswahili used in commercial centers
Literacy:
  50% (male 64%, female 37%) age 15 and over can read and write (1990 est.)
Labor force:
  3,600,000; agriculture 93%, government and services 5%, industry and
  commerce 2%; 49% of population of working age (1985)
Organized labor:
  NA

:Rwanda Government

Long-form name:
  Republic of Rwanda
Type:
  republic; presidential system in which military leaders hold key offices; on
  31 December 1990, the government announced a National Political Charter to
  serve as a basis for transition to a presidential/parliamentary political

system; the 1978 constitution was replaced in June 1991 via popular
referendum by a new constitution creating a multiparty system with a
president and prime minister

Capital: Kigali

Administrative divisions:
   10 prefectures (prefectures, singular - prefecture in French; plural - NA,
   singular - prefegitura in Kinyarwanda); Butare, Byumba, Cyangugu, Gikongoro,
   Gisenyi, Gitarama, Kibungo, Kibuye, Rigali, Ruhengeri

Independence:
   1 July 1962 (from UN trusteeship under Belgian administration)

Constitution:
   18 June 1991

Legal system:
   based on German and Belgian civil law systems and customary law; judicial
   review of legislative acts in the Supreme Court; has not accepted compulsory
   ICJ jurisdiction

National holiday:
   Independence Day, 1 July (1962)

Executive branch:
   president, prime minister, Council of Ministers (cabinet)

Legislative branch:
   unicameral National Development Council (Conseil National de Developpement)

Judicial branch:
   Constitutional Court (consists of the Court of Cassation and the Council of
   State in joint session)

Leaders:
  Chief of State:
   President Maj. Gen. Juvenal HABYARIMANA (since 5 July 1973)
  Head of Government:
   Prime Minister Sylvestre NSANZIMANA (since NA October 1991)

Political parties and leaders:
   Republican Revolutionary Movement for Democracy and Development (MRND),
Maj.
   Gen. Juvenal HABYARIMANA; formerly a one-party state, Rwanda legalized
   independent parties in mid-1991; since then, at least 10 new political
   parties have registered; President HABYARIMANA's political movement - the
   National Revolutionary Movement for Development (MRND) - reorganized itself
   as a political party and changed its name to the Republican National
   Movement for Democracy and Development (but kept the same initials - MRND);
   significant independent parties include: Democratic Republican Movement
   (MDR), leader NA; Liberal Party (PL), leader NA; Democratic and Socialist
   Party (PSD), leader NA; note - since October 1990, Rwanda has been involved
   in a low-intensity conflict with the Rwandan Patriotic Front/Rwandan
   Patriotic Army (RPF/RPA); the RPF/RPA is primarily an ethnically based
   organization

Suffrage:
   universal adult, exact age NA

Elections:
  President:

last held 19 December 1988 (next to be held NA December 1993); results - President Maj. Gen. Juvenal HABYARIMANA reelected

:Rwanda Government

National Development Council:
last held 19 December 1988 (next to be held NA December 1993); results - MRND is the only party; seats - (70 total) MRND 70

Member of:
ACCT, ACP, AfDB, ECA, CCC, CEEAC, CEPGL, FAO, G-77, GATT, IBRD, ICAO, IDA,
IFAD, IFC, ILO, IMF, INTELSAT, INTERPOL, IOC, ITU, LORCS, NAM, OAU, UN,
UNCTAD, UNESCO, UNIDO, UPU, WCL, WHO, WIPO, WMO, WTO

Diplomatic representation:
Ambassador Aloys UWIMANA; Chancery at 1714 New Hampshire Avenue NW, Washington, DC 20009; telephone (202) 232-2882

US:
Ambassador Robert A. FLATEN; Embassy at Boulevard de la Revolution, Kigali (mailing address is B. P. 28, Kigali); telephone [250] 75601 through 75603; FAX [250] 72128

Flag:
three equal vertical bands of red (hoist side), yellow, and green with a large black letter R
centered in the yellow band; uses the popular pan-African colors of Ethiopia; similar to the flag of Guinea, which has a plain yellow band

:Rwanda Economy

Overview:
Almost 50% of GDP comes from the agricultural sector; coffee and tea make up 80-90% of total exports. The amount of fertile land is limited, however, and deforestation and soil erosion have created problems. The industrial sector in Rwanda is small, contributing only 17% to GDP. Manufacturing focuses mainly on the processing of agricultural products. The Rwandan economy remains dependent on coffee exports and foreign aid. Weak international prices since 1986 have caused the economy to contract and per capita GDP to decline. A structural adjustment program with the World Bank began in October 1990. An outbreak of insurgency, also in October, has dampened any prospects for economic improvement.

GDP:
exchange rate conversion - $2.1 billion, per capita $300; real growth rate -6.8% (1990 est.)

Inflation rate (consumer prices):
4.2% (1990)

Unemployment rate: NA%

Budget:
revenues $391 million; expenditures $491 million, including capital expenditures of $225 million (1989 est.)

Exports:
$111.7 million (f.o.b., 1990 est.)
commodities:
coffee 85%, tea, tin, cassiterite, wolframite, pyrethrum

partners:
  Germany, Belgium, Italy, Uganda, UK, France, US
Imports:
  $279.2 million (f.o.b., 1990 est.)
  commodities:
  textiles, foodstuffs, machines and equipment, capital goods, steel,
  petroleum products, cement and construction material
  partners:
  US, Belgium, Germany, Kenya, Japan
External debt: $911 million (1990 est.)
Industrial production:
  growth rate 1.2% (1988); accounts for 17% of GDP
Electricity:
  30,000 kW capacity; 130 million kWh produced, 15 kWh per capita (1991)
Industries:
  mining of cassiterite (tin ore) and wolframite (tungsten ore), tin, cement,
  agricultural processing, small-scale beverage production, soap, furniture,
  shoes, plastic goods, textiles, cigarettes
Agriculture:
  accounts for almost 50% of GDP and about 90% of the labor force; cash crops
  - coffee, tea, pyrethrum (insecticide made from chrysanthemums); main food
  crops - bananas, beans, sorghum, potatoes; stock raising; self-sufficiency
  declining; country imports foodstuffs as farm production fails to keep up
  with a 3.8% annual growth in population
Economic aid:
  US commitments, including Ex-Im (FY70-89), $128 million; Western (non-US)
  countries, ODA and OOF bilateral commitments (1970-89), $2.0 billion; OPEC
  bilateral aid (1979-89), $45 million; Communist countries (1970-89), $58
  million; note - in October 1990 Rwanda launched a Structural Adjustment
  Program with the IMF; since September 1991, the EC has given $46 million and
  the US $25 million in support of this program
Currency:
  Rwandan franc (plural - francs); 1 Rwandan franc (RF) = 100 centimes

:Rwanda Economy

Exchange rates:
  Rwandan francs (RF) per US$1 - 121.40 (January 1992), 125.14 (1991), 82.60
  (1990), 79.98 (1989), 76.45 (1988), 79.67 (1987)
Fiscal year: calendar year

:Rwanda Communications

Highways:
  4,885 km total; 460 km paved, 1,725 km gravel and/or improved earth, 2,700
  km unimproved
Inland waterways:
  Lac Kivu navigable by shallow-draft barges and native craft
Civil air:
  2 major transport aircraft
Airports:
  8 total, 8 usable; 3 with permanent-surface runways; none with runways over
  3,659 m; 1 with runway 2,440-3,659 m;2 with runways 1,220-2,439 m

Telecommunications:
  fair system with low-capacity radio relay system centered on Kigali; broadcast stations - 2 AM, 1 (7 repeaters) FM, no TV; satellite earth stations - 1 Indian Ocean INTELSAT and 1 SYMPHONIE

:Rwanda Defense Forces

Branches:
  Army (including Air Wing), Gendarmerie
Manpower availability:
  males 15-49, 1,719,936; 876,659 fit for military service; no conscription
Defense expenditures:
  exchange rate conversion - $37 million, 1.6% of GDP (1988 est.)

Saint Helena Geography

Total area: 410 km2
Land area: 410 km2; includes Ascension, Gough Island, Inaccessible Island, Nightingale
  Island, and Tristan da Cunha
Comparative area: slightly more than 2.3 times the size of Washington, DC
Land boundaries:
  none
Coastline:
  60 km
Maritime claims:
 Exclusive fishing zone:
  200 nm
 Territorial sea:
  12 nm
Disputes:
  none
Climate:
  tropical; marine; mild, tempered by trade winds
Terrain:
  rugged, volcanic; small scattered plateaus and plains
Natural resources:
  fish; Ascension is a breeding ground for sea turtles and sooty terns; no minerals
Land use:
  arable land 7%; permanent crops 0%; meadows and pastures 7%; forest and woodland 3%; other 83%
Environment:
  very few perennial streams
Note:
  located 1,920 km west of Angola, about two-thirds of the way between South America and Africa; Napoleon Bonaparte's place of exile and burial; the remains were taken to Paris in 1840

:Saint Helena People

Population: 6,698 (July 1992), growth rate 0.3% (1992)
Birth rate: 10 births/1,000 population (1992)
Death rate: 7 deaths/1,000 population (1992)

Net migration rate: 0 migrants/1,000 population (1992)

Infant mortality rate: 40 deaths/1,000 live births (1992)

Life expectancy at birth: 72 years male, 76 years female (1992)

Total fertility rate: 1.2 children born/woman (1992)

Nationality:
  noun - Saint Helenian(s); adjective - Saint Helenian

Ethnic divisions:
  NA

Religions:
  Anglican majority; also Baptist, Seventh-Day Adventist, and Roman Catholic

Languages:
  English

Literacy:
  98% (male 97%, female 98%) age 15 and over can read and write (1987)

Labor force:
  NA

Organized labor:
  Saint Helena General Workers' Union, 472 members; crafts 17%, professional and technical 10%, service 10%, management and clerical 9%, farming and fishing 9%, transport 6%, sales 5%, and other 34%

:Saint Helena Government

Long-form name:
  none

Type:
  dependent territory of the UK

Capital: Jamestown

Administrative divisions:
  1 administrative area and 2 dependencies*; Ascension*, Saint Helena, Tristan da Cunha*

Independence:
  none (dependent territory of the UK)

Constitution:
  1 January 1967

Legal system:
  NA

National holiday:
  Celebration of the Birthday of the Queen (second Saturday in June), 10 June 1989

Executive branch:
  British monarch, governor, Executive Council (cabinet)

Legislative branch:
  unicameral Legislative Council

Judicial branch:
  Supreme Court

Leaders:
 Chief of State:
  Queen ELIZABETH II (since 6 February 1952)
 Head of Government:
  Governor A. N. HOOLE

Political parties and leaders:

Saint Helena Labor Party, leader NA; Saint Helena Progressive Party, leader NA; note - both political parties inactive since 1976

Suffrage:

NA

Elections:

Legislative Council:

last held October 1984 (next to be held NA); results - percent of vote by party NA; seats - (15 total, 12 elected) number of seats by party NA

Member of:

ICFTU

Diplomatic representation:

none (dependent territory of the UK)

Flag:

blue with the flag of the UK in the upper hoist-side quadrant and the Saint Helenian shield centered on the outer half of the flag; the shield features a rocky coastline and three-masted sailing ship

:Saint Helena Economy

Overview:

The economy depends primarily on financial assistance from the UK. The local population earns some income from fishing, the rearing of livestock, and sales of handicrafts. Because there are few jobs, a large proportion of the work force has left to seek employment overseas.

GDP:

$NA, per capita $NA; real growth rate NA%

Inflation rate (consumer prices):

-1.1% (1986)

Unemployment rate: NA%

Budget:

revenues $3.2 million; expenditures $2.9 million, including capital expenditures of NA (1984)

Exports:

$23.9 thousand (f.o.b., 1984)

commodities:

fish (frozen and salt-dried skipjack, tuna), handicrafts

partners:

South Africa, UK

Imports:

$2.4 million (c.i.f., 1984)

commodities:

food, beverages, tobacco, fuel oils, animal feed, building materials, motor vehicles and parts, machinery and parts

partners:

UK, South Africa

External debt: $NA

Industrial production:

growth rate NA%

Electricity:

9,800 kW capacity; 10 million kWh produced, 1,390 kWh per capita (1989)

Industries:
  crafts (furniture, lacework, fancy woodwork), fish
Agriculture:
  maize, potatoes, vegetables; timber production being developed; crawfishing
  on Tristan da Cunha
Economic aid:
  Western (non-US) countries, ODA and OOF bilateral commitments (1970-89),
  $198 million
Currency:
  Saint Helenian pound (plural - pounds); 1 Saint Helenian pound (#S) = 100
  pence
Exchange rates:
  Saint Helenian pounds (#S) per US$1 - 0.5799 (March 1992), 0.5652 (1991),
  0.6099 (1989), 0.5614 (1988), 0.6102 (1987); note - the Saint Helenian pound
  is at par with the British pound
Fiscal year: 1 April - 31 March

:Saint Helena Communications

Highways:
  87 km paved roads, 20 km earth roads on Saint Helena; 80 km paved roads on
  Ascension; 2.7 km paved roads on Tristan da Cunha
Ports:
  Jamestown (Saint Helena), Georgetown (Ascension)
Airports:
  1 with permanent-surface runway 2,440-3,659 m on Ascension
Telecommunications:
  1,500 radio receivers; broadcast stations - 1 AM, no FM, no TV; 550
  telephones in automatic network; HF radio links to Ascension, then into
  worldwide submarine cable and satellite networks; major coaxial submarine
  cable relay point between South Africa, Portugal, and UK at Ascension; 2
  Atlantic Ocean INTELSAT earth stations

:Saint Helena Defense Forces

Note: defense is the responsibility of the UK

Saint Kitts and Nevis Geography

Total area: 269 km2
Land area: 269 km2
Comparative area: slightly more than 1.5 times the size of Washington, DC
Land boundaries:
  none
Coastline:
  135 km
Maritime claims:
 Contiguous zone:
  24 nm
 Exclusive economic zone:
  200 nm
 Territorial sea:
  12 nm
Disputes:

Climate:

subtropical tempered by constant sea breezes; little seasonal temperature variation; rainy season (May to November)

Terrain:

volcanic with mountainous interiors

Natural resources:

negligible

Land use:

arable land 22%; permanent crops 17%; meadows and pastures 3%; forest and woodland 17%; other 41%

Environment:

subject to hurricanes (July to October)

Note:

located 320 km east-southeast of Puerto Rico

:Saint Kitts and Nevis People

Population: 40,061 (July 1992), growth rate 0.3% (1992)
Birth rate: 22 births/1,000 population (1992)
Death rate: 10 deaths/1,000 population (1992)
Net migration rate: -9 migrants/1,000 population (1992)
Infant mortality rate: 22 deaths/1,000 live births (1992)
Life expectancy at birth: 63 years male, 69 years female (1992)
Total fertility rate: 2.4 children born/woman (1992)
Nationality:

noun - Kittsian(s), Nevisian(s); adjective - Kittsian, Nevisian

Ethnic divisions:

mainly of black African descent

Religions:

Anglican, other Protestant sects, Roman Catholic

Languages:

English

Literacy:

98% (male 98%, female 98%) age 15 and over having ever attended school (1970)

Labor force:

20,000 (1981)

Organized labor:

6,700

:Saint Kitts and Nevis Government

Long-form name:

Federation of Saint Kitts and Nevis; formerly Federation of Saint Christopher and Nevis

Type:

constitutional monarchy

Capital: Basseterre

Administrative divisions:

14 parishs; Christ Church Nichola Town, Saint Anne Sandy Point, Saint George Basseterre, Saint George Gingerland, Saint James Windward, Saint John Capisterre, Saint John Figtree, Saint Mary Cayon, Saint Paul Capisterre,

Saint Paul Charlestown, Saint Peter Basseterre, Saint Thomas Lowland, Saint
Thomas Middle Island, Trinity Palmetto Point

Independence:
19 September 1983 (from UK)

Constitution:
19 September 1983

Legal system:
based on English common law

National holiday:
Independence Day, 19 September (1983)

Executive branch:
British monarch, governor general, prime minister, deputy prime minister,
Cabinet

Legislative branch:
unicameral House of Assembly

Judicial branch:
Eastern Caribbean Supreme Court

Leaders:
Chief of State:
Queen ELIZABETH II (since 6 February 1952), represented by Governor General
Sir Clement Athelston ARRINDELL (since 19 September 1983, previously
Governor General of the Associated State since NA November 1981)
Head of Government:
Prime Minister Dr. Kennedy Alphonse SIMMONDS (since 19 September 1983,
previously Premier of the Associated State since NA February 1980); Deputy
Prime Minister Michael Oliver POWELL (since NA)

Political parties and leaders:
People's Action Movement (PAM), Kennedy SIMMONDS; Saint Kitts and Nevis
Labor Party (SKNLP), Dr. Denzil DOUGLAS; Nevis Reformation Party (NRP),
Simeon DANIEL; Concerned Citizens Movement (CCM), Vance AMORY

Suffrage:
universal adult at age NA

Elections:
House of Assembly:
last held 21 March 1989 (next to be held by 21 March 1994); results -
percent of vote by party NA; seats - (14 total, 11 elected) PAM 6, SKNLP 2,
NRP 2, CCM 1

Member of:
ACP, C, CARICOM, CDB, ECLAC, FAO, IBRD, ICFTU, IDA, IFAD, IMF,
INTERPOL,
OAS, OECS, UN, UNCTAD, UNESCO, UNIDO, UPU, WCL, WHO

Diplomatic representation:
Minister-Counselor (Deputy Chief of Mission), Charge d'Affaires ad interim
Aubrey Eric HART; Chancery at Suite 608, 2100 M Street NW, Washington, DC
20037; telephone (202) 833-3550
US:
no official presence since the Charge resides in Saint John's (Antigua and
Barbuda)

:Saint Kitts and Nevis Government

Flag:
    divided diagonally from the lower hoist side by a broad black band bearing
    two white five-pointed stars; the black band is edged in yellow; the upper
    triangle is green, the lower triangle is red

:Saint Kitts and Nevis Economy

Overview:
    The economy has historically depended on the growing and processing of
    sugarcane and on remittances from overseas workers. In recent years, tourism
    and export-oriented manufacturing have assumed larger roles.
GDP:
    exchange rate conversion - $146.6 million, per capita $3,650; real growth
    rate 2.1% (1990)
Inflation rate (consumer prices):
    4.2% (1990)
Unemployment rate: 15% (1989)
Budget:
    revenues $38.1 million; expenditures $68 million, including capital
    expenditures of $31.5 million (1991)
Exports:
    $24.6 million (f.o.b., 1990)
  commodities:
    sugar, clothing, electronics, postage stamps
  partners:
    US 53%, UK 22%, Trinidad and Tobago 5%, OECS 5% (1988)
Imports:
    $103.2 million (f.o.b., 1990)
  commodities:
    foodstuffs, intermediate manufactures, machinery, fuels
  partners:
    US 36%, UK 17%, Trinidad and Tobago 6%, Canada 3%, Japan 3%, OECS 4%
(1988)
External debt: $26.4 million (1988)
Industrial production:
    growth rate 11.8% (1988 est.); accounts for 17% of GDP
Electricity:
    15,800 kW capacity; 45 million kWh produced, 1,117 kWh per capita (1991)
Industries:
    sugar processing, tourism, cotton, salt, copra, clothing, footwear,
    beverages
Agriculture:
    cash crop - sugarcane; subsistence crops - rice, yams, vegetables, bananas;
    fishing potential not fully exploited; most food imported
Economic aid:
    US commitments, including Ex-Im (FY85-88), $10.7 million; Western (non-US)
    countries, ODA and OOF bilateral commitments (1970-89), $67 million
Currency:
    East Caribbean dollar (plural - dollars); 1 EC dollar (EC$) = 100 cents
Exchange rates:

East Caribbean dollars (EC$) per US$1 - 2.70 (fixed rate since 1976)
Fiscal year: calendar year

:Saint Kitts and Nevis Communications

Railroads:
  58 km 0.760-meter gauge on Saint Kitts for sugarcane
Highways:
  300 km total; 125 km paved, 125 km otherwise improved, 50 km unimproved
  earth
Ports:
  Basseterre (Saint Kitts), Charlestown (Nevis)
Civil air:
  no major transport aircraft
Airports:
  2 total, 2 usable; 2 with permanent-surface runways; none with runways over
  3,659 m; 1 with runways 2,440-3,659 m; none with runways 1,220-2,439 m
Telecommunications:
  good interisland VHF/UHF/SHF radio connections and international link via
  Antigua and Barbuda and Saint Martin; 2,400 telephones; broadcast stations -
  2 AM, no FM, 4 TV

:Saint Kitts and Nevis Defense Forces

Branches:
  Royal Saint Kitts and Nevis Police Force, Coast Guard
Manpower availability:
  NA
Defense expenditures:
  exchange rate conversion - $NA, NA% of GDP

Saint Lucia Geography

Total area: 620 km2
Land area: 610 km2
Comparative area: slightly less than 3.5 times the size of Washington, DC
Land boundaries:
  none
Coastline:
  158 km
Maritime claims:
 Contiguous zone:
  24 nm
 Exclusive economic zone:
  200 nm
 Territorial sea:
  12 nm
Disputes:
  none
Climate:
  tropical, moderated by northeast trade winds; dry season from January to
  April, rainy season from May to August
Terrain:
  volcanic and mountainous with some broad, fertile valleys

Natural resources:
   forests, sandy beaches, minerals (pumice), mineral springs, geothermal
   potential
Land use:
   arable land 8%; permanent crops 20%; meadows and pastures 5%; forest and
   woodland 13%; other 54%; includes irrigated 2%
Environment:
   subject to hurricanes and volcanic activity; deforestation; soil erosion
Note:
   located 700 km southeast of Puerto Rico

:Saint Lucia People

Population: 151,774 (July 1992), growth rate 1.7% (1992)
Birth rate: 26 births/1,000 population (1992)
Death rate: 5 deaths/1,000 population (1992)
Net migration rate: -4 migrants/1,000 population (1992)
Infant mortality rate: 18 deaths/1,000 live births (1992)
Life expectancy at birth: 70 years male, 75 years female (1992)
Total fertility rate: 2.8 children born/woman (1992)
Nationality:
   noun - Saint Lucian(s); adjective - Saint Lucian
Ethnic divisions:
   African descent 90.3%, mixed 5.5%, East Indian 3.2%, Caucasian 0.8%
Religions:
   Roman Catholic 90%, Protestant 7%, Anglican 3%
Languages:
   English (official), French patois
Literacy:
   67% (male 65%, female 69%) age 15 and over having ever attended school
   (1980)
Labor force:
   43,800; agriculture 43.4%, services 38.9%, industry and commerce 17.7% (1983
   est.)
Organized labor:
   20% of labor force

:Saint Lucia Government

Long-form name:
   none
Type:
   parliamentary democracy
Capital: Castries
Administrative divisions:
   11 quarters; Anse-la-Raye, Castries, Choiseul, Dauphin, Dennery, Gros-Islet,
   Laborie, Micoud, Praslin, Soufriere, Vieux-Fort
Independence:
   22 February 1979 (from UK)
Constitution:
   22 February 1979
Legal system:
   based on English common law

National holiday:
  Independence Day, 22 February (1979)
Executive branch:
  British monarch, governor general, prime minister, Cabinet
Legislative branch:
  bicameral Parliament consists of an upper house or Senate and a lower house
  or House of Assembly
Judicial branch:
  Eastern Caribbean Supreme Court
Leaders:
  Chief of State:
  Queen ELIZABETH II (since 6 February 1952), represented by Acting Governor
  General Sir Stanislaus Anthony JAMES (since 10 October 1988)
  Head of Government:
  Prime Minister John George Melvin COMPTON (since 3 May 1982)
Political parties and leaders:
  United Workers' Party (UWP), John COMPTON; Saint Lucia Labor Party (SLP),
  Julian HUNTE; Progressive Labor Party (PLP), George ODLUM
Suffrage:
  universal at age 18
Elections:
  House of Assembly:
  last held 6 April 1987 (next to be held by 27 April 1992); results - percent
  of vote by party NA; seats - (17 total) UWP 10, SLP 7
Member of:
  ACCT (associate), ACP, C, CARICOM, CDB, ECLAC, FAO, G-77, IBRD, ICAO,
ICFTU,
  IDA, IFAD, IFC, ILO, IMF, IMO, INTERPOL, LORCS, NAM, OAS, OECS, UN,
UNCTAD,
  UNESCO, UNIDO, UPU, WCL, WHO, WMO
Diplomatic representation:
  Ambassador Dr. Joseph Edsel EDMUNDS; Chancery at Suite 309, 2100 M Street
  NW, Washington, DC 30037; telephone (202) 463-7378 or 7379; there is a Saint
  Lucian Consulate General in New York
  US:
  no official presence since the Ambassador resides in Bridgetown (Barbados)
Flag:
  blue with a gold isosceles triangle below a black arrowhead; the upper edges
  of the arrowhead have a white border

:Saint Lucia Economy

Overview:
  Since 1983 the economy has shown an impressive average annual growth rate of
  almost 5% because of strong agricultural and tourist sectors. Saint Lucia
  also possesses an expanding industrial base supported by foreign investment
  in manufacturing and other activities, such as in data processing. The
  economy, however, remains vulnerable because the important agricultural
  sector is dominated by banana production. Saint Lucia is subject to periodic
  droughts and/or tropical storms, and its protected market agreement with the
  UK for bananas may end in 1992.

GDP:
exchange rate conversion - $295 million, per capita $1,930; real growth rate
4.0% (1990 est.)
Inflation rate (consumer prices):
4.2% (1990)
Unemployment rate: 16.0% (1988)
Budget:
revenues $131 million; expenditures $149 million, including capital
expenditures of $71 million (FY90 est.)
Exports:
$127 million (f.o.b., 1990 est.)
commodities:
bananas 54%, clothing 17%, cocoa, vegetables, fruits, coconut oil
partners:
UK 51%, CARICOM 20%, US 19%, other 10%
Imports:
$270 million (c.i.f., 1990)
commodities:
manufactured goods 23%, machinery and transportation equipment 27%, food and
live animals 18%, chemicals 10%, fuels 6%
partners:
US 35%, CARICOM 16%, UK 15%, Japan 7%, Canada 4%, other 23%
External debt: $54.5 million (1989)
Industrial production:
growth rate 3.5% (1990 est.); accounts for 7% of GDP
Electricity:
32,500 kW capacity; 112 million kWh produced, 732 kWh per capita (1991)
Industries:
clothing, assembly of electronic components, beverages, corrugated boxes,
tourism, lime processing, coconut processing
Agriculture:
accounts for 16% of GDP and 43% of labor force; crops - bananas, coconuts,
vegetables, citrus fruit, root crops, cocoa; imports food for the tourist
industry
Economic aid:
Western (non-US) countries, ODA and OOF bilateral commitments (1970-89),
$120 million
Currency:
East Caribbean dollar (plural - dollars); 1 EC dollar (EC$) = 100 cents
Exchange rates:
East Caribbean dollars (EC$) per US$1 - 2.70 (fixed rate since 1976)

:Saint Lucia Communications

Highways:
760 km total; 500 km paved; 260 km otherwise improved
Ports:
Castries
Civil air:
no major transport aircraft
Airports:

2 total, 2 usable; 2 with permanent-surface runways; none with runways over 3,659 m; 1 with runways 2,440-3,659 m; 1 with runways 1,220-2,439

Telecommunications:
  fully automatic telephone system; 9,500 telephones; direct microwave link with Martinique and Saint Vincent and the Grenadines; interisland troposcatter link to Barbados; broadcast stations - 4 AM, 1 FM, 1 TV (cable)

:Saint Lucia Defense Forces

Branches:
  Royal Saint Lucia Police Force, Coast Guard

Manpower availability:
  NA

Defense expenditures:
  exchange rate conversion - $NA, NA% of GDP

Saint Pierre and Miquelon Geography

Total area: 242 km2

Land area: 242 km2; includes eight small islands in the Saint Pierre and the Miquelon groups

Comparative area: slightly less than 1.5 times the size of Washington, DC

Land boundaries:
  none

Coastline:
  120 km

Maritime claims:
 Exclusive economic zone:
  200 nm
 Territorial sea:
  12 nm

Disputes:
  focus of maritime boundary dispute between Canada and France

Climate:
  cold and wet, with much mist and fog; spring and autumn are windy

Terrain:
  mostly barren rock

Natural resources:
  fish, deepwater ports

Land use:
  arable land 13%; permanent crops 0%; meadows and pastures 0%; forest and woodland 4%; other 83%

Environment:
  vegetation scanty

Note:
  located 25 km south of Newfoundland, Canada, in the North Atlantic Ocean

:Saint Pierre and Miquelon People

Population: 6,513 (July 1992), growth rate 0.4% (1992)

Birth rate: 9 births/1,000 population (1992)

Death rate: 6 deaths/1,000 population (1992)

Net migration rate: 1 migrant/1,000 population (1992)

Infant mortality rate: 10 deaths/1,000 live births (1992)

Life expectancy at birth: 75 years male, 78 years female (1992)
Total fertility rate: 1.2 children born/woman (1992)
Nationality:
  noun - Frenchman(men), Frenchwoman(women); adjective - French
Ethnic divisions:
  originally Basques and Bretons (French fishermen)
Religions:
  Roman Catholic 98%
Languages:
  French
Literacy:
  99% (male 99%, female 99%) age 15 and over can read and write (1982)
Labor force:
  2,850 (1988)
Organized labor:
  Workers' Force trade union

:Saint Pierre and Miquelon Government

Long-form name:
  Territorial Collectivity of Saint Pierre and Miquelon
Type:
  territorial collectivity of France
Capital: Saint-Pierre
Administrative divisions:
  none (territorial collectivity of France)
Independence:
  none (territorial collectivity of France); note - has been under French
  control since 1763
Constitution:
  28 September 1958 (French Constitution)
Legal system:
  French law
National holiday:
  National Day, 14 July (Taking of the Bastille)
Executive branch:
  French president, commissioner of the Republic
Legislative branch:
  unicameral General Council
Judicial branch:
  Superior Tribunal of Appeals (Tribunal Superieur d'Appel)
Leaders:
  Chief of State:
  President Francois MITTERRAND (since 21 May 1981)
  Head of Government:
  Commissioner of the Republic Jean-Pierre MARQUIE (since February 1989);
  President of the General Council Marc PLANTEGENET (since NA)
Political parties and leaders:
  Socialist Party (PS); Union for French Democracy (UDF/CDS), Gerard GRIGNON
Suffrage:
  universal at age 18

Elections:
  General Council:
    last held September-October 1988 (next to be held NA September 1994);
    results - percent of vote by party NA; seats - (19 total) Socialist and
    other left-wing parties 13, UDF and right-wing parties 6
  French President:
    last held 8 May 1988 (next to be held NA May 1995); results - (second
    ballot) Jacques CHIRAC 56%, Francois MITTERRAND 44%
  French Senate:
    last held 24 September 1989 (next to be held NA September 1992); results -
    percent of vote by party NA; seats - (1 total) PS 1
  French National Assembly:
    last held 5 and 12 June 1988 (next to be held NA June 1993); results -
    percent of vote by party NA; seats - (1 total) UDF/CDS 1; note - Saint
    Pierre and Miquelon elects 1 member each to the French Senate and the French
    National Assembly who are voting members
Member of:
  FZ, WFTU
Diplomatic representation:
  as a territorial collectivity of France, local interests are represented in
  the US by France
Flag:
  the flag of France is used

:Saint Pierre and Miquelon Economy

Overview:
  The inhabitants have traditionally earned their livelihood by fishing and by
  servicing fishing fleets operating off the coast of Newfoundland. The
  economy has been declining, however, because the number of ships stopping at
  Saint Pierre has dropped steadily over the years. In March 1989, an
  agreement between France and Canada set fish quotas for Saint Pierre's
  trawlers fishing in Canadian and Canadian-claimed waters for three years.
  The agreement settles a longstanding dispute that had virtually brought fish
  exports to a halt. The islands are heavily subsidized by France. Imports
  come primarily from Canada and France.
GDP:
  exchange rate conversion - $60 million, per capita $9,500; real growth rate
  NA% (1991 est.)
Inflation rate (consumer prices):
  NA%
Unemployment rate: 9.6% (1990)
Budget:
  revenues $18.3 million; expenditures $18.3 million, including capital
  expenditures of $5.5 million (1989)
Exports:
  $25.5 million (f.o.b., 1990)
 commodities:
  fish and fish products, fox and mink pelts
 partners:
  US 58%, France 17%, UK 11%, Canada, Portugal

Imports:

$87.2 million (c.i.f., 1990)

commodities:

meat, clothing, fuel, electrical equipment, machinery, building materials

partners:

Canada, France, US, Netherlands, UK

External debt: $NA

Industrial production:

growth rate NA%

Electricity:

10,000 kW capacity; 25 million kWh produced, 3,970 kWh per capita (1989)

Industries:

fish processing and supply base for fishing fleets; tourism

Agriculture:

vegetables, cattle, sheep and pigs for local consumption; fish catch, 20,500 metric tons (1989)

Economic aid:

Western (non-US) countries, ODA and OOF bilateral commitments (1970-89), $500 million

Currency:

French franc (plural - francs); 1 French franc (F) = 100 centimes

Exchange rates:

French francs (F) per US$1 - 5.6397 (March 1992), 5.6421 (1991), 5.4453 (1990), 6.3801 (1989), 5.9569 (1988), 6.0107 (1987)

Fiscal year: calendar year

:Saint Pierre and Miquelon Communications

Highways:

120 km total; 60 km paved (1985)

Ports:

Saint Pierre

Civil air:

no major transport aircraft

Airports:

2 total, 2 usable; 2 with permanent-surface runways, none with runways over 2,439 m; 1 with runway 1,220-2,439 m

Telecommunications:

3,601 telephones; broadcast stations - 1 AM, 3 FM, no TV; radio communication with most countries in the world; 1 earth station in French domestic satellite system

:Saint Pierre and Miquelon Defense Forces

Note: defense is the responsibility of France

Saint Vincent and the Grenadines Geography

Total area: 340 km2

Land area: 340 km2

Comparative area: slightly less than twice the size of Washington, DC

Land boundaries:

Coastline:

84 km
Maritime claims:
 Contiguous zone:
  24 nm
 Exclusive economic zone:
  200 nm
 Territorial sea:
  12 nm
Disputes:
  none
Climate:
  tropical; little seasonal temperature variation; rainy season (May to
  November)
Terrain:
  volcanic, mountainous; Soufriere volcano on the island of Saint Vincent
Natural resources:
  negligible
Land use:
  arable land 38%; permanent crops 12%; meadows and pastures 6%; forest and
  woodland 41%; other 3%; includes irrigated 3%
Environment:
  subject to hurricanes; Soufriere volcano is a constant threat
Note:
  some islands of the Grenadines group are administered by Grenada

:Saint Vincent and the Grenadines People

Population: 115,339 (July 1992), growth rate 1.1% (1992)
Birth rate: 23 births/1,000 population (1992)
Death rate: 5 deaths/1,000 population (1992)
Net migration rate: -7 migrants/1,000 population (1992)
Infant mortality rate: 19 deaths/1,000 live births (1992)
Life expectancy at birth: 71 years male, 74 years female (1992)
Total fertility rate: 2.4 children born/woman (1992)
Nationality:
  noun - Saint Vincentian(s) or Vincentian(s); adjectives - Saint Vincentian
  or Vincentian
Ethnic divisions:
  mainly of black African descent; remainder mixed, with some white, East
  Indian, Carib Indian
Religions:
  Anglican, Methodist, Roman Catholic, Seventh-Day Adventist
Languages:
  English, some French patois
Literacy:
  96% (male 96%, female 96%) age 15 and over having ever attended school
  (1970)
Labor force:
  67,000 (1984 est.)
Organized labor:
  10% of labor force

:Saint Vincent and the Grenadines Government

Long-form name:
  none
Type:
  constitutional monarchy
Capital: Kingstown
Administrative divisions:
  6 parishes; Charlotte, Grenadines, Saint Andrew, Saint David, Saint George,
  Saint Patrick
Independence:
  27 October 1979 (from UK)
Constitution:
  27 October 1979
Legal system:
  based on English common law
National holiday:
  Independence Day, 27 October (1979)
Executive branch:
  British monarch, governor general, prime minister, Cabinet
Legislative branch:
  unicameral House of Assembly
Judicial branch:
  Eastern Caribbean Supreme Court
Leaders:
 Chief of State:
  Queen ELIZABETH II (since 6 February 1952), represented by Governor General
  David JACK (since 29 September 1989)
 Head of Government:
  Prime Minister James F. MITCHELL (since 30 July 1984)
Political parties and leaders:
  New Democratic Party (NDP), James (Son) MITCHELL; Saint Vincent Labor Party
  (SVLP), Vincent BEACHE; United People's Movement (UPM), Adrian
SAUNDERS;
  Movement for National Unity (MNU), Ralph GONSALVES; National Reform Party
  (NRP), Joel MIGUEL
Suffrage:
  universal at age 18
Elections:
 House of Assembly:
  last held 16 May 1989 (next to be held NA July 1994); results - percent of
  vote by party NA; seats - (21 total; 15 elected representatives and 6
  appointed senators) NDP 15
Member of:
  ACP, C, CARICOM, CDB, ECLAC, FAO, G-77, IBRD, ICAO, ICFTU, IDA,
IFAD, IMF,
  IMO, INTERPOL, IOC, ITU, LORCS, OAS, OECS, UN, UNCTAD, UNESCO,
UNIDO, UPU,
  WCL, WFTU, WHO
Diplomatic representation:
  Ambassador Kingsley LAYNE; 1717 Massachusetts Avenue, NW, Suite 102,

Washington, DC 20036; telephone NA
US:
no official presence since the Ambassador resides in Bridgetown (Barbados)
Flag:
three vertical bands of blue (hoist side), gold (double width), and green;
the gold band bears three green diamonds arranged in a V pattern
*** No entry for this item ***

:Saint Vincent and the Grenadines Economy

Overview:
Agriculture, dominated by banana production, is the most important sector of
the economy. The services sector, based mostly on a growing tourist
industry, is also important. The economy continues to have a high
unemployment rate of 30% because of an overdependence on the weather-plagued
banana crop as a major export earner. Government progress toward
diversifying into new industries has been relatively unsuccessful.
GDP:
exchange rate conversion - $146 million, per capita $1,300; real growth rate
5.9% (1989)
Inflation rate (consumer prices):
3.0% (1990)
Unemployment rate: 30% (1989 est.)
Budget:
revenues $62 million; expenditures $67 million, including capital
expenditures of $21 million (FY90 est.)
Exports:
$75 million (f.o.b., 1990)
commodities:
bananas, eddoes and dasheen (taro), arrowroot starch, tennis racquets, flour
partners:
UK 43%, CARICOM 37%, US 15%
Imports:
$130 million (f.o.b., 1990 est.)
commodities:
foodstuffs, machinery and equipment, chemicals and fertilizers, minerals and
fuels
partners:
US 42%, CARICOM 19%, UK 15%
External debt: $50.9 million (1989)
Industrial production:
growth rate 0% (1989); accounts for 14% of GDP
Electricity:
16,594 kW capacity; 64 million kWh produced, 560 kWh per capita (1991)
Industries:
food processing (sugar, flour), cement, furniture, clothing, starch, sheet
metal, beverage
Agriculture:
accounts for 15% of GDP and 60% of labor force; provides bulk of exports;
products - bananas, coconuts, sweet potatoes, spices; small numbers of
cattle, sheep, hogs, goats; small fish catch used locally

Economic aid:
  US commitments, including Ex-Im (FY70-87), $11 million; Western (non-US)
  countries, ODA and OOF bilateral commitments (1970-89), $81 million
Currency:
  East Caribbean dollar (plural - dollars); 1 EC dollar (EC$) = 100 cents
Exchange rates:
  East Caribbean dollars (EC$) per US$1 - 2.70 (fixed rate since 1976)
Fiscal year: calendar year (as of January 1991); previously 1 July - 30 June

:Saint Vincent and the Grenadines Communications

Highways:
  about 1,000 km total; 300 km paved; 400 km improved; 300 km unimproved
Ports:
  Kingstown
Merchant marine:
  407 ships (1,000 GRT or over) totaling 3,388,427 GRT/5,511,325 DWT; includes
  3 passenger, 2 passenger-cargo, 222 cargo, 22 container, 19 roll-on/roll-off
  cargo, 14 refrigerated cargo, 24 petroleum tanker, 7 chemical tanker, 4
  liquefied gas, 73 bulk, 13 combination bulk, 2 vehicle carrier, 1 livestock
  carrier, 1 specialized tanker; note - China owns 3 ships; a flag of
  convenience registry
Civil air:
  no major transport aircraft
Airports:
  6 total, 6 usable; 4 with permanent-surface runways; none with runways over
  2,439 m; 1 with runways 1,220-2,439 m
Telecommunications:
  islandwide fully automatic telephone system; 6,500 telephones; VHF/UHF
  interisland links from Saint Vincent to Barbados and the Grenadines; new SHF
  links to Grenada and Saint Lucia; broadcast stations - 2 AM, no FM, 1 TV
  (cable)

:Saint Vincent and the Grenadines Defense Forces

Branches:
  Royal Saint Vincent and the Grenadines Police Force, Coast Guard
Manpower availability:
  NA
Defense expenditures:
  exchange rate conversion - $NA, NA% of GDP

San Marino Geography

Total area: 60 km2
Land area: 60 km2
Comparative area: about 0.3 times the size of Washington, DC
Land boundaries:
  39 km; Italy 39 km
Coastline:
  none - landlocked
Maritime claims:
  none - landlocked
Disputes:

Climate:
  Mediterranean; mild to cool winters; warm, sunny summers
Terrain:
  rugged mountains
Natural resources:
  building stones
Land use:
  arable land 17%; permanent crops 0%; meadows and pastures 0%; forest and
  woodland 0%; other 83%
Environment:
  dominated by the Appenines
Note:
  landlocked; world's smallest republic; enclave of Italy

:San Marino People

Population: 23,404 (July 1992), growth rate 0.6% (1992)
Birth rate: 8 births/1,000 population (1992)
Death rate: 7 deaths/1,000 population (1992)
Net migration rate: 5 migrants/1,000 population (1992)
Infant mortality rate: 8 deaths/1,000 live births (1992)
Life expectancy at birth: 74 years male, 79 years female (1992)
Total fertility rate: 1.3 children born/woman (1992)
Nationality:
  noun - Sanmarinese (singular and plural); adjective - Sanmarinese
Ethnic divisions:
  Sanmarinese, Italian
Religions:
  Roman Catholic
Languages:
  Italian
Literacy:
  96% (male 96%, female 95%) age 14 and over can read and write (1976)
Labor force:
  about 4,300
Organized labor:
  Democratic Federation of Sanmarinese Workers (affiliated with ICFTU) has
  about 1,800 members; Communist-dominated General Federation of Labor, 1,400
  members

:San Marino Government

Long-form name:
  Republic of San Marino
Type:
  republic
Capital: San Marino
Administrative divisions:
  9 municipalities (castelli, singular - castello); Acquaviva, Borgo Maggiore,
  Chiesanuova, Domagnano, Faetano, Fiorentino, Monte Giardino, San Marino,
  Serravalle
Independence:

301 AD (by tradition)

Constitution:
8 October 1600; electoral law of 1926 serves some of the functions of a constitution

Legal system:
based on civil law system with Italian law influences; has not accepted compulsory ICJ jurisdiction

National holiday:
Anniversary of the Foundation of the Republic, 3 September

Executive branch:
two captains regent, Congress of State (cabinet); real executive power is wielded by the secretary of state for foreign affairs and the secretary of state for internal affairs

Legislative branch:
unicameral Great and General Council (Consiglio Grande e Generale)

Judicial branch:
Council of Twelve (Consiglio dei XII)

Leaders:
Co-Chiefs of State:
Captain Regent Edda CETCOLI and Captain Regent Marino RICCARDI (since 1 October 1991)
Head of Government:
Secretary of State Gabriele GATTI (since July 1986)

Political parties and leaders:
Christian Democratic Party (DCS), Piermarino MENICUCCI; San Marino Democratic Progressive Party (PPDS) formerly San Marino Communist Party (PCS), Gilberto GHIOTTI; San Marino Socialist Party (PSS), Remy GIACOMINI; Unitary Socialst Party (PSU); Democratic Movement (MD), Emilio Della BALDA; San Marino Social Democratic Party (PSDS), Augusto CASALI; San Marino Republican Party (PRS), Cristoforo BUSCARINI

Suffrage:
universal at age 18

Elections:
Great and General Council:
last held 29 May 1988 (next to be held by NA May 1993); results - percent of vote by party NA; seats - (60 total) DCS 27, PCS 18, PSU 8, PSS 7

Communists:
about 300 members

Member of:
CE, CSCE, ICAO, ICFTU, ILO, IMF (observer), IOC, IOM (observer), ITU, LORCS,
NAM (guest), UN, UNCTAD, UNESCO, UPU, WHO, WTO

Diplomatic representation:
San Marino maintains honorary Consulates General in Washington and New York and an honorary Consulate in Detroit

:San Marino Government

US:
no mission in San Marino, but the Consul General in Florence (Italy) is accredited to San Marino; Consulate General at Lungarno Amerigo Vespucci,

38, 50123 Firenze, Italy (mailing address is APO AE 09613; telephone [39] (55) 239-8276 through 8279 and 217-605; FAX [39] (55) 284-088

Flag:
  two equal horizontal bands of white (top) and light blue with the national coat of arms superimposed in the center; the coat of arms has a shield (featuring three towers on three peaks) flanked by a wreath, below a crown and above a scroll bearing the word

Flag:
  AS (Liberty)

:San Marino Economy

Overview:
  More than 2 million tourists visit each year, contributing about 60% to GDP. The sale of postage stamps to foreign collectors is another important income producer. The manufacturing sector employs nearly 40% of the labor force and agriculture less than 4%. The per capita level of output and standard of living are comparable to northern Italy.

GDP:
  purchasing power equivalent - $400 million, per capita $17,000; real growth rate NA% (1991 est.)

Inflation rate (consumer prices):
  6% (1990)

Unemployment rate: 6.5% (1985)

Budget:
  revenues $99.2 million; expenditures $NA, including capital expenditures of $NA (1983)

Exports:
  *** No entry for this item ***
  trade data are included with the statistics for Italy; commodity trade consists primarily of exchanging building stone, lime, wood, chestnuts, wheat, wine, baked goods, hides, and ceramics for a wide variety of consumer manufactures

Imports:
  see

External debt: $NA

Industrial production:
  growth rate NA%

Electricity:
  supplied by Italy

Industries:
  wine, olive oil, cement, leather, textile, tourism

Agriculture:
  employs less than 4% of labor force; products - wheat, grapes, corn, olives, meat, cheese, hides; small numbers of cattle, pigs, horses; depends on Italy for food imports

Economic aid:
  NA

Currency:
  Italian lira (plural - lire); 1 Italian lira (Lit) = 100 centesimi; also mints its own coins

Exchange rates:
    Italian lire (Lit) per US$1 - 1,248.4 (March 1992), 1,240.6 (1991), 1,198.1
    (1990), 1,372.1 (1989), 1,301.6 (1988), 1,296.1 (1987)
Fiscal year: calendar year

:San Marino Communications

Highways:
    104 km
Telecommunications:
    automatic telephone system completely integrated into Italian system; 11,700
    telephones; broadcast services from Italy; microwave and cable links into
    Italian networks; no communication satellite facilities

:San Marino Defense Forces

Branches:
    public security or police force of less than 50 people
Manpower availability:
    all fit men ages 16-60 constitute a militia that can serve as an army
Defense expenditures:
    exchange rate conversion - $NA, NA% of GDP

Sao Tome and Principe Geography

Total area: 960 km2
Land area: 960 km2
Comparative area: slightly less than 5.5 times the size of Washington, DC
Land boundaries:
    none
Coastline:
    209 km
Maritime claims:
    (measured from claimed archipelagic baselines)
 Exclusive economic zone:
    200 nm
 Territorial sea:
    12 nm
Disputes:
    none
Climate:
    tropical; hot, humid; one rainy season (October to May)
Terrain:
    volcanic, mountainous
Natural resources:
    fish
Land use:
    arable land 1%; permanent crops 20%; meadows and pastures 1%; forest and
    woodland 75%; other 3%
Environment:
    deforestation; soil erosion
Note:
    located south of Nigeria and west of Gabon near the Equator in the North
    Atlantic Ocean

Population: 132,338 (July 1992), growth rate 2.9% (1992)
Birth rate: 38 births/1,000 population (1992)
Death rate: 8 deaths/1,000 population (1992)
Net migration rate: 0 migrants/1,000 population (1992)
Infant mortality rate: 58 deaths/1,000 live births (1992)
Life expectancy at birth: 64 years male, 68 years female (1992)
Total fertility rate: 5.2 children born/woman (1992)
Nationality:
   noun - Sao Tomean(s); adjective - Sao Tomean
Ethnic divisions:
   mestico, angolares (descendents of Angolan slaves), forros (descendents of
   freed slaves), servicais (contract laborers from Angola, Mozambique, and
   Cape Verde), tongas (children of servicais born on the islands), and
   Europeans (primarily Portuguese)
Religions:
   Roman Catholic, Evangelical Protestant, Seventh-Day Adventist
Languages:
   Portuguese (official)
Literacy:
   57% (male 73%, female 42%) age 15 and over can read and write (1981)
Labor force:
   21,096 (1981); most of population engaged in subsistence agriculture and
   fishing; labor shortages on plantations and of skilled workers; 56% of
   population of working age (1983)
Organized labor:
   NA

:Sao Tome and Principe Government

Long-form name:
   Democratic Republic of Sao Tome and Principe
Type:
   republic
Capital: Sao Tome
Administrative divisions:
   2 districts (concelhos, singular - concelho); Principe, Sao Tome
Independence:
   12 July 1975 (from Portugal)
Constitution:
   5 November 1975, approved 15 December 1982
Legal system:
   based on Portuguese law system and customary law; has not accepted
   compulsory ICJ jurisdiction
National holiday:
   Independence Day, 12 July (1975)
Executive branch:
   president, prime minister, Council of Ministers (cabinet)
Legislative branch:
   unicameral National People's Assembly (Assembleia Popular Nacional)
Judicial branch:

Supreme Court

Leaders:

Chief of State:

President Miguel TROVOADA (since 4 April 1991)

Head of Government:

Prime Minister Noberto COSTA ALEGRE (since 16 May 1992)

Political parties and leaders:

Party for Democratic Convergence-Reflection Group (PCD-GR), Prime Minister Daniel Lima Dos Santos DAIO, secretary general; Movement for the Liberation of Sao Tome and Principe (MLSTP), Carlos da GRACA; Christian Democratic Front (FDC), Alphonse Dos SANTOS; Democratic Opposition Coalition (CODO), leader NA; other small parties

Suffrage:

universal at age 18

Elections:

President:

last held 3 March 1991 (next to be held NA March 1996); results - Miguel TROVOADA was elected without opposition in Sao Tome's first multiparty presidential election

National People's Assembly:

last held 20 January 1991 (next to be held NA January 1996); results - PCD-GR 54.4%, MLSTP 30.5%, CODO 5.2%, FDC 1.5%, other 8.3%; seats - (55 total) PCD-GR 33, MLSTP 21, CODO 1; note - this was the first multiparty election in Sao Tome and Principe

Member of:

ACP, AfDB, CEEAC, ECA, FAO, G-77, IBRD, ICAO, IDA, IFAD, ILO, IMF, INTERPOL,

ITU, LORCS, NAM, OAU, UN, UNCTAD, UNESCO, UNIDO, UPU, WHO, WMO, WTO

Diplomatic representation:

Ambassador Joaquim Rafael BRANCO; Chancery (temporary) at 801 Second Avenue,

Suite 603, New York, NY 10017; telephone (212) 697-4211

US:

Ambassador to Gabon is accredited to Sao Tome and Principe on a nonresident basis and makes periodic visits to the islands

:Sao Tome and Principe Government

Flag:

three horizontal bands of green (top), yellow (double width), and green with two black five-pointed stars placed side by side in the center of the yellow band and a red isosceles triangle based on the hoist side; uses the popular pan-African colors of Ethiopia

:Sao Tome and Principe Economy

Overview:

The economy has remained dependent on cocoa since the country gained independence nearly 15 years ago. Since then, however, cocoa production has gradually deteriorated because of drought and mismanagement, so that by 1987 output had fallen to less than 50% of its former levels. As a result, a shortage of cocoa for export has created a serious balance-of-payments problem. Production of less important crops, such as coffee, copra, and palm kernels, has also declined. The value of imports generally exceeds that of exports by a ratio of 4:1. The emphasis on cocoa production at the expense of other food crops has meant that Sao Tome has to import 90% of food needs. It also has to import all fuels and most manufactured goods. Over the years, Sao Tome has been unable to service its external debt, which amounts to roughly 80% of export earnings. Considerable potential exists for development of a tourist industry, and the government has taken steps to expand facilities in recent years. The government also implemented a Five-Year Plan covering 1986-90 to restructure the economy and reschedule external debt service payments in cooperation with the International Development Association and Western lenders.

GDP:
exchange rate conversion - $46.0 million, per capita $400; real growth rate 1.5% (1989)

Inflation rate (consumer prices):
36% (1989)

Unemployment rate: NA%

Budget:
revenues $10.2 million; expenditures $36.8 million, including capital expenditures of $22.5 million (1989)

Exports:
$4.4 million (f.o.b., 1990 est.)
commodities:
cocoa 85%, copra, coffee, palm oil
partners:
FRG, GDR, Netherlands, China

Imports:
$21.3 million (f.o.b., 1990 est.)
commodities:
machinery and electrical equipment 54%, food products 23%, other 23%
partners:
Portugal, GDR, Angola, China

External debt: $147 million (1990 est.)

Industrial production:
growth rate 7.1% (1986)

Electricity:
5,000 kW capacity; 10 million kWh produced, 80 kWh per capita (1991)

Industries:
light construction, shirts, soap, beer, fisheries, shrimp processing

Agriculture:
dominant sector of economy, primary source of exports; cash crops - cocoa (85%), coconuts, palm kernels, coffee; food products - bananas, papaya, beans, poultry, fish; not self-sufficient in food grain and meat

Economic aid:
US commitments, including Ex-Im (FY70-89), $8 million; Western (non-US) countries, ODA and OOF bilateral commitments (1970-89), $89 million

Currency:
dobra (plural - dobras); 1 dobra (Db) = 100 centimos

:Sao Tome and Principe Economy

Exchange rates:
  dobras (Db) per US$1 - 260.0 (November 1991), 122.48 (December 1988), 72.827
  (1987), 36.993 (1986)
Fiscal year: calendar year

:Sao Tome and Principe Communications

Highways:
  300 km (two-thirds are paved); roads on Principe are mostly unpaved and in
  need of repair
Ports:
  Sao Tome, Santo Antonio
Civil air:
  10 major transport aircraft
Airports:
  2 total, 2 usable; 2 with permanent-surface runways 1,220-2,439 m
Telecommunications:
  minimal system; broadcast stations - 1 AM, 2 FM, no TV; 1 Atlantic Ocean
  INTELSAT earth station

:Sao Tome and Principe Defense Forces

Branches:
  Army, Navy, National Police
Manpower availability:
  males 15-49, 30,188; 15,918 fit for military service
Defense expenditures:
  exchange rate conversion - $NA, NA% of GDP

Saudi Arabia Geography

Total area: 1,945,000 km2
Land area: 1,945,000 km2
Comparative area: slightly less than one-fourth the size of the US
Land boundaries:
  4,532 km total; Iraq 808 km, Jordan 742 km, Kuwait 222 km, Oman 676 km,
  Qatar 40 km, UAE 586 km, Yemen 1,458 km
Coastline:
  2,510 km
Maritime claims:
 Contiguous zone:
  18 nm
 Continental shelf:
  not specific
 Territorial sea:
  12 nm
Disputes:
  no defined boundaries with Yemen; location and status of Saudi Arabia's
  boundaries with Qatar and UAE are unresolved; Kuwaiti ownership of Qaruh and
  Umm al Maradim Islands is disputed by Saudi Arabia
Climate:
  harsh, dry desert with great extremes of temperature
Terrain:
  mostly uninhabited, sandy desert

Natural resources:
  crude oil, natural gas, iron ore, gold, copper
Land use:
  arable land 1%; permanent crops NEGL%; meadows and pastures 39%; forest and
  woodland 1%; other 59%; includes irrigated NEGL%
Environment:
  no perennial rivers or permanent water bodies; developing extensive coastal
  seawater desalination facilities; desertification
Note:
  extensive coastlines on Persian Gulf and Red Sea provide great leverage on
  shipping (especially crude oil) through Persian Gulf and Suez Canal

:Saudi Arabia People

Population: 17,050,934 (July 1992), growth rate 3.3% (1992); note - the population
  figure is based on growth since the last official Saudi census of 1974 that
  reported a total of 7 million persons and included foreign workers;
  estimates from other sources may be 15-30% lower
Birth rate: 39 births/1,000 population (1992)
Death rate: 6 deaths/1,000 population (1992)
Net migration rate: 0 migrants/1,000 population (1992)
Infant mortality rate: 59 deaths/1,000 live births (1992)
Life expectancy at birth: 65 years male, 68 years female (1992)
Total fertility rate: 6.7 children born/woman (1992)
Nationality:
  noun - Saudi(s); adjective - Saudi or Saudi Arabian
Ethnic divisions:
  Arab 90%, Afro-Asian 10%
Religions:
  Muslim 100%
Languages:
  Arabic
Literacy:
  62% (male 73%, female 48%) age 15 and over can read and write (1990 est.)
Labor force:
  5,000,000; about 60% are foreign workers; government 34%, industry and oil
  28%, services 22%, and agriculture 16%
Organized labor:
  trade unions are illegal

:Saudi Arabia Government

Long-form name:
  Kingdom of Saudi Arabia
Type:
  monarchy
Capital: Riyadh
Administrative divisions:
  14 emirates (imarat, singular - imarah); Al Bahah, Al Hudud ash Shamaliyah,
  Al Jawf, Al Madinah, Al Qasim, Al Qurayyat, Ar Riyad, Ash Sharqiyah, `Asir,
  Ha'il, Jizan, Makkah, Najran, Tabuk
Independence:
  23 September 1932 (unification)

Constitution:
none; governed according to Shari`a (Islamic law)
Legal system:
based on Islamic law, several secular codes have been introduced; commercial
disputes handled by special committees; has not accepted compulsory ICJ
jurisdiction
National holiday:
Unification of the Kingdom, 23 September (1932)
Executive branch:
monarch and prime minister, crown prince and deputy prime minister, Council
of Ministers
Legislative branch:
none
Judicial branch:
Supreme Council of Justice
Leaders:
 Chief of State and Head of Government:
King and Prime Minister FAHD bin `Abd al-`Aziz Al Sa`ud (since 13 June
1982); Crown Prince and Deputy Prime Minister `ABDALLAH bin `Abd al-`Aziz
Al
Sa`ud (half-brother to the King, appointed heir to the throne 13 June 1982)
Suffrage:
none
Elections:
none
Member of:
ABEDA, AfDB, AFESD, AL, AMF, CCC, ESCWA, FAO, G-19, G-77, GCC,
IAEA, IBRD,
ICAO, ICC, IDA, IDB, IFAD, IFC, ILO, IMF, IMO, INMARSAT, INTELSAT,
INTERPOL,
IOC, ISO, ITU, LORCS, NAM, OAPEC, OAS (observer), OIC, OPEC, UN,
UNCTAD,
UNESCO, UNIDO, UPU, WFTU, WHO, WIPO, WMO
Diplomatic representation:
Ambassador BANDAR Bin Sultan; Chancery at 601 New Hampshire Avenue NW,
Washington, DC 20037; telephone (202) 342-3800; there are Saudi Arabian
Consulates General in Houston, Los Angeles, and New York
 US:
Ambassador Charles W. FREEMAN, Jr.; Embassy at Collector Road M, Diplomatic
Quarter, Riyadh (mailing address is American Embassy, Unit 61307, Riyadh;
International Mail: P. O. Box 94309, Riyadh 11693; or APO AE 09803-1307);
telephone [966] (1) 488-3800; Telex 406866; there are US Consulates General
in Dhahran and Jiddah (Jeddah)
Flag:
green with large white Arabic script (that may be translated as There is no
God but God; Muhammad is the Messenger of God) above a white horizontal
saber (the tip points to the hoist side); green is the traditional color of
Islam

:Saudi Arabia Economy

847

Overview:
  The petroleum sector accounts for roughly 70% of budget revenues, 37% of
  GDP, and almost all export earnings. Saudi Arabia has the largest reserves
  of petroleum in the world, ranks as the largest exporter of petroleum, and
  plays a leading role in OPEC. For the 1990s the government intends to
  encourage private economic activity and to foster the gradual process of
  turning Saudi Arabia into a modern industrial state that retains traditional
  Islamic values.
GDP:
  exchange rate conversion - $104 billion, per capita $5,800; real growth rate
  1.5% (1991 est.)
Inflation rate (consumer prices):
  3% (1991 est.)
Unemployment rate: 0% (1989 est.)
Budget:
  revenues $40.3 billion; expenditures $48.3 billion, including capital
  expenditures of $NA (1992)
Exports:
  $44.3 billion (f.o.b., 1990)
 commodities:
  petroleum and petroleum products 85%
 partners:
  US 22%, Japan 22%, Singapore 7%, France 6%
Imports:
  $21.5 billion (f.o.b., 1990)
 commodities:
  manufactured goods, transportation equipment, construction materials,
  processed food products
 partners:
  US 16%, UK 14%, Japan 14%, FRG 7%
External debt: $18.9 billion (December 1989 est.)
Industrial production:
  growth rate -1.1% (1989 est.); accounts for 37% of GDP, including petroleum
Electricity:
  30,000,000 kW capacity; 60,000 million kWh produced, 3,300 kWh per capita
  (1991)
Industries:
  crude oil production, petroleum refining, basic petrochemicals, cement,
  small steel-rolling mill, construction, fertilizer, plastic
Agriculture:
  accounts for about 10% of GDP, 16% of labor force; fastest growing economic
  sector; subsidized by government; products - wheat, barley, tomatoes,
  melons, dates, citrus fruit, mutton, chickens, eggs, milk; approaching
  self-sufficiency in food
Economic aid:
  donor - pledged $64.7 billion in bilateral aid (1979-89)
Currency:
  Saudi riyal (plural - riyals); 1 Saudi riyal (SR) = 100 halalas
Exchange rates:
  Saudi riyals (SR) per US$1 - 3.7450 (fixed rate since late 1986), 3.7033

(1986)

Fiscal year: calendar year

:Saudi Arabia Communications

Railroads:
  886 km 1.435-meter standard gauge
Highways:
  74,000 km total; 35,000 km paved, 39,000 km gravel and improved earth
Pipelines:
  crude oil 6,400 km, petroleum products 150 km, natural gas 2,200 km,
  includes natural gas liquids 1,600 km
Ports:
  Jiddah, Ad Dammam, Ras Tanura, Jizan, Al Jubayl, Yanbu al Bahr, Yanbu al
  Sinaiyah
Merchant marine:
  81 ships (1,000 GRT or over) totaling 884,470 GRT/1,254,882 DWT; includes 1
  passenger, 7 short-sea passenger, 11 cargo, 14 roll-on/roll-off cargo, 3
  container, 6 refrigerated cargo, 5 livestock carrier, 24 petroleum tanker, 7
  chemical tanker, 1 liquefied gas, 1 specialized tanker, 1 bulk
Civil air:
  104 major transport aircraft available
Airports:
  211 total, 191 usable; 70 with permanent-surface runways; 14 with runways
  over 3,659 m; 37 with runways 2,440-3,659 m; 105 with runways 1,220-2,439 m
Telecommunications:
  good system with extensive microwave and coaxial and fiber optic cable
  systems; 1,624,000 telephones; broadcast stations - 43 AM, 13 FM, 80 TV;
  radio relay to Bahrain, Jordan, Kuwait, Qatar, UAE, Yemen, and Sudan;
  coaxial cable to Kuwait and Jordan; submarine cable to Djibouti, Egypt and
  Bahrain; earth stations - 3 Atlantic Ocean INTELSAT, 2 Indian Ocean
  INTELSAT, 1 ARABSAT, 1 INMARSAT

:Saudi Arabia Defense Forces

Branches:
  Land Force (Army), Navy, Air Force, Air Defense Force, National Guard, Coast
  Guard, Frontier Forces, Special Security Force, Public Security Force
Manpower availability:
  males 15-49, 5,619,147; 3,118,261 fit for military service; 133,314 reach
  military age (17) annually
Defense expenditures:
  exchange rate conversion - $14.5 billion, 13% of GDP (1992 budget)

Senegal Geography

Total area: 196,190 km2
Land area: 192,000 km2
Comparative area: slightly smaller than South Dakota
Land boundaries:
  2,640 km total; The Gambia 740 km, Guinea 330 km, Guinea-Bissau 338 km, Mali
  419 km, Mauritania 813 km
Coastline:
  531 km

Maritime claims:
  Contiguous zone:
    24 nm
  Continental shelf:
    edge of continental margin or 200 nm
  Exclusive fishing zone:
    200 nm
  Territorial sea:
    12 nm
Disputes:
    short section of the boundary with The Gambia is indefinite; the
    International Court of Justice (ICJ) on 12 November 1991 rendered its
    decision on the Guinea-Bissau/ Senegal maritime boundary in favor of Senegal
    - that decision has been rejected by Guinea-Bissau; boundary with Mauritania
Climate:
    tropical; hot, humid; rainy season (December to April) has strong southeast
    winds; dry season (May to November) dominated by hot, dry harmattan wind
Terrain:
    generally low, rolling, plains rising to foothills in southeast
Natural resources:
    fish, phosphates, iron ore
Land use:
    arable land 27%; permanent crops 0%; meadows and pastures 30%; forest and
    woodland 31%; other 12%; includes irrigated 1%
Environment:
    lowlands seasonally flooded; deforestation; overgrazing; soil erosion;
    desertification
Note:
    The Gambia is almost an enclave

:Senegal People

Population: 8,205,058 (July 1992), growth rate 3.1% (1992)
Birth rate: 44 births/1,000 population (1992)
Death rate: 13 deaths/1,000 population (1992)
Net migration rate: 0 migrants/1,000 population (1992)
Infant mortality rate: 80 deaths/1,000 live births (1992)
Life expectancy at birth: 54 years male, 57 years female (1992)
Total fertility rate: 6.2 children born/woman (1992)
Nationality:
    noun - Senegalese (singular and plural); adjective - Senegalese
Ethnic divisions:
    Wolof 36%, Fulani 17%, Serer 17%, Toucouleur 9%, Diola 9%, Mandingo 9%,
    European and Lebanese 1%, other 2%
Religions:
    Muslim 92%, indigenous beliefs 6%, Christian 2% (mostly Roman Catholic)
Languages:
    French (official); Wolof, Pulaar, Diola, Mandingo
Literacy:
    38% (male 52%, female 25%) age 15 and over can read and write (1990 est.)
Labor force:

2,509,000; 77% subsistence agricultural workers; 175,000 wage earners -
private sector 40%, government and parapublic 60%; 52% of population of
working age (1985)
Organized labor:
majority of wage-labor force represented by unions; however, dues-paying
membership very limited; major confederation is National Confederation of
Senegalese Labor (CNTS), an affiliate of the governing party

:Senegal Government

Long-form name:
Republic of Senegal
Type:
republic under multiparty democratic rule
Capital: Dakar
Administrative divisions:
10 regions (regions, singular - region); Dakar, Diourbel, Fatick, Kaolack,
Kolda, Louga, Saint-Louis, Tambacounda, Thies, Ziguinchor
Independence:
20 August 1960 (from France); The Gambia and Senegal signed an agreement on
12 December 1981 (effective 1 February 1982) that called for the creation of
a loose confederation to be known as Senegambia, but the agreement was
dissolved on 30 September 1989
Constitution:
3 March 1963, last revised in 1991
Legal system:
based on French civil law system; judicial review of legislative acts in
Supreme Court, which also audits the government's accounting office; has not
accepted compulsory ICJ jurisdiction
National holiday:
Independence Day, 4 April (1960)
Executive branch:
president, prime minister, Council of Ministers (cabinet)
Legislative branch:
unicameral National Assembly (Assemblee Nationale)
Judicial branch:
Supreme Court (Cour Supreme)
Leaders:
 Chief of State:
 President Abdou DIOUF (since 1 January 1981)
 Head of Government:
 Prime Minister Habib THIAM (since 7 April 1991)
Political parties and leaders:
Socialist Party (PS), President Abdou DIOUF; Senegalese Democratic Party
(PDS), Abdoulaye WADE; 13 other small uninfluential parties
Suffrage:
universal at age 18
Elections:
 President:
 last held 28 February 1988 (next to be held NA February 1993); results -
 Abdou DIOUF (PS) 73%, Abdoulaye WADE (PDS) 26%, other 1%

National Assembly:
>last held 28 February 1988 (next to be held NA February 1993); results - PS
>71%, PDS 25%, other 4%; seats - (120 total) PS 103, PDS 17

Other political or pressure groups:
>students, teachers, labor, Muslim Brotherhoods

Member of:
>ACCT, ACP, AfDB, CCC, CEAO, ECA, ECOWAS, FAO, FZ, G-77, GATT, IAEA, IBRD,
>ICAO, ICC, IDA, IDB, IFAD, IFC, ILO, IMF, IMO, INTELSAT, INTERPOL, IOC, ISO
>(correspondent), ITU, LORCS, NAM, OAU, OIC, PCA, UN, UNCTAD, UNESCO, UNIDO,
>UNIIMOG, UPU, WADB, WCL, WFTU, WHO, WIPO, WMO, WTO

Diplomatic representation:
>Ambassador Ibra Deguene KA; Chancery at 2112 Wyoming Avenue NW, Washington,
>DC 20008; telephone (202) 234-0540 or 0541

US:
>Ambassador Katherine SHIRLEY; Embassy on Avenue Jean XXIII at the corner of
>Avenue Kleber, Dakar (mailing address is B. P. 49, Dakar); telephone [221]
>23-42-96 or 23-34-24; FAX [221] 22-29-91

:Senegal Government

Flag:
>three equal vertical bands of green (hoist side), yellow, and red with a
>small green five-pointed star centered in the yellow band; uses the popular
>pan-African colors of Ethiopia

:Senegal Economy

Overview:
>The agricultural sector accounts for about 20% of GDP and provides
>employment for about 75% of the labor force. About 40% of the total
>cultivated land is used to grow peanuts, an important export crop. The
>principal economic resource is fishing, which brought in about $200 million
>or about 25% of total foreign exchange earnings in 1987. Mining is dominated
>by the extraction of phosphate, but production has faltered because of
>reduced worldwide demand for fertilizers in recent years. Over the past 10
>years tourism has become increasingly important to the economy.

GDP:
>exchange rate conversion - $5.0 billion, per capita $615; real growth rate
>3.6% (1990)

Inflation rate (consumer prices):
>2.0% (1990)

Unemployment rate: 3.5% (1987)

Budget:
>revenues $921 million; expenditures $1,024 million; including capital
>expenditures of $14 million (FY89 est.)

Exports:
>$814 million (f.o.b., 1990 est.)

commodities:
>manufactures 30%, fish products 27%, peanuts 11%, petroleum products 11%,

phosphates 10%
partners:
  France, other EC members, Mali, Ivory Coast, India
Imports:
  $1.05 billion (c.i.f., 1990 est.)
commodities:
  semimanufactures 30%, food 27%, durable consumer goods 17%, petroleum 12%,
  capital goods 14%
partners:
  France, other EC, Ivory Coast, Nigeria, Algeria, China, Japan
External debt: $2.9 billion (1990)
Industrial production:
  growth rate 4.7% (1989); accounts for 15% of GDP
Electricity:
  215,000 kW capacity; 760 million kWh produced, 100 kWh per capita (1991)
Industries:
  agricultural and fish processing, phosphate mining, petroleum refining,
  building materials
Agriculture:
  including fishing, accounts for 20% of GDP and more than 75% of labor force;
  major products - peanuts (cash crop), millet, corn, sorghum, rice, cotton,
  tomatoes, green vegetables; estimated two-thirds self-sufficient in food;
  fish catch of 299,000 metric tons in 1987
Economic aid:
  US commitments, including Ex-Im (FY70-89), $551 million; Western (non-US)
  countries, ODA and OOF bilateral commitments (1970-89), $5.23 billion; OPEC
  bilateral aid (1979-89), $589 million; Communist countries (1970-89), $295
  million
Currency:
  Communaute Financiere Africaine franc (plural - francs); 1 CFA franc (CFAF)
  = 100 centimes
Exchange rates:
  Communaute Financiere Africaine francs (CFAF) per US$1 - 269.01 (January
  1992), 282.11 (1991), 272.26 (1990), 319.01 (1989), 297.85 (1988), 300.54
  (1987)

:Senegal Economy

Fiscal year: 1 July - 30 June; note - in January 1993, Senegal will switch to a calendar
  year

:Senegal Communications

Railroads:
  1,034 km 1.000-meter gauge; all single track except 70 km double track Dakar
  to Thies
Highways:
  14,007 km total; 3,777 km paved, 10,230 km laterite or improved earth
Inland waterways:
  897 km total; 785 km on the Senegal, 112 km on the Saloum
Ports:
  Dakar, Kaolack, Foundiougne, Ziguinchor
Merchant marine:

2 ships (1,000 GRT and over) totaling 7,676 GRT/12,310 DWT; includes 1
cargo, 1 bulk
Civil air:
3 major transport aircraft
Airports:
25 total, 19 usable; 10 with permanent-surface runways; none with runways
over 3,659 m; 1 with runways 2,440-3,659 m; 15 with runways 1,220-2,439 m
Telecommunications:
above-average urban system, using microwave and cable; broadcast stations -
8 AM, no FM, 1 TV; 3 submarine cables; 1 Atlantic Ocean INTELSAT earth
station

:Senegal Defense Forces

Branches:
Army, Navy, Air Force, Gendarmerie, National Police
Manpower availability:
males 15-49, 1,814,452; 947,723 fit for military service; 88,271 reach
military age (18) annually
Defense expenditures:
exchange rate conversion - $100 million, 2% of GDP (1989 est.)

Serbia and Montenegro Geography

Total area: 102,350 km2
Land area: 102,136 km2: note - Serbia has a total area and a land area of 88,412 km2
while Montenegro has a total area of 13,938 km2 and a land area of 13,724
km2
Comparative area: slightly larger than Kentucky; note - Serbia is slightly larger than
Maine
while Montenegro is slightly larger than Connecticut
Land boundaries:
2,234 km total; Albania 287 km (114 km with Serbia, 173 km with Montenegro),
Bosnia and Hercegovina 527 km (312 km with Serbia, 215 km with Montenegro),
Bulgaria 318 km, Croatia (north) 239 km, Croatia (south) 15 km, Hungary 151
km, Macedonia 221 km, Romania 476 km; note - the internal boundary between
Montenegro and Serbia is 211 km
Coastline:
199 km; Montenegro 199 km, Serbia 0 km
Maritime claims:
none - landlocked
Contiguous zone:
NA nm
Continental shelf:
NA meter depth
Exclusive fishing zone:
NA nm
Exclusive economic zone:
NA nm
Territorial sea:
12 nm
Disputes:
Sandzak region bordering northern Montenegro and southeastern Serbia -

Muslims seeking autonomy; Vojvodina taken from Hungary and awarded to the former Yugoslavia (Serbia) by Treaty of Trianon in 1920; disputes with Bosnia and Herzegovina and Croatia over Serbian populated areas; Albanian minority in Kosovo seeks independence from Serbian Republic

Climate:
in the north, continental climate - cold winter and hot, humid summers with well distributed rainfall; central portion, continental and Mediterranean climate; to the south, Adriatic climate along the coast, hot, dry summers and autumns and relatively cold winters with heavy snowfall inland

Terrain:
extremely varied; to the north, rich fertile plains; to the east, limestone ranges and basins; to the southeast, ancient mountain and hills; to the southwest, extremely high shoreline with no islands off the coast; home of largest lake in former Yugoslavia, Lake Scutari

Natural resources:
oil, gas, coal, antimony, copper, lead, zinc, nickel, gold, pyrite, chrome

Land use:
arable land 30%; permanent crops 5%; meadows and pastures 20%; forest and woodland 25%; other 20%; includes irrigated 5%

Environment:
coastal water pollution from sewage outlets, especially in tourist related areas such as Kotor; air pollution around Belgrade and other industrial cities; water pollution along Danube from industrial waste dump into the Sava which drains into the Danube; subject to destructive earthquakes

Note:
controls one of the major land routes from Western Europe to Turkey and the Near East; strategic location along the Adriatic coast

:Serbia and Montenegro People

Population: 10,642,000 (July 1992), growth rate NA% (1991)
Birth rate: NA births/1,000 population (1992)
Death rate: NA deaths/1,000 population (1992)
Net migration rate: NA migrants/1,000 population (1992)
Infant mortality rate: NA deaths/1,000 live births (1992)
Life expectancy at birth: Serbia - 70.11 years male, 75.21 years female (1992); Montenegro - 76.33
years male, 82.27 years female (1992)
Total fertility rate: NA children born/woman (1992)
Nationality:
noun - Serbian(s) and Montenegrin(s); adjective - Serbian and Montenegrin
Ethnic divisions:
Serbs 63%, Albanians 14%, Montenegrins 6%, Hungarians 4%
Religions:
Orthodox 65%, Muslim 19%, Roman Catholic 4%, Protestant 1%, other 11%
Languages:
Serbo-Croatian 100%
Literacy:
89% (male 95%, female 83%) age 10 and over can read and write (1991 est.)
Labor force:
2,640,909; industry, mining 40%, agriculture 5% (1990)

Organized labor:
NA

:Serbia and Montenegro Government

Long-form name:
none
Type:
republic
Capital: Belgrade
Administrative divisions:
2 provinces (pokajine, singular - pokajina); and 2 automous provinces*;
Kosovo*, Montenegro, Serbia, Vojvodina*
Independence:
NA April 1992
Constitution:
NA April 1992
Legal system:
based on civil law system
National holiday:
NA
Executive branch:
president, vice president, prime minister, deputy prime minister
Legislative branch:
Parliament
Judicial branch:
NA
Leaders:
 Chief of State:
 President Dobric COSIC (since NA), Vice President Branko KOSTIC (since July
 1991); note - Slobodan MILOSEVIC is president of Serbia
 Head of Government:
 Prime Minister Milan PANIC (since 14 July 1992), Deputy Prime Minister
 Aleksandr MITROVIC (since March 1989)
Political parties and leaders:
former Communisty Party, Slobodan MILOSEVIC; Serbian Radical Party, Vojislav
SESELJ; Serbian Renewal Party, Vok DRASKOVIC
Suffrage:
at age 16 if employed, universal at age 18
Elections:
 President:
 NA
 Parliament:
 last held 4 June 1992 (next to be held NA); results - percent of vote by
 party NA; seats - (138 total) former Community Party 73, Radical Party 33,
 other 32
Communists:
NA
Other political or pressure groups:
NA
Member of:

CSCE, UN
Diplomatic representation:
none; US does not recognize Serbia and Montenegro
Flag:
NA

:Serbia and Montenegro Economy

Overview:
The swift collapse of the Yugoslav federation has been accompanied by bloody
ethnic warfare, the destabilization of republic boundaries, and the breakup
of important interrepublic trade flows. The situation in Serbia and
Montenegro remains fluid in view of the extensive political and military
strife. This new state faces major economic problems. First, like the other
former Yugoslav republics, Serbia and Montenegro depended on their sister
republics for large amounts of foodstuffs, energy supplies, and
manufactures. Wide varieties in climate, mineral resources, and levels of
technology among the six republics accentuated this interdependence, as did
the Communist practice of concentrating much industrial output in a small
number of giant plants. The breakup of many of the trade links, the sharp
drop in output as industrial plants lost suppliers and markets, and the
destruction of physical assets in the fighting all have contributed to the
economic difficulties of the republics. One singular factor in the economic
situation of Serbia and Montenegro is the continuation in office of a
Communist government that is primarily interested in political and military
mastery, not economic reform. A further complication is the major economic
sanctions by the leading industrial nations.
GDP:
exchange rate conversion - $44 billion, per capita $4,200; real growth rate
NA% (1990)
Inflation rate (consumer prices):
60% per month
Unemployment rate: 25-40%
Budget:
NA
Exports:
$4.4 billion (f.o.b., 1990)
commodities:
machinery and transport equipment 29%, manufactured goods 28.5%,
miscellaneous manufactured articles 13.5%, chemicals 11%, food and live
animals 9%, raw materials 6%, fuels and lubricants 2%, beverages and tobacco
1%
partners:
principally the other former Yugoslav republics; Italy, Germany, other EC,
the former USSR, East European countries, US
Imports:
$6.4 billion (c.i.f., 1990)
commodities:
machinery and transport equipment 26%, fuels and lubricants 18%,
manufactured goods 16%, chemicals 12.5%, food and live animals 11%,
miscellaneous manufactured items 8%, raw materials, including coking coal

857

for the steel industry, 7%, beverages, tobacco, and edible oils 1.5%
partners:
  principally the other former Yugoslav republics; the former USSR, EC
  countries (mainly Italy and Germany), East European countries, US
External debt: $4.2 billion (may assume some part of foreign debt of former Yugoslavia)
Industrial production:
  growth rate -20% or greater (1991 est.)
Electricity:
  8,633,000 kW capacity; 34,600 million kWh produced, 3,496 kWh per capita
  (1991)

:Serbia and Montenegro Economy

Industries:
  machine building (aircraft, trucks, and automobiles; armored vehicles and
  weapons; electrical equipment; agricultural machinery), metallurgy (steel,
  aluminum, copper, lead, zinc, chromium, antimony, bismuth, cadmium), mining
  (coal, bauxite, nonferrous ore, iron ore, limestone), consumer goods
  (textiles, footwear, foodstuffs, appliances), electronics, petroleum
  products, chemicals, and pharmaceuticals
Agriculture:
  the fertile plains of Vojvodina produce 80% of the cereal production of the
  former Yugoslavia and most of the cotton, oilseeds, and chicory; Vojvodina
  also produces fodder crops to support intensive beef and dairy production;
  Serbia proper, although hilly, has a well-distributed rainfall and a long
  growing season; produces fruit, grapes, and cereals; in this area, livestock
  production (sheep and cattle) and dairy farming prosper; Kosovo province
  produces fruits, vegetables, tobacco, and a small amount of cereals; the
  mountainous pastures of Kosovo and Montenegro support sheep and goat
  husbandry; Montenegro has only a small agriculture sector, mostly near the
  coast where a Mediterranean climate permits the culture of olives, citrus,
  grapes, and rice
Illicit drugs:
  NA
Economic aid:
  NA
Currency:
  Yugoslav New Dinar (plural - New Dinars); 1 Yugo New Dinar (YD) = 100 paras
Exchange rates:
  Yugoslav New Dinars (YD) per US $1 - 28.230 (December 1991), 15.162 (1990),
  15.528 (1989), 0.701 (1988), 0.176 (1987)
Fiscal year: calendar year

:Serbia and Montenegro Communications

Railroads:
  NA
Highways:
  46,019 km total (1990); 26,949 km paved, 10,373 km gravel, 8,697 km earth
Inland waterways:
  NA km
Pipelines:

crude oil 415 km, petroleum products 130 km, natural gas 2,110 km
Ports:
  maritime - Bar; inland - Belgrade
Merchant marine:
  43 ships (1,000 GRT or over) totaling 866,915 GRT/1,449,094 DWT; includes 19
  cargo, 5 container, 16 bulk carriers, 2 combination/ore carrier and 1
  passenger ship, under Serbian and Montenegrin flag; note - Montenegro also
  operates 3 bulk carriers under the flags of Panama and Saint Vincent and the
  Grenadines
Civil air:
  NA
Airports:
  NA
Telecommunications:
  700,000 telephones; broadcast stations - 26 AM, 9 FM, 18 TV; 2,015,000
  radios; 1,000,000 TVs; satellite ground stations - 1 Atlantic Ocean INTELSAT

:Serbia and Montenegro Defense Forces

Branches:
  Army, Navy, and Air Forces
Manpower availability:
  males 15-49, 2,545,357; NA fit for military service; 96,832 reach military
  age (18) annually (est.)
Defense expenditures:
  $NA, NA% of GDP

Seychelles Geography

Total area: 455 km2
Land area: 455 km2
Comparative area: slightly more than 2.5 times the size of Washington, DC
Land boundaries:
  none
Coastline:
  491 km
Maritime claims:
 Continental shelf:
  edge of continental margin or 200 nm
 Exclusive economic zone:
  200 nm
 Territorial sea:
  12 nm
Disputes:
  claims Tromelin Island
Climate:
  tropical marine; humid; cooler season during southeast monsoon (late May to
  September); warmer season during northwest monsoon (March to May)
Terrain:
  Mahe Group is granitic, narrow coastal strip, rocky, hilly; others are
  coral, flat, elevated reefs
Natural resources:
  fish, copra, cinnamon trees

Land use:
  arable land 4%; permanent crops 18%; meadows and pastures 0%; forest and
  woodland 18%; other 60%
Environment:
  lies outside the cyclone belt, so severe storms are rare; short droughts
  possible; no fresh water - catchments collect rain; 40 granitic and about 50
  coralline islands
Note:
  located north-northeast of Madagascar in the Indian Ocean

:Seychelles People

Population: 69,519 (July 1992), growth rate 0.8% (1992)
Birth rate: 23 births/1,000 population (1992)
Death rate: 7 deaths/1,000 population (1992)
Net migration rate: -8 migrants/1,000 population (1992)
Infant mortality rate: 15 deaths/1,000 live births (1992)
Life expectancy at birth: 65 years male, 75 years female (1992)
Total fertility rate: 2.4 children born/woman (1992)
Nationality:
  noun - Seychellois (singular and plural); adjective - Seychelles
Ethnic divisions:
  Seychellois (mixture of Asians, Africans, Europeans)
Religions:
  Roman Catholic 90%, Anglican 8%, other 2%
Languages:
  English and French (official); Creole
Literacy:
  85% (male NA%, female NA%) age 15 and over can read and write (1990)
Labor force:
  27,700; industry and commerce 31%, services 21%, government 20%,
  agriculture, forestry, and fishing 12%, other 16% (1985); 57% of population
  of working age (1983)
Organized labor:
  three major trade unions

:Seychelles Government

Long-form name:
  Republic of Seychelles
Type:
  republic
Capital: Victoria
Administrative divisions:
  23 administrative districts; Anse aux Pins, Anse Boileau, Anse Etoile, Anse
  Louis, Anse Royale, Baie Lazare, Baie Sainte Anne, Beau Vallon, Bel Air, Bel
  Ombre, Cascade, Glacis, Grand' Anse (on Mahe Island), Grand' Anse (on
  Praslin Island), La Digue, La Riviere Anglaise, Mont Buxton, Mont Fleuri,
  Plaisance, Pointe La Rue, Port Glaud, Saint Louis, Takamaka
Independence:
  29 June 1976 (from UK)
Constitution:
  5 June 1979

Legal system:
  based on English common law, French civil law, and customary law
National holiday:
  Liberation Day (anniversary of coup), 5 June (1977)
Executive branch:
  president, Council of Ministers
Legislative branch:
  unicameral People's Assembly (Assemblee du Peuple)
Judicial branch:
  Court of Appeal, Supreme Court
Leaders:
  Chief of State and Head of Government:
  President France Albert RENE (since 5 June 1977)
Political parties and leaders:
  ruling party - Seychelles People's Progressive Front (SPPF), France Albert
  RENE; note - in December 1991, President RENE announced that the Seychelles
  would begin an immediate transition to a multiparty political system;
  registration of new political parties was scheduled to begin in January 1992
Suffrage:
  universal at age 17
Elections:
  election of delegates to a multiparty constitutional conference is scheduled
  for June 1992
 President:
  last held 9-11 June 1989 (next to be held NA June 1994); results - President
  France Albert RENE reelected without opposition
 People's Assembly:
  last held 5 December 1987 (next to be held NA December 1992); results - SPPF
  was the only legal party; seats - (25 total, 23 elected) SPPF 23
Other political or pressure groups:
  trade unions, Roman Catholic Church
Member of:
  ACCT, ACP, AfDB, C, ECA, FAO, G-77, IBRD, ICAO, ICFTU, IFAD, IFC, ILO,
  IMF,
  IMO, INTERPOL, IOC, NAM, OAU, UN, UNCTAD, UNESCO, UNIDO, UPU,
  WCL, WHO, WMO
Diplomatic representation:
  Second Secretary, Charge d'Affaires ad interim Marc R. MARENGO; Chancery
  (temporary) at 820 Second Avenue, Suite 900F, New York, NY 10017; telephone
  (212) 687-9766
 US:
  Ambassador Richard W. CARLSON; Embassy at 4th Floor, Victoria House,
  Victoria (mailing address is Box 148, Victoria, and Victoria House, Box 251,
  Victoria, Mahe, Seychelles, or APO AE 09815-2501); telephone (248) 25256;
  FAX (248) 25189

:Seychelles Government

Flag:
  three horizontal bands of red (top), white (wavy), and green; the white band
  is the thinnest, the red band is the thickest

861

:Seychelles Economy

Overview:

In this small, open, tropical island economy, the tourist industry employs about 30% of the labor force and provides more than 70% of hard currency earnings. In recent years the government has encouraged foreign investment in order to upgrade hotels and other services. At the same time, the government has moved to reduce the high dependence on tourism by promoting the development of farming, fishing, and small-scale manufacturing.

GDP:

exchange rate conversion - $350 million, per capita $5,200; real growth rate -4.5% (1991 est.)

Inflation rate (consumer prices):

1.8% (1990 est.)

Unemployment rate: 9% (1987)

Budget:

revenues $180 million; expenditures $202 million, including capital expenditures of $32 million (1989)

Exports:

$40 million (f.o.b., 1990 est.)

commodities:

fish, copra, cinnamon bark, petroleum products (reexports)

partners:

France 63%, Pakistan 12%, Reunion 10%, UK 7% (1987)

Imports:

$186 million (f.o.b., 1990 est.)

commodities:

manufactured goods, food, tobacco, beverages, machinery and transportation equipment, petroleum products

partners:

UK 20%, France 14%, South Africa 13%, PDRY 13%, Singapore 8%, Japan 6% (1987)

External debt: $189 million (1991 est.)

Industrial production:

growth rate 7% (1987); accounts for 10% of GDP

Electricity:

30,000 kW capacity; 80 million kWh produced, 1,160 kWh per capita (1991)

Industries:

tourism, processing of coconut and vanilla, fishing, coir rope factory, boat building, printing, furniture, beverage

Agriculture:

accounts for 7% of GDP, mostly subsistence farming; cash crops - coconuts, cinnamon, vanilla; other products - sweet potatoes, cassava, bananas; broiler chickens; large share of food needs imported; expansion of tuna fishing under way

Economic aid:

US commitments, including Ex-Im (FY78-89), $26 million; Western (non-US) countries, ODA and OOF bilateral commitments (1978-89), $315 million; OPEC bilateral aid (1979-89), $5 million; Communist countries (1970-89), $60 million

Currency:

Seychelles rupee (plural - rupees); 1 Seychelles rupee (SRe) = 100 cents
Exchange rates:
  Seychelles rupees (SRe) per US$1 - 5.2946 (March 1992), 5.2893 (1991),
  5.3369 (1990), 5.6457 (1989), 5.3836 (1988), 5.6000 (1987)
Fiscal year: calendar year

:Seychelles Communications

Highways:
  260 km total; 160 km paved, 100 km crushed stone or earth
Ports:
  Victoria
Merchant marine:
  1 refrigerated cargo totaling 1,827 GRT/2,170 DWT
Civil air:
  1 major transport aircraft
Airports:
  14 total, 14 usable; 8 with permanent-surface runways; none with runways
  over 3,659 m; 1 with runways 2,440-3,659 m; none with runways 1,220-2,439 m
Telecommunications:
  direct radio communications with adjacent islands and African coastal
  countries; 13,000 telephones; broadcast stations - 2 AM, no FM, 2 TV; 1
  Indian Ocean INTELSAT earth station; USAF tracking station

:Seychelles Defense Forces

Branches:
  Army, Navy, Air Force, Presidential Protection Unit, Police Force, Militia
Manpower availability:
  males 15-49, 17,739; 9,096 fit for military service
Defense expenditures:
  exchange rate conversion - $12 million, 4% of GDP (1990 est.)

Sierra Leone Geography

Total area: 71,740 km2
Land area: 71,620 km2
Comparative area: slightly smaller than South Carolina
Land boundaries:
  958 km total; Guinea 652 km, Liberia 306 km
Coastline:
  402 km
Maritime claims:
 Territorial sea:
  200 nm
Disputes:
  none
Climate:
  tropical; hot, humid; summer rainy season (May to December); winter dry
  season (December to April)
Terrain:
  coastal belt of mangrove swamps, wooded hill country, upland plateau,
  mountains in east
Natural resources:

diamonds, titanium ore, bauxite, iron ore, gold, chromite

Land use:

arable land 25%; permanent crops 2%; meadows and pastures 31%; forest and woodland 29%; other 13%; includes irrigated NEGL%

Environment:

extensive mangrove swamps hinder access to sea; deforestation; soil degradation

:Sierra Leone People

Population: 4,456,737 (July 1992), growth rate -0.2% (1992)
Birth rate: 46 births/1,000 population (1992)
Death rate: 20 deaths/1,000 population (1992)
Net migration rate: -28 migrants/1,000 population (1992)
Infant mortality rate: 148 deaths/1,000 live births (1992)
Life expectancy at birth: 43 years male, 48 years female (1992)
Total fertility rate: 6.1 children born/woman (1992)
Nationality:

noun - Sierra Leonean(s); adjective - Sierra Leonean

Ethnic divisions:

native African 99% (Temne 30%, Mende 30%); Creole, European, Lebanese, and Asian 1%; 13 tribes

Religions:

Muslim 30%, indigenous beliefs 30%, Christian 10%, other or none 30%

Languages:

English (official); regular use limited to literate minority; principal vernaculars are Mende in south and Temne in north; Krio is the language of the resettled ex-slave population of the Freetown area and is lingua franca

Literacy:

21% (male 31%, female 11%) age 15 and over can read and write English, Mende, Temne, or Arabic (1990 est.)

Labor force:

1,369,000 (est.); agriculture 65%, industry 19%, services 16% (1981); only about 65,000 earn wages (1985); 55% of population of working age

Organized labor:

35% of wage earners

:Sierra Leone Government

Long-form name:

Republic of Sierra Leone

Type:

military government

Capital: Freetown

Administrative divisions:

Western Area and 3 provinces; Eastern, Northern, Southern

Independence:

27 April 1961 (from UK)

Constitution:

1 October 1991; amended September 1991

Legal system:

based on English law and customary laws indigenous to local tribes; has not accepted compulsory ICJ jurisdiction

National holiday:
  Republic Day, 27 April (1961)
Executive branch:
  National Provisional Ruling Council
Legislative branch:
  unicameral House of Representatives (suspended after coup of 29 April 1992)
Judicial branch:
  Supreme Court (suspended after coup of 29 April 1992)
Leaders:
  Chief of State and Head of Government:
    President Gen. Joseph Saidu MOMOH was ousted in coup of 29 April 1992;
    succeeded by Chairman of the National Provisional Ruling Council Valentine
    STRASSER (since 29 April 1992)
Political parties and leaders:
  status of existing political parties are unknown following 29 April 1992
  coup
Suffrage:
  universal at age 18
Elections:
  suspended after 29 April 1992 coup; Chairman STRASSER promises multi-party
  elections sometime in the future
Member of:
  ACP, AfDB, C, CCC, ECA, ECOWAS, FAO, G-77, GATT, IAEA, IBRD, ICAO,
  ICFTU,
  IDA, IDB, IFAD, IFC, ILO, IMF, IMO, INTERPOL, IOC, ITU, LORCS, NAM,
  OAU,
  OIC, UN, UNCTAD, UNESCO, UNIDO, UPU, WCL, WHO, WIPO, WMO, WTO
Diplomatic representation:
  Ambassador (vacant); Chancery at 1701 19th Street NW, Washington, DC 20009;
  telephone (202) 939-9261
  US:
  Ambassador Johnny YOUNG; Embassy at the corner of Walpole and Siaka Stevens
  Street, Freetown; telephone [232] (22) 226-481; FAX [232] (22) 225471
Flag:
  three equal horizontal bands of light green (top), white, and light blue

:Sierra Leone Economy

Overview:
  The economic and social infrastructure is not well developed. Subsistence
  agriculture dominates the economy, generating about one-third of GDP and
  employing about two-thirds of the working population. Manufacturing, which
  accounts for roughly 10% of GDP, consists mainly of the processing of raw
  materials and of light manufacturing for the domestic market. Diamond mining
  provides an important source of hard currency. The economy suffers from high
  unemployment, rising inflation, large trade deficits, and a growing
  dependency on foreign assistance. The government in 1990 was attempting to
  get the budget deficit under control and, in general, to bring economic
  policy in line with the recommendations of the IMF and the World Bank. Since
  March 1991, however, military incursions by Liberian rebels in southern and
  eastern Sierra Leone have severely strained the economy and have undermined

efforts to institute economic reforms.

GDP:
exchange rate conversion - $1.4 billion, per capita $330; real growth rate 3% (FY91 est.)

Inflation rate (consumer prices):
110% (1990)

Unemployment rate: NA%

Budget:
revenues $134 million; expenditures $187 million, including capital expenditures of $32 million (FY91 est.)

Exports:
$138 million (f.o.b., 1990)
commodities:
rutile 50%, bauxite 17%, cocoa 11%, diamonds 3%, coffee 3%
partners:
US, UK, Belgium, FRG, other Western Europe

Imports:
$146 million (c.i.f., 1990)
commodities:
capital goods 40%, food 32%, petroleum 12%, consumer goods 7%, light industrial goods
partners:
US, EC, Japan, China, Nigeria

External debt: $572 million (1990)

Industrial production:
NA

Electricity:
85,000 kW capacity; 185 million kWh produced, 45 kWh per capita (1991)

Industries:
mining (diamonds, bauxite, rutile), small-scale manufacturing (beverages, textiles, cigarettes, footwear), petroleum refinery

Agriculture:
accounts for over 30% of GDP and two-thirds of the labor force; largely subsistence farming; cash crops - coffee, cocoa, palm kernels; harvests of food staple rice meets 80% of domestic needs; annual fish catch averages 53,000 metric tons

Economic aid:
US commitments, including Ex-Im (FY70-89), $161 million; Western (non-US) countries, ODA and OOF bilateral commitments (1970-89), $848 million; OPEC bilateral aid (1979-89), $18 million; Communist countries (1970-89), $101 million

Currency:
leone (plural - leones); 1 leone (Le) = 100 cents

:Sierra Leone Economy

Exchange rates:
leones (Le) per US$1 - 476.74 (March 1992), 295.34 (1991), 144.9275 (1990), 58.1395 (1989), 31.2500 (1988), 30.7692 (1987)

Fiscal year: 1 July - 30 June

:Sierra Leone Communications

Railroads:
    84 km 1.067-meter narrow-gauge mineral line is used on a limited basis
    because the mine at Marampa is closed
Highways:
    7,400 km total; 1,150 km paved, 490 km laterite (some gravel), remainder
    improved earth
Inland waterways:
    800 km; 600 km navigable year round
Ports:
    Freetown, Pepel, Bonthe
Merchant marine:
    1 cargo ship totaling 5,592 GRT/9,107 DWT
Civil air:
    no major transport aircraft
Airports:
    12 total, 7 usable; 4 with permanent-surface runways; none with runways over
    3,659 m; 1 with runways 2,440-3,659 m; 3 with runways 1,220-2,439 m
Telecommunications:
    marginal telephone and telegraph service; national microwave system
    unserviceable at present; 23,650 telephones; broadcast stations - 1 AM, 1
    FM, 1 TV; 1 Atlantic Ocean INTELSAT earth station

:Sierra Leone Defense Forces

Branches:
    Army, Navy, National Police Force, Special Security Detachment
Manpower availability:
    males 15-49, 976,147; 472,112 fit for military service; no conscription
Defense expenditures:
    exchange rate conversion - $6 million, 0.7% of GDP (1988 est.)

Singapore Geography

Total area: 632.6 km2
Land area: 622.6 km2
Comparative area: slightly less than 3.5 times the size of Washington, DC
Land boundaries:
    none
Coastline:
    193 km
Maritime claims:
  Exclusive fishing zone:
    12 nm
  Territorial sea:
    3 nm
Disputes:
    two islands in dispute with Malaysia
Climate:
    tropical; hot, humid, rainy; no pronounced rainy or dry seasons;
    thunderstorms occur on 40% of all days (67% of days in April)
Terrain:
    lowland; gently undulating central plateau contains water catchment area and
    nature preserve

Natural resources:
  fish, deepwater ports
Land use:
  arable land 4%; permanent crops 7%; meadows and pastures 0%; forest and
  woodland 5%; other 84%
Environment:
  mostly urban and industrialized
Note:
  focal point for Southeast Asian sea routes

:Singapore People

Population: 2,792,092 (July 1992), growth rate 1.3% (1992)
Birth rate: 18 births/1,000 population (1992)
Death rate: 5 deaths/1,000 population (1992)
Net migration rate: 0 migrants/1,000 population (1992)
Infant mortality rate: 6 deaths/1,000 live births (1992)
Life expectancy at birth: 73 years male, 78 years female (1992)
Total fertility rate: 1.9 children born/woman (1992)
Nationality:
  noun - Singaporean(s); adjective - Singapore
Ethnic divisions:
  Chinese 76.4%, Malay 14.9%, Indian 6.4%, other 2.3%
Religions:
  majority of Chinese are Buddhists or atheists; Malays are nearly all Muslim
  (minorities include Christians, Hindus, Sikhs, Taoists, Confucianists)
Languages:
  Chinese, Malay, Tamil, and English (all official); Malay (national)
Literacy:
  88% (male 93%, female 84%) age 15 and over can read and write (1990 est.)
Labor force:
  1,485,800; financial, business, and other services 30.2%, manufacturing
  28.4%, commerce 22.0%, construction 9.0%, other 10.4% (1990)
Organized labor:
  210,000; 16.1% of labor force (1989)

:Singapore Government

Long-form name:
  Republic of Singapore
Type:
  republic within Commonwealth
Capital: Singapore
Administrative divisions:
  none
Independence:
  9 August 1965 (from Malaysia)
Constitution:
  3 June 1959, amended 1965; based on preindependence State of Singapore
  Constitution
Legal system:
  based on English common law; has not accepted compulsory ICJ jurisdiction
National holiday:

National Day, 9 August (1965)
Executive branch:
president, prime minister, two deputy prime ministers, Cabinet
Legislative branch:
unicameral Parliament
Judicial branch:
Supreme Court
Leaders:
Chief of State:
President WEE Kim Wee (since 3 September 1985)
Head of Government:
Prime Minister GOH Chok Tong (since 28 November 1990); Deputy Prime Minister
LEE Hsien Loong (since 28 November 1990); Deputy Prime Ministers ONG Teng
Cheong (since 2 January 1985) and LEE Hsien Loong
Political parties and leaders:
government:
People's Action Party (PAP), LEE Kuan Yew, secretary general;
opposition:
Workers' Party (WP), J. B. JEYARETNAM; Singapore Democratic Party (SDP),
CHIAM See Tong; National Solidarity Party (NSP), leader NA; Barisan Sosialis
(BS, Socialist Front), leader NA
Suffrage:
universal and compulsory at age 20
Elections:
President:
last held 31 August 1989 (next to be held NA August 1993); results -
President WEE Kim Wee was reelected by Parliament without opposition
Parliament:
last held 31 August 1991 (next to be held 31 August 1996); results - percent
of vote by party NA; seats - (81 total) PAP 77, SDP 3, WP 1
Communists:
200-500; Barisan Sosialis infiltrated by Communists; note - Communist party
illegal
Member of:
APEC, AsDB, ASEAN, C, CCC, CP, ESCAP, G-77, GATT, IAEA, IBRD, ICAO,
ICC,
ICFTU, IFC, ILO, IMF, IMO, INMARSAT, INTELSAT, INTERPOL, IOC, ISO,
ITU,
LORCS, NAM, UN, UNCTAD, UPU, WHO, WMO
Diplomatic representation:
Ambassador S. R. NATHAN; Chancery at 1824 R Street NW, Washington, DC
20009;
telephone (202) 667-7555
US:
Ambassador Robert D. ORR; Embassy at 30 Hill Street, Singapore 0617 (mailing
address is FPO AP 96534); telephone [65] 338-0251; FAX [65] 338-4550
:Singapore Government
Flag:
two equal horizontal bands of red (top) and white; near the hoist side of

the red band, there is a vertical, white crescent (closed portion is toward
the hoist side) partially enclosing five white five-pointed stars arranged
in a circle

:Singapore Economy

Overview:

Singapore has an open entrepreneurial economy with strong service and
manufacturing sectors and excellent international trading links derived from
its entrepot history. During the 1970s and early 1980s, the economy expanded
rapidly, achieving an average annual growth rate of 9%. Per capita GDP is
among the highest in Asia. The economy grew at a respectable 6.5% in 1991,
down from 8.3% in 1990, in part because of a slowdown in overseas demand and
lower growth in the financial and business services sector.

GDP:

exchange rate conversion - $38.3 billion, per capita $13,900; real growth
rate 6.5% (1991 est.)

Inflation rate (consumer prices):

3.4% (1991 est.)

Unemployment rate: 1.5% (1991 est.)

Budget:

revenues $9.8 billion; expenditures $9.0 billion, including capital
expenditures of $2.8 billion (FY91 est.)

Exports:

$57.8 billion (f.o.b., 1991 est.)

commodities:

includes transshipments to Malaysia - petroleum products, rubber,
electronics, manufactured goods

partners:

US 20%, Malaysia 15%, Japan 9%, Hong Kong 7%, Thailand 6%

Imports:

$65.8 billion (c.i.f., 1991 est.)

commodities:

includes transshipments from Malaysia - capital equipment, petroleum,
chemicals, manufactured goods, foodstuffs

partners:

Japan 21%, US 16%, Malaysia 15%, Taiwan 4%

External debt: $3.8 billion (1991 est.)

Industrial production:

growth rate 9% (1991 est.); accounts for 29% of GDP (1990)

Electricity:

4,000,000 kW capacity; 14,400 million kWh produced, 5,300 kWh per capita
(1990)

Industries:

petroleum refining, electronics, oil drilling equipment, rubber processing
and rubber products, processed food and beverages, ship repair, entrepot
trade, financial services, biotechnology

Agriculture:

occupies a position of minor importance in the economy; self-sufficient in
poultry and eggs; must import much of other food; major crops - rubber,
copra, fruit, vegetables

Economic aid:
  US commitments, including Ex-Im (FY70-83), $590 million; Western (non-US) countries, ODA and OOF bilateral commitments (1970-89), $1.0 billion
Currency:
  Singapore dollar (plural - dollars); 1 Singapore dollar (S$) = 100 cents
Exchange rates:
  Singapore dollars (S$) per US$1 - 1.6596 (March 1992), 1.7276 (1991), 1.8125 (1990), 1.9503 (1989), 2.0124 (1988), 2.1060 (1987)
Fiscal year: 1 April - 31 March

:Singapore Communications

Railroads:
  38 km of 1.000-meter gauge
Highways:
  2,597 km total (1984)
Ports:
  Singapore
Merchant marine:
  468 ships (1,000 GRT or over) totaling 8,751,619 GRT/14,195,718 DWT; includes 1 passenger-cargo, 126 cargo, 74 container, 7 roll-on/roll-off cargo, 5 refrigerated cargo, 18 vehicle carrier, 1 livestock carrier, 144 petroleum tanker, 5 chemical tanker, 4 combination ore/oil, 1 specialized tanker, 5 liquefied gas, 74 bulk, 2 combination bulk, 1 short-sea passenger; note - many Singapore flag ships are foreign owned
Civil air:
  38 major transport aircraft (est.)
Airports:
  10 total, 10 usable; 10 with permanent-surface runways; 2 with runways over 3,659 m; 4 with runways 2,440-3,659 m; 3 with runways 1,220-2,439 m
Telecommunications:
  good domestic facilities; good international service; good radio and television broadcast coverage; 1,110,000 telephones; broadcast stations - 13 AM, 4 FM, 2 TV; submarine cables extend to Malaysia (Sabah and peninsular Malaysia), Indonesia, and the Philippines; satellite earth stations - 1 Indian Ocean INTELSAT and 1 Pacific Ocean INTELSAT

:Singapore Defense Forces

Branches:
  Army, Navy, Air Force, People's Defense Force, Police Force
Manpower availability:
  males 15-49, 847,435; 626,914 fit for military service
Defense expenditures:
  exchange rate conversion - $1.7 billion, 4% of GDP (1990 est.)

Slovenia Geography

Total area: 20,296 km2
Land area: 20,296 km2
Comparative area: slightly larger than New Jersey
Land boundaries:
  998 km total; Austria 262 km, Croatia 455 km, Italy 199 km, Hungary 83 km
Coastline:

32 km
Maritime claims:
 Contiguous zone:
 NA nm
 Continental shelf:
 200 m or to depth of exploitation
 Exclusive economic zone:
 NA nm
 Exclusive fishing zone:
 NA nm
 Territorial sea:
 12 nm
Disputes:
    dispute with Croatia over fishing rights in the Adriatic; small vocal
    minority in northern Italy seeks the return of parts of southwestern
    Slovenia
Climate:
    Mediterranean climate on the coast, continental climate with mild to hot
    summers and cold winters in the plateaus and valleys to the east
Terrain:
    a short coastal strip on the Adriatic, an alpine mountain region adjacent to
    Italy, mixed mountain and valleys with numerous rivers to the east
Natural resources:
    lignite coal, lead, zinc, mercury, uranium, silver
Land use:
    arable land 10%; permanent crops 2%; meadows and pastures 20%; forest and
    woodland 45%; other 23%; includes irrigated 1%
Environment:
    Sava River polluted with domestic and industrial waste; heavy metals and
    toxic chemicals along coastal waters; near Koper, forest damage from air
    pollutants originating at metallurgical and chemical plants; subject to
    flooding and earthquakes

:Slovenia People

Population: 1,963,000 (July 1992), growth rate 0.2% (1992)
Birth rate: NA births/1,000 population (1992)
Death rate: NA deaths/1,000 population (1992)
Net migration rate: NA migrants/1,000 population (1992)
Infant mortality rate: NA deaths/1,000 live births (1992)
Life expectancy at birth: 70 years male, 78 years female (1992)
Total fertility rate: NA children born/woman (1992)
Nationality:
    noun - Slovene(s); adjective - Slovenia
Ethnic divisions:
    Slovene 91%, Croat 3%, Serb 2%, Muslim 1%, other 3%
Religions:
    Roman Catholic 94%, Orthodox Catholic 2%, Muslim 1%, other 3%
Languages:
    Slovenian 91%, Serbo-Croatian 7%, other 2%
Literacy:

99.2% (male 99.3%, female 99.1%) age 10 and over can read and write
Labor force:
786,036; 2% agriculture, manufacturing and mining 46%
Organized labor:
NA

:Slovenia Government

Long-form name:
Republic of Slovenia
Type:
emerging democracy
Capital: Ljubljana
Administrative divisions:
62 provinces (pokajine, singular - pokajina)
Independence:
25 June 1991; 15 January 1992 from Yugoslavia
Constitution:
adopted 23 December 1991, effective 23 December 1991
Legal system:
based on civil law system
National holiday:
NA
Executive branch:
president, 4 vice presidents
Legislative branch:
bicameral; consists of the State Assembly and the State Council; note - will
take effect after next election
Judicial branch:
NA
Leaders:
 Chief of State:
  President Milan KUCAN (since 22 April 1990); Vice President Matjaz KMECL
  (since 11 April 1990); Vice President Ivan OMAN (since 11 April 1990); Vice
  President Dusan PLUT (since 11 April 1990); Vice President Ciril ZLOBEC
  (since 11 April 1990)
 Head of Government:
  Prime Minister Janez DRNOVSEK (since 14 May 1992)
Political parties and leaders:
  Christian Democratic, Lozje PETERLE, chairman; Liberal Democratic, Janez
  DRNOVSEK, chairman; Social Democratic, Joze PUNIK, chairman; Socialist,
  Viktor ZAKELJ, chairman; Greens, Dusan PLUT, chairman; National Democratic,
  Rajko PIRNAT, chairman; Democratic Peoples Party, Marjan PODOBNIK, chair-
man;
  Reformed Socialists (former Communist Party), Ciril RIBICIC, chairman
Suffrage:
  at age 16 if employed, universal at age 18
Elections:
 President:
  last held NA (next to be held NA)
 State Assembly:

last held NA (next to be held NA);
State Council:
last held NA (next to be held NA)
Communists:
NA
Other political or pressure groups:
NA
Member of:
CSCE, IMF, UN
Diplomatic representation:
Representative Ernest PETRIC; Chancery at 1300 19th Street NW, Washington, DC 20036; telephone (202) 828-1650
US:
Ambassador Ignac GOLOB, Embassy at NA (mailing address is APO AE 09862); telephone NA

:Slovenia Government

Flag:
a three color flag, white (hoist side), blue, and red of equal width with the Slovenian seal (a shield with the image of Triglav in white against a blue background at the center; beneath it are two wavy blue lines depicting seas and rivers; around it, there are three six-sided stars arranged in an inverted triangle); the seal is located in the upper hoist side of the flag centered in the white and blue band

:Slovenia Economy

Overview:
Slovenia was by far the most prosperous of the old Yugoslav republics, with a per capita income more than twice the Yugoslav average, indeed not far below the levels in neighboring Austria and Italy. Because of its strong ties to Western Europe and the small scale of damage during internecine fighting in Yugoslavia, Slovenia has the brightest prospects among the former Yugoslav republics for economic reform and recovery over the next few years. The political and economic disintegration of Yugoslavia, however, has led to severe short-term dislocations in production, employment, and trade ties. For example, overall industrial production fell 10% in 1991; particularly hard hit were the iron and steel, machine-building, chemical, and textile industries. Meanwhile, fighting has continued in other republics leading to further destruction of long-established trade channels and to an influx of tens of thousands of Croatian refugees. As in other former Communist areas in Eastern Europe, economic reform has often sputtered not only because of the vested interests of old bosses in retaining old rules of the game but also because of the tangible losses experienced by rank-and-file people in the transition to a more market-oriented system. The key program for breaking up and privatizing major industrial firms has not yet begun. Bright spots for encouraging Western investors are Slovenia's comparatively well-educated work force, its developed infrastructure, and its Western business attitudes. Slovenia in absolute terms is a small economy, and a little Western investment would go a long way.
GDP:
$21 billion, per capita $10,700; real growth rate -10% (1991 est.)

Inflation rate (consumer prices):
   15-20% (1991 est.)
Unemployment rate: 10% (April 1992)
Budget:
   revenues $NA; expenditures $NA, including capital expenditures of $NA
Exports:
   $4,120 million (f.o.b., 1990)
  commodities:
   machinery and transport equipment 38%, other manufactured goods 44%,
   chemicals 9%, food and live animals 4.6%, raw materials 3%, beverages and
   tobacco less than 1%
  partners:
   principally the other former Yugoslav republics, Austria, and Italy
Imports:
   $4,679 million (c.i.f., 1990)
  commodities:
   machinery and transport equipment 35%, other manufactured goods 26.7%,
   chemicals 14.5%, raw materials 9.4%, fuels and lubricants 7%, food and live
   animals 6%
  partners:
   principally the other former Yugoslav republics, Germany, former USSR, US,
   Hungary, Italy, and Austria
External debt: $2.5 billion
Industrial production:
   industrial production has been declining at a rate of about 1% per month
   (1991-92), mostly because of lost markets in the other former Yugoslav
   republics
Electricity:
   2,900,000 kW capacity; 12,250 million kWh produced, 6,447 kWh per capita
   (1991)

:Slovenia Economy

Industries:
   ferrous metallurgy and rolling mill products, aluminum reduction and rolled
   products, lead and zinc smelting, electronics (including military
   electronics), trucks, electric power equipment, wood products, textiles,
   chemicals, machine tools
Agriculture:
   dominated by stock breeding (sheep and cattle) and dairy farming; main crops
   are potatoes, hops, hemp, and flax; although self-sufficient and having an
   export surplus in these commodities, Slovenia must import many other
   agricultural products and has a negative overall trade balance in this
   sector
Illicit drugs:
   NA
Economic aid:
   NA
Currency:
   Slovene Tolar (plural - Tolars); 1 Tolar (SLT) = 100 NA
Exchange rates:

Tolars (SLT) per US$1 - 28 (January 1992)

Fiscal year: calendar year

:Slovenia Communications

Railroads:
  NA
Highways:
  14,553 km total; 10,525 km paved, 4,028 km gravel
Inland waterways:
  NA
Pipelines:
  crude oil 290 km, natural gas 305 km
Ports:
  maritime - Koper
Merchant marine:
  0 ships (1,000 GRT or over) are under Slovenian flag; note - Slovenian
  owners control 21 ships (1,000 GRT or over) totaling 334,995 GRT/558,621
  DWT; includes 14 bulk carriers and 7 general cargo ships all under Saint
  Vincent and the Grenadines flag
Civil air:
  NA major transport aircraft
Airports:
  3 main airports
Telecommunications:
  130,000 telephones; broadcast stations - 6 AM, 5 FM, 7 TV; 370,000 radios;
  330,000 TVs

:Slovenia Defense Forces

Branches:
  Army, Navy, Air Force
Manpower availability:
  males 15-49, 444,030; NA fit for military service; 18,219 reach military age
  (18) annually
Defense expenditures:
  exchange rate conversion - 13.5 billion Slovene Tolars, 4.5% of GDP (1992);
  note - conversion of the military budget into US dollars using the current
  exchange rate could produce misleading results

Solomon Islands Geography

Total area: 28,450 km2
Land area: 27,540 km2
Comparative area: slightly larger than Maryland
Land boundaries:
  none
Coastline:
  5,313 km
Maritime claims:
  (measured from claimed archipelagic baselines)
 Exclusive economic zone:
  200 nm
 Territorial sea:

12 nm
Disputes:
  none
Climate:
  tropical monsoon; few extremes of temperature and weather
Terrain:
  mostly rugged mountains with some low coral atolls
Natural resources:
  fish, forests, gold, bauxite, phosphates
Land use:
  arable land 1%; permanent crops 1%; meadows and pastures 1%; forest and
  woodland 93%; other 4%
Environment:
  subject to typhoons, which are rarely destructive; geologically active
  region with frequent earth tremors
Note:
  located just east of Papua New Guinea in the South Pacific Ocean

:Solomon Islands People

Population: 360,010 (July 1992), growth rate 3.5% (1992)
Birth rate: 40 births/1,000 population (1992)
Death rate: 5 deaths/1,000 population (1992)
Net migration rate: 0 migrants/1,000 population (1992)
Infant mortality rate: 30 deaths/1,000 live births (1992)
Life expectancy at birth: 67 years male, 72 years female (1992)
Total fertility rate: 6.0 children born/woman (1992)
Nationality:
  noun - Solomon Islander(s); adjective - Solomon Islander
Ethnic divisions:
  Melanesian 93.0%, Polynesian 4.0%, Micronesian 1.5%, European 0.8%, Chinese
  0.3%, other 0.4%
Religions:
  almost all at least nominally Christian; Anglican 34%, Roman Catholic 19%,
  Baptist 17%, United (Methodist/Presbyterian) 11%, Seventh-Day Adventist 10%,
  other Protestant 5%
Languages:
  120 indigenous languages; Melanesian pidgin in much of the country is lingua
  franca; English spoken by 1-2% of population
Literacy:
  NA% (male NA%, female NA%)
Labor force:
  23,448 economically active; agriculture, forestry, and fishing 32.4%;
  services 25%; construction, manufacturing, and mining 7.0%; commerce,
  transport, and finance 4.7% (1984)
Organized labor:
  NA, but most of the cash-economy workers have trade union representation

:Solomon Islands Government

Long-form name:
  none
Type:

877

parliamentary democracy

Capital: Honiara

Administrative divisions:
  7 provinces and 1 town*; Central, Guadalcanal, Honiara*, Isabel, Makira,
  Malaita, Temotu, Western

Independence:
  7 July 1978 (from UK; formerly British Solomon Islands)

Constitution:
  7 July 1978

Legal system:
  common law

National holiday:
  Independence Day, 7 July (1978)

Executive branch:
  British monarch, governor general, prime minister, Cabinet

Legislative branch:
  unicameral National Parliament

Judicial branch:
  High Court

Leaders:
  Chief of State:
    Queen ELIZABETH II (since 6 February 1952), represented by Governor General
    Sir George LEPPING (since 27 June 1989, previously acted as governor general
    since 7 July 1988)
  Head of Government:
    Prime Minister Solomon MAMALONI (since 28 March 1989); Deputy Prime Minis-
ter
    Sir Baddeley DEVESI (since NA October 1990)

Political parties and leaders:
  People's Alliance Party (PAP); United Party (UP), leader NA; Solomon Islands
  Liberal Party (SILP), Bartholemew ULUFA'ALU; Nationalist Front for Progress
  (NFP), Andrew NORI; Labor Party (LP), Joses TUHANUKU

Suffrage:
  universal at age 21

Elections:
  National Parliament:
    last held 22 February 1989 (next to be held NA February 1993); results -
    percent of vote by party NA; seats - (38 total) PAP 13, UP 6, NFP 4, SILP 4,
    LP 2, independents 9

Member of:
  ACP, AsDB, C, ESCAP, FAO, G-77, IBRD, ICAO, IDA, IFAD, IFC, ILO, IMF,
IMO,
  IOC, ITU, SPC, SPF, UN, UNCTAD, UPU, WFTU, WHO, WMO

Diplomatic representation:
  Ambassador (vacant) resides in Honiara (Solomon Islands)
  US:
    the ambassador in Papua New Guinea is accredited to the Solomon Islands;
    Embassy at Mud Alley, Honiara (mailing address is American Embassy, P. O.
    Box 561, Honiara); telephone (677) 23890; FAX (677) 23488

Flag:

divided diagonally by a thin yellow stripe from the lower hoist-side corner; the upper triangle (hoist side) is blue with five white five-pointed stars arranged in an X pattern; the lower triangle is green

:Solomon Islands Economy

Overview:
About 90% of the population depend on subsistence agriculture, fishing, and forestry for at least part of their livelihood. Agriculture, fishing, and forestry contribute about 70% to GDP, with the fishing and forestry sectors being important export earners. The service sector contributes about 25% to GDP. Most manufactured goods and petroleum products must be imported. The islands are rich in undeveloped mineral resources such as lead, zinc, nickel, and gold. The economy suffered from a severe cyclone in mid-1986 that caused widespread damage to the infrastructure.

GDP:
exchange rate conversion - $200 million, per capita $600; real growth rate 6.0% (1990 est.)

Inflation rate (consumer prices):
10.2% (1990)

Unemployment rate: NA%

Budget:
revenues $44 million; expenditures $45 million, including capital expenditures of $22 million (1989 est.)

Exports:
$67.3 million (f.o.b., 1990)
commodities:
fish 46%, timber 31%, copra 5%, palm oil 5%
partners:
Japan 51%, UK 12%, Thailand 9%, Netherlands 8%, Australia 2%, US 2% (1985)

Imports:
$86.0 million (c.i.f., 1990)
commodities:
plant and machinery 30%, fuel 19%, food 16%
partners:
Japan 36%, US 23%, Singapore 9%, UK 9%, NZ 9%, Australia 4%, Hong Kong 4%, China 3% (1985)

External debt: $128 million (1988 est.)

Industrial production:
growth rate 0% (1987); accounts for 5% of GDP

Electricity:
21,000 kW capacity; 39 million kWh produced, 115 kWh per capita (1990)

Industries:
copra, fish (tuna)

Agriculture:
including fishing and forestry, accounts for about 70% of GDP; mostly subsistence farming; cash crops - cocoa, beans, coconuts, palm kernels, timber; other products - rice, potatoes, vegetables, fruit, cattle, pigs; not self-sufficient in food grains; 90% of the total fish catch of 44,500 metric tons was exported (1988)

Economic aid:

Western (non-US) countries, ODA and OOF bilateral commitments (1980-89),
$250 million

Currency:
  Solomon Islands dollar (plural - dollars); 1 Solomon Islands dollar (SI$) =
  100 cents

Exchange rates:
  Solomon Islands dollars (SI$) per US$1 - 2.8740 (March 1992), 2.7148 (1991),
  2.5288 (1990), 2.2932 (1989), 2.0825 (1988), 2.0033 (1987)

Fiscal year: calendar year

:Solomon Islands Communications

Highways:
  about 2,100 km total (1982); 30 km paved, 290 km gravel, 980 km earth, 800
  private logging and plantation roads of varied construction

Ports:
  Honiara, Ringi Cove

Civil air:
  no major transport aircraft

Airports:
  33 total, 30 usable; 2 with permanent-surface runways; none with runways
  over 2,439 m; 3 with runways 1,220-2,439 m

Telecommunications:
  3,000 telephones; broadcast stations - 4 AM, no FM, no TV; 1 Pacific Ocean
  INTELSAT earth station

:Solomon Islands Defense Forces

Branches:
  Police Force

Manpower availability:
  NA

Defense expenditures:
  exchange rate conversion - $NA, NA% of GDP

Somalia Geography

Total area: 637,660 km2
Land area: 627,340 km2
Comparative area: slightly smaller than Texas
Land boundaries:
  2,340 km total; Djibouti 58 km, Ethiopia 1,600 km, Kenya 682 km
Coastline:
  3,025 km
Maritime claims:
 Territorial sea:
  200 nm
Disputes:
  southern half of boundary with Ethiopia is a Provisional Administrative
  Line; territorial dispute with Ethiopia over the Ogaden; possible claims to
  Djibouti and parts of Ethiopia and Kenya based on unification of ethnic
  Somalis
Climate:
  desert; northeast monsoon (December to February), cooler southwest monsoon

(May to October); irregular rainfall; hot, humid periods (tangambili) between monsoons

Terrain:
mostly flat to undulating plateau rising to hills in north

Natural resources:
uranium and largely unexploited reserves of iron ore, tin, gypsum, bauxite, copper, salt

Land use:
arable land 2%; permanent crops NEGL%; meadows and pastures 46%; forest and woodland 14%; other 38%; includes irrigated 3%

Environment:
recurring droughts; frequent dust storms over eastern plains in summer; deforestation; overgrazing; soil erosion; desertification

Note:
strategic location on Horn of Africa along southern approaches to Bab el Mandeb and route through Red Sea and Suez Canal

:Somalia People

Population: 7,235,226 (July 1992), growth rate 2.1% (1992)
Birth rate: 46 births/1,000 population (1992)
Death rate: 13 deaths/1,000 population (1992)
Net migration rate: -12 migrants/1,000 population (1992)
Infant mortality rate: 115 deaths/1,000 live births (1992)
Life expectancy at birth: 56 years male, 57 years female (1992)
Total fertility rate: 7.1 children born/woman (1992)

Nationality:
noun - Somali(s); adjective - Somali

Ethnic divisions:
Somali 85%, rest mainly Bantu; Arabs 30,000, Europeans 3,000, Asians 800

Religions:
almost entirely Sunni Muslim

Languages:
Somali (official); Arabic, Italian, English

Literacy:
24% (male 36%, female 14%) age 15 and over can read and write (1990 est.)

Labor force:
2,200,000; very few are skilled laborers; pastoral nomad 70%, agriculture, government, trading, fishing, handicrafts, and other 30%; 53% of population of working age (1985)

Organized labor:
General Federation of Somali Trade Unions was controlled by the government prior to January 1991; the fall of SIAD regime may have led to collapse of Trade Union organization

:Somalia Government

Long-form name:
none

Type:
none

Capital: Mogadishu

Administrative divisions:

16 regions (plural - NA, singular - gobolka); Bakool, Banaadir, Bari, Bay, Galguduud, Gedo, Hiiraan, Jubbada Dhexe, Jubbada Hoose, Mudug, Nugaal, Sanaag, Shabeellaha Dhexe, Shabeellaha Hoose, Togdheer, Woqooyi Galbeed

Independence:
1 July 1960 (from a merger of British Somaliland, which became independent from the UK on 26 June 1960, and Italian Somaliland, which became independent from the Italian-administered UN trusteeship on 1 July 1960, to form the Somali Republic)

Constitution:
25 August 1979, presidential approval 23 September 1979

National holiday:
NA

Executive branch:
president, two vice presidents, prime minister, Council of Ministers (cabinet)

Legislative branch:
unicameral People's Assembly (Golaha Shacbiga)

Judicial branch:
Supreme Court

Leaders:
Chief of State:
Interim President ALI Mahdi Mohamed (since 27 January 1991)
Head of Government:
Prime Minister OMAR Arteh Ghalib (since 27 January 1991)

Political parties and leaders:
the United Somali Congress (USC) ousted the former regime on 27 January 1991; note - formerly the only party was the Somali Revolutionary Socialist Party (SRSP), headed by former President and Commander in Chief of the Army Maj. Gen. Mohamed SIAD Barre

Suffrage:
universal at age 18

Elections:
President:
last held 23 December 1986 (next to be held NA); results - President SIAD was reelected without opposition
People's Assembly:
last held 31 December 1984 (next to be held NA); results - SRSP was the only party; seats - (177 total, 171 elected) SRSP 171; note - the United Somali Congress (USC) ousted the regime of Maj. Gen. Mohamed SIAD Barre on 27 January 1991; the provisional government has promised that a democratically elected government will be established

Member of:
ACP, AfDB, AFESD, AL, AMF, CAEU, ECA, FAO, G-77, IBRD, ICAO, IDA, IDB, IFAD,
IFC, IGADD, ILO, IMF, IMO, INTELSAT, INTERPOL, IOC, IOM (observer), ITU,
LORCS, NAM, OAU, OIC, UN, UNCTAD, UNESCO, UNHCR, UNIDO, UPU, WHO, WIPO, WMO

Diplomatic representation:
Ambassador (vacant); Chancery at Suite 710, 600 New Hampshire Avenue NW,

Washington, DC 20037; telephone (202) 342-1575; there is a Somali Consulate
General in New York; note - Somalian Embassy ceased operations on 8 May 1991

:Somalia Government

US:
Ambassador (vacant); Embassy at K-7, AFGOI Road, Mogadishu (mailing address
is P. O. Box 574, Mogadishu); telephone [252] (01) 39971; note - US Embassy
evacuated and closed indefinitely in January 1991

Flag:
light blue with a large white five-pointed star in the center; design based
on the flag of the UN (Italian Somaliland was a UN trust territory)

:Somalia Economy

Overview:
One of the world's poorest and least developed countries, Somalia has few
resources. Agriculture is the most important sector of the economy, with the
livestock sector accounting for about 40% of GDP and about 65% of export
earnings. Nomads and seminomads who are dependent upon livestock for their
livelihoods make up more than half of the population. Crop production
generates only 10% of GDP and employs about 20% of the work force. The main
export crop is bananas; sugar, sorghum, and corn are grown for the domestic
market. The small industrial sector is based on the processing of
agricultural products and accounts for less than 10% of GDP. Greatly
increased political turmoil in 1991-92 has resulted in a substantial drop in
output, with widespread famine a grim fact of life.

GDP:
exchange rate conversion - $1.7 billion, per capita $210; real growth rate
-1.4% (1988)

Inflation rate (consumer prices):
210% (1989)

Unemployment rate: NA%

Budget:
revenues $190 million; expenditures $195 million, including capital
expenditures of $111 million (1989 est.)

Exports:
$58.0 million (f.o.b., 1990 est.)
commodities:
bananas, livestock, fish, hides, skins
partners:
US 0.5%, Saudi Arabia, Italy, FRG (1986)

Imports:
$249 million (c.i.f., 1990 est.)
commodities:
petroleum products, foodstuffs, construction materials
partners:
US 13%, Italy, FRG, Kenya, UK, Saudi Arabia (1986)

External debt: $1.9 billion (1989)

Industrial production:
growth rate -5.0% (1988); accounts for 5% of GDP

Electricity:
75,000 kW capacity; 60 million kWh produced, 10 kWh per capita (1991)

Industries:
　a few small industries, including sugar refining, textiles, petroleum
　refining
Agriculture:
　dominant sector, led by livestock raising (cattle, sheep, goats); crops -
　bananas, sorghum, corn, mangoes, sugarcane; not self-sufficient in food;
　fishing potential largely unexploited
Economic aid:
　US commitments, including Ex-Im (FY70-89), $639 million; Western (non-US)
　countries, ODA and OOF bilateral commitments (1970-89), $3.8 billion; OPEC
　bilateral aid (1979-89), $1.1 billion; Communist countries (1970-89), $336
　million
Currency:
　Somali shilling (plural - shillings); 1 Somali shilling (So. Sh.) = 100
　centesimi
Exchange rates:
　Somali shillings (So. Sh.) per US$1 - 3,800.00 (December 1990), 490.7
　(1989), 170.45 (1988), 105.18 (1987), 72.00 (1986)

:Somalia Economy

Fiscal year:　　calendar year

:Somalia Communications

Highways:
　15,215 km total; including 2,335 km paved, 2,880 km gravel, and 10,000 km
　improved earth or stabilized soil (1983)
Pipelines:
　crude oil 15 km
Ports:
　Mogadishu, Berbera, Chisimayu, Bosaso
Merchant marine:
　3 ships (1,000 GRT or over) totaling 6,913 GRT/8,718 DWT; includes 2 cargo,
　1 refrigerated cargo
Civil air:
　1 major transport aircraft
Airports:
　53 total, 40 usable; 7 with permanent-surface runways; 2 with runways over
　3,659 m; 6 with runways 2,440-3,659 m; 15 with runways 1,220-2,439 m
Telecommunications:
　minimal telephone and telegraph service; microwave and troposcatter system
　centered on Mogadishu connects a few towns; 6,000 telephones; broadcast
　stations - 2 AM, no FM, 1 TV; 1 Indian Ocean INTELSAT earth station;
　scheduled to receive an ARABSAT ground station

:Somalia Defense Forces

Branches:
　NA
Manpower availability:
　males 15-49, 1,673,542; 942,153 fit for military service
Defense expenditures:
　exchange rate conversion - $NA, NA% of GDP

South Africa Geography

Total area: 1,221,040 km2
Land area: 1,221,040 km2; includes Walvis Bay, Marion Island, and Prince Edward Island
Comparative area: slightly less than twice the size of Texas
Land boundaries:
  4,973 km total; Botswana 1,840 km, Lesotho 909 km, Mozambique 491 km, Namibia 1,078 km, Swaziland 430 km, Zimbabwe 225 km
Coastline:
  2,881 km
Maritime claims:
 Continental shelf:
  200 m (depth) or to depth of exploitation
 Exclusive fishing zone:
  200 nm
 Territorial sea:
  12 nm
Disputes:
  claim by Namibia to Walvis Bay exclave and 12 offshore islands administered by South Africa; South Africa and Namibia have agreed to jointly administer the area for an interim period; the terms and dates to be covered by joint administration arrangements have not been established at this time; and Namibia will continue to maintain a claim to sovereignty over the entire area
Climate:
  mostly semiarid; subtropical along coast; sunny days, cool nights
Terrain:
  vast interior plateau rimmed by rugged hills and narrow coastal plain
Natural resources:
  gold, chromium, antimony, coal, iron ore, manganese, nickel, phosphates, tin, uranium, gem diamonds, platinum, copper, vanadium, salt, natural gas
Land use:
  arable land 10%; permanent crops 1%; meadows and pastures 65%; forest and woodland 3%; other 21%; includes irrigated 1%
Environment:
  lack of important arterial rivers or lakes requires extensive water conservation and control measures
Note:
  Walvis Bay is an exclave of South Africa in Namibia; South Africa completely surrounds Lesotho and almost completely surrounds Swaziland

:South Africa People

Population: 41,688,360 (July 1992), growth rate 2.6% (1992); includes the 10 so-called
  homelands, which are not recognized by the US
Population: four independent homelands:
  Bophuthatswana 2,489,347, growth rate 2.86%; Ciskei 1,088,476, growth rate 2.99%; Transkei 4,746,796, growth rate 4.13%; Venda 718,207, growth rate 3.81%
 six other homelands:

Gazankulu 803,806, growth rate 3.96%; Kangwane 597,783, growth rate 3.60%; KwaNdebele 373,012, growth rate 3.40%; KwaZulu 5,748,950, growth rate 3.58%; Lebowa 2,924,584, growth rate 3.90%; QwaQwa 288,155, growth rate 3.60%

Birth rate: 34 births/1,000 population (1992)
Death rate: 8 deaths/1,000 population (1992)
Net migration rate: NEGL migrants/1,000 population (1992)
Infant mortality rate: 50 deaths/1,000 live births (1992)
Life expectancy at birth: 62 years male, 67 years female (1992)
Total fertility rate: 4.4 children born/woman (1992)
Nationality:
   noun - South African(s); adjective - South African
Ethnic divisions:
   black 75.2%, white 13.6%, Colored 8.6%, Indian 2.6%
Religions:
   most whites and Coloreds and about 60% of blacks are Christian; about 60% of Indians are Hindu; Muslim 20%
Languages:
   Afrikaans, English (both official); many vernacular languages, including Zulu, Xhosa, North and South Sotho, Tswana
Literacy:
   76% (male 78%, female 75%) age 15 and over can read and write (1980)
Labor force:
   11,000,000 economically active (1989); services 34%, agriculture 30%, industry and commerce 29%, mining 7% (1985)
Organized labor:
   about 17% of total labor force belongs to a registered trade union (1989); African unions represent 15% of black labor force

:South Africa Government

Long-form name:
   Republic of South Africa; abbreviated RSA
Type:
   republic
Capital: Pretoria (administrative); Cape Town (legislative); Bloemfontein (judicial)
Administrative divisions:
   4 provinces; Cape, Natal, Orange Free State, Transvaal; there are 10 homelands not recognized by the US - 4 independent (Bophuthatswana, Ciskei, Transkei, Venda) and 6 other (Gazankulu, Kangwane, KwaNdebele, KwaZulu, Lebowa, QwaQwa)
Independence:
   31 May 1910 (from UK)
Constitution:
   3 September 1984
Legal system:
   based on Roman-Dutch law and English common law; accepts compulsory ICJ jurisdiction, with reservations
National holiday:
   Republic Day, 31 May (1910)
Executive branch:
   state president, Executive Council (cabinet), Ministers' Councils (from the

three houses of Parliament)

Legislative branch:

tricameral Parliament (Parlement) consists of the House of Assembly (Volksraad; whites), House of Representatives (Raad van Verteenwoordigers; Coloreds), and House of Delegates (Raad van Afgevaardigdes; Indians)

Judicial branch:

Supreme Court

Leaders:

Chief of State and Head of Government:

State President Frederik W. DE KLERK (since 13 September 1989)

Political parties and leaders:

white political parties and leaders:

National Party (NP), Frederik W. DE KLERK (majority party); Conservative Party (CP), Dr. Andries P. TREURNICHT (official opposition party); Democratic Party (DP), Zach DE BEER

Colored political parties and leaders:

Labor Party (LP), Allan HENDRICKSE (majority party); Freedom Party; note - the Democratic Reform Party (DRP) and the United Democratic Party (UDP) were disbanded in May 1991

Indian political parties and leaders:

Solidarity, J. N. REDDY (majority party); National People's Party (NPP), Amichand RAJBANSI; Merit People's Party

Suffrage:

universal at age 18, but voting rights are racially based

Elections:

House of Assembly (whites):

last held 6 September 1989 (next to be held by NA March 1995); results - NP 58%, CP 23%, DP 19%; seats - (178 total, 166 elected) NP 103, CP 41, DP 34; note - by February 1992 because of byelections, changes in number of seats held by parties were as follows: NP 102, CP 42, DP 33, vacant 1

House of Representatives (Coloreds):

last held 6 September 1989 (next to be held no later than March 1995); results - percent of vote by party NA; seats - (85 total, 80 elected) LP 69, DRP 5, UDP 3, Freedom Party 1, independents 2; note - since the National Party became multiracial, by February 1992 many representatives from other parties have changed their allegiance causing the following changes in seating: LP 39, NP 38, Freedom Party 1, independents 7

:South Africa Government

House of Delegates (Indians):

last held 6 September 1989 (next to be held no later than March 1995); results - percent of vote by party NA; seats - (45 total, 40 elected) Solidarity 16, NPP 9, Merit People's Party 3, independents 6, other 6; note - due to delegates changing party affiliation, seating as of February 1992 is as follows: Solidarity 25, NPP 7, Merit People's Party 2, other 5, independents 5, vacancy 1

Communists:

South African Communist Party, Chris HANI, secretary general, and Joe SLOVO, national chairman

Other political or pressure groups:

African National Congress (ANC), Nelson MANDELA, president; Inkatha Freedom
Party (IFP), Mangosuthu BUTHELEZI, president; Pan-Africanist Congress (PAC),
Clarence MAKWETU, president

Member of:

BIS, CCC, ECA, GATT, IAEA, IBRD, ICAO (suspended), ICC, IDA, IFC, IMF,
INTELSAT, ISO, ITU (suspended), LORCS, SACU, UN, UNCTAD, WFTU, WHO,
WIPO,

WMO (suspended)

Diplomatic representation:

Ambassador Harry SCHWARZ; Chancery at 3051 Massachusetts Avenue NW,
Washington, DC 20008; telephone (202) 232-4400; there are South African
Consulates General in Beverly Hills (California), Chicago, Houston, and New
York

US:

Ambassador William L. SWING; Embassy at Thibault House, 225 Pretorius
Street, Pretoria; telephone [27] (12) 28-4266, FAX [27] (12) 21-92-78; there
are US Consulates General in Cape Town, Durban, and Johannesburg

Flag:

actually four flags in one - three miniature flags reproduced in the center
of the white band of the former flag of the Netherlands, which has three
equal horizontal bands of orange (top), white, and blue; the miniature flags
are a vertically hanging flag of the old Orange Free State with a horizontal
flag of the UK adjoining on the hoist side and a horizontal flag of the old
Transvaal Republic adjoining on the other side

:South Africa Economy

Overview:

Many of the white one-seventh of the South African population enjoy incomes,
material comforts, and health and educational standards equal to those of
Western Europe. In contrast, most of the remaining population suffers from
the poverty patterns of the Third World, including unemployment, lack of job
skills, and barriers to movement into higher-paying fields. Inputs and
outputs thus do not move smoothly into the most productive employments, and
the effectiveness of the market is further lowered by international
constraints on dealings with South Africa. The main strength of the economy
lies in its rich mineral resources, which provide two-thirds of exports.
Average growth of less than 2% in output in recent years falls far short of
the 5% to 6% level needed to absorb some 300,000 new entrants to the labor
force annually. Economic developments in the 1990s will be driven partly by
the changing relations among the various ethnic groups.

GDP:

exchange rate conversion - $104 billion, per capita $2,600; real growth rate
- 0.5% (1991 est.)

Inflation rate (consumer prices):

15.7% (March 1992)

Unemployment rate: 40% (1991); well over 50% in some homeland areas (1991 est.)

Budget:

revenues $29.4 billion; expenditures $35.0 billion, including capital
expenditures of $1.1 billion (FY93 est.)

Exports:

$24.0 billion (f.o.b., 1991)
commodities:
  gold 25-30%, minerals and metals 20-25%, food 5%, chemicals 3%
partners:
  Italy, Japan, US, FRG, UK, other EC members, Hong Kong
Imports:
  $18.8 billion (c.i.f., 1991)
commodities:
  machinery 32%, transport equipment 15%, chemicals 11%, oil, textiles,
  scientific instruments, base metals
partners:
  FRG, Japan, UK, US, Italy
External debt: $19.0 billion (December 1991)
Industrial production:
  growth rate NA%; accounts for about 40% of GDP
Electricity:
  46,000,000 kW capacity; 180,000 million kWh produced, 4,100 kWh per capita
  (1991)
Industries:
  mining (world's largest producer of platinum, gold, chromium), automobile
  assembly, metalworking, machinery, textile, iron and steel, chemical,
  fertilizer, foodstuffs
Agriculture:
  accounts for about 5% of GDP and 30% of labor force; diversified
  agriculture, with emphasis on livestock; products - cattle, poultry, sheep,
  wool, milk, beef, corn, wheat, sugarcane, fruits, vegetables;
  self-sufficient in food
Economic aid:
  NA
Currency:
  rand (plural - rand); 1 rand (R) = 100 cents

:South Africa Economy

Exchange rates:
  rand (R) per US$1 - 2.7814 (January 1992), 2.7563 (1991), 2.5863 (1990),
  2.6166 (1989), 2.2611 (1988), 2.0350 (1987)
Fiscal year: 1 April - 31 March

:South Africa Communications

Railroads:
  20,638 km route distance total; 35,079 km of 1.067-meter gauge trackage
  (counts double and multiple tracking as single track); 314 km of 610 mm
  gauge
Highways:
  188,309 km total; 54,013 km paved, 134,296 km crushed stone, gravel, or
  improved earth
Pipelines:
  crude oil 931 km, petroleum products 1,748 km, natural gas 322 km
Ports:
  Durban, Cape Town, Port Elizabeth, Richard's Bay, Saldanha, Mosselbaai,
  Walvis Bay

Merchant marine:
  5 ships (1,000 GRT or over) totaling 213,708 GRT/201,043 DWT; includes 4
  container, 1 vehicle carrier
Civil air:
  90 major transport aircraft
Airports:
  901 total, 732 usable; 132 with permanent-surface runways; 5 with runways
  over 3,659 m; 10 with runways 2,440-3,659 m; 224 with runways 1,220-2,439 m
Telecommunications:
  the system is the best developed, most modern, and has the highest capacity
  in Africa; it consists of carrier-equipped open-wire lines, coaxial cables,
  radio relay links, fiber optic cable, and radiocommunication stations; key
  centers are Bloemfontein, Cape Town, Durban, Johannesburg, Port Elizabeth,
  and Pretoria; over 4,500,000 telephones; broadcast stations - 14 AM, 286 FM,
  67 TV; 1 submarine cable; satellite earth stations - 1 Indian Ocean INTELSAT
  and 2 Atlantic Ocean INTELSAT

:South Africa Defense Forces

Branches:
  South African Defense Force (SADF; including Army, Navy, Air Force, Medical
  Services), South African Police (SAP)
Manpower availability:
  males 15-49, 10,051,202; 6,133,484 fit for military service; 420,275 reach
  military age (18) annually; obligation for service in Citizen Force or
  Commandos begins at 18; volunteers for service in permanent force must be
  17; national service obligation is one year; figures include the so-called
  homelands not recognized by the US
Defense expenditures:
  exchange rate conversion - $3.5 billion, about 3% of GDP (FY92)

South Georgia and the South Sandwich Islands Geography

Total area: 4,066 km2
Land area: 4,066 km2; includes Shag and Clerke Rocks, South Georgia, Bird Island,
South
  Sandwich Islands
Comparative area: slightly larger than Rhode Island
Land boundaries:
  none
Coastline:
  undetermined
Maritime claims:
  Territorial sea:
  12 nm
Disputes:
  administered by the UK, claimed by Argentina
Climate:
  variable, with mostly westerly winds throughout the year, interspersed with
  periods of calm; nearly all precipitation falls as snow
Terrain:
  most of the islands, rising steeply from the sea, are rugged and
  mountainous; South Georgia is largely barren and has steep, glacier-covered

mountains; the South Sandwich Islands are of volcanic origin with some active volcanoes

Natural resources:
  fish

Land use:
  arable land 0%; permanent crops 0%; meadows and pastures 0%; forest and woodland 0%; other 100%; largely covered by permanent ice and snow with some sparse vegetation consisting of grass, moss, and lichen

Environment:
  reindeer, introduced early in this century, live on South Georgia; weather conditions generally make it difficult to approach the South Sandwich Islands; the South Sandwich Islands are subject to active volcanism

Note:
  the north coast of South Georgia has several large bays, which provide good anchorage

:South Georgia and the South Sandwich Islands People

Population: no permanent population; there is a small military garrison on South Georgia, and the British Antarctic Survey has a biological station on Bird Island; the South Sandwich Islands are uninhabited

:South Georgia and the South Sandwich Islands Government

Long-form name:
  South Georgia and the South Sandwich Islands (no short-form name)

Type:
  dependent territory of the UK

Capital: none; Grytviken on South Georgia is the garrison town

Administrative divisions:
  none (dependent territory of the UK)

Independence:
  none (dependent territory of the UK)

Constitution:
  3 October 1985

Legal system:
  English common law

National holiday:
  Liberation Day, 14 June (1982)

Executive branch:
  British monarch, commissioner

Legislative branch:
  none

Judicial branch:
  none

Leaders:
  Chief of State:
  Queen ELIZABETH II (since 6 February 1952), represented by Commissioner William Hugh FULLERTON (since 1988; resident at Stanley, Falkland Islands)

:South Georgia and the South Sandwich Islands Economy

Overview:
  Some fishing takes place in adjacent waters. There is a potential source of

891

income from harvesting fin fish and krill. The islands receive income from postage stamps produced in the UK.

Budget:
revenues $291,777; expenditures $451,011, including capital expenditures of $NA (FY88 est.)

Electricity:
900 kW capacity; 2 million kWh produced, NA kWh per capita (1990)

:South Georgia and the South Sandwich Islands Communications

Highways:
NA

Ports:
Grytviken on South Georgia

Airports:
5 total, 5 usable; 2 with permanent-surface runways; 1 with runway 2,440-3,659 m

Telecommunications:
coastal radio station at Grytviken; no broadcast stations

:South Georgia and the South Sandwich Islands Defense Forces

Note: defense is the responsibility of the UK

Spain Geography

Total area: 504,750 km2
Land area: 499,400 km2; includes Balearic Islands, Canary Islands, and five places of sovereignty (plazas de soberania) on and off the coast of Morocco - Ceuta, Mellila, Islas Chafarinas, Penon de Alhucemas, and Penon de Velez de la Gomera

Comparative area: slightly more than twice the size of Oregon

Land boundaries:
1,903.2 km total; Andorra 65 km, France 623 km, Gibraltar 1.2 km, Portugal 1,214 km

Coastline:
4,964 km

Maritime claims:
 Exclusive economic zone:
 200 nm
 Territorial sea:
 12 nm

Disputes:
Gibraltar question with UK; Spain controls five places of sovereignty (plazas de soberania) on and off the coast of Morocco - the coastal enclaves of Ceuta and Melilla, which Morocco contests, as well as the islands of Penon de Alhucemas, Penon de Velez de la Gomera, and Islas Chafarinas

Climate:
temperate; clear, hot summers in interior, more moderate and cloudy along coast; cloudy, cold winters in interior, partly cloudy and cool along coast

Terrain:
large, flat to dissected plateau surrounded by rugged hills; Pyrenees in north

Natural resources:

coal, lignite, iron ore, uranium, mercury, pyrites, fluorspar, gypsum, zinc, lead, tungsten, copper, kaolin, potash, hydropower

Land use:

arable land 31%; permanent crops 10%; meadows and pastures 21%; forest and woodland 31%; other 7%; includes irrigated 6%

Environment:

deforestation; air pollution

Note:

strategic location along approaches to Strait of Gibraltar

:Spain People

Population: 39,118,399 (July 1992), growth rate 0.2% (1992)
Birth rate: 11 births/1,000 population (1992)
Death rate: 9 deaths/1,000 population (1992)
Net migration rate: NEGL migrants/1,000 population (1992)
Infant mortality rate: 7 deaths/1,000 live births (1992)
Life expectancy at birth: 74 years male, 81 years female (1992)
Total fertility rate: 1.4 children born/woman (1992)
Nationality:

noun - Spaniard(s); adjective - Spanish

Ethnic divisions:

composite of Mediterranean and Nordic types

Religions:

Roman Catholic 99%, other sects 1%

Languages:

Castilian Spanish; second languages include Catalan 17%, Galician 7%, Basque 2%

Literacy:

95% (male 97%, female 93%) age 15 and over can read and write (1990 est.)

Labor force:

14,621,000; services 53%, industry 24%, agriculture 14%, construction 9% (1988)

Organized labor:

less 10% of labor force (1988)

:Spain Government

Long-form name:

Kingdom of Spain

Type:

parliamentary monarchy

Capital: Madrid

Administrative divisions:

17 autonomous communities (comunidades autonomas, singular - comunidad autonoma); Andalucia, Aragon, Asturias, Canarias, Cantabria, Castilla-La Mancha, Castilla y Leon, Cataluna, Communidad Valencia, Extremadura, Galicia, Islas Baleares, La Rioja, Madrid, Murcia, Navarra, Pais Vasco; note - there are five places of sovereignty on and off the coast of Morocco (Ceuta, Mellila, Islas Chafarinas, Penon de Alhucemas, and Penon de Velez de la Gomera) with administrative status unknown

Independence:

1492 (expulsion of the Moors and unification)

Constitution:
  6 December 1978, effective 29 December 1978
Legal system:
  civil law system, with regional applications; does not accept compulsory ICJ
  jurisdiction
National holiday:
  National Day, 12 October
Executive branch:
  monarch, president of the government (prime minister), deputy prime
  minister, Council of Ministers (cabinet), Council of State
Legislative branch:
  bicameral The General Courts or National Assembly (Las Cortes Generales)
  consists of an upper house or Senate (Senado) and a lower house or Congress
  of Deputies (Congreso de los Diputados)
Judicial branch:
  Supreme Court (Tribunal Supremo)
Leaders:
 Chief of State:
  King JUAN CARLOS I (since 22 November 1975)
 Head of Government:
  Prime Minister Felipe GONZALEZ Marquez (since 2 December 1982); Deputy
Prime
  Minister Narcis SERRA (since 13 March 1991)
Political parties and leaders:
  principal national parties, from right to left - Popular Party (PP), Jose
  Maria AZNAR; Popular Democratic Party (PDP), Luis DE GRANDES; Social
  Democratic Center (CDS), Rafael Calvo ORTEGA; Spanish Socialist Workers
  Party (PSOE), Felipe GONZALEZ Marquez; Socialist Democracy Party (DS),
  Ricardo Garcia DAMBORENEA; Spanish Communist Party (PCE), Julio
ANGUITA;
  chief regional parties - Convergence and Unity (CiU), Jordi PUJOL Saley, in
  Catalonia; Basque Nationalist Party (PNV), Xabier ARZALLUS; Basque
  Solidarity (EA), Carlos GARAICOETXEA Urizza; Basque Popular Unity (HB), Jon
  IDIGORAS; Basque Left (EE), Kepa AULESTIA; Andalusian Party (PA), Pedro
  PACHECO; Independent Canary Group (AIC); Aragon Regional Party (PAR);
  Valencian Union (UV)
Suffrage:
  universal at age 18
Elections:
 Senate:
  last held 29 October 1989 (next to be held NA October 1993); results -
  percent of vote by party NA; seats - (208 total) PSOE 106, PP 79, CiU 10,
  PNV 4, HB 3, AIC 1, other 5
:Spain Government

 Congress of Deputies:
  last held 29 October 1989 (next to be held NA October 1993); results - PSOE
  39.6%, PP 25.8%, CDS 9%, Communist-led coalition (IU) 9%, CiU 5%, PNV 1.2%,
  HB 1%, PA 1%, other 8.4%; seats - (350 total) PSOE 175, PP 106, CiU 18, IU
  17, CDS 14, PNV 5, HB 4, other 11

Communists:

PCE membership declined from a possible high of 160,000 in 1977 to roughly 60,000 in 1987; the party gained almost 1 million voters and 10 deputies in the 1989 election; voters came mostly from the disgruntled socialist left; remaining strength is in labor, where it dominates the Workers Commissions trade union (one of the country's two major labor centrals), which claims a membership of about 1 million; experienced a modest recovery in 1986 national election, nearly doubling the share of the vote it received in 1982

Other political or pressure groups:

on the extreme left, the Basque Fatherland and Liberty (ETA) and the First of October Antifascist Resistance Group (GRAPO) use terrorism to oppose the government; free labor unions (authorized in April 1977) include the Communist-dominated Workers Commissions (CCOO); the Socialist General Union of Workers (UGT), and the smaller independent Workers Syndical Union (USO); the Catholic Church; business and landowning interests; Opus Dei; university students

Member of:

AG (observer), AsDB, BIS, CCC, CE, CERN, COCOM, CSCE, EBRD, EC, ECE, ECLAC,

EIB, ESA, FAO, G-8, GATT, IADB, IAEA, IBRD, ICAO, ICC, ICFTU, IDA, IEA, IFAD, IFC, ILO, IMF, IMO, INMARSAT, INTELSAT, INTERPOL, IOC, IOM (observer),

ISO, ITU, LAIA (observer), LORCS, NAM (guest), NATO, NEA, OAS (observer), OECD, PCA, UN, UNAVEM, UNCTAD, UNESCO, UNIDO, UPU, WCL, WEU, WHO, WIPO, WMO,

WTO

Diplomatic representation:

Ambassador Jaime de OJEDA; Chancery at 2700 15th Street NW, Washington, DC 20009; telephone (202) 265-0190 or 0191; there are Spanish Consulates General in Boston, Chicago, Houston, Los Angeles, Miami, New Orleans, New York, San Francisco, and San Juan (Puerto Rico)

US:

Ambassador Joseph ZAPPALA; Embassy at Serrano 75, 28006 Madrid (mailing address is APO AE 09642); telephone [34] (1) 577-4000, FAX [34] (1) 577-5735; there is a US Consulate General in Barcelona and a Consulate in Bilbao

Flag:

three horizontal bands of red (top), yellow (double width), and red with the national coat of arms on the hoist side of the yellow band; the coat of arms includes the royal seal framed by the Pillars of Hercules, which are the two promontories (Gibraltar and Ceuta) on either side of the eastern end of the Strait of Gibraltar

:Spain Economy

Overview:

Spain has done well since joining the EC in 1986. In accordance with its accession treaty, Spain has almost wholly liberalized trade and capital markets. Foreign and domestic investment has spurred average growth of 4% per year. Beginning in 1989, Madrid implemented a tight monetary policy to fight inflation - around 7% in 1989 and 1990. As a result growth slowed to

2.5% in 1991. Spanish policymakers remain concerned with inflation - still hovering at 6%. Government officials also are worried about 16% unemployment, although many people listed as unemployed work in the underground economy. Spanish economists believe that structural adjustments due to the ongoing integration of the European market are likely to lead to more displaced workers.

GDP:
  purchasing power equivalent - $487.5 billion, per capita $12,400; real growth rate 2.5% (1991 est.)

Inflation rate (consumer prices):
  5.9% (1991 est.)

Unemployment rate: 16.0% (1991 est.)

Budget:
  revenues $111.0 billion; expenditures $115.9 billion, including capital expenditures of $20.8 billion (1991 est.)

Exports:
  $60.1 billion (f.o.b., 1991)
  commodities:
  cars and trucks, semifinished manufactured goods, foodstuffs, machinery
  partners:
  EC 71.0%, US 4.9%, other developed countries 7.9%

Imports:
  $93.1 billion (c.i.f., 1990)
  commodities:
  machinery, transport equipment, fuels, semifinished goods, foodstuffs, consumer goods, chemicals
  partners:
  EC 60.0%, US 8.0%, other developed countries 11.5%, Middle East 2.6%

External debt: $45 billion (1991 est.)

Industrial production:
  growth rate 2.0% (1991 est.)

Electricity:
  46,589,000 kW capacity; 157,040 million kWh produced, 3,980 kWh per capita (1991)

Industries:
  textiles and apparel (including footwear), food and beverages, metals and metal manufactures, chemicals, shipbuilding, automobiles, machine tools, tourism

Agriculture:
  accounts for about 5% of GDP and 14% of labor force; major products - grain, vegetables, olives, wine grapes, sugar beets, citrus fruit, beef, pork, poultry, dairy; largely self-sufficient in food; fish catch of 1.4 million metric tons is among top 20 nations

Illicit drugs:
  key European gateway country for Latin American cocaine entering the European market

Economic aid:
  US commitments, including Ex-Im (FY70-87), $1.9 billion; Western (non-US) countries, ODA and OOF bilateral commitments (1970-79), $545.0 million; not currently a recipient

:Spain Economy

Currency:
peseta (plural - pesetas); 1 peseta (Pta) = 100 centimos

Exchange rates:
pesetas (Ptas) per US$1 - 104.79 (March 1992), 103.91 (1991), 101.93 (1990),
118.38 (1989), 116.49 (1988), 123.48 (1987)

Fiscal year: calendar year

:Spain Communications

Railroads:
15,430 km total; Spanish National Railways (RENFE) operates 12,691 km
1.668-meter gauge, 6,184 km electrified, and 2,295 km double track; FEVE
(government-owned narrow-gauge railways) operates 1,821 km of predominantly
1.000-meter gauge and 441 km electrified; privately owned railways operate
918 km of predominantly 1.000-meter gauge, 512 km electrified, and 56 km
double track

Highways:
150,839 km total; 82,513 km national (includes 2,433 km limited-access
divided highway, 63,042 km bituminous treated, 17,038 km intermediate
bituminous, concrete, or stone block) and 68,326 km provincial or local
roads (bituminous treated, intermediate bituminous, or stone block)

Inland waterways:
1,045 km, but of minor economic importance

Pipelines:
crude oil 265 km, petroleum products 1,794 km, natural gas 1,666 km

Ports:
Algeciras, Alicante, Almeria, Barcelona, Bilbao, Cadiz, Cartagena, Castellon
de la Plana, Ceuta, El Ferrol del Caudillo, Puerto de Gijon, Huelva, La
Coruna, Las Palmas (Canary Islands), Mahon, Malaga, Melilla, Rota, Santa
Cruz de Tenerife, Sagunto, Tarragona, Valencia, Vigo, and 175 minor ports

Merchant marine:
278 ships (1,000 GRT or over) totaling 2,915,409 GRT/5,228,378 DWT; includes
2 passenger, 9 short-sea passenger, 86 cargo, 13 refrigerated cargo, 15
container, 32 roll-on/roll-off cargo, 4 vehicle carrier, 48 petroleum
tanker, 14 chemical tanker, 7 liquefied gas, 3 specialized tanker, 45 bulk

Civil air:
210 major transport aircraft

Airports:
105 total, 99 usable; 60 with permanent-surface runways; 4 with runways over
3,659 m; 22 with runways 2,440-3,659 m; 25 with runways 1,220-2,439 m

Telecommunications:
generally adequate, modern facilities; 15,350,464 telephones; broadcast
stations - 190 AM, 406 (134 repeaters) FM, 100 (1,297 repeaters) TV; 22
coaxial submarine cables; 2 communications satellite earth stations
operating in INTELSAT (Atlantic Ocean and Indian Ocean); MARECS,
INMARSAT,
and EUTELSAT systems; tropospheric links

:Spain Defense Forces

Branches:
   Army, Navy, Air Force, Marines, Civil Guard, National Police, Coastal Civil
   Guard
Manpower availability:
   males 15-49, 10,205,741; 8,271,151 fit for military service; 337,407 reach
   military age (20) annually
Defense expenditures:
   exchange rate conversion - $8.7 billion, 2% of GDP (1991)

Spratly Islands Geography

Total area: NA but less than 5 km2
Land area: less than 5 km2; includes 100 or so islets, coral reefs, and sea mounts
   scattered over the South China Sea
Comparative area: undetermined
Land boundaries:
   none
Coastline:
   926 km
Maritime claims:
   undetermined
Disputes:
   all of the Spratly Islands are claimed by China, Taiwan, and Vietnam; parts
   of them are claimed by Malaysia and the Philippines; in 1984, Brunei
   established an exclusive economic zone, which encompasses Louisa Reef, but
   has not publicly claimed the island
Climate:
   tropical
Terrain:
   flat
Natural resources:
   fish, guano; undetermined oil and natural gas potential
Land use:
   arable land 0%; permanent crops 0%; meadows and pastures 0%; forest and
   woodland 0%; other 100%
Environment:
   subject to typhoons; includes numerous small islands, atolls, shoals, and
   coral reefs
Note:
   strategically located near several primary shipping lanes in the central
   South China Sea; serious navigational hazard

:Spratly Islands People

Population: no permanent inhabitants; garrisons

:Spratly Islands Government

Long-form name: none

:Spratly Islands Economy

Overview:
   Economic activity is limited to commercial fishing, proximity to nearby oil-
   and gas-producing sedimentary basins suggests the potential for oil and gas
   deposits, but the Spratlys region is largely unexplored, and there are no

reliable estimates of potential reserves; commercial exploitation has yet to
be developed.
Industries:
  none

:Spratly Islands Communications

Ports:
  no natural harbors
Airports:
  2 total, 2 usable; none with runways over 2,439 m; 1 with runways
  1,220-2,439 m

:Spratly Islands Defense Forces

Note:
  44 small islands or reefs are occupied by China, Malaysia, the Philippines,
  Taiwan, and Vietnam

Sri Lanka Geography

Total area: 65,610 km2
Land area: 64,740 km2
Comparative area: slightly larger than West Virginia
Land boundaries:
  none
Coastline:
  1,340 km
Maritime claims:
 Contiguous zone:
  24 nm
 Continental shelf:
  edge of continental margin or 200 nm
 Exclusive economic zone:
  200 nm
 Territorial sea:
  12 nm
Disputes:
  none
Climate:
  tropical; monsoonal; northeast monsoon (December to March); southwest
  monsoon (June to October)
Terrain:
  mostly low, flat to rolling plain; mountains in south-central interior
Natural resources:
  limestone, graphite, mineral sands, gems, phosphates, clay
Land use:
  arable land 16%; permanent crops 17%; meadows and pastures 7%; forest and
  woodland 37%; other 23%; includes irrigated 8%
Environment:
  occasional cyclones, tornados; deforestation; soil erosion
Note:
  only 29 km from India across the Palk Strait; near major Indian Ocean sea
  lanes

:Sri Lanka People

Population: 17,631,528 (July 1992), growth rate 1.2% (1992); note - about 120,000 people
   fled to India in 1991 because of fighting between government forces and
   Tamil insurgents; about 200,000 Tamils will be repatriated in 1992
Birth rate: 20 births/1,000 population (1992)
Death rate: 6 deaths/1,000 population (1992)
Net migration rate: -2 migrants/1,000 population (1992)
Infant mortality rate: 21 deaths/1,000 live births (1992)
Life expectancy at birth: 69 years male, 74 years female (1992)
Total fertility rate: 2.2 children born/woman (1992)
Nationality:
   noun - Sri Lankan(s); adjective - Sri Lankan
Ethnic divisions:
   Sinhalese 74%; Tamil 18%; Moor 7%; Burgher, Malay, and Veddha 1%
Religions:
   Buddhist 69%, Hindu 15%, Christian 8%, Muslim 8%
Languages:
   Sinhala (official); Sinhala and Tamil listed as national languages; Sinhala
   spoken by about 74% of population, Tamil spoken by about 18%; English
   commonly used in government and spoken by about 10% of the population
Literacy:
   86% (male 91%, female 81%) age 15 and over can read and write (1981)
Labor force:
   6,600,000; agriculture 45.9%, mining and manufacturing 13.3%, trade and
   transport 12.4%, services and other 28.4% (1985 est.)
Organized labor:
   about 30% of labor force, over 50% of which are employed on tea, rubber, and
   coconut estates

:Sri Lanka Government

Long-form name:
   Democratic Socialist Republic of Sri Lanka
Type:
   republic
Capital: Colombo
Administrative divisions:
   the administrative structure now includes 9 provinces - Central, Eastern,
   North, North Central, North Western, Sabaragamuwa, Southern, Uva, and
   Western and 24 districts - Amparai, Anuradhapura, Badulla, Batticaloa,
   Colombo, Galle, Gampaha, Hambantota, Jaffna, Kalutara, Kandy, Kegalla,
   Kurunegala, Mannar, Matale, Matara, Moneragala, Mullaittivu, Nuwara Eliya,
   Polonnaruwa, Puttalam, Ratnapura, Trincomalee, Vavuniya; note - in the
   future there may be only 8 provinces (combining the two provinces of North
   and Eastern into one province of North Eastern) and 25 districts (adding
   Kilinochchi to the existing districts)
Independence:
   4 February 1948 (from UK; formerly Ceylon)
Constitution:
   31 August 1978

Legal system:

a highly complex mixture of English common law, Roman-Dutch, Muslim, Sinhalese, and customary law; has not accepted compulsory ICJ jurisdiction

National holiday:

Independence and National Day, 4 February (1948)

Executive branch:

president, prime minister, Cabinet

Legislative branch:

unicameral Parliament

Judicial branch:

Supreme Court

Leaders:

Chief of State:

President Ranasinghe PREMADASA (since 2 January 1989)

Head of Government:

Prime Minister Dingiri Banda WIJETUNGE (since 6 March 1989)

Political parties and leaders:

United National Party (UNP), Ranasinghe PREMADASA; Sri Lanka Freedom Party (SLFP), Sirimavo BANDARANAIKE; Sri Lanka Muslim Congress (SLMC), M. H. M.

ASHRAFF; All Ceylon Tamil Congress (ACTC), Kumar PONNAMBALAM; People's

United Front (MEP, or Mahajana Eksath Peramuna), Dinesh GUNAWARDENE; Eelam

Democratic Front (EDF), Edward Sebastian PILLAI; Tamil United Liberation Front (TULF), leader (vacant); Eelam Revolutionary Organization of Students (EROS), Velupillai BALAKUMARAN; New Socialist Party (NSSP, or Nava Sama Samaja Party), Vasudeva NANAYAKKARA; Lanka Socialist Party/Trotskyite (LSSP,

or Lanka Sama Samaja Party), Colin R. de SILVA; Sri Lanka People's Party (SLMP, or Sri Lanka Mahajana Party), Ossie ABEYGUNASEKERA; Communist Party,

K. P. SILVA; Communist Party/Beijing (CP/B), N. SHANMUGATHASAN; note - the

United Socialist Alliance (USA) includes the NSSP, LSSP, SLMP, CP/M, and CP/B

Suffrage:

universal at age 18

Elections:

President:

last held 19 December 1988 (next to be held NA December 1994); results -

Ranasinghe PREMADASA (UNP) 50%, Sirimavo BANDARANAIKE (SLFP) 45%, other 5%

:Sri Lanka Government

Parliament:

last held 15 February 1989 (next to be held by NA February 1995); results -

UNP 51%, SLFP 32%, SLMC 4%, TULF 3%, USA 3%, EROS 3%, MEP 1%, other 3%;

seats - (225 total) UNP 125, SLFP 67, other 33

Other political or pressure groups:

Liberation Tigers of Tamil Eelam (LTTE) and other smaller Tamil separatist
groups; Janatha Vimukthi Peramuna (JVP or People's Liberation Front);
Buddhist clergy; Sinhalese Buddhist lay groups; labor unions

Member of:

AsDB, C, CCC, CP, ESCAP, FAO, G-24, G-77, GATT, IAEA, IBRD, ICAO, ICC,
ICFTU, IDA, IFAD, IFC, ILO, IMF, IMO, INMARSAT, INTELSAT, INTERPOL,
IOC,
ISO, ITU, LORCS, NAM, PCA, SAARC, UN, UNCTAD, UNESCO, UNIDO, UPU,
WCL, WFTU,
WHO, WIPO, WMO, WTO

Diplomatic representation:

Ambassador W. Susanta De ALWIS; Chancery at 2148 Wyoming Avenue NW,
Washington, DC 20008; telephone (202) 483-4025 through 4028; there is a Sri
Lankan Consulate in New York

US:

Ambassador Marion V. CREEKMORE, Jr.; Embassy at 210 Galle Road, Colombo 3
(mailing address is P. O. Box 106, Colombo); telephone [94] (1) 44180107,
FAX [94] (1) 43-73-45

Flag:

yellow with two panels; the smaller hoist-side panel has two equal vertical
bands of green (hoist side) and orange; the other panel is a large dark red
rectangle with a yellow lion holding a sword, and there is a yellow bo leaf
in each corner; the yellow field appears as a border that goes around the
entire flag and extends between the two panels

:Sri Lanka Economy

Overview:

Agriculture, forestry, and fishing dominate the economy, employing half of
the labor force and accounting for one quarter of GDP. The plantation crops
of tea, rubber, and coconuts provide about one-third of export earnings. The
economy has been plagued by high rates of unemployment since the late 1970s.
Economic growth, which has been depressed by ethnic unrest, accelerated in
1991 as domestic conditions began to improve.

GDP:

exchange rate conversion - $7.2 billion, per capita $410; real growth rate
5.0% (1991 est.)

Inflation rate (consumer prices):

10% (1991)

Unemployment rate: 14% (1991 est.)

Budget:

revenues $2.0 billion; expenditures $3.7 billion, including capital
expenditures of $500 million (1992)

Exports:

$2.3 billion (f.o.b., 1991)

commodities:

textiles and garment, teas, petroleum products, coconut, rubber,
agricultural products, gems and jewelry, marine products

partners:

US 25%, FRG, Japan, UK, Belgium, Taiwan, Hong Kong, China

Imports:

$3.0 billion (c.i.f., 1991)

commodities:

food and beverages, textiles and textile materials, petroleum, machinery and equipment

partners:

Japan, Iran, US 7.7%, India, Taiwan, Singapore, FRG, UK

External debt: $5.8 billion (1990)

Industrial production:

growth rate 8% (1991 est.); accounts for 20% of GDP

Electricity:

1,300,000 kW capacity; 4,200 million kWh produced, 240 kWh per capita (1990)

Industries:

processing of rubber, tea, coconuts, and other agricultural commodities; cement, petroleum refining, textiles, tobacco, clothing

Agriculture:

accounts for 26% of GDP and nearly half of labor force; most important staple crop is paddy rice; other field crops - sugarcane, grains, pulses, oilseeds, roots, spices; cash crops - tea, rubber, coconuts; animal products - milk, eggs, hides, meat; not self-sufficient in rice production

Economic aid:

US commitments, including Ex-Im (FY70-89), $1.0 billion; Western (non-US) countries, ODA and OOF bilateral commitments (1980-89), $5.1 billion; OPEC bilateral aid (1979-89), $169 million; Communist countries (1970-89), $369 million

Currency:

Sri Lankan rupee (plural - rupees); 1 Sri Lankan rupee (SLRe) = 100 cents

Exchange rates:

Sri Lankan rupees (SLRes) per US$1 - 43.112 (March 1992), 41.372 (1991), 40.063 (1990), 36.047 (1989), 31.807 (1988), 29.445 (1987)

Fiscal year: calendar year

:Sri Lanka Communications

Railroads:

1,948 km total (1990); all 1.868-meter broad gauge; 102 km double track; no electrification; government owned

Highways:

75,749 km total (1990); 27,637 km paved (mostly bituminous treated), 32,887 km crushed stone or gravel, 14,739 km improved earth or unimproved earth; several thousand km of mostly unmotorable tracks (1988 est.)

Inland waterways:

430 km; navigable by shallow-draft craft

Pipelines:

crude oil and petroleum products 62 km (1987)

Ports:

Colombo, Trincomalee

Merchant marine:

30 ships (1,000 GRT or over) totaling 310,173 GRT/489,378 DWT; includes 13 cargo, 6 refrigerated cargo, 5 container, 3 petroleum tanker, 3 bulk

Civil air:

8 major transport (including 1 leased)
Airports:
  14 total, 13 usable; 12 with permanent-surface runways; none with runways
  over 3,659 m; 1 with runways 2,440-3,659 m; 7 with runways 1,220-2,439 m
Telecommunications:
  good international service; 114,000 telephones (1982); broadcast stations -
  12 AM, 5 FM, 5 TV; submarine cables extend to Indonesia and Djibouti; 2
  Indian Ocean INTELSAT earth stations
:Sri Lanka Defense Forces

Branches:
  Army, Navy, Air Force, Police Force
Manpower availability:
  males 15-49, 4,709,203; 3,678,952 fit for military service; 177,554 reach
  military age (18) annually
Defense expenditures:
  exchange rate conversion - $432 million, 6% of GDP (1991)
\

Sudan Geography

Total area: 2,505,810 km2
Land area: 2,376,000 km2
Comparative area: slightly more than one-quarter the size of the US
Land boundaries:
  7,697 km total; Central African Republic 1,165 km, Chad 1,360 km, Egypt
  1,273 km, Ethiopia 2,221 km, Kenya 232 km, Libya 383 km, Uganda 435 km,
  Zaire 628 km
Coastline:
  853 km
Maritime claims:
  Contiguous zone:
   18 nm
  Continental shelf:
   200 m (depth) or to depth of exploitation
  Territorial sea:
   12 nm
Disputes:
  administrative boundary with Kenya does not coincide with international
  boundary; administrative boundary with Egypt does not coincide with
  international boundary
Climate:
  tropical in south; arid desert in north; rainy season (April to October)
Terrain:
  generally flat, featureless plain; mountains in east and west
Natural resources:
  small reserves of crude oil, iron ore, copper, chromium ore, zinc, tungsten,
  mica, silver, crude oil
Land use:
  arable land 5%; permanent crops NEGL%; meadows and pastures 24%; forest and
  woodland 20%; other 51%; includes irrigated 1%
Environment:

dominated by the Nile and its tributaries; dust storms; desertification
Note:
   largest country in Africa

:Sudan People

Population: 28,305,046 (July 1992), growth rate 3.1% (1992)
Birth rate: 44 births/1,000 population (1992)
Death rate: 13 deaths/1,000 population (1992)
Net migration rate: NEGL migrants/1,000 population (1992)
Infant mortality rate: 83 deaths/1,000 live births (1992)
Life expectancy at birth: 53 years male, 54 years female (1992)
Total fertility rate: 6.3 children born/woman (1992)
Nationality:
   noun - Sudanese (singular and plural); adjective - Sudanese
Ethnic divisions:
   black 52%, Arab 39%, Beja 6%, foreigners 2%, other 1%
Religions:
   Sunni Muslim (in north) 70%, indigenous beliefs 20%, Christian (mostly in
   south and Khartoum) 5%
Languages:
   Arabic (official), Nubian, Ta Bedawie, diverse dialects of Nilotic,
   Nilo-Hamitic, and Sudanic languages, English; program of Arabization in
   process
Literacy:
   27% (male 43%, female 12%) age 15 and over can read and write (1990 est.)
Labor force:
   6,500,000; agriculture 80%, industry and commerce 10%, government 6%; labor
   shortages for almost all categories of skilled employment (1983 est.); 52%
   of population of working age (1985)
Organized labor:
   trade unions suspended following 30 June 1989 coup; now in process of being
   legalized anew

:Sudan Government

Long-form name:
   Republic of the Sudan
Type:
   military; civilian government suspended and martial law imposed after 30
   June 1989 coup
Capital: Khartoum
Administrative divisions:
   9 states (wilayat, singular - wilayat or wilayah*); A'ali an Nil, Al Wusta*,
   Al Istiwa'iyah*, Al Khartum, Ash Shamaliyah*, Ash Sharqiyah*, Bahr al
   Ghazal, Darfur, Kurdufan
Independence:
   1 January 1956 (from Egypt and UK; formerly Anglo-Egyptian Sudan)
Constitution:
   12 April 1973, suspended following coup of 6 April 1985; interim
   constitution of 10 October 1985 suspended following coup of 30 June 1989
Legal system:
   based on English common law and Islamic law; as of 20 January 1991, the

Revolutionary Command Council imposed Islamic law in the six northern states of Al Wusta, Al Khartum, Ash Shamaliyah, Ash Sharqiyah, Darfur, and Kurdufan; the council is still studying criminal provisions under Islamic law; Islamic law will apply to all residents of the six northern states regardless of their religion; some separate religious courts; accepts compulsory ICJ jurisdiction, with reservations

National holiday:

Independence Day, 1 January (1956)

Executive branch:

executive and legislative authority vested in a 12-member Revolutionary Command Council (RCC); chairman of the RCC acts as prime minister; in July 1989, RCC appointed a predominately civilian 22-member cabinet to function as advisers

Legislative branch:

appointed 300-member Transitional National Assembly; note - as announced 1 January 1992 by RCC Chairman BASHIR, the Assembly assumes all legislative authority for Sudan until the eventual, unspecified resumption of national elections

Judicial branch:

Supreme Court, Special Revolutionary Courts

Leaders:

Chief of State and Head of Government:

Revolutionary Command Council Chairman and Prime Minister Lt. Gen. Umar Hasan Ahmad al-BASHIR (since 30 June 1989); Deputy Chairman of the Command Council and Deputy Prime Minister Maj. Gen. al-Zubayr Muhammad SALIH Ahmed

(since 9 July 1989)

Political parties and leaders:

none; banned following 30 June 1989 coup

Suffrage:

Elections:

Member of:

ABEDA, ACP, AfDB, AFESD, AL, AMF, CAEU, CCC, ECA, FAO, G-77, IAEA, IBRD,

ICAO, IDA, IDB, IFAD, IFC, IGADD, ILO, IMF, IMO, INTELSAT, INTERPOL, IOC,

ISO, ITU, LORCS, NAM, OAU, OIC, PCA, UN, UNCTAD, UNESCO, UNHCR, UNIDO, UPU,

WFTU, WHO, WIPO, WMO, WTO

Diplomatic representation:

Ambassador `Abdallah Ahmad `ABDALLAH; Chancery at 2210 Massachusetts Avenue

NW, Washington, DC 20008; telephone (202) 338-8565 through 8570; there is a Sudanese Consulate General in New York

:Sudan Government

US:

Ambassador James R. CHEEK (will be replaced summer of 1992); Embassy at

Shar'ia Ali Abdul Latif, Khartoum (mailing address is P. O. Box 699,
Khartoum, or APO AE 09829); telephone 74700 or 74611; Telex 22619

Flag:
three equal horizontal bands of red (top), white, and black with a green
isosceles triangle based on the hoist side

:Sudan Economy

Overview:
Sudan is buffeted by civil war, chronic political instability, adverse
weather, high inflation, and counterproductive economic policies. The
economy is dominated by governmental entities that account for more than 70%
of new investment. The private sector's main areas of activity are
agriculture and trading, with most private industrial investment predating
1980. The economy's base is agriculture, which employs 80% of the work
force. Industry mainly processes agricultural items. Sluggish economic
performance over the past decade, attributable largely to declining annual
rainfall, has reduced levels of per capita income and consumption. A high
foreign debt and huge arrearages continue to cause difficulties. In 1990 the
International Monetary Fund took the unusual step of declaring Sudan
noncooperative because of its nonpayment of arrearages to the Fund. Despite
subsequent government efforts to implement reforms urged by the IMF and the
World Bank, the economy remained stagnant in FY91 as entrepreneurs lack the
incentive to take economic risks.

GDP:
exchange rate conversion - $12.1 billion, per capita $450; real growth rate
0% (FY91 est.)

Inflation rate (consumer prices):
95% (FY91 est.)

Unemployment rate: 15% (FY91 est.)

Budget:
revenues $1.3 billion; expenditures $2.1 billion, including capital
expenditures of $505 million (FY91 est.)

Exports:
$325 million (f.o.b., FY91 est.)

commodities:
cotton 52%, sesame, gum arabic, peanuts

partners:
Western Europe 46%, Saudi Arabia 14%, Eastern Europe 9%, Japan 9%, US 3%
(FY88)

Imports:
$1.40 billion (c.i.f., FY91 est.)

commodities:
foodstuffs, petroleum products, manufactured goods, machinery and equipment,
medicines and chemicals, textiles

partners:
Western Europe 32%, Africa and Asia 15%, US 13%, Eastern Europe 3% (FY88)

External debt: $14.6 billion (June 1991 est.)

Industrial production:
growth rate NA%; accounts for 11% of GDP (FY89)

Electricity:

610,000 kW capacity; 905 million kWh produced, 40 kWh per capita (1991)
Industries:
  cotton ginning, textiles, cement, edible oils, sugar, soap distilling,
  shoes, petroleum refining
Agriculture:
  accounts for 35% of GDP and 80% of labor force; water shortages; two-thirds
  of land area suitable for raising crops and livestock; major products -
  cotton, oilseeds, sorghum, millet, wheat, gum arabic, sheep; marginally
  self-sufficient in most foods
Economic aid:
  US commitments, including Ex-Im (FY70-89), $1.5 billion; Western (non-US)
  countries, ODA and OOF bilateral commitments (1970-89), $5.1 billion; OPEC
  bilateral aid (1979-89), $3.1 billion; Communist countries (1970-89), $588
  million

:Sudan Economy

Currency:
  Sudanese pound (plural - pounds); 1 Sudanese pound (#Sd) = 100 piasters
Exchange rates:
  official rate - Sudanese pounds (#Sd) per US$1 - 90.1 (March 1992), 5.4288
  (1991), 4.5004 (fixed rate since 1987), 2.8121 (1987); note - free market
  rate 83 (December 1991)
Fiscal year: 1 July - 30 June

:Sudan Communications

Railroads:
  5,500 km total; 4,784 km 1.067-meter gauge, 716 km 1.6096-meter-gauge
  plantation line
Highways:
  20,000 km total; 1,600 km bituminous treated, 3,700 km gravel, 2,301 km
  improved earth, 12,399 km unimproved earth and track
Inland waterways:
  5,310 km navigable
Pipelines:
  refined products 815 km
Ports:
  Port Sudan, Swakin
Merchant marine:
  5 ships (1,000 GRT or over) totaling 42,277 GRT/59,588 DWT; includes 3
  cargo, 2 roll-on/roll-off cargo
Civil air:
  18 major transport aircraft
Airports:
  72 total, 57 usable; 8 with permanent-surface runways; none with runways
  over 3,659 m; 5 with runways 2,440-3,659 m; 31 with runways 1,220-2,439 m
Telecommunications:
  large, well-equipped system by African standards, but barely adequate and
  poorly maintained by modern standards; consists of microwave, cable, radio
  communications, and troposcatter; domestic satellite system with 14
  stations; broadcast stations - 11 AM, 3 TV; satellite earth stations - 1
  Atlantic Ocean INTELSAT and 1 ARABSAT

:Sudan Defense Forces

Branches:
   Army, Navy, Air Force, Air Defense Force
Manpower availability:
   males 15-49, 6,432,270; 3,949,518 fit for military service; 302,696 reach
   military age (18) annually
Defense expenditures:
   exchange rate conversion - $610 million, 7.2% of GDP (1989 est.)

Suriname Geography

Total area: 163,270 km2
Land area: 161,470 km2
Comparative area: slightly larger than Georgia
Land boundaries:
   1,707 km total; Brazil 597 km, French Guiana 510 km, Guyana 600 km
Coastline:
   386 km
Maritime claims:
 Exclusive economic zone:
   200 nm
 Territorial sea:
   12 nm
Disputes:
   claims area in French Guiana between Litani Rivier and Riviere Marouini
   (both headwaters of the Lawa); claims area in Guyana between New (Upper
   Courantyne) and Courantyne/Kutari Rivers (all headwaters of the Courantyne)
Climate:
   tropical; moderated by trade winds
Terrain:
   mostly rolling hills; narrow coastal plain with swamps
Natural resources:
   timber, hydropower potential, fish, shrimp, bauxite, iron ore, and small
   amounts of nickel, copper, platinum, gold
Land use:
   arable land NEGL%; permanent crops NEGL%; meadows and pastures NEGL%;
forest
   and woodland 97%; other 3%; includes irrigated NEGL%
Environment:
   mostly tropical rain forest

:Suriname People

Population: 410,016 (July 1992), growth rate 1.5% (1992)
Birth rate: 26 births/1,000 population (1992)
Death rate: 6 deaths/1,000 population (1992)
Net migration rate: -5 migrants/1,000 population (1992)
Infant mortality rate: 34 deaths/1,000 live births (1992)
Life expectancy at birth: 66 years male, 71 years female (1992)
Total fertility rate: 2.9 children born/woman (1992)
Nationality:
   noun - Surinamer(s); adjective - Surinamese

Ethnic divisions:
  Hindustani (East Indian) 37.0%, Creole (black and mixed) 31.0%, Javanese
  15.3%, Bush black 10.3%, Amerindian 2.6%, Chinese 1.7%, Europeans 1.0%,
  other 1.1%
Religions:
  Hindu 27.4%, Muslim 19.6%, Roman Catholic 22.8%, Protestant (predominantly
  Moravian) 25.2%, indigenous beliefs about 5%
Languages:
  Dutch (official); English widely spoken; Sranan Tongo (Surinamese, sometimes
  called Taki-Taki) is native language of Creoles and much of the younger
  population and is lingua franca among others; also Hindi Suriname Hindustani
  (a variant of Bhoqpuri) and Javanese
Literacy:
  95% (male 95%, female 95%) age 15 and over can read and write (1990 est.)
Labor force:
  104,000 (1984)
Organized labor:
  49,000 members of labor force

:Suriname Government

Long-form name:
  Republic of Suriname
Type:
  republic
Capital: Paramaribo
Administrative divisions:
  10 districts (distrikten, singular - distrikt); Brokopondo, Commewijne,
  Coronie, Marowijne, Nickerie, Para, Paramaribo, Saramacca, Sipaliwini,
  Wanica
Independence:
  25 November 1975 (from Netherlands; formerly Netherlands Guiana or Dutch
  Guiana)
Constitution:
  ratified 30 September 1987
Legal system:
  NA
National holiday:
  Independence Day, 25 November (1975)
Executive branch:
  president, vice president and prime minister, Cabinet of Ministers, Council
  of State; note - Commander in Chief of the National Army maintains
  significant power
Legislative branch:
  unicameral National Assembly (Assemblee Nationale)
Judicial branch:
  Supreme Court
Leaders:
  Chief of State and Head of Government:
  President Ronald VENETIAAN (since 16 September 1991); Vice President and
  Prime Minister Jules AJODHIA (since 16 September 1991)

910

Political parties and leaders:

traditional ethnic-based parties:

The New Front (NF), a coalition formed of four parties following the 24
December 1990 military coup - Progressive Reform Party (VHP), Jaggernath
LACHMON; National Party of Suriname (NPS), Henck ARRON; Indonesian Pea-
sants
Party (KTPI), Willie SOEMITA; and Suriname Labor Party (SPA) Fred DERBY;

promilitary:

National Democratic Party (NDP), Orlando VAN AMSON; Democratic Alternative
'91 (DA '91), Winston JESSURUN, a coalition of five parties formed in
January 1991 - Alternative Forum (AF), Gerard BRUNINGS, Winston JESSURUN;
Reformed Progressive Party (HPP), Panalal PARMESSAR; Party for Brotherhood
and Unity in Politics (BEP), Cipriano ALLENDY; Pendawalima, Marsha JAMIN;
and Independent Progressive Group, Karam RAMSUNDERSINGH;

leftists:

Revolutionary People's Party (RVP), Michael NAARENDORP; Progressive Workers
and Farmers (PALU), Iwan KROLIS

Suffrage:

universal at age 18

Elections:

President:

last held 6 September 1991 (next to be held NA May 1996); results - elected
by the National Assembly - Ronald VENETIAAN (NF) 80% (645 votes), Jules
WIJDENBOSCH (NDP) 14% (115 votes), Hans PRADE (DA '91) 6% (49 votes)

National Assembly:

last held 25 May 1991 (next to be held NA May 1996); results - percent of
vote NA; seats - (51 total) NF 30, NDP 12, DA '91 9

:Suriname Government

Member of:

ACP, CARICOM (observer), ECLAC, FAO, GATT, G-77, IADB, IBRD, ICAO,
ICFTU,
IFAD, ILO, IMF, IMO, INTERPOL, IOC, ITU, LAES, LORCS, NAM, OAS,
OPANAL, UN,
UNCTAD, UNESCO, UNIDO, UPU, WCL, WHO, WIPO, WMO

Diplomatic representation:

Ambassador Willem A. UDENHOUT; Chancery at Suite 108, 4301 Connecticut
Avenue NW, Washington, DC 20008; telephone (202) 244-7488 or 7490 through
7492; there is a Surinamese Consulate General in Miami

US:

Ambassador John (Jack) P. LEONARD; Embassy at Dr. Sophie Redmonstraat 129,
Paramaribo (mailing address is P. O. Box 1821, Paramaribo); telephone [597]
472900, 477881, or 476459; FAX [597] 410025

Flag:

five horizontal bands of green (top, double width), white, red (quadruple
width), white, and green (double width); there is a large yellow
five-pointed star centered in the red band

:Suriname Economy

Overview:
  The economy is dominated by the bauxite industry, which accounts for about
  70% of export earnings and 40% of tax revenues. The economy has been in
  trouble since the Dutch ended development aid in 1982. A drop in world
  bauxite prices which started in the late 1970s and continued until late 1986
  was followed by the outbreak of a guerrilla insurgency in the interior that
  crippled the important bauxite sector. Although the insurgency has since
  ebbed and the bauxite sector recovered, a military coup in December 1990
  reflected continued political instability and deterred investment and
  economic reform. High inflation, high unemployment, widespread black market
  activity, and hard currency shortfalls continue to mark the economy.
GDP:
  exchange rate conversion - $1.4 billion, per capita $3,400; real growth rate
  0% (1989 est.)
Inflation rate (consumer prices):
  50% (1989 est.)
Unemployment rate: 33% (1990)
Budget:
  revenues $466 million; expenditures $716 million, including capital
  expenditures of $123 million (1989 est.)
Exports:
  $549 million (f.o.b., 1989 est.)
  commodities:
  alumina, bauxite, aluminum, rice, wood and wood products, shrimp and fish,
  bananas
  partners:
  Norway 33%, Netherlands 20%, US 15%, FRG 9%, Brazil 5%, UK 5%, Japan 3%,
  other 10%
Imports:
  $331 million (f.o.b., 1989 est.)
  commodities:
  capital equipment, petroleum, foodstuffs, cotton, consumer goods
  partners:
  US 37%, Netherlands 15%, Netherlands Antilles 11%, Trinidad and Tobago 9%,
  Brazil 5%, UK 3%, other 20%
External debt: $138 million (1990 est.)
Industrial production:
  growth rate NA; accounts for 22% of GDP
Electricity:
  458,000 kW capacity; 2,018 million kWh produced, 5,015 kWh per capita (1991)
Industries:
  bauxite mining, alumina and aluminum production, lumbering, food processing,
  fishing
Agriculture:
  accounts for 11% of GDP; paddy rice planted on 85% of arable land and
  represents 60% of total farm output; other products - bananas, palm kernels,
  coconuts, plantains, peanuts, beef, chicken; shrimp and forestry products of
  increasing importance; self-sufficient in most foods
Economic aid:
  US commitments, including Ex-Im (FY70-83), $2.5 million; Western (non-US)

countries, ODA and OOF bilateral commitments (1970-89), $1.5 billion

Currency:
Surinamese guilder, gulden, or florin (plural - guilders, gulden, or florins); 1 Surinamese guilder, gulden, or florin (Sf.) = 100 cents

Exchange rates:
Surinamese guilders, gulden, or florins (Sf.) per US$1 - 1.7850 (fixed rate)

:Suriname Economy

Fiscal year: calendar year

:Suriname Communications

Railroads:
166 km total; 86 km 1.000-meter gauge, government owned, and 80 km 1.435-meter standard gauge; all single track

Highways:
8,300 km total; 500 km paved; 5,400 km bauxite gravel, crushed stone, or improved earth; 2,400 km sand or clay

Inland waterways:
1,200 km; most important means of transport; oceangoing vessels with drafts ranging up to 7 m can navigate many of the principal waterways

Ports:
Paramaribo, Moengo

Merchant marine:
3 ships (1,000 GRT or over) totaling 6,472 GRT/8,914 DWT; includes 2 cargo, 1 container

Civil air:
1 major transport aircraft

Airports:
46 total, 40 usable; 6 with permanent-surface runways; none with runways over 3,659 m; 1 with runways 2,440-3,659 m; 2 with runways 1,220-2,439 m

Telecommunications:
international facilities good; domestic microwave system; 27,500 telephones; broadcast stations - 5 AM, 14 FM, 6 TV, 1 shortwave; 2 Atlantic Ocean INTELSAT earth stations

:Suriname Defense Forces

Branches:
National Army (including Navy which is company-size, small Air Force element), Civil Police, People's Militia

Manpower availability:
males 15-49, 109,551; 65,250 fit for military service

Defense expenditures:
$NA, NA% of GDP

Svalbard Geography

Total area: 62,049 km2
Land area: 62,049 km2; includes Spitsbergen and Bjornoya (Bear Island)
Comparative area: slightly smaller than West Virginia
Land boundaries:
none
Coastline:
3,587 km

Maritime claims:

  Exclusive fishing zone:

  200 nm unilaterally claimed by Norway, not recognized by Russia

  Territorial sea:

  4 nm

Disputes:

  focus of maritime boundary dispute in the Barents Sea between Norway and
  Russia

Climate:

  arctic, tempered by warm North Atlantic Current; cool summers, cold winters;
  North Atlantic Current flows along west and north coasts of Spitsbergen,
  keeping water open and navigable most of the year

Terrain:

  wild, rugged mountains; much of high land ice covered; west coast clear of
  ice about half the year; fjords along west and north coasts

Natural resources:

  coal, copper, iron ore, phosphate, zinc, wildlife, fish

Land use:

  arable land 0%; permanent crops 0%; meadows and pastures 0%; forest and
  woodland 0%; other 100%; there are no trees and the only bushes are
  crowberry and cloudberry

Environment:

  great calving glaciers descend to the sea

Note:

  located 445 km north of Norway where the Arctic Ocean, Barents Sea,
  Greenland Sea, and Norwegian Sea meet

:Svalbard People

Population: 3,181 (July 1992), growth rate -3.9% (1992); about one-third of the
  population resides in the Norwegian areas (Longyearbyen and Svea on
  Vestspitsbergen) and two-thirds in the Russian areas (Barentsburg and
  Pyramiden on Vestspitsbergen); about 9 persons live at the Polish research
  station
Birth rate: NA births/1,000 population (1992)
Death rate: NA deaths/1,000 population (1992)
Net migration rate: NA migrants/1,000 population (1992)
Infant mortality rate: NA deaths/1,000 live births (1992)
Life expectancy at birth: NA years male, NA years female (1992)
Total fertility rate: NA children born/woman (1992)
Ethnic divisions:

  Russian 64%, Norwegian 35%, other 1% (1981)

Languages:

  Russian, Norwegian

Literacy:

  NA% (male NA%, female NA%)

Labor force:

  NA

Organized labor:

:Svalbard Government

Long-form name:
    none
Type:
    territory of Norway administered by the Ministry of Industry, Oslo, through
    a governor (sysselmann) residing in Longyearbyen, Spitsbergen; by treaty (9
    February 1920) sovereignty was given to Norway
Capital: Longyearbyen
Leaders:
  Chief of State:
    King HARALD V (since 17 January 1991)
  Head of Government:
    Governor Leif ELDRING (since NA)
Member of:
    none
Flag:
    the flag of Norway is used

:Svalbard Economy

Overview:
    Coal mining is the major economic activity on Svalbard. By treaty (9
    February 1920), the nationals of the treaty powers have equal rights to
    exploit mineral deposits, subject to Norwegian regulation. Although US, UK,
    Dutch, and Swedish coal companies have mined in the past, the only companies
    still mining are Norwegian and Russian. The settlements on Svalbard are
    essentially company towns. The Norwegian state-owned coal company employs
    nearly 60% of the Norwegian population on the island, runs many of the local
    services, and provides most of the local infrastructure. There is also some
    trapping of seal, polar bear, fox, and walrus.
Budget:
    revenues $13.3 million, expenditures $13.3 million, including capital
    expenditures of $NA (1990)
Electricity:
    21,000 kW capacity; 45 million kWh produced, 11,420 kWh per capita (1989)
Currency:
    Norwegian krone (plural - kroner); 1 Norwegian krone (NKr) = 100 ore
Exchange rates:
    Norwegian kroner (NKr) per US$1 - 6.5189 (March 1992), 6.4829 (1991), 6.2597
    (1990), 6.9045 (1989), 6.5170 (1988), 6.7375 (1987)

:Svalbard Communications

Ports:
    limited facilities - Ny-Alesund, Advent Bay
Airports:
    4 total, 4 usable; 1 with permanent-surface runways; none with runways over
    2,439 m; 1 with runways 1,220-2,439 m
Telecommunications:
    5 meteorological/radio stations; local telephone service; broadcast stations
    - 1 AM, 1 (2 repeaters) FM, 1 TV; satellite communication with Norwegian
    mainland

:Svalbard Defense Forces

Note: demilitarized by treaty (9 February 1920)

Swaziland Geography

Total area: 17,360 km2
Land area: 17,200 km2
Comparative area: slightly smaller than New Jersey
Land boundaries:
   535 km total; Mozambique 105 km, South Africa 430 km
Coastline:
   none - landlocked
Maritime claims:
   none - landlocked
Disputes:
   none
Climate:
   varies from tropical to near temperate
Terrain:
   mostly mountains and hills; some moderately sloping plains
Natural resources:
   asbestos, coal, clay, cassiterite, hydropower, forests, small gold and
   diamond deposits, quarry stone, and talc
Land use:
   arable land 8%; permanent crops NEGL%; meadows and pastures 67%; forest and
   woodland 6%; other 19%; includes irrigated 2%
Environment:
   overgrazing; soil degradation; soil erosion
Note:
   landlocked; almost completely surrounded by South Africa

:Swaziland People

Population: 913,008 (July 1992), growth rate 2.6% (1992)
Birth rate: 44 births/1,000 population (1992)
Death rate: 12 deaths/1,000 population (1992)
Net migration rate: -6 migrants/1,000 population (1992)
Infant mortality rate: 98 deaths/1,000 live births (1992)
Life expectancy at birth: 52 years male, 60 years female (1992)
Total fertility rate: 6.2 children born/woman (1992)
Nationality:
   noun - Swazi(s); adjective - Swazi
Ethnic divisions:
   African 97%, European 3%
Religions:
   Christian 60%, indigenous beliefs 40%
Languages:
   English and siSwati (official); government business conducted in English
Literacy:
   55% (male 57%, female 54%) age 15 and over can read and write (1976)
Labor force:
   195,000; over 60,000 engaged in subsistence agriculture; about 92,000 wage
   earners (many only intermittently), with agriculture and forestry 36%,
   community and social services 20%, manufacturing 14%, construction 9%, other

21%; 16,800 employed in South Africa mines (1990)
Organized labor:
  about 10% of wage earners

:Swaziland Government

Long-form name:
  Kingdom of Swaziland
Type:
  monarchy; independent member of Commonwealth
Capital: Mbabane (administrative); Lobamba (legislative)
Administrative divisions:
  4 districts; Hhohho, Lubombo, Manzini, Shiselweni
Independence:
  6 September 1968 (from UK)
Constitution:
  none; constitution of 6 September 1968 was suspended on 12 April 1973; a new
  constitution was promulgated 13 October 1978, but has not been formally
  presented to the people
Legal system:
  based on South African Roman-Dutch law in statutory courts, Swazi
  traditional law and custom in traditional courts; has not accepted
  compulsory ICJ jurisdiction
National holiday:
  Somhlolo (Independence) Day, 6 September (1968)
Executive branch:
  monarch, prime minister, Cabinet
Legislative branch:
  bicameral Parliament is advisory and consists of an upper house or Senate
  and a lower house or House of Assembly
Judicial branch:
  High Court, Court of Appeal
Leaders:
  Chief of State:
  King MSWATI III (since 25 April 1986)
  Head of Government:
  Prime Minister Obed DLAMINI (since 12 July 1989)
Political parties and leaders:
  none; banned by the Constitution promulgated on 13 October 1978
Suffrage:
  none
Elections:
  indirect parliamentary election through Swaziland's Tinkhundala System
  scheduled for November 1992
Member of:
  ACP, AfDB, C, CCC, ECA, FAO, G-77, IBRD, ICAO, ICFTU, IDA, IFAD, IFC,
ILO,
  IMF, INTELSAT, INTERPOL, IOC, ITU, LORCS, NAM, OAU, PCA, SACU,
SADCC, UN,
  UNCTAD, UNESCO, UNIDO, UPU, WHO, WIPO, WMO
Diplomatic representation:

Ambassador Absalom Vusani MAMBA; Chancery at 3400 International Drive NW, Washington, DC 20008; telephone (202) 362-6683

US:

Ambassador Stephen H. ROGERS; Embassy at Central Bank Building, Warner Street, Mbabane (mailing address is P. O. Box 199, Mbabane); telephone [268] 46441 through 5; FAX [268] 45959

Flag:

three horizontal bands of blue (top), red (triple width), and blue; the red band is edged in yellow; centered in the red band is a large black and white shield covering two spears and a staff decorated with feather tassels, all placed horizontally

:Swaziland Economy

Overview:

The economy is based on subsistence agriculture, which occupies most of the labor force and contributes nearly 25% to GDP. Manufacturing, which includes a number of agroprocessing factories, accounts for another quarter of GDP. Mining has declined in importance in recent years; high-grade iron ore deposits were depleted in 1978, and health concerns cut world demand for asbestos. Exports of sugar and forestry products are the main earners of hard currency. Surrounded by South Africa, except for a short border with Mozambique, Swaziland is heavily dependent on South Africa, from which it receives 75% of its imports and to which it sends about half of its exports.

GDP:

exchange rate conversion - $563 million, per capita $725; real growth rate 5.0% (1990 est.)

Inflation rate (consumer prices):

13% (1990)

Unemployment rate: NA%

Budget:

revenues $335.4 million; expenditures $360.5 million, including capital expenditures of $NA (FY93 est.)

Exports:

$557 million (f.o.b., 1990)

commodities:

soft drink concentrates, sugar, wood pulp, citrus, canned fruit

partners:

South Africa 50% (est.), EC, Canada

Imports:

$632 million (f.o.b., 1990)

commodities:

motor vehicles, machinery, transport equipment, petroleum products, foodstuffs, chemicals

partners:

South Africa 75% (est.), Japan, Belgium, UK

External debt: $290 million (1990)

Industrial production:

growth rate NA; accounts for 26% of GDP (1989)

Electricity:

60,000 kW capacity; 155 million kWh produced, 180 kWh per capita (1991)

Industries:
   mining (coal and asbestos), wood pulp, sugar
Agriculture:
   accounts for 23% of GDP and over 60% of labor force; mostly subsistence
   agriculture; cash crops - sugarcane, cotton, maize, tobacco, rice, citrus
   fruit, pineapples; other crops and livestock - corn, sorghum, peanuts,
   cattle, goats, sheep; not self-sufficient in grain
Economic aid:
   US commitments, including Ex-Im (FY70-89), $142 million; Western (non-US)
   countries, ODA and OOF bilateral commitments (1970-89), $518 million
Currency:
   lilangeni (plural - emalangeni); 1 lilangeni (E) = 100 cents
Exchange rates:
   emalangeni (E) per US$1 - 2.7814 (January 1992), 2.7563 (1991), 2.5863
   (1990), 2.6166 (1989), 2.2611 (1988), 2.0350 (1987); note - the Swazi
   emalangeni is at par with the South African rand
Fiscal year: 1 April - 31 March

:Swaziland Communications

Railroads:
   297 km (plus 71 km disused), 1.067-meter gauge, single track
Highways:
   2,853 km total; 510 km paved, 1,230 km crushed stone, gravel, or stabilized
   soil, and 1,113 km improved earth
Civil air:
   4 major transport aircraft
Airports:
   23 total, 21 usable; 1 with permanent-surfaced runways; none with runways
   over 3,659 m; 1 with runways 2,440-3,659 m; 1 with runways 1,220-2,439 m
Telecommunications:
   system consists of carrier-equipped open-wire lines and low-capacity
   microwave links; 17,000 telephones; broadcast stations - 7 AM, 6 FM, 10 TV;
   1 Atlantic Ocean INTELSAT earth station

:Swaziland Defense Forces

Branches:
   Umbutfo Swaziland Defense Force, Royal Swaziland Police Force
Manpower availability:
   males 15-49, 197,654; 114,204 fit for military service
Defense expenditures:
   exchange rate conversion - $11 million, about 2% of GNP (1989)

Sweden Geography

Total area: 449,964 km2
Land area: 410,928 km2
Comparative area: slightly smaller than California
Land boundaries:
   2,205 km total; Finland 586 km, Norway 1,619 km
Coastline:
   3,218 km
Maritime claims:

Continental shelf:
  200 m (depth) or to depth of exploitation
Exclusive fishing zone:
  200 nm
Territorial sea:
  12 nm
Disputes:
  none
Climate:
  temperate in south with cold, cloudy winters and cool, partly cloudy
  summers; subarctic in north
Terrain:
  mostly flat or gently rolling lowlands; mountains in west
Natural resources:
  zinc, iron ore, lead, copper, silver, timber, uranium, hydropower potential
Land use:
  arable land 7%; permanent crops 0%; meadows and pastures 2%; forest and
  woodland 64%; other 27%; includes irrigated NEGL%
Environment:
  water pollution; acid rain
Note:
  strategic location along Danish Straits linking Baltic and North Seas

:Sweden People

Population: 8,602,157 (July 1992), growth rate 0.4% (1992)
Birth rate: 13 births/1,000 population (1992)
Death rate: 11 deaths/1,000 population (1992)
Net migration rate: 2 migrants/1,000 population (1992)
Infant mortality rate: 6 deaths/1,000 live births (1992)
Life expectancy at birth: 75 years male, 81 years female (1992)
Total fertility rate: 1.9 children born/woman (1992)
Nationality:
  noun - Swede(s); adjective - Swedish
Ethnic divisions:
  homogeneous white population; small Lappish minority; foreign born or
  first-generation immigrants (Finns, Yugoslavs, Danes, Norwegians, Greeks,
  Turks) about 12%
Religions:
  Evangelical Lutheran 94%, Roman Catholic 1.5%, Pentecostal 1%, other 3.5%
  (1987)
Languages:
  Swedish, small Lapp- and Finnish-speaking minorities; immigrants speak
  native languages
Literacy:
  99% (male NA%, female NA%) age 15 and over can read and write (1979 est.)
Labor force:
  4,552,000 community, social and personal services 38.3%, mining and
  manufacturing 21.2%, commerce, hotels, and restaurants 14.1%, banking,
  insurance 9.0%, communications 7.2%, construction 7.0%, agriculture,
  fishing, and forestry 3.2% (1991)

Organized labor:
  80% of labor force (1990 est.)

:Sweden Government

Long-form name:
  Kingdom of Sweden
Type:
  constitutional monarchy
Capital: Stockholm
Administrative divisions:
  24 provinces (lan, singular and plural); Alvsborgs Lan, Blekinge Lan,
  Gavleborgs Lan, Goteborgs och Bohus Lan, Gotlands Lan, Hallands Lan,
  Jamtlands Lan, Jonkopings Lan, Kalmar Lan, Kopparbergs Lan, Kristianstads
  Lan, Kronobergs Lan, Malmohus Lan, Norrbottens Lan, Orebro Lan,
  Ostergotlands Lan, Skaraborgs Lan, Sodermanlands Lan, Stockholms Lan,
  Uppsala Lan, Varmlands Lan, Vasterbottens Lan, Vasternorrlands Lan,
  Vastmanlands Lan
Independence:
  6 June 1809, constitutional monarchy established
Constitution:
  1 January 1975
Legal system:
  civil law system influenced by customary law; accepts compulsory ICJ
  jurisdiction, with reservations
National holiday:
  Day of the Swedish Flag, 6 June
Executive branch:
  monarch, prime minister, Cabinet
Legislative branch:
  unicameral parliament (Riksdag)
Judicial branch:
  Supreme Court (Hogsta Domstolen)
Leaders:
 Chief of State:
  King CARL XVI GUSTAF (since 19 September 1973); Heir Apparent Princess
  VICTORIA Ingrid Alice Desiree, daughter of the King (born 14 July 1977)
 Head of Government:
  Prime Minister Carl BILDT (since 3 October 1991)
Political parties and leaders:
  ruling four-party coalition consists of the Moderate Party (conservative),
  Carl BILDT; Liberal People's Party, Bengt WESTERBERG; Center Party, Olof
  JOHANSSON; and the Christian Democratic Party, Alf SVENSSON; Social
  Democratic Party, Ingvar CARLSSON; New Democracy Party, Count Ian
  WACHTMEISTER; Left Party (VP; Communist), Lars WERNER; Swedish Com-
munist
  Party (SKP), Rune PETTERSSON; Communist Workers' Party, Rolf HAGEL;
Green
  Party, no formal leader
Suffrage:
  universal at age 18

Elections:
 Riksdag:
  last held 15 September 1991 (next to be held NA September 1994); results -
  Social Democratic Party 37.6%, Moderate Party (conservative) 21.9%, Liberal
  People's Party 9.1%, Center Party 8.5%, Christian Democrats 7.1%, New
  Democracy 6.7%, Left Party (Communist) 4.5%, Green Party 3.4%, other 1.2%;
  seats - (349 total) Social Democratic 138, Moderate Party (conservative) 80,
  Liberal People's Party 33, Center Party 31, Christian Democrats 26, New
  Democracy 25, Left Party (Communist) 16; note - the Green Party has no seats
  in the Riksdag because it received less than the required 4% of the vote
Communists:
  VP and SKP; VP, formerly the Left Party-Communists, is reported to have
  roughly 17,800 members and attracted 5.8% of the vote in the 1988 election;
  VP dropped the Communist label in 1990, but maintains a Marxist ideology

:Sweden Government

Member of:
  AfDB, AG (observer) AsDB, BIS, CCC, CE, CERN, CSCE, EBRD, ECE, EFTA,
ESA,
  FAO, G-6, G-8, G-9, G-10, GATT, IADB, IAEA, IBRD, ICAO, ICC, ICFTU, IDA,
  IEA, IFAD, IFC, ILO, IMF, IMO, INMARSAT, INTERPOL, INTELSAT, IOC,
IOM
  (observer), ISO, ITU, LORCS, NAM (guest), NC, NEA, NIB, OECD, PCA, UN,
  UNCTAD, UNESCO, UNFICYP, UNHCR, UNIDO, UNIFIL, UNIIMOG,
UNMOGIP, UNTSO, UPU,
  WHO, WIPO, WMO
Diplomatic representation:
  Ambassador Anders THUNBORG; Chancery at Suite 1200, 600 New Hampshire
Avenue
  NW, Washington, DC 20037; telephone (202) 944-5600; there are Swedish
  Consulates General in Chicago, Los Angeles, Minneapolis, and New York
 US:
  Ambassador Charles E. REDMAN; Embassy at Strandvagen 101, S-115 89
  Stockholm; telephone [46] (8) 783-5300; FAX [46] (8) 661-1964
Flag:
  blue with a yellow cross that extends to the edges of the flag; the vertical
  part of the cross is shifted to the hoist side in the style of the Dannebrog
  (Danish flag)

:Sweden Economy

Overview:
  Aided by a long period of peace and neutrality during World War I through
  World War II, Sweden has achieved an enviable standard of living under a
  mixed system of high-tech capitalism and extensive welfare benefits. It has
  essentially full employment, a modern distribution system, excellent
  internal and external communications, and a skilled labor force. Timber,
  hydropower, and iron ore constitute the resource base of an economy that is
  heavily oriented toward foreign trade. Privately owned firms account for
  about 90% of industrial output, of which the engineering sector accounts for
  50% of output and exports. In the last few years, however, this
  extraordinarily favorable picture has been clouded by inflation, growing

922

absenteeism, and a gradual loss of competitiveness in international markets. The new center-right government, facing a sagging economic situation which is unlikely to improve until 1993, is pushing full steam ahead with economic reform proposals to end Sweden's recession and to prepare for possible EC membership in 1995. The free-market-oriented reforms are designed to spur growth, maintain price stability, lower unemployment, create a more efficient welfare state, and further adapt to EC standards. The measures include: cutting taxes, particularly the value-added tax (VAT) and levies on new and small business; privatization; liberalizing foreign ownership restrictions; and opening the welfare system to competition and private alternatives, which the government will still finance. Growth is expected to remain flat in 1992, but increase slightly in 1993, while inflation should remain around 3% for the next few years. On the down side, unemployment may climb to slightly over 4% in 1993, and the budget deficit will reach nearly $9 billion in 1992.

GDP:
purchasing power equivalent - $147.6 billion, per capita $17,200; real growth rate -1.1% (1991)

Inflation rate (consumer prices):
8.0% (1991)

Unemployment rate: 2.7% (1991)

Budget:
revenues $67.5 billion; expenditures $78.7 billion, including capital expenditures of $NA (FY92 est.)

Exports:
$54.5 billion (f.o.b., 1991 est.)
commodities:
machinery, motor vehicles, paper products, pulp and wood, iron and steel products, chemicals, petroleum and petroleum products
partners:
EC, (FRG, UK, Denmark), US, Norway

Imports:
$50.2 billion (c.i.f., 1991 est.)
commodities:
machinery, petroleum and petroleum products, chemicals, motor vehicles, foodstuffs, iron and steel, clothing
partners:
EC 55.3%, US 8.4% (1990)

External debt: $10.7 billion (November 1991)

Industrial production:
growth rate -5.3% (1991)

Electricity:
39,716,000 kW capacity; 142,000 million kWh produced, 16,700 kWh per capita (1991)

:Sweden Economy

Industries:
iron and steel, precision equipment (bearings, radio and telephone parts, armaments), wood pulp and paper products, processed foods, motor vehicles

Agriculture:

animal husbandry predominates, with milk and dairy products accounting for 37% of farm income; main crops - grains, sugar beets, potatoes; 100% self-sufficient in grains and potatoes, 85% self-sufficient in sugar beets

Economic aid:
donor - ODA and OOF commitments (1970-89), $10.3 billion

Currency:
Swedish krona (plural - kronor); 1 Swedish krona (SKr) = 100 ore

Exchange rates:
Swedish kronor (SKr) per US$1 - 6.0259 (March 1992), 6.0475 (1991) 5.9188 (1990), 6.4469 (1989), 6.1272 (1988), 6.3404 (1987)

Fiscal year: 1 July - 30 June

:Sweden Communications

Railroads:
12,000 km total; Swedish State Railways (SJ) - 10,819 km 1.435-meter standard gauge, 6,955 km electrified and 1,152 km double track; 182 km 0.891-meter gauge; 117 km rail ferry service; privately owned railways - 511 km 1.435-meter standard gauge (332 km electrified); 371 km 0.891-meter gauge (all electrified)

Highways:
97,400 km (51,899 km paved, 20,659 km gravel, 24,842 km unimproved earth)

Inland waterways:
2,052 km navigable for small steamers and barges

Pipelines:
natural gas 84 km

Ports:
Gavle, Goteborg, Halmstad, Helsingborg, Kalmar, Malmo, Stockholm; numerous secondary and minor ports

Merchant marine:
186 ships (1,000 GRT or over) totaling 2,665,902 GRT/3,646,165 DWT; includes 10 short-sea passenger, 29 cargo, 3 container, 43 roll-on/roll-off cargo, 12 vehicle carrier, 2 railcar carrier, 33 petroleum tanker, 28 chemical tanker, 4 specialized tanker, 1 liquefied gas, 7 combination ore/oil, 12 bulk, 1 combination bulk, 1 refrigerated cargo

Civil air:
115 major transports

Airports:
254 total, 252 usable; 139 with permanent-surface runways; none with runways over 3,659 m; 10 with runways 2,440-3,659 m; 94 with runways 1,220-2,439 m

Telecommunications:
excellent domestic and international facilities; 8,200,000 telephones; mainly coaxial and multiconductor cables carry long-distance network; parallel microwave network carries primarily radio, TV and some telephone channels; automatic system; broadcast stations - 5 AM, 360 (mostly repeaters) FM, 880 (mostly repeaters) TV; 5 submarine coaxial cables; satellite earth stations - 1 Atlantic Ocean INTELSAT and 1 EUTELSAT

:Sweden Defense Forces

Branches:
Swedish Army, Swedish Navy, Swedish Air Force

Manpower availability:

males 15-49, 2,129,996; 1,858,944 fit for military service; 57,492 reach
military age (19) annually

Defense expenditures:
exchange rate conversion - $6.2 billion, about 4% of GDP (FY91)

Switzerland Geography

Total area: 41,290 km2
Land area: 39,770 km2
Comparative area: slightly more than twice the size of New Jersey
Land boundaries:
1,852 km total; Austria 164 km, France 573 km, Italy 740 km, Liechtenstein
41 km, Germany 334 km
Coastline:
none - landlocked
Maritime claims:
none - landlocked
Disputes:
none
Climate:
temperate, but varies with altitude; cold, cloudy, rainy/snowy winters; cool
to warm, cloudy, humid summers with occasional showers
Terrain:
mostly mountains (Alps in south, Jura in northwest) with a central plateau
of rolling hills, plains, and large lakes
Natural resources:
hydropower potential, timber, salt
Land use:
arable land 10%; permanent crops 1%; meadows and pastures 40%; forest and
woodland 26%; other 23%; includes irrigated 1%
Environment:
dominated by Alps
Note:
landlocked; crossroads of northern and southern Europe

:Switzerland People

Population: 6,828,023 (July 1992), growth rate 0.6% (1992)
Birth rate: 12 births/1,000 population (1992)
Death rate: 9 deaths/1,000 population (1992)
Net migration rate: 3 migrants/1,000 population (1992)
Infant mortality rate: 6 deaths/1,000 live births (1992)
Life expectancy at birth: 76 years male, 83 years female (1992)
Total fertility rate: 1.6 children born/woman (1992)
Nationality:
noun - Swiss (singular and plural); adjective - Swiss
Ethnic divisions:
total population - German 65%, French 18%, Italian 10%, Romansch 1%, other
6%; Swiss nationals - German 74%, French 20%, Italian 4%, Romansch 1%, other
1%
Religions:
Roman Catholic 47.6%, Protestant 44.3%, other 8.1% (1980)
Languages:

total population - German 65%, French 18%, Italian 12%, Romansch 1%, other 4%; Swiss nationals - German 74%, French 20%, Italian 4%, Romansch 1%, other 1%

Literacy:
99% (male NA%, female NA%) age 15 and over can read and write (1980 est.)

Labor force:
3,310,000; 904,095 foreign workers, mostly Italian; services 50%, industry and crafts 33%, government 10%, agriculture and forestry 6%, other 1% (1989)

Organized labor:
20% of labor force

:Switzerland Government

Long-form name:
Swiss Confederation

Type:
federal republic

Capital: Bern

Administrative divisions:
26 cantons (cantons, singular - canton in French; cantoni, singular - cantone in Italian; kantone, singular - kanton in German); Aargau, Ausser-Rhoden, Basel-Landschaft, Basel-Stadt, Bern, Fribourg, Geneve, Glarus, Graubunden, Inner-Rhoden, Jura, Luzern, Neuchatel, Nidwalden, Obwalden, Sankt Gallen, Schaffhausen, Schwyz, Solothurn, Thurgau, Ticino, Uri, Valais, Vaud, Zug, Zurich

Independence:
1 August 1291

Constitution:
29 May 1874

Legal system:
civil law system influenced by customary law; judicial review of legislative acts, except with respect to federal decrees of general obligatory character; accepts compulsory ICJ jurisdiction, with reservations

National holiday:
Anniversary of the Founding of the Swiss Confederation, 1 August (1291)

Executive branch:
president, vice president, Federal Council (German - Bundesrat, French - Conseil Federal, Italian - Consiglio Federale)

Legislative branch:
bicameral Federal Assembly (German - Bundesversammlung, French - Assemblee Federale, Italian - Assemblea Federale) consists of an upper council or Council of States (German - Standerat, French - Conseil des Etats, Italian - Consiglio degli Stati) and a lower council or National Council (German - Nationalrat, French - Conseil National, Italian - Consiglio Nazionale)

Judicial branch:
Federal Supreme Court

Leaders:
 Chief of State and Head of Government:
President Rene FELBER (1992 calendar year; presidency rotates annually); Vice President Adolf OGI (term runs concurrently with that of president)

Political parties and leaders:

Free Democratic Party (FDP), Bruno HUNZIKER, president; Social Democratic
Party (SPS), Helmut HUBACHER, chairman; Christian Democratic People's Party
(CVP), Eva SEGMULLER-WEBER, chairman; Swiss People's Party (SVP), Hans
UHLMANN, president; Green Party (GPS), Peter SCHMID, president; Automobile
Party (AP), DREYER; Alliance of Independents' Party (LdU), Dr. Franz JAEGER,
president; Swiss Democratic Party (SD), NA; Evangelical People's Party
(EVP), Max DUNKI, president; Workers' Party (PdA; Communist), Jean
SPIELMANN, general secretary; Ticino League, leader NA Liberal Party (LPS),
Gilbert COUTAU, president

Suffrage:
universal at age 18

Elections:
Council of States:
last held throughout 1991 (next to be held NA 1995); results - percent of
vote by party NA; seats - (46 total) FDP 18, CVP 16, SVP 4, SPS 3, LPS 3,
LdU 1, Ticino League 1

:Switzerland Government

National Council:
last held 20 October 1991 (next to be held NA October 1995); results -
percent of vote by party NA; seats - (200 total) FDP 44, SPS 42, CVP 37, SVP
25, GPS 14, LPS 10, AP 8, LdU 6, SD 5, EVP 3, PdA 2, Ticino League 2, other
2

Communists:
4,500 members (est.)

Member of:
AfDB, AG (observer), AsDB, BIS, CCC, CE, CERN, CSCE, EBRD, ECE, EFTA,
ESA,
FAO, G-8, G-10, GATT, IADB, IAEA, ICAO, ICC, ICFTU, IEA, IFAD, ILO, IMF,
IMO, INMARSAT, INTELSAT, INTERPOL, IOC, IOM, ISO, ITU, LORCS, NAM
(guest),
NEA, OAS (observer), OECD, PCA, UN (observer), UNCTAD, UNESCO,
UNHCR, UNIDO,
UPU, WCL, WHO, WIPO, WMO, WTO

Diplomatic representation:
Ambassador Edouard BRUNNER; Chancery at 2900 Cathedral Avenue NW,
Washington, DC 20008; telephone (202) 745-7900; there are Swiss Consulates
General in Atlanta, Chicago, Houston, Los Angeles, New York, and San
Francisco

US:
Ambassador Joseph B. GILDENHORN; Embassy at Jubilaeumstrasse 93, 3005
Bern;
telephone [41] (31) 437-011; FAX [41] (31) 437-344; there is a Branch Office
of the Embassy in Geneva and a Consulate General in Zurich

Flag:
red square with a bold, equilateral white cross in the center that does not
extend to the edges of the flag

:Switzerland Economy

Overview:
Switzerland's economic success is matched in few other nations. Per capita

output, general living standards, education and science, health care, and diet are unsurpassed in Europe. Economic stability helps promote the important banking and tourist sectors. Since World War II, Switzerland's economy has adjusted smoothly to the great changes in output and trade patterns in Europe and presumably can adjust to the challenges of the 1990s, particularly to the further economic integration of Western Europe and the amazingly rapid changes in East European political and economic prospects. After 8 years of growth, the economy experienced a mild recession in 1991 because monetary policy was tightened to combat inflation and because of the weak international economy. In the second half of 1992, however, Switzerland is expected to resume growth, despite inflation and unemployment problems. GDP growth for 1992 may be just under 1%, inflation should drop from 5.9% to 3.5%, and the trade deficit will continue to decline after dropping by over 15% to $5 billion, due to increased exports to Germany. Unemployment, however, is forecast to rise to 1.6% in 1992, up from 1.3% in 1991 and 0.5% in 1990.

GDP:
purchasing power equivalent - $147.4 billion, per capita $21,700; real growth rate -0.2% (1991 est.)

Inflation rate (consumer prices):
5.9% (1991)

Unemployment rate: 1.3% (1991)

Budget:
revenues $24.0 billion; expenditures $23.8 billion, including capital expenditures of $NA (1990)

Exports:
$62.2 billion (f.o.b., 1991 est.)
commodities:
machinery and equipment, precision instruments, metal products, foodstuffs, textiles and clothing
partners:
Western Europe 64% (EC 56%, other 8%), US 9%, Japan 4%

Imports:
$68.5 billion (c.i.f., 1991 est.)
commodities:
agricultural products, machinery and transportation equipment, chemicals, textiles, construction materials
partners:
Western Europe 78% (EC 71%, other 7%), US 6%

External debt: $NA

Industrial production:
growth rate 0.4% (1991 est.)

Electricity:
17,710,000 kW capacity; 59,070 million kWh produced, 8,930 kWh per capita (1991)

Industries:
machinery, chemicals, watches, textiles, precision instruments

Agriculture:
dairy farming predominates; less than 50% self-sufficient; food shortages - fish, refined sugar, fats and oils (other than butter), grains, eggs,

fruits, vegetables, meat

Economic aid:
donor - ODA and OOF commitments (1970-89), $3.5 billion

:Switzerland Economy

Currency:
Swiss franc, franken, or franco (plural - francs, franken, or franchi); 1
Swiss franc, franken, or franco (SwF) = 100 centimes, rappen, or centesimi

Exchange rates:
Swiss francs, franken, or franchi (SwF) per US$1 - 1.4037 (January 1992),
1.4340 (1991), 1.3892 (1990), 1.6359 (1989), 1.4633 (1988), 1.4912 (1987)

Fiscal year: calendar year

:Switzerland Communications

Railroads:
5,174 km total; 2,971 km are government owned and 2,203 km are nongovernment
owned; the government network consists of 2,897 km 1.435-meter standard
gauge and 74 km 1.000-meter narrow gauge track; 1,432 km double track, 99%
electrified; the nongovernment network consists of 710 km 1.435-meter
standard gauge, 1,418 km 1.000-meter gauge, and 75 km 0.790-meter gauge
track, 100% electrified

Highways:
62,145 km total (all paved), of which 18,620 km are canton and 1,057 km are
national highways (740 km autobahn); 42,468 km are communal roads

Inland waterways:
65 km; Rhine (Basel to Rheinfelden, Schaffhausen to Bodensee); 12 navigable
lakes

Pipelines:
crude oil 314 km, natural gas 1,506 km

Ports:
Basel (river port)

Merchant marine:
22 ships (1,000 GRT or over) totaling 325,234 GRT/576,953 DWT; includes 5
cargo, 2 roll-on/roll-off cargo, 3 chemical tanker, 2 specialized tanker, 9
bulk, 1 petroleum tanker

Civil air:
89 major transport aircraft

Airports:
66 total, 65 usable; 42 with permanent-surface runways; 2 with runways over
3,659 m; 5 with runways 2,440-3,659 m; 18 with runways 1,220-2,439 m

Telecommunications:
excellent domestic, international, and broadcast services; 5,890,000
telephones; extensive cable and microwave networks; broadcast stations - 7
AM, 265 FM, 18 (1,322 repeaters) TV; communications satellite earth station
operating in the INTELSAT (Atlantic Ocean and Indian Ocean) system

:Switzerland Defense Forces

Branches:
Army, Air Force, Frontier Guards, Fortification Guards

Manpower availability:
males 15-49, 1,798,632; 1,544,191 fit for military service; 43,952 reach

military age (20) annually

Defense expenditures:
  exchange rate conversion - $4.6 billion, about 2% of GDP (1990)

Syria Geography

Total area: 185,180 km2
Land area: 184,050 km2 (including 1,295 km2 of Israeli-occupied territory)
Comparative area: slightly larger than North Dakota
Land boundaries:
  2,253 km total; Iraq 605 km, Israel 76 km, Jordan 375 km, Lebanon 375 km,
  Turkey 822 km
Coastline:
  193 km
Maritime claims:
 Contiguous zone:
  6 nm beyond territorial sea limit
 Territorial sea:
  35 nm
Disputes:
  separated from Israel by the 1949 Armistice Line; Golan Heights is Israeli
  occupied; Hatay question with Turkey; periodic disputes with Iraq over
  Euphrates water rights; ongoing dispute over water development plans by
  Turkey for the Tigris and Euphrates Rivers
Climate:
  mostly desert; hot, dry, sunny summers (June to August) and mild, rainy
  winters (December to February) along coast
Terrain:
  primarily semiarid and desert plateau; narrow coastal plain; mountains in
  west
Natural resources:
  crude oil, phosphates, chrome and manganese ores, asphalt, iron ore, rock
  salt, marble, gypsum
Land use:
  arable land 28%; permanent crops 3%; meadows and pastures 46%; forest and
  woodland 3%; other 20%; includes irrigated 3%
Environment:
  deforestation; overgrazing; soil erosion; desertification
Note:
  there are 38 Jewish settlements in the Israeli-occupied Golan Heights

:Syria People

Population: 13,730,436 (July 1992), growth rate 3.8% (1992); in addition, there are at
  least 14,500 Druze and 14,000 Jewish settlers in the Israeli-occupied Golan
  Heights (1992 est.)
Birth rate: 44 births/1,000 population (1992)
Death rate: 7 deaths/1,000 population (1992)
Net migration rate: 0 migrants/1,000 population (1992)
Infant mortality rate: 45 deaths/1,000 live births (1992)
Life expectancy at birth: 65 years male, 67 years female (1992)
Total fertility rate: 6.9 children born/woman (1992)
Nationality:

noun - Syrian(s); adjective - Syrian
Ethnic divisions:
 Arab 90.3%; Kurds, Armenians, and other 9.7%
Religions:
 Sunni Muslim 74%, Alawite, Druze, and other Muslim sects 16%, Christian
 (various sects) 10%, tiny Jewish communities in Damascus, Al Qamishli, and
 Aleppo
Languages:
 Arabic (official), Kurdish, Armenian, Aramaic, Circassian; French widely
 understood
Literacy:
 64% (male 78%, female 51%) age 15 and over can read and write (1990 est.)
Labor force:
 2,400,000; miscellaneous and government services 36%, agriculture 32%,
 industry and construction 32%; majority unskilled; shortage of skilled labor
 (1984)
Organized labor:
 5% of labor force

:Syria Government

Long-form name:
 Syrian Arab Republic
Type:
 republic; under leftwing military regime since March 1963
Capital: Damascus
Administrative divisions:
 14 provinces (muhafazat, singular - muhafazah); Al Hasakah, Al Ladhiqiyah,
 Al Qunaytirah, Ar Raqqah, As Suwayda', Dar`a, Dayr az Zawr, Dimashq, Halab,
 Hamah, Hims, Idlib, Rif Dimashq, Tartus
Independence:
 17 April 1946 (from League of Nations mandate under French administration);
 formerly United Arab Republic
Constitution:
 13 March 1973
Legal system:
 based on Islamic law and civil law system; special religious courts; has not
 accepted compulsory ICJ jurisdiction
National holiday:
 National Day, 17 April (1946)
Executive branch:
 president, three vice presidents, prime minister, three deputy prime
 ministers, Council of Ministers (cabinet)
Legislative branch:
 unicameral People's Council (Majlis al-Chaab)
Judicial branch:
 Supreme Constitutional Court, High Judicial Council, Court of Cassation,
 State Security Courts
Leaders:
 Chief of State:
 President Hafiz al-ASAD (since 22 February 1971); Vice Presidents `Abd

al-Halim KHADDAM, Vice President Rif at al-ASAD, and Vice President Muham-mad
Zuhayr MASHARIQA (since 11 March 1984)
Head of Government:
Prime Minister Mahmud ZU`BI (since 1 November 1987); Deputy Prime Minister
Lt. Gen. Mustafa TALAS (since 11 March 1984); Deputy Prime Minister Salim
YASIN (since NA December 1981); Deputy Prime Minister Mahmud QADDUR (since
. NA May 1985)
Political parties and leaders:
ruling party is the Arab Socialist Resurrectionist (Ba`th) Party; the
Progressive National Front is dominated by Ba`thists but includes
independents and members of the Syrian Arab Socialist Party (ASP), Arab
Socialist Union (ASU), Syrian Communist Party (SCP), Arab Socialist Unionist
Movement, and Democratic Socialist Union Party
Suffrage:
universal at age 18
Elections:
President:
last held 2 December 1991 (next to be held December 1998); results -
President Hafiz al-ASAD was reelected for a fourth seven-year term with
99.98% of the vote
People's Council:
last held 22-23 May 1990 (next to be held NA May 1994); results - Ba`th
53.6%, ASU 3.2%, SCP 3.2%, Arab Socialist Unionist Movement 2.8%, ASP 2%,
Democratic Socialist Union Party 1.6%, independents 33.6%; seats - (250
total) Ba`th 134, ASU 8, SCP 8, Arab Socialist Unionist Movement 7, ASP 5,
Democratic Socialist Union Party 4, independents 84; note - the People's
Council was expanded to 250 seats total prior to the May 1990 election

:Syria Government

Communists:
Syrian Communist Party (SCP)
Other political or pressure groups:
non-Ba`th parties have little effective political influence; Communist party
ineffective; conservative religious leaders; Muslim Brotherhood
Member of:
ABEDA, AFESD, AL, AMF, CAEU, CCC, ESCWA, FAO, G-24, G-77, IAEA, IBRD, ICAO,
ICC, IDA, IDB, IFAD, IFC, ILO, IMF, IMO, INTELSAT, INTERPOL, IOC, ISO, ITU,
LORCS, NAM, OAPEC, OIC, UN, UNCTAD, UNESCO, UNIDO, UNRWA, UPU, WFTU, WHO,
WMO, WTO
Diplomatic representation:
Ambassador Walid MOUALEM; Chancery at 2215 Wyoming Avenue NW, Wash-ington, DC
20008; telephone (202) 232-6313
US:
Ambassador Christopher W. S. ROSS; Embassy at Abu Rumaneh, Al Mansur Street

932

No. 2, Damascus (mailing address is P. O. Box 29, Damascus); telephone [963] (11) 333052 or 332557, 330416, 332814, 332315, 714108, 337178, 333232; FAX [963] (11) 718-687

Flag:

three equal horizontal bands of red (top), white, and black with two small green five-pointed stars in a horizontal line centered in the white band; similar to the flag of Yemen, which has a plain white band and of Iraq, which has three green stars (plus an Arabic inscription) in a horizontal line centered in the white band; also similar to the flag of Egypt, which has a symbolic eagle centered in the white band

:Syria Economy

Overview:

Syria's state-dominated Ba`thist economy has benefited from the Gulf war, increased oil production, good weather, and economic deregulation. Economic growth averaged nearly 12% annually in 1990-91, buoyed by increased oil production and improved agricultural performance. The Gulf war of early 1991 provided Syria an aid windfall of several billion dollars from Arab, European, and Japanese donors. These inflows more than offset Damascus's war-related costs and will help Syria cover some of its debt arrears, restore suspended credit lines, and initiate selected military and civilian purchases. For the long run, Syria's economy is still saddled with a large number of poorly performing public sector firms; investment levels remain low; and industrial and agricultural productivity is poor. A major long-term concern is the additional drain of upstream Euphrates water by Turkey when its vast dam and irrigation projects are completed by mid-decade.

GDP:

exchange rate conversion - $30 billion, per capita $2,300; real growth rate 11% (1991 est.)

Inflation rate (consumer prices):

25% (1991 est.)

Unemployment rate: NA%

Budget:

revenues $5.4 billion; expenditures $7.5 billion, including capital expenditures of $2.9 billion (1991 est.)

Exports:

$3.6 billion (f.o.b., 1991 est.)

commodities:

petroleum 40%, farm products 13%, textiles, phosphates (1989)

partners:

USSR and Eastern Europe 42%, EC 31%, Arab countries 17%, US/Canada 2% (1989)

Imports:

$2.7 billion (f.o.b., 1991 est.)

commodities:

foodstuffs and beverages 21%, metal and metal products 16%, machinery 14%, textiles, petroleum products (1989)

partners:

EC 42%, USSR and Eastern Europe 13%, other Europe 13%, US/Canada 8%, Arab countries 6% (1989)

External debt: $5.2 billion in hard currency (1990 est.)

Industrial production:
   growth rate 6% (1991 est.); accounts for 17% of GDP

Electricity:
   3,005,000 kW capacity; 8,800 million kWh produced, 680 kWh per capita (1991)

Industries:
   textiles, food processing, beverages, tobacco, phosphate rock mining,
   petroleum

Agriculture:
   accounts for 27% of GDP and one-third of labor force; all major crops
   (wheat, barley, cotton, lentils, chickpeas) grown mainly on rainfed land
   causing wide swings in production; animal products - beef, lamb, eggs,
   poultry, milk; not self-sufficient in grain or livestock products

Economic aid:
   US commitments, including Ex-Im (FY70-81), $538 million; Western (non-US)
   ODA and OOF bilateral commitments (1970-89), $1.23 billion; OPEC bilateral
   aid (1979-89), $12.3 billion; former Communist countries (1970-89), $3.3
   billion

Currency:
   Syrian pound (plural - pounds); 1 Syrian pound (#S) = 100 piasters

:Syria Economy

Exchange rates:
   Syrian pounds (#S) per US$1 - 22.0 (promotional rate since 1991), 11.2250
   (fixed rate 1987-90), 3.9250 (fixed rate 1976-87)

Fiscal year: calendar year

:Syria Communications

Railroads:
   2,350 km total; 2,035 km standard gauge, 315 km 1.050-meter (narrow) gauge

Highways:
   28,000 km total; 22,000 km paved, 3,000 km gravel or crushed stone, 3,000 km
   improved earth

Inland waterways:
   672 km; minimal economic importance

Pipelines:
   crude oil 1,304 km, petroleum products 515 km

Ports:
   Tartus, Latakia, Baniyas

Merchant marine:
   29 ships (1,000 GRT or over) totaling 85,417 GRT/138,078 DWT; includes 25
   cargo, 1 roll-on/roll-off cargo, 1 vehicle carrier, 2 bulk

Civil air:
   35 major transport aircraft

Airports:
   104 total, 100 usable; 24 with permanent-surface runways; none with runways
   over 3,659 m; 21 with runways 2,440-3,659 m; 3 with runways 1,220-2,439 m

Telecommunications:
   fair system currently undergoing significant improvement; 512,600
   telephones; broadcast stations - 9 AM, 1 FM, 17 TV; satellite earth stations

- 1 Indian Ocean INTELSAT and 1 Intersputnik, 1 submarine cable; coaxial
cable and radio relay to Iraq, Jordan, Lebanon, and Turkey

:Syria Defense Forces

Branches:
Syrian Arab Army, Syrian Arab Navy, Syrian Arab Air Force, Syrian Arab Air
Defense Forces, Police and Security Force
Manpower availability:
males 15-49, 3,012,671; 1,691,660 fit for military service; 145,976 reach
military age (19) annually
Defense expenditures:
exchange rate conversion - $2.5 billion, 8% of GDP (1989)

Taiwan Geography

Total area: 35,980 km2
Land area: 32,260 km2; includes the Pescadores, Matsu, and Quemoy
Comparative area: slightly less than three times the size of Connecticut
Land boundaries:
none
Coastline:
1,448 km
Maritime claims:
 Exclusive economic zone:
200 nm
 Territorial sea:
12 nm
Disputes:
involved in complex dispute over the Spratly Islands with China, Malaysia,
Philippines, Vietnam, and possibly Brunei; Paracel Islands occupied by
China, but claimed by Vietnam and Taiwan; Japanese-administered
Senkaku-shoto (Senkaku Islands/Diaoyu Tai) claimed by China and Taiwan
Climate:
tropical; marine; rainy season during southwest monsoon (June to August);
cloudiness is persistent and extensive all year
Terrain:
eastern two-thirds mostly rugged mountains; flat to gently rolling plains in
west
Natural resources:
small deposits of coal, natural gas, limestone, marble, and asbestos
Land use:
arable land 24%; permanent crops 1%; meadows and pastures 5%; forest and
woodland 55%; other 15%; irrigated 14%
Environment:
subject to earthquakes and typhoons

:Taiwan People

Population: 20,878,556 (July 1992), growth rate 1.0% (1992)
Birth rate: 16 births/1,000 population (1992)
Death rate: 5 deaths/1,000 population (1992)
Net migration rate: NEGL migrants/1,000 population (1992)
Infant mortality rate: 6 deaths/1,000 live births (1992)

Life expectancy at birth: 72 years male, 78 years female (1992)
Total fertility rate: 1.8 children born/woman (1992)
Nationality:
  noun - Chinese (singular and plural); adjective - Chinese
Ethnic divisions:
  Taiwanese 84%, mainland Chinese 14%, aborigine 2%
Religions:
  mixture of Buddhist, Confucian, and Taoist 93%, Christian 4.5%, other 2.5%
Languages:
  Mandarin Chinese (official); Taiwanese (Miu) and Hakka dialects also used
Literacy:
  91.2% (male NA%, female NA%) age 15 and over can read and write (1990)
Labor force:
  7,900,000; industry and commerce 53%, services 22%, agriculture 15.6%, civil
  administration 7% (1989)
Organized labor:
  2,728,000 or about 44% (1991)

:Taiwan Government

Long-form name:
  none
Type:
  multiparty democratic regime; opposition political parties legalized in
  March, 1989
Capital: Taipei
Administrative divisions:
  the authorities in Taipei claim to be the government of all China; in
  keeping with that claim, the central administrative divisions include 2
  provinces (sheng, singular and plural) and 2 municipalities* (shih, singular
  and plural) - Fu-chien (some 20 offshore islands of Fujian Province
  including Quemoy and Matsu), Kao-hsiung*, T'ai-pei*, and Taiwan (the island
  of Taiwan and the Pescadores islands); the more commonly referenced
  administrative divisions are those of Taiwan Province - 16 counties (hsien,
  singular and plural), 5 municipalities* (shih, singular and plural), and 2
  special municipalities** (chuan-shih, singular and plural); Chang-hua,
  Chia-i, Chia-i*, Chi-lung*, Hsin-chu, Hsin-chu*, Hua-lien, I-lan,
  Kao-hsiung, Kao-hsiung**, Miao-li, Nan-t'ou, P'eng-hu, P'ing-tung,
  T'ai-chung, T'ai-chung*, T'ai-nan, T'ai-nan*, T'ai-pei, T'ai-pei**,
  T'ai-tung, T'ao-yuan, and Yun-lin; the provincial capital is at
  Chung-hsing-hsin-ts'un; note - Taiwan uses the Wade-Giles system for
  romanization
Constitution:
  25 December 1947, presently undergoing revision
Legal system:
  based on civil law system; accepts compulsory ICJ jurisdiction, with
  reservations
National holiday:
  National Day (Anniversary of the Revolution), 10 October (1911)
Executive branch:
  president, vice president, premier of the Executive Yuan, vice premier of

the Executive Yuan, Executive Yuan
Legislative branch:
  unicameral Legislative Yuan, unicameral National Assembly
Judicial branch:
  Judicial Yuan
Leaders:
  Chief of State:
  President LI Teng-hui (since 13 January 1988); Vice President LI Yuan-zu
  (since 20 May 1990)
  Head of Government:
  Premier (President of the Executive Yuan) HAO Po-ts'un (since 2 May 1990);
  Vice Premier (Vice President of the Executive Yuan) SHIH Ch'i-yang (since NA
  July 1988)
Political parties and leaders:
  Kuomintang (Nationalist Party), LI Teng-hui, chairman; Democratic Socialist
  Party and Young China Party controlled by Kuomintang; Democratic Progressive
  Party (DPP); Labor Party; 27 other minor parties
Suffrage:
  universal at age 20
Elections:
  President:
  last held 21 March 1990 (next to be held NA March 1996); results - President
  LI Teng-hui was reelected by the National Assembly
  Vice President:
  last held 21 March 1990 (next to be held NA March 1996); results - LI
  Yuan-zu was elected by the National Assembly

:Taiwan Government

  Legislative Yuan:
  last held 2 December 1989 (next to be held NA December 1992); results - KMT
  65%, DPP 33%, independents 2%; seats - (304 total, 102 elected) KMT 78, DPP
  21, independents 3
Elections:
  National Assembly:
  first National Assembly elected in November 1947 with a supplementary
  election in December 1986; second National Assembly elected in December 1991
Member of:
  expelled from UN General Assembly and Security Council on 25 October 1971
  and withdrew on same date from other charter-designated subsidiary organs;
  expelled from IMF/World Bank group April/May 1980; seeking to join GATT;
  attempting to retain membership in INTELSAT; suspended from IAEA in 1972,
  but still allows IAEA controls over extensive atomic development; APEC,
  AsDB, ICC, ICFTU, IOC
Diplomatic representation:
  none; unofficial commercial and cultural relations with the people of the US
  are maintained through a private instrumentality, the Coordination Council
  for North American Affairs (CCNAA) with headquarters in Taipei and field
  offices in Washington and 10 other US cities with all addresses and
  telephone numbers NA
US:

unofficial commercial and cultural relations with the people of Taiwan are
maintained through a private institution, the American Institute in Taiwan
(AIT), which has offices in Taipei at #7, Lane 134, Hsiu Yi Road, Section 3,
telephone [886] (2) 709-2000, and in Kao-hsiung at #2 Chung Cheng 3d Road,
telephone [886] (7) 224-0154 through 0157, and the American Trade Center at
Room 3207 International Trade Building, Taipei World Trade Center, 333
Keelung Road Section 1, Taipei 10548, telephone [886] (2) 720-1550

Flag:
red with a dark blue rectangle in the upper hoist-side corner bearing a
white sun with 12 triangular rays

:Taiwan Economy

Overview:
Taiwan has a dynamic capitalist economy with considerable government
guidance of investment and foreign trade and partial government ownership of
some large banks and industrial firms. Real growth in GNP has averaged about
9% a year during the past three decades. Export growth has been even faster
and has provided the impetus for industrialization. Agriculture contributes
about 4% to GNP, down from 35% in 1952. Taiwan currently ranks as number 13
among major trading countries. Traditional labor-intensive industries are
steadily being replaced with more capital- and technology-intensive
industries. Taiwan has become a major investor in China, Thailand,
Indonesia, the Philippines, and Malaysia. The tightening of labor markets
has led to an influx of foreign workers, both legal and illegal.

GNP:
purchasing power equivalent - $150.8 billion, per capita $7,380; real growth
rate 5.2% (1990)

Inflation rate (consumer prices):
4.1% (1990); 3.8% (1991 est.)

Unemployment rate: 1.7% (1990); 1.5% (1991 est.)

Budget:
revenues $30.3 billion; expenditures $30.1 billion, including capital
expenditures of $NA (FY91 est.)

Exports:
$67.2 billion (f.o.b., 1990)
commodities:
electrical machinery 18.2%, textiles 15.6%, general machinery and equipment
14.8%, basic metals and metal products 7.8%, foodstuffs 1.7%, plywood and
wood products 1.6% (1989)
partners:
US 36.2%, Japan 13.7% (1989)

Imports:
$54.7 billion (c.i.f., 1990)
commodities:
machinery and equipment 15.3%, basic metals 13.0%, chemical and chemical
products 11.1%, crude oil 5%, foodstuffs 2.2% (1989)
partners:
Japan 31%, US 23%, FRG 5% (1989)

External debt: $1.1 billion (December 1990 est.)

Industrial production:

growth rate 6.5% (1991 est.)

Electricity:
17,000,000 kW capacity; 76,900 million kWh produced, 3,722 kWh per capita (1991)

Industries:
electronics, textiles, chemicals, clothing, food processing, plywood, sugar milling, cement, shipbuilding, petroleum

Agriculture:
accounts for 4% of GNP and 16% of labor force (includes part-time farmers); heavily subsidized sector; major crops - vegetables, rice, fruit, tea; livestock - hogs, poultry, beef, milk, cattle; not self-sufficient in wheat, soybeans, corn; fish catch increasing, 1.4 million metric tons (1988)

Economic aid:
US, including Ex-Im (FY46-82), $4.6 billion; Western (non-US) countries, ODA and OOF bilateral commitments (1970-89), $500 million

Currency:
New Taiwan dollar (plural - dollars); 1 New Taiwan dollar (NT$) = 100 cents

:Taiwan Economy

Exchange rates:
New Taiwan dollars per US$1 - 25.000 (February 1992), 25.748 (1991), 27.108 (1990), 26.407 (1989) 28.589 (1988), 31.845 (1987)

Fiscal year: 1 July - 30 June

:Taiwan Communications

Railroads:
about 4,600 km total track with 1,075 km common carrier lines and 3,525 km industrial lines; common carrier lines consist of the 1.067-meter gauge 708 km West Line and the 367 km East Line; a 98.25 km South Link Line connection was completed in late 1991; common carrier lines owned by the government and operated by the Railway Administration under Ministry of Communications; industrial lines owned and operated by government enterprises

Highways:
20,041 km total; 17,095 km bituminous or concrete pavement, 2,371 km crushed stone or gravel, 575 km graded earth

Pipelines:
petroleum products 615 km, natural gas 97 km

Ports:
Kao-hsiung, Chi-lung (Keelung), Hua-lien, Su-ao, T'ai-tung

Merchant marine:
213 ships (1,000 GRT or over) totaling 6,491,539 GRT/9,082,118 DWT; includes 1 passenger, 42 cargo, 15 refrigerated cargo, 73 container, 17 petroleum tanker, 3 combination ore/oil, 1 specialized tanker, 58 bulk, 1 roll-on/roll-off, 2 combination bulk

Airports:
40 total, 39 usable; 36 with permanent-surface runways; 3 with runways over 3,659 m; 16 with runways 2,440-3,659 m; 8 with runways 1,220-2,439 m

Telecommunications:
best developed system in Asia outside of Japan; 7,800,000 telephones; extensive microwave transmission links on east and west coasts; broadcast stations - 91 AM, 23 FM, 15 TV (13 repeaters); 8,620,000 radios; 6,386,000

TVs (5,680,000 color, 706,000 monochrome); satellite earth stations - 1 Pacific Ocean INTELSAT and 1 Indian Ocean INTELSAT; submarine cable links to Japan (Okinawa), the Philippines, Guam, Singapore, Hong Kong, Indonesia, Australia, Middle East, and Western Europe

:Taiwan Defense Forces

Branches:
  Army, Navy (including Marines), Air Force, Taiwan General Garrison Headquarters, Ministry of National Defense
Manpower availability:
  males 15-49, 5,982,717; 4,652,586 fit for military service; about 180,706 currently reach military age (19) annually
Defense expenditures:
  exchange rate conversion - $9.16 billion, 4.5% of GNP (FY92)

Tajikistan Geography

Total area: 143,100 km2
Land area: 142,700 km2
Comparative area: slightly smaller than Wisconsin
Land boundaries:
  3,651 km total; Afghanistan 1,206 km, China 414 km, Kyrgyzstan 870 km, Uzbekistan 1,161 km
Coastline:
  none - landlocked
Maritime claims:
  none - landlocked
Disputes:
  boundary with China under dispute
Climate:
  midlatitude semiarid to polar in Pamir Mountains
Terrain:
  Pamir and Alay Mountains dominate landscape; western Fergana Valley in north, Kafirnigan and Vakhsh Valleys in southeast
Natural resources:
  significant hydropower potential, petroleum, uranium, mercury, small production of petroleum, brown coal, lead, zinc, antimony, tungsten
Land use:
  6% arable land; NA% permanent crops; NA% meadows and pastures; NA% forest and woodland; NA% other; includes NA% irrigated
Environment:
  NA
Note:
  landlocked

:Tajikistan People

Population: 5,680,242 (July 1992), growth rate 3.0% (1992)
Birth rate: 40 births/1,000 population (1992)
Death rate: 8 deaths/1,000 population (1992)
Net migration rate: -1 migrant/1,000 population (1992)
Infant mortality rate: 74 deaths/1,000 live births (1992)
Life expectancy at birth: 64 years male, 70 years female (1992)

Total fertility rate: 5.3 children born/woman (1992)
Nationality:
   noun - Tajik(s); adjective - Tajik
Ethnic divisions:
   Tajik 62%, Uzbek 24%, Russian 8%, Tatar 2%, other 4%
Religions:
   Sunni Muslim approximately 80%, Shi`a Muslim 5%
Languages:
   Tajik (official) NA%
Literacy:
   NA% (male NA%, female NA%) age 15 and over can read and write
Labor force:
   1,938,000; agriculture and forestry 43%, industry and construction 22%,
   other 35% (1990)
Organized labor:
   NA

:Tajikistan Government

Long-form name:
   Republic of Tajikistan
Type:
   republic
Capital: Dushanbe
Administrative divisions:
   3 oblasts (oblastey, singular - oblast') and one autonomous oblast*;
   Gorno-Badakhshan*; Kurgan-Tyube, Kulyab, Leninabad (Khudzhand); note - the
   rayons around Dushanbe are under direct republic jurisdiction; an oblast
   usually has the same name as its administrative center (exceptions have the
   administrative center name following in parentheses)
Independence:
   9 September 1991 (from Soviet Union); formerly Tajikistan Soviet Socialist
   Republic
Constitution:
   adopted NA April 1978
Legal system:
   based on civil law system; no judicial review of legislative acts
National holiday:
   NA
Executive branch:
   president, prime minister
Legislative branch:
   unicameral Supreme Soviet
Judicial branch:
   NA
Leaders:
   Chief of State:
   President Rakhman NABIYEV (since NA September 1991); note - a government of
   National Reconciliation was formed in May 1992; NABIYEV is titular head
   Head of Government:
   Prime Minister Akbar MIRZOYEV (since 10 January 1992); First Deputy Prime

Minister Davlat USMON

Political parties and leaders:

Tajik Democratic Party, Shodmon YUSUF, chairman; Rastokhez (Rebirth), Tohir ABDULJABAR, chairman; Islamic Revival Party, Sharif HIMMOT-ZODA, chairman

Suffrage:

universal at age 18

Elections:

President:

last held 27 October 1991 (next to be held NA); results - Rakhman NABIYEV, Communist Party 60%; Daolat KHUDONAZAROV, Democratic Party, Islamic Rebirth

Party and Rastokhoz Party 30%

Supreme Soviet:

last held 25 February 1990 (next to be held NA); results - Communist Party 99%, other 1%; seats - (230 total) Communist Party 227, other 3

Communists:

NA

Other political or pressure groups:

Kazi Kolon, Akbar TURAJON-SODA, Muslim leader

Member of:

CSCE, IMF, UN

Diplomatic representation:

NA

US:

Ambassador-designate Stan ESCUDERO; Embassy at Interim Chancery, #39 Ainii Street; Residences: Oktyabrskaya Hotel, Dushanbe (mailing address is APO AE 09862); telephone [8] (011) 7-3772-24-32-23

:Tajikistan Government

Flag:

NA; still in the process of designing one

:Tajikistan Economy

Overview:

Tajikistan has had the lowest standard of living and now faces the bleakest economic prospects of the 15 former Soviet republics. Agriculture is the main economic sector, normally accounting for 38% of employment and featuring cotton and fruits. Industry is sparse, bright spots including electric power and aluminum production based on the country's sizable hydropower resources and a surprising specialty in the production of metal-cutting machine tools. In 1991 and early 1992, disruptions in food supplies from the outside have severely strained the availability of food throughout the republic. The combination of the poor food supply, the general disruption of industrial links to suppliers and markets, and political instability have meant that the republic's leadership could make little progress in economic reform in 1991 and early 1992.

GDP:

$NA, per capita $NA; real growth rate -9% (1991 est.)

Inflation rate (consumer prices):

84% (1991)

Unemployment rate: 25% (1991 est.)
Budget:
  $NA
Exports:
  $706 million (1990)
  commodities:
  aluminum, cotton, fruits, vegetable oil, textiles
  partners:
  Russia, Kazakhstan, Ukraine, Uzbekistan
Imports:
  $1.3 billion (1990)
  commodities:
  chemicals, machinery and transport equipment, textiles, foodstuffs
  partners:
  NA
External debt: $650 million (end of 1991 est.)
Industrial production:
  growth rate -2.0% (1991)
Electricity:
  4,575,000 kW capacity; 17,500 million kWh produced, 3,384 kWh per capita
  (1991)
Industries:
  aluminum, zinc, lead, chemicals and fertilizers, cement, vegetable oil,
  metal-cutting machine tools, refrigerators and freezers
Agriculture:
  cotton, grain, fruits, grapes, vegetables; cattle, pigs, sheep and goats,
  yaks
Illicit drugs:
  illicit producers of cannabis and opium; mostly for domestic consumption;
  status of government eradication programs unknown; used as transshipment
  points for illicit drugs to Western Europe
Economic aid:
  NA
Currency:
  as of May 1992, retaining ruble as currency
Exchange rates:
  NA
Fiscal year: calendar year

:Tajikistan Communications

Railroads:
  480 km all 1.520-meter (broad) gauge (includes NA km electrified); does not
  include industrial lines (1990); 258 km between Dushanbe (Tajikistan) and
  Termez (Uzbekistan), connects with the railroad system of the other
  republics of the former Soviet Union at Tashkent in Uzbekistan
Highways:
  29,900 km total (1990); 24,400 km hard surfaced, 8,500 km earth
Inland waterways:
  NA km perennially navigable
Pipelines:

NA
Civil air:
  NA
Airports:
  NA
Telecommunications:
  poorly developed; telephone density NA; linked by landline or microwave with
  other CIS member states and by leased connections via the Moscow
  international gateway switch to other countries; satellite earth stations -
  Orbita and INTELSAT (TV receive only)

:Tajikistan Defense Forces

Branches:
  Republic Security Forces (internal and border troops), National Guard; CIS
  Forces (Ground, Air, and Air Defense)
Manpower availability:
  males 15-49, NA; NA fit for military service; NA reach military age (18)
  annually
Defense expenditures:
  $NA, NA% of GDP

Tanzania Geography

Total area: 945,090 km2
Land area: 886,040 km2; includes the islands of Mafia, Pemba, and Zanzibar
Comparative area: slightly larger than twice the size of California
Land boundaries:
  3,402 km total; Burundi 451 km, Kenya 769 km, Malawi 475 km, Mozambique 756
  km, Rwanda 217 km, Uganda 396 km, Zambia 338 km
Coastline:
  1,424 km
Maritime claims:
 Exclusive economic zone:
  200 nm
 Territorial sea:
  12 nm
Disputes:
  boundary dispute with Malawi in Lake Nyasa; Tanzania-Zaire-Zambia tripoint
  in Lake Tanganyika may no longer be indefinite since it is reported that the
  indefinite section of the Zaire-Zambia boundary has been settled
Climate:
  varies from tropical along coast to temperate in highlands
Terrain:
  plains along coast; central plateau; highlands in north, south
Natural resources:
  hydropower potential, tin, phosphates, iron ore, coal, diamonds, gemstones,
  gold, natural gas, nickel
Land use:
  arable land 5%; permanent crops 1%; meadows and pastures 40%; forest and
  woodland 47%; other 7%; includes irrigated NEGL%
Environment:

lack of water and tsetse fly limit agriculture; recent droughts affected marginal agriculture; Kilimanjaro is highest point in Africa

:Tanzania People

Population: 27,791,552 (July 1992), growth rate 3.4% (1992)
Birth rate: 49 births/1,000 population (1992)
Death rate: 15 deaths/1,000 population (1992)
Net migration rate: -1 migrant/1,000 population (1992)
Infant mortality rate: 103 deaths/1,000 live births (1992)
Life expectancy at birth: 50 years male, 55 years female (1992)
Total fertility rate: 7.0 children born/woman (1992)
Nationality:
    noun - Tanzanian(s); adjective - Tanzanian
Ethnic divisions:
    mainland - native African consisting of well over 100 tribes 99%; Asian,
    European, and Arab 1%
Religions:
    mainland - Christian 33%, Muslim 33%, indigenous beliefs 33%; Zanzibar -
    almost all Muslim
Languages:
    Swahili and English (official); English primary language of commerce,
    administration, and higher education; Swahili widely understood and
    generally used for communication between ethnic groups; first language of
    most people is one of the local languages; primary education is generally in
    Swahili
Literacy:
    46% (male 62%, female 31%) age 15 and over can read and write (1978)
Labor force:
    732,200 wage earners; 90% agriculture, 10% industry and commerce (1986 est.)
Organized labor:
    15% of labor force

:Tanzania Government

Long-form name:
    United Republic of Tanzania
Type:
    republic
Capital: Dar es Salaam; some government offices have been transferred to Dodoma,
    which is planned as the new national capital by the end of the 1990s
Administrative divisions:
    25 regions; Arusha, Dar es Salaam, Dodoma, Iringa, Kigoma, Kilimanjaro,
    Lindi, Mara, Mbeya, Morogoro, Mtwara, Mwanza, Pemba North, Pemba South,
    Pwani, Rukwa, Ruvuma, Shinyanga, Singida, Tabora, Tanga, Zanzibar
    Central/South, Zanzibar North, Zanzibar Urban/West, Ziwa Magharibi
Independence:
    Tanganyika became independent 9 December 1961 (from UN trusteeship under
    British administration); Zanzibar became independent 19 December 1963 (from
    UK); Tanganyika united with Zanzibar 26 April 1964 to form the United
    Republic of Tanganyika and Zanzibar; renamed United Republic of Tanzania 29
    October 1964
Constitution:

15 March 1984 (Zanzibar has its own Constitution but remains subject to provisions of the union Constitution)

Legal system:
based on English common law; judicial review of legislative acts limited to matters of interpretation; has not accepted compulsory ICJ jurisdiction

National holiday:
Union Day, 26 April (1964)

Executive branch:
president, first vice president and prime minister of the union, second vice president and president of Zanzibar, Cabinet

Legislative branch:
unicameral National Assembly (Bunge)

Judicial branch:
Court of Appeal, High Court

Leaders:
Chief of State:
President Ali Hassan MWINYI (since 5 November 1985); First Vice President John MALECELA (since 9 November 1990); Second Vice President Salmin AMOUR
(since 9 November 1990)
Head of Government:
Prime Minister John MALECELA (since 9 November 1990)

Political parties and leaders:
only party - Chama Cha Mapinduzi (CCM or Revolutionary Party), Ali Hassan MWINYI, party chairman

Suffrage:
universal at age 18

Elections:
President:
last held 28 October 1990 (next to be held NA October 1995); results - Ali Hassan MWINYI was elected without opposition
National Assembly:
last held 28 October 1990 (next to be held NA October 1995); results - CCM is the only party; seats - (241 total, 168 elected) CCM 168

Member of:
ACP, AfDB, C, CCC, EADB, ECA, FAO, FLS, G-6, G-77, GATT, IAEA, IBRD, ICAO,
IDA, IFAD, IFC, ILO, IMF, IMO, INTELSAT, INTERPOL, IOC, ISO, ITU, LORCS,
NAM, OAU, SADCC, UN, UNCTAD, UNESCO, UNHCR, UNIDO, UPU, WCL, WHO, WIPO, WMO,
WTO

:Tanzania Government

Diplomatic representation:
Ambassador-designate Charles Musama NYIRABU; Chancery at 2139 R Street NW, Washington, DC 20008; telephone (202) 939-6125
US:
Ambassador Edmund DE JARNETTE, Jr.; Embassy at 36 Laibon Road (off Baga-moyo

Road), Dar es Salaam (mailing address is P. O. Box 9123, Dar es Salaam); telephone [255] (51) 66010/13; FAX [255] (51)66701

Flag:

divided diagonally by a yellow-edged black band from the lower hoist-side corner; the upper triangle (hoist side) is green and the lower triangle is blue

:Tanzania Economy

Overview:

Tanzania is one of the poorest countries in the world. The economy is heavily dependent on agriculture, which accounts for about 47% of GDP, provides 85% of exports, and employs 90% of the work force. Industry accounts for 8% of GDP and is mainly limited to processing agricultural products and light consumer goods. The economic recovery program announced in mid-1986 has generated notable increases in agricultural production and financial support for the program by bilateral donors. The World Bank, the International Monetary Fund, and bilateral donors have provided funds to rehabilitate Tanzania's deteriorated economic infrastructure. Growth in 1991 was featured by a pickup in industrial production and a substantial increase in output of minerals led by gold.

GDP:

exchange rate conversion - $6.9 billion, per capita $260 (1989 est.); real growth rate 4.5% (1991 est.)

Inflation rate (consumer prices):

16.5% (1991 est.)

Unemployment rate: NA%

Budget:

revenues $495 million; expenditures $631 million, including capital expenditures of $118 million (FY90)

Exports:

$478 million (f.o.b., FY91 est.)

commodities:

coffee, cotton, sisal, tea, cashew nuts, meat, tobacco, diamonds, gold, coconut products, pyrethrum, cloves (Zanzibar)

partners:

FRG, UK, Japan, Netherlands, Kenya, Hong Kong, US

Imports:

$1.5 billion (c.i.f., FY91 est.)

commodities:

manufactured goods, machinery and transportation equipment, cotton piece goods, crude oil, foodstuffs

partners:

FRG, UK, US, Japan, Italy, Denmark

External debt: $5.2 billion (December 1991 est.)

Industrial production:

growth rate 4.2% (1988); accounts for 8% of GDP

Electricity:

405,000 kW capacity; 905 million kWh produced, 35 kWh per capita (1991)

Industries:

primarily agricultural processing (sugar, beer, cigarettes, sisal twine),

diamond and gold mining, oil refinery, shoes, cement, textiles, wood
products, fertilizer

Agriculture:
accounts for over 45% of GDP; topography and climatic conditions limit
cultivated crops to only 5% of land area; cash crops - coffee, sisal, tea,
cotton, pyrethrum (insecticide made from chrysanthemums), cashews, tobacco,
cloves (Zanzibar); food crops - corn, wheat, cassava, bananas, fruits, and
vegetables; small numbers of cattle, sheep, and goats; not self-sufficient
in food grain production

Economic aid:
US commitments, including Ex-Im (FY70-89), $400 million; Western (non-US)
countries, ODA and OOF bilateral commitments (1970-89), $9.8 billion; OPEC
bilateral aid (1979-89), $44 million; Communist countries (1970-89), $614
million

:Tanzania Economy

Currency:
Tanzanian shilling (plural - shillings); 1 Tanzanian shilling (TSh) = 100
cents

Exchange rates:
Tanzanian shillings (TSh) per US$1 - 236.01 (February (1992), 219.16 (1991),
195.06 (1990), 143.38 (1989), 99.29 (1988), 64.26 (1987)

Fiscal year: 1 July-30 June

:Tanzania Communications

Railroads:
3,555 km total; 960 km 1.067-meter gauge; 2,595 km 1.000-meter gauge, 6.4 km
double track, 962 km Tazara Railroad 1.067-meter gauge; 115 km 1.000-meter
gauge planned by end of decade

Highways:
total 81,900 km, 3,600 km paved; 5,600 km gravel or crushed stone; remainder
improved and unimproved earth

Inland waterways:
Lake Tanganyika, Lake Victoria, Lake Nyasa

Pipelines:
crude oil 982 km

Ports:
Dar es Salaam, Mtwara, Tanga, and Zanzibar are ocean ports; Mwanza on Lake
Victoria and Kigoma on Lake Tanganyika are inland ports

Merchant marine:
6 ships (1,000 GRT or over) totaling 19,185 GRT/22,916 DWT; includes 2
passenger-cargo, 2 cargo, 1 roll-on/roll-off cargo, 1 petroleum tanker

Civil air:
8 major transport aircraft

Airports:
104 total, 94 usable; 12 with permanent-surface runways; none with runways
over 3,659 m; 3 with runways 2,440-3, 659 m; 43 with runways 1,220-2,439 m

Telecommunications:
fair system operating below capacity; open wire, radio relay, and
troposcatter; 103,800 telephones; broadcast stations - 12 AM, 4 FM, 2 TV; 1
Indian Ocean and 1 Atlantic Ocean INTELSAT earth station

:Tanzania Defense Forces

Branches:

Tanzanian People's Defense Force (TPDF; including Army, Navy, and Air Force); paramilitary Police Field Force Unit; Militia

Manpower availability:

males 15-49, 5,747,542; 3,319,116 fit for military service

Defense expenditures:

exchange rate conversion - $119 million, about 2% of GDP (FY89 budget)

Thailand Geography

Total area: 514,000 km2
Land area: 511,770 km2
Comparative area: slightly more than twice the size of Wyoming
Land boundaries:

4,863 km total; Burma 1,800 km, Cambodia 803 km, Laos 1,754 km, Malaysia 506 km

Coastline:

3,219 km

Maritime claims:

Exclusive economic zone:

200 nm

Territorial sea:

12 nm

Disputes:

boundary dispute with Laos; unresolved maritime boundary with Vietnam

Climate:

tropical; rainy, warm, cloudy southwest monsoon (mid-May to September); dry, cool northeast monsoon (November to mid-March); southern isthmus always hot and humid

Terrain:

central plain; eastern plateau (Khorat); mountains elsewhere

Natural resources:

tin, rubber, natural gas, tungsten, tantalum, timber, lead, fish, gypsum, lignite, fluorite

Land use:

arable land 34%; permanent crops 4%; meadows and pastures 1%; forest and woodland 30%; other 31%; includes irrigated 7%

Environment:

air and water pollution; land subsidence in Bangkok area

Note.

controls only land route from Asia to Malaysia and Singapore

:Thailand People

Population: 57,624,180 (July 1992), growth rate 1.4% (1992)
Birth rate: 20 births/1,000 population (1992)
Death rate: 6 deaths/1,000 population (1992)
Net migration rate: 0 migrants/1,000 population (1992)
Infant mortality rate: 35 deaths/1,000 live births (1992)
Life expectancy at birth: 67 years male, 71 years female (1992)
Total fertility rate: 2.2 children born/woman (1992)

Nationality:
  noun - Thai (singular and plural); adjective - Thai
Ethnic divisions:
  Thai 75%, Chinese 14%, other 11%
Religions:
  Buddhism 95%, Muslim 3.8%, Christianity 0.5%, Hinduism 0.1%, other 0.6%
  (1991)
Languages:
  Thai; English is the secondary language of the elite; ethnic and regional
  dialects
Literacy:
  93% (male 96%, female 90%) age 15 and over can read and write (1990 est.)
Labor force:
  30,870,000; agriculture 62%, industry 13%, commerce 11%, services (including
  government) 14% (1989 est.)
Organized labor:
  309,000 union members (1989)

:Thailand Government

Long-form name:
  Kingdom of Thailand
Type:
  constitutional monarchy
Capital: Bangkok
Administrative divisions:
  72 provinces (changwat, singular and plural); Ang Thong, Buriram,
  Chachoengsao, Chai Nat, Chaiyaphum, Chanthaburi, Chiang Mai, Chiang Rai,
  Chon Buri, Chumphon, Kalasin, Kamphaeng Phet, Kanchanaburi, Khon Kaen,
  Krabi, Krung Thep Mahanakhon, Lampang, Lamphun, Loei, Lop Buri, Mae Hong
  Son, Maha Sarakham, Nakhon Nayok, Nakhon Pathom, Nakhon Phanom, Nakhon
  Ratchasima, Nakhon Sawan, Nakhon Si Thammarat, Nan, Narathiwat, Nong Khai,
  Nonthaburi, Pathum Thani, Pattani, Phangnga, Phatthalung, Phayao,
  Phetchabun, Phetchaburi, Phichit, Phitsanulok, Phra Nakhon Si Ayutthaya,
  Phrae, Phuket, Prachin Buri, Prachuap Khiri Khan, Ranong, Ratchaburi,
  Rayong, Roi Et, Sakon Nakhon, Samut Prakan, Samut Sakhon, Samut Songkhram,
  Sara Buri, Satun, Sing Buri, Sisaket, Songkhla, Sukhothai, Suphan Buri,
  Surat Thani, Surin, Tak, Trang, Trat, Ubon Ratchathani, Udon Thani, Uthai
  Thani, Uttaradit, Yala, Yasothon
Independence:
  1238 (traditional founding date); never colonized
Constitution:
  22 December 1978; new constitution approved 7 December 1991
Legal system:
  based on civil law system, with influences of common law; has not accepted
  compulsory ICJ jurisdiction; martial law in effect since 23 February 1991
  military coup
National holiday:
  Birthday of His Majesty the King, 5 December (1927)
Executive branch:
  monarch, interim prime minister, three interim deputy prime ministers,

interim Council of Ministers (cabinet), Privy Council; following the
military coup of 23 February 1991 a National Peace-Keeping Council was set
up

Legislative branch:
bicameral National Assembly (Rathasatha) consists of an upper house or
Senate (Vuthisatha) and a lower house or House of Representatives
(Saphaphoothan-Rajsadhorn)

Judicial branch:
Supreme Court (Sarndika)

Leaders:
Chief of State:
King PHUMIPHON Adunlayadet (since 9 June 1946); Heir Apparent Crown Prince
WACHIRALONGKON (born 28 July 1952)

Head of Government:
Prime Minister Anan PANYARACHUN (since 10 June 1992)

Political parties and leaders:
Justice Unity Party (Samakki Tham); Chart Thai Party; Solidarity Party; Thai
Citizens Party (TCP, Prachakorn Thai); Social Action Party (SAP); Democrat
Party (DP); Force of Truth Party (Palang Dharma); New Aspiration Party;
Rassadorn Party; Muanchon Party; Puangchon Chothai Party

Suffrage:
universal at age 21

:Thailand Government

Elections:
House of Representatives:
last held 22 March 1992 (next to be held by NA); results - percent of vote
by party NA; seats - (360 total) Samakki Tham 79, Chart Thai Party 74, New
Aspiration Party 72, DP 44, Palang Dharma 41, SAP 31, TCP 7, Solidarity
Party 6, Rassadorn 4, Muanchon 1, Puangchon Chotahi 1

Communists:
illegal Communist party has 500 to 1,000 members; armed Communist insurgents
throughout Thailand total 200 (est.)

Member of:
APEC, AsDB, ASEAN, CCC, CP, ESCAP, FAO, G-77, GATT, IAEA, IBRD,
ICAO, ICC,
ICFTU, IDA, IFAD, IFC, ILO, IMF, IMO, INTELSAT, INTERPOL, IOC, IOM,
ISO,
ITU, LORCS, PCA, UN, UNCTAD, UNESCO, UNHCR, UNIDO, UPU, WCL,
WHO, WIPO, WMO

Diplomatic representation:
Ambassador-designate PHIRAPHONG Kasemsi; Embassy at 2300 Kalorama Road
NW,
Washington, DC 20008; telephone (202) 483-7200; there are Thai Consulates
General in Chicago, Los Angeles, and New York

US:
Ambassador David F. LAMBERTSON; Embassy at 95 Wireless Road, Bangkok
(mailing address is APO AP 96546); telephone [66] (2) 252-5040; FAX [66] (2)
254-2990; there is a US Consulate General in Chiang Mai and Consulates in
Songkhla and Udorn

Flag:
  five horizontal bands of red (top), white, blue (double width), white, and
  red

:Thailand Economy

Overview:
  Thailand, one of the more advanced developing countries in Asia, enjoyed a
  year of 8% growth in 1991, although down from an annual average of 11%
  growth between 1987 and 1990. The increasingly sophisticated manufacturing
  sector benefited from export-oriented investment. The manufacturing and
  service sectors have accounted for the lion's share of economic growth.
  Thailand's traditional agricultural sector continued to become less
  important to the overall economy in 1991. The trade deficit continued to
  increase in 1991, to $11 billion; earnings from tourism and remittances grew
  marginally as a result of the Gulf War; and Thailand's import bill grew,
  especially for manufactures and oil. The government has followed fairly
  sound fiscal and monetary policies. Aided by increased tax receipts from the
  fast-moving economy; Bangkok recorded its fourth consecutive budget surplus
  in 1991. The government is moving ahead with new projects - especially for
  telecommunications, roads, and port facilities - needed to refurbish the
  country's overtaxed infrastructure. Political unrest and the military's
  shooting of antigovernment demonstrators in May 1992 have caused
  international businessmen to question Thailand's political stability.
  Thailand's general economic outlook remains good, however, assuming the
  continuation of the government's progrowth measures.
GNP:
  exchange rate conversion - $92.6 billion, per capita $1,630; real growth
  rate 8% (1991 est.)
Inflation rate (consumer prices):
  5.6% (1991 est.)
Unemployment rate: 4.1% (1991 est.)
Budget:
  revenues $17.9 billion; expenditures $17.9 billion, including capital
  expenditures of $5.0 billion (FY92 est.)
Exports:
  $27.5 billion (f.o.b., 1991)
 commodities:
  machinery and manufactures 62%, food 28%, crude materials 7% (1990)
 partners:
  US 23.4%, Japan 17.2%, Singapore 7.3%, Germany 5.3%, Hong Kong 4.8%, UK
  4.4%, Netherlands 4.3%, Malaysia, France, China (1990)
Imports:
  $39.0 billion (c.i.f., 1991)
 commodities:
  machinery and manufactures 67%, chemicals 10%, fuels 9%, crude materials 6%
  (1990)
 partners:
  Japan 30.2%, US 12%, Singapore 6.9%, Taiwan 5%, Germany 4.8%, China 3.2%,
  South Korea, Malaysia, UK (1990)
External debt: $25.1 billion (1990)

Industrial production:
  growth rate 14% (1990 est.); accounts for about 25% of GDP
Electricity:
  7,400,000 kW capacity; 37,500 million kWh produced, 660 kWh per capita
  (1991)
Industries:
  tourism is the largest source of foreign exchange; textiles and garments,
  agricultural processing, beverages, tobacco, cement, other light
  manufacturing, such as jewelry; electric appliances and components,
  integrated circuits, furniture, plastics; world's second-largest tungsten
  producer and third-largest tin producer

:Thailand Economy

Agriculture:
  accounts for 12% of GDP and 60% of labor force; leading producer and
  exporter of rice and cassava (tapioca); other crops - rubber, corn,
  sugarcane, coconuts, soybeans; except for wheat, self-sufficient in food
Illicit drugs:
  a minor producer, major illicit trafficker of heroin, particularly from
  Burma and Laos, and cannabis for the international drug market; eradication
  efforts have reduced the area of cannabis cultivation and shifted some
  production to neighboring countries; opium poppy cultivation has been
  affected by eradication efforts
Economic aid:
  US commitments, including Ex-Im (FY70-89), $870 million; Western (non-US)
  countries, ODA and OOF bilateral commitments (1970-89), $8.6 billion; OPEC
  bilateral aid (1979-89), $19 million
Currency:
  baht (plural - baht); 1 baht (B) = 100 satang
Exchange rates:
  baht (B) per US$1 - 25.614 (March 1992), 25.517 (1991), 25.585 (1990),
  25.702 (1989), 25.294 (1988), 25.723 (1987)
Fiscal year: 1 October-30 September

:Thailand Communications

Railroads:
  3,940 km 1.000-meter gauge, 99 km double track
Highways:
  44,534 km total; 28,016 km paved, 5,132 km earth surface, 11,386 km under
  development
Inland waterways:
  3,999 km principal waterways; 3,701 km with navigable depths of 0.9 m or
  more throughout the year; numerous minor waterways navigable by
  shallow-draft native craft
Pipelines:
  natural gas 350 km, petroleum products 67 km
Ports:
  Bangkok, Pattani, Phuket, Sattahip, Si Racha
Merchant marine:
  151 ships (1,000 GRT or over) totaling 628,225 GRT/957,095 DWT; includes 1
  short-sea passenger, 87 cargo, 11 container, 31 petroleum tanker, 9

liquefied gas, 2 chemical tanker, 3 bulk, 4 refrigerated cargo, 2
combination bulk, 1 passenger

Civil air:
41 (plus 2 leased) major transport aircraft

Airports:
115 total, 97 usable; 50 with permanent-surface runways; 1 with runways over
3,659 m; 13 with runways 2,440-3,659 m; 28 with runways 1,220-2,439 m

Telecommunications:
service to general public inadequate; bulk of service to government
activities provided by multichannel cable and radio relay network; 739,500
telephones (1987); broadcast stations - over 200 AM, 100 FM, and 11 TV in
government-controlled networks; satellite earth stations - 1 Indian Ocean
INTELSAT and 1 Pacific Ocean INTELSAT domestic satellite system being
developed

:Thailand Defense Forces

Branches:
Royal Thai Army, Royal Thai Navy (including Royal Thai Marine Corps), Royal
Thai Air Force, Paramilitary Forces

Manpower availability:
males 15-49, 16,361,393; 9,966,446 fit for military service; 612,748 reach
military age (18) annually

Defense expenditures:
exchange rate conversion - $2.7 billion, about 3% of GNP (1992 budget)

Togo Geography

Total area: 56,790 km2
Land area: 54,390 km2
Comparative area: slightly smaller than West Virginia
Land boundaries:
1,647 km total; Benin 644 km, Burkina 126 km, Ghana 877 km
Coastline:
56 km
Maritime claims:
Exclusive economic zone:
200 nm
Territorial sea:
30 nm
Disputes:
none
Climate:
tropical; hot, humid in south; semiarid in north
Terrain:
gently rolling savanna in north; central hills; southern plateau; low
coastal plain with extensive lagoons and marshes
Natural resources:
phosphates, limestone, marble
Land use:
arable land 25%; permanent crops 1%; meadows and pastures 4%; forest and
woodland 28%; other 42%; includes irrigated NEGL%
Environment:

hot, dry harmattan wind can reduce visibility in north during winter; recent droughts affecting agriculture; deforestation

:Togo People

Population: 3,958,863 (July 1992), growth rate 3.6% (1992)
Birth rate: 48 births/1,000 population (1992)
Death rate: 12 deaths/1,000 population (1992)
Net migration rate: 0 migrants/1,000 population (1992)
Infant mortality rate: 94 deaths/1,000 live births (1992)
Life expectancy at birth: 54 years male, 58 years female (1992)
Total fertility rate: 7.0 children born/woman (1992)
Nationality:
   noun - Togolese (singular and plural); adjective - Togolese
Ethnic divisions:
   37 tribes; largest and most important are Ewe, Mina, and Kabye; under 1%
   European and Syrian-Lebanese
Religions:
   indigenous beliefs about 70%, Christian 20%, Muslim 10%
Languages:
   French, both official and language of commerce; major African languages are
   Ewe and Mina in the south and Dagomba and Kabye in the north
Literacy:
   43% (male 56%, female 31%) age 15 and over can read and write (1990 est.)
Labor force:
   NA; agriculture 78%, industry 22%; about 88,600 wage earners, evenly divided
   between public and private sectors; 50% of population of working age (1985)
Organized labor:
   Federation of Togolese Workers (CNTT) was only legal labor union until
   Spring 1991; at least two more groups established since then: Labor
   Federation of Togolese Workers (CSTT) and the National Union of Independent
   Syndicates (UNSIT), each with 10-12 member unions; four other civil service
   unions have formed a loose coalition known as the Autonomous Syndicates of
   Togo (CTSA)

:Togo Government

Long-form name:
   Republic of Togo
Type:
   republic; under transition to multiparty democratic rule
Capital: Lome
Administrative divisions:
   21 circumscriptions (circonscriptions, singular - circonscription); Amlame
   (Amou), Aneho (Lacs), Atakpame (Ogou), Badou (Wawa), Bafilo (Assoli), Bassar
   (Bassari), Dapango (Tone), Kande (Keran), Klouto (Kloto), Pagouda (Binah),
   Lama-Kara (Kozah), Lome (Golfe), Mango (Oti), Niamtougou (Doufelgou), Notse
   (Haho), Pagouda, Sotouboua, Tabligbo (Yoto), Tchamba, Nyala, Tchaoudjo,
   Tsevie (Zio), Vogan (Vo); note - the 21 units may now be called prefectures
   (prefectures, singular - prefecture) and reported name changes for
   individual units are included in parentheses
Independence:
   27 April 1960 (from UN trusteeship under French administration, formerly

French Togo)

Constitution:
  1980 constitution nullified during national reform conference; transition
  constitution adopted 24 August 1991; multiparty draft constitution sent to
  High Council of the Republic for approval in November 1991, scheduled to be
  put to public referendum in NA 1992

Legal system:
  French-based court system

National holiday:
  Independence Day 27 April (1960)

Executive branch:
  president, prime minister, Council of Ministers (cabinet)

Legislative branch:
  National Assembly dissolved during national reform conference; 79-member
  interim High Council for the Republic (HCR) formed to act as legislature
  during transition to multiparty democracy; legislative elections scheduled
  to be held in NA

Judicial branch:
  Court of Appeal (Cour d'Appel), Supreme Court (Cour Supreme)

Leaders:
  Chief of State:
  President Gen. Gnassingbe EYADEMA (since 14 April 1967)
  Head of Government:
  interim Prime Minister Joseph Kokou KOFFIGOH (since 28 August 1991)

Political parties and leaders:
  Rally of the Togolese People (RPT) led by President EYADEMA was the only
  party until the formation of multiple parties was legalized 12 April 1991;
  more than 10 parties formed as of mid-May, though none yet legally
  registered; a national conference to determine transition regime took place
  10 July-28 August 1991

Suffrage:
  universal adult at age NA

Elections:
  President:
  last held 21 December 1986 (next to be held NA 1992); results - Gen. EYADEMA
  was reelected without opposition
  National Assembly:
  last held 4 March 1990; dissolved during national reform conference (next to
  be held April/May 1992); results - RPT was the only party; seats - (77
  total) RPT 77

:Togo Government

Member of:
  ACCT, ACP, AfDB, CEAO (observer), ECA, ECOWAS, Entente, FAO, FZ, G-77,
  GATT,
  IBRD, ICAO, ICC, IDA, IFAD, IFC, ILO, IMF, IMO, INTELSAT, INTERPOL,
  IOC,
  ITU, LORCS, NAM, OAU, UN, UNCTAD, UNESCO, UNIDO, UPU, WADB,
  WCL, WHO, WIPO,
  WMO, WTO

Diplomatic representation:

Ambassador Ellom-Kodjo SCHUPPIUS; Chancery at 2208 Massachusetts Avenue NW,

Washington, DC 20008; telephone (202) 234-4212 or 4213

US:

Ambassador Harmon E. KIRBY; Embassy at Rue Pelletier Caventou and Rue Vauban, Lome (mailing address is B. P. 852, Lome); telephone [228] 21-29-91 through 94 and 21-77-17; FAX [228] 21-79-52

Flag:

five equal horizontal bands of green (top and bottom) alternating with yellow; there is a white five-pointed star on a red square in the upper hoist-side corner; uses the popular pan-African colors of Ethiopia

:Togo Economy

Overview:

The economy is heavily dependent on subsistence agriculture, which accounts for about 35% of GDP and provides employment for 78% of the labor force. Primary agricultural exports are cocoa, coffee, and cotton, which together account for about 30% of total export earnings. Togo is self-sufficient in basic foodstuffs when harvests are normal. In the industrial sector phosphate mining is by far the most important activity, with phosphate exports accounting for about 40% of total foreign exchange earnings. Togo serves as a regional commercial and trade center. The government, over the past decade, with IMF and World Bank support, has been implementing a number of economic reform measures, that is, actively encouraging foreign investment and attempting to bring revenues in line with expenditures. Political unrest throughout 1991, however, has jeopardized the reform program and has disrupted vital economic activity.

GDP:

exchange rate conversion - $1.5 billion, per capita $400; real growth rate 2% (1990 est.)

Inflation rate (consumer prices):

1.0% (1990)

Unemployment rate: 2.0% (1987)

Budget:

revenues $330 million; expenditures $363 million, including capital expenditures of $101 million (1990 est.)

Exports:

$396 million (f.o.b., 1990)

commodities:

phosphates, cocoa, coffee, cotton, manufactures, palm kernels

partners:

EC 70%, Africa 9%, US 2%, other 19% (1985)

Imports:

$502 million (f.o.b., 1990)

commodities:

food, fuels, durable consumer goods, other intermediate goods, capital goods

partners:

EC 61%, US 6%, Africa 4%, Japan 4%, other 25% (1989)

External debt: $1.3 billion (1990 est.)

Industrial production:
  growth rate 4.9% (1987 est.); 6% of GDP
Electricity:
  179,000 kW capacity; 209 million kWh produced, 60 kWh per capita (1990)
Industries:
  phosphate mining, agricultural processing, cement, handicrafts, textiles, beverages
Agriculture:
  cash crops - coffee, cocoa, cotton; food crops - yams, cassava, corn, beans, rice, millet, sorghum; livestock production not significant; annual fish catch, 10,000-14,000 tons
Economic aid:
  US commitments, including Ex-Im (FY70-89), $132 million; Western (non-US) countries, ODA and OOF bilateral commitments (1970-89), $1.9 billion; OPEC bilateral aid (1979-89), $35 million; Communist countries (1970-89), $51 million
Currency:
  Communaute Financiere Africaine franc (plural - francs); 1 CFA franc (CFAF) = 100 centimes

:Togo Economy

Exchange rates:
  Communaute Financiere Africaine francs (CFAF) per US$1 - 281.99 (March 1992), 282.11 (1991), 272.26 (1990), 319.01 (1989), 297.85 (1988), 300.54 (1987)
Fiscal year: calendar year

:Togo Communications

Railroads:
  515 km 1.000-meter gauge, single track
Highways:
  6,462 km total; 1,762 km paved; 4,700 km unimproved roads
Inland waterways:
  50 km Mono River
Ports:
  Lome, Kpeme (phosphate port)
Merchant marine:
  3 ships (1,000 GRT or over) totaling 20,975 GRT/34,022 DWT; includes 2 roll-on/roll-off cargo, 1 multifunction large-load carrier
Civil air:
  3 major transport aircraft
Airports:
  9 total, 9 usable; 2 with permanent-surface runways; none with runways over 3,659 m; 2 with runways 2,440-3,659 m; none with runways 1,220-2,439 m
Telecommunications:
  fair system based on network of radio relay routes supplemented by open wire lines; broadcast stations - 2 AM, no FM, 3 (2 relays) TV; satellite earth stations - 1 Atlantic Ocean INTELSAT and 1 SYMPHONIE

:Togo Defense Forces

958

Branches:
  Army, Navy, Air Force, Gendarmerie
Manpower availability:
  males 15-49, 828,259; 435,113 fit for military service; no conscription
Defense expenditures:
  exchange rate conversion - $43 million, about 3% of GDP (1989)

Tokelau Geography

Total area: 10 km2
Land area: 10 km2
Comparative area: about 17 times the size of The Mall in Washington, DC
Land boundaries:
  none
Coastline:
  101 km
Maritime claims:
 Exclusive economic zone:
  200 nm
 Territorial sea:
  12 nm
Disputes:
  none
Climate:
  tropical; moderated by trade winds (April to November)
Terrain:
  coral atolls enclosing large lagoons
Natural resources:
  negligible
Land use:
  arable land 0%; permanent crops 0%; meadows and pastures 0%; forest and
  woodland 0%; other 100%
Environment:
  lies in Pacific typhoon belt
Note:
  located 3,750 km southwest of Honolulu in the South Pacific Ocean, about
  halfway between Hawaii and New Zealand

:Tokelau People

Population: 1,760 (July 1992), growth rate 0.7% (1992)
Birth rate: NA births/1,000 population (1992)
Death rate: NA deaths/1,000 population (1992)
Net migration rate: NA migrants/1,000 population (1992)
Infant mortality rate: NA deaths/1,000 live births (1992)
Life expectancy at birth: NA years male, NA years female (1992)
Total fertility rate: NA children born/woman (1992)
Nationality:
  noun - Tokelauan(s); adjective - Tokelauan
Ethnic divisions:
  all Polynesian, with cultural ties to Western Samoa
Religions:
  Congregational Christian Church 70%, Roman Catholic 28%, other 2%; on Atafu,

all Congregational Christian Church of Samoa; on Nukunonu, all Roman
Catholic; on Fakaofo, both denominations, with the Congregational Christian
Church predominant
Languages:
Tokelauan (a Polynesian language) and English
Literacy:
NA% (male NA%, female NA%)
Labor force:
NA
Organized labor:
NA

:Tokelau Government

Long-form name:
none
Type:
territory of New Zealand
Capital: none; each atoll has its own administrative center
Administrative divisions:
none (territory of New Zealand)
Independence:
none (territory of New Zealand)
Constitution:
administered under the Tokelau Islands Act of 1948, as amended in 1970
Legal system:
British and local statutes
National holiday:
Waitangi Day (Treaty of Waitangi established British sovereignty over New
Zealand), 6 February (1840)
Executive branch:
British monarch, administrator (appointed by the Minister of Foreign Affairs
in New Zealand), official secretary
Legislative branch:
Council of Elders (Taupulega) on each atoll
Judicial branch:
High Court in Niue, Supreme Court in New Zealand
Leaders:
 Chief of State:
 Queen ELIZABETH II (since 6 February 1952)
 Head of Government:
 Administrator Neil WALTER (since NA February 1988); Official Secretary
 Casimilo J. PEREZ, Office of Tokelau Affairs
Suffrage:
NA
Elections:
NA
Member of:
SPC
Diplomatic representation:
none (territory of New Zealand)

960

Flag:
  the flag of New Zealand is used

:Tokelau Economy

Overview:
  Tokelau's small size, isolation, and lack of resources greatly restrain
  economic development and confine agriculture to the subsistence level. The
  people must rely on aid from New Zealand to maintain public services, annual
  aid being substantially greater than GDP. The principal sources of revenue
  come from sales of copra, postage stamps, souvenir coins, and handicrafts.
  Money is also remitted to families from relatives in New Zealand.
GDP:
  exchange rate conversion - $1.4 million, per capita $800; real growth rate
  NA% (1988 est.)
Inflation rate (consumer prices):
  NA%
Unemployment rate: NA%
Budget:
  revenues $430,830; expenditures $2.8 million, including capital expenditures
  of $37,300 (FY87)
Exports:
  $98,000 (f.o.b., 1983)
 commodities:
  stamps, copra, handicrafts
 partners:
  NZ
Imports:
  $323,400 (c.i.f., 1983)
 commodities:
  foodstuffs, building materials, fuel
 partners:
  NZ
External debt: none
Industrial production:
  growth rate NA%
Electricity:
  200 kW capacity; 300,000 kWh produced, 180 kWh per capita (1990)
Industries:
  small-scale enterprises for copra production, wood work, plaited craft
  goods; stamps, coins; fishing
Agriculture:
  coconuts, copra; basic subsistence crops - breadfruit, papaya, bananas;
  pigs, poultry, goats
Economic aid:
  Western (non-US) countries, ODA and OOF bilateral commitments (1970-89), $24
  million
Currency:
  New Zealand dollar (plural - dollars); 1 New Zealand dollar (NZ$) = 100
  cents
Exchange rates:

New Zealand dollars (NZ$) per US$1 - 1.8245 (March 1992), l.7265 (1991), 1.6750 (1990), 1.6708 (1989), 1.5244 (1988), 1.6886 (1987)

Fiscal year: 1 April-31 March

:Tokelau Communications

Ports:
  none; offshore anchorage only
Airports:
  none; lagoon landings by amphibious aircraft from Western Samoa
Telecommunications:
  telephone service between islands and to Western Samoa

:Tokelau Defense Forces

Note: defense is the responsibility of New Zealand

Tonga Geography

Total area: 748 km2
Land area: 718 km2
Comparative area: slightly more than four times the size of Washington, DC
Land boundaries:
  none
Coastline:
  419 km
Maritime claims:
 Continental shelf:
  no specific limits
 Exclusive economic zone:
  200 nm
 Territorial sea:
  12 nm
Disputes:
  none
Climate:
  tropical; modified by trade winds; warm season (December to May), cool
  season (May to December)
Terrain:
  most islands have limestone base formed from uplifted coral formation;
  others have limestone overlying volcanic base
Natural resources:
  fish, fertile soil
Land use:
  arable land 25%; permanent crops 55%; meadows and pastures 6%; forest and
  woodland 12%; other 2%
Environment:
  archipelago of 170 islands (36 inhabited); subject to cyclones (October to
  April); deforestation
Note:
  located about 2,250 km north-northwest of New Zealand, about two-thirds of
  the way between Hawaii and New Zealand

:Tonga People

Population: 103,114 (July 1992), growth rate 0.8% (1992)
Birth rate: 26 births/1,000 population (1992)
Death rate: 7 deaths/1,000 population (1992)
Net migration rate: -11 migrants/1,000 population (1992)
Infant mortality rate: 22 deaths/1,000 live births (1992)
Life expectancy at birth: 65 years male, 70 years female (1992)
Total fertility rate: 3.7 children born/woman (1992)
Nationality:
   noun - Tongan(s); adjective - Tongan
Ethnic divisions:
   Polynesian; about 300 Europeans
Religions:
   Christian; Free Wesleyan Church claims over 30,000 adherents
Languages:
   Tongan, English
Literacy:
   100% (male 100%, female 100%) age 15 and over can read and write a simple
   message in Tongan or English (1976)
Labor force:
   NA; 70% agriculture; 600 engaged in mining
Organized labor:
   none

:Tonga Government

Long-form name:
   Kingdom of Tonga
Type:
   hereditary constitutional monarchy
Capital: Nuku`alofa
Administrative divisions:
   three island groups; Ha`apai, Tongatapu, Vava`u
Independence:
   4 June 1970 (from UK; formerly Friendly Islands)
Constitution:
   4 November 1875, revised 1 January 1967
Legal system:
   based on English law
National holiday:
   Emancipation Day, 4 June (1970)
Executive branch:
   monarch, prime minister, deputy prime minister, Council of Ministers
   (cabinet), Privy Council
Legislative branch:
   unicameral Legislative Assembly (Fale Alea)
Judicial branch:
   Supreme Court
Leaders:
  Chief of State:
   King Taufa'ahau TUPOU IV (since 16 December 1965)
  Head of Government:

Prime Minister Baron VAEA (since 22 August 1991); Deputy Prime Minister S. Langi KAVALIKU (since 22 August 1991)

Political parties and leaders:

Democratic Reform Movement, 'Akilisi POHIVA

Suffrage:

all literate, tax-paying males and all literate females over 21

Elections:

Legislative Assembly:

last held 14-15 February 1990 (next to be held NA February 1993); results - percent of vote NA; seats - (29 total, 9 elected) 6 proreform, 3 traditionalist

Member of:

ACP, AsDB, C, ESCAP, FAO, G-77, IBRD, ICAO, IDA, IFAD, IFC, IMF, INTERPOL,

IOC, ITU, LORCS, SPC, SPF, UNCTAD, UNESCO, UNIDO, UPU, WHO

Diplomatic representation:

Ambassador Siosaia a'Ulupekotofa TUITA resides in London

US:

the US has no offices in Tonga; the Ambassador to Fiji is accredited to Tonga and makes periodic visits

Flag:

red with a bold red cross on a white rectangle in the upper hoist-side corner

:Tonga Economy

Overview:

The economy's base is agriculture, which employs about 70% of the labor force and contributes 50% to GDP. Coconuts, bananas, and vanilla beans are the main crops and make up two-thirds of exports. The country must import a high proportion of its food, mainly from New Zealand. The manufacturing sector accounts for only 11% of GDP. Tourism is the primary source of hard currency earnings, but the island remains dependent on sizable external aid and remittances to offset its trade deficit.

GDP:

exchange rate conversion - $92 million, per capita $900; real growth rate 2.5% (FY90 est.)

Inflation rate (consumer prices):

8.9% (third quarter 1991)

Unemployment rate: NA%

Budget:

revenues $30.6 million; expenditures $48.9 million, including capital expenditures of $22.5 million (FY89 est.)

Exports:

$9.6 million (f.o.b., FY90 est.)

commodities:

coconut oil, desiccated coconut, copra, bananas, taro, vanilla beans, fruits, vegetables, fish

partners:

NZ 35%, Australia 22%, US 13%, Fiji 5% (FY90)

Imports:

$59.9 million (c.i.f., FY90 est.)
commodities:
food products, machinery and transport equipment, manufactures, fuels, chemicals
partners:
NZ 30%, Australia 23%, US 12%, Japan 7% (FY90)
External debt: $42.0 million (FY89)
Industrial production:
growth rate 15% (FY86); accounts for 11% of GDP
Electricity:
6,000 kW capacity; 8 million kWh produced, 80 kWh per capita (1990)
Industries:
tourism, fishing
Agriculture:
dominated by coconut, copra, and banana production; vanilla beans, cocoa, coffee, ginger, black pepper
Economic aid:
US commitments, including Ex-Im (FY70-89), $16 million; Western (non-US) countries, ODA and OOF bilateral commitments (1970-89), $258 million
Currency:
pa'anga (plural - pa'anga); 1 pa'anga (T$) = 100 seniti
Exchange rates:
pa'anga (T$) per US$1 - 1.2987 (January 1992), 1.2961 (1991), 1.2809 (1990), 1.2637 (1989), 1.2799 (1988), 1.4282 (1987)
Fiscal year: 1 July-30 June

:Tonga Communications

Highways:
198 km sealed road (Tongatapu); 74 km (Vava`u); 94 km unsealed roads usable only in dry weather
Ports:
Nukualofa, Neiafu, Pangai
Merchant marine:
4 ships (1,000 GRT or over) totaling 11,511 GRT/17,816 DWT; includes 2 cargo, 1 roll-on/roll-off cargo, 1 liquefied gas
Civil air:
no major transport aircraft
Airports:
6 total, 6 usable; 1 with permanent-surface runways; none with runways over 3,659 m; 1 with runways 2,440-3,659; 1 with runways 1,220-2,439 m
Telecommunications:
3,529 telephones; 66,000 radios; no TV sets; broadcast stations - 1 AM, no FM, no TV; 1 Pacific Ocean INTELSAT earth station

:Tonga Defense Forces

Branches:
Tonga Defense Force, Tonga Maritime Division, Royal Tongan Marines, Royal Tongan Guard, Police
Manpower availability:
NA

Defense expenditures:
  exchange rate conversion - $NA, NA% of GDP

Trinidad and Tobago Geography

Total area: 5,130 km2
Land area: 5,130 km2
Comparative area: slightly smaller than Delaware
Land boundaries:
  none
Coastline:
  362 km
Maritime claims:
  Continental shelf:
   outer edge of continental margin or 200 nm
  Exclusive economic zone:
   200 nm
  Territorial sea:
   12 nm
Disputes:
  none
Climate:
  tropical; rainy season (June to December)
Terrain:
  mostly plains with some hills and low mountains
Natural resources:
  crude oil, natural gas, asphalt
Land use:
  arable land 14%; permanent crops 17%; meadows and pastures 2%; forest and
  woodland 44%; other 23%; includes irrigated 4%
Environment:
  outside usual path of hurricanes and other tropical storms
Note:
  located 11 km from Venezuela

:Trinidad and Tobago People

Population: 1,299,301 (July 1992), growth rate 1.1% (1992)
Birth rate: 21 births/1,000 population (1992)
Death rate: 6 deaths/1,000 population (1992)
Net migration rate: -3 migrants/1,000 population (1992)
Infant mortality rate: 17 deaths/1,000 live births (1992)
Life expectancy at birth: 68 years male, 73 years female (1992)
Total fertility rate: 2.4 children born/woman (1992)
Nationality:
  noun - Trinidadian(s), Tobagonian(s); adjective - Trinidadian, Tobagonian
Ethnic divisions:
  black 43%, East Indian 40%, mixed 14%, white 1%, Chinese 1%, other 1%
Religions:
  Roman Catholic 32.2%, Hindu 24.3%, Anglican 14.4%, other Protestant 14%,
  Muslim 6%, none or unknown 9.1%
Languages:
  English (official), Hindi, French, Spanish

Literacy:
  95% (male 97%, female 93%) age 15 and over can read and write (1980)
Labor force:
  463,900; construction and utilities 18.1%; manufacturing, mining, and
  quarrying 14.8%; agriculture 10.9%; other 56.2% (1985 est.)
Organized labor:
  22% of labor force (1988)

:Trinidad and Tobago Government

Long-form name:
  Republic of Trinidad and Tobago
Type:
  parliamentary democracy
Capital: Port-of-Spain
Administrative divisions:
  8 counties, 3 municipalities*, and 1 ward**; Arima*, Caroni, Mayaro, Nariva,
  Port-of-Spain*, Saint Andrew, Saint David, Saint George, Saint Patrick, San
  Fernando*, Tobago**, Victoria
Independence:
  31 August 1962 (from UK)
Constitution:
  31 August 1976
Legal system:
  based on English common law; judicial review of legislative acts in the
  Supreme Court; has not accepted compulsory ICJ jurisdiction
National holiday:
  Independence Day, 31 August (1962)
Executive branch:
  president, prime minister, Cabinet
Legislative branch:
  bicameral Parliament consists of an upper house or Senate and a lower house
  or House of Representatives
Judicial branch:
  Court of Appeal, Supreme Court
Leaders:
 Chief of State:
 President Noor Mohammed HASSANALI (since 18 March 1987)
 Head of Government:
 Prime Minister Patrick Augustus Mervyn MANNING (since 17 December 1991)
Political parties and leaders:
  People's National Movement (PNM), Patrick MANNING; United National Congress
  (UNC), Basdeo PANDAY; National Alliance for Reconstruction (NAR), Carson
  CHARLES; Movement for Social Transformation (MOTION), David ABDULLAH;
  National Joint Action Committee (NJAC), Makandal DAAGA
Suffrage:
  universal at age 18
Elections:
 House of Representatives:
 last held 16 December 1991 (next to be held by December 1996);results - PNM
 32%, UNC 13%, NAR 2%; seats - (36 total) PNM 21, UNC 13, NAR 2

Communists:
  Communist Party of Trinidad and Tobago; Trinidad and Tobago Peace Council,
  James MILLETTE
Member of:
  ACP, C, CARICOM, CCC, CDB, ECLAC, FAO, G-24, G-77, GATT, IADB, IBRD,
  ICAO,
  ICFTU, IDA, IFAD, IFC, ILO, IMF, IMO, INTELSAT, INTERPOL, IOC, ISO,
  ITU,
  LAES, LORCS, NAM, OAS, OPANAL, UN, UNCTAD, UNESCO, UNIDO, UPU,
  WFTU, WHO,
  WIPO, WMO
Diplomatic representation:
  Ambassador Corinne BAPTISTE; Chancery at 1708 Massachusetts Avenue NW,
  Washington, DC 20036; telephone (202) 467-6490; Trinidad and Tobago has a
  Consulate General in New York
US:
  Ambassador Sally GROOMS-COWAL; Embassy at 15 Queen's Park West,
  Port-of-Spain (mailing address is P. O. Box 752, Port-of-Spain); telephone
  (809) 622-6372 through 6376, 6176; FAX (809) 628-5462

:Trinidad and Tobago Government

Flag: red with a white-edged black diagonal band from the upper hoist side

:Trinidad and Tobago Economy

Overview:
  Trinidad and Tobago's petroleum-based economy began to emerge from a lengthy
  depression in 1990 and 1991. The economy fell sharply through most of the
  1980s, largely because of the decline in oil prices. This sector accounts
  for 80% of export earnings and more than 25% of GDP. The government, in
  response to the oil revenue loss, pursued a series of austerity measures
  that pushed the unemployment rate as high as 22% in 1988. The economy showed
  signs of recovery in 1990, however, helped along by rising oil prices.
  Agriculture employs only about 11% of the labor force and produces about 3%
  of GDP. Since this sector is small, it has been unable to absorb the large
  numbers of the unemployed. The government currently seeks to diversify its
  export base.
GDP:
  exchange rate conversion - $4.9 billion, per capita $3,600; real growth rate
  0.7% (1990)
Inflation rate (consumer prices):
  11.1% (1990)
Unemployment rate: 21% (1990)
Budget:
  revenues $1.5 billion; expenditures $1.7 billion, including capital
  expenditures of $150 million (1991 est.)
Exports:
  $2.0 billion (f.o.b., 1990)
 commodities:
  includes reexports - petroleum and petroleum products 82%, steel products
  9%, fertilizer, sugar, cocoa, coffee, citrus (1988)
 partners:

US 54%, CARICOM 16%, EC 10%, Latin America 3% (1989)
Imports:
  $1.2 billion (c.i.f., 1990)
  commodities:
  raw materials and intermediate goods 47%, capital goods 26%, consumer goods
  26% (1988)
  partners:
  US 41%, Latin America 10%, UK 8%, Canada 5%, CARICOM 6% (1989)
External debt: $2.5 billion (1990)
Industrial production:
  growth rate 2.3%, excluding oil refining (1986); accounts for 40% of GDP,
  including petroleum
Electricity:
  1,176,000 kW capacity; 3,480 million kWh produced, 2,708 kWh per capita
  (1991)
Industries:
  petroleum, chemicals, tourism, food processing, cement, beverage, cotton
  textiles
Agriculture:
  highly subsidized sector; major crops - cocoa and sugarcane; sugarcane
  acreage is being shifted into rice, citrus, coffee, vegetables; poultry
  sector most important source of animal protein; must import large share of
  food needs
Economic aid:
  US commitments, including Ex-Im (FY70-89), $373 million; Western (non-US)
  countries, ODA and OOF bilateral commitments (1970-89), $518 million
Currency:
  Trinidad and Tobago dollar (plural - dollars); 1 Trinidad and Tobago dollar
  (TT$) = 100 cents

:Trinidad and Tobago Economy

Exchange rates:
  Trinidad and Tobago dollars (TT$) per US$1 - 4.2500 (March 1992), 4.2500
  (1991), 4.2500 (1990), 4.2500 (1989), 3.8438 (1988), 3.6000 (1987)
Fiscal year: calendar year

:Trinidad and Tobago Communications

Railroads:
  minimal agricultural railroad system near San Fernando
Highways:
  8,000 km total; 4,000 km paved, 1,000 km improved earth, 3,000 km unimproved
  earth
Pipelines:
  crude oil 1,032 km, petroleum products 19 km, natural gas 904 km
Ports:
  Port-of-Spain, Point Lisas, Pointe-a-Pierre
Civil air:
  14 major transport aircraft
Airports:
  6 total, 5 usable; 2 with permanent-surface runways; none with runways over
  3,659 m; 2 with runways 2,440-3,659 m; 1 with runways 1,220-2,439 m

Telecommunications:
   excellent international service via tropospheric scatter links to Barbados
   and Guyana; good local service; 109,000 telephones; broadcast stations - 2
   AM, 4 FM, 5 TV; 1 Atlantic Ocean INTELSAT earth station

:Trinidad and Tobago Defense Forces

Branches:
   Trinidad and Tobago Defense Force (Army), Coast Guard, Air Wing, Trinidad
   and Tobago Police Service
Manpower availability:
   males 15-49, 344,990; 248,912 fit for military service
Defense expenditures:
   exchange rate conversion - $59 million, 1-2% of GDP (1989 est.)

Tromelin Island Geography

Total area: 1 km2
Land area: 1 km2
Comparative area: about 1.7 times the size of The Mall in Washington, DC
Land boundaries:
   none
Coastline:
   3.7 km
Maritime claims:
  Contiguous zone:
   12 nm
  Continental shelf:
   200 m (depth) or to depth of exploitation
  Exclusive economic zone:
   200 nm
  Territorial sea:
   12 nm
Disputes:
   claimed by Madagascar, Mauritius, and Seychelles
Climate:
   tropical
Terrain:
   sandy
Natural resources:
   fish
Land use:
   arable land 0%; permanent crops 0%; meadows and pastures 0%; forest and
   woodland 0%; other - scattered bushes 100%
Environment:
   wildlife sanctuary
Note:
   located 350 km east of Madagascar and 600 km north of Reunion in the Indian
   Ocean; climatologically important location for forecasting cyclones

:Tromelin Island People

Population: uninhabited

:Tromelin Island Government

Long-form name:
  none
Type:
  French possession administered by Commissioner of the Republic Jacques
  DEWATRE (since NA July 1991), resident in Reunion
Capital: none; administered by France from Reunion

:Tromelin Island Economy

Overview: no economic activity

:Tromelin Island Communications

Ports:
  none; offshore anchorage only
Airports:
  1 with runway less than 1,220 m
Telecommunications:
  important meteorological station

:Tromelin Island Defense Forces

Note: defense is the responsibility of France

Tunisia Geography

Total area: 163,610 km2
Land area: 155,360 km2
Comparative area: slightly larger than Georgia
Land boundaries:
  1,424 km total; Algeria 965 km, Libya 459 km
Coastline:
  1,148 km
Maritime claims:
  Territorial sea:
  12 nm
Disputes:
  maritime boundary dispute with Libya; land boundary disputes with Algeria
  under discussion
Climate:
  temperate in north with mild, rainy winters and hot, dry summers; desert in
  south
Terrain:
  mountains in north; hot, dry central plain; semiarid south merges into the
  Sahara
Natural resources:
  crude oil, phosphates, iron ore, lead, zinc, salt
Land use:
  arable land 20%; permanent crops 10%; meadows and pastures 19%; forest and
  woodland 4%; other 47%; includes irrigated 1%
Environment:
  deforestation; overgrazing; soil erosion; desertification
Note:
  strategic location in central Mediterranean; only 144 km from Italy across
  the Strait of Sicily; borders Libya on east

:Tunisia People

Population: 8,445,656 (July 1992), growth rate 2.0% (1992)
Birth rate: 25 births/1,000 population (1992)
Death rate: 5 deaths/1,000 population (1992)
Net migration rate: 0 migrants/1,000 population (1992)
Infant mortality rate: 38 deaths/1,000 live births (1992)
Life expectancy at birth: 70 years male, 74 years female (1992)
Total fertility rate: 3.2 children born/woman (1992)
Nationality:
  noun - Tunisian(s); adjective - Tunisian
Ethnic divisions:
  Arab-Berber 98%, European 1%, Jewish less than 1%
Religions:
  Muslim 98%, Christian 1%, Jewish less than 1%
Languages:
  Arabic (official); Arabic and French (commerce)
Literacy:
  65% (male 74%, female 56%) age 15 and over can read and write (1990 est.)
Labor force:
  2,250,000; agriculture 32%; shortage of skilled labor
Organized labor:
  about 360,000 members claimed, roughly 20% of labor force; General Union of
  Tunisian Workers (UGTT), quasi-independent of Constitutional Democratic
  Party

:Tunisia Government

Long-form name:
  Republic of Tunisia; note - may be changed to Tunisian Republic
Type:
  republic
Capital: Tunis
Administrative divisions:
  23 governorates; Beja, Ben Arous, Bizerte, Gabes, Gafsa, Jendouba, Kairouan,
  Kasserine, Kebili, L'Ariana, Le Kef, Mahdia, Medenine, Monastir, Nabeul,
  Sfax, Sidi Bou Zid, Siliana, Sousse, Tataouine, Tozeur, Tunis, Zaghouan
Independence:
  20 March 1956 (from France)
Constitution:
  1 June 1959
Legal system:
  based on French civil law system and Islamic law; some judicial review of
  legislative acts in the Supreme Court in joint session
National holiday:
  National Day, 20 March (1956)
Executive branch:
  president, prime minister, Cabinet
Legislative branch:
  unicameral Chamber of Deputies (Majlis al-Nuwaab)
Judicial branch:
  Court of Cassation (Cour de Cassation)

Leaders:
  Chief of State:
  President Gen. Zine el Abidine BEN ALI (since 7 November 1987)
  Head of Government:
  Prime Minister Hamed KAROUI (since 26 September 1989)
Political parties and leaders:
  Constitutional Democratic Rally Party (RCD), President BEN ALI (official
  ruling party); Movement of Democratic Socialists (MDS), Mohammed MOUAADA;
  five other political parties are legal, including the Communist Party
Suffrage:
  universal at age 20
Elections:
  President:
  last held 2 April 1989 (next to be held NA April 1994); results - Gen. Zine
  el Abidine BEN ALI was reelected without opposition
  Chamber of Deputies:
  last held 2 April 1989 (next to be held NA April 1994); results - RCD 80.7%,
  independents/Islamists 13.7%, MDS 3.2%, other 2.4%; seats - (141 total) RCD
  141
Member of:
  ABEDA, ACCT, AfDB, AFESD, AL, AMF, AMU, CCC, ECA, FAO, G-77, GATT,
IAEA,
  IBRD, ICAO, ICC, ICFTU, IDA, IDB, IFAD, IFC, ILO, IMF, IMO, INMARSAT,
  INTELSAT, INTERPOL, IOC, ISO, ITU, LORCS, NAM, OAU, OIC, UN,
UNCTAD, UNESCO,
  UNHCR, UNIDO, UPU, WHO, WIPO, WMO, WTO
Diplomatic representation:
  Ambassador Ismail KHELIL; Chancery at 1515 Massachusetts Avenue NW,
  Washington DC 20005; telephone (202) 862-1850
  US:
  Ambassador John T. McCARTHY; Embassy at 144 Avenue de la Liberte, 1002
  Tunis-Belvedere; telephone [216] (1) 782-566; FAX [216] (1) 789-719
Flag:
  red with a white disk in the center bearing a red crescent nearly encircling
  a red five-pointed star; the crescent and star are traditional symbols of
  Islam

:Tunisia Economy

Overview:
  The economy depends primarily on petroleum, phosphates, tourism, and exports
  of light manufactures. Following two years of drought-induced economic
  decline, the economy made a strong recovery in 1990 as a result of a
  bountiful harvest, continued export growth, and higher domestic investment.
  Continued high inflation and unemployment have eroded popular support for
  the government, however, and forced Tunis to slow the pace of economic
  reform. Nonetheless, the government appears committed to implementing its
  IMF-supported structural adjustment program and to servicing its foreign
  debt.
GDP:
  exchange rate conversion - $10.9 billion, per capita $1,320; real growth

rate 3.5% (1991)

Inflation rate (consumer prices):
 8.2% (1991)

Unemployment rate: 15% (1991)

Budget:
 revenues $3.8 billion; expenditures $5.4 billion, including capital
 expenditures of $970 million (1992 est.)

Exports:
 $3.7 billion (f.o.b., 1991)
 commodities:
 hydrocarbons, agricultural products, phosphates and chemicals
 partners:
 EC 74%, Middle East 11%, US 2%, Turkey, USSR

Imports:
 $4.9 billion (f.o.b., 1991)
 commodities:
 industrial goods and equipment 57%, hydrocarbons 13%, food 12%, consumer
 goods
 partners:
 EC 67%, US 6%, Canada, Japan, Switzerland, Turkey, Algeria

External debt: $8.6 billion (1991)

Industrial production:
 growth rate 5% (1989); accounts for about 25% of GDP, including petroleum

Electricity:
 1,493,000 kW capacity; 4,210 million kWh produced, 530 kWh per capita (1989)

Industries:
 petroleum, mining (particularly phosphate and iron ore), tourism, textiles,
 footwear, food, beverages

Agriculture:
 accounts for 16% of GDP and one-third of labor force; output subject to
 severe fluctuations because of frequent droughts; export crops - olives,
 dates, oranges, almonds; other products - grain, sugar beets, wine grapes,
 poultry, beef, dairy; not self-sufficient in food; fish catch of 99,200
 metric tons (1987)

Economic aid:
 US commitments, including Ex-Im (FY70-89), $730 million; Western (non-US)
 countries, ODA and OOF bilateral commitments (1970-89), $5.2 billion; OPEC
 bilateral aid (1979-89), $684 million; Communist countries (1970-89), $410
 million

Currency:
 Tunisian dinar (plural - dinars); 1 Tunisian dinar (TD) = 1,000 millimes

Exchange rates:
 Tunisian dinars (TD) per US$1 - 0.9272 (March 1992), 0.9246 (1991), 0.8783
 (1990), 0.9493 (1989), 0.8578 (1988), 0.8287 (1987)

:Tunisia Economy

Fiscal year: calendar year

:Tunisia Communications

Railroads:
 2,115 km total; 465 km 1.435-meter (standard) gauge; 1,650 km 1.000-meter

gauge
Highways:
   17,700 km total; 9,100 km bituminous; 8,600 km improved and unimproved earth
Pipelines:
   crude oil 797 km, petroleum products 86 km, natural gas 742 km
Ports:
   Bizerte, Gabes, Sfax, Sousse, Tunis, La Goulette, Zarzis
Merchant marine:
   21 ships (1,000 GRT or over) totaling 160,069 GRT/218,791 DWT; includes 1
   short-sea passenger, 4 cargo, 2 roll-on/roll-off cargo, 2 petroleum tanker,
   6 chemical tanker, 1 liquefied gas, 5 bulk
Civil air:
   19 major transport aircraft
Airports:
   29 total, 26 usable; 13 with permanent-surface runways; none with runways
   over 3,659 m; 7 with runways 2,440-3,659 m; 7 with runways 1,220-2,439 m
Telecommunications:
   the system is above the African average; facilities consist of open-wire
   lines, coaxial cable, and radio relay; key centers are Sfax, Sousse,
   Bizerte, and Tunis; 233,000 telephones; broadcast stations - 7 AM, 8 FM, 19
   TV; 5 submarine cables; satellite earth stations - 1 Atlantic Ocean INTELSAT
   and 1 ARABSAT with back-up control station; coaxial cable to Algeria and
   Libya; radio relay to Algeria, and Libya

:Tunisia Defense Forces

Branches:
   Army, Navy, Air Force, paramilitary forces, National Guard
Manpower availability:
   males 15-49, 2,117,864; 1,217,819 fit for military service; 88,619 reach
   military age (20) annually
Defense expenditures:
   exchange rate conversion - $520 million, 5% of GDP (1992 budget)

   Turkey Geography

Total area: 780,580 km2
Land area: 770,760 km2
Comparative area: slightly larger than Texas
Land boundaries:
   2,627 km total; Armenia 268 km, Azerbaijan 9 km, Bulgaria 240 km, Georgia
   252 km, Greece 206 km, Iran 499 km, Iraq 331 km, Syria 822 km
Coastline:
   7,200 km
Maritime claims:
   Exclusive economic zone:
   in Black Sea only - to the maritime boundary agreed upon with the former
   USSR
   Territorial sea:
   6 nm in the Aegean Sea, 12 nm in Black Sea and Mediterranean Sea
Disputes:
   complex maritime and air (but not territorial) disputes with Greece in
   Aegean Sea; Cyprus question; Hatay question with Syria; ongoing dispute with

downstream riparians (Syria and Iraq) over water development plans for the
Tigris and Euphrates Rivers
Climate:
  temperate; hot, dry summers with mild, wet winters; harsher in interior
Terrain:
  mostly mountains; narrow coastal plain; high central plateau (Anatolia)
Natural resources:
  antimony, coal, chromium, mercury, copper, borate, sulphur, iron ore
Land use:
  arable land 30%; permanent crops 4%; meadows and pastures 12%; forest and
  woodland 26%; other 28%; includes irrigated 3%
Environment:
  subject to severe earthquakes, especially along major river valleys in west;
  air pollution; desertification
Note:
  strategic location controlling the Turkish straits (Bosporus, Sea of
  Marmara, Dardanelles) that link Black and Aegean Seas

:Turkey People

Population: 59,640,143 (July 1992), growth rate 2.1% (1992)
Birth rate: 27 births/1,000 populatition (1992)
Death rate: 6 deaths/1,000 population (1992)
Net migration rate: 0 migrants/1,000 population (1992)
Infant mortality rate: 55 deaths/1,000 live births (1992)
Life expectancy at birth: 68 years male, 72 years female (1992)
Total fertility rate: 3.4 children born/woman (1992)
Nationality:
  noun - Turk(s); adjective - Turkish
Ethnic divisions:
  Turkish 80%, Kurdish 17%, other 3% (est.)
Religions:
  Muslim (mostly Sunni) 99.8%, other (Christian and Jews) 0.2%
Languages:
  Turkish (official), Kurdish, Arabic
Literacy:
  81% (male 90%, female 71%) age 15 and over can read and write (1990 est.)
Labor force:
  20,700,000; agriculture 49%, services 30%, industry 15%; about 1,500,000
  Turks work abroad (1989)
Organized labor:
  10% of labor force

:Turkey Government

Long-form name:
  Republic of Turkey
Type:
  republican parliamentary democracy
Capital: Ankara
Administrative divisions:
  73 provinces (iller, singular - il); Adana, Adiyaman, Afyon, Agri, Aksaray,
  Amasya, Ankara, Antalya, Artvin, Aydin, Balikesir, Batman, Bayburt, Bilecik,

Bingol, Bitlis, Bolu, Burdur, Bursa, Canakkale, Cankiri, Corum, Denizli, Diyarbakir, Edirne, Elazig, Erzincan, Erzurum, Eskisehir, Gaziantep, Giresun, Gumushane, Hakkari, Hatay, Icel, Isparta, Istanbul, Izmir, Kahraman Maras, Karaman, Kars, Kastamonu, Kayseri, Kirikkale, Kirklareli, Kirsehir, Kocaeli, Konya, Kutahya, Malatya, Manisa, Mardin, Mugla, Mus, Nevsehir, Nigde, Ordu, Rize, Sakarya, Samsun, Siirt, Sinop, Sirnak, Sivas, Tekirdag, Tokat, Trabzon, Tunceli, Urfa, Usak, Van, Yozgat, Zonguldak

Independence:
29 October 1923 (successor state to the Ottoman Empire)

Constitution:
7 November 1982

Legal system:
derived from various continental legal systems; accepts compulsory ICJ jurisdiction, with reservations

National holiday:
Anniversary of the Declaration of the Republic, 29 October (1923)

Executive branch:
president, Presidential Council, prime minister, deputy prime minister, Cabinet

Legislative branch:
unicameral Grand National Assembly (Buyuk Millet Meclisi)

Judicial branch:
Court of Cassation

Leaders:
Chief of State:
President Turgut OZAL (since 9 November 1989)
Head of Government:
Prime Minister Suleyman DEMIREL (since 30 November 1991); Deputy Prime Minister Erdal INONU (since 30 November 1991)

Political parties and leaders:
Correct Way Party (DYP), Suleyman DEMIREL; Motherland Party (ANAP), Mesut YILMAZ; Social Democratic Populist Party (SHP), Erdal INONU; Refah Party (RP), Necmettin ERBAKAN; Democratic Left Party (DSP), Bulent ECEVIT; Nationalist Labor Party (MCP), Alpaslan TURKES; People's Labor Party (HEP), Feridun YAZAR; Socialist Unity Party (SBP), leader NA; Great Anatolia Party (BAP), leader NA; Democratic Center Party (DSP), Bedrettin DALAN; Grand National Party (GNP), leader NA

Suffrage:
universal at age 21

Elections:
Grand National Assembly:
last held 20 October 1991 (next to be held NA October 1996); results - DYP 27.03%, ANAP 24.01%, SHP 20.75%, RP 16.88%, DSP 10.75%, SBP 0.44%, independent 0.14%; seats - (450 total) DYP 178, ANAP 115, SHP 86, RP 40, MCP 19, DSP 7, other 5

:Turkey Government

Member of:
AsDB, BIS, CCC, CE, CERN (observer), COCOM, CSCE, EBRD, ECE, FAO, GATT,

IAEA, IBRD, ICAO, ICC, ICFTU, IDA, IDB, IEA, IFAD, IFC, ILO, IMF, IMO, INTELSAT, INTERPOL, IOC, IOM (observer), ISO, ITU, LORCS, NATO, NEA, OECD,
OIC, PCA, UN, UNCTAD, UNESCO, UNHCR, UNIDO, UNIIMOG, UNRWA, UPU, WHO, WIPO,
WMO, WTO

Diplomatic representation:
Ambassador Nuzhet KANDEMIR; Chancery at 1606 23rd Street NW, Washington, DC;
20008; telephone (202) 387-3200; there are Turkish Consulates General in Chicago, Houston, Los Angeles, and New York

US:
Ambassador Richard C. BARKLEY; Embassy at 110 Ataturk Boulevard, Ankara (mailing address is PSC 88, Box 5000, Ankara, or APO AE 09823); telephone [90] (4) 126 54 70; FAX [90] (4) 167-0057; there are US Consulates General in Istanbul and Izmir, and a Consulate in Adana

Flag:
red with a vertical white crescent (the closed portion is toward the hoist side) and white five-pointed star centered just outside the crescent opening

:Turkey Economy

Overview:
The impressive stream of benefits from the economic reforms that Turkey launched in 1980 have begun to peter out. Although real growth in per capita GDP averaged 5% annually between 1983 and 1988, recent economic performance has fallen substantially. Moreover, inflation and interest rates remain high, and a large budget deficit will continue to provide difficulties for a country undergoing a substantial transformation from a centrally controlled to a free market economy. Agriculture remains an important economic sector, employing about half of the work force, accounting for 18% of GDP, and contributing 19% to exports. The government has launched a multibillion-dollar development program in the southeastern region, which includes the building of a dozen dams on the Tigris and Euphrates Rivers to generate electric power and irrigate large tracts of farmland. The planned tapping of huge additional quantities of Euphrates water has raised serious concern in the downstream riparian nations of Syria and Iraq. The Turkish economy emerged from the Gulf War of early 1991 in stronger shape than Ankara had expected. Although the negative effects of the crisis were felt primarily in the politically sensitive southeast, aid pledges by the coalition allies of more than $4 billion have helped offset the burden.

GDP:
purchasing power equivalent - $198 billion, per capita $3,400; real growth rate 1.5% (1991 est.)

Inflation rate (consumer prices):
71.1% (1991)

Unemployment rate: 11.1% (1991 est.)

Budget:
revenues $41.9 billion; expenditures $49.7 billion, including capital expenditures of $9.9 billion (1992)

Exports:

$13.0 billion (f.o.b., 1990)
commodities:
  industrial products (steel, chemicals) 81%; fruits, vegetables, tobacco and
  meat products 19%
partners:
  EC countries 49%, US 7%, Iran 5%
Imports:
  $22.3 billion (c.i.f., 1990)
commodities:
  crude oil, machinery, transport equipment, metals, chemicals,
  pharmaceuticals, dyes, plastics, rubber, fertilizers, grain
partners:
  EC countries 49%, US 7%, Iran 5%
External debt: $49.0 billion (1990)
Industrial production:
  growth rate 10% (1990 est.); accounts for 29% of GDP
Electricity:
  14,400,000 kW capacity; 44,000 million kWh produced, 750 kWh per capita
  (1991)
Industries:
  textiles, food processing, mining (coal, chromite, copper, boron minerals),
  steel, petroleum, construction, lumber, paper
Agriculture:
  accounts for 18% of GDP and employs about half of working force; products -
  tobacco, cotton, grain, olives, sugar beets, pulses, citrus fruit, variety
  of animal products; self-sufficient in food most years

:Turkey Economy

Illicit drugs:
  one of the world's major suppliers of licit opiate products; government
  maintains strict controls over areas of opium poppy cultivation and output
  of poppy straw concentrate
Economic aid:
  US commitments, including Ex-Im (FY70-89), $2.3 billion; Western (non-US)
  countries, ODA and OOF bilateral commitments (1970-89), $10.1 billion; OPEC
  bilateral aid (1979-89), $665 million; Communist countries (1970-89), $4.5
  billion; note - aid for Persian Gulf war efforts from coalition allies
  (1991), $4.1 billion; aid pledged for Turkish Defense Fund, $2.5 billion
Currency:
  Turkish lira (plural - liras); 1 Turkish lira (TL) = 100 kurus
Exchange rates:
  Turkish liras (TL) per US$1 - 6,098.4 (March 1992), 4,171.8 (1991), 2,608.6
  (1990), 2,121.7 (1989), 1,422.3 (1988), 857.2 (1987)
Fiscal year: calendar year

:Turkey Communications

Railroads:
  8,401 km 1.435-meter gauge; 479 km electrified
Highways:
  49,615 km total; 26,915 km paved; 16,500 km gravel or crushed stone; 4,000
  km improved earth; 2,200 km unimproved earth (1985)

Inland waterways:
  about 1,200 km
Pipelines:
  crude oil 1,738 km, petroleum products 2,321 km, natural gas 708 km
Ports:
  Iskenderun, Istanbul, Mersin, Izmir
Merchant marine:
  353 ships (1,000 GRT or over) totaling 4,056,455 GRT/7,143,096 DWT; includes
  7 short-sea passenger, 1 passenger-cargo, 191 cargo, 1 container, 5
  roll-on/roll-off cargo, 3 refrigerated cargo, 1 livestock carrier, 37
  petroleum tanker, 9 chemical tanker, 3 liquefied gas, 10 combination
  ore/oil, 1 specialized tanker, 80 bulk, 4 combination bulk
Civil air:
  52 major transport aircraft (1991)
Airports:
  109 total, 104 usable; 65 with permanent-surface runways; 3 with runways
  over 3,659 m; 30 with runways 2,440-3,659 m; 27 with runways 1,220-2,439 m
Telecommunications:
  fair domestic and international systems; trunk radio relay network; limited
  open wire network; 3,400,000 telephones; broadcast stations - 15 AM; 94 FM;
  357 TV; 1 satellite ground station operating in the INTELSAT (2 Atlantic
  Ocean) and EUTELSAT systems; 1 submarine cable

:Turkey Defense Forces

Branches:
  Land Forces, Navy (including Naval Air and Naval Infantry), Air Force, Coast
  Guard, Gendarmerie
Manpower availability:
  males 15-49, 15,274,591; 9,330,851 fit for military service; 597,814 reach
  military age (20) annually
Defense expenditures:
  exchange rate conversion - $5.2 billion, 3-4% of GDP (1992 budget)

Turkmenistan Geography

Total area: 488,100 km2
Land area: 488,100 km2
Comparative area: slightly larger than California
Land boundaries:
  3,736 km total; Afghanistan 744 km, Iran 992 km, Kazakhstan 379 km,
  Uzbekistan 1,621 km
Coastline:
  0 km
note:
  Turkmenistan does border the Caspian Sea (1,768 km)
Maritime claims:
  none - landlocked
Disputes:
  none
Climate:
  subtropical desert
Terrain:

flat-to-rolling sandy desert with dunes; borders Caspian Sea in west
Natural resources:
  petroleum, natural gas, coal, sulphur, salt, magnesium
Land use:
  NA% arable land; NA% permanent crops; NA% meadows and pastures; NA% forest
  and woodland; NA% other; includes NA% irrigated
Environment:
  NA
Note:
  landlocked

:Turkmenistan People

Population: 3,838,108 (July 1992), growth rate 2.4% (1992)
Birth rate: 36 births/1,000 population (1992)
Death rate: 9 deaths/1,000 population (1992)
Net migration rate: -3 migrants/1,000 population (1992)
Infant mortality rate: 94 deaths/1,000 live births (1992)
Life expectancy at birth: 59 years male, 66 years female (1992)
Total fertility rate: 4.5 children born/woman (1992)
Nationality:
  noun - Turkmen(s); adjective - Turkmen
Ethnic divisions:
  Turkmen 72%, Russian 9%, Uzbek 9%, other 10%
Religions:
  Islam 85%, Eastern Orthodox 10%, unknown 5%
Languages:
  Turkmen 72%, Russian 12%, Uzbek 9%, other 7%
Literacy:
  NA% (male NA%, female NA) age 15 and over can read and write
Labor force:
  1,542,000; agriculture and forestry 42%, industry and construction 21%,
  other 37% (1990)
Organized labor:
  NA

:Turkmenistan Government

Long-form name:
  none
Type:
  republic
Capital: Ashgabat (Ashkhabad)
Administrative divisions:
  4 oblasts (oblastey, singular - oblast'); Balkan (Nebit-Dag), Chardzhou,
  Mary, Tashauz; note - the rayons around Ashgabat are under direct republic
  jurisdiction; all oblasts have the same name as their administrative center
  except Balkan Oblast, centered at Nebit-Dag
Independence:
  27 October 1991 (from the Soviet Union; formerly Turkmen Soviet Socialist
  Republic)
Constitution:
  adopted 18 May 1992

Legal system:
  NA
National holiday:
  Independence Day, 27 October (1991)
Executive branch:
  president, prime minister, two deputy prime ministers, Council of Ministers
Legislative branch:
  Majlis
Judicial branch:
  NA
Leaders:
 Chief of State:
  President Saparmurad NIYAZOV (since 21 June 1992)
 Head of Government:
  Prime Minister (vacant), Deputy Prime Ministers V. G. OCHERTSOV and Atta
  CHARYYEV (since NA 1991)
Political parties and leaders:
  Democratic Party (formerly Communist), Saparmurad NIYAZOV, chairman
  opposition:
  Democratic Party, Durdymorad KHODZHA Mukhammed, chairman
Suffrage:
  universal at age 18
Elections:
 President:
  last held 21 June 1992 (next to be held NA June 1997); results - Saparmurad
  NIYAZOV 99.5% (ran unopposed)
 Majlis:
  last held 7 January 1990 (next to be held NA 1995); results - percent of
  vote by party NA; seats - (175 total) elections not officially by party, but
  Communist Party members won nearly 90% of seats
Communists:
  renamed Democratic Party, 16 December 1990
Other political or pressure groups:
  Agzybirlik (Unity) Movement
Member of:
  CIS, CSCE, IBRD, IMF, NACC, UN, UNCTAD
Diplomatic representation:
  NA
 US:
  Ambassador-designate Joseph HULINGS; Embassy at Yubilenaya Hotel, Ashgabat
  (Ashkhabad) (mailing address is APO; AE 09862); telephone [8] (011)
  7-3630-24-49-08

:Turkmenistan Government

Flag:
  green field with five claret carpet gels (that is, a repeated carpet
  pattern) on the hoist side; a white crescent and five white stars in the
  upper left corner to the right of the carpet gels

:Turkmenistan Economy

Overview:

Like the other 15 former Soviet republics, Turkmenistan faces enormous problems of economic adjustment - to move away from Moscow-based central planning toward a system of decisionmaking by private enterpreneurs, local government authorities, and, hopefully, foreign investors. This process requires wholesale changes in supply sources, markets, property rights, and monetary arrangements. Industry - with 10% of the labor force - is heavily weighted toward the energy sector, which produced 11% of the ex-USSR's gas and 1% of its oil. Turkmenistan ranked second among the former Soviet republics in cotton production, mainly in the irrigated western region, where the huge Karakumskiy Canal taps the Amu Darya.

GDP:

purchasing power equivalent - NA, per capita $NA; real growth rate -0.6% (1991 est.)

Inflation rate (consumer prices):

85% (1991)

Unemployment rate:　20-25% (1991 est.)

Budget:

NA

Exports:

$239 million (1990)

commodities:

natural gas, oil, chemicals, cotton, textiles, carpets

partners:

Russia, Ukraine, Uzbekistan

Imports:

$970 million (1990)

commodities:

machinery and parts, plastics and rubber, consumer durables, textiles

partners:

NA

External debt:　$650 million (end of 1991 est.)

Industrial production:

growth rate 4.1% (1991)

Electricity:

3,170,000 kW capacity; 14,900 million kWh produced, 4,114 kWh per capita (1990)

Industries:

oil and gas, petrochemicals, fertilizers, food processing, textiles

Agriculture:

cotton, fruits, vegetables

Illicit drugs:

illicit producers of cannabis and opium; mostly for domestic consumption; status of government eradication programs unknown; used as transshipment points for illicit drugs to Western Europe

Economic aid:

NA

Currency:

As of May 1992, retaining ruble as currency

Exchange rates:

NA

Fiscal year: calendar year

:Turkmenistan Communications

Railroads:
  2,120 km all 1.520-meter gauge
Highways:
  23,000 km total (1990); 18,300 km hard surfaced, 4,700 km earth
Inland waterways:
  NA km
Pipelines:
  NA
Ports:
  inland - Krasnovodsk
Civil air:
  NA
Airports:
  NA
Telecommunications:
  poorly developed; telephone density NA; linked by landline or microwave to
  other CIS member states and Iran, and by leased connections via the Moscow
  international gateway switch to other countries; satellite earth stations -
  Orbita and INTELSAT (TV receive only)

:Turkmenistan Defense Forces

Branches:
  Republic Security Forces (internal and border troops), National Guard; CIS
  Forces (Ground, Air and Air Defense)
Manpower availability:
  males 15-49, NA; NA fit for military service; NA reach military age (18)
  annually
Defense expenditures:
  $NA, NA% of GDP

Turks and Caicos Islands Geography

Total area: 430 km2
Land area: 430 km2
Comparative area: slightly less than 2.5 times the size of Washington, DC
Land boundaries:
  none
Coastline:
  389 km
Maritime claims:
 Exclusive fishing zone:
  200 nm
 Territorial sea:
  12 nm
Disputes:
  none
Climate:
  tropical; marine; moderated by trade winds; sunny and relatively dry

Terrain:
  low, flat limestone; extensive marshes and mangrove swamps
Natural resources:
  spiny lobster, conch
Land use:
  arable land 2%; permanent crops 0%; meadows and pastures; 0%; forest and woodland 0%; other 98%
Environment:
  30 islands (eight inhabited); subject to frequent hurricanes
Note:
  located 190 km north of the Dominican Republic in the North Atlantic Ocean

:Turks and Caicos Islands People

Population: 12,697 (July 1992), growth rate 3.3% (1992)
Birth rate: 16 births/1,000 population (1992)
Death rate: 5 deaths/1,000 population (1992)
Net migration rate: 22 migrants/1,000 population (1992)
Infant mortality rate: 13 deaths/1,000 live births (1992)
Life expectancy at birth: 73 years male, 77 years female (1992)
Total fertility rate: 2.3 children born/woman (1992)
Nationality:
  no noun or adjectival forms
Ethnic divisions:
  majority of African descent
Religions:
  Baptist 41.2%, Methodist 18.9%, Anglican 18.3%, Seventh-Day Adventist 1.7%, other 19.9% (1980)
Languages:
  English (official)
Literacy:
  98% (male 99%, female 98%) age 15 and over having ever attended school (1970)
Labor force:
  NA; majority engaged in fishing and tourist industries; some subsistence agriculture
Organized labor:
  Saint George's Industrial Trade Union

:Turks and Caicos Islands Government

Long-form name:
  none
Type:
  dependent territory of the UK
Capital: Grand Turk (Cockburn Town)
Administrative divisions:
  none (dependent territory of the UK)
Independence:
  none (dependent territory of the UK)
Constitution:
  introduced 30 August 1976, suspended in 1986, and a Constitutional Commission is currently reviewing its contents

Legal system:
  based on laws of England and Wales with a small number adopted from Jamaica
  and The Bahamas
National holiday:
  Constitution Day, 30 August (1976)
Executive branch:
  British monarch, governor, Executive Council, chief minister
Legislative branch:
  unicameral Legislative Council
Judicial branch:
  Supreme Court
Leaders:
 Chief of State:
  Queen ELIZABETH II (since 6 February 1953), represented by Governor Michael
  J. BRADLEY (since 1987)
 Head of Government:
  Chief Minister Washington MISSIC (since NA 1991)
Political parties and leaders:
  People's Democratic Movement (PDM), Oswald SKIPPINGS; Progressive National
  Party (PNP), Washington MISSIC; National Democratic Alliance (NDA), Ariel
  MISSICK
Suffrage:
  universal at age 18
Elections:
 Legislative Council:
  last held on 3 April 1991 (next to be held NA); results - percent of vote by
  party NA; seats - (20 total, 13 elected) PNP 8, PDM 5
Member of:
  CDB
Diplomatic representation:
  as a dependent territory of the UK, the interests of the Turks and Caicos
  Islands are represented in the US by the UK
 US:
  none
Flag:
  blue with the flag of the UK in the upper hoist-side quadrant and the
  colonial shield centered on the outer half of the flag; the shield is yellow
  and contains a conch shell, lobster, and cactus

:Turks and Caicos Islands Economy

Overview:
  The economy is based on fishing, tourism, and offshore banking. Only
  subsistence farming - corn and beans - exists on the Caicos Islands, so that
  most foods, as well as nonfood products, must be imported.
GDP:
  purchasing power equivalent - $44.9 million, per capita $5,000; real growth
  rate NA% (1986)
Inflation rate (consumer prices):
  NA%
Unemployment rate: 12% (1989)

Budget:
  revenues $12.4 million; expenditures $15.8 million, including capital
  expenditures of $2.6 million (FY87)
Exports:
  $2.9 million (f.o.b., FY84)
  commodities:
  lobster, dried and fresh conch, conch shells
  partners:
  US, UK
Imports:
  $26.3 million (c.i.f., FY84)
  commodities:
  foodstuffs, drink, tobacco, clothing
  partners:
  US, UK
External debt: $NA
Industrial production:
  growth rate NA%
Electricity:
  9,050 kW capacity; 11.1 million kWh produced, 1,140 kWh per capita (1990)
Industries:
  fishing, tourism, offshore financial services
Agriculture:
  subsistence farming prevails, based on corn and beans; fishing more
  important than farming; not self-sufficient in food
Economic aid:
  Western (non-US) countries, ODA and OOF bilateral commitments (1970-89),
  $110 million
Currency:
  US currency is used
Exchange rates:
  US currency is used
Fiscal year: calendar year

:Turks and Caicos Islands Communications

Highways:
  121 km, including 24 km tarmac
Ports:
  Grand Turk, Salt Cay, Providenciales, Cockburn Harbour
Civil air·
  Air Turks and Caicos (passenger service) and Turks Air Ltd. (cargo service)
Airports:
  7 total, 7 usable; 4 with permanent-surface runways; none with runways over
  2,439 m; 4 with runways 1,220-2,439 m
Telecommunications:
  fair cable and radio services; 1,446 telephones; broadcast stations - 3 AM,
  no FM, several TV; 2 submarine cables; 1 Atlantic Ocean INTELSAT earth
  station

:Turks and Caicos Islands Defense Forces

Note: defense is the responsibility of the UK

Tuvalu Geography

Total area: 26 km2
Land area: 26 km2
Comparative area: about 0.1 times the size of Washington, DC
Land boundaries:
  none
Coastline:
  24 km
Maritime claims:
 Exclusive economic zone:
  200 nm
 Territorial sea:
  12 nm
Disputes:
  none
Climate:
  tropical; moderated by easterly trade winds (March to November); westerly
  gales and heavy rain (November to March)
Terrain:
  very low-lying and narrow coral atolls
Natural resources:
  fish
Land use:
  arable land 0%; permanent crops 0%; meadows and pastures 0%; forest and
  woodland 0%; other 100%
Environment:
  severe tropical storms are rare
Note:
  located 3,000 km east of Papua New Guinea in the South Pacific Ocean

:Tuvalu People

Population: 9,494 (July 1992), growth rate 1.8% (1992)
Birth rate: 28 births/1,000 population (1992)
Death rate: 9 deaths/1,000 population (1992)
Net migration rate: 0 migrants/1,000 population (1992)
Infant mortality rate: 34 deaths/1,000 live births (1992)
Life expectancy at birth: 61 years male, 64 years female (1992)
Total fertility rate: 3.1 children born/woman (1992)
Nationality:
  noun - Tuvaluans(s); adjective - Tuvaluan
Ethnic divisions:
  96% Polynesian
Religions:
  Church of Tuvalu (Congregationalist) 97%, Seventh-Day Adventist 1.4%, Baha'i
  1%, other 0.6%
Languages:
  Tuvaluan, English
Literacy:
  NA% (male NA%, female NA%)
Labor force:

NA
Organized labor:
  none

:Tuvalu Government

Long-form name:
  none
Type:
  democracy
Capital: Funafuti
Administrative divisions:
  none
Independence:
  1 October 1978 (from UK; formerly Ellice Islands)
Constitution:
  1 October 1978
National holiday:
  Independence Day, 1 October (1978)
Executive branch:
  British monarch, governor general, prime minister, deputy prime minister,
  Cabinet
Legislative branch:
  unicameral Parliament (Palamene)
Judicial branch:
  High Court
Leaders:
  Chief of State:
    Queen ELIZABETH II (since 6 February 1952), represented by Governor General
    Tupua LEUPENA (since 1 March 1986)
  Head of Government:
    Prime Minister Bikenibeu PAENIU (since 16 October 1989); Deputy Prime
    Minister Dr. Alesana SELUKA (since October 1989)
Political parties and leaders:
  none
Suffrage:
  universal at age 18
Elections:
  Parliament:
    last held 28 September 1989 (next to be held by NA September 1993); results
    - percent of vote NA; seats - (12 total)
Member of:
  ACP, C (special), ESCAP, SPC, SPF, UPU
Diplomatic representation:
  Ambassador (vacant)
  US:
    none
Flag:
  light blue with the flag of the UK in the upper hoist-side quadrant; the
  outer half of the flag represents a map of the country with nine yellow
  five-pointed stars symbolizing the nine islands

:Tuvalu Economy

Overview:
  Tuvalu consists of a scattered group of nine coral atolls with poor soil.
  The country has no known mineral resources and few exports. Subsistence
  farming and fishing are the primary economic activities. The islands are too
  small and too remote for development of a tourist industry. Government
  revenues largely come from the sale of stamps and coins and worker
  remittances. Substantial income is received annually from an international
  trust fund established in 1987 by Australia, New Zealand, and the UK and
  supported also by Japan and South Korea.

GNP:
  exchange rate conversion - $4.6 million, per capita $530; real growth rate
  NA% (1989 est.)

Inflation rate (consumer prices):
  3.9% (1984)

Unemployment rate: NA%

Budget:
  revenues $4.3 million; expenditures $4.3 million, including capital
  expenditures of $NA (1989)

Exports:
  $1.0 million (f.o.b., 1983 est.)
  commodities:
  copra
  partners:
  Fiji, Australia, NZ

Imports:
  $2.8 million (c.i.f., 1983 est.)
  commodities:
  food, animals, mineral fuels, machinery, manufactured goods
  partners:
  Fiji, Australia, NZ

External debt: $NA

Industrial production:
  growth rate NA

Electricity:
  2,600 kW capacity; 3 million kWh produced, 330 kWh per capita (1990)

Industries:
  fishing, tourism, copra

Agriculture:
  coconuts, copra

Economic aid:
  US commitments, including Ex-Im (FY70-87), $1 million; Western (non-US)
  countries, ODA and OOF bilateral commitments (1970-89), $101 million

Currency:
  Tuvaluan dollar and Australian dollar (plural - dollars); 1 Tuvaluan dollar
  ($T) or 1 Australian dollar ($A) = 100 cents

Exchange rates:
  Tuvaluan dollars ($T) or Australian dollars ($A) per US$1 - 1.3117 (March
  1992), 1.2835 (1991), 1.2799 (1990), 1.2618 (1989), 1.2752 (1988), 1.4267

(1987)

Fiscal year: NA

:Tuvalu Communications

Highways:
8 km gravel

Ports:
Funafuti, Nukufetau

Merchant marine:
1 passenger-cargo (1,000 GRT or over) totaling 1,043 GRT/450 DWT

Civil air:
no major transport aircraft

Airports:
1 with runway 1,220-2,439 m

Telecommunications:
broadcast stations - 1 AM, no FM, no TV; 300 radiotelephones; 4,000 radios; 108 telephones

:Tuvalu Defense Forces

Branches:
Police Force

Manpower availability:
NA

Defense expenditures:
exchange rate conversion - $NA, NA% of GNP

Uganda Geography

Total area: 236,040 km2
Land area: 199,710 km2
Comparative area: slightly smaller than Oregon

Land boundaries:
2,698 km total; Kenya 933 km, Rwanda 169 km, Sudan 435 km, Tanzania 396 km, Zaire 765 km

Coastline:
none - landlocked

Maritime claims:
none - landlocked

Disputes:
none

Climate:
tropical; generally rainy with two dry seasons (December to February, June to August); semiarid in northeast

Terrain:
mostly plateau with rim of mountains

Natural resources:
copper, cobalt, limestone, salt

Land use:
arable land 23%; permanent crops 9%; meadows and pastures 25%; forest and woodland 30%; other 13%; includes irrigated NEGL%

Environment:
straddles Equator; deforestation; overgrazing; soil erosion

Note:
  landlocked

:Uganda People

Population: 19,386,104 (July 1992), growth rate 3.7% (1992)
Birth rate: 51 births/1,000 population (1992)
Death rate: 14 deaths/1,000 population (1992)
Net migration rate: 0 migrants/1,000 population (1992)
Infant mortality rate: 91 deaths/1,000 live births (1992)
Life expectancy at birth: 50 years male, 52 years female (1992)
Total fertility rate: 7.2 children born/woman (1992)
Nationality:
  noun - Ugandan(s); adjective - Ugandan
Ethnic divisions:
  African 99%, European, Asian, Arab 1%
Religions:
  Roman Catholic 33%, Protestant 33%, Muslim 16%, rest indigenous beliefs
Languages:
  English (official); Luganda and Swahili widely used; other Bantu and Nilotic
  languages
Literacy:
  48% (male 62%, female 35%) age 15 and over can read and write (1990 est.)
Labor force:
  4,500,000 (est.); 50% of population of working age (1983)
Organized labor:
  125,000 union members

:Uganda Government

Long-form name:
  Republic of Uganda
Type:
  republic
Capital: Kampala
Administrative divisions:
  10 provinces; Busoga, Central, Eastern, Karamoja, Nile, North Buganda,
  Northern, South Buganda, Southern, Western
Independence:
  9 October 1962 (from UK)
Constitution:
  8 September 1967, in process of constitutional revision
Legal system:
  government plans to restore system based on English common law and customary
  law and reinstitute a normal judicial system; accepts compulsory ICJ
  jurisdiction, with reservations
National holiday:
  Independence Day, 9 October (1962)
Executive branch:
  president, vice president, prime minister, three deputy prime ministers,
  Cabinet
Legislative branch:
  unicameral National Resistance Council

992

Judicial branch:
   Court of Appeal, High Court
Leaders:
   Chief of State:
   President Lt. Gen. Yoweri Kaguta MUSEVENI (since 29 January 1986); Vice
   President Samson Babi Mululu KISEKKA (since NA January 1991)
   Head of Government:
   Prime Minister George Cosmas ADYEBO (since NA January 1991)
Political parties and leaders:
   only party - National Resistance Movement (NRM); note - the Uganda Patriotic
   Movement (UPM), Ugandan People's Congress (UPC), Democratic Party (DP), and
   Conservative Party (CP) are all proscribed from conducting public political
   activities
Suffrage:
   universal at age 18
Elections:
   National Resistance Council:
   last held 11-28 February 1989 (next to be held by January 1995); results -
   NRM was the only party; seats - (278 total, 210 indirectly elected) 210
   members elected without party affiliation
Other political or pressure groups:
   Uganda People's Front (UPF), Uganda People's Christian Democratic Army
   (UPCDA), Ruwenzori Movement
Member of:
   ACP, AfDB, C, CCC, EADB, ECA, FAO, G-77, GATT, IAEA, IBRD, ICAO,
ICFTU, IDA,
   IDB, IFAD, IFC, IGADD, ILO, IMF, INTELSAT, INTERPOL, IOC, ITU, LORCS,
NAM,
   OAU, OIC, PCA, UN, UNCTAD, UNESCO, UNHCR, UNIDO, UPU, WHO,
WIPO, WMO, WTO
Diplomatic representation:
   Ambassador Stephen Kapimpina KATENTA-APULI; 5909 16th Street NW, Wash-
ington,
   DC 20011; telephone (202) 726-7100 through 7102
   US:
   Ambassador Johnnie CARSON; Embassy at Parliament Avenue, Kampala (mailing
   address is P. O. Box 7007, Kampala); telephone [256] (41) 259792, 259793,
   259795

:Uganda Government

Flag:
   six equal horizontal bands of black (top), yellow, red, black, yellow, and
   red; a white disk is superimposed at the center and depicts a red-crested
   crane (the national symbol) facing the staff side

:Uganda Economy

Overview:
   Uganda has substantial natural resources, including fertile soils, regular
   rainfall, and sizable mineral deposits of copper and cobalt. The economy has
   been devastated by widespread political instability, mismanagement, and
   civil war since independence in 1962, keeping Uganda poor with a per capita

income of about $300. (GDP remains below the levels of the early 1970s, as does industrial production.) Agriculture is the most important sector of the economy, employing over 80% of the work force. Coffee is the major export crop and accounts for the bulk of export revenues. Since 1986 the government has acted to rehabilitate and stabilize the economy by undertaking currency reform, raising producer prices on export crops, increasing petroleum prices, and improving civil service wages. The policy changes are especially aimed at dampening inflation, which was running at over 300% in 1987, and boosting production and export earnings. During the period 1990-91, the economy turned in a solid performance based on continued investment in the rehabilitation of infrastructure, improved incentives for production and exports, and gradually improving domestic security.

GDP:
 exchange rate conversion - $5.6 billion, per capita $300; real growth rate 4.5% (1991 est.)

Inflation rate (consumer prices):
 35% (1991 est.)

Unemployment rate: NA%

Budget:
 revenues $365 million; expenditures $545 million, including capital expenditures of $165 million (FY89 est.)

Exports:
 $208 million (f.o.b., 1990)
 commodities:
 coffee 97%, cotton, tea
 partners:
 US 25%, UK 18%, France 11%, Spain 10%

Imports:
 $209 million (c.i.f., 1990)
 commodities:
 petroleum products, machinery, cotton piece goods, metals, transportation equipment, food
 partners:
 Kenya 25%, UK 14%, Italy 13%

External debt: $1.9 billion (1991 est.)

Industrial production:
 growth rate 7.0% (1990); accounts for 5% of GDP

Electricity:
 175,000 kW capacity; 315 million kWh produced, 15 kWh per capita (1991)

Industries:
 sugar, brewing, tobacco, cotton textiles, cement

Agriculture:
 mainly subsistence; accounts for 57% of GDP and over 80% of labor force; cash crops - coffee, tea, cotton, tobacco; food crops - cassava, potatoes, corn, millet, pulses; livestock products - beef, goat meat, milk, poultry; self-sufficient in food

Economic aid:
 US commitments, including Ex-Im (1970-89), $145 million; Western (non-US) countries, ODA and OOF bilateral commitments (1970-89), $1.4 billion; OPEC

bilateral aid (1979-89), $60 million; Communist countries (1970-89), $169 million

:Uganda Economy

Currency:
Ugandan shilling (plural - shillings); 1 Ugandan shilling (USh) = 100 cents
Exchange rates:
Ugandan shillings (USh) per US$1 - 1,031.3 (March 1992), 734.0 (1991), 428.85 (1990), 223.1 (1989), 106.1 (1988), 42.8 (1987)
Fiscal year: 1 July - 30 June

:Uganda Communications

Railroads:
1,300 km, 1.000-meter-gauge single track
Highways:
26,200 km total; 1,970 km paved; 5,849 km crushed stone, gravel, and laterite; remainder earth roads and tracks
Inland waterways:
Lake Victoria, Lake Albert, Lake Kyoga, Lake George, Lake Edward; Victoria Nile, Albert Nile; principal inland water ports are at Jinja and Port Bell, both on Lake Victoria
Merchant marine:
1 roll-on/roll-off (1,000 GRT or over) totaling 1,697 GRT
Civil air:
6 major transport aircraft
Airports:
35 total, 27 usable; 5 with permanent-surface runways; 1 with runways over 3,659 m; 3 with runways 2,440-3,659 m; 10 with runways 1,220-2,439 m
Telecommunications:
fair system with microwave and radio communications stations; broadcast stations - 10 AM, no FM, 9 TV; satellite communications ground stations - 1 Atlantic Ocean INTELSAT

:Uganda Defense Forces

Branches:
Army, Navy, Air Force
Manpower availability:
males 15-49, about 4,132,887; about 2,243,933 for military service
Defense expenditures:
$NA, NA% of GDP

Ukraine Geography

Total area: 603,700 km2
Land area: 603,700 km2
Comparative area: slightly smaller than Texas
Land boundaries:
4,558 km total; Belarus 891 km, Czechoslovakia 90 km, Hungary 103 km, Moldova 939 km, Poland 428 km, Romania (southwest) 169 km, Romania (west) 362 km, Russia 1,576 km
Coastline:
2,782 km
Maritime claims:

Contiguous zone:
  NA nm
Continental shelf:
  NA meter depth
Exclusive fishing zone:
  NA nm
Exclusive economic zone:
  NA nm
Territorial sea:
  NA nm
Disputes:
  potential border disputes with Moldova and Romania in northern Bukovina and
  southern Odessa oblast
Climate:
  temperate continental; subtropical only on the southern Crimean coast;
  precipitation disproportionately distributed, highest in west and north,
  lesser in east and southeast; winters vary from cool along the Black Sea to
  cold farther inland; summers are warm across the greater part of the
  country, hot in the south
Terrain:
  most of Ukraine consists of fertile plains (steppes) and plateaux, mountains
  being found only in the west (the Carpathians), and in the Crimean peninsula
  in the extreme south
Natural resources:
  iron ore, coal, manganese, natural gas, oil, salt, sulphur, graphite,
  titanium, magnesium, kaolin, nickel, mercury, timber
Land use:
  56% arable land; 2% permanent crops; 12% meadows and pastures; NA% forest
  and woodland; 30% other; includes 3% irrigated
Environment:
  air and water pollution, deforestation, radiation contamination around
  Chernobyl nuclear plant
Note:
  strategic position at the crossroads between Europe and Asia; second largest
  country in Europe

:Ukraine People

Population: 51,940,426 (July 1992), growth rate 0.2% (1992)
Birth rate: 14 births/1,000 population (1992)
Death rate: 12 deaths/1,000 population (1992)
Net migration rate: 1 migrant/1,000 population (1992)
Infant mortality rate: 22 deaths/1,000 live births (1992)
Life expectancy at birth: 65 years male, 75 years female (1992)
Total fertility rate: 2.0 children born/woman (1992)
Nationality:
  noun - Ukrainian(s); adjective - Ukrainian
Ethnic divisions:
  Ukrainian 73%, Russian 22%, Jewish 1%, other 4%
Religions:
  Ukrainian Autonomous Orthodox, Ukrainian Autocephalous Orthodox, Ukrainian

Catholic (Uniate), Protestant, Jewish
Languages:
Ukrainian, Russian, Romanian, Polish
Literacy:
NA%
Labor force:
25,277,000; industry and construction 41%, agriculture and forestry 19%, health, education, and culture 18%, trade and distribution 8%, transport and communication 7%, other 7% (1990)
Organized labor:
NA

:Ukraine Government

Long-form name:
none
Type:
republic
Capital: Kiev (Kyyiv)
Administrative divisions:
24 oblasts (oblastey, singular - oblast') and 1 autonomous republic* (avtomnaya respublika); Chernigov, Cherkassy, Chernovtsy, Dnepropetrovsk, Donetsk, Ivano-Frankovsk, Khar'kov, Kherson, Khmel'nitskiy, Kiev, Kirovograd, Krym (Simferopol')*, Lugansk, L'vov, Nikolayev, Odessa, Poltava, Rovno, Sumy, Ternopol', Vinnitsa, Volyn' (Lutsk), Zakarpat (Uzhgorod), Zaporozh'ye, Zhitomir; note - an oblast usually has the same name as its administrative center (exceptions have the administrative center name following in parentheses)
Independence:
24 August 1991; 1 December 1991 de facto from USSR; note - formerly the Ukrainian Soviet Socialist Republic in the Soviet Union
Constitution:
currently being drafted
Legal system:
based on civil law system; no judicial review of legislative acts
National holiday:
Independence Day, 24 August (1991)
Executive branch:
president, prime minister
Legislative branch:
unicameral Supreme Council
Judicial branch:
being organized
Leaders:
 Chief of State:
 President Leonid M. KRAVCHUK (since 5 December 1991)
 Head of Government:
 Prime Minister Vitol'd FOKIN (since 14 November 1991); two First Deputy Prime Ministers: Valentyn SYMONENKO and Konstantyn MASYK (since 21 May 1991); two Deputy Prime Ministers: Oleh SLEPICHEV and Viktor SYTNYK (since 21 May 1991)

Political parties and leaders:

Ukrainian Republican Party, Levko LUKYANENKO, chairman; Green Party, Yuriy
SHCHERBAK, chairman; Social Democratic Party, Andriy NOSENKO, chairman;
Ukrainian Democratic Party, Yuriy BADZO, chairman; Democratic Rebirth Party,
Oleksandr Volodymyr GRINEV, Oleksandr FILENKO, YEMETS, Miroslav
POPOVICH,
Sergei LYLYK, Oleksandr BAZYLYUK, Valeriy KHMELKO, leaders; People's
Party
of Ukraine, Leopold TABURYANSKIY, chairman; Peasant Democratic Party, Jer-
hiy
PLACHYNDA, chairman; Ukrainian Socialist Party, Oleksandr MOROZ, chairman

Suffrage:

universal at age 18

Elections:

President:

last held 1 December 1991 (next to be held NA 1996); results - Leonid
KRAVCHUK 61.59%, Vyacheslav CHERNOVIL 23.27%, Levko LUKYANENKO
4.49%,
Volodymyr GRINEV 4.17%, Iher YUKHNOVSKY 1.74%, Leopold
TABURYANSKIY 0.57%

Supreme Council:

last held 4 March 1990 (next scheduled for 1995, may be held earlier in late
1992 or 1993); results - percent of vote by party NA; seats - (NA total)
number of seats by party NA

:Ukraine Government

Communists:

Communist Party of Ukraine was banned by decree of the Supreme Council on 30
August 1991

Other political or pressure groups:

Ukraninan People's Movement for Restructuring (RUKH)

Member of:

CIS, CSCE, CE, ECE, IAEA, IMF, INMARSAT, IOC, ITU, NACC, PCA, UN,
UNCTAD,
UNESCO, UNIDO, UPU, WHO, WIPO, WMO

Diplomatic representation:

Ambassador Oleh H. BILORUS; Embassy at 1828 L Street, NW, Suite 711,
Washington, DC 20036; telephone (202) 296-6960

US:

Ambassador Roman POPADIUK; Embassy at ;10 Vul. Yuriy Kotsubinskoho, Kiev
(mailing address is APO AE 09862); telephone (044) 244-7349; FAX (044)
244-7350

Flag:

two horizontal bars of equal size: azure (sky blue) top half, golden yellow
bottom half (represents grainfields under a blue sky)

:Ukraine Economy

Overview:

Because of its size, geographic location, Slavic population, and rich
resources, the loss of Ukraine was the final and most bitter blow to the
Soviet leaders wishing to preserve some semblance of the old political,

military, and economic power of the USSR. After Russia, the Ukrainian republic was far and away the most important economic component of the former Soviet Union producing more than three times the output of the next-ranking republic. Its fertile black soil generated more than one fourth of Soviet agricultural output, and its farms provided substantial quantities of meat, milk, grain and vegetables to other republics. Likewise, its well-developed and diversified heavy industry supplied equipment and raw materials to industrial and mining sites in other regions of the USSR. In early 1992 the continued wholesale disruption of economic ties and the lack of an institutional structure necessary to formulate and implement economic reforms preclude a near-term recovery of output.

GDP:
$NA, per capita $NA; real growth rate -10% (1991 est.)

Inflation rate (consumer prices):
83% (1991 est.)

Unemployment rate: NA%

Budget:
not finalized as of May 1992

Exports:
$13.5 billion (1990)
commodities:
coal, electric power, ferrous and nonferrous metals, chemicals, machinery and transport equipment, grain, meat
partners:
Russia, Belarus, Kazakhstan

Imports:
$16.7 billion (1990)
commodities:
machinery and parts, transportation equipment, chemicals, textiles
partners:
none
*** No entry for this item ***

External debt: $10.4 billion (end of 1991 est.)

Industrial production:
growth rate -4.5% (1991)

Electricity:
NA kW capacity; 298,000 million kWh produced, 5,758 kWh per capita (1990)

Industries:
coal, electric power, ferrous and nonferrous metals, machinery and transport equipment, chemicals, food-processing

Agriculture:
grain, vegetables, meat, milk

Illicit drugs:
illicit producer of cannabis and opium; mostly for domestic consumption; status of government eradication programs unknown; used as transshipment points for illicit drugs to Western Europe

Economic aid:
$NA

:Ukraine Economy

Currency:
    as of August 1992 using ruble and Ukrainian coupons as legal tender; Ukraine plans to withdraw the ruble from circulation and convert to a coupon-based economy on 1 October 1992; Ukrainian officials claim this will be an interim move toward introducing a Ukrainian currency - the hryvnya - possibly as early as January 1993

Exchange rates:
    NA

Fiscal year: calendar year

:Ukraine Communications

Railroads:
    22,800 km all 1.500-meter gauge; does not include industrial lines (1990)

Highways:
    273,700 km total (1990); 236,400 km hard surfaced, 37,300 km earth

Inland waterways:
    NA km perennially navigable

Pipelines:
    NA

Ports:
    maritime - Berdyansk, Il'ichevsk Kerch', Kherson, Mariupol' (formerly Zhdanov), Nikolayev, Odessa, Sevastopol', Yuzhnoye; inland - Kiev

Merchant marine:
    338 ships (1,000 GRT or over) totaling 4,117,595 GRT/5,403,685 DWT; includes 221 cargo, 11 container, 9 barge carriers, 59 bulk cargo, 9 petroleum tanker, 2 chemical tanker, 3 liquefied gas, 24 passenger

Civil air:
    NA major transport aircraft

Airports:
    NA

Telecommunications:
    inheriting part of the former USSR system, Ukraine has about 7 million telephone lines (13.5 telephones for each 100 persons); as of 31 January 1990, 3.56 million applications for telephones could not be satisfied; international calls can be made via satellite, by landline to other CIS countries, and through the Moscow international switching center; satellite earth stations employ INTELSAT, INMARSAT, and Intersputnik

:Ukraine Defense Forces

Branches:
    Republic Security Forces (internal and border troops), National Guard; CIS Forces (Ground Navy, Air, and Defense)

Manpower availability:
    males 15-49, NA; NA fit for military service; NA reach military age (18) annually

Defense expenditures:
    $NA, NA% of GDP

United Arab Emirates Geography

Total area: 83,600 km2
Land area: 83,600 km2

Comparative area: slightly smaller than Maine
Land boundaries:
  1,016 km total; Oman 410 km, Saudi Arabia 586 km, Qatar 20 km
Coastline:
  1,448 km
Maritime claims:
 Continental shelf:
  defined by bilateral boundaries or equidistant line
 Exclusive economic zone:
  200 nm
 Territorial sea:
  3 nm (assumed), 12 nm for Ash Shariqah (Sharjah)
Disputes:
  boundary with Qatar is unresolved; no defined boundary with Saudi Arabia; no
  defined boundary with most of Oman, but Administrative Line in far north;
  claims two islands in the Persian Gulf occupied by Iran (Jazireh-ye Tonb-e
  Bozorg or Greater Tunb, and Jazireh-ye Tonb-e Kuchek or Lesser Tunb); claims
  island in the Persian Gulf jointly administered with Iran (Jazireh-ye Abu
  Musa or Abu Musa,)
Climate:
  desert; cooler in eastern mountains
Terrain:
  flat, barren coastal plain merging into rolling sand dunes of vast desert
  waste- land; mountains in east
Natural resources:
  crude oil and natural gas
Land use:
  arable land NEGL%; permanent crops NEGL%; meadows and pastures 2%; forest
  and woodland NEGL%; other 98%; includes irrigated NEGL%
Environment:
  frequent dust and sand storms; lack of natural freshwater resources being
  overcome by desalination plants; desertification
Note:
  strategic location along southern approaches to Strait of Hormuz, a vital
  transit point for world crude oil

:United Arab Emirates People

Population: 2,522,315 (July 1992), growth rate 5.4% (1992)
Birth rate: 29 births/1,000 population (1992)
Death rate: 3 deaths/1,000 population (1992)
Net migration rate: 27 migrants/1,000 population (1992)
Infant mortality rate: 23 deaths/1,000 live births (1992)
Life expectancy at birth: 70 years male, 74 years female (1992)
Total fertility rate: 4.7 children born/woman (1992)
Nationality:
  noun - Emirian(s), adjective - Emirian
Ethnic divisions:
  Emirian 19%, other Arab 23%, South Asian (fluctuating) 50%, other
  expatriates (includes Westerners and East Asians) 8%; less than 20% of the
  population are UAE citizens (1982)

Religions:
Muslim 96% (Shi`a 16%); Christian, Hindu, and other 4%
Languages:
Arabic (official); Persian and English widely spoken in major cities; Hindi,
Urdu
Literacy:
68% (male 70%, female 63%) age 10 and over but definition of literacy not
available (1980)
Labor force:
580,000 (1986 est.); industry and commerce 85%, agriculture 5%, services 5%,
government 5%; 80% of labor force is foreign
Organized labor:
trade unions are illegal

:United Arab Emirates Government

Long-form name:
United Arab Emirates (no short-form name); abbreviated UAE
Type:
federation with specified powers delegated to the UAE central government and
other powers reserved to member emirates
Capital: Abu Dhabi
Administrative divisions:
7 emirates (imarat, singular - imarah); Abu Zaby (Abu Dhabi), `Ajman, Al
Fujayrah, Ash Shariqah, Dubayy, Ra's al Khaymah, Umm al Qaywayn
Independence:
2 December 1971 (from UK; formerly Trucial States)
Constitution:
2 December 1971 (provisional)
Legal system:
secular codes are being introduced by the UAE Government and in several
member shaykhdoms; Islamic law remains influential
National holiday:
National Day, 2 December (1971)
Executive branch:
president, vice president, Supreme Council of Rulers, prime minister, deputy
prime minister, Council of Ministers
Legislative branch:
unicameral Federal National Council (Majlis Watani Itihad)
Judicial branch:
Union Supreme Court
Leaders:
 Chief of State:
president Shaykh Zayid bin Sultan Al NUHAYYAN, (since 2 December 1971),
ruler of Abu Dhabi; Vice President Shaykh Maktum bin Rashid al-MAKTUM (since
8 October 1990), ruler of Dubayy
 Head of Government:
Prime Minister Shaykh Maktum bin Rashid al-MAKTUM (since 8 October 1990),
ruler of Dubayy; Deputy Prime Minister Sultan bin Zayid Al NUHAYYAN (since
20 November 1990)
Political parties and leaders:

Suffrage:
  none
Elections:
  none
Other political or pressure groups:
  a few small clandestine groups may be active
Member of:
  ABEDA, AFESD, AL, AMF, CAEU, CCC, ESCWA, FAO, G-77, GCC, IAEA,
IBRD, ICAO,
  IDA, IDB, IFAD, IFC, ILO, IMF, IMO, INMARSAT, INTELSAT, INTERPOL,
IOC, ISO
  (correspondent), ITU, LORCS, NAM, OAPEC, OIC, OPEC, UN, UNCTAD,
UNESCO,
  UNIDO, UPU, WHO, WIPO, WMO, WTO
Diplomatic representation:
  Ambassador Muhammad bin Husayn Al SHAALI; Chancery at Suite 740, 600 New
  Hampshire Avenue NW, Washington, DC 20037; telephone (202) 338-6500
  US:
  Ambassador Edward S. WALKER, Jr.; Embassy at Al-Sudan Street, Abu Dhabi
  (mailing address is P. O. Box 4009, Abu Dhabi); telephone [971] (2) 336691,
  afterhours 338730; FAX [971] (2) 318441; there is a US Consulate General in
  Dubayy (Dubai)
Flag:
  three equal horizontal bands of green (top), white, and black with a thicker
  vertical red band on the hoist side

:United Arab Emirates Economy

Overview:
  The UAE has an open economy with one of the world's highest incomes per
  capita outside the OECD nations. This wealth is based on oil and gas, and
  the fortunes of the economy fluctuate with the prices of those commodities.
  Since 1973, when petroleum prices shot up, the UAE has undergone a profound
  transformation from an impoverished region of small desert principalities to
  a modern state with a high standard of living. At present levels of
  production, crude oil reserves should last for over 100 years.
GDP:
  exchange rate conversion - $33.7 billion, per capita $14,100 (1990); real
  growth rate 11% (1989)
Inflation rate (consumer prices):
  5.5% (1990 est.)
Unemployment rate: NEGL (1988)
Budget:
  revenues $3.8 billion; expenditures $3.7 billion, including capital
  expenditures of $NA (1989 est.)
Exports:
  $21.3 billion (f.o.b., 1990 est.)
  commodities:
  crude oil 65%, natural gas, reexports, dried fish, dates
  partners:

Japan 35%, Singapore 6%, US 4%, Korea 3%
Imports:
  $11.0 billion (f.o.b., 1990 est.)
 commodities:
  food, consumer and capital goods
 partners:
  Japan 14%, UK 10%, US 9%, Germany 9%
External debt: $11.0 billion (December 1989 est.)
Industrial production:
  NA
Electricity:
  5,800,000 kW capacity; 17,000 million kWh produced, 7,115 kWh per capita
  (1991)
Industries:
  petroleum, fishing, petrochemicals, construction materials, some boat
  building, handicrafts, pearling
Agriculture:
  accounts for 2% of GDP and 5% of labor force; cash crop - dates; food
  products - vegetables, watermelons, poultry, eggs, dairy, fish; only 25%
  self-sufficient in food
Economic aid:
  donor - pledged $9.1 billion in bilateral aid to less developed countries
  (1979-89)
Currency:
  Emirian dirham (plural - dirhams); 1 Emirian dirham (Dh) = 100 fils
Exchange rates:
  Emirian dirhams (Dh) per US$1 - 3.6710 (fixed rate)
Fiscal year: calendar year

:United Arab Emirates Communications

Highways:
  2,000 km total; 1,800 km bituminous, 200 km gravel and graded earth
Pipelines:
  crude oil 830 km, natural gas, including natural gas liquids, 870 km
Ports:
  Al Fujayrah, Khawr Fakkan, Mina' Jabal `Ali, Mina' Khalid, Mina' Rashid,
  Mina' Saqr, Mina' Zayid
Merchant marine:
  55 ships (1,000 GRT or over) totaling 1,033,866 GRT/1,772,646 DWT; includes
  18 cargo, 8 container, 3 roll-on/roll-off, 20 petroleum tanker, 4 bulk, 1
  refrigerated cargo, 1 vehicle carrier
Civil air:
  10 major transport aircraft
Airports:
  37 total, 34 usable; 20 with permanent-surface runways; 7 with runways over
  3,659 m; 5 with runways 2,440-3,659 m; 5 with runways 1,220-2,439 m
Telecommunications:
  adequate system of microwave and coaxial cable; key centers are Abu Dhabi
  and Dubayy; 386,600 telephones; broadcast stations - 8 AM, 3 FM, 12 TV;
  satellite communications ground stations - 1 Atlantic Ocean INTELSAT, 2

Indian Ocean INTELSAT and 1 ARABSAT; submarine cables to Qatar, Bahrain, India, and Pakistan; tropospheric scatter to Bahrain; microwave to Saudi Arabia

:United Arab Emirates Defense Forces

Branches:
Army, Navy, Air Force, Federal Police Force
Manpower availability:
males 15-49, 974,288; 533,673 fit for military service
Defense expenditures:
exchange rate conversion - $1.47 billion, 5.3% of GDP (1989 est.)

United Kingdom Geography

Total area: 244,820 km2
Land area: 241,590 km2; includes Rockall and Shetland Islands
Comparative area: slightly smaller than Oregon
Land boundaries:
360 km; Ireland 360 km
Coastline:
12,429 km
Maritime claims:
Continental shelf:
as defined in continental shelf orders or in accordance with agreed upon boundaries
Exclusive fishing zone:
200 nm
Territorial sea:
12 nm
Disputes:
Northern Ireland question with Ireland; Gibraltar question with Spain; Argentina claims Falkland Islands (Islas Malvinas); Argentina claims South Georgia and the South Sandwich Islands; Mauritius claims island of Diego Garcia in British Indian Ocean Territory; Rockall continental shelf dispute involving Denmark, Iceland, and Ireland (Ireland and the UK have signed a boundary agreement in the Rockall area); territorial claim in Antarctica (British Antarctic Territory)
Climate:
temperate; moderated by prevailing southwest winds over the North Atlantic Current; more than half of the days are overcast
Terrain:
mostly rugged hills and low mountains; level to rolling plains in east and southeast
Natural resources:
coal, crude oil, natural gas, tin, limestone, iron ore, salt, clay, chalk, gypsum, lead, silica
Land use:
arable land 29%; permanent crops NEGL%; meadows and pastures 48%; forest and woodland 9%; other 14%; includes irrigated 1%
Environment:
pollution control measures improving air, water quality; because of heavily indented coastline, no location is more than 125 km from tidal waters

1005

Note:
lies near vital North Atlantic sea lanes; only 35 km from France and now being linked by tunnel under the English Channel

:United Kingdom People

Population: 57,797,514 (July 1992), growth rate 0.3% (1992)
Birth rate: 14 births/1,000 population (1992)
Death rate: 11 deaths/1,000 population (1992)
Net migration rate: NEGL migrants/1,000 population (1992)
Infant mortality rate: 8 deaths/1,000 live births (1992)
Life expectancy at birth: 73 years male, 79 years female (1992)
Total fertility rate: 1.8 children born/woman (1992)
Nationality:
noun - Briton(s), British (collective pl.); adjective - British
Ethnic divisions:
English 81.5%, Scottish 9.6%, Irish 2.4%, Welsh 1.9%, Ulster 1.8%, West Indian, Indian, Pakistani, and other 2.8%
Religions:
Anglican 27.0 million, Roman Catholic 5.3 million, Presbyterian 2.0 million, Methodist 760,000, Jewish 410,000
Languages:
English, Welsh (about 26% of population of Wales), Scottish form of Gaelic (about 60,000 in Scotland)
Literacy:
99% (male NA%, female NA%) age 15 and over can read and write (1978 est.)
Labor force:
26,177,000; services 60.6%, manufacturing and construction 27.2%, government 8.9%, energy 2.1%, agriculture 1.2% (June 1991)
Organized labor:
40% of labor force (1991)

:United Kingdom Government

Long-form name:
United Kingdom of Great Britain and Northern Ireland; abbreviated UK
Type:
constitutional monarchy
Capital: London
Administrative divisions:
47 counties, 7 metropolitan counties, 26 districts, 9 regions, and 3 islands areas
England:
39 counties, 7 metropolitan counties*; Avon, Bedford, Berkshire, Buckingham, Cambridge, Cheshire, Cleveland, Cornwall, Cumbria, Derby, Devon, Dorset, Durham, East Sussex, Essex, Gloucester, Greater London*, Greater Manchester*, Hampshire, Hereford and Worcester, Hertford, Humberside, Isle of Wight, Kent, Lancashire, Leicester, Lincoln, Merseyside*, Norfolk, Northampton, Northumberland, North Yorkshire, Nottingham, Oxford, Shropshire, Somerset, South Yorkshire*, Stafford, Suffolk, Surrey, Tyne and Wear*, Warwick, West Midlands*, West Sussex, West Yorkshire*, Wiltshire
Northern Ireland:
26 districts; Antrim, Ards, Armagh, Ballymena, Ballymoney, Banbridge,

Belfast, Carrickfergus, Castlereagh, Coleraine, Cookstown, Craigavon, Down, Dungannon, Fermanagh, Larne, Limavady, Lisburn, Londonderry, Magherafelt, Moyle, Newry and Mourne, Newtownabbey, North Down, Omagh, Strabane
Scotland:
9 regions, 3 islands areas*; Borders, Central, Dumfries and Galloway, Fife, Grampian, Highland, Lothian, Orkney*, Shetland*, Strathclyde, Tayside, Western Isles*
Wales:
8 counties; Clwyd, Dyfed, Gwent, Gwynedd, Mid Glamorgan, Powys, South Glamorgan, West Glamorgan
Independence:
1 January 1801, United Kingdom established
Constitution:
unwritten; partly statutes, partly common law and practice
Dependent areas:
Anguilla, Bermuda, British Indian Ocean Territory, British Virgin Islands, Cayman Islands, Falkland Islands, Gibraltar, Guernsey, Hong Kong, Jersey, Isle of Man, Montserrat, Pitcairn Islands, Saint Helena, South Georgia and the South Sandwich Islands, Turks and Caicos Islands
Legal system:
common law tradition with early Roman and modern continental influences; no judicial review of Acts of Parliament; accepts compulsory ICJ jurisdiction, with reservations
National holiday:
Celebration of the Birthday of the Queen (second Saturday in June)
Executive branch:
monarch, prime minister, Cabinet
Legislative branch:
bicameral Parliament consists of an upper house or House of Lords and a lower house or House of Commons
Judicial branch:
House of Lords
Leaders:
Chief of State:
Queen ELIZABETH II (since 6 February 1952); Heir Apparent Prince CHARLES (son of the Queen, born 14 November 1948)
Head of Government:
Prime Minister John MAJOR (since 28 November 1990)

:United Kingdom Government

Political parties and leaders:
Conservative and Unionist Party, John MAJOR; Labor Party, John SMITH; Liberal Democrats (LD), Jeremy (Paddy) ASHDOWN; Scottish National Party, Alex SALMOND; Welsh National Party (Plaid Cymru), Dafydd Iwan WIGLEY;
Ulster
Unionist Party (Northern Ireland), James MOLYNEAUX; Democratic Unionist Party (Northern Ireland), Rev. Ian PAISLEY; Ulster Popular Unionist Party (Northern Ireland), James KILFEDDER; Social Democratic and Labor Party (SDLP, Northern Ireland), John HUME; Sinn Fein (Northern Ireland), Gerry ADAMS; Alliance Party (Northern Ireland), John ALDERDICE; Democratic Left,

Nina TEMPLE
Suffrage:
  universal at age 18
Elections:
  House of Commons:
  last held 9 April 1992 (next to be held by NA April 1997); results -
  Conservative 41.9%, Labor 34.5%, Liberal Democratic 17.9%, other 5.7%; seats
  - (651 total) Conservative 336, Labor 271, Liberal Democratic 20, other 24
Communists:
  15,961
Other political or pressure groups:
  Trades Union Congress, Confederation of British Industry, National Farmers'
  Union, Campaign for Nuclear Disarmament
Member of:
  AfDB, AG (observer), AsDB, BIS, C, CCC, CDB, CE, CERN, COCOM, CP, CSCE,
  EBRD, EC, ECA (associate), ECE, ECLAC, EIB, ESCAP, ESA, FAO, G-5, G-7, G-
10,
  GATT, IADB, IAEA, IBRD, ICAO, ICC, ICFTU, IDA, IEA, IFAD, IFC, ILO, IMF,
  IMO, INMARSAT, INTELSAT, INTERPOL, IOC, IOM (observer), ISO, ITU,
LORCS,
  NATO, NEA, OECD, PCA, SPC, UN, UNCTAD, UNFICYP, UNHCR, UNIDO,
UNRWA, UN
  Security Council, UN Trusteeship Council, UPU, WCL, WEU, WHO, WIPO, WMO
Diplomatic representation:
  Ambassador Sir Robin RENWICK; Chancery at 3100 Massachusetts Avenue NW,
  Washington, DC 20008; telephone (202) 462-1340; there are British Consulates
  General in Atlanta, Boston, Chicago, Cleveland, Houston, Los Angeles, New
  York, and San Francisco, and Consulates in Dallas, Miami, and Seattle
  US:
  Ambassador Raymond G. H. SEITZ; Embassy at 24/31 Grosvenor Square, London,
  W.1A1AE, (mailing address is FPO AE 09498-4040); telephone [44] (71)
  499-9000; FAX 409-1637; there are US Consulates General in Belfast and
  Edinburgh
Flag:
  blue with the red cross of Saint George (patron saint of England) edged in
  white superimposed on the diagonal red cross of Saint Patrick (patron saint
  of Ireland) which is superimposed on the diagonal white cross of Saint
  Andrew (patron saint of Scotland); known as the Union Flag or Union Jack;
  the design and colors (especially the Blue Ensign) have been the basis for a
  number of other flags including dependencies, Commonwealth countries, and
  others
Note:
  Hong Kong is scheduled to become a Special Administrative Region of China in
  1997

:United Kingdom Economy

Overview:
  The UK is one of the world's great trading powers and financial centers, and
  its economy ranks among the four largest in Europe. The economy is
  essentially capitalistic with a generous admixture of social welfare

1008

programs and government ownership. Prime Minister MAJOR has continued the basic thrust of THATCHER's efforts to halt the expansion of welfare measures and promote extensive reprivatization of the government economic sector. Agriculture is intensive, highly mechanized, and efficient by European standards, producing about 60% of food needs with only 1% of the labor force. Industry is a mixture of public and private enterprises, employing about 27% of the work force and generating 22% of GDP. The UK is an energy-rich nation with large coal, natural gas, and oil reserves; primary energy production accounts for 12% of GDP, one of the highest shares of any industrial nation. In mid-1990 the economy fell into recession after eight years of strong economic expansion, which had raised national output by one quarter. Britain's inflation rate, which has been consistently well above those of her major trading partners, declined significantly in 1991. Between 1986 and 1990 unemployment fell from 11% to about 6%, but crept back up to 8% in 1991 because of the economic slowdown. As a major trading nation, the UK will continue to be greatly affected by world boom or recession, swings in the international oil market, productivity trends in domestic industry, and the terms on which the economic integration of Europe proceeds.

GDP:
  purchasing power equivalent - $915.5 billion, per capita $15,900; real growth rate -1.9% (1991 est.)

Inflation rate (consumer prices):
  5.8% (1991)

Unemployment rate: 8.1% (1991)

Budget:
  revenues $435 billion; expenditures $469 billion, including capital expenditures of $NA (FY92 est.)

Exports:
  $186.4 billion (f.o.b., 1991)
  commodities:
  manufactured goods, machinery, fuels, chemicals, semifinished goods, transport equipment
  partners:
  EC 53.2% (FRG 12.7%, France 10.5%, Netherlands 7.0%), US 12.4%

Imports:
  $211.9 billion (c.i.f., 1991)
  commodities:
  manufactured goods, machinery, semifinished goods, foodstuffs, consumer goods
  partners:
  EC 52.2% (FRG 15.6%, France 9.3%, Netherlands 8.4%), US 11.5%

External debt: $10.5 billion (1990)

Industrial production:
  growth rate 0% (1991)

Electricity:
  98,000,000 kW capacity; 316,500 million kWh produced, 5,520 kWh per capita (1991)

:United Kingdom Economy

Industries:

  production machinery including machine tools, electric power equipment,
  equipment for the automation of production, railroad equipment,
  shipbuilding, aircraft, motor vehicles and parts, electronics and
  communications equipment, metals, chemicals, coal, petroleum, paper and
  paper products, food processing, textiles, clothing, and other consumer
  goods

Agriculture:

  accounts for only 1.5% of GDP and 1% of labor force; highly mechanized and
  efficient farms; wide variety of crops and livestock products produced;
  about 60% self-sufficient in food and feed needs; fish catch of 665,000
  metric tons (1987)

Economic aid:

  donor - ODA and OOF commitments (1970-89), $21.0 billion

Currency:

  British pound or pound sterling (plural - pounds); 1 British pound (#) = 100
  pence

Exchange rates:

  British pounds (#) per US$1 - 0.5799 (March 1992), 0.5652 (1991), 0.5603
  (1990), 0.6099 (1989), 0.5614 (1988), 0.6102 (1987)

Fiscal year: 1 April-31 March

:United Kingdom Communications

Railroads:

  Great Britain - 16,629 km total; British Railways (BR) operates 16,629 km
  1.435-meter (standard) gauge (4,205 km electrified and 12,591 km double or
  multiple track); several additional small standard-gauge and narrow-gauge
  lines are privately owned and operated; Northern Ireland Railways (NIR)
  operates 332 km 1.600-meter gauge, including 190 km double track

Highways:

  UK, 362,982 km total; Great Britain, 339,483 km paved (including 2,573 km
  limited-access divided highway); Northern Ireland, 23,499 km (22,907 paved,
  592 km gravel)

Inland waterways:

  2,291 total; British Waterways Board, 606 km; Port Authorities, 706 km;
  other, 979 km

Pipelines:

  crude oil (almost all insignificant) 933 km, petroleum products 2,993 km,
  natural gas 12,800 km

Ports:

  London, Liverpool, Felixstowe, Tees and Hartlepool, Dover, Sullom Voe,
  Southampton

Merchant marine:

  224 ships (1,000 GRT or over) totaling 3,905,571 GRT/4,840,862 DWT; includes
  7 passenger, 21 short-sea passenger, 37 cargo, 27 container, 14
  roll-on/roll-off, 10 refrigerated cargo, 1 vehicle carrier, 1 railcar
  carrier, 66 petroleum tanker, 2 chemical tanker, 9 liquefied gas, 1
  combination ore/oil, 1 specialized tanker, 26 bulk, 1 combination bulk

Civil air:

  618 major transport aircraft

Airports:
   498 total, 385 usable; 249 with permanent-surface runways; 1 with runways
   over 3,659 m; 37 with runways 2,440-3,659 m; 133 with runways 1,220-2,439 m
Telecommunications:
   technologically advanced domestic and international system; 30,200,000
   telephones; equal mix of buried cables, microwave and optical-fiber systems;
   excellent countrywide broadcast systems; broadcast stations - 225 AM, 525
   (mostly repeaters) FM, 207 (3,210 repeaters) TV; 40 coaxial submarine
   cables; 5 satellite ground stations operating in INTELSAT (7 Atlantic Ocean
   and 3 Indian Ocean), MARISAT, and EUTELSAT systems; at least 8 large
   international switching centers

:United Kingdom Defense Forces

Branches:
   Army, Royal Navy (including Royal Marines), Royal Air Force
Manpower availability:
   males 15-49, 14,462,820; 12,122,497 fit for military service; no
   conscription
Defense expenditures:
   exchange rate conversion - $42 billion, 4.3% of GDP (FY91)

United States Geography

Total area: 9,372,610 km2
Land area: 9,166,600 km2; includes only the 50 states and District of Colombia
Comparative area: about three-tenths the size of Russia; about one-third the size of
Africa;
   about one-half the size of South America (or slightly larger than Brazil);
   slightly smaller than China; about two and one-half times the size of
   Western Europe
Land boundaries:
   12,248.1 km; Canada 8,893 km (including 2,477 km with Alaska), Mexico 3,326
   km, Cuba (US naval base at Guantanamo) 29.1 km
Coastline:
   19,924 km
Maritime claims:
 Contiguous zone:
   12 nm
 Continental shelf:
   not specified
 Exclusive economic zone:
   200 nm
 Territorial sea:
   12 nm
Disputes:
   maritime boundary disputes with Canada (Dixon Entrance, Beaufort Sea, Strait
   of Juan de Fuca); US Naval Base at Guantanamo is leased from Cuba and only
   mutual agreement or US abandonment of the area can terminate the lease;
   Haiti claims Navassa Island; US has made no territorial claim in Antarctica
   (but has reserved the right to do so) and does not recognize the claims of
   any other nation; Marshall Islands claims Wake Island
Climate:

mostly temperate, but varies from tropical (Hawaii) to arctic (Alaska); arid
to semiarid in west with occasional warm, dry chinook wind

Terrain:
vast central plain, mountains in west, hills and low mountains in east;
rugged mountains and broad river valleys in Alaska; rugged, volcanic
topography in Hawaii

Natural resources:
coal, copper, lead, molybdenum, phosphates, uranium, bauxite, gold, iron,
mercury, nickel, potash, silver, tungsten, zinc, crude oil, natural gas,
timber

Land use:
arable land 20%; permanent crops NEGL%; meadows and pastures 26%; forest and
woodland 29%; other 25%; includes irrigated 2%

Environment:
pollution control measures improving air and water quality; acid rain;
agricultural fertilizer and pesticide pollution; management of sparse
natural water resources in west; desertification; tsunamis, volcanoes, and
earthquake activity around Pacific Basin; continuous permafrost in northern
Alaska is a major impediment to development

Note:
world's fourth-largest country (after Russia, Canada, and China)

:United States People

Population: 254,521,000 (July 1992), growth rate 0.8% (1992)
Birth rate: 14 births/1,000 population (1992)
Death rate: 9 deaths/1,000 population (1992)
Net migration rate: 2 migrants/1,000 population (1992)
Infant mortality rate: 10 deaths/1,000 live births (1992)
Life expectancy at birth: 72 years male, 79 years female (1992)
Total fertility rate: 1.8 children born/woman (1992)
Nationality:
noun - American(s); adjective - American
Ethnic divisions:
white 84.1%, black 12.4%, other 3.5% (1989)
Religions:
Protestant 56%, Roman Catholic 28%, Jewish 2%, other 4%, none 10% (1989)
Languages:
predominantly English; sizable Spanish-speaking minority
Literacy:
98% (male 97%, female 98%) age 25 and over having completed 5 or more years
of schooling (1989)
Labor force:
126,867,000 (includes armed forces and unemployed); civilian labor force
125,303,000 (1991)
Organized labor:
16,568,000 members; 16.1% of total wage and salary employment which was
102,786,000 (1991)

:United States Government

Long-form name:
United States of America; abbreviated US or USA

Type:
  federal republic; strong democratic tradition
Capital: Washington, DC
Administrative divisions:
  50 states and 1 district*; Alabama, Alaska, Arizona, Arkansas, California,
  Colorado, Connecticut, Delaware, District of Columbia*, Florida, Georgia,
  Hawaii, Idaho, Illinois, Indiana, Iowa, Kansas, Kentucky, Louisiana, Maine,
  Maryland, Massachusetts, Michigan, Minnesota, Mississippi, Missouri,
  Montana, Nebraska, Nevada, New Hampshire, New Jersey, New Mexico, New York,
  North Carolina, North Dakota, Ohio, Oklahoma, Oregon, Pennsylvania, Rhode
  Island, South Carolina, South Dakota, Tennessee, Texas, Utah, Vermont,
  Virginia, Washington, West Virginia, Wisconsin, Wyoming
Independence:
  4 July 1776 (from England)
Constitution:
  17 September 1787, effective 4 June 1789
Dependent areas:
  American Samoa, Baker Island, Guam, Howland Island; Jarvis Island, Johnston
  Atoll, Kingman Reef, Midway Islands, Navassa Island, Northern Mariana
  Islands, Palmyra Atoll, Puerto Rico, Virgin Islands, Wake Island
Legal system:
  based on English common law; judicial review of legislative acts; accepts
  compulsory ICJ jurisdiction, with reservations
National holiday:
  Independence Day, 4 July (1776)
Executive branch:
  president, vice president, Cabinet
Legislative branch:
  bicameral Congress consists of an upper house or Senate and a lower house or
  House of Representatives
Judicial branch:
  Supreme Court
Leaders:
 Chief of State and Head of Government:
  President George BUSH (since 20 January 1989); Vice President Dan QUAYLE
  (since 20 January 1989)
Political parties and leaders:
  Republican Party, Richard N. BOND, national committee chairman; Jeanie
  AUSTIN, co-chairman; Democratic Party, Ronald H. BROWN, national committee
  chairman; several other groups or parties of minor political significance
Suffrage:
  universal at age 18
Elections:
 President:
  last held 8 November 1988 (next to be held 3 November 1992); results -
  George BUSH (Republican Party) 53.37%, Michael DUKAKIS (Democratic Party)
  45.67%, other 0.96%
 Senate:
  last held 6 November 1990 (next to be held 3 November 1992); results -
  Democratic Party 51%, Republican Party 47%, other 2%; seats - (100 total)

1013

Democratic Party 56, Republican Party 44

House of Representatives:

last held 6 November 1990 (next to be held 3 November 1992); results -
Democratic Party 52%, Republican Party 44%, other 4%; seats - (435 total)
Democratic Party 267, Republican Party 167, Socialist 1

:United States Government

Communists:

Communist Party (claimed 15,000-20,000 members), Gus HALL, general
secretary; Socialist Workers Party (claimed 1,800 members), Jack BARNES,
national secretary

Member of:

AfDB, AG (observer), ANZUS, APEC, AsDB, BIS, CCC, COCOM, CP, CSCE,
EBRD,

ECE, ECLAC, FAO, ESCAP, G-2, G-5, G-7, G-8, G-10, GATT, IADB, IAEA,
IBRD,

ICAO, ICC, ICFTU, IDA, IEA, IFAD, IFC, ILO, IMF, IMO, INMARSAT,
INTELSAT,

INTERPOL, IOC, IOM, ISO, ITU, LORCS, NATO, NEA, OAS, OECD, PCA, SPC,
UN,

UNCTAD, UNHCR, UNIDO, UNRWA, UN Security Council, UN Trusteeship
Council,

UNTSO, UPU, WCL, WHO, WIPO, WMO, WTO

Diplomatic representation:

US Representative to the UN, Ambassador Thomas R. PICKERING; Mission at 799
United Nations Plaza, New York, NY 10017; telephone (212) 415-4050, after
hours (212) 415-4444; FAX (212) 415-4443

Flag:

thirteen equal horizontal stripes of red (top and bottom) alternating with
white; there is a blue rectangle in the upper hoist-side corner bearing 50
small white five-pointed stars arranged in nine offset horizontal rows of
six stars (top and bottom) alternating with rows of five stars; the 50 stars
represent the 50 states, the 13 stripes represent the 13 original colonies;
known as Old Glory; the design and colors have been the basis for a number
of other flags including Chile, Liberia, Malaysia, and Puerto Rico

Note:

since 18 July 1947, the US has administered the Trust Territory of the
Pacific Islands, but recently entered into a new political relationship with
three of the four political units; the Northern Mariana Islands is a
Commonwealth in political union with the US (effective 3 November 1986);
Palau concluded a Compact of Free Association with the US that was approved
by the US Congress but to date the Compact process has not been completed in
Palau, which continues to be administered by the US as the Trust Territory
of the Pacific Islands; the Federated States of Micronesia signed a Compact
of Free Association with the US (effective 3 November 1986); the Republic of
the Marshall Islands signed a Compact of Free Association with the US
(effective 21 October 1986)

:United States Economy

Overview:

The US has the most powerful, diverse, and technologically advanced economy in the world, with a per capita GDP of $22,470, the largest among major industrial nations. The economy is market oriented with most decisions made by private individuals and business firms and with government purchases of goods and services made predominantly in the marketplace. In 1989 the economy enjoyed its seventh successive year of substantial growth, the longest in peacetime history. The expansion featured moderation in wage and consumer price increases and a steady reduction in unemployment to 5.2% of the labor force. In 1990, however, growth slowed to 1% because of a combination of factors, such as the worldwide increase in interest rates, Iraq's invasion of Kuwait in August, the subsequent spurt in oil prices, and a general decline in business and consumer confidence. In 1991 output failed to recover, unemployment grew, and signs of recovery proved premature. Ongoing problems for the 1990s include inadequate investment in economic infrastructure, rapidly rising medical costs, and sizable budget and trade deficits.

GDP:
purchasing power equivalent - $5,673 billion, per capita $22,470; real growth rate -0.7% (1991)

Inflation rate (consumer prices):
4.2% (1991)

Unemployment rate: 6.6% (1991)

Budget:
revenues $1,054 billion; expenditures $1,323 billion, including capital expenditures of $NA (FY91)

Exports:
$428.1 billion (f.o.b., 1991 est.)
commodities:
capital goods, automobiles, industrial supplies and raw materials, consumer goods, agricultural products
partners:
Western Europe 27.3%, Canada 22.1%, Japan 12.1% (1989)

Imports:
$499.4 billion (c.i.f., 1991 est.)
commodities:
crude and partly refined petroleum, machinery, automobiles, consumer goods, industrial raw materials, food and beverages
partners:
Western Europe 21.5%, Japan 19.7%, Canada 18.8% (1989)

External debt: NA

Industrial production:
growth rate -1.9% (1991)

Electricity:
776,550,000 kW capacity; 3,020,000 million kWh produced, 12,080 kWh per capita (1990)

Industries:
leading industrial power in the world, highly diversified; petroleum, steel, motor vehicles, aerospace, telecommunications, chemicals, electronics, food processing, consumer goods, fishing, lumber, mining

Agriculture:
accounts for 2% of GDP and 2.8% of labor force; favorable climate and soils

1015

support a wide variety of crops and livestock production; world's second
largest producer and number one exporter of grain; surplus food producer;
fish catch of 5.0 million metric tons (1988)

:United States Economy

Illicit drugs:
illicit producer of cannabis for domestic consumption with 1987 production
estimated at 3,500 metric tons or about 25% of the available marijuana;
ongoing eradication program aimed at small plots and greenhouses has not
reduced production

Economic aid:
donor - commitments, including ODA and OOF, (FY80-89), $115.7 billion

Currency:
United States dollar (plural - dollars); 1 United States dollar (US$) = 100
cents

Exchange rates:
British pounds:
(#) per US$ - 0.5599 (March 1992), 0.5652 (1991), 0.5603 (1990), 0.6099
(1989), 0.5614 (1988), 0.6102 (1987)
Canadian dollars:
(Can$) per US$ - 1.1926 (March 1992), 1.1457 (1991), 1.1668 (1990), 1.1840
(1989), 1.2307 (1988), 1.3260 (1987)
French francs:
(F) per US$ - 5.6397, (March 1992), 5.6421 (1991), 5.4453 (1990), 6.3801
(1989), 5.9569 (1988), 6.0107 (1987)
Italian lire:
(Lit) per US$ - 1,248.4 (March 1992), 1,240.6 (1991), 1,198.1 (1990),
1.372.1 (1989), 1,301.6 (1988), 1,296.1 (1987)
Japanese yen:
(Y) per US$ - 132.70 (March 1992), 134.71 (1991), 144.79 (1990), 137.96
(1989), 128.15 (1988), 144.64 (1987)
German deutsche marks:
(DM) per US$ - 1.6611 (March 1992), 1.6595 (1991), 1.6157 (1990), 1.8800
(1989), 1.7562 (1988), 1.7974 (1987)

Fiscal year: 1 October - 30 September

:United States Communications

Railroads:
270,312 km
Highways:
6,365,590 km, including 88,641 km expressways
Inland waterways:
41,009 km of navigable inland channels, exclusive of the Great Lakes (est.)
Pipelines:
petroleum 275,800 km, natural gas 305,300 km (1985)
Ports:
Anchorage, Baltimore, Beaumont, Boston, Charleston, Chicago, Cleveland,
Duluth, Freeport, Galveston, Hampton Roads, Honolulu, Houston, Jacksonville,
Long Beach, Los Angeles, Milwaukee, Mobile, New Orleans, New York,
Philadelphia, Portland (Oregon), Richmond (California), San Francisco,
Savannah, Seattle, Tampa, Wilmington

Merchant marine:

396 ships (1,000 GRT or over) totaling 12,969 GRT/20,179 DWT; includes 3 passenger-cargo, 38 cargo, 25 bulk, 174 tanker, 13 tanker tug-barge, 14 liquefied gas, 129 intermodal; in addition, there are 231 government-owned vessels

Civil air:

8,252 commercial multiengine transport aircraft (weighing 9,000 kg and over) including 6,036 jet, 831 turboprop, 1,382 piston (December 1989)

Airports:

14,177 total, 12,417 usable; 4,820 with permanent-surface runways; 63 with runways over 3,659 m; 325 with runways 2,440-3,659 m; 2,524 with runways 1,220-2,439 m

Telecommunications:

182,558,000 telephones; broadcast stations - 4,892 AM, 5,200 FM (including 3,915 commercial and 1,285 public broadcasting), 7,296 TV (including 796 commercial, 300 public broadcasting, and 6,200 commercial cable); 495,000,000 radio receivers (1982); 150,000,000 TV sets (1982); satellite ground stations - 45 Atlantic Ocean INTELSAT and 16 Pacific Ocean INTELSAT

:United States Defense Forces

Branches:

Department of the Army, Department of the Navy (including Marine Corps), Department of the Air Force

Manpower availability:

males 15-49, 66,458,000; NA fit for military service

Defense expenditures:

exchange rate conversion - $323.5 billion, 5.7% of GNP (1991)

Uruguay Geography

Total area: 176,220 km2
Land area: 173,620 km2
Comparative area: slightly smaller than Washington State
Land boundaries:

1,564 km total; Argentina 579 km, Brazil 985 km

Coastline:

660 km

Maritime claims:

Continental shelf:

200 m (depth) or to depth of exploitation

Territorial sea:

200 nm (overflight and navigation permitted beyond 12 nm)

Disputes:

short section of boundary with Argentina is in dispute; two short sections of the boundary with Brazil are in dispute (Arroyo de la Invernada area of the Rio Quarai and the islands at the confluence of the Rio Quarai and the Uruguay)

Climate:

warm temperate; freezing temperatures almost unknown

Terrain:

mostly rolling plains and low hills; fertile coastal lowland

Natural resources:

soil, hydropower potential, minor minerals
Land use:
   arable land 8%; permanent crops NEGL%; meadows and pastures 78%; forest and
   woodland 4%; other 10%; includes irrigated 1%
Environment:
   subject to seasonally high winds, droughts, floods

:Uruguay People

Population: 3,141,533 (July 1992), growth rate 0.6% (1992)
Birth rate: 17 births/1,000 population (1992)
Death rate: 10 deaths/1,000 population (1992)
Net migration rate: -1 migrant/1,000 population (1992)
Infant mortality rate: 23 deaths/1,000 live births (1992)
Life expectancy at birth: 69 years male, 76 years female (1992)
Total fertility rate: 2.4 children born/woman (1992)
Nationality:
   noun - Uruguayan(s); adjective - Uruguayan
Ethnic divisions:
   white 88%, mestizo 8%, black 4%
Religions:
   Roman Catholic (less than half adult population attends church regularly)
   66%, Protestant 2%, Jewish 2%, nonprofessing or other 30%
Languages:
   Spanish
Literacy:
   96% (male 97%, female 96%) age 15 and over can read and write (1990 est.)
Labor force:
   1,355,000 (1991 est.); government 25%, manufacturing 19%, agriculture 11%,
   commerce 12%, utilities, construction, transport, and communications 12%,
   other services 21% (1988 est.)
Organized labor:
   Interunion Workers' Assembly/National Workers' Confederation (PIT/CNT) Labor
   Federation

:Uruguay Government

Long-form name:
   Oriental Republic of Uruguay
Type:
   republic
Capital: Montevideo
Administrative divisions:
   19 departments (departamentos, singular - departamento); Artigas, Canelones,
   Cerro Largo, Colonia, Durazno, Flores, Florida, Lavalleja, Maldonado,
   Montevideo, Paysandu, Rio Negro, Rivera, Rocha, Salto, San Jose, Soriano,
   Tacuarembo, Treinta y Tres
Independence:
   25 August 1828 (from Brazil)
Constitution:
   27 November 1966, effective February 1967, suspended 27 June 1973, new
   constitution rejected by referendum 30 November 1980
Legal system:

based on Spanish civil law system; accepts compulsory ICJ jurisdiction

National holiday:

Independence Day, 25 August (1828)

Executive branch:

president, vice president, Council of Ministers (cabinet)

Legislative branch:

bicameral General Assembly (Asamblea General) consists of an upper chamber or Chamber of Senators (Camara de Senadores) and a lower chamber or Chamber of Representatives (Camera de Representantes)

Judicial branch:

Supreme Court

Leaders:

Chief of State and Head of Government:

President Luis Alberto LACALLE (since 1 March 1990); Vice President Gonzalo AGUIRRE Ramirez (since 1 March 1990)

Political parties and leaders:

National (Blanco) Party, Carlos CAT; Colorado Party, Jorge BATLLE Ibanez; Broad Front Coalition, Liber SEREGNI Mosquera - includes Communist Party led by Jaime PEREZ and National Liberation Movement (MLN) or Tupamaros led by Eleuterio FERNANDEZ Huidobro; New Space Coalition consists of the Party of the Government of the People (PGP), Hugo BATALLA; Christian Democratic Party (PDC), leader NA; and Civic Union, Humberto CIGANDA

Suffrage:

universal and compulsory at age 18

Elections:

President:

last held 26 November 1989 (next to be held NA November 1994); results - Luis Alberto LACALLE Herrera (Blanco) 37%, Jorge BATLLE Ibanez (Colorado) 29%, Liber SEREGNI Mosquera (Broad Front) 20%

Chamber of Senators:

last held 26 November 1989 (next to be held NA November 1994); results - Blanco 40%, Colorado 30%, Broad Front 23% New Space 7%; seats - (30 total) Blanco 12, Colorado 9, Broad Front 7, New Space 2

Chamber of Representatives:

last held NA November 1989 (next to be held NA November 1994); results - Blanco 39%, Colorado 30%, Broad Front 22%, New Space 8%, other 1%; seats - (99 total) number of seats by party NA

Communists:

50,000

:Uruguay Government

Member of:

AG (observer), CCC, ECLAC, FAO, G-11, G-77, GATT, IADB, IAEA, IBRD, ICAO,

ICC, IFAD, IFC, ILO, IMF, IMO, INTELSAT, INTERPOL, IOC, IOM, ISO (correspondent), ITU, LAES, LAIA, LORCS, NAM (observer), OAS, OPANAL, PCA,

RG, UN, UNCTAD, UNESCO, UNIDO, UNIIMOG, UNMOGIP, UPU, WCL, WHO, WIPO, WMO,

WTO

Diplomatic representation:

Ambassador Eduardo MACGILLICUDDY; Chancery at 1918 F Street NW, Washington,

DC 20006; telephone (202) 331-1313 through 1316; there are Uruguayan Consulates General in Los Angeles, Miami, and New York, and a Consulate in New Orleans

US:

Ambassador Richard C. BROWN; Embassy at Lauro Muller 1776, Montevideo (mailing address is APO AA 34035); telephone [598] (2) 23-60-61 or 48-77-77; FAX [598] (2) 48-86-11

Flag:

nine equal horizontal stripes of white (top and bottom) alternating with blue; there is a white square in the upper hoist-side corner with a yellow sun bearing a human face known as the Sun of May and 16 rays alternately triangular and wavy

:Uruguay Economy

Overview:

The economy is slowly recovering from the deep recession of the early 1980s. In 1988 real GDP grew by only 0.5% and in 1989 by 1.5%. The recovery was led by growth in the agriculture and fishing sectors, agriculture alone contributing 20% to GDP, employing about 11% of the labor force, and generating a large proportion of export earnings. Raising livestock, particularly cattle and sheep, is the major agricultural activity. In 1991, domestic growth improved somewhat over 1990, but various government factors, including concentration on the external sector, adverse weather conditions, and greater attention to bringing down inflation and reducing the fiscal deficit kept output from expanding rapidly. In a major step toward greater regional economic cooperation, Uruguay joined Brazil, Argentina, and Paraguay in forming the Southern Cone Common Market (Mercosur). President LACALLE continues to press ahead with a broad economic reform plan to reduce state intervention in the economy, but he faces strong opposition.

GDP:

exchange rate conversion - $9.1 billion, per capita $2,935; real growth rate 2.3% (1991 est.)

Inflation rate (consumer prices):

60% (1992 est.)

Unemployment rate: 8.5% (1991 est.)

Budget:

revenues $1.2 billion; expenditures $1.4 billion, including capital expenditures of $165 million (1988)

Exports:

$1.6 billion (f.o.b., 1991)

commodities:

hides and leather goods 17%, beef 10%, wool 9%, fish 7%, rice 4%

partners:

Brazil, US, Argentina, Germany

Imports:

$1.3 billion (f.o.b., 1991)

commodities:

fuels and lubricants 15%, metals, machinery, transportation equipment, industrial chemicals

partners:

Brazil 23%, Argentina 17%, US 10%, EC 27.1% (1990)

External debt: $4.2 billion (1991 est.)

Industrial production:

growth rate -1.4% (1990), accounts for almost 25% of GDP

Electricity:

2,065,000 kW capacity; 5,677 million kWh produced, 1,819 kWh per capita (1991)

Industries:

meat processing, wool and hides, sugar, textiles, footwear, leather apparel, tires, cement, fishing, petroleum refining, wine

Agriculture:

large areas devoted to livestock grazing; wheat, rice, corn, sorghum; self-sufficient in most basic foodstuffs

Economic aid:

US commitments, including Ex-Im (FY70-88), $105 million; Western (non-US) countries, ODA and OOF bilateral commitments (1970-89), $420 million; Communist countries (1970-89), $69 million

Currency:

new Uruguayan peso (plural - pesos); 1 new Uruguayan peso (N$Ur) = 100 centesimos

:Uruguay Economy

Exchange rates:

new Uruguayan pesos (N$Ur) per US$1 - 2,732.8 (March 1992), 2,018.8 (1991), 1,171.0 (1990), 605.5 (1989), 359.4 (1988), 226.7 (1987)

Fiscal year: calendar year

:Uruguay Communications

Railroads:

3,000 km, all 1.435-meter (standard) gauge and government owned

Highways:

49,900 km total; 6,700 km paved, 3,000 km gravel, 40,200 km earth

Inland waterways:

1,600 km; used by coastal and shallow-draft river craft

Ports:

Montevideo, Punta del Este

Merchant marine:

3 ships (1,000 GRT or over) totaling 56,737 GRT/104,143 DWT; includes 1 cargo, 1 container, 1 petroleum tanker

Civil air:

11 major transport aircraft

Airports:

90 total, 83 usable; 16 with permanent-surface runways; none with runways over 3,659 m; 2 with runways 2,440-3,659 m; 16 with runways 1,220-2,439 m

Telecommunications:

most modern facilities concentrated in Montevideo; new nationwide microwave network; 337,000 telephones; broadcast stations - 99 AM, no FM, 26 TV, 9 shortwave; 2 Atlantic Ocean INTELSAT earth stations

Branches:
   Army, Navy (including Naval Air Arm, Coast Guard, and Marines), Air Force,
   Grenadier Guards, Police
Manpower availability:
   males 15-49, 745,728; 605,392 fit for military service; no conscription
Defense expenditures:
   exchange rate conversion - $168 million, 2.2% of GDP (1988)

Uzbekistan Geography

Total area: 447,400 km2
Land area: 425,400 km2
Comparative area: slightly larger than California
Land boundaries:
   6,221 km total; Afghanistan 137 km, Kazakhstan 2,203 km, Kyrgyzstan 1,099
   km, Tajikistan 1,161 km, Turkmenistan 1,621 km
Coastline:
   0 km
   note:
   Uzbekistan does border the Aral Sea (420 km)
Maritime claims:
   none - landlocked
Disputes:
   none
Climate:
   mostly mid latitude desert; semiarid grassland in east
Terrain:
   mostly flat-to-rolling sandy desert with dunes; Fergana valley in east
   surrounded by mountainous Tajikistan and Kyrgyzstan; shrinking Aral Sea in
   west
Natural resources:
   natural gas, petroleum, coal, gold, uranium, silver, copper, lead and zinc,
   tungsten, molybdenum
Land use:
   NA% arable land; NA% permanent crops; NA% meadows and pastures; NA% forest
   and woodland; NA% other; includes NA% irrigated
Environment:
   drying up of the Aral Sea is resulting in growing concentrations of chemical
   pesticides and natural salts
Note:
   landlocked

:Uzbekistan People

Population: 21,626,784 (July 1992), growth rate 2.4% (1992)
Birth rate: 34 births/1,000 population (1992)
Death rate: 7 deaths/1,000 population (1992)
Net migration rate: -2 migrants/1,000 population (1992); note - 179,000 persons left
Uzbekistan
   in 1990
Infant mortality rate: 65 deaths/1,000 live births (1992)

Life expectancy at birth: 64 years male, 70 years female (1992)
Total fertility rate: 4.2 children born/woman (1992)
Nationality:
  noun - Uzbek(s); adjective - Uzbek
Ethnic divisions:
  Uzbek 71%, Russian 8%, Tajik 5%, other 16%; note - includes 70% of Crimean
  Tatars since their World War II deportation
Religions:
  Muslim (mostly Sunnis) 75-80%, other (includes Farsi) 20-25%
Languages:
  Uzbek 85%, Russian 5%, other 10%
Literacy:
  NA%
Labor force:
  7,941,000; agriculture and forestry 39%, industry and construction 24%,
  other 37% (1990)
Organized labor:
  NA

:Uzbekistan Government

Long-form name:
  Republic of Uzbekistan
Type:
  republic
Capital: Tashkent (Toshkent)
Administrative divisions:
  11 oblasts (oblastey, singular - oblast') and 1 autonomous republic*
  (avtomnaya respublika); Andizhan, Bukhara, Dzhizak, Fergana, Karakalpakstan*
  (Nukus), Kashkadar'ya (Karshi), Khorezm (Urgench), Namangan, Samarkand,
  Surkhandar'ya (Termez), Syrdar'ya (Gulistan), Tashkent; note - an
  administrative division has the same name as its administrative center
  (exceptions have the administrative center name following in parentheses)
Independence:
  31 August 1991 from the Soviet Union; note - formerly Uzbek Soviet Socialist
  Republic in the Soviet Union
Constitution:
  NA
Legal system:
  NA
National holiday:
  NA
Executive branch:
  president
Legislative branch:
  unicameral Supreme Soviet
Judicial branch:
  NA
Leaders:
 Chief of State:
  President Islam KARIMOV (since 29 December 1991)

Head of Government:
Prime Minister Abdulhashim MUTALOV (since 13 January 1992)
Political parties and leaders:
People's Democratic Party of Uzbekistan (formerly Communist Party), Islam KARIMOV, chairman; ERK, Mukhammad SOLIKH, chairman
Suffrage:
universal at age 18
Elections:
President:
last held 29 December 1991 (next to be held NA December 1996); results - Islam KARIMOV 86%, Mukhammad SOLIKH 12%, other 2%
Supreme Soviet:
last held NA March 1990 (next to be held NA); results - percent of vote by party NA; seats - (500 total) Communist 450, ERK 10, other 40
Communists:
NA
Other political or pressure groups:
Birlik (Unity) Abdurakhim PULATOV, chairman; Islamic Renaissance Party, Abdulljon UTAEV, chairman
Member of:
CIS, CSCE, IMF, NACC, UN UNCTAD
Diplomatic representation:
NA
US:
Charge d'Affaires Michael MOZUR; Embassy at Hotel Uzbekistan, ;55 Chelendarskaya, Tashkent (mailing address is APO AE 09862); telephone [8] (011) 7-3712-33-15-74
:Uzbekistan Government

Flag:
three equal horizontal bands - blue (top), white, and green with a crescent moon and 12 stars in the upper hoist-side quadrant
:Uzbekistan Economy

Overview:
Although Uzbekistan accounted for only 3.4% of total Soviet output, it produced two-thirds of the USSR's cotton. Moscow's push for ever-increasing amounts of cotton included massive irrigation projects which caused extensive environmental damage to the Aral Sea and rivers of the republic. Furthermore, the lavish use of chemical fertilizers has caused extensive pollution and widespread health problems. Recently the republic has sought to encourage food production at the expense of cotton. The small industrial sector specializes in such items as agricultural machinery, mineral fertilizers, vegetable oil, and electrical cranes. Uzbekistan also has some important natural resources including gold (about 30% of Soviet production), uranium, and natural gas. The Uzbek government has encouraged land reform but has shied away from other aspects of economic reform.
GDP:
purchasing power equivalent - $NA, per capita $NA; real growth rate -0.9% (1991)
Inflation rate (consumer prices):

83% (1991)

Unemployment rate: NA

Budget:

revenues $NA; expenditures $NA, including capital expenditures of $NA

Exports:

$1.5 billion (1990)

commodities:

cotton, gold, textiles, chemical and mineral fertilizers, vegetable oil

partners:

Russia, Ukraine, Eastern Europe

Imports:

$3.5 billion (1990)

commodities:

machinery and parts, consumer durables, grain, other foods

partners:

principally other former Soviet republics

External debt: $2 billion (end of 1991 est.)

Industrial production:

growth rate 1.8% (1991)

Electricity:

11,400,000 kW capacity; 54,100 million kWh produced, 2,662 kWh per capita (1991)

Industries:

chemical and mineral fertilizers, vegetable oil, textiles

Agriculture:

cotton, with much smaller production of grain, fruits, vegetables, and livestock

Illicit drugs:

illicit producers of cannabis and opium; mostly for domestic consumption; status of government eradication programs unknown; used as transshipment points for illicit drugs to Western Europe

Economic aid:

$NA

Currency:

as of May 1992, retaining ruble as currency

Exchange rates:

NA

Fiscal year: calendar year

:Uzbekistan Communications

Railroads:

3,460 km all 1.520-meter gauge (includes NA km electrified); does not include industrial lines (1990)

Highways:

78,400 km total (1990); 67,000 km hard-surfaced, 11,400 km earth

Inland waterways:

NA km

Pipelines:

NA

Ports:

none - landlocked
Civil air:
  NA
Airports:
  NA
Telecommunications:
  poorly developed; telephone density NA; linked by landline or microwave with
  CIS member states and by leased connection via the Moscow international
  gateway switch to other countries; satellite earth stations - Orbita and
  INTELSAT (TV receive only)
:Uzbekistan Defense Forces

Branches:
  Republic Security Forces (internal and border troops), National Guard; CIS
  Forces (Ground, Air and Air Defense)
Manpower availability:
  males 15-49, NA; NA fit for military service; NA reach military age (18)
  annually
Defense expenditures:
  $NA, NA% of GDP

Vanuatu Geography

Total area: 14,760 km2
Land area: 14,760 km2; includes more than 80 islands
Comparative area: slightly larger than Connecticut
Land boundaries:
  0 km
Coastline:
  2,528 km
Maritime claims:
  (measured from claimed archipelagic baselines)
 Contiguous zone:
  24 nm
 Continental shelf:
  edge of continental margin or 200 nm
 Exclusive economic zone:
  200 nm
 Territorial sea:
  12 nm
Disputes:
  none
Climate:
  tropical; moderated by southeast trade winds
Terrain:
  mostly mountains of volcanic origin; narrow coastal plains
Natural resources:
  manganese, hardwood forests, fish
Land use:
  arable land 1%; permanent crops 5%; meadows and pastures 2%; forest and
  woodland 1%; other 91%
Environment:

subject to tropical cyclones or typhoons (January to April); volcanism causes minor earthquakes

Note:

located 5,750 km southwest of Honolulu in the South Pacific Ocean about three-quarters of the way between Hawaii and Australia

:Vanuatu People

Population: 174,574 (July 1992), growth rate 3.0% (1992)
Birth rate: 35 births/1,000 population (1992)
Death rate: 5 deaths/1,000 population (1992)
Net migration rate: 0 migrants/1,000 population (1992)
Infant mortality rate: 30 deaths/1,000 live births (1992)
Life expectancy at birth: 67 years male, 72 years female (1992)
Total fertility rate: 5.1 children born/woman (1992)
Nationality:

noun - Ni-Vanuatu (singular and plural); adjective - Ni-Vanuatu

Ethnic divisions:

indigenous Melanesian 94%, French 4%, remainder Vietnamese, Chinese, and various Pacific Islanders

Religions:

Presbyterian 36.7%, Anglican 15%, Catholic 15%, indigenous beliefs 7.6%, Seventh-Day Adventist 6.2%, Church of Christ 3.8%, other 15.7%

Languages:

English and French (official); pidgin (known as Bislama or Bichelama)

Literacy:

53% (male 57%, female 48%) age 15 and over can read and write (1979)

Labor force:

NA

Organized labor:

7 registered trade unions - largest include Oil and Gas Workers' Union, Vanuatu Airline Workers' Union

:Vanuatu Government

Long-form name:

Republic of Vanuatu

Type:

republic

Capital: Port-Vila

Administrative divisions:

11 island councils; Ambrym, Aoba/Maewo, Banks/Torres, Efate, Epi, Malakula, Paama, Pentecote, Santo/Malo, Shepherd, Tafea

Independence:

30 July 1980 (from France and UK; formerly New Hebrides)

Constitution:

30 July 1980

Legal system:

unified system being created from former dual French and British systems

National holiday:

Independence Day, 30 July (1980)

Executive branch:

president, prime minister, deputy prime minister, Council of Ministers

(cabinet)
Legislative branch:
unicameral Parliament; note - the National Council of Chiefs advises on
matters of custom and land
Judicial branch:
Supreme Court
Leaders:
Chief of State:
President Frederick TIMAKATA (since 30 January 1989)
Head of Government:
Prime Minister Maxime CARLOT (since 16 December 1991); Deputy Prime Minis-
ter
Sethy REGENVANU (since 17 December 1991)
Political parties and leaders:
Vanuatu Party (VP), Donald KALPOKAS; Union of Moderate Parties (UMP), Serge
VOHOR; Melanesian Progressive Party (MPP), Barak SOPE; National United Party
(NUP), Walter LINI; Tan Union Party (TUP), Vincent BOULEKONE; Nagriamel
Party, Jimmy STEVENS; Friend Melanesian Party, leader NA
Suffrage:
universal at age 18
Elections:
Parliament:
last held 2 December 1991 (next to be held by November 1995); note - after
election, a coalition was formed by the Union of Moderate Parties and the
National United Party to form new government on 16 December 1991; seats -
(46 total) UMP 19; NUP 10; VP 10; MPP 4; TUP 1; Nagriamel 1; Friend 1
Member of:
ACCT, ACP, AsDB, C, ESCAP, FAO, G-77, IBRD, ICAO, ICFTU, IDA, IFC, IMF,
IMO,
IOC, ITU, NAM, SPC, SPF, UN, UNCTAD, UNIDO, UPU, WFTU, WHO, WMO
Diplomatic representation:
Vanuatu does not have a mission in Washington
US:
the ambassador in Papua New Guinea is accredited to Vanuatu
Flag:
two equal horizontal bands of red (top) and green (bottom) with a black
isosceles triangle (based on the hoist side) all separated by a black-edged
yellow stripe in the shape of a horizontal Y (the two points of the Y face
the hoist side and enclose the triangle); centered in the triangle is a
boar's tusk encircling two crossed namele leaves, all in yellow

:Vanuatu Economy

Overview:
The economy is based primarily on subsistence farming which provides a
living for about 80% of the population. Fishing and tourism are the other
mainstays of the economy. Mineral deposits are negligible; the country has
no known petroleum deposits. A small light industry sector caters to the
local market. Tax revenues come mainly from import duties.
GDP:
exchange rate conversion - $142 million, per capita $900 (1988 est.); real

growth rate 6% (1990)
Inflation rate (consumer prices):
    5% (1990)
Unemployment rate: NA%
Budget:
    revenues $90.0 million; expenditures $103.0 million, including capital
    expenditures of $45.0 million (1989 est.)
Exports:
    $15.6 million (f.o.b., 1990 est.)
  commodities:
    copra 59%, cocoa 11%, meat 9%, fish 8%, timber 4%
  partners:
    Netherlands, Japan, France, New Caledonia, Belgium
Imports:
    $60.4 million (f.o.b., 1990 est.)
  commodities:
    machines and vehicles 25%, food and beverages 23%, basic manufactures 18%,
    raw materials and fuels 11%, chemicals 6%
  partners:
    Australia 36%, Japan 13%, NZ 10%, France 8%, Fiji 8%
External debt: $30 million (1990 est.)
Industrial production:
    growth rate NA%; accounts for about 10% of GDP
Electricity:
    17,000 kW capacity; 30 million kWh produced, 180 kWh per capita (1990)
Industries:
    food and fish freezing, wood processing, meat canning
Agriculture:
    accounts for 40% of GDP; export crops - copra, cocoa, coffee, and fish;
    subsistence crops - copra, taro, yams, coconuts, fruits, and vegetables
Economic aid:
    Western (non-US) countries, ODA and OOF bilateral commitments (1970-89),
    $606 million
Currency:
    vatu (plural - vatu); 1 vatu (VT) = 100 centimes
Exchange rates:
    vatu (VT) per US$1 - 112.55 (March 1992), 111.68 (1991), 116.57 (1990),
    116.04 (1989), 104.43 (1988), 109.85 (1987)
Fiscal year: calendar year

:Vanuatu Communications

Railroads:
    none
Highways:
    1,027 km total; at least 240 km sealed or all-weather roads
Ports:
    Port-Vila, Luganville, Palikoulo, Santu
Merchant marine:
    121 ships (1,000 GRT or over) totaling 2,093,443 GRT/3,168,822 DWT; includes
    26 cargo, 14 refrigerated cargo, 5 container, 11 vehicle carrier, 1

livestock carrier, 5 petroleum tanker, 2 chemical tanker, 3 liquefied gas,
51 bulk, 1 combination bulk, 1 passenger, 1 short-sea passenger; note - a
flag of convenience registry
Civil air:
no major transport aircraft
Airports:
33 total, 31 usable; 2 with permanent-surface runways; none with runways
over 3,659 m; 1 with runways 2,440-3,659 m; 2 with runways 1,220-2,439 m
Telecommunications:
broadcast stations - 2 AM, no FM, no TV; 3,000 telephones; satellite ground
stations - 1 Pacific Ocean INTELSAT

:Vanuatu Defense Forces

Branches:
no military forces; Vanuatu Police Force (VPF), paramilitary Vanuatu Mobile
Force (VMF)
Manpower availability:
males 15-49, NA; NA fit for military service
Defense expenditures:
$NA, NA% of GDP

Venezuela Geography

Total area: 912,050 km2
Land area: 882,050 km2
Comparative area: slightly more than twice the size of California
Land boundaries:
4,993 km total; Brazil 2,200 km, Colombia 2,050 km, Guyana 743 km
Coastline:
2,800 km
Maritime claims:
 Contiguous zone:
 15 nm
 Continental shelf:
 200 m (depth) or to depth of exploitation
 Exclusive economic zone:
 200 nm
 Territorial sea:
 12 nm
Disputes:
claims all of Guyana west of the Essequibo river; maritime boundary dispute
with Colombia in the Gulf of Venezuela
Climate:
tropical; hot, humid; more moderate in highlands
Terrain:
Andes mountains and Maracaibo lowlands in northwest; central plains
(llanos); Guyana highlands in southeast
Natural resources:
crude oil, natural gas, iron ore, gold, bauxite, other minerals, hydropower,
diamonds
Land use:
arable land 3%; permanent crops 1%; meadows and pastures 20%; forest and

woodland 39%; other 37%; includes irrigated NEGL%
Environment:
    subject to floods, rockslides, mudslides; periodic droughts; increasing
    industrial pollution in Caracas and Maracaibo
Note:
    on major sea and air routes linking North and South America

:Venezuela People

Population: 20,675,970 (July 1992), growth rate 2.4% (1992)
Birth rate: 27 births/1,000 population (1992)
Death rate: 4 deaths/1,000 population (1992)
Net migration rate: 1 migrant/1,000 population (1992)
Infant mortality rate: 23 deaths/1,000 live births (1992)
Life expectancy at birth: 71 years male, 78 years female (1992)
Total fertility rate: 3.3 children born/woman (1992)
Nationality:
    noun - Venezuelan(s); adjective - Venezuelan
Ethnic divisions:
    mestizo 67%, white 21%, black 10%, Indian 2%
Religions:
    nominally Roman Catholic 96%, Protestant 2%
Languages:
    Spanish (official); Indian dialects spoken by about 200,000 Amerindians in
    the remote interior
Literacy:
    88% (male 87%, female 90%) age 15 and over can read and write (1981 est.)
Labor force:
    5,800,000; services 56%, industry 28%, agriculture 16% (1985)
Organized labor:
    32% of labor force

:Venezuela Government

Long-form name:
    Republic of Venezuela
Type:
    republic
Capital: Caracas
Administrative divisions:
    21 states (estados, singular - estado), 1 territory* (territorios, singular
    - territorio), 1 federal district** (distrito federal), and 1 federal
    dependence*** (dependencia federal); Amazonas*, Anzoategui, Apure, Aragua,
    Barinas, Bolivar, Carabobo, Cojedes, Delta Amacuro, Dependencias
    Federales***, Distrito Federal**, Falcon, Guarico, Lara, Merida, Miranda,
    Monagas, Nueva Esparta, Portuguesa, Sucre, Tachira, Trujillo, Yaracuy,
    Zulia; note - the federal dependence consists of 11 federally controlled
    island groups with a total of 72 individual islands
Independence:
    5 July 1811 (from Spain)
Constitution:
    23 January 1961
Legal system:

based on Napoleonic code; judicial review of legislative acts in Cassation
Court only; has not accepted compulsory ICJ jurisdiction

National holiday:
Independence Day, 5 July (1811)

Executive branch:
president, Council of Ministers (cabinet)

Legislative branch:
bicameral Congress of the Republic (Congreso de la Republica) consists of an
upper chamber or Senate (Senado) and a lower chamber or Chamber of Deputies
(Camara de Diputados)

Judicial branch:
Supreme Court of Justice (Corte Suprema de Justica)

Leaders:
Chief of State and Head of Government:
President Carlos Andres PEREZ (since 2 February 1989)

Political parties and leaders:
Social Christian Party (COPEI), Hilarion CARDOZO, president, and Eduardo
FERNANDEZ, secretary general; Democratic Action (AD), Humberto CELLI,
president, and Luis ALFARO Ucero, secretary general; Movement Toward
Socialism (MAS), Argelia LAYA, president, and Freddy MUNOZ, secretary
general

Suffrage:
universal at age 18

Elections:
President:
last held 4 December 1988 (next to be held NA December 1993); results -
Carlos Andres PEREZ (AD) 54.6%, Eduardo FERNANDEZ (COPEI) 41.7%, other
3.7%
Senate:
last held 4 December 1988 (next to be held NA December 1993); results -
percent of vote by party NA; seats - (49 total) AD 23, COPEI 22, other 4;
note - 3 former presidents (1 from AD, 2 from COPEI) hold lifetime senate
seats
Chamber of Deputies:
last held 4 December 1988 (next to be held NA December 1993); results - AD
43.7%, COPEI 31.4%, MAS 10.3%, other 14.6%; seats - (201 total) AD 97, COPEI
67, MAS 18, other 19

Communists:
10,000 members (est.)

:Venezuela Government

Other political or pressure groups:
FEDECAMARAS, a conservative business group; Venezuelan Confederation of
Workers, the Democratic Action - dominated labor organization

Member of:
AG, CDB, CG, ECLAC, FAO, G-3, G-11, G-19, G-24, G-77, GATT, IADB, IAEA,
IBRD, ICAO, ICC, ICFTU, IFAD, IFC, ILO, IMF, IMO, INTELSAT, INTERPOL,
IOC,
IOM, ISO, ITU, LAES, LAIA, LORCS, NAM, OAS, OPANAL, OPEC, PCA, RG,
UN,

UNCTAD, UNESCO, UNHCR, UNIDO, UPU, WFTU, WHO, WIPO, WMO, WTO

Diplomatic representation:

Ambassador Simon Alberto CONSALVI Bottaro; Chancery at 1099 30th Street NW, Washington, DC 20007; telephone (202) 342-2214; there are Venezuelan Consulates General in Baltimore, Boston, Chicago, Houston, Miami, New Orleans, New York, Philadelphia, San Francisco, and San Juan (Puerto Rico)

US:

Ambassador Michael Martin SKOL; Embassy at Avenida Francisco de Miranda and Avenida Principal de la Floresta, Caracas (mailing address is P. O. Box 62291, Caracas 1060-A, or APO AA 34037); telephone [58] (2) 285-2222; FAX [58] (2) 285-0336; there is a US Consulate in Maracaibo

Flag:

three equal horizontal bands of yellow (top), blue, and red with the coat of arms on the hoist side of the yellow band and an arc of seven white five-pointed stars centered in the blue band

:Venezuela Economy

Overview:

Petroleum is the cornerstone of the economy and accounted for 23% of GDP, 80% of central government revenues, and 80% of export earnings in 1991. President PEREZ introduced an economic readjustment program when he assumed office in February 1989. Lower tariffs and price supports, a free market exchange rate, and market-linked interest rates threw the economy into confusion, causing an 8% decline in GDP in 1989. However, the economy recovered part way in 1990, and grew by 9.2% in 1991, led by the petroleum sector.

GDP:

exchange rate conversion - $52.3 billion, per capita $2,590; real growth rate 9.2% (1991 est.)

Inflation rate (consumer prices):

30.7% (1991 est.)

Unemployment rate: 9.3% (1991 est.)

Budget:

revenues $13.2 billion; expenditures $13.1 billion, including capital expenditures of $NA (1991)

Exports:

$15.1 billion (f.o.b., 1991 est.)

commodities:

petroleum 80%, bauxite and aluminum, iron ore, agricultural products, basic manufactures

partners:

US 50.7%, Europe 13.7%, Japan 4.0% (1989)

Imports:

$10.2 billion (f.o.b., 1991 est.)

commodities:

foodstuffs, chemicals, manufactures, machinery and transport equipment

partners:

US 44%, FRG 8.0%, Japan 4%, Italy 7%, Canada 2% (1989)

External debt: $30.9 billion (1991)

Industrial production:

growth rate 5.4% (1991 est.); accounts for one-fourth of GDP, including petroleum

Electricity:
20,128,000 kW capacity; 55,753 million kWh produced, 2,762 kWh per capita (1991)

Industries:
petroleum, iron-ore mining, construction materials, food processing, textiles, steel, aluminum, motor vehicle assembly

Agriculture:
accounts for 6% of GDP and 16% of labor force; products - corn, sorghum, sugarcane, rice, bananas, vegetables, coffee, beef, pork, milk, eggs, fish; not self-sufficient in food other than meat

Illicit drugs:
illicit producer of cannabis and coca leaf for the international drug trade on a small scale; however, large quantities of cocaine transit the country from Colombia

Economic aid:
US commitments, including Ex-Im (FY70-86), $488 million; Communist countries (1970-89), $10 million

Currency:
bolivar (plural - bolivares); 1 bolivar (Bs) = 100 centimos

Exchange rates:
bolivares (Bs) per US$1 - 65.39 (March 1992), 56.82 (1991), 46.90 (1990), 34.68 (1989), 14.50 (fixed rate 1987-88)

:Venezuela Economy

Fiscal year: calendar year

:Venezuela Communications

Railroads:
542 km total; 363 km 1.435-meter standard gauge all single track, government owned; 179 km 1.435-meter gauge, privately owned

Highways:
77,785 km total; 22,780 km paved, 24,720 km gravel, 14,450 km earth roads, and 15,835 km unimproved earth

Inland waterways:
7,100 km; Rio Orinoco and Lago de Maracaibo accept oceangoing vessels

Pipelines:
crude oil 6,370 km; petroleum products 480 km; natural gas 4,010 km

Ports:
Amuay Bay, Bajo Grande, El Tablazo, La Guaira, Puerto Cabello, Puerto Ordaz

Merchant marine:
57 ships (1,000 GRT or over) totaling 790,108 GRT/1,257,637 DWT; includes 1 short-sea passenger, 1 passenger cargo, 22 cargo, 1 container, 2 roll-on/roll-off, 17 petroleum tanker, 1 chemical tanker, 2 liquefied gas, 8 bulk, 1 vehicle carrier, 1 combination bulk

Civil air:
56 major transport aircraft

Airports:
308 total, 287 usable; 135 with permanent-surface runways; none with runways over 3,659 m; 14 with runways 2,440-3,659 m; 88 with runways 1,220-2,439 m

Telecommunications:

modern and expanding; 1,440,000 telephones; broadcast stations - 181 AM, no FM, 59 TV, 26 shortwave; 3 submarine coaxial cables; satellite ground stations - 1 Atlantic Ocean INTELSAT and 3 domestic

:Venezuela Defense Forces

Branches:

Ground Forces (Army), Naval Forces (including Navy, Marines, Coast Guard), Air Forces, Armed Forces of Cooperation (National Guard)

Manpower availability:

males 15-49, 5,365,880; 3,884,558 fit for military service; 210,737 reach military age (18) annually

Defense expenditures:

exchange rate conversion - $1.95 billion, 4% of GDP (1991)

Vietnam Geography

Total area: 329,560 km2
Land area: 325,360
Comparative area: slightly larger than New Mexico
Land boundaries:

3,818 km total; Cambodia 982 km, China 1,281 km, Laos 1,555 km

Coastline:

3,444 km; excludes islands

Maritime claims:

Contiguous zone:

24 nm

Continental shelf:

edge of continental margin or 200 nm

Exclusive economic zone:

200 nm

Territorial sea:

12 nm

Disputes:

maritime boundary with Cambodia not defined; involved in a complex dispute over the Spratly Islands with China, Malaysia, Philippines, Taiwan, and possibly Brunei; unresolved maritime boundary with Thailand; maritime boundary dispute with China in the Gulf of Tonkin; Paracel Islands occupied by China but claimed by Vietnam and Taiwan

Climate:

tropical in south; monsoonal in north with hot, rainy season (mid-May to mid-September) and warm, dry season (mid-October to mid-March)

Terrain:

low, flat delta in south and north; central highlands; hilly, mountainous in far north and northwest

Natural resources:

phosphates, coal, manganese, bauxite, chromate, offshore oil deposits, forests

Land use:

arable land 22%; permanent crops 2%; meadows and pastures 1%; forest and woodland 40%; other 35%; includes irrigated 5%

Environment:

occasional typhoons (May to January) with extensive flooding

:Vietnam People

Population: 68,964,018 (July 1992), growth rate 2.0% (1992)

Birth rate: 29 births/1,000 population (1992)

Death rate: 8 deaths/1,000 population (1992)

Net migration rate: -1 migrant/1,000 population (1992)

Infant mortality rate: 47 deaths/1,000 live births (1992)

Life expectancy at birth: 63 years male, 67 years female (1992)

Total fertility rate: 3.6 children born/woman (1992)

Nationality:

noun - Vietnamese (singular and plural); adjective - Vietnamese

Ethnic divisions:

predominantly Vietnamese 85-90%; Chinese 3%; ethnic minorities include
Muong, Thai, Meo, Khmer, Man, Cham; other mountain tribes

Religions:

Buddhist, Confucian, Taoist, Roman Catholic, indigenous beliefs, Islamic,
Protestant

Languages:

Vietnamese (official), French, Chinese, English, Khmer, tribal languages
(Mon-Khmer and Malayo-Polynesian)

Literacy:

88% (male 92%, female 84%) age 15 and over can read and write (1990 est.)

Labor force:

32.7 million; agricultural 65%, industrial and service 35% (1990 est.)

Organized labor:

reportedly over 90% of wage and salary earners are members of the Vietnam
Federation of Trade Unions (VFTU)

:Vietnam Government

Long-form name:

Socialist Republic of Vietnam; abbreviated SRV

Type:

Communist state

Capital: Hanoi

Administrative divisions:

50 provinces (tinh, singular and plural), 3 municipalities* (thanh pho,
singular and plural); An Giang, Ba Ria-Vung Tau, Bac Thai, Ben Tre, Binh
Dinh, Binh Thuan, Can Tho, Cao Bang, Dac Las, Dong Nai, Dong Tay, Gia Lai,
Ha Bac, Ha Giang, Ha Noi*, Ha Tay, Ha Tinh, Hai Hung, Hai Phong*, Ho Chi
Minh*, Hoa Binh, Khanh Hoa, Kien Giang, Kon Tum, Lai Chau, Lam Dong, Lang
Son, Lao Cai, Long An, Minh Hai, Nam Ha, Nghe An, Ninh Binh, Ninh Thuan, Phu
Yen, Quang Binh, Quang Nam-Da Nang, Quang Ngai, Quang Ninh, Quang Tri, Soc
Trang, Son La, Song Be, Tay Ninh, Thai Binh, Thanh Hoa, Thua Thien, Tien
Giang, Tra Vinh, Tuyen Quang, Vinh Long, Vinh Phu, Yen Bai; note -
diacritical marks are not included

Independence:

2 September 1945 (from France)

Constitution:

18 December 1980; new Constitution to be approved Spring 1992

Legal system:
  based on Communist legal theory and French civil law system
National holiday:
  Independence Day, 2 September (1945)
Executive branch:
  president, prime minister, deputy prime minister, Council of Ministers
Legislative branch:
  unicameral National Assembly (Quoc-Hoi)
Judicial branch:
  Supreme People's Court
Leaders:
  Chief of State:
  President Vo Chi CONG (since 18 June 1987)
  Head of Government:
  Prime Minister Vo Van KIET (since 9 August 1991); Deputy Prime Minister Phan
  Van KHAI (since 10 August 1991)
Political parties and leaders:
  only party - Vietnam Communist Party (VCP), DO MUOI
Suffrage:
  universal at age 18
Elections:
  National Assembly:
  last held 19 April 1987 (next to be held 19 July 1992); results - VCP is the
  only party; seats - (496 total) VCP or VCP-approved 496; note - number of
  seats under new government 395
Communists:
  nearly 2 million
Member of:
  ACCT, AsDB, ESCAP, FAO, G-77, IAEA, IBEC, IBRD, ICAO, IDA, IFAD, IFC,
IIB,
  IMF, IMO, INTELSAT, IOC, ISO, ITU, LORCS, NAM, UN, UNCTAD, UNESCO,
UNIDO,
  UPU, WCL, WFTU, WHO, WIPO, WMO, WTO
Diplomatic representation:
  none
Flag:
  red with a large yellow five-pointed star in the center

:Vietnam Economy

Overview:
  This is a formerly centrally planned, developing economy with extensive
  government ownership and control of productive facilities. The economy is
  primarily agricultural; the sector employs about 70% of the labor force and
  accounts for half of GNP. Rice is the staple crop; substantial amounts of
  maize, sorghum, cassava, and sweet potatoes are also grown. The government
  permits sale of surplus grain on the open market. Most of the mineral
  resources are located in the north, including coal, which is an important
  export item. Oil was discovered off the southern coast in 1986 with
  production reaching 70,000 barrels per day in 1991 and expected to increase
  in the years ahead. Following the end of the war in 1975, heavy-handed

1037

government measures undermined efforts at an efficient merger of the
agricultural resources of the south and the industrial resources of the
north. The economy remains heavily dependent on foreign aid and has received
assistance from UN agencies, France, Australia, Sweden, and Communist
countries. Inflation, although down from recent triple-digit levels, is
still a major weakness and is showing signs of accelerating upwards again.
Per capita output is among the world's lowest. Since late 1986 the
government has sponsored a broad reform program that seeks to turn more
economic activity over to the private sector.

GNP:
  exchange rate conversion - $15 billion, per capita $220; real growth rate
  2.5% (1991 est.)
Inflation rate (consumer prices):
  80% (1991 est.)
Unemployment rate: 30% (1991 est.)
Budget:
  revenues $551 million; expenditures $830 million, including capital
  expenditures of $58 million (1990)
Exports:
  $1.8 billion (f.o.b., 1991)
  commodities:
  agricultural and handicraft products, coal, minerals, crude petroleum, ores,
  seafood
  partners:
  Japan, Singapore, Thailand, Eastern Europe, USSR
Imports:
  $1.9 billion (c.i.f., 1991)
  commodities:
  petroleum products, steel products, railroad equipment, chemicals,
  medicines, raw cotton, fertilizer, grain
  partners:
  Japan, Singapore, Thailand, Eastern Europe, USSR
External debt: $16.8 billion (1990 est.)
Industrial production:
  growth rate -3.6% (1989); accounts for 30% of GNP
Electricity:
  3,300,000 kW capacity; 9,200 million kWh produced, 140 kWh per capita (1991)
Industries:
  food processing, textiles, machine building, mining, cement, chemical
  fertilizer, glass, tires, oil, fishing
Agriculture:
  accounts for half of GNP; paddy rice, corn, potatoes make up 50% of farm
  output; commercial crops (rubber, soybeans, coffee, tea, bananas) and animal
  products other 50%; since 1989 self-sufficient in food staple rice; fish
  catch of 943,100 metric tons (1989 est.)

:Vietnam Economy

Economic aid:
  US commitments, including Ex-Im (FY70-74), $3.1 billion; Western (non-US)
  countries, ODA and OOF bilateral commitments (1970-89), $2.9 billion; OPEC

bilateral aid (1979-89), $61 million; Communist countries (1970-89), $12.0 billion

Currency:
new dong (plural - new dong); 1 new dong (D) = 100 xu

Exchange rates:
new dong (D) per US$1 - 11,100 (May 1992), 8,100 (July 1991), 7,280 (December 1990), 3,996 (March 1990), 2,047 (1988), 225 (1987); note - 1985-89 figures are end of year

Fiscal year: calendar year

:Vietnam Communications

Railroads:
3,059 km total; 2,454 1.000-meter gauge, 151 km 1.435-meter (standard) gauge, 230 km dual gauge (three rails), and 224 km not restored to service after war damage

Highways:
about 85,000 km total; 9,400 km paved, 48,700 km gravel or improved earth, 26,900 km unimproved earth

Inland waterways:
about 17,702 km navigable; more than 5,149 km navigable at all times by vessels up to 1.8 meter draft

Pipelines:
petroleum products 150 km

Ports:
Da Nang, Haiphong, Ho Chi Minh City

Merchant marine:
89 ships (1,000 GRT or over) totaling 400,430 GRT/643,877 DWT; includes 73 cargo 4 refrigerated cargo, 1 roll-on/roll-off, 8 petroleum tanker, 3 bulk; note - Vietnam owns 11 cargo ships (1,000 GRT or over) totaling 134,719 DWT under the registries of Panama and Malta

Civil air:
controlled by military

Airports:
100 total, 100 usable; 50 with permanent-surface runways; 10 with runways 2,440-3,659 m; 20 with runways 1,220-2,439 m

Telecommunications:
25 telephones per 10,000 persons (1991); broadcast stations - 16 AM, 1 FM, 2 TV; 2,300,000 TV sets; 6,000,000 radio receivers; 3 satellite earth stations

:Vietnam Defense Forces

Branches:
Ground, Navy (including Naval Infantry), Air Force

Manpower availability:
males 15-49, 16,839,400; 10,739,128 fit for military service; 787,026 reach military age (17) annually

Defense expenditures:
exchange rate conversion - $NA, NA% of GNP

Virgin Islands Geography

Total area: 352 km2
Land area: 349 km2

Comparative area: slightly less than twice the size of Washington, DC
Land boundaries:
  none
Coastline:
  188 km
Maritime claims:
  Contiguous zone:
    12 nm
  Continental shelf:
    200 m (depth)
  Exclusive economic zone:
    200 nm
  Territorial sea:
    12 nm
Disputes:
  none
Climate:
  subtropical, tempered by easterly tradewinds, relatively low humidity,
  little seasonal temperature variation; rainy season May to November
Terrain:
  mostly hilly to rugged and mountainous with little level land
Natural resources:
  sun, sand, sea, surf
Land use:
  arable land 15%; permanent crops 6%; meadows and pastures 26%; forest and
  woodland 6%; other 47%
Environment:
  rarely affected by hurricanes; subject to frequent severe droughts, floods,
  earthquakes; lack of natural freshwater resources
Note:
  important location 1,770 km southeast of Miami and 65 km east of Puerto
  Rico, along the Anegada Passage - a key shipping lane for the Panama Canal;
  Saint Thomas has one of the best natural, deepwater harbors in the Caribbean

:Virgin Islands People

Population: 98,942 (July 1992), growth rate -1.0% (1992)
Birth rate: 21 births/1,000 population (1992)
Death rate: 5 deaths/1,000 population (1992)
Net migration rate: -26 migrants/1,000 population (1992)
Infant mortality rate: 13 deaths/1,000 live births (1992)
Life expectancy at birth: 74 years male, 77 years female (1992)
Total fertility rate: 2.7 children born/woman (1992)
Nationality:
  noun - Virgin Islander(s); adjective - Virgin Islander; US citizens
Ethnic divisions:
  West Indian (45% born in the Virgin Islands and 29% born elsewhere in the
  West Indies) 74%, US mainland 13%, Puerto Rican 5%, other 8%; black 80%,
  white 15%, other 5%; Hispanic origin 14%
Religions:
  Baptist 42%, Roman Catholic 34%, Episcopalian 17%, other 7%

Languages:
English (official), but Spanish and Creole are widely spoken
Literacy:
NA% (male NA%, female NA%)
Labor force:
45,500 (1988)
Organized labor:
90% of the government labor force

:Virgin Islands Government

Long-form name:
Virgin Islands of the United States
Type:
organized, unincorporated territory of the US administered by the Office of
Territorial and International Affairs, US Department of the Interior
Capital: Charlotte Amalie
Administrative divisions:
none (territory of the US)
Independence:
none (territory of the US)
Constitution:
Revised Organic Act of 22 July 1954
Legal system:
based on US
National holiday:
Transfer Day (from Denmark to US), 31 March (1917)
Executive branch:
US president, popularly elected governor and lieutenant governor
Legislative branch:
unicameral Senate
Judicial branch:
US District Court handles civil matters over $50,000, felonies (persons 15
years of age and over), and federal cases; Territorial Court handles civil
matters up to $50,000 small claims, juvenile, domestic, misdemeanors, and
traffic cases
Leaders:
 Chief of State and Head of Government:
 President George BUSH (since 20 January 1989); Governor Alexander A.
 FARRELLY (since 5 January 1987); Lieutenant Governor Derek M. HODGE (since
5
 January 1987)
Political parties and leaders:
 Democratic Party, Marilyn STAPLETON; Independent Citizens' Movement (ICM),
 Virdin C. BROWN; Republican Party, Charlotte-Poole DAVIS
Suffrage:
 universal at age 18
Elections:
 Governor:
 last held 6 November 1990 (next to be held November 1994); results -
 Governor Alexander FARRELLY (Democratic Party) 56.5% defeated Juan LUIS

(independent) 38.5%
Senate:
  last held 6 November 1990 (next to be held 3 November 1992); results -
  percent of vote by party NA; seats - (15 total) number of seats by party NA
US House of Representatives:
  last held 6 November 1990 (next to be held 3 November 1992); results - Ron
  DE LUGO reelected as nonvoting delegate seats - (1 total); seat by party NA;
  note - the Virgin Islands elects one nonvoting representative to the US
  House of Representatives
Member of:
  ECLAC (associate), IOC, applied for associate membership in OECS in February
  1990
Diplomatic representation:
  none (territory of the US)
Flag:
  white with a modified US coat of arms in the center between the large blue
  initials V and I; the coat of arms shows an eagle holding an olive branch in
  one talon and three arrows in the other with a superimposed shield of
  vertical red and white stripes below a blue panel

:Virgin Islands Economy

Overview:
  Tourism is the primary economic activity, accounting for more than 70% of
  GDP and 70% of employment. The manufacturing sector consists of textile,
  electronics, pharmaceutical, and watch assembly plants. The agricultural
  sector is small, most food being imported. International business and
  financial services are a small but growing component of the economy. The
  world's largest petroleum refinery is at Saint Croix.
GDP:
  purchasing power equivalent - $1.2 billion, per capita $11,000; real growth
  rate NA% (1987)
Inflation rate (consumer prices):
  NA%
Unemployment rate: 2.0% (1990)
Budget:
  revenues $364.4 million; expenditures $364.4 million, including capital
  expenditures of $NA (FY90)
Exports:
  $2.2 billion (f.o.b., 1988)
  commodities:
  refined petroleum products
  partners:
  US, Puerto Rico
Imports:
  $3.7 billion (c.i.f., 1988)
  commodities:
  crude oil, foodstuffs, consumer goods, building materials
  partners:
  US, Puerto Rico
External debt: $NA

Industrial production:
  growth rate 12%
Electricity:
  358,000 kW capacity; 532 million kWh produced, 5,360 kWh per capita (1990)
Industries:
  tourism, petroleum refining, watch assembly, rum distilling, construction,
  pharmaceuticals, textiles, electronics
Agriculture:
  truck gardens, food crops (small scale), fruit, sorghum, Senepol cattle
Economic aid:
  Western (non-US) countries, ODA and OOF bilateral commitments (1970-89), $42
  million
Currency:
  US currency is used
Exchange rates:
  US currency is used
Fiscal year: 1 October - 30 September

:Virgin Islands Communications

Highways:
  856 km total
Ports:
  Saint Croix - Christiansted, Frederiksted; Saint Thomas - Long Bay, Crown
  Bay, Red Hook; Saint John - Cruz Bay
Airports:
  2 total, 2 usable; 2 with permanent-surface runways 1,220-2,439 m;
  international airports on Saint Thomas and Saint Croix
Telecommunications:
  44,280 telephones; broadcast stations - 4 AM, 8 FM, 4 TV; modern system
  using fiber-optic cable, submarine cable, microwave radio, and satellite
  facilities; 98,000 radios; 63,000 TV (1988)

:Virgin Islands Defense Forces

Note: defense is the responsibility of the US

Wake Island Geography

Total area: 6.5 km2
Land area: 6.5 km2
Comparative area: about 11 times the size of The Mall in Washington, DC
Land boundaries:
  none
Coastline:
  19.3 km
Maritime claims:
 Contiguous zone:
  12 nm
 Continental shelf:
  200 m (depth)
 Exclusive economic zone:
  200 nm
 Territorial sea:

12 nm
Disputes:
  claimed by the Republic of the Marshall Islands
Climate:
  tropical
Terrain:
  atoll of three coral islands built up on an underwater volcano; central
  lagoon is former crater, islands are part of the rim; average elevation less
  than four meters
Natural resources:
  none
Land use:
  arable land 0%; permanent crops 0%; meadows and pastures 0%; forest and
  woodland 0%; other 100%
Environment:
  subject to occasional typhoons
Note:
  strategic location 3,700 km west of Honolulu in the North Pacific Ocean,
  about two-thirds of the way between Hawaii and the Northern Mariana Islands;
  emergency landing location for transpacific flights

:Wake Island People

Population: no indigenous inhabitants; 381 temporary population (US Air Force personnel,
  civilian weather service personnel, and US and Thai contractors) (January
  1992); note - population peaked about 1970 with over 1,600 persons during
  the Vietnam conflict

:Wake Island Government

Long-form name:
  none
Type:
  unincorporated territory of the US administered by the US Air Force (under
  an agreement with the US Department of Interior) since 24 June 1972
Capital: none; administered from Washington, DC
Flag:
  the US flag is used

:Wake Island Economy

Overview:
  Economic activity is limited to providing services to US military personnel
  and contractors located on the island. All food and manufactured goods must
  be imported.
Electricity:
  supplied by US military

:Wake Island Communications

Ports:
  none; because of the reefs, there are only two offshore anchorages for large
  ships
Airports:
  1 with permanent-surface runways 2,440-3,659 m

Telecommunications:
  underwater cables to Guam and through Midway to Honolulu; 1 Autovon circuit off the Overseas Telephone System (OTS); Armed Forces Radio/Television Service (AFRTS) radio and television service provided by satellite; broadcast stations - 1 AM, no FM, no TV
Note:
  formerly an important commercial aviation base, now used only by US military and some commercial cargo planes

:Wake Island Defense Forces

Note: defense is the responsibility of the US

Wallis and Futuna Geography

Total area: 274 km2
Land area: 274 km2; includes Ile Uvea (Wallis Island), Ile Futuna (Futuna Island), Ile Alofi, and 20 islets
Comparative area: slightly larger than Washington, DC
Land boundaries:
  none
Coastline:
  129 km
Maritime claims:
 Exclusive economic zone:
  200 nm
 Territorial sea:
  12 nm
Disputes:
  none
Climate:
  tropical; hot, rainy season (November to April); cool, dry season (May to October)
Terrain:
  volcanic origin; low hills
Natural resources:
  negligible
Land use:
  arable land 5%; permanent crops 20%; meadows and pastures 0%; forest and woodland 0%; other 75%
Environment:
  both island groups have fringing reefs
Note:
  located 4,600 km southwest of Honolulu in the South Pacific Ocean about two-thirds of the way from Hawaii to New Zealand

:Wallis and Futuna People

Population: 17,095 (July 1992), growth rate 3.0% (1992)
Birth rate: 27 births/1,000 population (1992)
Death rate: 6 deaths/1,000 population (1992)
Net migration rate: 8 migrants/1,000 population (1992)
Infant mortality rate: 29 deaths/1,000 population (1992)
Life expectancy at birth: 70 years male, 71 years female (1992)

Total fertility rate: 3.6 children born/woman (1992)
Nationality:
  noun - Wallisian(s), Futunan(s), or Wallis and Futuna Islanders; adjective -
  Wallisian, Futunan, or Wallis and Futuna Islander
Ethnic divisions:
  almost entirely Polynesian
Religions:
  largely Roman Catholic
Languages:
  French, Wallisian (indigenous Polynesian language)
Literacy:
  50% (male 50%, female 51%) at all ages can read and write (1969)
Labor force:
  NA
Organized labor:
  NA

:Wallis and Futuna Government

Long-form name:
  Territory of the Wallis and Futuna Islands
Type:
  overseas territory of France
Capital: Mata Utu (on Ile Uvea)
Administrative divisions:
  none (overseas territory of France)
Independence:
  none (overseas territory of France)
Constitution:
  28 September 1958 (French Constitution)
Legal system:
  French
National holiday:
  Taking of the Bastille, 14 July (1789)
Executive branch:
  French president, chief administrator; note - there are three traditional
  kings with limited powers
Legislative branch:
  unicameral Territorial Assembly (Assemblee Territoriale)
Judicial branch:
  none; justice generally administered under French law by the chief
  administrator, but the three traditional kings administer customary law and
  there is a magistrate in Mata Utu
Leaders:
 Chief of State:
  President Francois MITTERRAND (since 21 May 1981)
 Head of Government:
  Chief Administrator Robert POMMIES (since 26 September 1990)
Political parties and leaders:
  Rally for the Republic (RPR); Union Populaire Locale (UPL); Union Pour la
  Democratie Francaise (UDF); Lua kae tahi (Giscardians); Mouvement des

Radicaux de Gauche (MRG)
Suffrage:
  universal adult at age 18
Elections:
  Territorial Assembly:
  last held 15 March 1987 (next to be held NA March 1992); results - percent
  of vote by party NA; seats - (20 total) RPR 7, UPL 5, UDF 4, UNF 4
  French Senate:
  last held NA September 1989 (next to be held by NA September 1992); results
  - percent of vote by party NA; seats - (1 total) RPR 1
  French National Assembly:
  last held 12 June 1988 (next to be held by NA September 1992); results -
  percent of vote by party NA; seats - (1 total) MRG 1
Member of:
  FZ, SPC
Diplomatic representation:
  as an overseas territory of France, local interests are represented in the
  US by France
Flag:
  the flag of France is used

:Wallis and Futuna Economy

Overview:
  The economy is limited to traditional subsistence agriculture, with about
  80% of the labor force earning its livelihood from agriculture (coconuts and
  vegetables), livestock (mostly pigs), and fishing. About 4% of the
  population is employed in government. Revenues come from French Government
  subsidies, licensing of fishing rights to Japan and South Korea, import
  taxes, and remittances from expatriate workers in New Caledonia. Wallis and
  Futuna imports food, fuel, clothing, machinery, and transport equipment, but
  its exports are negligible, consisting of copra and handicrafts.
GDP:
  exchange rate conversion - $25 million, per capita $1,500; real growth rate
  NA% (1991 est.)
Inflation rate (consumer prices):
  NA%
Unemployment rate: NA%
Budget:
  revenues $2.7 million; expenditures $2.7 million, including capital
  expenditures of $NA (1983)
Exports:
  negligible
 commodities:
  copra, handicrafts
 partners:
  NA
Imports:
  $13.3 million (c.i.f., 1984)
 commodities:
  foodstuffs, manufactured goods, transportation equipment, fuel

partners:
France, Australia, New Zealand
External debt: $NA
Industrial production:
growth rate NA%
Electricity:
1,200 kW capacity; 1 million kWh produced, 70 kWh per capita (1990)
Industries:
copra, handicrafts, fishing, lumber
Agriculture:
dominated by coconut production, with subsistence crops of yams, taro, bananas, and herds of pigs and goats
Economic aid:
Western (non-US) countries, ODA and OOF bilateral commitments (1970-89), $118 million
Currency:
Comptoirs Francais du Pacifique franc (plural - francs); 1 CFP franc (CFPF) = 100 centimes
Exchange rates:
Comptoirs Francais du Pacifique francs (CFPF) per US$1 - 102.53 (March 1992), 102.57 (1991), 99.0 (1990), 115.99 (1989), 108.30 (1988), 109.27 (1987); note - linked at the rate of 18.18 to the French franc
Fiscal year: NA

:Wallis and Futuna Communications

Highways:
100 km on Ile Uvea, 16 km sealed; 20 km earth surface on Ile Futuna
Inland waterways:
none
Ports:
Mata-Utu, Leava
Airports:
2 total; 2 usable; 1 with permanent-surface runways; none with runways over 2,439 m; 2 with runways 1,220-2,439 m
Telecommunications:
225 telephones; broadcast stations - 1 AM, no FM, no TV

:Wallis and Futuna Defense Forces

Note: defense is the responsibility of France

:West Bank Header

Note:
The war between Israel and the Arab states in June 1967 ended with Israel in control of the West Bank and the Gaza Strip, the Sinai, and the Golan Heights. As stated in the 1978 Camp David Accords and reaffirmed by President Bush's post-Gulf crisis peace initiative, the final status of the West Bank and the Gaza Strip, their relationship with their neighbors, and a peace treaty between Israel and Jordan are to be negotiated among the concerned parties. Camp David further specifies that these negotiations will resolve the respective boundaries. Pending the completion of this process, it is US policy that the final status of the West Bank and the Gaza Strip

1048

has yet to be determined. In the view of the US, the term West Bank describes all of the area west of the Jordan River under Jordanian administration before the 1967 Arab-Israeli war. However, with respect to negotiations envisaged in the framework agreement, it is US policy that a distinction must be made between Jerusalem and the rest of the West Bank because of the city's special status and circumstances. Therefore, a negotiated solution for the final status of Jerusalem could be different in character from that of the rest of the West Bank.

West Bank Geography

Total area: 5,860 km2
Land area: 5,640 km2; includes West Bank, East Jerusalem, Latrun Salient, Jerusa-
lem No
  Man's Land, and the northwest quarter of the Dead Sea, but excludes Mt.
  Scopus
Comparative area: slightly larger than Delaware
Land boundaries:
  404 km total; Israel 307 km, Jordan 97 km
Coastline:
  none - landlocked
Maritime claims:
  none - landlocked
Disputes:
  Israeli occupied with status to be determined
Climate:
  temperate, temperature and precipitation vary with altitude, warm to hot
  summers, cool to mild winters
Terrain:
  mostly rugged dissected upland, some vegetation in west, but barren in east
Natural resources:
  negligible
Land use:
  arable land 27%, permanent crops 0%, meadows and pastures 32%, forest and
  woodland 1%, other 40%
Environment:
  highlands are main recharge area for Israel's coastal aquifers
Note:
  landlocked; there are 175 Jewish settlements in the West Bank and 14
  Israeli-built Jewish neighborhoods in East Jerusalem

:West Bank People

Population: 1,362,464 (July 1992), growth rate 3.1% (1992); in addition, there are
  95,000 Jewish settlers in the West Bank and 132,000 in East Jerusalem (1992
  est.)
Birth rate: 35 births/1,000 population (1992)
Death rate: 6 deaths/1,000 population (1992)
Net migration rate: 2 migrants/1,000 population (1992)
Infant mortality rate: 37 deaths/1,000 live births (1992)
Life expectancy at birth: 68 years male, 71 years female (1992)
Total fertility rate: 4.5 children born/woman (1992)
Nationality:

NA
Ethnic divisions:
   Palestinian Arab and other 88%, Jewish 12%
Religions:
   Muslim (predominantly Sunni) 80%, Jewish 12%, Christian and other 8%
Languages:
   Arabic, Israeli settlers speak Hebrew, English widely understood
Literacy:
   NA% (male NA%, female NA%)
Labor force:
   NA; excluding Israeli Jewish settlers - small industry, commerce, and
   business 29.8%, construction 24.2%, agriculture 22.4%, service and other
   23.6% (1984)
Organized labor:
   NA

:West Bank Government

Long-form name:
   none
Note:
   The West Bank is currently governed by Israeli military authorities and
   Israeli civil administration. It is US policy that the final status of the
   West Bank will be determined by negotiations among the concerned parties.
   These negotiations will determine how the area is to governed.

:West Bank Economy

Overview:
   Economic progress in the West Bank has been hampered by Israeli military
   administration and the effects of the Palestinian uprising (intifadah).
   Industries using advanced technology or requiring sizable investment have
   been discouraged by a lack of local capital and restrictive Israeli
   policies. Capital investment consists largely of residential housing, not
   productive assets that would enable local firms to compete with Israeli
   industry. A major share of GNP is derived from remittances of workers
   employed in Israel and Persian Gulf states, but such transfers from the Gulf
   dropped dramatically after Iraq invaded Kuwait in August 1990. In the wake
   of the Persian Gulf crisis, many Palestinians have returned to the West
   Bank, increasing unemployment, and export revenues have plunged because of
   the loss of markets in Jordan and the Gulf states. Israeli measures to
   curtail the intifadah also have pushed unemployment up and lowered living
   standards. The area's economic outlook remains bleak.
GNP:
   exchange rate conversion - $1.3 billion, per capita $1,200; real growth rate
   -10% (1990 est.)
Inflation rate (consumer prices):
   11% (1991 est.)
Unemployment rate: 15% (1990 est.)
Budget:
   revenues $31.0 million; expenditures $36.1 million, including capital
   expenditures of $NA (FY88)
Exports:

$150 million (f.o.b., 1988 est.)
commodities:
NA
partners:
Jordan, Israel
Imports:
$410 million (c.i.f., 1988 est.)
commodities:
NA
partners:
Jordan, Israel
External debt: $NA
Industrial production:
growth rate 1% (1989); accounts for about 4% of GNP
Electricity:
power supplied by Israel
Industries:
generally small family businesses that produce cement, textiles, soap, olive-wood carvings, and mother-of-pearl souvenirs; the Israelis have established some small-scale modern industries in the settlements and industrial centers
Agriculture:
accounts for about 15% of GNP; olives, citrus and other fruits, vegetables, beef, and dairy products
Economic aid:
NA
Currency:
new Israeli shekel (plural - shekels) and Jordanian dinar (plural - dinars); 1 new Israeli shekel (NIS) = 100 new agorot and 1 Jordanian dinar (JD) = 1,000 fils

:West Bank Economy

Exchange rates:
new Israeli shekels (NIS) per US$1 - 2.4019 (March 1992), 2.2791 (1991), 2.0162 (1990), 1.9164 (1989), 1.5989 (1988), 1.5946 (1987); Jordanian dinars (JD) per US$1 - 0.6760 (January 1992), 0.6810 (1991), 0.6636 (1990), 0.5704 (1989), 0.3709 (1988), 0.3387 (1987)
Fiscal year: previously 1 April - 31 March; FY91 was 1 April - 31 December, and since 1
January 1992 the fiscal year has conformed to the calendar year

:West Bank Communications

Highways:
small road network, Israelis developing east-west axial highways to service new settlements
Airports:
2 total, 2 usable; 2 with permanent-surface runways; none with runways over 2,439 m; 1 with runways 1,220-2,439 m
Telecommunications:
open-wire telephone system currently being upgraded; broadcast stations - no AM, no FM, no TV

Branches:
  NA
Manpower availability:
  males 15-49, NA; NA fit for military service
Defense expenditures:
  exchange rate conversion - $NA, NA% of GDP

Western Sahara Geography

Total area: 266,000 km2
Land area: 266,000 km2
Comparative area: slightly smaller than Colorado
Land boundaries:
  2,046 km total; Algeria 42 km, Mauritania 1,561 km, Morocco 443 km
Coastline:
  1,110 km
Maritime claims:
  contingent upon resolution of sovereignty issue
Disputes:
  claimed and administered by Morocco, but sovereignty is unresolved and the
  UN is attempting to hold a referendum on the issue; the UN-administered
  cease-fire has been currently in effect since September 1991
Climate:
  hot, dry desert; rain is rare; cold offshore currents produce fog and heavy
  dew
Terrain:
  mostly low, flat desert with large areas of rocky or sandy surfaces rising
  to small mountains in south and northeast
Natural resources:
  phosphates, iron ore
Land use:
  arable land NEGL%; permanent crops 0%; meadows and pastures 19%; forest and
  woodland 0%; other 81%
Environment:
  hot, dry, dust/sand-laden sirocco wind can occur during winter and spring;
  widespread harmattan haze exists 60% of time, often severely restricting
  visibility; sparse water and arable land

:Western Sahara People

Population: 201,467 (July 1992), growth rate 2.6% (1992)
Birth rate: 48 births/1,000 population (1992)
Death rate: 20 deaths/1,000 population (1992)
Net migration rate: -2 migrants/1,000 population (1992)
Infant mortality rate: 159 deaths/1,000 live births (1992)
Life expectancy at birth: 43 years male, 45 years female (1992)
Total fertility rate: 7.1 children born/woman (1992)
Nationality:
  noun - Sahrawi(s), Sahraoui(s); adjective - Sahrawian, Sahraouian
Ethnic divisions:
  Arab and Berber

Religions:
  Muslim
Languages:
  Hassaniya Arabic, Moroccan Arabic
Literacy:
  NA% (male NA%, female NA%)
Labor force:
  12,000; 50% animal husbandry and subsistence farming
Organized labor:
  NA

:Western Sahara Government

Long-form name:
  none
Type:
  legal status of territory and question of sovereignty unresolved; territory
  contested by Morocco and Polisario Front (Popular Front for the Liberation
  of the Saguia el Hamra and Rio de Oro), which in February 1976 formally
  proclaimed a government in exile of the Sahrawi Arab Democratic Republic
  (SADR); territory partitioned between Morocco and Mauritania in April 1976,
  with Morocco acquiring northern two-thirds; Mauritania, under pressure from
  Polisario guerrillas, abandoned all claims to its portion in August 1979;
  Morocco moved to occupy that sector shortly thereafter and has since
  asserted administrative control; the Polisario's government in exile was
  seated as an OAU member in 1984; guerrilla activities continued
  sporadically, until a UN-monitored cease-fire was implemented 6 September
  1991
Capital: none
Administrative divisions:
  none (under de facto control of Morocco)
Leaders:
  none
Member of:
  none
Diplomatic representation:
  none

:Western Sahara Economy

Overview:
  Western Sahara, a territory poor in natural resources and having little
  rainfall, has a per capita GDP of roughly $300. Pastoral nomadism, fishing,
  and phosphate mining are the principal sources of income for the population.
  Most of the food for the urban population must be imported. All trade and
  other economic activities are controlled by the Moroccan Government.
GDP:
  $60 million, per capita $300; real growth rate NA% (1991 est.)
Inflation rate (consumer prices):
  NA%
Unemployment rate: NA%
Budget:
  revenues $NA; expenditures $NA, including capital expenditures of $NA

Exports:
  $8 million (f.o.b., 1982 est.)
  commodities:
  phosphates 62%
  partners:
  Morocco claims and administers Western Sahara, so trade partners are
  included in overall Moroccan accounts
Imports:
  $30 million (c.i.f., 1982 est.)
  commodities:
  fuel for fishing fleet, foodstuffs
  partners:
  Morocco claims and administers Western Sahara, so trade partners are
  included in overall Moroccan accounts
External debt: $NA
Industrial production:
  growth rate NA%
Electricity:
  60,000 kW capacity; 79 million kWh produced, 425 kWh per capita (1989)
Industries:
  phosphate, fishing, handicrafts
Agriculture:
  limited largely to subsistence agriculture; some barley is grown in
  nondrought years; fruit and vegetables are grown in the few oases; food
  imports are essential; camels, sheep, and goats are kept by the nomadic
  natives; cash economy exists largely for the garrison forces
Economic aid:
  NA
Currency:
  Moroccan dirham (plural - dirhams); 1 Moroccan dirham (DH) = 100 centimes
Exchange rates:
  Moroccan dirhams (DH) per US$1 - 8.889 (March 1992), 8.071 (1991), 8.242
  (1990), 8.488 (1989), 8.209 (1988), 8.359 (1987)
Fiscal year: NA

:Western Sahara Communications

Highways:
  6,200 km total; 1,450 km surfaced, 4,750 km improved and unimproved earth
  roads and tracks
Ports:
  El Aaiun, Ad Dakhla
Airports:
  13 total, 13 usable; 3 with permanent-surface runways; none with runways
  over 3,659 m; 3 with runways 2,440-3,659 m; 5 with runways 1,220-2,439 m
Telecommunications:
  sparse and limited system; tied into Morocco's system by microwave,
  tropospheric scatter, and 2 Atlantic Ocean INTELSAT earth stations linked to
  Rabat, Morocco; 2,000 telephones; broadcast stations - 2 AM, no FM, 2 TV

:Western Sahara Defense Forces

Branches:
  NA
Manpower availability:
  NA
Defense expenditures:
  exchange rate conversion - $NA, NA% of GDP

Western Samoa Geography

Total area: 2,860 km2
Land area: 2,850 km2
Comparative area: slightly smaller than Rhode Island
Land boundaries:
  none
Coastline:
  403 km
Maritime claims:
 Exclusive economic zone:
  200 nm
 Territorial sea:
  12 nm
Disputes:
  none
Climate:
  tropical; rainy season (October to March), dry season (May to October)
Terrain:
  narrow coastal plain with volcanic, rocky, rugged mountains in interior
Natural resources:
  hardwood forests, fish
Land use:
  arable land 19%; permanent crops 24%; meadows and pastures NEGL%; forest and
  woodland 47%; other 10%
Environment:
  subject to occasional typhoons; active volcanism
Note:
  located 4,300 km southwest of Honolulu in the South Pacific Ocean about
  halfway between Hawaii and New Zealand

:Western Samoa People

Population: 194,992 (July 1992), growth rate 2.4% (1992)
Birth rate: 34 births/1,000 population (1992)
Death rate: 6 deaths/1,000 population (1992)
Net migration rate: -4 migrants/1,000 population (1992)
Infant mortality rate: 40 deaths/1,000 live births (1992)
Life expectancy at birth: 65 years male, 70 years female (1992)
Total fertility rate: 4.4 children born/woman (1992)
Nationality:
  noun - Western Samoan(s); adjective - Western Samoan
Ethnic divisions:
  Samoan; Euronesians (persons of European and Polynesian blood) about 7%,
  Europeans 0.4%
Religions:

Christian 99.7% (about half of population associated with the London
Missionary Society; includes Congregational, Roman Catholic, Methodist,
Latter Day Saints, Seventh-Day Adventist)

Languages:
Samoan (Polynesian), English

Literacy:
97% (male 97%, female 97%) age 15 and over can read and write (1971)

Labor force:
38,000; 22,000 employed in agriculture (1987 est.)

Organized labor:
Public Service Association (PSA)

:Western Samoa Government

Long-form name:
Independent State of Western Samoa

Type:
constitutional monarchy under native chief

Capital: Apia

Administrative divisions:
11 districts; A`ana, Aiga-i-le-Tai, Atua, Fa`asaleleaga, Gaga`emauga,
Gagaifomauga, Palauli, Satupa`itea, Tuamasaga, Va`a-o-Fonoti, Vaisigano

Independence:
1 January 1962 (from UN trusteeship administered by New Zealand)

Constitution:
1 January 1962

Legal system:
based on English common law and local customs; judicial review of
legislative acts with respect to fundamental rights of the citizen; has not
accepted compulsory ICJ jurisdiction

National holiday:
National Day, 1 June

Executive branch:
chief, Executive Council, prime minister, Cabinet

Legislative branch:
unicameral Legislative Assembly (Fono)

Judicial branch:
Supreme Court, Court of Appeal

Leaders:
Chief of State:
Chief Susuga Malietoa TANUMAFILI II (Co-Chief of State from 1 January 1962
until becoming sole Chief of State on 5 April 1963)

Head of Government:
Prime Minister TOFILAU Eti Alesana (since 7 April 1988)

Political parties and leaders:
Human Rights Protection Party (HRPP), TOFILAU Eti, chairman; Samoan National
Development Party (SNDP), VA'AI Kolone, chairman

Suffrage:
universal adult over age 21, but only matai (head of family) are able to run
for the Legislative Assembly

Elections:

1056

Legislative Assembly:
last held NA February 1991 (next to be held by NA February 1994); results -
percent of vote by party NA; seats - (47 total) HRPP 30, SNDP 14,
independents 3
Member of:
ACP, AsDB, C, ESCAP, FAO, G-77, IBRD, ICFTU, IDA, IFAD, IFC, IMF, IOC,
ITU,
LORCS, SPC, SPF, UN, UNCTAD, UNESCO, UPU, WHO
Diplomatic representation:
Ambassador Fili (Felix) Tuaopepe WENDT; Chancery (temporary) at suite 510,
1155 15th Street NW, Washington, DC 20005; telephone (202) 833-1743
US:
the ambassador to New Zealand is accredited to Western Samoa (mailing
address is P.O. Box 3430, Apia); telephone (685) 21-631; FAX (685) 22-030
Flag:
red with a blue rectangle in the upper hoist-side quadrant bearing five
white five-pointed stars representing the Southern Cross constellation

:Western Samoa Economy

Overview:
Agriculture employs more than half of the labor force, contributes 50% to
GDP, and furnishes 90% of exports. The bulk of export earnings comes from
the sale of coconut oil and copra. The economy depends on emigrant
remittances and foreign aid to support a level of imports several times
export earnings. Tourism has become the most important growth industry, and
construction of the first international hotel is under way.
GDP:
exchange rate conversion - $115 million, per capita $690 (1989); real growth
rate -4.5% (1990 est.)
Inflation rate (consumer prices):
15% (1990)
Unemployment rate: NA%; shortage of skilled labor
Budget:
revenues $95.3 million; expenditures $95.4 million, including capital
expenditures of $41 million (FY92)
Exports:
$9 million (f.o.b., 1990)
commodities:
coconut oil and cream 54%, taro 12%, copra 9%, cocoa 3%
partners:
NZ 28%, American Samoa 23%, Germany 22%, US 6% (1990)
Imports:
$75 million (c.i.f., 1990)
commodities:
intermediate goods 58%, food 17%, capital goods 12%
partners:
New Zealand 41%, Australia 18%, Japan 13%, UK 6%, US 6%
External debt: $83 million (December 1990 est.)
Industrial production:
growth rate -4% (1990 est.); accounts for 14% of GDP

Electricity:
  29,000 kW capacity; 45 million kWh produced, 240 kWh per capita (1990)
Industries:
  timber, tourism, food processing, fishing
Agriculture:
  accounts for 50% of GDP; coconuts, fruit (including bananas, taro, yams)
Economic aid:
  US commitments, including Ex-Im (FY70-89), $18 million; Western (non-US)
  countries, ODA and OOF bilateral commitments (1970-89), $306 million; OPEC
  bilateral aid (1979-89), $4 million
Currency:
  tala (plural - tala); 1 tala (WS$) = 100 sene
Exchange rates:
  tala (WS$) per US$1 - 2,4284 (March 1992), 2,3975 (1991), 2.3095 (1990),
  2.2686 (1989), 2.0790 (1988), 2.1204 (1987)
Fiscal year: calendar year

:Western Samoa Communications

Highways:
  2,042 km total; 375 km sealed; remainder mostly gravel, crushed stone, or
  earth
Ports:
  Apia
Merchant marine:
  1 roll-on/roll-off ship (1,000 GRT or over) totaling 3,838 GRT/5,536 DWT
Civil air:
  3 major transport aircraft
Airports:
  3 total, 3 usable; 1 with permanent-surface runways; none with runways over
  3,659 m; 1 with runways 2,440-3,659 m; none with runways 1,220-2,439 m
Telecommunications:
  7,500 telephones; 70,000 radios; broadcast stations - 1 AM, no FM, no TV; 1
  Pacific Ocean INTELSAT ground station

:Western Samoa Defense Forces

Branches:
  Department of Police and Prisons
Manpower availability:
  males 15-49, NA; NA fit for military service
Defense expenditures:
  exchange rate conversion - $NA, NA% of GDP

World Geography

Total area: 510,072,000 km2
Land area: 148,940,000 km2 (29.2%)
Comparative area: land area about 16 times the size of the US
Land boundaries:
  442,000 km
Coastline:
  356,000 km
Maritime claims:

range from 3 to 200 nm; 1 claim is rectangular; 112 states claim a 12 nm limit; note - boundary situations with neighboring states prevent many countries from extending their fishing or economic zones to a full 200 nm; 41 nations and other areas are landlocked and include Afghanistan, Andorra, Armenia, Austria, Azerbaijan, Belarus, Bhutan, Bolivia, Botswana, Burkina, Burundi, Central African Republic, Chad, Czechoslovakia, Hungary, Kazakhstan, Kyrgyzstan, Laos, Lesotho, Liechtenstein, Luxembourg, Macedonia, Malawi, Mali, Moldova, Mongolia, Nepal, Niger, Paraguay, Rwanda, San Marino, Swaziland, Switzerland, Tajikistan, Turkmenistan, Uganda, Uzbekistan, Vatican City, West Bank, Zambia, Zimbabwe

Contiguous zone:

39 states claim contiguous zone, 33 of which have 24 nm limits

Continental shelf:

approximately 78 states have specific continental shelf claims, the limit of 42 claims is based on depth (200 m) plus exploitability, 21 claims define the continental shelf as 200 nm or to the edge of the continental margin

Exclusive fishing zone:

23 claims with limits ranging from 12 nm to 200 nm

Exclusive Economic Zone (EEZ):

83 states claim an EEZ, with most limits being 200 nm

Territorial sea:

claims range from 3 to 200 nm, 112 states claim a 12 nm limit; note - 41 nations and miscellaneous areas are landlocked and comprise Afghanistan, Andorra, Armenia, Austria, Azerbaijan, Bhutan, Bolivia, Botswana, Burkina, Burundi, Byelarus, Central African Republic, Chad, Czechoslovakia, Hungary, Kazakhstan, Kyrgyzstan, Laos, Lesotho, Liechtenstein, Luxembourg, Macebia, Zimbabwe

Disputes:

major international land boundary or territorial diputes - Bahrain-Qatar, Chad-Libya, China-India, China-Russia, Ecuador-Peru, El Salvador-Honduras, Israel-Jordan, Israel-Syria, Japan-Russia, North Korea-South Korea, Saudi Arabia-Yemen, South China Sea

Climate:

two large areas of polar climates separated by two rather narrow temperate zones from a wide equatorial band of tropical to subtropical climates

Terrain:

highest elevation is Mt. Everest at 8,848 meters and lowest depression is the Dead Sea at 392 meters below sea level; greatest ocean depth is the Marianas Trench at 10,924 meters

Natural resources:

the rapid using up of nonrenewable mineral resources, the depletion of forest areas and wetlands, the extinction of animal and plant species, and the deterioration in air and water quality (especially in Eastern Europe and the former USSR) pose serious long-term problems that governments and peoples are only beginning to address

Land use:

arable land 10%; permanent crops 1%; meadows and pastures 24%; forest and woodland 31%; other 34%; includes irrigated 1.6%

World Geography

Environment:
   large areas subject to severe weather (tropical cyclones), natural disasters
   (earthquakes, landslides, tsunamis, volcanic eruptions), overpopulation,
   industrial disasters, pollution (air, water, acid rain, toxic substances),
   loss of vegetation (overgrazing, deforestation, desertification), loss of
   wildlife resources, soil degradation, soil depletion, erosion

:World People

Population: 5,515,617,484 (July 1992), growth rate 1.7% (1992)
Birth rate: 26 births/1,000 population (1992)
Death rate: 9 deaths/1,000 population (1992)
Infant mortality rate: 63 deaths/1,000 live births (1992)
Life expectancy at birth: 61 years male, 65 years female (1992)
Total fertility rate: 3.3 children born/woman (1992)
Literacy:
   74% (male 81%, female 67%) age 15 and over can read and write (1990 est.)
Labor force:
   2.24 billion (1992)
Organized labor:
   NA

:World Government

Administrative divisions:
   187 sovereign nations plus 72 dependent, other, and miscellaneous areas
Legal system:
   varies by individual country; 182 are parties to the United Nations
   International Court of Justice (ICJ or World Court)
Diplomatic representation:
   there are 178 members of the UN

:World Economy

Overview:
   Aggregate world output in 1991 increased by 1.3%, in contrast to estimated
   2% growth in 1990 and 3% growth in 1989. In 1991, the developed countries
   grew by 2.5% and the LDCs by 3.5%, these gains being offset by a 10-15% drop
   in the former Communist-dominated areas of the USSR and Eastern Europe. As
   usual, results among individual countries differed widely. In the developed
   group, Japan led with 4.5%, the West European members averaged 1.2%, and the
   recession-plagued United States lagged,with GDP down 0.7%. As for the 15
   former Soviet republics and the seven nations of Eastern Europe, output
   plummeted in many economic sectors because of fundamental changes in the
   rules of the game and in the channels of production and exchange. China and
   the Four Dragons performed well in 1991 but many of the other developing
   countries are mired in poverty and political instability. For the world as a
   whole, the addition of nearly 100 million people each year to an already
   overcrowded globe will exacerbate the problems of pollution,
   desertification, underemployment, epidemics, and famine.
GWP (gross world product):
   purchasing power equivalent - $25 trillion, per capita $4,600; real growth
   rate 1.3% (1991 est.)
Inflation rate (consumer prices):

developed countries 5%; developing countries 50%, with wide variations (1991 est.)

Unemployment rate: NA%

Exports:

$3.34 trillion (f.o.b., 1991 est.)

commodities:

the whole range of industrial and agricultural goods and services

partners:

in value, about 75% of exports from developed countries

Imports:

$3.49 trillion (c.i.f., 1991 est.)

commodities:

the whole range of industrial and agricultural goods and services

partners:

in value, about 75% of imports by the developed countries

External debt: $1.0 trillion for less developed countries (1991 est.)

Industrial production:

growth rate 3% (1990 est.)

Electricity:

2,864,000,000 kW capacity; 11,450,000 million kWh produced, 2,150 kWh per capita (1990)

Industries:

industry worldwide is dominated by the onrush of technology, especially in computers, robotics, telecommunications, and medicines and medical equipment; most of these advances take place in OECD nations; only a small portion of non-OECD countries have succeeded in rapidly adjusting to these technological forces, and the technological gap between the industrial nations and the less-developed countries continues to widen; the rapid development of new industrial (and agricultural) technology is complicating already grim environmental problems

:World Economy

Agriculture:

the production of major food crops has increased substantially in the last 20 years. The annual production of cereals, for instance, has risen by 50%, from about 1.2 billion metric tons to about 1.8 billion metric tons; production increases have resulted mainly from increased yields rather than increases in planted areas; while global production is sufficient for aggregate demand, about one-fifth of the world's population remains malnourished, primarily because local production cannot adequately provide for large and rapidly growing populations, which are too poor to pay for food imports; conditions are especially bad in Africa where drought in recent years has exacerbated the consequences of all other factors

Economic aid:

NA

:World Communications

Railroads:

239,430 km of narrow gauge track; 710,754 km of standard gauge track; 251,153 km of broad gauge track; includes about 190,000 to 195,000 km of electrified routes of which 147,760 km are in Europe, 24,509 km in the Far

East, 11,050 km in Africa, 4,223 km in South America, and only 4,160 km in
North America; fastest speed in daily service is 300 km/hr attained by
France's SNCF TGV-Atlantique line

Ports:
  Mina al Ahmadi (Kuwait), Chiba, Houston, Kawasaki, Kobe, Marseille, New
  Orleans, New York, Rotterdam, Yokohama
Merchant marine:
  23,596 ships (1,000 GRT or over) totaling 386,736,000 GRT/637,493,000 DWT;
  includes 348 passenger-cargo, 12,441 freighters, 5,446 bulk carriers, and
  5,361 tankers (January 1991)
Civil air:
  14,500-16,000 major transport aircraft with gross take-off weight of 9,000
  kg (20,000 lbs) or more (1992 est.)

:World Defense Forces

Branches:
  ground, maritime, and air forces at all levels of technology
Manpower availability:
  males 15-49, 1,400,000,000; NA fit for military service
Defense expenditures:
  $1.0 trillion, 4% of total world output; decline of 5-10% (1991 est.)

Yemen Geography

Total area: 527,970 km2
Land area: 527,970 km2; includes Perim, Socotra, the former Yemen Arab Republic
(YAR or
  North Yemen), and the former People's Democratic Republic of Yemen (PDRY or
  South Yemen)
Comparative area: slightly larger than twice the size of Wyoming
Land boundaries:
  1,746 km total; Oman 288 km, Saudi Arabia 1,458 km
Coastline:
  1,906 km
Maritime claims:
 Contiguous zone:
  North - 18 nm; South - 24 nm
 Continental shelf:
  North - 200 meters (depth); South - edge of continental margin or 200 nm
 Exclusive economic zone:
  200 nm
 Territorial sea:
  12 nm
Disputes:
  undefined section of boundary with Saudi Arabia; Administrative Line with
  Oman; there is a proposed treaty with Oman (which has not yet been formerly
  accepted) to settle the Yemeni-Omani boundary
Climate:
  mostly desert; hot and humid along west coast; temperate in western
  mountains affected by seasonal monsoon; extraordinarily hot, dry, harsh
  desert in east
Terrain:

narrow coastal plain backed by flat-topped hills and rugged mountains;
dissected upland desert plains in center slope into the desert interior of
the Arabian Peninsula
Natural resources:
crude oil, fish, rock salt, marble; small deposits of coal, gold, lead,
nickel, and copper; fertile soil in west
Land use:
arable land 6%; permanent crops NEGL%; meadows and pastures 30%; forest and
woodland 7%; other 57%; includes irrigated NEGL%
Environment:
subject to sand and dust storms in summer; scarcity of natural freshwater
resources; overgrazing; soil erosion; desertification
Note:
controls Bab el Mandeb, the strait linking the Red Sea and the Gulf of Aden,
one of world's most active shipping lanes

:Yemen People

Population: 10,394,749 (July 1992), growth rate 3.3% (1992)
Birth rate: 51 births/1,000 population (1992)
Death rate: 16 deaths/1,000 population (1992)
Net migration rate: -3 migrants/1,000 population (1992)
Infant mortality rate: 118 deaths/1,000 live births (1992)
Life expectancy at birth: 49 years male, 52 years female (1992)
Total fertility rate: 7.3 children born/woman (1992)
Nationality:
noun - Yemeni(s); adjective - Yemeni
Ethnic divisions:
North - Arab 90%, Afro-Arab (mixed) 10%; South - almost all Arabs; a few
Indians, Somalis, and Europeans
Religions:
North - Muslim almost 100% (45% Sunni and 55% Zaydi Shi`a); NEGL Jewish;
South - Sunni Muslim, some Christian and Hindu
Languages:
Arabic
Literacy:
38% (male 53%, female 26%) age 15 and over can read and write (1990 est.)
Labor force:
North - NA number of workers with agriculture and herding 70%, and
expatriate laborers 30% (est.); South - 477,000 with agriculture 45.2%,
services 21.2%, construction 13.4%, industry 10.6%, commerce and other 9.6%
(1983)
Organized labor:
North - NA; South - 348,200 and the General Confederation of Workers of the
People's Democratic Republic of Yemen had 35,000 members

:Yemen Government

Long-form name:
Republic of Yemen
Type:
republic
Capital: Sanaa

Administrative divisions:
  17 governorates (muhafazat, singular - muhafazah); Abyan, `Adan, Al Bayda',
  Al Hudaydah, Al Jawf, Al Mahrah, Al Mahwit, Dhamar, Hadramawt, Hajjah, Ibb,
  Lahij, Ma'rib, Sa`dah, San`a', Shabwah, Ta`izz
Independence:
  Republic of Yemen was established on 22 May 1990 with the merger of the
  Yemen Arab Republic {Yemen (Sanaa) or North Yemen} and the Marxist-
dominated
  People's Democratic Republic of Yemen {Yemen (Aden) or South Yemen};
  previously North Yemen had become independent on NA November 1918 (from the
  Ottoman Empire) and South Yemen had become independent on 30 November 1967
  (from the UK); the union is to be solidified during a 30-month transition
  period, which coincides with the remainder of the five-year terms of both
  legislatures
Constitution:
  16 April 1991
Legal system:
  based on Islamic law, Turkish law, English common law, and local customary
  law; does not accept compulsory ICJ jurisdiction
National holiday:
  Proclamation of the Republic, 22 May (1990)
Executive branch:
  five-member Presidential Council (president, vice president, two members
  from northern Yemen and one member from southern Yemen), prime minister
Legislative branch:
  unicameral House of Representatives
Judicial branch:
  North - State Security Court; South - Federal High Court
Leaders:
  Chief of State and Head of Government:
  President `Ali `Abdallah SALIH (since 22 May 1990, the former president of
  North Yemen); Vice President Ali Salim al-BIDH (since 22 May 1990, and
  Secretary General of the Yemeni Socialist Party); Presidential Council
  Member Salim Salih MUHAMMED; Presidential Council Member Kadi Abdul-
Karim
  al-ARASHI; Presidential Council Member Abdul-Aziz ABDUL-GHANI; Prime
  Minister Haydar Abu Bakr al-`ATTAS (since 22 May 1990, former president of
  South Yemen)
Political parties and leaders:
  General People's Congress, `Ali `Abdallah SALIH; Yemeni Socialist Party
  (YSP; formerly South Yemen's ruling party - a coalition of National Front,
  Ba`th, and Communist Parties), Ali Salim al-BIDH; Yemen Grouping for Reform
  or Islaah, Abdallah Husayn AHMAR
Suffrage:
  universal at age 18
Elections:
  House of Representatives:
  last held NA (next to be held NA November 1992); results - percent of vote
  NA; seats - (301); number of seats by party NA; note - the 301 members of
  the new House of Representatives come from North Yemen's Consultative

Assembly (159 members), South Yemen's Supreme People's Council (111 members), and appointments by the New Presidential Council (31 members)

Communists:

small number in North, greater but unknown number in South

:Yemen Government

Other political or pressure groups:

conservative tribal groups, Muslim Brotherhood, leftist factions - pro-Iraqi Ba`thists, Nasirists, National Democratic Front (NDF)

Member of:

ACC, AFESD, AL, AMF, CAEU, ESCWA, FAO, G-77, IBRD, ICAO, IDA, IDB, IFAD,

IFC, ILO, IMF, IMO, INTELSAT, INTERPOL, IOC, ITU, LORCS, NAM, OIC, UN,

UNCTAD, UNESCO, UNIDO, UPU, WFTU, WHO, WIPO, WMO, WTO

Diplomatic representation:

Ambassador Muhsin Ahmad al-AYNI; Chancery at Suite 840, 600 New Hampshire Avenue NW, Washington, DC 20037; telephone (202) 965-4760 or 4761; there is a Yemeni Consulate General in Detroit and a Consulate in San Francisco

US:

Ambassador Arthur H. HUGHES; Embassy at Dhahr Himyar Zone, Sheraton Hotel District, Sanaa (mailing address is P. O. Box 22347 Sanaa, Republic of Yemen or Sanaa - Department of State, Washington, DC 20521-6330); telephone [967] (2) 238-842 through 238-852; FAX [967] (2) 251-563

Flag:

three equal horizontal bands of red (top), white, and black; similar to the flag of Syria which has two green stars and of Iraq which has three green stars (plus an Arabic inscription) in a horizontal line centered in the white band; also similar to the flag of Egypt which has a symbolic eagle centered in the white band

:Yemen Economy

Overview:

Whereas the northern city Sanaa is the political capital of a united Yemen, the southern city Aden, with its refinery and port facilities, is the economic and commercial capital. Future economic development depends heavily on Western-assisted development of promising oil resources. South Yemen's willingness to merge stemmed partly from the steady decline in Soviet economic support.

Overview:

North:

The low level of domestic industry and agriculture have made northern Yemen dependent on imports for virtually all of its essential needs. Large trade deficits have been made up for by remittances from Yemenis working abroad and foreign aid. Once self-sufficient in food production, northern Yemen has become a major importer. Land once used for export crops - cotton, fruit, and vegetables - has been turned over to growing qat, a mildly narcotic shrub chewed by Yemenis which has no significant export market. Oil export revenues started flowing in late 1987 and boosted 1988 earnings by about $800 million.

South:

This has been one of the poorest Arab countries, with a per capita GNP of about $500. A shortage of natural resources, a widely dispersed population, and an arid climate have made economic development difficult. The economy has grown at an average annual rate of only 2-3% since the mid-1970s. The economy had been organized along socialist lines, dominated by the public sector. Economic growth has been constrained by a lack of incentives, partly stemming from centralized control over production decisions, investment allocation, and import choices.

GDP:
exchange rate conversion - $5.3 billion, per capita $545; real growth rate NA% (1990 est.)

Inflation rate (consumer prices):
North:
16.9% (1988)
South:
0% (1989)

Unemployment rate: North:
13% (1986)
South:
NA%

Budget:
North:
revenues $1.4 billion; expenditures $2.2 billion, including capital expenditures of $590 million (1988 est.)
South:
revenues and grants $435 million; expenditures $1.0 billion, including capital expenditure of $460 million (1988 est.)

Exports:
North:
$606 million (f.o.b., 1989)
commodities:
crude oil, cotton, coffee, hides, vegetables
partners:
FRG 29%, US 26%, Netherlands 12%
South:
$113.8 million (f.o.b., 1989 est.)
commodities:
cotton, hides, skins, dried and salted fish

:Yemen Economy

partners:
Japan, North Yemen, Italy
Imports:
North:
$1.3 billion (f.o.b., 1988)
Imports:
commodities:
textiles and other manufactured consumer goods, petroleum products, sugar, grain, flour, other foodstuffs, and cement
partners:

Saudi Arabia 12%, France 6%, US 5%, Australia 5% (1985)
South:
  $553.9 million (f.o.b., 1989 est.)
commodities:
  grain, consumer goods, crude oil, machinery, chemicals
partners:
  USSR, UK, Ethiopia
External debt: $5.75 billion (December 1989 est.)
Industrial production:
North:
  growth rate 2% in manufacturing (1988)
South:
  growth rate NA% in manufacturing
Electricity:
  700,000 kW capacity; 1,200 million kWh produced, 120 kWh per capita (1991)
Industries:
  crude oil production and petroleum refining; small-scale production of
  cotton textiles and leather goods; food processing; handicrafts; fishing;
  small aluminum products factory; cement
Agriculture:
North:
  accounted for 26% of GDP and 70% of labor force; farm products - grain,
  fruits, vegetables, qat (mildly narcotic shrub), coffee, cotton, dairy,
  poultry, meat, goat meat; not self-sufficient in grain
South:
  accounted for 17% of GNP and 45% of labor force; products - grain, qat
  (mildly narcotic shrub), coffee, fish, livestock; fish and honey major
  exports; most food imported
Economic aid:
  US commitments, including Ex-Im (FY70-89), $389 million; Western (non-US)
  countries, ODA and OOF bilateral commitments (1970-89), $2.0 billion; OPEC
  bilateral aid (1979-89), $3.2 billion; Communist countries (1970-89), $2.4
  billion
Currency:
  North Yemeni riyal (plural - riyals); 1 North Yemeni riyal (YR) = 100 fils;
  South Yemeni dinar (plural - dinars); 1 South Yemeni dinar (YD) = 1,000 fils
Exchange rates:
  North Yemeni riyals (YR) per US$1 - 12,1000 (June 1992), 12.0000 (1991),
  9.7600 (1990), 9.7600 (January 1989), 9.7717 (1988), 10.3417 (1987); South
  Yemeni dinars (YD) per US$1 - 0.3454 (fixed rate)
Fiscal year: calendar year

:Yemen Communications

Highways:
  15,500 km; 4,000 km paved, 11,500 km natural surface (est.)
Pipelines:
  crude oil 644 km, petroleum products 32 km
Ports:
  Aden, Al Hudaydah, Al Khalf, Mocha, Nishtun, Ra's Kathib, Salif
Merchant marine:

3 ships (1,000 GRT or over) totaling 4,309 GRT/6,568 DWT; includes 2 cargo, 1 petroleum tanker

Civil air:

11 major transport aircraft

Airports:

46 total, 40 usable; 10 with permanent-surface runways; none with runways over 3,659 m; 20 with runways 2,440-3,659 m; 11 with runways 1,220-2,439 m

Telecommunications:

since unification in 1990, efforts are being made to create a national domestic civil telecommunications network and to revitalize the infrastructure of a united Yemen; the network consists of microwave, cable and troposcatter; 65,000 telephones (est.); broadcast stations - 4 AM, 1 FM, 10 TV; satellite earth stations - 2 Indian Ocean INTELSAT, 1 Atlantic Ocean INTELSAT, 1 Intersputnik, 2 ARABSAT; microwave to Saudi Arabia, and Djibouti

:Yemen Defense Forces

Branches:

Army, Navy, Air Force, Police

Manpower availability:

males 15-49, 1,981,710; 1,127,391 fit for military service; 130,405 reach military age (14) annually

Defense expenditures:

exchange rate conversion - $1.06 billion, 20% of GDP (1990)

Zaire Geography

Total area: 2,345,410 km2

Land area: 2,267,600 km2

Comparative area: slightly more than one-quarter the size of US

Land boundaries:

10,271 km total; Angola 2,511 km, Burundi 233 km, Central African Republic 1,577 km, Congo 2,410 km, Rwanda 217 km, Sudan 628 km, Uganda 765 km, Zambia

1,930 km

Coastline:

37 km

Maritime claims:

 Exclusive fishing zone:

200 nm

 Territorial sea:

12 nm

Disputes:

Tanzania-Zaire-Zambia tripoint in Lake Tanganyika may no longer be indefinite since it is reported that the indefinite section of the Zaire-Zambia boundary has been settled; long section with Congo along the Congo River is indefinite (no division of the river or its islands has been made)

Climate:

tropical; hot and humid in equatorial river basin; cooler and drier in southern highlands; cooler and wetter in eastern highlands; north of Equator - wet season April to October, dry season December to February; south of Equator - wet season November to March, dry season April to October

1068

Terrain:
   vast central basin is a low-lying plateau; mountains in east
Natural resources:
   cobalt, copper, cadmium, crude oil, industrial and gem diamonds, gold,
   silver, zinc, manganese, tin, germanium, uranium, radium, bauxite, iron ore,
   coal, hydropower potential
Land use:
   arable land 3%; permanent crops NEGL%; meadows and pastures 4%; forest and
   woodland 78%; other 15%; includes irrigated NEGL%
Environment:
   dense tropical rain forest in central river basin and eastern highlands;
   periodic droughts in south
Note:
   straddles Equator; very narrow strip of land that controls the lower Congo
   River and is only outlet to South Atlantic Ocean

:Zaire People

Population: 39,084,400 (July 1992), growth rate 3.3% (1992)
Birth rate: 45 births/1,000 population (1992)
Death rate: 13 deaths/1,000 population (1992)
Net migration rate: 0 migrants/1,000 population (1992)
Infant mortality rate: 97 deaths/1,000 live births (1992)
Life expectancy at birth: 52 years male, 56 years female (1992)
Total fertility rate: 6.1 children born/woman (1992)
Nationality:
   noun - Zairian(s); adjective - Zairian
Ethnic divisions:
   over 200 African ethnic groups, the majority are Bantu; four largest tribes
   - Mongo, Luba, Kongo (all Bantu), and the Mangbetu-Azande (Hamitic) make up
   about 45% of the population
Religions:
   Roman Catholic 50%, Protestant 20%, Kimbanguist 10%, Muslim 10%, other
   syncretic sects and traditional beliefs 10%
Languages:
   French (official), Lingala, Swahili, Kingwana, Kikongo, Tshiluba
Literacy:
   72% (male 84%, female 61%) age 15 and over can read and write (1990 est.)
Labor force:
   15,000,000; agriculture 75%, industry 13%, services 12%; wage earners 13%
   (1981); population of working age 51% (1985)
Organized labor:
   National Union of Zairian Workers (UNTZA) was the only officially recognized
   trade union until April 1990; other unions are now in process of seeking
   official recognition

:Zaire Government

Long-form name:
   Republic of Zaire
Type:
   republic with a strong presidential system
Capital: Kinshasa

Administrative divisions:
  10 regions (regions, singular - region) and 1 town* (ville); Bandundu,
  Bas-Zaire, Equateur, Haut-Zaire, Kasai-Occidental, Kasai-Oriental,
  Kinshasa*, Maniema, Nord-Kivu, Shaba, Sud-Kivu
Independence:
  30 June 1960 (from Belgium; formerly Belgian Congo, then Congo/Leopoldville,
  then Congo/Kinshasa)
Constitution:
  24 June 1967, amended August 1974, revised 15 February 1978; amended April
  1990; new constitution to be promulgated in 1992
Legal system:
  based on Belgian civil law system and tribal law; has not accepted
  compulsory ICJ jurisdiction
National holiday:
  Anniversary of the Regime (Second Republic), 24 November (1965)
Executive branch:
  president, prime minister, Executive Council (cabinet)
Legislative branch:
  unicameral Legislative Council (Conseil Legislatif)
Judicial branch:
  Supreme Court (Cour Supreme)
Leaders:
  Chief of State:
  President Marshal MOBUTU Sese Seko Kuku Ngbendu wa Za Banga (since 24
  November 1965)
  Head of Government:
  Prime Minister Jean NGUZ a Karl-i-Bond (since 26 November 1991)
Political parties and leaders:
  sole legal party until January 1991 - Popular Movement of the Revolution
  (MPR); other parties include Union for Democracy and Social Progress (UDPS),
  Etienne TSHISEKEDI wa Mulumba; Democratic Social Christian Party (PDSC),
  Joseph ILEO; Union of Federalists and Independent Republicans (UFERI), NGUZ
  a Karl-I-Bond; and Congolese National Movement-Lumumba (MNC-L)
Suffrage:
  universal and compulsory at age 18
Elections:
  President:
  last held 29 July 1984 (next to be scheduled by ongoing National
  Conference); results - President MOBUTU was reelected without opposition
  Legislative Council:
  last held 6 September 1987 (next to be scheduled by ongoing National
  Conference); results - MPR was the only party; seats - (210 total) MPR 210;
  note - MPR still holds majority of seats but some deputies have joined other
  parties
Member of:
  ACCT, ACP, AfDB, APC, CCC, CEEAC, CEPGL, CIPEC, ECA, FAO, G-19, G-24,
G-77,
  GATT, IAEA, IBRD, ICAO, ICC, IDA, IFAD, IFC, ILO, IMF, IMO, INTELSAT,
  INTERPOL, IOC, ITU, LORCS, NAM, OAU, PCA, UN, UNCTAD, UNESCO,
UNHCR, UNIDO,

UPU, WCL, WHO, WIPO, WMO, WTO
Diplomatic representation:
  Ambassador TATANENE Manata; Chancery at 1800 New Hampshire Avenue NW,
  Washington, DC 20009; telephone (202) 234-7690 or 7691
:Zaire Government

US:
  Ambassador Melissa F. WELLS; Embassy at 310 Avenue des Aviateurs, Kinshasa
  (mailing address is APO AE 09828); telephone [243] (12) 21532, 21628; FAX
  [243] (12) 21232; the US Consulate General in Lubumbashi was closed and
  evacuated in October 1991 because of the poor security situation
Flag:
  light green with a yellow disk in the center bearing a black arm holding a
  red flaming torch; the flames of the torch are blowing away from the hoist
  side; uses the popular pan-African colors of Ethiopia

:Zaire Economy

Overview:
  In 1990, in spite of large mineral resources Zaire had a GDP per capita of
  only about $260, putting it among the desperately poor African nations. The
  country's chronic economic problems worsened in 1991, with copper and cobalt
  production down 20-30%, inflation near 8,000% in 1991 as compared with 100%
  in 1987-89, and IMF and most World Bank support suspended until the
  institution of agreed-on changes. Agriculture, a key sector of the economy,
  employs 75% of the population but generates under 25% of GDP. The main
  potential for economic development has been the extractive industries.
  Mining and mineral processing account for about one-third of GDP and
  three-quarters of total export earnings. Zaire is the world's largest
  producer of diamonds and cobalt.
GDP:
  exchange rate conversion - $9.8 billion, per capita $260; real growth rate
  -3% (1990 est.)
Inflation rate (consumer prices):
  8,000% (1991)
Unemployment rate: NA%
Budget:
  revenues $685 million; expenditures $1.1 billion, does not include capital
  expenditures mostly financed by donors (1990)
Exports:
  $2.2 billion (f.o.b., 1989 est.)
 commodities:
  copper 37%, coffee 24%, diamonds 12%, cobalt, crude oil
 partners:
  US, Belgium, France, FRG, Italy, UK, Japan, South Africa
Imports:
  $2.1 billion (f.o.b., 1989 est.)
 commodities:
  consumer goods, foodstuffs, mining and other machinery, transport equipment,
  fuels
 partners:
  South Africa, US, Belgium, France, FRG, Italy, Japan, UK

External debt: $7.9 billion (December 1990 est.)
Industrial production:
  growth rate -7.3%; accounts for almost 30% of GDP (1989)
Electricity:
  2,580,000 kW capacity; 6,000 million kWh produced, 160 kWh per capita (1991)
Industries:
  mining, mineral processing, consumer products (including textiles, footwear,
  and cigarettes), processed foods and beverages, cement, diamonds
Agriculture:
  cash crops - coffee, palm oil, rubber, quinine; food crops - cassava,
  bananas, root crops, corn
Illicit drugs:
  illicit producer of cannabis, mostly for domestic consumption
Economic aid:
  US commitments, including Ex-Im (FY70-89), $1.1 billion; Western (non-US)
  countries, ODA and OOF bilateral commitments (1970-89), $6.9 billion; OPEC
  bilateral aid (1979-89), $35 million; Communist countries (1970-89), $263
  million
Currency:
  zaire (singular and plural); 1 zaire (Z) = 100 makuta
Exchange rates:
  zaire (Z) per US$1 - 111,196 (March 1992), 15,587 (1991), 719 (1990), 381
  (1989), 187 (1988), 112 (1987)

:Zaire Economy

Fiscal year: calendar year

:Zaire Communications

Railroads:
  5,254 km total; 3,968 km 1.067-meter gauge (851 km electrified); 125 km
  1.000-meter gauge; 136 km 0.615-meter gauge; 1,025 km 0.600-meter gauge;
  limited trackage in use because of civil strife
Highways:
  146,500 km total; 2,800 km paved, 46,200 km gravel and improved earth;
  97,500 unimproved earth
Inland waterways:
  15,000 km including the Congo, its tributaries, and unconnected lakes
Pipelines:
  petroleum products 390 km
Ports:
  Matadi, Boma, Banana
Merchant marine:
  2 ships (1,000 GRT or over) totaling 22,921 GRT/30,332 DWT; includes 1
  passenger cargo, 1 cargo
Civil air:
  45 major transport aircraft
Airports:
  284 total, 239 usable; 24 with permanent-surface runways; 1 with runways
  over 3,659 m; 6 with runways 2,440-3,659 m; 73 with runways 1,220-2,439 m
Telecommunications:

barely adequate wire and microwave service; broadcast stations - 10 AM, 4
FM, 18 TV; satellite earth stations - 1 Atlantic Ocean INTELSAT, 14 domestic

:Zaire Defense Forces

Branches:
  Army, Navy, Air Force, paramilitary National Gendarmerie, Civil Guard,
  Special Presidential Division
Manpower availability:
  males 15-49, 8,521,292; 4,333,492 fit for military service
Defense expenditures:
  exchange rate conversion - $49 million, 0.8% of GDP (1988)

Zambia Geography

Total area: 752,610 km2
Land area: 740,720 km2
Comparative area: slightly larger than Texas
Land boundaries:
  5,664 km total; Angola 1,110 km, Malawi 837 km, Mozambique 419 km, Namibia
  233 km, Tanzania 338 km, Zaire 1,930 km, Zimbabwe 797 km
Coastline:
  none - landlocked
Maritime claims:
  none - landlocked
Disputes:
  quadripoint with Botswana, Namibia, and Zimbabwe is in disagreement;
  Tanzania-Zaire-Zambia tripoint in Lake Tanganyika may no longer be
  indefinite since it is reported that the indefinite section of the
  Zaire-Zambia boundary has been settled
Climate:
  tropical; modified by altitude; rainy season (October to April)
Terrain:
  mostly high plateau with some hills and mountains
Natural resources:
  copper, cobalt, zinc, lead, coal, emeralds, gold, silver, uranium,
  hydropower potential
Land use:
  arable land 7%; permanent crops NEGL%; meadows and pastures 47%; forest and
  woodland 27%; other 19%; includes irrigated NEGL%
Environment:
  deforestation; soil erosion; desertification
Note:
  landlocked

:Zambia People

Population: 8,745,284 (July 1992), growth rate 3.5% (1992)
Birth rate: 48 births/1,000 population (1992)
Death rate: 11 deaths/1,000 population (1992)
Net migration rate: -2 migrants/1,000 population (1992)
Infant mortality rate: 77 deaths/1,000 live births (1992)
Life expectancy at birth: 55 years male, 59 years female (1992)
Total fertility rate: 6.9 children born/woman (1992)

Nationality:
  noun - Zambian(s); adjective - Zambian
Ethnic divisions:
  African 98.7%, European 1.1%, other 0.2%
Religions:
  Christian 50-75%, Muslim and Hindu 24-49%, remainder indigenous beliefs 1%
Languages:
  English (official); about 70 indigenous languages
Literacy:
  73% (male 81%, female 65%) age 15 and over can read and write (1990 est.)
Labor force:
  2,455,000; agriculture 85%; mining, manufacturing, and construction 6%;
  transport and services 9%
Organized labor:
  about 238,000 wage earners are unionized

:Zambia Government

Long-form name:
  Republic of Zambia
Type:
  multiparty system; on 17 December 1990, President Kenneth KAUNDA signed into
  law the constitutional amendment that officially reintroduced the multiparty
  system in Zambia ending 17 years of one-party rule
Capital: Lusaka
Administrative divisions:
  9 provinces; Central, Copperbelt, Eastern, Luapula, Lusaka, Northern,
  North-Western, Southern, Western
Independence:
  24 October 1964 (from UK; formerly Northern Rhodesia)
Constitution:
  NA August 1991
Legal system:
  based on English common law and customary law; judicial review of
  legislative acts in an ad hoc constitutional council; has not accepted
  compulsory ICJ jurisdiction
National holiday:
  Independence Day, 24 October (1964)
Executive branch:
  president, Cabinet
Legislative branch:
  unicameral National Assembly
Judicial branch:
  Supreme Court
Leaders:
  Chief of State and Head of Government:
  President Frederick CHILUBA (since 31 October 1991)
Political parties and leaders:
  Movement for Multiparty Democracy (MMD), Frederick CHILUBA; United National
  Independence Party (UNIP), none; elections pending

Suffrage:
  universal at age 18
Elections:
  President:
    last held 31 October 1991 (next to be held mid-1995); results - Frederick
    CHILUBA 84%, Kenneth KAUNDA 16%
  National Assembly:
    last held 31 October 1991 (next to be held mid-1995); results - percent of
    vote by party NA; seats - (150 total) MMD 125, UNIP 25
Member of:
  ACP, AfDB, C, CCC, ECA, FAO, FLS, G-19, G-77, GATT, IAEA, IBRD, ICAO,
IDA,
  IFAD, IFC, ILO, IMF, INTELSAT, INTERPOL, IOC, ITU, LORCS, NAM, OAU,
SADCC,
  UN, UNCTAD, UNESCO, UNIDO, UNIIMOG, UPU, WCL, WHO, WIPO, WMO,
WTO
Diplomatic representation:
  Ambassador (vacant); Chancery at 2419 Massachusetts Avenue NW, Washington,
  DC 20008; telephone (202) 265-9717 through 9721
  US:
  Ambassador Gordon L. STREEB; Embassy at corner of Independence Avenue and
  United Nations Avenue, Lusaka (mailing address is P. O. Box 31617, Lusaka);
  telephone [2601] 228-595, 228-601, 228-602, 228-603; FAX [2601] 251-578
Flag:
  green with a panel of three vertical bands of red (hoist side), black, and
  orange below a soaring orange eagle, on the outer edge of the flag

:Zambia Economy

Overview:
  The economy has been in decline for more than a decade with falling imports
  and growing foreign debt. Economic difficulties stem from a sustained drop
  in copper production and ineffective economic policies. In 1991 real GDP
  fell by 2%. An annual population growth of more than 3% has brought a
  decline in per capita GDP of 50% over the past decade. A high inflation rate
  has also added to Zambia's economic woes in recent years.
GDP:
  exchange rate conversion - $4.7 billion, per capita $600; real growth rate
  -2% (1991)
Inflation rate (consumer prices):
  100% (1991)
Unemployment rate: NA%
Budget:
  revenues $665 million; expenditures $767 million, including capital
  expenditures of $300 million (1991 est.)
Exports:
  $1.1 billion (f.o.b., 1991)
  commodities:
  copper, zinc, cobalt, lead, tobacco
  partners:
  EC, Japan, South Africa, US, India

Imports:
  $1.3 billion (c.i.f., 1991)
  commodities:
  machinery, transportation equipment, foodstuffs, fuels, manufactures
  partners:
  EC, Japan, Saudi Arabia, South Africa, US
External debt: $8 billion (December 1991)
Industrial production:
  growth rate -2% (1991); accounts for 50% of GDP
Electricity:
  2,775,000 kW capacity; 12,000 million kWh produced, 1,400 kWh per capita
  (1991)
Industries:
  copper mining and processing, transport, construction, foodstuffs,
  beverages, chemicals, textiles, and fertilizer
Agriculture:
  accounts for 17% of GDP and 85% of labor force; crops - corn (food staple),
  sorghum, rice, peanuts, sunflower, tobacco, cotton, sugarcane, cassava;
  cattle, goats, beef, eggs
Economic aid:
  US commitments, including Ex-Im (1970-89), $4.8 billion; Western (non-US)
  countries, ODA and OOF bilateral commitments (1970-89), $4.8 billion; OPEC
  bilateral aid (1979-89), $60 million; Communist countries (1970-89), $533
  million
Currency:
  Zambian kwacha (plural - kwacha); 1 Zambian kwacha (ZK) = 100 ngwee
Exchange rates:
  Zambian kwacha (ZK) per US$1 - 128.2051 (March 1992), 61.7284 (1991),
  28.9855 (1990), 12.9032 (1989), 8.2237 (1988), 8.8889 (1987)
Fiscal year: calendar year

:Zambia Communications

Railroads:
  1,266 km, all 1.067-meter gauge; 13 km double track
Highways:
  36,370 km total; 6,500 km paved, 7,000 km crushed stone, gravel, or
  stabilized soil; 22,870 km improved and unimproved earth
Inland waterways:
  2,250 km, including Zambezi and Luapula Rivers, Lake Tanganyika
Pipelines:
  crude oil 1,724 km
Ports:
  Mpulungu (lake port)
Civil air:
  12 major transport aircraft
Airports:
  117 total, 104 usable; 13 with permanent-surface runways; 1 with runways
  over 3,659 m; 4 with runways 2,440-3,659 m; 22 with runways 1,220-2,439 m
Telecommunications:
  facilities are among the best in Sub-Saharan Africa; high-capacity microwave

connects most larger towns and cities; broadcast stations - 11 AM, 5 FM, 9
TV; satellite earth stations - 1 Indian Ocean INTELSAT and 1 Atlantic Ocean
INTELSAT

:Zambia Defense Forces

Branches:
    Army, Air Force, Police, paramilitary
Manpower availability:
    males 15-49, 1,818,545; 953,718 fit for military service
Defense expenditures:
    exchange rate conversion - $NA, NA% of GDP

Zimbabwe Geography

Total area: 390,580 km2
Land area: 386,670 km2
Comparative area: slightly larger than Montana
Land boundaries:
    3,066 km total; Botswana 813 km, Mozambique 1,231 km, South Africa 225 km,
    Zambia 797 km
Coastline:
    none - landlocked
Maritime claims:
    none - landlocked
Disputes:
    quadripoint with Botswana, Namibia, and Zambia is in disagreement
Climate:
    tropical; moderated by altitude; rainy season (November to March)
Terrain:
    mostly high plateau with higher central plateau (high veld); mountains in
    east
Natural resources:
    coal, chromium ore, asbestos, gold, nickel, copper, iron ore, vanadium,
    lithium, tin, platinum group metals
Land use:
    arable land 7%; permanent crops NEGL%; meadows and pastures 12%; forest and
    woodland 62%; other 19%; includes irrigated NEGL%
Environment:
    recurring droughts; floods and severe storms are rare; deforestation; soil
    erosion; air and water pollution
Note:
    landlocked

:Zimbabwe People

Population: 11,033,376 (July 1992), growth rate 2.9% (1992)
Birth rate: 40 births/1,000 population (1992)
Death rate: 8 deaths/1,000 population (1992)
Net migration rate: -3 migrants/1,000 population (1992)
Infant mortality rate: 59 deaths/1,000 live births (1992)
Life expectancy at birth: 60 years male, 64 years female (1992)
Total fertility rate: 5.4 children born/woman (1992)
Nationality:

noun - Zimbabwean(s); adjective - Zimbabwean

Ethnic divisions:
African 98% (Shona 71%, Ndebele 16%, other 11%); white 1%, mixed and Asian 1%

Religions:
syncretic (part Christian, part indigenous beliefs) 50%, Christian 25%, indigenous beliefs 24%, a few Muslim

Languages:
English (official); Shona, Sindebele

Literacy:
67% (male 74%, female 60%) age 15 and over can read and write (1990 est.)

Labor force:
3,100,000; agriculture 74%, transport and services 16%, mining, manufacturing, construction 10% (1987)

Organized labor:
17% of wage and salary earners have union membership

:Zimbabwe Government

Long-form name:
Republic of Zimbabwe

Type:
parliamentary democracy

Capital: Harare

Administrative divisions:
8 provinces; Manicaland, Mashonaland Central, Mashonaland East, Mashonaland West, Masvingo (Victoria), Matabeleland North, Matabeleland South, Midlands

Independence:
18 April 1980 (from UK; formerly Southern Rhodesia)

Constitution:
21 December 1979

Legal system:
mixture of Roman-Dutch and English common law

National holiday:
Independence Day, 18 April (1980)

Executive branch:
executive president, 2 vice presidents, Cabinet

Legislative branch:
unicameral Parliament

Judicial branch:
Supreme Court

Leaders:
 Chief of State and Head of Government:
Executive President Robert Gabriel MUGABE (since 31 December 1987); Co-Vice President Simon Vengai MUZENDA (since 31 December 1987); Co-Vice President Joshua M. NKOMO (since 6 August 1990)

Political parties and leaders:
Zimbabwe African National Union-Patriotic Front (ZANU-PF), Robert MUGABE; Zimbabwe African National Union-Sithole (ZANU-S), Ndabaningi SITHOLE; Zimbabwe Unity Movement (ZUM), Edgar TEKERE; Democratic Party (DP), Emmanuel

MAGOCHE

Suffrage:
  universal at age 18

Elections:
  Executive President:
  last held 28-30 March 1990 (next to be held NA March 1996); results - Robert
  MUGABE 78.3%, Edgar TEKERE 21.7%
  Parliament:
  last held 28-30 March 1990 (next to be held NA March 1995); results -
  percent of vote by party NA; seats - (150 total, 120 elected) ZANU-PF 117,
  ZUM 2, ZANU-S 1

Member of:
  ACP, AfDB, C, CCC, ECA, FAO, FLS, G-77, GATT, IAEA, IBRD, ICAO, IDA,
  IFAD,
  IFC, ILO, IMF, INTELSAT, INTERPOL, IOC, IOM (observer), ITU, LORCS,
  NAM,
  OAU, PCA, SADCC, UN, UNCTAD, UNESCO, UNIDO, UPU, WCL, WHO,
  WIPO, WMO, WTO

Diplomatic representation:
  Counselor (Political Affairs), Head of Chancery, Ambassador Stanislaus
  Garikai CHIGWEDERE; Chancery at 1608 New Hampshire Avenue NW, Washing-
  ton, DC
  20009; telephone (202) 332-7100
  US:
  Ambassador Edward Gibson LANPHER; Embassy at 172 Herbert Chitapo Avenue,
  Harare (mailing address is P. O. Box 3340, Harare); telephone [263] (4)
  794-521

:Zimbabwe Government

Flag:
  seven equal horizontal bands of green, yellow, red, black, red, yellow, and
  green with a white equilateral triangle edged in black based on the hoist
  side; a yellow Zimbabwe bird is superimposed on a red five-pointed star in
  the center of the triangle

:Zimbabwe Economy

Overview:
  Agriculture employs three-fourths of the labor force and supplies almost 40%
  of exports. The manufacturing sector, based on agriculture and mining,
  produces a variety of goods and contributes 35% to GDP. Mining accounts for
  only 5% of both GDP and employment, but supplies of minerals and metals
  account for about 40% of exports. Wide year-to-year fluctuations in
  agricultural production over the past six years have resulted in an uneven
  growth rate, one that on average has matched the 3% annual increase in
  population. Helped by an IMF/World Bank structural adjustment program,
  output rose 3.5% in 1991. A drought beginning toward the end of 1991
  suggests rough going for 1992.

GDP:
  exchange rate conversion - $7.1 billion, per capita $660; real growth rate
  3.5% (1991 est.)

Inflation rate (consumer prices):

1079

25% (1991 est.)

Unemployment rate: at least 30% (1991 est.)

Budget:
   revenues $2.7 billion; expenditures $3.3 billion, including capital
   expenditures of $330 million (FY91)

Exports:
   $1.8 billion (f.o.b., 1991 est.)
  commodities:
   agricultural 35% (tobacco 20%, other 15%), manufactures 20%, gold 10%,
   ferrochrome 10%, cotton 5%
  partners:
   Europe 55% (EC 40%, Netherlands 5%, other 15%), Africa 20% (South Africa
   10%, other 10%), US 5%

Imports:
   $1.6 billion (c.i.f., 1991 est.)
  commodities:
   machinery and transportation equipment 37%, other manufactures 22%,
   chemicals 16%, fuels 15%
  partners:
   EC 31%, Africa 29% (South Africa 21%, other 8%), US 8%, Japan 4%

External debt: $2.96 billion (December 1989 est.)

Industrial production:
   growth rate 5% (1991 est.); accounts for 35% of GDP

Electricity:
   3,650,000 kW capacity; 7,500 million kWh produced, 700 kWh per capita (1991)

Industries:
   mining, steel, clothing and footwear, chemicals, foodstuffs, fertilizer,
   beverage, transportation equipment, wood products

Agriculture:
   accounts for 11% of GDP and employs 74% of population; 40% of land area
   divided into 4,500 large commercial farms and 42% in communal lands; crops -
   corn (food staple), cotton, tobacco, wheat, coffee, sugarcane, peanuts;
   livestock - cattle, sheep, goats, pigs; self-sufficient in food

Economic aid:
   US commitments, including Ex-Im (FY80-89), $389 million; Western (non-US)
   countries, ODA and OOF bilateral commitments (1970-89), $2.6 billion; OPEC
   bilateral aid (1979-89), $36 million; Communist countries (1970-89), $134
   million

Currency:
   Zimbabwean dollar (plural - dollars); 1 Zimbabwean dollar (Z$) = 100 cents

:Zimbabwe Economy

Exchange rates:
   Zimbabwean dollars (Z$) per US$1 - 4.3066 (March 1992), 3.4282 (1991),
   2.4480 (1990), 2.1133 (1989), 1.8018 (1988), 1.6611 (1987)

Fiscal year: 1 July - 30 June

:Zimbabwe Communications

Railroads:
   2,745 km 1.067-meter gauge; 42 km double track; 355 km electrified

Highways:

85,237 km total; 15,800 km paved, 39,090 km crushed stone, gravel,
stabilized soil: 23,097 km improved earth; 7,250 km unimproved earth
Inland waterways:
  Lake Kariba is a potential line of communication
Pipelines:
  petroleum products 8 km
Civil air:
  12 major transport aircraft
Airports:
  491 total, 401 usable; 22 with permanent-surface runways; 2 with runways
  over 3,659 m; 3 with runways 2,440-3,659 m; 32 with runways 1,220-2,439 m
Telecommunications:
  system was once one of the best in Africa, but now suffers from poor
  maintenance; consists of microwave links, open-wire lines, and radio
  communications stations; 247,000 telephones; broadcast stations - 8 AM, 18
  FM, 8 TV; 1 Atlantic Ocean INTELSAT earth station

:Zimbabwe Defense Forces

Branches:
  Zimbabwe National Army, Air Force of Zimbabwe, Zimbabwe National Police
  (including Police Support Unit, Paramilitary Police), People's Militia
Manpower availability:
  males 15-49, 2,355,965; 1,456,829 fit for military service
Defense expenditures:
  exchange rate conversion - $412.4 million, about 6% of GDP (FY91 est.)
****

Notes, Definitions, and Abbreviations

Text (264 nations, dependent areas, and other entities)

Afghanistan
Albania
Algeria
American Samoa
Andorra
Angola
Anguilla
Antarctica
Antigua and Barbuda
Arctic Ocean
Argentina
Armenia
Aruba
Ashmore and Cartier
Islands
Atlantic Ocean
Australia
Austria
Azerbaijan

Bahamas, The
Bahrain
Baker Island
Bangladesh
Barbados
Bassas da India
Belarus
Belgium
Belize
Benin
Bermuda
Bhutan
Bolivia
Bosnia and Hercego-
vina
Botswana
Bouvet Island
Brazil
British Indian Ocean
Territory
British Virgin Islands

Brunei
Bulgaria
Burkina
Burma
Burundi
Cambodia
Cameroon
Canada
Cape Verde
Cayman Islands
Central African Re-
public
Chad
Chile
China (also see sepa-
rate Taiwan entry)
Christmas Island
Clipperton Island
Cocos (Keeling) Isl-
ands
Colombia

Comoros
Congo
Cook Islands
Coral Sea Islands
Costa Rica
Croatia
Cuba
Cyprus
Czechoslovakia

Denmark
Djibouti
Dominica
Dominican Republic

Ecuador
Egypt
El Salvador
Equatorial Guinea
Estonia
Ethiopia
Europa Island

Falkland Islands (Islas Malvinas)
Faroe Islands
Fiji
Finland
France
French Guiana
French Polynesia
French Southern and Antarctic Lands

Gabon
Gambia, The
Gaza Strip
Georgia
Germany
Ghana
Gibraltar
Glorioso Islands
Greece
Greenland
Grenada
Guadeloupe
Guam
Guatemala
Guernsey
Guinea
Guinea-Bissau
Guyana

Haiti
Heard Island and McDonald Islands
Honduras
Hong Kong
Howland Island
Hungary

Iceland
India
Indian Ocean
Indonesia
Iran
Iraq
Ireland
Israel (also see separate Gaza Strip and West Bank entries)
Italy
Ivory Coast

Jamaica
Jan Mayen
Japan
Jarvis Island
Jersey
Johnston Atoll
Jordan (also see separate West Bank entry)
Juan de Nova Island

Kazakhstan
Kenya
Kingman Reef
Kiribati
Korea, North
Korea, South
Kuwait
Kyrgyzstan

Laos
Latvia
Lebanon
Lesotho
Liberia
Libya
Liechtenstein
Lithuania
Luxembourg

Macau
Macedonia
Madagascar

Malawi
Malaysia
Maldives
Mali
Malta
Man, Isle of
Marshall Islands
Martinique
Mauritania
Mauritius
Mayotte
Mexico
Micronesia, Federated States of
Midway Islands
Moldova
Monaco
Mongolia
Montserrat
Morocco
Mozambique

Namibia
Nauru
Navassa Island
Nepal
Netherlands
Netherlands Antilles
New Caledonia
New Zealand
Nicaragua
Niger
Nigeria
Niue
Norfolk Island
Northern Mariana Islands
Norway

Oman

Pacific Islands, Trust Territory of the (Palau)
Pacific Ocean
Pakistan
Palmyra Atoll
Panama
Papua New Guinea
Paracel Islands
Paraguay
Peru
Philippines

Pitcairn Islands
Poland
Portugal
Puerto Rico
Qatar
Reunion
Romania
Russia
Rwanda
Saint Helena
Saint Kitts and Nevis
Saint Lucia
Saint Pierre and Miquelon
Saint Vincent and the Grenadines
San Marino
Sao Tome and Principe
Saudi Arabia
Senegal
Serbia and Montenegro
Seychelles
Sierra Leone
Singapore
Slovenia
Solomon Islands

Somalia
South Africa
South Georgia and the South Sandwich Islands
Spain
Spratly Islands
Sri Lanka
Sudan
Suriname
Svalbard
Swaziland
Sweden
Switzerland
Syria
Taiwan (follows Zimbabwe)
Tajikistan
Tanzania
Thailand
Togo
Tokelau
Tonga
Trinidad and Tobago
Tromelin Island
Tunisia
Turkey
Turkmenistan
Turks and Caicos Islands

Tuvalu
Uganda
Ukraine
United Arab Emirates
United Kingdom
United States
Uruguay
Uzbekistan
Vanuatu
Vatican City
Venezuela
Vietnam
Virgin Islands
Wake Island
Wallis and Futuna
West Bank
Western Sahara
Western Samoa
World
Yemen
Zaire
Zambia
Zimbabwe
Taiwan

Appendixes

A: The United Nations System
B: Abbreviations for International Organizations and Groups
C: International Organizations and Groups
D: Weights and Measures
E: Cross-Reference List of Geographic Names

Standard Time Zones of the World

Notes, Definitions, and Abbreviations

There have been some significant changes in this edition. The Soviet Union, Yugoslavia, and the Iraq - Saudi Arabia Neutral Zone have been dropped. All 15 former Soviet republics have been added - Armenia, Azerbaijan, Belarus, Estonia, Georgia, Kazakhstan, Kyrgyzstan, Latvia, Lithuania, Moldova, Russia, Tajikistan, Turkmenistan, Ukraine, and Uzbekistan. Bosnia and Hercegovina, Croatia, Macedonia, Serbia and Montenegro, and Slovenia have replaced Yugoslavia. Three maps on areas of special interest have been added this year - two maps on the Commonwealth of Independent States (European States and Central Asian States) and a map of Ethnic Groups in Eastern Europe.

Abbreviations: (see Appendix B for international organizations and groups)

avdp.: avoirdupois

c.i.f.: cost, insurance, and freight

CY: calendar year

DWT: deadweight ton

est.: estimate

Ex-Im: Export-Import Bank of the United States

f.o.b.: free on board

FRG: Federal Republic of Germany (West Germany); used for information dated before 3 October 1990 or CY91

FY: fiscal year

GDP: gross domestic product

GDR: German Democratic Republic (East Germany); used for information dated before 3 October 1990 or CY91

GNP: gross national product

GRT: gross register ton

km: kilometer

km2: square kilometer

kW: kilowatt

kWh: kilowatt hour

m: meter

NA: not available

NEGL: negligible

nm: nautical mile

NZ: New Zealand

ODA: official development assistance

OOF: other official flows

PDRY: People's Democratic Republic of Yemen [Yemen (Aden) or South Yemen]; used for information dated before 22 May 1990 or CY91

UAE: United Arab Emirates

UK: United Kingdom

US: United States

USSR: Union of Soviet Socialist Republics (Soviet Union); used for information dated before 25 December 1991

YAR: Yemen Arab Republic [Yemen (Sanaa) or North Yemen]; used for information dated before 22 May 1990 or CY91

Administrative divisions: The numbers, designatory terms, and first-order administrative divisions are generally those approved by the US Board on Geographic Names (BGN). Changes that have been reported but not yet acted on by BGN are noted.

Area: Total area is the sum of all land and water areas delimited by international boundaries and/or coastlines. Land area is the aggregate of all surfaces delimited by international boundaries and/or coastlines, excluding inland water bodies (lakes, reservoirs, rivers). Comparative areas are based on total area equivalents. Most entities are compared with the entire US or one of the 50 states. The smaller entities are compared with Washington, DC (178 km2, 69 miles2) or the Mall in Washington, DC (0.59 km2, 0.23 miles2, 146 acres).

Birth rate: The average annual number of births during a year per 1,000 population at midyear; also known as crude birth rate.

Dates of information: In general, information available as of 1 January 1992 was used in the preparation of this edition. Population figures are estimates for 1 July 1992, with population growth rates estimated for mid-1992 through mid-1993. Major political events have been updated through 30 June 1992. Military age figures are for 1992.

Death rate: The average annual number of deaths during a year per 1,000 population at midyear; also known as crude death rate.

Diplomatic representation: The US Government has diplomatic relations with 176 nations (the US has not yet established full diplomatic relations with Bosnia and Hercegovina, Croatia, and Slovenia). The US has diplomatic relations with 167 of the 178 UN members - the exceptions are Angola, Bhutan, Bosnia and Hercegovina, Croatia, Cuba, Iran, Iraq, North Korea, Slovenia, and Vietnam. In addition, the US has diplomatic relations with 9 nations that are not in the UN - Andorra, Kiribati, Monaco, Nauru, San Marino, Switzerland, Tonga, Tuvalu, and Vatican City.

Disputes: This category includes a wide variety of situations that range from traditional bilateral boundary disputes to unilateral claims of one sort or another. Every international land boundary dispute in the ``Guide to Interna- tional Boundaries,'' a map published by the Department of State, is included. References to other situations may also be included that are border or frontier relevant, such as maritime disputes, geopolitical questions, or irredentist issues. However, inclusion does not necessarily constitute official acceptance or recognition by the US Government.

Economic aid: This entry refers to bilateral commitments of official develop- ment assistance (ODA), which is defined as government grants that are administered with the promotion of economic development and welfare of LDCs as their main objective and are concessional in character and contain a grant element of at least 25%, and other official flows (OOF) or transactions by the official sector whose main objective is other than development motivated or whose grant element is below the 25% threshold for ODA. OOF transactions include official export credits (such as Eximbank credits), official equity and portfolio investment, and debt reorganization by the official sector that does not meet concessional terms. Aid is considered to have been committed when agreements are initialed by the parties involved and constitute a formal declaration of intent.

Entities: Some of the nations, dependent areas, areas of special sovereignty, and governments included in this publication are not independent, and others are not officially recognized by the US Government. ``Nation'' refers to a people politically organized into a sovereign state with a definite territory. ``Dependent'' area refers to a broad category of political entities that are associated in some way with a nation. Names used for page headings are usually the short-form names as approved by the US Board on Geographic Names. The long-form name is included in the ``Government'' section, and an entry of ``none'' indicates a long-form name does not exist. In some instances, no short-form name exists - then the long-form name must serve for all usages. There are 264 entities in The World Factbook that may be categorized as follows:

NATIONS

177 UN members (excluding Yugoslavia)

11 nations that are not members of the UN - Andorra, Georgia, Kiribati, Macedonia, Monaco, Nauru, Serbia and Montenegro, Switzerland, Tonga, Tuvalu, Vatican City (Holy See)

OTHER

1 Taiwan

DEPENDENT AREAS

6 Australia - Ashmore and Cartier Islands, Christmas Island, Cocos (Keeling) Islands, Coral Sea Islands, Heard Island and McDonald Islands, Norfolk Island

2 Denmark - Faroe Islands, Greenland

16 France - Bassas da India, Clipperton Island, Europa Island, French Guiana, French Polynesia, French Southern and Antarctic Lands, Glorioso Islands, Guadeloupe, Juan de Nova Island, Martinique, Mayotte, New Caledonia, Reunion, Saint Pierre and Miquelon, Tromelin Island, Wallis and Futuna

2 Netherlands - Aruba, Netherlands Antilles

3 New Zealand - Cook Islands, Niue, Tokelau

3 Norway - Bouvet Island, Jan Mayen, Svalbard

1 Portugal - Macau

16 United Kingdom - Anguilla, Bermuda, British Indian Ocean Territory, British
Virgin Islands, Cayman Islands, Falkland Islands, Gibraltar, Guernsey,
Hong Kong, Isle of Man, Jersey, Montserrat, Pitcairn Islands, Saint Helena,
South Georgia and the South Sandwich Islands, Turks and Caicos Islands

15 United States - American Samoa, Baker Island, Guam, Howland Island, Jarvis
Island, Johnston Atoll, Kingman Reef, Midway Islands, Navassa Island, Northern
Mariana Islands, Palmyra Atoll, Puerto Rico, Trust Territory of the Pacific
Islands (Palau), Virgin Islands, Wake Island

MISCELLANEOUS

6 Antarctica, Gaza Strip, Paracel Islands, Spratly Islands, West Bank, Western Sahara

OTHER ENTITIES

4 oceans - Arctic Ocean, Atlantic Ocean, Indian Ocean, Pacific Ocean

1 World

264 total

note: The US Government does not recognize the four so-called independent homelands of Bophuthatswana, Ciskei, Transkei, and Venda in South Africa.

Gross domestic product (GDP): The value of all goods and services produced domestically.

Gross national product (GNP): The value of all goods and services produced domestically plus income earned abroad, minus income earned by foreigners from domestic
production.

GNP/GDP methodology: In the ``Economy'' section, GNP/GDP dollar estimates for the
OECD countries, the former Soviet republics, and the East European countries are derived from purchasing power parity (PPP) calculations rather than from conversions at
official currency exchange rates. The PPP method normally involves the use of international dollar price weights, which are applied to the quantities of goods and services
produced in a given economy. In addition to the lack of reliable data from the majority
of countries, the statistician faces a major difficulty in specifying, identifying, and allowing for the quality of goods and services. The division of a PPP GNP/GDP estimate
in dollars by the corresponding estimate in the local currency gives the PPP conversion
rate. One thousand dollars will buy the same market basket of goods in the US as one
thousand dollars - converted to the local currency at the PPP conversion rate - will buy
in the other country. GNP/GDP estimates for the LDCs, on the other hand, are based on
the conversion of GNP/GDP estimates in local currencies to dollars at the official currency exchange rates. One caution: the proportion of, say, defense expenditures as a
percent of GNP/GDP in local currency accounts may differ substantially from the proportion when GNP/GDP accounts are expressed in PPP terms, as, for example, when an
observer estimates the dollar level of Russian or Japanese military expenditures; similar
problems exist when components are expressed in dollars under currency exchange rate
procedures. Finally, as academic research moves forward on the PPP method, we hope
to convert all GNP/GDP estimates to this method in future editions of The World Factbook.

Growth rate (population): The annual percent change in the population, resulting from a surplus (or deficit) of births over deaths and the balance of migrants entering and leaving a country. The rate may be positive or negative.

Illicit drugs: There are five categories of illicit drugs - narcotics, stimulants, depressants (sedatives), hallucinogens, and cannabis. These categories include many drugs legally produced and prescribed by doctors as well as those illegally produced and sold outside medical channels.

Cannabis (Cannabis sativa) is the common hemp plant, which provides hallucinogens with some sedative properties, and includes marijuana (pot, Acapulco gold, grass, reefer), tetrahydrocannabinol (THC, Marinol), hashish (hash), and hashish oil (hash oil).

Coca (Erythroxylon coca) is a bush, and the leaves contain the stimulant cocaine. Coca is not to be confused with cocoa, which comes from cacao seeds and is used in making chocolate, cocoa, and cocoa butter.

Cocaine is a stimulant derived from the leaves of the coca bush.

Depressants (sedatives) are drugs that reduce tension and anxiety and include chloral hydrate, barbiturates (Amytal, Nembutal, Seconal, phenobarbital), benzodiazepines (Librium, Valium), methaqualone (Quaalude), glutethimide (Doriden), and others (Equanil, Placidyl, Valmid).

Drugs are any chemical substances that effect a physical, mental, emotional, or behavioral change in an individual.

Drug abuse is the use of any licit or illicit chemical substance that results in physical, mental, emotional, or behavioral impairment in an individual.

Hallucinogens are drugs that affect sensation, thinking, self-awareness, and emotion.

Hallucinogens include LSD (acid, microdot), mescaline and peyote (mexc, buttons, cactus), amphetamine variants (PMA, STP, DOB), phencyclidine (PCP, angel dust, hog), phencyclidine analogues (PCE, PCPy, TCP), and others (psilocybin, psilocyn).

Hashish is the resinous exudate of the cannabis or hemp plant (Cannabis sativa).

Heroin is a semisynthetic derivative of morphine.

Marijuana is the dried leaves of the cannabis or hemp plant (Cannabis sativa).

Narcotics are drugs that relieve pain, often induce sleep, and refer to opium, opium derivatives, and synthetic substitutes. Natural narcotics include opium (paregoric, parepectolin), morphine (MS-Contin, Roxanol), codeine (Tylenol w/codeine, Empirin w/codeine, Robitussan A-C), and thebaine. Semisynthetic narcotics include heroin (horse, smack), and hydromorphone (Dilaudid). Synthetic narcotics include meperidine or Pethidine (Demerol, Mepergan), methadone (Dolophine, Methadose), and others (Darvon, Lomotil).

Opium is the milky exudate of the incised, unripe seedpod of the opium poppy.

Opium poppy (Papaver somniferum) is the source for many natural and semisynthetic narcotics.

Poppy straw concentrate is the alkaloid derived from the mature dried opium poppy.

Qat (kat, khat) is a stimulant from the buds or leaves of Catha edulis that is chewed or drunk as tea.

Stimulants are drugs that relieve mild depression, increase energy and activity, and include cocaine (coke, snow, crack), amphetamines (Desoxyn,

Dexedrine), phenmetrazine (Preludin), methylphenidate (Ritalin), and others (Cylert, Sanorex, Tenuate).

Infant mortality rate: The number of deaths to infants under one year old in a given year per 1,000 live births occurring in the same year.

Land use: Human use of the land surface is categorized as arable land - land cultivated for crops that are replanted after each harvest (wheat, maize, rice); permanent crops - land cultivated for crops that are not replanted after each harvest (citrus, coffee, rubber); meadows and pastures - land permanently used for herbaceous forage crops; forest and woodland - land under dense or open stands of trees; and other - any land type not specifi- cally mentioned above (urban areas, roads, desert). The percentage figure for irrigated land refers to the portion of the entire amount of land area that is artificially supplied with water.

Leaders: The chief of state is the titular leader of the country who represents the state at official and ceremonial funcions but is not involved with the day-to-day activities of the government. The head of government is the administrative leader who manages the day-to-day activities of the government. In the UK, the monarch is the chief of state, and the Prime Minister is the head of government. In the US, the President is both the chief of state and the head of government.

Life expectancy at birth: The average number of years to be lived by a group of people all born in the same year, if mortality at each age remains constant in the future.

Literacy: There are no universal definitions and standards of literacy. Unless otherwise noted, all rates are based on the most common definition - the ability to read and write at a specified age. Detailing the standards that individual countries use to assess the ability to read and write is beyond the scope of this publication.

Maps: All maps will be available only in the printed version for the fore- seeable future.

Maritime claims: The proximity of neighboring states may prevent some national claims from being fully extended.

Merchant marine: All ships engaged in the carriage of goods. All commercial vessels (as opposed to all nonmilitary ships), which excludes tugs, fishing vessels, offshore oil rigs, etc.; also, a grouping of merchant ships by nationality or register.

Captive register - A register of ships maintained by a territory, possession, or colony primarily or exclusively for the use of ships owned in the parent country; also referred to as an offshore register, the offshore equivalent of an internal register. Ships on a captive register will fly the same flag as the parent country, or a local variant of it, but will be subject to the maritime laws and taxation rules of the offshore territory. Although the nature of a captive register makes it especially desirable for ships owned in the parent country, just as in the internal register, the ships may also be owned abroad. The captive register then acts as a flag of convenience register, except that it is not the register of an independent state.

Flag of convenience register - A national register offering registration to a merchant ship not owned in the flag state. The major flags of convenience (FOC) attract ships to their register by virtue of low fees, low or nonexistent taxation of profits, and liberal manning requirements. True FOC registers are characterized by having relatively few of the ships registered actually owned in the flag state. Thus, while virtually any flag can be used for ships under a given set of circumstances, an FOC register is one where the majority of the merchant fleet is owned abroad. It is also referred to as an open register.

Flag state - The nation in which a ship is registered and which holds legal jurisdiction over operation of the ship, whether at home or abroad. Differences in flag state maritime legislation determine how a ship is manned and taxed and whether a foreign-owned ship may be placed on the register.

Internal register - A register of ships maintained as a subset of a national register. Ships on the internal register fly the national flag and have that nationality but are subject to a separate set of maritime rules from those on the main national register. These differences usually include lower taxation of profits, manning by foreign nationals, and, usually, ownership outside the flag state (when it functions as an FOC register). The Norwegian International Ship Register and Danish International Ship Register are the most notable examples of an internal register. Both have been instrumental in stemming flight from the national flag to flags of convenience and in attracting foreign-owned ships to the Norwegian and Danish flags.

Merchant ship - A vessel that carries goods against payment of freight; commonly used to denote any nonmilitary ship but accurately restricted to commercial vessels only.

Register - The record of a ship's ownership and nationality as listed with the maritime authorities of a country; also, the compendium of such individual ships' registrations. Registration of a ship provides it with a nationality and makes it subject to the laws of the country in which registered (the flag state) regardless of the nationality of the ship's ultimate owner.

Money figures: All are expressed in contemporaneous US dollars unless otherwise indicated.

Net migration rate: The balance between the number of persons entering and leaving a country during the year per 1,000 persons (based on midyear population). An excess of persons entering the country is referred to as net immigration (3.56 migrants/1,000 population); an excess of persons leaving the country as net emigration (-9.26 migrants/1,000 population).

Population: Figures are estimates from the Bureau of the Census based on statistics from population censuses, vital registration systems, or sample surveys pertaining to the recent past, and on assumptions about future trends.

Total fertility rate: The average number of children that would be born per woman if all women lived to the end of their childbearing years and bore children according to a given fertility rate at each age.

Years: All year references are for the calendar year (CY) unless indicated as fiscal year (FY).

Note: Information for the US and US dependencies was compiled from material in the public domain and does not represent Intelligence Community estimates. The Handbook of International Economic and Environmental Statistics, published annually in September by the Central Intelligence Agency, contains detailed economic information for the Organization for Economic Cooperation and Development (OECD) countries, Eastern Europe, the newly independent republics of the former nations of Yugoslavia and the Soviet Union, and selected other countries. The Handbook can be obtained wherever The World Factbook is available.

Appendix A:

The United Nations System

The UN is composed of six principal organs and numerous subordinate agencies and bodies as follows:

1) Secretariat

2) General Assembly:
UNCHS United Nations Center for Human Settlements (Habitat)
UNCTAD United Nations Conference on Trade and Development
UNDP United Nations Development Program
UNEP United Nations Environment Program
UNFPA United Nations Population Fund
UNHCR United Nations Office of High Commissioner for Refugees
UNICEF United Nations Children's Fund
UNITAR United Nations Institute for Training and Research
UNRWA United Nations Relief and Works Agency for Palestine
        Refugees in the Near East
UNSF United Nations Special Fund
UNU United Nations University
WFC World Food Council
WFP World Food Program

3) Security Council:
UNAVEM United Nations Angola Verification Mission
UNDOF United Nations Disengagement Observer Force
UNFICYP United Nations Force in Cyprus
UNIFIL United Nations Interim Force in Lebanon
UNIIMOG United Nations Iran-Iraq Military Observer Group
UNMOGIP United Nations Military Observer Group in India and
        Pakistan
UNTSO United Nations Truce Supervision Organization

4) Economic and Social Council (ECOSOC):
Specialized agencies
  FAO Food and Agriculture Organization of the United Nations
  IBRD International Bank for Reconstruction and Development
  ICAO International Civil Aviation Organization
  IDA International Development Association
  IFAD International Fund for Agricultural Development
  IFC International Finance Corporation
  ILO International Labor Organization
  IMF International Monetary Fund
  IMO International Maritime Organization
  ITU International Telecommunication Union
  UNESCO United Nations Educational, Scientific, and Cultural
        Organization
  UNIDO United Nations Industrial Development Organization
  UPU Universal Postal Union
  WHO World Health Organization
  WIPO World Intellectual Property Organization
  WMO World Meteorological Organization
        Related organizations

GATT General Agreement on Tariffs and Trade
IAEA International Atomic Energy Agency
Regional commissions
ECA Economic Commission for Africa
ECE Economic Commission for Europe
ECLAC Economic Commission for Latin America and the Caribbean
ESCAP Economic and Social Commission for Asia and the Pacific
ESCWA Economic and Social Commission for Western Asia
Functional commissions
Commission on Human Rights
Commission on Narcotic Drugs
Commission for Social Development
Commission on the Status of Women
Population Commission
Statistical Commission

5) Trusteeship Council

6) International Court of Justice (ICJ)

Appendix B

Abbreviations for International Organizations and Groups

ABEDA Arab Bank for Economic Development in Africa
ACC Arab Cooperation Council
ACCT Agency for Cultural and Technical Cooperation
ACP African, Caribbean, and Pacific Countries
AfDB African Development Bank
AFESD Arab Fund for Economic and Social Development
AG Andean Group
AL Arab League
ALADI Asociacion Latinoamericana de Integracion; see Latin
    American Integration Association (LAIA)
AMF Arab Monetary Fund
AMU Arab Maghreb Union
ANZUS Australia-New Zealand-United States Security Treaty
APEC Asia Pacific Economic Cooperation
AsDB Asian Development Bank
ASEAN Association of Southeast Asian Nations

BAD Banque Africaine de Developpement;
    see African Development Bank (AfDB)
BADEA Banque Arabe de Developpement Economique en Afrique;
    see Arab Bank for Economic Development in Africa (ABEDA)
BCIE Banco Centroamericano de Integracion Economico; see Central
    American Bank for Economic Integration (BCIE)
BDEAC Banque de Developppment des Etats de l'Afrique Centrale; see
    Central African States Development Bank (BDEAC)
Benelux Benelux Economic Union
BID Banco Interamericano de Desarvollo; see Inter-American
    Development Bank (IADB)
BIS Bank for International Settlements

BOAD Banque Ouest-Africaine de Developpement; see West African Development Bank (WADB)

C Commonwealth

CACM Central American Common Market

CAEU Council of Arab Economic Unity

CARICOM Caribbean Community and Common Market

CCC Customs Cooperation Council

CDB Caribbean Development Bank

CE Council of Europe

CEAO Communaute Economique de l'Afrique de l'Ouest; see West African Economic Community (CEAO)

CEEAC Communaute Economique des Etats de l'Afrique Centrale; see Economic Community of Central African States (CEEAC)

CEMA Council for Mutual Economic Assistance; also known as CMEA or Comecon; abolished 1 January 1991

CEPGL Communaute Economique des Pays des Grands Lacs; see Economic Community of the Great Lakes Countries (CEPGL)

CERN Conseil Europeen pour la Recherche Nucleaire; see European Organization for Nuclear Research (CERN)

CG Contadora Group

CIS Commonwealth of Independent States

CMEA Council for Mutual Economic Assistance (CEMA); also known as Comecon; abolished 1 January 1991

COCOM Coordinating Committee on Export Controls

Comecon Council for Mutual Economic Assistance (CEMA); also known as CMEA; abolished 1 January 1991

CP Colombo Plan

CSCE Conference on Security and Cooperation in Europe

DC developed country

EADB East African Development Bank

EBRD European Bank for Reconstruction and Development

EC European Community

ECA Economic Commission for Africa

ECAFE Economic Commission for Asia and the Far East; see Economic and Social Commission for Asia and the Pacific (ESCAP)

ECE Economic Commission for Europe

ECLA Economic Commission for Latin America; see Economic Commission for Latin America and the Caribbean (ECLAC)

ECLAC Economic Commission for Latin America and the Caribbean

ECOSOC Economic and Social Council

ECOWAS Economic Community of West African States

ECWA Economic Commission for Western Asia; see Economic and Social Commission for Western Asia (ESCWA)

EFTA European Free Trade Association

EIB European Investment Bank

Entente Council of the Entente

ESA European Space Agency

ESCAP Economic and Social Commission for Asia and the Pacific

ESCWA Economic and Social Commission for Western Asia

FAO Food and Agriculture Organization
FLS Front Line States
FZ Franc Zone

G-2 Group of 2
G-3 Group of 3
G-5 Group of 5
G-6 Group of 6 (not to be confused with the Big Six)
G-7 Group of 7
G-8 Group of 8
G-9 Group of 9
G-10 Group of 10
G-11 Group of 11
G-15 Group of 15
G-19 Group of 19
G-24 Group of 24
G-30 Group of 30
G-33 Group of 33
G-77 Group of 77
GATT General Agreement on Tariffs and Trade
GCC Gulf Cooperation Council

Habitat see United Nations Center for Human Settlements (UNCHS)
HG Hexagonal Group

IADB Inter-American Development Bank
IAEA International Atomic Energy Agency
IBEC International Bank for Economic Cooperation
IBRD International Bank for Reconstruction and Development
ICAO International Civil Aviation Organization
ICC International Chamber of Commerce
ICEM Intergovernmental Committee for European Migration; see
        International Organization for Migration (IOM)
ICFTU International Confederation of Free Trade Unions
ICJ International Court of Justice
ICM Intergovernmental Committee for Migration; see
        International Organization for Migration (IOM)
ICRC International Committee of the Red Cross
IDA International Development Association
IDB Islamic Development Bank
IEA International Energy Agency
IFAD International Fund for Agricultural Development
IFC International Finance Corporation
IGADD Inter-Governmental Authority on Drought and Development
IIB International Investment Bank
ILO International Labor Organization
IMCO Intergovernmental Maritime Consultative Organization; see
        International Maritime Organization (IMO)
IMF International Monetary Fund
IMO International Maritime Organization
INMARSAT International Maritime Satellite Organization
INTELSAT International Telecommunications Satellite Organization

INTERPOL International Criminal Police Organization
IOC International Olympic Committee
IOM International Organization for Migration
ISO International Organization for Standardization
ITU International Telecommunication Union

LAES Latin American Economic System
LAIA Latin American Integration Association
LAS League of Arab States; see Arab League (AL)
LDC less developed country
LLDC least developed country
LORCS League of Red Cross and Red Crescent Societies

MERCOSUR Southern Cone Common Market
MTCR Missile Technology Control Regime

NACC North Atlantic Cooperation Council
NAM Nonaligned Movement
NATO North Atlantic Treaty Organization
NC Nordic Council
NEA Nuclear Energy Agency
NIB Nordic Investment Bank
NIC newly industrializing country; see newly industrializing
    economy (NIE)
NIE newly industrializing economy
NSG Nuclear Suppliers Group

OAPEC Organization of Arab Petroleum Exporting Countries
OAS Organization of American States
OAU Organization of African Unity
OECD Organization for Economic Cooperation and Development
OECS Organization of Eastern Caribbean States
OIC Organization of the Islamic Conference
OPANAL Agency for the Prohibition of Nuclear Weapons in Latin America
    and the Caribbean
OPEC Organization of Petroleum Exporting Countries

PCA Permanent Court of Arbitration

RG Rio Group

SAARC South Asian Association for Regional Cooperation
SACU Southern African Customs Union
SADCC Southern African Development Coordination Conference
SELA Sistema Economico Latinoamericana; see Latin American Economic
    System (LAES)
SPC South Pacific Commission
SPF South Pacific Forum

UDEAC Union Douaniere et Economique de l'Afrique Centrale; see
    Central African Customs and Economic Union (UDEAC)
UN United Nations
UNAVEM United Nations Angola Verification Mission
UNCHS United National Center for Human Settlements (also
    known as Habitat)
UNCTAD United Nations Conference on Trade and Development

UNDOF United Nations Disengagement Observer Force
UNDP United Nations Development Program
UNEP United Nations Environment Program
UNESCO United Nations Educational, Scientific, and Cultural
    Organization
UNFICYP United Nations Force in Cyprus
UNFPA United Nations Fund for Population Activities; see UN Population
    Fund (UNFPA)
UNHCR United Nations Office of the High Commissioner for Refugees
UNICEF United Nations International Children's Emergency Fund; see
    United Nations Children's Fund (UNICEF)
UNIDO United Nations Industrial Development Organization
UNIFIL United Nations Interim Force in Lebanon
UNIIMOG United Nations Iran-Iraq Military Observer Group
UNMOGIP United Nations Military Observer Group in India and Pakistan
UNRWA United Nations Relief and Works Agency for Palestine Refugees
    in the Near East
UNTSO United Nations Truce Supervision Organization
UPU Universal Postal Union
USSR/EE USSR/Eastern Europe

WADB West African Development Bank
WCL World Confederation of Labor
WEU Western European Union
WFC World Food Council
WFP World Food Program
WFTU World Federation of Trade Unions
WHO World Health Organization
WIPO World Intellectual Property Organization
WMO World Meteorological Organization
WP Warsaw Pact (members met 1 July 1991 to dissolve the alliance)
WTO World Tourism Organization

ZC Zangger Committee

note: not all international organizations and groups have abbreviations

Appendix C:

International Organizations and Groups

****

advanced developing countries

Note - another term for those less developed countries (LDCs) with particularly rapid
industrial development; see newly industrializing economies (NIEs)
****

African, Caribbean, and Pacific Countries (ACP)

established - 1 April 1976

aim - members have a preferential economic and aid relationship with the EC

members - (69) Angola, Antigua and Barbuda, The Bahamas,
Barbados, Belize, Benin, Boswana, Burkina, Burundi, Cameroon,
Cape Verde, Central African Republic, Chad, Comoros, Congo,

Djibouti, Dominica, Dominican Republic, Equatorial Guinea,
Ethiopia, Fiji, Gabon, The Gambia, Ghana, Grenada, Guinea,
Guinea-Bissau, Guyana, Haiti, Ivory Coast, Jamaica, Kenya,
Kiribati, Lesotho, Liberia, Madagascar, Malawi, Mali, Mauritania,
Mauritius, Mozambique, Namibia, Niger, Nigeria, Papua New Guinea,
Rwanda, Saint Kitts and Nevis, Saint Lucia, Saint Vincent and the
Grenadines, Sao Tome and Principe, Senegal, Seychelles, Sierra
Leone, Solomon Islands, Somalia, Sudan, Suriname, Swaziland,
Tanzania, Togo, Tonga, Trinidad and Tobago, Tuvalu, Uganda,
Vanuatu, Western Samoa, Zaire, Zambia, Zimbabwe
****

African Development Bank (AfDB), also known as Banque Africaine de Developpement (BAD)

established - 4 August 1963

aim - to promote economic and social development

regional members - (51) Algeria, Angola, Benin, Botswana,
Burkina, Burundi, Cameroon, Cape Verde, Central African Republic,
Chad, Comoros, Congo, Djibouti, Egypt, Equatorial Guinea,
Ethiopia, Gabon, The Gambia, Ghana, Guinea, Guinea-Bissau, Ivory
Coast, Kenya, Lesotho, Liberia, Libya, Madagascar, Malawi, Mali,
Mauritania, Mauritius, Morocco, Mozambique, Namibia, Niger,
Nigeria, Rwanda, Sao Tome and Principe, Senegal, Seychelles,
Sierra Leone, Somalia, Sudan, Swaziland, Tanzania, Togo, Tunisia,
Uganda, Zaire, Zambia, Zimbabwe

nonregional members - (25) Argentina, Australia, Austria,
Belgium, Brazil, Canada, China, Denmark, Finland, France,
Germany, India, Italy, Japan, South Korea, Kuwait, Netherlands,
Norway, Portugal, Saudi Arabia, Sweden, Switzerland, UK, US,
Yugoslavia
****

Agence de Cooperation Culturelle et Technique (ACCT)

Note - see Agency for Cultural and Technical Cooperation (ACCT)
****

Agency for Cultural and Technical Cooperation (ACCT)

Note - acronym from Agence de Cooperation Culturelle et Technique

established - 21 March 1970

aim - to promote cultural and technical cooperation among French- speaking countries

members - (32) Belgium, Benin, Burkina, Burundi, Canada, Central
African Republic, Chad, Comoros, Congo, Djibouti, Dominica,
France, Gabon, Guinea, Haiti, Ivory Coast, Lebanon, Luxembourg,
Madagascar, Mali, Mauritius, Monaco, Niger, Rwanda, Sao Tome and
Principe, Senegal, Seychelles, Togo, Tunisia, Vanuatu, Vietnam,
Zaire

associate members - (7) Cameroon, Egypt, Guinea-Bissau, Laos, Mauritania, Morocco,
Saint Lucia

participating governments - (2) New Brunswick (Canada), Quebec (Canada)

****

Agency for the Prohibition of Nuclear Weapons in Latin America and the Caribbean (OPANAL)

Note - acronym from Organismo para la Proscripcion de las Armas Nucleares en la America Latina y el Caribe (OPANAL)

established - 14 February 1967

aim - to encourage the peaceful uses of atomic energy and prohibit nuclear weapons

members - (24) Antigua and Barbuda, The Bahamas, Barbados, Bolivia, Chile, Colombia, Costa Rica, Dominican Republic, Ecuador, El Salvador, Grenada, Guatemala, Haiti, Honduras, Jamaica, Mexico, Nicaragua, Panama, Paraguay, Peru, Suriname, Trinidad and Tobago, Uruguay, Venezuela

****

Andean Group (AG)

established - 26 May 1969, effective 16 October 1969

aim - to promote harmonious development through economic integration

members - (5) Bolivia, Colombia, Ecuador, Peru, Venezuela

associate member - (1) Panama

observers - (26) Argentina, Australia, Austria, Belgium, Brazil, Canada, Costa Rica, Denmark, Egypt, Finland, France, Germany, India, Israel, Italy, Japan, Mexico, Netherlands, Paraguay, Spain, Sweden, Switzerland, UK, US, Uruguay, Yugoslavia

Note - The US view is that the Socialist Federal represents its continuation. Republic of Yugoslavia (SFRY) has dissolved and that none of the successor republics

****

Arab Bank for Economic Development in Africa (ABEDA)

Note - also known as Banque Arabe de Developpement Economique en Afrique (BADEA)

established - 18 February 1974

effective - 16 September 1974

aim - to promote economic development

members - (16 plus the Palestine Liberation Organization) Algeria, Bahrain, Iraq, Jordan, Kuwait, Lebanon, Libya, Mauritania, Morocco, Oman, Qatar, Saudi Arabia, Sudan, Syria, Tunisia, UAE, Palestine Liberation Organization; note - these are all the members of the Arab League except Djibouti, Somalia, and Yemen

****

Arab Cooperation Council (ACC)

established - 16 February 1989

aim - to promote economic cooperation and integration, possibly leading to an Arab Common Market

members - (4) Egypt, Iraq, Jordan, Yemen

****

Arab Fund for Economic and Social Development (AFESD)

established - 16 May 1968

aim - to promote economic and social development

members - (20 plus the Palestine Liberation Organization)
Algeria, Bahrain, Djibouti, Egypt (suspended from 1979 to 1988),
Iraq, Jordan, Kuwait, Lebanon, Libya, Mauritania, Morocco, Oman,
Qatar, Saudi Arabia, Somalia, Sudan, Syria, Tunisia, UAE, Yemen,
Palestine Liberation Organization

****

Arab League (AL)

Note - also known as League of Arab States (LAS)

established - 22 March 1945

aim - to promote economic, social, political, and military cooperation

members - (20 plus the Palestine Liberation Organization)
Algeria, Bahrain, Djibouti, Egypt, Iraq, Jordan, Kuwait, Lebanon,
Libya, Mauritania, Morocco, Oman, Qatar, Saudi Arabia, Somalia,
Sudan, Syria, Tunisia, UAE, Yemen, Palestine Liberation
Organization

****

Arab Maghreb Union (AMU)

established - 17 February 1989

aim - to promote cooperation and integration among the Arab states of northern Africa

members - (5) Algeria, Libya, Mauritania, Morocco, Tunisia

****

Arab Monetary Fund (AMF)

established - 27 April 1976

effective - 2 February 1977

aim - to promote Arab cooperation, development, and integration in monetary and economic affairs

members - (19 plus the Palestine Liberation Organization)
Algeria, Bahrain, Egypt, Iraq, Jordan, Kuwait, Lebanon, Libya,
Mauritania, Morocco, Oman, Qatar, Saudi Arabia, Somalia, Sudan,
Syria, Tunisia, UAE, Yemen, Palestine Liberation Organization

****

Asia Pacific Economic Cooperation (APEC)

established - NA November 1989

aim - to promote trade and investment in the Pacific basin

members - (15) all ASEAN members (Brunei, Indonesia, Malaysia, Philippines, Singapore, Thailand) plus Australia, Canada, China, Hong Kong, Japan, South Korea, NZ,
Taiwan, US

****

Asian Development Bank (AsDB)

established - 19 December 1966

aim - to promote regional economic cooperation

regional members - (35) Afghanistan, Australia, Bangladesh, Bhutan, Burma, Cambodia, China, Cook Islands, Fiji, Hong Kong, India, Indonesia, Japan, Kiribati, South Korea, Laos, Malaysia, Maldives, Marshall Islands, Federated States of Micronesia, Mongolia, Nepal, NZ, Pakistan, Papua New Guinea, Philippines, Singapore, Solomon Islands, Sri Lanka, Taiwan, Thailand, Tonga, Vanuatu, Vietnam, Western Samoa

nonregional members - (15) Austria, Belgium, Canada, Denmark, Finland, France, Germany, Italy, Netherlands, Norway, Spain, Sweden, Switzerland, UK, US

****

Asociacion Latinoamericana de Integracion (ALADI)

Note - see Latin American Integration Association (LAIA)

****

Association of Southeast Asian Nations (ASEAN)

established - 9 August 1967

aim - regional economic, social, and cultural cooperation among the non-Communist countries of Southeast Asia

members - (6) Brunei, Indonesia, Malaysia, Philippines, Singapore, Thailand

observer - (1) Papua New Guinea

****

Australia Group

established - 1984

aim - to consult on and coordinate export controls related to chemical and biological weapons

members - (22) Australia, Austria, Belgium, Canada, Denmark, Finland, France, Germany, Greece, Ireland, Italy, Japan, Luxembourg, Netherlands, NZ, Norway, Portugal, Spain, Sweden, Switzerland, UK, US

****

Australia - New Zealand - United States Security Treaty (ANZUS)

established - 1 September 1951, effective 29 April 1952

aim - trilateral mutual security agreement, although the US suspended security obligations to NZ on 11 August 1986

members - (3) Australia, NZ, US

****

Banco Centroamericano de Integracion Economico (BCIE)

Note - see Central American Bank for Economic Integration (BCIE)

****

Banco Interamericano de Desarvollo (BID)

Note - see Inter-American Development Bank (IADB)

****

Bank for International Settlements (BIS)

established - 20 January 1930

effective - 17 March 1930

aim - to promote cooperation among central banks in international financial settlements

members - (29) Australia, Austria, Belgium, Bulgaria, Canada, Czechoslovakia, Denmark, Finland, France, Germany, Greece, Hungary, Iceland, Ireland, Italy, Japan, Netherlands, Norway, Poland, Portugal, Romania, South Africa, Spain, Sweden, Switzerland, Turkey, UK, US, Yugoslavia

****

Banque Africaine de Developpement (BAD)

Note - see African Development Bank (AfDB)

****

Banque Arabe de Developpement Economique en Afrique (BADEA)

Note - see Arab Bank for Economic Development in Africa (ABEDA)

****

Banque de Developpement des Etats de l'Afrique Centrale (BDEAC)

Note - see Central African States Development Bank (BDEAC)

****

Banque Ouest-Africaine de Developpement (BOAD)

Note - see West African Development Bank (WADB)

****

Benelux Economic Union (Benelux)

Note - acronym from Belgium, Netherlands, and Luxembourg

established - 3 February 1958

effective - 1 November 1960

aim - to develop closer economic cooperation and integration

members - (3) Belgium, Luxembourg, Netherlands

****

Big Seven

Note - membership is the same as the Group of 7

established - NA

aim - to discuss and coordinate major economic policies

members - (7) Big Six (Canada, France, Germany, Italy, Japan, UK) plus the US

****

Big Six

Note - not to be confused with the Group of 6

established - NA

aim - economic cooperation

members - (6) Canada, France, Germany, Italy, Japan, UK
****

Caribbean Community and Common Market (CARICOM)

established - 4 July 1973

effective - 1 August 1973

aim - to promote economic integration and development, especially among the less developed countries

members - (13) Antigua and Barbuda, The Bahamas, Barbados, Belize, Dominica, Grenada, Guyana, Jamaica, Montserrat, Saint Kitts and Nevis, Saint Lucia, Saint Vincent and the Grenadines, Trinidad and Tobago

associate members - (2) British Virgin Islands, Turks and Caicos Islands

observers - (10) Anguilla, Bermuda, Cayman Islands, Dominican Republic, Haiti, Mexico, Netherlands Antilles, Puerto Rico, Suriname, Venezuela
****

Caribbean Development Bank (CDB)

established - 18 October 1969

effective - 26 January 1970

aim - to promote economic development and cooperation

regional members - (20) Anguilla, Antigua and Barbuda, The Bahamas, Barbados, Belize, British Virgin Islands, Cayman Islands, Colombia, Dominica, Grenada, Guyana, Jamaica, Mexico, Montserrat, Saint Kitts and Nevis, Saint Lucia, Saint Vincent and the Grenadines, Trinidad and Tobago, Turks and Caicos Islands, Venezuela

nonregional members - (5) Canada, France, Germany, Italy, UK
****

Cartagena Group

Note - see Group of 11
****

Central African Customs and Economic Union (UDEAC)

Note - acronym from Union Douaniere et Economique de l'Afrique Centrale

established - 8 December 1964

effective - 1 January 1966

aim - to promote the establishment of a Central African Common Market

members - (6) Cameroon, Central African Republic, Chad, Congo, Equatorial Guinea, Gabon
****

Central African States Development Bank (BDEAC)

Note - acronym from Banque de Developpement des Etats de l'Afrique Centrale

established - 3 December 1975

aim - to provide loans for economic development

members - (9) Cameroon, Central African Republic, Chad, Congo, Equatorial Guinea, France, Gabon, Germany, Kuwait
****

Central American Bank for Economic Integration (BCIE)
Note - acronym from Banco Centroamericano de Integracion Economico
established - 13 December 1960
aim - to promote economic integration and development
members - (5) Costa Rica, El Salvador, Guatemala, Honduras, Nicaragua
****

Central American Common Market (CACM)
established - 13 December 1960
effective - 3 June 1961
aim - to promote establishment of a Central American Common Market
members - (5) Costa Rica, El Salvador, Guatemala, Honduras, Nicaragua
****

centrally planned economies
Note - a term applied mainly to the traditionally Communist states that looked to the former USSR for leadership; most are now evolving toward more democratic and market-oriented systems; also known formerly as the Second World or as the Communist countries; through the 1980s, this group included Albania, Bulgaria, Cambodia, China, Cuba, Czechoslovakia, GDR, Hungary, North Korea, Laos, Mongolia, Poland, Romania, USSR, Vietnam, Yugoslavia
****

Colombo Plan (CP)
established - 1 July 1951
aim - to promote economic and social development in Asia and the Pacific
nembers - (26) Afghanistan, Australia, Bangladesh, Bhutan, Burma, Cambodia, Canada, Fiji, India, Indonesia, Iran, Japan, South Korea, Laos, Malaysia, Maldives, Nepal, NZ, Pakistan, Papua New Guinea, Philippines, Singapore, Sri Lanka, Thailand, UK, US
****

Commission for Social Development
established - 21 June 1946 as the Social Commission, renamed 29 July 1966
aim - ECOSOC organization dealing with social development programs
members - (31) selected on a rotating basis from all regions
****

Commission on Human Rights
established - 18 February 1946
aim - ECOSOC organization dealing with human rights
members - (43) selected on a rotating basis from all regions
****

Commission on Narcotic Drugs

established - 16 February 1946

aim - ECOSOC organization dealing with illicit drugs

members - (38) selected on a rotating basis from all regions with emphasis on producing and processing countries

****

Commission on the Status of Women

established - 21 June 1946

aim - ECOSOC organization dealing with women's rights

members - (32) selected on a rotating basis from all regions

****

Commonwealth (C)

established - 31 December 1931

aim - voluntary association that evolved from the British Empire and that seeks to foster multinational cooperation and assistance

members - (48) Antigua and Barbuda, Australia, The Bahamas, Bangladesh, Barbados, Belize, Botswana, Brunei, Canada, Cyprus, Dominica, The Gambia, Ghana, Grenada, Guyana, India, Jamaica, Kenya, Kiribati, Lesotho, Malawi, Malaysia, Maldives, Malta, Mauritius, Namibia, NZ, Nigeria, Pakistan, Papua New Guinea, Saint Kitts and Nevis, Saint Lucia, Saint Vincent and the Grenadines, Seychelles, Sierra Leone, Singapore, Solomon Islands, Sri Lanka, Swaziland, Tanzania, Tonga, Trinidad and Tobago, Uganda, UK, Vanuatu, Western Samoa, Zambia, Zimbabwe

special members - (2) Nauru, Tuvalu

****

Commonwealth of Independent States (CIS)

established - 8 December 1991

effective - 21 December 1991

aim - to coordinate intercommonwealth relations and to provide a mechanism for the orderly dissolution of the USSR

members - (11) Armenia, Azerbaijan, Belarus, Kazakhstan, Kyrgyzstan, Moldova, Russia, Tajikistan, Turkmenistan, Ukraine, Uzbekistan

****

Communaute Economique de l'Afrique de l'Ouest (CEAO)

Note - see West African Economic Community (CEAO)

****

Communaute Economique des Etats de l'Afrique Centrale (CEEAC)

Note - see Economic Community of Central African States (CEEAC)

****

Communaute Economique des Pays des Grands Lacs (CEPGL)

Note - see Economic Community of the Great Lakes Countries (CEPGL)
****

Communist countries

Note - traditionally the Marxist-Leninist states with authoritarian governments and command economies based on the Soviet model; most of the successor states are no longer Communist; see centrally planned economies
****

Conference on Security and Cooperation in Europe (CSCE)

established - NA November 1972

aim - discusses issues of mutual concern and reviews implementation of the Helsinki Agreement

members - (52) Albania, Armenia, Austria, Azerbaijan, Belarus, Belgium, Bosnia and Hercegovina, Bulgaria, Canada, Croatia, Cyprus, Czechoslovakia, Denmark, Estonia, Finland, France, Georgia, Germany, Greece, Hungary, Iceland, Ireland, Italy, Kazakhstan, Kyrgyzstan, Latvia, Liechtenstein, Lithuania, Luxembourg, Malta, Moldova, Monaco, Netherlands, Norway, Poland, Portugal, Romania, Russia, San Marino, Slovenia, Spain, Sweden, Switzerland, Tajikistan, Turkey, Turkmenistan, Ukraine, UK, US, Uzbekistan, Vatican City, Yugoslavia
****

Conseil Europeen pour la Recherche Nucleaire (CERN)

Note - see European Organization for Nuclear Research (CERN)
****

Contadora Group (CG) - Note - was established 5 January 1983 (on the Panamanian island of Contadora) to reduce tensions and conflicts in Central America but evolved into the Rio Group (RG); members included Colombia, Mexico, Panama, Venezuela
****

Cooperation Council for the Arab States of the Gulf

Note - see Gulf Cooperation Council (GCC)
****

Coordinating Committee on Export Controls (COCOM)

established - NA 1949

aim - to control the export of strategic products and technical data from member countries to proscribed destinations<ATT>

members - (17) Australia, Belgium, Canada, Denmark, France, Germany, Greece, Italy, Japan, Luxembourg, Netherlands, Norway, Portugal, Spain, Turkey, UK, US

cooperating countries - (8) Austria, Finland, Ireland, South Korea, NZ, Singapore, Sweden, Switzerland
****

Council for Mutual Economic Assistance (CEMA)

Note - also known as CMEA or Comecon, was established 25 January 1949 to promote the development of socialist economies and was abolished 1 January 1991; members included Afghanistan (observer), Albania (had not participated since 1961 break with USSR), Angola (observer), Bulgaria, Cuba, Czechoslovakia, Ethiopia (observer), GDR, Hungary, Laos (observer), Mongolia, Mozambique (observer), Nicaragua (observer), Poland, Romania, USSR, Vietnam, Yemen (observer), Yugoslavia (associate)

****

Council of Arab Economic Unity (CAEU)

established - 3 June 1957

effective - 30 May 1964

aim - to promote economic integration among Arab nations

members - (11 plus the Palestine Liberation Organization) Egypt, Iraq, Jordan, Kuwait, Libya, Mauritania, Somalia, Sudan, Syria, UAE, Yemen, Palestine Liberation Organization

****

Council of Europe (CE)

established - 5 May 1949

effective - 3 August 1949

aim - to promote increased unity and quality of life in Europe

members - (28) Austria, Belgium, Belarus, Cyprus, Czechoslovakia, Denmark, Finland, France, Germany, Greece, Hungary, Iceland, Ireland, Italy, Liechtenstein, Luxembourg, Malta, Netherlands, Norway, Poland, Portugal, San Marino, Spain, Sweden, Switzerland, Turkey, Ukraine, UK

****

Council of the Entente (Entente)

established - 29 May 1959

aim - to promote economic, social, and political coordination

members - (5) Benin, Burkina, Ivory Coast, Niger, Togo

****

Customs Cooperation Council (CCC)

established - 15 December 1950

aim - to promote international cooperation in customs matters

members - (108) Algeria, Angola, Argentina, Australia, Austria, The Bahamas, Bangladesh, Belgium, Bermuda, Botswana, Brazil, Bulgaria, Burkina, Burundi, Cameroon, Canada, Central African Republic, Chile, China, Congo, Cuba, Cyprus, Czechoslovakia, Denmark, Egypt, Ethiopia, Finland, France, Gabon, The Gambia, Germany, Ghana, Greece, Guatemala, Guyana, Haiti, Hong Kong, Hungary, Iceland, India, Indonesia, Iran, Iraq, Ireland, Israel, Italy, Ivory Coast, Jamaica, Japan, Jordan, Kenya, South Korea, Lebanon, Lesotho, Liberia, Libya, Luxembourg, Madagascar, Malawi, Malaysia, Mali, Malta, Mauritania, Mauritius, Mexico, Morocco, Mozambique, Nepal, Netherlands, NZ, Niger, Nigeria, Norway,

Pakistan, Paraguay, Peru, Philippines, Poland, Portugal, Romania, Rwanda, Saudi Arabia, Senegal, Sierra Leone, Singapore, South Africa, Spain, Sri Lanka, Sudan, Swaziland, Sweden, Switzerland, Syria, Tanzania, Thailand, Togo, Trinidad and Tobago, Tunisia, Turkey, Uganda, UAE, UK, US, Uruguay, Yugoslavia, Zaire, Zambia, Zimbabwe

****

developed countries (DCs)

Note - the top group in the comprehensive but mutually exclusive hierarchy of developed countries (DCs), former USSR/Eastern Europe (former USSR/EE), and less developed countries (LDCs); includes the market-oriented economies of the mainly democratic nations in the Organization for Economic Cooperation and Development (OECD), Bermuda, Israel, South Africa, and the European ministates; also known as the First World, high-income countries, the North, industrial countries; generally have a per capita GNP/GDP in excess of $10,000 although some OECD countries and South Africa have figures well under $10,000 and two of the excluded OPEC countries have figures of more than $10,000. The 34 DCs are: Andorra, Australia, Austria, Belgium, Bermuda, Canada, Denmark, Faroe Islands, Finland, France, Germany, Greece, Iceland, Ireland, Israel, Italy, Japan, Liechtenstein, Luxembourg, Malta, Monaco, Netherlands, NZ, Norway, Portugal, San Marino, South Africa, Spain, Sweden, Switzerland, Turkey, UK, US, Vatican City

****

developing countries

Note - an imprecise term for the less developed countries with growing economies; see less developed countries (LDCs)

****

East African Development Bank (EADB)

established - 6 June 1967

effective - 1 December 1967

aim - to promote economic development

members - (3) Kenya, Tanzania, Uganda

****

Economic and Social Commission for Asia and the Pacific (ESCAP)

established - 28 March 1947 as Economic Commission for Asia and the Far East (ECAFE)

aim - to promote economic development as a regional commission for the UN's ECOSOC

members - (39) Afghanistan, Australia, Bangladesh, Bhutan, Brunei, Burma, Cambodia, China, Fiji, France, India, Indonesia, Iran, Japan, North Korea, South Korea, Laos, Malaysia, Maldives, Mongolia, Nauru, Nepal, Netherlands, NZ, Pakistan, Papua New Guinea, Philippines, Russia, Singapore, Solomon Islands, Sri Lanka, Thailand, Tonga, Tuvalu, UK, US, Vanuatu, Vietnam, Western Samoa associate members - (10) American Samoa, Cook Islands, Guam, Hong Kong, Kiribati, Marshall Islands, Federated States of Micronesia, Niue, Northern Mariana Islands, Trust Territory of the Pacific Islands (Palau)

****

Economic and Social Commission for Western Asia (ESCWA)

established - 9 August 1973 as Economic Commission for Western Asia (ECWA)

aim - to promote economic development as a regional commission for the UN's ECOSOC

members - (12 and the Palestine Liberation Organization) Bahrain, Egypt, Iraq, Jordan, Kuwait, Lebanon, Oman, Qatar, Saudi Arabia, Syria, UAE, Yemen, Palestine Liberation Organization

****

Economic and Social Council (ECOSOC)

established - 26 June 1945

effective - 24 October 1945

aim - to coordinate the economic and social work of the UN; includes five regional commissions (see Economic Commission for Africa, Economic Commission for Europe, Economic Commission for Latin America and the Caribbean, Economic and Social Commission for Asia and the Pacific, Economic and Social Commission for Western Asia) and six functional commissions (see Commission for Social Development, Commission on Human Rights, Commission on Narcotic Drugs, Commission on the Status of Women, Population Commission, and Statistical Commission)

members - (54) selected on a rotating basis from all regions

****

Economic Commission for Africa (ECA)

established - 29 April 1958

aim - to promote economic development as a regional commission of the UN's ECOSOC

members - (52) Algeria, Angola, Benin, Botswana, Burkina, Burundi, Cameroon, Cape Verde, Central African Republic, Chad, Comoros, Congo, Djibouti, Egypt, Equatorial Guinea, Ethiopia, Gabon, The Gambia, Ghana, Guinea, Guinea-Bissau, Ivory Coast, Kenya, Lesotho, Liberia, Libya, Madagascar, Malawi, Mali, Mauritania, Mauritius, Morocco, Mozambique, Namibia, Niger, Nigeria, Rwanda, Sao Tome and Principe, Senegal, Seychelles, Sierra Leone, Somalia, South Africa (suspended), Sudan, Swaziland, Tanzania, Togo, Tunisia, Uganda, Zaire, Zambia, Zimbabwe

****

Economic Commission for Asia and the Far East (ECAFE) <p>see Economic and Social Commission for Asia and the Pacific (ESCAP)

****

Economic Commission for Europe (ECE)

established - 28 March 1947

aim - to promote economic development as a regional commission of the UN's ECOSOC

members - (33) Albania, Austria, Belarus, Belgium, Bulgaria, Canada, Cyprus, Czechoslovakia, Denmark, Finland, France, Germany, Greece, Hungary, Iceland, Ireland, Italy, Luxembourg, Malta, Netherlands, Norway, Poland, Portugal, Romania, Russia, Spain, Sweden, Switzerland, Turkey, UK, Ukraine, US, Yugoslavia

****

Economic Commission for Latin America (ECLA) <p>see Economic Commission for Latin America and the Caribbean (ECLAC)

****

Economic Commission for Latin America and the Caribbean (ECLAC)

established - 25 February 1948 as Economic Commission for Latin America (ECLA)

aim - to promote economic development as a regional commission of the UN's ECOSOC

members - (41) Antigua and Barbuda, Argentina, The Bahamas, Barbados, Belize, Bolivia, Brazil, Canada, Chile, Colombia, Costa Rica, Cuba, Dominica, Dominican Republic, Ecuador, El Salvador, France, Grenada, Guatemala, Guyana, Haiti, Honduras, Jamaica, Mexico, Netherlands, Nicaragua, Panama, Paraguay, Peru, Portugal, Puerto Rico, Saint Kitts and Nevis, Saint Lucia, Saint Vincent and the Grenadines, Spain, Suriname, Trinidad and Tobago, UK, US, Uruguay, Venezuela

associate members - (5) Aruba, British Virgin Islands, Montserrat, Netherlands Antilles, Virgin Islands

****

Economic Commission for Western Asia (ECWA)

Note - see Economic and Social Commission for Western Asia (ESCWA)

****

Economic Community of Central African States (CEEAC) - acronym from Communaute Economique des Etats de l'Afrique Centrale

established - 18 October 1983

aim - to promote regional economic cooperation and establish a Central African Common Market

members - (10) Burundi, Cameroon, Central African Republic, Chad, Congo, Equatorial Guinea, Gabon, Rwanda, Sao Tome and Principe, Zaire

observer - (1) Angola

****

Economic Community of the Great Lakes Countries (CEPGL)

Note - acronym from Communaute Economique des Pays des Grands Lacs

established - 26 September 1976

aim - to promote regional economic cooperation and integration

members - (3) Burundi, Rwanda, Zaire

****

Economic Community of West African States (ECOWAS)

established - 28 May 1975

aim - to promote regional economic cooperation

members - (16) Benin, Burkina, Cape Verde, The Gambia, Ghana, Guinea, Guinea-Bissau, Ivory Coast, Liberia, Mali, Mauritania, Niger, Nigeria, Senegal, Sierra Leone, Togo

****

European Bank for Reconstruction and Development (EBRD)

established - 15 April 1991

aim - to facilitate the transition of seven centrally planned economies in Europe (Bulgaria, Czechoslovakia, Hungary, Poland, Romania, former USSR, and former Yugoslavia) to market economies by committing 60% of its loans to privatization

members - (35) Albania, Australia, Austria, Belgium, Canada, Cyprus, Denmark, European Community (EC), Egypt, European Investment Bank (EIB), Finland, France, Germany, Greece, Iceland, Ireland, Israel, Italy, Japan, South Korea, Liechtenstein, Luxembourg, Malta, Mexico, Morocco, Netherlands, NZ, Norway, Portugal, Spain, Sweden, Switzerland, Turkey, UK, US; note - includes all 24 members of the OECD and the EC as an institution

****

European Community (EC)

established - 8 April 1965

effective - 1 July 1967

aim - a fusing of the European Atomic Energy Community (Euratom), the European Coal and Steel Community (ESC), and the European Economic Community (EEC or Common Market); the EC plans to establish a completely integrated common market in 1992 and an eventual federation of Europe

members - (12) Belgium, Denmark, France, Germany, Greece, Ireland, Italy, Luxembourg, Netherlands, Portugal, Spain, UK

associate member - (1) Czechoslovakia

****

European Free Trade Association (EFTA)

established - 4 January 1960

effective - 3 May 1960

aim - to promote expansion of free trade

members - (6) Austria, Finland, Iceland, Norway, Sweden, Switzerland

****

European Investment Bank (EIB)

established - 25 March 1957

effective - 1 January 1958

aim - to promote economic development of the EC

members - (12) Belgium, Denmark, France, Germany, Greece, Ireland, Italy, Luxembourg, Netherlands, Portugal, Spain, UK

****

European Organization for Nuclear Research (CERN)

Note - acronym retained from the predecessor organization Conseil Europeen pour la Recherche Nucleaire

established - 1 July 1953

effective - 29 September 1954

aim - to foster nuclear research for peaceful purposes only

members - (16) Austria, Belgium, Denmark, Finland, France, Germany, Greece, Italy, Netherlands, Norway, Poland, Portugal, Spain, Sweden, Switzerland, UK

observers - (2) Turkey, Yugoslavia

****

European Space Agency (ESA)

established - 31 July 1973

effective - 1 May 1975

aim - to promote peaceful cooperation in space research and technology

members - (13) Austria, Belgium, Denmark, France, Germany, Ireland, Italy, Netherlands, Norway, Spain, Sweden, Switzerland, UK

associate member - (1) Finland

****

First World

Note - another term for countries with advanced, industrialized economies; this term is fading from use; see developed countries (DCs)

****

Food and Agriculture Organization (FAO)

established - 16 October 1945

aim - UN specialized agency to raise living standards and increase availability of agricultural products

members - (157) all UN members except Armenia, Azerbaijan, Belarus, Bosnia and Hercegovina, Brunei, Croatia, Estonia, Kazakhstan, Kyrgyzstan, Latvia, Liechtenstein, Lithuania, Marshall Islands, Federated States of Micronesia, Moldova, Russia, San Marino, Singapore, Slovenia, South Africa, Tajikistan, Turkmenistan, Ukraine, Uzbekistan; other members are Cook Islands, Switzerland, Tonga

****

Former USSR/Eastern Europe (former USSR/EE)

Note - the middle group in the comprehensive but mutually exclusive hierarchy of developed countries (DCs), former USSR/Eastern Europe (former USSR/EE), and less developed countries (LDCs); these countries are in political and economic transition and may well be grouped differently in the near future; this includes Albania, Armenia,

Azerbaijan, Belarus, Bosnia and Hercegovina, Bulgaria, Croatia, Czecholovakia, Estonia, Georgia, Hungary, Kazakhstan, Kyrgyzstan, Latvia, Lithuania, Moldova, Poland, Romania, Russia, Slovenia, Tajikistan, Turkmenistan, Uzbekistan, Yugoslavia
****

Four Dragons

Note - the four small Asian less developed countries (LDCs) that have experienced unusually rapid economic growth; also known as the Four Tigers; this group includes Hong Kong, South Korea, Singapore, Taiwan
****

Four Tigers

Note - another term for the Four Dragons; see Four Dragons
****

Franc Zone (FZ)

established - NA

aim - monetary union among countries whose currencies are linked to the French franc

members - (15) Benin, Burkina, Cameroon, Central African Republic, Chad, Comoros, Congo, Equatorial Guinea, France, Gabon, Ivory Coast, Mali, Niger, Senegal, Togo; note - France includes metropolitan France, the four overseas departments of France (French Guiana, Guadeloupe, Martinique, Reunion), the two territorial collectivities of France (Mayotte, Saint Pierre and Miquelon), and the three overseas territories of France (French Polynesia, New Caledonia, Wallis and Futuna)
****

Front Line States (FLS)

established - NA

aim - to achieve black majority rule in South Africa

members - (7) Angola, Botswana, Mozambique, Namibia, Tanzania, Zambia, Zimbabwe
****

General Agreement on Tariffs and Trade (GATT)

established - 30 October 1947

effective - 1 January 1948

aim - to promote the expansion of international trade on a nondiscriminatory basis

members - (98) Antigua and Barbuda, Argentina, Australia, Austria, Bangladesh, Barbados, Belgium, Belize, Benin, Botswana, Brazil, Burkina, Burma, Burundi, Cameroon, Canada, Central African Republic, Chad, Chile, Colombia, Congo, Cuba, Cyprus, Czechoslovakia, Denmark, Dominican Republic, Egypt, Finland, France, Gabon, The Gambia, Germany, Ghana, Greece, Guatemala, Guyana, Haiti, Hong Kong, Hungary, Iceland, India, Indonesia, Ireland, Israel, Italy, Ivory Coast, Jamaica, Japan, Kenya, South Korea, Kuwait, Lesotho, Luxembourg, Madagascar, Malawi, Malaysia, Maldives, Malta, Mauritania, Mauritius, Mexico, Morocco, Netherlands, NZ, Nicaragua, Niger, Nigeria, Norway, Pakistan, Peru, Philippines, Poland, Portugal, Romania, Rwanda, Senegal,

Sierra Leone, Singapore, South Africa, Spain, Sri Lanka, Suriname, Sweden, Switzerland, Tanzania, Thailand, Togo, Trinidad and Tobago, Tunisia, Turkey, Uganda, UK, US, Uruguay, Yugoslavia, Zaire, Zambia, Zimbabwe

****

Group of 2 (G-2)

established - informal term that came into use about 1986

aim - bilateral economic cooperation between the two most powerful economic giants

members - (2) Japan, US

****

Group of 3 (G-3)

established - NA October 1990

aim - mechanism for policy coordination

members - (3) Colombia, Mexico, Venezuela

****

Group of 5 (G-5)

established - 22 September 1985

aim - the five major non-Communist economic powers

members - (5) France, Germany, Japan, UK, US

****

Group of 6 (G-6)

Note - not to be confused with the Big Six

established - 22 May 1984

aim - seeks to achieve nuclear disarmament

members - (6) Argentina, Greece, India, Mexico, Sweden, Tanzania

****

Group of 7 (G-7)

Note - membership is the same as the Big Seven

established - 22 September 1985

aim - the seven major non-Communist economic powers

members - (7) Group of 5 (France, Germany, Japan, UK, US) plus Canada and Italy

****

Group of 8 (G-8)

established - NA October 1975

aim - the developed countries (DCs) that participated in the Conference on International Economic Cooperation (CIEC), held in several sessions between NA December 1975 and 3 June 1977

members - (8) Australia, Canada, EC (as one member), Japan, Spain, Sweden, Switzerland, US

****

Group of 9 (G-9)

established - NA

aim - informal group that meets occasionally on matters of mutual interest

members - (9) Austria, Belgium, Bulgaria, Denmark, Finland, Hungary, Romania, Sweden, Yugoslavia

****

Group of 10 (G-10)

Note - also known as the Paris Club

established - NA October 1962

aim - wealthiest members of the IMF who provide most of the money to be loaned and act as the informal steering committee; name persists in spite of the addition of Switzerland on NA April 1984

members - (11) Belgium, Canada, France, Germany, Italy, Japan, Netherlands, Sweden, Switzerland, UK, US

****

Group of 11 (G-11)

Note - also known as the Cartagena Group

established - 22 June 1984, in Cartagena, Colombia

aim - forum for largest debtor nations in Latin America

members - (11) Argentina, Bolivia, Brazil, Chile, Colombia, Dominican Republic, Ecuador, Mexico, Peru, Uruguay, Venezuela

****

Group of 15 (G-15)

Note - byproduct of the Non-Aligned Movement

established - 1989

aim - to promote economic cooperation among developing nations; to act as the main political organ for the Non-Aligned Movement

members - (15) Algeria, Argentina, Brazil, Egypt, India, Indonesia, Jamaica, Malaysia, Mexico, Nigeria, Peru, Senegal, Venezuela, Yugoslavia, Zimbabwe

****

Group of 19 (G-19)

established - NA October 1975

aim - the less developed countries (LDCs) that participated in the Conference on International Economic Cooperation (CIEC) held in several sessions between NA December 1975 and 3 June 1977

members - (19) Algeria, Argentina, Brazil, Cameroon, Egypt, India, Indonesia, Iran, Iraq, Jamaica, Mexico, Nigeria, Pakistan, Peru, Saudi Arabia, Venezuela, Yugoslavia, Zaire, Zambia

****

Group of 24 (G-24)

established - NA January 1972

aim - to promote the interests of developing countries in Africa, Asia, and Latin America within the IMF

members - (24) Algeria, Argentina, Brazil, Colombia, Egypt,
Ethiopia, Gabon, Ghana, Guatemala, India, Iran, Ivory Coast,
Lebanon, Mexico, Nigeria, Pakistan, Peru, Philippines, Sri Lanka,
Syria, Trinidad and Tobago, Venezuela, Yugoslavia, Zaire
****

Group of 30 (G-30)

established - NA 1979

aim - to discuss and propose solutions to the world's economic problems

members - (30) informal group of 30 leading international bankers, economists, financial experts, and businessmen organized by Johannes Witteveen (former managing
director of the IMF)
****

Group of 33 (G-33)

established - NA 1987

aim - to promote solutions to international economic problems

members - (33) leading economists from 13 countries
****

Group of 77 (G-77)

established - NA October 1967

aim - to promote economic cooperation among developing countries; name persists in
spite of increased membership

members - (127 plus the Palestine Liberation Organization)
Afghanistan, Algeria, Angola, Antigua and Barbuda, Argentina, The
Bahamas, Bahrain, Bangladesh, Barbados, Belize, Benin, Bhutan,
Bolivia, Botswana, Brazil, Brunei, Burkina, Burma, Burundi,
Cambodia, Cameroon, Cape Verde, Central African Republic, Chad,
Chile, Colombia, Comoros, Congo, Costa Rica, Cuba, Cyprus,
Djibouti, Dominica, Dominican Republic, Ecuador, Egypt, El
Salvador, Equatorial Guinea, Ethiopia, Fiji, Gabon, The Gambia,
Ghana, Grenada, Guatemala, Guinea, Guinea-Bissau, Guyana, Haiti,
Honduras, India, Indonesia, Iran, Iraq, Ivory Coast, Jamaica,
Jordan, Kenya, North Korea, South Korea, Kuwait, Laos, Lebanon,
Lesotho, Liberia, Libya, Madagascar, Malawi, Malaysia, Maldives,
Mali, Malta, Mauritania, Mauritius, Mexico, Mongolia, Morocco,
Mozambique, Namibia, Nepal, Nicaragua, Niger, Nigeria, Oman,
Pakistan, Panama, Papua New Guinea, Paraguay, Peru, Philippines,
Qatar, Romania, Rwanda, Saint Kitts and Nevis, Saint Lucia, Saint
Vincent and the Grenadines, Sao Tome and Principe, Saudi Arabia,
Senegal, Seychelles, Sierra Leone, Singapore, Solomon Islands,
Somalia, Sri Lanka, Sudan, Suriname, Swaziland, Syria, Tanzania,
Thailand, Togo, Tonga, Trinidad and Tobago, Tunisia, Uganda, UAE,
Uruguay, Vanuatu, Venezuela, Vietnam, Western Samoa, Yemen,
Yugoslavia, Zaire, Zambia, Zimbabwe, Palestine Liberation
Organization
****

Gulf Cooperation Council (GCC)

Note - also known as the Cooperation Council for the Arab States of the Gulf

established - 25-26 May 1981

aim - to promote regional cooperation in economic, social, political, and military affairs

members - (6) Bahrain, Kuwait, Oman, Qatar, Saudi Arabia, UAE

****

Habitat

Note - see United Nations Center for Human Settlements (UNCHS)

****

Hexagonal Group

Note - HG - the old Pentagonal Group plus one)

established - July 1991

aim - to form an economic and political cooperation group for the region between the Adriatic and the Baltic Seas

members - (6) Austria, Czechoslovakia, Hungary, Italy, Poland, Yugoslavia

****

high-income countries

Note - another term for the industrialized countries with high per capita GNPs/GDPs; see developed countries (DCs)

****

industrial countries

Note - another term for the developed countries; see developed countries (DCs)

****

Inter-American Development Bank (IADB)

Note - also known as Banco Interamericano de Desarvollo (BID)

established - 8 April 1959

effective - 30 December 1959

aim - to promote economic and social development in Latin America

members - (44) Argentina, Austria, The Bahamas, Barbados, Belgium, Bolivia, Brazil, Canada, Chile, Colombia, Costa Rica, Denmark, Dominican Republic, Ecuador, El Salvador, Finland, France, Germany, Guatemala, Guyana, Haiti, Honduras, Israel, Italy, Jamaica, Japan, Mexico, Netherlands, Nicaragua, Norway, Panama, Paraguay, Peru, Portugal, Spain, Suriname, Sweden, Switzerland, Trinidad and Tobago, UK, US, Uruguay, Venezuela, Yugoslavia

****

Inter-Governmental Authority on Drought and Development (IGADD)

established - NA January 1986

aim - to promote cooperation on drought-related matters

members - (6) Djibouti, Ethiopia, Kenya, Somalia, Sudan, Uganda

****

International Atomic Energy Agency (IAEA)

established - 26 October 1956

effective - 29 July 1957

aim - to promote peaceful uses of atomic energy

members - (115) Afghanistan, Albania, Algeria, Argentina,
Australia, Austria, Bangladesh, Belarus, Belgium, Bolivia,
Brazil, Bulgaria, Burma, Cambodia, Cameroon, Canada, Chile,
China, Colombia, Costa Rica, Cuba, Cyprus, Czechoslovakia,
Denmark, Dominican Republic, Ecuador, Egypt, El Salvador,
Estonia, Ethiopia, Finland, France, Gabon, Germany, Ghana,
Greece, Guatemala, Haiti, Hungary, Iceland, India, Indonesia,
Iran, Iraq, Ireland, Israel, Italy, Ivory Coast, Jamaica, Japan,
Jordan, Kenya, North Korea, South Korea, Kuwait, Latvia, Lebanon,
Liberia, Libya, Liechtenstein, Lithuania, Luxembourg, Madagascar,
Malaysia, Mali, Mauritius, Mexico, Monaco, Mongolia, Morocco,
Namibia, Netherlands, NZ, Nicaragua, Niger, Nigeria, Norway,
Pakistan, Panama, Paraguay, Peru, Philippines, Poland, Portugal,
Qatar, Romania, Russia, Saudi Arabia, Senegal, Sierra Leone,
Singapore, South Africa, Spain, Sri Lanka, Sudan, Sweden,
Switzerland, Syria, Tanzania, Thailand, Tunisia, Turkey, Uganda,
Ukraine, UAE, UK, US, Uruguay, Vatican City, Venezuela, Vietnam,
Yugoslavia, Zaire, Zambia, Zimbabwe

****

International Bank for Economic Cooperation (IBEC)

Note - established in 22 October 1963; aim was to promote
economic cooperation and development - members were Bulgaria,
Cuba, Czechoslovakia, East Germany, Hungary, Mongolia, Poland,
Romania, USSR, Vietnam; now a Russian bank with a new charter

****

International Bank for Reconstruction and Development (IBRD)

Note - also known as the World Bank

established - 22 July 1944

effective - 27 December 1945

aim - UN specialized agency that initially promoted economic rebuilding after World
War II and now provides economic development loans

members - (156) all UN members except Armenia, Azerbaijan,
Brunei, Cuba, Estonia, Kazakhstan, North Korea, Kyrgyzstan,
Latvia, Liechtenstein, Lithuania, Marshall Islands, Federated
States of Micronesia, Moldova, San Marino, Tajikistan,
Turkmenistan, Ukraine, Uzbekistan; other members are Kiribati,
Tonga

****

International Chamber of Commerce (ICC)

established - NA 1919

aim - to promote free trade and private enterprise and to represent business interests at national and international levels

members - (58 national councils) Argentina, Australia, Austria, Belgium, Brazil, Burkina, Cameroon, Canada, Colombia, Cyprus, Denmark, Ecuador, Egypt, Finland, France, Gabon, Germany, Greece, Iceland, India, Indonesia, Iran, Ireland, Israel, Italy, Ivory Coast, Japan, Jordan, South Korea, Lebanon, Luxembourg, Madagascar, Mexico, Morocco, Netherlands, Nigeria, Norway, Pakistan, Portugal, Saudi Arabia, Senegal, Singapore, South Africa, Spain, Sri Lanka, Sweden, Switzerland, Syria, Taiwan, Togo, Tunisia, Turkey, UK, US, Uruguay, Venezuela, Yugoslavia, Zaire

****

International Civil Aviation Organization (ICAO)

established - 7 December 1944

effective - 4 April 1947

aim - UN specialized agency to promote international cooperation in civil aviation

members - (164) all UN members except Armenia, Azerbaijan, Belarus, Bosnia and Hercegovina, Croatia, Dominica, Estonia, Kazakhstan, Kyrgyzstan, Latvia, Liechtenstein, Lithuania, Moldova, Saint Kitts and Nevis, Slovenia, Tajikistan, Turkmenistan, Ukraine, Uzbekistan, Western Samoa; other members are Cook Islands, Kiribati, Monaco, Nauru, Switzerland, Tonga

****

International Committee of the Red Cross (ICRC)

established - NA 1863

aim - to provide humanitarian aid in wartime

members - (25 individuals) all Swiss nationals

****

International Confederation of Free Trade Unions (ICFTU)

established - NA December 1949

aim - to promote the trade union movement

members - (144 national organizations in the following 103 areas) Antigua and Barbuda, Argentina, Australia, Austria, The Bahamas, Bangladesh, Barbados, Basque Country, Belgium, Bermuda, Botswana, Brazil, Bulgaria, Burkina, Canada, Central African Republic, Chad, Chile, Colombia, Costa Rica, Curacao, Cyprus, Czechoslovakia, Denmark, Dominica, Dominican Republic, Ecuador, El Salvador, Estonia, Falkland Islands, Fiji, Finland, France, French Polynesia, The Gambia, Germany, Greece, Grenada, Guatemala, Guyana, Honduras, Hong Kong, Iceland, India, Indonesia, Israel, Italy, Jamaica, Japan, Kiribati, South Korea, Lebanon, Lesotho, Liberia, Luxembourg, Madagascar, Malawi, Malaysia, Malta, Mauritius, Mexico, Montserrat, Morocco, Netherlands, New Caledonia, NZ, Nicaragua, Norway, Pakistan, Panama, Papua New Guinea, Peru, Philippines, Poland, Portugal,

Puerto Rico, Russia, Saint Helena, Saint Kitts and Nevis, Saint
Lucia, Saint Vincent and the Grenadines, San Marino, Seychelles,
Sierra Leone, Singapore, Spain, Sri Lanka, Suriname, Swaziland,
Sweden, Switzerland, Taiwan, Thailand, Tonga, Trinidad and
Tobago, Tunisia, Turkey, Uganda, UK, US, Vatican City, Venezuela,
Western Samoa

****

International Court of Justice (ICJ)

Note - also known as the World Court

established - 26 June 1945

effective - 24 October 1945

aim - primary judicial organ of the UN

members - (15 judges) elected by the General Assembly and Security Council to
represent all principal legal systems

****

International Criminal Police Organization (INTERPOL)

established - 13 June 1956

aim - to promote international cooperation between criminal police authorities

members - (152) Albania, Algeria, Andorra, Angola, Antigua and
Barbuda, Argentina, Aruba, Australia, Austria, The Bahamas,
Bahrain, Bangladesh, Barbados, Belgium, Belize, Benin, Bolivia,
Botswana, Brazil, Brunei, Burkina, Burma, Burundi, Cambodia,
Cameroon, Canada, Cape Verde, Central African Republic, Chad,
Chile, China, Colombia, Congo, Costa Rica, Cuba, Cyprus, Denmark,
Djibouti, Dominica, Dominican Republic, Ecuador, Egypt,
Equatorial Guinea, Ethiopia, Fiji, Finland, France, Gabon, The
Gambia, Germany, Ghana, Greece, Grenada, Guatemala, Guinea,
Guyana, Haiti, Honduras, Hungary, Iceland, India, Indonesia,
Iran, Iraq, Ireland, Northern Ireland, Israel, Italy, Ivory
Coast, Jamaica, Japan, Jordan, Kenya, Kiribati, South Korea,
Kuwait, Laos, Lebanon, Lesotho, Liberia, Libya, Liechtenstein,
Luxembourg, Madagascar, Malawi, Malaysia, Maldives, Mali, Malta,
Mauritania, Mauritius, Mexico, Monaco, Morocco, Mozambique,
Nauru, Nepal, Netherlands, Netherlands Antilles, NZ, Nicaragua,
Niger, Nigeria, Norway, Oman, Pakistan, Panama, Papua New Guinea,
Paraguay, Peru, Philippines, Portugal, Qatar, Romania, Russia,
Rwanda, Saint Kitts and Nevis, Saint Lucia, Saint Vincent and the
Grenadines, Sao Tome and Principe, Saudi Arabia, Senegal,
Seychelles, Sierra Leone, Singapore, Somalia, Spain, Sri Lanka,
Sudan, Suriname, Swaziland, Sweden, Switzerland, Syria, Tanzania,
Thailand, Togo, Tonga, Trinidad and Tobago, Tunisia, Turkey,
Uganda, UAE, UK, US, Uruguay, Venezuela, Yemen, Yugoslavia,
Zaire, Zambia, Zimbabwe

****

International Development Association (IDA)

established - 26 January 1960

effective - 24 September 1960

aim - UN specialized agency and IBRD affiliate that provides economic loans for low income countries

members - (136) Part I - (22 more economically advanced countries) Australia, Austria, Belgium, Canada, Denmark, Finland, France, Germany, Iceland, Ireland, Italy, Japan, Kuwait, Luxembourg, Netherlands, NZ, Norway, South Africa, Sweden, UAE, UK, US

members - Part II - (114 less developed nations) Afghanistan, Algeria, Argentina, Bangladesh, Belize, Benin, Bhutan, Bolivia, Botswana, Brazil, Burkina, Burma, Burundi, Cambodia, Cameroon, Cape Verde, Central African Republic, Chad, Chile, China, Colombia, Comoros, Congo, Costa Rica, Cyprus, Djibouti, Dominica, Dominican Republic, Ecuador, Egypt, El Salvador, Equatorial Guinea, Ethiopia, Fiji, Gabon, The Gambia, Ghana, Greece, Grenada, Guatemala, Guinea, Guinea-Bissau, Guyana, Haiti, Honduras, Hungary, India, Indonesia, Iran, Iraq, Israel, Ivory Coast, Jordan, Kenya, Kiribati, South Korea, Laos, Lebanon, Lesotho, Liberia, Libya, Madagascar, Malawi, Malaysia, Maldives, Mali, Mauritania, Mauritius, Mexico, Morocco, Mozambique, Nepal, Nicaragua, Niger, Nigeria, Oman, Pakistan, Panama, Papua New Guinea, Paraguay, Peru, Philippines, Poland, Rwanda, Saint Kitts and Nevis, Saint Lucia, Saint Vincent and the Grenadines, Sao Tome and Principe, Saudi Arabia, Senegal, Sierra Leone, Solomon Islands, Somalia, Spain, Sri Lanka, Sudan, Swaziland, Syria, Tanzania, Thailand, Togo, Tonga, Trinidad and Tobago, Tunisia, Turkey, Uganda, Vanuatu, Vietnam, Western Samoa, Yemen, Yugoslavia, Zaire, Zambia, Zimbabwe

****

International Energy Agency (IEA)

established - 15 November 1974

aim - established by the OECD to promote cooperation on energy matters, especially emergency oil sharing and relations between oil consumers and oil producers

members - (21) Australia, Austria, Belgium, Canada, Denmark, Germany, Greece, Ireland, Italy, Japan, Luxembourg, Netherlands, NZ, Norway, Portugal, Spain, Sweden, Switzerland, Turkey, UK, US

****

International Finance Corporation (IFC)

established - 25 May 1955

effective - 20 July 1956

aim - UN specialized agency and IBRD affiliate that helps private enterprise sector in economic development

members - (133) Afghanistan, Antigua and Barbuda, Argentina, Australia, Austria, The Bahamas, Bangladesh, Barbados, Belgium, Belize, Benin, Bolivia, Botswana, Brazil, Burkina, Burma, Burundi, Cameroon, Canada, Chile, China, Colombia, Congo, Costa Rica, Cyprus, Denmark, Djibouti, Dominica, Dominican Republic, Ecuador, Egypt, El Salvador, Ethiopia, Fiji, Finland, France,

Gabon, The Gambia, Germany, Ghana, Greece, Grenada, Guatemala,
Guinea, Guinea-Bissau, Guyana, Haiti, Honduras, Hungary, Iceland,
India, Indonesia, Iran, Iraq, Ireland, Israel, Italy, Ivory
Coast, Jamaica, Japan, Jordan, Kenya, Kiribati, South Korea,
Kuwait, Lebanon, Lesotho, Liberia, Libya, Luxembourg, Madagascar,
Malawi, Malaysia, Maldives, Mali, Mauritania, Mauritius, Mexico,
Morocco, Mozambique, Nepal, Netherlands, NZ, Nicaragua, Niger,
Nigeria, Norway, Oman, Pakistan, Panama, Papua New Guinea,
Paraguay, Peru, Philippines, Portugal, Romania, Rwanda, Saint
Lucia, Saudi Arabia, Senegal, Seychelles, Sierra Leone,
Singapore, Solomon Islands, Somalia, South Africa, Spain, Sri
Lanka, Sudan, Swaziland, Sweden, Syria, Tanzania, Thailand, Togo,
Tonga, Trinidad and Tobago, Tunisia, Turkey, Uganda, UAE, UK, US,
Uruguay, Vanuatu, Venezuela, Vietnam, Western Samoa, Yemen,
Yugoslavia, Zaire, Zambia, Zimbabwe

****

International Fund for Agricultural Development (IFAD)

established - NA November 1974

aim - UN specialized agency that promotes agricultural development

members - (144) Category I - (21 industrialized aid contributors)
Australia, Austria, Belgium, Canada, Denmark, Finland, France,
Germany, Greece, Ireland, Italy, Japan, Luxembourg, Netherlands,
NZ, Norway, Spain, Sweden, Switzerland, UK, US

members - Category II - (12 petroleum-exporting aid contributors) Algeria, Gabon,
Indonesia, Iran, Iraq, Kuwait, Libya, Nigeria, Qatar, Saudi Arabia, UAE, Venezuela

members - Category III - (111 aid recipients) Afghanistan,
Angola, Antigua and Barbuda, Argentina, Bangladesh, Barbados,
Belize, Benin, Bhutan, Bolivia, Botswana, Brazil, Burkina, Burma,
Burundi, Cameroon, Cape Verde, Central African Republic, Chad,
Chile, China, Colombia, Comoros, Congo, Costa Rica, Cuba, Cyprus,
Djibouti, Dominica, Dominican Republic, Ecuador, Egypt, El
Salvador, Equatorial Guinea, Ethiopia, Fiji, The Gambia, Ghana,
Grenada, Guatemala, Guinea, Guinea-Bissau, Guyana, Haiti,
Honduras, India, Israel, Ivory Coast, Jamaica, Jordan, Kenya,
North Korea, South Korea, Laos, Lebanon, Lesotho, Liberia,
Madagascar, Malawi, Malaysia, Maldives, Mali, Malta, Mauritania,
Mauritius, Mexico, Morocco, Mozambique, Nepal, Nicaragua, Niger,
Oman, Pakistan, Panama, Papua New Guinea, Paraguay, Peru,
Philippines, Portugal, Romania, Rwanda, Saint Kitts and Nevis,
Saint Lucia, Saint Vincent and the Grenadines, Sao Tome and
Principe, Senegal, Seychelles, Sierra Leone, Solomon Islands,
Somalia, Sri Lanka, Sudan, Suriname, Swaziland, Syria, Tanzania,
Thailand, Togo, Tonga, Trinidad and Tobago, Tunisia, Turkey,
Uganda, Uruguay, Vietnam, Western Samoa, Yemen, Yugoslavia,
Zaire, Zambia, Zimbabwe

****

International Investment Bank (IIB)

Note - established on 7 July 1970; to promote economic development; members were Bulgaria, Cuba, Czechoslovakia, East Germany, Hungary, Mongolia, Poland, Romania, USSR, Vietnam; now a Russian bank with a new charter

****

International Labor Organization (ILO)

established - 11 April 1919 (affiliated with the UN 14 December 1946)

aim - UN specialized agency concerned with world labor issues

members - (150) all UN members except Armenia, Azerbaijan, Bhutan, Bosnia and Hercegovina, Brunei, Croatia, Estonia, The Gambia, Kazakhstan, Kyrgyzstan, Latvia, Liechtenstein, Lithuania, Maldives, Marshall Islands, Federation of Micronesia, Moldova, Oman, Saint Kitts and Nevis, Saint Vincent and the Grenadines, San Marino, Slovenia, South Africa, Tajikistan, Turkmenistan, Uzbekistan, Vanuatu, Vietnam, Western Samoa; other member is Switzerland

****

International Maritime Organization (IMO)

Note - name changed from Intergovernmental Maritime Consultative Organization (IMCO) on 22 May 1982

established - 17 March 1958

aim - UN specialized agency concerned with world maritime affairs

members - (135) Algeria, Angola, Antigua and Barbuda, Argentina, Australia, Austria, The Bahamas, Bahrain, Bangladesh, Barbados, Belgium, Belize, Benin, Bolivia, Brazil, Brunei, Bulgaria, Burma, Cambodia, Cameroon, Canada, Cape Verde, Chile, China, Colombia, Congo, Costa Rica, Cuba, Cyprus, Czechoslovakia, Denmark, Djibouti, Dominica, Dominican Republic, Ecuador, Egypt, El Salvador, Equatorial Guinea, Ethiopia, Fiji, Finland, France, Gabon, The Gambia, Germany, Ghana, Greece, Guatemala, Guinea, Guinea-Bissau, Guyana, Haiti, Honduras, Hungary, Iceland, India, Indonesia, Iran, Iraq, Ireland, Israel, Italy, Ivory Coast, Jamaica, Japan, Jordan, Kenya, North Korea, South Korea, Kuwait, Lebanon, Liberia, Libya, Luxembourg, Madagascar, Malawi, Malaysia, Maldives, Malta, Mauritania, Mauritius, Mexico, Monaco, Morocco, Mozambique, Nepal, Netherlands, NZ, Nicaragua, Nigeria, Norway, Oman, Pakistan, Panama, Papua New Guinea, Peru, Philippines, Poland, Portugal, Qatar, Romania, Russia, Saint Lucia, Saint Vincent and the Grenadines, Sao Tome and Principe, Saudi Arabia, Senegal, Seychelles, Sierra Leone, Singapore, Solomon Islands, Somalia, Spain, Sri Lanka, Sudan, Suriname, Sweden, Switzerland, Syria, Tanzania, Thailand, Togo, Trinidad and Tobago, Tunisia, Turkey, UAE, UK, US, Uruguay, Vanuatu, Venezuela, Vietnam, Yemen, Yugoslavia, Zaire

associate members - (2) Hong Kong, Macao

****

International Maritime Satellite Organization (INMARSAT)

established - 3 September 1976

effective - 26 July 1979

aim - to provide worldwide communications for maritime and other applications

members - (63) Algeria, Argentina, Australia, Bahrain, Belarus, Belgium, Brazil, Bulgaria, Cameroon, Canada, Chile, China, Colombia, Cuba, Czechoslovakia, Denmark, Egypt, Finland, France, Gabon, Germany, Greece, India, Indonesia, Iran, Iraq, Ireland, Israel, Italy, Japan, South Korea, Kuwait, Liberia, Malaysia, Monaco, Mozambique, Netherlands, NZ, Nigeria, Norway, Oman, Pakistan, Panama, Peru, Philippines, Poland, Portugal, Qatar, Romania, Russia, Saudi Arabia, Singapore, Spain, Sri Lanka, Sweden, Switzerland, Tunisia, Turkey, Ukraine, UAE, UK, US, Yugoslavia

****

International Monetary Fund (IMF)

established - 22 July 1944

effective - 27 December 1945

aim - UN specialized agency concerned with world monetary stability and economic development

members - (156) all UN members except Armenia, Azerbaijan, Belarus, Bosnia and Hercegovina, Brunei, Croatia, Cuba, Estonia, Kazakhstan, North Korea, Kyrgyzstan, Latvia, Liechtenstein, Lithuania, Marshall Islands, Federated States of Micronesia, Moldova, Russia, San Marino, Slovenia, Tajikistan, Turkmenistan, Ukraine, Uzbekistan; other members are Kiribati and Tonga

****

International Olympic Committee (IOC)

established - 23 June 1894

aim - to promote the Olympic ideals and administer the Olympic games: 1992 Winter Olympics in Albertville, France (8-23 February); 1992 Summer Olympics in Barcelona, Spain (25 July-9 August); 1994 Winter Olympics in Lillehammer; Norway (12-27 February); 1996 Summer Olympics in Atlanta, United States (20 July-4 August); 1998 Winter Olympics in Nagano, Japan (date NA)

members - (167) Afghanistan, Albania, Algeria, American Samoa, Andorra, Angola, Antigua and Barbuda, Argentina, Aruba, Australia, Austria, The Bahamas, Bahrain, Bangladesh, Barbados, Belarus, Belgium, Belize, Benin, Bermuda, Bhutan, Bolivia, Botswana, Brazil, British Virgin Islands, Brunei, Bulgaria, Burkina, Burma, Cameroon, Canada, Cayman Islands, Central African Republic, Chad, Chile, China, Colombia, Congo, Cook Islands, Costa Rica, Cuba, Cyprus, Czechoslovakia, Denmark, Djibouti, Dominican Republic, Ecuador, Egypt, El Salvador, Equatorial Guinea, Ethiopia, Fiji, Finland, France, Gabon, The Gambia, Germany, Ghana, Greece, Grenada, Guam, Guatemala, Guinea, Guyana, Haiti, Honduras, Hong Kong, Hungary, Iceland, India, Indonesia,

Iran, Iraq, Ireland, Israel, Italy, Ivory Coast, Jamaica, Japan, Jordan, Kenya, North Korea, South Korea, Kuwait, Laos, Lebanon, Lesotho, Liberia, Libya, Liechtenstein, Luxembourg, Madagascar, Malawi, Malaysia, Maldives, Mali, Malta, Mauritania, Mauritius, Mexico, Monaco, Mongolia, Morocco, Mozambique, Nepal, Netherlands, Netherlands Antilles, NZ, Nicaragua, Niger, Nigeria, Norway, Oman, Pakistan, Panama, Papua New Guinea, Paraguay, Peru, Philippines, Poland, Portugal, Puerto Rico, Qatar, Romania, Russia, Rwanda, Saint Vincent and the Grenadines, San Marino, Saudi Arabia, Senegal, Seychelles, Sierra Leone, Singapore, Solomon Islands, Somalia, Spain, Sri Lanka, Sudan, Suriname, Swaziland, Sweden, Switzerland, Syria, Taiwan, Tanzania, Thailand, Togo, Tonga, Trinidad and Tobago, Tunisia, Turkey, Uganda, Ukraine, UAE, UK, US, Uruguay, Vanuatu, Venezuela, Vietnam, Virgin Islands, Western Samoa, Yemen, Yugoslavia, Zaire, Zambia, Zimbabwe

****

International Organization for Migration (IOM) - established as Provisional Intergovernmental Committee for the Movement of Migrants from Europe; renamed Intergovernmental Committee for European Migration (ICEM) on 15 November 1952; renamed Intergovernmental Committee for Migration (ICM) in November 1980; current name adopted 14 November 1989

established - 5 December 1951

aim - to facilitate orderly international emigration and immigration

members - (39) Argentina, Australia, Austria, Bangladesh, Belgium, Bolivia, Canada, Chile, Colombia, Costa Rica, Cyprus, Denmark, Dominican Republic, Ecuador, El Salvador, Germany, Greece, Guatemala, Honduras, Israel, Italy, Kenya, South Korea, Luxembourg, Netherlands, Nicaragua, Norway, Panama, Paraguay, Peru, Philippines, Portugal, Sri Lanka, Sweden, Switzerland, Thailand, US, Uruguay, Venezuela

observers - (25) Belize, Brazil, Cape Verde, Egypt, Finland, France, Ghana, Guinea-Bissau, Hungary, Japan, Mexico, NZ, Pakistan, San Marino, Somalia, Sovereign Military Order of Malta, Spain, Turkey, Uganda, UK, Vatican City, Vietnam, Yugoslavia, Zambia, Zimbabwe

****

International Organization for Standardization (ISO)

established - NA February 1947

aim - to promote the development of international standards

members - (72 national standards organizations) Albania, Algeria, Argentina, Australia, Austria, Bangladesh, Belgium, Brazil, Bulgaria, Canada, Chile, China, Colombia, Cuba, Cyprus, Czechoslovakia, Denmark, Egypt, Ethiopia, Finland, France, Germany, Ghana, Greece, Hungary, India, Indonesia, Iran, Iraq, Ireland, Israel, Italy, Ivory Coast, Jamaica, Japan, Kenya, North

Korea, South Korea, Malaysia, Mexico, Mongolia, Morocco,
Netherlands, NZ, Nigeria, Norway, Pakistan, Papua New Guinea,
Peru, Philippines, Poland, Portugal, Russia, Saudi Arabia,
Singapore, South Africa, Spain, Sri Lanka, Sudan, Sweden,
Switzerland, Syria, Tanzania, Thailand, Trinidad and Tobago,
Tunisia, Turkey, UK, US, Venezuela, Vietnam, Yugoslavia

correspondent members - (14) Bahrain, Barbados, Brunei, Guinea, Hong Kong, Iceland, Jordan, Kuwait, Malawi, Mauritius, Oman, Senegal, UAE, Uruguay

****

International Red Cross and Red Crescent Movement

established - NA 1928

aim - to promote worldwide humanitarian aid through the International Committee of the Red Cross (ICRC) in wartime, and League of Red Cross and Red Crescent Societies (LORCS) in peacetime

members - (9) 2 representatives from ICRC, 2 from LORCS, and 5 from national societies elected by the international conference of the International Red Cross and Red Crescent Movement

****

International Telecommunication Union (ITU)

established - 9 December 1932

effective - 1 January 1934

affiliated with the UN - 15 November 1947

aim - UN specialized agency concerned with world telecommunications

members - (164) all UN members except Armenia, Azerbaijan, Bosnia and Hercegovina, Croatia, Dominica, Estonia, Kazakhstan, Kyrgyzstan, Latvia, Lithuania, Marshall Islands, Federation of Micronesia, Moldova, Saint Kitts and Nevis, Saint Lucia, Seychelles, Slovenia, Tajikistan, Turkmenistan, Uzbekistan; other members are Kiribati, Monaco, Nauru, Switzerland, Tonga, Vatican City

****

International Telecommunications Satellite Organization (INTELSAT)

established - 20 August 1971

effective - 12 February 1973

aim - to develop and operate a global commercial telecommunications satellite system

members - (118) Afghanistan, Algeria, Angola, Argentina,
Australia, Austria, The Bahamas, Bangladesh, Barbados, Belgium,
Benin, Bolivia, Brazil, Burkina, Cameroon, Canada, Central
African Republic, Chad, Chile, China, Colombia, Congo, Costa
Rica, Cyprus, Denmark, Dominican Republic, Ecuador, Egypt, El
Salvador, Ethiopia, Fiji, Finland, France, Gabon, Germany, Ghana,
Greece, Guatemala, Guinea, Haiti, Honduras, Iceland, India,
Indonesia, Iran, Iraq, Ireland, Israel, Italy, Ivory Coast,
Jamaica, Japan, Jordan, Kenya, South Korea, Kuwait, Lebanon,
Libya, Liechtenstein, Luxembourg, Madagascar, Malawi, Malaysia,
Mali, Mauritania, Mauritius, Mexico, Monaco, Morocco, Mozambique,

Nepal, Netherlands, NZ, Nicaragua, Niger, Nigeria, Norway, Oman, Pakistan, Panama, Papua New Guinea, Paraguay, Peru, Philippines, Portugal, Qatar, Rwanda, Saudi Arabia, Senegal, Singapore, Somalia, South Africa, Spain, Sri Lanka, Sudan, Swaziland, Sweden, Switzerland, Syria, Tanzania, Thailand, Togo, Trinidad and Tobago, Tunisia, Turkey, Uganda, UAE, UK, US, Uruguay, Vatican City, Venezuela, Vietnam, Yemen, Yugoslavia, Zaire, Zambia, Zimbabwe

****

Islamic Development Bank (IDB)

established - 15 December 1973

aim - to promote Islamic economic aid and social development

members - (43 plus the Palestine Liberation Organization) Afghanistan, Algeria, Bahrain, Bangladesh, Benin, Brunei, Burkina, Cameroon, Chad, Comoros, Djibouti, Egypt, Gabon, The Gambia, Guinea, Guinea-Bissau, Indonesia, Iran, Iraq, Jordan, Kuwait, Lebanon, Libya, Malaysia, Maldives, Mali, Mauritania, Morocco, Niger, Oman, Pakistan, Qatar, Saudi Arabia, Senegal, Sierra Leone, Somalia, Sudan, Syria, Tunisia, Turkey, Uganda, UAE, Yemen, Palestine Liberation Organization

****

Latin American Economic System (LAES) - , also known as Sistema Economico Latinoamericana (SELA)

established - 17 October 1975

aim - to promote economic and social development through regional cooperation

members - (26) Argentina, Barbados, Bolivia, Brazil, Chile, Colombia, Costa Rica, Cuba, Dominican Republic, Ecuador, El Salvador, Grenada, Guatemala, Guyana, Haiti, Honduras, Jamaica, Mexico, Nicaragua, Panama, Paraguay, Peru, Suriname, Trinidad and Tobago, Uruguay, Venezuela

****

Latin American Integration Association (LAIA) - , also known as Asociacion Latinoamericana de Integracion (ALADI)

established - 12 August 1980

effective - 18 March 1981

aim - to promote freer regional trade

members - (11) Argentina, Bolivia, Brazil, Chile, Colombia, Ecuador, Mexico, Paraguay, Peru, Uruguay, Venezuela

****

League of Arab States (LAS)
Note - see Arab League (AL)

****

League of Red Cross and Red Crescent Societies (LORCS)
established - 5 May 1919

aim - to provide humanitarian aid in peacetime

members - (147) Afghanistan, Albania, Algeria, Angola, Argentina, Australia, Austria, The Bahamas, Bahrain, Bangladesh, Barbados, Belgium, Belize, Benin, Bolivia, Botswana, Brazil, Bulgaria, Burkina, Burma, Burundi, Cambodia, Cameroon, Canada, Cape Verde, Central African Republic, Chad, Chile, China, Colombia, Congo, Costa Rica, Cuba, Czechoslovakia, Denmark, Djibouti, Dominica, Dominican Republic, Ecuador, Egypt, El Salvador, Ethiopia, Fiji, Finland, France, The Gambia, Germany, Ghana, Greece, Grenada, Guatemala, Guinea, Guinea-Bissau, Guyana, Haiti, Honduras, Hungary, Iceland, India, Indonesia, Iran, Iraq, Ireland, Italy, Ivory Coast, Jamaica, Japan, Jordan, Kenya, North Korea, South Korea, Kuwait, Laos, Lebanon, Lesotho, Liberia, Libya, Liechtenstein, Luxembourg, Madagascar, Malawi, Malaysia, Mali, Mauritania, Mauritius, Mexico, Monaco, Mongolia, Morocco, Mozambique, Nepal, Netherlands, NZ, Nicaragua, Niger, Nigeria, Norway, Pakistan, Panama, Papua New Guinea, Paraguay, Peru, Philippines, Poland, Portugal, Qatar, Romania, Russia, Rwanda, Saint Lucia, Saint Vincent and the Grenadines, San Marino, Sao Tome and Principe, Saudi Arabia, Senegal, Sierra Leone, Singapore, Somalia, South Africa, Spain, Sri Lanka, Sudan, Suriname, Swaziland, Sweden, Switzerland, Syria, Tanzania, Thailand, Togo, Tonga, Trinidad and Tobago, Tunisia, Turkey, Uganda, UAE, UK, US, Uruguay, Venezuela, Vietnam, Western Samoa, Yemen, Yugoslavia, Zaire, Zambia, Zimbabwe

associate members - (2) Equatorial Guinea, Gabon

****

least developed countries (LLDCs)

Note - that subgroup of the less developed countries (LDCs) initially identified by the UN General Assembly in 1971 as having no significant economic growth, per capita GNPs/GDPs normally less than $500, and low literacy rates; also known as the undeveloped countries. The 41 LLDCs are: Afghanistan, Bangladesh, Benin, Bhutan, Botswana, Burkina, Burma, Burundi, Cape Verde, Central African Republic, Chad, Comoros, Djibouti, Equatorial Guinea, Ethiopia, The Gambia, Guinea, Guinea-Bissau, Haiti, Kiribati, Laos, Lesotho, Malawi, Maldives, Mali, Mauritania, Mozambique, Nepal, Niger, Rwanda, Sao Tome and Principe, Sierra Leone, Somalia, Sudan, Tanzania, Togo, Tuvalu, Uganda, Vanuatu, Western Samoa, Yemen

****

less developed countries (LDCs)

Note - the bottom group in the comprehensive but mutually exclusive hierarchy of developed countries (DCs), former USSR/Eastern Europe (former USSR/EE), and less developed countries (LDCs); mainly countries with low levels of output, living standards, and technology; per capita GNPs/GDPs are generally below $5,000 and often less than $1,000; however, the group also includes a number of countries with high per capita incomes, areas of advanced technology, and rapid rates of growth; includes the advanced developing countries, developing countries, Four Dragons (Four Tigers), least developed countries (LLDCs), low-income countries, middle-income countries, newly industrializing economies (NIEs), the South, Third World, underdeveloped

countries, undeveloped countries. The 173 LDCs are: Afghanistan, Algeria, American Samoa, Angola, Anguilla, Antigua and Barbuda, Argentina, Aruba, The Bahamas, Bahrain, Bangladesh, Barbados, Belize, Benin, Bhutan, Bolivia, Botswana, Brazil, British Virgin Islands, Brunei, Burkina, Burma, Burundi, Cambodia, Cameroon, Cape Verde, Cayman Islands, Central African Republic, Chad, Chile, China, Christmas Island, Cocos Islands, Colombia, Comoros, Congo, Cook Islands, Costa Rica, Cuba, Cyprus, Czechoslovakia, Djibouti, Dominica, Dominican Republic, Ecuador, Egypt, El Salvador, Equatorial Guinea, Ethiopia, Falkland Islands, Fiji, French Guiana, French Polynesia, Gabon, The Gambia, Gaza Strip, Ghana, Gibraltar, Greenland, Grenada, Guadeloupe, Guam, Guatemala, Guernsey, Guinea, Guinea-Bissau, Guyana, Haiti, Honduras, Hong Kong, India, Indonesia, Iran, Iraq, Ivory Coast, Jamaica, Jersey, Jordan, Kenya, Kiribati, North Korea, South Korea, Kuwait, Laos, Lebanon, Lesotho, Liberia, Libya, Macau, Madagascar, Malawi, Malaysia, Maldives, Mali, Isle of Man, Marshall Islands, Martinique, Mauritania, Mauritius, Mayotte, Mexico, Federated States of Micronesia, Mongolia, Montserrat, Morocco, Mozambique, Namibia, Nauru, Nepal, Netherlands Antilles, New Caledonia, Nicaragua, Niger, Nigeria, Niue, Norfolk Island, Northern Mariana Islands, Oman, Trust Territory of the Pacific Islands (Palau), Pakistan, Panama, Papua New Guinea, Paraguay, Peru, Philippines, Pitcairn Islands, Puerto Rico, Qatar, Reunion, Rwanda, Saint Helena, Saint Kitts and Nevis, Saint Lucia, Saint Pierre and Miquelon, Saint Vincent and the Grenadines, Sao Tome and Principe, Saudi Arabia, Senegal, Seychelles, Sierra Leone, Singapore, Solomon Islands, Somalia, Sri Lanka, Sudan, Suriname, Swaziland, Syria, Taiwan, Tanzania, Thailand, Togo, Tokelau, Tonga, Trinidad and Tobago, Tunisia, Turks and Caicos Islands, Tuvalu, UAE, Uganda, Uruguay, Vanuatu, Venezuela, Vietnam, Virgin Islands, Wallis and Futuna, West Bank, Western Sahara, Western Samoa, Yemen, Zaire, Zambia, Zimbabwe
****

low-income countries

Note - another term for those less developed countries with below-average per capita GNPs/GDPs; see less developed countries (LDCs)
****

middle-income countries

Note - another term for those less developed countries with above-average per capita GNPs/GDPs; see less developed countries (LDCs)
****

Missile Technology Control Regime (MTCR)

established - April 1987

aim - to arrest missile proliferation by controlling the export of key missile technologies and equipment

members - (20) Australia, Austria, Belgium, Canada, Denmark, Finland, France, Germany, Italy, Japan, Luxembourg, Netherlands, NZ, Norway, Portugal, Spain, Sweden, Switzerland, UK, US
****

newly industrializing countries (NICs)

Note - former term for the newly industrializing economies; see newly industrializing economies (NIEs)
****

newly industrializing economies (NIEs)

Note - that subgroup of the less developed countries (LDCs) that has experienced particularly rapid industrialization of their economies; formerly known as the newly industrializing countries (NICs); also known as advanced developing countries; usually includes the Four Dragons (Hong Kong, South Korea, Singapore, Taiwan) plus Brazil and Mexico

****

Nonaligned Movement (NAM)

established - 1-6 September 1961

aim - political and military cooperation apart from the traditional East or West blocs

members - (101 plus the Palestine Liberation Organization)
Afghanistan, Algeria, Angola, Argentina, The Bahamas, Bahrain,
Bangladesh, Barbados, Belize, Benin, Bhutan, Bolivia, Botswana,
Burkina, Burundi, Cambodia, Cameroon, Cape Verde, Central African
Republic, Chad, Colombia, Comoros, Congo, Cuba, Cyprus, Djibouti,
Ecuador, Egypt, Equatorial Guinea, Ethiopia, Gabon, The Gambia,
Ghana, Grenada, Guinea, Guinea-Bissau, Guyana, India, Indonesia,
Iran, Iraq, Ivory Coast, Jamaica, Jordan, Kenya, North Korea,
Kuwait, Laos, Lebanon, Lesotho, Liberia, Libya, Madagascar,
Malawi, Malaysia, Maldives, Mali, Malta, Mauritania, Mauritius,
Mongolia, Morocco, Mozambique, Namibia, Nepal, Nicaragua, Niger,
Nigeria, Oman, Pakistan, Panama, Peru, Qatar, Rwanda, Saint
Lucia, Sao Tome and Principe, Saudi Arabia, Senegal, Seychelles,
Sierra Leone, Singapore, Somalia, Sri Lanka, Sudan, Suriname,
Swaziland, Syria, Tanzania, Togo, Trinidad and Tobago, Tunisia,
Uganda, UAE, Vanuatu, Venezuela, Vietnam, Yemen, Yugoslavia,
Zaire, Zambia, Zimbabwe, Palestine Liberation Organization

observers - (9) Antigua and Barbuda, Brazil, Costa Rica, Dominica, El Salvador, Mexico, Papua New Guinea, Philippines, Uruguay

guests - (11) Australia, Austria, Dominican Republic, Finland, Greece, Portugal, Romania, San Marino, Spain, Sweden, Switzerland

****

Nordic Council (NC)

established - 16 March 1952

effective - 12 February 1953

aim - to promote regional economic, cultural, and environmental cooperation

members - (5) Denmark, Finland, Iceland, Norway, Sweden; note - Denmark includes Faroe Islands and Greenland

****

Nordic Investment Bank (NIB)

established - 4 December 1975

effective - 1 June 1976

aim - to promote economic cooperation and development

members - (5) Denmark, Finland, Iceland, Norway, Sweden

****

North

Note - a popular term for the rich industrialized countries
generally located in the northern portion of the Northern
Hemisphere; the counterpart of the South; see developed countries
(DCs)

****

North Atlantic Cooperation Council (NACC) - an extension of NATO

established - 8 November 1991

effective - 20 December 1991

aim - to form a forum to discuss cooperation concerning mutual political and security
issues

members - (35) Armenia, Azerbaijan, Belarus, Belgium, Bulgaria,
Canada, Czechoslovakia, Denmark, Estonia, France, Germany,
Greece, Hungary, Iceland, Italy, Kazakhstan, Kyrgyzstan, Latvia,
Lithuania, Luxembourg, Moldova, Netherlands, Norway, Poland,
Portugal, Romania, Russia, Spain, Tajikistan, Turkey,
Turkmenistan, Ukraine, UK, US, Uzbekistan

****

North Atlantic Treaty Organization (NATO)

established - 17 September 1949

aim - mutual defense and cooperation in other areas

members - (16) Belgium, Canada, Denmark, France, Germany, Greece, Iceland, Italy,
Luxembourg, Netherlands, Norway, Portugal, Spain, Turkey, UK, US

****

Nuclear Energy Agency (NEA)

established - NA 1958

aim - associated with OECD, seeks to promote the peaceful uses of nuclear energy

members - (23) Australia, Austria, Belgium, Canada, Denmark,
Finland, France, Germany, Greece, Iceland, Ireland, Italy, Japan,
Luxembourg, Netherlands, Norway, Portugal, Spain, Sweden,
Switzerland, Turkey, UK, US

****

Nuclear Suppliers Group (NSG)

Note - also known as the London Suppliers Group

established - 1974

aim - to establish guidelines on exports of enrichment and processing plant assistance
and nuclear exports to countries of proliferation concern and regions of conflict and
instability

members - (27) Australia, Austria, Belgium, Bulgaria, Canada,
Czechoslovakia, Denmark, Finland, France, Germany, Greece,
Hungary, Ireland, Italy, Japan, Luxembourg, Netherlands, Norway,

Poland, Portugal, Romania, Russia, Spain, Sweden, Switzerland, UK, US

****

Organismo para la Proscripcion de las Armas Nucleares en la America Latina y el Caribe (OPANAL)

Note - see Agency for the Prohibition of Nuclear Weapons in Latin America and the Caribbean (OPANAL)

****

Organization for Economic Cooperation and Development (OECD)

established - 14 December 1960, effective 30 September 1961

aim - to promote economic cooperation and development

members - (24) Australia, Austria, Belgium, Canada, Denmark, Finland, France, Germany, Greece, Iceland, Ireland, Italy, Japan, Luxembourg, Netherlands, NZ, Norway, Portugal, Spain, Sweden, Switzerland, Turkey, UK, US

special member - (1) Yugoslavia

****

Organization of African Unity (OAU)

established - 25 May 1963

aim - to promote unity and cooperation among African states

members - (50) Algeria, Angola, Benin, Botswana, Burkina, Burundi, Cameroon, Cape Verde, Central African Republic, Chad, Comoros, Congo, Djibouti, Egypt, Equatorial Guinea, Ethiopia, Gabon, The Gambia, Ghana, Guinea, Guinea-Bissau, Ivory Coast, Kenya, Lesotho, Liberia, Libya, Madagascar, Malawi, Mali, Mauritania, Mauritius, Mozambique, Niger, Nigeria, Rwanda, Sahrawi Arab Democratic Republic, Sao Tome and Principe, Senegal, Seychelles, Sierra Leone, Somalia, Sudan, Swaziland, Tanzania, Togo, Tunisia, Uganda, Zaire, Zambia, Zimbabwe

****

Organization of American States (OAS)

established - 30 April 1948

effective - 13 December 1951

aim - to promote peace and security as well as economic and social development

members - (35) Antigua and Barbuda, Argentina, The Bahamas, Barbados, Belize, Bolivia, Brazil, Canada, Chile, Colombia, Costa Rica, Cuba (excluded from formal participation since 1962), Dominica, Dominican Republic, Ecuador, El Salvador, Grenada, Guatemala, Guyana, Haiti, Honduras, Jamaica, Mexico, Nicaragua, Panama, Paraguay, Peru, Saint Kitts and Nevis, Saint Lucia, Saint Vincent and the Grenadines, Suriname, Trinidad and Tobago, US, Uruguay, Venezuela

observers - (25) Algeria, Austria, Belgium, Belize, Cyprus, EC, Egypt, Equatorial Guinea, Finland, France, Germany, Greece,

Guyana, Israel, Italy, Japan, South Korea, Morocco, Netherlands, Pakistan, Portugal, Saudi Arabia, Spain, Switzerland, Vatican City

****

Organization of Arab Petroleum Exporting Countries (OAPEC)

established - 9 January 1968

aim - to promote cooperation in the petroleum industry

members - (11) Algeria, Bahrain, Egypt, Iraq, Kuwait, Libya, Qatar, Saudi Arabia, Syria, Tunisia, UAE

****

Organization of Eastern Caribbean States (OECS)

established - 18 June 1981

effective - 4 July 1981

aim - to promote political, economic, and defense cooperation

members - (8) Antigua and Barbuda, British Virgin Islands, Dominica, Grenada, Montserrat, Saint Kitts and Nevis, Saint Lucia, Saint Vincent and the Grenadines

****

Organization of Petroleum Exporting Countries (OPEC)

established - 14 September 1960

aim - to coordinate petroleum policies

members - (13) Algeria, Ecuador, Gabon, Indonesia, Iran, Iraq, Kuwait, Libya, Nigeria, Qatar, Saudi Arabia, UAE, Venezuela

****

Organization of the Islamic Conference (OIC)

established - 22-25 September 1969

aim - to promote Islamic solidarity and cooperation in economic, social, cultural, and political affairs

members - (47 plus the Palestine Liberation Organization) Afghanistan (suspended), Albania, Algeria, Azerbaijan, Bahrain, Bangladesh, Benin, Brunei, Burkina, Cameroon, Chad, Comoros, Djibouti, Egypt, Gabon, The Gambia, Guinea, Guinea-Bissau, Indonesia, Iran, Iraq, Jordan, Kazakhstan, Kuwait, Lebanon, Libya, Malaysia, Maldives, Mali, Mauritania, Morocco, Niger, Nigeria, Oman, Pakistan, Qatar, Saudi Arabia, Senegal, Sierra Leone, Somalia, Sudan, Syria, Tunisia, Turkey, Uganda, UAE, Yemen, Palestine Liberation Organization<ATT>

observer - (1) Turkish-Cypriot administered area of Cyprus

****

Paris Club

Note - see Group of 10

****

Permanent Court of Arbitration (PCA)

established - NA 1899

aim - to facilitate the settlement of international disputes

members - (75) Argentina, Australia, Austria, Belarus, Belgium, Bolivia, Brazil, Bulgaria, Burkina, Cambodia, Cameroon, Canada, Chile, China, Colombia, Cuba, Czechoslovakia, Denmark, Dominican Republic, Ecuador, Egypt, El Salvador, Fiji, Finland, France, Germany, Greece, Guatemala, Haiti, Honduras, Hungary, Iceland, India, Iran, Iraq, Israel, Italy, Japan, Laos, Lebanon, Luxembourg, Malta, Mauritius, Mexico, Netherlands, NZ, Nicaragua, Nigeria, Norway, Pakistan, Panama, Paraguay, Peru, Poland, Portugal, Romania, Russia, Senegal, Spain, Sri Lanka, Sudan, Swaziland, Sweden, Switzerland, Thailand, Turkey, Uganda, Ukraine, UK, US, Uruguay, Venezuela, Yugoslavia, Zaire, Zimbabwe

****

Population Commission

established - 3 October 1946

aim - ECOSOC organization dealing with population matters

members - (27) selected on a rotating basis from all regions

****

Rio Group (RG)

established - NA 1988

aim - a consultation mechanism on regional Latin American issues

members - (11) Argentina, Bolivia, Brazil, Chile, Colombia, Ecuador, Mexico, Paraguay, Peru, Uruguay, Venezuela; note - Panama was expelled in 1988

****

Second World

Note - another term for the traditionally Marxist-Leninist states with authoritarian governments and command economies based on the Soviet model; the term is fading from use; see centrally planned economies

****

socialist countries

Note - in general, countries in which the government owns and plans the use of the major factors of production; note - the term is sometimes used incorrectly as a synonym for Communist countries

****

South

Note - a popular term for the poorer, less industrialized countries generally located south of the developed countries; the counterpart of the North; see less developed countries (LDCs)

****

South Asian Association for Regional Cooperation (SAARC)

established - 8 December 1985

aim - to promote economic, social, and cultural cooperation

members - (7) Bangladesh, Bhutan, India, Maldives, Nepal, Pakistan, Sri Lanka
****

South Pacific Commission (SPC)

established - 6 February 1947

effective - 29 July 1948

aim - to promote regional cooperation in economic and social matters

members - (27) American Samoa, Australia, Cook Islands, Fiji, France, French Polynesia, Guam, Kiribati, Marshall Islands, Federated States of Micronesia, Nauru, New Caledonia, NZ, Niue, Northern Mariana Islands, Trust Territory of the Pacific Islands (Palau), Papua New Guinea, Pitcairn Islands, Solomon Islands, Tokelau, Tonga, Tuvalu, UK, US, Vanuatu, Wallis and Futuna, Western Samoa
****

South Pacific Forum (SPF)

established - 5 August 1971

aim - to promote regional cooperation in political matters

members - (15) Australia, Cook Islands, Fiji, Kiribati, Marshall Islands, Federated States of Micronesia, Nauru, NZ, Niue, Papua New Guinea, Solomon Islands, Tonga, Tuvalu, Vanuatu, Western Samoa

observer - (1) Trust Territory of the Pacific Islands (Palau)
****

Southern African Customs Union (SACU)

established - 11 December 1969

aim - to promote free trade and cooperation in customs matters

members - (9) Bophuthatswana, Botswana, Ciskei, Lesotho, Namibia, South Africa, Swaziland, Transkei, Venda
****

Southern African Development Coordination Conference (SADCC)

established - 1 April 1980

aim - to promote regional economic development and reduce dependence on South Africa

members - (10) Angola, Botswana, Lesotho, Malawi, Mozambique, Namibia, Swaziland, Tanzania, Zambia, Zimbabwe
****

Southern Cone Common Market
****

(MERCOSUR)

established - 26 March 1991

aim - regional economic cooperation

members - (4) Argentina, Brazil, Paraguay, Uruguay

****

Statistical Commission

established - 21 June 1946

aim - ECOSOC organization dealing with development and standardization of national statistics

members - (25) selected on a rotating basis from all regions
****

Third World

Note - another term for the less developed countries; the term is fading from use; see less developed countries (LDCs)
****

underdeveloped countries

Note - refers to those less developed countries with the potential for above-average economic growth; see less developed countries (LDCs)
****

undeveloped countries

Note - refers to those extremely poor less developed countries (LDCs) with little prospect for economic growth; see least developed countries (LLDCs)
****

Union Douaniere et Economique de l'Afrique Centrale (UDEAC)

Note - see Central African Customs and Economic Union (UDEAC)
****

United Nations (UN)

established - 26 June 1945

effective - 24 October 1945

aim - to maintain international peace and security as well as promote cooperation involving economic, social, cultural and humanitarian problems

members - (178) Afghanistan, Albania, Algeria, Angola, Antigua and Barbuda, Argentina, Armenia, Australia, Austria, Azerbaijan, The Bahamas, Bahrain, Bangladesh, Barbados, Belarus, Belgium, Belize, Benin, Bhutan, Bolivia, Bosnia and Hercegovina, Botswana, Brazil, Brunei, Bulgaria, Burkina, Burma, Burundi, Cambodia, Cameroon, Canada, Cape Verde, Central African Republic, Chad, Chile, China, Colombia, Comoros, Congo, Costa Rica, Croatia, Cuba, Cyprus, Czechoslovakia, Denmark, Djibouti, Dominica, Dominican Republic, Ecuador, Egypt, El Salvador, Equatorial Guinea, Estonia, Ethiopia, Fiji, Finland, France, Gabon, The Gambia, Germany, Ghana, Greece, Grenada, Guatemala, Guinea, Guinea-Bissau, Guyana, Haiti, Honduras, Hungary, Iceland, India, Indonesia, Iran, Iraq, Ireland, Israel, Italy, Ivory Coast, Jamaica, Japan, Jordan, Kazakhstan, Kenya, North Korea, South Korea, Kuwait, Kyrgyzstan, Laos, Latvia, Lebanon, Lesotho, Liberia, Libya, Liechtenstein, Lithuania, Luxembourg, Madagascar, Malawi, Malaysia, Maldives, Mali, Malta, Marshall Islands,

Mauritania, Mauritius, Mexico, Federated States of Micronesia, Moldova, Mongolia, Morocco, Mozambique, Namibia, Nepal, Netherlands, NZ, Nicaragua, Niger, Nigeria, Norway, Oman, Pakistan, Panama, Papua New Guinea, Paraguay, Peru, Philippines, Poland, Portugal, Qatar, Romania, Russia, Rwanda, Saint Kitts and Nevis, Saint Lucia, Saint Vincent and the Grenadines, San Marino, Sao Tome and Principe, Saudi Arabia, Senegal, Seychelles, Sierra Leone, Singapore, Slovenia, Solomon Islands, Somalia, South Africa, Spain, Sri Lanka, Sudan, Suriname, Swaziland, Sweden, Syria, Tajikistan, Tanzania, Thailand, Togo, Trinidad and Tobago, Tunisia, Turkmenistan, Turkey, Uganda, Ukraine, UAE, UK, US, Uruguay, Uzbekistan, Vanuatu, Venezuela, Vietnam, Western Samoa, Yemen, Yugoslavia, Zaire, Zambia, Zimbabwe; note - all UN members are represented in the General Assembly

observers - (3 and the Palestine Liberation Organization) Monaco, Switzerland, Vatican City, Palestine Liberation Organization

****

United Nations Angola Verification Mission (UNAVEM)

established - 20 December 1988

aim - established by the UN Security Council to verify the withdrawal of Cuban troops from Angola

members - (10) Algeria, Argentina, Brazil, Congo, Czechoslovakia, India, Jordan, Norway, Spain, Yugoslavia

****

United Nations Center for Human Settlements (UNCHS or Habitat)

established - 12 October 1978

aim - to assist in solving human settlement problems

members - (88) selected on a rotating basis from all regions

****

United Nations Children's Fund (UNICEF)

Note - acronym retained from the predecessor organization UN International Children's Emergency Fund

established - 11 December 1946

aim - to help establish child health and welfare services

members - (41) selected on a rotating basis from all regions

****

United Nations Conference on Trade and Development (UNCTAD)

established - 30 December 1964

aim - to promote international trade

members - (181) all UN members plus Monaco, Switzerland, Tonga, Vatican City

****

United Nations Development Program (UNDP)

established - 22 November 1965

aim - to provide technical assistance to stimulate economic and social development

members - (48) selected on a rotating basis from all regions

****

United Nations Disengagement Observer Force (UNDOF)

established - 31 May 1974

aim - established by the UN Security Council to observe the 1973 Arab-Israeli ceasefire

members - (4) Austria, Canada, Finland, Poland

****

United Nations Educational, Scientific, and Cultural Organization (UNESCO)

established - 16 November 1945

effective - 4 November 1946

aim - to promote cooperation in education, science, and culture

members - (159) all UN members except Armenia, Azerbaijan, Bosnia and Hercegovina, Brunei, Croatia, Estonia, Kazakhstan, Kyrgyzstan, Latvia, Liechtenstein, Lithuania, Marshall Islands, Federated States of Micronesia, Moldova, Singapore, Slovenia, Solomon Islands, South Africa, Tajikistan, Turkmenistan, UK, US, Uzbekistan, Vanuatu; other members are Cook Islands, Kiribati, Monaco, Switzerland, Tonga

associate members - (3) Aruba, British Virgin Islands, Netherlands Antilles

****

United Nations Environment Program (UNEP)

established - 15 December 1972

aim - to promote international cooperation on all environmental matters

members - (58) selected on a rotating basis from all regions

****

United Nations Force in Cyprus (UNFICYP)

established - 4 March 1964

aim - established by the UN Security Council to serve as a peacekeeping force beween Greek Cypriots and Turkish Cypriots in Cyprus

members - (8) Australia, Austria, Canada, Denmark, Finland, Ireland, Sweden, UK

****

United Nations General Assembly

established - 26 June 1945

effective - 24 October 1945

aim - primary deliberative organ in the UN

members - (178) all UN members are represented in the General Assembly

****

United Nations Industrial Development Organization (UNIDO)

established - 17 November 1966

effective - 1 January 1967

aim - UN specialized agency that promotes industrial development especially among the members

members - (150) all UN members except Antigua and Barbuda, Armenia, Australia, Azerbaijan, Bosnia and Hercegovina, Brunei, Burma, Cambodia, Chad, Croatia, Djibouti, Estonia, Iceland, Kazakhstan, Kyrgyzstan, Latvia, Liberia, Liechtenstein, Lithuania, Marshall Islands, Federated States of Micronesia, Moldova, Singapore, Slovenia, Solomon Islands, South Africa, Tajikistan, Turkmenistan, Uzbekistan, Western Samoa; other members are Switzerland, Tonga
****

United Nations Interim Force in Lebanon (UNIFIL)

established - 19 March 1978

aim - established by the UN Security Council to confirm the withdrawal of Israeli forces, restore peace, and reestablish Lebanese authority in southern Lebanon

members - (9) Fiji, Finland, France, Ghana, Ireland, Italy, Nepal, Norway, Sweden
****

United Nations Iran-Iraq Military Observer Group (UNIIMOG)

established - 9 August 1988

aim - established by the UN Security Council to observe the 1988 Iran-Iraq ceasefire

members - (25) Argentina, Australia, Austria, Bangladesh, Canada, Denmark, Finland, Ghana, Hungary, India, Indonesia, Ireland, Italy, Kenya, Malaysia, NZ, Nigeria, Norway, Poland, Senegal, Sweden, Turkey, Uruguay, Yugoslavia, Zambia
****

United Nations Military Observer Group in India and Pakistan (UNMOGIP)

established - 13 August 1948

aim - established by the UN Security Council to observe the 1949 India-Pakistan cease-fire

members - (8) Belgium, Chile, Denmark, Finland, Italy, Norway, Sweden, Uruguay
****

United Nations Office of the High Commissioner for Refugees (UNHCR)

established - 3 December 1949

effective - 1 January 1951

aim - to try to ensure the humanitarian treatment of refugees and find permanent solutions to refugee problems

members - (43) Algeria, Argentina, Australia, Austria, Belgium, Brazil, Canada, China, Colombia, Denmark, Finland, France, Germany, Greece, Iran, Israel, Italy, Japan, Lebanon, Lesotho, Madagascar, Morocco, Namibia, Netherlands, Nicaragua, Nigeria, Norway, Pakistan, Somalia, Sudan, Sweden, Switzerland, Tanzania,

Thailand, Tunisia, Turkey, Uganda, UK, US, Vatican City, Venezuela, Yugoslavia, Zaire

****

United Nations Population Fund (UNFPA)

Note - acronym retained from predecessor organization UN Fund for Population Activities

established - NA July 1967

aim - to promote assistance in dealing with population problems

members - (51) selected on a rotating basis from all regions

****

United Nations Relief and Works Agency for Palestine Refugees in the Near East (UNRWA)

established - 8 December 1949

aim - to provide assistance to Palestinian refugees

members - (10) Belgium, Egypt, France, Japan, Jordan, Lebanon, Syria, Turkey, UK, US

****

United Nations Secretariat

established - 26 June 1945

effective - 24 October 1945

aim - primary administrative organ of the UN

members - Secretary General appointed for a five-year term by the General Assembly on the recommendation of the Security Council

****

United Nations Security Council

established - 26 June 1945

effective - 24 October 1945

aim - to maintain international peace and security

permanent members - (5) China, France, Russia, UK, US

nonpermanent members - (10) elected for two-year terms by the UN General Assembly; Austria (1991-92), Belgium (1991-92), Cuba (1990-91), Ecuador (1991-92), India (1991-92), Ivory Coast (1990- 91), Romania (1990-91), Yemen (1990-91), Zaire (1990-91), Zimbabwe (1991-92)

****

United Nations Truce Supervision Organization (UNTSO)

established - NA May 1948

aim - initially established by the UN Security Council to supervise the 1948 Arab-Israeli ceasefire and subsequently extended to work in the Sinai, Lebanon, Jordan, Afghanistan, and Pakistan

members - (19) Argentina, Australia, Austria, Belgium, Canada, Chile, China, Denmark, Finland, France, Ireland, Italy, Netherlands, NZ, Norway, Russia, Sweden, Switzerland, US

****

United Nations Trusteeship Council

established - 26 June 1945

effective - 24 October 1945

aim - to supervise the administration of the UN trust territories; only one of the original 11 trusteeships remains - the Trust Territory of the Pacific Islands (Palau)

members - (5) China, France, Russia, UK, US

****

Universal Postal Union (UPU)

established - 9 October 1874, affiliated with the UN 15 November 1947

effective - 1 July 1948

aim - UN specialized agency that promotes international postal cooperation

members - (168) all UN members except Antigua and Barbuda, Armenia, Azerbaijan, Bosnia and Hercegovina, Estonia, Kazakhstan, Kyrgyzstan, Latvia, Lithuania, Marshall Islands, Federated States of Micronesia, Moldova, Namibia, Slovenia, South Africa, Tajikistan, Turkmenistan, Uzbekistan; other members are Kiribati, Monaco, Nauru, Netherlands Antilles, Switzerland, Tonga, Tuvalu, UK Overseas Territories, Vatican City

****

Warsaw Pact (WP)

Note - was established 14 May 1955 to promote mutual defense; members met 1 July 1991 to dissolve the alliance; member states were Bulgaria, Czechoslovakia, Hungary, Poland, Romania, and the USSR

****

West African Development Bank (WADB)

Note - also known as Banque Ouest-Africaine de Developpement (BOAD)

established - 14 November 1973

aim - to promote economic development and integration

members - (7) Benin, Burkina, Ivory Coast, Mali, Niger, Senegal, Togo

****

West African Economic Community (CEAO)

Note - acronym from Communaute Economique de l'Afrique de l'Ouest

established - 3 June 1972

aim - to promote regional economic development

members - (7) Benin, Burkina, Ivory Coast, Mali, Mauritania, Niger, Senegal

observer - (1) Togo

****

Western European Union (WEU)

established - 23 October 1954

effective - 6 May 1955

aim - mutual defense and progressive political unification

members - (10) Belgium, France, Germany, Greece, Italy, Luxembourg, Netherlands, Portugal, Spain, UK

****

World Bank <p>see International Bank for Reconstruction and Development (IBRD)

****

World Bank Group

Note - includes International Bank for Reconstruction and Development (IBRD), International Development Association (IDA), and International Finance Corporation (IFC)

****

World Confederation of Labor (WCL)

established - 19 June 1920 as the International Federation of Christian Trade Unions (IFCTU), renamed 4 October 1968

aim - to promote the trade union movement

members - (96 national organizations) Algeria, Angola, Antigua and Barbuda, Argentina, Aruba, Austria, Bangladesh, Belgium, Belize, Benin, Bolivia, Bonaire Island, Botswana, Brazil, Burkina, Cameroon, Canada, Cape Verde, Central African Republic, Chad, Chile, Colombia, Costa Rica, Cuba, Curacao, Cyprus, Dominica, Dominican Republic, Ecuador, El Salvador, France, French Guiana, Gabon, The Gambia, Ghana, Grenada, Guadaloupe, Guatemala, Guinea, Guyana, Haiti, Honduras, Hong Kong, Indonesia, Italy, Ivory Coast, Jamaica, Kenya, Lesotho, Liechtenstein, Luxembourg, Madagascar, Malaysia, Mali, Martinique, Mauritius, Mexico, Montserrat, Namibia, Netherlands, Nicaragua, Niger, Nigeria, Pakistan, Panama, Paraguay, Peru, Philippines, Poland, Portugal, Puerto Rico, Rwanda, Saint Kitts and Nevis, Saint Lucia, Saint Martin, Saint Vincent and the Grenadines, Senegal, Seychelles, Sierra Leone, Spain, Sri Lanka, Suriname, Switzerland, Tanzania, Thailand, Togo, UK, US, Uruguay, Venezuela, Vietnam, Zaire, Zambia, Zimbabwe

****

World Court <p>see International Court of Justice (ICJ)

****

World Federation of Trade Unions (WFTU)

established - NA 1945

aim - to promote the trade union movement

members - (67) Afghanistan, Angola, Argentina, Australia, Austria, Bahrain, Bangladesh, Bolivia, Brazil, Burkina, Cambodia, Chile, Colombia, Congo, Costa Rica, Cuba, Cyprus, Dominican Republic, Ecuador, El Salvador, Ethiopia, France, The Gambia, Guatemala, Guinea-Bissau, Guyana, Haiti, Honduras, India, Indonesia, Iran, Iraq, Jamaica, Japan, Jordan, North Korea, Kuwait, Laos, Lebanon, Madagascar, Mauritius, Mongolia, Namibia, Nepal, Nicaragua, Oman, Pakistan, Panama, Papua New Guinea, Peru,

Philippines, Puerto Rico, Russia, Saint Vincent and the
Grenadines, Saudi Arabia, Senegal, Solomon Islands, South Africa,
Sri Lanka, Sudan, Syria, Trinidad and Tobago, Uruguay, Venezuela,
Vietnam, Yemen, Zaire
****

World Food Council (WFC)

established - 17 December 1974

aim - ECOSOC organization that studies world food problems and recommends solutions

members - (36) selected on a rotating basis from all regions
****

World Food Program (WFP)

established - 24 November 1961

aim - ECOSOC organization that provides food aid to assist in development or disaster relief

members - (30) selected on a rotating basis from all regions
****

World Health Organization (WHO)

established - 22 July 1946

effective - 7 April 1948

aim - UN specialized agency concerned with health matters

members - (164) all UN members except Armenia, Azerbaijan,
Belize, Bosnia and Hercegovina, China, Croatia, Estonia,
Kazakhstan, Kyrgyzstan, Latvia, Liechtenstein, Lithuania,
Marshall Islands, Federated States of Micronesia, Moldova,
Slovenia, Tajikistan, Turkmenistan, Uzbekistan; other members are
Cook Islands, Kiribati, Monaco, Switzerland, Tonga
****

World Intellectual Property Organization (WIPO)

established - 14 July 1967

effective - 26 April 1970

aim - UN specialized agency concerned with the protection of literary, artistic, and scientific works

members - (125) Algeria, Angola, Argentina, Australia, Austria,
The Bahamas, Bangladesh, Barbados, Belarus, Belgium, Benin,
Brazil, Bulgaria, Burkina, Burundi, Cameroon, Canada, Central
African Republic, Chad, Chile, China, Colombia, Congo, Costa
Rica, Cuba, Cyprus, Czechoslovakia, Denmark, Ecuador, Egypt, El
Salvador, Fiji, Finland, France, Gabon, The Gambia, Germany,
Ghana, Greece, Guatemala, Guinea, Guinea-Bissau, Haiti, Honduras,
Hungary, Iceland, India, Indonesia, Iraq, Ireland, Israel, Italy,
Ivory Coast, Jamaica, Japan, Jordan, Kenya, North Korea, South
Korea, Lebanon, Lesotho, Liberia, Libya, Liechtenstein,
Luxembourg, Madagascar, Malawi, Malaysia, Mali, Malta,

Mauritania, Mauritius, Mexico, Monaco, Mongolia, Morocco, Netherlands, NZ, Nicaragua, Niger, Norway, Pakistan, Panama, Paraguay, Peru, Philippines, Poland, Portugal, Qatar, Romania, Russia, Rwanda, Saudi Arabia, Senegal, Sierra Leone, Singapore, Somalia, South Africa, Spain, Sri Lanka, Sudan, Suriname, Swaziland, Sweden, Switzerland, Tanzania, Thailand, Togo, Trinidad and Tobago, Tunisia, Turkey, Uganda, Ukraine, UAE, UK, US, Uruguay, Vatican City, Venezuela, Vietnam, Yemen, Yugoslavia, Zaire, Zambia, Zimbabwe

****

World Meteorological Organization (WMO)

established - 11 October 1947

effective - 4 April 1951

aim - specialized UN agency concerned with meteorological cooperation

members - (162) all UN members except Armenia, Azerbaijan, Bhutan, Bosnia and Hercegovina, Croatia, Equatorial Guinea, Estonia, Grenada, Kazakhstan, Kyrgyzstan, Latvia, Liechtenstein, Lithuania, Moldova, Namibia, Poland, Saint Kitts and Nevis, Saint Vincent and the Grenadines, Slovenia, Tajikistan, Turkmenistan, Uzbekistan, Western Samoa; South Africa is included although WMO membership is suspended; other members are British Caribbean Territories, French Polynesia, Hong Kong, Slovenia, Netherlands Antilles, New Caledonia, Switzerland

****

World Tourism Organization (WTO)

established - 2 January 1975

aim - promote tourism as a means of contributing to economic development, international understanding, and peace

members - (102) Afghanistan, Algeria, Angola, Argentina, Australia, Austria, Bangladesh, Belgium, Benin, Bolivia, Brazil, Burkina, Burundi, Cambodia, Cameroon, Canada, Chad, Chile, China, Colombia, Congo, Cuba, Cyprus, Dominican Republic, Ecuador, Egypt, Ethiopia, Finland, France, Gabon, The Gambia, Germany, Ghana, Greece, Grenada, Guinea, Haiti, Hungary, India, Indonesia, Iran, Iraq, Israel, Italy, Ivory Coast, Jamaica, Japan, Jordan, Kenya, Kiribati, North Korea, South Korea, Kuwait, Laos, Lebanon, Lesotho, Libya, Madagascar, Malawi, Maldives, Mali, Malta, Mauritania, Mauritius, Mexico, Mongolia, Morocco, Nepal, Netherlands, Niger, Nigeria, Pakistan, Panama, Peru, Portugal, Romania, Russia, Rwanda, San Marino, Sao Tome and Principe, Senegal, Sierra Leone, Spain, Sri Lanka, Sudan, Switzerland, Syria, Tanzania, Togo, Tunisia, Turkey, Uganda, UAE, US, Uruguay, Venezuela, Vietnam, Yemen, Yugoslavia, Zaire, Zambia, Zimbabwe

associate members - (4) Aruba, Macau, Netherlands Antilles, Puerto Rico

permanent observer - (1) Vatican City

****

Zangger Committee (ZC)

established - early 1970s

aim - to establish guidelines for the export control provisions of the nuclear Non-Proliferation Treaty

members - (23) Australia, Austria, Belgium, Canada, Czechoslovakia, Denmark, Finland, Germany, Greece, Hungary, Ireland, Italy, Japan, Luxembourg, Netherlands, Norway, Poland, Romania, Russia, Sweden, Switzerland, UK, US

Appendix D: Weights and Measures Mathematical Notation Mathematical Power Name 10^{18} or 1,000,000,000,000,000,000 one quintillion 10^{15} or 1,000,000,000,000,000 one quadrillion 10^{12} or 1,000,000,000,000 one trillion 10^{9} or 1,000,000,000 one billion 10^{6} or 1,000,000 one million 10^{3} or 1,000 one thousand 10^{2} or 100 one hundred 10^{1} or 10 ten 10^{0} or 1 one 10^{-1} or 0.1 one tenth 10^{-2} or 0.01 one hundredth 10^{-3} or 0.001 one thousandth 10^{-6} or 0.000 001 one millionth 10^{-9} or 0.000 000 001 one billionth 10^{-12} or 0.000 000 000 001 one trillionth 10^{-15} or 0.000 000 000 000 001 one quadrillionth 10^{-18} or 0.000 000 000 000 000 001 one quintillionth Metric Interrelationships Conversions from a multiple or submultiple to the basic units of meters, liters, or grams can be done using the table. For example, to convert from kilometers to meters, multiply by 1,000 (9.26 kilometers equals 9,260 meters) or to convert from meters to kilometers, multiply by 0.001 (9,260 meters equals 9.26 kilometers) Prefix Symbol Length, Area Volume weight, capacity exa E 10^{18} 10^{36} 10^{54} peta P 10^{15} 10^{30} 10^{45} tera T 10^{12} 10^{24} 10^{36} giga G 10^{9} 10^{18} 10^{27} mega M 10^{6} 10^{12} 10^{18} hectokilo hk 10^{5} 10^{10} 10^{15} myria ma 10^{4} 10^{8} 10^{12} kilo k 10^{3} 10^{6} 10^{9} hecto h 10^{2} 10^{4} 10^{6} basic unit - 1 meter, 1 meter^{2} 1 meter^{3} 1 gram, 1 liter deci d 10^{-1} 10^{-2} 10^{-3} centi c 10^{-2} 10^{-4} 10^{-6} milli m 10^{-3} 10^{-6} 10^{-9} decimilli dm 10^{-4} 10^{-8} 10^{-12} centimilli cm 10^{-5} 10^{-10} 10^{-15} micro u 10^{-6} 10^{-12} 10^{-18} nano n 10^{-9} 10^{-18} 10^{-27} pico p 10^{-12} 10^{-24} 10^{-36} femto f 10^{-15} 10^{-30} 10^{-45} atto a 10^{-18} 10^{-36} 10^{-54}

Equivalents

Unit Metric Equivalent US Equivalent acre 0.404 685 64 hectares 43,560 feet^{2} acre 4,046,856 4 meters^{2} 4,840 yards^{2} acre 0.004 046 856 4 0.001 562 5 miles^{2}, kilometers^{2} statute are 100 meters^{2} 119.599 yards^{2} barrel (petroleum, US) 158.987 29 liters 42 gallons barrel (proof spirits, 151.416 47 liters 40 gallons US) barrel (beer, US) 117.347 77 liters 31 gallons bushel 35.239 07 liters 4 pecks cable 219.456 meters 120 fathoms chain (surveyor's) 20.116 8 meters 66 feet cord (wood) 3.624 556 meters^{3} 128 feet^{3} cup 0.236 588 2 liters 8 ounces, liquid (US) degrees, celsius (water boils at 100. multiply by 1.8 and add degrees C, freezes at 0. C) 32 to obtain .F degrees, fahrenheit subtract 32 and divide by (water boils at 212 .F, 1.8 to obtain .C freezes at 32 .F) dram, avoirdupois 1.771 845 2 grams 0.062 5 ounces, avoirdupois dram, troy 3.887 934 6 grams 0.125 ounces, troy dram, liquid (US) 3.696 69 milliliters 0.125 ounces, liquid fathom 1.828 8 meters 6 feet foot 30.48 centimeters foot 0.304 8 meters 0.333 333 3 yards foot 0.000 304 8 kilometers 0.000 189 39 miles, statute foot^{2} 929.030 4 centimeters^{2} 144 inches^{2} foot 2 0.092 903 04 meters^{2} 0.111 111 1 yards^{2} foot^{3} 28.316 846 592 liters 7.480 519 gallons foot^{3} 0.028 316 847 meters^{3} 1,728 inches^{3} furlong 201.168 meters 220 yards gallon, liquid (US) 3.785 411 784 liters 4 quarts, liquid gill (US) 118.294 118 milliliters 4 ounces, liquid grain 64.798 91 milligrams 0.002 285 71 ounces, advp. gram 1,000 milligrams 0.035 273 96 ounces, advp. hand (height of horse) 10.16 centimeters 4 inches hectare 10,000 meters^{2} 2.471 053 8 acres hundredweight, long 50.802 345 kilograms 112 pounds, avoirdupois hundredweight, short 45.359 237 kilograms 100 pounds, avoirdupois inch 2.54 centimeters 0.083 333 33 feet inch2 6.451 6 centimeters^2 0.006 944 44 feet^2 inch3 16.387 064 centimeters^3 0.000 578 7 feet^3 inch3 16.387 064 milliliters 0.029 761 6 pints, dry inch3 16.387 064 milliliters 0.034 632 0 pints, liquid kilogram 0.001 tons, metric 2.204 623 pounds, avoirdupois kilometer 1,000 meters 0.621 371 19 miles, statute kilometer^2 100 hectares 247.105 38 acres kilometer^2 1,000,000 meters^2 0.386 102 16 miles^2, statute knot (1 nautical 1.852 kilometers/hour 1.151 statute miles/hour mi/hr) league, nautical 5.559 552 kilometers 3 miles, nautical league, statute 4.828.032 kilometers 3 miles, statute link (surveyor's) 20.116 8 centimeters 7.92 inches liter 0.001 meters^3 61.023 74 inches^3 liter 0.1 dekaliter 0.908 083 quarts, dry liter 1,000 milliliters 1.056 688 quarts, liquid meter 100 centimeters 1.093 613 yards meter^2 10,000 centimeters^2 1.195 990 yards^2 meter^3 1,000 liters 1.307 951 yards^3 micron 0.000 001 meter 0.000 039 4 inches mil 0.025 4 millimeters 0.001 inch mile, nautical 1.852 kilometers 1.150 779 4 miles, statute mile^2, nautical 3.429 904 kilometers^2 1.325 miles^2, statute mile, statute 1.609 344 kilometers 5,280 feet or 8 furlongs mile^2, statute 258.998 811 hectares 640 acres or 1 section mile^2, statute 2.589 988 11 kilometers^2 0.755 miles^2, nautical minim (US) 0.061 611 52 milliliters 0.002 083 33 ounces, liquid ounce, avoirdupois 28.349 523 125 grams 437.5 grains ounce, liquid (US) 29.573 53 milliliters 0.062 5 pints, liquid ounce, troy 31.103 476 8 grams 480 grains pace 76.2 centimeters 30 inches peck 8.809 767 5 liters 8 quarts, dry pennyweight 1.555 173 84 grams 24 grains pint, dry (US) 0.550 610 47 liters 0.5 quarts, dry pint, liquid (US) 0.473 176 473 liters 0.5 quarts, liquid point (typographical) 0.351 459 8 millimeters 0.013 837 inches pound, avoirdupois 453.592 37 grams 16 ounces, avourdupois pound, troy 373.241 721 6 grams 12 ounces, troy quart, dry (US) 1.101 221 liters 2 pints, dry quart, liquid (US) 0.946 352 946 liters 2 pints, liquid quintal 100 kilograms 220.462 26 pounds, avdp. rod 5.029 2 meters 5.5 yards scruple 1.295 978 2 grams 20 grains section (US) 2.589 988 1 kilometers^2 1 mile2, statute or 640 acres span 22.86 centimeters 9 inches stere 1 meter3 1.307 95 yards^3 tablespoon 14.786 76 milliliters 3 teaspoons teaspoon 4.928 922 milliliters 0.333 333 tablespoons ton, long or 1,016.046 909 kilograms 2,240 pounds, avoirdupois deadweight

ton, metric 1,000 kilograms 2,204.623 pounds, avoirdupois ton, metric 1,000 kilograms 32,150.75 ounces, troy ton, register 2.831 684 7 meters^3 100 feet^3 ton, short 907.184 74 kilograms 2,000 pounds, avoirdupois township (US) 93.239 572 kilometers^2 36 miles^2, statute yard 0.914 4 meters 3 feet yard^2 0.836 127 36 meters^2 9 feet^2 yard^3 0.764 554 86 meters^3 27 feet^3 yard^3 764.554 857 984 liters 201.974 gallons

****

Appendix E

Cross-Reference List of Geographic Names

This list indicates where various names including all United States Foreign Service Posts, alternate names, former names, and political or geographical portions of larger entities can be found in The World Factbook. Spellings are not necessarily those approved by the United States Board on Geographic Names (BGN). Alternate names are included in parentheses; additional information is included in brackets.

Name Entry in The World Factbook

Abidjan [US Embassy] Ivory Coast
Abu Dhabi [US Embassy] United Arab Emirates

Acapulco [US Consular Agency] Mexico
Accra [US Embassy] Ghana
Adana [US Consulate] Turkey
Addis Ababa [US Embassy] Ethiopia
Adelaide [US Consular Agency] Australia
Adelie Land (Terre Adelie) Antarctica
  [claimed by France]
Aden Yemen
Aden, Gulf of Indian Ocean
Admiralty Islands Papua New Guinea
Adriatic Sea Atlantic Ocean
Aegean Islands Greece
Aegean Sea Atlantic Ocean
Afars and Issas, French Djibouti
  Territory of the (F.T.A.I.)
Agalega Islands Mauritius
Aland Islands Finland
Alaska United States
Alaska, Gulf of Pacific Ocean
Aldabra Islands Seychelles
Alderney Guernsey
Aleutian Islands United States
Alexander Island Antarctica
Alexandria [US Consulate General] Egypt
Algiers [US Embassy] Algeria
Alhucemas, Penon de Spain
Alma-Ata Kazakhstan
Alphonse Island Seychelles
Amami Strait Pacific Ocean
Amindivi Islands India
Amirante Isles Seychelles
Amman [US Embassy] Jordan
Amsterdam [US Consulate General] Netherlands
Amsterdam Island (Ile Amsterdam) French Southern and Antarctic Lands
Amundsen Sea Pacific Ocean
Amur China; Russia
Andaman Islands India
Andaman Sea Indian Ocean
Anegada Passage Atlantic Ocean
Anglo-Egyptian Sudan Sudan
Anjouan Comoros
Ankara [US Embassy] Turkey
Annobon Equatorial Guinea
Antananarivo [US Embassy] Madagascar
Antipodes Islands New Zealand
Antwerp [US Consulate General] Belgium
Aozou Strip [claimed by Libya] Chad
Aqaba, Gulf of Indian Ocean
Arabian Sea Indian Ocean
Arafura Sea Pacific Ocean

Argun China; Russia
Ascension Island Saint Helena
Ashgabat (Ashkhabad) Turkmenistan
Ashkhabad [Interim Chancery] Turkmenistan
Assumption Island Seychelles
Asuncion [US Embassy] Paraguay
Asuncion Island Northern Mariana Islands
Atacama Chile
Athens [US Embassy] Greece
Attu United States
Auckland [US Consulate General] New Zealand
Auckland Islands New Zealand
Australes Iles (Iles Tubuai) French Polynesia
Axel Heiberg Island Canada
Azores Portugal
Azov, Sea of Atlantic Ocean

Bab el Mandeb Indian Ocean
Babuyan Channel Pacific Ocean
Babuyan Islands Philippines
Baffin Bay Arctic Ocean
Baffin Island Canada
Baghdad Iraq
Baku Azerbaijan
Baky (Baku) Azerbaijan
Balabac Strait Pacific Ocean
Balearic Islands Spain
Balearic Sea (Iberian Sea) Atlantic Ocean
Bali [US Consular Agency] Indonesia
Bali Sea Indian Ocean
Balintang Channel Pacific Ocean
Balintang Islands Philippines
Balleny Islands Antarctica
Balochistan Pakistan
Baltic Sea Atlantic Ocean
Bamako [US Embassy] Mali
Banaba (Ocean Island) Kiribati
Bandar Seri Begawan [US Embassy] Brunei
Banda Sea Pacific Ocean
Bangkok [US Embassy] Thailand
Bangui [US Embassy] Central African Republic
Banjul [US Embassy] Gambia, The
Banks Island Canada
Banks Islands (Iles Banks) Vanuatu
Barcelona [US Consulate General] Spain
Barents Sea Arctic Ocean
Barranquilla [US Consulate] Colombia
Bashi Channel Pacific Ocean
Basilan Strait Pacific Ocean
Bass Strait Indian Ocean

Batan Islands Philippines
Bavaria (Bayern) Germany
Beagle Channel Atlantic Ocean
Bear Island (Bjornoya) Svalbard
Beaufort Sea Arctic Ocean
Bechuanaland Botswana
Beijing [US Embassy] China
Beirut [US Embassy] Lebanon
Belau Pacific Islands, Trust Territory of the
                    (Palau)
Belem [US Consular Agency] Brazil
Belep Islands (Iles Belep) New Caledonia
Belfast [US Consulate General] United Kingdom
Belgian Congo Zaire
Belgrade [US Embassy] Yugoslavia
Belize City [US Embassy] Belize
Belle Isle, Strait of Atlantic Ocean
Bellinghausen Sea Pacific Ocean
Belmopan Belize
Belorussia Belarus
Bengal, Bay of Indian Ocean
Bering Sea Pacific Ocean
Bering Strait Pacific Ocean
Berkner Island Antarctica
Berlin [US Branch Office] Germany
Berlin, East Germany
Berlin, West Germany
Bern [US Embassy] Switzerland
Bessarabia Romania; Moldova
Bijagos, Arquipelago dos Guinea-Bissau
Bikini Atoll Marshall Islands
Bilbao [US Consulate] Spain
Bioko Equatorial Guinea
Biscay, Bay of Atlantic Ocean
Bishbek [Interim Chancery] Kyrgyzstan
Bishop Rock United Kingdom
Bismarck Archipelago Papua New Guinea
Bismarck Sea Pacific Ocean
Bissau [US Embassy] Guinea-Bissau
Bjornoya (Bear Island) Svalbard
Black Rock Falkland Islands (Islas Malvinas)
Black Sea Atlantic Ocean
Boa Vista Cape Verde
Bogota [US Embassy] Colombia
Bombay [US Consulate General] India
Bonaire Netherlands Antilles
Bonifacio, Strait of Atlantic Ocean
Bonin Islands Japan
Bonn [US Embassy] Germany
Bophuthatswana South Africa

Bora-Bora French Polynesia
Bordeaux [US Consulate General] France
Borneo Brunei; Indonesia; Malaysia
Bornholm Denmark
Bosporus Atlantic Ocean
Bothnia, Gulf of Atlantic Ocean
Bougainville Island Papua New Guinea
Bougainville Strait Pacific Ocean
Bounty Islands New Zealand
Brasilia [US Embassy] Brazil
Brazzaville [US Embassy] Congo
Bridgetown [US Embassy] Barbados
Brisbane [US Consulate] Australia
British East Africa Kenya
British Guiana Guyana
British Honduras Belize
British Solomon Islands Solomon Islands
British Somaliland Somalia
Brussels [US Embassy, US Mission Belgium
  to European Communities, US
  Mission to the North Atlantic
  Treaty Organization (USNATO)]
Bucharest [US Embassy] Romania
Budapest [US Embassy] Hungary
Buenos Aires [US Embassy] Argentina
Bujumbura [US Embassy] Burundi
Byelorussia Belarus

Cabinda Angola
Cabot Strait Atlantic Ocean
Caicos Islands Turks and Caicos Islands
Cairo [US Embassy] Egypt
Calcutta [US Consulate General] India
Calgary [US Consulate General] Canada
California, Gulf of Pacific Ocean
Campbell Island New Zealand
Canal Zone Panama
Canary Islands Spain
Canberra [US Embassy] Australia
Cancun [US Consular Agency] Mexico
Canton (Guangzhou) China
Canton Island Kiribati
Cape Town [US Consulate General] South Africa
Caracas [US Embassy] Venezuela
Cargados Carajos Shoals Mauritius
Caroline Islands Micronesia, Federated States of;
                        Pacific Islands, Trust Territory of the
Caribbean Sea Atlantic Ocean
Carpentaria, Gulf of Pacific Ocean
Casablanca [US Consulate General] Morocco

Cato Island Australia
Cebu [US Consulate] Philippines
Celebes Indonesia
Celebes Sea Pacific Ocean
Celtic Sea Atlantic Ocean
Central African Empire Central African Republic
Ceuta Spain
Ceylon Sri Lanka
Chafarinas, Islas Spain
Chagos Archipelago (Oil Islands) British Indian Ocean Territory
Channel Islands Guernsey; Jersey
Chatham Islands New Zealand
Cheju-do Korea, South
Cheju Strait Pacific Ocean
Chengdu [US Consulate General] China
Chesterfield Islands New Caledonia
  (Iles Chesterfield)
Chiang Mai [US Consulate General] Thailand
Chihli, Gulf of (Bo Hai) Pacific Ocean
China, People's Republic of China
China, Republic of Taiwan
Choiseul Solomon Islands
Christchurch [US Consular Agency] New Zealand
Christmas Island [Indian Ocean] Australia
Christmas Island [Pacific Ocean] Kiribati
  (Kiritimati)
Chukchi Sea Arctic Ocean
Ciskei South Africa
Ciudad Juarez [US Consulate Mexico
  General]
Cochabamba [US Consular Agency] Bolivia
Coco, Isla del Costa Rica
Cocos Islands Cocos (Keeling) Islands
Colombo [US Embassy] Sri Lanka
Colon [US Consular Agency] Panama
Colon, Archipielago de Ecuador
  (Galapagos Islands)
Commander Islands Russia
  (Komandorskiye Ostrova)
Conakry [US Embassy] Guinea
Congo (Brazzaville) Congo
Congo (Kinshasa) Zaire
Congo (Leopoldville) Zaire
Con Son Islands Vietnam
Cook Strait Pacific Ocean
Copenhagen [US Embassy] Denmark
Coral Sea Pacific Ocean
Corn Islands (Islas del Maiz) Nicaragua
Corsica France
Cosmoledo Group Seychelles

Cote d'Ivoire Ivory Coast
Cotonou [US Embassy] Benin
Crete Greece
Crooked Island Passage Atlantic Ocean
Crozet Islands (Iles Crozet) French Southern and Antarctic Lands
Curacao [US Consulate General] Netherlands Antilles
Cusco [US Consular Agency] Peru

Dahomey Benin
Daito Islands Japan
Dakar [US Embassy] Senegal
Daman (Damao) India
Damascus [US Embassy] Syria
Danger Atoll Cook Islands
Danish Straits Atlantic Ocean
Danzig (Gdansk) Poland
Dao Bach Long Vi Vietnam
Dardanelles Atlantic Ocean
Dar es Salaam [US Embassy] Tanzania
Davis Strait Atlantic Ocean
Deception Island Antarctica
Denmark Strait Atlantic Ocean
D'Entrecasteaux Islands Papua New Guinea
Devon Island Canada
Dhahran [US Consulate General] Saudi Arabia
Dhaka [US Embassy] Bangladesh
Diego Garcia British Indian Ocean Territory
Diego Ramirez Chile
Diomede Islands Russia [Big Diomede]; United States
                    [Little Diomede]
Diu India
Djibouti [US Embassy] Djibouti
Dodecanese Greece
Doha [US Embassy] Qatar
Douala [US Consulate General] Cameroon
Dover, Strait of Atlantic Ocean
Drake Passage Atlantic Ocean
Dubai [US Consulate General] United Arab Emirates
Dublin [US Embassy] Ireland
Durango [US Consular Agency] Mexico
Durban [US Consulate General] South Africa
Dushanbe Tajikistan
Dusseldorf [US Consulate General] Germany
Dutch East Indies Indonesia
Dutch Guiana Suriname

East China Sea Pacific Ocean
Easter Island (Isla de Pascua) Chile
Eastern Channel (East Korea Pacific Ocean
  Strait or Tsushima Strait)
East Germany (German Democratic Germany

Republic)
East Korea Strait (Eastern Pacific Ocean
  Channel or Tsushima Strait)
East Pakistan Bangladesh
East Siberian Sea Arctic Ocean
East Timor (Portuguese Timor) Indonesia
Edinburgh [US Consulate General] United Kingdom
Elba Italy
Ellef Ringnes Island Canada
Ellesmere Island Canada
Ellice Islands Tuvalu
Elobey, Islas de Equatorial Guinea
Enderbury Island Kiribati
Enewetak Atoll (Eniwetok Atoll) Marshall Islands
England United Kingdom
English Channel Atlantic Ocean
Eniwetok Atoll Marshall Islands
Epirus, Northern Albania; Greece
Eritrea Ethiopia
Essequibo [claimed by Venezuela] Guyana
Etorofu Russia[de facto]

Farquhar Group Seychelles
Fernando de Noronha Brazil
Fernando Po (Bioko) Equatorial Guinea
Finland, Gulf of Atlantic Ocean
Florence [US Consulate General] Italy
Florida, Straits of Atlantic Ocean
Formosa Taiwan
Formosa Strait (Taiwan Strait) Pacific Ocean
Fort-de-France Martinique
  [US Consulate General]
Frankfurt am Main Germany
  [US Consulate General]
Franz Josef Land Russia
Freetown [US Embassy] Sierra Leone
French Cameroon Cameroon
French Indochina Cambodia; Laos; Vietnam
French Guinea Guinea
French Sudan Mali
French Territory of the Afars Djibouti
  and Issas (F.T.A.I.)
French Togo Togo
Friendly Islands Tonga
Frunze (Bishkek) Kyrgyzstan
Fukuoka [US Consulate] Japan
Funchal [US Consular Agency] Portugal
Fundy, Bay of Atlantic Ocean
Futuna Islands (Hoorn Islands) Wallis and Futuna

Gaborone [US Embassy] Botswana
Galapagos Islands (Archipielago Ecuador
  de Colon)
Galleons Passage Atlantic Ocean
Gambier Islands (Iles Gambier) French Polynesia
Gaspar Strait Indian Ocean
Geneva [Branch Office of the US Switzerland
  Embassy, US Mission to European
  Office of the UN and Other
  International Organizations]
Genoa [US Consulate General] Italy
George Town [US Consular Agency] Cayman Islands
Georgetown [US Embassy] Guyana
German Democratic Republic Germany
  (East Germany)
German Federal Republic of Germany
  (West Germany)
Gibraltar, Strait of Atlantic Ocean
Gilbert Islands Kiribati
Goa India
Gold Coast Ghana
Golan Heights Syria
Good Hope, Cape of South Africa
Goteborg [US Consulate General] Sweden
Gotland Sweden
Gough Island Saint Helena
Grand Banks Atlantic Ocean
Grand Cayman Cayman Islands
Grand Turk [US Consular Agency] Turks and Caicos Islands
Great Australian Bight Indian Ocean
Great Belt (Store Baelt) Atlantic Ocean
Great Britain United Kingdom
Great Channel Indian Ocean
Greater Sunda Islands Brunei; Indonesia; Malaysia
Green Islands Papua New Guinea
Greenland Sea Arctic Ocean
Grenadines, Northern Saint Vincent and the Grenadines
Grenadines, Southern Grenada
Guadalajara Mexico
 [US Consulate General]
Guadalcanal Solomon Islands
Guadalupe, Isla de Mexico
Guangzhou [US Consulate General] China
Guantanamo [US Naval Base] Cuba
Guatemala [US Embassy] Guatemala
Gubal, Strait of Indian Ocean
Guinea, Gulf of Atlantic Ocean
Guayaquil [US Consulate General] Ecuador

Ha'apai Group Tonga
Habomai Islands Russia[de facto]
Hague,The [US Embassy] Netherlands
Haifa [US Consular Agency] Israel
Hainan Dao China
Halifax [US Consulate General] Canada
Halmahera Indonesia
Hamburg [US Consulate General] Germany
Hamilton [US Consulate General] Bermuda
Hanoi Vietnam
Harare [US Embassy] Zimbabwe
Hatay Turkey
Havana [US post not maintained, Cuba
  representation by US Interests
  Section (USINT) of the Swiss
  Embassy]
Hawaii United States
Heard Island Heard Island and McDonald Islands
Helsinki [US Embassy] Finland
Hermosillo [US Consulate] Mexico
Hispaniola Dominican Republic; Haiti
Hokkaido Japan
Holy See, The Vatican City
Hong Kong [US Consulate General] Hong Kong
Honiara [US Consulate] Solomon Islands
Honshu Japan
Hormuz, Strait of Indian Ocean
Horn, Cape (Cabo de Hornos) Chile
Horne, Iles de Wallis and Futuna
Horn of Africa Ethiopia; Somalia
Hudson Bay Arctic Ocean
Hudson Strait Arctic Ocean

Inaccessible Island Saint Helena
Indochina Cambodia; Laos; Vietnam
Inner Mongolia (Nei Mongol) China
Ionian Islands Greece
Ionian Sea Atlantic Ocean
Irian Jaya Indonesia
Irish Sea Atlantic Ocean
Islamabad [US Embassy] Pakistan
Islas Malvinas Falkland Islands (Islas Malvinas)
Istanbul [US Consulate General] Turkey
Italian Somaliland Somalia
Iwo Jima Japan
Izmir [US Consulate General] Turkey

Jakarta [US Embassy] Indonesia
Japan, Sea of Pacific Ocean
Java Indonesia
Java Sea Indian Ocean

Jeddah [US Consulate General] Saudi Arabia
Jerusalem [US Consulate General] Israel; West Bank
Johannesburg South Africa
 [US Consulate General]
Juan de Fuca, Strait of Pacific Ocean
Juan Fernandez, Isla de Chile
Juventud, Isla de la Cuba
 (Isle of Youth)

Kabul [US Embassy now closed] Afghanistan
Kaduna [US Consulate General] Nigeria
Kalimantan Indonesia
Kamchatka Peninsula Russia
 (Poluostrov Kamchatka)
Kampala [US Embassy] Uganda
Kampuchea Cambodia
Karachi [US Consulate General] Pakistan
Kara Sea Arctic Ocean
Karimata Strait Indian Ocean
Kathmandu [US Embassy] Nepal
Kattegat Atlantic Ocean
Kauai Channel Pacific Ocean
Keeling Islands Cocos (Keeling) Islands
Kerguelen, Iles French Southern and Antarctic Lands
Kermadec Islands New Zealand
Khabarovsk Russia
Khartoum [US Embassy] Sudan
Khmer Republic Cambodia
Khuriya Muriya Islands Oman
 (Kuria Muria Islands)
Khyber Pass Pakistan
Kiel Canal (Nord-Ostsee Kanal) Atlantic Ocean
Kiev [Chancery] Ukraine
Kigali [US Embassy] Rwanda
Kingston [US Embassy] Jamaica
Kinshasa [US Embassy] Zaire
Kirghiziya Kyrgyzstan
Kiritimati (Christmas Island) Kiribati
Kishinev (Chicsinau) Moldova
Kithira Strait Atlantic Ocean
Kodiak Island United States
Kola Peninsula Russia
 (Kol'skiy Poluostrov)
Kolonia [US Special Office] Micronesia, Federated States of
Korea Bay Pacific Ocean
Korea, Democratic People's Korea, North
 Republic of
Korea, Republic of Korea, South
Korea Strait Pacific Ocean
Koror [US Special Office] Pacific Islands, Trust Territory of

Kosovo Yugoslavia
Kowloon Hong Kong
Krakow [US Consulate] Poland
Kuala Lumpur [US Embassy] Malaysia
Kunashiri (Kunashir) Russia [de facto]
Kuril Islands Russia [de facto]
Kuwait [US Embassy] Kuwait
Kwajalein Atoll Marshall Islands
Kyushu Japan
Kyyiv (Kiev) Ukraine

Labrador Canada
Laccadive Islands India
Laccadive Sea Indian Ocean
La Coruna [US Consular Agency] Spain
Lagos [US Embassy] Nigeria
Lahore [US Consulate General] Pakistan
Lakshadweep India
La Paz [US Embassy] Bolivia
La Perouse Strait Pacific Ocean
Laptev Sea Arctic Ocean
Las Palmas [US Consular Agency] Spain
Lau Group Fiji
Leningrad see Saint Petersburg Russia
 [US Consulate General]
Lesser Sunda Islands Indonesia
Leyte Philippines
Liancourt Rocks Korea, South
 [claimed by Japan]
Libreville [US Embassy] Gabon
Ligurian Sea Atlantic Ocean
Lilongwe [US Embassy] Malawi
Lima [US Embassy] Peru
Lincoln Sea Arctic Ocean
Line Islands Kiribati; Palmyra Atoll
Lisbon [US Embassy] Portugal
Lombok Strait Indian Ocean
Lome [US Embassy] Togo
London [US Embassy] United Kingdom
Lord Howe Island Australia
Louisiade Archipelago Papua New Guinea
Loyalty Islands (Iles Loyaute) New Caledonia
Lubumbashi [US Consulate General] Zaire
Lusaka [US Embassy] Zambia
Luxembourg [US Embassy] Luxembourg
Luzon Philippines
Luzon Strait Pacific Ocean
Lyon [US Consulate General] France

Macao Macau
Macedonia Bulgaria

Macquarie Island Australia
Madeira Islands Portugal
Madras [US Consulate General] India
Madrid [US Embassy] Spain
Magellan, Strait of Atlantic Ocean
Maghreb Algeria, Libya, Mauritania, Morocco,
      Tunisia
Mahe Island Seychelles
Maiz, Islas del (Corn Islands) Nicaragua
Majorca (Mallorca) Spain
Majuro [US Special Office] Marshall Islands
Makassar Strait Pacific Ocean
Malabo [US Embassy] Equatorial Guinea
Malacca, Strait of Indian Ocean
Malaga [US Consular Agency] Spain
Malagasy Republic Madagascar
Male [US post not maintained, Maldives
 representation from Colombo,
 Sri Lanka]
Mallorca (Majorca) Spain
Malpelo, Isla de Colombia
Malta Channel Atlantic Ocean
Malvinas, Islas Falkland Islands (Islas Malvinas)
Managua [US Embassy] Nicaragua
Manama [US Embassy] Bahrain
Manaus [US Consular Agency] Brazil
Manchukuo China
Manchuria China
Manila [US Embassy] Philippines
Manipa Strait Pacific Ocean
Mannar, Gulf of Indian Ocean
Manua Islands American Samoa
Maputo [US Embassy] Mozambique
Maracaibo [US Consulate] Venezuela
Marcus Island (Minami-tori-shima) Japan
Mariana Islands Guam; Northern Mariana Islands
Marion Island South Africa
Marmara, Sea of Atlantic Ocean
Marquesas Islands French Polynesia
 (Iles Marquises)
Marseille [US Consulate General] France
Martin Vaz, Ilhas Brazil
Mas a Tierra Chile
 (Robinson Crusoe Island)
Mascarene Islands Mauritius; Reunion
Maseru [US Embassy] Lesotho
Matamoros [US Consulate] Mexico
Mazatlan [US Consulate] Mexico
Mbabane [US Embassy] Swaziland
McDonald Islands Heard Island and McDonald Islands

Medan [US Consulate] Indonesia
Mediterranean Sea Atlantic Ocean
Melbourne [US Consulate General] Australia
Melilla Spain
Mensk (Minsk) Belarus
Merida [US Consulate] Mexico
Messina, Strait of Atlantic Ocean
Mexico [US Embassy] Mexico
Mexico, Gulf of Atlantic Ocean
Milan [US Consulate General] Italy
Minami-tori-shima Japan
Mindanao Philippines
Mindoro Strait Pacific Ocean
Minicoy Island India
Minsk Byelarus
Mogadishu [US Embassy] Somalia
Moldovia Moldova
Mombasa [US Consulate] Kenya
Mona Passage Atlantic Ocean
Monrovia [US Embassy] Liberia
Montego Bay [US Consular Agency] Jamaica
Montenegro Serbia and Montenegro
Monterrey [US Consulate General] Mexico
Montevideo [US Embassy] Uruguay
Montreal [US Consulate General, Canada
  US Mission to the International
  Civil Aviation Organization
  (ICAO)]
Moravian Gate Czechoslovakia
Moroni [US Embassy] Comoros
Mortlock Islands Micronesia, Federated States of
Moscow [US Embassy] Russia
Mozambique Channel Indian Ocean
Mulege [US Consular Agency] Mexico
Munich [US Consulate General] Germany
Musandam Peninsula Oman; United Arab Emirates
Muscat [US Embassy] Oman
Muscat and Oman Oman
Myanma, Myanmar Burma

Naha [US Consulate General] Japan
Nairobi [US Embassy] Kenya
Nampo-shoto Japan
Naples [US Consulate General] Italy
Nassau [US Embassy] Bahamas, The
Natuna Besar Islands Indonesia
N'Djamena [US Embassy] Chad
Netherlands East Indies Indonesia
Netherlands Guiana Suriname
Nevis Saint Kitts and Nevis

New Delhi [US Embassy] India
Newfoundland Canada
New Guinea Indonesia; Papua New Guinea
New Hebrides Vanuatu
New Siberian Islands Russia
New Territories Hong Kong
New York, New York [US Mission United States
 to the United Nations (USUN)]
Niamey [US Embassy] Niger
Nice [US Consular Agency] France
Nicobar Islands India
Nicosia [US Embassy] Cyprus
Nightingale Island Saint Helena
North Atlantic Ocean Atlantic Ocean
North Channel Atlantic Ocean
Northeast Providence Channel Atlantic Ocean
Northern Epirus Albania; Greece
Northern Grenadines Saint Vincent and the Grenadines
Northern Ireland United Kingdom
Northern Rhodesia Zambia
North Island New Zealand
North Korea Korea, North
North Pacific Ocean Pacific Ocean
North Sea Atlantic Ocean
North Vietnam Vietnam
Northwest Passages Arctic Ocean
North Yemen (Yemen Arab Republic) Yemen
Norwegian Sea Atlantic Ocean
Nouakchott [US Embassy] Mauritania
Novaya Zemlya Russia
Nuevo Laredo [US Consulate] Mexico
Nyasaland Malawi

Oahu United States
Oaxaca [US Consular Agency] Mexico
Ocean Island (Banaba) Kiribati
Ocean Island (Kure Island) United States
Ogaden Ethiopia; Somalia
Oil Islands (Chagos Archipelago) British Indian Ocean Territory
Okhotsk, Sea of Pacific Ocean
Okinawa Japan
Oman, Gulf of Indian Ocean
Ombai Strait Pacific Ocean
Oporto [US Consulate] Portugal
Oran [US Consulate] Algeria
Oresund (The Sound) Atlantic Ocean
Orkney Islands United Kingdom
Osaka-Kobe [US Consulate General] Japan
Oslo [US Embassy] Norway
Otranto, Strait of Atlantic Ocean

Ottawa [US Embassy] Canada
Ouagadougou [US Embassy] Burkina
Outer Mongolia Mongolia

Pagan Northern Mariana Islands
Palau Pacific Islands, Trust Territory of the
Palawan Philippines
Palermo [US Consulate General] Italy
Palk Strait Indian Ocean
Palma de Mallorca Spain
  [US Consular Agency]
Pamirs China; Tajikistan
Panama [US Embassy] Panama
Panama Canal Panama
Panama, Gulf of Pacific Ocean
Paramaribo [US Embassy] Suriname
Parece Vela Japan
Paris [US Embassy, US Mission to France
  the Organization for Economic
  Cooperation and Development
  (OECD), US Observer Mission at
  the UN Educational, Scientific,
  and Cultural Organization
  (UNESCO)]
Pascua, Isla de (Easter Island) Chile
Passion, Ile de la Clipperton Island
Pashtunistan Afghanistan; Pakistan
Peking (Beijing) China
Pemba Island Tanzania
Pentland Firth Atlantic Ocean
Perim Yemen
Perouse Strait, La Pacific Ocean
Persian Gulf Indian Ocean
Perth [US Consulate] Australia
Pescadores Taiwan
Peshawar [US Consulate] Pakistan
Peter I Island Antarctica
Philip Island Norfolk Island
Philippine Sea Pacific Ocean
Phoenix Islands Kiribati
Pines, Isle of Cuba
  (Isla de la Juventud)
Piura [US Consular Agency] Peru
Pleasant Island Nauru
Ponape (Pohnpei) Micronesia
Ponta Delgada [US Consulate] Portugal
Port-au-Prince [US Embassy] Haiti
Port Louis [US Embassy] Mauritius
Port Moresby [US Embassy] Papua New Guinea
Porto Alegre [US Consulate] Brazil

Port-of-Spain [US Embassy] Trinidad and Tobago
Port Said [US Consular Agency] Egypt
Portuguese Guinea Guinea-Bissau
Portuguese Timor (East Timor) Indonesia
Poznan [US Consulate] Poland
Prague [US Embassy] Czechoslovakia
Praia [US Embassy] Cape Verde
Pretoria [US Embassy] South Africa
Pribilof Islands United States
Prince Edward Island Canada
Prince Edward Islands South Africa
Prince Patrick Island Canada
Principe Sao Tome and Principe
Puerto Plata [US Consular Agency] Dominican Republic
Puerto Vallarta Mexico
  [US Consular Agency]
Pusan [US Consulate] South Korea
P'yongyang Korea, North

Quebec [US Consulate General] Canada
Queen Charlotte Islands Canada
Queen Elizabeth Islands Canada
Queen Maud Land Antarctica
  [claimed by Norway]
Quito [US Embassy] Ecuador

Rabat [US Embassy] Morocco
Ralik Chain Marshall Islands
Rangoon [US Embassy] Burma
Ratak Chain Marshall Islands
Recife [US Consulate] Brazil
Redonda Antigua and Barbuda
Red Sea Indian Ocean
Revillagigedo Island United States
Revillagigedo Islands Mexico
Reykjavik [US Embassy] Iceland
Rhodes Greece
Rhodesia Zimbabwe
Rhodesia, Northern Zambia
Rhodesia, Southern Zimbabwe
Riga [Interim Chancery] Latvia
Rio de Janeiro Brazil
  [US Consulate General]
Rio de Oro Western Sahara
Rio Muni Equatorial Guinea
Riyadh [US Embassy] Saudi Arabia
Robinson Crusoe Island Chile
  (Mas a Tierra)
Rocas, Atol das Brazil
Rockall [disputed] United Kingdom
Rodrigues Mauritius

Rome [US Embassy, US Mission to Italy
  the UN Agencies for Food and
  Agriculture (FODAG)]
Roncador Cay Colombia
Roosevelt Island Antarctica
Ross Dependency Antarctica
  [claimed by New Zealand]
Ross Island Antarctica
Ross Sea Antarctica
Rota Northern Mariana Islands
Rotuma Fiji
Ryukyu Islands Japan

Saba Netherlands Antilles
Sabah Malaysia
Sable Island Canada
Sahel Burkina; Cape Verde; Chad; The Gambia;
                    Guinea-Bissau; Mali; Mauritania;
                    Niger; Senegal
Saigon (Ho Chi Minh City) Vietnam
Saint Brandon Mauritius
Saint Christopher and Nevis Saint Kitts and Nevis
Saint George's [US Embassy] Grenada
Saint George's Channel Atlantic Ocean
Saint John's [US Embassy] Antigua and Barbuda
Saint Lawrence, Gulf of Atlantic Ocean
Saint Lawrence Island United States
Saint Lawrence Seaway Atlantic Ocean
Saint Martin Guadeloupe
Saint Martin (Sint Maarten) Netherlands Antilles
Saint Paul Island Canada
Saint Paul Island United States
Saint Paul Island French Southern and Antarctic Lands
  (Ile Saint-Paul)
Saint Peter and Saint Paul Rocks Brazil
  (Penedos de Sao Pedro e
  Sao Paulo)
Saint Petersburg Russia
  [US Consulate General]
Saint Vincent Passage Atlantic Ocean
Saipan Northern Mariana Islands
Sakhalin Island (Ostrov Sakhalin) Russia
Sala y Gomez, Isla Chile
Salisbury (Harare) Zimbabwe
Salvador de Bahia Brazil
  [US Consular Agency]
Salzburg [US Consulate General] Austria
Sanaa [US Embassy] Yemen
San Ambrosio Chile
San Andres y Providencia, Colombia

Archipielago
San Bernardino Strait Pacific Ocean
San Felix, Isla Chile
San Jose [US Embassy] Costa Rica
San Luis Potosi Mexico
 [US Consular Agency]
San Miguel Allende Mexico
 [US Consular Agency]
San Salvador [US Embassy] El Salvador
Santa Cruz [US Consular Agency] Bolivia
Santa Cruz Islands Solomon Islands
Santiago [US Embassy] Chile
Santo Domingo [US Embassy] Dominican Republic
Sao Luis [US Consular Agency] Brazil
Sao Paulo [US Consulate General] Brazil
Sao Pedro e Sao Paulo, Brazil
 Penedos de
Sapporo [US Consulate General] Japan
Sapudi Strait Indian Ocean
Sarawak Malaysia
Sardinia Italy
Sargasso Sea Atlantic Ocean
Sark Guernsey
Scotia Sea Atlantic Ocean
Scotland United Kingdom
Scott Island Antarctica
Senyavin Islands Micronesia, Federated States of
Seoul [US Embassy] Korea, South
Serbia Serbia and Montenegro
Serrana Bank Colombia
Serranilla Bank Colombia
Severnaya Zemlya (Northland) Russia
Seville [US Consular Agency] Spain
Shag Island Heard Island and McDonald Islands
Shag Rocks Falkland Islands (Islas Malvinas)
Shanghai [US Consulate General] China
Shenyang [US Consulate General] China
Shetland Islands United Kingdom
Shikoku Japan
Shikotan (Shikotan-to) Japan
Siam Thailand
Sibutu Passage Pacific Ocean
Sicily Italy
Sicily, Strait of Atlantic Ocean
Sikkim India
Sinai Egypt
Singapore [US Embassy] Singapore
Singapore Strait Pacific Ocean
Sinkiang (Xinjiang) China
Sint Eustatius Netherlands Antilles

Sint Maarten (Saint Martin) Netherlands Antilles
Skagerrak Atlantic Ocean
Slovakia Czechoslovakia
Society Islands French Polynesia
  (Iles de la Societe)
Socotra Yemen
Sofia [US Embassy] Bulgaria
Solomon Islands, northern Papua New Guinea
Solomon Islands, southern Solomon Islands
Soloman Sea Pacific Ocean
Songkhla [US Consulate] Thailand
Sound, The (Oresund) Atlantic Ocean
South Atlantic Ocean Atlantic Ocean
South China Sea Pacific Ocean
Southern Grenadines Grenada
Southern Rhodesia Zimbabwe
South Georgia South Georgia and the South
                Sandwich Islands
South Island New Zealand
South Korea Korea, South
South Orkney Islands Antarctica
South Pacific Ocean Pacific Ocean
South Sandwich Islands South Georgia and the South
                Sandwich Islands
South Shetland Islands Antarctica
South Tyrol Italy
South Vietnam Vietnam
South-West Africa Namibia
South Yemen (People's Democratic Yemen
  Republic of Yemen)
Soviet Union Armenia, Azerbaijan, Byelarus, Estonia,
                Georgia, Kazakhstan, Kyrgyzstan,
                Latvia, Lithuania, Moldova, Russia,
                Tajikistan, Turkmenistan, Ukraine,
                Uzbekistan
Spanish Guinea Equatorial Guinea
Spanish Sahara Western Sahara
Spitsbergen Svalbard
Stockholm [US Embassy] Sweden
Strasbourg [US Consulate General] France
Stuttgart [US Consulate General] Germany
Suez, Gulf of Indian Ocean
Sulu Archipelago Philippines
Sulu Sea Pacific Ocean
Sumatra Indonesia
Sumba Indonesia
Sunda Islands (Soenda Isles) Indonesia; Malaysia
Sunda Strait Indian Ocean
Surabaya [US Consulate] Indonesia
Surigao Strait Pacific Ocean

Surinam Suriname
Suva [US Embassy] Fiji
Swains Island American Samoa
Swan Islands Honduras
Sydney [US Consulate General] Australia

Tahiti French Polynesia
Taipei Taiwan
Taiwan Strait Pacific Ocean
Tallin [Interim Chancery] Estonia
Tampico [US Consular Agency] Mexico
Tanganyika Tanzania
Tangier [US Consulate General] Morocco
Tarawa Kiribati
Tartar Strait Pacific Ocean
Tashkent [Interim Chancery] Uzbekistan
Tasmania Australia
Tasman Sea Pacific Ocean
Taymyr Peninsula Russia
 (Poluostrov Taymyra)
Tegucigalpa [US Embassy] Honduras
Tehran [US post not maintained, Iran
 representation by Swiss Embassy]
Tel Aviv [US Embassy] Israel
Terre Adelie (Adelie Land) Antarctica
 [claimed by France]
Thailand, Gulf of Pacific Ocean
Thessaloniki Greece
 [US Consulate General]
Thurston Island Antarctica
Tibet (Xizang) China
Tbilisi Georgia
Tierra del Fuego Argentina; Chile
Tijuana [US Consulate General] Mexico
Timor Indonesia
Timor Sea Indian Ocean
Tinian Northern Mariana Islands
Tiran, Strait of Indian Ocean
Tobago Trinidad and Tobago
Tokyo [US Embassy] Japan
Tonkin, Gulf of Pacific Ocean
Toronto [US Consulate General] Canada
Torres Strait Pacific Ocean
Toshkent (Tashkent) Uzbekistan
Trans-Jordan Jordan
Transkei South Africa
Transylvania Romania
Trieste [US Consular Agency] Italy
Trindade, Ilha de Brazil
Tripoli [US post not maintained, Libya

representation by Belgian
Embassy]
Tristan da Cunha Group Saint Helena
Trobriand Islands Papua New Guinea
Trucial States United Arab Emirates
Truk Islands Micronesia
Tsugaru Strait Pacific Ocean
Tuamotu Islands (Iles Tuamotu) French Polynesia
Tubuai Islands (Iles Tubuai) French Polynesia
Tunis [US Embassy] Tunisia
Turin [US Consulate] Italy
Turkish Straits Atlantic Ocean
Turkmeniya Turkmenistan
Turks Island Passage Atlantic Ocean
Tyrol, South Italy
Tyrrhenian Sea Atlantic Ocean

Udorn [US Consulate] Thailand
Ulaanbaatar Mongolia
Ullung-do Korea, South
Unimak Pass [strait] Pacific Ocean
Union of Soviet Socialist Armenia, Azerbaijan, Byelarus, Estonia,
  Republics Georgia, Kazakhstan, Kyrgyzstan,
                    Latvia, Lithuania, Moldova, Russia,
                    Tajikistan, Turkmenistan, Ukraine,
                    Uzbekistan
United Arab Republic Egypt; Syria
Upper Volta Burkina
USSR Armenia, Azerbaijan, Byelarus, Estonia,
                    Georgia, Kazakhstan, Kyrgyzstan,
                    Latvia, Lithuania, Moldova, Russia,
                    Tajikistan, Turkmenistan, Ukraine,
                    Uzbekistan
Vaduz [US post not maintained, Liechtenstein
  representation from Zurich,
  Switzerland]
Vakhan Corridor (Wakhan) Afghanistan
Valencia [US Consular Agency] Spain
Valletta [US Embassy] Malta
Vancouver [US Consulate General] Canada
Vancouver Island Canada
Van Diemen Strait Pacific Ocean
Vatican City [US Embassy] Vatican City
Velez de la Gomera, Penon de Spain
Venda South Africa
Veracruz [US Consular Agency] Mexico
Verde Island Passage Pacific Ocean
Victoria [US Embassy] Seychelles
Vienna [US Embassy, US Mission Austria
  to International Organizations

in Vienna (UNVIE)]
Vientiane [US Embassy] Laos
Vilnius [Interim Chancery] Lithuania
Volcano Islands Japan
Vostok Island Kiribati
Vrangelya, Ostrov Russia
 (Wrangel Island)
Wakhan Corridor Afghanistan
 (now Vakhan Corridor)
Wales United Kingdom
Walvis Bay South Africa
Warsaw [US Embassy] Poland
Washington, DC [The Permanent United States
 Mission of the USA to the
 Organization of American
 States (OAS)]
Weddell Sea Atlantic Ocean
Wellington [US Embassy] New Zealand
Western Channel Pacific Ocean
 (West Korea Strait)
West Germany (Federal Republic Germany
 of Germany)
West Korea Strait Pacific Ocean
 (Western Channel)
West Pakistan Pakistan
Wetar Strait Pacific Ocean
White Sea Arctic Ocean
Windhoek Namibia
Windward Passage Atlantic Ocean
Winnipeg [US Consular Agency] Canada
Wrangel Island (Ostrov Vrangelya) Russia [de facto]
Yaounde [US Embassy] Cameroon
Yap Islands Micronesia
Yellow Sea Pacific Ocean
Yemen (Aden) [People's Democratic Yemen
 Republic of Yemen]
Yemen Arab Republic Yemen
Yemen, North [Yemen Arab Yemen
 Republic]
Yemen (Sanaa) [Yemen Arab Yemen
 Republic]
Yemen, People's Democratic Yemen
 Republic of
Yemen, South [People's Democratic Yemen
 Republic of Yemen]
Yerevan Armenia
Youth, Isle of Cuba
 (Isla de la Juventud)
Yucatan Channel Atlantic Ocean

Yugoslavia Bosnia and Hercegovina; Croatia;
  Macedonia; Serbia and Montenegro;
  Slovenia

Zagreb [US Consulate General] Yugoslavia
Zanzibar Tanzania
Zurich [US Consulate General] Switzerland

End of the Project Gutenberg EBook of The 1992 CIA World Factbook, by United States. Central Intelligence Agency.